HANDBOOK OF READING RESEARCH

VOLUME II

Rebecca Barr

Michael L. Kamil

Peter B. Mosenthal

P. David Pearson

 LAWRENCE ERLBAUM ASSOCIATES, PUBLISHERS
Mahwah, New Jersey

Originally published 1991.

Lawrence Erlbaum Associates, Inc., Publishers
10 Industrial Avenue
Mahwah, New Jersey 07430

Library of Congress Cataloging-in-Publication Data

Handbook of reading research / [edited by] Rebecca Barr ... [et al.].
    p.   cm.
  Originally published: New York : Longman, c1991.
  Reprinted from vol. 2 of the original 2 vol. ed.
  "Volume II." No more published.
  Includes bibliographical references and index.
  ISBN 0-8058-2416-2 (pbk.)
  1. Reading. 2. Reading--Research--Methodology. I. Barr,
Rebecca.
  LB1050.H278 1996
  428.4'072--dc20   96-10470
                                                CIP

Books published by Lawrence Erlbaum Associates are printed
on acid-free paper, and their bindings are chosen
for strength and durability.

Printed in the United States of America

10 9 8 7 6 5 4

CONTENTS

PREFACE

To collect the essential knowledge of the field of reading is an unattainable goal. Those of us who participate in such an effort become parties to the myth that the goal can be attained. By opening the pages of this book, you, as a reader, have opted for the convenience of seeing the field represented in a single space (and time) and decided, consciously or unconsciously, to live with the illusion that any living endeavor, such as a field of inquiry, can be represented as a static set of truths. As writers, we made the same compromise when we set pen to paper. But you know and we know that this static image is only an illusion. And we make the compromise because we fully expect that our partners in this communicative act know that these chapters represent points of departure rather than final destinations. Those of us who wrote them know each chapter invites its own destruction; the very act of reading any review should encourage readers to question the adequacy of the representation and to begin to contemplate better representations. Such is the nature of progress.

Since this is the second handbook of research in the field of reading, comparisons with the first handbook are inevitable and instructive. The most obvious difference is in organization. In Volume II, we decided to offer readers an examination of literacy through a variety of lenses, some to permit a microscopic view and others, a panoramic view. Part One, edited by Rebecca Barr, is labelled *Society and Literacy*; obviously, this is the widest lens that we provide. Part Two, *Task and Format Variables in Reading Research*, is edited by Michael Kamil; its chapters more or less define the range of activities that we have culturally determined to be a part of this enterprise we call literacy. Part Three, *Constructs of Reading Process*, edited by Peter Mosenthal, focuses more on the processes that individuals engage in when they perform this act we call reading. Part Four, *Literacy and Schooling*, edited by David Pearson, takes us into the environment in which the knowledge that comprises literacy is passed on from one generation to the next. The last section, an Epilogue to the whole enterprise of reading research, consists of a single chapter by Peter Mosenthal and Michael Kamil entitled *Understanding Progress in Reading Research*. Our overall plan is to start with the broadest possible societal view of literacy; then to look inward, first to the materials and tasks of literacy and then within the individual; and finally to work our way out, first to the context of schooling and then to a philosophical reflection upon this enterprise in which we are engaged. This conceptual structure contrasts with that of Volume I, in which our substructure was *Methodological Issues, Basic Processes: The State of the Art*, and *Instructional Practices: The State of the Art*.

The makeup of each of the four main sections was established through an extensive set of meetings among the four editors and conversations with research leaders in the field. Among other factors, we considered bodies of work in each area, major contributors who might be willing to write the chapters, and the internal logic of each section. We hope that our choices are compelling, appropriate, and appealing. In addition to some intended coherence within sections, there are some between-section connections; for example, there are two chapters each on vocabulary and comprehension, one each for basic processes and instruction.

The composition of sections was also influenced by two other decisions we made at the outset of our planning of Volume II in 1986. First, we decided not to repeat chapters just for the sake of complete coverage. None of the methodological chapters from Volume I are repeated in Volume II. Readers can still benefit, we believe, from the insights of Venezky's history, Calfee and Piontkowski's experimental guidelines, Hall and Guthrie's ethnographic advice, and Massaro's modeling techniques. We do not wish to claim that there have been no methodological advances in the past decade; only that these chapters still provide good points of departure. The same logic was applied to certain other chapters in Volume I; for example, Anderson and Armbruster's studying chapter or Ortony's metaphor chapter are quite relevant today. And, because of changes in research traditions, there is no advantage in repeating them. Research that might have fit in a repetition of either has found a new home in Volume II. It was, by the way, in the process of comparing our first to our second effort that we finally understood that what we had created was not a second edition of the same book, but another volume in a continuing effort.

Second, we decided not to ask any of the Volume I authors to write the same (or a comparable) chapter in Volume II. Many of the authors from Volume I wrote chapters in Volume II, but they all played a different role. New perspectives, we decided, should take precedence over authorial continuity.

The development of Volume II also provided an opportunity to compensate for important omissions in Volume I. We knew, for example, that areas like secondary reading, response to literature, graphic displays, vocabulary, and reading disability were woefully underrepresented in Volume I. Thus, in Volume II, each of those areas is included as a separate chapter; in fact, the latter two are represented, not by one, but by two chapters. In 1978, when Volume I was conceptualized, the concept of reading-writing relationships was little more than a rhetorical aphorism; by 1986, when we met to create an outline for Volume II, the debate centered on whether we needed one or two chapters. Between 1978 and 1986, scholars from a variety of disciplines had brought the tools of their fields to the study of literacy as a social phenomenon. This social context work had expanded so rapidly that we soon realized, as we worked on our outline, that an entire section was needed in order to represent the study of *Society and Literacy*.

Another kind of change involved unpacking topics to a greater degree than we had in Volume I. In Volume II, we often provide several chapters where only a single chapter was provided in Volume I; the best example is in the area of text comprehension. Represented by a single chapter in Volume I, there are separate chapters for narrative, expository, and procedural text in Volume II. Discussion of instructional effects appeared in a single chapter in Volume I; Volume II provides separate chapters on teacher's instructional actions and on teacher and school effects.

In the preface to the first volume of the *Handbook*, published in 1984, we discussed the rationale for the *Handbook* and the process through which it was conceived, nurtured, and born. One of our confessions in that preface was that the *Handbook* was obsolete the very instant it appeared in print. Chapters that should have been included were not. Reading research, we found, moves at such a frenetic pace that between the moments of conceptualization and publication, particular fields of inquiry had risen to a level which justified a separate chapter. But even for the chapters that were included, that frenetic pace in the field guaranteed instant obsolescence.

It is now 1990, and the same obsolescence that plagued us in 1984 worries us once again. There are fields that did not seem appropriate as separate chapters then, but they do now. For example, in 1990, we would probably add a separate chapter on multicultural perspectives on literacy and, perhaps, one that examines the economic bases and consequences of literacy. Also, as occurred in Volume I, we did ask for some chapters that were just never completed; we wanted a chapter which examined the social contexts of literacy instruction; it was assigned, but it never arrived.

In the end, the final source of obsolescence stems from our very progress. Many of the authors in Volume II will readily tell you that their chapter would be much different if they could begin writing it today—"so much has happened since I turned it over to the editors," they will say.

A volume like this cannot be undertaken, let alone completed, without the assistance and support of many professional colleagues. There are two key members of the editorial staff at Longman Publishing Group in White Plains, New York, who have devoted as much time and energy to this volume as we have. Ray O'Connell acted as our developmental editor, alternately playing the role of cheerleader, coach, and taskmaster. Marie-Josée Schorp managed to survive the frustration of keeping the volume to a very ambitious production schedule; more remarkably, she did this with incredible wit, acumen, and forbearance. At times, we even looked forward to correcting our inaccurate reference lists. The other group of people who deserve special mention are the literally thousands of literacy researchers whose work we have cited. Without their efforts, there would be no insights and understandings, no theories and models, and no body of knowledge to summarize in a handbook.

For all the flaws, omissions, obsolescences, and shortcomings, we could not be more pleased with the outcome. We offer you a volume that represents the labor and thought of many individuals; one, we believe, that contributes substantially to scholarship in our field. We repeat what we said in the preface to Volume I: *We hope that those of you who read it learn half as much as those of us who wrote it.*

CONTRIBUTORS

Richard L. Allington is professor of education in the Department of Reading at the State University of New York at Albany. He is a member of the editorial advisory boards of *Reading Research Quarterly, Journal of Educational Psychology, Elementary School Journal*, and *Remedial and Special Education*. Dr. Allington's research interests are in remedial and special education program design, delivery, and evaluation, with an emphasis on effective instructional processes used with children who do not find learning to read easy.

Donna Alvermann is an associate professor of reading education and a fellow in the Institute for Behavioral Research at the University of Georgia. She received her Ph.D. in reading from Syracuse University. Her current research focuses on classroom dialogue and content reading instruction at the secondary school level. She contributes frequently to the professional literature and is the author of a chapter on reading teacher education in the *Handbook of Research on Teacher Education* (Macmillan, in press).

Richard C. Anderson is director of the Center for the Study of Reading at the University of Illinois, where he is also professor of psychology, educational psychology, and elementary and early childhood education. Anderson is an honors graduate of Harvard College and earned his doctorate from the Harvard Graduate School of Education. He has received the Distinguished Research Award from the International Reading Association and the Oscar S. Causey Award for outstanding contributions to reading research from the National Reading Conference. Anderson has been elected to the National Academy of Education, and he has been president of the American Educational Research Association, an organization that has twice awarded him the Palmer O. Johnson Award for outstanding educational research. Anderson has published over a hundred articles on topics in psycholinguistics, human learning and memory, and reading instruction. He has authored or edited nine books. The three most recent ones are *Learning to Read in American Schools, Foundations for a Literate America*, and *Becoming a Nation of Readers*.

Rebecca Barr is a professor of education and associate dean of doctoral programs at National-Louis University. She received her Ph.D. in educational psychology and reading from the University of Chicago. She then taught at the University of British Columbia and at the University of Chicago before coming to National-Louis University. Her current research centers on classroom instruction and ability grouping. Dr. Barr is the author of many articles and several books among which are *How Schools Work* (with R. Dreeben, University of Chicago Press, 1983), *Reading Diagnosis for Teachers: An Instructional Approach* (with M. Sadow and C. Blachowicz, Longman, 1985, 1990), and *Teaching Reading in Elementary Classrooms: Developing Independent Readers* (with B. Johnson, Longman, 1990).

Richard Beach is professor of English education at the University of Minnesota. His research interests are in the areas of response to literature and in composition, with a particular interest in developmental differences in reading and writing. He is coeditor of *New Directions in Composition Research* (Guilford) and *Becoming Readers and Writers During Adolescence and Adulthood* (Ablex, in press), and coauthor of *Teaching Literature in the Secondary School* (Harcourt Brace Jovanovich, in press).

Isabel L. Beck is professor of education in the School of Education and senior scientist at the Learning Research and Development Center at the University of Pittsburgh. She received her Ph.D. in education at the University of Pittsburgh. Her research interests have involved the relationship between cognitive processes and instruction in the areas of decoding, vocabulary, and comprehension. She is a frequent contributor to the professional literature.

Susan Bovair is a graduate student in experimental psychology at the University of Michigan. She is the coauthor of several papers with David Kieras. Her research interests include comprehension of technical prose, mental models, and the acquisition and use of procedural knowledge.

Dr. John D. Bransford is centennial professor of psychology and of education and research scientist at the Learning Technology Center, Peabody College of Vanderbilt University. Dr. Bransford has published extensively in the fields of cognitive psychology and education, has authored numerous research articles and books, and is internationally recognized for his work on thinking and learning. Most recently, his research has focused on issues of situated learning, problem solving and instruction with learning-handicapped children, and on ways technology can be used to help these children overcome their difficulties. He has been instrumental in the development of the concept of anchored instruction and its implementation in the Jasper Woodbury mathematics problem solving series. Dr. Bransford is currently the co-principal investigator on an OSE project exploring videodisc-based instruction for improving learning-handicapped children's mathematical problem solving.

Lillian Bridwell-Bowles is director of the Program in Composition and Communication and of the Center of Interdisciplinary Studies of Writing at the University of Minnesota where she is an associate professor of English. She completed her doctoral work at the University of Georgia. She is the coeditor of *New Directions in Composition Research* and of two other books on computers and writing, as well as author of dozens of articles on composing processes, writing assessment, and computer applications in writing.

Robert Calfee is an experimental cognitive psychologist with research interests in the effect of schooling on the intellectual potential of individuals and groups. He earned his degrees at UCLA, did post-graduate work at Stanford, and spent five years in psychology at the University of Wisconsin, Madison. In 1969 he returned to Stanford University, where he is presently a professor in the Committee on Psychological Studies in the School of Education. His interests have evolved over the past two decades from a focus on assessment of beginning literacy skills to a concern with the broader reach of the school as a literate environment. His theoretical efforts are directed toward the nature of human thought processes and the influence of language and literacy in the development of problem solving and communication. His research activities include *Project READ, The Inquiring School,* and *Literacy for the Year 2000.* These projects all combine theoretical and practical facets directed toward understanding and facilitating school change. He has also written critical papers in recent years on the effects of testing and educational indicators, on ability grouping, and on textbooks.

Patricia A. Carpenter is Lee & Marge Gregg professor of psychology at Carnegie Mellon University, where she has been on the faculty since receiving her Ph.D. in psychology from Stanford. Her research is on cognitive processes in reading and individual differences, and often uses the time course and sequence of the reader's eye fixations in modeling cognitive processes. She is coauthor with Marcel Just of *The Psychology of Reading and Language Comprehension* (1987), and served as coeditor of the *Journal of Memory and Language* from 1984 to 1988.

Jeanne S. Chall is professor of education and director of the Reading Laboratory and the Adult Literacy Initiative, Harvard University. She received her Ph.D. from Ohio State University and currently directs the graduate programs in reading at the Harvard Graduate School of Education. Among her many publications are *Readability: An Appraisal of Research and Application* (1958), *Learning to Read: The Great Debate* (1967 and 1983), and *Stages of Reading Development* (1983). She is coauthor, with Edgar Dale, of the Dale–Chall Readability Formula (1948 and in press) and coeditor, with John B. Carroll, of *Toward a Literature Society* (1958).

Meredyth Daneman is an associate professor of psychology at the University of Toronto. She received her Ph.D. in cognitive psychology from Carnegie-Mellon University. She was an assistant professor for two years at the University of Waterloo before assuming her current position in Toronto. Her research focuses on individual differences in reading comprehension ability, and in particular, on the role of working memory in accounting for these differences.

Martha Bridge Denckla, M.D. is a professor of neurology and pediatrics at the Johns Hopkins University School of Medicine, and director of the Developmental Neurobehavior Clinic at the

Kennedy Institute, Baltimore, Maryland. Trained in behavioral neurology by Dr. Norman Geschwind, Dr. Denckla has worked at Columbia- and Harvard-affiliated hospitals in the field of learning disabilities (research and clinical aspects) for over 20 years. Her interests within developmental behavioral neurology cover the spectrum of the nonretardation-associated cognitive deficits, from dyslexia (the mildest) to autism (the most severe).

Robert Dreeben is professor of education at the University of Chicago and does research in the sociology of education. He is author of *On What Is Learned in School*, Addison-Wesley, 1968 and coauthor with Rebecca Barr of *How Schools Work*, University of Chicago Press, 1983.

Rad Drew of Drew and Associates is an instructional designer and a consultant who performs literacy task analysis and instructor training for workplace literacy programs. He has participated in a variety of literacy research and literacy instruction projects.

Gerald G. Duffy is a professor of education and senior researcher in the Institute for Research on Teaching at Michigan State University. A former classroom teacher, he received his doctorate from Northern Illinois University and now coordinates the Master's level literacy program at MSU. His research focuses on instructional effectiveness at both the classroom and staff development levels, particularly from the perspective of putting teachers in control of their own instructional actions. Dr. Duffy is widely published in the literacy field and is a coauthor (with L. Roehler) of *Improving Classroom Reading Instruction: A Decision-Making Approach*, published in 1989 by Random House. In addition, Dr. Duffy is president of the National Reading Conference.

Linnea C. Ehri is a professor of education at the University of California, Davis. She received her Ph.D. in educational psychology from the University of California, Berkeley. She has published several research studies dealing with cognitive and language development, and reading and spelling acquisition. Her studies in reading have focused upon how children learn to read words, what linguistic capabilities children need to move into word reading, how spelling contributes to word reading, the impact of knowing word spellings on how words are pronounced, and how automatic word reading skill develops.

Linda G. Fielding is an assistant professor of education at the University of Iowa. She previously was on the faculty of the State University of New York at Albany, and is a former middle-school reading and language arts teacher. She received her Ph.D. from the University of Illinois at Urbana-Champaign. She teaches courses in developmental and remedial reading and children's literature. Her research interests include reading comprehension instruction and the role of children's literature in the activities and learning of good and poor readers in elementary school.

Philip Foster is professor of education and sociology at the State University of New York at Albany. He received his Ph.D. in education and sociology from the University of Chicago and is a former director of the Comparative Education Center at that institution. Before coming to Albany he was professor of education and head of school at Macquarie University, Australia. His research interests focus upon problems of education and socioeconomic change with particular reference to the less developed countries. He is a former president of the Comparative and International Education Society and a frequent contributor to the professional literature.

Jonathan M. Golding is an assistant professor of psychology at the University of Kentucky. He received his Ph.D. from the University of Denver, and did postgraduate work at Memphis State University. His research interests are in inferential processes during reading, question answering, and working memory capacity during reading.

Arthur C. Graesser is a professor of psychology and mathematical sciences at Memphis State University. He received his Ph.D. in psychology from the University of California, San Diego. His current research interests are in the areas of knowledge representation, text comprehension, inference processing, question answering and asking, and human–computer interaction.

Vincent Greaney is a research fellow at the Educational Research Centre, St. Patrick's College, Dublin. After training as a primary school teacher, he received a B.A. from University College, Dublin, an M. Litt. from Trinity College, Dublin, and M.Ed. and Ph.D. degrees from Boston College. His research interests include reading, evaluation, and assessment. He is a board member of the International Reading Association and a member of the editorial advisory board of *Reading Research Quarterly* and the *Journal of Research in Reading.*

John T. Guthrie is professor of curriculum and instruction and director of the Center for Educational Research and Development at the University of Maryland, College Park. He was previously the research director for the International Reading Association. His interests include cognitive processes in document reading, reading assessment, and literacy activities.

Shirley Brice Heath received her Ph.D. from Columbia University in 1970 and is professor of linguistics and English and, by courtesy, of anthropology and education at Stanford University. She is also a special fellow for research and development at the Stanford Humanities Center. Her research interests include spoken and written language, first- and second-language acquisition, language planning, and the ethnography of communication. Among her publications are *Telling Tongues: Language Policy in Mexico, Colony to Nation,* (1972), *Language in the USA* (edited with Charles A. Ferguson, 1981), and *Ways With Words: Language, Life, and Work in Communities and Classrooms,* (1983). Named a MacArthur fellow in 1984, she has also been an NEH and Guggenheim fellow, and in 1988–1989, was a fellow at the Center for Advanced Study in the Behavioral Sciences.

Mary Hegarty is an assistant professor of psychology at the University of California, Santa Barbara. She received her B.A. and M.A. from University College, Dublin and her Ph.D. from Carnegie Mellon University. Her research interests include comprehension of text and graphics, spatial cognition, and individual differences in cognition.

Elfrieda H. Hiebert is associate professor of education at the University of Colorado at Boulder, where she teaches undergraduate and graduate courses in reading and writing. She received her Ph.D. from the University of Wisconsin. Her current research interests include teacher-based assessment and young children's acquisition of literacy in home and school contexts.

Dr. James V. Hoffman is assistant dean for Teacher Education and professor of reading education at the University of Texas at Austin. He received his Ph.D. in reading education from the University of Missouri at Kansas City. He is associate editor for *The Reading Research Quarterly* and served as president-elect (1988) and as president (1989) for the National Reading Conference. His current research is focused on the structuring of academic tasks in classrooms and its relationship to effective teaching.

Susan Hynds is associate professor of English education at Syracuse University, where she directs the English education program and the Writing Consultation Center. She received her Ph.D. from Vanderbilt University and has taught English, speech, and drama in grades 6 to 12 prior to her career as a university teacher. She was a former finalist in the National Council of Teachers of English Promising Researcher competition (1984). She is currently coediting two books: *Perspectives on Talk and Learning* (with Donald Rubin, NCTE forthcoming) and *Becoming Readers and Writers in Adolescence and Adulthood* (with Richard Beach, Ablex, forthcoming). Her research interests include social-cognitive aspects of response to literature and collaborative writing. Other publications have appeared or are forthcoming in *Research in the Teaching of English, The Journal of Reading, The Journal of Teaching Writing, The Review of Education,* and *Contemporary Psychology.*

Peter H. Johnston is an associate professor in the reading department at the State University of New York at Albany. He was an elementary school teacher in his native New Zealand where he also completed his undergraduate and masters degrees. He received his Ph.D. in educational psychology from the University of Illinois at Urbana-Champaign. His research on reading difficulties was recognized by the International Reading Association with the Albert J. Harris Award in 1986. His major research interests are focused on the political and instructional aspects of assessment of literacy, and on the elimination of disabling conditions for teachers and learners.

Connie Juel is an associate professor at the University of Texas at Austin. She is associate editor of *Reading Research Quarterly.* She received her Ph.D. in educational psychology from Stanford University in 1977. One of her main research interests is literacy acquisition, particularly in school settings.

Marcel Adam Just is D.O. Hebb Professor of Psychology at Carnegie-Mellon University, where he has served on the faculty since receiving Ph.D. in 1972 from Stanford University. His research has been in the areas of language comprehension, visual cognition, and individual differences in cognitive processes. He is coauthor with Patricia Carpenter of *The Psychology of Reading and Language Comprehension*, published in 1987, as well as coeditor on two earlier comprehension books, *Cognitive Processes in Comprehension* (in 1977 with Carpenter) and *New Methods in Reading Comprehension Research* (in 1984 with David Kieras). He served as coeditor of the *Journal of Memory and Language* from 1984 to 1988.

Michael L. Kamil is visiting professor of education at The Ohio State University. He received his Ph.D. in experimental psychology at the University of Wisconsin, Madison. His research interests are in the application of computer technology to reading and writing instruction, instructional decision making and classroom processes, and theories and models of reading. Currently, he is coauthoring a monograph on standards for research libraries in reading and English education. He has been editor of *Journal of Reading Behavior* and of the *National Reading Conference Yearbook* and was a coeditor of the first *Handbook of Reading Research*. He received the Milton D. Jacobson Readability Research Award for research on cloze techniques and the Albert J. Kingston award for distinguished service to the National Reading Conference. He was the head of the reading program at the University of Illinois at Chicago and directed the reading clinics at Purdue University and Arizona State University.

David E. Kieras is an associate professor with joint appointments in the Technical Communication Program and the Computer Science Department in the College of Engineering, and the Psychology Department at the University of Michigan. He received his Ph.D. in cognitive psychology from the University of Michigan in 1974, and held a post-doctoral fellowship at Carnegie-Mellon University from 1974 to 1976. His research interests include the comprehension of technical prose and the acquisition and use of procedural knowledge and mental models in interacting with equipment. His basic approach is to use cognitive simulation models to clarify and define the theoretical issues and then attempt to account for experimental data with the models.

Walter Kintsch is professor of psychology and director of the Institute of Cognitive Science at the University of Colorado at Boulder. He has an undergraduate degree from the Teacher College at Feldkirch, Austria, and received his Ph.D. in 1960 from the University of Kansas. He is currently the editor of *Psychological Review*, and the former editor of the *Journal of Verbal Behavior* and *Verbal Learning*. His research interests focus on the psychology of language comprehension, reading, and writing processes.

Marjorie Y. Lipson is an associate professor of education at the University of Vermont. She received her Ph.D. in curriculum and instruction (reading) at the University of Michigan. Her research interests are in explorations of the factors influencing reading ability and disability and in instruction design to empower readers. She has published articles in reading education and research journals, serves on the boards of several of these journals, is coeditor (with Peter Winograd and Karen Wixson) of *Improving Basal Reading Instruction* (Teacher's College Press, 1988), and is currently working on a book (with Karen Wixson) entitled *Assessment and Instruction of Reading (Dis)ability*, to be published by Scott, Foresman.

Debra L. Long is a doctoral student in the area of cognitive psychology at Memphis State University. Her research interests include inference processing, discourse processing, text comprehension and question answering.

Margaret G. McKeown is a research associate at the Learning Research and Development Center, University of Pittsburgh. She earned her Ph.D. in education at the University of Pittsburgh. Her current research interests include vocabulary acquisition in school-age children, and the effect of learner and text characteristics on learning in verbal domains. She is the editor (with M. E. Curtis) of *The Nature of Vocabulary Acquisition* (Erlbaum, 1987).

Timothy P. McNamara is assistant professor of psychology at Vanderbilt University. He received his Ph.D. from Yale University in 1984. His interests include the psychology of language, computational modeling of cognitive processes, and applications of research on cognition to education. McNamara is a recipient of a Spencer Fellowship from the National Academy of Education.

Larry Mikulecky is professor of education and director of the Learning Skills Center at Indiana University. For the past decade, he has done research to examine various aspects of literacy in the workplace. He is currently involved with research projects funded by the Department of Labor, Ford/UAW, and the American Bankers' Association.

Diana Miller is a doctoral candidate and university graduate fellow in cognitive psychology at Vanderbilt University. One line of her research focuses on reading comprehension processes and their accompanying mental representations. Another line of research examines individual differences in concept representation. Other interests include language acquisition and expert-novice performance.

David W. Moore is an associate professor of education in the department of Curriculum and Instruction at the University of Northern Iowa. He earned his Ph.D. in reading education at the University of Georgia. His research interest is in reading and writing in the content areas. He contributes frequently to the professional literature.

Peter B. Mosenthal is a professor in the Reading and Language Arts Center at Syracuse University. He received his M.A. in linguistics and Ph.D. in humanities education and educational psychology from Ohio State University. His current work includes modeling the processes that underlie prose, document, and quantitative literacy, exploring the discourse practices of researchers and the implications of these practices for defining progress in social-science research, and developing a CAT/CAI prototype system to teach and assess adult literacy.

William E. Nagy is a senior scientist at the Center for the Study of Reading at the University of Illinois, Urbana-Champaign. He received his Ph.D. in linguistics from the University of California, San Diego. His research interests are vocabulary acquisition and instruction.

Scott Paris is professor of psychology and education at the University of Michigan. He received his Ph.D. from Indiana University, taught at Purdue University, and has been a visiting scholar in Australia and New Zealand. His research focuses on children's cognitive development, learning, motivation, and reading. He is a coauthor of two textbooks, *Psychology* and *Developmental Psychology Today* and the author of educational materials entitled *Reading and Thinking Strategies*. Currently, he serves on the editorial boards of *Reading Research Quarterly, Journal of Educational Psychology, Educational Psychologist*, and *Developmental Review*.

P. David Pearson is a professor in the Department of Curriculum and Instruction at the University of Illinois at Urbana-Champaign and has been Dean of the College of Education since August of 1989. Prior to becoming Dean, professor Pearson served as codirector of the Center for the Study of Reading, where he continues to pursue a line of research related to reading instruction and reading assessment policies and practices.

Alan C. Purves, director of the Center for Writing and Literacy and professor of education and humanities at the State University of New York, Albany, received his B.A. from Harvard and his M.A. and Ph.D. in English from Columbia University. He has taught at Columbia and Barnard Colleges, the University of Illinois and at Indiana University before coming to Albany. He has served in many professional organizations and has held office in the National Council of Teachers of English and the International Association for the Evaluation of Educational Achievement (IEA), of which he is currently chairman. He has written or edited some twenty-five books and seventy articles dealing with literature, written composition, reading, and measurement. Among his titles are *The Selected Essays of Theodore Spencer, Literature Education in Ten Countries, Evaluation of Learning in Literature, Achievement in Reading and Literature: The United States in International Perspective, Becoming Readers in a Complex Society, The Idea of Culture and General Education*, and *Writing Across Cultures*.

David Reinking was a teacher in elementary and middle schools until he entered a doctoral program at the University of Minnesota where he received his Ph.D. After serving on the faculty of Rutgers University, he moved to the University of Georgia where he is currently an associate professor of education and codirector of the Reading/Language Arts Computer Resource Center. His research interests are focused on how texts displayed electronically may affect reading. In addition to conducting research related to computers, he has edited a book on the topic, developed computer-based materials for reading instruction, and taught numerous courses and inservice sessions that prepare teachers to use computers for reading and writing instruction effectively.

Laura R. Roehler is a professor of education and senior researcher in the Institute for Research on Teaching at Michigan State University. A former classroom teacher, she received her doctorate from Michigan State University, where she currently coordinates an all-University development team to reform teacher education and create professional development schools. Her research focuses on instructional effectiveness at both the classroom and staff development levels, particularly from the perspective of putting teachers in control of their own instructional actions. Dr. Roehler is widely published in the literacy field and is coauthor (with G. Duffy) of *Improving Classroom Reading Instruction: A Decision-Making Approach*, published in 1989 by Random House.

Timothy Shanahan is associate professor of education in the College of Education at the University of Illinois at Chicago. He teaches undergraduate and graduate courses in reading and writing instruction. His research interests include the study of reading-writing relationships, assessment of reading, and the learning of functional uses of literacy. He coauthored *Understanding Research in Reading and Writing* with Michael L. Kamil and Judith Langer (Allyn & Bacon, 1985), and coedited *Approaches to the Informal Evaluation of Reading* with John J. Pikulski (International Reading Association, 1982). He is senior coauthor of the McGraw-Hill Reading series. In 1983, he received the Milton D. Jacobson Readability Research Award presented by the International Reading Association. Shanahan received his Ph.D. in reading from the University of Delaware in 1980.

Patrick Shannon is a professor of education at the University of Minnesota, Duluth. He received his Ph.D. from the University of Minnesota, Twin Cities, in 1981. His current research interests concern societal effects on how literacy is defined, who is considered literate, what is written and read, and how literacy is taught at school. Shannon is the author of *Broken Promises: Reading Instruction in 20th-Century America* (Bergin & Garvey, 1988) and coauthor of *Report Card on Basal Readers* (Owens, 1988).

James R. Squire is an executive consultant for Silver, Burdett & Ginn, retired after 20 years as senior vice president, publisher, and editor-in-chief of Ginn and Company. He has been president of the National Conference on Research in English (1984), executive secretary of the National Council of Teachers of English (1960–1968), professor of English at the University of Illinois (1959–1968), lecturer, associate director of teacher education, and supervisor of the teaching of English, University of California, Berkeley (1951–1959). Among his several publications, the most recent is *The Dynamics of Language Learning* (1987), an appraisal of future directions in research for NCTE and NCRE.

Keith E. Stanovich is professor of psychology and education at Oakland University, Rochester, Michigan. His research interests are in the areas of literacy studies, the cognitive processes of reading, literate intelligence, individual differences in reading, and the cognitive consequences of literacy. He received the Albert J. Harris Award from the International Reading Association in 1988. His 1980 article in *Reading Research Quarterly* on interactive-compensatory models of reading is a *Current Contents* Citation Classic. He is the editor of the volume *Children's Reading and the Development of Phonological Awareness*. Since 1986, he has been the associate editor of the journal *Merrill-Palmer Quarterly*. He has served on the editorial boards of *Journal of Educational Psychology, Journal of Experimental Child Psychology, Reading Research Quarterly, Journal of Reading Behavior, Journal of Learning Disabilities*, and *The Reading Teacher*.

Elizabeth Sulzby is associate professor of education and faculty associate in linguistics at the University of Michigan. She received her B.A. in philosophy and English from Birmingham-Southern College, her M.Ed. in reading from the College of William and Mary, and her Ph.D. in reading from the University of Virginia. At Michigan, she is affiliated with the Center for Research in Learning and Schooling and the Combined Program in Education and Psychology. Her research area is emergent literacy and she edited, with William H. Teale, *Emergent literacy: Writing and reading*. She is the president of the IRA Special Interest Group, Literacy Development in Young Children, and Chair of the NCTE Committee on Early Childhood Testing. Prior to going to Michigan, she taught education for nine years at Northwestern University and was co-director of the Interdepartmental Program in Language and Cognition.

William H. Teale is associate professor of education at the University of Texas at San Antonio. He received his Ed.D. in reading education and English education from the University of Virginia. He completed post-doctoral work at the Laboratory of Comparative Human Cognition, University of California, San Diego, and was on the faculty of La Trobe University in Australia. His research focuses on the emergent literacy of young children. He is currently editor of *Language Arts*.

Robert J. Tierney is a professor of education at The Ohio State University. His research has focused on issues pertaining to the nature of meaning-making across various modes including reading, writing, and multimedia. He is especially interested in how these issues relate to student learning and classroom practices. He began his professional career as a classroom teacher in Australia and received his Ph.D. from the University of Georgia. For the past several years he has worked at universities and research centers in the United States (University of Arizona, University of Illinois–Center for the Study of Reading, Harvard University, University of California–Center for the Study of Writing). He has published numerous research articles dealing with the study of literacy and literacy instruction. He has also authored and edited books on a wide range of literacy topics.

Julianne C. Turner is a graduate student in the Combined Program in Education and Psychology at the University of Michigan. She received an M.Ed. from Boston University and was a classroom teacher for 13 years. She has supervised student teachers and has been a reading consultant during the past five years. Her interests include cognitive and motivational aspects of reading, classroom instruction, and reading assessment.

Dr. Frank Vellutino is a professor in both the department of psychology and the department of educational psychology at State University of New York at Albany. He is also director of the university's Child Research and Study Center. He is a cognitive psychologist who is especially interested in the reading process. He and his colleagues have systematically studied the cognitive and linguistic foundations of reading and reading disability and have written several research papers and book chapters summarizing this work. He is best known for his research in the study of dyslexia, and his book, *Dyslexia: Theory and Research* (MIT Press, 1981), has been well received.

Richard L. Venezky is Unidel professor of educational studies and professor of computer and information sciences at the University of Delaware. He received his B.E.E. and his M.A. (in linguistics) from Cornell University, and his Ph.D. in linguistics from Stanford University. Before coming to the University of Delaware he was professor and chairman of computer sciences at the University of Wisconsin, Madison. His research interests include writing systems, literacy, and the design of intelligent computing systems for knowledge access and instruction.

Robert Waller is lecturer in textual communication research at the Open University in England. He received his Ph.D. from the University of Reading. He has published research articles and book chapters on the relationship between typography, language, and the reading process and he is editor of *Information Design Journal*. He coedited (with Thomas M. Duffy) *Designing Usable Texts* (Academic Press, 1985).

Barbara A. Wasik is currently an associate research scientist at the Center for Research on Elementary and Middle Schools at Johns Hopkins University. She received her Ph.D. in developmental psychology from Temple University. Her current research focus is on developing effective tutoring programs for remedial readers. This focus is part of a larger interest in the metacognitive and motivational aspects of reading, and how remedial and normally achieving readers differ along these dimensions.

Charles A. Weaver, III, is assistant professor in psychology at the University of Colorado at Denver. He received a B.S. degree from Baylor University in 1984, and completed his Ph.D. from the University of Colorado, Boulder, in 1988, studying under Professor Walter Kintsch. His research interests include text comprehension processes, specifically understanding and solving algebra word problems, the formation of mental models from text, and comprehension monitoring.

Rose-Marie Weber is an associate professor in the reading department with a joint appointment in linguistics at the State University of New York at Albany. She received her doctorate in linguistics at Cornell University, where she was a research associate with Project Literacy before teaching at McGill University. She has had extensive field experience in Latin America. Her research interests include reading across languages, adult literacy, classroom interaction, and word recognition strategies.

Karen K. Wixson is an associate professor of education at the University of Michigan. Prior to receiving her doctorate in reading at Syracuse University, she was a remedial reading and learning disabilities teacher. Dr. Wixson conducts research and publishes widely in the areas of reading assessment and instruction. Her current projects include coauthoring a forthcoming diagnosis and remediation text, and being codirector of the project between the Michigan Department of Education and the Michigan Reading Association to revise statewide objectives and tests in reading.

PART ONE

Society and Literacy

Section Editor: Rebecca Barr

1 THE SENSE OF BEING LITERATE: HISTORICAL AND CROSS-CULTURAL FEATURES

Shirley Brice Heath

It is the huge, high harmony that sounds
A little and a little, suddenly,
By means of a separate sense. It is and it
Is not and, therefore, is.

from "A Primitive Like an Orb"
Wallace Stevens*

Any "separate sense" that enables individuals both to feel and to create harmony within their daily world comes in different forms and works in different ways. In the relatively few remaining traditional societies that have not experienced penetration by the institutions of industrial and urban growth, individuals depend on their primary senses to keep harmony in their daily lives (Goody, 1987). They listen for and feel climatic warnings, watch for signs of anger in their neighbors, or read footprints and bark thickness both to recount and predict animal behaviors.

In industrialized nations, neither direct experience nor reliance on immediate sensory feedback can go far enough toward giving a sense of harmony. The world is now the village—touched daily by global economic forces and geopolitical concerns. Here the writings of others—distant in history, geography, and profession—provide information, recommend actions, and promote political and philosophical orientations. Having access to such knowledge and being able to display it in appropriate oral and written forms suggest that an individual is in control and has power. Thus, the idea prevails in the Western world that harmony comes most readily for those who can call on their literateness to help them stabilize and control their world.

This chapter considers the very broad question of what having a sense of being literate means historically and cross-culturally. In this chapter, being literate goes beyond having *literacy skills* that enable one to disconnect from the interpretation or production of a text as a whole, discrete elements, such as letters, graphemes, words, grammar rules, main ideas, and topic sentences. The sense of being literate derives from the ability to exhibit *literate behaviors*. Through these, individuals can compare, sequence, argue with, interpret, and create extended chunks of spoken and written language in response to a written text in which communication, reflection, and interpretation are grounded.

Though we make some statements about this issue in the Western world in general, the focus of discussion in this chapter will be on the United States. In the first

---

* From *The Collected Poems of Wallace Stevens.* Copyright © 1955 by Alfred A. Knopf, Inc. Reproduced by permission.

section, we take up the historical bases for the development and promotion of literate behaviors as highly interpersonal and interdependent. The second section briefly contrasts these bases with some principles of learning in formal education, especially in terms of what these mean among minorities within the United States in the late twentieth century. A topic for special consideration here is ways that schools link critical thinking with literacy skills. The third section presents the conditions of learning language and defining thinking for some minority groups within the United States. The chapter closes with a suggested research and teacher education agenda that will move attention beyond literacy skills to literate behaviors.

Since at least the height of Greek civilization, those individuals who have looked upon themselves as literate have differed markedly from those who have used reading and writing merely as tools to achieve somewhat limited ends within narrow occupational roles. Being learned has continued to be central to being literate, with the implication that the learning that makes an individual literate goes beyond matters of daily sustenance and labor. In the Middle Ages, knowing Latin well enough to read, write, and speak it, regardless of the vernacular one spoke, marked an individual as literate. By the end of the sixteenth century, however, the term came to be not so much a marker of self-identity as a descriptor to dichotomize the population into literates who could read in the vernacular languages and illiterates who could not. It was also during this period that the Anglo world began the trend toward blaming those who did not learn to read and to speak preferred dialects for their lack of individual initiative (Jones, 1953). By the end of the nineteenth century, the term *literacy* emerged to refer primarily to measures of certain skills of reading and writing among large populations.

For individuals, being literate continues to carry the meaning of having achieved learning through special efforts to gain access to knowledge not generally available in the direct experiences of daily life. This focus on individual initiative in developing a sense of being literate fits well with the American drive "to become one's own person, almost to give birth to oneself" and to be leery of communal associations that might constrict individualism (Bellah, Madsen, Sullivan, Swidler, & Tipton, 1985, p. 82). For Americans, the fact that being able to read enables the individual to transcend time and space and to liberate the mind and spirit has been a critical component of a literate life (Cremin, 1970). By the end of the nineteenth century, the ability to write extended discourse, rather than merely provide a signature or engage in numerical calculations, clearly connoted the possibility of an unencumbered private self free from the limitations of the immediate environment. The state of being literate removes the individual from dependence on only immediate senses and direct contacts.

Yet since the days of Cicero, those who have been most literate have also been drawn to create opportunities to organize themselves into communities of literates and to talk within these groups about what they learned from what they read and how their writing might spread knowledge and promote actions among others. These close communal associations around texts—especially those of religious or legal content—have encouraged individuals to pursue their own private reflections about the life of the individual within the state and, indeed, within the cosmos. For those cut off by gender, race, or class from frequent face-to-face interactions with established and elite contemporary and contiguous communities, writing has provided a channel of communication for building communal links on paper. Women, blacks, and others with limited access often substituted their journals, diaries, and letters for direct oral exchange with a community of like-minded literates.

When formal schooling for the masses emerged in the United States as the primary institution for the spread of literacy, both communal reinforcements for being a literate individual and its strong base of support through oral communication began to diminish (Ong, 1983, pp. 126–129). Both the artifacts and personnel of schools supported sequenced approaches to learning to read and write that defined intelligence largely through the acquisition of knowledge transmitted in schools and displayed in solo performances. In its drive to instruct, measure, and prescribe the individual, the school jettisoned much of the learning in communities and the linkages between private self and public commitments that had supported literate behaviors for centuries. Measures of literateness became closely tied to individual achievements in reaching the higher levels of the formal education pyramid (Oxenham, 1980).

Ironically, even as national governments and theorists of modernization stressed strong connections between schooling and the national political and economic welfare, they followed educational models of developed nations to place extraordinary emphasis on individuals as solo learners in public schools. In developing nations around the world in the twentieth century, the larger polity and its bureaucratic replicas at local levels have promoted the benefits that could result from individuals competing against each other for academic excellence within schools (Hayes, 1965; Experimental World Literacy Program, 1973). Only in the 1960s did some national literacy campaigns and out-of-school programs begin to break this school model by linking reading and writing to social relations and new sets of cultural practices (Arnove & Graff, 1987; Friere & Macedo, 1987).

When, in the last quarter of the 20th century, critics within the developed nations pointed out the failure of schools to move large numbers of students beyond a minimal level of competence in literacy, national political figures stressed the current shortcomings of schooling and chided educators for letting standards slide from past eras of mythical high achievement. Their reference points for earlier levels of reading and writing, as well as the conditions for learning and practicing reading and writing, were often more myth than fact and often failed to consider the historical conditions for literate learning before and beyond schools (Miller, 1988). Critics of national levels of literacy focused almost completely on schools and hardly at all on the earlier important roles that literate behaviors had played in other societal institutions, such as family, church, and community organizations.

Implicit in these critiques and appeals to the national conscience has been the assumption that individuals and institutions alike hold similar notions about what being literate means. Yet few studies of the contributions of schools to national literacy levels have moved beyond definitions of literacy to consider *literate attributes* (but see Carnegie Forum, 1986). Educators and social scientists who attempted to identify literate attributes often shifted the focus from *being* to *having*, and literacy skills— discrete and mechanistic tools that make certain actions possible—went into definitions that focused on acquisition—*learning to read*—and not on retention or expansion of abilities, knowledge, and habits associated with *reading and writing to learn*.

Yet those who have a sense of being literate readily acknowledge that their capabilities extend beyond recognizing and recreating (either orally or in writing) words, sounds, and letters to include presentation of self-in-revision interdependent with other speakers and readers as well as with a variety of written texts. The literateness of any individual is also only somewhat stable; it is dynamic, iterative, and sometimes erratic and daring in its representations. On some occasions, those who think of themselves as literate can read a poem and see through it to both personal and universal meanings; at other times, the poet's words fall like dry chips with no connection to life. A word spelled or even identified and pronounced correctly at one point slips away into uncertainty on other occasions. Literates do not trust with certainty that the right words will come to sum up the essence of a meeting or to launch a charity campaign. Those who assume a sense of being literate in modern postindustrial nations know that they depend on far more than separate and individual skills for their literate identities. Being literate depends on an essential harmony of core language behaviors and certain critical supporting social relations and cultural practices.

LESSONS FROM HISTORY

Any sociocultural identification that extends into the core values of a society and its individuals has deep historical roots. Within those Western democracies that came early to industrial and urban life, ideals about the relationship of literacy to economic progress for the nation and social advancement for the individual became tightly intertwined with industrial growth and political stability. Compulsory graded schooling, national textbooks, and a cadre of professional teachers became natural companions to factories, election processes, and an expanded market for consumer goods. As former colonies became independent nations in the nineteenth and twentieth centuries, they followed the example of industrialized nations and hired teachers, built schools, and distributed basic texts to the young in the hope of increasing worker production and consumer interest to build the nation's role in the world marketplace.

Yet closer looks at the history of literacy in the industrialized nations of the West make it clear that developing a sense of being literate rather than simply acquiring the rudimentary literacy skills of reading and writing entailed far more than schools alone could give (see R. L. Venezky, "The Development of Literacy in the Industrialized Nations of the West," p. 46 of this volume). What has supported the development of a sense of being literate—of going beyond mere acquisition of reading and writing skills to expand these abilities with no apparent practical payoffs? In recent decades, when the school has centered literacy instruction on competition among autonomous, self-responsible individuals, what communal reinforcements have there been for literate behaviors?

Some hints of the subtle factors involved have come from historical studies of the development of habits of reading and of reading communities. Those who developed a sense of being literate were communities of elite groups, holding themselves and their knowledge and power apart from the masses. Churchmen, political leaders, and intellectuals—males released from responsibility for their own daily sustenance—came together to make meaning of written words. They did so through long periods of time for talking about what the texts meant, for generating ideas and actions not explicitly written in the text. Their habits of reading and talking were intertwined with specific ways of verifying and thinking about knowledge, because they were at leisure to become a community of talkers who could go beyond what texts said to what they meant for action, ideas, and ideology (Clanchy, 1979; Eisenstein, 1979; Stock, 1983).

In the Middle Ages, the church protected elite special-interest groups that were committed to write, to cultivate the forms of language for written texts, and to debate the meaning of what they had learned through reading. Before the advent of printing, scribes laboriously provided the texts that elites studied and interpreted for the populace through the church and institutions of learning. Bishops and kings guarded the written word in the armor of specialized vocations and long terms of institutionalized learning that depended upon an existence apart from the daily exigencies of providing for a family, quarreling with the local innkeeper, or deciding on the site of the local well.

Until the end of the fourteenth century in Europe, a few elites were able to secure reading and writing for themselves. The limited technology for spreading written materials and the knowledge of Latin, which was available only through privileged birth into learned families or through institutional learning, shut out all but the clerical and intellectual monopolies.

By the fifteenth century, the advent of printing removed the need to rely on individual scribes to reproduce texts and made possible the spread of both liberating and practical values gained from reading to ambitious peasants and members of the merchant class (Cressy, 1980; Darnton, 1984; Davis, 1965; Eisenstein, 1979; Ginzburg, 1976). The dissemination of books and the skills needed to read and benefit from them depended on both individuals and institutions. Disparate groups, from printers and booksellers to astronomers and life scientists, cooperated to alter earlier patterns of isolated masters and pupils at work on single problems or branches of study. Artists, scholars, learners, and printers helped supplement Latin texts with improved maps, drawings of human and celestial bodies, and the language of number. Literary artists and political pamphleteers stepped away from Latin to write in the languages of the people. The Reformation spread the expectations of the masses for religious texts available in the same form of speech in which they reprimanded their children and discussed changes in the weather.

Any sizable spread of reading depended on accompanying changes in the architecture and operation of institutions such as the church, as well as shifts in the economy that permitted greater leisure time for the masses. Moreover, individuals had to value information and experience from afar—from beyond their own direct individual experience. Initially, such efforts were random. Inns and farmhouses, as well as printers' stalls, became stopovers for wandering scholars, who mingled with local students and journeymen. Talk of planetary positions, new herbs and flowers, drawings of the human body, revised maps of distant parts of the globe, and the vernacular scriptural texts filled the backrooms of printers' shops (Eisenstein, 1979). The most industrious devoted their leisure time to self-learning with handbooks and do-it-yourself guides to everything from medicine to pronunciation (Davis, 1965; Dobson, 1968).

Gradually, forces within society began to agitate for the removal of children from the work force. As urbanization and industrialization spread, and large portions of the population in the Western world were no longer involved solely in agricultural work, working-class children (as well as the offspring of the affluent, who had for decades hired private tutors or sent their children to special schools) became available for removal from work and families for several hours each day. Within schools, top students emulated the habits of elite literate communities before them; they read, studied, and gathered in groups to talk about the meanings of what they had read. Rites of passage within formal education focused on oral disputation and oral rhetorical skills well into the nineteenth century (Hoskin, 1982). At the lower levels of schooling, nongraded and volunteer schools provided cross-age groups with similar opportunities for oral arguments, verbal games of wit, and recitation. At home in the evenings and on weekends, some families began to incorporate school-based learning into their leisure time: they read together, played games of challenge, and planned community events that featured local participants in drama and readings, as well as athletic events and seasonal parades. Women formed literary clubs to come together in groups to talk about the meaning of literary and historical texts. Protestant churches came increasingly to sponsor Sunday schools and to bring groups of all ages together for Bible study and moral and social training (Boyer, 1978).

SCHOOLING FOR SCIENTIFIC MANAGEMENT

Increased standardization in factory life and bureaucratization in government paralleled changes in formal schooling, especially in the United States. Throughout the first half of the 20th century, schools shifted swiftly and strongly away from oral to written performance, from teacher-based testing to standardized testing, from nongraded schooling to established grade levels. Textbooks with guides for teachers' activities and state-mandated testing programs pushed reading for pleasure or for the consideration of actions out of the classroom and into the leisure time of families and the activities of community organizations. Reading within a group of other readers who wanted to talk about learning or taking action from books became a privilege of those who did so either in their spare time or as a regular part of their daily work (Kaestle, 1985).

Similarly, schools shifted away from general writing classes to courses of study that highlighted school compositions that individuals wrote in isolation, solely in connection with coursework and for the audience of teacher. These compositions came to be subject to rules and principles similar to those of grammar and spelling: parts of a composition were prescribed, specific components mandated, and the organization of writing a reflection of the organizational capacities and powers of logical thinking in the writer (Applebee, 1974; Heath, 1989; Myers, 1986; Piche, 1967; Stewart, 1985).

Late 19th-century educators had proudly claimed school as the place where pupils learned to think, and they had frequently argued that children not only learned to think in schools but also learned there to value both the process of thinking and giving attention to that process. The state could expect to benefit from educating citizens who could think logically as they made choices in the nation. The dialectic methods of Socrates and Plato, supplemented by Aristotelian emphasis on inductive and deductive reasoning and the role of logic in learning, were especially held out as practices and principles for students in the American democracy to emulate.

Specific approaches in curricular materials were made available primarily to older students who were invited into courses on logic that advertised their benefits for facilitating rational thinking. English courses in high school and college became the place to learn "organized thinking" as a result of attention to clarity, conciseness, and precision in expression. Courses in English composition steadfastly proclaimed their value for instilling "critical reading" and rational thinking (McPeck, 1981).[1]

By the end of the 19th century, the responsibility of popular education for creating independent-thinking citizens was a matter of considerable debate and public media attention. Charles W. Eliot, then president of Harvard University, argued in favor of school programs geared to make students think: "There are many educated people who have little better protection against delusions and sophisms than the uneducated; for the simple reason that their education though prolonged and elaborate was still not of a kind to *train their judgment and reasoning power*" (Eliot, 1892, p. 425; emphasis not in the original).

In the early decades of the 20th century, the sometimes contradictory strands of judgment or evaluation and logical reasoning were intertwined in the talk of educators and laymen. However, none yet acknowledged that authority and agreed-upon criteria were far more abundant for logical thinking than for judgment and evaluation. Philosophers could be more certain about sound logic than poets or politicians could be about good lyrics or desirable platforms. Curricular materials of secondary-level classes across the nation carried the heavy assertion that judgment and reasoning went hand in hand with good expression, and those who learned to criticize and write well were felt to have more intelligence, morality, and industry than those who did not. In *Democracy and Education* (1916), John Dewey urged the important role of schools in promoting "good habits of thinking"; he declared "all which the school can or need do for pupils, so far as their minds are concerned (that is, leaving out certain specialized muscular abilities) is to develop their ability to think" (1916, p. 8).[2]

After the Civil War, schools in the urban north felt the first major influx of unschooled immigrants and southern blacks. Schools and factories responded to the strange languages and unfamiliar backgrounds of these students with rigid prescriptions of subjects to be learned and ways to display knowledge through certain kinds of writing and standardized test performance. Focus on the individual learner intensified, as did links between "good language" and acceptable character, discipline, and allegiance as a citizen. The sharing of knowledge through events so casual and unpredictable as conversations in small groups within classrooms could not fit new prescriptions for education as a science, which focused on knowledge imparted and managed for the individual. Key terms of both manufacturing and schooling came to be "standards," "management," "control," "rational," and "predictable." World War I intensified a focus on predictable habits, standard English, familiarity with approved literary and political readings, and adherence to set patterns of classroom behavior that centered on academic competition among individuals (Heath, 1982).

Critical Thinking through Reading and Writing

Behind the kind of reading and writing schools wanted by the 1940s lay certain expectations about thinking. A test of critical thinking, followed by recommended approaches to its general development (Watson & Glazer, 1980; originally developed in 1940), brought the attention of both subject area and reading specialists to critical thinking. But within the next two decades, most of the writing on critical thinking linked its development almost exclusively with reading and writing. The focus on "the correct assessing of statements" (Ennis, 1962, p. 83) centered on students' abilities to handle definition, explanation, justification, and deductive logic as they reacted to written texts—their own and that of their textbooks. Composition textbooks, as well as programs of reading instruction and literature study, followed promotions of critical thinking that benefited from separating written assignments into description, exposition, argumentation, and persuasion (Barell, 1983).

The public clamor of the 1970s and 1980s over weakened fundamentals and low levels of literacy brought intensified efforts to link reading and writing with critical thinking as "basic skills." Step-by-step approaches to the acquisition of each of these followed in numerous textbooks, prepackaged curricula, and teacher guides, as well as publications of the national professional organizations of teachers of reading and of English and social studies. Table 1.1 abbreviates the lists of skills that have appeared in major pedagogical treatments of critical thinking since the 1950s.

What follows below are a priori conditions that make the display of these skills possible. These out-of-awareness assumptions underlie critical thinking and emerge as children learn to use language and as they are socialized within their own family and community through the use of language (Schieffelin & Ochs, 1986a, 1986b).

1. A critical thinker acts out of a disposition to think and speak as an individual pitting his or her judgments against those of another individual or individuals.
2. A critical thinker may counter, complement, compare, or supplement information given by others as well as appraise the manner of construction of facts others used to present the information.
3. A critical thinker lays claim to a specific knowledge base out of which assertions and counterassertions to the knowledge presented by others are made. Thus one

TABLE 1.1   Some Critical Thinking Skills

I

1. Identifying central issues.
2. Recognizing underlying assumptions.
3. Evaluating evidence or authority by:
   a. Recognizing stereotypes and clichés.
   b. Recognizing bias and emotional factors in a presentation.
   c. Distinguishing between verifiable and unverifiable data.
   d. Distinguishing between relevant and nonrelevant.
   e. Distinguishing between essential and incidental.
   f. Recognizing the adequacy of data.
   g. Determining whether facts support a generalization.
   h. Checking consistency.
4. Drawing warranted conclusions.

—Paul Dressel and Lewis B. Mayhew, 1954

II

1. Determining relevance of material.
2. Evaluating reliability of authors.
3. Differentiating between fact and opinion.
4. Examining assumptions.
5. Checking (the accuracy of) data.
6. Detecting inconsistencies.

—Dorothy McClure Fraser and Edith West, 1961

III

1. Grasping the meaning of a statement.
2. Judging whether there is ambiguity in a line of reasoning.
3. Judging whether certain statements contradict each other.
4. Judging whether a conclusion necessarily follows.
5. Judging whether a statement is specific enough.
6. Judging whether a statement is actually the application of a certain principle.
7. Judging whether an observation statement is reliable.
8. Judging whether an inductive conclusion is warranted.
9. Judging whether the problem has been identified.
10. Judging whether something is an assumption.
11. Judging whether a definition is adequate.
12. Judging whether a statement made by an alleged authority is acceptable.

—Robert H. Ennis, 1961

IV

1. Determining the probable accuracy of an inference (including identifying the inference).
2. Recognizing assumptions.
3. Deducing conclusions.
4. Interpreting information.
5. Evaluating the strength of an argument (in terms of relevance and importance to a question).

—Goodwin Watson and Edward M. Glaser, 1980

TABLE 1.1 (continued)

V

Determining if:
1. A statement follows from the premises.
2. Something is an assumption.
3. An observation statement is reliable.
4. An alleged authority is reliable.
5. A simple generalization is warranted.
6. A hypothesis is warranted.
7. A theory is warranted.
8. An argument depends on an equivocation.
9. A statement is overvague or overspecific.
10. A reason is relevant.

—*Robert H. Ennis, 1966/1982*

VI

1. Distinguishing between statements of fact and statements of opinion.
2. Discriminating between statements of fact and statements of motive.
3. Determining the difficulty of proof.
4. Recognizing biased statements.
5. Drawing inferences.
6. Evaluating sources of information.

—*Horace T. Morse and George H. McCune,*
revised by Lester E. Brown and Ellen Cook, 1971

VII

1. Separating statements of fact from statements of value.
2. Distinguishing hypotheses from evidence.
3. Recognizing stated and unstated assumptions.
4. Recognizing logical inconsistency in an argument.
5. Distinguishing hypotheses from warranted conclusions.
6. Recognizing irrelevancy.
7. Recognizing logical fallacies.
8. Recognizing bias or frame of reference.
9. Recognizing organizing techniques or principles.
10. Recognizing persuading techniques.

—*Jean Fair, 1977*

VIII

1. Finding information.
2. Detecting bias (especially in terms of unreliability and overgeneralizing).
3. Evaluating a line of reasoning.
4. Weighing evidence.
5. Finding unstated assumptions.
6. Identifying ambiguous statements.
7. Identifying equivocal statements.

—*Bryce Hudgins, 1977*

Note: From "Critical Thinking: What Is It?" by B. K. Beyer. (1985). *Social Education, 49,* p. 273. Reprinted by permission from the National Council for the Social Studies.

who acts as a critical thinker takes on a social role that calls for frequent verbal displays of knowledge.

4. A critical thinker both assesses an ongoing exchange and projects a mental image of a sequenced future situation, moving back and forth between the current scene and the mentally constructed future outcome of the ongoing process.

5. A critical thinker focuses on the actual process of reflective thinking about a subject, action, or problem. Critical thinking is thinking about thinking while in the very process of expressing one's thought.

More simply put, a critical thinker in these programs is an individualist, a reflective skeptic, a questioner, a doubter, an arguer, and an observing bystander.

But what promotes the integration of verbal display of knowledge with the critical stance in an individual? Clearly, those who perform critical thinking emerge most predictably only as a result of learning certain attitudes, language uses, and orientations toward social roles in early socialization practices. The primary sociocultural group in which such performers are born must value individualism; combative, information-based rhetoric exchanged among individuals; and acceptance of attention by partici- pants to something more than their own immediate and direct sensory experiences. The social organization of the group must be more than open to change; it must value change as a phenomenon unto itself.

Learning to Use Language the Mainstream Way

Only certain types of language socialization practices provide such values and habits among those who are identified as mainstream and thus enculturate their young to fundamental beliefs and customs that undergird the school's criteria for successful displays of reading, writing, and critical thinking. Mainstreamers view infants as indi- viduals and orient them to see themselves as individuals who have the right and obligation to voice their judgments against those of others, so long as they respect rules and roles in doing so.

Children from mainstream, school-oriented, upwardly mobile aspiring groups initially believe and accept propositions until their own life experiences create alterna- tive perceptions. Through questioning, they test their propositions on parents, who value their children's display of knowledge about the world. Restrictions of age, setting, situation, and brute power soon begin to apply as 2-year-olds move from a world of all no's to the abundant questioning and sharing of experiences of 3- and 4-year-olds. Much of the early book reading and game playing that mainstream parents do with their children encourages youngsters to compare, complement, and supplement the informa- tion of the books they read (Heath, 1983; Taylor, 1983).

As they reach 8 to 10 years of age, they take up activities sponsored by community organizations; there they gain specific knowledge that their parents do not share (e.g., the events of the church's backpacking trip, the team's assessment of last night's soccer game). They increasingly participate in events and groups in which they can lay claim to a specific knowledge base out of which they can make assertions and counter the assertions of others. At home and in community-based activities, youngsters learn to display knowledge, consider its relevance for action, and challenge the ideas of others in gradually molded acceptable verbal forms.

Hence, without explicit teaching about the need to approach information from others conditionally, mainstream children learn in their everyday worlds acceptable ways to express their skepticism about what others tell them regarding areas over which they as children can claim expertise. They learn to weigh information from others against their own experiences. But these children learn more than this on their way to becoming critical thinkers; they learn to think about how they will argue their position with more evidence than just their own previous experiences. They learn that they must separate their experience from the proposition or general principle they wish to maintain; and they must, more often than not, structure their argument while in the midst of receiving information from others. Mainstream, literate-oriented families prepare their children to disengage from their own experience to attend to general argumentative principles by modeling talk about the language of argument within households (e.g., "But that doesn't make sense. You just said X. You can't now say Y!"). Moreover, a central ideal of mainstream homes—"don't get so involved that you can't stand back and look at what's going on"—is frequently voiced, if not consistently followed. Early involvement by mainstream youngsters in community organizations gives extended opportunities for their participation in discussions that focus not only on decisions but also on decision making. Mainstream organizations for youth pride themselves in providing opportunities for youngsters to "have their say" and be heard by their fellow team or club members (Heath & McLaughlin, 1987).

These redundant, repetitive, and multiply reinforced ways of socializing mainstream children as individual knowers and verbal contestants provide the bedrock discourse forms that sustain what schools define as critical thinking. The irony is that those who can practice them in school, more often than not, have to *learn* them outside school—through family and community life. Opportunities to practice them within schools come most frequently in advanced academic classes or in extracurricular activities of schools. The building blocks of such thinking as applied to reading and writing include questions that pinpoint reasons of evaluation or aesthetic judgment, brief narratives of evidence punctuated by counterassertions, and recasts in outline form or logical equation of prior arguments against those immediately at hand. The end-of-chapter questions that depend on this kind of thinking occur most frequently in upper-level textbooks or in the extra-credit sections of teachers' manuals. Demonstrating this kind of thinking takes considerable oral participation as preparation for written displays; moreover, performances of critical thinking do not fall into predictable patterns. Thus it is the rare classroom questioning session or standardized or criterion-referenced test that can accommodate more than a minimal display of critical thinking (Langer & Applebee, 1987; Smith, Meux, Coombs, Nuthall, & Precians, 1967; Cazden, 1988).

Clearly the language socialization of children who receive from their home and community life sustained reinforcement for demonstrating critical thinking and for responding to information with a literate orientation differs from that of nonmainstream groups. Many such groups carry marked ethnic, racial, and linguistic identities; have limited participation in the full range of professional and occupational roles of society; and are overly represented among the urban and rural poor of the United States. Moreover, numerous cultural features of their lives can work against their children learning in their language socialization the fundamentals of critical thinking outlined above. For example, many sociocultural groups traditionally orient their young to group membership and adherence to age and gender roles rather than to individual status. Community-valued institutions, such as the church, may underscore age and gender roles, as well as particular or literal readings of written materials. Any interpretation that sets up the views of the individual against those of the group or of those in authority may be widely discouraged or even punished.

Some communities may value an argumentative stance or challenging pose only for males and place a high value on metaphoric, highly rhetorical verbal combat (Baugh, 1983; Smitherman, 1977). Some groups may reinforce combative, individualistic verbal performance, but only of a restricted range of genres, such as songs in which the singer casts his words into those of a character who debates the adversary. Clearly, not all cultures identify one particular kind of thinking that members label "critical thinking"; and indeed, many sociocultural groups would not include "thinking" as a phenomenon to be discussed as an activity unto itself.

Hence it is clear that students from many minority communities will be at a disadvantage in classrooms and on certain types of tasks that expect their thinking, as demonstrated through oral and written language, to bear certain characteristics. As the research on cooperative learning has clearly demonstrated, some cultural groups place much higher value on learning in groups and the downplaying of individual displays of knowledge than other groups (Kagan, 1986; Slavin, 1983).

SOCIOCULTURAL VARIETY
IN LANGUAGE SOCIALIZATION

What are some specific examples of ways that nonmainstream cultures within the United States socialize their children to thinking, learning, and using spoken and written language? Are there initially some broad areas of contrast that could make a difference in the orientation of youngsters to the ways that schools prescribe and value language and thinking?

Generalizations most helpful to educators who ask these questions contrast specifically the orientations of certain nonmainstream groups to definitions or activities that are highly valued by schools. In the section above, we laid out some major criteria for demonstrating critical thinking that exist within school materials and programs. Here it may be useful to summarize briefly the kinds of language displays most prominently featured in schools as evidence of appropriate learning from reading and writing (Applebee, 1981; Cazden, 1988; Goodlad, 1984).

The major forms for the display of information and skills in academic performance consist of *labels* and *recounts*. Schools expect students to know how to do the following with language:

1.   Use language to label and describe objects, events, and information that nonintimates present them. The most common form of request for such labels and description is the *known-information question*, one for which the teacher already knows the answer ("Can you tell me the name of the most important battle of the American Revolution?" "Who is the central character in this story?").
2.   Recount or recast past events or information shared with or given by nonintimates in a predictable order and format. Teachers ask for such recounts by questions ("Where have we seen this before?" "What did we read the other day in the chapter on transportation?") and shape answers and their order to fit their prior expectations ("Wait, don't get to the point too fast. Isn't there something else in there that led to that outcome?").

In addition, students should know how to follow directions from oral and written sources without sustained personal reinforcement. They should also know the language of "common courtesy" in sustaining harmonious social interactions; teachers have classroom management rules for talk (e.g., only one person talks at a time; no interrupting), as well as space and property control to reinforce their expected norms for individuals ("Peter, if you want to use the stapler, you must ask." "Lauren, don't stand in front of Roberto when I'm trying to talk to him").

Reading abilities extend beyond the recall of labels and the shaping of recounts to the acceptance of information from written sources as prime for transfer to other situations; information gained in a unit on economic depression in the nineteenth century should transfer to an understanding of the Great Depression in the United States in the 1930s. In other words, students should know how to request and to clarify information as they move information across areas of study. They should view such information as extending beyond the authority of one particular person or specific occasion to similar situations and general use (e.g., "Remember the other day when we read in the science book about the invention of the cotton gin? What did that mean for the economy of the South?").

As students advance to higher-order tasks and higher grade levels or move into honors classes, they are expected to use language to display their merging of book knowledge with both their own experience and through particular analytical perspectives. Thus they show evidence that they can create new information, integrate ideas in innovative ways, and evaluate or analyze knowledge gained from books. Teachers expect students to accomplish such integration as individuals, with relatively little small-group interaction to test and develop ideas orally. Students write their book reports, term papers, or research papers as individuals, just as they take their tests as solo performers.

Within many nonmainstream groups of the United States, these academic uses of language fly in the face of everyday behaviors. For example, among black and Mexican-origin working-class communities, the following features of language use predominate (Heath, 1983, 1985, 1986; Slaughter, 1989):

1. Children learn the names and features of objects, events, or situations in the day-to-day process of interactions and not in "lessoned" contexts or through specific queries from adults.
2. Questions adults ask of children are more frequently yes-no questions or playful and teasing queries than requests for recounts of information already known to adults.
3. Narratives or stories stress persons as actors and the quality of events. Most narratives are jointly created by several speakers with frequent interruptions, overlap of turns at talk, and embellishment of details.

Though black and Mexican-origin working-class communities differ widely on many other features of language use (such as gender expectations related to talk and characteristics of talk that are more highly valued than others), both groups share these three features of language use. In addition, both groups place primary reliance on teaching by demonstration and apprenticeship in both home and community learning, with oral language support for evaluation of performers rather than performance. Children learn by watching and participating in appropriately assigned sociocultural roles. Adults learn new tasks demanded by the incorporation of new artifacts or the intrusion of additional bureaucratic institutions in their lives through dependence on group-nominated mediators, known for their abilities to perform in such situations. Adults expect talents to be differentially distributed across the community. All community members need not learn to do all tasks equally well, so long as they remain group members and can rely on mediators of various sorts within the group.

Moreover, members of these groups share two other features of social organization. They place high value on within-group reliance, which often leads to avoidance of extensive excursions into sustained participation in mainstream institutions. They thus cut themselves off from intense involvement in institutions such as the school or in other mainstream occupational groups that often repeat and reinforce, as well as rely on, many school-taught practices. These self-protective behaviors, in turn, contribute to group histories of powerlessness relative to surrounding groups that dominate through control of capital and access to certain types of socioeconomic or political participation. Moreover, these and other nonmainstream groups depend far more on a sense of identity as a member of a group or within a particular age- or gender-determined role than on a sense of being literate—of being an individual with access to sources of information and practiced ways of thinking and reasoning.[3]

A RESEARCH AND TEACHER EDUCATION AGENDA

The cognitive and behavioristic theories that have dominated the Western psychology of learning and thinking, and especially their approaches to the teaching of reading and writing, have kept researchers from focusing on the cultural and historical contexts in which individuals of different societies learn. These theories have related concepts or structures to individuals by outlining formal characteristics or steps in thinking processes instead of considering the cultural and historical world of the thinker and the thinking subject as continuous. Table 1.2 summarizes the essential differences between these two approaches to thinking.

The cultural-historical tradition draws primarily from the work of historians, anthropologists, and psychologists pursuing a sociocultural approach to mind (principally within the formulations set out by Soviet psychologist L. S. Vygotsky). Studies of patterns of learning among groups around the world have documented something of the range of human possibilities for cultural and linguistic expression. No sociocultural group demonstrates all the behaviors or values that lie within human capabilities; thus each group will in some ways be deficient in, or even exhibit a total absence of, certain forms of cultural and linguistic habits that other groups may exhibit. Under conditions in which members of one group judge it necessary or desirable to learn the habits of another, they can certainly do so. Yet all sociocultural groups will not find it equally easy to adopt new habits, and some habits will be less accessible and more difficult to learn than others for particular groups. For groups that have left few if any written records, ethnohistorians complement the ethnographic work of cultural anthropologists to give us descriptions of the current patterns of learning among bands, tribes, marginal or migrant communities, and nonmainstream sectors of nations around the world. For those groups whose past has been partially preserved in written records, social historians analyze these documents, as well as other artifactual evidence, to write of the evolution of those groups for whom writing and reading have been integral to their power within their community or nation (for a review of three generations of this historical work, see Graff, 1987; 1988).

Such work allows us to identify the socialization habits of various groups whose approaches to learning and displaying knowledge differ from those of mainstream institutions, such as the school. However, in the contemporary era in modern complex nations, anthropologists have an especially difficult and sensitive task when they set out to identify such features of nonmainstream groups. Attitudinal and behavioral characteristics that support socialization habits lie deeply embedded in private practices that are not open to scrutiny by the public. When nonmainstreamers work within mainstream institutions, they have to learn to function without drawing attention to them-

TABLE 1.2   The Cultural-Historical and the Cognitive-Behaviorist
Approaches to Thinking

THE CULTURAL-HISTORICAL TRADITION	THE COGNITIVE-BEHAVIORIST TRADITION
1. The point of departure for study is the content of thinking.	The point of departure for study is the function / structure of thinking.
2. Thinking is seen as an activity that includes motivation, action, and emotion, all of which have to be studied as a whole.	Thinking is studied as a separate function of the subject divided from other functions, where motivation is seen as a source outside the content of thinking.
3. There is no conceptualized border between the world to be thought of and the thinking subject because the content is in the objective world but only receives status through the thinking process of the individual.	The subject is conceptually separated from the world so that thinking has to be related to the impressions that the individual receives of the world.
4. There is a distinction between two types of thinking: Empirical and theoretical thinking. Theoretical thinking is based upon the inner determining relations of objects. Empirical thinking is based on common attributes. The relation between these two modes of thinking is that empirical thinking precedes theoretical thinking in development. Through the process of teaching, the child acquires theoretical thinking and this type of thinking then dominates empirical thinking.	There is a distinction between convergent and divergent thinking. Divergent thinking is a form of fantasizing. The main characteristic of convergent thinking is its goal orientation and its logical character operating with the common traits of objects. The relation between these two modes of thinking is that convergent thinking in the child's development gradually becomes the dominant mode of thinking, perhaps with divergent thinking as a phase in the thinking process.
5. The concepts of thinking have the social and historical genesis of the objects as their preliminaries.	The concepts of thinking have sensoric aspects of the world as preliminaries.
6. Schooling is seen as the necessary condition for the development of theoretical thinking. Teaching is seen as a necessity for guidance into the essentials of a scientific area.	Schooling develops convergent thinking (empirical thinking). Teaching is seen as a means that can give the pupil the knowledge for his own discovering activities in relation to the subject area.
7. The goals of teaching are to give the pupil models of the objects of the scientific area taught and a method so that the child can move inside these models.	The goals of teaching are to give the pupil the facts of the scientific area and to develop his thinking so that it can be characterized by the rules of logic.
8. The development of thinking in the child is one side of the coin; the child's acquisition of the concepts of society is the other. So, concept acquisition and development of thinking is the same process where inner contradictions in the content of the concepts determine development.	Development of thinking is seen as stage-specific, either characterized by differences in structure or by differences in representational modes, where structural or functional conflicts determine development.

continued

TABLE 1.2   (*continued*)

THE CULTURAL-HISTORICAL TRADITION	THE COGNITIVE-BEHAVIORIST TRADITION
9. The essence of the concept is explored in a uniting object-system by analyzing the content of the system. The function of the concepts is to find new aspects of the objects so that the relation between the objects in the system can be explained.	The concepts are related to each other in a hierarchical way, where sensual aspects are always the primaries for concepts on an abstract level. The sole function of the concept is classification, so that the individual can have an unambiguous system regarding the world around him.
10. The concepts of an object-system have to be related to the history and the development of the scientific area. A scientific area is a system in change because science is renewed as a system in relation to the development of society. The characterization of science is at the same time the main characteristic of thinking as an activity of the individual.	The hierarchical organization of a concept is related to the Aristotelian rules of logic. And science is seen as one-dimensional in its development, without any relation in content to the development of society.

Note: From "Two Approaches to Thinking and Knowledge Acquisition," by M. Hedegaard (1986). *Quarterly Newsletter of the Laboratory of Comparative Human Cognition, 8,* 7, p. 60. Reprinted by permission.

selves. Moreover, a faith in economic and social rewards motivates individuals to assimilate rapidly to those behavioral norms that are easily identifiable as marking mainstream membership. As they do so, specific habits that nonmainstreamers may regard as marking the boundaries of their group from others become more private and take place during rites that express common history and religious intensification. Thus, in place of overt boundary markers that distinguish those minority sociocultural groups from each other and from the mainstream in the United States or other culturally plural nations, anthropologists must describe instead their degrees of integration into the economic, political, and social life of the mainstream.

Only with long-term participant observation can anthropologists study the primary-group socialization practices through which these groups enculturate their young, and minority groups carefully protect themselves against outsiders' access to the intimate daily affairs of their families and community institutions (Heath, 1989). The goal of accounts of participant observers must be to identify features that are present in the daily life of these groups and not to report that a particular group does *not* do or have X. Such reporting implies that X is the expected norm, and the group should therefore exhibit such a behavior or have such an artifact.

Through descriptions of degrees of integration to the values and habits of mainstream institutions as well as detailed accounts of deep-seated socialization and intensification practices, anthropologists can, along with historians, provide data for comparative analyses. Such analyses allow the extraction of those ways of believing, behaving, and using language that most frequently occur within these groups. This knowledge, set against clear descriptions of the daily habits of classrooms, such as critical thinking, extended literacy, and argumentative discourse, can illustrate some hint of the range of ways that humans define, display, and evaluate information in coordination with their communities' different ways of distributing roles and status (e.g., Ochs, 1988).

All such studies underline the fact that different ways of assessing and displaying knowledge come with different ways of learning to talk. As young children learn the sounds and grammatical combinations of their mother tongue, they learn also how to package or classify what they perceive and feel (Schieffelin & Ochs, 1986a; Ochs & Schieffelin, 1984). Middle-class mainstream families of communities in which most children go to school prepare their young children for the special ways of using language that the school rewards. Parents simplify their language into baby talk, giving special intonation and unique vocabulary items in their talk to children. Adults ask children questions that focus their attention on labels, require that they learn to say what they mean, and insist on the recounting of shared and known knowledge in prescribed ways. Adults expect children to retell real events in chronological order; fanciful alterations and additions have to be announced as stories. Gradually as children grow older, through their experiences with books, they learn to separate the knowledge of books from real-world experiences; the illustrations and antics of pigs in storybooks bear little relation to the real animals raised for slaughterhouses. Children learn also to offer accounts of their own experiences and to fashion such information in ways that are organized to allow the listener to predict the structure of the telling if not the content (Cochran-Smith, 1984; Heath, 1983; Taylor, 1983; Teale & Sulzby, 1986).

Yet not in all cultural groups do children learn language in ways that prepare them for the particular uses of language that formal instruction rewards. In many societies, peers and older siblings have primary care-giving responsibilities; no specially constructed baby talk is reserved for infants (Heath, 1983). For example, in numerous agricultural communities within the United States and elsewhere, children as young as 3 years of age join their siblings in their daily activities. Children learn labels in the midst of their functional involvement with what they represent. Debates about the meaning of what has been said center first on instrumental goals: obtaining food and accomplishing tasks. Flights of imagination and accounts of one's individual experiences come in oral forms, with no storied tales or expositions from books to model their structures. Yet the first years of schooling break these patterns of using language for functional purposes and instead present "lesson" language.

These differences in learning to use language in the preschool years spring from different perceptions of the roles parents and children have to play and the means of physical sustenance (Ochs & Schieffelin, 1984). In addition, these values are subject to considerable influence from institutions beyond the family, such as the church, voluntary associations (e.g., Boy Scouts, soccer clubs, gangs), and mercantile and administrative interests representing centers of power beyond the local community (Heath, 1985, 1986). Such organizations include oral and written language uses that complement those of the school: special names, predesignated meanings, uniform interpretations, and recitation around a written text in a standard dialect or language.

A considerable amount of historical evidence points to the creative potential of giving readers and writers expanded opportunities to interpret texts orally and to negotiate their meanings in communal settings. In addition, as the end of the twentieth century nears, an increasing proportion of business leaders are calling for collaborative learning and improved approaches to learning and transmitting knowledge in the workplace. Support for the benefits of sharing knowledge, promoting oral exchange of information, and placing a premium on learning by observation, apprenticing, and reciprocal teaching comes also from researchers in cognitive science.

In the 1980s surveys of employers across a wide variety of businesses and industries indicated that expectations of what workers should be able to do have changed with the rapid growth of service-oriented jobs and with the increased role of computers in communication and information production. Employers want workers who know how to learn and are "well-grounded in fundamental knowledge and who have mastered concepts and skills that create an intellectual framework to which new knowledge can be added" (National Academy, 1984, p. 17). Individuals should be able to draw inferences from a variety of types of information (written and oral), to understand and transmit instructions, to develop alternatives and reach conclusions, and to "express their ideas intelligibly and effectively." These skills are adequate for entry-level work, but advancement in many organizations depends on the ability to compose tables and reports, consult source materials, handle mathematical concepts, control complex equipment, and address groups. What many employers now expect of computers—multifunctional and interactive capacities—they also expect of humans in the workplace. Collaborative problem identification and solution depends on rapid information exchange, creativity, and risk taking. Researchers from within industry and technology point out that the full advantage of technology comes only with closer attention to the social dimensions of communication, idea building, and problem solving (Blomberg, 1987).

Cognitive scientists began to join with anthropologists in the 1970s to study forms of social participation that have positive effects on reasoning and that redistribute knowledge through a group involved in collaboration (Doise & Mugny, 1984). In dyads or groups, individuals learn metacognitive strategies through participating in situations that promote reflecting on past performance, taking turns leading a dialogue based on a text, and reviewing past group performances with other members (Palinscar & Brown, 1984; Scardamalia, Bereiter, & Steinbach, 1984). Research has shown the power of using examples as points of reflection and in analogical reasoning; and cognitive scientists and linguists continue to point out ways in which conversation works to build shared references, to convey alternative logics in argumentation, and to support conclusions (Wertsch, 1985).

The paradox is that much that surrounds language and learning in schools works against students' developing and expanding the kinds of communicative and collaborative skills that a growing number of workplaces demand and that research on cognition suggests have strong potential. The insistence of schools on individualizing literacy and on making displays of critical thinking proceed along predictable routes has ignored traditional oral habits and an alternative sense of identity from minority group members. Ironically, many of these traditional minority patterns now match the demands and needs of employers in the late twentieth century far better than those of most classrooms. Businesses value reciprocal teaching, in which learners exchange and create information; new learners in many occupations, ranging from bricklayers to file clerks and junior executives, go through a brief period of apprenticeship with others before assuming full responsibility for their tasks. Labels and features of situations, objects, and types of encounters come through observing, listening, and hearing anecdotes or illustrations from others far more frequently than through lists of labels and calls for recounts of given information (Barbee, 1986; Mikulecky, 1982; Mikulecky & Winchester, 1983; Mikulecky & Ehlinger, 1986). The adaptability, keen interpretive talents, and group collaboration natural to many minority groups within the United States work against their school success; yet these characteristics better match some criteria that employers view as desirable than do work patterns and habits of language and learning that the schools value.

The challenge in research and teacher education is twofold: (1) to learn more about alternative and expanded genres of language and patterns of learning across cultures and situations; and (2) to enable teachers to observe, analyze, and consider the implications of alternative ways of learning and displaying knowledge in classrooms. Thousands of studies of classrooms have described language and learning there—especially conditions surrounding the teaching of reading and writing. Very few studies have described in detail the language and learning of low-income minority children of color. Such studies could tell us much about specific alternative language habits and situations of learning; we could then add these to the repertoire of language habits and ways of learning that have been documented within cognitive-behaviorist traditions that focused on the individual—and primarily on subjects drawn from mainstream middle-class communities.

We need to know more about alternative ways of learning and of using language in order to *add* these ways to those already valued in the classroom. The goal is *not* to use this knowledge about minorities' ways of using language and habits of learning to tailor classrooms to fit the daily habits of each minority group. Instead, schools must be able to incorporate some of these additional ways in order to facilitate learning about learning by *all* students. Moreover, studies that point out cross-cultural differences in behaviors fundamental to schooling—such as language use, habits of critical thinking, concepts of time and space, gender relations, and valuations of written information—should serve primarily as evidence that the language and thought skills valued by the school do not come naturally with developmental growth. John Dewey noted that reflective thinking is not an innate capacity but a learned ability. Students who can participate in a range of opportunities for different types of learning—multiple intelligences (Gardner, 1983; Sternberg, 1985)—will have the chance to adapt their learning habits to future needs and conditions.

Teachers must, however, also participate in learning through a variety of ways and must be allowed in their own professional education to display learning in ways other than short answers, standardized tests, and brief essays. Future teachers need opportunities in their education to observe quality teachers who exhibit a variety of teaching and learning styles. They need to learn to record what they see; to check their observations with teacher and students; and to consider the match among their observations, other teachers' perceptions, and student views of the learning and teaching taking place. Beyond such observations and analyses of situations of learning, future teachers should be encouraged to develop abilities to observe themselves and to record what is happening in their classrooms (Atwell, 1987; Goswami & Stillman, 1987; Newkirk & Atwell, 1988). By intuitive direction, many teachers continuously reassess conditions for learning in their classroom and use these data to make decisions on matters ranging from desk arrangement to types of reading assigned. Teachers engage in trying to explain what is happening in their classrooms; and in order to explain, they continuously seek out more phenomena that will shed light on patterns and deviations in events (Duckworth, 1987).

In addition, teacher education must instill a reward system based on collaborative learning through reading, talking, and writing among teachers. Currently, teachers are isolated within their classrooms, with little opportunity to talk about their solo efforts to learn; consequently, their own conditions for learning mirror those they provide their students. Teachers, like their students, learn to fear cooperation with each other because of insecurities about evaluation. If teachers are to equip their students to go beyond receiving knowledge to critiquing and creating it, they must be able to model such behaviors. Accomplished modeling comes only after opportunities to play meaningful roles in collaborative learning over a long period of time. As teachers learn from and with each other, they can gain confidence in identifying problems, as well as solving them.

Teachers whose education has enabled them to work in collaborative learning have some incentive to strip away outmoded terms for describing students and labels that fix and stabilize knowledge. They can rearrange practices, revise expectations in the light of altered contexts for learning, and throw away routinized predictors. Teachers can replace these with a spirit of intuition and intuitive knowledge gained from observing, recording, and reflecting on evidence from their own classrooms and from their own learning.

The special challenge within the United States at the end of the twentieth century is the diversity of nonmainstream learners within classrooms, as well as the clear signals from the economy that new ways of expanding production are needed. Throughout much of the history of U.S. schooling, educators have been fearful of the diversity of human potential played out in different sociocultural and language minority communities. Educators and the public's idea of what schools should do to increase literacy have not admitted the widened range of habits of displaying knowledge and conceiving of mind that characterize being literate. We must find the incentive to reexamine traditional positions on the issues of direction, rate, agent, substance, and identity in learning.

It has been the continued learning and creating of opportunities to expand with others what one has read through talk, action, and reflection that has formed the core of the sense of being literate since the classical era of Greek civilization. It is this separate sense that the poet Wallace Stevens speaks of as providing the harmony that builds and ebbs, that is and is not. Being literate enables individuals to work on problems never before seen, demonstrate contemplation, and entice apprentices. It is the sense of being literate that enables teachers and students to stop thinking about learning and to think learning instead.

NOTES

1. Though discussions of being critical, critical writing, and engaging in criticism (especially literary) sometimes include informal references to critical thinking, the discussion here considers only those writings that have used this term to apply to a specialized type of thinking related to the hierarchical ordering of concepts and Aristotelian rules of logic. The term "critical thinking" appears for the first time as a separate entry in Volume 19 of *Education Index* (1968–1969). A subentry for appraisal of the Watson-Glazer Critical Thinking Tests, devised in 1940 and revised periodically, appears first in Volume 20 (1969–1970). Programs to teach critical thinking and discussions of its value have come most frequently from English and language arts teachers since the term first appeared in *Education Index*; social studies teachers constitute the second largest subject group. It is useful to compare educators' use of the term with that of humanists, who most often equate it with creative or inventive thinking—going "beyond what has been thought, said, done before . . ." (Commission on the Humanities, 1980, p. 31). Educators do not, in general, equate either inventive thinking or literary and other artistic criticism with logical, reflective, or critical thinking. Instead they tend to link critical thinking with problem-solving heuristics that characterize science (e.g., Scriven, 1976, and pedagogical programs elaborated in a special issue of *Educational Leadership* published in 1984).
2. A review of the links between writing and reading and the development of "straight," or "clear," thinking in early American education appears in Heath (1982). For a twentieth-century version of these links, see Beardsley (1950). Since the 1970s, the trend of English educators to tie their field to the teaching of critical thinking has been particularly evident; see, for example, Aronowitz (1977); D'Angelo (1970, 1971); George (1984); Grinols (1984); Madison (1971); Olson (1984); Petrosky (1982). Between 1969 and 1986, approximately one-third of all bibliographic entries under "critical thinking" in *Education Index* refer to publications that treat the teaching of reading and/or writing. This view is turned upside down when the emphasis is placed on the power of belief; Elbow (1986) urges writers to set critical thinking against methodological belief in order to learn to embrace the contraries that mark the sort of understanding that leads to creative transfer of concepts and skills.
3. The philosopher Walter Benjamin, in his essay, "The Storyteller," talks of the demise of storytelling and the communicability of experience. The rise of the middle class and the progress of modern journalism have led to the preference for information that can lay claim to immediate verifiability and can be

understood without any context or history beyond itself. Benjamin writes ". . . no event any longer comes to us without already being shot through with explanation. In other words, by now almost nothing that happens benefits storytelling; almost everything benefits information" (Benjamin, 1969, 89).

REFERENCES

Applebee, A. (1974). *Tradition and reform in the teaching of English: A history.* Urbana, IL: National Council of Teachers of English.

Applebee, A. (1981). *Writing in the secondary school: English and the content areas.* Urbana, IL: National Council of Teachers of English.

Arnove, R. F., & Graff, H. J. (Eds.). (1987). *National literacy campaigns: Historical and comparative perspectives.* New York: Plenum.

Aronowitz, S. (1977). Mass culture and the eclipse of reason: The implications for pedagogy. *College English,* 38, 768–774.

Atwell, N. (1987). *In the middle: Writing, reading, and learning with adolescents.* Portsmouth, NH: Boynton/ Cook Heinemann.

Barbee, D. E. (1986). *Methods of providing vocational skills to individuals with low literacy levels: The U.S. experience.* Geneva: International Labour Office.

Barell, J. (1983). Reflections on critical thinking in secondary schools. *Educational Leadership, 40,* 45–49.

Baugh, J. (1983). *Black street speech: Its history, structure, and survival.* Austin: University of Texas Press.

Beardsley, M. C. (1950). *Thinking straight: A guide for readers and writers.* New York: Prentice-Hall.

Bellah, R. N., Madsen, R., Sullivan, W. M., Swidler, A., & Tipton, S. M. (1985). *Habits of the heart: Individualism and commitment in American life.* New York: Harper & Row.

Benjamin, W. (1969). *Illuminations.* New York: Schocken Books.

Beyer, B. K. (1985). Critical thinking: What is it? *Social Education, 49* (4), 270–276.

Blomberg, J. (1987). Social interaction and office communication: Effects on user's evaluation of new technologies. In R. E. Kraut (Ed.), *Technology and the transformation of white-collar work.* Hillsdale, NJ: Erlbaum.

Boyer, P. (1978). *Urban masses and moral order in America: 1820–1920.* Cambridge, MA: Harvard University Press.

Carnegie Forum on Education and the Economy. (1986). *A nation prepared: Teachers for the 21st century.* New York: Author.

Cazden, C. B. (1988). *Classroom discourse: The language of teaching and learning.* Portsmouth, NH: Heinemann.

Clanchy, M. T. (1979). *From memory to written record: English, 1066–1307.* Cambridge, MA: Harvard University Press.

Cochran-Smith, M. (1984). *The making of a reader.* Norwood, NJ: Ablex.

Commission on the Humanities. (1980). *The humanities in American life.* Berkeley: University of California Press.

Cremin, L. A. (1970). *American education: The colonial experience 1607–1783.* New York: Harper & Row.

Cressy, D. (1980). *Literacy and the social order.* Cambridge, Eng.: Cambridge University Press.

D'Angelo, E. (1970). The teaching of critical thinking through literature. *Elementary English, 47,* 633–637.

D'Angelo, E. (1971). *The teaching of critical thinking.* Amsterdam: Gruner.

Darnton, R. (1984). *The great cat massacre and other episodes in French cultural history.* New York: Basic Books.

Davis, N. Z. (1965). *Society and culture in early modern France.* Stanford, CA: Stanford University Press.

Dewey, J. (1916). *Democracy and education.* New York: Macmillan.

Dobson, E. J. (1968). *English pronunciation, 1500–1700. Vol. 1, Survey of the sources* (2nd ed.). Oxford, Eng.: Clarendon Press.

Doise, W., & Mugny, G. (1984). *The social development of the intellect.* Oxford, Eng.: Pergamon Press.

Duckworth, E. (1987). *"The having of wonderful ideas" and other essays on teaching and learning.* New York: Teachers College Press.

Elbow, P. (1986). *Embracing contraries: Explorations in learning and teaching.* New York: Oxford University Press.

Eliot, C. W. (1892). Wherein popular education has failed. *Forum, 14,* 425–426.

Eisenstein, E. (1979). *The printing press as an agent of change* (2 vols.). Cambridge, Eng.: Cambridge University Press.

Ennis, R. H. (1962). A concept of critical thinking: A proposed basis for research in the teaching and evaluation of critical thinking ability. *Harvard Educational Review, 32*(1), 81–111.

Experimental World Literacy Program. (1973). *Practical guide to functional literacy.* Paris: UNESCO.

Freire, P., & Macedo, D. (1987). *Literacy: Reading the word and the world.* South Hadley, MA: Bergin & Garvey.

Gardner, H. (1983). *Frames of mind: The theory of multiple intelligences*. New York: Basic Books.

George, D. (1984). Creating contexts: Using the research paper to teach critical thinking. *English Journal, 73*, 27–32.

Ginzburg, C. (1976). *The cheese and the worms: The cosmos of a sixteenth-century miller*. Harmondsworth, Eng.: Penguin.

Goodlad, J. (1984). *A place called school: Prospects for the future*. New York: McGraw-Hill.

Goody, J. (1987). *Interface of literacy and the oral word*. Cambridge, Eng.: Cambridge University Press.

Goswami, D., & Stillman, P. R. (Eds.). (1987). *Reclaiming the classroom: Teacher research as an agency for change*. Upper Montclair, NJ: Boynton/Cook.

Graff, H. J. (1987). *The legacies of literacy*. Bloomington: Indiana University Press.

Graff, H. J. (1988). Whither the history of literacy? The future of the past. *Communication, 11*, 5–22.

Grinols, A. B. (1984). *Critical thinking: Reading across the curriculum*. Ithaca, NY: Cornell University Press.

Hayes, A. S. (Ed.). (1965). *Recommendations of the Work Conference on Literacy held for the Agency for International Development*. Washington, DC: Center for Applied Linguistics.

Heath, S. B. (1982). Toward an ethnohistory of writing in American education. In M. F. Whiteman (Ed.), *Writing: The nature, development, and teaching of written communication. Vol. 1, Variation in Writing: Functional and linguistic-cultural differences*. Hillsdale, NJ: Erlbaum.

Heath, S. B. (1983). *Ways with words: Language, life, and work in communities and classrooms*. Cambridge, Eng.: Cambridge University Press.

Heath, S. B. (1985). Language policies: Patterns of retention and maintenance. In W. Connor (Ed.), *Mexican-Americans in comparative perspective*. Washington, DC: Urban Institute.

Heath, S. B. (1986). Sociocultural contexts of language development. In *Beyond language: Social and cultural factors in schooling language minority students*. Sacramento: Bilingual Education Office, California State Department of Education.

Heath, S. B. (1989). Oral and literate traditions among black Americans living in poverty. *American Psychologist, 44*(2), 367–379.

Heath, S. B. (1989). Talking the text in teaching composition. In S. deCastell, A. Luke, and C. Luke (Eds.), *Language, authority, and criticism: Readings on the school textbook*. London: Falmer Press.

Heath, S. B., & McLaughlin, M. W. (1987). A child resource policy: Moving beyond dependence on school and family. *Phi Delta Kappan*, April, pp. 576–580.

Hedegaard, M. (1986). Two approaches to thinking and knowledge acquisition. *Quarterly Newsletter of the Laboratory of Comparative Human Cognition, 8*(2), 58–63.

Hoskin, K. (1982). Examinations and the schooling of science. In R. MacLeod (Ed.), *Days of judgment*. London: Nafferton Books.

Jones, R. F. (1953). *The triumph of the English language*. Stanford, CA: Stanford University Press.

Kaestle, C. (1985). The history of literacy and the history of readers. *Review of Research in Education, 12*, 11–53.

Kagan, S. (1986). Cooperative learning and sociocultural factors in schooling. In *Beyond language: Social and cultural factors in schooling language minority students*. Sacramento: Bilingual Education Office, California State Department of Education.

Langer, J. A., & Applebee, A. N. (1987). *How writing shapes thinking: A study of teaching and learning*. NCTE Research Report No. 22. Urbana, IL: National Council of Teachers of English.

McPeck, J. E. (1981). *Critical thinking and education*. New York: St. Martin's Press.

Madison, J. P. (1971). Critical thinking in the English classroom. *English Journal, 60*(8), 1133–1140, 1144.

Mikulecky, L. (1982). Job literacy: The relationship between school preparation and workplace actuality. *Reading Research Quarterly, 17*, 400–419.

Mikulecky, L., & Ehlinger, J. (1986). The influence of metacognitive aspects of literacy on job performance of electronics technicians. *Journal of Reading Behavior, 18*, 41–62.

Mikulecky, L., & Winchester, D. (1983). Job literacy and job performance among nurses at varying employment levels. *Adult Education Quarterly, 34*, 1–15.

Miller, G. (1988). The challenge of universal literacy. *Science, 241*, 1293–1299.

Myers, G. (1986). Reality, consensus, and reform in the rhetoric of composition teaching. *College English, 48*, 154–174.

National Academy of Sciences. (1984). *High schools and the changing workplace: The employers' view*. Washington, DC: National Academy Press.

Newkirk, T., & Atwell, N. (Eds.). (1988). *Understanding writing: Ways of observing, learning, and teaching K-8* (2nd ed.). Portsmouth, NH: Heinemann.

Ochs, E. (1988). *Culture and language development: Language acquisition and language socialization in a Samoan village*. Cambridge, Eng.: Cambridge University Press.

Ochs, E., & Schieffelin, B. (1984). Three developmental stories and their implications. In R. A. Shweder & R. A. Levine (Eds.), *Culture theory: Essays on mind, self, and emotion*. New York: Cambridge University Press.

Olson, C. B. (1984). Fostering critical thinking skills through writing. *Educational Leadership, 42*, 28–39.

Ong, W. (1983). Literacy and orality in our times. In W. B. Horner (Ed.), *Composition & literature: Bridging the gap*. Chicago: University of Chicago Press.

Oxenham, J. (1980). *Literacy: Writing, reading, and social organization*. London: Routledge & Kegan Paul.

Palincsar, A. S., & Brown, A. L. (1984). Reciprocal teaching of comprehension-fostering and comprehension-monitoring activities. *Cognition and Instruction, 1*(2), 117–175.

Petrosky, A. R. (1982). Critical thinking and writing. *English Education, 14*, 3–46.

Piche, G. (1967). Revision and reform in the secondary school curriculum. Ph.D. dissertation, University of Minnesota.

Scardamalia, M., Bereiter, C., & Steinbach, R. (1984). Teachability of reflective processes in written composition. *Cognitive Science, 8*, 173–190.

Schieffelin, B. B., & Ochs, E. (Eds.). (1986a). *Language socialization across cultures*. Cambridge, Eng.: Cambridge University Press.

Schieffelin, B. B., & Ochs, E. (1986b). Language socialization. *Annual Review of Anthropology, 15*, 163–91.

Scriven, M. (1976). *Reasoning*. New York: McGraw-Hill.

Slaughter, D. T. (Ed.). (1989). *Black children and poverty*. San Francisco: Jossey-Bass.

Slavin, R. E. (1983). *Cooperative learning*. New York: Longman.

Smith, B. O., Meux, M., Coombs, J., Nuthall, G., & Precians, R. (1967). *A Study of the strategies of teaching*. Urbana, IL: College of Education [ERIC ED 029 165].

Smitherman, G. (1977). *Talkin' and testifyin': The language of black America*. Boston: Houghton Mifflin.

Sternberg. R. J. (1985). *Beyond IQ: A triarchic theory of human intelligence*. Cambridge, Eng.: Cambridge University Press.

Stevens, W. (1982). A primitive like an orb. *Wallace Stevens: The collected poems*. New York: Vintage.

Stewart, D. (1985). The status of composition and rhetoric in American colleges, 1880–1902: An MLA perspective. *College English, 47*, 734–746.

Stock, B. (1983). *Implications of literacy*. Cambridge, Eng.: Cambridge University Press.

Taylor, D. (1983). *Family literacy: Young children learning to read and write*. Exeter, NH: Heinemann.

Teale, W. H., & Sulzby, E. (Eds.). (1986). *Emergent literacy: Writing and reading*. Norwood, NJ: Ablex.

Watson, G., & Glazer, E. M. (1980). *Watson-Glazer Critical Thinking Appraisal*. New York: Harcourt, Brace & World.

Wertsch, J. V. (1985). *Culture, communication, and cognition*. Cambridge, Eng.: Cambridge University Press.

2 LITERACY AND SOCIETY WITH PARTICULAR REFERENCE TO THE NON-WESTERN WORLD

Philip Foster and Alan Purves

In the past several decades there has been an increasing interest in the relationship between predominantly oral cultures and those with substantial literacy. This concern has arisen within a variety of disciplines, most notably anthropology and psychology, although literary critics, rhetoricians, and linguists have also been involved. The reasons behind this interest are many, among them the decline in absolute number of nonliterate cultures; the rise of new "oral" technologies that have been seen to threaten the written culture; an atmosphere of neo-Rousseauian anti-imperialism that has called into question the colonizing of societies and the imposition on those cultures; and an increasing realization that the most revolutionary of human inventions was written—and particularly alphabetic—language.

Earlier anthropologists and linguists accepted the dictum that written language was simply transcribed speech. Rhetoric dealt in oral language and particularly formal presentations; when rhetoricians turned to writing, they tended to treat it in terms appropriate to oratory or drama. The same was true of linguists, particularly the structural linguists who followed de Saussure (1916) and Bloomfield (1933). It was not until the postwar era and the influence of some of the Prague linguists like Vachek (1973) that it became acceptable to see written language as having a set of structures and rules of its own, with few counterparts in oral discourse. This extreme view has itself been challenged (Tannen, 1982; Akinnaso, 1981, 1985).

Similarly, literary theorists came to the conclusion that many literary works had to be dealt with as written texts and should not be seen in the light of oral forms of discourse. The novel was the great testimony to the difference between oral and written literary art (Watt, 1957), but other forms such as the essay and the visual poem also defied the traditional approach (Wann, 1939).

As these changes in perception emerged, there also grew to be a realization that such inventions as telephone, radio, and, particularly, television, were changing the ways in which society acquired information and communicated (McLuhan, 1964). Some even saw written language as being on the way out; and its exit could be documented in ways that had not been true of its entrance. The scholarly community could chart a change and through it look at earlier changes that had brought written language into human history. They did so by turning to history and to anthropology, particularly the study of nonliterate cultures—if they could find them (Clifford, 1986).

The characterizations of the differences between oral and literate cultures have been several. One view was that the oral culture might be "traditional" or "savage" but not because of the lack of written language (Lévi-Strauss, 1966). Literacy was a concomitant of an emerging civilization but not a major constituent of the difference between the barbarian and the civilized. The work of such scholars as Innis (1951), Havelock (1976), and Goody (1977, 1986) in the past three decades, as well as the work of Ong (1982) and McLuhan (1962) on the effects of printing on the structure of human discourse, have called in question that earlier thinking and suggested that indeed oral and written cultures were quite distinct and that written language more than any other human invention transformed society from that of the hunter-gatherer to the agricultural and mercantile world that forms the basis of "civilization" (Murdock & Provost, 1980). It is difficult to assert that the invention of written language was the sole cause, of course, yet certainly it was one of the concomitants of the transformation, which is the subject of this chapter. In the first section, we shall outline the major features of the difference between oral and written cultures as these differences have come to be generalized across history and across the globe. In the second section, we will outline some of the ways in which the transformation has manifested itself in three autonomous cultures; and in the third, we will contrast the differences in this regard between autonomous and postcolonial societies.

ORAL AND LITERATE CULTURES

In her recent history of writing, Gaur (1985) begins by saying that all writing is information storage. In so saying, she makes a distinction crucial to an understanding of the distinction between oral and literate cultures: the distinction between *knowledge* (that which is retained within individual memory), and *information* (that which is external to memory but accessible to one or more individuals). Writing is, therefore, social; the amount of information is greater than can be retained by any one person or even a community (Scribner & Cole, 1981; Heath, 1983). This early information was usually commercial (Schmandt-Besserat, 1981) and concerned itself with prices and amounts of goods traded or transported, and the need arose at a time when the society moved from the individual and self-sufficient farm or the village to a more complex town society with specialized vocations and the movement of goods (Braudel, 1979). Thereafter other forms of information came to be included in written language, most of it public or commercial but some of it private and literary.

In these early societies, these arose a subgroup of writers and readers—*scribes*—who perfected and controlled the techniques of writing and the forms of written language (Gelb, 1963). They often controlled entry into their group and legitimated the standards and traditions of literate activity. The size of this group in relation to the total population has varied, but its role has remained in all literate societies; we call them by such names as tax consultants (Tornebohm, 1973).

Written language has allowed different forms of discourse and therewith different effects in shaping society. As Goody (1977) has observed, the advent of written language brought with it a variety of forms that were unknown or at least unwieldy in oral societies: the list, the table, and the recipe or prescription. Each of these allowed information to be stored in a palpable, ordered, and semipermanent form. Each allowed people recourse and access to storehouses of information that were not available to them earlier. These forms of writing allowed for the transcription of history as opposed to legend, law as opposed to tradition, and religion as opposed to cult. As Goody (1986) has proceeded to observe, written language allowed religions and secular states to spread and to maintain greater continuity from past to present. It is the fact of written language, for example, that allows for there to be laws and therefore arguments concerning original intent in discussing the United States Constitution and that allows for there to be scripture and therefore religious fundamentalism in the Christian and Muslim worlds (Purves & Purves, 1986). The ramifications of written language occur within the commercial, political, and religious worlds; and they have helped create and perpetuate the modern state, as well as mercantilism (if not capitalism) and theocracy (Wagner, 1987). There is some controversy as to whether it was the advent of the printing press that enhanced the rise of the modern world as much as it was the creation of an invisible monetary system (Braudel, 1979); but it seems clear that for the West, printing brought with it both the Protestant Reformation and much of the cultural renaissance, as well as the spread of literacy (Steinberg, 1961).

Large-scale states are dependent upon hierarchical bureaucratic structures for their administration; thus literacy became the basis upon which these states have maintained themselves both spatially and temporally (Goody, 1986). Moreover, legal written codes governing the resolution of disputes are not only essential for the polity's survival but provide the framework within which routine commercial contracts can be effected. Literacy and numeracy are thus crucial to the recording of transactions and estimates of profit and loss. Finally, one observes in many societies the transition to a *written* form of cosmology and myth initially rooted in the oral tradition (Lord, 1987). Religious texts thus have provided not only an ostensibly unchangeable body of doctrine but have enshrined the codes governing ritual and have often prescribed patterns of social interaction—for example, marriage.

Another point of controversy concerns whether science as we know it could exist without the advent of written language. It seems clear to Goody and others that some form of written notation was necessary for the advance of mathematics, geometry, and much science. Some have gone further, however, and argued that science could advance only with a phonetic system of writing (Logan, 1986), and that the difference between writing systems helps explain why scientific advances occurred primarily in the West and why Chinese science remained relatively primitive.

We can claim that some societies have been historically characterized by a relatively high level of literacy and may be regarded as having *written cultures* whether or not they can be seen as traditional or modern, industrial or preindustrial, or Western or non-Western (Murdock & Provost, 1980). Although it is true that literacy as a *mass* phenomenon has been usually associated with processes of industrialization, this has been by no means always the case (Scribner & Cole, 1981; Cole, 1985); and thus we have commenced with a discussion of some basic differences in the nature of oral and written cultures, irrespective of where these cultures might stand on some other social or economic continuum.

However, we must recognize that, in another sense, beyond this very general level, the meaning of literacy is also contingent upon the social and economic context in which it occurs (Goody & Watt, 1968). Thus in the next sections we focus upon some more specific structural or sociological implications of literacy. Here we found it useful to distinguish between those societies with generally indigenous (or at least pre-Western) traditions of literacy and those where literacy has been essentially a concomitant of Western influence or colonial overrule. Further, in both types of situation literacy may be restricted on a de jure or de facto basis; and hence we must explore the social implications of variable levels in the diffusion of literacy.

PREINDUSTRIAL SOCIETIES WITH INDIGENOUS
TRADITIONS OF LITERACY

This section concerns itself with a selection of non-Western preindustrial societies that possessed some form of literary culture. Under this rubric we will focus upon the societies or preindustrial states of East Asia (e.g., imperial China, Japan), Southeast Asia (e.g., Thailand), and South Asia (the Indian subcontinent), along with the Islamic societies of the Middle East and the Maghrib.

In many of these societies literacy often resulted from the borrowing of scripts and orthographies from neighboring cultures—for example, Thailand, whose script is derived from South Indian Devanagram; or Japan, where the written language was initially based on Chinese ideographs. However, the source of a written language was perhaps less important than its subsequent degree of diffusion and its function or meaning within a new societal or cultural context.

Estimates of the levels of literacy that obtained in these societies in the pre-Western period must always be subject to conjecture. Indeed, the definition of literacy itself may be ambiguous: In many societies the ability to read sacred scriptures, for example, did not imply comprehension of their content; nor was the ability to read with comprehension always associated with writing skills, particularly in those areas where reading and writing were taught consecutively rather than concurrently (Clammer, 1976). However, a useful distinction can be made between *restricted* and *universal* *traditions* of literacy. In some societies or states, literacy was formally or legally restricted to particular categories of functionary or social strata; and its acquisition was, in variable degree, denied to the bulk of the population. Thus the mastery of sacred texts could be confined to largely endogamous castes or where state business was conducted through skills monopolized by administrative cadres whose membership was largely based on lineage and descent. As Goody observes, "Such restrictive practices tend to arise wherever people have an interest in maintaining a monopoly of their sources of power" (Goody, 1968, p. 12).

It is unlikely, however, that de jure distinctions could be effectively maintained, given the function of literacy in a widening variety of contexts. For example, with the growth of trading networks and the emergence of new merchant classes, literacy and numeracy became vital to the economy; and it is difficult to see how formal restrictions on the acquisition of literacy could be sustained in a society, given any degree of social or economic change. What did occur in some societies, however, was the parallel maintenance of an esoteric literary tradition and a widespread diffusion of literacy based upon more cursive scripts and simplified orthographies.

It seems likely, then, that de facto restrictions on literacy were far more important in these societies than de jure impediments. Thus, even where no formal prohibitions against literacy existed, and where indeed there was a belief that its universal acquisition was permissible and even desirable, logistical constraints frequently operated to confine literacy to a minority of the population (Scribner & Cole, 1981).

Universal literacy has been achievable only within the framework of those societies where the provision of schooling has been seen as an essentially public responsibility and where the state or religious institution has been willing to provide the infrastructure and support for the development of a formal educational system. In other words, where literacy was perceived in functional terms (whether religious, economic, or social) by an increasing proportion of the population, educational institutions emerged to meet increasing demand. However, such institutions were rarely able to provide universal literacy, with the result that even where a putative majority of the population was literate, there were considerable inequalities in its diffusion both geographically and socially. Thus, while it is clearly misleading to assume that widespread literacy of a more than rudimentary sort has been historically associated only with the emergence of the contemporary nation-state, it is true that the notion of universal literacy as an achievable and necessarily publicly supported goal is of largely 19-century Western origin.

Further, in many societies literacy was restricted in extent as a result of the high direct and opportunity costs involved in its acquisition (Blaug, 1966). Even where monetary costs or "gifts in kind" were low or nonexistent, it is apparent that in terms of time outlays and productivity foregone, opportunity costs were high in agricultural societies, particularly those that were more heavily dependent on family-based child labor. Moreover, such opportunity costs were necessarily higher in regions where literacy was achieved through mastery of more complex ideographic sets of characters than in others where alphabetic or partially alphabetic scripts prevailed.

Conjoined with the problem of the level of literacy is that of its primary *function* or *meaning* in preindustrial societies or states. As implied earlier, the number of social characteristics of literate individuals must, in large measure, be related to the major context in which literacy was utilized. In these societies literacy was associated with one or more of the following activities: administration, law, and long-distance trade or commerce, which necessarily involved partial economic monetization and religion. In order to emphasize certain divergent patterns in terms of these functions, we now delineate several case studies, while recognizing that such cursory treatment inevitably involves oversimplification.

Imperial China

Imperial China provides the clearest example of a close nexus between restricted literacy and the existence of a protobureaucratic, highly centralized state. The Ch'in dynasty (246–207 B.C.) witnessed the first successful attempt to establish the dominance of the center over the periphery in order to counter the fissiparous tendencies so evident throughout early Chinese history. This necessitated the creation of a hierarchy of officeholders who were theoretically members of the emperor's household (Weber, 1958a). Entry to this hierarchy required not only literacy but the mastery of an increasingly voluminous body of philosophic discourse and commentary. We refer to this administrative structure as protobureaucratic in the sense that there was an administrative hierarchy, access to which was governed by differential levels of achievement; but, in some contrast to contemporary bureaucratic structures, the content of the educational process was designed not to engender functionally specific skills but rather to produce morally enlightened and cultivated generalists.

A major outcome of this system was the creation of a basic division in Chinese society between the gentry (literati) and commoners (Ho, 1962). The former group, who probably never constituted more than 2 percent of the population, consisted of both a small number of actual administrative officeholders who had passed several or all levels of the hierarchy of examinations and had received appointments; and a far larger number of "candidates," who were not officeholders but who had succeeded in passing the first-stage examinations. Collectively the gentry class constituted a powerful status group and were the bearers of a "high culture," which distinguished them from the peasants, artisans, and trading classes. Although literacy was not confined to the gentry (since local schools existed in many villages and townships and basic literacy could be acquired even by those of peasant origin), a massive cultural gap existed between those who were literate to the level required by the ordinary demands of trade or craft and those whose literacy linked them to the high culture of imperial China.

Much research on literacy in imperial China has focused upon the relationship between social status, social mobility (particularly in terms of entry into the hierarchy of officeholders), and literacy, where the latter involved mastery of a complex ideographic script. Though there is controversy concerning the amount of time required to achieve it, there can be no doubt that it involved a far more lengthy and difficult process than that associated with the acquisition of literacy in an alphabetic script (Gough, 1968).

Yet it has been established that the Chinese literati were well aware of the existence of syllabaries and, more important, alphabetic scripts of Indian or Tibetan derivation that would have made reading and writing skills far more accessible to the bulk of the population. Two general sets of reasons have been advanced for their reluctance to employ these forms: The first rests upon a sociological "conflict" perspective, and the second derives from more immediately functional considerations.

The conflict perspective suggests that the difficulty of acquiring literacy in an ideographic script militated successfully against the entry of commoners (particularly peasants) into the ranks of the literati; and thus the gentry class attempted to maintain their monopoly of power through the de facto existence of restricted literacy, even though formal access to the examination system was open to all males of "respectable family." There is evidence that the literati attempted from time to time to control entry to their ranks and maintain a quasi-castelike status, as in those periods when their own offspring were exempt from the first-level examinations and thus could automatically acquire gentry status (though not incumbency as officeholders) (Marsh, 1961). However, there is no direct historical evidence that the gentry consciously saw the maintenance of an ideographic script as a device for restricting upward mobility from the lower orders.

The functional reasons derive from an understanding of the divergence between the written and spoken languages. Since China encompasses a number of major spoken and mutually unintelligible languages (not merely dialects), the written classical language (*wen-yen*) provided a common idiom for law and administration. Though various dialects of spoken Mandarin were widely diffused, they could hardly be regarded as universal; and without greater linguistic uniformity, *wen-yen* necessarily became the basis for the control of the polity. Thus, the utilization of an alphabetic script would necessarily have involved an attempt by authority to enforce the dissemination of, for example, Peking Mandarin as the universal spoken language of the empire. This attempt was not made, and it is difficult to see how it could have been made without the growth of a state-controlled and publicly supported nationwide system of schools.

Whatever post-hoc interpretations may be given for the continued employment of a complex ideographic system, the system itself did not prevent mobility into the ranks of the literati from the peasant, artisan, and commercial classes (Yang, 1956). Although aggregate rates of social mobility were low in imperial China (in the sense that only a tiny proportion of individuals changed their status over their lifetime), the evidence is that the ranks of the gentry were permeable. Though the degree of permeability varied over various dynastic periods, there was a gradual circulation within the elite through downward mobility and upward mobility from talented males of peasant origin. Thus over a span of several generations the gentry never constituted a closed caste, though entry to it necessarily presupposed a total assimilation of and identification with an exclusive high culture based on mastery of literary *wen-yen* (Marsh, 1961).

In emphasizing the association between script, polity, and social status in the

Chinese case study, we do not ignore the importance of literacy in other spheres. Though political exigencies stimulated major developments in historiography and legal codification in the empire, the importance of literacy to the aesthetic spheres of narrative literature and poetry cannot be neglected. Indeed, the persistence of literary *wen-yen* derived, in part, from its aesthetic appeal since calligraphic elegance was an intrinsic part of literary appreciation. Further, the literary language was crucial in the preservation of religious traditions and texts and in the important spheres of science and technology, and magic and divination. Finally, long-distance trade and commerce throughout the empire presupposed literacy among the merchant classes; and it is in the commercial sphere that there first developed popular forms of the written language based on a simplified script. However, this discussion has emphasized the importance of a tradition of de facto restricted literacy in a preindustrial society wherein there was a particularly close nexus between the written language and the political, social, and legal structure.

Pre-Moghul India

Pre-Moghul India provides a major contrast with the Chinese experience. India, like China, exhibited a pattern of restricted literacy conjoined with an even more differentiated social structure; but, in this case, the reasons for restricted literacy were markedly different. In the Chinese case the complexity of the ideographic system militated against widespread literacy, but in India most languages were written in semisyllabic or partially alphabetic scripts usually requiring the mastery of some 40 or 50 letters, thus enabling the far easier acquisition of reading and writing skills. The explanation for limited literacy in India must be found in the nature of the caste system and the patterns of religious belief that legitimized that system. Thus the potentialities of protoalphabetic scripts that could have led to widespread literacy were, in fact, limited by religious tradition.

Though its actual origins are still the subject of controversy, the caste system derived its legitimacy from sacred scriptures. In broadest terms, the caste system comprised a hierarchy of five supercastes (Varnas), including Brahmans (priests, law givers, and scholars), Kshattriyas (secular rulers and warriors), Vaishyas (merchants and craftsmen), and Sudras (manual laborers). The Untouchables, with an even lower ranking than the Sudras, were in the strictest sense exterior to the caste system. In fact, the association between caste and occupation was far looser than is often supposed (Brahmans could be found over a whole range of economic activities); and the Varnas themselves nowhere constituted a direct basis for social action (Gough, 1968). In practice, they dissolved into literally thousands of geographically based and culturally diverse castes (Jatis), which constituted the basis for patterns of face-to-face interaction between individuals and groups. However, the element that undergirded the whole structure was the notion of varying levels of purity among castes that determined ritual obligations and life-style and, most important, governed access to the sacred literature (both in its written and oral forms) (Weber, 1958b).

In India, then, the impetus to the development of literacy lay not in the imperatives of the state (unlike China, India enjoyed only relatively short periods of unification under centralized authority), but in the need to write down the sacred scriptures. Again, unlike China, Hindu society initially extolled the virtues and superiority of the oral to the written tradition. Thus, for lengthy periods the whole corpus of Indian religious cosmology and ritual was transmitted orally (and ostensibly unchanged) from generation to generation, often with the injunction that it should *not* be written down.

Clearly, access to an esoteric oral tradition was related to caste rank and, in turn, confirmed the ritual and social superiority of the "twice-born castes" (comprising the first three Varnas).

It was only very slowly that a massive body of religious oral tradition was finally committed to written form; and initially, written texts were regarded as constituting no more than an aide-mémoire to oral recitation. The rationale for the commitment of oral texts to writing was essentially conservative and designed to transmit an unchanging corpus of religious knowledge and ritual forms to subsequent generations. Literacy was not associated with the idea of change but rather with the perpetuation of ancient religious belief and forms of social organization.

Once the sacred texts were written, however, they were rendered more available to lower castes; certain bodies of literature were regarded as being legitimately accessible to those groups, while other materials, notably the Vedic literature in both the oral and written forms, were explicitly forbidden. Thus, the pattern of restricted literacy in India can only be understood in terms of the religious tradition that undergirded a social structure composed of endogamous castes. In any event, it would seem that literacy was widespread among the twice-born castes but very narrowly diffused among the Sudras or Untouchables (Gough, 1968).

Other significant differences are apparent between India and China. First, the latter was unified through possession of a common written script that transcended differences in the spoken language. To be sure, written Sanskrit was widely diffused and represented the older traditions of Indian religious thought, but India also witnessed the emergence of a religious literature based on a large number of local languages or vernaculars and written in different protoalphabetic scripts. Thus written forms did not perform the same politically unifying function as did *wen-yen* in the Chinese context.

Second, since the spread of literacy was not primarily associated with statecraft, Indian writings never developed the strong traditions of historiography so evident in China, although they did evidence a major concern with jurisprudence designed to adumbrate the religious, ritual, and social obligations of individuals and groups in their interaction with each other. Finally, the impetus to scientific and technological innovation evident in China was constrained by the Indian religious tradition, though that same tradition stimulated advances in mathematics and astronomy.

In emphasizing the nexus between a tradition of restricted literacy, religion, and caste structure, however, we do not ignore the importance of literacy in the secular context. Although India did not develop the elaborate bureaucratic administrative structures so characteristic of imperial China, literacy was significant in public administration; and Brahmans, like the clergy in medieval Europe, were often employed as senior officials in Hindu courts. Finally, literacy was important in trade and commerce, though it has been observed that the egalitarian traditions of Buddhism and Jainism were more attractive to the merchant and trading castes, resulting in widespread literacy in the vernacular and a rejection of some of the older Vedic traditions.

Literacy in the Early Islamic World

Our final case study represents a pattern of restricted literacy in a cluster of preindustrial societies not always initially linked by common culture or language but by possession of a shared religious tradition. As with pre-Moghul India, literacy in the Islamic world derived from religious rather than secular impulses; but the reasons for the development of a pattern of restricted literacy were very different. An understanding of the situation requires both a discussion of the nature of Arabic as a written language and its central role in the Islamic religious tradition.

Arabic is a Semitic language whose written form derives from an early alphabetic Phoenician script employing only 28 characters. The script was relatively simple to learn, and thus the reason for restricted literacy in early Islamic societies is not to be found in the problems of mastering an intrinsically difficult writing system.

Arabic might have remained a minor written language confined to the Arabian Peninsula had it not been for the rise of Islam in the 7th century. The prophetic vision of Muhammad was only written down in fragments by accompanying scribes to be used as aides-mémoires to oral recitation. With the death of many of the Prophet's immediate entourage, the need for a single unified text became imperative; and thus a commission appointed by Caliph Uthman succeeded in A.D. 650 in producing an accepted, standardized version of the Qur'an (the Word of God speaking to Man) consisting of 114 Suras.

Along with its description of God's imminent judgment, the Qur'an laid down the rules that should govern the conduct of all believers; but only one standardized version of Arabic text (with limited variation in lettering style) was authorized, and oral recitation could be given only in a standard dialect of spoken Arabic. Moreover, since Arabic was literally the "language of God," the Qur'an could be read or recited *only* in that language; for example, 10th- and 11th-century translations into Persian or Turkish written in Arabic script were unequivocally rejected by the orthodox.

Several social and political characteristics of Islam should also be noted. First, of all the "religions of the book," Islam remains the most egalitarian and universalistic, with no distinctions among believers in terms of race, ethnicity, or economic status. This egalitarianism constituted part of the vital force that led it to become initially the religion of the Arabic world, with a subsequent spread to other parts of Asia and the Maghrib and thence to the Indian subcontinent.

Second, Islam never countenanced the emergence of a priestly caste or class, as in pre-Moghul India and medieval Europe, that constituted a vicarate standing between man and God. Thus, the Ulama (learned men) who were dominant in both religion and politics obtained recognition only through criteria of personal achievement: they exerted moral and intellectual influence but not on the basis of any preordained status, and their political role largely derived from the fact that Islam admitted of no distinction between religion and the state.

Third, literacy in Arabic, even of a rudimentary sort, was an important element of religious belief and practice for *all* believers, and this was conjoined with a generally high regard for the importance of learning and scholarship. Thus, in the very earliest years of Islam, schools were established for the teaching of moral behavior and knowledge of the Qur'an, along with the provision of basic literacy and rudimentary arithmetical skills. Alongside these schools, there emerged a powerful tradition of higher education provided within a number of distinguished urban universities. These institutions were responsible for the production of the Ulama class and, during the Golden Age of Islam, preserved much Greek and Roman knowledge through translation.

Given the initially egalitarian and open nature of Islamic social structure and its emphasis on learning and mastery of "the Book," reasons must be given for the restricted provision of literacy in the Islamic world, since its limited diffusion did not rest on the difficulty of the orthography and script nor upon the existence of a priestly caste or administrative class with any claim to a monopoly on an esoteric body of literature or skills.

So long as Islam was confined to the Arab-speaking world or to groups speaking related Semitic languages, Qur'anic literacy might not have been difficult to achieve. However, the Arab Empire expanded to incorporate major groups who spoke neither Arabic nor any Semitic tongue but rather Indo-European or Turkic languages. For these non-Semitic groups, literacy in the Qur'an involved not only mastery of a script but comprehension of the language. It is impossible to assess the level of that comprehension among non-Semitic groups; but it is clear that, even where children entered lower-level schools (Mektebs), learning rarely went beyond the ability to master Arabic script and subsequently to read passages from the Qur'an without comprehension. Much "reading" may, in fact, have been recitation, as appears to have been the case in Protestant Europe, which had a similar emphasis on "reading" the Bible. A gradual transition to comprehension was likely to occur only with the small minority who went on to more advanced schools (Medressehs); and even here, there was no clear route between lower-level institutions and the universities of the Islamic world.

Discussions concerning literacy in the early Islamic period have tended to exaggerate its extent, since the work of many scholars has concentrated on Islamic elites and the traditions of orthodox Islam. Although Islam began as the religion of a primarily rural, agriculturally based people, it became an essentially urban religion with the expansion of the Arab Empire. Arab minorities established themselves in cities that subsequently became major centers of literacy and learning, but these centers of the great Islamic tradition existed alongside massive rural communities where literacy was not widespread and where Islamic belief coexisted with older pre-Islamic and often animistic religious traditions.

Recent research has tended to stress this disjunction between the "great" and "folk" traditions of Islam (Geertz, 1960). Within the first context, functional literacy was vital to a comprehension of the Qur'an; but in the latter the Qur'an was often associated with pre-Islamic practices wherein knowledge of "the Book" did not require comprehension but rather the ability to read, without comprehension, passages that were presumed to have an intrinsic magical efficacy (Goody, 1968).

Thus, within the empire, literacy in Arabic was vital to orthodox Islam and important for those minorities involved in the law, administration, commerce, and trade; but for the bulk of the population, real functional literacy in Arabic must have been quite limited. Moreover, with the decline of Arab power and the subsequent rise of the Ottoman Empire, Arabic remained encapsulated with the orthodox religious tradition of the minority. Henceforth, Ottoman, which was essentially Persian with an admixture of Turkish and Arabic words written in a modified classical Arabic script, became the medium of the administrative elite.

Summary and Conclusions

Our discussion has attempted to show that the origin of the demand for literacy in preindustrial non-Western societies was often very different from that characterizing most contemporary societies. Although it is possible to point to basic differences in the nature of literate and nonliterate cultures, it is still crucial to examine the specific meanings attributed to literacy in a variety of social and historical contexts. Literacy in imperial China cannot be understood without reference to political exigencies and the problems of the script itself. By contrast, in pre-Moghul India and the Islamic world, the meaning of literacy was inseparable from religiously inspired imperatives, although the outcomes were very different. As the next section will show, these earlier traditions still exert a powerful influence on the language and literacy policies of those states that now constitute the heirs to these "great traditions."

PREINDUSTRIAL SOCIETIES IN THE CONTEMPORARY WORLD: THE NATION-STATE AND THE WESTERN IMPACT

Given the fact that some preindustrial societies of varying degrees of social, political, and cultural complexity exhibited widespread patterns of "indigenous" literacy, it is clear that in the contemporary context formidable problems occur in those societies where the mass diffusion of literacy has been associated with the rise of the modern nation-state and either Western influence or direct Western colonial overrule. The distinction between Western schooling and literacy has been noted by Scribner and Cole (1981); Cole (1985) notes that it is the former that is associated with our notions of intelligent behavior and economic progress. It is also useful to make a distinction between societies such as those described in earlier sections with pre-European traditions of literacy which, in fact, contend with newer patterns that are associated with the emergence of Western-type schooling and other societies or states with essentially pre-Western oral traditions. Among the former we may include, for example, the states of the Middle East and the Maghrib, and South and Southeast Asia, while most of sub-Saharan Africa provides the clearest example of the second cluster.

Literacy and Socioeconomic Change

It can be argued that the spread of formal schooling and a general rise in literacy levels has usually been associated with rather similar patterns of social and economic change in all societies, whether they were ostensibly colonial or not. Generally, the demand for Western-type schooling and literacy has been associated with economic transformation (Foster, 1987). This transformation has everywhere involved a greater monetization of local economies and their linkage with national or international markets, the development of Western-style systems of national administration, and a greater degree of urbanization of local populations (Lerner, 1958). In fact, schooling and literacy tend to have a distinctive ecology: the incidence of schooling is nearly always associated with the development of new transport networks, the rise of modern urban centers, and the emergence of a monetized economy (Fuller, Edwards, & Gorman, 1987). Given differential rates of economic change within most of these societies, it follows that schooling and literacy will be similarly unevenly diffused (Foster, 1980). Exceptions exist but the sharp differences between literacy levels in urban as opposed to rural areas exemplify this situation. Thus, while it seems incontrovertible that literacy and schooling play a major role in facilitating economic growth, it is also evident that the demand for literacy and schooling tends to emerge when structural economic change is *already* underway (Foster, 1987).

Moreover, those economic transformations that are linked to the demand for literacy are associated with correlative changes in the social and cultural spheres. As noted, social status in most preindustrial societies was based in variable degrees on criteria of descent and lineage. However, as economic change continues, new status structures tend to emerge, wherein individual or group social rank depends in large measure upon possession of a Western-type occupation to which access is largely governed by level of formal education. Literacy and schooling are thus inevitably linked to the emergence of new social class structures that, in many respects, resemble their Western counterparts (Foster, 1977). In most of these societies, then, status structures tend to be dualistic in nature: rank in one context may be based on descent or in part on possession of a traditional education, while in another context it will be increasingly dependent on modern schooling. Within different cultural contexts, individuals or groups may shuttle between these different traditions: Both traditional and modern literacy and schooling may have instrumental value, but their meaning will vary within different social and cultural situations. This situation is exemplified in those societies where, as noted earlier, older traditions of literacy contend with newer forms derived from Western influence or overrule.

The Language/Literacy Issue

In many preindustrial societies that now constitute nation-states, the literacy problem is compounded by that of linguistic fragmentation. For the most part, the older nation-states of the Western world were characterized by a high degree of linguistic uniformity, with notable exceptions like the former Austro-Hungarian and Russian empires. Although in Western states with ostensibly monolingual traditions, the demands of minorities for the recognition of their own linguistic heritage has escalated, such developments do not usually challenge the continued existence of the polity. In older multilingual states, lively traditions of literacy in minority languages may coexist with a more general consensus concerning the dominant language of the polity and economy: there is a general recognition of the distinction between literacy in the language of culture and tradition and literacy in the language of power.

Within many of the preindustrial new states, however, the situation is more precarious since no broad consensus exists as to what constitutes the national language. In a few new nations, substantial linguistic uniformity has made the language/literacy issue one of limited importance but this is unusual. Conversely, there is only one example, that of the Republic of Indonesia, where the problem of extreme linguistic diversification has led to the successful adoption and diffusion of an essentially alien language of *non-European* origin as the vehicle of national literacy. Bahasa Indonesia is not an artificial language in the sense that it is a variant of Malay, but it is the mother tongue of only a tiny minority of Indonesians. However, its spoken and written forms have been modified within the Indonesian context; and its promulgation as a viable written national language has surmounted the language/literacy issue. The reasons for the remarkable success of the policy are by no means clear, but successful adoption of Bahasa Indonesia after independence was preceded by many years of effort by early Indonesian nationalists to establish it as the medium of nationalist literature in the face of Dutch opposition (Diah, 1982). Perhaps the only parallel to the Indonesian case is that of Israel, where Hebrew, which had survived only within a ritual and religious context, was "recreated" in modified form to constitute the spoken and written medium of a modern nation-state.

These situations are, however, unusual: more frequently, the new nation-states exhibit a multilingual heritage that may range from extreme linguistic fragmentation (e.g., Nigeria), through states exhibiting a multilingual pattern where one language is dominant (Iran), to others where several major indigenous languages seem evenly balanced in terms of their distribution (Kenya). To add to this complexity, it is apparent that in those states with a colonial past, there is controversy concerning the status of the language of the former colonial power and whether, *faute de mieux*, this must become the national language and thus the universal medium of literacy. In discussing issues of literacy and literacy policy in these states, then, we must acknowledge that they are confounded with those of language policy and that as such they introduce more political than educational issues. Once again, we examine variant situations through presentation of a number of case studies, commencing with nation-states exhibiting pre-European patterns of literacy and concluding with others having essentially pre-European oral traditions.

The Nation-States of the Contemporary Islamic World

With long-established traditions of literacy associated with the study of the Qur'an, Islamic education now contends with newer types of formal education whose content is sometimes transmitted in a Western language. The outcome, so far as literacy is concerned, depends in some measure on whether or not Arabic is the primary language of these Islamic societies or states. Classical spoken and written Arabic differs markedly from the various local variants of spoken colloquial Arabic; but in those areas of the Maghrib and the Middle East where Arabic is the spoken and written medium, conflict is less severe. In spite of the frequent existence of linguistic minorities, there is an acceptance that Arabic will remain the national language of most states, and literacy will be achieved in some version of the classical written form (Ezzaki, Spratt, & Wagner, 1987). What is occurring is that new national systems of education have emerged whose organization and content is predominantly Western but where the medium of instruction is Arabic. At the same time, these schools coexist with older institutions whose organization is very different and whose content is based on Qur'anic traditions. How far these two traditions can be accommodated with one another is difficult to predict, though there are increasing attempts to meld an essentially Western-type structure of schooling with a part-Western and part-Qur'anic curriculum.

At least in the Arabic-speaking societies, there is a general consensus that basic literacy will be achieved in Arabic; but the situation is far more complex in those states with overwhelmingly Islamicized populations but where Arabic is not predominantly spoken. This, for example, is the case in Iran, where Indo-European Farsi constitutes the accepted national language; Indonesia, with the dominance of Bahasa; and Pakistan, where Urdu, originally a lingua franca comprising Persian, Hindi, and Arabic elements, has been recognized as the national medium. Thus, basic literacy is acquired in the national language in the state system of schools, while at the same time, there exists a network of Qur'anic institutions based initially on the learning of classical Arabic forms. It must be stressed that Iran, for example, and Pakistan see themselves as Islamic states; but the drive for national universal literacy cannot be easily linked to the Arabic language. It is possible that Qur'anic schools in these nations may remain as a separate system, wherein at lower levels, memorization of passages in the Qur'an will in no sense imply any substantive literacy in Arabic. General literacy, therefore, may be achieved in a national language or in one of a cluster of other languages used as the medium of instruction in Western-type schools—though once again, there may be attempts to include Qur'anic elements within the curriculum.

Thus, within the Islamic world, Iran, for example, and Pakistan exemplify the problems of non-Arabic-speaking polities with a multilingual heritage. As with the Arab states, there is a desire to maintain Qur'anic traditions, with a recognition that Arabic can never become the national medium of literacy. Moreover, in the case of Pakistan, the continued importance of English in both commerce and administration has required that English still be recognized as an additional national language.

The Republic of India

This nation-state provides another variant of the language/literacy dilemma; once again, one cannot speak of a solution but rather of a compromise between the numerous pre-European traditions of literacy and language that has produced an unstable situation, made even more complicated by the variable diffusion of English, the language of the former colonial power.

We have described the nature and extent of literacy in early India; but during the

ensuing Moghul period, Persian became the language of the imperial court and administration and "overlay," as it were, earlier traditions of literacy in Sanskrit and the
vernaculars. From the late 18th century, the gradual extension of British overrule
introduced a new dimension into an already complex linguistic situation. Increasingly,
English became the language of administration and assumed a major role in trade and
commerce. Thus, literacy in English was valued as a means of access to positions in
commerce and administration but did not displace older traditions of literacy in local
Indian languages, which remained important in the religious and aesthetic spheres.

At independence in 1948, a small minority had achieved literacy in English, while
there was a variable but still narrow diffusion of literacy in local languages among the
bulk of the population. Understandably, national self-esteem suggested that an Indian
language should replace English as the official spoken and written medium of the new
state, but no consensus existed as to what this should be. Indeed, support for English
remained strong in the Indian "rimland," or those portions of the littoral that had first
been exposed to British influence and where English had made the greatest inroads
(Rudolph & Rudolph, 1972). However, the bulk of the population was concentrated in
the heartland of northern and central India, which was both economically less developed than the rimland and where English was far less diffused as a medium. This
asymmetrical relationship between political influence and economic development led to
the demand that a standardized form of Hindi should be the written and spoken
medium of the republic, but this proposal met and continues to meet with opposition.

Since federal educational policy lays down that all children have the right to be
taught initially in their mother tongue or a recognized language, it is apparent that extra
burdens have been placed on southerners, who speak a cluster of languages (mainly
Kanada, Telugu, and Malayalam) that are totally unrelated to the Sanskritically derived
languages of the north and center. Thus, a child in the heartland must become literate
in his or her own vernacular or recognized language and then in standard Hindi, which,
however, is often related to that mother tongue. Moreover, further progress in the
educational system requires some literacy in English at secondary and higher levels.
However, in the south literacy in the local language and then English is supplemented
by the Hindi requirement. Paradoxically, given the educational traditions of the south,
Hindi is in some respects a more "alien" language than is English.

Since independence, a succession of educational commissions has recommended
the replacement of English by "standard" Hindi as the national medium; but because of
persistent opposition and the logistical problems involved, the formal date of transition
has been constantly deferred. Thus English remains a de facto national language, while
Hindi has maintained a very slow if gathering momentum. For the indefinite future, a
situation of linguistic "diglossia" (Fishman, 1967) will prevail, with a minority of the
population possessing some literacy in English and the remainder increasingly having a
degree of facility in a local vernacular, one or the other of the 14 languages recognized
by the federal constitution. That this degree of "linguistic pandemonium" has survived
with a degree of compromise reflects the consensual nature of Indian politics and the
reluctance of the federal government to adopt more coercive language and literacy
policies (Harrison, 1960).

China

If literacy policy in India reflects a compromise rather than a solution, contemporary
China might be moving toward a significant resolution of the language/literacy issue. In
the imperial period, a linguistically divided nation was unified by a common written
literary language (*wen-yen*) that bore little or no relation to spoken forms. During this

earlier period, there were sporadic attempts to bring the written language into closer relation with spoken vernaculars; but the movement did not gain real momentum until after the foundation of the republic, when, along with an effort to simplify the written ideographs, there was a reasonably successful effort to write in the vernacular. However, the vernacular in question was Mandarin; and although this was widely spoken, it was still necessary for non-Mandarin speakers (e.g., in Shanghai or Canton) to learn the Mandarin idiom.

Thus, although a simplified ideographic script was fairly widely diffused, a more definitive solution required a far more profound and essentially twofold reform. The reform first involved a systematic attempt to diffuse a standard form of spoken Mandarin throughout the nation; this step necessarily depended upon the establishment of a national system of schooling largely effected in the post-1949 period. Second, the standardized spoken language had to be associated with the development of a romanized alphabetic script (Pinyin). Current efforts to diffuse standard spoken Mandarin along with Pinyin through the school system are meeting with considerable success; and within a few decades, China will be unified through near-universal literacy in a common spoken language and an easily acquired alphabetic script. It must not be assumed, however, that Pinyin will displace either the simplified or more complex ideographic traditions. Pinyin may become the written language of state and commerce; but older formal or simplified written forms will, for the forseeable future, inevitably remain significant in literature and the arts.

We have examined the language/literacy issue in a selected number of preindustrial societies that now constitute modern nation-states and where older traditions of literacy now exist alongside efforts to spread literacy in a national language. In view of their own traditions, some of these states have rejected the use of a European language as the national medium, though there is frequently controversy as to which vernacular is to be elevated to the status of the national language. However, even in these states, the issue of literacy in a European tongue has by no means been resolved. At lower levels of the educational system, policies to spread literacy in an indigenous language may be politically acceptable and economically viable. However, at secondary and postsecondary levels, the need for access to more advanced materials, particularly in the areas of science and technology, mandates literacy in a Western language; and except for those areas that were subject to French, Russian, Spanish, or Portuguese overrule or direct influence, that language is almost inevitably English. A local language may be the medium of instruction in primary schools, but there must be an increasing transition to literacy in a Western language at secondary and university levels. For example, literacy in Arabic may be general throughout the Middle East or Maghrib, but mastery of French or English remains the key to maximal social mobility. Likewise, Hindi may conceivably be accepted as the national language of India, but it is extremely unlikely that it can ever displace English, albeit a distinct version of English (Kachru, 1982). Paradoxically, even in states that have never experienced direct colonial overrule, literacy in a Western language is crucial for that minority of students who proceed to secondary or university education; and thus in China, efforts to diffuse Pinyin are paralleled by increasing emphasis on the mastery of English at postprimary levels.

A few Western languages remain the languages of power; and while national self-esteem may be frustrated by this situation, a total transition to literacy in an indigenous language is usually rendered impossible by the basic economics of literacy: so long as secondary and higher education remain narrowly diffused and nation-states relatively small, the size of the internal market can never justify the publication of advanced materials in a local language. Larger states such as China might move toward publication in Pinyin, or smaller states linked by a common linguistic tradition (such as Arabic) might establish joint publishing enterprises to service a larger internal market; but there are few signs of such developments. Thus, in a world characterized by an increasing level of direct intercommunication, literacy in a major Western language remains imperative for a minority of local populations in all these nation-states.

Nation-States with a Pre-European Oral Tradition

A continued and, indeed, increasing demand for literacy in a Western language is even more obvious in that cluster of nation-states that derive from societies that had no indigenous traditions of literacy prior to the colonial episode. Within this category we include most of the new microstates of the Pacific, particularly Papua New Guinea, which is distinguished by an extreme degree of linguistic fragmentation (700 languages spoken in a population of approximately 3 million) (Burke, 1974). With the exception of those areas subject to Islamic influence and the Amharic portion of Ethiopia, we also include the new states of sub-Saharan Africa, which are composed of clusters of culturally diverse peoples with oral traditions, who have been artificially grouped together as a result of earlier colonial mapmaking. These new nations are linguistically divided to the extent that only one indigenous sub-Saharan African state, Somalia, is now unified by a common spoken indigenous language. Thus literacy in the subcontinent was largely a consequence of Western colonialism. Since the current situation in these new states is a direct consequence of prior colonial educational policies, it can only be understood in terms of divergences in those policies.

During the colonial period there was, in fact, considerable controversy concerning the language of instruction within the newly established African schools. By the end of the colonial period, however, the educational policies of the major colonial powers were firmly established. Within French territories, French was used as the medium of instruction from the first day of primary school onward; and thus, at the official level, there was no attempt to develop orthographies of African languages, although there is evidence that some of these languages existed in unofficial written form in communication among Africans who had some literacy in French and who thus utilized the French orthography as a medium (UNESCO, 1953).

With a few exceptions, British policy rested on the axiom that, as far as possible, all children should be initially taught in their own mother tongue, with English introduced as a subject in the upper grades of primary school, and complete transition to English at secondary and postsecondary levels. However, the mother tongue principle could not be adhered to in territories characterized by extreme linguistic fragmentation; in practice, there was an effort to develop orthographies and printed materials in selected major African languages in each colony (UNESCO, 1953). This task was rendered easier where a language constituted a lingua franca over wide areas and was already spoken by large numbers of Africans for whom it was not a mother tongue. This was the case, for example, with Hausa in northern Nigeria, Twi in Ghana, and Swahili in East Africa (particularly Tanganyika).

Belgian policy in some respects paralleled that of the British. There was an attempt to provide very basic instruction in a selected number of local languages; indeed, by 1960 the then Belgian Congo exhibited higher levels of literacy than any other colonial territory (UNESCO, 1953). However, the Belgian administration made no real effort to provide secondary or postsecondary schooling and, until very late in the colonial period, education beyond the primary level was only available in a tiny cluster of vocational schools and seminaries, wherein French usually became the medium of instruction. Finally, in Portuguese territories, where different mission school systems tended initially to pursue divergent policies, there was ultimately a move toward using

Portuguese as the medium of instruction at all levels, largely as a result of the greater influence of Portuguese-based Catholic missions.

Though the political decolonization of sub-Saharan Africa is now virtually complete, it is fair to say that the new African states have adhered to colonial precedents with respect to the language/literacy issue (Foster, 1971). Over the past two or three decades, there has been a massive expansion of enrollments at all levels in African educational systems; but this has not been associated with any major new initiatives concerning the medium of instruction in the schools: literacy rates have everywhere risen, but it has been literacy in the language or languages selected by the former colonial regimes. The reasons are clear enough: ethnic tensions within most of these nations have made it quite impossible for any regime to elevate an African language, however widely spoken, to the status of a national language over the bitter opposition of other often sizeable linguistic minorities. Indeed, in view of its potentially disastrous political consequences, a consensus seems to have emerged in most states that the language/literacy issue should not constitute a priority item on the national agenda. Thus, in only one country, Tanzania, has a local language been effectively recognized as the national language, and here the circumstances are unique. At the time of independence in 1963, Swahili, originally a coastal language, had already established itself as a lingua franca spoken by approximately 60 percent of the Tanzanian population, while the remainder of that population overwhelmingly spoke some cognate Bantu tongue. Thus, it was not too difficult to establish Swahili throughout the primary school system, although there was some need to promulgate a standard spoken and written version. This fortunate situation hardly obtains in any other African nation; and in neighboring Kenya, where Swahili is also widely spoken, it is noteworthy that attempts to effectively establish it as the national language are likely to fail (UNESCO, 1987).

Political issues aside, there is an equally cogent reason why African states cannot effectively modify earlier colonial policies. Mastery of the language of the former colonial power is essential at secondary and postsecondary levels; and, as in most other multilingual states, the economic problems associated with the use of any African language as a medium at anything beyond the primary school are insuperable. Moreover, there is a widespread recognition among African populations themselves that literacy in French or English remains the key to occupational success; and, paradoxically, there is public pressure both to extend and improve the quality of instruction in the spoken and written language of the former metropole. Thus, while the rhetoric of nationalism in most states emphasizes the need for literacy in an African national language, economic and political realities increase the demand for literacy in a Western tongue.

As with India, the situation in middle Africa represents a compromise, not a solution. In some nations Africans will perhaps achieve literacy in an African language and some may also achieve very rudimentary skills in a European tongue. In others literacy will *only* be acquired in a European language, but real facility in that language is likely to be confined for the forseeable future to that minority which has proceeded beyond the primary school level.

CONCLUSION

From this brief survey, we may return to the general principles about the societal impact of literacy as set forth by scholars such as Ong and Goody. It would seem that literacy must be seen less as a single concept and more as a multivalent phenomenon. In many societies, both past and present, a number of people learn a rudimentary form of literacy in order to transact business or to participate in certain forms of religious ritual. In general, this sort of literacy allows for a society to progress towards a "town" (as opposed to village) life, and it appears to be accompanied by a certain amount of specialized labor. Literacy in this case may be in an indigenous language or in a language associated with a particular religion.

In most societies, however, there is another level of literacy that is associated with a smaller educated or scribal class and the development of complex city-states or nations (Purves, 1987). As some of these nations expanded, they often took their literate language with them and thus created a major lingua franca (e.g., Chinese, Sanskrit, Latin, French, Portuguese, Russian, Spanish, and English among the world languages; and Bahasa, German, and Swahili among the regional ones). This level of literacy is accompanied by the establishment of laws, bureaucracies, standard weights and measures, and other manifestations of commercial or cultural uniformity. Some of these manifestations (e.g., the metric system) have become worldwide. The facts of earlier colonialism and of global communication and interdependence have led to the diminution of subnational or even national literacy systems and the dominance of a few literate languages. This dominance and the selection of the language in which a people will be schooled to a high level of literacy is often a complex political question and one that has brought with it a goodly amount of bloodshed.

It is this level of literacy, too, that has brought about the equation of literacy and education in the minds of many. Scribner and Cole (1981) have shown that the two are not synonymous, for indeed people can be literate at the rudimentary level without manifesting the signs of being educated. Training in the more advanced literacy brings with it the various other attributes of a literate culture that we have noted. This training appears to be in the activities of an urbanized intelligentsia that has become increasingly cosmopolitan and increasingly subdivided into specialized communities (Heath, 1983; Tornebohm, 1973). The group differs from the earlier priests or scribes of India, China, or Islam in the types of learning they have acquired but not in their essential separation from and control over the larger polity.

Although the history of written language and the contrast between oral and written language has been of great interest to the anthropologist and the cultural psychologist, there has of late been a mistaken assumption that ontogeny recapitulates phylogeny and that from the nature of the cultural shift people might glean insights into individual development. Some have suggested that the child's early progress is from an oral to a textual culture and have sought to draw instructional lessons (Olson, 1977; Dickinson, 1987). The analogy could not be further from the truth, as we have shown. Moreover, it is a mistake to assume that today's child inhabits an oral world. In the Western nations certainly and most probably around the globe, the environment is replete with print and text. They are in garbage cans, along the side of every street and road, and on the television tube. Like it or not, our culture is a print culture, and the child begins to inhabit the world of print almost at the same time as it begins to inhabit the world of oral language. Although there is much of interest to educational policy makers in the various ways by which a society becomes literate, the application of these findings to the instruction of the individual is at best remote. The current research on emergent literacy (covered elsewhere in this volume), which shows that children at very early ages have a sense of what a text is when it is read aloud to them or when they attempt to fashion one, clearly supports the idea that children are well aware that they inhabit a literate culture. They are also aware of the differences between oral and written discourse. Educational policy makers, therefore, must take into account the nature and history of oral and literate cultures, but they should not assume that the child is a "primitive."

REFERENCES

Akinnaso, F. N. (1981). On the difference between writing and speech. *Language and Speech, 25,* 97–125.
Akinnaso, F. N. (1985). On the similarities between spoken and written language. *Language and Speech, 28,* 323–359.
Blaug, M. (1966). Literacy and economic development. *School Review, 74,* 393–418.
Bloomfield, L. (1933). *Language.* New York: Holt.
Braudel, F. (1979). *Civilisation materielle: Economie et capitalism, XVe-XVIIIe siecle [A history of capitalism in the West (1981)].* Paris: A Colin.
Burke, E. (1975). Language and early education in Papua New Guinea. In J. Brammall & R. J. May (Eds.), *Education in Melanesia* (pp. 268–273). Canberra: Australian National University.
Clammer, J. R. (1976). *Literacy and social change: A case study of Fiji.* Leiden: E. J. Brill.
Clifford, J. (1986). On ethnographic allegory. In J. Clifford & G. G. Marcus (Eds.), *Writing culture: The poetics and politics of ethnography.* Berkeley: University of California Press.
Cole, M. (1985). Education and the third world: A critical discussion and some experimental data. In E. Bok, J. P. P. Haanen, & M. A. Walters (Eds.), *Education for cognitive development.* The Hague: SVO/SCO.
deSaussure, F. (1916). *Cours de linguistique general.* Lausanne: Payot.
Diah, M. (1982). *National language policy and the writing curriculum in Indonesia: A case study.* Unpublished dissertation. Urbana, IL.
Dickinson, D. K. (1987). Oral language, literacy skills, and response to literature. In J. R. Squire (Ed.), *The dynamics of language learning: Research in reading and English* (pp. 147–183). Urbana, IL: National Conference on Research in English.
Ezzaki, A., Spratt, J. E., and Wagner, D. A. (1987). Childhood literacy acquisition in rural Morocco: Effects of language differences and Quranic preschooling. In D. Wagner (Ed.), *The future of literacy in a changing world* (pp. 159–173). New York: Pergamon.
Fishman, J. (1967). Bilingualism with and without diglossia. Diglossia without bilingualism. *Journal of Social Issues, 23,* 29–38.
Foster, P. (1971). Problems of literacy in sub-Saharan Africa. In T. Sebeok (Ed.), *Current trends in linguistics* (Vol. 7) (pp. 587–617). The Hague: Mouton.
Foster, P. (1977). Education and social differentiation in less-developed countries. *Comparative Education Review, 21* (2/3), 211–229.
Foster, P. (1980). Regional disparities in educational development: Some critical observations. In G. Carron & T. N. Chau (Eds.), *Regional disparities in educational development: A controversial issue* (pp. 19–48). Paris: IIEP.
Foster, P. (1987). The contribution of education to development. In G. Psacharopoulos (Ed.), *The economics of education: Research and studies* (pp. 93–100). New York: Pergamon Press.
Fuller, B., Edwards, J. H. Y., & Gorman, K. (1987). Does rising literacy spark economic growth? Commercial expansion in Mexico. In D. Wagner (Ed.), *The future of literacy in a changing world* (pp. 319–340). New York: Pergamon Press.
Gaur, A. (1985). *A history of writing.* New York: Scribner's.
Geertz, C. (1960). *The religion of Java.* Glencoe, IL: Free Press.
Gelb, I. (1963). *A study of writing.* Chicago: University of Chicago Press.
Goody, J. (1968). Restricted literacy in Northern Ghana. In J. Goody (Ed.), *Literacy in traditional societies* (pp. 199–246). Cambridge, Eng.: Cambridge University Press.
Goody, J. (1977). *The domestication of the savage mind.* Cambridge, Eng.: Cambridge University Press.
Goody, J. (1986). *The logic of writing and the organization of society* (pp. XVII, 1–213). Cambridge, Eng.: Cambridge University Press.
Goody, J., & Watt, I. (1968). The consequences of literacy. In J. Goody (Ed.), *Literacy in traditional societies* (pp. 27–68). Cambridge, Eng.: Cambridge University Press.
Gough, K. (1968). Implications of literacy in traditional China and India. In J. Goody (Ed.), *Literacy in traditional societies* (pp. 70–84). Cambridge, Eng.: Cambridge University Press.
Harrison, S. (1960). *India: The most dangerous decade.* Princeton, NJ: Princeton University Press.
Havelock, E. (1976). *Origins of Western literacy.* Toronto: University of Toronto Press.
Heath, S. B. (1983). *Ways with words.* New York: Cambridge University Press.
Ho, Ping-ti (1962). *The ladder of success in imperial China: Aspects of social mobility, 1368–1911.* New York: Columbia University Press.
Innis, H. (1951). *The bias of communication.* Oxford, Eng.: Oxford University Press.
Kachru, B. (1982). *The other tongue: English across cultures.* Urbana, IL: University of Illinois Press.
Lerner, D. (1958). *The passing of traditional society.* Glencoe, IL: Free Press.
Lévi-Strauss, C. (1966). *The savage mind.* Chicago: University of Chicago Press.
Logan, R. K. (1986). *The alphabet effect: The impact of the phonetic alphabet on the development of Western civilization.* New York: Morrow.
Lord, A. B. (1987). Characteristics of orality. *Oral Tradition, 2,* 54–72.
McLuhan, H. M. (1962). *The Gutenberg galaxy.* Toronto: University of Toronto Press.

McLuhan, H. M. (1964). *Understanding media*. Toronto: University of Toronto Press.

Marsh, R. M. (1961). *The Mandarins: The elites in China*. Glencoe, IL: Free Press.

Murdock, C. P., & Provost, C. (1980). The measurement of cultural complexity in H. Barry & A. Schlegel (Eds.), *Cross-cultural samples and codes* (pp. 147–148). Pittsburgh: Pittsburgh University Press.

Ong, W. J. (1982). *Orality and literacy: The technologizing of the word*. London and New York: Methuen.

Olson, D. (1977). From utterance to text: The bias of language in speech and writing. *Harvard Educational Review, 47*, 257–281.

Purves, A. C., & Purves, W. (1986). Perspectives: Culture, text models, and the activity of writing. *Research in the Teaching of English, 19*, 174–197.

Purves, A. C. (1987). Literacy, culture, and community. In D. A. Wagner (Ed.), *The future of literacy in a changing world* (pp. 216–232). Oxford, Eng.: Pergamon.

Rudolph S. H., & Rudolph L. (Eds.). (1972). *Education and politics in India: Studies in organization, society, and polity*. Cambridge, MA: Harvard University Press.

Schmandt-Besserat, D. (1981). Decipherment of the earliest tablets. *Science, 211*, 283–285.

Scribner, S., & Cole, M. (1981). *The psychology of literacy*. Cambridge, MA.: Harvard University Press.

Steinberg, S. H. (1961). *Five hundred years of printing*. London: Penguin.

Tannen, D. (1982). Oral and literate strategies in spoken and written narratives. *Language, 58*, 1–21.

Tornebohm, H. (1973). Perspectives on inquiring systems. Department of Theory of Science, University of Gothenburg, Report No. 53.

UNESCO (1953). The use of vernacular languages in education. Monographs on Fundamental Education, No. 8. Paris: Author.

UNESCO (1987). *Education and training policies in sub-Saharan Africa*. Paris: Author.

Vachek, F. (1973). *Written language: General problems and problems of English*. The Hague: Mouton.

Wann, L. (1939). *Century readings in the English essay*. New York: Appleton-Century Crofts.

Watt, I. (1957). *The rise of the novel: Studies in DeFoe, Richardson, and Fielding*. London: Chatto and Windus.

Wagner, D. (Ed.). (1987). *The future of literacy in a changing world*. Oxford, Eng.: Pergamon Press.

Weber, M. (1958a). The Chinese literati. In H. Gerth & C. Wright Mills (Eds.), *From Max Weber: Essays in sociology*. Oxford, Eng.: Oxford University Press.

Weber, M. (1958b). India: The Brahman and the castes. In H. Gerth & C. Wright Mills (Eds.), *From Max Weber: Essays in sociology*. Oxford, Eng.: Oxford University Press.

Yang, L. S. (1956). Powerful families of Eastern Han. In E. Zen Sun & J. De Francis (Eds.), *Chinese social history*. Washington, DC: American Council of Learned Societies.

3 THE DEVELOPMENT OF LITERACY IN THE INDUSTRIALIZED NATIONS OF THE WEST

Richard L. Venezky

Literacy represents both a national aspiration and a set of human practices anchored in space and time. From this dual existence literacy has acquired both a sociopolitical dimension, associated with its role within society and the ways in which it is deployed for political, cultural, and economic ends; and a psychological dimension, associated with cognitive and affective properties that lead to greater or lesser individual motivation for and competence with writing and print. These dimensions have developed over the past 1,000 years as literacy in the Western world changed from being the private possession of scribes and clerics, practiced primarily within the circumscribed domains of religion and government, to a near-universal tool of the masses, utilizable within every facet of daily life.

In parallel with this downward and outward spread of literacy within society have also occurred changes in literacy practices. As the manuscript page, with its often perceptually complex graphical style, its unspaced arrangement of words, and its irregular orthography was replaced over time by the printed page, with its increasing legibility of print and regularity of spelling, and as exposure to literacy practices began at earlier ages and received more regular and intensive practice through a lifetime, reading for the average literate changed from a slow, oral production to a more rapid, silent practice.

The goal of this chapter is to trace these complex changes within the histories of the Western industrialized nations, primarily from the rise of feudalism until the end of the first quarter of this century, when most of these nations had attained—or were close to attaining—universal literacy. This is not intended to be a comprehensive chronicle of literacy within the countries of interest, but instead a perspective for viewing literacy development, with emphasis on those issues of theory and methodology that are of interest to readers of this text. The primary focus here is the practice of literacy, its expansion over time, and the evidence for both the quantity and quality of literacy at different periods in Western history. Little attention is given to speculations on the consequences of literacy (e.g., Goody & Watt, 1968; Stock, 1983; Eisenstein, 1979) or on conspiracy theories, particularly those that posit manipulation of children through reading practices or of the masses through literacy expectations (e.g., Graff, 1979).

This chapter, like a classical symphony, is divided into four major sections. In the first, Preliminaries, the major theme of the chapter is introduced and a few secondary themes played out: how literacy has been defined over time, what threads can be

I am grateful to Rebecca Barr, John Craig, and Robert Hampel for their thoughtful comments on earlier drafts of this paper.

stretched between the modern psychological study of reading and the history of literacy, and an obligatory note on the sources for this work. In the second section, Problems of Evidence, the forms of evidence that can be adduced for the study of literacy are classified and dissected, their values and foibles laid bare. The third section, General Development, finally gets down to the progression of literacy across the centuries, leaping, sometimes like falling water across the rocks, from country to country and time period to time period, through religious influences, the Renaissance, the rise of the vernaculars, the Industrial Revolution, and the modern era. Then, in a brief coda, a research agenda is offered for closing the many gaps uncovered in the earlier sections.

PRELIMINARIES

Common Threads in Literacy Expansion

The perspective adopted here, in brief, is that literacy is a response to the needs of collective society; and therefore the most immediate social change that promotes wider literacy is the expansion of writing and print into areas of everyday life where previously it did not exist or where its role was more restricted. Therefore one of the most important goals of historical studies on literacy is to understand the mechanisms by which first handwritten and later printed materials were generated, distributed, and used. Scholarship centered on what the French call *L'histoire du livre*. What has come to be called the "history of the book" in Anglo-American circles has quickened in the past decade; and a large body of material on Western print culture, including new theories on the nature of print and its use, has appeared (e.g., Kaestle, 1985; Darnton, 1983; Spufford, 1981; Marker, 1985).

But the expansion of writing and print is only the first part of this perspective. Equally important to this notion is the answer to the question of what has driven this expansion over the past 1,000 years or so. What are the differences between, for example, the English worlds of King John (of Magna Carta fame) and the last years of Queen Victoria, or the French worlds of King Philip and Georges Clemenceau that make print more important in the 20th century than in earlier times? In other words, "The problem . . . is not simply how and why people became literate. It is rather why the printed word in its various forms assumes significance in the lives of individuals and societies" (Laqueur, 1983, p. 44).

Among the changes most often cited as direct causes of the spread of literacy are the development of the market economy (Thomas, 1986), the Reformation (Haile, 1976, p. 817), and the expansion of schooling (Spufford, 1981, p. 19; Craig, 1981, p. 171). All three are important components of the transformation of Europe from feudalism to modern, industrial nationhood, but they cannot fully explain the profound change that has occurred in the role of literacy in individual lives. The Reformation, the market economy, schooling, industrialization, and many other factors contributed to the outward expansion of the physical and mental space of the ordinary citizen and thus have driven the continual incursion of print into everyday life. So long as most individuals saw their lives as permanently rooted to an ancestral farm or village, their occupations and social statuses determined inexorably by heredity, and their relationship to Scripture and the supernatural mediated by others, there was little need for literacy. What happened at a distance from the daily perimeter of their existence was usually not of major interest, and if it were it could easily be transmitted orally by local officials, clerics, or travelers who might happen by.

But as political awareness and power developed, the desire to know what was happening in distant political centers increased. Similarly, the market economy created a need not only to communicate with shippers and merchants who were far away, but also to monitor events in those places that might affect the nature or quantity of what one produced. The change in relationship between individual and Scripture that resulted from the Reformation expanded the mental world of the devout. Where once the village priest provided verse and interpretation, now each individual, at least within the new Protestant faiths, was directly responsible for these. These and other changes expanded continually the mental and physical space within which the ordinary person lived, making communication beyond the immediately observable world both necessary and desirable. The printing press and schooling were important components of this change process, but they did not by themselves drive the spread of literacy; instead, their separate importances derived also from the outward expansion of personal space, as will be discussed more fully below.

An alternative view to the one presented here could be created around the idea of empowerment: that each stage in the expansion of literacy among the masses gave power to yet another group of people—that is, entrée to social, political, or economic benefits that previously had not been enjoyed. But this is too general and too hasty a conclusion. Literacy may have been acquired in some instances to maintain position in a changing environment, rather than to acquire new privilege. Literacy may then have been only one of a number of skills required for promotion in society; or it may have been an enabling skill that, if not followed by the acquisition of additional skills, gave no special returns. The notion of personal space, although not yet as precise as it might be, is neutral towards power, control, and even advantage, at least in the traditional senses of these terms. The use of literacy for personal enjoyment, for example, gives no special powers to the reader, yet represents a major expansion of personal space and a large step for the integration of print into everyday life.

This, then, is the framework within which almost 1,000 years of literacy development will be traced. This perspective might, in a loose sense, be called a theory of *literacy expansion*. It predicts that social changes which enlarge individual space offer the greatest opportunity for the spread of print culture and that where print culture expands, literacy expands. The domain to which this theory applies is Europe and America, from feudal times until the 19th and early 20th centuries, when almost all industrialized nations had accepted basic education and universal literacy as national interests.

Exceptions to the theory of literacy expansion presented here can be found, particularly where literacy was promoted for limited ends. In late 17th-century Sweden, for example, reading ability was pressed on the population by church and state to ensure that everyone could "read, sing, and pray the holy 'Word' of God from books printed in Gothic type" (Johansson, 1987, p. 65). Through regular parish examinations, fines for parents who failed to teach their children, and denial of Communion and marriage rights to those adults who could not read and recite the catechism, reading ability rose above 90 percent by the mid-18th century. This form of literacy, like the semiliteracy based upon reading that the Catholic Church promoted in 19th-century France (Furet & Ozouf, 1982, p. 220), did not represent an individual response to social needs. It was imposed from without to preserve tradition rather than to adjust to new needs.[1] Even today, however, literacy is used by some primarily to confirm cherished beliefs rather than to gain access to new ideas and information (e.g., Heath, 1980, p. 129). However, the literacy expansion theory can account for the major trends that have accompanied literacy development in the West, at least up to recent times. Perhaps more important, it also provides a perspective through which testable hypotheses can be generated and better theories built.

What is Literacy?

Literacy has meant different things at different times and in different places. The modern terms "literate" and "illiterate" both derive from the Latin *literatus*, which for Cicero was a learned person. In the Middle Ages a literatus was one who could read, write, and perhaps speak Latin, regardless of what his competence might have been in the vernacular (Stock, 1983, p. 27). After 1300, however, literacy in the vernacular became increasingly more common (Clanchy, 1979, pp. 182 ff.). In addition, due to the breakdown of learning during the Middle Ages, literatus came to mean minimal ability in reading. Although the term "literacy" does not occur in the English lexicon until near the end of the 19th century, the modern concepts of literate and illiterate date from the last half of the 16th century. Remnants of the classical definition survived, nevertheless, until at least the end of the 18th century, when Lord Chesterfield wrote that an illiterate was one "ignorant of Greek and Latin" (cited in *Oxford English Dictionary*, 1933, s.v. "illiterate").

Unfortunately, the literate/illiterate dichotomy that pervades the historical literature on literacy disguises the continual nature of literacy ability. Almost no attempt has been made to estimate the actual levels of reading or writing ability that might have resulted in the past from different exposures to instruction and practice, or that might have been required at different times, in spite of Schofield's (1968, p. 314) call to do this in an oft-cited paper on the evidence for historical literacy. Cremin (1970, pp. 448–449) suggested a beginning to this discrimination by differentiating between marginal ("inert") literacy and self-sustaining ("liberating") literacy, but the techniques for making this distinction have not been explored.

The exclusion of writing from the early definitions of literacy resulted primarily from the complexities inherent in the preparation of writing surfaces, inks, and quills. Furet and Ozouf (1982, p. 76) point out that "We are inclined to forget, today, that for a long time writing was really a technical exercise, involving instruments, muscular gymnastics and a knack." (Whether writing today requires significantly more than eye-hand coordination, plus mastery of appropriate graphical conventions, has not been properly addressed by the current research on writing.) According to Cippola (1969, p. 8), writing over the past 500 years "is strictly and almost inevitably connected with the condition of urbanization and commercial intercourse." In 15th-century England, for example, where literacy had begun to spread to the masses, writing (and accounting) remained the possession of a small group of professionals (Fisher, 1977, p. 896).

The addition of writing to the definition of literacy appears to be a contribution of the Reformation. Without writing, literacy is restricted to a passive activity, dependent upon the will of others. Entry to the market economy requires writing, as do those other activities that mark the modern person—for example, pursuit of personal efficacy and self-directed relationships with the traditional sources of social and political influence (Inkeles & Smith, 1974, p. 290).

For those who read but cannot write, Cipolla (1969, p. 11) proposes the term "semiliterate." Cipolla also uses this term for those who read and write poorly, but this suggests that sufficient information is available to distinguish at least two levels of reading ability for earlier times, an issue that will be discussed more fully below. In this chapter, literacy, unless qualified otherwise, will assume both reading and writing.

Psychology and History

Literacy qua literacy is a cognitive skill, categorically similar to numeracy, bookkeeping, and chess playing. This is not to deny literacy's sociopolitical dimension, but instead to reinforce the relevance of psychology to the study of literacy acquisition and literacy performance. As a cognitive skill, literacy can be viewed as two related complex processes: reading and writing. For the former an enormous research literature is available, from which a few empirically derived conclusions can be drawn. For example, the process of reading involves (1) a set of lower-level skills for detecting and recognizing letters and other word parts and for assembling these into wholes for matching against an internal lexicon, and (2) a set of higher-level skills for deriving and integrating meanings. For efficient reading the lower-level skills must work rapidly and autonomously, although how much so for different reading tasks remains to be explored. The higher-level skills must integrate local and global text information with information from long-term memory, although the degree of such integration depends upon the text and the task (Perfetti, 1985).

We also invoke developmental data on reading, but these apply primarily to children. From these data we can estimate such reading characteristics as oral and silent reading rates, degree of subvocalization, average eye fixation span, and types of oral reading errors for learners at different points in their reading development (e.g., Taylor, 1937; Hardyck & Petrinovich, 1970; Judd & Buswell, 1922; Biemiller, 1970; Barr, 1975). One of the challenges in the historical analysis of literacy is to relate such conclusions from the modern psychological study of reading to the estimation of reading ability in earlier times. For example, what oral reading rate might we expect of a 6-year-old child in 16th-century Paris after 20 to 30 hours of tutoring with a Latin Psalter as the only reading text? How well would the average accountant in late 15th-century Milan, trained in reading black-letter Gothic script, read documents written in roman script or printed in the then emerging roman italic font (Febvre & Martin, 1958, pp. 80 ff.)?

Thomas (1986, pp. 100 ff.) hypothesizes that during the 16th to the 18th centuries an ability to read Gothic did not necessarily guarantee an ability to read roman, and that some could read print but not handwriting. A professional in early 16th-century Europe might be expected to read documents written in either Latin or the local vernacular, and either handwritten in any of the four popular scripts of the time or printed, with a comparable number of options for type styles. For such an individual, how much exposure to these various graphic forms would be required before word recognition became automatic in each? Would the Stroop effect be equally strong across all forms of writing and print, or would it reflect differential exposure (Stroop, 1935)?[2] And would frequency effects in word recognition be unique to each writing/printing style, or common within a language?

These questions and many others are generally not answerable with the marginal trace that remains of earlier reading habits. Dead men neither give interviews nor do they respond to tachistoscopic exposures of letters and words. Even the gross characteristics of reading in earlier times are not well understood. Oral reading predominated at least to the time of Chaucer among proficient readers, and perhaps to the end of the 19th century for most elementary schools (Hendrickson, 1929–1930; Saeger, 1982; Crosby, 1936; Venezky, 1987). Whether this was the result of limited practice opportunities, low legibility of script and early print, or social convention, we do not know. For most modern readers, continually bombarded with print, word recognition is overlearned for all but the least common words. But the nobility of pre-Gutenberg Europe might not encounter more than a page or two per day of handwritten text, containing perhaps not more than 400 words total, on the average. These pages might be in a highly legible hand or in a barely decipherable scrawl, and they might be in Latin or in a vernacular. Under these conditions it is unlikely that any but a small minority of copyists, scholars, professors, and the like would gain sufficient exposure to writing to read silently.

Certainly the perceptual conditions for reading were different from today, but how different they were has not been carefully studied. For example, eyeglasses were introduced into Europe in the late 13th or early 14th century (Rosen, 1956), but their acquisition by the masses probably came much later. Artificial lighting for sustained reading on overcast days or at night was severely limited until at least the 1780s, when the Argand lamp was invented. However, as late as the third quarter of the 19th century, many university libraries in America did not utilize artificial lighting for safety reasons and therefore closed at or near sundown.

With sometimes no more than signatures as evidence for literacy, we can at best make crude comparisons across regions and times. Converging evidence can sometimes be marshalled, however, to make estimations beyond these crude comparisons; and the modern psychological findings can probably be applied significantly more than they have been so far to establish upper and lower bounds on abilities.

A Note on Sources

Among the sources of information on the development of literacy in the West, Cipolla (1969) remains the most comprehensive, in spite of its age and limited size. Kaestle (1985) provides an introduction to current scholarly thinking on the development of literacy plus a sketch of its development in the West. Clanchy (1979) is essential for understanding the transition of English society from memory to written record during the period from 1066 to 1307; it is exemplary for its documentation of the expansion of writing into public and private life. Also useful, especially for alternative viewpoints, are Houston (1983) and Graff (1986). Other works exist on specific countries, generally limited to a few centuries; and some, like Brooks (1985), which covers the rise of literacy in Russia from 1861 to 1917, and Chartier (1987), which deals with print in early modern France, attempt to explore the uses of literacy in society. The majority, however, are concerned primarily with the quantity of literacy as revealed by signatures on official documents, and therefore reveal little about the ways in which literacy entered peoples' lives. Almost all of the works cited here are in English and are generally available. For direct quotations, paraphrases, and data, and for ideas that might be difficult to locate within a work, page references are given; otherwise, only the work itself is referenced. No up-to-date bibliography on the history of literacy in the Western industrialized countries is available, but Graff (1981) covers a large percentage of what was available up to the time he published.

PROBLEMS OF EVIDENCE

The archaeologist works with remnants of physical objects, revealing over time both products and the technologies that produced them. From a few postholes and a charcoal deposit, a pit house is reconstructed and its construction techniques identified; from a few pot shards, a complete vessel is drawn, its construction and firing procedures determined, and often even the sources of its constituents located. The historian, working with both the archaeologist's findings and written records, reconstructs societies and cultures, traces their growth and decline, the raising of their young, and the other everyday events that stitched their lives from awakening to bedding down. From these assemblages of materials, people, and events, the more adventuresome attempt to recover mental capacities, attitudes, and beliefs.

It is at this point that the student of historical literacy enters. His or her task, at least as defined so far, has been to determine the presence or absence of a specific learned ability in specified populations that arrayed themselves across the historical landscape. But since reading is an ephemeral act that leaves no discernible trace, the evidence for earlier literacy levels must be gathered from indirect indicators and connected to the process of interest by inference, presumption, and other tenuous threads of faith. While this evidence presents many difficulties in interpretation, it does not appear so weak as to justify Eisenstein's (1979, p. 414) decision in her study of the printing press ". . . to sidestep problems associated with literacy rates whenever possible since inadequate data and uncertain criteria make all general statements suspect."

The central weakness in the marshalling and deployment of evidence for historical literacy has been in the restricted goal that most historians of literacy have accepted, that of assigning a single statistic to each group of interest, representing percentage of literacy or illiteracy. Most commonly, this single statistic has been based on the number of people who signed a will, court deposition, marriage certificate, or other document with a signature rather than a mark. While some like Auwers (1980, p. 206) have noted that the use of signatures as literacy indicators reduces a continuous variable to a dichotomous one, most studies have focused on quantity rather than quality of literacy (e.g., Lockridge, 1974; Cressy, 1980; Furet & Ozouf, 1982). A small number of studies, as will be discussed later, have attempted to reconstruct the uses of literacy in everyday life for particular periods and groups, and thus demonstrate actual literacy practices rather than simply the potential ability to read or write.

Types of Evidence

Historical indicators of literacy ability can be classed in three groups, based upon whether they are evidence for literacy ability, or for opportunity for literacy practice, or for exposure to literacy training. For convenience these will be referred to as *ability*, *practice*, and *training*. Each draws upon different sources of information, and each presents its own problems not only of linkage to actual literacy but also of validity and reliability.

Ability

Direct assessment.   Performance data ostensibly give the most direct evidence of literacy abilities; however, until the development of mental testing in the early part of this century and literacy testing in particular, direct assessment measures of literacy were crude at best. The earliest reading assessments on record were done for benefit of clergy, beginning in 14th-century England but probably earlier in France (Gabel, 1928–29, p. 67). Since clerics charged with certain crimes (mostly felonies) were to be tried in ecclesiastical rather than secular courts, a crude test of clericy was developed, based upon the reading aloud of a verse from the Bible. One who passed this examination was assumed to be a cleric, since clerics were the vast majority of the literate in medieval and feudal England. Presumably, one escaped the gallows through satisfactory reading ability. It was possible, especially when the same passage was used repeatedly for benefit-of-clergy tests, to pass through memorization rather than true reading ability; and cases are reported where such memorization was revealed (Gabel, 1928–1929, p. 71n).

Reading aloud, generally from a religious text or school reader, was the most common direct assessment technique for reading ability until the end of the 19th century. It was, for example, the principal technique used in Sweden in the 17th through the early 19th century for nationwide reading tests (Johansson, 1987). While the Swedish records do not note any criteria for judging reading ability, some parish records indicate more than simple literate-illiterate; one even divides reading ability into five levels: cannot read, has begun to read, reads a little, reads acceptably, and can read (Johansson, 1987, p. 83). Rice (1893), who tested schoolchildren in the major U.S. cities during the 1880s and 1890s on a variety of school subjects, also used oral performance as his test of reading ability.

Tests for writing were rare prior to the 20th century. The Swiss military was among the first to assess writing ability, beginning in the last decades of the 19th century (Cipolla, 1969, p. 12). Writing of letters, along with understanding of newspaper articles, were among the tests given by the U.S. military during World War I to about 1.5 million soldiers and sailors (Gray, 1925, p. 14; Gray & Munroe, 1929, pp. 21–22). In these tests, about 25 percent of all tested failed the reading and writing components.

Self-report.   Besides direct assessment techniques, two indirect methods have been used by historians: self-report and analysis of writing samples. The U.S. Census has used self-report to determine literacy since 1840, although the questions asked and the criterion levels employed have varied. Self-report was also used in other national censuses and by the French military in the 19th century (Furet & Ozouf, 1982). While self-report may overestimate reading ability, limited empirical data are available on this issue. In addition, we have incomplete information in many cases on the questions asked and on the scoring procedures.

Analysis of writing samples.   Writing samples, particularly signatures from wills, court depositions, pensioner rolls, oaths, and the like, are the most often used evidence for literacy levels. Other writing samples such as diaries, letters, graffiti, and epitaphs are rarer and generally not comparable across countries and time periods. They are, therefore, difficult to use for quantitative comparisons, but are invaluable for tracing the general spread of literacy practices.

On the validity and reliability of signatures as predictors of literacy, a vigorous debate has developed over the past 20 years (Schofield, 1968; Cremin, 1970; Lockridge, 1974; Cressy, 1980; Rachal, 1987), even though they were used as evidence for literacy rates at least as early as the first decade of this century (e.g., Bruce, 1910). The issues in this debate, aside from the quality of literacy that might be implied and how it might have been utilized, center on (1) whether or not signing was always learned *after* reading was acquired, and (2) whether or not those who could write always signed rather than marked. Although the issues specific to signatures will be discussed more extensively in a following section, certain problems pertain both to signatures and to the other forms of writing.

One problem is ascertaining whose literacy is reflected by a signature, letter, or other form of writing: that of the ostensible owner or that of a scrivener, copyist, or other surrogate. Another is deciding which literacy skills are reflected by a particular literacy act. A letter, diary entry, or other connected text can with high certainty be taken as evidence for both reading and writing ability. A signature, on the other hand, becomes an indicator of writing only through the assumption that signing is acquired only after full writing ability is learned; and it becomes an indicator of reading ability only through the assumption that signing is learned after reading ability is acquired. These assumptions, as will be discussed in the section on signatures, may have been true for some eras and some countries, but not for others.

Contemporary reports.   Finally, literacy performance has been judged by contemporaries who have recorded their observations about the characteristics of a people. The Frenchman Alexis de Tocqueville, traveling through the United States in the early 1830s, was one such observer, recording that New Englanders were better educated than those from the West and the South (Tocqueville, 1840/1963, p. 315). Similarly, Sir Joshua Fitch, an English inspector of training colleges, reported from visits to the United States in the 1880s that American schools stressed silent reading (Fitch, 1900, pp. 46–47). Altick (1957, ch. 7) reports similar evaluations for 19th century England, as does Brooks (1985, ch. 1) for late 19th- and early 20th-century Russia. But without knowing the capabilities, interests, and audience of the reporters, little credence can be given to such reports.

Opportunity for Practice

A second approach to estimating the extent or quantity of literacy is through assessment of opportunity for literacy practices, such as purchase or possession of books, subscriptions to newspapers and magazines, or borrowing of books from a library. Gilmore's (1982) study of literacy in the Connecticut Valley in the late 18th and early 19th centuries uses, among other indicators of literacy, references to books in probate inventories. Similar evidence for England has been reported by Johnston (1983), who analyzed the contents of wills from the diocese of Worcester from 1699 to 1713; Jayne (1956), who surveyed private book collections in England from 1500 to 1640; and Dyer (1973) and Clark (1976), both of whom studied book ownership in parts of England in the period from the mid-16th to the mid-17th century.

Evidence centered at greater and greater distances from the readers' hands has also been adduced. The development of libraries and their spread throughout Europe and the United States is often cited as evidence for the spread of literacy. Other types of distant evidence center around the production and distribution of books. Spufford (1981, ch. 4), for example, uses sizes of publisher inventories for chapbooks and the extent of the distribution network for cheap printed materials as two of several types of evidence for the extent of reading in 17th-century England. She recognized, nevertheless, the lack of a critical link between production/distribution and ownership. "What we cannot do, however, is to close the argument convincingly by showing the humble reader actually in possession of ballads and chapbooks" (Spufford, 1981, p. 45).

As important as book ownership is for demonstrating the spread of literacy practices, it has limitations as a quantitative indicator of literacy. Book ownership has varied through the centuries not only according to the interests and reading abilities of any population, but also according to income levels, church and government censorship, prices, and distribution. Clark (1976), is analyzing book ownership in the county of Kent (England) in the period from 1560 to 1640, concluded that expansion of ownership during this period was due to three factors: a rising standard of living, increased literacy skills, and an improved sales network for books. Clark found, for example, that the chances for book ownership were uniformly high throughout this period for estates with goods valued £500 or above, and uniformly low for those valued below £24. Book ownership in the United States rose after the Revolutionary War due to increases in discretionary income and time, as well as to an improved transportation system for commercial goods.

Even the possession of books, when it can be clearly established, does not guarantee reading ability. Bibles, in particular, might be possessed as totems or obtained as gifts, or even purchased by illiterates with the expectation that literate visitors might read aloud from them (Bauml, 1980). Probate inventories as evidence of book ownership offer a number of special but not necessarily debilitating problems for determining the extent of literacy. They are class biased and highly selective for the types of books mentioned, particularly in the United States and England. Expensive texts are often mentioned but ephemeral items (e.g., almanacs, primers, ballads, chapbooks) rarely are. Then, books of especial value to a family might be distributed before the death of the owner of the household and therefore escape mention in the probate inventory.

Of equal interest to books for demonstrating the spread of literacy but more difficult to locate are those indicators of reading and writing that are by-products of these acts or are adjustments to the environment that result from them. Among the most innovative uses of such evidence is Clanchy's (1979, p. 43) compilations of the amounts of sealing wax used by the English Royal Chancery in the 13th century. From an average of 3.63 pounds per week in the interval 1226–1230, consumption increased to 31.90 pounds per week for the interval 1265–1271. If we assume that the average amount of wax required to seal a document remained constant over this period (and also assuming constant weight and wastage), then the Chancery increased by ninefold its document production from 1226–1230 until 1265–1271.

Environmental evidence for change in literacy practices is described by Thomas (1986, pp. 112 ff.), who claims that church congregations in Europe began to read in churches in the 15th century. Part of the evidence for this is found in design changes in church interiors from this period that made them brighter and therefore more conducive to reading of manuscript and print, including the replacement of stained glass with clearer glass after the Reformation. Saeger (1982, pp. 396 f.) also describes architectural change as evidence for shifts in literacy practices, but in this case changes in library interiors that signaled a switch from oral to silent reading.

In summary, opportunity-for-practice evidence rarely can be used alone to establish quantity of literacy. It does, however, provide convergent evidence for the spread of literacy into specific areas and classes of society.

Training

Exposure to literacy training is, next to ability measures, the most often used evidence for literacy. In general, the assumption is made that the spread of schooling, as marked by numbers of students in attendance, number of teachers employed, expenditures for education, or other tangible markers of schooling indicates a spread of literacy. The U.S. Census, for example, has assumed at various times that a fixed number of years of schooling (e.g., four) was a sufficient indicator of literacy, a practice used in a number of other countries (UNESCO, 1957; Furet & Ozouf, 1982). Spufford (1981, ch. 3) presents data on the numbers of schoolteachers in 19th-century England as evidence of increased literacy abilities. The relationship of schooling and literacy in the history of industrialized countries is discussed by Anderson (1965), who cites various types of evidence for the existence in earlier times of schooling, including community complaints over the short supply of teachers and controversies over who has the right to be a teacher (1965, p. 352). Cipolla (1969, pp. 24 ff.) discusses at length the use of formal education statistics as estimators of literacy levels, including proportion of economic resources allocated for education and ratio of teachers to population. Similar issues on the schooling-literacy relationship are discussed by Rachal (1987).

Although schooling records can provide positive evidence for capacity to read and write, a variety of cautions need to be observed. First, quality of schooling varied considerably across and within countries, regions, and time periods. For example, the quality of schooling for the English working class in the first half of the 19th century, and for the Papal States in the middle of the 19th century was generally low; but for Holland and Prussia at roughly this same time, it was considered good (Cipolla, 1969, pp. 31 ff.). After extensive study of the American district school of the 18th and 19th centuries, opinion is still divided on its quality (cf. Greene, 1965; Fuller, 1982; Johnson, 1904/1963; Cremin, 1970). Similar problems attend the evaluation of the rural schools in Scotland (Webb, 1954). Craig (1981, p. 179) speculates that urban schooling was probably more effective than rural schooling, perhaps because of higher attendance rates and a longer school year. Years of formal schooling, particularly from the middle of the 19th century (in most industrialized countries), may be a reasonable predictor of literacy; but in some countries like Russia, compulsory schooling was not instituted nationally until the 20th century (Brooks, 1985).

Schooling also applied differentially within and across populations. Except for Sweden (Johansson, 1987), boys were more likely than girls to receive schooling prior to the middle of the 19th century. Even when girls were sent to school, they often encountered a different curriculum from boys. For example, in William Gilpin's school in Hampshire parish (England) in the late 18th century, boys were taught reading, writing, and arithmetic, while girls were taught reading, knitting, and sewing (Adamson, 1929, p. 38). In the American South prior to the end of the Civil War, slaves received little or no education, and in most of the slave states the teaching of reading and writing to them was outlawed (Webber, 1978).

Whatever the outcomes of formal schooling, it is important to consider the percentages of any population that received their literacy instruction out of school. In one province of Moscow in 1883–1884, among 7,123 literate factory workers, only 38 percent reported learning to read in a village, town, or district school. The remainder learned to read outside of school (36%), or in a factory school (10%), or were taught by clergy (9%), or during military service (Cipolla, 1969, p. 25). Increases in the supply of teachers or in expenditures for education will be misleading as indicators of increased literacy if high proportions of the population are learning to read outside of school. Nevertheless, assuming a reasonable constant-quality factor, education and literacy are closely linked in most industrialized countries, at least from the middle of the 19th century.

Signatures as Evidence

The general case in favor of signatures as a measure of literacy is that (1) they are the only historical data that meet Schofield's (1968, pp. 317 ff.) requirements of a widely applicable and standard measure; (2) they are useful for comparative studies regardless of what their exact relationship to literacy is (Schofield, 1968); and (3) when other indicators of literacy are available along with signatures, the latter appear to change in relation to changes in these alternative variables (Cressy, 1980, pp. 42 ff.). Both Cressy (1980) and Schofield (1968) draw upon signatures in English records from relative modern times, but Furet and Ozouf (1982) arrive at similar conclusions from French data, based on comparisons of (1) self-report of literacy among army conscripts, (2) census data on reading and writing ability in the general population, and (3) signatures on marriage certificates (*actes de mariage*).

Schofield's (1968) requirements are by modern standards of scholarship overly conservative. What is required is comparability across regions, people, and time, which could be accomplished with different measures if they could be reliably anchored. Signatures, although they may represent the same skill across people, place, and time, may not bear the same relationship to what they proxy—that is, reading and writing— and therefore may not be comparable across all points on the historical spectrum.

Other reservations about the value of signatures come from a variety of sources. Data from a number of countries and a number of time periods demonstrate that high reading ability coexisted with low writing ability. This is especially true of the Scandinavian countries from the late 17th through the early 19th centuries, when state and church combined to enforce the teaching of reading but not of writing. Johansson (1987) has published extensive evidence on the separate developments of reading and writing in Sweden prior to the middle 1800s; and Smout (1982, p. 122) makes similar claims for Denmark, where most could read by the late 18th century, but where writing was not taught extensively until after the educational acts of 1814. In these situations signatures would grossly underestimate reading ability. Data on the disparity between reading and writing ability are also provided by West (1970, p. 130) for northern England in the year 1840. In a tabulation of the literacy abilities of 843 miners, only 67 percent of those who could read could also write. Since the number who could write represented about 50% of the total population, West suggested using a multiple of 1.49 to convert writer totals to reader totals when writing ability is in this same range.

The source of signatures is an additional factor in considering the reliability and validity of this form of evidence. Bruce (1910), who studied signing patterns in 17th-century Virginia, preferred signatures on court depositions to those on jury inquests and deeds of conveyance because the former tended to include all classes in society except slaves, while the other two were biased toward members of the middle and upper classes. Schofield (1968) prefers English signatures resulting from the Protestation Oath of 1642 (males over 18), the Test Oath of 1723 (everyone over 18), and the Anglican marriage register, although the latter omits several religious groups.

Auwers (1980), who studied female literacy in Windsor, Connecticut, 1640–1799, used mainly signatures on deeds; while Lockridge (1974), who studied literacy in pre-19th-century New England, used signatures on wills exclusively. Cressy (1980, p. 62), a strong advocate of signatures as evidence for literacy, nevertheless warns against the use of signatures from documents that are typically endorsed by nonrepresentative samples of the population. Wills, in particular, he found to be "chronically afflicted by social bias" (1980, p. 106), as were marriage license records (1980, p. 109). While using a variety of document types, Cressy agrees with Bruce (1910) that court deposition records, at least those produced by the ecclesiastical administration in England, offer the least bias for signatures of all available records.

Data on schooling practices in several countries show not only a read first-then write instructional pattern, but also disparities in writing ability based on sex. In Scotland in the middle of the 18th century, for example, among 109 men and women who indicated that they could read, many more men than women could write (Smout, 1982). Eklof (1983, p. 117) reports that the 19th-century Russian peasant showed little interest in educating girls, thus leading to the assumption that Russian women, at least until compulsory schooling was enforced, lagged behind Russian men both in reading and writing.

Adding to the uncertainty about the value of signatures is the distinction made by Gilmore (1982) between signing and writing. From data collected on book possession, signatures, and other indicators from the Connecticut Valley in the late 18th and early 19th centuries, Gilmore concluded that signing was learned first, followed by reading and then writing. If this were true, then signatures could grossly overestimate literacy levels. Although Gilmore's sequence has been challenged (cf. Monaghan, 1983), his separation of signing and writing still raises questions about the assumption made in most other studies that signing and writing are identical.

Missing from the discussion so far has been any concern for changes over a lifetime in literacy abilities and practices. The modern practice of beginning schooling between the ages of 5 and 7 should not be assumed for earlier times. Prior to mass public schooling, people acquired schooling when they needed it or when it was convenient. A family in a remote area of the American Tidewater of the late 18th century might hire a tutor for a few months of the winter to teach all of its children at once, and a 15-year-old in preindustrial Italy might be taught to read and write through an apprenticeship that requires by contract that these skills be taught along with the specified trade. Thus, some of those who marked marriage certificates in 17th-century France may have learned to read and write later in their lives. But alternatively, some of those who signed their names may have lost the ability to read and write later on through disuse. We have little empirical data on loss of these abilities in healthy individuals, but suspect that there is a level of reading and writing that must be reached before literacy becomes self-sustaining. In studies done for UNESCO in the 1950s, a fifth-grade level was claimed to be necessary for this stage of literacy (UNESCO, 1957). Soltow and Stevens (1981) claim that four years of formal schooling was required in mid-19th-century Ohio for literacy to become self-sustaining. Nevertheless, the rise of literacy levels throughout Europe and North America at times when formal schooling for most was far less than four years might be interpreted as an indication that literacy practice and not formal instruction per se is the critical factor in literacy attainment and literacy maintenance. In a recent study of the literacy abilities of young adults in the United States, Kirsch and Jungeblut (1986) found that literacy abilities improved with practice outside of school, regardless of the amount of schooling received. For the rise of literacy in Russia prior to World War I, Brooks (1985) holds that the types of literature available for the general population had a significant influence on the improvement of reading skills.

GENERAL DEVELOPMENT

From Church Monopoly to Lay Property

The general development of literacy in the industrialized West is a diffusion from a church monopoly to a possession of the nobility, from the nobility to the higher professions, from the higher to the lower professions, and eventually to the laboring class. Overlaid with this spreading out, like a subordinate theme in a symphony, are the patterns that characterize most of the progression to modernity: literacy came first to men and then to women, and it came to the towns and cities before it came to the rural areas. And its progress was neither steady nor linear. Up to the 19th and early 20th centuries, the expansion of the written word, whether by manuscript or printed form, drove the expansion of literacy. Then, beginning mostly in the 19th century, governments found it within their best interests to provide a basic education to all their citizens as a necessity for productive participation in civic, economic, and military affairs.

While the expansion of print into everyday life was driven at all times by complex needs, bureaucratic, economic, and religious pressures dominated at different times. In medieval Europe literacy was a closely guarded monopoly of the church, which used it sparingly for religious and government affairs. Pockets of lay literacy existed among the nobility, and an exceptional ruler like King Alfred in 9th-century England could read and perhaps write (Galbraith, 1935); but the need for lay literacy was highly limited and made all the more difficult by the dominion of Latin throughout most of Europe (Havelock, 1976).

But already in the 9th century, a gradual expansion of reading ability could be discerned as the higher and lower nobility began to access written information in charters, royal writs, medicinal recipes, and the like (Bauml, 1980). This process was greatly accelerated in the 11th and 12th centuries as towns and cities came to dominate over the countryside. With the increased division of labor that is intrinsic to urban society, daily life became increasingly more complex, requiring greater amounts of record keeping, administration, and communication. This in turn created a greater need for literate semiprofessionals to fill economic, administrative, and military positions (Bishop, 1968, pp. 42 f.; Strayer, 1965, p. 63). Education at all levels expanded to meet this need, resulting in a higher percentage of the young learning basic reading on one end of the ability scale, and the establishment of universities to meet training needs on the other end of the scale.

The origins of modern mass literacy have been located in these developments, particularly in the 12th and 13th centuries, when society shifted from reliance on memory to reliance on written records—or in Clanchy's (1979) words, "from sacred script to practical literacy." According to Clanchy (1979, p. 263), "Only in the 12th century did the number of documents, and the number of persons who understood them, begin to increase at a fast rate under the pressures of emerging bureaucracy. Practical business was the foundation of this new literacy."

This increase in practical literacy can be gauged not only in the increase in bureaucratic and economic documents that appear decade after decade from this period onward, but also in such indirect indicators as the simplification and standardization of document forms; a changeover from tedious, time-consuming monastic hands to faster cursive hands; and the use of seals to authenticate royal documents. Perhaps under the pressure of this large increase in the demand for writing materials, papermaking plants began to appear in Europe. Paper was known in Europe since the 12th century, when it was brought by merchants from China via the Arab countries. In spite of occasional edicts against its use (due to its fragility compared to parchment), the use of paper spread; and by the early 14th century several papermakers were established near Fabriano (Febvre & Martin, 1958, p. 30). At about the same time the art of grinding glass for spectacles was perfected in Europe (Cipolla, 1980, p. 175). With the decline of feudalism in the late 13th century, a new reading public developed, consisting of state officials, lawyers, lay advisors at court, and later, rich merchants. They, along with the nobility and the clergy, created a demand for subject matter texts, moral treatises, literature, romances, and other genres (Febvre & Martin, 1958). One dimension of this demand can be estimated by the more than 2,000 copies of Aristotle's works that have survived from the 13th and 14th centuries alone.

Literacy spread rapidly in the 14th, 15th, and 16th centuries in selected professions and in selected areas of Europe. By 1332, for example, judges in Venice had to be able to read and write; and by 1338 approximately 40 percent of the children in Florence between the ages of 5 and 14 attended school (Cipolla, 1969, pp. 42–46). By 1478 English goldsmiths would no longer accept apprentices who could not read and write (Anderson, 1965, p. 347). In the 15th century, wealthy tradesmen began to establish schools unattached to religious orders, thus accelerating the secularization of education; and by the middle of the 16th century school systems had expanded dramatically in Germany (Strauss, 1984), England (Adamson, 1929), and northeastern France and the Low Countries (Cipolla, 1969). Literacy continued through this period to be driven by practical utility, appearing first and to the highest degree in those trades most closely associated with the market economy (Thomas, 1986), and in areas where new technologies were forcing change, such as navigation and warfare. Early evidence for the entry of print into commercial life can be seen in the news-reporting service that developed in 14th- and 15th-century Nuremberg, bringing written accounts of news from places with commercial ties to the city (Houston, 1983). Yet economics was not the only impetus for literacy. In Scotland, Sweden, and Switzerland, for example, illiteracy was low in spite of backward economies (Houston, 1983).

The Role of Vernaculars

One of the complicating factors in determining literacy until roughly the end of the 17th century is the role that Latin played in religion, government, and the higher professions. As was mentioned earlier, a literate person, or literatus, was one who read, wrote, and perhaps spoke Latin regardless of his competence in the vernacular. So long as Latin remained the official language of church and government, the chasm between the ruling class and those ruled was maintained, resulting in what Havelock (1976, p. 75) calls *craft literacy*. Beginning around 1300, the vernacular languages, both in speech and in writing, began to acquire increasing importance in everyday life and slowly began to challenge Latin in the more regulated areas.

The movement towards the acceptance of vernacular for official use began in Italy before the Renaissance and spread quickly to France, where by 1539 French had become the official language of the Courts of Justice (Febvre & Martin, 1958). In England, where French (which dominated after the Norman Conquest), Latin, and English were all in use, the court language after 1300 was increasingly spoken English and written French (Fisher, 1977, p. 873). Parliament was addressed in English as early as 1362, and probably earlier; and English began to be used for the official administrative transactions of Chancery after 1420. The period from 1420 to 1460, according to Fisher (1977, p. 898), was crucial for the adoption of English in government, business, and private transactions. The Brewers' Company of London, which decided to switch its record keeping in 1422 from Latin and French to English (Adamson, 1929, p. 40 f.), was typical of many English enterprises that found this switch necessary because few of the middling ranks could read Latin or French.

The replacement of Latin by the vernaculars can be traced also through book titles, which provide a conservative estimate of vernacular popularity. In early 16th-century France, as an example, two-thirds of all books published were written in Latin. By the 1780s only one book in 20 in France was written in Latin and only one in 11 in Germany (Gray, 1969, p. 60). The legitimacy that Dante's *Divina Commedia* gave to Italian and Chaucer's *Canterbury Tales* gave to English in the 14th century spread over the centuries from popular literature to business and government and finally to science and religion. Hobbes's use of English for philosophical works and Descartes' use of French for science mark the distance that the vernaculars had traveled from the medieval dominion of Latin to the 17th century. The triumph of the vernacular languages in the 16th and 17th centuries appears to have been aided by the diffusion of literacy among the middling ranks as well as the nobility, but at the same time served as an impetus to the further spread of literacy among the lower classes.

Religious Factors

The introduction of printing in the middle of the 15th century and its rapid spread throughout Europe over the next decades had an impact on literacy, the full extent of which has yet to be determined. But whatever this might have been, printing was not a cause for increased literacy so much as it was an expediter for other pressures that led to a greater need for access to written materials. One of these pressures was clearly religion. Beginning with Luther's Reformation in the first quarter of the 16th century, which substituted the Word of God for the authority of the church, access to print became not only a requirement for the Protestant faithful but a necessity for those caught up in the ensuing ecclesiastical disputes.

Most writers on the history of literacy place the Reformation at or near the top of their lists of the causes of literacy expansion in Europe after the early 1500s (e.g., Stone,

1969; Cipolla, 1969). Haile (1976, p. 817) summarizes this consensus with the claim that "From a secular viewpoint surely the most far-reaching effect of Luther's activities was the radical increase in literacy from the 1520s on through the rest of the century."

Luther's views were circulated quickly throughout Europe in pamphlets, posters, handbills, and broadsheets, all of which were in use before this time for the circulation of information to the masses. Some of Luther's works were reprinted as early as 1519 in France, leading two years later to the French Parliament's ban on the printing or sale of unauthorized writings on Scripture (Febvre & Martin, 1958, p. 297). In time the Protestant areas of Europe acquired significantly higher literacy than the Catholic areas, with the exception of certain German-speaking Catholic enclaves. By the late 19th century in Prussia, Catholic illiteracy was twice as high as that of Protestants; and in Ireland and Italy the disparities were as great, if not greater (Cipolla, 1969, pp. 72 ff.).

Where Protestantism appeared, literacy and learning were seen to thrive. "Calvinist states like Geneva and the Dutch Republic were avid for learning, and England, with its vigorous Puritan strain, already had developed a substantial reading public in the seventeenth century" (Gay, 1969, p. 58). The influence of the Lutheran church in the Scandinavian countries, which was described earlier, brought near-universal reading ability there by the middle of the 18th century (Johansson, 1987). Nevertheless, the tidy causal chain leading from Luther to Protestantism to literacy does not lie unchallenged. Strauss (1984) points out that after about 1525 Luther began to doubt the wisdom of allowing the general population to interpret Scripture on its own. After this time, Luther advocated "expert guidance" in such matters and in 1529 published his *Greater Catechism* and *Smaller Catechism*, which introduced a more authoritative approach to scriptural interpretation than individual Bible reading. Nevertheless, the groundwork for mass literacy had been established, and Luther's shift in emphasis probably did little to stall its expansion to the Lutheran faithful.

The expansion of the German school system with both local and national assistance was, according to Strauss (1984), the main cause of the spread of literacy in 16th-century Germany. Similarly, Houston (1982) disputes claims that Calvinist Protestantism was the primary cause of increased literacy in Scotland, claiming instead socioeconomic causes (but cf. Smout, 1982). In general, the areas that embraced Protestantism tended to be economically well-off compared to the areas that retained Catholicism. Then, some areas (e.g., Italy) displayed regional differences in literacy that far exceeded religious differences, thus confounding any simple relationship between religion and literacy in preindustrial Europe.

Whether or not religious differences can account for variations in literacy abilities, by the middle of the 17th century religious works represented almost 50 percent of all titles printed in Europe and religious reading had become a powerful impetus to the acquisition of literacy for all faiths. Long after the forces of the Reformation and Counter-Reformation had quieted, religion continued to provide a motivation for the spread of print. Lockridge (1974) argues that conservative Protestantism was the primary impetus for increased literacy in 17th- and 18th-century New England, and Spufford (1981) makes similar arguments for the expansion of the English reading public in the 17th century. In the late 18th and early 19th centuries Bible and religious tract societies sprang up in Europe and the United States, driven by the evangelical spirit of religious regeneration (Bronner, 1967). Between 1804 and 1819 the British and Foreign Bible Society printed over 2.5 million copies of Testaments and Bibles; by 1861 the Religious Tract Society in England was annually printing over 20 million copies of tracts and over 13 million copies of periodicals (Altick, 1957, pp. 99 ff.). Most of these were distributed door to door throughout England by local tract and Bible societies, but many in the early part of the 19th century were supplied to American tract societies (Nord, 1984).

Altick (1957, p. 99) considers evangelical religion, along with utilitarianism, to be the "most potent influences upon the social and cultural tone of nineteenth-century England." To the evangelicals Bible reading was an end unto itself, requiring only limited reading ability. Pronunciation without comprehension was sufficient. The intent of the tract societies was to bring approved reading materials to the masses, rekindling their lagging faith in the revealed word and its contemporary prescriptions for the conduct of their daily lives. However, those who accepted and read these little pamphlets may not have been as attracted to the wholesome messages of Christian virtue as they were to the opportunity to practice reading with cheap materials that were written in a simple style.

Religious curiosity as an individual motivation for access to print fits the general hypothesis presented here for the expansion of literacy. The thirst for new religious experiences or for challenging what one already believes can expand one's personal space. But reading and rereading for confirmation of firmly held belief, and the teaching of reading for the sole purpose of conversion to a particular faith, as practiced by many missionary societies, are problematic for this framework. In the latter case, literacy is taught to constrain rather than to expand, just as in early 19th-century France, where the Catholic church allowed what Furet and Ozouf (1982, pp. 308 f.) called *semiliteracy* based on reading alone for promotion of religiosity rather than for modernization. Nevertheless, literacy once attained becomes a personal property with the potential for deployment wherever and whenever the individual desires.

The Commercial Revolution and the Printed Book

With the Renaissance, Europe gained a renewed interest in learning and in secular learning in particular. During the period from roughly 1450 until the end of the first quarter of the 17th century, education expanded throughout most of Western Europe and literacy increased, at least as evidenced by dramatic increases in signature rates. The remainder of the 17th century, however, was marked by economic and educational stagnation, particularly in France, England, Germany, Italy, and Spain, where wars (civil and otherwise) and economic declines limited resources and administrative support for schooling. Only the Low Countries and Scandinavia appear to have been unaffected by these forces (Cipolla, 1969). But the bases upon which modern European literacy is established continued to develop throughout this period. The importance of trade forced the entry of practical matters into the classical curriculum, and practical texts such as handbooks and almanacs, which first appeared in volume in the 16th century, were printed and distributed in increasingly large numbers. Information, which once had been a monopoly of the clerics and the nobility, became common property through the availability of such cheap materials, thus widening further the world to which the common person had access (Anderson, 1965).

The rapid spread of printed materials after the middle of the 15th century and the concomitant rise in the size of the reading public led in the 16th century to widespread attempts to restrict access to particular types of information. In England Henry VIII forbade laborers and women to read an English Bible (Adamson, 1929, p. 46), while in France at roughly the same time a variety of methods for information control were attempted, including hanging for those caught publishing a seditious book (Darnton, 1972, pp. 252 ff.). By the end of the 16th century, England had restricted the number of commercial presses allowed to operate in the country, limited the number of impressions that could be made from a single setting of type (for most types of books), and had begun issuing *patents* or *rights of privilege* to selected booksellers, giving rights for selling specified categories of print. Both secular and ecclesiastical control of printing and of book distribution continued in Europe and the United States for a number of centuries; and while the United States eliminated interference with the press with the First Amendment to the Constitution (1791), England did not drop government control until the 1830s, France until 1870, and the area now occupied by West Germany, not until after World War II (Feather, 1986).

The progression of the masses towards literacy should not be viewed as an unbroken movement forward, however, with unrelenting pressure for access to print. For centuries after print became the primary communication medium of most facets of government, economics, and the higher trades and professions, illiterates could still manage their daily lives without major inconvenience. Scriveners and semiprofessional letter writers could be hired. Proclamations were read aloud in public places, as were newspapers in taverns, military barracks, and in the workplace (Schofield, 1968, pp. 312–313; Webb, 1955, pp. 33–34; Chartier, 1987, pp. 230–231). Between the illiterate, who was print-unaware, and the literate there existed (and continue to exist) those who neither read nor wrote, but who were aware of many of the functions of print and who engaged in some of them through intermediaries. These people also were aware of many of the spatial properties of print and of documents: they recognized books, posters, newspapers, and the other common text types, and may even have recognized fields within these, although they were not able to read their contents (e.g., the title of a newspaper). Learning to read in a preliterate society and learning to read in a society awash in print may be vastly different experiences and have different cognitive consequences. Part of the agenda for understanding the spread of literacy should include more careful attention to the mediation of literacy for the illiterate, including the growth of negative attitudes towards illiterates, which are recorded for England from at least the end of the 17th century (Thomas, 1986, pp. 117 f.).

The Industrial Revolution

The Industrial Revolution, which began in Europe in the middle of the 18th century, had a multifaceted relationship to literacy. On the one hand the countries with the highest literacy rates were the first to foster industrialization, yet one of the first effects of the early phases of the Industrial Revolution was to stagnate education and the spread of literacy (Craig, 1981, p. 178). Cipolla (1969, p. 102) sees the Industrial Revolution as the direct result of the efforts of "literate craftsmen and amateur scientists." Economists tend to agree that a modest level of literacy was a necessary condition for the early stages of Western industrialization, but they do not agree that it was a sufficient condition (Anderson & Bowman, 1976, p. 4). They argue, in addition, that only those at the center of technological and organizational change were required to have practical and intellectual skills.

The early factories required few technical skills from the majority of their workers, and therefore industrialization in its early stages produced little pressure for higher literacy. In towns where factories located, the migration of low-literacy rural workers to the new jobs led in some cases to noticeably lower overall literacy rates. In addition, by offering employment for children, the new factories raised the opportunity cost for education—that is, the amount of income that a family would lose by sending a child to school rather than to work in the factory (Cipolla, 1980, p. 931). This in part explains the stagnation in education that accompanied the Industrial Revolution, at least until the mid-19th century. In time, the increased complexity of production led to a higher demand for literate workers. But literacy was also encouraged by many factory owners on moral grounds or out of the belief that literacy would be the "route to obedience and docility" (Thomas, 1986, p. 118).

Opposing these latter trends were overt attempts to restrict mass access to print, particularly in France and England. In England opposition to both education of the masses and the unconstrained distribution of print was strong during the first half of the 19th century (West, 1970, ch. 9). Advertising duties on newspapers and excise taxes on paper were not removed until the 1860s; and free, government-sponsored education was not instituted until 1870. Censorship of specific titles and authors continued, carried to its most absurd extreme in Vienna in 1777, where the *Catalogue of Forbidden Books* listed itself. This Hapsburg Index had apparently become for some a reliable guide to the most interesting reading (Gay, 1969, p. 70). Nevertheless, private support for education continued, and the net effect of the opposition to literacy was apparently small.

The Transition to the Modern Era

Urban and rural education expanded in the 19th century throughout Western Europe and North America, spurred on both by local and national governments and by private organizations. In concord with increased schooling, new papermaking, printing, and transportation techniques dramatically reduced the costs for producing and shipping books, thus improving access to print for the masses (Barbier, 1983; Barnes, 1983; Brooks, 1985; Moran, 1978; Nord, 1984). Cheap literature (e.g., the French *feuilleton*, the British "penny dreadful," the American "dime novel") flooded the boarding houses, military camps, railroad stations, and general stores (Denning, 1987). By the end of the third quarter of the 19th century, Denmark, Sweden, The Netherlands, Germany, and Switzerland had near-universal enrollment in primary schooling, a position reached by most of the other industrialized countries by World War I (Craig, 1981).

By the early 20th century, the United States, England, Scotland, Switzerland, Scandinavia, the Low Countries, France, and Germany were approaching universal literacy. Northern Italy was headed in this direction, but southern Italy, the countries of eastern Europe, Russia, Spain, Portugal, Greece, and Turkey lagged far behind (Cipolla, 1969, p. 97). UNESCO (1957, pp. 13–17) estimated that in 1950 illiteracy for those 15 years old and older was below 5 percent for North America and all of Europe—except the southern portion, where it averaged around 20 percent. Russian illiteracy was estimated to be between 5 percent and 10 percent, but limited data were available for making this judgment.

A RESEARCH AGENDA

We cannot recover any more of the past than what has been bequeathed us, but we can make better use of available historical data and of opportunities for new research. The research literature on literacy is nearly blank on the skills required for writing and their normal development through and after schooling. It is also deficient on the development of reading and writing in adults. Should we assume the same stages of development for reading ability in adults as we do for children, or are different paths taken? The research literature also is silent on learning to read handwriting, and about the loss of literacy abilities through disuse.

From the historical record we can strive for a clearer picture of the uses of literacy in everyday life from period to period and region to region. What did a typical shopkeeper in 16th-century London read on a daily basis? What were the document types, their syntax, their discourse structures, and their vocabulary? Were shopkeepers in 16th-century Milan and Mainz confronted with significantly different literacy tasks? What is needed is a coherent picture of everyday writing and print and their uses throughout the history of the West. Studies are needed on the spread of eyeglasses among the masses and on the development of artificial lighting for reading, as well as on signatures and book inventories. Besides knowing how many might have been able to read, we should attempt to learn what people read, where they read, and under what conditions.

For the period before printing, imitative experiments might be used to gain insight into the complexities of reading manuscripts under prevailing lighting conditions; of preparing quill, ink, and parchment; and in reading documents for different types of information. The general outlines of literacy growth are probably as well established now as they can be, given the limitations on available evidence. The remaining challenge is to understand the functions of literacy at different periods and among different people, and how handwritten and printed materials entered into these worlds.

NOTES

1. The consequences of such literacy programs, however, were probably not significantly different from those with more open-ended goals.
2. The Stroop effect refers to the interference that printed color words cause in naming ink colors. In a typical experiment, several lists of words are prepared, with each list word printed in a selected color. Typically, several lists are composed of color terms and several of noncolor terms. Some of the color term lists are printed with ink colors that disagree with the words and some with ink colors that agree (word by word). The noncolor words are printed in randomly selected colors. For control, a list of ink bars roughly the size of printed words is often used. The task for each subject is to name the ink colors in each list as quickly as possible. The words themselves are not to be read. The time for reading each list is recorded. Almost all subjects can name the ink colors more quickly for either noncolor words (e.g., chair, floor) printed in different colors, or color words printed in agreeing colors (e.g., the word "blue" printed with blue ink) than for color words printed in nonagreeing colors (e.g., the word "blue" printed with red ink). This effect is remarkably persistent across age groups and resists extinction with training.

REFERENCES

Adamson, J. W. (1929). The extent of literacy in England in the fifteenth and sixteenth centuries. *The Library, 10,* 163–193.

Altick, R. D. (1957). *The English common reader.* Chicago: University of Chicago Press.

Anderson, C. A. (1965). Literacy and schooling on the development threshold: Some historical cases. In C. A. Anderson & M. J. Bowman (Eds.), *Education and economic development* (pp. 347–362). Chicago: Aldine.

Anderson, C. A., & Bowman, M. J. (1976). Education and economic modernization in historical perspective. In L. Stone (Ed.), *Schooling and society: Studies in the history of education* (pp. 3–19). Baltimore and London: Johns Hopkins University Press.

Auwers, L. (1980). Reading the marks of the past: Exploring female literacy in colonial Windsor, Connecticut. *Historical Methods, 13* (4), 204–214.

Barbier, F. (1983). The publishing industry and printed output in nineteenth-century France. In K. E. Carpenter (Ed.), *Books and society in history* (pp. 199–230). New York: R. R. Bowker.

Barnes, J. J. (1983). Depression and innovation in the British and American book trade, 1819–1939. In K. E. Carpenter (Ed.), *Books and society in history* (pp. 231–248). New York: Bowker.

Barr, R. (1975). The effect of instruction on pupil reading strategies. *Reading Research Quarterly, 10,* 555–582.

Bauml, F. H. (1980). Varieties and consequences of medieval literacy and illiteracy. *Speculum, 55* (2), 237–265.

Biemiller, A. (1970). The development of the use of graphic and contextual information as children learn to read. *Reading Research Quarterly*, 6, 75–96.

Bishop, M. (1968). *The middle ages*. Boston: Houghton Mifflin.

Bronner, E. B. (1967). Distributing the printed word: The Tract Association of Friends, 1816–1966. *Pennsylvania Magazine of History and Biography*, 91, 344–348.

Brooks, J. (1985). *When Russia learned to read: Literacy and popular literature, 1861–1971*. Princeton, NJ: Princeton University Press.

Bruce, P. A. (1910). *Institutional history of Virginia in the seventeenth century* (Vol. 1). New York: Putnam's.

Chartier, R. (1987). *The cultural uses of print in early modern France* (L. G. Cochrane, Trans.). Princeton, NJ: Princeton University Press.

Cipolla, C. M. (1969). *Literacy and development in the West*. Baltimore: Penguin Books.

Cipolla, C. M. (1980). *Before the Industrial Revolution: European society and economy, 1000–1700* (2nd ed.). New York: Norton.

Clanchy, M. T. (1979). *From memory to written record: England, 1066–1307*. Cambridge, MA: Harvard University Press.

Clark, P. (1976). The ownership of books in England, 1560–1640: The example of some Kentish townsfolk. In L. Stone (Ed.), *Schooling and society: Studies in the history of education* (pp. 95–111). Baltimore: Johns Hopkins University Press.

Craig, J. E. (1981). The expansion of education. *Review of Research in Education*, 9, 151–213.

Cremin, L. A. (1970). *American education: The colonial experience, 1607–1783*. New York: Harper & Row.

Cressy, D. (1980). *Literacy and the social order: Reading and writing in Tudor and Stuart England*. Cambridge, Eng.: Cambridge University Press.

Crosby, R. (1936). Oral delivery in the Middle Ages. *Speculum*, 11, 88–110.

Darnton, R. (1972). Reading, writing, and publishing in eighteenth-century France. In F. Gilbert and S. R. Graubard (Eds.), *Historical studies today* (pp. 238–280). New York: Norton.

Darnton, R. (1983). What is the history of books? In K. E. Carpenter (Ed.), *Books and society in history* (pp. 3–26). New York: Bowker.

Denning, M. (1987). *Mechanic accents: Dime novels and working-class culture in America*. London and New York: Verso.

Dyer, A. D. (1973). *The city of Worcester in the sixteenth century*. Leicester, Eng.: Leicester University Press.

Eisenstein, E. L. (1979). *The printing press as an agent of change*. Cambridge, Eng.: Cambridge University Press.

Eklof, B. (1983). Schooling and literacy in late imperial Russia. In D. P. Resnick (Ed.), *Literacy in historical perspective* (pp. 105–128). Washington, DC: Library of Congress.

Feather, J. P. (1986). The book in history and the history of the book. In J. Y. Cole (Ed.), *The history of books and libraries: Two views* (pp. 1–16). Washington, DC: Library of Congress.

Febvre, L., & Martin, H. (1958). *The coming of the book*. London: Verso.

Fisher, J. H. (1977). Chancery and the emergence of standard written English in the fifteenth century. *Speculum*, 52, 870–899.

Fitch, J. (1900). *Educational aims and methods*. New York: Macmillan.

Fuller, W. E. (1982). *The old country school*. Chicago: University of Chicago Press.

Furet, F., & Ozouf, J. (1982). *Reading and writing: Literacy in France from Calvin to Jules Ferry*. Cambridge, Eng.: Cambridge University Press.

Gabel, L. C. (1928–1929). Benefit of clergy in England in the later Middle Ages. *Smith College Studies in History*, 14 (1–4) (whole issue), 1–148.

Galbraith, V. H. (1935). The literacy of medieval English kings. *Proceedings of the British Academy*, 21, 201–238.

Gay, P. (1969). *The Enlightenment: An interpretation*. New York: Knopf.

Gilmore, W. (1982). Elementary literacy on the eve of the industrial revolution: Trends in rural New England, 1760–1830. *Proceedings of the American Antiquarian Society*, 92 (1), 87–178.

Goody, J., & Watt, I. (1968). The consequences of literacy. In J. Goody (Ed.), *Literacy in traditional societies* (pp. 27–68). Cambridge, Eng.: Cambridge University Press.

Graff, H. J. (1979). *The literacy myth*. New York: Academic Press.

Graff, H. J. (1981). Reflections on the history of literacy: Overview, critique, and proposals. *Humanities in Society*, 4, 303–333.

Graff, H. J. (1986). *The legacies of literacy: Continuities and contradictions in Western society and culture*. Bloomington: IN.: Indiana University Press.

Gray, W. S. (1925). Report of the National Committee on Reading. *Twenty-fourth yearbook of the National Society for the Study of Education, Part 1*. Bloomington, IL: Public School Publishing Co.

Gray, W. S., & Munroe, R. (1929). *The reading interests and habits of adults: A preliminary report*. New York: Macmillan.

Greene, M. (1965). *The public school and the private vision*. New York: Random House.

Haile, H. G. (1976). Luther and literacy. *Publications of the Modern Language Association*, 91, 816–828.

Hardyck, C. D., & Petrinovich, L. F. (1970). Subvocal speech and comprehension level as a function of the difficulty level of reading material. *Journal of Verbal Learning and Verbal Behavior*, 9, 647–652.

Havelock, E. A. (1976). *Origins of Western literacy*. Toronto: Ontario Institute for Studies in Education.
Heath, S. B. (1980). The functions and uses of literacy. *Journal of Communication, 30,* 123–133.
Hendrickson, G. L. (1929–1930). Ancient reading. *Classical Journal, 25,* 182–196.
Houston, R. A. (1982). The literacy myth? Illiteracy in Scotland, 1630–1760. *Past and Present, 96,* 81–102.
Houston, R. A. (1983). Literacy and society in the West, 1500–1800. *Social History, 8,* 269–293.
Inkeles, A., & Smith, D. H. (1974). *Becoming modern: Individual change in six developing countries.* Cambridge, MA: Harvard University Press.
Jayne, S. R. (1956). *Library catalogues of the English Renaissance.* Berkeley: University of California Press.
Johansson, E. (1987). Literacy campaigns in Sweden. In R. F. Arnove & H. J. Graff (Eds.), *National literacy campaigns* (pp. 65–98). New York: Plenum Press.
Johnson, C. (1963). *Old-time schools and school books.* New York: Dover. (Original work published 1904)
Johnston, J. A. (1983). Books in wills. *Local Historian, 15* (8), 478–482.
Judd, C. H., & Buswell, G. T. (1922). *Silent reading: A study of the various types.* Supplementary Educational Monographs, No. 23. Chicago: University of Chicago Press.
Kaestle, C. F. (1985). The history of literacy and the history of readers. In E. W. Gordon (Ed.), *Review of Research in Education, 12,* 11–53.
Kirsch, I. S., & Jungeblut, A. (1986). *Literacy: Profiles of America's young adults.* Report No. 16–PL–02. Princeton, NJ: National Assessment of Educational Progress.
Laqueur, T. W. (1983). Toward a cultural ecology of literacy in England, 1600–1850. In D. P. Resnick (Ed.), *Literacy in historical perspective* (pp. 43–57). Washington, DC: Library of Congress.
Lockridge, K. A. (1974). *Literacy in colonial New England.* New York: Norton.
Marker, G. (1985). *Publishing, printing, and the origins of intellectual life in Russia, 1700–1800.* Princeton, NJ: Princeton University Press.
Monaghan, E. J. (1983). *A common heritage: Noah Webster's blue-back speller.* Hamden, CT: Archon Books.
Moran, J. (1978). *Printing presses: History and development from the 15th century to modern times.* Berkeley: University of California Press.
Nord, D. P. (1984). The evangelical origins of mass media in America, 1815–1835. *Journalism Monographs, 88,* 1–30.
Perfetti, C. A. (1985). *Reading ability.* New York: Oxford University Press.
Rachal, J. R. (1987). Measuring English and American historical literacy: A review of methodological approaches. *International Journal of Lifelong Education, 6* (3), 185–198.
Rice, J. M. (1893). *The public school system of the United States.* New York: Century Co.
Rosen, E. (1956). The invention of eyeglasses. *Journal of the History of Medicine, 11,* 13–46, 183–218.
Saeger, P. (1982). Silent reading: Its impact on late medieval script and society. *Viator, 13,* 367–414.
Schofield, R. S. (1968). The measurement of literacy in preindustrial England. In J. Goody (Ed.), *Literacy in traditional societies* (pp. 311–325). Cambridge, Eng.: University of Cambridge Press.
Smout, T. C. (1982). New evidence on popular religion and literacy in eighteenth-century Scotland. *Past and Present, 97,* 114–127.
Soltow, L., & Stevens, E. (1981). *The rise of literacy and the common school in the United States: A socioeconomic analysis to 1870.* Chicago: University of Chicago Press.
Spufford, M. (1981). *Small books and pleasant histories.* London: Methuen.
Stock, B. (1983). *The implications of literacy: Written language and models of interpretation in the eleventh and twelfth centuries.* Princeton, NJ: Princeton University Press.
Stone, L. (1969). Literacy and education in England, 1640–1900. *Past and Present, 42,* 69–139.
Strauss, G. (1984). Lutheranism and literacy: A reassessment. In K. von Greyerz (Ed.), *Religion and society in early modern Europe* (pp. 109–123). London: George Allen & Unwin.
Strayer, J. R. (1965). *Feudalism.* Huntington, NY: Robert E. Krieger.
Stroop, J. R. (1935). Studies in interference in serial verbal reactions. *Journal of Experimental Psychology, 18,* 643–661.
Taylor, E. A. (1937). *Controlled reading.* Chicago: University of Chicago Press.
Thomas, K. (1986). The meaning of literacy in early modern England. In G. Baumann (Ed.), *The written work: Literacy in transition* (pp. 97–131). Oxford, Eng.: Clarendon Press.
Tocqueville, A. de. (1963). *Democracy in America.* New York: Knopf. (First English edition 1840)
UNESCO (1957). *World illiteracy at mid-century: A statistical study.* Paris: UNESCO.
Venezky, R. L. (1987). Steps toward a modern history of American reading instruction. *Review of Research in Education, 13,* 129–167.
Webb, R. K. (1954). Literacy among the working classes in nineteenth-century Scotland. *Scottish Historical Review, 33,* 100–114.
Webb, R. K. (1955). *The British working-class reader, 1790–1848: Literacy and social tension.* London: George Allen & Unwin.
Webber, T. (1978). *Deep like the rivers: Education in the slave quarter community, 1831–1865.* New York: Norton.
West, E. G. (1970). *Education and the state* (2nd ed.). London: Institute of Economic Affairs.

4 LITERACY ACTS

John T. Guthrie and Vincent Greaney

$\mathbf{T}$he aim of this chapter is to account as fully as possible for the literacy activities of people. Central to this goal is the notion that literacy is a conscious action. It is a personal choice with consequences for the individual and the society. Thus, literacy activities will be examined in terms of how they contribute to the personal and societal accomplishments of adults and how they are affected by educational and psychological factors in childhood.

One approach to understanding literacy is to impose the frame used by cultural anthropologists to apprehend such aspects of a culture as marriage, ritual, death, sport, or talk. When Charles Frake (1980) traveled from Berkeley to study the Subanum, a primitive tribe of the Philippines, he found it necessary to explain the phenomenon of talk. Talk was not universal, uniform, or unidimensional. Frake accounted for oral communication in this particular social group by posing the following questions: What kinds of it are there? How are they distributed in the population? What factors determine their occurrence? The present chapter addresses these questions to literacy.

Literacy acts have rarely been studied as a dimension of the contemporary social milieu. To devise a framework for this inquiry, we raise two questions.

1. What kinds of literacy activity exist? This refers to the issues of what people read and how much time they spend doing it. The content, volume, and preferences for reading will be examined.
2. What are the uses and purposes of literacy acts? The extent that literacy is utilized to acquire knowledge, fulfill school assignments, gain a job, reaffirm a sense of worth, enhance cognitive capacity for more mature reading, or fulfill other cultural functions will be discussed.

ADULT LITERACY ACTIVITY

Content and Volume

Literacy activity is indispensable to citizens as they negotiate their paths through society, despite the increasing role of television and video. As people attend school, work, or pursue private concerns, they make informed choices. They consume written information in newspapers, books, charts, newsletters, computer printouts, and other forms. Political leaders, for example, focus on particular sections of particular newspapers (Weiss, 1974). Rarely does anyone read any of these types of materials in toto. A national sample of adults reported reading the newspaper for a median of 35 minutes daily (Sharon, 1973–1974). Few people, however, read the whole newspaper. Further, high school graduates read a mean of 5.5 out of 13 possible sections of newspapers, parts of 2.5 magazines, and 15 different document types (Kirsch & Jungblut, 1986). Because adult reading is heterogeneous and diverse, we organized this literature into the situations in which reading occurs, and the purposes for which it is conducted.

We suggest that distinctive social contexts give rise to qualitatively different literacy activities. In brief, we propose that the situation leads to the development of a purpose for reading. The purpose or goal dictates a selection of content and subject matter. These contents, as objects of the purpose for reading, require cognitive processes of the individual. In the following sections we will describe three types of situations: leisure, occupational, and community. For each situation we examine evidence on the amount of reading that has been observed. More important than sheer volume, however, is the way that literacy is represented within each situation in terms of its purpose, content, and cognitive process. Relativity little attention will be given to cognitive process in this chapter, since that topic will be treated by other authors in different sections of this volume.

Leisure Reading

How much time is given to reading? In 1971 Sharon (1973–1974) supervised an interview study of a nationally representative sample of 5,067 United States adults aged 16 or older. The interview included questions about reading newspapers, magazines, books, mail, and documents that are encountered in work, shopping, commuting, and other activities. The amount of time spent reading was found to be distributed among the population in a negatively decelerated form. A relatively large percentage of individuals, about 30 percent, read for about one hour per day or less, and a relatively small proportion read for three hours per day or more.

Although the distribution of reading activity was highly skewed, the average amount of time American adults spent reading was 106 minutes. Relatively few people spent three on more hours per day, and a plurality spent one hour per day or less. In that study, on a "typical day" 73 percent of readers reported reading newspapers, 39 percent reported reading magazines, 33 percent reported reading books, and 33 percent reported reading at work.

Measuring the amount of time individuals spend reading at leisure, however, poses measurement problems (Guthrie & Seifert, 1984; Nell, 1988). A question such as "How much time did you spend reading today?" tends to yield an underestimate because reading activity is often below the threshold of awareness. Extensive studies by Szalai (1972) show that about one-third of leisure reading is secondary to another activity such as cooking, waiting for the doctor, or planning a vacation. A second reason for underestimates is that people visualize reading as enjoying a novel by the fireside (Waples, 1938). Examining production schedules at work is not included unless it is explicitly cued. Further, reading entails scanning and searching. For example, Stamm and Jacoubovitch (1980) have shown that a sample of adults in a metropolitan area, reading on a Thursday afternoon, inspected an average of 53 headlines, 25 articles, 8 photographs, 6 outlines, 7 cartoons, and one table. People tended to read two headlines for each article, to avoid tables, and to scan photos. These patterns shifted from Thursday to Saturday. On Saturday the percentage of headlines decreased and the percentage of articles within the paper increased, resulting in a doubling of the text/headline ratio from Thursday to Saturday. These findings illustrate that "reading a newspaper" is not a simple process. Because the contents (Burgoon, Burgoon, & Wilkinson, 1983) and the types of materials vary, the amount of time spent is a more appropriate measure of the volume of activity than the amount of material that is read (Bogart, 1981).

Given these measurement constraints, it is not surprising that relatively few studies of leisure reading time have been conducted. At the adult level Sharon (1973–1974) reported that adults in the United States read newspapers and books for a median of 82 minutes per day. A similar finding was reported by Guthrie and Seifert (1983). While the Sharon (1973–1974) study contained guided interviews of a national sample of adults, the latter study randomly sampled households in a small community. The community was selected to be similar to the U.S. population in terms of the number of years of schooling and frequency of four occupational groups. A personal interview approach examined reading comprehensively. Reading at leisure, school, and work were inventoried, including time spent with newspapers, books, magazines, and other brief documents. The median amount of time spent reading by wage earners in this community was 157 minutes, which is about 2.6 hours daily. The median amount of time spent reading newspapers and books was 39 minutes and 24 minutes per day respectively. The total of 63 minutes per day is reasonably similar to the Sharon figure for newspaper and book reading, considering that in the Sharon study the median time was calculated on the 33 percent of individuals who reported book reading and the 73 percent who reported newspaper reading. It should be noted that the amount of time reading newspapers and books is suggested as an approximation of the amount of leisure reading activity. Age and income tend to increase both newspaper and book reading (Burgoon & Burgoon, 1980), and newspaper reading declined slightly from 1970 to 1980 (Robinson, 1980).

A number of studies have examined purposes for leisure reading. Lain (1986), for instance, sent a questionnaire to a stratified sample of individuals in a county in the Midwest and obtained a 67 percent response rate. A factor analysis of responses to questions about reasons for adult newspaper reading revealed three factors: surveillance, companionship, and stimulation. Surveillance referred to knowing about metropolitan events, national events, and new sales in the marketplace. Companionship referred to overcoming loneliness and feeling companionable. Stimulation referred to having information for conversation, hearing exciting things, and seeing one's ideas confirmed. Different purposes are predicted by different demographic factors. For example, younger respondents reported greater surveillance than older. Age, however, was not related to reading for companionship and stimulation. Surveillance was more important for males; the reverse was true in the case of companionship. These findings were corroborated by Grunig (1979) for representative samples of adults in two eastern U.S. cities.

A comparison between purposes for leisure reading and occupational reading was made by Kirsch and Guthrie (1984a), who studied 99 individuals across five occupational categories in a high-technology company. At the outset a series of 12 case studies was conducted over a one-year period. The following purposes for reading were identified: knowledge acquisition, specific information, evaluation, keeping abreast, regulation, construction, social interaction, excitement, relaxation, affirmation, and aesthetic. Subsequently, all were subjected to a two-hour interview. Situations, contents, and purposes for reading were ascertained. The amounts of time spent for each purpose and each content domain in each situation were recorded. At leisure the prevailing purposes were: (1) relaxation (23 minutes per day), (2) keeping abreast (19 minutes per day), and (3) reading to gain knowledge (14 minutes per day). Relaxation was reported to be the main purpose for reading fiction and also for news in magazines, sports in the newspaper, and information about hobbies in magazines. In contrast, locating specific information was the primary purpose for occupational literacy. This purpose was distinguished from knowledge acquisition because it referred to search for facts, numbers, or details rather than learning interconnected ideas in a substantive subject matter. Search for specific information occurred for an average of 48 minutes per day. The materials associated with this purpose were training manuals, books on science, business correspondence, diagrams, and other brief documents.

The content of adult leisure reading has been examined by Guthrie, Seifert, and Kirsch (1986), who recorded the time spent reading books, magazines, newspapers, and other documents. Based on guided interviews, it was found that adults spent an average of 26 minutes per day reading fiction. Mean daily time devoted to reading about news and business was 15 minutes; sports and recreation was read 14 minutes; society and science was read 14 minutes; reference material was read 9 minutes; and brief documents such as personal correspondence were read 2 minutes. The total amount of time spent in leisure reading in this study was 80 minutes per day. A relatively high standard deviation (43 minutes) suggests that the top one-third are reading two hours per day at leisure or more. Other studies confirm the prevalence of reading fiction for relaxation at leisure (McKlroy, 1968).

Occupational Reading

Reading at work is not only pervasive but is embedded within the structure of most occupations (Guthrie & Kirsch, 1987). An initial estimate of the amount of time spent reading at work in a representative national sample of U.S. adults was a median of 61 minutes per day (Sharon, 1973–1974). The mean is likely to be higher because the data were skewed due to the high amounts of reading time accounted for by a few individuals. Another estimate of time spent reading at work has been made by Mikulecky (1982), who surveyed 150 individuals from 31 businesses in a midwestern town. Occupational categories included professional, technical, clerical, sales, services, agricultural, fisherman, and blue collar. Professional workers reported a mean reading time of 162 minutes per day in occupational settings; comparable times for middle-level and blue-collar workers were 168 and 97 minutes respectively. Guthrie, Seifert, and Kirsch (1986) reported that the average amount of time spent reading at work for individuals across a broad range of occupations from professional to unskilled was 127 minutes per day. Clerical workers spent more time than other categories of employees, followed by technicians and skilled workers, managers and professional, and semiskilled/service workers.

Community Literacy

In our framework, *community literacy* refers to reading that is associated with participation in neighborhood activities and in government, church, and social organizations (Bloome, 1983; Heath, 1980). Reading may take place outside the site of the organization (such as reading a hymnal in church) or within another location (such as reading a church newsletter at home). Community reading activity is distinguished from leisure reading because it is generated by a specific organization of interest to the reader and is likely to implicate relationships and obligations with regard to the organization. Community literacy activity is distinguished from occupational in the obvious sense that it does not entail economic benefits as a primary consequence of reading activity. Although the school may be considered an institution of the community, school literacy is of such importance that it is not included within the domain of community literacy (Bickel & Milton, 1983).

Forms of community literacy are exemplified most vividly in Reder and Green's (1983) depiction of literacy in an Alaskan fishing village. They illustrated that one form of literacy is associated with the Russian Orthodox church, in which the Cyrillic script is used. Another form of literacy, however, is associated with government and commercial transactions in which the script is English. They note that "the city office is the [English] literacy hub of the village. It is there that outside visitors report when they enter Seal Bay. The walls are literally covered with signs, letters, official certifications, and other written materials."

Fingeret (1983) has documented that neighborhood literacy encompasses joint reading of income tax forms, bank statements, bills, and other written forms of commercial information exchange. Sharon (1973–1974) reported that individuals spent a median of 16 minutes per day reading about club and church activities and 17 minutes per day reading brief documents such as notices, advertisements, and schedules for shopping, theater, or recreational events in which they were active participants.

Community literacy consists basically of reading brief documents such as signs, notices, newsletters, and schedules for the goal of obtaining specific information that is valuable for participating in the organization referenced in the document. Reading community literature, especially newspapers, may facilitate the social integration of individuals into a community (Stamm and Weis, 1986; Lain, 1986). Reder and Green (1983) show that literacy specialists are used by the Alaskan community to negotiate legal arrangements with organizations of the United States and Canada. Intense scrutiny of legal documents demands reading and reasoning. In addition, social and religious organizations of the village are maintained by written regulations. Notices of church activities in the form of letters, posters, and articles are often tacked on the sanctuary doors for people to read upon entering and leaving church during the Thursday night services in honor of St. Herman of Alaska.

Community literacy is often collaborative. Fingeret (1983) reported that exchanges of skills and resources between literate and marginally literate individuals are frequent. For example, an illiterate barber exchanges haircuts for bus tickets and help with forms that need to be filled out. A plumber exchanges repairs for assistance with income tax forms. And a housewife exchanges errands for writing letters and completing applications for welfare. Collaborative study of the Bible in Puerto Rican communities occurs among people whose literacy is highly variable, according to Shuman (1983). Shuman contends that among low-income Puerto Rican adolescents and adults, a low level of reading and writing competencies was rarely a source of stigma. Collaboration was a means for managing literacy demands, but did not determine social status. In addition the social integration of individuals into a community has been suggested by Stamm and Weis (1986) and Lain (1986) to be facilitated by reading community literature and newspapers.

Purposes and Influences

Knowledge Gain

Knowledge gain is a traditionally established and socially sanctioned use of literacy. There is universal agreement that people should use literacy to acquire information. This role of literacy is expanding, despite the transmission of information through television, radio, and audio tapes. Our conceptual framework suggests that a person who is an active user of literacy for the purpose of gaining knowledge will be more knowledgeable than a person who is less inclined to use literacy for this purpose.

Studies of the relationship between literacy activity and knowledge gain have been more conspicuous in the discipline of journalism than in psychology or education. Tan and Gunter (1979) administered a questionnaire to 93 high school seniors. They reported the frequency of reading about local and state government and politics, national government and politics, and international affairs. Reading these contents was assumed to be undertaken for the purpose of gaining information. The frequencies of reading sports, comics, and movie sections in the newspaper were obtained and assumed to occur for the purpose of entertainment. Television viewing was likewise subdivided into information and entertainment categories. Frequency of reading a newspaper for information was correlated significantly (.35) with grades in history and civics, when other media consumption variables were held constant. Frequency of reading the newspaper in total did not correlate with grades in these two subjects. These data suggest that students who more actively use literacy for gaining knowledge about politics are indeed more well versed in history and national affairs.

In a related study, Homlov (1982) tested 101 high school students on knowledge of municipal politics. Student information about city affairs was significantly predicted by their rated probability of reading about these issues. Total newspaper reading time did not predict knowledge levels, but topic-relevant reading was associated with political information.

Use of literacy for knowledge gain is likely to be enhanced by an awareness of differentiated purposes for reading. Measures of this awareness and its relation to knowledge levels have taken two forms in the journalistic literature. One measure of information seeking is the frequency that a person requests specific information, such as a pamphlet, about a specific topic, such as a political candidate. Chaffee and McLeod (1973) found this measure of information seeking, among 240 residents of a midwestern town, to be significantly associated with differences in levels of political knowledge among voters. Political knowledge was tested by the ability of respondents to name all of the candidates in a state election, their parties, and their positions. The study documents that frequency of requesting and reading political information, in fact, correlates with amount of political knowledge.

Awareness of the knowledge-oriented uses of the media was examined by Katz, Gurevitch, and Haas (1973). They reported that individuals who desired to strengthen their knowledge, information, and understanding about the state, society, and world tended to select current newspapers during leisure time. In contrast, individuals who wished to increase their knowledge or understanding of themselves or to enjoy other vicarious experiences selected books of fiction and literature. These findings exemplify a line of research known as *uses and gratifications studies* within the communications field. The general theory is that individuals are aware of their needs for information, aesthetics/entertainment, and confidence/belief. Such awareness leads to differential selection of reading material or other media, such as television programs or cinema. In sum, "gratifications" occur when "needs" are met with appropriate "sources."

Personal Empowerment

Personal empowerment refers to an individual's sense of being capable of participating, contributing, or accomplishing a desired goal. Individuals may be empowered if they believe that they are competent in a pursuit such as math or ballet, or that they can experience affects such as excitement or empathy. For example, political empowerment refers to the belief in one's ability to learn about political issues and act on that knowledge. An active user of literacy who gains political knowledge will be more fully empowered in the political arena.

Elliott and Rosenberg (1987) studied political empowerment as a function of reading activity. They randomly sampled adults in a major U.S. city and completed telephone interviews with 332 respondents. A measure of the sense of empowerment was obtained by questioning the respondents' beliefs about their competence to make informed choices on scientific and technological issues. Three blocks of predictor variables were obtained: (1) a science news reading block, which was composed of variables measuring newspaper reading of science news, newspaper reading of space news, newspaper reading of medical news, amount of reading in science magazines, and viewing television science programs; (2) general news reading, which was measured by variables that tapped newspaper use for political news, reading news magazines, and viewing television news; (3) demographic variables, including sex, educational attainment, political conservatism, and technological exposure. Commonality analysis revealed that empowerment was uniquely predicted by the amount of science reading, when total news reading and demographic variables were held constant. Approximately 50 percent of the explained variance was uniquely attributable to the level of relevant literacy activity. In sum, it appears that a sense of empowerment, or self-efficacy, in political and civic matters is more strongly predicted by use of literacy for learning about these topics than by background factors.

Personal empowerment may relate to a religious or social identity as well as a sense of competency about science and technology. Adoni and Shadmi (1980) studied a nationally representative sample of 841 high school students in Israel. They measured cognitive and political values regarding Israeli society and the Jewish people, the perceived usefulness of books in developing these values, the number of books read in the last three months, and demographic variables. The correlation between the dominance of the political content in books that were read and the perceived usefulness of books in developing values was significant (.16–.40)[1]. Individuals who stated that "books were useful in enabling the reader to feel part of the Jewish people" or that they read "to learn and understand the history of the Jewish people" or "to feel part of Israeli society" were significantly more likely to read books that contained a large amount of information about society and citizenship in Israel than individuals with opposing views. In other words, high school students who believed that books were a useful instrument in developing national values selected, and were impressed by, books in which political content was salient and national values were central. Chaffee and McLeod (1973) also observed that reading political material affected political and social values and beliefs.

Participation in Society

Society is an amalgam of groups, many of which have civic, religious, recreational, and political agendas. Shared ideas, beliefs, causes, and personal needs provide the drawing power of these groups. Normally, the process of sharing must extend beyond face-to-face communication to the reading and writing of substantive and organizational information. Literacy activity has occasionally been studied as a mediator between the individual and the group, between the person and the social system. Is literacy activity associated with the amount of societal participation? What is the evidence?

Correlations between amount of literacy activity and degree of societal participation have been reported by a few investigators. Hirschman (1981) found that the number of issues of newspapers and magazines read by individuals in a given year was significantly correlated with the number of different business, community, recreational, religious, and social groups in which they participated. Less direct evidence has been reported by Lain (1986), who showed that likelihood of subscribing to a local newspaper correlated .51 with degree of community integration, which was measured by length of residence in the current dwelling, home ownership, and other indices of community attachment. Furthermore, from two developing urban centers of Guatemala, Sexton (1979) reported a path analysis in which literacy use mediated between education and modernity. Higher levels of educational attainment produced higher amounts of literacy use, which resulted in modern medical practices, participation in new religious groups, and aspiration to join advanced occupational levels.

Connections between literacy activity and social group participation have been shown to be independent of age, education, demographic, and occupational factors. Lain (1986) showed that newspaper subscribing and community integration were independent of chronological age. After controlling for educational attainment, sex, occupational status, childhood magazine use, and parental socioeconomic status (SES), Hirschman (1981) found that the amount of literacy activity correlated significantly (.20) with level of societal participation.

In the pragmatic perspective that we propose, literacy activity is expected to have a specific rather than a generalized influence on group participation. Reading about a particular topic (such as gardening) is expected to be associated with commitment to a relevant social or business organization (such as a garden club). From telephone interviews with a random sample of 202 residents of an eastern city, Grunig (1979) reported the correlations between rated probability of reading certain topics and amount of time spent in related activities. Time spent in child care correlated .26 with likelihood of reading an article on child psychology. Time spent in community activities correlated .14 with probability of reading an article on civic organizations. Time spent in business management groups correlated .13 with reading an article on labor. These data and other studies (Weis, 1974) suggest a connection between literacy activities pertaining to a topic and societal/personal expenditures of time in the same area.

The relationship between literacy activity and group participation was further examined by Stamm and Weis (1986), who studied a random sample of 491 rural households within a diocese. They showed that the amount of church participation, indicated by number of church groups in which individuals were active, was increased by subscribing to church newspapers. However, church newspaper reading was not related to general volunteer work outside of the diocese. These studies suggest that effective contributors to societal groups are information seekers who use literacy to gain substantive and organizational knowledge that undergirds their processes of group engagement.

Occupational Effectiveness

The volume of occupational reading activity is relatively high. Mikulecky (1982) and Sharon (1973–1974) reported that adults spent approximately 60 to 120 minutes per day reading in the workplace. They also reported a weak positive relationship between time spent reading and occupational level. These studies, however, did not subdivide reading into different content domains and merely questioned workers about general estimates of time. Their procedures tend to obscure the amount and diversity of literacy activity. Amount of occupational reading in six content domains by four occupational subgroups was analyzed by Guthrie, Siefert, and Kirsch (1986) through a combination of case studies, guided interviews, and questionnaires. Managers and professionals spent 15 minutes per day reading scientific materials for the purpose of knowledge gain, whereas other subgroups reported negligible amounts of this type of literacy activity. Technicians and skilled workers spent 50 minutes per day reading reference materials such as manuals for the purpose of extracting specific information to solve problems, whereas other subgroups spent about 15 minutes per day or less in this literacy activity. Clerical workers spent 166 minutes reading brief documents such as letters, charts, schedules, and tables. In addition, semiskilled and service workers spent 98 minutes per day reading brief documents for the purpose of locating specific information to guide their work activities. Multivariate analyses of variance for reading time showed that the predominant content domain varied significantly across occupational subgroups. These findings support Resnick's (1987) view that "to be truly skillful outside school, people must develop situation-specific forms of competence" (p. 15).

Purposes for reading in occupational settings are dominated by the search for specific information to perform concrete tasks and solve problems defined by occupational responsibility. Kirsch and Guthrie (1984a) found that the purpose of locating specific information in written materials required a mean of 48 minutes per day for individuals across four occupational groups. Reading to regulate one's ongoing behavior in a semiroutine or production situation consumed 24 minutes per day; reading to construct or repair objects consumed 21 minutes per day; reading to evaluate the work of other individuals consumed 21 minutes per day; and reading to acquire knowledge that was not linked to immediate problem-solving or troubleshooting activity consumed 9 minutes per day. It should be noted that the standard deviation for this latter category was 52 minutes per day, an indication that a few individuals spend many hours per day reading for knowledge acquisition, whereas the majority spend no time reading for this goal.

Goals of reading activity in occupational settings were first delineated by Sticht (1975), who suggested the distinction of "reading to do" versus "reading to learn." Mikulecky (1982) quantified the frequency with which individuals read for these goals. He found that "reading to do" was most frequent for blue-collar workers; "reading to do" was also highly frequent among middle-level workers; and "reading to do plus learn" was the most frequent objective in reading performed by professionals. These data concur with the Kirsch and Guthrie (1984) findings. These two studies indicate that semiskilled and service workers in technical companies spend an average of one and one-half hours per day reading brief documents for the purpose of behavioral regulations and manual activities. Technicians and skilled workers also read brief documents (such as schedules, tables, and directions) largely for the purpose of obtaining specific information. Professionals read for a smaller amount of time, but the time is more highly concentrated on learning and knowledge acquisition than on behavioral guidance.

These findings illustrate that knowledge acquisition, which has been widely studied as a framework for understanding reading, is appropriate for a small segment of occupational literacy. Bazerman (1985) has shown how physicists in a research laboratory select and filter new knowledge from their research fields for the purposes tailored to their research and development programs. Information search, retrieval, and application are needed for this type of occupational reading. As Guthrie (1988) and Mikulecky and Ehlinger (1986) have illustrated, these goals require metacognitive activity. Cognitive models of reasoning appear to be more suitable than language-based models in accounting for success in occupational literacy tasks (Mikulecky & Winchester, 1983).

Literacy processes within occupational contexts are more distinct from literacy in school contexts than many psychologists and educators have assumed (Resnick, 1987). Several investigators have reported that typical job reading tasks place substantial metacognitive demands on workers (Mikulecky & Winchester, 1983; Scribner, 1984). Process analyses of document reading tasks in occupational settings show that aspects of problem solving such as goal setting, categorizing, inferencing, and integrating are intrinsic to these tasks (Guthrie, 1988). These findings suggest that the use of literacy in occupational settings may be more unique to these contexts than educators have recognized. As a consequence, teaching transferable reading skills may require reevaluation and innovation (Resnick, 1987; Sticht, 1975).

CHILDREN'S LITERACY ACTIVITIES

Content Preferences

Preschool

At a very early stage children in developed countries are normally introduced to picture books. At this age level, from the point of view of appeal, illustrations are of particular importance (Cappa, 1957). Later, stories are read aloud and popular ones such as A. A. Milne's *Winnie the Pooh* tend to be reread many times (Soderberg, 1971). Picture books, nursery rhymes (Bamberger, 1975), fairy tales, folktales, animal stories, and, in more recent times, stories based on well-known television characters are most popular (Mason & Blanton, 1971). A Japanese study (Takagi, 1980) revealed that the most popular books had stories that were happy, full of life, complicated, well illustrated, and full of movement. The content of fairy tales has prompted much debate. Proponents argue that exposure to fairy tales helps young children master their fears (e.g., Bettelheim, 1975) and prepares them for the pain and grief of real life. Others have objected to the efforts to "Disneyfy" some of the folktales by censoring references to sickness, deformity, violence, pain, and death (MacAogain, 1986).

Elementary School

Throughout the elementary grades, interest in reading (as indicated by measures such as time devoted to reading, book purchases, and library records) varies according to sex, age, and reading ability. Classification of reading material for children is quite subjective—for example, the same book could be classified as "nature," "science," "exploration," "history," or "adventure." In general, reading interests include adventure, fantasy, mystery, sports and games, humor, and especially animals (Carter, 1986; Chiu, 1984; Robinson & Weintraub, 1973). The children's book markets have become increasingly international (Chambers, 1980); international copublishing agreements involving children's books are common (Gault, 1982). Among young British elementary pupils, book reading proved to be much more popular than comic reading (James, 1987). Southgate, Arnold, and Johnson (1981) considered that many of the books, especially nonfiction, selected by young readers (age 7 to 9) were quite difficult. The same study noted that girls far outnumbered boys in expressing enjoyment of "happy" stories and fairy tales. During the middle grades, the range of children's reading interests appears to expand (Robinson & Weintraub, 1973). Mystery stories are particularly popular (Ashley, 1970; Heather, 1981a). Series books (e.g., Hardy Boys, Nancy Drew, Enid Blyton), despite their literary inadequacies (Huck, 1976), are popular in many countries (e.g., Binder, 1976; Ellis, 1968; Gopinathan, 1978; Gorman, White, Orchard, & Tate, 1981; Price, Powell, & Griffith, 1987). Pronounced sex differences in reading interests were recorded in the 1920s (Terman & Lima, 1926; Washburne & Vogel, 1926) and in much more recent studies. Boys tend to show a preference for books on science, sports, and transportation, while girls appear to favor books on people and fantasy (Huus, 1979; Meisel & Glass, 1970). Boys tend to dislike love stories and stories published for girls, while girls tend to dislike books with violent themes (Ashley, 1970).

Toward the end of elementary school, boys, although still preferring fiction to nonfiction, show a greater interest in nonfiction than girls (Heather, 1981b). Lists of favorite books (Elley & Tolley, 1972; Gorman & White, in press; Maxwell, 1977) may not be very useful since "popular" books are not read with any pronounced frequency. Indeed, the most frequently cited book in one study (Gorman & White, in press) was the only book selected by more than one percent of the respondents, apart from one book linked to a popular television series.

Comics have been the target of severe criticism, most notably in Wertham's (1954) *The Seduction of the Innocent*. The low intellectual status accorded comics may well stem from a "Victorian tradition of literacy which decreed pictures as unrespectable—a form of neopuritanism. Pictures were too easy" (Perry & Aldridge, 1967, 9). Comic books are widely read by children throughout the world. A U.S. review (Witty & Sizemore, 1955) concluded that 90 percent of children between ages 8 and 13 read comics frequently. In England, Wales, and Northern Ireland, almost half of the 11-year-olds sampled in a large-scale study preferred reading comics and annuals to other sorts of books; this tendency was more pronounced among boys (Gorman, White, Orchard, & Tate, 1982a). Sex was identified as the major discriminator in a series of 13 variables (which included achievement, home background, and library membership) between predominantly book readers and predominantly comic readers (Greaney, 1980); boys tended to read more comic books. A Scottish survey (Maxwell, 1977) concluded that the students spent as much time reading comics as reading in school. The popularity of comics seems to diminish sharply around the ages of 11 and 12, especially among boys in Great Britain (Brown, 1987) and among girls in Sweden (Flodin, Hedinsson, & Roe, 1982). Dorrell and Carrol (1981) reported that the presence of comics in a library led to an increase of 82 percent in library use and of 30 percent in the circulation of noncomic books.

While many comic books have reasonable levels of reading difficulty (Thorndike, 1941; Wright, 1979), and even in some cases sophisticated dialogue (Krashen, 1987), a number of studies have reported that pictures do not appear to contribute to the acquisition of vocabulary (Braun, 1969; Singer, Samuels, & Spiroff, 1974). Indeed, preference for reading comic books and annuals to other sorts of books has been shown to be negatively related to reading achievement (Gorman et al., 1981), or to show a weak positive (.13) correlation with achievement (Greaney, 1980).

Reading newspapers does not appear to be an important feature of the reading behavior of elementary school age children (Greaney, 1980; Johnson, 1963; Schramm, Lyle & Parker, 1961). The limited available evidence suggests that newspaper reading has greater appeal to boys than to girls (Flodin et al., 1982; Norvell, 1966). Amount of time spent reading the newspaper tends to increase with age (Elley & Tolley, 1972; Johnson, 1963). For example, a British survey (Brown, 1987) established that the percentage of boys who claimed to have read or looked at a newspaper the previous day increased from 27 percent for the 8 to 9 age group to 53 percent for the 12 to 13 age group. Comparable figures for girls were 20 percent and 47 percent.

Poems that involve either rhyme (Pittman, 1966), humor (Gorman et al., 1981), animals, or everyday experience tend to be liked (Avegno, 1956); poems that lack a story line or that are difficult to understand are unpopular. In comparison with other forms of reading, poetry tended to be less popular (Elley & Tolley, 1972; Robinson & Weintraub, 1973; Schulte, 1969). In two separate surveys of 11-year-olds, 60 percent (Gorman et al., 1981) and 43 percent (Gorman et al., 1982a) agreed with the statement "I like reading poems." Girls were more likely than boys to agree with the statement.

Secondary School

Following transfer to postprimary school, there seems to be an overall decline in interest in independent reading (Gorman, et al., 1982a). Interest in book reading in particular appears to decrease; at the same time, however, there is a marked level of reading activity in magazines and newspapers (James, 1987).

While some topics such as adventure and mystery have maintained a high readership throughout this century, the popularity of other topics has varied, reflecting political, technological, and social changes. In the late 1930s and 1940s, school stories were popular with both sexes, while girls tended to read books related to home life (e.g., Jenkinson, 1940; Norvell, 1950). Studies carried out around 1950 were reviewed by Robinson and Weintraub (1973). They tended to show interest in violence, love, glamour, sport, careers, and stories with a historical background. Yarlott and Harpin's (1971) study of pupils in selective secondary schools found that girls preferred romance, historical novels, and seriously themed novels, while boys selected masculine writers, science fiction, sport, history, and war. Personal experience, biography, humor, hobbies, and sex were popular in the 1970s (Carlsen, Manna, & Yoder, 1977; Elliot & Steinbellner, 1979; Wendelin & Zinc, 1983), while boys in particular had developed an interest in "spy and sex" stories (e.g., James Bond).

Squire and Applebee's (1966, 1968) comparative studies of reading interests of United States and British students reported similar preferences with regard to book titles. *Lord of the Flies* was mentioned most frequently in both samples. Where differences occurred, they appeared to reflect differences in social attitudes in the two countries. In teenage books, differences in the treatment of sexual, social, and political issues found in some countries restrict the likelihood of this material being available to readers in other cultures or political systems. As boys get older they tend to become much more interested in nonfiction material (Gorman et al., 1982b; Taylor, 1973), while girls maintain their interest in fiction books. Adult authors are read at an ever-increasing rate (Chambers, 1980). A Dutch study, for instance, established that 73 percent of 14 to 17-year-olds borrowed books from the library (Tellegen-VanDelft & Zanger, 1987). Students at this level should have little difficulty reading popular adult material; a readability survey of the 10 best-sellers for 1974 reported a mean readability level of 7.4 (Monteith, 1980).

Data from the National Assessment of Educational Progress in the United States (Walberg & Tsai, 1983, 1984) indicated that 43 percent of 13-year-olds and 49 percent of 17-year-olds use the paper as a source of information "every day." Interest in particular aspects of the paper may be a function of geographical location. New Zealand students (Elley & Tolley, 1972), for example, ranked world news highest, followed by local news and sports (boys) and TV/radio (girls), while U.S. students appear to have a preference for comic strips, sports (especially boys), and local news (Elliot & Steinbellner, 1979; Vaughan, 1963). Males appear to devote more time to newspaper reading than do females (e.g., Brown, 1987; Flodin, et al., 1982). By the time a person reaches the late teens, the newspaper-reading habit appears to be fixed and is dependent on the tradition of newspaper reading in the home (Stone & Wetherington, 1979). Access to newspapers is also a function of geographical location. In this respect Japan, the German Democratic Republic, and the Scandinavian countries are much better serviced than other developed countries (e.g., United States) and, in particular, the developing countries. According to UNESCO data (1986), the production rate of daily general interest papers in Japan is more than twice that of the United States.

The beginning of the postprimary school years seems to coincide with a rapid decrease in interest in comic book reading (Flodin et al., 1982; James, 1987; Whitehead, Capey, & Maddres, 1975; Wright, 1979). Among girls, however, one form of comic—teen romances—has proved popular. Parrish and Atwood (1985) reported all ninth graders had read at least five teen romances. Greaney and Kellaghan (1984) observed that romance comics accounted for virtually all reading of comics carried out by girls living in a disadvantaged inner-city area.

Comic books appear to give way to magazines (James, 1987). Teenage magazine reading appears to cover an extensive range of interests (Gorman, White, Orchard, & Tate, 1983). Teenagers purchase magazines written specifically for this age group as well as magazines published for adults (James, 1987; Norvell, 1966). While both boys and girls are interested in magazines devoted to popular teenage culture, especially music, considerable sex differences in magazine-reading interests have been recorded (Norvell, 1966; Robinson & Weintraub, 1973). Girls appear to favor magazines devoted to fashion, home and beauty care, and courtship, while boys' interests tend to be directed towards factual material (Gorman, et al., 1983), especially sport (Vaughan, 1963) and cars and electronics (Elley & Tolley, 1972; Gorman et al., 1983).

A number of studies have highlighted the relative lack of popularity of poetry among 16-year-olds. Girls appear to be much more favorably disposed to poetry (Gorman et al., 1982b; Vaughan, 1963). Poetry seems to be less popular at the postprimary stage than it had been at the primary (Elley & Tolley, 1972). Yarlott and Harpin (1971) commented on the widespread indifference to poetry among 16-year-olds. Girls appear to be much more favorably disposed to poetry (Gorman et al., 1982b; Jenkinson, 1940) than boys. Short, easy-to-understand, humorous poems are most popular (Gorman et al., 1981, 1982a, 1982b, 1983). Liking for poetry does not appear to be related to achievement (Gorman & White, in press).

Volume and Frequency of Reading

School

Despite the fact that reading occupies significant time slots in most school days, research evidence suggests that the actual amount of time children spend reading in the average classroom is small, perhaps as little as seven or eight minutes per day at the primary level and 15 minutes per day at the middle-grade level (Dishaw, 1977). Pupils are afforded little opportunity to read for enjoyment (Lamme, 1976; Spiegel, 1981). Large amounts of the class reading period tend to be devoted to questioning (Squire, 1969) and to workbook exercises and "meaningless seatwork" (Durkin, 1984). While many teachers might be favorably disposed toward voluntary classroom reading, they tend to assign a higher priority to skills development (Holdaway, 1979; Killeen, 1986; Morrow, 1985a). There is also evidence to suggest that teachers may feel uneasy if their pupils are "only reading" (Lunzer & Gardner, 1979).

Research findings indicate that where teachers encourage pupils to read for extended time periods in classrooms, pupils perform as well or better on traditional achievement measures as those in comparison groups (Greaney, 1970; Southgate, Arnold, & Johnson, 1981). Furthermore, systematic approaches to encouraging independent reading in the classroom have resulted in positive long-term effects on reading behavior outside of the school context (Greaney & Clarke, 1975; La Brandt, 1961). Independent reading outside of the classroom has been credited with most of the yearly vocabulary growth of pupils in middle grades (Nagy, Herman, & Anderson, 1985). Some researchers, however, while recognizing the value of broad reading, advocate the need for instruction on skills (Anderson, Hiebert, Scott, & Wilkinson, 1984), especially for weaker pupils (e.g., Chall, 1987).

Leisure

How much reading do children do outside of school? Methods of determining volume and frequency of children's reading include examination of library records, children's daily diaries, children's recollections over longer time periods, and parents' recollections. The validity of some of the research findings is questionable. Recall, for instance, has limitations and number of books may be quite different from number of books read.

Available evidence from a number of countries (Anderson, et al., 1984; Gopinathan, 1978; Greaney, 1980) suggests that large percentages of children devote little or no time to leisure reading. For instance, in one large-scale study of fifth graders, 22 percent did not devote any time to leisure reading (Greaney, 1980). Over a one-year period fourth-grade students in one U.S. study reported reading an average of 23.5 books a year, while students in both fifth and sixth grade read an average of 19.5 books per year (Lamme, 1976). British findings indicate that children read approximately three books per month and that there has been little increase in the amount of book reading between the mid-fifties (Himmelweit, Oppenheim, & Vince, 1958) and the early seventies (Whitehead, Capey, & Maddren, 1975). A Scottish survey (Maxwell, 1977) reported that children in the 8 to 15 age group read an average of 1.5 books and slightly over four comics and/or newspapers per week. An eight-month Irish study (Greaney, 1970) reported sixth-grade pupils in a control group borrowing 23 and completing seven books; the completion rate for comparable pupils in a program designed to encourage leisure reading was three times as great.

At the secondary level, the frequency of reading for enjoyment appears to diminish. In particular, as students get older, frequency of book reading appears to decrease while reading of magazines and newspapers increases (Heather, 1981b; James, 1987). A reanalysis of National Assessment of Educational Performance (NAEP) data revealed that 72 percent of 13-year-olds read for pleasure at least once a week (Walberg & Tsai, 1984), the figure for 17-year-olds was 67 percent (Walberg & Tsai, 1983). A Japanese survey (Sakamoto & Makita, 1973) of second-year junior high school students found that 38 percent had not read a complete book in the months prior to the survey. Disadvantaged youth in an Irish study (Greaney & Kellaghan, 1984) did relatively little leisure reading; slightly over 60 percent had not read a book over a three-month period. Among 13- and 14-year-old English students, over a one-month period, 20 percent had read at most one book; in contrast, 79 percent had read comics, 74 percent magazines, and 94 percent newspapers (Pugh, 1969). A high rate of newspaper reading was also recorded in a British national survey (Brown, 1987); 70 percent of 14- and 15-year-olds had read or looked at a newspaper the previous day. Whitehead, et al. (1977) found that subjects who were age 14 and above read an average of 1.95 books per month. Volume of reading by 10- to 19-year-olds in New Zealand is quite high (Guthrie, 1981). Here the amount of material read per person per month was slightly over 23 daily newspapers, 3.7 weekly newspapers, and over 7 magazines. Book reading was not included in this study.

Studies that report time devoted to leisure reading should be interpreted with some caution. First, a variety of research methodologies has been used. Second, some studies fail to distinguish between reading as a primary or secondary (e.g., while watching television) activity. Third, the time period surveyed varies from "last night" to much longer periods. Fourth, statistics for average time can mask the fact that distributions for leisure activities are generally highly skewed; very often the average is derived from scores of large numbers of nonreaders and avid readers. For example, in one study that reported a mean reading time of 48.9 minutes over a three-day period to reading books, a total of 44 percent did not read books while at the other extreme 6.4 percent of the pupils devoted at least three hours of their leisure activity to book reading (Greaney, 1980).

Whether or not young people devote less time to reading than their predecessors is unclear. Certainly adults in Britain appear to spend less time reading books. Luckham (1988), on the basis of a comparison of eleven surveys of adult reading habits, concluded that there had been a substantial drop in time devoted to reading books between 1943 and 1985. A U.S. study reported that between 1978 and 1983 the proportion of young people under 21 years of age who read regularly declined from 75 percent to 63 percent (Book Industry Study Group, 1984). Turning to Britain, the results of two studies (Jenkinson, 1940; Taylor, 1973) suggest that there has been a decline in the amount of time given to book reading among secondary-level pupils; since one of these studies (Taylor, 1973), however, was based on data from a small sample of schools, its results should be interpreted with considerable caution.

At the preschool level, parents regularly devote time to reading to their children, particularly prior to bedtime (Clarke, 1976; Morrow, 1983; Sakamoto & Makita, 1973). Prater (1985) noted that the great majority of working parents of 3-, 4-, and 5-year-olds spend at least 15 minutes reading aloud to their children at least several times a week. At the elementary school level, children's personal reading tends to be of a sporadic nature (Greaney & Hegarty, 1987; Southgate et al., 1981). Clearly, for most children independent reading is not a conspicuous feature of their use of leisure time. Fielding, Wilson, and Anderson (1986) established that 50 percent of the fifth-grade children in their study read books for an average of four minutes per day or less, 30 percent read two minutes per day or less, while 10 percent had never read a book over a period of time ranging from two to six months. Other studies of fifth graders yielded comparable results (Long & Henderson, 1973; Neuman, 1986). Two Irish studies (Greaney, 1980; Greaney & Hegarty, 1987) reported that fifth-grade pupils devoted 5 percent and 7.2 percent respectively of available leisure time to reading. At the secondary school level, students appear to devote less time to reading. Results from the NAEP study indicated the percentage reading for at least one hour per day was 40 percent for nine-year-olds, 26 percent for 13-year-olds, and 24 percent for 17-year-olds (Searls, Mead, & Ward, 1985).

Influences and Correlates

At the outset it should be recognized that the development of independent reading seems to depend not on one factor but on a series of factors. Before attempting to identify these factors, however, a number of caveats are in order. First, in most of the published studies, variations in patterns of independent reading have been explained in terms of variations in other variables based on data collected in developed countries. By examining conditions in less-developed countries, we can identify critical factors that we might otherwise take for granted. These potentially critical factors include the presence or absence of schools, age of withdrawal from school, availability of reading material, and the status of reading within a community. Second, many of the studies on leisure reading leave much to be desired from the points of view of design and analysis and sampling. There is a dearth of longitudinal studies. In particular, many studies have focused on simple bivariate relationships. Multivariable studies in which possibly relevant variables are considered simultaneously are required. Concentration on bivariate relationships fails to highlight that students who score highly on one variable (e.g., achievement) tend to score highly on others (e.g., ability, reading interest). Third, children's independent reading tends to be sporadic, depending on factors such as climatic conditions, availability of appropriate material, school homework, and alternative attractions. Thus, it is unreasonable to expect high correlations between predictive measures and amount of reading activity.

Age

Terman and Lima's (1926) claim over 60 years ago that children read most toward the end of primary school appears to have stood the test of time. Separate British studies reported that 11-year-olds had more favorable attitudes than 15-year-olds (Gorman et al., 1983), and that 13-year-olds (Heather, 1981b) read more than 15-year-olds. In the United States, a review of evidence (Robinson & Weintraub, 1973) concluded that the peak of book reading occurs at grade seven. A Swedish study (Flodin et al., 1982) reported that book reading increased from ages 11 to 13 but dropped substantially between ages 13 and 15. Reading of comics, especially by girls, also declines with age (Flodin et al., 1982; Maxwell, 1977).

Sex

Studies in the United States (Robinson & Weintraub, 1973), England and Wales (Whitehead et al., 1977), Scotland (Maxwell, 1977), Sweden (Flodin et al., 1982), Ireland (Greaney, 1980), and Singapore (Gopinathan, 1978) have indicated that girls tend to devote more time to reading than boys. A 1940 British study also observed that girls read more than boys (Jenkinson, 1940). Boys, however, appear to do more comic book reading than girls (Flodin et al., 1982; Greaney, 1980); though in England and Wales, girls appear to do more periodical (mainly comic books) reading than boys (Whitehead et al., 1977)—perhaps a function of the greater supply of comics that address themselves specifically to girls (Murdock & Phelps, 1973). Boys also appear to devote more time to newspapers than girls (Brown, 1987; Flodin et al., 1982; Norvell, 1966). Judging by the results of a British survey (James, 1987), the difference between the sexes in time spent book reading appears to increase with age; by age 16 or 17, more than twice as many females (29%) as males had read books for pleasure "yesterday."

General Availability of Printed Material

Children tend to obtain reading material from whatever source is most readily available (Ingham, 1981). For example, one study of 15-year-olds revealed a high incidence of reading of newspapers purchased by their parents (Gorman & White, in press; see also Jenkinson, 1940); while a study of pupils, grades 4 to 6, found that seven of the ten most widely known magazines were adult, a reflection of the extent of the availability of these magazines in the home (Norvell, 1966). A study of kindergartners revealed that high level of reported enjoyment in reading is associated with general availability of reading material in the home (Morrow, 1983). Adjacency to a public library (Heyns, 1978), the presence or absence of class or school libraries, and the opportunity of borrowing from friends (Carter, 1986) have been identified as factors related to book usage.

At a global level, children in developing countries face considerable disadvantages from the point of view of access to material. Not only are they less likely, due to economic circumstances, to be confronted with environmental print (e.g., signs and advertisements), they are also less likely to have access to books or newspapers. UNESCO (1986) figures suggest that in comparison with the developing world, the developed world publishes in excess of eight times as many books and sells almost ten times as many newspapers per unit of population. In developing countries, books may be unavailable in the first language; furthermore, the subject matter and illustrations in many books are often alien to the cultural backgrounds of young readers (Alemna, 1982; Osa, 1986).

Library Membership

For many the local public or school library is the major source of books. Library membership among children appears to reflect parental interest and use of libraries (Greaney & Hegarty, 1987; Heather, 1981). The extent to which library membership prompts children to devote time to independent reading or simply reflects interest in reading is problematic. Among kindergarten children, frequency of visits to the library appears to be associated with level of interest in reading (Morrow, 1983). Studies have established a relationship between time spent reading and library membership (Greaney, 1980; Whitehead et al., 1977) and also number of books borrowed (Long & Henderson, 1973). Over a period as brief as a summer program, regular library usage correlated significantly with number of books read (Heyns, 1978), the relationship being more pronounced among the more disadvantaged. Squire and Applebee's (1966, 1968) studies in the United States and in Great Britain indicated that students in the 1960s preferred public to school libraries as the source for their personal reading. A 1965 Danish requirement that each municipality maintain a public library with a children's section resulted in the immediate beneficiaries reading more in the 1980s than other generations (Tellegen-VanDelft & Zanger, 1987). Library membership is an expression of family values and a concrete requisite for wide reading activity.

Enrolling a child in the local public library is an obvious expression of parental interest in fostering the reading habit. In a separate analysis of the results of the previous study (Greaney & Hegarty, 1987), it was found that after the effects of library membership, reading achievement, and sex had been taken into account, home emphasis on reading did not correlate significantly with time devoted to reading. Some of the effects of home emphasis appear to operate through library membership. Heyns (1978) arrived at a similar conclusion in her study of summer learning; she reported that the relationship between parental background and leisure reading was almost entirely mediated by the presence and use of public libraries. Clearly, libraries appear to serve a compensatory role; their availability seems to be most influential in the case of children who do not or cannot purchase books (Heyns, 1978). In addition to public libraries, the presence of a school library appears to have its most positive effect on children from families where the support for reading is relatively poor (Rodriguez-Trujillo, 1986).

Home

Socioeconomic status is usually defined in terms of income, level of education, occupation, or composites of these variables. Studies have established that amount of reading is related to socioeconomic status (e.g., Guthrie & Seifert, 1984; Himmelweit & Swift, 1976; Neuman, 1986; Walberg & Tsai, 1984), to family size (Greaney, 1980; Whitehead et al., 1975), and to living conditions (Ingham, 1981). Among kindergartners reading interest appears to be related to level of parental education (Morrow, 1983).

Parental verbal interaction, including reading to the child, has been shown to be related to knowledge of letters at age 6 (Hess et al., 1982) and to proficiency in reading (Hess & Holloway, 1984; Moon & Wells, 1979). Furthermore, children with early experience of books tend to have an increased interest in learning to read and begin to read early (Durkin, 1966; Feitelson & Goldstein, 1986). Indeed many of them learn to read for themselves before enrolling in formal school, even though parents may not have had this objective in mind at the outset (Durkin, 1966; Morrow, 1985b; Taylor, 1983; Teale, 1984). Frequency of early reading to a child has also been shown to be related to the amount of time a child devotes subsequently to voluntary leisure reading (Neuman, 1986; Ingham, 1981) and to reading interest (Chaffee, McLeod, & Atkin, 1971; Morrow, 1983). It is interesting to note that none of the infrequent readers in a study (Ingham, 1981) of 9- to 13-year-olds had stories read to them, whereas all of the parents of avid readers had read to their children or told them stories when they were quite young.

Parents of children who devote time to reading tend to have relatively structured life-styles as evidenced by the imposition of rules regarding use of television (Whitehead et al., 1975; Fielding, Wilson, & Anderson, 1986) and time when children were expected home or had to be in bed (Fielding et al., 1986). Parents of avid readers also set aside some time for themselves to read and thereby act as models for their children (Clarke, 1976; Heather, 1981b; Ingham, 1981; Whitehead et al., 1975). Parents of kindergarten children with a high interest in reading were more likely to read novels than parents of low-interest children. Guthrie (1981) attributed the level of reading achievement among New Zealand pupils to the high volume of reading in the adult population. At the college level, Spiegel (1981) reported that the parents of remedial students read less than the parents of nonremedials. Furthermore, remedial students were read to less often as children and had a smaller number and variety of books in the home.

Children who are consistently active readers have access both to materials and also opportunities to read. There is evidence to suggest that avid readers have books immediately available to them in their homes (Durkin, 1966; Marjoribanks & Walberg, 1976; Neuman, 1986; Taylor, 1983). Studies in the United States (Fielding et al., 1986), Great Britain (Gorman et al., 1981; Price et al., 1987), and Ireland (Greaney, 1980) suggest that much of children's leisure reading is carried out in the bedroom, especially in bed. The relatively favorable circumstances of children in developed countries are brought into sharp focus when contrasted with the environmental situations facing children in many developing countries. In these latter countries children are less likely to have access to appropriate reading materials or to have an opportunity to read.

Earlier, we made reference to studies which noted that both reading achievement and amount of leisure reading correlated significantly with socioeconomic status (SES). There has been a growing appreciation (see Marjoribanks, 1979) that traditional measures of SES, such as occupation and/or level of education, do not explain adequately the effects of the child's environment on his or her mental scholastic development. They do little to explain how homes are effective, since they tend to focus on what parents "are" and not on what they "do." Studies that attempted to describe home background as a series of subenvironments or home processes have been more successful in explaining children's abilities and achievements than traditional SES measures (see Hansen, 1969; Kellaghan, 1977; Laosa & Siegel, 1982; Marjoribanks, 1979; Marjoribanks & Walberg, 1976; Neuman, 1986).

Over the years a series of studies has identified home variables that have a direct or indirect influence on reading behavior. These are parental interest in reading (Clay, 1976; Neuman, 1986; O'Rourke, 1979; Spiegel, 1981), provision of space or opportunity for reading (Gorman et al., 1981; Greaney, 1980; Southgate et al., 1981), availability of reading materials (Fielding et al., 1986; Gopinathan, 1978; Morrow, 1983; Spiegel, 1981; Teale, 1978; Walberg & Tsai, 1984), parental reading habits (Clarke, 1976; Durkin, 1966; Morrow, 1983; Rodriguez-Trujillo, 1986; Spiegel, 1981; Wiseman, 1967), reading with the child (Briggs & Elkind, 1977; Brzeinski, 1964; Clay, 1976; Hess et al., 1982; Hess & Holloway, 1979; Morrow, 1983; Southgate, et al., 1981; Spiegel, 1981), and purchasing of reading materials (Briggs & Elkind, 1977; Clark, 1976; Durkin, 1966). In a study of the reading activities of fifth graders, measures of these home variables were combined to form an overall home emphasis on reading variable (Greaney & Hegarty, 1987). It was found that press for reading correlated more highly with both time devoted to book reading and with reading achievement than did socioeconomic status as measured by father's occupation. This finding suggests that amount of leisure reading is related to the existence of a positive home environment and in particular to the value placed on reading in the home.

Reading Achievement

A positive relationship between amount of leisure reading and reading achievement has been reported in a number of studies (Greaney, 1980; Greaney & Hegarty, 1987; Long & Henderson, 1973; Walberg & Tsai, 1983, 1984; Whitehead, et al., 1975). On the other hand, a study (Morrow & Weinstein, 1986) of second graders found that achievement was not related to use of a classroom library center. In addition to book reading, a certain level of reading competence seems to be associated with comic book reading (Greaney, 1980). The relationship between reading achievement and time appears to operate independently of socioeconomic status (Greaney, 1980; Heyns, 1978). Fielding, Wilson, and Anderson (1986) noted that the first few minutes per day of reading were associated with sharp increases in reading achievement; subsequently the law of diminishing returns appeared to operate.

Teaching Method

Teachers have been relatively successful in helping to ensure that most children master basic reading skills. In many instances, however, they have not afforded children an opportunity to practice these literacy skills by allowing them to read for enjoyment (Holdaway, 1979; Spiegel, 1981). Cullinan (1987) and Huck (1976) have argued that the development of the independent reading habit should be fostered within the school's reading program. There is evidence to suggest that teachers may lack knowledge of children's books (Wendelin, 1981), or even when books are available, that they may fail to encourage their pupils to read them (Ingham, 1981). Where teachers make systematic efforts to foster programs involving self-selection of reading materials or sustained silent reading, the results have tended to be positive (see Krashen, in press, for a review of studies), especially when the programs last for a year or more. Although many of the successful teaching approaches vary, they tend to have one common element: pupils are permitted to read self-selected material during the reading period. In Austria, for example, the "lure into reading" approach (Bamberger, 1975) permitted the child to read for up to 20 minutes per day from a selection of books arranged according to difficulty level. In New Zealand, teachers were provided with storybooks and school journals usually written by local authors and containing topics of local relevance (Watson, 1987). The advantages of the teacher reading privately in front of the class, thereby serving as a role model, were noted in one ethnographic-type study (Pluck, Ghafaugari, Glynn, & McNaughton, 1984). Well-presented classroom library corners have led to an increase in the voluntary use of the library (Morrow & Weinstein, 1986). Other studies have indicated that children appear to like the opportunity to read for themselves during the reading period (Gorman et al., 1981; Greaney, 1970; Southgate et al., 1981); and where they are given the opportunity to read something that interests them, their learning power increases substantially.

Alternative Time Demands

Homework demands vary considerably across cultures. Japanese (Chichii, 1981) children, for instance, appear to devote considerably more time to this activity than, for instance, do children in the United States (Walberg & Tsai, 1984). Despite the significant part played by homework assignments in the life of the child and its consequent impact on family life (Pope, 1978), it has been the focus of relatively little research interest (Coulter, 1985). It is recognized, however, that the homework reading demands are considerable (Bond & Smith, 1966; Lunzer & Gardner, 1979) and vary according to the nature of the homework assignment.

It may be argued that young people may read frequently because they are less involved in other activities than their colleagues. Research evidence (Greaney, 1980; Ingham, 1981) suggests that the opposite is the case. Avid readers of books and comics in fact spend less time being "inactive" or "lying about" than their colleagues (Greaney, 1980).

In very many Western countries, television absorbs a substantial portion of leisure time. According to Finn (1980), the average 18-year-old in the United States spends more time watching television than attending school. Studies in Great Britain (e.g., Ingham, 1981; Whitehead et al., 1975), Ireland (Greaney, 1980), New Zealand (Elley & Tolley, 1972), and the United States (Neuman, 1986) have reported a lack of a relationship between amount of time reading and time spent watching television; many avid readers watch a lot of television, while other children neither watch much television nor read. Heather (1981b), however, noted that there was a "slight" tendency for those who watched a lot of television to devote less time to reading. This does not mean that television viewing has no effect on time given to reading. Obviously frequent television viewing limits the amount of time available for other activities such as reading. There may be a different form of relationship between television and reading. Japanese evidence (Ogawa, 1986) suggests that older students' interests in topics are stable over media; students interested in academic and technical books tended to be interested in educational television programs, while those interested in mystery novels and science fiction showed a preference for more popular television programs. In some instances, however, the popular television series based on books (e.g., "Batman," "Superman," Waugh's *Brideshead Revisited*, or Attenborough's *Life on Earth*) have helped promote the sales of these comics and books (James, 1987).

Attitude

Attitude to reading refers to feelings towards reading and aspects of reading. An individual's attitude to reading is dependent on perceptions of the value of reading and on the level of satisfaction or pleasure derived from prior reading experiences. Considerable research attention has been focused on the measurement of reading attitude (e.g., Ashov & Fischbach, 1973; Estes, 1971; Ewing & Johnstone, 1981; Gorman et al., 1981, 1982a, 1982b, 1983; Lewis, 1979; Moore & Lemons, 1982; Roettger, Szymezuk, & Millard, 1979; Wallbrown & Blaha, 1981).

Young people tend to have favorable attitudes to reading (Chiu, 1984; Gorman et al., 1981; Walberg & Tsai, 1983, 1984). High scores on a number of aspects of reading attitude are associated with higher levels of reading achievement (Gorman et al., 1981, 1982a, 1982b, 1983; Greaney & Hegarty, 1987; Roettger et al., 1979; Walberg & Tsai, 1984). Girls tend to have more favorable attitudes to reading than boys (Ashov & Fishbach, 1973; Chiu, 1984; Greaney & Hegarty, 1987), and younger children of both sexes have a more positive attitude than older children (Gorman & White, in press). Greaney and Hegarty (1987) identified attitude to reading as a significant correlate of amount of book reading, even after controlling for sex, library membership, reading achievement, and press for reading in the home.

Interest

Reading interest refers to a tendency to attend selectively to reading as an activity and to reading materials. It need not necessarily find expression in actual reading (Waples & Tyler, 1931). Research has established that level of reading interest is related to level of pupil comprehension (Asher, Hymel &, Wigfield, 1978; Asher & Markell, 1974; Schnayer, 1969) and time spent by kindergarten pupils looking at books (Morrow, 1983). When students are presented with interesting reading material, there is evidence (Anderson, Mason, & Shirley, 1984) to suggest that the interest factor accounts for more variance in recall than measures of readability or verbal ability. Among second-language learners, significant improvement in reading comprehension was achieved by those who had access to high-interest books (Elley & Mangubhai, 1983). Other studies, however, have drawn attention to the fact that among poor readers, interest alone is not sufficient to persuade them to complete a book (Anderson, Higgins, & Wurster, 1985; Mork, 1973).

Purpose

Various motives for independent reading have been identified (Alerup, 1985; Gorman, et al., 1983; Greaney & Neuman, 1983, 1988; Landheer, 1957; Lewis & Teale, 1980, 1982). While there may be some disagreement regarding the number of motives, there is general agreement that children engage in independent reading for utilitarian, diversionary or escapist, and in particular for enjoyment reasons. These three motives for reading were identified in a 15-nation study of fifth and eighth graders' reasons for reading (Greaney & Neuman, 1988). Reading for a utilitarian motive includes reading to achieve educational and vocational goals (Lewis & Teale, 1980; Razzanno, 1985). Other examples include reading to know more about religion (Watson, 1987; Graff, 1987) and culture (Adoni & Shadmi, 1980). Interestingly enough, the results of one study (Greaney & Hegarty, 1987) suggest that reading for a utilitarian motive may not be related to amount of leisure-time reading; in fact it was established that those who claimed to read for a utilitarian reason tended to have relatively low reading achievement and verbal ability scores.

The *diversionary function of reading* refers to reading to fill time when there is nothing else to do or reading to distract oneself from personal worries. Typical examples of this are reading while flying or in a waiting room or when "there is nothing on television." While this function may appear negative in tone, Tellegen-VanDelft and Zanger (1987) argue that it is healthy, that we need to be able to escape from the frenetic pace of modern life.

Reading for enjoyment would probably have been frowned on by some in earlier times. A review (Ellis, 1968) of a child's magazine that flourished from 1866 to 1885 included a reference to the fact that parents "need not fear an overflowing of mere amusement" (p. 78). Reading for enjoyment allows the reader to engage in something that is interesting and exciting. For young readers it allows them to identify with and become absorbed in stories by helping them "into another world and have an adventure" (Greaney & Neuman, 1988). Reading for enjoyment is associated with reading achievement, ability, freedom to select, perceptions of the importance of reading, home reading press, and sex (Greaney & Hegarty, 1987; Walberg & Tsai, 1983). Not surprisingly, reading for enjoyment correlates significantly with amount of leisure-time reading (Greaney & Hegarty, 1987; Robinson, 1977). Between the ages of 11 and 15, Gorman et al. (1982a) reported that reading for enjoyment appears to yield ground to reading for a utilitarian motive, especially to reading for self-improvement.

In addition to these three motives, ethnographers have emphasized a social function: people read because of a desire to discuss things they have read with other people (Taylor, 1983). Closely related is the status-conferring motive and the need to read best-sellers and other books for the purpose of dialogue (Mann & Burgoyne, 1969).

Among young readers, level of interest in particular material may be related to physical characteristics of a book such as the type, cover, amount of illustration (Bamberger, 1975; Brinton & Ingham, 1984; Rodriguez-Trujillo, 1986), or prior knowledge of the author or of the content area (Heather, 1981; Ingham, 1981). Interest may be manifested by rereading books (Whitehead et al., 1977) or by reading other books in a series (Ingham, 1981).

SUMMARY AND FUTURE RESEARCH

A full account of literacy activity will address the questions that have guided this review: (1) What types of it can be identified, and how much time is spent on the different types? (2) What are the uses or roles of these various kinds of literacy, and (3) Which factors influence these types, amounts, and uses of literacy? The existing empirical literature emphasizes some aspects intensively; whereas others receive little study. Sufficient research has been completed, however, to provide important insights into the nature of literacy activity.

Adult literacy activity is characterized by the (a) time spent, or volume; (b) content, or subject matter; (c) form, or genre; (d) use, or function; and (e) situation, or social context. Time spent is a prominent feature in this account because engaged time reflects personal values and cultural pressures. If a group spends a relatively high amount of time reading history, it is safe to infer that they personally value history, are socially compelled to know history, or participate in a school or occupational setting in which knowing history is necessary. From the time perspective, the prevailing literacy activity of adults is searching brief documents such as tables, schedules, charts, memos, bulletins, computer programs, and other material aside from books, magazines, and newspapers. The information age compels this type of literacy, and its expansion in the future seems likely. Searching documents dominates occupational and community settings.

In addition to document reading, adults spend considerable time reading fiction and literature. These literacy activities occur almost exclusively in home-leisure situations and tend to vary according to educational attainment and occupational level. Reading news of the government, community, or special interests, usually in newspapers and magazines during leisure, constitutes the third priority for adults; and time devoted to this latter activity is relatively free of socioeconomic influence.

The uses, functions, or purposes for adult literacy may be conceptualized as knowledge gain, participation in society, personal empowerment, and occupational effectiveness. Searching brief documents is mandatory for competence in the workplace and beneficial to participation in societal groups and organizations. Reading fiction and literature seems to enhance the sense of enjoyment and empowerment of individuals. Reading articles on news, science, and contemporary problems enhances the information level of individuals. Increased amounts of time devoted to reading for these different purposes consistently facilitates the fulfillment of those roles for literacy.

The types, amounts, and uses of children's reading at the elementary school level contrast with those of adults on many dimensions. In school, a relatively small amount of time is allocated for book reading, while the time devoted to improving specific skills appears to be substantial. Children's reading preferences vary according to age, sex, and personal interest. The amount of independent reading for both boys and girls is positively correlated with the availability of printed material, ownership of a library card, reading achievement level, methods of reading instruction, recreational interests, language/literacy interactions, parental example, and home values. Children's self-generated purposes for reading have been classified as utilitarian, diversionary, and enjoyment. The amount of reading for enjoyment is influenced by achievement level. In secondary school, amount of book reading generally declines and newspaper reading increases slightly. Magazines tend to replace comic books. The transition from secondary school to higher education or occupational settings is characterized by increases in time spent reading, complexity of material, and diversity of reading purpose.

Understanding literacy activity more fully requires a deeper analysis of context. Like all acts, literacy occurs in a milieu. As a case in point, Bill James is a 12-year-old in a midwestern town. One November morning he woke up while the first snow was falling. After pulling on his blue jeans and a sweatshirt, he read the comics ("Peanuts," "Tank McNamara") for ten minutes with his breakfast. He threw his unfinished homework in a bookbag and caught the school bus. In first-period English he orally read "The Sea" by Williams. He copied homework assignments from the blackboard. Through social studies, art, and arithmetic classes he completed 12 sundry workbook pages, read three articles in the *Encyclopaedia Britannica*, followed eight steps of written directions for glazing paint, and asked his friend to interpret four fraction multiplication problems. He departed school with three subjects for homework. After playing 30 minutes of indoor basketball at the YMCA, he relaxed at home, reading two articles in a sport magazine and listening to a recording of "Graceland." In the evening he wrote a two-page paper on the port cities of Europe from the notes on the encyclopedia articles. He despaired of completing the arithmetic assignment and found a Clint Eastwood western on television after searching the cable television guide. He drifted to sleep, imagining himself gliding down a ski slope.

Understanding what led this lad to each literacy decision at each point in his day, describing how these decisions influence his development, and identifying the joint contributions of Bill's teachers, parents, and peers will contribute vital data to the conceptual framework for literacy acts.

REFERENCES

Adoni, H., & Shadmi, E. (1980). The portrait of the citizen as a young reader: The functions of books in the political socialization of youth in Israel. *Reading Research Quarterly, 16*(1), 121–137.

Alemna, A. A. (1982). Factors affecting the reading habits of African children. *School Librarian, 30,* 107–111.

Alerup, P. (1985). *Why I like to read: Statistical analysis of questionnaire data.* Copenhagen: Institute for Educational Research.

Anderson, G., Higgins, D., & Wurster, S. (1985). Differences in the free-reading books selected by high, average, and low achievers. *Reading Teacher, 39*(3), 326–330.

Anderson, R. C., Hiebert, E. H., Scott, J. A., & Wilkinson, I. A. (1984). *Becoming a nation of readers: The report of the Commission on Reading.* Washington, DC: National Institute of Education.

Anderson, R. C., Mason, J., & Shirley, L. (1984). The reading group: An experimental investigation of a labyrinth. *Reading Research Quarterly, 20,* 6–38.

Asher, S., Hymel, S., & Wigfield, A. (1978). Influence of topic interest on children's reading comprehension. *Journal of Reading Behavior, 10*(1), 35–47.

Asher, S. R., & Markell, R. A. (1974). Sex differences in comprehension of high- and low-interest material. *Journal of Educational Psychology, 66,* 680–687.

Ashley, L. F. (1970). Children's reading interests and individualized reading. *Elementary English, 47,* 1088–1096.

Ashov, E. N., & Fischbach, T. J. (1973). An investigation of primary pupils' attitudes toward reading. *Journal of Experimental Education, 41,* 1–7.

Avegno, T. S. (1956). Intermediate-grade children's choices. *Elementary English, 33,* 428–432.

Bamberger, R. (1975). *Promoting the reading habit.* Paris: UNESCO.

Bazerman, C. (1985). Physicists reading physics: Schema-laden purposes and purpose-laden schema. *Written Communication, 2*(1), 3–23.

Bettelheim, B. (1975). *The uses of enchantment: The meaning and importance of fairy tales.* Harmondsworth, Eng.: Penguin.

Bickel, R., & Milton, S. (1983). The social circumstances of illiteracy: Interpretation and exchange in a class-based society. *Urban Review, 15*(4), 203–215.

Binder, L. (1976). Evaluation of progress in spare-time reading. In J. E. Merritt (Ed.), *New horizons in reading* (pp. 215–219). Newark, DE: International Reading Association.

Bloome, D. (1983). Reading as a social process. *Advances in Reading/Language Research, 2,* 165–195.

Bogart, L. (1981). *Press and public: Who reads what, when, where, and why in American newspapers.* Hillsdale, NJ: Erlbaum.

Bond, G. W., & Smith, G. H. (1966). Homework in the elementary school. *National Elementary Principal, 45,* 46–56.

Book Industry Study Group. (1984). *The 1983 consumer research study on reading and book purchasing.* New York: Book Industry Group.

Braun, C. (1969). Interest loading and modality effects on textual response acquisition. *Reading Research Quarterly, 4,* 428–444.

Briggs, C., & Elkind, D. (1977). Characteristics of early readers. *Perceptual and Motor Skills, 44,* 1231–1237.

Brinton, P., & Ingham, J. (1984). What do kids think of the books in our schools? *Reading, 18,* 107–114.

Brown, M. (1987). A study of children's reading habits conducted for W. H. Smith. Unpublished manuscript. London: Author.

Brzeinski, J. (1964). Beginning reading in Denver. *Reading Teacher, 18,* 16–21.

Burgoon, J. K., & Burgoon, M. (1980). Predictors of newspaper readership. *Journalism Quarterly, 57*(4), 589–596.

Burgoon, J. K., Burgoon, M., & Wilkinson, M. (1983). Dimensions of content readership in 10 newspaper markets. *Journalism Quarterly, 60*(1), 74–80.

Cappa, D. (1957). Sources of appeal in children's kindergarten books. *Elementary English, 34,* 259.

Carlsen, G. R., Manna, T., & Yoder, J. (1977). Books for young adults: The 1976 BYA book poll. *English Journal, 66,* 62–67.

Carter, C. J. (1986). Young people and books: A review of the research into young people's reading habits. *Journal of Librarianship, 18,* 1–22.

Chaffee, S. H., & McLeod, J. M. (1973). Individual vs. social predictors of information seeking. *Journalism Quarterly, 50*(2), 237–245.

Chaffee, S., McLeod, J., & Atkin, C. (1971). Parental influences on adolescent media use. *American Behavioral Scientist, 14*(3), 323–340.

Chall, J. (1987). Reading and early childhood education: The critical issues. *Principal, 66,* 6–9.

Chambers, N. (1980). *The signal approach to children's books.* London: Kestrel.

Chichii, K. (1981). Encouraging broad reading among junior high school students in Japan. *Journal of Reading, 24,* 587–590.

Chiu, L. (1984). Children's attitudes toward reading and reading interest. *Perceptual and Motor Skills, 58*(3), 960–962.

Clarke, M. (1976). *Young fluent readers: What can they teach us?* London: Heinemann Educational.

Clay, M. (1976). Early childhood and cultural diversity in New Zealand. *Reading Teacher, 29,* 333–342.

Coulter, F. (1985). Homework. In T. Husen & T. N. Postlethwaite (Eds.), *The international encyclopedia of education* (pp. 2289–2294). Oxford, Eng.: Pergamon.

Cullinan, B. E. (Ed.) (1987). *Children's literature in the reading program.* Newark, DE: International Reading Association.

Dishaw, M. (1977). *Description of allocated time to content areas for the A-B period.* (Beginning Teacher Evaluation Study Tech. Note IV–11a). San Francisco: Far West Regional Laboratory for Educational Research and Development. Cited in R. C. Anderson, E. H. Hiebert, J. A. Scott, & T. A. Wilkinson (1984), *Becoming a nation of readers: The report of the Commission on Reading.* Washington, DC: National Institute of Education.

Dorrell, L., & Carroll, E. (1981). Spiderman at the library. *School Library Journal, 27,* 17–19.

Durkin, D. (1966). *Children who read early: Two longitudinal studies.* New York: Teachers College Press.

Durkin, D. (1984). Is there a match between what elementary teachers do and what basal reader manuals recommend? *Reading Teacher, 37,* 734–744.

Elley, W. B., & Mangubhai, F. (1983). The impact of reading in second language learning. *Reading Research Quarterly, 19,* 53–67.

Elley, W. B., & Tolley, C. W. (1972). *Children's reading interests.* Wellington: New Zealand Council for Educational Research and the Wellington Council of the International Reading Association.

Elliot, P. G., & Steinbellner, L. L. (1979). Reading preferences of urban and suburban secondary students: Topics and media. *Journal of Reading, 23*(2), 121–125.

Elliott, W. R., & Rosenberg, W. L. (1987). Media exposure and beliefs about science and technology. *Communication Research, 14*(2), 164–188.

Ellis, A. (1968). *A history of children's reading and literature*. Oxford, Eng.: Pergamon.

Estes, T. H. (1971). A scale to measure attitudes toward reading. *Journal of Reading, 15*, 135–138.

Ewing, J., & Johnstone, M. (1981). *Attitudes to reading*. Dundee, Scot.: Dundee College of Education.

Feitelson, D., & Goldstein, Z. (1986). Patterns of book ownership and reading to young children in Israeli school-oriented and nonschool-oriented families. *Reading Teacher, 9*, 924–930.

Fielding, L., Wilson, P., & Anderson, R. (1986). A new focus on free reading: The role of trade books in reading instruction. In T. Raphael & R. Reynolds (Eds.), *The contexts of school-based literacy* (pp. 149–160. New York: Random House.

Fingeret, A. (1983). Social network: A new perspective on independence and illiterate adults. *Adult Education Quarterly, 33*(3), 133–146.

Finn, P. (1980). Developing critical television viewing skills. *Educational Forum, 44*, 473–482.

Flodin, B., Hedinsson, E., & Roe, K. (1982). *Primary school panel: A descriptive report*. Lunds: Sociologiska Institutionen, Lunds Universitet.

Frake, C. O. (1980). Notes on queries in ethnography. In C. Frake (Ed.), *Language and cultural description* (pp. 26–45). Stanford, CA: Stanford University Press.

Gault, M. (1982). *The future of the book. Part II: The changing role of reading*. Paris: UNESCO.

Gopinathan, S. (1978). *A measure of reading: IE survey of reading interests and habits*. Singapore: Institute of Education.

Gorman, T., & White, J. (in press). Pupils' views about reading and writing.

Gorman, T. P., White, J., Orchard, I., & Tate, A. (1981). *Language performance in schools: Primary survey report No. 1*. London: Her Majesty's Stationary's Office.

Gorman, T. P., White, J., Orchard, I., & Tate, A. (1982a). *Language performance in schools: Primary survey report No. 2*. London: Her Majesty's Stationary's Office.

Gorman, T. P., White, J., Orchard, I., & Tate, A. (1982b). *Language performance in schools: Primary survey report No. 1*. London: Her Majesty's Stationary's Office.

Gorman, T. P., White, J., Orchard, I., & Tate, A. (1983). *Language performance in schools: Secondary survey report No. 2*. London: Her Majesty's Stationary's Office.

Graff, H. J. (1987). *The legacies of literacy*. Bloomington: Indiana University Press.

Greaney, V. (1970). A comparison of individualized and basal reader approach to reading instruction. *Irish Journal of Education, 4*(1), 19–29.

Greaney, V. (1980). Factors related to amount and type of leisure-time reading. *Reading Research Quarterly, 15*, 337–357.

Greaney, V., & Clarke, M. (1975). A longitudinal study of the effects of two reading methods on leisure-time reading habits. In D. Moyle (Ed.), *Reading: What of the future?* (pp. 107–114). London: Ward Lock.

Greaney, V., & Hegarty, M. (1987). Correlates of leisure-time reading. *Journal of Research in Reading, 10*, 3–20.

Greaney, V., & Kellaghan, T. (1984). Long-term effects on leisure reading of a home-school program for disadvantaged children. Paper presented at the Tenth World Congress on Reading. Hong Kong.

Greaney, V., & Neuman, S. (1983). Functions of reading: A cross-cultural perspective. *Reading Teacher, 37*, 158–63.

Greaney, V., & Neuman, S. (1988). The functions of reading: A cross-cultural perspective. Unpublished paper. Dublin: Educational Research Centre.

Grunig, J. (1979). Time budgets, level of involvement, and use of the mass media. *Journalism Quarterly, 56*(2), 248–261.

Guthrie, J. (1981). Reading in New Zealand: Achievement and volume. *Reading Research Quarterly, 17*(1), 6–27.

Guthrie, J. T. (1988). Locating information in documents: Examination of a cognitive model. *Reading Research Quarterly, 23*(2), 178–199.

Guthrie, J. T., & Kirsch, I. (1987). Distinctions between reading comprehension and locating information in text. *Journal of Educational Psychology, 79*(3), 220–227.

Guthrie, J. T., & Seifert, M. (1983). Profiles of reading activity in a community. *Journal of Reading, 126*(6), 498–508.

Guthrie, J., & Seifert, M. (1984). *Measuring readership: Rationale and technique*. Paris: UNESCO.

Guthrie, J. T., Seifert, M., & Kirsch, I. W. (1986). Effects of education, occupation, and setting on reading practices. *American Educational Research Journal, 23*(1), 151–160.

Hansen, H. S. (1969). The impact of the home literary environment on reading attitude. *Elementary English, 46*, 17–24.

Heath, S. (1980). The functions and uses of literacy. *Journal of Communication, 30*(1), 123–133.

Heather, P. (1981a). *CSUS Occasional Paper* (BCR & DD Report No. 5650). Sheffield, Eng.: University of Sheffield, Centre for Research on User Studies.

Heather, P. (1981b). *Young people's reading: A study of the leisure reading of 13–15 year olds*. Sheffield, Eng.: University of Sheffield, Centre for Research on User Studies.

Hess, R., & Holloway, S. (1979). *The intergenerational transmission of literacy*. Washington, DC: Department of Health, Education and Welfare, National Institute of Education. Stanford University.

Hess, R. D., & Holloway, S. (1984). Family and school as educational institutions. In R. D. Parke (Ed.), *The family* (pp. 179–222). Chicago: University of Chicago Press.

Hess, R. D., Holloway, S., Price, G. G., & Dickson, W. P. (1982). Family environments and the acquisition of reading skills: Toward a more precise analysis. In L. M. Laosa & I. E. Sigel (Eds.), *Family learning environments for children* (pp. 87–113). New York: Plenum Press.

Heyns, B. (1978). *Summer learning and the effects of schooling*. New York: Academic Press.

Himmelweit, H. T., Oppenheim, A., & Vince, P. (1958). *Television and the child*. London: Oxford University Press.

Himmelweit, H., & Swift, B. (1976). Continuities and discontinuities in media and usage and taste: A longitudinal study. *Journal of Social Issues, 32*, 133–156.

Hirschman, E. C. (1981). Social and cognitive influences on information exposure: A path analysis. *Journal of Communication, 31*(1), 76–87.

Holdaway, D., (1979). *The foundation of literacy*. New York: Ashton Scholastic.

Homlov, P. G. (1982). Motivation for reading different content domains. *Communication Research, 9*(2), 314–320.

Huck, C. S. (1976). *Children's literature in the elementary school*. New York: Holt, Rinehart & Winston.

Huus, H. (1979). A new look at children's interests. In J. E. Shapiro, (Ed.), *Using literature and poetry affectively* (pp. 37–45). Newark, DE: International Reading Association.

Ingham, J. (1981). *Books and reading development: The Bradford Book Flood Experiment*. London: Heinemann Educational.

James, C. (1987). Book buying for and by children. *Proceedings of the children's market symposium*. London: Publishers Association.

Jenkinson, A. J. (1940). *What do boys and girls read?* (2nd ed.). London: Methuen.

Johnson, L. V. (1963). Children's newspaper reading. *Elementary English, 40*, 428–432.

Katz, E., Gurevitch, M., & Haas, H. (1973). On the use of the mass media for important things. *American Sociological Review, 38*, 164–181.

Kellaghan, T. (1977). *The evaluation of an intervention programme for disadvantaged children*. Slough, Eng.: National Foundation for Educational Research.

Killeen, J. (1986). Approaches to the teaching of English in Dublin City Schools. In V. Greaney & B. Molloy (Eds.), *Dimensions of reading* (pp. 63–76). Dublin: Educational Company.

Kirsch, I., & Guthrie, J. T. (1984a). Adult reading practices for work and leisure. *Adult Education Quarterly, 34*(4), 213–232.

Kirsch, I., & Guthrie, J. T. (1984b). Prose comprehension and text search as a function of reading volume. *Reading Research Quarterly, 19*(3), 331–342.

Kirsch, I. S., & Jungblut, A. (1986). *Literacy: Profiles of America's young adults* (Report No. 16–PL–02). Princeton, NJ: National Assessment of Educational Progress.

Krashen, S. D. (1987). *Comic book reading and language development*. Victoria, BC: Abel.

La Brant, L. C. (1961). The use of communication media. In M. Willis (Ed.), *The guinea pigs after twenty years*. Columbus: Ohio State University Press.

Lain, L. (1986). Steps toward a comprehensive model of newspaper readership. *Journalism Quarterly, 63*(1), 69–74.

Lamme, L. (1976). Are reading habits and abilities related? *Reading Teacher, 30*(1), 21–27.

Landheer, B. (1957). *The social functions of libraries*. New York: Scarecrow.

Laosa, L. M., & Siegel, I. E. (Eds.). (1982). *Families as learning environments for children*. New York: Plenum Press.

Lewis, J. (1979). A reading attitude inventory for elementary school pupils. *Educational and Psychological Measurement, 39*, 511–513.

Lewis, R., & Teale, W. (1980). Another look at secondary school students' attitudes toward reading. *Journal of Reading Behavior, 12*, 187–201.

Lewis, R., & Teale, W. (1982). Primary school students' attitudes toward reading. *Journal of Research in Reading, 5*, 113–122.

Long, H., & Henderson, E. H. (1973). Children's use of time: Some personal and social correlates. *Elementary School Journal, 23*, 193–199.

Luckham, B. (1988). Reading patterns and trends for young people. Unpublished manuscript, University of Manchester.

Lunzer, E., & Gardner, K. (Eds.). (1979). *The effective use of reading*. London: Heinemann Educational Books.

MacAogain, E. (1986). Oral and written language. In V. Greaney & B. Molloy (Eds.), *Dimensions of reading* (pp. 25–41). Dublin: Educational Company.

McKlroy, E. W. (1968). Subject variety in adult reading: II. Characteristics of readers of ten categories of books. *Library Quarterly, 38*(3), 261–269.

Mann, P., & Burgoyne, J. L. (1969). *Books and reading*. London: Andre Deutsch.

Marjoribanks, K. (1979). *Families and their learning environments: An empirical analysis*. London: Routledge & Kegan Paul.

Marjoribanks, K., & Walberg, H. J. (1976). Family socialization and adolescent behavior: A canonical analysis. *Alberta Journal of Educational Research, 22*(4), 334–344.

Mason, G. E., & Blanton, W. E. (1971). Story content for beginning reading instruction. *Elementary English, 48*, 793–796.

Maxwell, J. (1977). *Reading progress from 8 to 15*. Slough, Eng.: National Foundation for Educational Research.

Meisel, S., & Glass, G. G. (1970). Voluntary reading interests and the interest content of basal readers. *Reading Teacher, 23*, 655–659.

Mikulecky, L. (1982). Job Literacy: The relationship between school preparation and workplace actuality. *Reading Research Quarterly, 17*(3), 400–419.

Mikulecky, L., & Ehlinger, J. (1986). The influence of metacognitive aspects of literacy on job performance of electronics technicians. *Journal of Reading Behavior, 18*(1), 41–62.

Mikulecky, L., & Winchester, D. (1983). Job literacy and job performance among nurses at varying employment levels. *Adult Education Quarterly, 34*(1), 1–15.

Monteith, M. (1980). How well does the average American read? Some facts, figures, and opinions. *Journal of Reading, 23*(5), 460–464.

Moon, C., & Wells, G. (1979). The influence of home on learning to read. *Journal of Research in Reading, 2,* 53–62.

Moore, S. C., & Lemons, R. (1982). Measuring reading attitudes: Three dimensions. *Reading World, 22*(1), 48–57.

Mork, T. A. (1973). The ability of children to select reading materials at their own instructional level. In W. H. MacGinitie (Ed.), *Assessment problems in reading* (pp. 87–95). Newark, DE: International Reading Association.

Morrow, L. M. (1983). Home and school correlates of early interest in literature. *Journal of Educational Research, 76*(4), 221–230.

Morrow, L. M. (1985a). Attitudes of teachers, principals, and parents toward promoting voluntary reading in the elementary school. *Reading Research and Instruction, 25*, 116–130.

Morrow, L. M. (1985b). *Promoting voluntary reading in school and home*. Fastback 225. Bloomington, NJ: Phi Delta Kappan.

Morrow, L., & Weinstein, C. (1986). Encouraging voluntary reading: The impact of a literature program on children's use of library centers. *Reading Research Quarterly, 21*(3), 330–346.

Murdock, G., & Phelps, G. (1973). *Mass media and the secondary school*. New York: Macmillan.

Nagy, W. E., Herman, P., & Anderson, R. C. (1985). Learning words from context. *Reading Research Quarterly, 20*(2), 233–253.

Nell, V. (1988). The psychology of reading for pleasure: Needs and gratifications. *Reading Research Quarterly, 23*(1), 6–51.

Neuman, S. (1986). The home environment and fifth-grade students' leisure reading. *Elementary School Journal, 86*(3), 333–343.

Norvell, G. W. (1966). The challenge of periodicals in education. *Elementary English, 43*, 402–408.

Norvell, G. W. (1950). *The reading interest of young people*. Boston: Heath.

Ogawa, T. (1986). Reading and other leisure activities of Japanese adolescents. Paper presented to the Eleventh World Congress on Reading. London.

O'Rourke, W. J. (1979). Are parents an influence on adolescent reading habits? *Journal of Reading, 22*, 340–343.

Osa, O. (1986). The young Nigerian youth literature. *Journal of Reading, 30*, 100–104.

Parrish, B., & Atwood, K. (1985). Enticing readers: The teen romance craze. *California Reader, 18*, 22–27.

Perry, G., & Aldridge, A. (1967). *The Penguin book of comics: A slight history*. Harmondsworth, Eng.: Penguin Books.

Pittman, G. (1966). Young children enjoy poetry. *Elementary English, 43*, 247–251.

Pluck, M. L., Ghafaugari, E., Glynn, T., & McNaughton, S. (1984). Teacher and parent modelling of recreational reading. *New Zealand Journal of Educational Studies, 19*, 114–23.

Pope, L. (1978). A new look at homework. *Teacher, 96*, 94–99.

Prater, N. J. (1985). Who's reading to the children? Paper presented at the Annual Conference of the National Association for the Education of Young Children. New Orleans. Available from *Resources in Education, 21* (1986), ED 264–023.

Price, E., Powell, R. S., & Griffith, C. L. (1987). *Welsh reading survey*. Slough, Eng.: National Foundation for Educational Research.

Pugh, A. K. (1969). Some neglected aspects of reading in secondary school. *Reading. 3*, 3–10.

Razzanno, B. W. (1985). Creating the library habit. *Library Journal, 110*, 111–114.

Reder, S., & Green, K. R. (1983). Contrasting patterns of literacy in an Alaskan fishing village. *International Journal of the Sociology of Language, 42*, 9–39.

Resnick, L. B. (1987). Learning in school and out. *Educational Researcher, 16*(9), 13–21.

Robinson, J. (1977). *How Americans use time*. New York: Praeger.

Robinson, J. P. (1980). The changing reading habits of the American public. *Journal of Communication, 30*(1), 141–152.

Robinson, H. M., & Weintraub, S. (1973). Research related to children's interests and to developmental values of reading, *Library Trends, 22*, 81–108.

Rodriguez-Trujillo, N. (1986). Effect of availability of reading materials on reading behavior of primary school students. Paper presented to the 32nd Annual Conference of the International Reading Association, Philadelphia.

Roettger, D., Szymezuk, M., & Millard, R. (1979). Validation of a reading attitude scale for elementary students and an investigation of the relationship between attitude and achievement. *Journal of Educational Research, 72,* 138–142.

Sakamoto, T., & Makita, K. (1973). Japan. In J. Downing (Ed.), *Comparative reading* (pp. 440–466). New York: Macmillan.

Schnayer, S. W. (1969). Relationships between reading interest and reading comprehension. In J. A. Figurel (Ed.), *Reading and realism* (pp. 698–702). Newark, DE: International Reading Association.

Schramm, W., Lyle, J., & Parker, E. B. (1961). *Television in the lives of our children.* Stanford, CA: Stanford University Press.

Schulte, E. S. (1969). Independent reading interests of children in grades four, five, and six. In J. A. Figurel (Ed.) *Reading and realism* (pp. 728–732). Newark, DE: International Reading Association.

Scribner, S. (1984). Studying working intelligence. In B. Rogoff & J. Lave (Eds.), *Everyday cognition: Its development in social context* (pp. 9–41). Cambridge, MA: Harvard University Press.

Searls, D. T., Mead, N. A., & Ward. B. (1985). The relationship of students' reading skills to TV watching, leisure time reading, and homework. *Journal of Reading, 29,* 158–162.

Sexton, J. (1979). Education and acculturation in highland Guatemala. *Anthropology and Education Quarterly, 10*(2), 80–92.

Sharon, A. T. (1973–1974). What do adults read? *Reading Research Quarterly, 9*(2), 148–169.

Shuman, A. (1983). Collaborative literacy in an urban multiethnic neighborhood. *International Journal of the Sociology of Language, 42,* 69–81.

Singer, H., Samuels, S. J., & Spiroff, J. (1974). The effect of pictures and contextual conditions on learning responses to printed words. *Reading Research Quarterly, 4,* 555–567.

Soderberg, R. (1971). Reading in early childhood. Stockholm: Almquist & Wiksell. Cited in H. Robinson & S. Weintraub (1973), Research related to children's interests, *Library Trends, 22,* 81–108.

Southgate, V., Arnold, H., & Johnson, S. (1981). *Extending beginning reading.* London: Heinemann Educational.

Spiegel, D. L. (1981). *Reading for pleasure: Guidelines.* Newark, DE: International Reading Association.

Squire, J. R. (1969). What does research reveal about attitudes toward reading? *English Journal, 58,* 523–532.

Squire, J. R., & Applebee, R. K. (1966). *A study of English programs in selected high schools which consistently educate outstanding students in English.* Urbana, IL: University of Illinois Press.

Squire, J. R., & Applebee, R. K. (1968). *A study of the teaching of English in selected British secondary schools.* Urbana, IL: University of Illinois Press.

Stamm, K. R., & Jacoubovitch, M. (1980). How much do they read in the daily newspaper: A measurement study. *Journalism Quarterly, 57*(2), 234–242.

Stamm, K., & Weis, R. (1986). The newspaper and community integration: A study of ties to a local church community. *Communication Research, 13*(1), 125–137.

Sticht, T. (1975). *Reading for working.* Alexandria, VA: HumRRO.

Stone, G., & Wetherington, R. (1979). Confirming the newspaper reading habit. *Journalism Quarterly, 56,* 554–556, 566.

Szalai, A. (Ed.). (1972). *The use of time: Daily activities of urban and suburban populations in twelve countries.* The Hague: Mouton.

Takagi, K. (1980). Interests in picture books of Japanese 5-year-olds. *Reading Teacher, 33,* 442–444.

Tan, A. S., & Gunter, D. (1979). Media use and academic achievement of Mexican-American high school students. *Journalism Quarterly, 56*(4), 827–831.

Taylor, D. (1983). *Family literacy: Young children learning to read and write.* Exeter, NH: Heinemann Educational Books.

Taylor, J. J. (1973). The voluntary book-reading habits of secondary school pupils. *Use of English, 25,* 5–12, 16.

Teale, W. (1978). Positive environments for learning to read: What studies of early reading tell us. *Language Arts, 55,* 922–932.

Teale, W. (1984). Reading to young children: Its significance for literacy development. In H. Goelman, A. Oberg, & F. Smith (Eds.), *Awakening to literacy* (pp. 110–121). London: Heinemann Educational.

Tellegen-Van Delft, S. B., & DeZanger, J. (1987). The promotion of reading and literacy. Paper presented to the International Conference "Books and literacy: A response to new developments," Amsterdam.

Terman, L. M., & Lima, M. (1926). *Children's reading.* New York: Appleton.

Thorndike, R. (1941). Words and the comics. *Journal of Experimental Education, 10,* 110–113.

UNESCO. (1986). *Statistical Yearbook.* Paris: Author.

Vaughan, B. I. (1963). Reading interests of eighth-grade students. *Journal of Developmental Reading, 6,* 149–155.

Walberg, H. J., & Tsai, S. (1983). Reading achievement and attitude productivity among 17-year-olds. *Journal of Reading Behavior, 15*(3), 41–53.

Walberg, H. J., & Tsai, S. (1984). Reading achievement and diminishing returns to time. *Journal of Educational Psychology, 76,* 442–451.

Wallbrown, F. H., & Blaha, J. (1981). Behavioral correlates for eight dimensions of reading attitude. *Measurement and Evaluation in Guidance, 14*(3), 158–167.

Waples, D. (1938). *People and print: Social aspects of reading in the Depression.* Chicago: University of Chicago Press.

Waples, D., & Tyler, R. W. (1931). *What people want to read about.* Chicago: University of Chicago Press.

Washburne, C., & Vogel, M. (1926). *Winnetaka graded book list*. Chicago: American Library Association.

Watson, D. (1987). *Report card on basal readers*. Draft report. National Council of Teachers of English, 1987 (to be updated).

Weiss, C. H. (1974). What America's leaders read. *Public Opinion Quarterly*, *38*(1), 1–22.

Wendelin, K. (1981). Teachers' memories and opinions of children's books: A research update. *Language Arts*, *58*(4), 416–424.

Wendelin, K., & R. Zinc. (1983). How students make book choices. *Reading Horizons*, *23*(2), 84–88.

Wertham, F. (1954). *Seduction of the innocent*. New York: Rinehart.

Whitehead, F., Capey, A. C., Maddren, W. (1975). *Children's reading interests*. London: Evans and Methuen.

Whitehead, F., Capey, A. C., Maddren, W., & Wellings, A. (1977). *Children and their books*. London: Macmillan Education.

Wiseman, S. (1967). *Children and their primary schools*. London: Great Britain Department of Education and Science.

Witty, P. A., & Sizemore, R. A. (1955). Reading the comics: A summary of studies and an evaluation, III. *Elementary English*, *32*, 109–114.

Wright, G. (1979). The comic book: A forgotten medium in the classroom. *Reading Teacher*, *33*, 158–151.

Yarlott, G., & Harpin, W. S. (1971). 1,000 responses to English literature—2. *Educational Research*, *13*, 87–97.

5 LINGUISTIC DIVERSITY AND READING IN AMERICAN SOCIETY

Rose-Marie Weber

English is the paramount language of the United States, a given in most public and private situations. In these times, literacy in the language is mandatory for acquiring full-fledged recognition as an American. To become a citizen of the country, immigrants are required to demonstrate their ability to read and write English, just as children growing up as citizens in the 50 states are required to read and write English. When the United States became a nation, the former colonies included speakers of many languages other than English, including indigenous American languages, and were flanked by French and Spanish colonies to the west and southwest. The first century or so of territorial expansion and Atlantic immigration brought many instances of the use of writing in the various languages, even for official purposes in state governments and public schools (Kloss, 1977). In the 20th century, however, English has had few rivals at the instrument of law and government, commerce and industry, arts and sciences, communications, and public education. Nowadays, the stature of English as the national language is reinforced by the continuing expansion of English as a world language, learned by hundreds of millions as a second language (Kachru, 1982). It is the most widely read language in the world, ranking first in the number of book titles published annually (Gage, 1986).

Against this background of English, linguistic diversity in the United States nevertheless prevails (Ferguson & Heath, 1981; Grosjean, 1982; Sagarin & Kelly, 1985). Pacific Islanders, Native Alaskans, and American Indians still maintain a wide variety of languages; and descendants of the French and Spanish colonists, including Puerto Ricans, carry on their linguistic traditions in communities across the country. Immigrants continue to enter the country in large numbers, although at a more modest level than in earlier periods of our history, and contribute to the diversity. The general pattern of immigrants in the century has been for the immigrants themselves to add English to their mother tongue, for the next generation to be bilingual for different purposes, and for the third generation to acquire English only. Nevertheless, many languages are maintained through innumerable individual and community efforts. The 1980 Census reported that nearly 23 million persons five years or older in the population of 226.5 million spoke languages other than English at home. Of the 23 million, nearly half spoke Spanish and about three-quarters of these spoke English well enough to consider themselves bilingual (Wardhaugh, 1987).

At the same time classical and modern foreign languages have a traditional place in the standard curriculum in secondary and higher education for their cultural and literary value, contributing as well to the linguistic diversity in the nation. About a quarter of secondary school students are enrolled in foreign language courses (Center for Education Statistics, 1987); the most commonly taught are Spanish, French, Ger-

Warm thanks are due many colleagues for their contributions and reactions to this chapter, especially John G. Barnitz, Elizabeth B. Bernhardt, and Rosalind Horowitz.

man, and Latin. After years of declining interest, their study is being fostered by policy favoring languages as tools of communication in a changing world (Ambach, 1987; Rhodes & Oxford, 1988). Further, a variety of languages such as classical Arabic and Papago are learned and maintained for their value in religious practice and as sources of traditional wisdom.

With respect to literacy, the various languages in the United States differ in their form, their uses, and the values placed on them. Each language has its own history and characteristics that impinge on how its written form is learned and maintained. There are some that are major world languages whose form and use as a written language have been elaborately developed to complement their spoken varieties. They have a standard orthography, widespread conventions of printing, and established styles of written discourse serving a variety of purposes in law, government, technology, commerce, press, popular literature, and so on. Further, they have long been taught to small children so that they carry traditions of instruction, such as the way in which words are broken down into smaller parts for teaching. These languages include Spanish, French, German, and Chinese. It is notable, however, that the varieties of the languages spoken in the United States may differ in such ways from the international standards taught in the schools that students learning to read their home languages may encounter structural differences and negative valuation of their linguistic knowledge.

There are other languages—the classical and religious languages—that are essentially learned and maintained only through reading ancient texts and are valued for their association with devotion, learning, and their contribution of learned words to modern languages. Still other languages, in contrast, have been developed in only limited ways as written languages. These include Pacific Island, Native Alaskan, and American Indian languages, as well as immigrant languages with relatively brief histories like Haitian Creole. Such languages differ from one another in having been developed as a written language for religious texts, public announcements, keeping of records, and the like and may still be in the process of establishing orthographic conventions, accommodating dialectal variation, and setting conventions regarding textual form and organization. For religious, aesthetic, and political reasons, not all such languages are considered appropriate for written development and modern schooling by their speakers (e.g., Brandt, 1982). But if they have been chosen for bilingual education, they may have required the development of instructional materials and conventions of teaching.

In the view of American education, knowledge of a mother tongue other than English has been perceived until recently as a liability to learning, a factor in low intelligence, and an indicator of poverty and questionable academic potential. That view shifted with the social climate that warmed to ethnic diversity several decades ago, supported by research offering the possibility that bilingualism, rather than a burden, may be a cognitive benefit (Hakuta, 1986). It is uncertain, however, what values will be associated with languages other than English in the future, given the resistance to them reflected by the movement to make English the only language for conducting public affairs (Marshall, 1986).

In the light of the linguistic diversity in the United States, this chapter will review major areas of research regarding reading and learning to read when more than one language is involved for the reader. One major area concerns learning to read by children who do not know English well and are starting out and progressing in their first language, in English only, or in both languages. For the most part, this research has concentrated on children participating in bilingual education programs or receiving specific instruction in English as a second language. Related to this area is research on children learning to read in a second language other than English.

The other major area of research to be reviewed concerns reading a second language by students far beyond the beginning stages of literacy. This area includes, on the one hand, reading a foreign language by students in secondary schools and college who are already literate in English and, on the other hand, reading English as a second language by advanced students, generally international students who have come to study at U.S. universities and are highly literate in their first or other language. Research and professional activities for these various students, incidentally, are organized along somewhat different lines—bilingual education, foreign language education, and English as a second language—and touch on literacy theory and practice at different points. Yet all such students face the psychological complexity of crossing linguistic lines as they read and become fluent readers.

The research on reading across languages in this chapter will be limited to the experience of the United States, except to take advantage of influential contributions made by colleagues in Canada. It will accordingly disregard the accomplishments of researchers who have studied literacy in other multilingual settings around the world and have, in many ways, influenced the work reported on here (e.g., Alderson & Urquhart, 1984). It will also be virtually limited to reading and therefore skirt issues of writing a second language in relation to reading, in spite of their mutual relevance (Carrell, 1987; Zamel, 1987). The efforts in American research on reading across languages are scattered, interpretations are often contentious, and findings are not always cumulative in the various lines of inquiry. As Hymes (1981) has pointed out, the commitment to research on linguistic diversity in the United States ebbs and flows with the national political climate.

The degree of proficiency in a language and the conditions of acquisition, use, and even loss in spoken or written form all contribute to the picture of linguistic diversity in the country and in an individual's repertoire. They are central factors in research on reading. For the sake of convenience, however, terms such as *bilingual, mother tongue, first language, native speaker, second language*, and *foreign language* will be used in this chapter in conventional ways, with little attention to the issues raised in attempting to define them precisely.

Two especially notable dimensions of linguistic diversity in American life will be passed over here, despite their social significance and the research on them with respect to literacy. One is regional and social dialect variation within English. Studies of dialect variation have concentrated on the phonology, morphology, and syntax of vernacular Black English, in particular, as a source of difficulty in learning to read because it differs from standard English as represented in writing. Evidence for reading problems directly due to such structural discrepancies, however, remains problematic (Sims, 1982; Anastasiow, Hanes, & Hanes, 1982). Other research has gone on to concentrate on the educational consequences of social dialects in use—for instance, the disadvantage that children skilled in constructing narratives may suffer in becoming literate when the narratives are not in harmony with school traditions (Michaels, 1981); or, on the other hand, the advantage that students may have in understanding figurative written language because of their special oral abilities (Delain, Pearson, & Anderson, 1985). Furthermore, studies on minority children's use of language during reading lessons, exemplified by their responses to teachers' questioning (Au, 1980; Heath, 1982), has led to rethinking the source of their difficulty in learning to read.

The other significant dimension of linguistic diversity neglected here is the range of manual/visual linguistic systems used by the deaf: American Sign Language and other systems that are more structurally similar to English (Wilbur, 1987). Achievement in fluent reading is generally low among deaf people, especially those who lost their hearing before learning the spoken language; yet literacy plays important functions in their lives (Maxwell, 1985). Researchers have explored the ability of deaf children learning to read in the light of research on the linguistic abilities of the learners and have drawn explicit comparisons to children learning to read a second language (King & Quigley, 1985). The incidence, problems, and educational alternatives for deaf children from backgrounds other than English have also received attention (Delgado, 1984).

LEARNING TO READ ACROSS LANGUAGES

How children learn to read is a complicated process made more complicated by the presence of more than one language. The psychological intricacies of becoming literate multiply across languages, whether children are taught to read in the language they are only learning to speak, whether they are taught in the language they already speak as a foundation for reading in a second language, or whether they are taught to read in two languages at the same time. Growth in reading ability is further complicated by the values placed on the languages and the opportunities for children to read in them. For the most part, research has addressed such matters in programs providing bilingual education and English as a second language for linguistic minority children in the United States, but it has also considered the experience of English-speaking children learning to read in minority languages.

Bilingual education in our public schools was born of the civil rights movement in our nation. It grew from the conviction that children who do not speak and understand English easily could benefit from compensatory instruction that would enable them to attain equal access to education without discrimination. Federal legislation in the form of the Civil Rights Act of 1964 and the Bilingual Education Act, Title VII of the Elementary and Secondary Education Act of 1968 and subsequent amendments, as well as the Supreme Court case *Lau v. Nichols* of 1974 gave rise to regulations and recommendations for compliance that have been brought to bear on instructional practice for children with limited English proficiency. Funds have been made available through Title VII on a competitive basis to implement programs in the schools, to provide technical assistance, and through other legislation, to serve immigrant and refugee children. At the same time, about half the states in the nation, especially those with large concentrations of non-English-speaking citizens and immigrants, have enacted legislation mandating or permitting special efforts to develop programs, prepare teachers, adjust testing requirements, and otherwise take into account the linguistic barriers for students who do not yet know English (Ambert & Melendez, 1985; Bennett, 1987; Ramirez, 1985; Rossell & Ross, 1986). In the mid-1980s, it was estimated that 1.5 million students in the schools were considered limited in English proficiency by their school districts. Of those being served, close to 200,000 were being served through Title VII, roughly twice as many through immigrant and refugee programs, and the great majority under state and local programs (Government Accounting Office, 1987b; cf. Bennett, 1987).

Across the nation, much effort has been concentrated on providing specific instruction in speaking English as a second language for such children. This has been the main approach when students are few in number or speak a variety of languages in a given school. But the most widely implemented program, specified as federal policy under Title VII until the mid-1980s and broadly adopted in the states, has been *transitional bilingual education*, designed to provide beginning instruction in the children's mother tongue as a foundation for early school learning before a shift to full instruction in English. In such a transitional bilingual education program, reading and math are typically taught in the mother tongue and possibly in English for two or three years, while spoken English is taught as well. To avoid segregating the children from others and to strengthen their English, other subjects and activities are conducted in English. The complexities of such programs have been documented for various linguistic backgrounds—in particular, American Indian (Spolsky, 1978), Asian- and Pacific-American (Chu-Chang, 1983), and Hispanic (Escobedo, 1983).

In the mid-1980s, 40 percent of first-grade children with limited English proficiency were estimated to be in transitional bilingual programs. About a quarter of the first graders were in maintenance programs where the mother tongue was to be used for a time even after the children became proficient in English. Another quarter received instruction only in English as a second language (Young et al., 1984). Although two languages are used for instruction in bilingual programs, there has been a good deal of variation from one program to another with respect to the time and systematic attention allocated to each, as might be expected from community to community. But by and large, English has tended to dominate instruction in bilingual programs, even in settings allocated for the mother tongue (Garcia, 1986; Wong Fillmore, Ammon, McLaughlin, & Ammon, 1985; Young et al., 1984).

The academic rationale for bilingual education in this country rests on several working assumptions. On the one hand, children need time to learn a second language and can benefit from direct instruction in its pronunciation, structure, vocabulary, and use. Therefore, instruction in English as a second language is called for. On the other hand, children can progress normally through learning subject matter and develop strategies for school learning in their mother tongue; they benefit only partially from instruction in subjects that are taught in a weaker language. Their general linguistic and cognitive potential may well be fostered by allowing development of their capacities in their first language. Further, their academic potential is more likely to be nourished if their language and ways of being in the world are affirmed in school. Therefore, mother tongue instruction is recommended (Cummins, 1981; Garcia, 1986; Wong Fillmore & Valadez, 1986).

As to reading, the rationale for a bilingual program rests on the assumptions that learning to read is fundamentally a single achievement transferable across languages and that it is beneficial to separate learning to read from learning to speak the second language, English. Having made a start on learning to read in their mother tongue, children can reorganize and carry much of their learning over to reading the second language. They can become confident in their knowledge that print is an alternative form of their language, that sentences and texts are comprehensible and interpretable, and that certain graphic features count in differentiating words from one another. If their language is written with the Roman alphabet, they can learn specific conventions of spacing and layout as well as many correspondences between letters and sounds, although spelling patterns and some correspondences will differ. At the same time, through instruction in English as a subject and through other school activities in English, they can acquire the fundamentals of spoken English as a base for making sense of written English and for creating their own texts.

Much of the research on bilingual programs has focused on spoken proficiency in English—the degree of its achievement, the conditions for its achievement, the course of its development, the level required for success in academic subjects, and the ways it can best be evaluated (Alatis & Staczek, 1985). Related to this concern for spoken English has been an important assumption about learning to read, specifically, that progress in reading is directly dependent on progress in the spoken language. Learning the spoken form of the second language is primary, learning to read the language is secondary. Until recently, this has been a long-standing notion in American second-language instruction, supported by mechanistic principles of language learning and reinforced by a narrow conception of reading as translating symbols to speech. Although the dependence of reading on speech has been questioned (e.g., Goodman, Goodman, & Flores, 1979; Natalicio, 1979), the notion has had important consequences for the design of programs. Most important, it has led to basing the academic transition from reading the mother tongue to reading English on speaking ability rather than reading ability (Ovando & Collier, 1985). In the research on bilingual education, it has contributed to giving stronger recognition to speaking English than to reading English, both as a variable and as an object of study, despite the centrality of literacy to schooling. Furthermore, spoken-language proficiency as a variable has hardly been explicitly related to reading development. For instance, research on the speech acts in classrooms, including the quality and quantity of English that children hear and give their attention, only mentions reading in passing (e.g., Ramirez, 1986; Wong Fillmore, Ammon, McLaughlin, & Ammon, 1985). By and large, the working assumption seems to be that reading does not make much of an impact on the growing knowledge of the spoken language. The possibility that a learner's knowledge may be confirmed, elaborated, or extended through experience with the written language has not been directly addressed.

Effectiveness of Programs

Given the commitment to provide appropriate instruction for linguistic minority students, research has been undertaken to evaluate the effectiveness of bilingual education. Clear findings are desirable, especially because in some areas minority students comprise an increasing proportion of the children entering elementary schools. Reviews of the research on effectiveness (e.g., Baker & de Kanter, 1983; Rossell & Ross, 1986) show that this work has largely concentrated on the choice of language for classroom instruction as the main variable. Most studies have thus compared transitional bilingual education programs involving the use of the mother tongue with *submersion programs* involving the immediate introduction of reading and content area instruction in English, with or without instruction in spoken English as a second language. They have compared the approaches on measures of achievement, usually standardized tests in English, but also have flagged minority children's ability to read their mother tongue as a potential educational benefit.

The research on effectiveness has generated extraordinary controversy (Government Accounting Office, 1987a; Secada, 1987). As reviews of the research have shown (Baker and de Kanter, 1983; Rossell & Ross, 1986; Willig, 1985), many studies are of poor quality, suffering from both subtle and glaring methodological flaws so that they have been deemed unacceptable as social science evidence for the evaluation of effectiveness. Time and again the researchers did not assemble randomly assigned groups (or failed to take that fact into consideration in their analysis), reported comparisons in unacceptable terms such as grade level scores on standardized tests, did not allow adequate time before measuring achievement, or did not distinguish between spoken or written English in referring to such variables as English vocabulary. Because of this, the results of reviews inquiring into the effectiveness of transitional bilingual education have been inconclusive. Some well-designed studies show its superiority, as measured by standardized tests of achievement and spoken-English proficiency (e.g., Kaufman, 1968; Legaretta, 1979), but others clearly do not (e.g., Stern, 1975). The interpretations of the research findings and the evaluative reviews often reflect the beliefs of many professionals in the salutary effects of bilingual education for linguistic minority students. Some educators are satisfied that while the superiority of transitional bilingual education has not been established, neither has its inferiority, and that the experience afforded minority students of learning in their mother tongue has intrinsic cultural and cognitive value. Favored policy seems to have guided the interpretation of the outcomes of many studies (Rossell & Ross, 1986).

It is worth noting that the methodology of the evaluative reviews has itself stirred debate. Taking a narrative approach to studies carried out in the 1970s, Baker and de Kanter (1983) came down against transitional bilingual education as the primary model for schools to follow, since there was little support for its benefits. Reviewing the same set of studies (except for several exclusions) with meta-analytic techniques, Willig (1985, 1987) saw stronger positive effects and therefore greater reason to support it. Unlike others on the effectiveness of bilingual education, Willig isolated reading for attention, concluding that the children in bilingual programs were gaining in reading English at a faster rate than students in submersion programs and at a faster rate than might be anticipated from speculation based on experience elsewhere (1985, 310).

An offshoot among the studies of effectiveness is the attention given to *immersion programs* in the United States (Genesee, 1985). These efforts to teach a second language by direct, functional use of the language to the near exclusion of the mother tongue were initiated in Canada when English-speaking communities wanted their children to master the minority language, French. When immersion begins in the kindergarten and continues into first grade, it involves teaching children to read only in the language that they are acquiring. Reading and writing in their familiar mother tongue are introduced later (e.g., Kendall, Lajeunesse, Chmilar, Shapson, & Shapson, 1987). The research on the Canadian experience, much of it longitudinal, has been carefully planned, executed, and interpreted within the social and political context of Canada. The general findings have confirmed that children can benefit from immersion, speaking far more flexibly than children given lessons in spoken French as a second language; they also learn to read French adequately. Furthermore, their overall ability in mother tongue English literacy, as measured by achievement tests administered within a year or so of beginning English language arts instruction, does not suffer (Genesee, 1983; Swain & Lapkin, 1981). The American efforts in such programs generally support the findings that immersion provides an enriching experience for English-speaking children, including disadvantaged children, and that reading skills are effectively transferred from the newly acquired second language to reading English (Cohen, 1985; Genesee, 1985).

The immersion approach in Canada was designed to bring children a second language without endangering their first, which is the majority language of the nation and the dominant language of school instruction. Immersion is often distinguished from submersion, the conventional approach to teaching minority children, which develops the majority language and ignores the first. An alternative to submersion is *structured immersion*, the general use of English adjusted to the children's level, along with assistance in the mother tongue at moments judged relevant by the teacher or aide. Structured immersion has apparently become widespread in nominally transitional bilingual programs (Young et al., 1984). The value of this approach has support from an aspect of the Canadian immersion studies—that is, that intense time on the task of using the language functionally contributes to learning. Therefore, the sooner that children hear, speak, read, and write English, the sooner they will become proficient in English (Rossell & Ross, 1986). Structured immersion also has been considered especially appropriate when children from a range of linguistic backgrounds attend the same school. A structured immersion program based on principles of direct instruction in the academic subjects, including reading, resulted in superior achievement for such diverse children, in contrast to a transitional bilingual program (Gersten, 1985).

In the American bilingual education literature on effectiveness, it is notable that there is little systematic concern for other aspects of educational efforts that might have played a part in children's success, such as scheduling, time allocated, point of introduction of second-language reading, as in Canadian research (Swain & Lapkin, 1981); or for such factors as differential treatment, the nature of the language in contrast to English, or convergence in the reading curriculum of the respective languages. A six-year longitudinal study conducted by Mace-Matluck, Hoover, and Calfee (1984, 1985), however, considered a range of practices associated with gains, especially quality and quantity of reading instruction. Recent efforts on a national scale take into account background language, family and home characteristics (including time spent reading at home), academic aptitude, time alloted for reading in the respective languages, and other factors to be examined over a period of years (Young et al., 1986).

Interdependence

Apart from the study of effectiveness, research efforts in bilingual reading have to some extent reflected research trends in first-language reading, particularly in the turn to qualitative methods to explore children's learning in and out of classrooms, the nature of instruction, and the relevance of writing to reading. Since more than one language is involved, these issues inevitably touch on questions about the interdependence of the languages in both their spoken and written forms (Horowitz, 1984)—specifically, how literacy in the second language, English, may be related to literacy in the first language, on the one hand, and to the knowledge of oral English on the other.

Edelsky (1986), for example, studying the Spanish and English writing development of first, second, and third graders in a whole-language program through a year, considered these relations. She analyzed the children's written productions against the background of their experience with spoken English and with print from books and from one another's writing. She observed that the children generally applied their literacy knowledge from the first to the second language. They often showed similar syntactic and pragmatic styles across the languages. Yet they kept the languages apart and developed separate orthographic systems, now and then transferring inappropriate elements from Spanish, apparently to solve orthographic problems in English. Although generally agreeing that one must be orally fluent in a language before one can read and write in it, Edelsky found evidence that countered the generalization. Some children with little apparent proficiency in English surprisingly took to writing it. This may be because English print is generally more available in the environment and given higher priority.

Studies such as Edelsky's and those reported in Rigg and Enright (1986) complement other observations of children reading and writing in and out of school. They led Hudelson (1984) and Barrera (1983) to challenge principles that have guided practice and the preparation of materials for literacy instruction in English as a second language. These principles include the following: children should be asked to read only what they have practiced saying; they should read only orthographically controlled materials; and they should write messages with words that they can already read. In contrast, Hudelson (1984) describes the ways in which children abandon the constraints of structured materials when given the opportunity. For instance, they take advantage of the print in their environment; they necessarily bring their experience to bear on understanding print in the classroom; and they read and write expressions in English before they appear to have much oral control over them.

The relationship between first- and second-language literacy has been examined with respect to the minute-to-minute quality of the instruction in children's respective languages. Moll and Diaz (1985, 1987), for example, focused on the interaction in lessons for Spanish-dominant children during lessons in a maintenance bilingual program. They approached the academic consequences of the instruction within the tradition of microethnography, viewing interaction as accomplishments of the participants, and in the tradition of the sociohistorical Vygotskian school, articulating the role of interaction in learning and development. Three children in one study were Spanish-dominant fourth graders in a low-ability English reading group, but in high, middle, and low Spanish reading groups. In a typical English lesson, the Anglo teacher concentrated on the pronunciation and meaning of individual words, and the children showed difficulty expressing their understanding. In lessons led by the researchers, on the other hand, the children had the opportunity to speak in Spanish and showed that their ability to comprehend English texts—one they read and one they heard—was higher than one would surmise from the typical lesson. Moll and Diaz view reading as a unified ability to interpret and construct meaning from texts across languages. They remind us that, in Vygotskian terms, instruction must be at the proximal level to be effective and go on to assert—provocatively—that for reading instruction to be proximal in English, it should not be limited by decoding skills in it, but should rather be aimed at the level of understanding shown in the first language.

The contribution of story schemata to such understanding was raised in a study by Goldman, Reyes, and Varnhagen (1984), who compared the comprehension of fables across languages. When students had an opportunity to recall fables read in their second language and answer questions about them in the first, they showed as high comprehension as when they read the fables in their first.

A quasi-experimental approach to the relation between spoken and written forms of the respective languages was taken by Tregar and Wong (1984). They compared students' reading proficiency in English to their reading proficiency in their native language, on the one hand, and to their oral proficiency in English on the other. The students were Cantonese-speaking and Spanish-speaking learners in elementary (grades 3 to 5) and middle school (6 to 8) bilingual programs who received reading instruction in English as well as their first languages. Tregar and Wong specifically asked, for example, whether student scores on a reading cloze test in English correlated higher with scores on a reading cloze test in their first language or with scores on a test of oral English. The results showed that what predicted English reading better for both language groups at the elementary level were the reading scores in the first language, confirming the effort to foster reading abilities in English by developing them in the first language. But oral English predicted English reading better in the middle grades, suggesting that programs for early adolescents, given their variable experience before entering the bilingual program, may call for a different instructional strategy. In a study also focusing only on oral proficiency in relation to reading, McConnell (1985) investigated the achievement of younger Spanish-speaking children in comparable bilingual programs, one in a Texas community, where Spanish is maintained, and the other in Washington State, where families are quick to shift to English. Although progress in oral English was significantly faster for the children in Washington, their superiority was not reflected in their English reading achievement, which was about equal for both groups.

It is notable that there is little research examining the word recognition strategies of learners as they learn to read more than one language that would delineate the course of their mastery, ascertain the interdependence of the languages, and determine in what sense one learns to read only once. An important exception is Kendall et al.'s (1987) study of Canadian first and second graders' application of reading skills from one language to another. In this case, however, the children were applying skills learned in their second language to their mother tongue, since they were English speakers but receiving instruction in French as part of an immersion program. Citing the unsatisfying results of group-administered standardized tests for tracing the growth of reading ability, Kendall and her colleagues administered Mason and McCormick's (1979) Letter and Word Recognition Test as well as an oral reading and comprehension test that provided measures of rate, accuracy, and recall. They compared the immersion children on these English tests to a group receiving normal instruction in English, noting the degree to which the immersion group approximated the English-only group on the various subtests. Their detailed analysis showed that while the immersion children did not have as much mastery over the details of English word recognition and its place in comprehension as the comparison group, they successfully transferred much of their French reading skills and knowledge to reading their mother tongue. By the end of second grade, they screened out French skills that were not applicable to English. The integration and separation of children's reading abilities, in its complexity, may take a different course at a different rate when children are moving from their stronger first language to their second language. Classroom observation studies in American programs have not provided comparable details.

Other Matters

Since their inception, bilingual programs have faced the challenge of developing curricula and seeking out appropriate materials for the students. For some language groups, materials were imported, at least at the outset. For others, particularly the native American languages, materials were developed locally. In the case of Spanish, American commercial publishers have developed materials that conform to the pattern set by basal reader series in English. Freeman (1988) analyzed six Spanish basal programs published in the mid-1980s, concluding that the instructional emphasis is on word identification, often in exercises on isolated sentences. Progression is from part to whole and in small steps (cf. Barrera, 1983). Four of the six take the syllable as the unit for instruction in decoding, in accord with widespread practice in the Spanish-speaking world, given the phonological structure of the language. How such materials are coordinated with English materials for developing reading in bilingual children is not clear. It is worth noting that in current English basal series, the Spanish-language background of potential students is recognized in teachers' manuals by encouraging them to refer to vocabulary and expressions in Spanish.

The relationship between home environment and reading acquisition is another line of research that has been taken up with respect to linguistic minority students. Attempts to explain the low achievement of some minority groups have been based on qualitative approaches to the social organization and interaction patterns that emphasize the discontinuities in knowledge and values between home and school (Jacob & Jordan, 1987). Along these lines, Trueba (1984) studied the forms, functions, and values of texts in the homes of bilingual Hispanic students in grades 5 through 12, noting qualitative differences among the individuals. Along different lines, Goldenberg (1987) sought out the continuities between home and school in a study of immigrant Hispanic parents' interest and involvement in their first-grade children's learning Spanish word recognition skills in a bilingual program. Goldenberg's interviews and observations led him to conclude that the parents who helped their children with sound-letter correspondences contributed directly to the children's progress in the school program, fostering continuity, and that the others shared high aspirations and would have helped had they received greater support from the school. In a different context, Fishman, Riedler-Berger, Koling, and Steele (1985) explored in detail various dimensions of ethnic all-day schools intended to strengthen and safeguard the ethnolinguistic communities. In spite of the emphasis on writing over speaking the ethnic language in school, they found little evidence of out-of-school activities in literacy and little in-school attention given to home and community.

The importance of providing information on bilingual reading to those professionals responsible for identifying students as learning disabled led Miramontes (1987) to compare good and poor Hispanic students reading in both Spanish and English. She analyzed a sample of oral reading errors of four groups of students: good readers and poor readers identified as learning disabled, some of whom had begun learning to read in Spanish and some in English. Among the findings, good readers who had learned Spanish reading first showed more evidence of attention to graphic clues in their English than the good readers who had learned English first, perhaps reflecting the high concentration on graphic cues in Spanish instruction. Further, poor readers instructed in Spanish made errors that were similar to the errors of good readers in type and adherence to the text, casting doubt on their classification as learning disabled. In an exploratory study also underlining the need for sensitive assessment of language minority students, Ammon (1987) concentrated on the performance patterns of poor bilingual readers from Hispanic and Chinese backgrounds. Examining responses to items from standardized reading tests of English and following up with case analyses of individual problem readers on a variety of tasks, she speculated on the recurrent but dysfunctional strategies that they applied.

In a different vein, Collier (1987) focused on the length of time that learners in a program of English as a second language took to achieve parity with native English counterparts on standardized achievement tests in subject areas as well as reading. She examined the performance of a large sample of advantaged children from 75 different language backgrounds with respect to their age, English proficiency, and native language skills at the point when they entered the program. She found that children 8 to 11 years old achieved the 50th percentile on national norms the fastest, requiring 2 to 5 years in all subjects. Children younger than 8 years needed more time, and those aged 12 to 15 years needed even more, requiring 6 to 8 years. It is worth noting that the reading scores, which most directly reflect students' knowledge of English, were lower than the scores in the subject areas for each age group, confirming that becoming literate in a second language is a lengthy and complex process.

The research on children learning to read in bilingual programs has unevenly covered a range of issues of interest in the field of reading. Generally, the concern for outcomes and descriptions of bilingual programs has outweighed interest in the path that children follow in learning to read within programs. Despite the variety of research on reading, many questions remain as to how reading fits in a learner's acquisition of a second language; how bilingual readers coordinate different yet overlapping orthographic, syntactic, semantic, and pragmatic knowledge; how they grow in their ability to coordinate their knowledge; and how they construct their reading abilities in the face of different instruction across languages.

SECOND-LANGUAGE READING

Research on reading a second language has dealt mainly with reading in academic settings by mature learners who are already fluent readers in a first language. It has concentrated on the psychology of reading, on the one hand, by students in secondary school and college studying a foreign language as an academic subject and, on the other hand, by international students improving their English to profit from advanced studies at U.S. universities. Although many other people in the country learn to read English informally and still others study English as a second language in formal settings such as adult basic education programs, their development toward literacy is only beginning to attract research.

The direction of research on second-language reading in academic and laboratory settings follows recent trends in first-language reading, especially comprehension, and addresses perennial questions in second-language learning, especially the relevance of knowledge of the language to reading (MacLean, 1985). At the same time, interest continues in the psychology of bilingualism and the place that reading may have in the mental representation and processing of more than one language.

In contrast to the work in academic settings, a handful of studies have examined reading and writing as social practice in the everyday life of ethnic communities in the United States where other languages play a part along with English. Reder (1987) has analyzed, compared, and contrasted several communities: an Eskimo village in Alaska, Hmong immigrants on the West Coast, and partially settled Hispanic migrants in the Pacific Northwest as they face growing demands for literacy. In the spirit of research on the social aspects of literacy and their relation to the cognitive in other parts of the world, he explored in detail the social and historical foundations of literacy development; the distribution of literacy skills; the meanings attached to being literate; and the range of literate practices in economic, religious, and educational activities. Each language has its value and function in these matters that contribute to community members' learning, rejection, or refinement of literate skills. In a similar vein, Delgado-Gaitan (1987) studied a community of Mexican immigrants in California, focusing on adults who were acquiring literacy and English in a formal setting. Comparing what they read at home and at school in both Spanish and English, she elicited the values that they placed on their growing literacy in the context of their daily lives and their aspirations for the future. Needless to say, such social considerations tend to be set aside, if not taken for granted, in the research that focuses on cognitive processing by students in the mainstream.

Reading is of course central to learning and using second languages in formal educational settings (Rivers, 1987; Dubin, Eskey, & Grabe, 1986). Yet the sorts of knowledge and processes that it entails have received relatively minor attention in theory and practice, even though it is largely through written materials that students encounter the new language. The assumption seems to be that reading will follow from knowing the structure of the language and knowing how to read in the first language. With respect to instruction in English as a second language directed to students who need reading and listening comprehension for advanced studies, the complex relations among text structures, background knowledge, linguistic proficiency, and rapid, accurate word identification are not systematically addressed. With respect to foreign language instruction, the emphasis is often on learning to speak and to understand speech, even though the standard curriculum moves toward reading literature. In large part, classroom exercises and homework put the written language to the service of the spoken form (cf. Beatie, Martin, & Oberst, 1984). An exception here is the teaching of Latin, which concentrates on the grammar of the written language, but presumes reading ability in English.

The greater emphasis given to the spoken over the written form is apparent, for example, in two important trends in theory and practice. One is the theoretical perspective known as *second-language acquisition*, which guides much of the research on second-language learning; it derives from the theory, findings, and implications of research on first-language acquisition (e.g., Gass & Madden, 1985; Beebe, 1987). Broadly speaking, it holds that learners are similar to one another in that they construct their knowledge of the second language in orderly ways that depend to a great extent on the structure of the language and their fundamental human capacities for acquiring its characteristics; they differ from one another by the situations, particularly interaction with other speakers, that foster the natural sequence. How reading—and knowing how to read—might enter into this development to organize, reinforce, and enrich knowledge has hardly been approached.

The other trend emphasizing speech is the *proficiency movement*, which has recently come to influence much of U.S. foreign language instruction (e.g., Byrnes & Canale, 1987). This general approach emphasizes developing the ability to communicate in the second language not only with acceptable pronunciation and grammar, but also in ways that are appropriate to the new speech community and functional in typical life circumstances. When reading is directly addressed, the approach encourages the use of authentic texts that commonly occur in the other culture, since such texts have communicative intent behind them and are not composed or edited for pedagogical purposes. Such characteristics allow learners to construct meaning in rich contexts (Swaffar, 1985). Again, the part that the written form of the language might play in helping students learn vocabulary, syntax, and the interpretation of texts is largely taken for granted.

Comprehension

The most significant line of inquiry in second-language reading has developed with respect to comprehension. The theoretical advances that led to viewing fluent reading as an interactive process have energized and extended the domain of research on second-language reading (e.g., Carrell, Devine, & Eskey,1988; Swaffar, 1988). Much of it has served to demonstrate that understanding functional and literary texts in full measure cannot be accomplished solely through knowledge of the linguistic structure of the second language, as earlier models had suggested (Barnitz, 1985). Rather, the research has moved to explore the influence of background knowledge—some of it culturally specific—that may be taken for granted in second-language texts and the rhetorical structures that are favored in the language (Barnitz, 1986; Bernhardt, 1984). It has also continued to address other factors that enter into second-language reading, especially the extent of learners' knowledge of the second language and the limits it may place on comprehension. But still other factors, such as first-language reading ability, breadth of experience in the second language, and the influence of first-language orthography, lexicon, and syntax on the second, complicate the study of reading comprehension across languages and make generalizations difficult.

Furthermore, methodological problems arise in this research by virtue of the involvement of two or more languages. To take one example, asking subjects to read orally in their second language may lead to unwarranted conclusions, especially since the discrepancy in comprehension between oral and silent reading has been shown to be remarkably high (Bernhardt, 1983). To take another example, a favorite method for measuring comprehension, examining influences on it, and drawing comparisons across groups has been to have subjects read a passage and write or tell as much as they can remember from it. The degree and quality of understanding is inferred from the propositions or the idea units expressed in the recalls (e.g., Johnson, 1982; Connor, 1984; Bernhardt, 1986). In this way, for example, Carrell (1983) concluded that, in contrast to readers who were native speakers of English, non-native readers showed little positive effect from the background knowledge made available to them in the experiment. The interpretation of such comparative findings based on recall protocols, however, needs to be questioned. Since non-native readers may be asked to write their recall of the passage in their weaker second language, they may be limited in their ability to demonstrate their level of understanding. In one study of reading, Lee (1986b) found that learners of Spanish included significantly more of the content in their protocols in English, their first language, than in their protocols in Spanish. In another study (1986a), he showed that when readers recalled in their native language they revealed subtle differences in the use of knowledge sources provided in the experimental materials that hardly surfaced when they recalled in their second language.

The contribution of background knowledge to comprehension has been demonstrated by a range of experiments that have manipulated relevant sources of knowledge under varying treatment conditions and measured their influence (Barnitz, 1986). Hudson (1982), for example, made the case that inducing a schema for a reading passage through vocabulary and pictures can override limitations of linguistic knowledge, especially for beginning and intermediate students in English. In a similar vein, Floyd and Carrell (1987) gave intermediate learners of English as a second language two training sessions between pre- and posttests on a topic, the celebration of the Fourth of July, and compared their performance to a control group of such students, demonstrating that the instruction facilitated comprehension. On the other hand, Johnson (1982) showed a lack of significant effect for exposure to vocabulary on the topic of Halloween; direct experience with the holiday festivities was more important to making familiar information easier to understand in a text.

Complementing the studies on the significance of content schemata on second-language reading are studies on *formal schemata*, the knowledge of rhetorical organization of texts that readers bring to bear on their understanding. Such work confirms that the rhetorical organization of expository texts in English influences the recall by learners of English as a second language as well as by native readers (Carrell, 1984; Barnitz, 1986). Furthermore, it takes into account the findings of contrastive rhetoric. Experience as well as systematic comparisons across languages have revealed that the favorite rhetorical organization in expository texts differs from one language to another and so may play an important part in readers' comprehension (Kaplan, d'Anglejan, Cowan, Kachru, & Tucker, 1983). Studies do not unequivocally support its influence in reading, however. In one study along these lines, for example, Connor (1984) analyzed the recall of an expository text with respect to the quantity and quality of propositions and their relationship to one another in terms of rhetorical predicates. She compared native English speakers with speakers of Japanese and Spanish, asking whether there would be differences in recall of superordinate and subordinate ideas by the learners of English that could be attributed to the first language. The three groups unexpectedly did not differ from one another in the recall of superordinate ideas. Yet the learners of English reported fewer subordinate ideas than the native readers (perhaps because they were writing in their weaker language) and differed from one another by language group with respect to discourse features in their writing.

The strategies that second-language readers may use to search out and reflect on meaning have also been studied in several ways. Block (1986), for example, asked learners of English to think aloud in English as they read English texts. The participants were speakers of Spanish and Chinese who were roughly equivalent in English, and native speakers of English who were in a remedial reading course. Block was interested in the nature and effectiveness of the participants' strategies as expressed in the verbal reports from one language group to another. The readers fell into two groups on the basis of distinctive patterns of strategy use. One group, the *integrators*, drew information together, showed awareness of text structure, and monitored their understanding effectively. The other group, the *nonintegrators*, made fewer attempts to draw information together and referred to personal experiences more frequently. The integrators were, by and large, more successful on other experimental tasks and in their academic achievement. Language background, however, did not play a part in the differences.

Other studies eliciting strategies from participants yielded findings particular to the situation. Hosenfeld (1984), for instance, asked ninth graders studying foreign languages to reflect retrospectively about what they had been taught to do as they read. Their responses showed up questionable strategies in the light of current thinking on fluent reading. Walker (1983) asked learners of English to think aloud as they came across nonwords that had been inserted in texts so as to ascertain the hierarchy of strategies that readers use to establish the meaning of unknown words.

Taking up another issue, Devine (1988) examined learners' strategies as a manifestation of their internalized model of reading and concluded that such models have significant influence on comprehension in a second language. On the basis of the Burke (1978) interview, learners of English as a second language differed from one another in being sound-, word-, or meaning-centered in their internalized model of reading. By and large, their model predicted their performance in oral reading and recall of texts. For instance, sound-centered readers enacted their concern for sound in their oral reading errors, which closely approximated the target word in letters and sounds, but they showed relatively weak understanding in their retellings. On the basis of case studies, Devine went on to suggest that readers' internalized models may be especially powerful in relation to proficiency, a meaning-centered model allowing the reader to defy the limits set by their linguistic knowledge.

The research on reading comprehension in both first and second languages has suggested alternatives to the standard practice of providing passages and comprehension questions in foreign language instruction (e.g., Hosenfeld, Arnold, Kirchofer, Laciura, & Wilson, 1981; Bernhardt, 1986). In particular, Barnett (1988) designed and implemented an instructional experiment for first- and second-year college students of French, incorporating such matters as providing background information, encouraging guessing, helpful students infer word meanings, and fostering global comprehension. Although the experimental classes outperformed the control classes on a multiple-choice standardized reading test and student reactions tended to support the greater effectiveness, the differences were not significant. Like studies on the effectiveness of bilingual education, this one points up the problem of changing instruction without changing the assessment. In a different vein, Lambert (1986) has explored how *subtitling*, the provision of a visual script with auditory dialogue, might contribute to learning a second language, specifically French by English-speaking upper elementary students. He and his collaborators compared the performance of learners whose instruction in French varied by several conditions that included listening to spoken dialogue in French while reading coordinated scripts in English and, on the other hand, listening to dialogue in English, their first language, while reading scripts in French. On composite measures students surprisingly showed benefits from hearing English while reading French, suggesting unconventional ways to supplement instruction.

Other Matters

The close examination of reading performance shows that in general second-language learners do not perform as economically or with as much understanding in their second language as they do in their first. They read more slowly, make more errors in oral reading, and perform with lower accuracy on tasks such as rational cloze (Clarke, 1981; Cziko, 1980). The sources of weaker performance have been examined in several respects. Cziko (1980), for instance, observed differences in the quality of oral errors associated with less proficiency. Similarly, Clarke (1981) provided evidence focusing on contextual acceptability of errors, suggesting that insufficient knowledge of the second language "short-circuits" performance. In more positive terms, Barnett (1986) attempted to ascertain whether control of grammar or range of vocabulary was the more important aspect of knowledge contributing to comprehension by English-speaking learners of French. Her equivocal results suggest that the distinction may not be as separable in processing by readers as the conventions of instruction that separate vocabulary and grammar might imply.

Apart from knowledge of the second language, the source of differences among learners in second-language reading ability may be grounded in differences in first-language reading ability. When Clarke (1981), for instance, ranked readers by reading ability as measured by cloze scores in both Spanish and English, their second language, they maintained their ranks across languages. Still other sources of differences among second-language readers may derive from the specific knowledge and strategies that they mastered in reading their first language. Imperfect perceptual learning of a new writing system and underdeveloped new strategies for word recognition, some of them grounded in first-language reading, have hardly been examined as possible constraints on fluent reading of second-language texts. This issue was raised by Brown and Haynes (1985), working within a component skills approach to characterizing the reading process. Examining students' performance on a set of skills that included visual discrimination of alphabetic letter patterns, pronouncing letter strings, as well as overall proficiency, they found that the students from Japanese-, Arabic-, and Spanish-language backgrounds differed in their performance in English. In particular, Japanese students showed advantages in speed and low error rates over Spanish- and Arabic-speaking students in ways that defied easy explanations, but indicated that the nature of the bottom-up demands of the first language will influence learning the second. In an experiment on the learning of word recognition strategies, Hayes (1988) manipulated phonological, graphic, and semantic aspects of Chinese characters to compare native speakers and English-speaking learners in their use of such information, concluding that learners relied relatively more on visual-processing strategies than native speakers.

It should be noted that even fluent bilinguals, people who are equally articulate in each language and are highly skilled and practiced in reading both, usually read more slowly in their second language. The French-English bilinguals studied in Montreal by Favreau and Segalowitz (1982) typically read their second language at the rate of 60 percent to 70 percent of their first. The possible sources of unequal reading ability that cannot be explained by less knowledge of the second language have been reviewed by Segalowitz (1986). In a set of experiments, he and colleagues also dismissed the possibility that the strategic use of syntactic, semantic, or textual knowledge might be implicated, but rather found evidence suggesting that the source was in the way that the basic processing apparatus functions. In the second language, for instance, bilinguals showed reduced automaticity of word recognition and less efficiency in using phonological coding in memory. A fluent bilingual's slower reading may lie in the inefficiency with which information at lower levels is provided to the higher interpretive levels.

The growth of reading ability in a second language has not been systematically traced through longitudinal studies; generalizations offered about the development of reading ability and the interplay of transfer and proficiency are largely based on cross-sectional studies comparing beginning, intermediate, and advanced students (e.g., Bernhardt, 1987; Cziko, 1980; Devine, 1981). An exception is presented by Devine (1987). She was concerned about the growth of reading ability in relation to the development of language proficiency in learners of English. Over the course of an academic year, they showed gains in the development of oral reading strategies and comprehension, along with gains in proficiency in English as measured holistically, but not as measured by discrete point tests of grammar and vocabulary.

McLeod and McLaughlin (1986), although using a cross-sectional design comparing beginning and advanced readers learning English with native readers, were concerned to explain patterns in the growth of second-language reading in information-processing terms. They argue for the significance of *restructuring*, a discontinuity in the development of strategies for acquiring a complex skill like reading. It would seem that comprehension should improve steadily as decoding becomes automatic and frees capacity for processing the complexities of syntax and semantics. This expectation was supported by performance on a cloze test; mean scores by beginning, advanced, and native readers were equally distant from one another. But it was not supported by oral reading. The errors of the advanced learners were no more "meaningful" than the beginners', suggesting that in the second language the advanced learners had not yet reached the point of restructuring in their semantic and syntactic competencies. Such a hypothesis clearly requires more convincing empirical evidence, but points up the cognitive complexities that second-language reading implicates.

A different direction in research on cognitive strategies has been taken by Bernhardt (1987). Using measures of eye movement, she analyzed the reading performance in German of native speakers and two groups of non-native university students, one highly experienced in the language and the other relatively inexperienced. The native and non-native experienced readers read with shorter and somewhat fewer fixations and with higher comprehension than the inexperienced readers, as might be expected. Further, the groups differed by other, more unexpected patterns. For instance, the native and experienced readers devoted a good deal of fixation time to function words such as case-marking articles and prepositions, while the inexperienced readers devoted relatively longer times to content words, as has been shown in eye movement studies of native English readers. Here is evidence pointing to the possibility that experienced bilingual readers adapt their perceptual and cognitive strategies to meet the demands of the languages in question.

Finally, reading has played a part in research on the psychology of bilingualism. Much of the research on bilingualism, like psycholinguistic research in general, is conducted through experimental tasks involving reading. Conclusions are drawn from the experiments which presumably would also be drawn from experiments involving speech. One of the central issues, for instance, concerns the separation and interdependence of the two languages. A way of addressing this issue has been to ask how the organization of each language in bilinguals may differ from the organization of the same language in monolinguals. To take one example, Mack (1986) concluded that French-English bilinguals, in spite of their long-time proficiency in both languages, perform differently from English monolinguals and show the dependence of one language on the other. She drew her conclusion from their performance on a lexical decision task and on grammaticality judgments in print, yet did not limit her conclusion to the organization of each language in its written form.

An area of reading research specifically focused on bilinguals' organization and processing of different languages has concerned orthography and the role it plays in the reading process. In this connection, a good deal of work has addressed the status of phonological recoding in the fluent reading of languages with a non-alphabetic orthography compared to reading with an alphabetic orthography, usually involving experiments on groups of monolinguals reading in their respective languages (Hung & Tzeng, 1981). There is, however, a slender line of research on bilinguals reading in both of their languages. Fang, Tzeng, and Alva (1981), for instance, studied Chinese-English and Spanish-English bilinguals on a version of the Stroop color-naming task. In this task, a subject must name the color of the ink used to write a color word and often suffers interference from the name that is written. Fang, Tzeng, and Alva set up inter-language and intra-language conditions, asking Chinese-English bilinguals to name colors in either Chinese or English on an English version or on a Chinese version. In the inter-language condition, when subjects responded in Chinese on the English version or vice versa, they showed a reduced interference effect compared to the intra-language condition, as did the Spanish-English bilinguals in the Spanish-English versions. But the reduction of interference was greater for the Chinese-English bilinguals than for the Spanish-English bilinguals, implicating the differential effects of the Chinese non-alphabetic orthography and the Spanish alphabetic orthography in relation to English. Bilingual processing seems to be strongly affected by orthography, and yet the research in the area is very tentative (Hatsuike, Tzeng, & Hung, 1986; Hayes, 1988; Koda, 1987).

In sum, the research on second-language reading has recently been dominated by the concern for comprehension. The attempts to explore the nature of the reading process across languages have been conducted mainly through the analysis of oral reading errors, the cloze technique—as problematic as it is—and, in accord with an expanded view of comprehension, immediate recall and verbal reports. The knowledge and strategies that readers already skilled in their first language may bring to recognizing words, learning words, and accessing meaning in the second language have been given scant attention and invite methodological innovation. All in all, the picture is limited, but holds implications for improved instruction as well as for an understanding of becoming bilingual.

CONCLUSIONS

The predominance of English in U.S. society is apparent from the research on reading in more than one language. It is seen in the descriptions of bilingual programs that confirm the push toward reading English as soon as possible in all but a few settings, but only occasionally note mother tongue maintenance as a powerful value. It is also apparent from the research activities themselves, which rarely focus on knowledge and use of children's mother tongue and neglect the various languages that children know to concentrate on limited English proficiency. With respect to older readers learning a second language, the work on reading English as a second language has gained impetus, has expanded to a wide range of issues, and has been enriched by research from abroad. Further, it is being complemented, qualified, and reinforced by considerable research programs under way in reading the various foreign languages.

Research on reading and learning to read more than one language can be seen largely as an extension of inquiry undertaken in first-language reading. The effort to measure the effectiveness of our bilingual programs as a basis for policy is a familiar one on the American scene, in spite of the wide gulfs between the learning that goes on in classrooms and the way that such learning is assessed. The effort to examine activities in classrooms and the day-to-day performance of children reflects the interest in taking into account their multifaceted experience as they refine their linguistic abilities in print and, in the case of linguistic diversity, across languages. The effort to understand how readers understand written texts in a second language, like the effort to understand comprehension of speech and comprehension of first-languages texts, is based on a view of reading as a complex cognitive process relating textual information to knowledge structures, especially linguistic, in both controlled and automatic ways that can be shaped by instruction as well as experience. All in all, the research confirms our expectation that, given the universality of human capacity for linguistic processing, reading in a second language is like reading in the first, but subject to differences in linguistic structure, differently organized similarities in structure, differential knowledge of the language and ability to process it, as well as cultural disparities in the content and use for print. In ways that need to be systematically captured, the research on literacy in a social context leads us to conclude that the values associated with a particular language influence the core of cognitive processing and how it is acquired.

The research efforts have generally concentrated on issues close to the problems faced by practitioners in educational programs. But the current picture is fragmented and underdeveloped, if not controversial, with respect to most issues and many remain largely unexamined. For instance, there is little research in sorting out the difficulties of children who are learning English from those who are native speakers in remedial programs, especially in the light of proposed explanations for severe disabilities. Furthermore, there is little interest in the development of word recognition and, especially in the case of closely related languages, the ability to coordinate, inhibit, and build on abilities in the first language. As limited as it is, the research on reading nevertheless holds implications for understanding how bilingual cognition operates: how humans are able to learn, keep apart, and pass back and forth between more than one linguistic system, whether spoken or written.

REFERENCES

Alatis, J. E., & Staczek, J. J. (Eds.). (1985). *Perspectives on bilingualism and bilingual education.* Washington, DC: Georgetown University Press.

Alderson, J. C., & Urquhart, A. H. (Eds.). (1984). *Reading in a foreign language.* New York: Longman.

Ambach, G. M. (1987). Incorporating an international dimension in educational reform: Strategies for success. In J. M. Darcey (Ed.), *The language teacher: Commitment and collaboration* (pp. 63–74). Middlebury, VT: Northeast Conference on the Teaching of Foreign Languages.

Ambert, A. N., & Melendez, S. E. (1985). *Bilingual education: A sourcebook.* New York: Teachers College Press.

Ammon, M. S. (1987). Patterns of performance among bilingual children who score low in reading. In S. R. Goldman & H. T. Trueba (Eds.), *Becoming literate in English as a second language* (pp. 71–105). Norwood, NJ: Ablex.

Anastasiow, N. J., Hanes, M. L., & Hanes, M. D. (1982). *Language and reading strategies for poverty children.* Baltimore: University Park Press.

Au, K. H. (1980). Participation structures in reading lessons: Analysis of a culturally appropriate instructional event. *Anthropology and Education Quarterly, 11,* 91–115.

Baker, K. A., & de Kanter, A. A. (1983). Federal policy and the effectiveness of bilingual education. In K. Baker & A. de Kanter (Eds.), *Bilingual education: A reappraisal of federal policy* (pp. 33–86). Lexington, MA: Lexington Books.

Barnett, M. A. (1986). Syntactic and lexical/semantic skill in foreign language reading: Importance and interaction. *Modern Language Journal, 70,* 343–349.

Barnett, M. A. (1988). Teaching reading strategies: How methodology affects language course articulation. *Foreign Language Annals, 21,* 109–119.

Barnitz, J. G. (1985). *Reading development of nonnative speakers of English.* Orlando, FL: Harcourt Brace Jovanovich. (ERIC document ED 256 182)

Barnitz, J. G. (1986). Toward understanding the effects of cross-cultural schemata and discourse structure on second language comprehension. *Journal of Reading Behavior, 18,* 95–116.

Barrera, R. B. (1983). Bilingual reading in the primary grades: Some questionable views and practices. In T. H. Escobedo (Ed.), *Early childhood bilingual education* (pp. 164–184). New York: Teachers College Press.

Beatie, B. A., Martin, L. & Oberst, B. S. (1984). Reading in the first-year college textbook: A syllabus guide for textbook authors, publishers, reviewers, and instructors. *Modern Language Journal, 68,* 203–211.

Beebe, L. M. (Ed.). (1987). *Issues in second language acquisition.* New York: Newbury House.

Bennett, W. J. (1987). *The condition of bilingual education in the nation: 1986* (A report from the Secretary of Education to the President and Congress). Washington, DC: U.S. Department of Education.

Bernhardt, E. B. (1983). Three approaches to reading comprehension in intermediate German. *Modern Language Journal, 67,* 111–115.

Bernhardt, E. B. (1984). Toward an information processing perspective in foreign language reading. *Modern Language Journal, 68,* 322–331.

Bernhardt, E. B. (1986). Reading in the foreign language. In B. Wing (Ed.), *Listening, reading, writing: Analysis and application* (pp. 93–115). Middlebury, VT: Northeast Conference on the Teaching of Foreign Languages.

Bernhardt, E. B. (1987). Cognitive processes in L2: An examination of reading behaviors. In J. Lantolf & A. Labarca (Eds.), *Research in second language learning: Focus on the classroom* (pp. 35–50). Norwood, NJ: Ablex.

Block, E. (1986). The comprehension strategies of second language readers. *TESOL Quarterly, 20,* 463–494.

Brandt, E. A. (1982). A research agenda for Native American languages. In F. Barkin, E. A. Brandt, & J. Ornstein-Galicia (Eds.), *Bilingualism and language contact: Spanish, English, and Native American Languages.* New York: Teachers College Press.

Brown, T. L., & Haynes, M. (1985). Literacy background and reading developing in a second language. In T. H. Carr (Ed.), *The development of reading skills* (pp. 19–34). San Francisco: Jossey-Bass.

Burke, C. (1978). The reading interview. Unpublished guide. Indiana University Reading Program, Bloomington.

Byrnes, H., & Canale, M. (Eds.). (1987). *Defining and developing proficiency: Guidelines, implementations, and concepts.* Lincolnwood, IL: National Textbook Company/American Council on the Teaching of Foreign Languages.

Carrell, P. L. (1983). Three components of background knowledge in reading comprehension. *Language Learning, 33,* 183–207.

Carrell, P. L. (1984). The effects of rhetorical organization on ESL readers. *TESOL Quarterly, 18,* 441–469.

Carrell, P. L. (1987). Text as interaction: Some implications of text analysis and reading research for ESL composition. In U. Connor and R. B. Kaplan (Eds.), *Writing across languages: Anaysis of L2 text* (pp. 45–55). Reading, MA: Addison-Wesley.

Carrell, P. L., Devine, J., & Eskey, D. (1988). *Interactive approaches to second language reading.* New York: Cambridge University Press.

Center for Education Statistics (1987). *Digest of Educational Statistics.* Washington, DC: Office of Educational Research and Instruction.

Chu-Chang, M. (Ed.) (1983). *Asian- and Pacific-American perspectives in bilingual education.* New York: Teachers College Press.

Clarke, M. A. (1981). Reading in Spanish and English: Evidence from adult ESL students. In S. Hudelson (Ed.), *Learning to read in different languages* (pp. 69–92). Washington, DC: Center for Applied Linguistics. (Reprinted from *Language Learning,* 1979, *29,* 121–150.)

Cohen, A. (1985). Bilingual education. In M. Celce-Mercia (Ed.), *Beyond basics: Issues and research in TESOL* (pp. 167–192). Rowley, MA: Newbury House.

Collier, V. P. (1987). Age and acquisition of second language for academic purposes. *TESOL Quarterly, 21,* 617–641.

Connor, U. (1984). Recall of text: Differences between first and second language readers. *TESOL Quarterly, 18,* 239–256.

Cummins, J. (1981). The role of primary language in promoting educational success for language minority students. In California State Department of Education, *Schooling and language minority students: A theoretical framework* (pp. 3–50). Los Angeles: California State University Evaluation, Dissemination, and Assessment Center.

Cziko, G. A. (1980). Language competence and reading strategies: A comparison of first- and second-language oral reading errors. *Language Learning, 30,* 101–116.

Delain, M. T., Pearson, P. D., & Anderson, R. C. (1985). Reading comprehension and creativity in black language use: You stand to gain by playing the sounding game. *American Educational Research Journal, 22,* 155–173.

Delgado, G. L. (Ed.). (1984). *The Hispanic deaf: Issues and challenges for bilingual special education.* Washington, DC: Gallaudet College Press.

Delgado-Gaitan, C. (1987). Mexican adult literacy. In S. R. Goldman & H. T. Trueba (Eds.), *Becoming literate in English as a second language* (pp. 9–32). Norwood, NJ: Ablex.

Devine J. (1981). Developmental patterns in native and non-native reading acquisition. In S. Hudelson (Ed.), *Learning to read in different languages* (pp. 103–114). Washington, DC: Center for Applied Linguistics.

Devine, J. (1987). General language competence and adult second language reading. In J. Devine, P. L. Carrell, & D. E. Eskey (Eds.), *Research on reading English as a second language* (pp. 73–86). Washington, DC: Teaching English to Speakers of Other Languages.

Devine, J. (1988). A case study of two readers: Models of reading and reading performance. In P. L. Carrell, J. Devine, & D. E. Eskey (Eds.), *Interactive approaches to second language reading* (pp. 127–139). New York: Cambridge University Press.

Dubin, F., Eskey, D. E. & Grabe, W. (Eds.) (1986). *Teaching second language reading for academic purposes.* Reading, MA: Addison-Wesley.

Edelsky, C. (1986). *Writing in a bilingual program. Había una vez.* Norwood, NJ: Ablex.

Escobedo, T. H. (Ed.) (1983). *Early childhood bilingual education: A Hispanic perspective.* New York: Teachers College Press.

Fang, S.-P., Tzeng, O. J. L., & Alva, L. (1981). Intralanguage vs. interlanguage Stroop effects in two types of writing systems. *Memory and Cognition, 9,* 609–617.

Favreau, M., & Segalowitz, N. S. (1982). Second language reading in fluent bilinguals. *Applied Psycholinguistics, 3*, 329–341.

Fishman, J. A., Riedler-Berger, C., Koling, P., & Steele, J. M. (1985). Ethnocultural dimensions in the acquisition and retention of biliteracy: A comparative ethnography of four New York City schools. In J. Fishman, M. H. Gertner, E. G. Lowy, & W. G. Milan (Eds.), *The rise and fall of the ethnic revival: Perspectives on language and ethnicity* (pp. 377–441). New York: Mouton.

Floyd, P., & Carrell, P. L. (1987). Effects on ESL reading of teaching cultural content schemata. *Language Learning, 37*, 89–108.

Ferguson, C. A., & Heath, S. B. (Eds.). (1981). *Language in the USA*. New York: Cambridge University Press.

Freeman, Y. (1988). Do Spanish methods and materials reflect current understanding of the reading process? *Reading Teacher, 41*, 654–663.

Gage, W. (1986). The world balance of languages. In J. A. Fishman, A. Tabouret-Keller, M. Clyne, B. Krishnamurti, & M. Abdulaziz (Eds.), *The Fergusonian impact: Vol. 2. Sociolinguistics and sociology of language* (pp. 371–383). Berlin: Mouton de Gruyter.

Garcia, E. G. (1986). Bilingual development and early bilingual education. *American Journal of Education, 95*, 96–121.

Gass, S. M., & Madden, C. G. (Eds.). (1985). *Input in second language acquisition*. Rowley, MA: Newbury House.

Genesee, F. (1983). Bilingual education of majority language children: The immersion experiments in review. *Applied Psycholinguistics, 4*, 1–46.

Genesee, F. (1985). Second language learning through immersion: A review of U.S. programs. *Review of Educational Research, 55*, 541–561.

Gersten, R. (1985). Structured immersion for language minority students: Results of a longitudinal evaluation. *Educational Evaluation and Policy Analysis, 7*, 187–196.

Goldenberg, C. N. (1987). Low-income Hispanic parents' contributions to their first-grade children's word recognition skills. *Anthropology and Education Quarterly, 18*, 149–179.

Goldman, S. R., Reyes, M., & Varnhagen, C. K. (1984). Understanding fables in first and second languages. *NABE Journal, 8* (2), 35–66.

Goodman, K., Goodman, Y., & Flores, B. (1979). *Reading in the bilingual classroom*. Rosslyn, VA: National Clearinghouse of Bilingual Education.

Government Accounting Office (1987a). *Bilingual education: A new look at the research evidence* (GAO/PEMD-87-12BR). Washington, DC: Author. (ED 282 949)

Government Accounting Office (1987b). *Bilingual education: Information on limited English proficient students* (GAO/HRD-87-85BR). Washington, DC: Author. (ED 284 438)

Grosjean, F. (1982). *Life with two languages*. Cambridge, MA: Harvard University Press.

Hakuta, K. (1986). *Mirror of language*. New York: Basic Books.

Hatsuike, R., Tzeng, O., & Hung, D. (1986). Script effects and cerebral lateralization: The case of Chinese characters. In J. Vaid (Ed.), *Language processing in bilinguals: Psychological and neuropsychological perspectives* (pp. 275–288). Hillsdale, NJ: Erlbaum.

Hayes, E. B. (1988). Encoding strategies used by native and non-native readers of Chinese Mandarin. *Modern Language Journal, 72*, 188–195.

Heath, S. B. (1982). Questioning at home and at school: A comparative study. In G. Spindler (Ed.), *Doing the ethnography of schooling* (pp. 105–131). New York: Holt, Rinehart & Winston.

Horowtiz, R. (1984). Orality and literacy in bilingual-bicultural contexts. *NABE Journal, 8*(3), 11–26.

Hosenfeld, C. (1984). Case studies of ninth-grade readers. In J. C. Alderson & A. H. Urquhart (Eds.), *Reading in a foreign language* (pp. 231–249). New York: Longman.

Hosenfeld, C., Arnold, V., Kirchofer, J., Laciura, J., & Wilson, L. (1981). Second language reading: A curricular sequence for teaching reading strategies. *Foreign Language Annals, 14*, 415–422.

Hudelson, S. (1984). Kan yu ret an rayt en Ingles: Children become literate in English as a second language. *TESOL Quarterly, 18*, 221–238.

Hudson, T. (1982). The effects of induced schemata on the "short circuit" in L2 reading: Nondecoding factors in L2 reading performance. *Language Learning, 32*, 1–31.

Hung, D. L., & Tzeng, O. J. L. (1981). Orthographic variations and visual information processing. *Psychological Bulletin, 90*, 377–414.

Hymes, D. H. (1981). Foreword. In C. A. Ferguson & S. B. Heath (Eds.), *Language in the USA* (pp. v–ix). New York: Cambridge University Press.

Jacob, E., & Jordan, C. (Eds.). (1987). Explaining the school performance of minority students. (Theme issue.) *Anthropology and Education Quarterly, 18* (4)

Johnson, P. (1982). Effects on reading comprehension of building background knowledge. *TESOL Quarterly, 15*, 169–181.

Kachru, B. (1982). *The other tongue: English across cultures*. Urbana: University of Illinois Press.

Kaplan, R. B., d'Anglejan, A., Cowan, J. R., Kachru, B. B., & Tucker, G. R. (Eds.). (1983). *Annual Review of Applied Linguistics III*. Rowley, MA: Newbury House.

Kaufman, M. (1968). Will instruction in reading Spanish affect ability in reading English? *Journal of Reading, 11*, 521–527.

Kendall, J. R., Lajeunesse, G., Chmilar, P., Shapson, L. R., & Shapson, S. M. (1987). English reading skills of French immersion students in kindergarten and grades 1 and 2. *Reading Research Quarterly, 22*, 135–160.

King, C. M., & Quigley, S. P. (1985). *Reading and deafness.* San Diego: College-Hill Press.

Kloss, H. (1977). *The American bilingual tradition.* Rowley, MA: Newbury House.

Koda, K. (1987). Cognitive strategy transfer in second language reading. In Devine, J., Carrell, P. L., & Eskey, D. E. (Eds.), *Research in reading English as a second language* (pp. 127–144). Washington, DC: Teachers of English to Speakers of Other Languages.

Lambert, W. E. (1986). Pairing first- and second-language speech and writing in ways that aid language acquisition. In J. Vaid (Ed.), *Language processing in bilinguals: Psycholinguistic and neurological perspectives* (pp. 65–96). Hillsdale, NJ: Erlbaum.

Lee, J. F. (1986a). Background knowledge and L2 reading. *Modern Language Journal, 70*, 350–354.

Lee, J. F. (1986b). On the use of the recall task to measure L2 reading comprehension. *Studies in Second Language Acquisition, 8*, 83–93.

Legarreta, D. (1979). The effects of program models on language acquisition by Spanish-speaking children. *TESOL Quarterly 13*, 521–534.

Mace-Matluck, B. J., Hoover, W. A., & Calfee, R. C. (1984). *Teaching reading to bilingual children study* (Vols. 1–8). Austin, TX: Southwest Educational Development Laboratory. (ED 267 624)

Mace-Matluck, B. J., Hoover, W. A., & Calfee, R. C. (1985). *Language, literacy, and instruction in bilingual settings.* Austin, TX: Southwest Educational Development Laboratory. (ED 273 430)

Mack, M. (1986). A study of semantic and syntactic processing in monolinguals and early bilinguals. *Journal of Psycholinguistic Research, 15*, 463–488.

McConnell, B. B. (1985). Bilingual education and language shift. In L. Elias-Olivares, E. A. Leone, R. Cisneros & J. Gutierrez (Eds.), *Spanish language use and public life in the United States.* Berlin: Mouton.

McLeod, B., & McLaughlin, B. (1986). Restructuring or automaticity? Reading in a second language. *Language Learning, 36*, 109–123.

MacLean, M. (1985). Reading in a second/foreign language: A bibliography 1974–1984. *Canadian Modern Language Review, 42*, 56–66.

Marshall, D. (1986). The question of an official language: Language rights and the English Language Amendment. *International Journal of the Sociology of Language, 60*, 7–75.

Mason, J., & McCormick, C. (1979). *Testing the development of reading and linguistic awareness* (Technical Report No. 126). Champaign-Urbana: University of Illinois, Center for the Study of Reading.

Maxwell, M. (1985). Some functions and uses of literacy in the deaf community. *Language in Society, 14*, 205–221.

Michaels, S. (1981). "Sharing time": Children's narrative styles and differential access to literacy. *Language in Society, 10*, 423–442.

Miramontes, O. (1987). Oral reading miscues of Hispanic good and learning disabled students: Implications for second language reading. In S. R. Goldman & H. T. Trueba (Eds.), *Becoming literate in English as a second language* (pp. 127–154). Norwood, NJ: Ablex.

Moll, L. C., & Diaz, S. (1985). Ethnographic pedagogy: Promoting effective bilingual instruction. In E. E. Garcia & R. V. Padilla (Eds.), *Advances in bilingual education research.* Tucson: University of Arizona Press.

Moll, L. C., & Diaz, S. (1987). Change as the goal of educational research. *Anthropology and Education Quarterly, 18*, 300–311.

Natalicio, D. S. (1979). Reading and the bilingual child. In L. B. Resnick & P. A. Weaver (Eds.), *Theory and practice of early reading: Vol 1* (pp. 131–149). Hillsdale, NJ: Erlbaum.

Ovando, C. J., & Collier, V. P. (1985). *Bilingual and ESL classrooms: Teaching in multicultural contexts.* New York: McGraw-Hill.

Ramirez, A. G. (1985). *Bilingualism through schooling: Cross-cultural education for minority and majority students.* Albany: State University of New York Press.

Ramirez, J. D. (1986). Comparing structured English immersion and bilingual education: First-year results of a national study. *American Journal of Education, 95*, 122–148.

Reder, S. M. (1987). Comparative aspects of functional literacy development: Three ethnic American communities. In D. Wagner (Ed.), *The future of literacy in a changing world* (pp. 250–270). New York: Pergamon Press.

Rigg, P., & Enright, D. S. (1986). *Children and ESL.* Washington, DC: Teachers of English to Speakers of Other Languages.

Rivers, W. (Ed.). (1987). *Interactive language teaching.* New York: Cambridge University Press.

Rhodes, N. C., & Oxford, R. L. (1988). Foreign languages in elementary and secondary schools: Results of a national survey. *Foreign Language Annals, 21*, 51–69.

Rossell, C., & Ross, J. M. (1986). The social science evidence on bilingual education. *Journal of Law and Education, 15*, 385–419.

Sagarin, E., & Kelly, R. J. (1985). Polylingualism in the United States of America: A multitude of tongues and a monolingual majority. In W. Beer & J. E. Jacob (Eds.), *Language policy and language unity* (pp. 20–44). Totowa, NJ: Rowman and Allenheld.

Secada, W. G. (1987). This is 1987, not 1980: A comment on a comment. *Review of Educational Research, 57,* 377–384.

Segalowitz, N. S. (1986). Skilled reading in the second language. In J. Vaid (Ed.), *Language processing in bilinguals: Psycholinguistic and neurological perspectives* (pp. 3–19). Hillsdale, NJ: Erlbaum.

Sims, R. (1982). Dialect and reading: Toward redefining the issues. In J. A. Langer and M. T. Smith-Burke (Eds.), *Reader meets author/bridging the gap* (pp. 232–236). Newark, DE: International Reading Association.

Spolsky, B. (1978). American Indian bilingual education. In B. Spolsky & R. L. Cooper (Eds.), *Case studies in bilingual education* (pp. 332–361). Rowley, MA: Newbury House.

Stern, C. (1975). *Final report of the Compton Unified School District's Title VII bilingual-bicultural project: September 1969 through June 1975.* Compton City: CA: Compton City Schools.

Swaffar, J. K. (1985). Reading authentic texts in a foreign language: A cognitive model. *Modern Language Journal, 69,* 15–34.

Swaffar, J. K. (1988). Readers, texts, and second languages: The interactive processes. *Modern Language Journal, 72,* 123–149.

Swain, M., & Lapkin, S. (1981). *Evaluating bilingual education: A Canadian case study.* Avon, Engl.: Multilingual Matters.

Tregar, B., & Wong, B. F. (1984). The relationship between native and second language reading comprehension and second language oral ability. In C. Rivera (Ed.), *Placement procedures in bilingual education: Education and policy issues* (pp. 152–164). Clevedon, Engl.: Multilingual Matters.

Trueba, H. T. (1984). The forms, functions, and values of literacy: Reading for survival in a barrio as a student. *NABE Journal, 9*(1), 21–40.

Walker, L. J. (1983). Word identification strategies in reading a foreign language. *Foreign Language Annals, 16,* 293–299.

Wardhaugh, R. (1987). *Languages in competition: Dominance, diversity, and decline.* New York: Blackwell.

Wilbur, R. (1987). *American Sign Language: Linguistic and applied dimensions* (2nd ed.). Boston: Little Brown.

Willig, A. C. (1985). A meta-analysis of selected studies on the effectiveness of bilingual education. *Review of Educational Research, 55,* 269–317.

Willig, A. C. (1987). Examining bilingual education research through meta-analysis of bilingual education. *Review of Educational Research, 57,* 363–376.

Wong Fillmore, L., Ammon, P., McLaughlin, B., & Ammon, M. S. (1985). *Learning English through bilingual instruction.* Final Report to National Institute of Education (400-80-0030). (ED 259 579)

Wong Fillmore, L., & Valadez, C. (1986). Teaching bilingual learners. In M. C. Wittrock (Ed.), *Handbook of research on teaching* (3rd ed.), (pp. 648–685). New York: Macmillan.

Young, M. B., Hopstock, P. J., Goldsamt, M. R., Rudes, B. A., Bauman, J. E., Fleischman, H. L., Burkheimer, G. J., Zehler, A., Ratner, M., & Shaycoft, M. F. (1984). *LEP students: Characteristics and school services. The descriptive phase of the National Longitudinal Evaluation of the effectiveness of services for language-minority limited-English-proficient students.* Arlington, VA: Development Associates (ED 259 564)

Young, M. B., Shaycoft, M. F., Hopstock, P. J., Zehler, A., Ratner, M., Rivera, C., & Rudes, B. A. (1986). *Instructing children with limited English ability. Year One Report of the National Longitudinal Evaluation of the effectiveness of services of language-minority limited-English-proficient students.* Arlington, VA: Development Associates.

Zamel, V. (1987). Recent research on writing pedagogy. *TESOL Quarterly, 21,* 697–715.

6 THE PUBLISHING INDUSTRY AND TEXTBOOKS

Jeanne S. Chall and James R. Squire

T he development of school publishing in the United States parallels in many ways the development of curriculum and instruction in reading. From the colonial schools through the state schools and academies of the early 19th century and ultimately to our modern public schools, the teaching of reading has been our largest single educational enterprise and has received more attention than any other subject.

This chapter surveys current characteristics of school publishing in the United States, particularly with respect to the publishing of reading textbooks and the historical development of such materials. Current characteristics of reading textbooks and their research bases are then examined: content, level of difficulty, instructional design, graphic design, and the ways books are selected. Finally, the chapter looks at some current conditions influencing educational publishing of reading textbooks.

EDUCATIONAL PUBLISHING

Current Characteristics

Close to 40 educational publishers generated sales of instructional materials of $1.6 billion from U.S. public and private schools in 1986. In addition, many smaller publishers offered supplementary items (Association of American Publishers, 1987), so total educational sales were close to $2 billion. Today's schools presently expend around $34.17 per pupil per year for textbooks and related materials; but in 1986 such expenditures ranged from a high of $68 per pupil in Washington, D.C., to a low of $19 per pupil in Utah (AAP, 1987).

Eleven percent of all textbook expenditures occur in California and 7.3 percent in Texas—the two states often alleged to dominate textbook decisions because of the size of their markets. However, sales are spread more evenly throughout the country, with the 10 largest states accounting for only half of the industry revenues (AAP, 1987). Approximately half the revenues are achieved in "open territory," where local schools and teachers select instructional materials directly; half in the South and West, where statewide committees prescreen textbooks and determine a limited number (from 5 to 10) that can then be purchased. Although the number of states engaged in statewide adoptions (21) has not changed for 15 years, the importance of these states to the industry has grown as the American population has moved south and west and the percent of the total textbook market in these regions has climbed from 40 to around 50 percent.

120

Of roughly $1 billion expended by elementary schools on textbooks and related materials in 1986, some 43.6 percent was spent on reading instructional materials, more than twice the total dollars expended in elementary school mathematics (16.6%). Much less was expended on elementary social studies (7%), elementary science and health (8.6%), elementary language arts (8.9%), and spelling (7.1%). Indeed, reading and language arts, when combined with spelling and literature, account for about 60 percent of the instructional dollars, just as total language arts teaching dominates instructional time throughout the first six years of schooling (AAP, 1987, F-4). And these totals do *not* include expenditures for library books, newspapers, and other materials not directly associated with reading instruction.

History of Readers and Textbook Publishing

How did this educational industry grow to its present position of prominence in elementary school reading instruction? The origins date back to colonial America. Goodman, Freeman, Murphy, and Shannon, P. (1988); Graham (1978); Venezky (1988); and Woodward (1985), among others, have studied the history of reading textbooks; but more revealing, perhaps, are comments on readers in histories of reading instruction published by Gray (1984), Smith (1934/1986), Venezky (1983), and Elson (1972). Also instructive is a study of the life work of William S. Gray, one of the early leaders in the development of today's readers (Mavrogenes, 1985).

The first widely used reader was the *New England Primer*, which emphasized alphabetic rhymes, pictures, and religious content. Then Noah Webster's *American Spelling Book*, initially published in 1798, became the most popular reader through the first quarter of the 19th century, reaching a total distribution in excess of 24 million. Its content had a moral focus, and its teaching methodology stressed sounding and "standard" American pronunciation and spelling (Smith, 1934/1986; Venezky, 1983).

The content of readers changed throughout various periods of history. Before 1775, their content was primarily religious; from about 1775 to 1825, religious and secular elements received equal emphasis; from 1825 to 1875, moralistic and secular values seemed prominent; from 1875 to 1915 literary values predominated; since 1915, many different objectives have dictated the content of readers, with the greatest emphasis since 1920 on "realistic experience" (Gray, 1984).

Although the McGuffey readers are widely regarded as setting the standard for reading textbooks used in the 19th century, Venezky (1988) recently pointed out the importance of Samuel Wood, a publisher of children's books in New York City, who compiled the first graded series of readers between 1808 and 1810. Used in the Lancastrian charity schools sponsored by the Society of Friends, which had a rigid monitorial system with well-defined levels of reading ability, Wood's readers rejected fiction, fairy stories, and military adventures and stressed what he felt children should read. As a Quaker, he stressed the morality and knowledge that the Quakers believed to be important; hence, his books were heavily religious but also filled with practical knowledge. His books sold widely but were not revised and gradually became noncompetitive.

By the time of the first appearance of the readers authored by William Holmes McGuffey between 1836 and 1844, an emphasis on moralistic content and on alphabetic/phonetic methods had been well established (Smith, 1934/1986). For the next 50 years, the *McGuffey Eclectic Readers*—graded with controlled introduction of vocabulary, sentence length, word repetition, and reading instruction built around oral reading and elocutionary principles, and a section of advice for teachers—became the most widely used reading textbooks in the history of America, "the schoolbooks for millions" (Bohning, 1986). The *McGuffey Readers* were the norm, but several other graded programs were produced during the century, following the McGuffey mold (Venezky, 1988). Over 122 million copies of the *McGuffey Readers* were sold, and from 1836 to 1920 more than half the schoolchildren of America learned to read from these books.

During the long dominance of the *McGuffey Readers*, few competitive reader programs were successfully introduced; but this condition changed by the late 19th century, when publisher-initiated rather than author-initiated series emerged (Venezky, 1988). New publishers appeared and each developed its own reading program. Moralistic and informational selections decreased; so did elocutionary rules. In their place came Mother Goose rhymes, folktales, and other belles lettres. Longer reading selections chosen for literary rather than oratorical features became the norm. By the 1920s and 1930s, another change in content could be seen: realistic stories about children of similar age and background to most of the children using the books. Publishers thus tried to appeal to the interests of young readers.

The 1920s also saw the emergence of reading readiness programs and of the *preprimer*, designed to use only a limited number of high-frequency words during beginning reading, an application of the growing use of a sight, or whole-word, approach to beginning reading. Torn between the desire to provide well-written selections in beginning basal texts and the limited word recognition abilities of children learning to read, authors and publishers created preprimers with stories told mainly by pictures.

The rise of scientific research in education furthered the development of the form of the basal reader (Goodman et al., 1988). With research pointing to the greater effectiveness of systematic approaches to instruction as compared to less structured ones, teacher's manuals began to receive greater prominence (Gray, 1984). By the 1940s and 1950s, most basal reading series continued the use of graded readers with a readiness program, carefully controlled introduction of vocabulary in the primary-level books, and control of readability for levels three or four and above (Gray, 1984; Smith, 1934/1986). Workbooks related to basic instruction were introduced early in the century and, when Arthur Gates's research reported the power of using related workbooks to provide systematic practice of skills as well as controlled vocabulary for ease in learning, the so-called *basal reader approach* to teaching reading had become well established (Gates, 1926; Thorndike, 1921). Smith reports these features largely dominated 16 sets of basal readers in use in 1926 (Smith, 1934/1986).

Many of the authors of these basal reading programs, then as now (William S. Gray, Arthur Gates, and David H. Russell particularly), were the leading researchers and reading educators. Of these early leaders, William S. Gray was especially influential, since the Elson-Gray readers, which he first coauthored for Scott Foresman in 1929, became through subsequent revisions the dominant and most influential series in U.S. publishing between 1930 and 1970. Gray's "Dick and Jane" series, as it was commonly called, is even today a legendary series, widely imitated by other publishers (see Chall, 1966/1983a, for an analysis of the 1950 and 1960 editions of the series, grades one to three). Small wonder, since more than 200 million Americans learned to read with these readers; and the pattern of whole-word methods, controlled vocabulary, word repetition, stress on comprehension, and specific instructions in a teacher's manual set the pattern for programs offered by a dozen other publishers (Mavrogenes, 1985).

By the mid-1960s, around 18 educational publishers were serving schools through publication of eight-year basal reading programs, and more than 95 percent of all elementary schoolteachers used these materials in their classrooms (Chall, 1967/1983a; Cronbach, Biersted, McMurray, Schramm, & Spaulding, 1955).

But the nature of the content and methods readers continued to change. Chall's synthesis of research on phonics from 1910 to 1965, together with her analysis of the methods used in basal readers published in the late 1960s and 1970s (Chall, 1967/1983a), led to an increase in the teaching of phonics in basal readers, a development also supported by findings in the First-Grade Reading Studies (Bond & Dykstra, 1967). A growth of concern with accountability during the 1970s encouraged the strengthening of testing programs and the preparation of children for such tests in the basal reading programs. The teaching effectiveness research of recent years has increased the emphasis on direct instruction (Duffy, Roehler, & Reinsmoen, 1983; Gutherie, Martuza, & Serfect, 1979). The problems in learning to read faced by children of lower socioeconomic groups and by minority children have led both to the creation of special reading programs for such children, such as the Palo Alto Reading Program, published by Harcourt Brace Jovanovich, and DISTAR, published by Science Research Associates, and to strengthening provisions for meeting individual needs in the general program. The concern with minorities has also resulted in greater representation in stories and illustrations of different ethnic and minority groups. And, recently, schools have been seeking more literary values in basal selections (California State Department of Education, 1987; Goodman et al., 1988).

Publishing Basal Reading Programs

Basal reading programs, with their diverse ancillary materials, such as workbooks and tests, account for at least two-thirds of all expenditures for reading instruction and are used in more than 95 percent of all school districts through grade six. About 66 percent of teachers in grades seven and eight also use basals (Institutional Tracking Service, 1980). Whether the use of basals will decline as more teachers seem to embrace some aspects of "whole-language" procedures for teaching reading is not yet known. But at the time of this writing, it appears that basal readers or some form of a structured text will probably continue to dominate U.S. classroom instruction.

Twelve national publishers currently publish K-8 basal reading programs, a significantly smaller number than in the recent past, resulting from corporate consolidation, acquisition, and merger (Bowker, 1988). Indeed, the cost of investing in a basal reading program is so great and the return on investment so slow (requiring up to eight years after work begins on a program because of adoption cycles), that a program failure can seriously weaken even a major publisher and render it vulnerable to takeover.

Of the current twelve basal publishers, the top five combined secure more than 80 percent of industry reading revenues. Although the market leaders change somewhat from year to year, depending on the recency of a revision and on success in particular large adoptions, the same publishers have generally dominated the basal reading market for the past quarter century.

Although publishers of basal programs and their authors and consultants play a significant role in defining the character of today's basal series, other groups and agencies are also influential: (1) the schools themselves as consumers—administrators and teachers who must respond to both the academic and social demands of the local community: (2) the academic community that does the research; interprets it for publishers, reading specialists, administrators, and teachers; and educates and trains teachers in the uses of textbooks (Austin, 1961); (3) the research and development laboratories at the various universities, particularly those in language research centers that focus specifically on the teaching of reading; (4) the test makers (commercial as well as state and national assessment groups), whose concentration on some skills and processes, and not others, directs (or misdirects) the focus of some of today's instructional programs (Squire, 1988); (5) the outside developers employed by publishers to create program materials to specification. At present writing, at least eleven such commercial developers are currently at work in the industry as well as numerous individuals who contract for outside work.

A complete basal reading program today can consist of as many as 150 to 200 separate items: primers and readers (two or more a grade until grade three); teachers' editions of each primer or reader; a workbook and teacher's edition of a workbook for each pupil book; a program-related end-of-book test and sometimes a diagnostic pretest or series of unit tests for each level; extra drill-and-practice sheets often available in spirit or photographic duplication form as well as in print, and sometimes in computer formats; recordings, cassettes, flash cards, charts, language games, "big books," and often classroom libraries of program-related titles for independent reading, or related programs for teaching spelling or writing in relation to reading. Few schools purchase all of these materials, of course, but salespeople find that their availability is important to a program that wishes to remain competitive.

The development of a total reading program can require up to five years prior to publication—a time period that has been decreasing with more efficient product-development procedures but is still so lengthy as to prevent an early response to new research findings or to new market trends. However, revisions with fewer changes or new copyright editions tend to be published every three years, if not more frequently, since some school board regulations prohibit use of public monies to purchase materials that are more than three years old. Often the changes are modest and almost indistinguishable since extensive changes require substantial investment. Increasingly, however, publishers find they must invest millions of dollars in order to remain competitive about every three years, rather than every six.

The total investment by a publisher to bring a complete basal program to the market has been estimated to range from $15 million to $35 million, including editorial and authorship costs, permission fees, research and field testing, printing and distribution costs, promotion and sales training, and warehousing. Since the first dollar in sales is seldom returned until a year after publication (schools begin to select textbooks a year in advance of purchase), and six years must pass after publication until every school has had an opportunity to purchase, the high risk/low return involved in educational publishing becomes manifest. According to industry data, the average school publisher achieved 17.8 percent return on all publishing efforts in 1985 (or something less than 9% profit after taxes), with smaller publishers (those with sales below $30 million) reporting only a 6.6 percent return before taxes (3.3 % profit after taxes), and the larger (revenues about $80 million) yielding 22.7 percent (11.4% profit after taxes). At a time when the federal government guarantees a return of 6 percent to 8 percent in nonrisk savings accounts, profits not in excess of 10 percent are not designed to stimulate widespread investment, particularly during the periods of high inflation that this country experienced between 1970 and 1984. Given the high total investment in basal reading programs, one can understand why reading publishing is dominated by a relatively limited number of large companies (small publishers, for example, seldom can expend 41 percent of their funds in marketing and distribution of textbooks), and why the industry is basically conservative.

Since the average cost for "installing" a new basal reading program has been estimated to be in excess of $30 per pupil by the AAP (1987), one can realize why reading programs are changed infrequently. The high cost of a basal series also militates against installing such programs during the same year as language arts or spelling series.

And yet at $30 per pupil, cost is relatively low when compared to the per-pupil cost of some computer-based reading programs, normally several times the cost of basal readers. Teachers report that they generally use basal programs in conjunction with other materials, such as juvenile or library books for children (40%). Some schools also adopt multiple basals (around 28%). As of 1980, only 30 percent reported using a single basal program (ITS, 1980); but the percentage of single basal adoptions has increased in recent years as more and more administrators are concerned with the high mobility of urban students, accountability, and the increasing use of local, state, and national proficiency tests, and turn to systematic districtwide instructional programs as solutions.

Supplementary materials for instruction in reading comprise about one-third of the total industry sales and consist of independent workbooks and "skill drill" activities, kits for class or group activities, flash cards and charts, graded books for individual reading, "big books," sometimes "take home" books for parent reading, puppets and other manipulatives, pictures, language games, recordings, audio and video cassettes, and computer programs. Although most basals provide similar ancillary materials, many schools and teachers purchase quantities of materials independent of basals, particularly phonics workbooks, worksheets and, more recently, skill drill activities in comprehension and meaning vocabulary for extra practice.

Increasingly, ancillary materials, as well as program segments, have been made available for use on microcomputers, but at this time industry statistics indicate only selective uses of computers in teaching reading. However, there are increasing attempts made to produce total programs. The IBM *Writing to Read* is an example of such a program for beginning reading. Tested by Educational Testing Service (ETS), it was reported to produce "better" results in the kindergarten and first grade than did more "traditional" programs (Murphy & Appel, 1984).

BASAL READING PROGRAMS

Content of Student Books

A look at the content of today's readers—the stories, the themes, their length—reveals definite changes as one moves from those for the early grades to those for the intermediate and upper grades. Generally, the stories tend to get longer, become more mature in theme, and more difficult linguistically. The books for the first grade—preprimers, primers, and first readers—tend to be highly simplified, written specifically for the series. By the second grade, they contain more original stories, although some adapting and shortening continues. Less and less major adaptation occurs after grade two. Although Goodman and associates (1988) and Davidson (1984) have criticized the extent and quality of adaptations even in the later grades, many of these represent abridgements of longer quality works and modifications or deletions required to conform to social mores—for example, the elimination of slang or objectionable sexist or racist terms.

Today's readers are particularly strong in introducing children to literature. A recent analysis of basal reader content demonstrates the high preponderance of literature of quality in today's textbooks (Farr, 1988). It would appear that the criticism of the quality of the content in readers, mounted first during the academic reform effort of the

1950s and 1960s, has persisted, although the content has changed appreciably in the direction of literature of high quality.

Growth in understanding the role that reading materials can play in furthering instructional intent has led during the past twenty-five years to demands for improved textbook content. Ruth Strickland (1964) was one of the first to call for children's literature of better quality in basal readers when she noted that the simplicity of the prose sentence patterns in primer stories might impact adversely on children's growth in language. Chall's (1967/1983a) analyses of the vocabulary control used in basal readers warned that they had gone much below the standards suggested by experimental research and that such controls limited the level and quality of the selections included in the readers. Bettelheim and Zelan (1982), Bruce (1984), and Zimet (1972a, 1972b), expressed similar concerns.

With the recent publication of Hirsch's best-seller, *Cultural Literacy* (1988), basals will in all probability be examining their selections more carefully, particularly in the readers for grade four and upwards, when background knowledge becomes of greater importance for the development of comprehension. The National Association of Education Progress (NAEP) assessment of what children know about literature and history (Applebee, Langer & Mullis, 1987), and the publicity accorded Ravitch and Finn's recommendations in this area (1988), assure that the development of background knowledge in literature and history will receive renewed emphasis (see, for example, Squire, 1986). It should be noted, of course, that concern for background knowledge is hardly a new concept in reading, and is the basis for the major distinction between beginning reading and more mature reading. See in this connection Chall's *Stages of Reading Development* (1983b).

The quality of writing in the preprimers and primers has particularly received considerable criticism. Some writers have called for ignoring vocabulary and readability specifications and for relying instead on "regular" literature. Most of these proposals have ignored the possibility that the best writers of children's books have written excellent materials to vocabulary specifications. See the picture books of Patty Wolcutt, who uses as few as 10 different words to tell a story; and Dr. Seuss's *The Cat in the Hat*, which uses about 200 common words. It would seem to be possible to have both "quality" and "control" if publishers and editors would have a greater understanding of it.

Level of Difficulty

One characteristic of a modern basal reading series is its sequencing or grading, with each book designed to be suitable in content, appeal, and difficulty for children within each grade from the first to the sixth, or eighth, grade. As the discussion on the history of textbooks indicated, grading of textbooks became well established in the 19th century with the grading of schools, as U.S. education moved away from one-room schools. In graded schools students are promoted by year or half-year; and the proper grading of the textbooks has been of first importance, since it is no longer common as it once was in one-room schools, to have a student move to the next harder textbook when the more elementary ones were completed. The sequencing of readers has been a practice widespread for more than 100 years; but, from about the 1940s, when schools began to promote by age (i.e., social promotion rather than by achievement only), the problem of selecting a single text appropriate for most students in a grade became even greater, since a wide achievement range began to appear in most grades and widened in the higher grades (Chall, Conard & Harris, 1977).

Two developments occurring in the 1920s promoted an increased interest in the assessment of difficulty. One was the influx of new students in junior and senior high schools who came from families who, themselves, had not gone as far in school, and who were less well prepared for their academic studies than those who preceded them. Many of the new students, teachers reported, found their textbooks too difficult (see Chall, 1988a, for greater detail).

Another development was the publication of tools for estimating difficulty objectively—for example, Thorndike's *Teacher's Word Book*, which contained the 10,000 most frequent words of the English language used in print, and which made possible estimates of the difficulty of the words used in texts (Thorndike, 1921). These developments led to two kinds of studies: those dealing with the *vocabulary difficulty* (and density) and those dealing with *readability* (the comprehension difficulty of texts) (Chall, 1988; Klare, 1983). Both the vocabulary and the readability studies sought objective means of measuring the difficulty of text for learning to read and for comprehending and learning from textbooks, newspapers, novels, and so on. The vocabulary studies concentrated mainly on primary-level reading textbooks, while the readability studies were focused more on the comprehensibility of readers and content texts written for students of middle and upper elementary grades, high school, college, and adults. Both kinds of studies found that the textbooks of the 1920s and 1930s—the basal readers and the content texts—were too difficult for most students in the grades for whom they were intended (Chall, 1967/1983a), Analyses of the vocabularies and the readability of texts published after these early studies show that the textbooks did, indeed, become easier.

However, Chall (1967/1983a), in a review of this research, could find only one study, by Gates (1930), designed to determine experimentally optimal difficulty of vocabulary in a first-grade basal reader. Gates tried out materials of varying vocabulary loads and found these to be optimal: 35 repetitions for those of average ability, 20 for above average, and 40 to 55 for those below average. Chall (1967/1983a) further found that Gates's vocabulary standards had been met by most basal readers in the late 1930s. And yet the vocabulary loads of the primary basal readers continued to decline until the middle of the 1960s (Chall, Conard & Harris, 1977). Compulsory elementary schooling had long been in effect and a better match of difficulty to ability would already have been made. Perhaps the large number of immigrant children entering the elementary grades in the 1920s brought about the need for less-demanding readers. But, interestingly, this is not mentioned in the research literature on vocabulary difficulty (Chall, 1988). Another, more likely, hypothesis is the change from a heavier phonic to a heavier sight-word approach for the teaching of beginning reading in the 1920s and extending to the late 1960s and early 1970s. The decline in teaching phonics and the greater emphasis on sight recognition may have resulted in a need for lower vocabulary loads in the reading textbooks, particularly in the primary grades. That this hypothesis has some validity is seen in the changes over time in the words in basal readers from 1920 to the early 1980s. They decreased substantially from the 1920s to the 1960s, the years when sight-word approaches were predominant (Chall, 1967/1983a). From the late 1960s to the early 1980s, when the amount of phonics instruction increased, the vocabulary loads increased (Chall, 1967/1983a).

Visual Design: Typography and Illustration

Along with content and level of difficulty, the attractiveness of basal readers influences selection and use. It is common knowledge among publishers that textbooks must first pass "the thumb test," the initial, cursory examination used by teachers and members of textbook selection committees as a screen to arrive at a manageable number for serious study. This "thumbing through" rarely takes more than a few minutes, yet the art, illustration, typeface, and overall page layout take on maximum importance.

Given the importance of the visual design in customer acceptance, it is surprising that so little educational research has seriously addressed the problem. Tinker (1963) was one of the first to concern himself with typography (legibility) and reading efficiency. (See Houghton & Willows, 1987; and Tinker, 1963, for a review of early studies.) Individuals in England have addressed such considerations for the past two decades (Spencer, 1968). Recent studies have been spotty. Frase and Schwartz (1979) manipulated two typographic designs to determine which facilitated comprehension. Wendt demonstrated that changing column width and type size can affect reader response (Wendt, 1979, 1982). And Willows has addressed the issue of type, layout, and overall visual design (Willows, 1978a).

Data reported over more than 70 years seem to confirm that page layout and type size can make a difference in reading efficiency and comprehension. A number of more recent exploratory studies, although far from definitive, suggest that graphic cues can facilitate learning (Hartley, 1985, Hartley & Trueman, 1981; Pelletti, 1974; Shebilski & Rotondo, 1981; Waller, 1980). Studies of visual layout should be undertaken jointly by textbook designers and educational researchers to improve tomorrow's books, the more so as data are accumulated on teachers' and students' reactions to various visual designs.

The role of art and illustration in textbooks seems to have concerned researchers more than the study of typeface. A few studies of the attitudes of readers toward illustration have been reported (Gray & Leary, 1935; Poulos, 1969), and publishers regularly test such reactions as they develop programs. Woodward (1986) observes that the increase in illustration frequently results in a simplification of learning. However, one looks in vain for studies of the relationship of art style (e.g., realistic, fanciful, photographic, surreal, and so on) and learning, even though any cursory review of selected basal readers or social studies textbooks over the years will indicate that attitudes toward and styles of illustration change from decade to decade.

Do illustrations affect comprehension? If so, how? First asked fifty years ago, these questions have long interested researchers (Brody, 1980; Brody & Ligenza, 1979; Duchastel, 1980a, 1980b; Flagg, Weaver, Fenton, Gelatti, & Pray, 1980; Goodykoontz, 1936; Green & Olson, 1985; Guttman, Levin, & Pressy, 1977; Koenke, 1987; Miller, 1937; Schallert, 1980; Thomas, 1976; Weintraub, 1960; Willows, 1978a, 1978b; Willows, 1980). Most researchers report that illustration can either facilitate or hinder comprehension, depending on the nature of the visual, its location, the level of the reading materials, and the extent to which it is designed to direct readers to the instructional focus rather than detract from it. Legenza and Knafle (1978) report the three key components of illustrations that have the greatest appeal to elementary school children: number of actions in an illustration, the number of children, and the number of people. The evidence is mixed, but it appears that a key factor is the way in which the illustration is used in teaching. Is it provided to stimulate learning? Or merely to enhance attractiveness? And does the increase in illustration over recent decades, reported by Chall, Conard, and Harris (1977), militate against effective learning or does it enhance learning?

One of the more widely discussed studies on the role of illustration in beginning reading materials was by Samuels (1968), who reported that color illustration can negatively impact children's learning to read at the primer level and direct attention away from words (see also Montare, Elman, & Cohen, 1977). Samuels recommended the use of black-and-white illustration. However, whether teachers will select a basal series that contains only black-and-white art is a moot question. At least one publisher of a laboratory-developed reading program found strong customer reaction against the use of black-and-white illustrations at the primer level (Southwest Regional Laboratories, 1976). This may well be an example of teacher preferences controlling practice, rather than research findings.

Although the research on the value of illustrations is far from clear, Chall (1967/1983a) found the number of full-color illustrations in basal readers growing from 1920 to 1983 and an increase in illustration in content area textbooks from 1940 to 1970. As the number of pictures increased, the challenge or level of difficulty declined (Chall, Conard, & Harris, 1977). More recently, Bryant (1980) reported that humorous illustration in textbooks has little effect on comprehension but has a negative impact on reader acceptance of the plausibility of the text, even though such humor adds to a text's appeal. Woodward (1986, 1988) criticized the photographs in social studies textbooks as being more cosmetic than instructional, a criticism often made informally with respect to basal reading series. How basal readers as well as those in the content areas can best integrate content, illustration, and instruction offers an area of research that is still in need of study. This is of great importance since the number of full-color illustrations in textbooks keeps growing and the costs of texts rise; it would seem to be essential that we know more about whether or how they contribute to learning.

A recent study of how maps, charts, and graphs in readers and social studies books are used for instruction stresses that visual displays are seldom pointed out to students, nor are the students encouraged to construct their own charts, graphs, and maps—a pedagogical strategy almost mandatory for conceptual understanding (Hunter, Crismore, & Pearson, 1986). Early work had demonstrated the usefulness of constructing maps for learning geography, but the new analysis seems to break ground in considering how the visuals can be used in teaching important study skills. More attention to the instructional uses of illustration may result from this recent effort.

Instructional Design

Widespread concern with instruction (as distinct from curriculum) emerged in the 1950s and 1960s with the creation of research and development centers by the U.S. Office of Education—and subsequently the National Institute of Education and the Department of Education—giving rise to a codification of procedures for instructional product development. Many criteria emerged from federally sponsored attempts to produce better textbooks in areas of compelling national need (e.g., Anderson & Jones, 1981; Baker & Schutz, 1971; Basista et al., 1976; Dick & Carey, 1985; Hartley, 1985; Jonassen, 1985; Kemp, 1985). Basically, these reports summarize the practical experience of developers of instructional products—either in university or governmental laboratories—who attempt to make product development more systematic and learning more predictable.

The work of research-trained developers is an important dimension of research in instructional materials, because in studying how instruction should be designed (e.g., congruence of objective, learning activity, and test; varying massed and spaced practice), these developers were also specifying how instructional products should be used. Their work has been especially powerful in its impact on such recent school emphases as mastery learning in reading and on applying findings from the "teaching effectiveness" studies, where systematic emphasis on teaching basic skills is important. These reports in combination have also influenced the ways in which commercial instructional materials are developed and evaluated. For a time, researchers published learner verification studies that demonstrated the effectiveness of instructional materials (Ball, 1979; Cronnell, 1978; Humes, 1978). Much of the work of practitioners, like Madeleine Hunter and Ethna Reid, finds its roots in the studies of instructional design, as do the evaluative studies by Educational Products Information Exchange (EPIE) and some of the research at the Center for the Study of Reading and the Institute for Research on Teaching (Schmidt, Caw, Byers, & Buchmann, 1984). Stahl and Miller (1989), for example, recently analyzed the research on the effectiveness of basals and experiential whole-language approaches; and, while they found neither was clearly superior, the whole-language/language-experience approaches seemed more effective in kindergarten, with the basals more effective for teaching reading in later grades. Further, Barr and Sadow (1989), in a provocative new study of the uses of fourth-grade basals, hypothesize that the design of a basal reading program influences the way in which it is used and the extent to which teachers encourage extended reading in the classroom.

Some of these researchers have attempted to create guidelines for constructing effective texts (Hartley, 1985). Others have explored the instructional effectiveness of including certain instructional strategies as coherence (Beck, McKeown & Omanson, 1984); teaching phonics (Beck & McCaslin, 1978); teaching comprehension of main idea (Baumann & Serra 1984; Baumann, 1986); anaphora (Baumann, 1985); ideational bonds (Glynn & DiVesta, 1978); remodeling reading activities (Lange, 1979); instructional strategies as questioning (Armbruster, 1987; McGraw & Grotelueschen, 1971); metadiscourse and use of refutation (Hynd & Alvermann, 1986); embedding headings and processing aids (Holly et al., 1981); and remodeling reading activities (Lange, 1979). Almost all of these studies demonstrated ways in which instructional materials could be designed to achieve predictable learning outcomes.

Teachers' Manuals for Basal Readers

The teachers' manuals of basal readers encompass many contradictions. While viewed as the core of a basal reading program, since they contain the instructional system for teaching reading, they are also given away at no cost to teachers. Although the teachers for whom they are designed have, through the years, obtained more professional education in teaching generally, and in teaching reading in particular, the manuals have become longer, providing more and more specific instructions (Chall, 1967/1983a; Woodward, 1985). Although the basal manuals are the responsibility of scholars, researchers, and experienced practitioners, they normally do not undergo critical peer review. These manuals have come under increasing attack as not being research based, and as being too long and too "scripted." They have also been criticized as containing too many questions and exercises that permit too little time for the reading of stories.

The research on teachers' manuals of basal reading programs seems to fall into two kinds: studies of manuals to reveal the teaching as well as the research emphasis of the basal readers; and secondly the extent of teacher autonomy expected in the manuals. Thus, Chall's (1967/1983a) analysis of the manuals of two widely used basal series for grades one to three published in the late 1950s and early 1960s found a strong emphasis on the teaching of meaning and comprehension, with relatively little systematic teaching of decoding. An analysis and synthesis of the relevant research indicated, however, that a stronger decoding rather than comprehension emphasis produced better results. It is important to note that by the early 1970s, a few years after the publication of these findings, most basal series increased the amount of decoding taught, then began to teach it earlier and more systematically (Chall, 1967/1983a). Although the quantity and timing of phonics increased, the basal readers differed as to whether they taught phonics analytically or synthetically (Beck & Block, 1979).

A similar, more recent analysis of the basal reachers' manuals for the intermediate grades by Durkin (1981, 1984) found little emphasis on the teaching of comprehension and word meanings. Subsequently, studying teacher use of manuals in teaching reading, she reported that much of the prereading and questioning aids that were provided tended to be ignored by teachers (Durkin, 1983, 1984).

Teaching methods utilized in succeeding grades of the primary school change as much in methods as in content. For example, Chall (1966/1983a) found in an analysis of the manuals of widely used readers published in 1956 and 1962 that the questions based on pictures decreased from about 30 percent in the preprimers to 8 percent in the grade three (level 2) books. Comprehension questions on selections increased from 23 percent in preprimers to 69 percent in the grade three (level 2) books. The follow-up activities, however, showed little difference by grade, with about 28 percent reading comprehension activities in the preprimer to 31 percent in the grade three and (level 2) books; 19 percent phonics and structured analysis activities in the preprimer and 16 percent in the grade three (level 2) books. No comparable data are available for follow-up activities suggested in the teacher's manuals for the 1970s and 1980s. However, an analysis of basal reader tests reported in the Report Card on Basal Readers (Goodman et al., 1988) found about 60 percent of the first-grade basal tests (of six publishers) tested words and phonics, as compared to 50 percent of the third-grade tests and about 30 percent in the grade five tests. Language study and literary understanding were tested more at the higher than the lower grades.

Popp (1975) also found more phonics in the basal readers in the 1970s. An analysis of the reading score trends on the National Assessment of Educational Progress seems to indicate that the heavier code emphasis in the basal readers published in the 1970s probably did contribute to the significant gains in reading achievement among 9-year-olds from 1970 to 1980. In a cohort analysis of NAEP scores in relation to the provision of literacy experiences in school and home, Chall (1983c) suggested that the stronger beginning reading programs—earlier reading at home and in kindergarten; "Sesame Street" and "The Electric Company"; Head Start; and a stronger, more challenging reading program in grade one, with earlier and more systematic teaching of phonics—contributed to the significant gains in reading, particularly among the minority and low socioeconomic status (SES) children, confirming that the instructional improvements of the 1970s based on the research of the 1960s had a beneficial effect on all children—especially those at risk.

An analysis of 1984 and 1986 NAEP scores for 9-year-olds indicates that the significant gains have not held up when compared to 1970 scores, and that this lack of gain may stem from a reemphasis on comprehension and word meaning in the early grades as a result of the growing concern for developing higher thought processes at the beginning levels, and with whole-language approaches that do not teach phonics directly and systematically (Chall, 1989).

More recent research on the manuals accompanying basal readers, which focuses on the amount and kind of instructions to teachers, finds that the manuals "overscript" the teacher. Shannon (1983) made a particularly strong argument against the weighty manuals because they "deskill teachers." He suggests that "the organization of reading instruction around commercial materials has reduced teachers' and students' roles in that instruction . . . " (p. 307). Based on the assumption that effective teachers of reading need to make the substantive curricular and instructional decisions, Duffy, Roehler, and Reinsmoen (1983) hypothesize that "decision making is impeded by the expectations under which elementary school teachers work, particularly the expectation that basal textbook instruction should conform to certain centrally imposed procedures" (p. 357).

They continue: "There is a fundamental conflict between the expectations set for basal textbook use by 'master developers' and the need for teachers to make their own decisions about subject matter and instruction" (pp. 361–362). Their recommendation to "master developers"—text publishers, creators of assessment tests, or district administrators—is that the message they send to teachers must be changed. "They must communicate that the centrally imposed directives are flexible conceptual guidelines, not scripts to be followed by rote. Instructor's manuals for basal reading textbooks, for instance, must be written so that they are not random sequences of tasks to be completed but conceptually consistent guides that encourage and promote teacher modification" (p. 364). Some of the most recent reading programs seem to be beginning to apply these recommendations. (See, for example, the programs published in 1988 by Open Court and Silver Burdett & Ginn.) Unfortunately, few studies have examined the materials and studied their use in classrooms.

Woodward (1985) made essentially the same point after comparing the teacher guides of the 1920s to those in the 1980s. He notes the "overdesign" of the modern basal and suggests that in its attempt to provide a foolproof way of teaching reading, it has emphasized more and more the administrative, nonteaching, and nonprofessional role of the teacher. Woodward also found that the earlier fifth-grade guidebooks had a greater emphasis on oral reading and they asked students to read more. "The manuals of the 1920s, 1930s, 1940s, and 1950s provided no scripts. Teachers were expected to make professional decisions about how to teach reading. Few answers to the proposed questions were provided" (p. 16).

Similar changes in teachers' editions and guidebooks from 1920 to 1962 were noted by Chall (1967/1983a) for first-grade teachers. The number of pages in the teachers' manuals increased from 157 in 1920 to 256 pages in 1962; and the number of words of instruction to the teacher for an average lesson (story and follow-up) increased from 561 words in 1920 to 2,000 in 1962. Thus, from 1920 to 1962, the first-grade teacher received more and more suggestions and directions for each lesson. If we remember that during this period the practice of teachers dividing classes into three reading groups and preparing a different lesson for each group became widespread, we realize that the amount of instruction for every lesson increased still further, more than tripling the teacher's instructional task (Gates, 1949, 173).

CONTENT AREA TEXTBOOKS

Textbooks for every subject taught in the elementary school have been introduced by U.S. publishers during the past 100 years and are adopted by schools, as are the basal reading programs. Almost all of these programs—in mathematics, social studies, English, science, and health—appear in graded sequences of titles. Content analyses of such textbook offerings have yielded continued insights into the strengths and weaknesses of subject teaching. (See, for example, the general review of such research by Squire, 1988.) Educational Development Corporation recently analyzed the usability of selected textbooks in science and social studies and called a conference of publishers to present recommendations for improving the textbooks (Ciborowski, 1988). Essentially, these dealt with ways content textbooks could prepare students for learning (focusing instruction, activating prior knowledge, previewing vocabulary and structure); engage students in learning (study strategies, experimental activities, metacognition); and help students demonstrate competence and extend knowledge.

Subject matter textbooks, from the first studies in the 1920s until the past decade, have been reported to be too difficult for most students. The evidence from research, together with the experience of teachers, resulted in the development of easier textbooks grade for grade. In a study commissioned by the Panel on the Scholastic Aptitude Test (SAT) Score Decline, which analyzed textbooks in relation to the declining SAT scores, Chall, Conard, and Harris (1977) found a decline in difficulty of elementary and high school textbooks—readers, social studies, literature, grammar, and composition texts—as judged by a variety of measures: readability formulas, level of maturity, difficulty of questions, original literature versus adapted, and ratio of pictures to text. Only the basal readers were found to be more difficult from the middle 1960s to 1970s. This was explained by the introduction during the late 1960s and early 1970s of stronger phonics programs in most basal reading series, which made possible the use of larger vocabularies (Chall, 1967/1983a).

The decline in textbook difficulty, when related to the decline in SAT scores, suggested an association between the two—the more difficult the texts, the higher the SAT scores of those who used them. It was further suggested that the textbooks had become too easy for the optimal development of reading, particularly of students reading on grade level and above. The analysis of textbooks published during the 1970s showed that many for the eleventh and twelfth grades were written on a ninth- or tenth-grade reading level, while the reading passages on the SAT were written on the eleventh- or twelfth-grade grade level. A change in the difficulty of textbooks was suggested. Although easier books may lead to better comprehension, they might also, if too easy, lead to slower reading development. The study also found a narrow range of difficulty of books on the same subject and grade, making it particularly difficult for meeting the needs of students reading two or more reading levels below their grade placement, a group for whom the available textbooks were too difficult.

Why the five or six decades of decline in difficulty? Many reasons can be suggested: the early expressed needs of teachers for easier books for a changing population; the research that confirmed the need; the development of analytical tools to assess the difficulty of the books; competition among publishers to produce easier books; and acceptance by teachers, administrators, and adoption committees that "easier is better."

Unfortunately, the research evidence was based mainly on comparisons and averages of difficulty among published books rather than on experimental tests on students. What was needed were experimental data on the effects on learning of different kinds of vocabularies, readability levels, and organization on different students in different settings. With the growing consensus that the easier books were the better books, textbooks inevitably became easier over time without strong evidence of increasing effectiveness.

It is of significance that the beginnings of both vocabulary and readability measurement research had their roots in changing social conditions and in attempts to solve the educational problems arising from them. The educational philosophy of the schools and of most researchers was dedicated to providing an education for all, the lower as well as the higher achievers; and they sought ways to assess materials objectively for a better match to the abilities of students. Thus, while their research started with the desire to find a better match of students and texts (by objective means), it also had a strong mission behind it: to develop and use textbooks suitable for *all* children in each grade.

Recently, Anderson and Armbruster (1986), Armbruster (1984, 1985, 1986), Armbruster and Anderson (1981), and Armbruster and Gudbrandsen (1986) have studied the effects of various organizational factors on "considerate texts." Their work has been influential on social studies textbooks. Beck, McKeown, and Omanson (1984) and others demonstrated that revisions in selections to improve coherence resulted in greater reader understanding. Baumann also has demonstrated how passages in content readers rewritten to improve clarity can also increase comprehensibility (1986). A similar study by Graves and Slater (1986) dealt with secondary school textbooks. See the recent International Reading Association monograph on readability (Zakaluk & Samuels, 1988), which includes references and discussions of the recent research and uses of such stylistic factors of readability as cohesion, organization, and focusing.

Text Structure

Considerable attention has also been directed recently to the structure of expository texts, particularly with respect to using structural clues for facilitating the readability of texts as well as facilitating the learning from them (Anderson & Armbruster, 1986; Binkley, 1987; Britton & Black, 1985; Mayer, 1975, 1977; Meyer & Rice, 1984). Much of this attention has been directed to textbooks in the social studies, to the structure of their paragraphs, and to the structural design principles of longer texts (Calfee & Chambliss, 1986; Calfee & Curley, 1984; Mason & Osborn, 1983). Some researchers have noted that non-narrative expository prose makes different demands than literature (Donlan, 1976). Hence, the recent increase (in reading programs) in including nonliterary, non-narrative selections and content area reading passages in basal reading programs (Venezky, Kaestle, & Sum, 1987).

Many of the studies of text structure, particularly those dealing with expository prose and content area textbooks, indicate that teaching children about the structure of texts will facilitate reading comprehension (Armbruster, 1986; Barnett, 1984; Jones, Ariran & Katims, 1984). Hence, lessons on reading in the content areas increasingly deal with the structure of prose written in social studies, science, and other subject fields. It should also be noted that the greater use in the intermediate and upper elementary grades of special and abstract vocabularies in basal readers and especially in content textbooks has brought a renewed interest and an emphasis on the teaching of vocabulary. (See Chall, 1983b; Chall & Snow, 1988; Dale & O'Rourke, 1971, 1981; Stahl & Fairbanks, 1986. Also, for various studies in text structure, see Brennan, Bridge & Winograd, 1986; Mandler, 1978; Mandler & Johnson, 1977; Stein, 1978).

TEXTBOOK SELECTION PROCEDURES

The procedures used by state agencies and large school districts to select textbooks and other instructional materials have long been criticized but only recently have they been studied systematically.

More than 100 years ago, the State Commissioner of Education in New York expressed concern about the variation in textbooks, both in content and in quality (Edmondson, 1930); and the issue has been raised periodically over the years (Burnett, 1950, 1952; Dodd, 1928; Duke, 1985; English, 1980; Jensen, 1931; Keith, 1981, 1985; Komoski, 1978; Maxwell, 1921, 1930; National Education Association & Association of American Publishers, 1972; Robbins, 1980; Tidwell, 1928).

Much of the concern has focused on state adoptions of textbooks in the South and West—presently in 21 states representing close to 50 percent of the dollar market—as sales have increased substantially during the past 25 years with the population moving south and west. This adoption market thus has been growing in size, even though there has been no change in the number of adoptions for two decades.

Nor are textbook adoptions limited to states. Most large city districts—Buffalo, Hartford, Chicago, Milwaukee Archdiocese, and St. Louis, for example—follow similar procedures. According to a national market survey conducted in 1980, more than three-quarters of school superintendents reported new reading programs adopted regularly every five years or so (ITS, 1980).

Any review of studies of adoption procedures published over the past 75 years, such as those listed above, will document the gradual liberalization of requirements, as almost all states moved from single basal reader adoptions, judged inappropriate by critics for meeting the individual needs of children, to multiple listing of five or more texts from which schools could choose those most appropriate for local use. Publishers refer to such action by states as "granting a hunting license." In other words, book representatives still have to sell to local districts, but normally only can sell those titles that are listed. (In a few adoption states, schools are permitted to use a small percentage of textbook funds, say 15 percent to 20 percent, to purchase nonlisted materials to satisfy special needs.) However, a strong trend during recent years has been a movement toward a single basal adoption in large districts (ITS, 1980). Administrators claim that use of a single reading program throughout the district provides more consistency in instruction.

Adoption of textbooks on a regular cycle, every five to eight years, assures that children in the states involved will have fresh materials, and schools will have reasonable funding for instructional materials on a regular basis. This does not always happen when adoptions are not regularly scheduled. Publishers, particularly, have been aware of abuses in *open territory*, or nonlisting regions, where funding for instructional materials is seldom budgeted on any regular basis, and adoptions can easily be passed over and delayed. Many reports of young people using older textbooks have come from such open territory states.

On the other hand, the procedures regulating most selection of textbooks require decision making in full view of public and press ("sunshine" laws), and provide an open invitation to textbook critics who wish to complain publicly about the books being considered. Among those critics have been those who claim that the methods of teaching used by the readers are not optimal—that they do not contain enough phonics or the right phonics (Hinds, 1987). Critics have also presented negative views on the selections used in the books in states that provide for open citizen hearings like California and Texas (Jenkinson, 1979; Last, 1982), although similar objections can emerge in any district.

Another fact about the adoption process, rarely studied by critics until recently, is that procedures followed in large city districts within open territory states, such as the districts of Chicago, Milwaukee, Baltimore, the Hartford Archdiocese, and others, are remarkably similar to those followed in state adoptions (Follett, 1985). And the dollars involved in districts as large as Detroit, for example, frequently exceed those involved in states the size of Mississippi. According to a 1980 survey, too, the teachers in state adoption areas consider largely the same basal program attributes as those in open territory: 44.4 percent of the schools say they look first at the strength of the skills program. Other important factors are reading level (40.0%), content relationship to district program (40.0%), achievement of reliable outcomes (31.1%), supportive material (31.1%), and provision for individuals and small group instruction (31.1%) (ITS, 1980).

Public criticism of the readers used in the schools began to increase in the 1970s, and publishers then were wont to point out the variety in U.S. textbooks in level of challenge, quality, and content made available through the U.S. free enterprise system (Dessauer, 1985; Squire, 1981). The fact is that for the past 40 years, between 10 and 15 basal series have been submitted for consideration in every adoption, and despite similarity in format, the programs seem to vary in content, literary quality, instructional design, level of challenge, and emphasis on instruction. (See, for example, analyses of different readers by Beck & Block [1979], Durkin [1981, 1984], and others.) However, a comparison of the primary readers of the two most widely used basal readers published during the late 1950s and early 1960s found considerable similarities in methods and content, although they did differ considerably from a newer series that introduced phonics earlier, used more words, and introduced literary selections earlier (Chall, 1967/1983a). The so-called "basal reader approach" can be accurately used to refer to the formatting of instruction; that is, the basal program is carried by pupil books, workbooks and teachers' editions (manuals). In this sense, the programs are, indeed, more alike than different. Thus, the process of selection is still an important one. Concerns of this kind have directed attention to adoption procedures. These procedures, as studied during the last decade, have turned out to be varied and complex, even though the National Education Association and the Association of American Publishers had made attempts to educate school people about textbooks (1972). These associations pointed to the declining expenditures for instructional materials (then as now less than one percent of total school expenditures), and suggested criteria to be considered in evaluating school textbooks. Not always were selectors found to be informed about new developments in learning and teaching; on occasion they were found to lack familiarity with the basic content of the textbooks they were trying to select. Some committees heard presentations from the publishers represented; others did not. Some were trained for the task of selecting instructional materials; others were not. Some had adequate released time to undertake the task; more did not.

Farr and colleagues undertook a systematic study of procedures that guided the reading adoption in Indiana, then expanded the research to other states. Almost all procedures in the adoptions that Farr reviewed seemed to lack disciplined, systematic approaches (Farr, Courtland, Harris, Tarr, & Treece, 1983; Powell, 1985; Tulley, 1983; Tulley & Farr, 1985). The Indiana findings with respect to the selection of reading programs have been similar to those reported in other states (Marshall, 1987; Winograd, 1987; Winograd & Osborn, 1985), have been summarized and interpreted in various journals (Bernstein, 1985; Dessauer, 1985), and have even served as the focus for a national conference of the National Association of State Boards of Education (Cody, 1986).

However, a 1987 study of procedures in large urban districts reported that schools were satisfied with the processes used for selection of textbooks and with the textbooks that had been selected (Wernersbach, 1987). Lang (1985) also reports that procedures in Virginia and in the Arlington schools are organized, workable, and contribute to better education. Subsequent studies report the growing importance of the initial proclamation or call for adoption when specifications are detailed (Last, 1982), as well as concern with text organization and a new emphasis on pedagogical soundness. However, despite this overall concern with pedagogy, few investigators found selectors concerned with the research base of a program or with results of publishers' field tests or with market studies. Again and again, researchers found that selectors considered textbooks from reputable publishing houses to be of "equal quality." Hence, qualitative discriminations are not always made (Follett, 1985; Winograd, 1987).

Dependent upon the decisions made by schools in selecting readers—more than 80 percent of the choices are now made by classroom teachers—publishers follow adoptions with care. Those program attributes highly regarded by teachers—manuals that are easy to use, for example, or selections and illustrations that appeal to children—become widely emulated in subsequent revisions.

Given the amount of criticism of textbook selection in reading, it is helpful to note that during the past several years, the Center for the Study of Reading at the University of Illinois at Urbana-Champaign has been developing and testing new guidelines for the selection of readers (Osborn, Jones, & Stein, 1985). Studies suggest that adoptions are most successful when the committee is enthusiastic, has time for reflection, is provided with some staff development, and has good leadership (Dole, 1987). However, studies also indicate repeatedly that selection committees assume excellence in pedagogy in all widely used published programs, and spend little time examining the quality of instruction in the programs being considered.

CONDITIONS INFLUENCING
TEXTBOOK PUBLISHING

Adoption Criteria

Specific requirements of various adopting agencies continue to influence the kind and quality of textbooks published; and the larger the adoption unit, the greater the influence. Most states and large school districts specify not only the content desired in textbooks, but the physical specifications as well—for example, the quality of paper, bindings, and so on. Specific demands, such as the recent stress in California for literature-centered reading programs (California State Department of Education, 1987) will, in all probability, influence the preparation of materials when publishers have time to prepare for these adaptations. Similarly, most school districts with published lists of learning objectives in reading or in any subject area ask publishers to submit a correlation of program learning goals with district or state objectives to ensure reasonable coverage in instructional materials of the desired scope and sequence. Still, the fact that even successful programs are likely to secure only a portion of sales in any state when five programs are selected deters publishers from responding to any parochial regional requests.

Educational Trends

Almost any dimension of content or pedagogy that attracts widespread professional attention seems likely to generate a study of textbooks, and particularly of basal reading programs, since the readers are used by virtually all children and all teachers. Indeed, comparisons of content in basal programs over time has been used as a way of studying historical changes in values (see in this connection Chall, 1967/1983a).

General evaluative studies that compare reading programs have been published from time to time (EPIE, 1974; Wrightstone & Lazar, 1957). Making such analyses widely available to the profession could support sound selection decisions. Two studies have been so influential that they require separate mention: Chall's analysis (1967/1983a) of beginning reading programs that resulted in changes in the decoding component in more challenging books and in more mature content of selections, grade for grade; and Durkin's review of the teaching of comprehension in basal readers, which resulted in increased attention to comprehension (Durkin, 1984). Osborn found that the workbooks provided with basal reading series frequently violated basic instructional principles and did not systematically provide practice in applying concepts and skills taught in the lessons, findings subsequently supported by Anderson (Anderson, Hiebert, Scott, & Wilkinson, 1985; Osborn, 1984a, 1984b). Also influential were the studies of Chall et al. (1977) on the importance of the level of challenge of instructional material in relation to the reading level of students. Findings from such studies have been widely disseminated in the reports on SAT score decline, in *A Nation at Risk* (1983), and in interpretations of recent NAEP assessments (Applebee, Langer & Mullis, 1987; Chall, 1989). These studies have been enormously influential in improving recent reading texts, the more so since they have been so widely publicized to editors, textbook selectors, and administrators (Apple, 1985; Chall, Conrad, & Harris, 1977: Lerner, 1982; Osborn, Jones, & Stein, 1985; Tyson-Bernstein & Woodward, 1986; Woodward, 1985).

One result of the widespread concern with improving the instructional quality of textbooks was the rise of Educational Products Information Exchange (EPIE), an agency established to evaluate texts and regularly publish a newsletter on textbook quality, which prepared comparative evaluations of textbooks in various fields and argued for field-tested learner verification of textbook effectiveness. Having learner verification data was a criterion for selection adopted in one or two states for a time and in an occasional school district, but not widely emulated throughout the country. Some publishers continue to engage in effectiveness studies as a way of improving materials, and an occasional school administrator asks for data on effectiveness; but the concern is not widespread, and few publishers can recall an adoption that turned on data of effectiveness of use (Squire, 1988).

The most recent curricular trend to influence basal reading programs has been the integration of reading and language arts and the use of writing to support reading (Applebee, Langer, & Mullis, 1987; Langer, 1987). Research on emergent literacy (readiness) (Teale & Sulzby, 1986) and generally on the reading-writing connection (Langer, 1987; Wittrock, 1983) seems to have fanned the trend. The reports and interpretations of the recent national assessment in reading, writing, and literacy also stress the metacognitive aspects of reading comprehension and the process of writing rather than the teaching of specific skills (Applebee, Langer, & Mullis, 1987). See also the recent analysis and interpretation of NAEP findings by Chall (1989) that question the value of instruction on higher cognitive processes during the first stages of reading and show the importance for both early and later progress of strong early reading programs.

Reports from the National Academy of Education (Anderson et al., 1985) and Durkin's study of the kindergarten (1987) suggest that children in our schools engage too much in skill drills, too little in reading books and in oral and written activities that give them an opportunity to apply and practice skills taught in the instructional program. Chall (1989) suggests that the current emphasis on silent reading, comprehension, and metacognition in the primary grades may also be taking time away from the reading of connected texts.

Committed to much heavier emphases on oral language and writing, particularly at early levels, whole-language proponents have called for the elimination of basal readers because of the literary quality, which they find wanting, and the attention to skill development (see, for example, Goodman et al., 1988). However, advocates of whole language have yet to provide compelling research evidence demonstrating the effectiveness of such approaches in teaching children to read. Indeed, research over the past 70 years shows that structured, systematic teaching in the early grades produces the better results. Still, the demands for more emphasis on oral language and writing are beginning to affect the basal readers (Stahl & Miller, 1988; study reported above).

Advocacy Groups

School textbooks have always been a subject of public concern, the more so during periods of public criticism of schooling. Jenkinson (1979) identified more than 200 outside groups attempting to influence schoolbooks in one state alone. Although articulate defenders like Jenkinson and the People for the American Way have emerged publicly only during the past decade, objections to selected textbooks have been voiced by some groups throughout our history and on some occasions have been answered.

Concern about eliminating prejudice from readers as a means of improving intergroup relations first surfaced during the late 1940s (Steward, 1950; Wilson, 1948). Attention to international understanding was also studied in textbooks published at that time (Quillan, 1948). Such analyses resulted in the elimination of the more objectionable stereotypes, such as ethnic humor; but not until the 1960s did concern for multiethnicity and the fair depiction of black Americans, native Americans, and other minority groups transform textbooks. Indeed, until the mid-1960s, white characters and illustrations were required by schools in many districts, and publishers not infrequently maintained dual editions of textbooks. For example, special editions for black children had disappeared before the end of the 1960s (Squire, 1981), although concern about the multiethnicity of content and illustrations continues. Culture-fair treatment of black Americans, however, expanded during the early 1970s to embrace Hispanic-Americans, Asian-Americans, the role of females, the depiction of the elderly, the handicapped, and similar minority or nonprivileged groups (Arnold-Gerrity, 1978; Bachman, 1976; Britton & Lumpkin, 1976; Dance, 1974; Garcia, 1976; Jay, 1973; Kane, 1971; Sadker, Sadker, & Garies, 1980). These concerns, often expressed by human relations committees, who in some districts monitored the selection of reading programs, changed the face of American instructional materials (Cole & Sticht, 1981; Jenkinson, 1979). Even a cursory comparison of readers published in 1988 with those published twenty-five years ago will reveal the impact of these activities.

Analysis of textbook content has also covered many topics. At various times concerned groups have analyzed the treatment of Jewish cultural history and the Holocaust; the presentation of alternative life-styles; the inclusion of situational ethics and secular humanism; the expression of U.S. free enterprise; the presentation of morality and ethical considerations; the appropriateness of language in textbooks; the nutritional quality of the food mentioned or illustrated; the teaching of religion, creationism and evolution; the teaching of poetry; the teaching of cultural literacy (Hirsch, 1987; Ravitch & Finn, 1988); and a host of other issues (Doyle, 1984; Hefley, 1976; Jenkinson, 1987; Shapiro, 1985; Woodward, 1985). Still, when the Committee on Freedom to Read studied parent objections to schoolbooks in 1981, only 15 percent of the challenges were raised about textbooks or the printed materials used for instruction. The group concluded that educational publishers had learned to tailor textbooks to fit customer requirements (Association of American Publishers, American Library Association & Association for Supervision and Curriculum Development, 1981). Some call this *precensorship*. It is an inevitable part of educational publishing—developing texts that respond to perceived customer needs—and virtually all major publishers conduct market studies to ascertain these needs, even though this research is largely unreported in public documents.

Yet, major controversy continues concerning efforts to censor schoolbooks (Last, 1982). Possibly the most intensive studies of schoolbook censorship were those that emerged from the community uprising against the language arts textbooks selected in Kanawha County, West Virginia, during the mid-1970s, where the lack of parental involvement in text selection and the selection of language arts textbooks with contemporary illustrations, liberal standards for language, and urban-oriented content for use in a conservative area inflamed local passions (Hillocks, 1978; Moffett, 1988).

Market Research

Publishers do not readily adapt materials to satisfy every advocacy group, evaluative study, or educational trend. Rather, they weigh the ways in which teachers and school leaders respond to each concern before determining changes that schools will accept in programs. Thus, today's publisher relies heavily on market research to assess those dimensions of educational programs of greatest importance to teachers. Questionnaires, interviews, consultant panels, and field tryouts of materials have been used for such purposes; but gaining importance during recent years has been a reliance on focus groups of classroom teachers pulled together in various geographical areas to evaluate proposed new textbook manuscripts. As Venezky has indicated (1988), such teacher groups—usually selected randomly by independent research teams—heavily influence the development of new programs. Small wonder, since 80 percent of today's purchasing decisions are made by teachers; and a program must be competitive in 80 percent of all markets if it is to be competitive at all (Squire, 1988).

To Conclude

We have presented some concerns in educational publishing, with particular reference to the publishing of reading textbooks and related instructional materials. We have surveyed the research on reading textbooks as well as the uses of the research and the effects of these uses. Much is known about reading textbooks from historical and educational research, and most of it points to the central importance of reading textbooks in the teaching and learning of reading—from colonial times to the present. Research has played an increasing role in the design, selection, and use of reading textbooks in the classroom. However, the large investments and competition among publishers have made the role of marketing, of state and local adoption committees, and of teacher preferences equally, if not more, influential in the design and content of readers. There is considerable debate today as to whether the readers, as we know them, are the best instructional form for most children and teachers. The current ferment, hopefully, will lead to more sensitive inquiries important to the development and use of quality textbooks.

REFERENCES

Anderson, L. W., & Jones, B. F. (1981). Designing instructional strategies which facilitate learning for mastery. *Educational Psychology, 16*, 121–138.
Anderson, R., Hiebert, E., Scott, J., & Wilkinson, I. (1985). *Becoming a nation of readers.* Champaign, IL.: National Academy of Education, National Institute of Education, Center for the Study of Reading.
Anderson, T. H., & Armbruster, B. B. (1986). Readable textbooks; or, selecting a textbook is not like buying a pair of shoes. In J. Orasamu (Ed.), *Reading comprehension: From research to practice* (pp. 151–162). Hillsdale, NJ: Erlbaum.
Apple, M. W. (1985). Making knowledge legitimate: Power, profit and the textbook. In A. Molnar (Ed.), *Current thoughts on curriculum* (pp. 73–89). Alexandria, VA: Association for Supervision and Curriculum Development.
Applebee, A. N., Langer, J., & Mullis, I. (1987). *Learning to be literate in America: Reading, writing, and reasoning.* Princeton, NJ: Educational Testing Service.
Armbruster, B. B. (1984). The problem of inconsiderate text. In G. Duffy, L. Roehler, & J. Mason (Eds.), *Comprehension instruction: Perspectives and suggestions* (p. 203). New York: Longman.
Armbruster, B. (1985). Content-area textbooks: A research perspective. In J. Osborne, P. T. Wilson, & R. C. Anderson (Eds.), *Reading education: Foundations for a literate America.* Lexington, MA: Lexington Books.
Armbruster, B. (1986). Schema theory and the design of content-area textbooks. *Educational Psychologist, 21*, 253–267.
Armbruster, B. (1987). Name that date: Questions in social studies programs. Paper presented at the American Educational Research Association, Washington, DC.
Armbruster, B., & Anderson, T. H. (1981). *Content-area textbooks.* Reading Report No. 23, University of Illinois, Center for the Study of Reading.
Armbruster, B., & Gudbrandsen, B. (1986). Reading comprehension instructions in social studies programs. *Reading Research Quarterly, 21*, 36–48.
Arnold-Gerrity, D. (1978). Sex stereotyping of women and girls in elementary textbooks and its implication for future work force participation. A paper presented at North Central Sociological Association. (ERIC ED 191 087)
Association of American Publishers. (1987). *Annual industry statistics.* Washington, DC: Author.
Association of American Publishers, American Library Association, & Association for Supervision and Curriculum Development. (1981). *Limiting what students shall read.* Washington, DC: Author.

Austin, Mary. (1961). *The torchlighters*. Cambridge, MA: Harvard University Press.

Bachman, S. (1976). Comparative textbook analysis. *Education and Culture, 31,* 33–37.

Baker, R. L., & Schutz, R. E. (Eds.). (1971). *Instructional product development*. New York: VanNostrand Reinhold.

Ball, E. H. (1979). *Prepublication learner verification report for "Language Basics Plus": A basic language arts program*. E.R.I.C. Research Report. (ERIC ED 178 863)

Barnett, J. E. (1984). Facilitating retention through instruction about text structure. *Journal of Reading Behavior, 16* 1–13.

Barr, R., & Sadow, M. W. (1989). Influence of basal programs on fourth-grade reading instruction. *Reading Research Quarterly, 14*(1), 44–71.

Basista, E., et al. (1986). *How to prepare material for new literates*. Newark, DE: International Reading Association.

Baumann, J. F. (1985). Anaphora in basal reader selections: How frequently do they occur? Paper presented at National Reading Conference.

Baumann, J. F. (1986). Effect of rewritten content passages on middle-grade students' comprehension of main ideas: Making the inconsiderate considerate. *Journal of Reading Behavior, 18,* 1–21.

Baumann, J. F., & Serra, J. K. (1984). The frequency and placement of main ideas in social studies textbooks: A modified replication of Braddock's research on topic sentences. *Journal of Reading Behavior, 16,* 27–40.

Beck, I. L., & Block, K. (1979). An analysis of two beginning reading programs: Some facts and some opinions. In L. B. Resnick and P. Weaver (Eds.), *Theory and practice of early reading* (Vol. 1). Pittsburgh: University of Pittsburgh, Learning Research and Development Center.

Beck, I. L., & McCaslin, E. S. (1978). *An analysis of dimensions that affect the development of code-breaking activity in eight beginning reading programs*. Pittsburgh: University of Pittsburgh, Learning Research and Development Center.

Beck, I. L., McKeown, M. G., McCaslin, E. S., & Burkes, A. M. (1979). *Instructional dimensions that may affect reading comprehension: Examples from two commercial reading programs*. Pittsburgh: University of Pittsburgh, Learning Research and Development Center.

Beck, I. L., McKeown, M., & Omanson, R. C. (1984). Improving the comprehensibility of stories: The effects of revisions that improve coherence. *Reading Research Quarterly, 19,* 263–277.

Bernstein, H. T. (1985). The new politics of textbook adoption. *Phi Delta Kappan, 66,* 463–466.

Bettelheim, B., & Zelan, K. (1982). *On learning to read: The child's fascination with meaning*. New York: Knopf.

Binkley, M. (1987). The impact of rewriting world history textbooks for low-achieving students. Paper presented at the American Educational Research Association, Washington, DC.

Bohning, Gerry. (1986). The McGuffey eclectic readers: 1836–1986. *Reading Teacher, 40,* 263–289.

Bond, G., & Dykstra, R. (1967). The cooperative research program in first-grade reading instruction. *Reading Research Quarterly, 2,* 5–141.

Bowker, R. R. Company. (1987, 1988). *Literary marketplace: The directory of American book publishing*. New York: Author.

Brennan, A. D., Bridge, C., & Winograd, P. N. (1986). The effects of structural variation on children's recall of basal reader stories. *Reading Research Quarterly, 21,* 91–107.

Britton, B. K., & Black, J. B. (Eds.). (1985). *Understanding expository text*. Hillsdale, NJ: Erlbaum.

Britton, G. E., & Lumpkin, M. C. (1976). *For sale: Subliminal bias in textbooks*. Reports prepared at Oregon State University. (ERIC ED 140 279)

Brody, P. J. (1980). Research on pictures and instructional texts: Difficulties and directions. Paper presented at Association for Educational Communications and Technology. (ERIC ED 196 422)

Brody, P. J., & Ligenza, A. (1976). The effects of picture-type and picture location on comprehension. Paper presented at Association for Educational Communications and Technology. (ERIC ED 172 797)

Bruce, B. (1984). A new point of view on children's stories. In R. C. Anderson, J. Osborn, & R. J. Tierney (Eds.), *Learning to read in American schools: Basal readers and content texts*. Hillsdale, NJ: Erlbaum.

Bryant, J. (1980). Humorous illustrations in textbooks: Effect on information acquisition, appeals, and motivation. Paper presented at Speech Communication Association. (ERIC ED 196 077)

Burnett, L. W. (1950). Textbook provisions in the several states. *Journal of Education Research, 43,* 357–366.

Burnett, L. W. (1952). State textbook policies. *Phi Delta Kappan, 33,* 257–261.

Calfee, R. C., & Chambliss, M. J. (1986). *The structural design features of large texts*. Palo Alto, CA: Stanford University Press.

Calfee, R. C., & Curley, R. G. (1984). Structures of prose in the content areas. In J. Flood (Ed.), *Understanding reading comprehension*. Newark, DE: International Reading Association.

California State Department of Education. (1987). *Handbook for planning an effective literature program: Kindergarten through grade twelve*. Sacramento: Author.

Chall, J. S. (1967/1983a). *Learning to read: The great debate* (rev. ed.). New York: McGraw-Hill.

Chall, J. S. (1983b). *Stages of reading development*. New York: McGraw-Hill.

Chall, J. S. (1983c). Literacy: Trends and explanations. *Educational Researcher, 12,* 3–8.

Chall, J. S. (1988). The beginning years. In B. L. Zakaluk & S. J. Samuels (Eds.), *Readability: Its past, present, and future*. Newark, DE: International Reading Association.

Chall, J. S. (1989). Could the decline be real? Recent trends in reading instruction and support in the U.S. In E. Haertel et al., *Report of the NAEP Technical Review Panel on the 1986 reading anomaly, the accuracy of NAEP trends, and issues raised by state-level NAEP comparisons*: Washington, DC: National Center for Education Statistics and U.S. Department of Education.

Chall, J. S., Conard, S., & Harris, S. (1977). *An analysis of textbooks in relation to declining SAT scores*. New York: College Entrance Examination Board.

Chall, J. S., & Snow, C. E. (1988). School influences on the reading development of low-income children. *Harvard Education Letter, 4*, 1–4.

Ciborowski, J. (1988). *Improving textbook usability*. Newton, MA: Education Development Center.

Cody, C. B. (1986). *A policymaker's guide to textbook selection*. Alexandria, VA: National Association of State Boards of Education.

Cole, J. Y., & Sticht, T. G. (Eds.). (1981). *Textbooks in American society*. Washington, DC: Library of Congress.

Cronbach, L., Bierstedt, R., McMurray, F., Schramm, W., & Spaulding, N. B. (1955). *Text materials in modern education*. Urbana: University of Illinois Press.

Cronnell, B. (1978). *Proficiency verification system (PVS): Skill indices for spelling*. Technical Note 3-78-13, Southwest Regional Laboratory, Los Alamitos, CA. (ERIC ED 172 250).

Dale, E., & O'Rourke, J. (1971). *Techniques of teaching vocabulary*. Menlo Park, CA: Benjamin/Cummings.

Dale, E., & O'Rourke, J. (1981). *The living word vocabulary*. Chicago: World Book/Childcraft International.

Dance, E. H. (1974). To each his own truth. *New York Times Educational Supplement* (November 21).

Davidson, A. (1984). Readability—appraising text difficulty. In R. C. Anderson, J. Osborn, & R. J. Tierney (Eds.), *Learning to read in American schools*. Hillsdale, NJ: Erlbaum.

Dessauer, J. P. (Ed.). (1985). School adoptions and textbook quality. *Book Research Quarterly, 1*, 3–81.

Dick, W., & Carey, L. (1985). *The systematic design of instruction*. Glenview, IL: Scott Foresman.

Dodd, Clarence T. (1928). *State control of textbooks*. New York: Teachers College, Columbia University.

Dole, J. A. (1987). Improving the textbook selection process: Case studies of the textbook adoption guidelines project. Paper presented at the American Educational Research Association, Washington, DC.

Donlan, D. (1976). *Textbook writing in three content areas*. Research report, University of California at Riverside. (ERIC ED 123 635.)

Doyle, D. (1984). The unsacred texts. *American Educator* (summer), 8–13.

Duchastel, P. C. (1980a). *Research on illustrations in instructional text*. Occasional Paper No. 3, American College, Bryn Mawr, PA.

Duchastel, P. C. (1980b). Research on illustrations in text: Issues and perspectives. *Educational Communication and Technology, 28*, 283–287.

Duffy, G., Roehler, L., & Reinsmoen, T. (Eds.). (1983). *Comprehension instruction: Perspective and suggestions*. New York: Longman.

Duke, C. R. (1985). A look at current statewide adoptions procedures. Paper presented at National Council of Teachers of English. (ERIC ED 254 854).

Durkin, D. (1981). Reading comprehension instruction in five basal reader series. *Reading Research Quarterly, 16*, 515–544.

Durkin, D. (1983). *Is there a match between what elementary teachers do and what basal manuals recommend?* Technical Report No. 44, University of Illinois, Center for the Study of Reading.

Durkin, D. (1984). Do basal manuals teach reading comprehension? In R. C. Anderson, J. Osborn, & R. J. Tierney (Eds.), *Learning to read in American schools: Basal readers and content texts*. Hillsdale, NJ: Erlbaum.

Durkin, D. (1987). Teaching and testing in kindergarten. *Reading Teacher, 40*, 766–770.

Edmonson, J. B., et al. (1930). The textbook in American education. *National Society for the Study of Education Yearbook, 30*.

Educational Products Information Exchange. (1979). *Students' knowledge of textbook content at the start and end of the school year*. New York: Author. (NIE-G-79-0DE3)

Educational Products Information Exchange Institute. (1974). *Selecting and evaluating beginning reading materials*. Product Report No. 62/63, EPIE Institute, New York.

Elson, R. M. (1972). *Guardians of tradition: American schoolbooks of the nineteenth century*. Lincoln: University of Nebraska Press.

English, R. (1980). The politic of textbook adoption. *Phi Delta Kappan, 62*, 272–278.

Farr, R. (1988). The changing basal reader. *Educational Leadership, 45*, 86.

Farr, R., Courtland, M. C., Harris, P., Tarr, J., & Treece, L. (1983). *A case study of the Indiana state reading adoption process*. Bloomington: Indiana University Press.

Flagg, B. N., Weaver, P. A., Fenton, T., Gelatti, R., & Pray, R. (1980). Children's use of pictures in comprehending written text. Paper presented at American Educational Research Association. (NIE-G-78-0053)

Follett, R. (1985). The textbook adoption process. *Book Research Quarterly, 1*, 19–22.

Frase, L. T., & Schwartz, J. (1979). Typographical cues that facilitate comprehension. *Journal of Educational Psychology, 71*, 197–206.

Garcia, J. (1976). Images of named and nonwhite ethnic groups as presented in selected eighth-grade U.S. history textbooks. Paper presented at Inter-American Congress of Psychology. (ERIC ED 145 379)

Gates, Arthur. (1949). *The improvement of reading*. New York: Macmillan.

Gates, Arthur. (1926). *A reading vocabulary for the primary grades.* New York: Teachers College, Columbia University.

Gates, Arthur. (1930). *Interest and ability in reading.* New York: Macmillan.

Glynn, S. M., & DiVesta, F. J. (1978). Development of ideational bonds in text and relational and locative cues. Paper presented at Eastern Educational Research Association. (ERIC ED 158 267)

Goodman, K. S., Freeman, Y., Murphy, S., & Shannon, P. (1988). *Basal reader report card.* Des Moines, IA: Richard Owen.

Goodykoontz, B. (1936). The relations of pictures to reading comprehension. *Elementary English Reading Review, 13,* 125–130.

Graham, G. (1978). *A present and historical analysis of basal reading series.* Unpublished doctoral dissertation, University of Virginia.

Graves, M. F., & Slater, W. H. (1986). Could textbooks be better written and would it make a difference? *American Educator, 10,* 36–42.

Gray, William S. (1984). *Reading.* Newark, DE: International Reading Association.

Gray, W. S., & Leary, B. E. (1935). *What makes a book readable?* Chicago: University of Chicago Press.

Green, G. M., & Olson, M. S. (1985). *Interactions of text and illustration in beginning reading.* Technical Report No. 355. University of Illinois, Center for the Study of Reading.

Gutherie, J. T., Martuza, V., & Seifert, M. (1979). Impacts of instructional time in reading. In L. B. Resnick & P. Weaver (Eds.), *Theory and practice of early reading.* Hillsdale, NJ: Erlbaum.

Guttmann, J., Levin, J. R., & Pressley, M. (1977). Pictures, partial pictures, and young children's oral prose learning. *Journal of Educational Psychology, 69,* 473–480.

Hartley, J. (1985). *Designing instructional text* (2nd ed.). London: Kogan Page; New York: Nicols.

Hartley, J., & Trueman, M. (1981). The effects of changes in layout and changes in wording on preferences for instructional text. *Visible Language, 15,* 13–31.

Hefley, J. C. (1976). *Are textbooks harming your children?* Milford, MI: Mott Media.

Hillocks, G., Jr. (1978). Books and bombs: Ideological conflict and the schools—a case study of the Kanawha County book protest. *School Review, 76,* 632–651.

Hinds, M. S. (1987). We must do more (conference report). *Reading Informer, 15*(1), 40–41.

Hirsch, E. D., Jr. (1987). *Cultural literacy: What every American needs to know.* Boston: Houghton Mifflin.

Holly, C. D., et al. (1981). Using intact and embedded headings as processing aids with non-narrative text. *Contemporary Educational Psychology, 6,* 227–236.

Houghton, H., & Willows, D. (Eds.). (1987). *Psychology of illustration (2 vols.).* New York: Springer-Verlag.

Humes, A. (1978). *Proficiency verification systems (PVS): Skill indices for language arts.* Technical Note, Southwest Regional Laboratory, Los Alamitos. (ERIC ED 172 143)

Hunter, B., Crismore, A., & Pearson, P. D. (1986). *Visual displays in basal readers and social studies textbooks.* Urban, IL: Center for the Study of Reading.

Hynd, C., & Alvermann, D. E. (1986). The role of refutation text in overcoming difficulty with science concepts. *Journal of Reading, 29,* 440–446.

Institutional Tracking Service. (1980). *Reading/Language arts.* White Plains, NY: Author.

Jay, W. T. (1973). *Sex stereotyping in selected mathematics textbooks for grades two, four, and six.* Ed.D. dissertation, University of Oregon. (ERIC ED 087 627)

Jenkinson, E. B. (1979). *Censors in the classroom: The mind benders.* Carbondale, IL: Southern Illinois Press.

Jenkinson, E. B. (1987). The significance of the decision in "Scopes II." *Phi Delta Kappan,* (February), 445–450.

Jensen, F. A. (1931). *Current procedures in selecting textbooks.* Philadelphia: Lippincott.

Jonassen, D. H. (1985). *The technology of text.* Englewood Cliffs, NJ: Educational Technology Publications.

Jones, B. F., Ariran, R., & Katims, M. (1984). Teaching cognitive strategies and text structures within language arts programs. In J. Segal, S. Chipman, & R. Glaser (Eds.), *Thinking and learning skills: Relating basic research to practice.* Hillsdale, NJ: Erlbaum.

Kane, M. B. (1971). Minorities: What the textbooks don't say. *Current, 129,* 13–16.

Keith, S. (1981). *Politics of textbook selection* (Research Report No. 81-AT). Palo Alto, CA: Stanford University, Institute for Research on Educational Finance and Governance.

Keith, S. (1985). Choosing textbooks: A study of instructional materials selection processes for public education. *Book Research Quarterly, 1,* 24–37.

Kemp, J. E. (1985). *The instructional design process.* New York: Harper & Row.

Klare, G. R. (1983). Readability. In P. D. Pearson et al (Eds.), *Handbook of research on reading.* New York: Longman.

Koenke, K. (1987). Pictures in reading materials: What do we know about them? *Reading Teacher, 40,* 902–905.

Komoski, P. K. (1978). The realities of choosing and using instructional materials. *Educational Leadership, 36,* 46–50.

Lang, L. Z. (1985). The adoption of reading textbooks in Virginia and its application to the Arlington public schools. *Book Research Quarterly, 1,* 49–72.

Lange, B. (1979). ERIC/RCS: Modeling and remodeling textbook reading activities. *Journal of Reading, 23,* 170–173.

Langer, Judith. (1987). *Children's reading and writing.* Norwood, NJ: Ablex.

Last, E. (1982). *The Texas textbook protestors defend literature and education.* Doctoral dissertation, University of Wisconsin. (ERIC ED 257 071)

Legenza, A., & Knafle, J. D. (1978). *The effective components of children's pictures.* Paper presented at National Reading Conference. (ERIC ED 165 134)

Lerner, B. (1982). American education: How are we doing? *Public Interest, 69,* 59–82.

Mandler, J. M. (1978). A code in the node: The use of story schema in retrieval. *Discourse Processes, 1,* 14–35.

Mandler, J. M., & Johnson, N. S. (1977). Remembrance of things passed. Story structure and recall. *Cognitive Psychology, 9,* 111–115.

Marshall, J. D. (1987). *State-level textbook decision-making: The way things were in Texas*: Paper presented at American Educational Research Association, Washington, DC.

Mason, J., & Osborn, J. (1983). When do children begin reading to learn? In *A survey of reading practices in grades two to five* (Technical Report No. 261). Urbana: University of Illinois, Center for the Study of Reading.

Mavrogenes, N. A. (1985). *William Scott Gray: Leader of teachers and shaper of American reading instruction.* Doctoral dissertation, University of Chicago.

Maxwell, C. R. (1921, 1930). *The selection of textbooks.* Boston: Houghton Mifflin.

McGraw, B., & Grotelueschen, A. (1971). *The direction of the effect of questions in prose materials.* Urbana: University of Illinois, Center for Instructional Research. (ERIC ED 061 539)

Meyer, B. J. (1975). *The organization of prose and its effects on memory.* New York: Elsevier.

Meyer, B. J. (1977). The structure of prose: Effects on learning and memory and implication for educational practice. In R. C. Anderson, R. J. Spiro, & W. E. Montague (Eds.), *Schooling and the acquisition of knowledge.* Hillsdale, NJ: Erlbaum.

Meyer, B. J., & Rice, G. E. (1984). The structure of text. In P. D. Pearson (Ed.) *Handbook of reading research* (Vol. 1) (pp. 319–351). New York: Longman.

Miller, W. A. (1937). Reading with and without pictures. *Elementary School Journal, 38,* 676–682.

Moffett, J. (1988). *Storm in the mountains.* Carbondale: Southern Illinois University Press.

Montare, A., Elman, E., & Cohen, J. (1977). Words and pictures: A test of Samuels' findings. *Journal of Reading Behavior, 40,* 397–407.

Murphy, R. T., & Appel, L. R. (1984). *Evaluation of the Writing to Read instructional system (second-year report).* Princeton, NJ: Educational Testing Service.

National Education Association & Association of American Publishers. (1972). *Selecting instructional materials for purchase.* Washington, DC: Author.

Osborn, J. (1984a). *Evaluating workbooks* (Reading Education Report No. 52). Urbana: University of Illinois, Center for the Study of Reading.

Osborn, J. (1984b). The purposes, uses, and contents of workbooks and some guidelines for publishers. In R. C. Anderson, J. Osborn, & R. L. Tierney (Eds.)., *Learning to read in American schools: Basal readers and content texts.* Hillsdale, NJ: Erlbaum.

Osborn, J., Jones, B. F., & Stein, M. (1985). The case for improving textbooks. *Educational Leadership* (April), 9–16.

Pelletti, J. C. (1974). The effect of graphic roles in elementary social studies texts on cognitive achievement. *Theory and Research in Social Education, 11,* 79–93.

Popp, H. M. (1975). Current practices in the teaching of beginning reading. In J. B. Carroll & J. S. Chall (Eds.), *Toward a literate society.* New York: McGraw-Hill.

Poulos, N. (1969). Negro attitudes toward textbook illustration. *Journal of Negro Education, 38,* 177–181.

Powell, D. A. (1985). Selection of textbooks on the district level: Is this a rational process? *Book Review Quarterly, 1,* 23–35.

Quillan, I. J. (1948). *Textbook improvement and international understanding.* Washington, DC: American Council on Education.

Ravitch, Diane, & Finn, Chester E. (1988). *What do our seventeen-year-olds know?* A report of the First National Assessment of History and Literature. New York: Harper & Row.

Robbins, R. H. (1980). Choosing the right basic reader. *Curriculum Review, 19,* 395–399.

Sadker, M. P., Sadker, D. M., & Garies, R. S. (1980). Sex bias in reading and language arts teacher education texts. *Reading Teacher, 33,* 350–537.

Samuels, S. J. (1968). Effects of pictures on learning to read, comprehension, and attitudes. *Review of Educational Research, 40,* 397–407.

Schallert, D. (1980). The role of illustrations in reading comprehension. In R. Spiro, W. Brewer, & B. C. Bruce (Eds.), *Theoretical issues in reading comprehension.* Hillsdale, NJ: Erlbaum.

Schmidt, W. H., Caw, J., Byers, J. L., & Buchmann, M. (1984). Content of basal text selections: Implications for comprehension instruction. In G. Duffy, L. R. Roehler, & J. Mason (Eds.), *Comprehension instruction: Perspectives and suggestions.* New York: Longman.

Shannon, P. (1983). The use of commercial reading materials in American elementary schools. *Reading Research Quarterly, 19,* 68–85.

Shapiro, S. (1985). An analysis of poetry teaching procedures in sixth-grade basal manuals. *Reading Research Quarterly, 20,* 368–381.

Shebilski, W. L., & Rotondo, J. A. (1981). Typographical and spatial clues that facilitate learning from textbooks. *Visible Language, 15*, 41–54.

Smith, N. B. (1934/1986). *American reading instruction.* Newark, DE: International Reading Association. (Originally published in 1934; revised periodically by the author until 1965, then by collaborators.)

Southwest Regional Laboratories. (1976). *Communication skills program.* Lexington, MA: Ginn.

Squire, J. R. (1981). Publishers, social pressures, and textbooks. In J. Cole & T. Sticht (Eds.), *The textbook in American society* (pp. 27–30). Washington DC: Library of Congress.

Squire, J. R. (1986). The current crisis in literature. *English Journal, 74*(8), 18–21.

Squire, J. R. (1988). Textbooks: Are we asking the right questions? In P. Jackson (Ed.), *Contributing to educational change.* Berkeley, CA: McCutcheon.

Stahl, S. A., & Fairbanks, M. M. (1986). The effects of vocabulary instruction: A model-based meta-analysis. *Review of Educational Research, 56*, 72–110.

Stahl, S. A., & Miller, P. D. (1989). Whole language and language experience approaches for beginning reading: A quantitative research synthesis. *Review of Educational Research, 59*, 87–116.

Stein, N. L. (1978). *How children understand stories: A developmental analysis* (Technical Report No. 69). Urbana: University of Illinois, Center for the Study of Reading.

Steward, M. D. (1950). *Prejudice in textbooks.* Washington, DC: American Council on Education.

Strickland, R. G. (1964). The contribution of structural linguistics to the teaching of reading, writing, and grammar in the elementary school. *Bulletin of the Indiana University School of Education, 40*(1).

Teale, W. A., & Sulzby, E. (1986). *Emergent literacy: Reading and writing.* Norwood, NJ: Ablex.

Thomas, J. L. (1976). *The use of pictorial illustration in illustration: Current findings and implications for further research.* (E.R.I.C. Research report. (ERIC ED 160 108).

Thorndike, Edward. (1921). *A teacher's word book.* New York: Teachers College, Columbia University.

Tidwell, C. J. (1928). *State control of textbooks.* New York: Columbia University Press.

Tinker, M. A. (1963). *Legibility of print.* Ames: Iowa State University Press.

Tulley, M. (1983). *A descriptive study of selected state-level textbook adoption policies.* Doctoral dissertation, Indiana University.

Tulley, M., & Farr, R. (1985). Textbook adoptions: Insight, impact, and potential. *Book Research Quarterly, 1*, 4–11.

Tyson-Bernstein, H., & Woodward, A. (1986). The great textbook machine and prospects for reform. *Social Education, 50*, 41–45.

Venezky, Richard. (1983). The history of reading research. In P. David Pearson (Ed.), *Handbook of research in reading* (Vol. 1) (pp. 3–38). New York: Longman.

Venezky, R. (1988). *The American reading script and its nineteenth-century origins.* First Marilyn Sadow Memorial Lecture, University of Chicago (April).

Venezky, R., Kaestle, C. F., & Sum, A. M. (1987). *The subtle danger.* Princeton, NJ: Educational Testing Service.

Waller, R. (1980). *Typography for graphic communication and typographic access structures for educational texts and graphic aspects of complex texts.* Evaluative report, Open University, England. (ERIC ED 271 152)

Webster, Noah. (1798). *The American spelling book.* Boston: Isaiah Thomas and Ebenezer Andrews. Now available from Bureau of Publications, New York: Teachers College, Columbia University.

Weintraub, S. (1960). *The effect of pictures on the comprehension of a second-grade basal reader.* Doctoral dissertation, University of Illinois.

Wendt, D. (1979). An experimental approach to the improvement of the typographic design of textbooks. *Visible Language, 13*, 108–133.

Wendt, D. (1982). Improving the legibility of textbooks: Effect of working and typographic design. *Visible Language, 16*, 88–93.

Wernersbach, R. (1987). *Textbook adoption procedures in public schools of large urban districts.* Doctoral dissertation, University of Cincinnati.

Willows, D. M. (1978a). A picture is not always worth a thousand words: Pictures as distractors in reading. *Journal of Educational Research, 70*, 255–262.

Willows, D. M. (1978b). Individual difference in distraction by pictures in a reading situation. *Journal of Educational Psychology, 70*, 837–847.

Willows, D. M. (1980). Effects of picture salience on reading comprehension of illustrated and nonillustrated aspects of texts. Paper presented at American Educational Research Association (April).

Wilson, H. E. (1948). *Intergroup relations in teaching material.* Washington, DC: A.C.E.

Winograd, P. (1987). Adopting textbooks in Kentucky: A retrospective view. Paper presented to American Educational Research Association.

Winograd, P., & Osborn, J. (1985). How adoption of reading textbooks works in Kentucky: Some problems and some solutions. *Book Research Quarterly, 1* 3–22.

Wittrock, Merlin. (1983). *Generative reading comprehension.* Lexington, MA: Ginn.

Woodward, A. (1985). Taking teaching out of teaching and reading out of learning to read: A historical study of reading textbook teachers' guides, 1920–1980. Paper presented at American Educational Research Association.

Woodward, A. (1986). Photographs in textbooks: More than pretty pictures? Paper presented at American Educational Research Association, San Francisco.

Woodward, A. (1988). Stress on visuals weakens texts. *Education Week, 7,* 19.

Wrightstone, J. W., & Lazar, M. (1957). *A study of preprimers through third-grade readers in eleven basic readings series.* New York: Bureau of Educational Research, Board of Education of City of New York.

Zakaluk, B. L., & Samuels, J. (Eds.). (1988). *Readability: Its past, present, and future.* Newark, DE: International Reading Association.

Zimet, S. G. (1972a). Attitudes and values in primers from the United States and twelve other countries. *Journal of Social Psychology, 84,* 167–174.

Zimet, S. G. (1972b). *What children read in school.* New York: Grune and Stratton.

7 POLITICS, POLICY, AND READING RESEARCH

Patrick Shannon

In an analysis of *What Works: Research about Teaching and Learning* (U.S. Department of Education, 1986), Gene V. Glass (1987) argues that the Reagan administration selected among educational research findings in order to prepare a document that would promote its conservative vision of schooling among state and local jurisdictions. Although he deplores this use of educational research, Glass acknowledges that such selectivity may be the rule rather than the exception concerning the negotiations, development, and implementation of educational policy, regardless of who is in the White House, the state house, or the school boardroom. Glass's criticism is important for reading researchers because it identifies several layers of the inherent politics of educational policy making and research—a subject long neglected within the reading research community. Through an extension of Glass's underlying logic, we can see both an agenda and a process for examining the development of educational policy and its effects on the structure and process of reading education in schools.

First, Glass admits that the interpretation of educational research depends heavily upon the political assumptions of the interpreters. That is, he states that others do not agree with his assessment of *What Works* because they overlook its politics, find it politically expedient to endorse the document, or share its conservative assumption about human nature, ideal social organizations, and the role of schooling.

Second, Glass implies that groups who seek to influence educational policy do so as much for political reasons as they do to reach pedagogic goals. As evidence, he criticizes the promotion by *What Works* of research findings that require little governmental involvement or support (e.g., more homework, more phonics), while ignoring "more heavily documented," but costly findings that run contrary to the department's conservative philosophy (e.g., cooperative learning, smaller class size, and so on).

Third, Glass considers the power relations among the individuals or groups who seek to influence educational policy. Specifically, he worries about the abilities of school districts and state officials who disagree with the thrust of *What Works* to withstand the pressure of the federal government when it operates outside regular legislative channels as an independent pressure group. His concern is heightened by the fact that 300,000 copies of *What Works* were in circulation within three months of its printing.

Finally, Glass implies that education research itself is political, although he does not state this explicitly. The implication is embedded in the ease with which he classifies educational research as being supportive of conservative or liberal politics. If the research studies were not based on the same assumptions about human nature and society as the political philosophies, then it would be much more difficult for Glass to make his points about the selection of research to support political goals.

From start to finish, then, Glass maintains that the policy-making process is replete with political activity: the definition of the problems, the intended solution, the research to support that solution, the research itself, and the negotiations of the specifics for the completed document are all political in nature. With this assertion, Glass sets the task for anyone who attempts to identify and explain not only the content and consequences of an educational policy, but also its explicit and implicit politics. With the addition of politics to policy analyses, we gain perspective on the origins, maintenance, and consequences of educational policy, which can no longer be discussed as the natural evolution of scientific progress, neutral or benign. Rather, with political discussions included, specific policies can be identified as particular historic constructions negotiated among people with unequal power and authority to make decisions, often pursuing differing visions of how we should live together in and out of schools. That is, from these analyses, we lose some of the fatalism which suggests that educators must work with the policies in place and within the current structure because "this is the way things are." The addition of politics lends a sense of possibility for a better future—however defined—to the consideration of reading education in schools.

The purpose of this chapter is to apply Glass's logic to an analysis of the research and writing concerning educational policy that affects the structure and process of reading instruction in public schools. There are as many conceptions of the relationship among educational policy, reading research, and reading instruction as there are political views. Toward these ends, I divide the chapter into four sections. In the first section, I begin with a brief historical overview of the federal government's involvement in education and delve deeper into the Elementary and Secondary Education Act to demonstrate the political nature of the debate on policy matters. The second section presents a review of the direct and indirect state governmental influence over reading programs, with a longer discussion of differing interpretations of state minimum competence tests for reading. Third, I present a discussion of independent pressure groups' influence concerning reading programs, ending with an overview of censorship in schools.

The section reviews are neither summative nor analytical concerning the factors affecting reading education policy. Because of the paucity of research in this area (many important policy issues and agents who directly or indirectly affect reading education have been largely ignored by reading researchers), the discussion is speculative, suggesting what might be fruitful avenues for reading research. In order to provide examples of various political orientations for the three main topics, I follow Glass's classification scheme: conservative, liberal, and socialist.

- A *conservative* seeks to preserve the established social order by maintaining private property and explicit moral standards. On balance, conservatives reject governmental intervention into private matters, suggestions of social engineering, and moral and political permissiveness.
- A *liberal* accepts the established social order but acknowledges some flaws that warrant governmental intervention in order to ensure some minimum level of social welfare that will in turn lead to social progress for all individuals. Liberals value science as the lever for that progress. On balance, liberals are suspicious of attacks on individual liberties as granted in the Bill of Rights, moral and social intolerance, and egalitarianism.
- A *socialist* rejects the present social structure and its infrastructure because it enables a minority elite to exploit the majority through the control of economic and cultural capital. On balance, socialists support a redistribution of that capital; individual freedom through participation in collective political control; and immediate, aggressive enforcement of laws to prevent discrimination based on class, gender, or race.

In the fourth section, I pose topics for further research and use a tripartite scheme concerning educational paradigms in order to discuss suggested avenues for research concerning reading education policy. Although these categories do not break down easily along traditional political lines, they provide an interesting way to look at and think about the relationship between policy for reading programs and research on that policy.

FEDERAL GOVERNMENTAL INVOLVEMENT

Although the U.S. Constitution does not mention education, thereby making it a state's right under the Tenth Amendment, members of the federal government have been interested in schooling in general and reading instruction in particular since the country's beginning. Thomas Jefferson expressed this interest in his call for universal public schooling (for all white males) in literacy, arithmetic, and history. "If a nation expects to be ignorant and free in a state of civilization, it expects what never was and will never be" (Jefferson, 1893, 221). From its rhetorical beginnings, federal attempts, first to influence research and later to intervene directly in schooling, have grown until they now can be portrayed as "the overriding issue in the support and control of elementary and secondary education" (Kaestle & Smith, 1982, p. 384). Of course, whether or not this growth is considered beneficial to the public depends on whom one reads (Aronowitz & Giroux, 1985; Bell, 1986; Clark & Astuto, 1986).

At present, the federal government uses three ways to influence the organization and practices of schooling. First, federal officials use indirect means to persuade state and local agencies to change their educational policy (Jung & Kirst, 1986). For example, since 1876, the federal commissioners and later secretaries of the Department of Education have written and spoken directly to the public concerning the important issues of the day in order to present the administration's agenda for education (see Lannie, 1974, concerning Henry Barnard, the first commissioner; Keppel, 1966; Bennett, 1986). Second, the federal government has attempted to direct reading research and programs to needed areas through the Cooperative Research Act of 1954. The funding of large research projects—such as the so-called first-grade studies (Bond & Dykstra, 1967), their follow-up in second grade (Dykstra, 1968), and the planned variation research for preschool and elementary school curricula (Rivlin & Timpane, 1975)—has had prolonged effects on reading research, if not on reading programs (Anderson, Hiebert, Scott, & Wilkinson, 1985). Finally, legislation provides a third means of influence for federal officials. From the indirect effects of the National Defense Education Act of 1958, which forced local school superintendents to seek additional state funds for reading programs in order to achieve some sort of parity with the federal funds promoting mathematics and science, to the school assessability legislation of the 1960s and 1970s, to the consolidation of federal programs during the 1980s, federally mandated programs have made increasing demands on the organization and process of reading instruction in local districts.

The Elementary and Secondary Education Act

Perhaps the most examined aspect of federal involvement in reading programs is the Title I section of the Elementary and Secondary Education Act (ESEA) of 1965, its subsequent refunding, and its transformation into Chapter 1 of the Education Consolidation and Improvement Act of 1981 (see Calfee & Drum, 1979; and Glass & Smith, 1977, for reviews of this literature). It seems impossible to write about Title I without referring to the politics of educational policy, and an analysis of three commentaries on the ESEA and literacy development will serve as my first example of the politics of research on reading education policy.

Even before its inception, the idea of ESEA was at the center of the dispute between state and federal control of education. Kaestle and Smith (1982) argue that the compromise to direct the funds toward the education of the poor rather than toward improved schooling for minority students was the condition that allowed the bill to make its way into law (because Southern representatives dropped their opposition to the bill). Title I of the original act was also open to political interpretation. For example, Senator Robert Kennedy saw this portion of the act as schools finally giving service to powerless individuals in local communities who had often been ignored by school officials; and therefore he insisted that the ESEA legislation carry a reporting requirement that would make school administrators responsive to parents of poor children (McLaughlin, 1975). On the other hand, officials in the Program Evaluation Section of the Department of Health, Education, and Welfare, who were ultimately responsible for overseeing the funding and implementation of the act, saw Title I and the requirement for evaluation and reporting as an experiment to determine the most efficient approaches to educating poor children; they therefore sought to "develop program goals that could be stated, measured, and evaluated in cost-benefit terms" (House, 1978). These two interpretations of the intent of the legislation set the parameters of the liberal and conservative positions respectively.

The Conservative Position

A conservative position concerning ESEA can be represented by a short article on the cost-effectiveness of all compensatory education (Mullin & Summers, 1983). Mullin and Summers begin their report by suggesting that the goals for compensatory education are sufficiently murky to warrant the imposition of net gain scores on achievement tests as the "necessary, if not sufficient, outcomes of education" (p. 339). Through a thorough review of the results and research methods of 47 studies culled in a painstaking manner from the hundreds of articles written on compensatory education, Mullin and Summers conclude that the educational benefits claimed for such programs are grossly overstated. In fact, when methodological problems in the studies are accounted for, "the burden of evidence does not support sustained effects of compensatory education" (p. 341). Nor do they find any connection between cost of a program and its effectiveness: "No approach and no program characteristic was consistently found to be effective. And those that were identified as effective in specific studies were not necessarily the costlier ones" (p. 342). Overall, they conclude, "It is difficult to marshal arguments in favor of spending more money on compensatory education programs" (p. 342). If school officials are not willing to modify their programs accordingly, then "sweeping, across-the-board cuts in funding may be the alternative" (p. 342).

Several factors make Mullin and Summers's study politically conservative. First, they perceive concern for the ESEA Title I program to be more of an economic problem than a moral or even an educational one. That is, they seem more disturbed over the costs of the programs than the welfare and the academic achievement of poor students. They wonder implicitly if the federal government should be involved at all in this matter. This is most noticeably indicated when they acknowledge that program effectiveness might be defined in many ways but offer little rationale for why readers of their article should accept a correlation between test points and dollars as that definition, and it is also noticeable during their call for funding cuts rather than programmatic change. Clearly, for Mullin and Summers, the ESEA Title I experiment in social engineering has failed, and they seem willing to accept the consequences of reduced funding for educating the poor. And while they mention reading programs only in terms of the test scores they produce, Mullins and Summers seem willing to return poor students to regular classroom reading programs, where they will remain in the lower reading groups receiving substandard treatment (Allington, 1983; Shannon, 1985).

The Liberal Position

A liberal position is presented in Allington's (1986) review of research on compensatory reading instruction. He begins, "Compensatory instruction for readers who are experiencing difficulty in acquiring reading ability is a good idea" (p. 270). However, he argues that Title I programs are poorly implemented in terms of program structure (too many pull-out programs), curriculum (little congruence between regular classroom and Title I content), instructional time (too little time on task), focus (not enough academic coverage), and evaluation (poor models used). Moreover, "in this case and, unfortunately, too many others, the level of commitment [of local school officials to Title I goals] seemingly ends with the expenditure of federal funds available" (p. 272). According to Allington, poor implementation and the lack of commitment account for the marginal results gained from Title I reading programs. However, rather than use his conclusions to argue for a reduction in federal involvement as do Mullin and Summers, Allington remains firm on his original commitment to compensatory education and makes 13 suggestions, based largely on school and teacher effectiveness research, that he believes will enable Title I teachers to realize the initial promise of the ESEA program. Ironically, some of the research Allington cites was originally funded under ESEA Title I or Title IV-C (Minter, 1982). Allington ends with a call for action: "Compensatory reading programs can be improved; it is time to initiate the changes indicated" (p. 286).

What makes Allington's review a liberal document? First, he assumes that federal involvement in public schooling is a legitimate act, and that were it not for the federal government many local school officials would ignore this concern. These assumptions direct his line of reasoning throughout the article. Second, he paraphrases Robert Kennedy's original concern for the program: that local school officials would gladly take the money but would half-heartedly pursue the program's goals without federal evaluation. Additionally, Allington's enthusiasm for reorganizing Title I programs around school and teacher effectiveness research suggests that he shares Kennedy's belief that reading achievement tests will tell us all that is worth telling about compensatory programs (House, 1978). Third, implicit in his review is Allington' moral concern for the Title I program. He implies that poor students have the right to an effective education, one that will not stop at equal access but will ensure equal outcomes. In sum, Allington sees Title I as a service program for the poor.

The Socialist Position

A socialist position on ESEA is offered in Kozol's *Illiterate America* (1985), in which he discusses the personal and social costs of adult illiteracy among one-third of the U.S. population. At first glance, this book does not seem concerned with compensatory education at all. However, careful consideration of Kozol's argument suggests that he is pessimistic concerning whether Project Head Start or Title I programs can break the cycle of illiteracy in poor communities because schools too frequently cannot make literate students out of children of illiterate parents. "Illiteracy does not breed illiteracy. But it does set up the preconditions for perpetuation of the lack of reading skills within successive generations" (p. 59). Illiteracy among the poor, Kozol argues, is a vestige of an "unjust social order" in which one class benefits from the misery of another. He questions the government's recent concern for the literacy of the poor, particularly the goals of functional literacy programs, and presents an extended discussion of the need of business to raise the literacy capabilities of the lowest levels of workers in order to keep them productive. Such concerns and programs will simply perpetuate the social status quo, Kozol maintains. As a countersolution, he calls simultaneously for adult literacy in order for poor adults to use written language to participate fully in American society and for programs to develop full employment to break the cycle of poverty.

While the conservative and liberal conceptions of ESEA and reading instruction for the poor locate literacy problems within the student or the educational system and ignore poverty itself as a contributing factor, Kozol, as a socialist, argues that the injustice of the U.S. social order is ultimately to blame for students' difficulty in learning to read. Kozol sees the unequal distribution of literacy as a function of the unequal distribution of wealth and power in society. His suggested programs for developing civic and aesthetic literacy are offered to help poor adults empower themselves at work and in their community, as well as enable them to support the development of their children's literacy. With universal adult literacy, active participation in civic responsibilities, and full employment, Kozol projects a drastic reduction in the literacy problems at schools. From his perspective, federal ESEA funds would be better spent on adult literacy projects and programs to promote full employment.

STATE INTERVENTION

Well before the ratification of the U.S. Constitution, colonial governments tied literacy education directly to schooling through legislation. As early as 1642, the Massachusetts Bay Colony gave government officials the right to inquire into the private matters of families and apprentices to determine if parents and masters were fulfilling their responsibilities toward children "especially of [children's] ability to read and understand the principles of religion and the capital laws of this country" (as quoted in Cubberley, 1934, p. 17). Variation among colonies and, later, states was the rule until the success of the common school movement in the mid-19th century (Cohen, 1974). Despite considerable resistance to this centralization of educational autonomy, "state aid and regulation came to be accepted in principle by the majority of northerners by 1860 and of southerners by the early twentieth century" (Kaestle & Smith, 1982, p. 387). Ironically, the last to accept state regulation have been at the forefront of the centralization of textbook adoption, evaluation, and curricula since the 1920s. Based on questionnaires and interviews with the "educational policy elites" in six states, policy making is now largely the domain of "insiders" (state legislators, state education officials, and governors and their staffs), with only marginal influence from "outsiders" (Marshall, Mitchell, & Wirt, 1985).

The centralization of authority, funding, and regulation has considerable consequences for the reading programs currently offered in American schools as more and more components become the concern of the state rather than the district.

Curriculum. Curriculum was traditionally a state concern only to ensure a balanced program in elementary and secondary schools; however, several state legislatures have recently specified skills to be included in the reading curricula of public schools across the state (Wise, 1979). For example, House Bill 246 in Texas set the "essential elements" of reading curricula for that state (Killian, 1984); and Florida and South Carolina, among others, have established detailed outlines of the reading skills to be mastered before students may progress to the next grade level (Odden & Odden, 1984). Even states that adopt a less skills-oriented approach to reading curricula (e.g.,

California Department of Public Instruction, 1987) are much more detailed in their curricular requirements than they were even 10 years ago.

Textbooks.   Textbooks and reading curricula are closely associated in American schools (Shannon, 1988). Some argue that the state textbook adoption policies of Texas and California unduly influence the reading curricula in other states because textbook publishers tailor their textbooks to meet the requirements set by these populous, and therefore potentially lucrative, markets (Bowler, 1978; Follett, 1985; Muther, 1985; Squires, 1985), and because school personnel rely heavily on these textbooks to provide the curriculum, materials, and instruction for reading lessons (Educational Products Information Exchange, 1977). The putative advantages of such state adoption policies (e.g., lower prices and increased uniformity) have recently been carefully analyzed (see Farr, Tulley, & Powell, 1987, for a review of this literature).

Teacher certification.   Teacher certification has been a state prerogative in some states for over 150 years and for as little as 40 years in others. Prior to the 1920s, teacher certification was largely a matter of passing an examination offered by a local school board (see Cubberley, 1906, for a discussion of these tests). Between the 1920s and 1980, successful completion of normal school or teacher's college replaced examinations as the primary means of gaining certification (Cremin, 1980). These decentralized approaches have been challenged recently in 27 states with legislation requiring prospective teachers to pass literacy tests before entry into teacher education programs and in 45 states in which teachers must successfully complete a teacher certification test (Anrig, 1986). These examinations test prospective teachers' knowledge of literacy and instruction primarily through multiple-choice formats.

Instruction.   Instruction is a relatively new state concern stimulated by legislators' perceptions of declining student achievement (Odden & Anderson, 1986). The intent of these instructional initiatives is to tie instruction closely to students' scores on achievement and/or criterion-referenced tests (Bracey, 1987; Cuban, 1986; Popham, 1987). For example, Maryland's School Improvement Through Instruction Process Program, Missouri's Instructional Management System, and Arkansas's Program for Effective Teaching promote active learning (Robinson & Good, 1987), mastery learning (Levine & Associates, 1985), and the Madeline Hunter Model (Hunter, 1982), respectively, each requiring closer supervision of all teachers' instructional efforts based on components designed to raise test scores (Cruse, 1985; Samidifer, 1985).

Evaluation.   Evaluation of reading programs can take many forms (e.g., adequacy of library facilities, education of teacher, and so forth). Foremost among the methods now used to evaluate reading programs, teachers, and students is the minimum competence test for reading, required in nearly every state (National Governors' Association, 1986). Almost half of these states tie their testing programs to student promotion; others use them to determine areas in need of additional support (Popham, 1985).

Minimum Competence Tests

Although most agree that the minimum competence test has a considerable impact on classroom reading programs (Klein, 1984), its value for students and society is often debated (Jaeger & Tittle, 1980). This issue serves as the second example of the politics of research on educational policy affecting reading programs.

The Conservative Position

Finn (1982) presents a *conservative position* in this debate. In his brief article, he argues that educational standards have drastically declined over the last 20 years as educators have been more concerned with equal access to schooling than with the quality of that schooling. He chides the public for making too many demands on the educational system, which should focus its attention solely on the development of intellect and character. In order to regain these lost standards, Finn offers 12 prescriptions for public schools. Prescription 1 suggests that decisions for promotion and graduation be made solely on student's achievement: "The way to start this reform—and some communities and a few whole states have already begun—is to confer the high school diploma only on boys and girls who can demonstrate mastery of a body of knowledge and a range of skills" (p. 33). Prescription 3 suggests that tests be the means of demonstration and that competency examinations are "not a bad idea" throughout the curriculum and across the grades. Acknowledging that some students will undoubtedly fail such tests, Finn recommends that appropriate remedial programs be arranged; and he concludes that "being rigorous does not mean being cruel. But a society that allows no one to fail is a society that has lost the meaning of success" (p. 33).

Finn's position can be considered conservative because he bases his argument on a perceived need to return to traditional educational standards in order to preserve the American way of life. For example, in explaining his rationale for raising standards through testing, he suggests that "the kind of society we want to inhabit . . ., the productivity and competitiveness of our national economy . . ., knowledge transmission from one generation to the next . . ., and our sense of national security and national purpose" (p. 33) are all contingent on the improvement and verification of educational standards. Finn implies that the failed attempts at social engineering through the educational legislation and federal court decisions of the 1960s and 1970s are the primary reasons for the educational decline, and that charges of elitism made against minimum competence and other forms of testing only serve to perpetuate America's decline toward a third-world status. Finally, Finn champions the cause of individualism in his suggestion that some must fail so that others may succeed.

The Liberal Position

Wixson, Peters, Weber, and Roeber (1987) describe a *liberal position* concerning reading competency tests in their essay on the development of a new assessment device for Michigan. This work began with a scheduled review of the definitions and objectives of a previous competency test. At that time, a committee of state officials, school personnel, and university faculty decided that Michigan's definition of reading no longer reflected the accepted scientific thinking concerning reading and instruction. Through the efforts of this review committee, a new, more scientific definition was composed based on an interactive view of reading; and new instructional objectives were written for each grade level based on research on the characteristics of good readers. Later, committees of school personnel developed test items from these new objectives, and the various levels of the test were to be field tested for full implementation in 1989. Wixson et al. conclude by describing the unique coalition that typically allowed "outsiders of policy making" (teachers, school personnel, and university researchers) to affect the thoughts and actions of state policy makers.

Wixson et al.'s liberalism is almost entirely implicit. First, they accept the right of the state to evaluate, and therefore generally direct, the reading programs of individual schools in order to preserve some level of standardization of programs across the state.

Their objection to the present system of competency tests is based solely on its unscientific nature and its consequent inability to perform its evaluative function correctly. Should the old test continue to be used, there would be unscientific, and by implication, unjust decisions made concerning reading programs, teachers, and students. They find this possibility intolerable and take appropriate actions to make sure that a scientifically valid test was substituted. However, they go well beyond this. By extension, they propose a form of social engineering by using the test to change the instructional goals and behaviors of teachers across Michigan as they hone their reading programs and instruction to meet the demands of the new test. Wixson et al. accept this outcome because it may be the most efficient way to reach their scientific goal.

The Socialist Position

Rome (1986) offers a socialist position on testing, with specific reference to the "damaging" effects of minimum competency examinations, in his introduction to a special issue of *Radical Teacher* on standardization. "In this issue, we will look at ways in which standardized testing is playing an increasingly important role in the sorting of students to their appropriate place in the social structure" (p. 1). Rome argues that minimum competency tests are used for three major reasons for this task: their simplicity, their pseudo-objectivity, and their technological aura. Rather than address "the complexity of social and economic problems which must be dealt with" (p. 1), state agencies and school districts design tests that will demonstrate to the public that improvements are being made (e.g., test scores are increasing), without ameliorating the unequal reading achievement among students from different social classes. Although the tests are written by experts and scored by machine, "the questions betray the reality that these tests are largely written by and for the white, preferably male, elite" (p. 3). And while they suggest scientific rigor and technological efficiency, "the hidden agenda of narrowing educational options emphasizing authoritarian relations in the school and increasing the dropout rate attempts to produce a more manageable, marketable educational product" (p. 2). "But what these tests really reveal is the effects of poverty, of past and present discrimination, of unequal schooling, and of the whole collection of social inequalities that make the notion of fair and objective testing irrelevant" (p. 3).

Rome's position is socialist because of his underlying assumption that minimum competency tests are used to sort individuals according to their social class origins in order to perpetuate the current social order in schools and society. Rome argues that this form of discrimination is cloaked in a scientific aura in order that school and state officials may pretend that this sorting function is part of the natural order of things. The basic means with which this sorting is accomplished is through the design and content of the tests, which, Rome maintains, are based on middle-class experience and language and which relegate lower-class whites, women, and minority students to a lower status at school and later in society. Finally, Rome doubts the possibility of equitable evaluation because of the injustice of everyday life, but he offers alternative forms of evaluation and calls for collective action to combat the unjust effects of minimum competency and other standardized tests.

THE INFLUENCE OF PRESSURE GROUPS

With the increasing centralization of schooling in the late 19th and throughout the 20th centuries, local citizens' influence on educational policy began to wane as policy decision making moved further away from the local schoolhouse to state and federal educational agencies. In order to maintain some level of influence, citizens forged groups representing various segments of society, mounting unevenly successful campaigns for change for various causes (see Katznelson & Weir, 1985, for an example of how groups formed and operated).

Corporate society is represented among these pressure groups by philanthropic foundations (Arnove, 1982) and business and industrial organizations (Cuban, 1984). For example, philanthropic foundations are the second-largest single source of funding for educational research and programming outside of the federal government (Arnove, 1982). Many important literacy education studies were and are conducted under their auspices (e.g., the Carnegie Foundation funded Austin & Morrison, 1963; Barton & Wilder, 1964; Chall, 1967; and Gray & Monroe, 1929, among many others). The Ford Foundation provided the funds and expertise for the nation's first attempt at a fifth-year professional teacher education program in the 1950s (Colvard, 1964), and the Carnegie Foundation's *A Nation Prepared* (1986) seeks improvements in teacher education programs along similar lines. These two foundations were the original sponsors of the National Assessment of Educational Progress (NAEP), the NAEP's first administrative home at the Education Commission of the State, and the NAEP's most recent home at the Educational Testing Service (Buss, 1982).

Ironically, business groups (e.g., the Committee for Economic Development, 1985) now seek to replace vocational education with liberal arts studies for all high school students and to supplant scientific management practices with bottom-up administrative practices—the exact reverse of their successful lobbying efforts during the first two decades of the 20th century. In what is referred to as "concerned self-interest" (Levine, 1986a), business offers expertise (Levine, 1986b), money (Cuban, 1983), management schemes (Rogers, Talbot, & Cosgrove, 1984), and free curricular materials (Apple, 1982). In return, business expects improved policy and practice concerning school productivity, well-prepared workers, and an open market for school-related products (Doyle & Levine, 1985).

The education profession is represented by professional organizations, teacher education reform groups, teacher associations, unions, and collectives among other groups. For example, the International Reading Association (IRA) and the National Council of Teachers of English (NCTE) have large memberships, distinguished histories (Hook, 1979; Jerrolds, 1977), and considerable networks of teachers at state and local levels across the United States. These groups lobby at the state and federal level and disseminate policy-related resolutions concerning how literacy should be taught in public schools. The Holmes Group (1986), the National Council for Accreditation of Teacher Education (1985), and other teacher education reform groups seek to influence reading education policy indirectly through the "upgrading" of educational standards at colleges of education. In 46 states that permit teachers to bargain collectively, the recent calls for changes in teachers' working conditions will be negotiated with local unions and associations. Although traditionally these groups have been more interested in economic issues and job security than in curricular and instructional concerns (Jessup, 1985; Johnson, 1984), Johnson and Nelson (1987) predict that their interests will broaden when the reform proposals meet the impending teacher shortage.

Citizens concerned with educational policy have formed independent research organizations, parent groups, and religious and political associations (Bastian, Fruchter, Gitkill, Greer, & Haskins, 1985). For example, Design for Change, a Chicago-based research group, was largely responsible for the Chicago Public Schools' retesting of and reclassifying over 10,000 students, many of whom had been mistakenly placed in special education programs because of faulty testing procedures and placement criteria (1982); Chicago Public Schools replaced the Chicago Mastery Learning Reading program because Designs for Change found that very few inner-city high school graduates could read at or above grade level (1985). The New Jersey Institute for Citizen Involvement in Education, a parent organization formed originally to combat reduced funding for education, conducts "parent/activist" workshops, which have lobbied successfully at the district level to promote policy based on school and teacher effectiveness research (Fruchter, Silvestri, & Green, 1985). Religious and political groups such as the Moral Majority, Eagle Forum, and People for the American Way argue over whose definition of appropriate knowledge will be validated in the textbooks and library books at school—the third example of the politics of reading educative policy.

Censorship

The history of the struggle over the content of children's and adolescents' reading material is nearly as long as the history of schooling in the United States. An argument concerning which version of the Bible would be read at school resulted in the burning of Quaker books and the refusal to publish papal doctrines in the Massachusetts Bay Colony during the mid-17th century (Bryson & Delty, 1982). Despite this long history, the study of censorship remains a new and complex issue because the typical responses of the past (the more conservative the group, the more stridently in favor of censorship; the more liberal the group, the more stridently against censorship) can no longer be the anticipated responses from advocacy groups.

The Traditional Conservative Position

A traditional conservative position on censorship is found in the Gablers' (1985) *What Are They Teaching Our Children?*, a mixture of homilies, careful text analyses, research reports, citations of law and court cases, and Bible quotations. Although the Gablers are incorporated as their own pressure group, Educational Research Analysts, their work is also frequently used by conservative groups across the country in their efforts to remove what they consider to be antifamily, anti-Christian, and anti-American content from school textbooks. The Gablers exhort parents to read carefully their children's school books, to identify objectionable material, and then to band together to force officials to remove that material from school shelves. They do not mince words:

> We can avert the disaster that surely awaits us if humanistic educators win. We must reverse these trends. We must restore schools and textbooks to sanity. We must save our children. Not all at one time. Not all in one place. Not by denying our differences, but by working for common goals in our own communities and states. (p. 160)

Although the extent of its influence has not been fully studied, Educational Research Analysts has successfully influenced textbook selection in Texas and engendered some levels of self-censorship among teachers, librarians, and publishers across the United States (Piasecki, 1982).

The Neoconservative Position

A neoconservative position is offered in Thomas's *Book Burning* (1983), in which he, as vice president of Moral Majority, uses the First Amendment to accuse school officials and "establishment" publishers of censoring Christian and traditional content from school textbook and library books. Evoking a traditionally liberal position (the right of all sides to be heard on any issue), Thomas documents the contradiction between school officials' recent rhetoric on the need for a balanced treatment for all issues and their systematic rejection of prolife, profamily, pro-Christian, and pro-American information from both schoolbooks and curriculum. For example, he discusses the irony of the American Civil Liberties Union's current position on teaching only one theory of origins (evolution), when Clarence Darrow, representing that organization at the Scopes Trial in 1925, argued the "bigotry" of teaching only one theory (creationism). To complete this role reversal, Thomas contends that the Moral Majority could not possibly be censors in public schools because "censorship by definition is an act of suppression carried out from a position of power" (p. xi), and Christian America is currently separated from power by a misinterpretation of the U.S. Constitution.

The Liberal Position

A liberal position is presented by the American Library Association (ALA), which currently leads the way in activism against the censorship of books. Ironically, until 1939, the ALA advocated that librarians avoid controversial issues in order to be considered neutral; at the same time, it endorsed librarians as moral censors in order to redirect the interests of the "masses." For example, the Board of Examiners for the Boston Public Library in 1875 suggested that "there is a vast range of ephemeral literature, exciting and fascinating, apologetic of vice, confusing distinctions between plain right and wrong . . . which it is not the business of a town library to supply" (Geller, 1984, p. 23). Official ALA policy on censorship did not change until 1939, when direct reaction to European fascism led to the acceptance of the Library Bill of Rights, drafted at the national convention in San Francisco. More than a manifesto against censorship concerning alternative points of view, it marked librarians' rejection of the guise of neutrality and began their open advocacy of democratic ideals to combat "inclinations in many part of the world of growing intolerance, suppression of speech, and censorship affecting the rights of minorities and individuals" (ALA, 1939, p. 60).

For the last 50 years, the ALA has officially championed the traditional liberal position, arguing forcefully for the end of all censorship of books and for the reader's right to choose reading materials (see Oboler, 1980, for a history of this period). The ALA's Intellectual Freedom Committee and its legal defense arm, the Freedom to Read Foundation, offer a censorship hotline, ALA position packets, legal and economic support for those in trouble, and the *Newsletter on Intellectual Freedom*. The *Newsletter* provides information concerning censorship in schools across the United States— celebrating victories when censorship is defeated and plotting strategies for a continued struggle when censorship is upheld. Through the ALA's (1983) attempt to establish a national grassroots network in order to further their cause, a colloquium of lawyers, publishers, librarians, and noted civil libertarians was held to discuss reactive strategies to a rising number of censorship challenges to books in school classrooms and libraries and to propose proactive policy strategies that would frustrate censors in their efforts to challenge schoolbooks in court.

The Socialist Position

A socialist position on censorship is offered by the Council on Interracial Books for Children (CIBC), with its strident objections to the biases of school textbooks in favor of the status quo, and against "the myth that the United States is all white, all Christian, all middle class, who all live in nuclear, suburban families" (CIBC, 1979, p. 43). Using the "equal protection under the law" clause from the Fourteenth Amendment, the CIBC calls for the demographics of textbook characters to reflect the actual demographics of the current United States (e.g., 50 percent female, over 20 percent minority, 10 percent disabled). The CIBC recognize that their suggestions require considerable change in textbooks, with some current information being eliminated in order to provide space for the new "antibiased" information. However, they maintain that these acts do not constitute censorship because the changes only make the textbooks comply with federal laws and because the CIBC does not recommend that all of the current biased information be cut—what remains can serve as fodder for teaching students to detect bias when they read. "We have no desire to see children's books that would solely help the dominated get a bigger piece of the pie. We don't like the pie, period" (CIBC, 1976, p. 2). Rather than censorship, the CIBC suggests that their concerns for school textbooks are really just "public interest criticism."

Beyond a concern for equitable treatment, the CIBC offers many educational services to inform parents, teachers, and students concerning the social injustices promoted in children's books.

> The value system that dominates in these books is very white, very contemptuous of females except in traditional roles, and very oriented to the needs of the upper class. It is very geared to individual achievement rather than community well-being. It is a value system that can serve only to keep people of color, poor people, women, and other dominated groups "in their places" because directly or indirectly it makes children—our future adults—think that this is the way it should be. (CIBC, 1976, p. 2)

In addition to workshops, books, and pamphlets, the CIBC developed *Guidelines for Parents, Educators, and Librarians* (1976), in which it explains through example the criteria for judging children's and adolescents' books to be antibiased, nonbiased, or biased. In their *Bulletin*, published eight times a year, the CIBC reviews current books, using these criteria. Because they have championed the rights of oppressed groups since 1966, they recommend only antibiased books, and they have maintained a list of objectionable books since 1976. The CIBC may promote self-censorship among teachers, librarians, and publishers during their selection of texts in order to avoid charges of bias (Donaldson, 1981).

In the first three sections, we have seen that the politics endemic to policy research, development, and implementation that Glass identified in general also holds true for reading education in particular. Whether at the state or federal level, policy makers and legislators engage in selective readings of reading research and community needs, often in order to substantiate their own political philosophies. Pressure groups' attempts to influence local, state, and federal officials are really political arguments concerning what knowledge should be validated at school and how reading programs should be organized and run to ensure that their constituents learn to read. Even reading education policy and other reading research and commentary are reflections of differing political convictions and contexts within the reading education community. Altogether, these conclusions argue for broader research parameters in order to include political analyses along with the psychological and instructional studies that now predominate in reading research.

READING EDUCATION POLICY

Unfortunately, we have few sophisticated answers to even the most basic policy questions that could be posed about federal, state, and citizen influences on the organization and process of reading instruction. Despite the obvious relevance of law and policy to teachers' and students' work during reading lessons, few reading researchers have tackled these complex, yet vital, concerns through systematic inquiries. Most often, just as I have done in this chapter, reading researchers rely on general analyses of educational policy, hypothesizing what these findings might mean for reading education. However, as we have learned in recent studies of classroom instruction, environmental context, including subject matter, makes a considerable difference in the thoughts and behaviors of lesson participants. It seems intuitively correct, then, to assume that hypothesizing from general education studies is of somewhat limited value. What we need is specific information concerning the formation of educational legislation and policies and the consequences of these policies on the day-to-day functioning of reading lessons in American schools.

To begin with, who are the insiders of reading education policy and legislation at the state and local levels, and why are they effective in evoking or preventing change? How does reading education and research become a priority for policy change, for legislation, or for research and program funding? For specific policies (e.g., the recent California Language Arts Initiative) or laws (e.g., Texas House Bill 246), what were the immediate and long-term motivating events? Who actually wrote these and other policies and bills, and what resources did they use to inform their work? Why do anachronistic policies like state textbook adoption persist, despite a lack of evidence of their benefit or utility? How are federal and state policies and laws translated into local policies, and why is there so much variation among districts? Finally, can any generalizations beyond civics class banalities be made across school districts and states?

Which agencies and organizations influence the legislative and policy-making process? For instance, what does it mean to the reading policy of local districts when the president and the secretary of education endorse phonics instruction as what works in primary grades? What influences do philanthropic foundations have on who teaches reading, how it is taught, and how it is evaluated and studied? Without answers to this set of questions, we cannot begin to address the larger issue of whether or not the influx of large amounts of privately controlled money is good for public institutions. How effective are the International Reading Association (IRA) or the National Council of Teachers of English (NCTE) in influencing policy decisions at the federal, state, and local levels? Do independent research groups, parent organizations, and citizen associations influence or prevent change in local and state policies?

What are the consequences of reading legislation and policy for teachers, students, and researchers? For example, what does it mean to teachers' sense of professionalism to have one standard curriculum for an entire state and one means of evaluation? What do these mean for students of varying abilities and different social classes? What are the effects of teacher certification tests on reading methods classes at universities, on prospective teachers' conceptions of literacy and instruction, and on their subsequent teaching? Given the problematic status of medical education (Schon, 1983; Spiro, 1987), what are the possible outcomes of modeling preservice teachers' practica after hospital residency? What were—and are—the long-term implications of the NDEA's funding of new curricular materials in the early 1960s or its forcing local districts to rely more heavily on state funding to keep some parity between reading instruction and science and mathematics programs? What are the effects of Title I (Chapter 1) on the regular classroom programs for the children who remain with their classroom teacher? How have federal requests for proposals for research and subsequent funding affected the trends in reading research and program development? What are the trade-offs for reading education and research if business and industry become their partners? The short answer to each of these question is "we just don't know."

Of course, this is not an exhaustive list of questions, and others may have their own ideas concerning which ones are fundamental. The point is that we have little information for answering these or most other policy questions beyond speculation. What does the lack of answers mean to the reading research community? Quite honestly, I think it limits substantially our ability to participate meaningfully in policy development. Perhaps it is an exaggeration, but only a slight one I fear, to say that often we don't know with whom to talk, when to talk to them, or even what to talk about. Without reading researchers acknowledging the importance of, and being intimately involved in, the development of reading education policy, it is likely that teacher and students will have to suffer through repetitions of our past mistakes.

These points are readily apparent to some researchers, who call for increased effort to sort out the legislative policy issues that face us. Their suggestions for needed research can be separated along paradigmatic lines in order to highlight the opportunities and constraints each offers our efforts to gain a better grasp of the development and consequences of reading education policy. More than just rules for the collection and analysis of data, educational paradigms provide different ways to think, see, feel, and act toward the world, offering researchers emotional and political attachments as well as technical advice (Tuthill & Ashton, 1983). By adopting a tripartite scheme for identifying educational research (Mosenthal, 1985; Popkewitz, 1984; Soltis, 1984), we can see how researchers working within the assumptions of different scientific traditions could choose to study different questions, to adopt different agendas for future research, and to set different criteria for productive policy research. My intention here is to give some indication of what we can and cannot expect from differing types of research.

Policy-Driven Research

Guthrie (1984, 1987) suggests that reading researchers use their expertise in conducting experiments and program evaluations to obtain empirically valid, straightforward solutions to the complex, practical problems facing reading programs (e.g., What is a successful reading program? How do we train teachers to deliver such a program? and so on). He labels this work *policy-driven research* (1987, p. 320) and argues that reading researchers can raise their status among policy makers as the primary source of the kinds of data necessary to develop informed policy. Relying heavily on the American Psychological Association's past efforts to render psychological research more practically relevant, Guthrie advises reading researchers to reevaluate vigorously the body of accepted knowledge now practiced in schools in order to promote methods that continue to receive research support and to eliminate methods that have been discredited by research, to disseminate their findings in clear language through popular media to allow policy makers greater access to them, and to take responsibility for drawing policy and instructional implications from their work in order to avoid controversy and to ensure that proper applications are made.

Both Wixson et al. (1987) and Mullin and Summers (1983) in their work, which I described in the first two sections of the chapter, are examples of policy-driven research. Wixson et al. relate the ongoing research project in Michigan to develop state-level reading policy, curricula, and competence tests based on the latest scientific evidence. Starting with a scheduled review of the state's definition of reading in 1983, which set the state's curricular goals and its procedures for testing student competence to the final field testing in 1988, Wixson et al. describe Michigan's broad-based efforts involving citizens, teachers, school administrators, state educational officials, and reading researchers to reeducate school personnel and policy makers alike in order to ensure that the best scientific findings are institutionalized in state reading policy. Mullin and

Summers offer another manner of reevaluating current school practices through the cost-benefit analysis of federal policy concerning compensatory education program for the poor. Not only is their report clear, data based, and directed toward a major issue in reading education, but they conclude unequivocally that compensatory programs are not worth the money spent on them.

Guthrie's suggestions and these two examples follow a common set of paradigmatic assumptions that were adapted from physical sciences. That is, they seek lawlike generalizations about reading and reading instruction that are judged to be value and context free, that are predicated on the analytic identification of important components of the complex phenomenon being studied, and that are best explained through the language of mathematics and deductive reasoning (Mosenthal, 1985, labels this type of research a *literal approach*; Popkewitz, 1984, calls it *empirical/analytic science*; and Soltis, 1984, calls it *empirical inquiry*). These assumptions and beliefs about social reality direct advocates of policy-driven research toward the study of questions about the consequences of reading education policy. More precisely, policy-driven researchers are best equipped to develop apparatuses to measure the effects of specific, well-defined policies and practices and to analyze those effects statistically. Although they might find interesting questions concerning how policy is formed, who forms it, and what it means in political and social terms, these researchers are unlikely to find these types of questions high priorities because such questions are considered to be value laden, they do not lend themselves easily to measurement and deductive logic, and they are process rather than product oriented.

Policy Communications Research

Mitchell and Green (1986) suggest that reading researchers cannot answer many questions about reading education policy because "social science cannot provide 'answers' to problems which are more political in nature than educational" (p. 404). They contend that more productive research would focus on the negotiation aspects of policy making and implementation, particularly the differing frames of mind and expectations various groups of participants bring to the policy bargaining table. Such research would investigate how these participants make sense of their daily work and how the rules they use when conducting that work independently can construct barriers to open and effective communications during reading education policy discussions. For example, they suggest that researchers are most concerned with the quality of their research, its impact on colleagues, and its contribution to theory building; while policy makers and practitioners, by the nature of their immediate accountability to the public, must be most concerned with the effectiveness and efficiency of policy deliberations, implementations, and results. A "bad fit" between perspectives means that reading researchers are considered too tentative and somewhat irrelevant to the framing of policy concerning practical matters.

According to Mitchell and Green, the most immediate need for policy communications research is the identification of patterns of behavior and the symbols used among groups who typically participate in reading education policy development at the federal, state, and local level. Such identification is necessary in order to educate "information brokers" (p. 400), who understand the frames of mind, the expectations, and the language of all sides in the debate and can act as facilitators if negotiations break down. Although very little of this type of research has been initiated to date, perhaps the closest example is Wallat's (1987) attempt to explain Florida policy makers' intentions in the recent spate of literacy legislation (e.g., the Education Accountability Act of 1978, the Raise Achievement in Secondary Education law, and the Gordon Writing Act).

Moreover, she tries to convince reading researchers that they still have a role to play in local interpretation of these policies by analyzing the language of the bills—for example, "As new research is conducted, particularly in areas and at levels where present research is fragile, it is expected that the Florida Performance Measurement System will be regularly updated to reflect the best professional knowledge" (Florida Coalition for the Measurement of Performance Measurement System, 1983, p. iii).

The paradigmatic assumptions that Mitchell and Green's suggestions and Wallat's research follow are quite different from those of policy-driven research. Relying on inductive logic and naturalistic research methods to conduct their investigations of entire policy events, policy communications researchers believe that the social world differs from the physical world in that it is constructed through human intentions and negotiations that result in social norms and rules for acceptable behavior in specific contexts. Although inclined to examine the intersubjective meanings of policy development and implementation, policy communication researchers still seek objectivity and value-free conclusions during their studies (Mosenthal, 1985, and Soltis, 1984, call this paradigm *interpretive inquiry*; and Popkewitz, 1984, labels it *symbolic science*). Because of these assumptions, policy communications researchers are more likely to address the process questions concerning reading education policy. For example, they might be most successful in identifying who are the successful agents in policy development, why their communications skills were effective, and what their success means to teachers and students on a daily basis after the policy has been implemented.

Critical Policy Research

Apple (1986) maintains that current educational policy and recent proposals for the reform of schools must be understood as historical and political phenomena, which should be considered microcosms of the current social relations in Western society. Using the political economy of textbook production and use as his example, Apple implies that reading education policies are unduly influenced by unequal class, gender, and race relations; by the state's need to legitimize itself through its public institutions; and by business and industrial interests. The result is unequal and unjust distribution of policy benefits. However, because these policies are based on social relations of the past, the inequalities of participation and benefits often appear appropriate, benign, or "just the way it is" to current participants. That is, the subordinate groups come to accept the dominant groups' definitions and rules of behavior as the natural way of conducting policy development and implementation. Apple suggests that the task facing critical researchers is to combine ethics, morality, politics, and science in order to demonstrate clearly who benefits from current policy, how they work to maintain their privilege while appearing to promote change, and what the de facto disenfranchised should and can do about the injustice. Rejecting what he considers to be the false guise of value-free research expected in the other paradigms, Apple argues that, above all, critical policy researchers should be advocates and activists for teachers' and students' rights to control their work during reading lessons.

The socialist position in each of the extended discussions offered earlier can serve as example of critical policy research. Kozol (1985) attempts to explain how federal literacy policies condemn many poor Americans to a life of illiteracy that ensures the perpetuation of their current social class status. Rome (1986) outlines how reading competency tests and other standardized tests are used to structure inequality in schools and later life by directing a disproportionate number of lower-class students into ineffective remedial and vocational programs. Finally, the CIBC (1976) presents an empirically based argument that the selection policies for children's books posed by conservatives (more pro-Christian, pro-American and fewer antifamily, humanistic books) and by liberals (selection based solely on literary merit) leaves racist, sexist, and classist stories on school library shelves, and tells minority, female, and poor students that their lives are not valued at school. In each case, the researchers combine a language of hope through proposals for changed based on the collective efforts of concerned teachers and affected groups with their language of critique.

In a way, the assumptions of critical policy research begin where those of policy communications research end. Although critical researchers agree that social reality is constructed, they believe that the negotiations of that social reality are not conducted among equals because social, economic, and political circumstances have given certain segments of society license to assert greater influence over the outcomes (Popkewitz, 1984, and Soltis, 1984, call this *critical science*; Mosenthal, 1985, labels it an *evaluative approach*). In their attempts to identify how this imbalance of power exerts itself in specific situations, critical policy researchers use history to access the past policy negotiations and social relations that set the parameters for the current negotiations; they employ survey and statistical analyses to gather information about how the larger social structure affects all reading policies; and they utilize naturalistic methods to understand how both the powerful and the powerless cope with policy negotiations and the consequent situations. This sense of injustice and the advocacy position in favor of teachers and students leads critical policy researchers to select questions that illuminate the power relations of reading policy and programs (e.g., How influential are educational publishers on state and local policy decisions? What are the influences of philanthropic foundations on reading research and programs?) and that can expose the contradictions in reading education policy as opportunities for change (e.g., What does one curriculum and evaluation structure for a state mean for lower-class and minority students? Why do anachronistic policies persist?).

SUMMARY

Each of these paradigms points reading researchers in a different direction in their quest to better understand reading education policy. Policy-driven research asks reading researchers to find the answers to the questions current policy makers pose in order to become recognized as the primary source of valued information. Policy communications research directs reading researchers to examine the socially constructed rules of language and behavior of the various groups participating in reading education policy development and implementation in order to ensure that reading researchers are heard in the process. Critical policy research leads reading researchers to look dialectically at current policies and decide what they offer and what they deny us. Each perspective offers a partial explanation of the current state of reading education policy. Although the positions may seem complementary at the topic level, a synthesis to achieve a broader perspective may be difficult to form. First, they are based on widely different assumptions about reality and on conflicting criteria for productive research. Second, the political beliefs of advocates of each position may mediate against even transparadigmatic reading, let alone joint research efforts.

I have attempted to make three points in this chapter. First, educational policy in general and reading education policy in particular are political matters from conception to implementation and maintenance, which suggests that there is much to be gained from including systematic political analyses in reading education policy studies. Second, the consideration of reading education policy—from research reports to essays—is also a political matter, relying on the same sets of assumptions about human nature, social organization, and civic responsibility as those who write about policy issues for other social institutions. Finally, too little attention is devoted to reading education policy, given the importance of reading in schooling and society and the importance of policy issues on the organization and process of reading instruction in U.S. schools

REFERENCES

Allington, R. (1983). The reading instruction provided readers of differing reading abilities. *Elementary School Journal, 83,* 548–559.

Allington, R. (1986). Policy constraints and effective compensatory reading instruction: A review. In J. Hoffman (Ed.), *Effective teaching of reading: Research and practice* (pp. 261–289). Newark, DE: International Reading Association.

American Library Association. (1939). Library's Bill of Rights. *Library Association's Bulletin, 33,* 60–61.

American Library Association. (1983). *Censorship litigation and the schools.* Chicago: Author.

Anderson, R., Hiebert, E., Scott, J., & Wilkinson, I. (1985). *Becoming a nation of readers.* Washington, DC: National Institute for Education.

Anrig, G. (1986). Teacher education and teacher testing: The rush to mandate. *Phi Delta Kappan, 67,* 447–451.

Apple, M. (1982). *Education and power.* Boston: Routledge & Kegan Paul.

Apple, M. (1986). *Teachers and texts: A political economy of class and gender relations in education.* Boston: Routledge & Kegan Paul.

Arnove, R. (1982). Foundation and the transfer of knowledge. In R. Arnove (Ed.), *Philanthropy and cultural imperialism* (pp. 305–330). Bloomington: Indiana University Press.

Aronowitz, S., & Giroux, H. (1959). *Education under siege: The conservative, liberal, and radical debate over schooling.* South Hadley, MA: Bergin & Garvey.

Austin, M., & Morrison, C. (1963). *The first R.* New York: Wiley.

Barton, A., & Wilder, D. (1964). Research and practice in the teaching of reading. In M. Miles (Ed.), *Innovations in education* (pp. 361–398). New York: Teachers College Press.

Bastian, A., Fruchter, N., Gitkill, M., Greer, C., & Haskins, K. (1985). *Choosing equality: The case for democratic schooling.* Philadelphia: Temple University Press.

Bell, T. (1986). Education policy development in the Reagan administration. *Phi Delta Kappan, 67,* 487–493.

Bennett, W. (1986). *First lessons: A report on elementary education in America.* Washington, DC: U.S. Department of Education.

Bond, G., & Dykstra, R. (1967). The cooperative research program in first-grade reading instruction. *Reading Research Quarterly, 2,* 5–142.

Bowler, M. (1978). Textbook publishers try to please all, but first they woo the heart of Texas. *Reading Teacher, 31,* 514–518.

Bracey, G. (1987). Measurement-driven instruction: Catchy phrase, dangerous practice. *Phi Delta Kappan, 68,* 683–686.

Bryson, J., & Delty, E. (1982). *The legal aspects of censorship of public school library and instructional materials.* Charlottesville, VA: Michie.

Buss, D. (1982). The Ford Foundation in public education: Emerging patterns. In R. Arnove (Ed.), *Philanthropy and cultural imperialism* (pp. 31–360). Bloomington: Indiana University Press.

Calfee, R., & Drum, P. (Eds.). (1979). *Teaching reading in compensatory classes.* Newark, DE: International Reading Association.

California Department of Public Instruction. (1987). *English language arts model curriculum guide (for kindergarten through grade eight).* Sacramento: Author.

Carnegie Foundation. (1986). *A nation prepared: Teachers for the 21st century.* New York: Author.

Chall, J. (1967). *Learning to read: The great debate.* New York: McGraw-Hill.

Clark, D., & Astuto, T. (1986). The significance and permanence of changes in federal educational policy. *Educational Researcher, 15,* 4–13.

Cohen, S. (1974). *A history of colonial education, 1607–1776.* New York: Wiley.

Colvard, R. (1964). The college and the Arkansas Purchase controversy. In M. Miles (Ed.), *Innovation in education* (pp. 117–156). New York: Teachers College Press.

Committee for Economic Development. (1985). *Investing in our children.* Washington, DC: American Enterprise Institutes.

Council on Interracial Books for Children. (1976). *Human (and antihuman) values in children's books.* New York: Author.

Council on Interracial Books for Children. (1979). Textbooks: A social responsibility. *Publishers Weekly, 216,* 43–44.

Cremin, L. (1980). *American education: The colonial experience.* New York: Harper & Row.

Cruse, K. (1985). Test scores rise in Texas. *Phi Delta Kappan, 66,* 629–631.

Cuban, L. (1983). Corporate involvement in the public school: A practitioner-academic's perspective. *Teachers College Record*, 85, 183–203.

Cuban, L. (1984). *How teachers taught, 1890–1980*. New York: Longman.

Cuban, L. (1986). Persistent instruction: Another look at constituency in the classroom. *Phi Delta Kappan, 68*, 7–11.

Cubberly, E. (1906). *The certification of teachers*. The fifth yearbook of the National Society for the Scientific Study of Education, Part II. Chicago: University of Chicago Press.

Cubberly, E. (1934). *Public education in the United States*. Boston: Houghton Mifflin.

Design for Change. (1985). *Caught in the web*. Chicago: Author.

Design for Change. (1985). *The bottom line*. Chicago: Author.

Donaldson, K. (1981). Shoddy and pernicious books and youthful parity: Literacy and moral censorship, then and now. *Library Quarterly*, 51, 4–19.

Doyle, D., & Levine, M. (1985). Business and the public schools: Observations on the policy statement of the committee for economic development. *Phi Delta Kappan*, 67, 113–118.

Dykstra, R. (1968). Summary of the second-grade phase of the cooperative research program in primary reading instruction. *Reading Research Quarterly*, 4, 49–70.

Educational Products Information Exchange. (1977). *Report on a national survey of the nature and the quality of instructional materials most used by teachers and learners* (Tech. Rep. No. 76). New York: EPIE Institute.

Farr, R., Tulley, M., & Powell, D. (1987). The evaluation and selection of basal readers. *Elementary School Journal*, 87, 267–281.

Finn, C., Jr. (1982). A call for quality education. *American Education, 18*, 31–36.

Florida Coalition for the Development of a Performance Measurement System. (1983). *Domains: The knowledge base for the Florida performance measurement system*. Tallahassee FL: Office of Teacher Education, Certification, and Inservice Staff Development.

Follett, R. (1985). The school textbook adoption process. *Book Research Quarterly, 1*, 19–23.

Fruchter, N., Silvestri, K., & Green, H. (1985). Public policy and public schools: A training program for parents. *Urban Education, 20*, 199–203.

Gabler, M., & Gabler, N. (1985). *What are they teaching our children?* Wheaton, IL: Victor.

Geller, E. (1984). *Forbidden books in American public libraries, 1876–1939*. Westport, CT: Greenwood.

Glass, G. (1987). What works: Politics and research. *Educational Researcher, 16*, 5–10.

Glass, G. & Smith, N. (1977). *Pull out in compensatory education*. Washington, DC: Department of Health, Education, and Welfare.

Gray, W. S., & Monroe, R. (1929). *The reading interests and habits of adults*. New York: Macmillan.

Guthrie, J. (1984). Policy studies. *Journal of Reading, 27*, 670–672.

Guthrie, J. (1987). Policy development in reading education. In D. Bloome (Ed.), *Literacy and schooling* (pp. 310–324). Norwood, NJ: Ablex.

Holmes Group Executive Board. (1986). *Tomorrow's teachers*. East Lansing, MI: Holmes Group.

Hook, J. N. (1979). *A long way together*. Urbana, IL: National Council of Teachers of English.

House, E. (1978). Evaluations as scientific management in U.S. school reform. *Comparative Educational Review, 22*, 388–401.

Hunter, M. (1982). *Mastery teaching*. Los Angeles: TIP Publications.

Jaeger, R., & Tittle, C. (Eds.). (1980). *Minimum competency achievement testing: Motives, models, measures, and consequences*. Berkeley, CA: McCutchan.

Jefferson, T. (1893). A bill for the more general diffusion of knowledge. In P. Ford (Ed.), *The writings of Thomas Jefferson* (p. 221). New York: Putnam.

Jerrolds, B. (1977). *Reading reflections: The history of the International Reading Association*. Newark, DE: International Reading Association.

Jessup, D. K. (1985). *Teachers, unions, and change: A comparative study*. New York: Praeger.

Johnson, S. M. (1984). *Teacher unions in schools*. Philadelphia: Temple University Press.

Johnson, S. M., & Nelson, N. (1987). Teaching reform in an active voice. *Phi Delta Kappan, 68*, 591–598.

Jung, R., & Kirst, M. (1986). Beyond mutual adaption, into the bully pulpit: Recent research on the federal role in education. *Educational Administration Quarterly, 22*, 80–109.

Kaestle, C., & Smith, M. (1982). The federal role in elementary and secondary education, 1940–1980. *Harvard Educational Review, 52*, 384–408.

Katznelson, I., & Weir, M. (1985). *Schooling for all*. New York: Basic Books.

Keppel, F. (1966). *The necessary revolution in American education*. New York: Harper & Row.

Killian, M. (1984). Local control—the vanishing myth in Texas. *Phi Delta Kappan, 66*, 192–195.

Klein, K. (1984). Minimum competency testing: Shaping and reflecting curricula. *Phi Delta Kappan, 65*, 565–567.

Kozol, J. (1985). *Illiterate America*. New York: Anchor/Doubleday.

Lannie, V. (1974). *Henry Barnard: American educator*. New York: Teachers College Press.

Levine, D., & Associates. (1985). *Improving student achievement through mastery learning*. San Francisco: Jossey-Bass.

Levine, M. (Ed.). (1986a). *The private sector in the public school*. Washington, DC: American Enterprise Institute.

Levine, M. (1986b). Business and the public schools. *Educational Leadership, 43,* 47–48.
McLaughlin, M. (1975). *Evaluation and reform.* Cambridge, MA: Ballinger.
Marshall, C., Mitchell, D., & Wirt, F. (1985). Influence, power, and policy making. *Peabody Journal of Education, 62,* 61–89.
Minter, T. (1982). The importance of the federal role in improving educational practice: Lessons from a big-city school system. *Harvard Educational Review, 52,* 500–513.
Mitchell, B., & Green, J. (1986). Of searchers, solons, and soldiers: How do educational research, policy, and practice relate. In J. Niles & R. Lalik (Eds.), *Solving problems in literacy* (pp. 395–405). Rochester, NY: National Reading Conference.
Mosenthal, P. (1985). Defining progress in educational research. *Educational Researcher, 14,* 3–9.
Mullin, S., & Summers, A. (1983). Is more better: The effectiveness of spending on compensatory education. *Phi Delta Kappan, 64,* 339–347.
Muther, C. (1985). What every textbook evaluator should know. *Educational Leadership, 42,* 4–8.
National Council for Accreditation of Teacher Education. (1985). *Redesign.* Washington, DC: Author.
National Governers' Association. (1986). *Time for results: The Governors' 1991 Report on Education.* Washington, DC: Author.
Oboler, E. (1980). *Defending intellectual freedom: The library and the censor.* New York: Wilson.
Odden, A., & Anderson, B. (1986). How successful state education improvement programs work. *Phi Delta Kappan, 67,* 582–585.
Odden, A., & Odden, E. (1984). Education reform, school improvement, and state policy. *Educational Leadership, 42,* 13–19.
Piasecki, F. (1982). *Norma and Mel Gabler: The development and causes of their involvement concerning the curricular appropriateness of school textbook context.* An unpublished doctoral dissertation, North Texas State University, Denton, TX.
Popham, W. J. (1985). Measurement-driven instruction. *Phi Delta Kappan, 66,* 628–634.
Popham, W. J. (1987). The merits of measurement-driven instruction. *Phi Delta Kappan, 68,* 679-682.
Popkewitz, T. (1984). *Paradigm and ideology in educational research.* Philadelphia: Falmer.
Rivlin, A., & Timpane, P. M. (Eds.). (1975). *Planned variation in education: Should we give up or try harder?* Washington, DC: Brookings Institution.
Robinson, R., & Good, T. (1987). *Becoming an effective reading teacher.* New York: Harper & Row.
Rogers, V., Talbot, C., & Cosgrove, E. (1984). Excellence: Some lessons from America's best run companies. *Educational Leadership, 41,* 39–41.
Rome, S. (1986). Introduction to the standardization issue. *Radical Teacher, 31,* 1–4.
Samidifer, P. (1985). Success in South Carolina. *Phi Delta Kappan, 66,* 632–633.
Schon, D. (1983). *The reflective practitioner.* San Francisco: Jossey-Bass.
Shannon, P. (1985). Reading instruction and social class. *Language Arts, 62,* 604–612.
Shannon, P. (1988). *Broken promises: Reading instruction in twentieth-century America.* South Hadley, MA: Bergin & Garvey.
Soltis, J. (1984). On the nature of educational research. *Educational Researcher, 18,* 5–10.
Spiro, R. (1987). *A researcher looks at the report card on basal readers.* A paper presented at the 1987 meeting of the National Council of Teachers of English, Los Angeles.
Squires, J. (1985). Textbooks to the forefront. *Book Research Quarterly, 1,* 12–18.
Thomas, G. (1983). *Book burning.* Westchester, IL: Crossways.
Tuthill, D., & Ashton, P. (1983). Improving educational research through the development of educational paradigms. *Educational Researcher, 12,* 6–14.
U.S. Department of Education. (1986). *What works: Research about teaching and learning.* Washington, DC: Author.
Wallat, C. (1987). Literacy, language, and schooling: State policy implications. In D. Bloome (Ed.) *Literacy and schooling* (pp. 291–309). Norwood, NJ: Ablex.
Wise, A. (1979). *Legislating learning.* Berkeley: University of California Press.
Wixson, K., Peters, C., Weber, E., & Roeber, E. (1987). New directions in statewide reading assessment. *Reading Teacher, 40,* 749–754.

Task and Format Variables in Reading Research

Section Editor: Michael L. Kamil

PART TWO

Task and Context
Variables in
Reading Research

8 NARRATIVE REPRESENTATION AND COMPREHENSION

Arthur Graesser, Jonathan M. Golding, and Debra L. Long

When people engage in conversations and interact socially, they frequently convey narratives of interesting experiences. These narratives refer to event sequences that either the speaker experienced, another person experienced, or a fictitious character would experience. Listeners want to know what happened (the plot) and why it is important (the point). Narratives are designed to satisfy a number of communicative objectives such as making a point, entertaining the listeners, griping, provoking an argument, or preventing embarrassing silences. In contrast, conversations are rarely sustained by definitions, comparison/contrasts, logical arguments, and other forms of expository discourse.

This chapter begins with a discussion of the special status of narrative in theories of discourse processing, language use, and literacy. Next, we attempt to define what narrative is, based on considerations from several different fields: cognitive psychology, artificial intelligence, computational linguistics, literary criticism, and anthropology. Finally, we discuss some major theories of narrative representation and comprehension in cognitive science. *Representation* has been at the center of recent theoretical debates in cognitive science, so it will receive primary billing throughout the chapter.

WHY IS NARRATIVE SPECIAL?

Narrative discourse has a special status in theories of discourse processing, language use, and literacy. Narrative discourse is easy to comprehend and to remember, compared to other discourse genres such as definition, description, exposition, and persuasion (Freedle & Hale, 1979; Graesser, 1981; Graesser & Riha, 1984; Spiro & Taylor, 1987). Whereas stories, folktales, and other types of narrative are read substantially more quickly than expository passages (e.g., encyclopedia articles), scores on recall tests and comprehension tests are substantially higher for the narrative genre. Knowledge about story structure is acquired before school age (Stein & Glenn, 1979), whereas the structural compositions of other genres require formal training. These empirical facts obviously have important implications for cognitive theories and for educational practice.

What explains the privileged status of narrative discourse in the cognitive system? One obvious answer is that the content of narrative discourse is more familiar to the

This research was partially funded by a contract from the Office of Naval Research (N100014-88-K-0110) awarded to the first author.

reader than is the content associated with other genres. However, such a simple dimension (i.e., content familiarity) does not readily explain the advantages of the narrative genre. Graesser and Riha (1984) have reported a strong advantage of narrative over expository text, even when there is control over the familiarity of the topics covered in the text. Moreover, it is easy to comprehend very novel, if not bizarre, narrative texts. Some stories have characters who violate normal properties of animate beings (e.g., entities that are half man and half machine; monsters that are half reptile and half bird). Inanimate objects may acquire capabilities of animate sentient beings (e.g., trees that can walk and talk; brooms that can fly). An adult's normal conception of physical and social reality is sometimes uprooted in fantasy and science fiction. Of course, there are limits on what can pass for a comprehensible fictive world within a given culture (Jacquenod, 1987). It is difficult for a normal person in the United States to understand a passage that is organized around an exotic social system or principles of magic (Bartlett, 1932; Kintsch & Greene, 1978). Nevertheless, there is some validity to the claim that stories can be quite easy to comprehend and recall, yet also violate many dimensions of knowledge in a culture.

There is another sense of familiarity that may better explain why narrative is easy to comprehend and remember. Narrative discourse depicts *event sequences* that people in a culture directly enact or experience. The events involve both (a) intentional actions that people perform in the pursuit of goals and (b) events that unfold in the material world. Such event sequences constitute the core content of what children and adults experience in everyday life. According to Nelson (1986), the representation of everyday event sequences is the primary form of world knowledge in children. Nelson and others (Mandler, 1984; Piaget, 1952) claim that more abstract mental representations and systems of reasoning (e.g., taxonomic, causal, conditional, disjunctive) are derived from event knowledge. Assuming that event knowledge constitutes the primary foundation of knowledge in the cognitive system, it is not surprising that narrative discourse has substantial advantages over other genres.

Another advantage of narrative is that it is close to the heart of oral literacy, the language of the mother tongue. Differences between written and spoken language have recently been documented in substantial detail (Chafe, 1985; Chafe & Danielewicz, 1987; Horowitz & Samuels, 1987; Mazzie, 1987; Redeker, 1984; Tannen, 1985, 1988) and are briefly summarized below.

1. *Involvement.* In spoken language the speaker is involved face-to-face with an actual listener and perhaps an audience. Written language is depersonalized and detached from social-communicative interaction. The writer pitches the text for an abstract ideal reader.

2. *Context.* Spoken language is produced in a context that is shared by the particular speech participants, at a specific time and location. In contrast, the writer and reader of written text are "decontextualized."

3. *Explicitness.* Ideas tends to be explicit in written language. The writer assumes that there is a minimal level of shared knowledge between writer and reader so the content must be expressed by explicit linguistic elements. In spoken language, the speech participants have established more *mutual knowledge* (i.e., knowledge that speech participants assume that they share) because of the common context that they experience.

4. *Error and feedback.* Whereas written language is polished, speakers ordinarily have error-ridden performances with misfires, restarts, vague expressions, hedges, and repairs. Speech is fundamentally a cooperative venture that corrects the errors. The listener provides feedback to the speaker about the adequacy of

referring expressions, coherence, and mutual knowledge. The listener may even fill in what the speaker is trying to say.

5. *Integration.* Spoken language is fragmented, very often with sequences of ideas that are connected by "and." Written language integrates more idea units within a clause through the use of nominalizations, embedded constituents, prepositional phrases, adjectives, and other linguistic devices that encourage dense packaging of information. Consequently, the syntactic complexity of the discourse is higher in written than spoken language (although see Halliday, 1987, for a challenge to this generalization).

To some extent, many of the above differences between oral and written language may be attributed to the fact that the narrative genre is very prevalent in oral language. For example, Mazzie (1987) reported that discourse genre is much more important than modality (spoken versus written) and the sender/receiver relationship (individual real audience versus multiple imagined audience).

Narrative plays a critical role in several skills associated with cognitive development, language acquisition, reading, and writing (Fitzgerald & Teasley, 1983, 1986; Galda, 1984; Horowitz & Samuels, 1987; Lehr, 1987; Mandler, 1984; Nelson, 1986; Olson, 1985; Sachs, Goldman & Chaille, 1984; Singer & Donlan, 1982; Wells, 1985; Winograd & Johnston, 1987). For example, a volume edited by Nelson (1986) documented many of the ways that cognitive development is critically dependent on event knowledge. Many children's narratives are fictitious event sequences that allow them to explore alternative possible worlds. This exploration ranges from children passively listening to stories to children enacting hypothetical scripts in dramatic play. Symbolic play requires mastery of a number of basic skills, including role taking, negotiating with partners, planning, and sequencing. Whether children enact narratives or simply comprehend stories, they achieve some independence from their immediate everyday surroundings and learn to decontextualize their cognitive processes. As a consequence, the children can (a) rely on mental representations instead of the immediate environment when they speak, (b) decenter from the present time, (c) formulate hypothetical and optional possibilities for events, and (d) abstract general features of events (French, 1986). Moreover, these central cognitive abilities are acquired in the context of play and enjoyable experiences.

Narrative discourse is a popular testbed for psychological investigations of inference generation. Compared to expository text, narrative discourse invites substantially more knowledge-based inferences (Graesser, 1981; Graesser & Clark, 1985). There is a higher density of mutual knowledge associated with narrative text, as we discussed earlier (Chafe, 1985; Tannen, 1988). The comprehender relies on this mutual knowledge to fill in the gaps between fragments of explicit code. This mutual knowledge is established by virtue of shared experiences among the participants in the communicative exchange (Clark & Marshall, 1981) or by world knowledge structures that are elicited by the text (Abelson & Black, 1986; Graesser & Clark, 1985; Schank & Abelson, 1977). The conceptual foundation of narrative rests on event sequences and experiences that once again are familiar to individuals in a culture, so there is a rich source of world knowledge for constructing meaning. In contrast, expository text is written to convey new information to readers. When expository prose is constructed, the writer attempts to be very explicit about concepts, ideas, and relationships between ideas; there is a reluctance to expect the reader to fill in the conceptual gaps. Indeed, there are many linguistic and psychological models of expository text comprehension that have few if any assumptions about inferences (Britton & Black, 1985; Kintsch & van Dijk, 1978; Meyer, 1985).

There has been some debate about *which* categories of inferences are generated when narrative text is comprehended (Beach & Brown, 1987; Graesser & Bower, 1990; Graesser & Clark, 1985; Uleman, in press). For example, comprehenders normally infer the goals and motives behind those actions performed by main characters in the plot (Graesser & Clark, 1985; Graesser & Nakamura, 1982; Morrow, Greenspan, & Bower, 1987; Seifert, Robertson, & Black, 1985; Yekovich & Walker, 1987). In contrast, ongoing states that enable events do not tend to be generated automatically during comprehension (Graesser, Haberlandt, & Koizumi, 1987; Seifert, Robinson, & Black, 1985). Comprehenders automatically generate inferences that are needed to establish coherence among the clauses at a particular point in the text; however, specific expectations about subsequent episodes (not yet read) do not tend to be automatically generated during comprehension (Duffy, 1986; Graesser & Clark, 1985; Potts, Keenan, & Golding, 1988; Singer & Ferreira, 1983). Available research has hardly resolved the question of which inferences are truly comprehension generated. Nevertheless, narrative text will probably constitute the primary genre for testing theories of inference generation.

Narrative has been studied much more extensively than the other discourse genres. Narrative has received considerable attention in cognitive psychology, education, discourse processing, and artificial intelligence, as this chapter will show. In addition to these fields, narrative has been extensively investigated in anthropology (Frazer, 1907–1915; Hansen, 1983; Lévi-Strauss, 1955; Propp, 1969), sociology (Goffman, 1974; Labov, 1972; Polanyi, 1985; Shiffrin, 1985), and literary criticism (Adams & Searle, 1986; Martin, 1986; Tompkins, 1980). For centuries, scholars have accumulated insights and wisdom about the components and properties of narrative. Clearly, there is a rich conceptual and theoretical foundation for investigations of narrative in cognitive science.

WHAT IS NARRATIVE?

Scholars have offered precise definitions of narrative, but there is no prevailing consensus among the fields and individuals within each field (Chatman, 1978; Foster-Harris, 1974; Frye, 1971; Martin, 1986). In psychology, there has been some debate over the necessary and sufficient features of storyhood (i.e., what makes discourse a story) and the features of an interesting story (de Beaugrande & Colby, 1979; Brewer & Lichtenstein, 1972; Brewer, 1985; Stein & Policastro, 1984). In the fields of literature and literary criticism, there has been a never-ending controversy over the proper category system for classifying narratives (e.g., myths, epics, legends, fables, folktales, short stories, novels, tragedy, comedy, irony, and so on). As with most natural concepts (and categories), it is worthwhile to identify the typical features and the prototypical exemplars of concepts that are inherently fuzzy. It is probably futile to postulate necessary and sufficient features of each concept, with sharp boundaries among concepts (Smith & Medin, 1981). Consequently, the goal of this section is to offer an eclectic, nontechnical, noncontroversial description of narrative.

Narratives are expressions of event-based experiences that (a) are either stored in memory or cognitively constructed, (b) are selected by the teller/writer to transmit to the audience/reader, and (c) are organized in knowledge structures that can be anticipated by the audience (for a similar definition, see Heath & Branscombe, 1986). This general definition embraces both actual and fictitious experiences. The definition emphasizes that narrative is embedded in a communicative interchange between speaker and listener, writer and reader, playwright and audience, or film creator and viewer. The definition discards unrelated event sequences which cannot be packaged into knowledge structures that are familiar to members of a culture. In addition to this general definition of narrative, narratives normally involve additional components and dimensions, which are presented below.

Characters.   *Characters* are normally animate beings that have goals and motives for performing actions. However, inanimate beings can serve as characters as long as they can have animate qualities, such as performing intentional actions or experiencing emotion. Through *characterization*, main characters may be elaborated with a rich configuration of goals, motives, traits, beliefs, attitudes, and emotions. Supporting characters have minimal characterization; they serve to flesh out the social world surrounding the main characters. The characterization of a main character is either distributed throughout the narrative or is concentrated at the point when the character is first introduced.

Temporal and spatial placements.   The event-based experience in a narrative occurs within a particular time period and spatial location (e.g., "Once upon a time in a far-off land . . ." or "last Friday at a McDonald's restaurant . . ."). This setting information normally is at the beginning of the narrative so the reader can construct a visual image of the spatial scenario and can identify the social norms associated with the situation.

Complications and major goals of main characters.   The *complication* is a problem or conflict that a main character encounters. The complication initiates a *major goal* to solve the problem or conflict. For example, the complication may consist of a disease that hits a small town; this initiates a main goal for a hero to cure the disease. In simple short narratives, a single complication and goal is presented at the beginning of the narrative, and the plot subsequently unfolds to resolve the complication. In long narratives, such as novels and films, there are multiple complications and goals, involving several characters throughout the narrative.

Plots and resolutions of complications.   The *plot* consists of a series of episodes that eventually resolve the complication. Interesting narratives have a number of barriers and challenges en route to the solution. The construction of the plot is quite tricky for a number of reasons. First, the plot configuration is constrained by several components that will be discussed shortly (e.g., affect, theme, the point of the narrative). Second, plots are layered structures. There may be complex embedded plans enacted by a single character; there may be complex social interactions with transfers of control between characters (Mandler, 1984; Ryan, 1986; Trabasso & van den Broek, 1985). Third, interesting plots normally have multiple characters, with each having a goal structure that influences other characters; the goals of characters may compete, clash, or mutually facilitate each other (Wilensky, 1983a). Fourth, plans get revised as the plot unfolds. It would appear to be a nontrivial feat to coordinate the goals, plans, emotions, and knowledge states of the various characters during plot construction. Fortunately, however, archetypal and culture-specific plot configurations are used repeatedly in any given culture.

Affect patterns.   One reason that narratives are told is to entertain the comprehender. Part of the entertainment is an entrapment of the comprehender's emotions and level of arousal. The plot structure plays a central role in manipulating *affective responses* such as surprise, suspense, or curiosity (Brewer & Lichtenstein, 1980; Brewer, 1985). Jokes and other forms of humorous text are carefully crafted to elicit salient emotional responses from the comprehender (Graesser, Long, & Mio, 1990; Long & Graesser, 1988). In many narratives, arousal continues to build as the plot unfolds, reaching a peak at the climax and quickly returning to a calm at the resolution phase. According to Foster-Harris (1974), the plot inverts, reverses, or twists the problem picture so that a new picture abruptly emerges; at the point of resolution, seemingly irreconcilable elements are reconciled, combined, and unified. These cognitive transformations have a direct impact on the comprehender's emotions and arousal levels (Mandler, 1976). Instead of segregating cognition and affect (or plot from the reader's emotional response), it is important to trace how the two systems are inextricably bound.

Points, morals, and themes.   Plot configurations are designed to make a *point.* There are many different kinds of points that a speaker/writer might convey in a communicative interchange. Some points consist of a moral, virtue, or value that is embraced in a culture: justice, equality, loyalty, honor, or honesty (Foster-Harris, 1974; Graesser, Millis, & Long, 1986). Some points uncover clever or interesting planning strategies that a main character implements to achieve a goal—for example, effective timing, perseverance, cooperation, and efficient resource management (Dyer, 1983; Lehnert, Dyer, Johnson, Yang, & Harley, 1983; Wilensky, 1983a). Other points are comments or gripes about a chaotic, uncontrollable, or absurd world (e.g., fate, luck, coincidence). Some points are universal whereas others are culture specific. Some points are very context specific—that is, poignantly relevant to a specific conversation among speech participants at a specific time and place. Folktales and written narratives tend to be at the decontextualized end of the continuum.

A literary narrative may have multiple points that address components of narrative other than plot (Martin, 1986). For example, the speaker/writer might want to comment on a character's beliefs, goals, or traits. The speaker/writer might comment on another author, on conventional uses of language, and on the process of communication itself. In a sense, the writer is engaging in multiple dialogues with multiple audiences (Bahktin, 1981) by implicitly or explicitly commenting on different components of narrative.

Points of view and perspectives.   It is important to distinguish between the experiential event structure and the discourse structure of a narrative. The *experiential event structure* consists of a series of events arranged in temporal order with respect to the real or imagined world. The *discourse structure* consists of the sequential order of event-statements in the narrative. The author has the freedom to omit, embellish, and rearrange events through the use of flashbacks, flashforwards, and embedded narratives. Films and experimental literature try out novel transformations of the experiential event sequence. Consequently, a family of different discourse structures can capture a single experiential event structure. Each discourse structure emphasizes a different truth or point by casting the narrative from a distinct perspective.

For purposes of illustrating some literary devices that manipulate point of view, consider written narratives. According to Prince (1980), the writer designs the text with a particular *narrator* (i.e., abstract person telling the story) and *narratee* (i.e., abstract person listening to the narrator); there essentially is a one-sided conversation between the narrator and the narratee. It is appropriate to consider the narrator as a separate entity from the writer. Also, the narratee is a separate entity from the real reader (i.e., the person holding the book), the virtual reader (i.e., the reader that the writer thinks he or she is writing for), and the ideal reader (i.e., one who understands the text perfectly). Consequently, there are at least three levels of conversation in most written narratives: (1) between writer and reader, (2) between narrator and narratee, and (3) between one character and another character.

Point of view may be manipulated by associating the narrator either with the writer, with a character, with both the writer and a character, or with neither. Given that there are many alternative combinations of point of view, only a few contrasts are provided here. Consider the following two renditions of a character named George who steals some diamonds.

1. George snuck quietly into the room and took the diamonds out of the safe.
2. I snuck quietly into the room and took the diamonds out of the safe.
3. "I snuck quietly into the room and took the diamonds out of the safe."

In rendition 1, the narrator is addressing the narratee and is referring to the character George in third person. In rendition 2, the narrator is taking the point of view of the character named George, so George is referred to in first person. In rendition 3, one character in the story is talking to another character in the story; whether the narrator is taking the point of view of George is entirely ambiguous.

There are other ways of manipulating point of view (Martin, 1986). The writer might associate the narratee with one of the characters (e.g., I saw you sneak into the room and steal the diamonds). The writer might associate the narrator with an animal (e.g., as in Harlan Ellison's *The Boy and His Dog*) or even an object (e.g., George came walking into the room, opened the door to my home, grabbed me, and slipped me into his pocket). A very important way of varying point of view is to manipulate access to the minds of characters. When the writer restricts his description to the overt actions of characters in third person, there is no direct access to what the characters are thinking. In contrast, when the narrator is associated with a character, there is normally unrestricted access to the thoughts of that character. There are still other ways of manipulating point of view. The writer can manipulate the time frame of the experience. The experience occurs either in the past (i.e., I/George snuck into the room), in the present (I sneak into the room/George sneaks into the room), or in yet other tenses (George had snuck into the room). The writer may manipulate an imaginary camera at different regions in the spatial setting as events in the narrative unfold (Black, Turner, & Bower, 1979). Normally the camera moves with the main character because the main character serves as the spatial and temporal reference point. However, other camera arrangements are possible, particularly in a culture where novels are targeted for screenplays.

Point of view is a comparatively complex component of narrative. It is currently inspiring lively debates in literature and the film industry. It should be noted that point of view is rarely declared explicitly by the writer. Instead, the reader infers the various perspectives on the basis of subtle linguistic features such as (a) the mood, voice, and tense of verbs; (b) type of pronouns and referring expressions; (c) quotation marks; and (d) deictic elements (Chatman, 1978; Martin, 1986; Morrow, Greenspan, & Bower, 1987).

Oral, written, and filmed narrative.   It is important to recognize the differences between these three media forms. For example, *oral narratives* include accounts, recounts, eventcasts, and stories in specific discourse contexts. Stories are fictitious whereas accounts, recounts, and eventcasts refer to actual experiences. Stories may be preserved through an oral tradition and perhaps be captured in writing (such as myths, folktales, and fables). Stories in the oral tradition have a simple "good form" composition compared to narratives that were originally created in writing or in film (Mandler, 1984; Propp, 1969).

Written narrative is comparatively complex in plot and in form. Indeed, writers often are in search of new inventions and new forms in order to challenge the prevailing conventions. For example, a Shakespearian plot may be displaced to a modern setting in a novel. Instead of having a rich, action-packed, adventurous plot (as in the 19th-century American novel), the novelist might construct a bland, unexciting plot along with a rich description of the mental experiences of a character (e.g., novels by Sartre). In a *parody*, the writer might mimic the style of another author in an effort to make fun of that author's art form; this technique involves *intertextuality*, the strategy of transporting patterns from other texts. The invention of a new plot configuration or a new form exposes new truths and represents life in all its diversity. Of course, the reader needs to master the appropriate literary skills in order to detect what otherwise would be subtle nuances.

Filmed narrative has a number of distinctive codes and formal devices at its disposal (Brewer, 1985; Cole & Keyssar, 1985). A brief visual scenario in a film can often convey what would require dozens of pages in a novel. However, a novel can provide a detailed description of a character's beliefs and conscious experiences, whereas it would be difficult to capture this material on film. At a film's disposal are facial expressions, overt actions, special camera effects, flashbacks, and verbal commentaries by the narrator. With all these features, however, film has inherent limitations on what it can convey about a character's mental world.

Fiction, nonfiction, and possible worlds.   There is an interesting paradox about novels. Novels are fiction, yet a distinguishing characteristic of novels is their truth to reality (Martin, 1986). Similarly, stories depict fictive worlds, yet the point of the story captures some truth about social values, morals, virtues, or planning strategies. There is always the question of where the truth resides in a particular narrative.

There obviously are constraints on the fictive worlds that entertain readers in a particular culture. A randomly configured world simply will not do the trick (Jacquenod, 1987). The comprehender must be able to infer the motives of characters and the causal relationships among events. The comprehender must be able to have some social-normative foundation for expectations about subsequent events. For example, in Western culture (a) a *departure* generates an expectation about a *return*, (b) a *promise* to fulfill a contract implies that the promiser intends to complete the *action*, (c) a *goal* results in an attempt to *achieve* the goal, and (d) ordering food in a restaurant generates the expectation that the customer will pay for the food. When fictive worlds are constructed, there clearly are constraints. One theoretical challenge is to identify the systematic regularities that explain the constraints. For example, the constraints may be explained to some extent by systems of modal logic (Dolezel, 1976; von Wright, 1971) such as *alethic logic* (involving necessity, possibility, and impossibility), *deontic logic* (permission, prohibition, obligation), *axiological logic* (goodness, badness, indifference), *epistemic logic* (knowledge, belief, ignorance), and the logic underlying *goal-oriented planning strategies*.

It should be obvious that there are many components, levels, dimensions, and perspectives of narrative. The cognitive representation of narrative is therefore expected to be a complex, multifaceted configuration of knowledge. The subsequent sections cover some theories of narrative representation that dissect one or more of these levels. The focus is primarily on the representational aspects of narrative because many of the research efforts and debates have centered on the problem of representation. Consequently, the concerns here will address (a) the units of code, (b) the composition and content of the units, (c) the structural relationships among units, (d) mappings between different levels of representation, and (e) cognitive procedures that operate on the representations in various behavioral tasks. In addition to specifying the representational foundations of each theory, we will present relevant empirical evidence. Consequently, the reader should acquire some idea of each theory's strengths, limitations, and inspirations for future research.

STORY GRAMMARS

Story grammars constitute the oldest theory of narrative representation in modern cognitive science and have guided most of the empirical research during the last decade. The story grammars developed in cognitive psychology (Mandler, 1984; Mandler & Johnson, 1977; Rumelhart, 1977; Stein & Glenn, 1979; Thorndyke, 1977) have roots in structuralism and formal linguistics (van Dijk, 1972; Lévi-Strauss, 1955). They provided the first powerful formalisms and principled methods of analyzing stories into meaningful parts. Aside from Kintsch and van Dijk's general psychological theory of text representation (van Dijk & Kintsch, 1983; Kintsch & van Dijk, 1978), the story grammars were the only game in cognitive psychology between 1974 and 1979. Remnants of the original story grammars continue to be alive and well today.

A *story grammar* is a formal device for capturing the important properties of a story schema. In this context, a *story schema* is a cognitive structure that guides the comprehension of a specific class of stories. The scope is intentionally limited to very simple "good form" stories in the oral tradition (i.e., myths, folktales, fables). These stories have (a) a single main protagonist who encounters a problem-solving situation, (b) a goal that the protagonist attempts to achieve, (c) a plot that unravels how the protagonist attempts to achieve the goal, and (d) an outcome regarding whether the goal was achieved. Members of a culture allegedly possess a story schema that guides comprehension of all texts within this scope. There are separate schemas for texts in other genres, registers, and subclasses of narratives (Grishman & Kittredge, 1987; Meyer, 1985).

The existing story grammars have a number of common formal components. For one, there is a set of rewrite rules that capture structural regularities. For example, the rewrite rules below are a subset of Mandler's most recent grammar (Mandler, 1987).

1. Story → Setting + Episode*
2. Episode → Beginning + Complex Reaction + Goal Path + Ending
3. Complex Reaction → Simple Reaction + Goal
4. Goal Path → Attempt + Outcome
5. Beginning → an event that initiates the Complex Reaction
6. Simple Reaction → an emotional or cognitive response
7. Goal → a state that a character wants to achieve
8. Attempt → an intentional action or plan of a character
9. Outcome → a consequence of the Attempt, specifying whether or not the goal is achieved
10. Ending → a reaction
11. Beginning → Episode*
12. Outcome → Episode*
13. Ending → Episode*
14. Setting → description of the characters, time, and location

(An asterisk means one or more instances of constituent.)

Rewrite rule 1 specifies the major constituents of a story: the Setting and one or more Episodes. In Thorndyke's (1977) grammar, the first rewrite rule indicates that a story contains four components (Setting + Theme + Plot + Resolution); this embellishment imposes more constraints on what constitutes a story.

Rewrite rules 2–4 specify the constituents of an Episode unit in Mandler's grammar. The node categories of Mandler's Episode unit are similar to, but not exactly the same as, those in the grammar of Stein and Glenn (1979):

Episode → Initiating Event + Internal Response
+ Attempt + Consequence + Reaction

Rules 5–10 and 14 specify what types of information can be assigned to the terminal node categories when text is interpreted. Clearly, there are semantic and conceptual constraints on the text information that can be assigned to the particular terminal node categories. For example, a Simple Reaction would involve an emotional or cognitive response (*the princess was frightened*) but not an intentional action (*the princess ran away*); an Attempt would involve an action but not an emotional or cognitive response. Listed below are some example text statements in a story that may be attached to the seven node categories:

> *Setting:* Once upon a time there was a lovely princess who lived in a castle near a forest.
> *Beginning:* One day the princess was walking in the woods and she encountered a large ugly dragon.
> *Simple Reaction:* The princess was startled and frightened.
> *Goal:* The princess wanted to escape from the dragon.
> *Attempt:* When she started to run away.
> *Outcome:* The dragon breathed fire in her path.
> •
> •
> •
> *Ending:* The princess was happy to be home again.

Rules 11–13 specify that one or more Episodes may be embedded in some of the node categories (Beginning, Outcome, Ending). In order to illustrate embedding, Figure 8.1 shows an abstract story structure that contains both outcome-embedded Episodes (i.e., Episode 3 is embedded in Episode 2, which in turn is embedded in Episode 1) and an ending-embedded Episode (i.e., Episode 4 is embedded in Episode 1). These rules of recursive embedding allow for some complex plot configurations. In stories with ending-embedded Episodes, the events of one Episode lead to a character's formulating a new goal. For example, a hero might fail to achieve a goal in the first Episode, so the hero formulates a new goal in the embedded Episode. Alternatively, a new protagonist adopts a goal that the previous protagonist abandons. In stories with outcome-embedded Episodes, the first Episode is interrupted by the second embedded Episode and gets finished subsequently in the story. For example, the protagonist fails to achieve the goal (e.g., slay the dragon) after his first attempt, so he formulates a subgoal (e.g., get assistance from warriors) which is associated with the embedded Episode; the subgoal ultimately gets achieved and thereafter eventually leads to the successful achievement of the main goal.

Most story grammars specify conceptual relations between node categories within an Episode. In Mandler's grammar, for example, the Beginning node *causes* a Complex Reaction, which in turn *causes* a Goal Path. The Simple Reaction *causes* the Goal. In contrast, the Setting and Episode are simply related by *and*. In multiEpisode stories, successive Episodes are also connected by different types of conceptual relations. Sometimes Episodes are weakly related by *and then*, whereas others are related by *causes*.

When a story grammar is applied to a particular story, it assigns a hierarchical constituent structure (i.e., Figure 8.1) to the explicit information in the text. The explicit phrases, clauses, and statements in text are segmented and then assigned to the terminal node categories of the grammar. Interesting stories normally have multiple Episodes. The various Episodes are interrelated structurally according to the con-

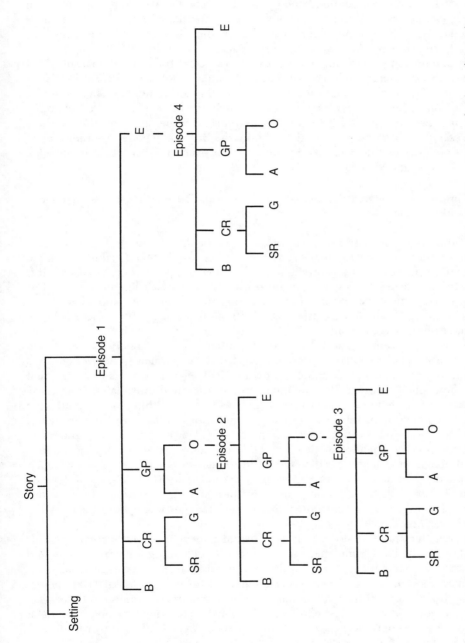

B = Beginning; CR = Complex Reaction; SR = Simple Reaction; G = Goal; GP = Goal Path; A = Attempt; O = Outcome; E = Ending.

FIGURE 8.1 An example story structure that would be generated by Mandler's (1987) story grammar.

straints of the grammar. a story is said to be *parsed* if the explicit text can be assigned to the grammatical categories and a single tree structure interrelates all of the explicit text. One computational test of a story grammar is whether it can assign a tree structure to every story that should be accommodated by the story schema. The grammar fails when no structure can be assigned to a perfectly good story that falls within the scope of the story schema. A second computational test of a grammar is whether "nonstories" are appropriately rejected by the story grammar (Black & Wilensky, 1979).

Story grammars become more complex when there are transformational rules that delete, move, and change node constituents (Mandler & Johnson, 1977). The most common types of transformational rules delete nodes that are redundant. For example, Simple Reaction nodes (*princess is frightened*) can often be inferred from the Beginning node (*the princess encountered a dragon*). Sometimes even the main goal (*the princess wanted to escape the dragon*) can be inferred from the Beginning node. Another type of transformation changes the order of constituents. For example, consider the following rendition of the example story.

> . . . the princess encountered a dragon and was frightened. The princess ran away in order to escape the dragon.

In this rendition the Goal (*escape the dragon*) is articulated after the Attempt (*the princess ran away*), yet the grammar's rewrite rules declare that the Goal is articulated before the Attempt. Specific transformational rules allow this permutation to occur. It is important to emphasize, however, that there usually are surface linguistic characteristics which signal the reader that there is a transformation (e.g., the *in order to* connective, a change in the tense of the verb). Without these linguistic surface cues, the reader would often become confused.

Now that we have introduced the key assumptions of story grammars, we should discuss some aspects of narrative representation that story grammars are not equipped to explain. Story grammars presuppose the existence of relevant word knowledge that underlies the explicit text, but the grammars are not designed to explain any of these representations. Consequently, story grammars have little or nothing to say about what makes a plot configuration interesting. They do not aspire to capture the conceptual constraints that are required in plots involving revenge, for example. Story grammars are not able to predict what knowledge-based inferences are generated during comprehension (although they might predict the node categories of inferences at particular points in a story). In addition, story grammars are not able to explain (a) systematic fluctuations in point of view, (b) how the point of a story gets computed, (c) reader affect, and (d) how story composition is influenced by the pragmatic aspects of the communicative interchange.

Although the scope of story grammars would appear to be rather narrow, this theoretical orientation has stimulated considerable research in cognitive psychology and education. Story grammars generate predictions about patterns of passage recall, passage summarization, importance ratings of statements, clustering of passage statements, and reading time. Some of the predictions have been confirmed, whereas others have seen little support. Of those predictions that have been confirmed by empirical data, there has been some controversy over whether the data can be explained by representations at other levels of code instead of the story grammars per se.

The most popular test of a story grammar assesses how well the grammar predicts the relative importance of text statements. The importance of a statement has been measured in three ways: (a) the mean importance rating for the statement, averaging over subjects; (b) the likelihood of recalling the statement in a recall task; and (c) the likelihood of including the statement in a summary of the story. We refer to these measures as *importance ratings, recall scores,* and *summarization scores,* respectively. Although there are some systematic differences among these measures (with respect to the predicted and obtained patterns of data), the similarities far outweigh the differences.

Early tests of the story grammars evaluated the hypothesis that superordinate information in a hierarchy is more important (or accessible from memory) than relatively subordinate information (Rumelhart, 1977; Thorndyke, 1977; Yekovich & Thorndyke, 1981). For example, the Episodes in Figure 8.1 should yield the following ordering in relative importance: Episode 1 > Episodes 2 and 4 > Episode 3. This relationship between importance and hierarchical level was supported in some stories, but the finding was ultimately not reliable. For example, the main goal in a passage is very superordinate in the hierarchy, yet it is often not included in a recall protocol because it can readily be inferred from other text statements (Mandler, 1984; Whaley, 1981). An Episode may be deeply embedded in a hierarchy but may involve a critical action that solves a very convoluted plot; nodes from such an Episode would have comparatively high importance and accessibility.

The hierarchy-importance relationship does consistently occur when (a) a single character enacts a recursively embedded plan (with multiple outcome-embedded Episodes) and (b) none of the Episodes has unpredictable or interesting Outcome nodes. Yet this particular hierarchy-importance relationship is also predicted by theories of *mundane planning* (Graesser, 1978, 1981; Lichtenstein & Brewer, 1980). For example, in a passage about washing dishes, main actions at the superordinate level (*wipe dishes, rinse dishes*) are more important than instrumental actions at the subordinate level (*walk to the sink, get a dishrag, turn on the water*). Moreover, the hierarchy-importance relationship is threatened when Outcomes involve interesting or unpredictable consequences that radically affect the plot (van den Broek & Trabasso, 1986). It would appear that the overarching principle is that of *inferability*. That is, a statement tends *not* to be important if it can be inferred readily from other text statements. In summary, the predicted hierarchy-importance relationship was a disappointment when the story grammars were first tested. There were too many disconfirmations in the data. The successes were not unique predictions of story grammars because other theories of narrative representation would explain them.

A second prediction of the story grammars consisted of the *node category effect*. Recall scores have exhibited the following pattern of means among the story grammar categories: Major Setting & Initiating Events & Consequences > Attempts > Internal Responses & Reactions (Mandler, 1984; Mandler & deForest, 1979; Mandler & Johnson, 1977; Stein & Glenn, 1979). This pattern appears to be rather consistent across cultures and age groups. Unfortunately, however, the node category effects may be attributable to content features of the statements. For example, the category effects disappear when content is controlled and recall is scored according to a gist criterion (Nezworski, Stein, & Trabasso, 1982). The node category effects either disappear or are radically attenuated when there is control over structural centrality (i.e., the number of other statements that a statement is directly connected to conceptually) and over content features that are described later (van den Broek & Trabasso, 1986; Omanson, 1982; Trabasso & van den Broek, 1985; Trabasso & Sperry, 1985). Once again, the inferability principle is quite relevant to the node category effect. Internal Responses and Reactions can often be inferred from the Attempts and Outcomes. For example, when one character attacks another character, the second character is normally frightened; when a difficult Goal is eventually satisfied by a successful Outcome, the obvious Consequent is that the character is happy. These inferences emerge from world knowledge that we have about motives, emotions, social action, and so on. Once again, there may be nothing particularly distinctive about the node category effect; it may fall out naturally from the inferability principle and our world knowledge.

According to the story grammars, there is a canonical order in which statements are articulated. This canonical order is directly derived from the order of node categories within a given Episode unit (acknowledging that causes precede effects) and the relationships between Episodes in Episode sequences. The fact that recall caters to the canonical order has been verified in a number of ways (Mandler, 1984; Mandler & Goodman, 1982; Stein & Glenn, 1979; Stein & Nezworski, 1978). First, the order in which statements are recalled follows the canonical order. Second, when the text departs from the canonical order, recall becomes difficult, even when deviations are disambiguated with explicit connectives (e.g., Y occurred *after* X) and other linguistic signalling devices. Third, textual deviations from the canonical order tend to be recalled in the proper canonical order. Fourth, inversions of statements within a story grammar node category tend to be more frequent than inversions of statements from different node categories. Fifth, reading time for story statements increases when there are deviations from canonical order. Once again, however, it should be acknowledged that these predictions are also generated by theories of planning and social action (Lichtenstein & Brewer, 1980; Omanson, 1982). Predictions about canonical order are not a unique attribute of story grammars.

Clustering analyses provide mixed support for the constituent structures generated by story grammars (Mandler, 1987; Pollard-Gott, McCloskey, & Todres, 1979). In these analyses subjects are presented the story statements in canonical order. The subjects mark locations in the text that correspond to conceptual boundaries. Mandler reported that subjects honored the terminal categories (i.e., they rarely put a mark between statements that were in the same node category). Moreover, when a hierarchical clustering analysis was applied to the subjects' judgments, there were systematic differences between different story structures (then-connected, outcome-embedded versus ending-embedded Episodes). However, there was not good agreement among subjects at intermediate levels of structure, particularly in the case of outcome-embedded stories. It should be noted that these tests were conducted on short passages with two Episodes. Additional research is needed on longer passages with more complex plot configurations.

Reading time data appear to support the existence of Episode constituents (Haberlandt, 1980; Mandler & Goodman, 1982). Reading times for sentences are longer at the beginning and at the end of Episodes, compared to sentences in the middle. At the end of an Episode boundary, the readers know the Episode is finished, so they wrap up the constituent with some sort of summary interpretation. At the beginning of the Episode, there is a topic shift that adds to reading time. Extra time is also needed to consolidate the previous Episode.

Virtually all of the predictions of the story grammars could be explained by content features that are outside the scope of story grammars. The content features would involve world knowledge about planning, motives, social action, and causality. However, this fact does not entirely undermine the utility of the story grammars. The units, constituents, and structures of story grammars seem to be at the crossroads of important structures and procedures in the cognitive system. Story grammars draw together dozens of interesting and disparate empirical trends in a single theory. All things being equal, the story grammars are an improvement over an alternative theory that focuses on world knowledge, unless the alternative theory is well grounded. To some extent, nevertheless, this grounding is supplied by the subsequent theories discussed in this section.

CAUSAL NETWORKS

This section discusses a causal network theory of narrative representation that was developed by Trabasso and his associates (van den Broek, 1988; van den Broek & Trabasso, 1986; Trabasso & van den Broek, 1985; Trabasso, van den Broek, & Lui, 1988; Trabasso, Secco, & van den Broek, 1983; Trabasso & Sperry, 1985). Trabasso's causal network theory adopts the node categories of the story grammars (or at least similar categories) but makes radically different assumptions about the structural organization of nodes and Episodes. Whereas the story grammars generate strictly hierarchical tree structures, Trabasso's narrative representations are network structures that substantially deviate from strict hierarchies. An important virtue of Trabasso's theory is that it explicitly identifies the logical and conceptual foundations for constructing each causal link in the structure. Therefore, the nodes in the structure are "wired" according to rigorous theoretical criteria.

Before discussing the key assumptions of Trabasso's causal network theory, a few words should be devoted to the scope of the theory. Whereas story grammars are confined to stories in the oral tradition that are organized around a single protagonist trying to solve a problem, Trabasso's theory can be applied to a much broader class of narratives. It is difficult to evaluate the exact scope of the narratives that Trabasso's theory can handle. Perhaps this question will be answered in subsequent studies. As with the story grammars, Trabasso's theory is designed to explain the organization of the *textbase*—that is, the explicit propositions and clauses in the text. Trabasso assumes that the construction of the textbase critically depends on background world knowledge (which he calls the "circumstances" and the "causal field") and that a situation model is continuously being updated during comprehension. However, the properties of world knowledge and the situation model are not explicated in his theory. The theory is also not designed to account for inference generation, story points, pragmatics, and reader affect.

Figure 8.2 shows an example causal network for a story with an outcome-embedding structure. Stories with outcome-embedded structures were investigated extensively by the researchers pursuing story grammars. The nodes (e.g., S11, E11, and so on) consist of statements. The statements are assigned to categories similar to those of the story grammars: Setting (S), Initiating Event (E), Reaction (R), Goal (G), Attempt

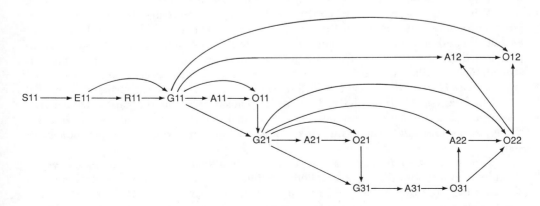

FIGURE 8.2   An outcome embedding structure in Trabasso's causal network theory.

(A), and Outcome (O). The subscripts refer to the level of embedding (the first digit) and the nth Episode of an Episode sequence within a given level (the second digit). Thus, G12 is the second goal of the first level (i.e., the most superordinate level), and G21 is the first goal of the second level. The main Episode in a story would contain the following nodes: S11, E11, R11, G11, A11, and O11. The structure produced by a story grammar would have two Episodes embedded within the Outcome node of the main Episode: [Episode 21 (G21, A21, and O21)] and [Episode 22 (A22 and O22)]. One Episode would be embedded within the Outcome node of Episode 21: [Episode 31 (G31, A31, and O31)]. Therefore, it is possible to translate a causal network into a story grammar structure whenever the narrative text can be accommodated by a story grammar. It is important to recognize that the causal network has a much more complex wiring than the elegant tree structures generated by story grammars.

The causal connection between a pair of nodes must satisfy a number of logical and conceptual constraints. There is a *temporal constraint* that captures the general law that the cause must precede the effect. The source node (without the arrowhead) occurs or exists prior to the end node (with the arrowhead). For example, E11 in figure 8.2 precedes R11 chronologically. There is a *necessity constraint* that establishes that the source node is necessary for the end node (e.g., E11 is necessary for R11). According to the necessity test, A is necessary for B if it passes the counterfactual test: If not A, then not B. Stated differently, if A is negated in the circumstances associated with the narrative, then B would not occur or exist. Finally, there is a *sufficiency constraint* when evaluating whether two nodes are causally linked. Node A is sufficient (in the circumstances) for node B in the sense that if A is put into the situation at that point in the narrative and events proceed in a normal fashion, then node B will occur.

In order to illustrate the temporal, necessity, and sufficiency constraints, consider the following two events in the context of a typical fairy tale about a dragon kidnapping a princess:

A.   The dragon grabbed the princess.
B.   The princess screamed.

We would argue that event A causes event B because it satisfies all three constraints. The princess screams after being grabbed by the dragon (i.e., A before B). If the dragon never grabbed the princess, the princess would not have screamed (i.e., A is necessary for B). If the dragon grabbed the princess in the context of a kidnapping, it would be natural for the princess to scream (i.e., A is sufficient for B).

When causal networks are constructed, the investigator first segments text into elementary statement nodes that depict either states or events. The second step is to evaluate whether each pair is causally connected. Thus, if there are N nodes in a passage, then $[N \times (N - 1)]/2$ judgments would be made. Third, a principle of *transitivity* permits sequencing in event chains. That is, if A causes B and B causes C and A causes C, then the "A causes C" link would be deleted from the structure because it can be inferred via transitivity. Fourth, the causal links may be categorized if the researcher so desires. For example, a "motivational link" would connect a goal and an action; a "psychological causation" link would connect an event with a psychological state.

One final point to make about Trabasso's model is that it makes some well-specified claims about the process of constructing the networks during comprehension. Trabasso has proposed a General Recursive Transition Network (GRTN), which specifies the alternative node categories which would be expected at each point *within* an Episode. For example, if Goal G is encountered in an Episode, the subsequent node in the text would either be an Attempt or an Outcome (but not a Setting, Initiating Event, or a Reaction). When a Reaction is encountered, then the subsequent node category would be a Goal.

Recursive transition networks have become a very popular formalism for sentence syntax in computational linguistics (Grishman, 1986). A major virtue of this formalism is that it provides a principled foundation for tracing expectations when sequential input gets interpreted. It is important to acknowledge three points about Trabasso's application of this formalism. First, the expectations that get generated are strictly at a node *category* level (S, E, R, G, A, versus O), not at a deep conceptual level. The network would not be able to expect, for example, that a king repays the hero after the hero saves the princess. Second, the principle of inferability ends up deleting some of the nodes without a loss of information. For example, Goals may be inferred from Attempts or Outcomes and Reactions may be inferred from Goals or Outcomes. These deletions are contingent on deep conceptual constraints rather than being applied automatically according to a syntactic rule system. As a consequence, Trabasso's GRTN may be difficult to test by comparing (a) sequences of node categories in the texts with (b) permissible node sequences according to the theory. Third, it is unclear how this GRTN will fare with narratives that lie outside the scope of simple narratives in the oral tradition. That is, will it accommodate irregular, transformed narratives that are characteristic of print and literature? Although the GRTN does face these limitations, it is a substantial improvement over the story grammars in specifying how structures get created during comprehension.

Trabasso's causal network theory has been tested by collecting data on the importance of text statements—that is, the importance ratings, recall scores, and summary scores (Goldman & Varnhagen, 1986; see above references with Trabasso). Three variables derived from the causal networks are able to predict statement importance: (1) node category, (2) number of causal links that radiate from a node, and (3) whether or not a node is on a "critical path." Regression analyses and multivariate analyses were used to segregate the independent contributions of these three variables. Although all three variables were not unique predictors in all passages, each of these variables was significant in at least some passages. The node category effect essentially confirms earlier tests of story grammars. The second variable is measured by simply counting the number of causal arcs that directly radiate to or from a given node. As the number of causal connections increases, statements are more important, as reflected in importance ratings, recall, and summarization (see also Graesser, 1978, 1981; Graesser & Clark, 1985). The third variable specifies whether or not a text statement lies on the narrative's critical path—that is, the main causal chain that extends from the beginning of the plot to the end of the plot. Nodes on the critical path tend to be important compared to "dead-end" nodes that extend from the critical path (see also Black & Bower, 1980; Omanson, 1982; Schank, 1975). Given that the above three variables predict the importance of statements in some but not all passages, an important next step for future research is to identify those types of passages and those conditions in which these variables are critical.

There is also some evidence that the causal networks play a predictive role in question-answering and question-asking tasks (Nicholas & Trabasso, 1980; Trabasso, van den Broek, & Lui, 1988). For example, when passage nodes are probed with why-questions, the answers include nodes on paths of causal antecedents (i.e., backward causal arcs). When comprehenders were asked to generate questions during comprehension, the categories of questions were predicted by constraints associated with the node categories. Once again, however, Trabasso's account of questioning predicts node categories but not node content. It does not penetrate the deeper levels of analysis that would account for particular inferences and variations of answers *within* node categories.

One undeveloped aspect of Trabasso's model addresses the order in which the nodes from a causal network get articulated. Presumably, output order can be derived systematically from these structures. For example, the output ordering would map directly onto the critical path, starting at the beginning and pursuing forward causal arcs to the end. How would the dead-end nodes be inserted into this main chronology? Do complications arise when there are loops and embedded Episodes? It would be useful to have a set of rules for producing nodes in the correct (chronological) order and to compare predictions of the causal network with predictions of other theories.

One future direction for this model is to expand its scope from representing the explicit textbase to representing world knowledge and the situation model (i.e., the mental representation of the situation, experience, world, or state of affairs characterized by the text). Certainly, causality is a key component of the world knowledge and the situation model. There is no reason to confine Trabasso's illuminating analysis of causality to the textbase.

CONCEPTUAL GRAPH STRUCTURES

Graesser has developed and tested a theory of narrative comprehension that represents the knowledge in the form of a *conceptual graph structure* (Graesser, 1981; Graesser & Clark, 1985; Graesser, Robertson, & Anderson, 1981; Graesser, Robertson, Lovelace, & Swinehart, 1980). The form of the conceptual graph structures is similar to Trabasso's causal networks, except that the node categories are different and there is an expanded set of arc categories. Differences between these two representational systems in part reflect the fact that Graesser attempted to incorporate many of the relations in Schank's conceptual dependency theory (Schank, 1975; Schank & Abelson, 1977). Another source of the difference is that Graesser attempted to account for passages in the expository genre (Graesser & Goodman, 1984) in addition to narrative text. Aside from these differences at the representational level, there are four salient characteristics of Graesser's theory of comprehension.

1. The theory assumes that a large number of knowledge-based inferences are generated during narrative comprehension and are incorporated in the passage representation. Therefore, the distinction between an explicit textbase and a situation model is considerably less discrete, if nonexistent.
2. The model offers a detailed explanation of the interaction between world knowledge and the construction of the passage representation. Relevant world knowledge structures are identified as being in working memory at particular points in the text. For example, the text statement *the princess cried* would activate knowledge structures for PRINCESS and CRYING. Graesser has mapped out the content and structure of these world knowledge structures (called GKSs, which stands for *generic knowledge structure*). The theory specifies how the GKSs are integrated with the explicit text as text statements are incrementally interpreted.
3. The theory explains what information in the active GKSs are passed down to the passage structure during comprehension. Whereas hundreds of "statement nodes" are activated in the GKSs that occupy working memory, there is a convergence on only a small subset (i.e., the passage inferences) when a particular text statement is comprehended. The tricky phenomenon to explain is how this convergence occurs.
4. The model accounts for the process of constructing passage representations as statements are incrementally interpreted during comprehension.

Although Graesser's theory attempts to account for world knowledge, inferences, and the construction of passage representations during comprehension, it does not account for pragmatics, story points, and reader affect.

Figure 8.3 shows an example conceptual graph structure that depicts an excerpt from a story about a dragon kidnapping three daughters of a czar. The nodes in rectangles (2, 3, 7, 8, 20) correspond to explicit text statements, whereas the nodes in ovals are knowledge-based inferences. According to Graesser and Clark (1985), the ratio of inference nodes per explicit node is approximately four to one in narrative text (but less than two to one in expository text). Each statement node is a proposition-like unit that is categorized as either a state, event, goal, or style specification (e.g., an event occurred *slowly*). An intentional action is not a primitive node category in this representation; instead, an action is an amalgamation of a goal node (e.g., node 7, *dragon wanted to kidnap the daughters*) and an event/state, which declares that the goal is achieved (node 8, *the dragon kidnapped the daughters*).

The arcs in Figure 8.3 specify how the nodes are conceptually related. There are nine arc categories in Graesser and Clark's (1985) representational system. Figure 8.3 contains six of the arc categories: Reason (R), Initiate (I), Outcome (O), Manner (M), Consequence (C), and Implies (Im). The arcs are directed (forward versus backward) in a nonarbitrary fashion. Graesser has explicitly articulated the semantic and conceptual constraints that must be satisfied in order to link two nodes with an arc in a particular category and direction. For example, Event 2 (*the daughters forgot the time*) is linked to Event 3 (*the daughters stayed too long*) by a forward Consequence arc; in order for this directed arc to be constructed, Event 2 must temporally precede Event 3 and must bear some causal relationship with Event 3. Indeed, it would pass Trabasso's test of causality. As yet another example, consider the forward Reason arc that relates Goal 7 (*dragon kidnap daughters*) with Goal 10 (*dragon kill daughters*). The construction of this arc must satisfy some specific rules of composition. One constraint is that Reason arcs may relate only Goal nodes; linking an Event to a Goal via a Reason arc would violate the rules of composition. A second constraint is that the source Goal is conceptually subordinate to the end Goal. As a consequence, it makes sense to say the "the dragon kidnapped the daughters *in order to* kill them," but it does not make sense to say "the dragon killed the daughters in order to kidnap them." A third constraint is that the source node is achieved in time prior to the end node. As a consequence, kidnapping would precede killing, rather than vice versa. It is beyond the scope of this article to specify the rules of composition associated with each arc category. It suffices to say that Graesser and Clark (1985) have articulated these constraints in detail.

World knowledge is also represented in the form of conceptual graph structures. World knowledge is housed in a large set of generic knowledge structures (GKSs) and specific knowledge structures in the cognitive system. When a specific passage is comprehended, several GKSs are triggered through pattern recognition processes. For example, the following GKSs would be among the set of GKSs that would be activated in the context of Figure 8.3: KIDNAP, DRAGON, DAUGHTER, FOREST, FAIRY TALE, and TIME. Each of these GKSs consists of a conceptual graph structure, with the same format, node categories, and arcs as those for passage representations. According to Graesser and Clark (1985), a GKS is a very rich knowledge structure that contains dozens if not hundreds of nodes. The noun-arguments of statement nodes in a GKS are typically more abstract than those in a passage structure. For example, one Event node in the GKS for KIDNAP is *victim becomes frightened*. This node would be passed as an inference to the passage structure (Event 19, *daughters were frightened*). The noun-argument slot for *victim* in the GKS corresponds to the noun-argument slot *daughters* in the passage structure. By virtue of this "argument substitution," it is possible to identify

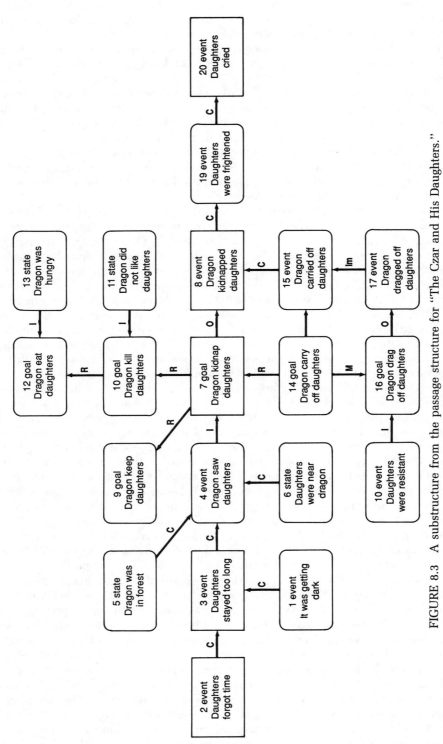

FIGURE 8.3   A substructure from the passage structure for "The Czar and His Daughters."

correspondences between nodes in the GKSs and nodes in the passage representations. Therefore, it is possible to map nodes and structures in the GKSs onto nodes and structures in passage representations. This permits detailed analyses of how the text and world knowledge get integrated during comprehension.

During the course of developing and testing this theory of comprehension, Graesser performed an extensive set of analyses on verbal protocols. These analyses mapped out empirically the content and structure of both the passage representations and the GKSs that were relevant to the passages. The method of collecting these verbal protocols will not be discussed here, other than to say that they involved very systematic means of questioning subjects. The upshot of these analyses was that very specific hypotheses about comprehension could be induced and/or tested by systematically inspecting these knowledge structures that were mapped out empirically.

Graesser traced how the passage representations dynamically evolved as passages were comprehended, statement by statement. That is, given that passage statements 1 to N are comprehended and that a temporary structure is created, how is this temporary structure modified when statement $N + 1$ is interpreted? What new inferences are generated and what old inferences are pruned out? Graesser discovered, for example, that structures are rarely reorganized during narrative comprehension; instead, erroneous nodes from the temporary structure get pruned and new nodes get appended. Graesser traced how each GKS in working memory furnishes inferences when a particular passage statement is comprehended. Graesser found that 80 percent or more of the passage inferences are inherited directly from GKSs that are activated in working memory. The other 20 percent are unique nodes that are constructed by virtue of several GKSs and passage nodes interacting with each other in working memory. Graesser and Clark (1985) also reported that 73 percent of the passage inferences come from "word-activated" GKSs—that is, from content words that are explicitly mentioned in the text. The increment from 73 percent to 80 percent is due to "pattern-activated" GKSs that are indirectly triggered (e.g., FAIRY TALE).

As discussed earlier, a central challenge in the model is to explain how comprehension mechanisms converge on a relatively small set of inferences that are relevant to a text. Graesser's empirical data analyses underscored the importance of convergence. The narratives that Graesser studied contained approximately 25 explicit statement nodes. The passage representation consisted of these 25 explicit nodes plus approximately 100 knowledge-based inference nodes. Such a passage would trigger approximately 35 GKSs, with 150 nodes in each GKS; this yields $35 \times 150 = 5,250$ potential inference nodes. Consequently, convergence mechanisms prune down the node space from 5,250 potential inferences to only 100 actual knowledge-based inferences! How does this occur?

Graesser's model explains how comprehension mechanisms converge on the comparatively small set of knowledge-based inferences. There are four components to the convergence mechanism. First, there is a set of assumptions about which GKSs are in working memory at any given point in the text. These *working memory occupancy assumptions* limit the number to about 5 to 7 GKSs when a particular text statement is being comprehended. Thus, when a particular passage statement is comprehended, only 5 to 7 GKSs (instead of 35 GKSs) serve as background knowledge to furnish inferences. Second, an *intersection principle* cuts down the node space further. According to the intersection principle, nodes from different structures may intersect (i.e., match, overlap). Intersecting nodes (and nodes that are structurally proximate to the intersecting nodes) have a high likelihood of being knowledge-based inferences. Third, *constraint propagation mechanisms* prune out nodes when there are conceptual incompatibilities among nodes. A set of priority rules specify a relative ordering of structures in working memory: (1) passage structure > GKS, (2) word-activated GKS > pattern-activated GKS, and (3) active verb GKS > noun GKS. Nodes in a low-priority structure are pruned out when they are incompatible with nodes in a structure of higher priority. Fourth, coherence-based nodes have a higher likelihood of being inferences than do elaborative nodes. Coherence-based nodes are bridging inferences that fill the conceptual gaps between the prior passage context and statement $N + 1$. Elaborative inferences are not needed for coherence; they radiate from the main passage structure (explicit nodes plus coherence-based bridging inferences). Once again, Graesser and Clark (1985) report some data from the verbal protocols that confirm each of these components of the convergence mechanism.

Graesser reported several analyses that test claims about which knowledge-based inferences are generated during comprehension. Most of these analyses were based on detailed inspections of question-answering protocols, recall intrusions, or inferences that emerge in summaries. These claims have recently been tested in studies that collect reading times on text segments (Graesser, Haberlandt, & Koizumi, 1987) and lexical decisions tasks (Long, Golding, Graesser, & Clark, 1990). Other than these two studies, however, Graesser's claims about inference processing have not been adequately tested by studies that collect processing time measures during comprehension (e.g., sentence reading times, gaze durations, lexical decision latencies for test words, reaction times for decisions on secondary tasks). Such measures are regarded as providing more direct windows to on-line comprehension processes.

As with the previous theories of narrative comprehension and representation, Graesser's model has successfully accounted for recall and summarization data. The model postulates a *Central Content Selector*, which contains a set of rules that predict which text statements are central, intermediate, or noncentral to the narrative. These rules have substantial similarity to the previous models (e.g., superordinate goals > subordinate goals; physical states/events > internal states/events; nodes with many causal connections > dead-end nodes). Unfortunately, the predictions of Graesser's model have never been directly compared to the predictions of the story grammars and Trabasso's causal network theory, so its relative status is uncertain. Graesser's model also predicts the order in which nodes get articulated. But once again, such data are comparatively uninformative because all of the theories predict that recall order closely corresponds to the chronological order of events.

In the context of recall and summarization, Graesser's model has one virtue that cannot be handled by the story grammars and Trabasso's causal network theory. Graesser's model predicts what knowledge-based inferences are likely to surface in summarization protocols and recall protocols (as intrusions). For example, a summary or recall protocol might have the statement 'character 1 repays character 2," even though this statement was never explicitly stated in the original text. The fact that Graesser's model can predict specific intrusions with some success could only occur because the model seriously focuses on inference mechanisms. The other models are essentially mute when it comes to predicting specific inferences.

One final virtue of Graesser's model is that it can account for question-answering data. After subjects read the narrative passages, statements in the text are queried with a variety of different questions (i.e., why, how, when, where, what enabled, what are the consequences, etc.). For each question, there is a distribution of answers that subjects produce empirically. Graesser's model of question answering can successfully predict which nodes occur in the answer distributions (Golding & Graesser, 1987; Graesser, 1978, 1981; Graesser et al., 1980; Graesser et al., 1981; Graesser & Murachver, 1985). For example, consider the question *why did the dragon kidnap the daughters?* in the context of Figure 8.3. Theoretical answers would include superordinate goals (in order to keep the daughters, in order to kill the daughters, in order to eat the daughters) and goal initiators (because the dragon saw the daughters, because the dragon did not like the daughters, because the dragon was hungry); theoretical answers would *not* include subordinate goals (in order to carry off the daughters, in order to drag off the daughters). In contrast, theoretical answers to *how did the dragon kidnap the daughters?* would include subordinate goals/actions but not superordinate goals and goal initiators; thus, a good answer would be "by dragging them off" but not "by eating them."

Graesser's conceptual graph structures have demonstrated an important utility in that they are capable of representing many different kinds of knowledge structures (narrative text, expository text, world knowledge structures), and they provide functionally important distinctions in many different tasks (recall, summarization, question answering, inferencing). It can be argued that the utility of a representational system increases to the extent that the same system persists unmodified in the face of many behavioral tasks and many types of text (Abelson & Black, 1986; Graesser, 1981; Reiser & Black, 1982). However, Graesser's model is in desperate need of more rigorous and decisive empirical tests, with comparisons to other models. How well does it compare to other models when it comes to recall scores (for each passage statement), summary scores, importance ratings, output order, and subjective clustering of statement nodes? Can reading times and other on-line processing measures be explained by the theory's predictions about which inferences are generated during comprehension? Is there any way to test the detailed assumptions about the convergence mechanisms (i.e., the working memory occupancy assumptions, the intersection principle, constraint propagation)? Tests of the model need to expand from the verbal protocol analyses to more traditional and defensible experimental methods.

SCRIPTS AND PLANS

Schank and Abelson (1977) introduced the concept of a *script* as a special type of generic knowledge structure that corresponds to frequently enacted activities. For example, there is a RESTAURANT script, which houses typical knowledge about eating at a restaurant. Figure 8.4 presents some of the knowledge that would be included in a RESTAURANT script. There are roles (e.g., customer, waiter), props (tables, menu), entry conditions (being hungry), results (being full), and configurations of actions that are segregated into scenes (e.g., entering the restaurant, ordering food, eating food, paying the bill). In Schank and Abelson's theory, the actions are decomposed into a common set of primitive predicates. For example, PTRANS stands for location change; "S PTRANS S to table" can be articulated as "the customer went to a table." The purpose of translating action verbs into primitive predicates need not concern us in this chapter. The important point is that scripts are packages of generic knowledge that have slots (roles, props, entry conditions, and so on), typical values that fill the slots, and structured sequences of actions that unfold in a particular order.

When a RESTAURANT script is triggered during the comprehension of a passage, the script knowledge guides the course of interpreting the text, of generating inferences, and of generating expectations about subsequent actions in the text. When text input matches content in the generic script, the script successfully interprets the input. For example, the text statement "the customer looked at the tables" would match the script node "S ATTEND eyes TO tables." This text statement would be bound to the abstract action description in the script during the process of interpretation. One or more expectations would be generated at this point, such as "S PTRANS S TO table."

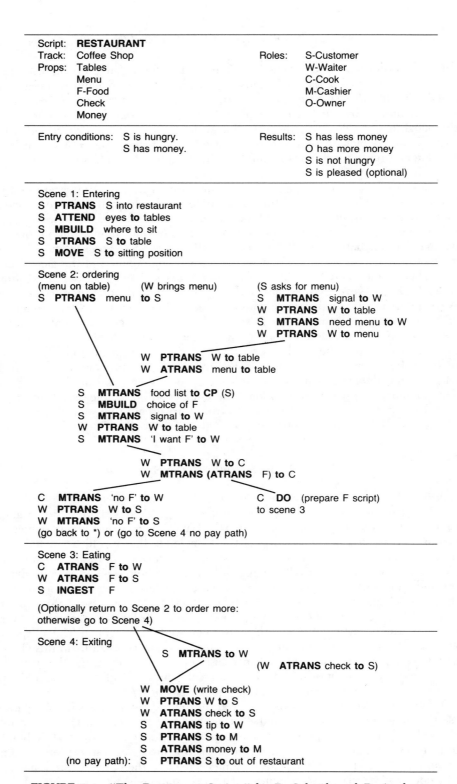

Script: **RESTAURANT**
Track: Coffee Shop
Props: Tables
      Menu
      F-Food
      Check
      Money

Roles: S-Customer
      W-Waiter
      C-Cook
      M-Cashier
      O-Owner

Entry conditions: S is hungry.
      S has money.

Results: S has less money
      O has more money
      S is not hungry
      S is pleased (optional)

Scene 1: Entering
S **PTRANS** S into restaurant
S **ATTEND** eyes **to** tables
S **MBUILD** where to sit
S **PTRANS** S **to** table
S **MOVE** S **to** sitting position

Scene 2: ordering
(menu on table)   (W brings menu)   (S asks for menu)
S **PTRANS** menu **to** S
      S **MTRANS** signal **to** W
      W **PTRANS** W **to** table
      S **MTRANS** need menu **to** W
      W **PTRANS** W **to** menu

    W **PTRANS** W **to** table
    W **ATRANS** menu **to** table

S **MTRANS** food list **to CP** (S)
S **MBUILD** choice of F
S **MTRANS** signal **to** W
W **PTRANS** W **to** table
S **MTRANS** 'I want F' **to** W

    W **PTRANS** W **to** C
    W **MTRANS (ATRANS** F) **to** C

C **MTRANS** 'no F' **to** W   C **DO** (prepare F script)
W **PTRANS** W **to** S   to scene 3
W **MTRANS** 'no F' **to** S
(go back to *) or (go to Scene 4 no pay path)

Scene 3: Eating
C **ATRANS** F **to** W
W **ATRANS** F **to** S
S **INGEST** F

(Optionally return to Scene 2 to order more:
otherwise go to Scene 4)

Scene 4: Exiting
    S **MTRANS to** W
      (W **ATRANS** check **to** S)

    W **MOVE** (write check)
    W **PTRANS** W **to** S
    W **ATRANS** check **to** S
    S **ATRANS** tip **to** W
    S **PTRANS** S **to** M
    S **ATRANS** money **to** M
(no pay path): S **PTRANS** S **to** out of restaurant

FIGURE 8.4 "The Restaurant Script," by R. Schank and R. Avelson. *Source*: From *Scripts, plans, goals, and understanding*. Lawrence Erlbaum Associates, Inc. 1979.

Subsequent text statements would perhaps confirm this expectation. Alternatively, the expectation either would be filled in as an inference or would be disconfirmed by the subsequent text. When the text input fails to match anything in the script, then the comprehender must construct a novel interpretation by activating other scripts and piecing together a structure that "explains" as much of the input as possible.

In order to concretize the role of scripts in comprehension, computer programs have been written that are designed to comprehend text, paraphrase text, generate inferences, and answer questions in a manner that bears some similarity to that of humans. Most of these programs have been developed by Schank and Abelson and their students (Cullingford, 1979; Dyer, 1983; Lehnert, 1978; Schank & Abelson, 1977; Schank & Riesbeck, 1981; Wilensky, 1983a).

Script theory also inspired a tremendous amount of empirical research that has attempted to account for memory, reading time, and the activation of script elements in scripted passages (Abbott, Black, & Smith, 1985; Bower, Black, & Turner, 1979; Graesser, Gordon, & Sawyer, 1979; Graesser & Nakamura, 1982; Haberlandt & Bingham, 1982; Sharkey, 1986; Yekovich & Walker, 1987). The original concept of a script has been modified somewhat as a result of these studies and some computational issues in artificial intelligence (Abelson, 1981; Abelson & Black, 1986; Schank, 1982). For example, the original concept of a script was too rigid, in the sense that the same sequence of main actions would always get encoded whenever a RESTAURANT script was activated. In the revised theory, a scripted passage is more dynamically constructed so that a main script action or a subchunk of actions does not necessarily get encoded. For example, if there is no mention of any action associated with entering the restaurant, the "entering" subchunk would not get encoded.

One of the important characteristics of scripts is that they furnish many inferences and expectations by default. If the passage states that *the customer entered the restaurant* and that *the customer sat down*, then there would be an inference that "the customer went to the table." This inference is passed down from the generic script and is encoded in the passage representation by default. The fact that these inferences are filled in by default has implications for memory (Bower, et al., 1979; Graesser, et al., 1979; Graesser & Nakamura, 1982). When subjects are asked to recall passages after comprehension, they often recall the inferences that were filled by default; these are called *intrusions*. In recognition tests, subjects often decide that these inferences had been presented in the passage even though they had not; these are called *false alarms*. Given that subjects find it difficult to decide whether or not typical script items were presented or merely inferred, there is very poor memory discrimination for very typical script items. In contrast, there is much better memory discrimination for actions that are either inconsistent with a script or irrelevant to the script.

Script theory offers some predictions about which typical actions in a scripted passage tend to be recalled. It is assumed that the actions in a script are organized hierarchically. The superordinate action/plan descriptions correspond to the main actions (entering the restaurant, ordering food, eating the food, paying the bill); subordinate descriptions include instrumental actions (walking to the door, looking at the waitress, lifting a fork, grasping the wallet). It is predicted and generally found that the more superordinate actions are recalled more often and appear more often in summary protocols (Black & Bower, 1980; Graesser, 1978, 1981).

Script theories predict patterns of reading time for actions in script passages. For example, reading times are predicted to be faster for script-typical actions than for script-irrelevant or script-inconsistent actions. Indeed, data support this prediction (Bellezza & Bower, 1981; Haberlandt & Bingham, 1982).

Some interesting questions in current psychological research address the activation of scripts, the deactivation of scripts, and the activation of elements within scripts (Sharkey, 1986; Sharkey & Mitchell, 1985; Sharkey & Sharkey, 1987; Yekovich & Walker, 1987). Under what conditions do scripts get activated in working memory? Scripts obviously are triggered by specific labels associated with the script (i.e., the word "restaurant" activates RESTAURANT) but there is no consensus on what aspects of the stimulus trigger scripts in a pattern-activated fashion. How do scripts become deactivated? According to Sharkey's research, several unrelated statements must occur in the text before a script gets deactivated. Moreover, the deactivation is to a large extent under strategic control of the comprehender. Which elements in a script are activated when a script enters working memory? According to research by Yekovich and Walker, the central script actions are automatically activated, whereas the peripheral actions are activated only when there is some text input that triggers it in a data-driven fashion. Thus, *customer eats* would always be activated; *customer lifts fork* would not be activated unless there is text input that makes this information relevant (e.g., "the steak was tough so the customer reached for some utensils").

It is important to acknowledge that the scope of script theory is not particularly broad. The actions in the narrative passages must generally conform to the content of a generic script. Unless there are events that deviate from the generic script, such passages are extremely dull. As soon as one expands the theory to include interesting narrative, the passages tend to include (a) several scripts instead of only one central organizing script and (b) several events and actions that deviate from the activated scripts. For this reason, the students of Schank and Abelson shifted their efforts to the novel plans of story characters and interesting plot configurations. Whereas the program SAM (Script Applier Mechanism) was restricted to scripts, the program PAM (Plan Applier Mechanism) attempted to account for the novel plans that story characters enact (Wilensky, 1983a). Narratives are more interesting when they involve these novel plans than when they merely involve familiar script content.

There is some psychological research that has investigated whether plan-based narratives are organized around hierarchical plan structures (Brewer & Dupree, 1983; Foss & Bower, 1986; Lichtenstein & Brewer, 1980; Means & Voss, 1985; Spilich, Vesonder, Chiesi, & Voss, 1979; Voss & Bisanz, 1985). Superordinate plans tend to be recalled more often than subordinate plans. The time to judge whether a particular action is relevant to a goal increases as a function of structural distance in the goal hierarchy.

STORY POINTS, PLOT UNITS, AND THEMATIC AFFECT UNITS

The theories of narrative in this section seriously dissect the content of plot configurations to a greater extent than any of the previous theories. Until this point, there have been no substantial recommendations on what makes an interesting narrative that is worthwhile telling in a communicative interchange. The theories in this section were developed at Yale by students of Schank and Abelson: (1) Wilensky's theory of story points (Wilensky, 1982, 1983a), (2) Lehnert's plot unit theory (Lehnert, 1981, 1982), and Dyer's analysis of thematic affect units (Dyer, 1983; Lehnert, Dyer, Johnson, Yang, & Harley, 1983). In the spirit of the Yale school, these theorists offer a systematic analysis of the plot *content*; this contrasts the emphasis on *structure* in the story grammars, Trabasso's causal networks, and Graesser's conceptual graph structures. Unlike the dull narratives that were generated in Schank and Abelson's analysis of scripts and plans, the present theories would sustain the attention of an adult comprehender.

Wilensky's (1982, 1983a) theory begins with the observation that storytellers ordinarily tell narratives in order to make a point to the listener. A theory of narrative representation should somehow account for this fundamental fact. There are two basic types of point: external and internal. An *external point* is the contextually specific goal that the storyteller has for telling the story—for example, convincing the listener of something, impressing the listener, getting the listener to react emotionally (see Schank, Collins, Davis, Johnson, Lytinen, & Reiser, 1982). An *internal point* is a part of the story itself that generates interest. Wilensky focused on the internal points rather than the external points.

According to Wilensky, a story with a point depicts a human dramatic situation that is intimately bound to the characters' goals. Characters encounter problems and there are nontrivial solutions that end up resolving the problems. Wilensky has carefully mapped out the alternative configurations of goals either within a character or between characters. A *goal conflict* occurs within a single character. Examples of goal conflicts include resource limitations (e.g., a character does not have time to both date a woman and work in an ambitious job) and states that are mutually exclusive (e.g., being married and being free to date several people). An interesting story would present a clever or nonobvious resolution to the conflict (e.g., dating several people, but deceiving the spouse that the job is taking up most of one's time). *Goal competition* involves a clash of goals between two or more characters. For example, two characters might want the same job. The problem may be resolved by an external event that removes the competition (one character suddenly gets a large inheritance), by antiplanning (one character spreads bad rumors about the other character), or by easing the competition. *Goal subsumption* occurs when a character plans for several goals at once (e.g., getting money opens the doors to many opportunities). Still other goal configurations include *goal facilitation* (i.e., one goal facilitates the achievement of another goal within a character) and *goal concord* (a consequence of alliances between characters). A story point expresses a novel, informative, or interesting solution to a goal configuration that involves incompatible goals.

The major contribution of Wilensky's theory of story points is his illuminating, comprehensive analysis of goals, goal configurations, and solution plans. Unfortunately, however, there have been very few attempts to test his theory by collecting data from human subjects. Given that Wilensky is in the field of artificial intelligence, he elected to focus more on computational issues than on empirical tests. There is some evidence that the story point theory can predict recall of text statements (Wilensky, 1983b), but there were essentially no comparisons to other theories. Perhaps a more serious problem with the theory is that it could account for the story points of only a small subset of narratives. Wilensky's goal-based analysis did not go the distance in accounting for the story points of most narratives. In particular, a more complete account was needed to trace the emotions of story characters. Consequently, the subsequent theories in the Yale school began to examine character "affect" in greater detail.

Lehnert's plot unit analysis centered around patterns of affect within characters and between characters (Lehnert, 1981, 1982). In her analysis, those statements that are relevant to the plot (i.e., events, actions, states, goals) are assigned to one of three *affect states*: positive event, (+), negative event (−), or a mental state with a neutral affect (M). There are four categories of directed arcs that relate pairs of affect states:

1. Motivation (m) must point to a mental state.
2. Actualization (a) must point from a mental state to an event.
3. Termination (t) either connects two mental states or connects two events.
4. Equivalence (e) either connects two mental states or connects two events.

There are 36 possible state-link-state combinations, given that there are three possible affect states and four possible arcs ($3 \times 4 \times 3 = 36$). However, given the rules of composition stated above, only 15 of these 36 combinations are legal. These 15 combinations are called *primitive plot units*. Table 8.1 presents these 15 plot units, along with a label that succinctly conveys the meaning of each plot unit and an example for each unit.

Complex plot units are built up from primitive plot units. Some complex plot units are confined within a single character. For example, there is a complex plot unit for "fleeting success," which consists of two primitive plot units: success and loss. Other examples are listed below.

> Intentional Problem Resolution = problem & success & resolution
> Starting Over = success & loss & problem & resolution

In most interesting plots, however, the complex plot units involve multiple characters, with cross-character causal links. A positive affect state for one character may be a negative affect state for another character. Consequently, there are variations in the point of view among the different characters. We will not present these complex structures in this chapter, but some of the titles of these complex plot configurations are honored/denied/bungled request, effective/ineffective/bungled coercion, promised request honored/bungled, double cross, problem resolution by effective coercion, simultaneous exchange, reneged promise, retaliation, and sabotage. Each of these complex plot units has a unique configuration of the 15 primitive plot units.

In some respects, Lehnert's approach to analyzing plot is similar to Propp's (1969) approach to analyzing Russian folktales. According to Propp, most Russian folktales can be characterized by an organization and combination of 31 basic motifs (e.g., violation, trickery, lack, receipt of magical agent). However, it is important to acknowledge that Lehnert's analyses are computationally more rigorous. The plot units are generated systematically and constrained by well-formed rules of combination. Complex plot units are neither generated haphazardly nor discovered empirically; instead, they are products of rules and constraints. Whereas legal configurations can be segregated from illegal configurations in Lehnert's system, Propp never had the computational foundation to be that decisive.

There have been a few empirical studies that have tested the psychological validity of Lehnert's plot unit analysis. Lehnert (1982) has accounted for the verbal protocols that subjects give when they are asked to summarize a sample of narrative passages. Reiser, Black, and Lehnert (1985) reported that complex plot units are psychologically valid constituents because they are used when subjects generate stories and when they sort stories into categories. When subjects are given a story and are asked to write a similar story, they produce the appropriate plot structure to a greater extent than they produce similar properties of characters. When subjects are asked to sort a set of passages into categories and there are exemplars from different complex plot units, they honor the complex plot configurations. Gee and Grosjean (1984) reported that the theoretical chunks derived from plot unit analysis successfully predict pauses in story writing and pauses in the reading of stories. These few studies exhaust the available evidence for the plot unit analysis. Clearly, there is a need for more empirical research that collects reading times, recall, summaries, and importance ratings for a diverse sample of narratives. There need to be more systematic comparisons among theories of narrative.

Nevertheless, Lehnert's plot unit analysis did not go the distance in accounting for interesting plots that are worthwhile to tell. Lehnert and Dyer introduced *Thematic Affect Units* (called TAUs) in order to go one step further in explaining the content of plots (Dyer, 1983; Lehnert, Dyer, Johnson, Yang, & Harley, 1983). TAUs are similar to complex plot units in that they have a strong affective component and they involve

TABLE 8.1   Lehnert's Primitive Plot Units

Problem	$(- \xrightarrow{m} M)$	You get fired so you apply for a job.
Motivation	$(M \xrightarrow{m} M)$	You want to buy a car so you apply for a loan.
Success	$(M \xrightarrow{a} +)$	You ask for a raise and you get one.
Failure	$(M \xrightarrow{a} -)$	You propose marriage but the person declines.
Change of mind	$(M \xleftarrow{t} M)$	You want to propose marriage but then decide against it.
Loss	$(+ \xleftarrow{t} -)$	Your big income tax refund ends up being a mistake.
Mixed Blessing	$(+ \xleftarrow{e} -)$	You fall in love but the person is insanely jealous.
Perseverance	$(M \xleftarrow{e} M)$	You get married again.
Resolution	$(- \xleftarrow{t} +)$	Your broken car starts working again.
Hidden Blessing	$(- \xleftarrow{e} +)$	You get audited but they end up owing you money.
Enablement	$(+ \xrightarrow{m} M)$	You get a raise so you spend the money.
Negative tradeoff	$(- \xleftarrow{t} -)$	You get fired so you don't have to do some boring work.
Positive tradeoff	$(+ \xleftarrow{t} +)$	You get a raise and then inherit a fortune.
Complex positive event	$(+ \xleftarrow{e} +)$	A gift is indicative of a close relationship.
Complex negative event	$(- \xleftarrow{e} -)$	Your house burns down and you aren't covered.

Note: Plot units: A narrative summarization strategy, by W. G. Lehert, from *Strategies for natural learning processes*, W. G. Lehert and M. H. Ringle (eds). Hillsdale, NJ: Lawrence Erlbaum Associates, Inc., 1982. *Chapter 9*.

variations from standard goal/plan processing (i.e., a plan goes wrong or an unexpected event occurs). However, TAUs are thematic in nature, often representing adages that describe how people respond to planning failures. For example, the TAU for "Hidden Blessing" may be captured by the adage "every cloud has a silver lining." Other example TAU-based adages are "counting your chickens before they hatch," "closing the barn door after the horse is gone," and "the pot calling the kettle black." Dyer and Lehnert have identified dozens of TAUs. They have dissected the configuration of goal and affect elements associated with each TAU. As a consequence, they can explain a diverse array of emotions that characters experience in narrative text: anger, eagerness, hope, worry, happiness, disappointment, gratitude, relief, embarrassment, and so on.

Lehnert and Dyer have developed a computer program that comprehends narrative texts which instantiate specific TAU's. This program, called *BORIS*, is capable of generating inferences and answering questions about a passage. One virtue of BORIS is that its processing mechanism integrates many types of world knowledge structures: TAUs, scripts, plans, person stereotypes, and so on. Therefore, in addition to providing an important contribution to plot analysis, the theory is rigorous computationally. Unfortunately, there have been very few psychological tests of the theory. Seifert, Dyer, and Black (1986) found some support for TAU units in story production tasks and story-sorting tasks. Seifert, McKoon, Abelson, and Ratcliff (1986) identified conditions under which a particular TAU is accessed during narrative comprehension and utilized to direct comprehension of the text in a top-down fashion. A thematically similar story may be accessed and used to guide processing of the current narrative, but only if the previous story was extensively prestudied and the comprehender was strategically tuned to relate the two narratives. Therefore, it has not been empirically demonstrated that it is easy to identify specific TAUs via pattern recognition during comprehension.

The series of computer models developed by the Yale school constitutes a landmark contribution to our understanding of interesting narratives. Unfortunately, there is precious little empirical data from psychology that has tested the models of Wilensky, Lehnert, and Dyer. This is one hot direction for future experimental research. Given that their theoretical framework offers the first serious foundation for analyzing interesting narrative, studies need to be conducted that assess interestingness ratings for stories. What aspects of the goal configurations, plot units, or TAUs can predict how interesting narratives are? How do these theories compare to other theories of narrative in predicting summarization, recall, importance ratings of statements, and other data that researchers have frequently collected? Yet another empirical question addresses the scope of these stories. What proportion of naturalistic stories have plots that can be explained by the Yale theories? In fact, nearly all of the narrative passages they have studied were generated by the researchers. More attention needs to be devoted to ecologically valid narratives.

THEORIES THAT ADDRESS PRAGMATICS AND READER AFFECT

The previous theories of narrative representation have analyzed the structure and content of the text. Unfortunately, they have not advanced our understanding of the pragmatic context in which a story is told or a story is read. The theories have essentially been mute about the writer/reader relationship, the storyteller/listener relationship, the common ground among speech participants, social parameters, and the emotions that the narrative elicits in the reader (called *reader affect*). Yet these pragmatic levels are very critical. Writers create stories to involve the reader emotionally, and it is the reader's intention to be so involved. People read narratives for enjoyment; this involvement is voluntary and personal. Consequently, the previous theories of narrative are incomplete at a very basic level.

Researchers have long acknowledged the important role of pragmatics and reader affect, but only recently have they begun to study it systematically and scientifically. For example, there are some informative discussions of reader affect in the fields of education (Mosenthal, 1987; Winograd & Johnston, 1987), cognitive science (Brewer, 1985), and literary criticism (Tompkins, 1980). In Europe, there is a new emerging discipline on the empirical study of literature that investigates reader affect and communication processes when literature is read (Hauptmeier, Meutsch, & Viehoff, 1987; Meutsch, 1986; Schmidt, 1981). Brewer's Structural Affect Theory relates particular discourse structures to affective states in the reader, such as suspense, curiosity, and surprise (Brewer, 1985; Brewer & Lichtenstein, 1980; Jose & Brewer, 1984). In the fields of sociology and linguistics, there have been some attempts to understand pragmatic components in conversational storytelling (Goffman, 1974; Polanyi, 1985; Sachs, et al., 1984; Shiffrin, 1985; Tannen, 1988).

For the most part, the above efforts at understanding pragmatics and reader affect are observational and theoretically sketchy. There is no large body of empirical data that tests well-articulated theoretical claims. There is no general theory of pragmatics or reader affect that ties together the dozens of interesting empirical observations that the sociologists and linguists have made. There needs to be more serious attention devoted to some computationally rigorous specifications of (a) the representation of the context-specific, pragmatic interactions between speaker/listener or reader/writer, (b) the linkages between the pragmatic representations in (a) and the narrative representations, and (c) the cognitive procedures and strategies associated with (a) and (b). The field of artificial intelligence has some models of pragmatics with the desired computational rigor (Allen, 1983, 1987; Bruce, 1982; Cohen & Perrault, 1979; Newman & Bruce, 1986), but these need to be applied to narrative text and storytelling.

In closing, we would like to point out some trends that are associated with attempts to penetrate deeper levels of code. Our survey of cognitive science research on narrative has progressed from abstract event structures, to world knowledge and inferences, to content analyses of interesting plot structures (that specify characters' goals and affective states), to pragmatics and reader affect. At each step, researchers have been stimulated by theories that are computationally rigorous and that provide predictions that can be tested empirically. However, as the field has progressed toward these greater depths, the representations and computations have become more complex and at times more nebulous. We believe that it is important to strive for, if not achieve, some computational rigor at the deeper levels. We hope that empirical researchers will not be frightened away by its complexity.

REFERENCES

Abbott, V., Black, J. B., & Smith, E. E. (1985). The representation of scripts in memory. *Journal of Memory and Language, 24,* 179–199.

Abelson, R. P. (1981). The phychological status of the script concept. *American Psychologist, 36,* 715–729.

Abelson, R. P., & Black, J. B. (1986). Introduction. In J. A. Galambos, R. P. Abelson, & J. B. Black (Eds.), *Knowledge structures.* Hillsdale, NJ: Erlbaum.

Adams, H., & Searle, L. (1986). *Critical theory since 1965.* Tallahassee: University Press of Florida.

Allen, J. (1983). Recognizing intentions from natural language utterances. In M. Brady & R. C. Berwick (Eds.), *Computational models of discourse.* Cambridge, MA: MIT Press.

Allen, J. (1987). *Natural language understanding.* Menlo Park, CA: Benjiman/Cummings.

Bahktin, M. M. (1981). *The dialogic imagination.* Austin: University of Texas Press.

Bartlett, F. C. (1932). *Remembering.* Cambridge, Eng.: Cambridge University Press.

Beach, R., & Brown, R. (1987). Discourse comprehension and literary inference: Toward a theoretical model. In R. J. Tierney, P. L. Anders, & J. N. Mitchell (Eds.), *Understanding readers' understanding.* Hillsdale, NJ: Erlbaum.

Beaugrande, R. de, & Colby, B. (1979). Narrative models of action and interaction. *Cognitive Science, 3,* 43–66.

Bellezza, F. S., & Bower, G. H. (1981). The representation and processing characteristics of scripts. *Bulletin of the Psychonomic Society, 18,* 1–4.

Black, J. B., & Bower, G. H. (1980). Story understanding as problem solving. *Poetics, 9,* 223–250.

Black, J. B., & Wilensky, R. (1979). An evaluation of story grammars. *Cognitive Science, 3,* 213–230.

Bower, G. H., Black, J. B., & Turner, T. J. (1979). Scripts in memory for text. *Cognitive Psychology, 11,* 177–220.

Black, J. B., Turner, T. J., & Bower, G. H. (1979). Point of view in narrative comprehension, memory, & production. *Journal of Memory and Language, 18,* 187–198.

Brewer, W. F. (1985). The story schema: Universal and culture-specific properties. In D. R. Olson, N. Torrance, & A. Hildyard (Eds.), *Literacy, language, and learning: The nature and consequences of reading and writing.* London: Cambridge University Press.

Brewer, W. F., & Dupree, P. A. (1983). Use of a plan schemata in the recall and recognition of goal-directed actions. *Journal of Experimental Psychology: Learning, Memory, and Cognition, 9,* 117–129.

Brewer, W. F., & Lichtenstein, E. H. (1980). Event schemas, story schemas, and story grammars. In J. Long & A. D. Baddeley (Eds.), *Attention and performance IX.* Hillsdale, NJ: Erlbaum.

Britton, B., & Black, J. B. (1985). *Understanding expository text.* Hillsdale, NJ: Erlbaum.

Bruce, B. C. (1982). Natural communication between person and computer. In W. G. Lehnert & M. H. Ringle (Eds.), *Strategies for natural language processing.* Hillsdale, NJ: Erlbaum.

Chafe, W. (1985). Linguistic differences produced by differences between speaking and writing. In D. R. Olson, A. Hildyard, & N. Torrance (Eds.), *Literacy, language, and learning: The nature and consequences of reading and writing.* London: Cambridge University Press.

Chafe, W., & Danielewicz, J. (1987). Properties of spoken and written language. In R. Horowitz & S. J. Samuels (Eds.), *Comprehending oral and written language.* New York: Academic Press.

Chatman, S. (1978). *Story and discourse: Narrative structure in fiction and film.* Ithaca, NY: Cornell University Press.

Clark, H. H., & Marshall, C. R. (1981). Definite reference and mutual knowledge. In A. K. Joshi, B. L. Webber, & I. A. Sag (Eds.), *Elements of discourse understanding.* Cambridge, Eng.: Cambridge University Press.

Cohen, P. R., & Perrault, C. R. (1979). Elements of a plan-based theory of speech acts. *Cognitive Science, 3,* 177–212.

Cole, M., & Keyssar, H. (1985). The concept of literacy in print and film. In D. R. Olson, N. Torrance, & A. Hildyard (Eds.), *Literacy, language, and learning: The nature and consequences of reading and writing.* London: Cambridge University Press.

Cullingford, R. E. (1979). Integrating knowledge sources for computer "understanding" in tasks. In *Proceedings of the 1979 International Conference on Cybernetics and Society.* Denver, CO. Pp. 746–752.

Dolezel, L. (1976). Narrative modalities. *Journal of Literary Semantics, 5,* 5–14.

Duffy, S. A. (1986). Role of expectations in sentence integration. *Journal of Experimental Psychology: Learning, Memory, and Cognition, 12,* 208–219.

Dyer, M. G. (1983). *In-depth understanding: A computer model of integrated processing for narrative comprehension.* Cambridge, MA: MIT Press.

Fitzgerald, J., & Teasley, A. (1983). Effects of instruction in narrative structure on children's writing. Paper presented at the annual meeting of the National Reading Conference, Austin, TX, Nov. 29–Dec. 3, 1983.

Fitzgerald, J., & Teasley, A. B. (1986). Effects of instruction in narrative structure on children's writing. *Journal of Educational Psychology, 78,* 424–432.

Foss, C. C., & Bower, G. H. (1986). Understanding actions in relation to goals. In N. E. Sharkey (Ed.), *Advances in cognitive science.* New York: Ellis Horwood.

Foster-Harris, W. (1974). *The basic patterns of plot.* Norman, OK: University of Oklahoma Press.

Frazer, J. G. (1907–1915). *The golden bough.* (Vols. 1–12). London: Macmillan.

Freedle, R., & Hale, G. (1979). Acquisition of new comprehension schemata for expository prose by transfer of a narrative schema. In R. O. Freedle (Ed.), *New directions in discourse processing.* Norwood, NJ: Ablex.

French, L. A. (1986). The language of events. In K. Nelson (Ed.), *Event knowledge: Structure and function in development.* Hillsdale, NJ: Erlbaum.

Frye, N. (1971). *The critical path.* Bloomington: Indiana University Press.

Galda, L. (1984). Narrative competence: Play, storytelling, and story comprehension. In A. Pellegrini & T. Yawkey (Eds.), *The development of oral and written language in social contexts.* Norwood, NJ: Ablex.

Gee, J. P., & Grosjean, F. (1984). Empirical evidence for narrative structure. *Cognitive Science, 8,* 59–85.

Goffman, E. (1974). *Frame analysis: An essay on the organization of experience.* Cambridge, MA: Harvard University Press.

Golding, J., & Graesser, A. C. (1987). Answering why-questions: Test of a psychological model of question answering. In *Proceedings of the Cognitive Science Society Conference* (pp. 945–951). Hillsdale, NJ: Erlbaum.

Goldman, S. R., & Varnhagen, C. K. (1986). Memory for embedded and sequential story structures. *Journal of Memory and Language, 25,* 401–418.

Graesser, A. C. (1978). How to catch a fish: The memory and representation of common procedures. *Discourse Processes, 1,* 72–89.

Graesser, A. C. (1981). *Prose comprehension beyond the word.* New York: Springer-Verlag.

Graesser, A. C., & Bower, G. H. (Eds.). (1990). *The psychology of learning and motivation* (Vol. 25). New York: Academic Press.

Graesser, A. C., & Clark, L. F. (1985). *Structures and procedures of implicit knowledge.* Norwood, NJ: Ablex.

Graesser, A. C., & Goodman, S. M. (1984). Implicit knowledge, question answering, and the representation of expository text. In B. Britton & J. B. Black (Eds.), *Understanding expository text.* Hillsdale, NJ: Erlbaum.

Graesser, A. C., Gordon, S. E., & Sawyer, J. D. (1979). Memory for typical and atypical actions in scripted activities: Test of a script pointer + tag hypothesis. *Journal of Verbal Learning and Verbal Behavior, 18,* 319–332.

Graesser, A. C., Haberlandt, K., & Koizumi, D. (1987). How is reading time influenced by knowledge-based inferences and world knowledge? In B. K. Britton & S. M. Glynn (Eds.), *Executive control processes in reading*. Hillsdale, NJ: Erlbaum.

Graesser, A. C., Long, D. L., & Mio, J. (1990). Humor and wit in comprehension. *Poetics, 18*, 143–164.

Graesser, A. C., Millis, K., & Long, D. L. (1986). The construction of knowledge structures and inferences during text comprehension. In N. E. Sharkey (Ed.), *Advances in cognitive science* (Vol. 1). London: Ellis Horwood.

Graesser, A. C., & Murachver, T. (1985). Symbolic procedures of question answering. In A. C. Graesser & J. B. Black (Eds.), *The psychology of questions*. Hillsdale, NJ: Erlbaum.

Graesser, A. C., & Nakamura, G. V. (1982). The impact of a schema on comprehension and memory. In G. H. Bower (Ed.), *The psychology of learning and motivation: Advances in research and theory*. New York: Academic Press.

Graesser, A. C., & Riha, J. R. (1984). An application of multiple regression techniques to sentence reading times. In D. Kieras & M. Just (Eds.), *New methods in comprehension research*. Hillsdale, NJ: Erlbaum.

Graesser, A. C., Robertson, S. P., & Anderson, P. A. (1981). Incorporating inferences in narrative representations: A study of how and why. *Cognitive Psychology, 13*, 1–26.

Graesser, A. C., Robertson, S. P., Lovelace, E., & Swinehart, D. (1980). Answers to why-questions expose the organization of story plot and predict recall of actions. *Journal of Verbal Learning and Verbal Behavior, 19*, 110–119.

Grishman, R. (1986). *Computational linguistics: An introduction*. Cambridge, Eng.: Cambridge University Press.

Grishman, R., & Kittredge, R. (Eds.). (1987). *Analyzing language in restricted domains: Sublanguage description and processing*. Hillsdale, NJ: Erlbaum.

Haberlandt, K. (1980). Story grammar and reading time of story constituents. *Poetics, 9*, 99–116.

Haberlandt, D., & Bingham, G. (1982). The role of scripts in the comprehension and retention of texts. *Text, 2*, 29–46.

Halliday, M. A. K. (1987) Spoken and written modes of meaning. In R. Horowitz & S. J. Samuels (Eds.), *Comprehending oral and written language*. New York: Academic Press.

Hansen, W. F. (1983). Greek mythology and the study of the ancient Greek oral story. *Journal of Folklore Research, 20*, 101–112.

Hauptmeier, H., Meutsch, D., & Viehoff, R. (1987). *Literary understanding from an empirical point of view*. Seigen, West Germany: Lumis-Schriften 14.

Heath, S. B., & Branscombe, A. M. (1986). The book as narrative prop in language acquisition. In B. B. Schieffelin & P. Gilmore (Eds.), *The acquisition of literacy: Ethnographic perspectives*. Norwood, NJ: Ablex.

Horowitz, R., & Samuels, S. J. (Eds.). (1987). *Comprehending oral and written language*. New York: Academic Press.

Jacquenod, C. (1987). Concerning the interpretation of fictional literary texts. In *Proceedings of the International Conference for the Empirical Study of Literature*. Siegen University, Siegen, West Germany, Dec. 9–12, 1987.

Jose, P., & Brewer, S. (1984). Development of story liking: Character identification, suspense, and outcome resolution. *Developmental Psychology, 20*, 911–924.

Kintsch, W., & Greene, E. (1978). The role of culture-specific schemata in the comprehension and recall of stories. *Discourse Processes, 1*, 1–13.

Kintsch, W., & van Dijk, T. A. (1978). Toward a model of text comprehension and production. *Psychological Review, 85*, 363–394.

Labov, W. (1972). The transformation of experience in narrative syntax. In *The social stratification of English in New York City*. Philadelphia: University of Pennsylvania Press.

Lehnert, W. G. (1978). *The process of question answering*. Hillsdale, NJ: Erlbaum.

Lehnert, W. G. (1981). Plot units and narrative summarization. *Cognitive Science, 5*, 293–331.

Lehnert, W. G. (1982). Plot units: A narrative summarization strategy. In W. G. Lehnert & M. H. Ringle (Eds.), *Strategies for natural language processing*. Hillsdale, NJ: Erlbaum.

Lehnert, W. G., Dyer, M. G., Johnson, P. N., Yang, C. J., & Harley, S. (1983). BORIS—An experiment in in-depth understanding of narratives. *Artificial Intelligence, 20*, 15–22.

Lehr, F. (1987). Story grammar. *The Reading Teacher, 31*, 550–552.

Lévi-Strauss, C. (1955). The structural study of myth. *Journal of American Folklore, 68*, 428–444.

Lichtenstein, E. H., & Brewer, W. F. (1980). Memory for goal-directed events. *Cognitive Psychology, 12*, 412–445.

Long, D. L., & Graesser, A. C. (1988). Wit and humor in discourse processing. *Discourse Processes, 11*, 35–60.

Long, D. L., Golding, J., Graesser, A. C., & Clark, L. F. (1990). Inference generation during story comprehension: A comparison of goals, events, and states. In A. C. Graesser & G. H. Bower (Eds.), *The psychology of learning and motivation* (Vol. 25). New York: Academic Press.

Mandler, G. (1976). *Mind and emotion*. New York: Wiley.

Mandler, J. M. (1984). *Stories, scripts, and scenes: Aspects of schema theory*. Hillsdale, NJ: Erlbaum.

Mandler, J. M. (1987). On the psychological reality of story structure. *Discourse Processes, 10*, 1–29.

Mandler, J. M., & deForest, M. (1979). Is there more than one way to read a story? *Child Development, 50*, 886–889.

Mandler, J. M., & Goodman, M. S. (1982). On the psychological validity of story structure. *Journal of Verbal Learning and Verbal Behavior, 21,* 507–523.

Mandler, J. M., & Johnson, N. S. (1977). Remembrance of things parsed: Story structure and recall. *Cognitive Psychology, 9,* 111–151.

Martin, W. (1986). *Recent theories of narrative.* London: Cornell University Press.

Mazzie, C. A. (1987). An experimental investigation of the determinants of implicitness in spoken and written discourse. *Discourse Processes, 10,* 31–42.

Means, M. L., & Voss, J. F. (1985). Star wars: A developmental study of expert and novice knowledge structures. *Journal of Memory and Language, 24,* 746–757.

Meutsch, D. (1986). Mental models in literary discourse: Towards the integration of linguistic and psychological levels of description. *Poetics, 15,* 307–331.

Meyer, B. J. F. (1985). Prose analysis: Purposes, procedures, and problems. In B. K. Britton & J. B. Black (Eds.), *Understanding expository text.* Hillsdale, NJ: Erlbaum.

Morrow, D. G., Greenspan, S. L., & Bower, G. H. (1987). Accessibility and situation models in narrative comprehension. *Journal of Memory and Language, 26,* 165–187.

Mosenthal, J. (1987). The reader's affective response to narrative text. In R. J. Tierney, P. L. Anders, & J. N. Mitchel (Eds.), *Understanding readers' understanding.* Hillsdale, NJ: Erlbaum.

Nelson, E. (Ed.). (1986). *Event knowledge: Structure and function in development.* Hillsdale, NJ: Erlbaum.

Newman, D., & Bruce, B. C. (1986). Interpretation and manipulation in human plans. *Discourse Processes, 9,* 167–195.

Nezworski, T., Stein, N. L., & Trabasso, T. (1982). Structure versus content in children's recall. *Journal of Verbal Learning and Verbal Behavior, 21,* 196–206.

Nicholas, D. W., & Trabasso, T. (1980). Towards a taxonomy of inferences. In F. Wilkening, J. Becker, & T. Trabasso (Eds.), *Information integration by children.* Hillsdale, NJ: Erlbaum.

Olson, D. (1985). Computers as tools of the intellect. *Educational Researchers, 14* (5), 5–7.

Omanson, R. C. (1982). An analysis of narratives: Identifying central, supportive, and distracting content. *Discourse Processes, 5,* 195–224.

Piaget, J. (1952). *The origins of intelligence in children.* New York: International University Press.

Polanyi, L. (1985). *Telling the American story: A structural and cultural analysis of conversational story-telling.* Norwood, NJ: Ablex.

Pollard-Gott, L., McCloskey, M., & Todres, A. K. (1979). Subjective story structure. *Discourse Processing, 2,* 251–282.

Potts, G. R., Keenan, J. M., & Golding, J. M. (1988). Assessing the occurrence of elaborative inferences: Lexical decision versus naming. *Journal of Memory and Language, 27,* 399–415.

Prince, G. (1980). Introduction to the study of the narratee. In J. P. Tompkins (Ed.), *Reader response criticism: From formalism to post-structuralism.* Baltimore: Johns Hopkins University Press.

Propp, V. (1969). *Morphology of the folktale.* Austin, TX: University of Texas Press.

Redeker, G. (1984). On differences between spoken and written language. *Discourse Processes, 7,* 43–55.

Reiser, B. J., & Black, J. B. (1982). Processing and structural models of comprehension. *Text, 2,* 225–252.

Reiser, B. J., Black, J. B., & Lehnert, W. G. (1985). Thematic knowledge structures in the understanding and generation of narratives. *Discourse Processes, 8,* 357–389.

Rumelhart, D. E. (1977). Understanding and summarizing brief stories. In D. LaBerge & S. J. Samuels (Eds.), *Basic processes in reading: Perception and comprehension.* Hillsdale, NJ: Erlbaum.

Ryan, M. (1986). Embedded narratives and the structure of plans. *Text, 6,* 107–142.

Sachs, J., Goldman, J., & Chaille, C. (1984). Planning in pretend play: Using language to coordinate narrative development. In A. Pellegrini & T. Yawkey (Eds.), *The development of oral and written language in social contexts.* Norwood, NJ: Ablex.

Schank, R. C. (1975). The structure of episodes in memory. In D. G. Bobrow & A. Collins (Eds.), *Representation and understanding.* New York: Academic Press.

Schank, R. C. (1982). Reminding and memory organization: An introduction to MOPs. In W. G. Lehnert & M. H. Ringle (Eds.), *Strategies for natural language processing.* Hillsdale, NJ: Erlbaum.

Schank, R. C. & Abelson, R. (1977). *Scripts, plans, goals, and understanding.* Hillsdale, NJ: Erlbaum.

Schank, R. C., Collins, G. C., Davis, E., Johnson, P. N., Lytinen, S., & Reiser, B. J. (1982). What's the point? *Cognitive Science, 5,* 255–276.

Schank, R. C., & Reisbeck, C. K. (1981). *Inside computer understanding.* Hillsdale, NJ: Erlbaum.

Schmidt, S. J. (1981). Empirical studies in literature: Introductory remarks. *Poetics, 10,* 317–336.

Seifert, C. M., Dyer, M. G., & Black, J. B. (1986). Thematic knowledge in story understanding. *Text, 6,* 393–426.

Seifert, C. M. McKoon, G. Abelson, R. P., & Ratcliff, R. (1986). Memory connections between thematically similar episodes. *Journal of Experimental Psychology: Learning, Memory, and Cognition, 12,* 219–231.

Seifert, C. M., Robertson, S. P., & Black, J. B. (1985). Types of inferences generated during reading. *Journal of Memory and Language, 24,* 405–422.

Sharkey, N. E. (1986). A model of knowledge-based expectations in text comprehension. In J. A. Galambos, R. P. Abelson, & J. B. Black (Eds.), *Knowledge structures.* Hillsdale, NJ: Erlbaum.

Sharkey, N. E., & Mitchell, D. C. (1985). Word recognition in a functional context: The use of scripts in reading. *Journal of Memory and Language, 2,* 253–270.

Sharkey, N. E., & Sharkey, A. J. C. (1987). What is the point of integration? The loci of knowledge-based facilitation in sentence processing. *Journal of Memory and Language, 26*, 255–276.

Shiffrin, D. (1985). Multiple constraints on discourse options: A qualitative analysis of causal sequences. *Discourse Processes, 8*, 281–303.

Singer, H., & Donlan, D. (1982). *Reading and learning from text.* Hillsdale, NJ: Erlbaum.

Singer, M., & Ferreira, F. (1983). Inferring consequences in story comprehension. *Journal of Verbal Learning and Verbal Behavior, 22*, 437–448.

Smith, E. E., & Medin, D. L. (1981). *Categories and concepts.* Cambridge, MA: Harvard University Press.

Spilich, G. J., Vesonder, G. J., Chiesi, H. L., & Voss, J. F. (1979). Test processing of domain-related information for individuals with high- and low-domain knowledge. *Journal of Verbal Learning and Verbal Behavior, 18*, 275–290.

Spiro, R. J., & Taylor, B. M. (1987). On investigating children's transition from narrative to expository discourse: The multidimensional nature of psychological text classification. In R. J. Tierney, P. L. Anders, & J. N. Mitchell (Eds.), *Understanding readers' understanding.* Hillsdale, NJ: Erlbaum.

Stein, N. L., & Glenn, C. G. (1979). An analysis of story comprehension in elementary school children. In R. O. Freedle (Ed.), *New directions in discourse processing* Vol. 2. Norwood, NJ: Ablex.

Stein, N. L., & Nezworski, G. (1978). The effects of organization and instructional set on story memory. *Discourse Processes, 1*, 177–193.

Stein, N. L., & Policastro, T. (1984). The story: A comparison between children's and teacher's viewpoints. In H. Mandel, N. L. Stein, & T. Trabasso (Eds.), *Learning and comprehension of text.* Hillsdale, NJ: Erlbaum.

Tannen, D. (1985). Relative focus on involvement in oral and written discourse. In D. R. Olson, N. Torrance, & A. Hildyard (Eds.), *Literacy, language, and learning: The nature and consequences of reading and writing.* Cambridge, Eng.: Cambridge University Press.

Tannen, D. (Ed.). (1988). *Linguistics in context: Connecting observation and understanding.* Norwood, NJ: Ablex.

Thorndyke, P. W. (1977). Cognitive structures in comprehension and memory of narrative discourse. *Cognitive Psychology, 9*, 77–110.

Tompkins, J. P. (1980). *Reader response criticism: From formalism to post-structuralism.* Baltimore, MD: Johns Hopkins University Press.

Trabasso, T., & van den Broek, P. (1985). Causal thinking and the representation of narrative events. *Journal of Memory and Language, 24*, 612–630.

Trabasso, T., van den Broek, P., & Lui, L. (1988). A model for generating questions that assess and promote comprehension. *Questioning Exchange, 2*, 25–38.

Trabasso, T., Secco, T., & van den Broek, P. (1983). Causal cohesion and story coherence. In H. Mandl, N. L. Stein, & T. Trabasso (Eds.), *Learning and comprehension of text.* Hillsdale, NJ: Erlbaum.

Trabasso, T., & Sperry, L. L. (1985). Causal relatedness and importance of story events. *Journal of Memory and Language, 24*, 595–611.

Uleman, J. S. (in press). A framework for thinking intentionally about unintended thoughts. In J. S. Uleman & J. A. Bargh (Eds.), *Unintended thought: The limits of awareness, intentions, and control.* New York: Guilford.

van den Broek, P. (1988). The effects of causal relations and hierarchical position on the importance of story statements. *Journal of Memory and Language, 27*, 1–22.

van den Broek, P., & Trabasso, T. (1986). Causal networks vs. goal hierarchies in summarizing text. *Discourse Processes, 9*, 1–15.

van Dijk, T. A. (1972). *Some aspects of text grammars: A study in theoretical linguistics and poetics.* The Hague: Mouton.

van Dijk, T. A., & Kintsch, W. (1983). *Strategies of discourse comprehension.* New York: Academic Press.

Voss, J. F., & Bisanz, G. L. (1985). Knowledge and the processing of narrative and expository texts. In B. K. Britton & J. B. Black (Eds.), *Understanding expository text.* Hillsdale, NJ: Erlbaum.

Wells, G. (1985). Oral and literate competencies in the early school years. In D. Olson, N. Torrance, & A. Hildyard (Eds.), *Literacy, language and learning: The nature and consequences of reading and writing.* Cambridge, Eng.: Cambridge University Press.

Whaley, J. F. (1981). Reader's expectations for story structure. *Reading Research Quarterly, 17*, 90–114.

Wilensky, R. (1982). Points: A theory of the structure of stories in memory. In W. G. Lehnert & M. H. Ringle (Eds.), *Strategies for natural language processing.* Hillsdale, NJ: Erlbaum.

Wilensky, R. (1983a). *Planning and understanding.* Cambridge, MA: Addison, Wesley.

Wilensky, R. (1983b). Story grammars versus story points. *Behavioral and Brain Sciences, 6*, 579–623.

Winograd, P., & Johnston, P. (1987). Some considerations for advancing the teaching of reading comprehension. *Educational Psychologist, 22*, 213–230.

Wright, G. H. von (1971). *Explanation and understanding.* Ithaca, NY: Cornell University Press.

Yekovich, F. R., & Thorndyke, P. W. (1981). An evaluation of alternative functional models of narrative schemata. *Journal of Verbal Learning and Verbal Behavior, 20*, 454–469.

Yekovich, F. R., & Walker, C. H. (1987). The activation and use of scripted knowledge in reading about activities. In B. K. Britton & S. M. Glynn (Eds.), *Executive control processes in reading.* Hillsdale, NJ: Erlbaum.

9 TOWARD A MODEL OF ACQUIRING PROCEDURES FROM TEXT

Susan Bovair and David E. Kieras

INTRODUCTION

Understanding how procedures are acquired from text is of both practical and theoretical importance, whether the focus is on the mental processes involved in acquisition, or on how differences in the text affect these processes. From a practical point of view, understanding this process, termed *procedure acquisition* in this paper, is important because all of us follow procedures from written instructions frequently in our daily lives. We fill out forms, assemble children's toys, follow recipes, and are given instructions for using everything from frozen lasagna to home computers. In addition, following procedures is typically a part of our jobs. Sticht (1977) found that in the U.S. Navy, 75 percent of the reading on the job was what he called *reading to do*, where people read in order to carry out some task.

The Need for Research on Procedural Text

There is a body of practically-oriented research on the issue of how usable procedural text or instructions normally are, and whether they can be improved. This research makes clear the value of research on procedural text and also shows the weakness of our current understanding.

Do People Read Instructions?

One problem with procedural text in daily life is that people often do not read it when they should. Although many people normally read instructions, a sizable minority does not. For example, 75 percent of the subjects interviewed by Wright (1981) said that they would read all of the instructions for a videocassette recorder or item of similar complexity, but this means that a quarter of the people would not. In addition, for most other consumer items, 30 percent to 40 percent of people said that they would not read any instructions. This means that at least a quarter of the people buying an item are likely not to read the instructions for it.

One reason that people do not read instructions may be because they do not feel that they need go to the trouble. If they think that there is an easier way to do the task, then they may not bother with the instructions. For example, Barnard, Wright, and Wilcox (1979) found that 30 percent of 200 undergraduates at Cambridge University

Work on this paper was supported by the Office of Naval Research, Cognitive Sciences Program, under contract number N00014-85-K-0138, NR 667-543.

filled out a simple one-question form the wrong way. They were asked to mark which one of three alternatives applied to them, but instead many deleted (marked through), the alternatives that did not apply. It seems more likely that these subjects simply did not read the instructions and instead guessed at how they should answer, than that they did read the instructions but were unable to understand them. Another example is the experiments by LeFevre and Dixon (1986), where subjects presented with instructions and an example that contradicted each other, ignored the instructions and followed the example. People may have learned from experience that instructions are often hard to understand and follow, and this may explain why they often prefer to use other strategies like guessing or following an example. Understanding the procedure acquisition process is not likely to be directly useful in motivating people to read instructions, but if it leads to an improvement in procedure instructions, then people may be more likely to read them.

Can People Follow the Instructions That They Read?

The problem of people not understanding the information they are given is a serious one. Kammann (1975) cites studies by the Bell Telephone Company that found that the instructions for dialing that are provided in the telephone book are correctly applied only 62 percent of the time. He suggests a rule of thumb: even when instructions are used, they are understood only about two-thirds of the time.

Wright (1981) has suggested that problems with understanding procedural text fall into three basic categories: The first is content; sometimes the information in the instructions is wrong. The second is presentation; the language and illustrations used in the instructions may be hard to understand. The third is structure; information may not be appropriately organized for the task. Thus, good procedural text has good content, presentation, and structure; but it is not easy to specify how to determine that a piece of procedural text has these qualities. While a specific piece of procedural text can be improved, it may not be clear which improvements actually made a difference. For example, Felker and Rose (1981) rewrote the FCC radio rules for recreational boaters into "clear English" and showed improvements in both the speed and accuracy of people's application of the rules. However, the fact that the rewritten rules were simply shorter, reducing the original 49 pages of material to 11, may have produced the better performance, rather than the new style of the material. In addition, even professional writers cannot always improve performance with a document. Duffy, Curran, and Sass (1983) found that new versions of technical prose prepared by three different technical writing companies failed to show improvement over the original.

Thus, even the community of practical technical writers cannot reliably improve a text or specify how it would be done. The need for further research and theoretical development is painfully clear.

Theoretical Value of Studying Procedural Text

While understanding procedure acquisition has practical importance, procedural text and the processes of procedure acquisition have distinctive qualities that make them interesting to study from a theoretical viewpoint. One quality is that when reading instructions to carry out some task, a reader's processing of the text is likely to be different from the processing involved when reading stories. Kieras (1981) showed that the task that readers are required to perform can affect how they read a text, so that reading for comprehension involves different amounts and types of processing from reading to identify a main idea. Reading in order to be able to execute some procedure is also likely to have characteristic ways of processing. Another distinctive quality of procedural text is that problems in understanding can be revealed directly in performance. The reader must use the knowledge from the text in order to do something, and so examining what the reader does can be used to assess what the reader acquired.

There is a severely limited amount of research on procedure acquisition. This is surprising, given the practical importance and the theoretical interest of procedure acquisition. The lack of research in this area is unexpected and not easy to understand; it is an important area, instructions are frequently poorly written, and there is no reason to think that procedures are any less theoretically interesting than stories. The dearth of research means that rather than simply review existing literature, this paper will focus on theoretical analysis and will try to outline a theory of procedure acquisition. The current lack of such a theory means that the sparse empirical research seems incoherent because studies cannot easily be related to each other or generalized to situations beyond those studied. Outlining a model of the acquisition of procedures from text will be the first step toward providing a perspective for existing work and will suggest where more research would be fruitful.

Scope of This Paper

In order to present a clear picture of the model, with its strengths and limitations, it is important to define procedure acquisition and to specify what kinds of written material and what aspects of the procedure acquisition process the model is concerned with. The kind of text of interest is *procedural text*, which is text intended to convey a procedure. Procedural text may vary in its level of procedural detail, ranging from a complete, detailed procedure that can be executed more or less directly from the text, through instructions that demand more inferences to be made by the reader, all the way to text that provides only general knowledge about the task and expects readers to infer the actual procedure by themselves. This paper will consider both text that presents incomplete procedures and thus demands some inference, and text that attempts to provide a complete, detailed procedure. However, text that does not try to present an explicit procedure will not be considered because, in this case, the reader's task is problem solving rather than procedure acquisition.

Because a reader's strategies and performance are different with different tasks, it is important to define what tasks are relevant. For the purposes of this discussion, procedure acquisition tasks include (a) reading instructions and performing each step as it is read; (b) reading a whole procedure through and then remembering it long enough to perform it; and (c) reading a procedure and memorizing it for performance later. While instructions may be hard to follow simply because they are poorly written, the task itself may be difficult and complex; such a procedure may be hard to acquire however well the text is written. While procedure complexity certainly deserves study, the writer of procedural text typically has no control over it. Thus, we will focus on effects of how procedural text is written and not on the effects of different kinds of procedures.

The rest of this paper is organized as follows: First, the theoretical model will be described, first in overview, and then some of the theoretical properties of the processes in the model will be described in some detail. Second, using the model as a framework, the relevant studies in the research literature will be surveyed based on what processes in the model each study addresses. A brief conclusion will summarize further research directions and practical implications.

A MODEL OF PROCEDURE ACQUISITION

Our goal is to outline a model of procedure acquisition that constitutes the first steps toward a theory. The model has been suggested both by some research (such as Kieras & Bovair, 1986) and theoretical considerations (notably Anderson, 1983, 1987). In this paper, we will outline the model and describe it in more detail and will then use it as a framework to interpret existing data. The model will also be used to identify gaps in our current understanding of procedure acquisition and to suggest how such gaps may be filled.

The model of procedure acquisition to be outlined was first described in Kieras and Bovair (1986) and is illustrated in Figure 9.1. It distinguishes two major comprehension processes: the basic reading comprehension process, and a procedure comprehension process. The procedure comprehension process consists of three sub-processes: procedure construction, immediate transfer, and an acquisition monitor. Finally, there is a procedure interpreter that actually executes a procedure once its representation has been built. The model assumes that the basic reading comprehension process produces a propositional representation of the input text (cf. Kintsch, 1974). Procedure comprehension processes then use the propositional representation to construct a correct representation of the procedure that can be executed by the interpreter. Once the interpreter can correctly execute the procedure, then knowledge compilation processes (Anderson, 1983, 1987) can begin to operate. Since knowledge compilation takes place after the procedure comprehension processes it is not discussed in detail.

Knowledge Representation in the Model

Procedural and Declarative Knowledge

The model assumes a distinction between procedural and declarative knowledge, along the lines of Anderson (1976). Declarative knowledge consists of a network of propositions in the form of HAM or ACT structure (Anderson & Bower, 1973; Anderson 1976, 1983), while procedural knowledge is represented as production rules (Anderson 1976, 1983). Like propositions, production rules are a good representation for knowledge because they provide a modular representation consisting of discrete components that are of roughly the same "size," and can be counted and used to make quantitative predictions. Examples of the use of production rules in this way may be found in Kieras and Bovair (1986), and Bovair, Kieras, and Polson (1988).

Examples of procedure text and the corresponding production rules are shown in Tables 9.1 and 9.2 (cf. Kieras and Bovair, 1986). The syntax of the production rules in Table 9.2 is (*Name IF (condition) THEN (action)*), where the condition tests for information in working memory, and everything in the action part of the rule will be executed if the condition is satisfied. In Table 9.2, the first rule is named *Start*. Its condition will be satisfied if the goal to do the procedure is present in working memory, and the note that the procedure is being done is not present. If the condition of this rule is satisfied, then the action will be executed, resulting in the goal of doing the first step and the note that the procedure is being done being added to working memory. This changes working memory so that the condition of the first rule is no longer satisfied, but now the condition of the second rule in Table 9.2 is satisfied.

Thus, each production rule modifies working memory in a way that "triggers," or *fires*, the next rule in the sequence. To correctly represent a procedure, the production

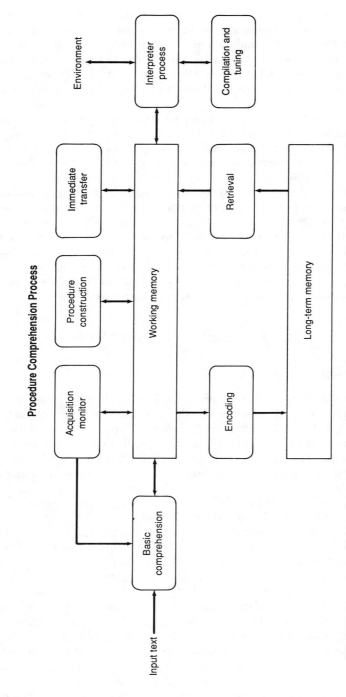

FIGURE 9.1 An outline of a process model for acquiring a procedure from text. *Source:* The acquisition of procedures from text: A production system analysis of transfer of training, by David E. Kieras and Susan Bovair. *Journal of Memory and Language, 25* (5), October 1986.

TABLE 9.1   Example of Procedural Text

If the command is to do the X procedure, then
Step 1: Press the red button
Step 2: If the red light is on, set the selector to X.
Step 3: If the blue light is on, then the system is ready.
Step 4: If the white light is on and the green light is off, press the blue button.

---

rules have to have a properly coordinated set of conditions and actions. Generating the correct set of rules from the input propositions is the job of the procedure comprehension process.

Acquiring a procedure from text is closely related to the process of acquiring procedures in general, which has been studied under the label of *acquisition of cognitive skill* (Anderson, 1981). Learning the procedures for a word-processing pro-

TABLE 9.2   Production Rules for Example Procedure

(Start   IF   ((GOAL DO X PROCEDURE)
              (NOT (NOTE DOING X PROCEDURE)))
     THEN ((ADD GOAL DO STEP ONE)
              (ADD NOTE DOING X PROCEDURE)))

(Step1 IF   ((GOAL DO X PROCEDURE)
              (GOAL DO STEP ONE))
    THEN ((PRESS RED BUTTON)
             (DELETE GOAL DO STEP ONE)
             (ADD GOAL DO STEP TWO)))

(Step2 IF   ((GOAL DO X PROCEDURE)
              (GOAL DO STEP TWO)
              (LOOK RED LIGHT ON))
     THEN ((SET SELECTOR TO X)
             (DELETE GOAL DO STEP TWO)
             (ADD DO STEP THREE)))

(Step3 IF   ((GOAL DO X PROCEDURE)
              (GOAL DO STEP THREE)
              (LOOK BLUE LIGHT ON))
    THEN ((DELETE GOAL DO STEP THREE)
             (ADD DO STEP FOUR)
             (ADD NOTE SYSTEM READY))

(Step4 IF   ((GOAL DO X PROCEDURE)
              (GOAL DO STEP FOUR
              (NOTE SYSTEM READY)
              (LOOK WHITE LIGHT ON)
              (LOOK GREEN LIGHT OFF))
     THEN ((PRESS BLUE BUTTON)
             (DELETE GOAL DO STEP FOUR)
             (ADD GOAL FINISH)))

(Finish IF   ((GOAL DO PROCEDURE)
              (GOAL FINISH)
     THEN ((DELETE GOAL FINISH)
             (DELETE GOAL DO PROCEDURE)
             (DELETE NOTE DOING PROCEDURE)))

---

gram to the point where they can be executed rapidly and without effort is an example of the acquisition of a cognitive skill. Anderson (1976, 1983) proposed that there are three stages in the skill acquisition process, as had Fitts (1964) before him. The first is the *declarative stage*, where a declarative representation of relevant knowledge is used by skill-independent production rules to produce behavior. In Anderson's model, knowledge of a procedure is assumed to be initially in declarative form. During this stage, the procedure can only be executed in a conscious, controlled way that often involves some degree of problem solving.

In Anderson's second stage, the *knowledge compilation stage*, the skill has been practiced enough that it can be executed with much less effort. At this stage the skill is represented as production rules, with each step represented in a separate rule; and when given the initial goal and appropriate context information, the rules run with no pause for problem solving. The third stage is the *tuning stage*. With practice, the rules become more and more efficient, steps are collapsed into one another, and the procedure is executed rapidly and with little effort.

Our model of procedure acquisition concentrates on the declarative stage of skill acquisition, where the text is translated into a declarative representation of the procedure. Although the later stages of skill acquisition are obviously important, they are assumed to be the result of practice and experience rather than reading the initial text, and therefore of less interest for this paper. Thus, the focus here will be on the text and how readers can generate a procedure from it, not on how people can remember a procedure over a long period of time, or how they improve in performance with practice. In this context, it is interesting to note that if we take Sticht's (1977) reading-to-do tasks as being largely procedural, then much real-world procedure acquisition is also concerned with generating and immediately following a procedure from text, rather than memorizing the procedures; Sticht found that 80 percent of reading on the job is for tasks that the reader has already done before.

Declarative Representations of Procedures

The model assumes that a procedure is first represented in declarative form and becomes represented as production rules only after the procedure has been acquired and practiced. However, it is both possible and convenient to describe this declarative form *as if* it were a set of production rules. This characterization is possible because the content of a procedure can be represented in either form, and convenient because a set of production rules can be easily checked for completeness and correctness by trying to execute them. Thus, it is useful to think of the reader as constructing a declarative version of the production rules that are needed to execute the procedure. Once a complete and correct declarative representation of the procedure has been constructed, then the true procedural representation can be constructed. Thus, although the initial representation of a procedure is easily expressed as production rules, the actual representation is assumed to be declarative.

The main thrust of this assumption is one of maintaining theoretical traditions and clarity; it seems accepted that declarative representations can be constructed and manipulated by complex, knowledge-driven, inferential processes, such as comprehension and problem-solving, while developing procedural knowledge is governed by more elementary, automatic mechanisms. If we assume that the reader temporarily represents a procedure as a declarative isomorph of the procedural production rules, it is easy to integrate standard theoretical reading mechanisms with standard theoretical cognitive skill mechanisms. Of course, other formats for the declarative representation of a procedure are possible; we have adopted production rule isomorphs only because of their formal adequacy and direct relationship to the assumed format of procedural knowledge. It would be worthwhile to construct a full simulation model of the procedure acquisition process to determine the viability of this representation and to explore alternatives.

Following the GOMS model of procedural knowledge proposed by Card, Moran, and Newell (1983), the model assumes that procedures are organized hierarchically in terms of *goals* and subgoals. For each goal, there is a procedure, called a *method*, for accomplishing the goal. A method consists of steps that can be either elementary actions, termed *operators*, or assertions of subgoals that need to be accomplished. The mapping between GOMS models and production rules is provided by Bovair, Kieras, and Polson (1988), and all of the example procedures and methods used in this paper follow the conventions described.

Processes Involved in Learning Procedures from Text

Reading Comprehension.

The reading comprehension process in this model of procedure acquisition is assumed to be the same as for any other reading task and consists of reading processes like those described in Just and Carpenter (1987a). Thus, this process will have problems with procedural text similar to those it would have with technical prose or narrative text. The reading comprehension process reads and processes the instructions one sentence at a time, parsing each sentence, and doing the basic referential and semantic analysis needed to create the propositional representation for each sentence in working memory. A typical referential analysis might involve simply attaching the label for a particular object to the appropriate concept. Thus, a knob might be referred to as *the tuning knob*, and this label must be attached to an instance of the concept KNOB. Note that for a procedure to be executed, the actual physical objects referred to must also be identified in the environment, so that the specified action can actually be performed. But it is not clear if identifying the external referent occurs during the reading comprehension process or if it occurs later.

Procedure Comprehension Processes.

In our model, the procedure comprehension processes build a declarative representation of the procedure from the propositional representation of the procedure text. Procedure comprehension is similar to what Just and Carpenter (1987a) describe as text-level processes in reading comprehension, in which schemas are used to integrate the text; for example, in comprehending narrative text, such processes use inference to fill in the causal chain of events. While establishing the causal and temporal chain is particularly important in stories, it may also be an important part of constructing a procedure. The idea that there are procedure comprehension processes that take place after reading comprehension is somewhat similar to the distinction proposed by van Dijk and Kintsch (1983) between the processes that produce the text base and those that produce the situation model.

Procedure comprehension consists of three major sub-processes. This first is the *procedure construction* process, which takes the representation of the text and constructs the declarative form of production rules. The others are the *immediate transfer* process, which checks to see if newly constructed rules are already known, and the *acquisition monitor* process, which monitors whether a new rule has been fully learned.

Procedure construction.   Our model assumes that the propositional representation of the text is used to construct an executable propositional representation of the procedure; but our understanding of the procedure construction process is quite limited, and it is not clear just how this construction takes place or what stages might be involved. It is possible to describe a general outline of the process; but in order to work out the details, a simulation model would need to be built and more research performed.

The assumptions of the model provide the framework within which procedure construction can be characterized. The theoretical problem is to determine how the production rules are constructed based on the information in the text. In other words, just how is text like that in Table 9.1 translated into rules like those in Table 9.2? Procedure construction involves heavy use of implicit information; for example, for each step in the procedure, the information about the goal, the current context, and the next step are all typically implicit but need to be explicitly encoded into the condition and action of a production rule. Problem solving may be required to infer missing information and details of the actions to be performed if they are not stated explicitly.

We can elaborate on some of these construction processes. In deciding what the goal of a procedure is, the reader is likely to be influenced by a variety of cues in the procedure text. Sometimes the goals will be stated explicitly: *If the goal is to do the MA procedure, then* . . . , but it may be signaled more indirectly, as in Table 9.1 by means of a short lead-in phrase such as *if the command is to do the X procedure* . . . or a heading. In the absence of more specific statements of the goal of the procedure, readers may simply assume that the end state of a procedure is the goal state.

The reader of procedural text must also generate rules that will perform the correct actions in the right order. The text may directly help the reader by using labels such as Step 1: as in the example in Tables 9.1 and 9.2, in which the step labels are incorporated into the rule conditions and actions. Also, production rules can have several elementary actions in a single rule. This would mean that a statement such as *Press button A and press button B* would be translated into one rule with both button pushes in its action. On the other hand, a useful assumption for newly learned procedures is that there is only one such action to a rule (Bovair, Kieras, & Polson, 1988). However, even when a single action is explicitly indicated in the procedure statement, there may be more than one step implied, and therefore more than one rule will need to be built. For example, Step 2 in Table 9.1 appears to correspond directly to a single production rule, as shown in Table 9.2. But it can also be interpreted as conveying two steps. The first is performing the actions to determine the state of the light (e.g., finding and looking at the light), while a second is setting the selector. This means that two production rules would need to be built to represent this step, one that checks the light and stores its state in working memory, and one that tests the state of the light and acts accordingly.

In a further complication, what seems to be a single step may actually be a whole method rather than a single rule. For example, Dixon (1982) used statements like *The left knob should be turned in order to set the alpha meter to 20.* Apparently, this could easily be translated to:

(IF ((GOAL SET ALPHA METER TO 20)) THEN ((TURN LEFT KNOB)))

However, this simple translation is not correct, because simply turning the left knob will not get the meter set to 20; the knob must be turned while the meter is monitored. When the right value is reached, the knob turning is stopped; if the meter overshoots, then the knob is turned in the opposite direction, and so forth. This single statement seems more accurately characterized as the user having the goal of setting the meter, and executing knob-turning and meter-monitoring methods in order to accomplish that goal.

Immediate transfer.   Based on the results in Kieras and Bovair (1986), there is an immediate transfer process that compares the representation of the current rule to the already-known rules. If the current rule is new, then it must be maintained in working memory and encoded into long-term memory, which takes time. If the current rule is the same as, or very similar to, an existing rule, then at most small modifications of the existing rule will be required, and these take very little time. This immediate transfer process is responsible for large savings in the time to learn new procedures if they have steps in common with previously read or learned procedures (Kieras, Tibbits, & Bovair, 1984; Kieras & Bovair, 1986; Bovair, Kieras, & Polson, 1988).

Acquisition monitor.   Finally, procedure comprehension also seems to involve an executive control process (Schumacher, 1987) that monitors the acquisition of the steps of the procedure. Kieras and Bovair (1986) had subjects learn procedures from a step-by-step, self-paced presentation and found that the reading time for each step of a procedure remained high until the subject could execute the step without error. At this point, when the step is apparently learned, the reading time for the step decreases sharply. Thus the subject allocates more time to steps not yet acquired and less time to acquired steps. This ability to allocate time between new and known material was also found by Johnson and Kieras (1983), who studied the effects of prior knowledge on reading and recall of simple expository text and found that subjects concentrated their time on the unknown information. The acquisition monitor process must be able to distinguish known from unknown steps to decide which information should be studied in more detail.

Executing and Debugging Procedures

Once the declarative version of a procedure has been constructed, then a procedure interpreter process accesses the representation and executes the procedure. This execution will succeed if the declarative representation has been correctly constructed. After this stage has been reached, the processes of skill acquisition that create a procedural knowledge representation of the procedure may begin.

FACTORS AFFECTING PERFORMANCE
IN ACQUIRING PROCEDURES FROM TEXT

Performance Measures

In assessing performance with procedural text, the task chosen will affect processing and thus performance measures. For example, there is some evidence that reading to execute a single step immediately may be different from reading to execute the whole procedure later (Dixon, 1982). There is also evidence that subjects asked to read procedural text for recall may read it differently from when they read for immediate execution (Dixon, 1982; Kintsch, 1986). The model outlined here suggests that tasks differ because they call different processes into play. If subjects are presented with procedural text to be recalled, they may simply memorize it as text and not as a procedure, thus involving only the reading comprehension and text-encoding processes. Procedures presented one step at a time for immediate execution of each step will involve both reading comprehension and procedure comprehension processes. However, the procedure comprehension stage will not need to integrate the procedure steps into a whole procedure, nor will the procedure have to be encoded into long-term memory.

If the concern is to assess how well procedural text allows the reader to actually perform the procedure, the best measures of success will be how quickly and accurately the reader can perform the procedure. In addition, reading time is a useful measure of both reading comprehension and procedure comprehension processes. Because verbal recall of a procedure may not involve much of the procedure comprehension processes, it has little value as a measure in the study of procedural text, in contrast to its role in much reading research. Measuring how well the procedures can be executed after a delay is a far more useful measure of retention.

Given the limited number of measures and tasks that are typically used in the study of procedural text, it may be difficult to distinguish the different processing stages that the model predicts from each other. For example, it may be hard to distinguish reading comprehension and procedure comprehension from each other, given that reading time reflects both processes. However, the syntactic complexity of the text should affect reading comprehension, while the complexity of the procedure should affect procedure comprehension; and so it may be possible to distinguish the procedures with an appropriately designed study.

Factors Affecting Reading Comprehension of Procedural Text

Reading comprehension effects in procedure acquisition are hard to assess by themselves because it is difficult to separate them from the effects of procedure comprehension or even execution. One reason for this is that experiments are typically not designed to study reading comprehension of procedural text separately from the other stages, frequently using overall measures that include all three stages. Basic comprehension should not be a source of execution problems unless a procedure is so incomprehensibly written that it is hard to construct a complete procedure at all, and so execution measures are not likely to reveal much about the basic comprehension stage. Even when more direct measures of reading comprehension such as reading times are collected, they can be affected by both procedure comprehension and reading comprehension.

One way to alleviate our inability to distinguish basic comprehension from procedure comprehension is to make the reasonable assumption that procedural text has the same reading comprehension processes and problems as other technical prose. Some factors that affect the comprehension of technical prose have been summarized by Kieras and Dechert (1985). One example that is well known from the comprehension literature is that negatives are harder to comprehend than affirmatives; the same is true of procedural text. Jones (1966) investigated the use of the qualifying negative *except* on the performance of a task. In one experiment, subjects were given the command *Mark the numbers 1, 3, 4, 6, 7* for a long string of digits 1 through 8, arranged randomly. Subjects seeing this command were faster and made fewer errors than subjects who saw the equivalent command *Mark all the numbers except 2, 5, 8*, although the number of items to be remembered is smaller. File and Jew (1973) gave airline passengers waiting for their flight some emergency instructions to be recalled that were presented in either written or oral form, were either affirmative or negative, and were either active or passive. Subjects tended to recall in an affirmative, active form, regardless of how the material had been presented, and their recall was better when the instructions had been presented in the affirmative form; but there was no difference between active and passive presentation.

While slower performance on instructions containing negations may be due to effects on reading comprehension, it may also be that it is more difficult to construct a procedure if it is presented in a negative form. One way to explain the results, from a study by Wright and Wilcox (1979), is as procedure construction effects. They found that while affirmative forms were always better, two negations could sometimes produce faster and more accurate performance than one. Subjects were required to perform one of two tasks, and the instructions contained either zero, one, or two negations. In the single-button task, the subject was required to either respond by pressing a button or not respond at all, based on the instruction and a presented letter. For example, *Do not press if the letter is P* has a single negation, while *Do not press unless the letter is P* has two. In the two-button task, the subject had to choose between one button or another, such as, *Press the right-hand button if the picture is a circle; press the left-hand button if not.* Wright and Wilcox found that in the single-button task, two negations in the instructions produced faster, more accurate performance than only one, but that one negation was better than two in the two-button task. If these effects were due only to reading comprehension effects, both tasks should show the expected pattern that two negations were harder than one.

The Wright and Wilcox effects may be a result of the way negations in text are translated into production rules. A production rule with a negated *action* is impossible, because the action is executed only if the rule condition is met; so a statement with a single negation like *Do not press if the letter is P* cannot be translated into

IF ((letter present) (letter is P)) THEN (NOT (press)).

Rather, in order to be executed it has to be transformed into

IF ((letter present) (NOT (letter is P))) THEN (press).

A statement containing two negative elements like *Do not press unless the letter is P* can be simply recoded into an affirmative form and then directly translated into

IF ((letter present) (letter is P)) THEN (press).

Simply recoding the whole statement into the affirmative form may be relatively easy, compared to moving the negation from the action to the condition. However, this may only be true for the single-button task; in the two-button task, the subject may attempt to construct a rule for each button, and this may remove the advantage for the double negative.

Although procedural text may have reading comprehension problems similar to those of other technical prose, such as difficulty with negative forms, it is likely to have characteristic reading comprehension problems as well. For example, procedural text seems to be especially prone to problems with reference. Wright (1981) suggests that people make errors with phrases used to qualify numbers, such as *at least* or *not more than* because they seem to concentrate on the number and disregard the qualifier. Such problems may arise either because of the difficulty of establishing the meaning of such open-ended terms, or the difficulty of building a procedure with them. Fisher (1981) analyzed the errors made on functional literacy tests, which are in large part tests of ability to use procedural text. For example, an item on such a test might be *Look at the program for a Business Administration course. Circle the term in which the subject "Salesmanship" is given.* Fisher found that 20 percent of the errors made on such items could be interpreted as a result of the reader failing to take into account a word, part of a word, or phrase in the instructions. For example, subjects might be given *lieutenant-general* in the instructions but circle examples of *general* in the material. Also, 16 percent of the errors were a result of the subjects giving more information than was requested, as when they were given *fruit dishes* and they circle both fruit and vegetable dishes. As Just and Carpenter (1987b) point out, these results suggest that a total of 36% of the errors may be a result of interpreting a referent too broadly. Just and Carpenter (1987b) have suggested that errors due to referential difficulties in procedural text could arise because the vocabulary used in procedural text is more likely to contain unknown terms, and these may lead to semantic and referential problems. For example, if the components are novel in an assembly task, the user may not know what a referent looks like. The presence of unknown terms may also explain why subjects interpret referents too broadly; for example, they may not know the difference between *lieutenant-general* and *general* and assume that these are different names for the same thing. Such problems may be obscured in ordinary reading tasks and materials but are unavoidable in procedural tasks, where subjects have to demonstrate their understanding overtly.

Factors Affecting Procedure Comprehension

Knowledge Required for Procedure Acquisition

Instructions do not spell out a procedure in the detail needed to actually construct and execute it. Readers must therefore try to infer these details from other knowledge. In many situations, a subject must build a procedure that includes many details of exactly what must be done that are usually not included in the instructions. For example, consider a step from the Smith and Goodman (1984) assembly task, *Now you are to wrap one end of the wire around one of the short bolts.* Before readers can actually carry this step out, they must find a short bolt and pick it up, then decide how to wrap the wire, and then select the part of the bolt where the wire should be wrapped.

The physical objects involved in the procedure can be a source of knowledge about how to perform various actions; how to operate a control is often suggested by the shape of the control, and the labels can suggest when to operate it. Instructions usually assume that the reader has at least some appropriate domain knowledge; for example, readers are usually assumed to know what a child's wagon looks like, or how to use a screwdriver, or turn a knob. If the objects and the prior knowledge support the required inferences, then inferring the necessary details will be quick, and constructing and executing the procedure will be easy. But if the knowledge is not available, then readers must try to fill in the gaps by engaging in problem solving, with varying levels of success. For example, although detailed procedures are often called "recipes," actual cooking recipes assume knowledge of cooking methods and equipment. If a reader does not know how to execute the *simmer* method, then the chicken cacciatore is likely to end up burnt. A direction like *add the softened butter* may cause problems for the cooking novice, because he or she has to figure out how to get the butter softened before executing the adding step. Because readers vary so much in their knowledge, even procedures that appear well specified may still demand major problem-solving efforts by some readers. For example, although the procedures used in Kieras and Bovair (1986) were intended to provide all the executable detail, some subjects thought that the lights on the control panel were push buttons and became very confused when pushing them had no effect.

If readers have the appropriate background knowledge, they may still be able to construct a correct procedure even when the propositional representation derived from the instructional text is defective. For example, in a study by Mohammed and Swales (1984), subjects used the manufacturer's instructions to set the time and the alarm on a digital alarm clock. Their subjects were either native or non-native speakers of English with either a science or a non-science background. The striking result was that non-native speakers with a science background were faster than native speakers of English with a non-science background. This result implies that it is not basic comprehension that is critical in using instructions but the ability to infer the details needed to construct correct procedures.

If knowledge needed to infer some detail used in constructing a procedure is not available, then the reader may not be able to do some step in the procedure. The problem may be identified at any stage in the process of procedure acquisition. For example, if a step in some procedure requires a reader to *Degauss the CRT*, then the reader must know how to degauss something, what the CRT is, and where to find it. When does the reader find out that he or she does not have this knowledge? The reader may be able to tell either during reading, because these words are unfamiliar, or during procedure construction, when he or she cannot construct a degaussing method from the instructions. But the reader may have to wait until procedure execution for it to become clear that how to degauss the CRT is not apparent from the execution context. For example, there is no push button on the device labeled *CRT Degauss*. Thus, frequently the reader may recognize a lack of knowledge in the reading comprehension or procedure comprehension stages, but sometimes the procedure must be executed in order for problems to become obvious.

Thus, the execution stage is the last chance to map the text onto the world, and so problems found here tend to be those that were not anticipated during procedure construction, and they may not be solvable by rereading the instructions. For example, readers may find that they do not know where a particular knob is. In addition, determining the correct sequence of steps is typically done during procedure construction; but if the text does not specify the order of steps, and the reader does not have the knowledge needed to infer it, then the correct order may have to be determined during execution by trial and error.

Supporting Inferences Needed to Construct an Executable Procedure

In the absence of useful cues from the physical objects, or appropriate background knowledge, the reader of procedural text may be able to make the proper inferences if the text itself contains the necessary information. Wright (1981) gives the example of a patient who has to decide how faithfully to follow the prescription orders given by the doctor or pharmacist, and how to interpret instructions such as "take two tablets a day." Providing information about the consequences of not following the orders, or about what the drug is supposed to do may help the patient make these decisions. Thus, whenever a reader must make inferences in order to construct a procedure, providing an explanation may help the inference processes.

While readers may not be able to make the correct inferences because of lack of knowledge, they also may not realize that the inferences they are making are incorrect. Evidence for this comes from a study by Kieras, Tibbits, and Bovair (1984), who compared experts and novices in a device operation task. The instructions were presented either in a linear step-by-step form or in a hierarchical menu, where making a menu choice gave the reader the appropriate step-by-step instructions. The hierarchical menu resulted in faster, more accurate performance if the subject was familiar with the device, but step-by-step instructions were better if the device was unfamiliar. With step-by-step instructions, lack of knowledge is not a problem because relatively few inferences are needed; but the hierarchical menu system apparently tempted subjects to try to infer parts of the instructions, and their lack of knowledge sometimes led them astray.

Explanatory material that can be used to support inferences in procedure construction can be divided into two main types. The first can be described as *how-it-works information* about components of the system and their relationships, while the second is *goal structure information* that explains why the steps are done in terms of what is accomplished. For example, in directions for assembling an electrical device, information about how electric circuits work is how-it-works information (Smith & Goodman, 1984). In providing goal structure information, a reader might be directed to assemble two float devices and a small connector bar and then might be told that this is done in order to make the base of a crane (Konoske & Ellis, 1986).

The helpfulness of a how-it-works explanation was demonstrated by Kieras and Bovair (1984), who found that subjects given a mental model of a device performed better during step-by-step training of the operating procedures for the device, compared to subjects who received only the procedure training. This experiment required the subjects to read through all the steps in the procedure before attempting to execute them from memory, and subjects were both faster and more accurate when they were given the mental model. In addition, the mental model was especially useful to subjects who were required to infer the operating procedures. The advantage for the mental model may be attributed to an improvement in memory for the procedures, due to these subjects being able to reconstruct the procedure by inference from the how-it-works knowledge. But the model may have also helped subjects infer the procedure so that they did not need to spend as much time on procedure construction. In addition, a similar study by Smith and Spoehr (1985) found that per-syllable reading times for instruction steps were faster for subjects given a device model, suggesting that the explanation benefited reading comprehension or procedure comprehension or both.

The value of goal structure information was shown by Smith and Goodman (1984). They provided subjects with instructions for a circuit assembly task that were either step-by-step directions with little explanation (the *linear* condition), or that had additional explanatory material. This material was either pure goal structure knowledge (the *structural* condition), or a mixture of goal structure and how-it-works information (the *functional* condition). They found that reading time and errors were worst for step-by-step instructions, and that the structural condition showed the best recall and transfer to a similar circuit, with the functional condition close behind. This implies that the goal structure information is the most useful for procedure construction, although clearly these results are too sketchy to resolve the issue of the merits of goal structure versus how-it-works information. Konoske and Ellis (1986) performed similar experiments in which they provided subjects with step-by-step instructions for the assembly of a model crane that seem to have been either with no explanation or with goal structure explanations. Subjects with goal structure information performed better both initially and after one month. However, in one experiment, the subjects were U.S. Navy personnel with mechanical experience, and for these subjects, there was no advantage for the explanatory information. This suggests that subjects who have the requisite domain knowledge benefit less from explanatory material.

Evidence of the organizing value of goal structure information is provided by Dixon (1987a), who had subjects draw pictures using components described in the instructions; for example, *This will be a picture of a wagon. Draw a long rectangle with two circles underneath.* He found that when information about what the picture will be is presented first, the directions are read faster. When the presentation order is reversed, Dixon suggests that readers buffer the information about the picture components until they find the organizing goal information, and try to guess the relations between the component steps. The guessing hypothesis is supported by the fact that most of the reading time difference comes when reading the components, and that the size of the effect is related to how difficult it is to guess relationships between components presented by themselves.

Another view of explanatory material proposed by Reder, Charney, and Morgan (1986) is that it consists of *elaborations*, which are typically either examples that provide specific instances of a procedure, or *analogies* that try to relate the new procedure to one the reader already knows. The study by Reder et al. (1986) suggests that providing such elaborations in a procedural text helps during reading only if readers do not know what task they will be asked to perform. In this study, subjects read general information on computers and computer commands, and then did tasks that required issuing several commands in sequence. Subjects were either provided with elaborations in the text or not, and were told what the task would be either before or after reading. If the task instructions were given after reading, the time per task and the efficiency (measured by the total number of commands issued, and the number of commands compared to the minimum required) were best for the elaborated manual. If task instructions were given first, it did not matter if the text contained elaborations or not. This is consistent with the interpretation that the elaborations helped subjects remember the information required to construct later-specified procedures; if the readers knew the procedure specifications prior to reading, they could apparently select the relevant material for encoding while reading, meaning that the elaborations are less useful. In a second experiment, where the elaborations were divided into elaborations of command syntax and of computer concepts, syntax elaboration showed improved performance, but the conceptual elaboration did not. This second experiment provides more support for the idea that it is goal structure information like command syntax that helps, not the general, conceptual how-it-works information. Note that this is consistent with the point argued in Kieras and Bovair (1984), that the explanatory material has to support the inference of specific procedures to be useful.

Examples seem to be especially important in procedural text. An example provides an instance of a complete, executable procedure; and it may be far more efficient to translate the example into a procedure and modify it where necessary, than to build a whole new procedure from the text. This may explain the result from a study by LeFevre and Dixon (1986), who found that when subjects were asked to answer series completion or classification questions, given an example and instructions that contradicted each other, they followed the example. However, conclusions drawn from this study must be limited because the example and test problems used were both pictorial, while the instructions were in the form of text. Subjects may prefer the pictorial example because it is in the same modality as the test problem and so seems simpler. However, most users of computer reference manuals would probably testify to the extreme usefulness of examples compared to descriptive text; this is clearly a topic in desperate need of further research.

In addition to being presented early in the instructions, goals need to be clearly signaled to the reader by being made explicit. Dixon, Faries, and Gabrys (1988) have shown that readers who are relatively unfamiliar with the task to be performed are more affected by text form than readers familiar with the task. Using recipes as their instructions, they found that explicit forms such as *soften the butter* rather than implicit ones like *blend the softened butter . . .* were read more quickly and were more likely to be remembered by subjects unfamiliar with cooking. The explicit form may signal to low-knowledge readers that they need to do something to get the butter softened, and that the statement is in fact the goal of a method and therefore important. With the implicit form, they may not realize this.

Procedure Construction

Importance of Procedure Construction

Constructing a procedure from the representation of the text is perhaps the single most important step in acquiring a procedure. Holland, Rose, Dean, and Dory (1985) attempted to characterize good instructions compared to poor ones for the tasks of tying a necktie or assembling a model car. They found that the good and bad instructions could not be distinguished by text characteristics likely to affect reading comprehension such as length of text or length of sentences; indeed, some of the best instructions had the most complex syntax and sentence structure. The important differences between good and bad instructions seemed to be those of content; in particular, poor instructions omitted important details like the orientation of parts in the assembly task, and often included the wrong level of detail. For example, in the task of tying a necktie, it is useful to be told how the tie should look after each step, but details of the exact positions of the hands are confusing.

Organizing Information to Aid Procedure Construction

One important issue is how to present the information so that a procedure can be constructed as efficiently as possible. There are many potential organizations for presenting procedures, and the preferred ones must be those that facilitate the construction process. Spoehr, Morris, and Smith (1983) have pointed out that the organization of information may be studied at two levels: the *micro-level*, where the contents of a single step are the focus; and the *macro-level*, where the focus is on understanding how the steps can be best organized.

With regard to macro-organization, our model assumes that procedures are organized hierarchically, with the hierarchy determined by the goal structure. This implies that instructions should have a hierarchical structure. Gordon, Munro, Rigney, and Lutz (1978) looked at the structure of stories, instructions, and definitions, using their own analyses of the text structure of each type of text. They defined rewrite rules to express the text structure for each type of text, and generated the corresponding tree diagrams. They found that definitions have little structure, while stories and instructions are hierarchical, with stories having a more hierarchical structure than instructions. This structure difference may arise because stories have both a strong temporal and causal structure, while procedures may have less causal structure. Gordon, Munro, Rigney, and Lutz (1978) found that the degree of structure appears to be important for how well the text is remembered, as the strongly constrained stories are recalled best and the unconstrained definitions recalled the least. The intermediate level of structure observed for instructions seems to suffice for short procedures, but long ones impose a greater load on memory and their recall is poor.

A hierarchical structure for procedures in memory is also suggested by Graesser (1978), who studied memory for common procedures, such as how to wash a car or catch a fish. One group of subjects generated the procedures from their own knowledge, another group answered *why?* questions about them, and the third group listened to the procedures and tried to recall them. It is important to note that although subjects listened to the procedures before recalling them, such very familiar procedures were clearly not acquired or learned in the usual sense; and so this study actually examined the structure of already-known procedures. Graesser scaled the hierarchy and relational density, using the answers to the *why?* questions, and found that statements higher in the hierarchy, related to many other statements, were better recalled. If procedures are stored in memory in hierarchical form, as this work suggests, then presenting them in this form may assist in the process of constructing the procedure.

A relatively well-researched aspect of organization is the order in which elements of a procedure are presented. The best order may be the one where the procedure elements are presented in the order in which they are used in executing the procedure; this idea is what Dixon (1982) calls the *use-order principle*. At the level of the complete procedure, this seems obvious; if the steps of a procedure are not presented in the order in which they are to be executed, then the reader will have to put them into the correct order; and this may well be difficult, as suggested by results reported in Kieras (1985). But the use-order principle may also hold at the level of individual steps. A step will be easier to construct if its elements are presented in the order in which they are used in the task.

There are several studies of micro-organization effects. Smith and Spoehr (1985) found that reading a procedure step in an assembly task is faster when information about the action, actor, and object in the step is presented first rather than orientation, location, or modality. In this case, the actor, action, and object information probably is needed first, while orientation, location, and modality provide the details of the operations to be performed. Dixon (1982) presented single steps in various orders of their action or condition components, which he labeled in a somewhat confusing manner. A "condition" could be a "consequence" of the action, as in *Turn the knob so that the meter reads 20*, or an "antecedent" of the action, as in *if the blue light is on, press the button*. He found that for both types of condition, presenting the action first produces faster reading than putting the condition first. On the other hand, Spoehr, Morris, and Smith (1983), using the same meter-setting task, distinguished more clearly Dixon's types into the forms *antecedent condition*, *action*, and *consequent of the action*. They used all six possible orders of antecedent condition, action, and consequent and found that the order antecedent, action, consequent was read the fastest. Dixon (1982, 1987c) argued that his result supports the idea that actions are of primary importance in building a procedure, while Spoehr, Morris, and Smith argued that their result supports the use-order principle. The reader first has to determine whether to do something, then what to do, and then what the final state should be (when to stop turning the knob). Spoehr, Morris, and Smith suggest that one reason for the difference between their results and those of Dixon (1982) is that his results averaged the antecedent-first and consequent-first conditions, giving an apparent advantage to the action-first condition. The nature of the task to be performed may also affect the preferred order; for example, Dixon (1987b) has found that when subjects were looking for a particular light to be either on or off, then action-second sentences were read faster than action-first. He also found that while action-first pairs are generally read faster if the task is to execute the step, antecedent-action pairs are read faster if the task is verbal recall.

One possible problem with these studies of micro-level order is differences in comprehensibility produced by the order manipulations. For example, in the Spoehr,

Morris, and Smith (1983) study, the order of the components is confounded with comprehensibility of the instructions; *So that the gamma meter reads 20 if the sigma indicator is on turn the right knob* seems rather more difficult to read than *if the indicator is on turn the right knob so that the gamma meter reads 20*, not because of the use-order issues but due to violations of normal English sentence structure.

The apparently contradictory results on micro-level order present a confusing picture; the optimum order is not clear, nor is it clear why the results can be so different for apparently similar tasks. Perhaps conceptualizing the task differently might help. In performing a task from instructions, the reader must construct a procedure with the steps in the correct order for execution. Thus, presenting the steps in their execution order, according to the use-order principle, should help the reader to construct the procedure, leading to shorter reading times, and possibly fewer errors and shorter execution times as well. But labeling parts of the procedure with arbitrarily-defined labels, such as antecedent, action, or consequent, does not seem a particularly useful way to think about the content of the instructions. As discussed above, there may be several production rules that need to be built for a single condition or consequent; so it is not obvious that the steps conforming to such labels will be related in a simple way to how they are used in constructing a procedure.

Immediate Transfer and Acquisition Monitor Processes

Immediate Transfer

As described by Kieras and Bovair (1986), the immediate transfer process can be responsible for large savings in the time to acquire new procedures. But it is not clear if the content or organization of the procedural text would affect these savings. The transferability of steps depends on their similarity, which is basically determined by the procedures themselves rather than how they are presented. But it is possible that the instructions could help transfer by emphasizing the similarity of steps or hinder it by obscuring the similarity.

According to Kieras and Bovair (1986), the transfer process is quite limited; subjects can transfer steps that are either the same, or that have only a single minor point of difference in their goal. This implies that the transfer process may be quite sensitive to differences in how the procedure is written. For example, using different terms to refer to the same object may hamper the transfer process. Foltz, Davies, Polson, and Kieras (1988) found that simply changing the name of a procedure from *Delete* to *Erase* produced a failure to transfer. Because of a small change in how the procedure was described, readers treated a procedure as new that in fact was virtually the same as a previously learned one.

Acquisition Monitor

The work by Kieras and Bovair (1986) mentioned above is one of the few pieces of evidence for the acquisition monitor process. Readers spend more time reading a step that has not been acquired, and less on a step that they have just learned. However, these results provide no indication of how the acquisition monitor process occurs or what might affect it. Another piece of evidence for the process is the result described above that in tying a necktie it helps to tell the reader how a tie should look after every step (Holland, Rose, Dean, & Dory 1985), which suggests that the acquisition monitor can use such information to check for correct acquisition of the procedure steps.

Factors Affecting Execution of Procedures

Some instructions may allow more efficient, faster-executing procedures to be generated than others. The work by Wright and Wilcox (1979) mentioned above is a possible example. In that study, instructions for a button-pushing task were sometimes easier with two negations than one. As discussed above, this result could be due to differences in the ease of constructing the procedures. But an execution time effect of number of negations in also possible. For example, Dixon (1987b) found that execution is faster if subjects must check to see if a light is *on* than if it is *off*, although reading times are similar.

Another potentially important factor in the execution of procedures is how well they can be remembered. If a procedure is easier to remember, then it is likely to be easier and faster to execute. A memory failure means that the reader will have to try to reconstruct the procedure through inference or trial and error, and this will take longer and produce more errors. Thus, assisting memory for a procedure by supporting reconstruction should result in improved execution performance. An example of this can be found in the mental model work of Kieras and Boviar (1984) mentioned above. Subjects who were provided with a mental model of the device executed the procedures faster and with fewer errors both immediately and after a week. The mental model may have helped retention by enabling reconstruction of steps that had been forgotten. A similar advantage for providing a model was found by Smith and Spoehr (1985) in an experiment where subjects performed a step immediately after reading it. Subjects provided with a model showed a small increase in execution accuracy.

Facilitation of retention and recall may explain some of the results obtained by Eylon and Reif (1984). Subjects were given information and training on deriving an argument in physics. Subjects who were given the goal structure of the arguments were better able to recall the argument than subjects who were simply given the steps without information about the goals. If the goal structure was presented as a deductive hierarchy, subjects recalled better on deductive problems; but if the goals were based on a historical organization, they recalled better on historical problems. Thus the explicit presentation of the goal structure facilitated the recall of procedures. Smith and Goodman (1985) found a related effect of explanatory material on transfer to new procedures. Subjects given information about the goals had better execution accuracy on a transfer task than subjects given only linear step-by-step instructions.

Comparison to Nontextual Instructions

There are important aspects of procedural text and instructions that are outside the scope of the model. For example, Booher (1975) found differences in performance between pictorial and text presentation for the same procedure, but the model can explain this difference only in very general terms. One of the interesting differences in performance between pictorial and text presentation is that time to complete a procedure such as *Set the power switch to ON position on the control panel. Check that power indicator illuminates*, was faster when presented with a picture consisting of a series of icons, but fewer errors are made with text. In particular, pictures were better for presenting static objects, while text was better for presenting the actual actions to be taken. Booher's results suggest that part of the difference between text and pictorial procedures may lie in the procedure comprehension stage; the pictorial presentation may result in faster performance because fewer inferences may need to be made in order to generate the procedure. For example, Stone and Glock (1981) found that one advantage of pictures is that they help eliminate orientation errors. However, the fact that text is better than pictures (Booher, 1975) for action steps implies that certain types of information are difficult to extract from a picture, causing errors. This may be why both Booher (1975) and Stone and Glock (1981) found that pictures and text together result in the best performance.

The *flowchart* is another visual form of presentation for procedures; it usually produces better performance than text. A flowchart may help procedure construction because only relevant information needs to be processed, and it may help execution because it relieves memory load. Kammann (1975) found that multibranch flowcharts are both faster and have fewer errors than text. In addition, performance with multibranch flowcharts is better than with binary flowcharts. Because Kammann measured only total time to do the task, no distinction can be drawn between construction and execution effects. Wright and Reid (1973) found that an algorithm presented as a flowchart produced fewer errors than prose. Holland and Rose (1981) compared performance with text versions of instructions such as *If you are a parent or a homeowner, and not both under 26 or a veteran, mark Box A*, to that with two algorithmic versions, one being a flowchart, the other being a verbal version in list form such as

(1)   If you are a parent, then go to (2), otherwise skip to the next question,
(2)   If you are a homeowner, then go to (3).

Performance with prose presentation was the worst both in terms of response time (which included both reading and execution time) and accuracy, while an algorithm presented as a flowchart was the best, having a particular advantage on the more difficult problems.

CONCLUSIONS

Future Research Needs

The most fundamental need in future research on acquiring procedures from text is simply an urgent need for much more research on this type of text. The new research should use more refined paradigms that allow the stages and processes involved to be isolated; studies using gross measures such as the total time to perform a task are simply not very informative.

With regard to the model outline here, many issues at each stage of the model need to be addressed. For example, the distinction between reading and procedure comprehension needs to be further clarified. While the surface form of the text can be considered separately from the form of the procedure, it may serve as an important cue to guide procedure construction. One important issue is how the procedure content is signaled or conveyed in English; several possible cues were discussed as part of the procedure construction process, and it is important to establish the roles such cues play. For example, the work discussed here suggests that identifying the goal structure is important in building a procedure; it could act like a macrostructure (Kintsch & van Dijk, 1978) in ordinary comprehension. Also, since the theme of a paragraph can be signaled to readers by initial mention (Kieras, 1980), initial mention may also signal the top-level goal of a procedure.

Another problem that needs more work is the apparent difficulty of reference in procedural text. The problems pointed out by Fisher (1981), Wright (1981), and Just and Carpenter (1987b), such as interpreting a referent too broadly by ignoring qualifiers, are potentially serious; and yet little is known about why people have such problems and what improvements to procedural text could prevent referential problems.

Practical Applications of Current and Future Research

Both the work described here and potential future research have important and useful practical implications. For example, one conclusion that can be drawn from the work described here is that the procedure comprehension stage—and in particular the procedure construction process—is the critical one. This implies that writers of procedural text should concentrate on ensuring that the procedure construction goes smoothly.

For example, procedural text should above all be correct and should provide all the steps of a procedure. It is probably wise to assume that the reader has less knowledge rather than more, and provide some detail. Readers can typically ignore details that they already know (Kieras, Tibbits, & Bovair, 1984), although some types of detail, such as the actual position of the hands in operation tasks, are likely to be confusing (Holland, Rose, Dean, & Dory, 1985). However, if important details are missing, readers may not be able to infer them without extensive problem solving. Providing a goal structure organization for the text is likely to be helpful (Graesser, 1978; Eylon & Reif, 1984), as will explanations that provide information directly useful in constructing the procedure, such as an effective mental model. (Kieras & Bovair, 1984).

REFERENCES

Anderson, J. R. (1976). *Language, memory and thought.* Hillsdale, NJ: Erlbaum.

Anderson, J. R. (Ed.). (1981). *Cognitive skills and their acquisition.* Hillsdale, NJ: Erlbaum.

Anderson, J. R. (1983). *The architecture of cognition.* Cambridge, MA: Harvard University Press.

Anderson, J. R. (1987). Skill acquisition: Compilation of weak-method problem solutions. *Psychological Review, 94,* 192–210.

Anderson, J. R., & Bower, G. H. (1973). *Human associative memory.* Washington, DC: Winston.

Barnard, P. J., Wright, P., & Wilcox, P. (1979). Effect of response instructions and question style on the ease of completing forms. *Journal of Occupational Psychology, 52,* 209–266.

Booher, H. R. (1975). Relative comprehensibility of pictorial information and printed words in proceduralized instructions. *Human Factors, 17,* 266–277.

Bovair, S., Kieras, D. E., & Polson, P. G. (1988). The acquisition and performance of text editing skill: A production system analysis (Technical Report No. 28). Ann Arbor: University of Michigan.

Card, S. K., Moran, T. P., & Newell, A. (1983). *The psychology of human-computer interaction.* Hillsdale, NJ: Erlbaum.

Dixon, P. (1982). Plans and written directions for complex tasks. *Journal of Verbal Learning and Verbal Behavior, 21,* 70–84.

Dixon, P. (1987a). The processing of organizational and component step information in written directions. *Journal of Memory and Language, 26,* 24–35.

Dixon, P. (1987b). The structure of mental plans for following directions. *Journal of Experimental Psychology: Learning, Memory, and Cognition, 13,* 18–26.

Dixon, P. (1987c). Actions and procedural directions. In R. S. Tomlin (Ed.), Coherence and grounding in discourse. *Typological studies in language* (Vol 11). Amsterdam: John Bejamins B. V.

Dixon, P., Faries, J., & Gabrys, G. (1988). The role of explicit action statements in understanding and using written directions. *Journal of Memory and Language, 27,* 649–667.

Duffy, T. M., Curran, T. E., & Sass, D. (1983). Document design for technical job tasks: An evaluation. *Human Factors, 25,* 143–160.

Eylon, B., & Reif, F. (1984). Effects of knowledge organization on task performance. *Cognition and instruction, 1*(1), 5–44.

Felker, D. B., & Rose, A. M. (1981). The evaluation of a public document: The case of FCC's marine radio rules for recreational boaters (Technical Report No. 11). Washington, DC: American Institutes for Research, Document Design Project.

Fitts, P. M. (1964). Perceptual-motor skill learning. In A. W. Melton (Ed.), *Categories of Human Learning.* New York: Academic Press.

File, S. E., & Jew, A. (1973). Syntax and the recall of instructions in a realistic situation. *British Journal of Psychology, 64,* 65–70.

Fisher, D. L. (1981). Functional literacy tests: A model of question-answering and an analysis of errors. *Reading Research Quarterly, 16,* 418–448.

Foltz, P. E., Davies, S. E., Polson, P. G., & Kieras, D. E. (1988). Transfer between menu systems. *Proceedings of the CHI 1988 Conference on Human Factors in Computing Systems.* Washington, DC: ACM.

Gordon, L., Munro, A., Rigney, J. W., & Lutz, K. A. (1978). *Summaries and recalls for three types of texts* (Technical Report No. 85). Los Angeles: University of Southern California.

Graesser, A. C. (1978). How to catch a fish: the memory and representation of common procedures. *Discourse Processes, 1,* 72–89.

Holland, M., & Rose, A. (1981). *A comparison of prose and algorithms for presenting complex instructions* (Technical Report No. 17). Washington, DC: Document Design Project.

Holland, V. M., Rose, A. M., Dean, R. A., & Dory, S. L. (1985). *Processes involved in writing effective procedural instructions* (Technical Report No. 1). Washington, DC: American Institutes for Research.

Johnson, W., & Kieras, D. E. (1983). Representation-saving effects of prior knowledge in memory for simple technical prose. *Memory and Cognition, 11,* 456–466.

Jones, S. (1966). The effect of a negative qualifier in an instruction. *Journal of Verbal Learning and Verbal Behavior. 5,* 497–501.

Just, M. A., & Carpenter, P. A. (1987a). *The psychology of reading and language comprehension.* Newton, MA: Allyn & Bacon.

Just, M. A., & Carpenter, P. A. (1987b). Unpublished chapter draft.

Kammann, M. R. (1975). The comprehensibility of printed instructions and the flowchart alternative. *Human Factors, 17,* 90–113.

Kieras, D. E. (1980). Initial mention as a signal to thematic content in technical passages. *Memory and Cognition, 8(4),* 345–353.

Kieras, D. E. (1985). *Improving the comprehensibility of a simulated technical manual* (Technical Report No. 20, TR-85/ONR-20). Ann Arbor: University of Michigan, Technical Communication. (DTIC AD A157482).

Kieras, D. E. (1981). Component processes in the comprehension of simple prose. *Journal of Verbal Learning and Verbal Behavior, 20,* 1–23.

Kieras, D. E., & Bovair, S. (1984). The role of a mental model in learning to operate a device. *Cognitive Science. 8,* 255–273.

Kieras, D. E., & Bovair, S. (1986). The acquisition of procedures from text: A production-system analysis of transfer of training. *Journal of Memory and Language, 25,* 507–524.

Kieras, D. E., & Dechert, C. (1985). *Rules for comprehensible technical prose: A survey of the psycholinguistic literature* (Technical Report No. 24). Ann Arbor: University of Michigan.

Kieras, D. E., Tibbits, M., & Bovair, S. (1984). *How experts and nonexperts operate electronic equipment from written instructions* (Technical Report No. 14, UARZ/DP/TR-83/ONR-14). Tucson, AZ: University of Arizona.

Kintsch, W. (1974). *The representation of meaning in memory.* Hillsdale, NJ: Erlbaum.

Kintsch, W. (1986). Learning from text. *Cognition and Instruction. 3(2),* 87–108.

Kintsch, W., & van Dijk, T. A. (1978). Toward a model of text comprehension and production. *Psychological Review, 85,* 363–394.

Konoske, P. J., & Ellis, E. G. (1986). *Cognitive factors in learning and retention of procedural tasks* (Technical Report No. NPRDC 87–14). San Diego, CA: Navy Personnel Research and Development Center.

LeFevre, J., & Dixon, P. (1986). Do written instructions need examples? *Cognition and Instruction, 3 (1),* 1–30.

Mohammed, M. A. H., & Swales, J. M. (1984). Factors affecting the successful reading of technical instructions. *Reading in a Foreign Language, 2,* 206–217.

Reder, L. M., Charney, D. H., & Morgan, K. I. (1986) The role of elaborations in learning a skill from an instructional text. *Memory and Cognition, 14(1),* 64–78.

Schumacher, G. M. (1987). Executive control studying. In B. K. Britton and S. M. Glynn (Eds.), *Executive control processes in reading.* Hillsdale, NJ: Erlbaum.

Smith, E. E., & Goodman, L. (1984). Understanding written instructions: The role of an explanatory schema. *Cognition and Instruction, 14,* 359–396.

Smith, E. E., & Spoehr, K. T. (1985). *Basic processes and individual differences in understanding and using instructions* (BBN Report No. 3029). Cambridge, MA: Bolt, Beranek, & Newman.

Spoehr, K. T., Morris, M. E., & Smith, E. E. (1983). *Comprehension of instructions for operating devices* (BBN Report No. 5712). Cambridge, MA: Bolt, Beranek, & Newman.

Sticht, T. G. (1977). Comprehending reading at work. In M. A. Just & P. A. Carpenter (Eds.), *Cognitive processes in comprehension.* Hillsdale, NJ: Erlbaum.

Stone, D. E., & Glock, M. D. (1981). How do young adults read directions with and without pictures? *Journal of Educational Psychology, 72,* 419–426.

Van Dijk, T. A., & Kintsch, W. (1983). *Strategies of discourse comprehension.* New York: Academic Press.

Wright, P. (1981). "The instructions clearly state . . ." Can't people read? *Applied Ergonomics, 12,* 131–141.

Wright, P., & Reid, F. (1973). Written information: Some alternatives to prose for expressing the outcomes of complex contingencies. *Journal of Applied Psychology, 57,* 160–166.

Wright, P., & Wilcox, P. (1979). When two no's nearly make a yes: A study of conditional imperatives. In P. A. Kolers, M. E. Wrolstad, & H. Bouma (Eds.), *Processing of visible language.* New York: Plenum.

10 EXPOSITORY TEXT

Charles A. Weaver, III
and Walter Kintsch

P sychological models of text comprehension have traditionally focused on two major types of texts: *expository texts*, which comprise textbooks, training manuals, software documentation, and so forth; and *narrative texts*, whose purpose is more to entertain than to inform. Obviously, it is impossible to draw absolute boundaries, and similarities of processing abound (even a classic narrative text, such as the *Wizard of Oz*, tries to educate us—after all, "there is no place like home"). However, the main thrust of expository texts is to communicate information so that the reader might learn something. The main focus of narrative texts is to tell a story, so that the reader will be entertained. This chapter deals with current models of expository text comprehension and attempts to integrate current research with existing theoretical models.

The research on expository text has, in essence, both a very long and a very short history. The history is long in the sense that rhetoric has been a formal academic discipline since antiquity. However, research into the cognitive aspects of what is now called expository text began in earnest only in the last 20 years or so. The cognitive revolution of the late 1950s opened the door for psychologists to study natural language. In the last 15 years, language comprehension has received much attention in the psychological literature. A number of global theories of text comprehension have been developed (Kintsch & van Dijk, 1978; Just & Carpenter, 1980; Perfetti, 1985; van Dijk & Kintsch, 1983) that tackle the difficult problems observed in text comprehension. While a great deal of progress has been made in such diverse areas as improving readability formulas (Amirin & Jones, 1982; Chall, 1984; Duffy & Waller, 1985; Davidson & Green, 1988), isolating comprehension difficulties associated with mathematical word problems (Cummins, Kintsch, Reusser, & Weimer, 1988; Kintsch & Greeno, 1985), and formulating systematic approaches for authors of technical prose (Kieras & Dechert, 1985; Dee-Lucas & Larkin, 1988), it is fair to say that the scientific study of reading and comprehension is still in its relative infancy.

Research in the perceptual facets of reading processes can be traced to experiments performed in the late 1800s by James M. Cattell, an American who worked as an assistant in Wilhelm Wundt's laboratory in Leipzig. In 1886, Cattell published some important work on the time involved in seeing and recognizing objects. While this was intended primarily as work in general perceptual processes, it soon became apparent that it would have a great impact on the study of reading processes. For example, one of Cattell's findings was that subjects could read a series of connected words (i.e., sentences) in half the time it took them to read unconnected words. Upon returning to America, Cattell established a laboratory at Columbia University, and from this lab came such students as Edward Thorndike and Walter Dearborn.

Three major studies summarizing the early work on reading processes were published around the turn of the century. Quantz (1897) published his work from the University of Wisconsin and postulated stage-by-stage reading processes not dissimilar from current information-processing notions. The work covered a number of important areas, from the rate at which people read to the eye-voice span. Since much of the instruction in reading at the time centered upon oral reading, a great deal of emphasis was placed on the latter series of findings.

Dearborn's work, performed at Columbia under Cattell's direction, provided an exhaustive review of the research involving eye movements and perceptual span. He was the first to observe the effects of pronounceability on reading. When subjects read unpronounceable words, their reading rates suffered dramatically. Furthermore, Dearborn established the link between fixation time and reading rate—the more fixations made by a reader, the slower the reading rate. The "golden era" of perceptual research in reading essentially came to an end with the publication of Huey's (1908) volume, *The Psychology and Pedagogy of Reading*.

Between the publication of Huey's research and the natural language revolution during the 1960s, very little significant work was done. Behaviorism dominated psychology, and research on text comprehension was restricted to readily observable variables such as word frequency and sentence length. One notable exception, however, was Frederick C. Bartlett's 1932 book, *Remembering*. Bartlett presented a passage, taken from on old Indian folk tale, to his colleagues and students, and he had them recall it hours, days, even years later. The story structure (as well as its content) was foreign to his British subjects, and Bartlett noticed some fascinating consistencies in the types of errors his subjects would make. First of all, very few used the exact wording, though the use of paraphrase in recall was hardly news. More important, though, these subjects had a tendency to misrecall the passage by making it more like the texts they were used to reading. For example, rather than recalling that something black came from the mouth of one of the warriors—an idea quite foreign to these readers—the subjects might say, "The warrior vomited" or "Smoke came from the warrior's mouth." In other words, the readers were reconstructing the passage from their memories, combining the actual passage with their interpretation of the events. Since the British readers had no previous experience with these peculiar Indian folktales, they tended to force them into preexisting knowledge structures—which Barlett called a *schema*—and thus, when reconstructing the information, they would use their previous schematic knowledge as a guide. The recalls, then, were a mixture of Indian folklore reinterpreted in a British manner.

Barlett's insights concerning the role of preexisting schemata and the reconstructive nature of comprehension were largely underappreciated in a field still dominated by the Ebbinghaus tradition of nonsense syllables. Current thinking was that since natural texts had so many preexisting associations it would be impossible to directly study true memory for verbal material this way. Many of Bartlett's conceptions and insights on comprehension are now incorporated into modern cognitive theories of comprehension and cognition, such as Minsky's (1975) *frames*, the *scripts* of Schank and his colleagues (Schank & Abelson, 1977), and the notions of *schemata* in reading, as in Anderson (1984).

The basic idea of a schema drives the comprehension process for such computer-based systems of comprehension as FRUMP (DeJong, 1979), which has at its core a series of newspaper-type story scripts. As FRUMP reads a wire service report of a news story, it attempts to fit the incoming information into one of the preexisting schemata. Once this match has been successful, FRUMP is able to summarize these stories and answer certain types of questions about them—in short, make use of these knowledge structures in a fashion similar to that of humans. Of course, should FRUMP receive some other type of input, it will often force it into one of the schemata, even if that is not what was intended by the writer. For example, a story of an old woman making a bank deposit is hardly newsworthy of a UPI report. However, if given a two-paragraph description of the transaction, FRUMP may very well conclude that a robbery took place, since there are a number of common features associated with the two actions (e.g., money is given from the teller to the patron, the patron leaves through the front door, and so forth.). FRUMP makes use of the real-world constraint that bank transactions do not make the wire service reports while robberies do.

Obviously, a program like FRUMP has serious limitations. It takes one single aspect of text understanding—top-down processing—and tries to do the whole job that way. There was never any question that this is not what human readers do, nor does this approach work well enough in practice. As a design experiment, one can learn a lot from pushing an idea to its limit, but in the long run we need to study in more detail what human readers actually do. Real readers employ top-down strategies when necessary, but in conjunction with a great deal of bottom-up processing of information. In the next section we shall discuss the current status of the research directed at a better understanding of reading comprehension processes.

THE COGNITIVE REVOLUTION
IN TEXT COMPREHENSION

Bartlett's schema theory was merely one of the factors that combined in the late 1950s and 1960s to redirect and renew the research on text comprehension. Indeed, this research was closely connected to and paralleled the rise of cognitive psychology and cognitive science. Gardner (1985) presents an excellent discussion of how this all came about. We shall restrict ourselves here to mentioning those factors that were directly responsible for the emergence of modern research on text comprehension.

Chomsky's approach to the study of language (Chomsky, 1957) was an important in this respect as it was for the development of cognitive science in general. His followers quickly transcended his limited focus on the sentence level and syntax (e.g., the "text grammar" approach of van Dijk, 1972; the emphasis on semantics, as in Fillmore, 1968). Shortly thereafter, the interest in natural language processing within the new artificial-intelligence (AI) community began to have a powerful impact on the study of text comprehension (e.g., Schank, 1972), in part by reestablishing the central role of the schema concept. A third determining influence came from the information-processing psychology that was developing at the same time (Anderson & Bower, 1972; Kintsch, 1974: Norman & Rumelhart, 1975).

Thus, linguists provided the idea of a generative, rule-based system; AI the computational techniques to work with such systems; and psychology the emphasis on language processing, rather than language as a fixed product. Below we describe those systems of text analysis that are most suited for expository texts, and are most widely used in educational research. In the following section we turn from text analysis to questions about how the text is processed. Finally, we discuss the practical implications of these developments under the headings of "readability" and "unsolved problems."

TEXT ANALYSIS

As psychologists and linguists accepted the legitimacy of studying natural language, the need came about for formal ways of analyzing texts. It was clear that variables beyond the traditional units of word difficulty and sentence length were critical to comprehension. Additionally, as formal models of the comprehension process were developed, some way of analyzing texts had to be developed to test these models. In the early 1970s a number of studies concerning text variables appeared. Studies published by Crothers (1972), Frederiksen (1975), Kintsch (1974), and Meyer (1975), among others, demonstrated effects of text structure on the comprehension process.

Perhaps the best-known and most widely used text analysis systems were developed by Kintsch (1974; Kintsch & van Dijk, 1978) and Meyer (1975). (Other researchers, such as Frederiksen [1975, 1979], Crothers [1972], and Graesser [1981] have also developed text analysis systems, but those will be only briefly discussed here.) The Kintsch system uses the notion of propositions as the basic unit of meaning. Propositions can be considered as the smallest unit of text that can logically be proven false. Texts are assumed to be broken down into propositions, which consist of predicates and arguments. Predicates are typically the relationship between objects, while the arguments are the objects and concepts mentioned in the text. For example, the sentence

John hit the ball

would be encoded propositionally as

HIT (John, Ball)

"Hit" is the relationship involved—the *predicate*—while "John" and "ball" are the *objects* of the relationship. Sentences can obviously consist of multiple propositions, such as

John hit the big red ball

which is encoded propositionally as

Hit (John, ball)
    big (ball)
    red (ball)

Notational variants for representing propositions, in part graphically, have been proposed by Schank (1972) and Norman & Rumelhart (1975). Propositions are considered to be units of meaning. Propositions directly derived from a text have been termed *micropropositions*, since they refer to the smallest definable text units, and completely represent the microstructure of the text. Kintsch and van Dijk (1978; van Dijk, 1980) also define *macropropositions* as propositions that contain only top-level "gist" information. Macropropositions are critically important for the understanding and long-term recall of text.

According to van Dijk (1980) there are a number of macro-operators that work on the micropropositions of the text to create the macrostructure. For example, the macroprocess of deletion removes all but the most important propositions, which leaves a superordinate proposition that captures only the top-level meaning of a passage. While the global meaning of a text (though not the exact words used) can be completely reconstructed from the micropropositions, the entire text cannot be reconstructed from the macropropositions, as the detail information is not encoded in the macropropositions and quickly fades.

One important property of propositions is that they only preserve the meaning of a text, not the actual surface form. The two sentences

John hit the ball
  and
The ball was hit by John

both express the same proposition (in Chomskian terms, they have the same *deep structure*, while having different *surface structures*). Thus, while there is a one-to-one mapping from the text to the propositions, there is no such mapping from the propositions to the text. Though many studies demonstrate the importance of surface structures (e.g., Keenan, MacWhinney, & Mayhew, 1977), in general the meaning of the passage is encoded rather than the exact words (Sachs, 1967).

The propositions representing the meaning of a text are linked together, usually by argument overlap, to form a hierarchical textbase. Important information tends to be at the top of this hierarchy (as well as stored in the macrostructure), while detailed information is at the lower levels. Only explicitly mentioned propositions are represented in this hierarchy, as well as inferences needed to maintain coherence (*bridging inferences*). Available evidence tends to support this practice; bridging inferences are made at the time of encoding (reading) since they are necessary to maintain coherence, but elaborative inferences are typically made during the recall phase (Kintsch, 1974).

Patterns of recall are such that top-level propositions are generally recalled better (Kintsch & Keenan, 1973; Meyer, 1975). This has been termed the "levels effect" of recall. Additionally, with time the lower-level propositions tend to be forgotten much more rapidly than do the higher-level propositions. Kintsch and van Dijk (1978) have demonstrated this effect. After 30 days, the only material that was recalled was the summary-type information: information that was not only stored in the top levels of the microstructure but also was represented in the macrostructure.

A large body of evidence suggests the psychological reality of propositions (Kintsch, Kozminsky, Streby, McKoon, & Keenan, 1975; McKoon & Ratcliff, 1980). Kintsch and Keenan (1973) took sentences that had the same number of words but varying numbers of propositions. For example, the sentence

Romulus, the legendary founder of Rome, took the women of the Sabine by force

contains four propositions. However, the sentence

Cleopatra's downfall lay in her mistrust of the fickle political figures of Rome

contains the same number of words, but eight propositions. When measuring the time to read each sentence, Kintsch and Keenan found that the second sentence took longer. In fact, they were able to estimate the reading time per proposition at about one second.

Meyer's system (1975) differs from the Kintsch system in a number of key respects. First, the unit of analysis is no longer the proposition but the *idea unit*. These idea units capture not only the expressed, explicit content of the passage (such as is contained in Kintsch's proposition), but also the inferred relationships implied by the text. This allows her system not only to represent the microproposition level (which is coded propositionally), but also to form a clear macrostructure, independent of the microstructure, that expresses the higher-order rhetorical relationships in the text.

Other systems for text analysis have also been developed (e.g., Crothers, 1972; Frederiksen, 1975, 1977; Graesser, 1981). Crother's system provides a remarkably detailed analysis of the text passage, but is limited to texts no longer than a few paragraphs. The Frederiksen system segments prose into *concepts* that have a more horizontal, network-like quality—they are not hierarchical, as are the Kintsch and Meyer representations. Such a system is designed for analysis of recall situations in which many inferences are drawn.

Graesser's (1981) system of text analysis breaks down the text into what he calls the "conceptual graph structure," which, like the Frederiksen system, results in a network of relations and not a hierarchy. Like Meyer's system, the conceptual graph structure of a text includes inferences and elaborations of the text, not just the explicit content. However, this network of inferences and elaborations is far more complex and exhaustive than in other analysis systems. While many traditional systems have included some mechanism to incorporate inferences necessary for maintaining coherence ("bridging inferences"), Graesser's system often expresses as many as 12 to 15 implicit inferences for every expressly mentioned statement in the passage. The great majority of these inferences would fall into the category of *elaborate inferences,* for which the available data seem to indicate are made at the time of inference and not at the time of encoding. Once these inferences are generated, the units are segmented into lexical propositions and then connected through structural and logical relationships. The result of such an analysis is that the ultimate representation of the text is a very rich, interconnected network capable of superior inferencing, and is suitable for many AI applications. However, it does not appear to be an accurate description of the mechanism by which readers generate their inferences. Thus, most researchers tend to use either the Kintsch system (and its close relatives, such as the one developed by Bovair and Kieras [1985]) or the Meyer system. A brief comparison of the two systems should provide a guide to their relative strengths and weaknesses.

Of the two major systems (Kintsch and Meyer), research has shown that the Meyer system may be somewhat more sensitive to developmental differences (Bieger & Dunn, 1980), and also that the hierarchy produced from using the Meyer system was the best predictor of recall (Meyer, 1985). However, the Kintsch system is considerably easier to use, and predictions of recall using this system are also quite accurate. Meyer (1985) formally compared the two systems and found that, while there was an advantage for her system in somewhat less accurate recall situations (such as long-term recall or recall from children), and that her system was better for passages which contained a number of logical relations, the overall correlation between the predictions made by the two systems was .96.

Meyer has produced a number of well-written, detailed comparisons examining the two approaches, which go into considerably more detail than space allows here. They are presented, among other places, in Meyer and Rice (1984) and Meyer (1985). The interested reader is referred to those papers.

Text analysis is not restricted to the local, microstructure level. Macrostructures play an equally important role (Meyer, 1975; van Dijk, 1980). Kintsch (1982) has listed a number of the most important rhetorical schemata upon which the macrostructures of expository texts tend to be based.

The systems described here were developed for more or less the same purposes (to analyze reading problems and recall). To a considerable extent, they can be considered as notational variants; and which system is best to use depends on the task to be analyzed.

The research described so far is primarily concerned with text analysis. The question asked is: How does one characterize the salient aspects of a text for purposes of doing psychological research on understanding and memory, or for instructional purposes? What are the appropriate independent and dependent variables for experiments using textual materials; how does one score recall? What properties of a text are most relevant in instructional contexts? During the last decade, interest has shifted from this kind of question to a concern not just with the text itself, but with what the reader does with the text. The process of comprehension, rather than the analysis of the text, has become the focus of the research effort.

PROCESS MODELS:
THE READER-TEXT INTERACTION

For most purposes it is not sufficient just to analyze a text. What matters is how a reader responds to that text. That the reader-text interaction, and not just the text alone, is crucial in comprehension has been argued for a long time by educators and literary scholars (e.g., Rosenblatt, 1978). The most significant contribution of modern research on text comprehension was to provide computational models that describe explicitly and in detail the processes involved in the reader-text interaction. Thus, aspects of the reader-text interaction can be described just as objectively, and in principle, measured just as precisely as characteristics of the text itself. Referring to a comprehension problem or a peculiar text interpretation, as a result of the reader-text interaction, need no longer be hand waving, but can be based on specifiable reader and text characteristics and known processing mechanisms.

A few examples must suffice here to illustrate this point. It is well known that very old persons read and remember a text differently from college students. But wherein lies the difference? Spillich (1983) has been able to attribute this difference to the fact that the available short-term memory capacity during reading is larger in the college-student population than for old people. Other than that, however, healthy old people read in the same way as college students (unlike senile old people, whose reading strategies are markedly different).

As a second example, consider the commonplace observation that the structure of a reader's preexisting knowledge affects how a text is understood and remembered. Mannes and Kintsch (1987) have not just shown this to be indeed the case but have supplied a detailed theoretical explanation as to how these effects arise—with some rather nonintuitive pedagogical consequences, which will be discussed later.

Or, as a final example, take the demonstration that making readers work harder by giving them a willfully difficult text to read can be beneficial under certain circumstances (Kintsch, E., 1990): by having a theoretical understanding of the processes involved, such an observation ceases to be an isolated, perhaps aberrant fact, but becomes a systematic piece of knowledge whose preconditions and implications are reasonably well understood.

Models of discourse processing have been presented by, among others, Kintsch and van Dijk (1978; also van Dijk & Kintsch, 1983; Kintsch, 1988) and Just and Carpenter (1980). It is not possible to describe these models adequately here. Instead, we shall focus on their implications for assessing the difficulty of understanding expository texts, recalling and summarizing them, and learning from such texts.

Information-Processing Constraints
on Text Comprehension

Text characteristics that are important for comprehension (such as sentence length, a coherent microstructure, a clearly signalled macrostructure) have long been recognized. The reader's information-processing capabilities provide similar constraints. We give two examples.

Effective comprehension requires a balanced allotment of limited attentional resources. If normally automated components of the process begin to absorb too much of these resources, controlled attention-demanding subprocesses will suffer (van Dijk & Kintsch, 1983). Thus, it is not just a matter of whether a person can do something, but how easy it is: if all my attention goes to the vocabulary and syntax level—say, because I am reading a text in a language that I do not know well—I may not be able to form a coherent macrostructure, and hence be able to recall what I have read.

During reading, temporary storage of information in a short-term memory buffer is generally required. Buffer capacity varies, and hence the reader's ability to bridge incoherent portions of a text. We have already mentioned the study by Spillich (1983), which shows that the differences in recall between college students and old (but not senile) people can be accounted for by the larger capacity of the short-term memory buffer for college students.

Knowledge Use in Discourse Comprehension

Discourse comprehension requires not only a large set of processing strategies, ranging from the perceptual level to the linguistic and discourse level, but also quite specific content knowledge in the domain of the text. The most sophisticated processing strategies will not be of much help if a text deals with a totally foreign domain. In general, understanding is impossible without a considerable amount of knowledge activation. All theories of discourse comprehension agree on this point. How this activation occurs is, however, currently a matter of dispute. The dominant schema view holds that comprehension is basically predictive and expectation driven. We understand because we have activated an appropriate knowledge structure (schema, script, frame), which we then use to organize the new information and connect it with what we already know (see the references on schema theory given above). Computationally what this implies is that the comprehender must have available very sensitive rules that will work properly in many different contexts. Such rules will necessarily be very complex.

Kintsch (1988) has proposed an alternative view, in which much simpler rules can be used. In his view, the context effects in comprehension do not come about because context controls the process in a top-down fashion, but comprehension is conceived as a bottom-up process. The rules are general and not very smart (but robust), so that they will generate many irrelevant or even false products. But since what is generated are not unrelated items but nodes in a network, an integration process can be used to sort out the irrelevant items. What belongs together in the network that has been generated will strengthen each other when activation is spread around the network, while unrelated items will die off, and contradictory ones will be suppressed. Thus, the rules that construct the items in the network do not have to be too refined—the network will cleanse itself of misconstructions.

Creating a coherent mental representation of a text—that is, understanding it—in this view becomes more a matter of constraint satisfaction than deliberate problem solving. There are all kinds of constraints that must be mutually satisfied: syntactic constraints that operate at the sentence level as well as at the discourse level, rhetorical constraints, and semantic constraints that derive from the nature of the text itself; constraints that arise from the knowledge base of the reader into which the text must be integrated; and constraints from the pragmatic situation of the reader—goals and task demands. Most of these are weak and not decisive by themselves, but in their totality they determine the outcome of comprehension.

Textbases and Situation Models

The mental representation of a text that not only includes the textual information itself but has become integrated into the reader's knowledge has been called by van Dijk & Kintsch (1983) the *situation model*. Thus, one type of mental representation that is formed in the process of comprehension is the *textbase* (including a microstructure, macrostructure, and rhetorical schema). It represents the memory for the text itself and controls the reader's ability to reproduce the text in any form at a later date—that is, such common laboratory tests as recognition, recall, summarization, and so on. In the situation model, the text has lost its identity; the macrostructure the author has chosen matters only insofar as it has influenced the original processing of it. What is crucial at this level is how the information contained in the text relates to the reader's previous knowledge structures. Where and when the text was read, and what its structure (the episodic memory trace of the text) was is not retained at this level of representation. It is this situational representation, however, that determines how the textual information combined with other knowledge can be used in inferencing and how it modifies existing knowledge structures.

In other words, the textbase—the episodic memory trace—is important when we are concerned with the specific text and whether it is evaluated by a summarization task, recognition, or recall. When we are concerned with what the reader has learned from the text, how he or she will be able to use the textual information in new situations, it is the situation model that matters.

Mannes and Kintsch (1987) have demonstrated experimentally the importance of this distinction. They have shown that under certain conditions it is easy to acquire a good textbase, and hence to recall and summarize a text. But these conditions may not be optimal for the formation of a situation model, so that subjects actually learn less from the text (in the sense of being able to use the knowledge they have acquired in new problem-solving tasks) than when the initial comprehension was made a little bit more difficult. We shall return to this point below, because it is of great significance for education: our goal is not usually to make comprehension easy, or to enable students to recall a text well, but to use the text for the transmission of information that then can be used in a variety of new contexts. At least with expository texts, educators are not so much concerned about textbases but about situation models: learning from texts, not comprehension or text recall, is the goal.

Rhetorical Structure of Expository Texts

Much of what has been said above holds for narratives and other types of texts equally well as for expository texts. The crucial difference between text types is at the level of rhetorical structure. The structure of narratives, for instance, can be described in terms of episodes of the form *setting-complication-resolution*, or alternatively in terms of story grammars, or causal event chains, and so on. Expository texts are typically described in terms of such schemata as classification, illustration, comparison and contrast, and procedural description. The following list shows an analysis of rhetorical schemata proposed by Kintsch (1982).

RHETORICAL SCHEMATA FOR EXPOSITORY TEXTS

A. **General-particular relations**
   1. *Identification* "What is it? Specify in space-time."
   2. *Definition*
      a. "What is it? Specify in semantic relations."
      b. Form of definer = (often) genus + differentiate, recursively
      c. Evaluation criteria: common ground, convertible, and not circular
   3. *Classification*
      a. Form of classification is A = Union A_1.

      b. Classification is recursive
      c. Evaluation Criteria:
        —at each level only a single criterion for classification is used
        —at each level, the classification must be exhaustive
        —and mutually exclusive.

  4. *Illustration*
      a. Reasoning is from particular to general.
      b. Evaluation criterion: Is the particular instance a prototype?

B. Object-object relations
  5. *Comparison and contrast*
      a. Form of comparison: X similar Y or x_1 similar y_1, for $x_1 < X$
      b. Form contrast: X different Y, or organized by attribute
      c. Purpose of comparison (contrast) is to compare to something familiar, or to illustrate a principle (new or old).
      d. Evaluation criterion: Is similarity (contrast) significant?

C. Object-part relations
  6. *Analysis*
      technical analysis with purpose of providing information, as distinguished from ordinary analysis that intends to create an experience
  6.1 *Structural analysis*
      a. "How is it put together?"
      b. List parts
      c. Relations among parts
  6.2 *Functional analysis*
      a. "How does it work?"
      b. Functional relations among components of a process—sequence of events in time
  6.3 *Causal analysis*
      a. "What caused this?"
      b. "What consequences does this have?"
      c. Form of causal analysis: A cause B and A cause B
        —if many connections, look for immediate one
        —if many connections, look for interesting one
        —complex causes
      d. Evaluation criterion: association versus cause

That readers actually use schema-appropriate strategies for expository texts has been demonstrated by Kintsch and Yarbrough (1982). These authors had students read essays that were well-structured examples of some of the text types shown above, or essays that were equivalent in their content but for which the cues that alert readers to their structure were deleted, and for which the order of their paragraphs deviated from the idea rhetorical form. Performance differed, depending upon whether tests were used that evaluated macro- or microprocesses. If local comprehension was measured (by means of a cloze test), performance was identical for the two versions. If global comprehension was measured (by means of topic and main-point questions), the students performed better after reading the good versions of the texts than after reading the poor versions.

The rhetorical form of a text is a conventional macrostructure, and students familiar with this convention are better able to form macrostructures when they read texts that are well-structured rhetorically, and which signal this structure clearly. It is important to note, however, that this effect was observed only when comprehension tests sensitive to macroprocesses were used.

READABILITY

One of the first goals adopted by educational psychologists was to rate the difficulty of various school texts. Which texts are appropriate for fourth-grade students? Which are more appropriate for high school students? Soon these formulas were being applied to such matters as the readability of insurance forms. Were the formulas good enough to warrant such widespread use?

Early work tended to focus primarily on such simple ideas as vocabulary difficulty and frequency (Gray & Leary, 1935). Application thus merely followed the basic research trends: the factors included in the early readability measures were the same ones as those studied in the laboratory during the behaviorist era—objective, but very superficial measures, basically word frequency and sentence length. Eventually, readability formulas were developed that could be applied to any given text (Vogel & Washburne, 1928; Dale & Chall, 1948; Flesch, 1948; Klare, 1963, 1974/1975, 1984), commonly utilizing word difficulty, sentence length, and number of syllables per word. These formulas were generally successful, at least to a point, and provided a reference from which texts could be compared. They soon became widely used not only in research settings but also in educational and other applied settings. Standardized testing procedures also made wide use of these formulas.

Perhaps such widespread use was not warranted. After all, these formulas analyzed but a few variables, and cases where the formulas failed were abundant. However, the limitations of the formulas—the fact that they analyzed only a few components—were also their most attractive feature: they were easy to use. Thus, these criticisms, even when recognized by the researchers, did not alter the popularity of readability formulas.

Since most of the formulas make use of at least two easily definable factors—word difficulty (usually measured by word frequency) and sentence length—it is instructive to look at the evidence supporting the relative merits of the two predictors. Such words as "caveman" and "girlish" occur very infrequently, according to published norms (*American Heritage Word Frequency Book*, by Carroll, Davies, & Richman, 1972). Surely their relative infrequency is not reflective of word difficulty. Even the youngest children can easily read and understand the word "caveman." Furthermore, it has been shown (Beck, McCaslin, & McKeown, 1980) that in some cases the use of difficult words can actually improve comprehension. Freebody and Anderson (1983) directly manipulated word frequency to determine its effect on comprehension. They substituted, for example, words like "minute" and "descending" for "tiny" and "falling," and then assessed the corresponding effect on reading. They found that this vocabulary manipulation accounted for quite a small bit of the variance (less than 5%) and that a fairly large number of substitutions were necessary in order to produce a considerable decrease in comprehension.

Furthermore, studies by Davidson, Wilson, and Herman (1985) indicate that sentence length alone accounts for a small percentage of the variance of the comprehension of individual texts. Since sentence length is correlated with a number of other factors, such as complexity of clause structure, and so on, it is not surprising that there is some contribution. In fact, sentence length would be highly correlated with such information-processing variables as number of propositions in the working memory buffer (Miller & Kintsch, 1980). However, the unique contribution of sentence length does not appear to be great.

Though the traditional approach to developing readability formulas is alive and well, recent developments in reading research have uncovered a great deal of new information. Traditional formulas assessed the readability of the text in isolation, and readability was essentially considered to be a property of a given text (see Ballstaedt & Mandl, 1988; Bruce, Rubin, & Starr, 1981; Duffy, 1985; Klare, 1976). Furthermore, most of these readability formulas consider only sentence length and word difficulty. A number of recent criticisms have pointed out these flaws (Bruce, 1984; Rubin, 1984).

Additionally, newer approaches have focused not only on the text itself but also on the text in the reading environment. This would allow for the text to be evaluated as part of a context, with a reader who has limited cognitive resources, differing goals and levels of motivation, etc. For example, Kintsch and Vipond (1979), using the Kintsch and van Dijk (1978) model of text comprehension, determined that one of the major determinants of readability was the number of bridging inferences required within a given passage. This approach was carried out theoretically by Miller and Kintsch (1980). Collins, Brown, and Larkin (1980) demonstrated the top-down effects of schemata on readability. In a passage that initially is interpreted as a man trying to buy a movie ticket, readers are greatly thrown off by the fact that "she"—presumably the cashier at the movie ticket window—refuses to take the man's money. This is quite inconsistent with our movie schema. However, once the passage is reinterpreted, and it becomes clear that the woman involved is not the cashier but the man's date, comprehension proceeds normally. Traditional analyses would have rated the passage quite readable, since the sentences were short and the words familiar, but the top-down effect (similar to linguistic "garden path" sentences) make the passage difficult to comprehend.

The effects of prior knowledge on readability have been well documented in the research of Spillich, Vesonder, Chiesi, and Voss (1979). In their research, subjects— those who were either high or low in baseball knowledge—were presented baseball passages (play-by-play game descriptions) to comprehend. Not surprisingly, the high-knowledge subjects comprehended the passages much better.

Another overlooked variable in readability is the effect of interestingness (Anderson, Shirey, Wilson, & Fielding, 1986). Children were presented sentences that they found interesting and some that they found comparatively uninteresting. When ratings of interestingness were compared with traditional readability measures it was found that interestingness accounted for greater than 25 times the variance that readability did!

However, readability formulas are still in widespread use. While it is hoped that refinement of these formulas to reflect current research on comprehension and learning will lead to more accurate formulas, it is clear that in the meantime, older, less reliable formulas will still be common. To this end, Bruce, Rubin, and Starr (1981) have proposed that readability formulas be used only when the following criteria are met:

1. The material will be freely read, and reading time will not be determined by "external factors" such as experimental control or (in their example) captions that are presented along with television programs (for the hearing impaired).
2. The text is "honestly written": that is, not directly written in such a way to satisfy the criteria of readability formulas.
3. The higher-level features of a text, such as organization and intention, correlate with the sentence and word features. As current formulas make little use of the top-level information, such material is otherwise ignored.

4. The purpose of the reading is similar to that of the readers in the validation studies. If the two groups are reading with different strategies, then the formula may not be valid across the situations.
5. The formulas are applied across a large number of texts, and individual texts are not singled out. Bruce, Rubin and Starr emphasize that readability scores are composite averages and may not apply to specific texts.
6. The population of readers is the same in the "real-world" setting as it was in the validation studies. If a text is to be used as a remedial text, it should not be validated on a group of average readers.

UNSOLVED PROBLEMS

The theoretical case against readability formulas has been argued many times (e.g., from the present perspective by Kintsch & Vipond, 1979). Their merits are undeniable: at best these formulas provide a scandalous oversimplification, more frequently a serious distortion. Nevertheless, as we have just shown, they continue to be used. It is the only game in town, and as long as the modern research described earlier in this chapter does not provide viable alternatives, there is not much else to do.

Why has cognitive science research on text comprehension failed, so far, to provide a viable alternative? And what would such an alternative look like if we had it? We have argued above that actually quite a bit is known about discourse processing, though of course, many important questions remain to be answered. But why has what we do know not led to the development of alternatives to readability formulas?

The answer to these questions has two parts. First of all, most of the cognitive science research discussed above has dealt with the formation of textbases: the factors affecting comprehension, the ability to summarize and recall the text. That is where current knowledge is concentrated. A great deal is known about how to construct comprehensible, recallable, and summarizable texts for given populations (e.g. Kieras, 1985a, 1985b, 1985c). However, while this knowledge is quite adequate for laboratory research on discourse processing, simple, easy-to-use procedures for practical applications have not yet been developed. When using a text in an experiment, often a relatively brief text, it does not matter whether the procedures for text analysis are time-consuming, require expertise, and so on. The purposes to which readability formulas are put, in contrast, matter a great deal. What would be necessary, therefore, is to embark on a large-scale effort directed toward the development of practical methods of text analysis that allow nonexperts to do with relatively little effort what only experts can do today with considerable effort. While such an enterprise would be nontrivial, it is certainly feasible.

Unfortunately, the problem is a little more complicated than that, for making texts comprehensible and recallable is not the only, or even major, goal of instruction. Learning from text, using textual information for new tasks and various purposes, is a more important goal. As we have indicated in our discussion on textbases and situation models, these two goals are not identical. Satisfying the first does not necessarily satisfy the second. We know (to a certain degree) how to satisfy the first goal, but as yet we know very little about the second. Current research is at a stage where we have been able to clearly identify the goal—but little more. Thus, before we worry too much about the transfer from basic cognitive research to readability-type applications, the research community still has to get further ahead with its task. When we know as much about learning from texts as about recalling texts, then the time has come for a concerted effort to transfer this laboratory to practice. For the moment, however, we cannot foresee a substantial change in the current state of affairs—where readability measures have no connection to the cognitive science research on text comprehension.

REFERENCES

Amirin, M. R., & Jones, B. F. (1982). Toward a new definition of readability. *Educational Psychologist, 17,* 13–30.

Anderson, R. C. (1984). Role of the reader's schema in comprehension, learning, and memory. In R. C. Anderson, J. Osborn, & R. J. Tierney (Eds.), *Learning to read in American schools* (pp. 243–258). Hillsdale, NJ: Erlbaum.

Anderson, J. R., & Bower, G. H. (1972). *Human associative memory.* Washington, DC: Winston.

Anderson, R. C., Shirey, L., Wilson, P., & Fielding, L. (1986). Interestingness of children's reading material. In R. Snow & M. Farr (Eds.), *Aptitude learning and instruction.* Hillsdale, NJ: Erlbaum.

Ballstaedt, S. P., & Mandl, H. (1988). The assessment of comprehension. In U. Ammon, N. Diffman, & K. J. Mattheier (Eds.), *Sociolinguistics: An international handbook of the science of language and society.* Berlin, New York: de Gruyter.

Bartlett, F. C. (1932). *Remembering.* Cambridge, Eng.: Cambridge University Press.

Beck, I., McCaslin, E., & McKeown, M. G. (1980). *The rational design of a program to teach vocabulary to fourth-grade students.* Pittsburgh: University of Pittsburgh, Learning Research and Development Center.

Bieger, G. R., & Dunn, B. R. (1980, April). *Sensitivity to developmental differences in the recall of prose: A comparison of two prose grammars.* Paper presented at the Annual Meeting of the American Educational Research Association, Boston, MA.

Bovair, S., & Kieras, D. E. (1985). A guide to propositional analysis for research on technical prose. In B. K. Britton & J. B. Black (Eds.), *Understanding expository text.* Hillsdale, NJ: Erlbaum.

Bruce, B. C. (1984). A new point of view on children's stories. In R. C. Anderson, J. Osborne, & R. T. Tierney (Eds.), *Learning to read in American schools: Basal readers and content texts.* Hillsdale, NJ: Erlbaum.

Bruce, B., Rubin, A., & Starr, K. (1981). *Why readability formulas fail.* Champaign, IL: Center for the Study of Reading.

Carroll, J. B., Davies, P., & Richman, B. (1972). *The American Heritage word frequency book.* Boston: Houghton Mifflin.

Chall, J. S. (1984). Readability and prose comprehension continuities and discontinuities. In J. S. Flood (Ed.), *Understanding reading comprehension: Cognition, language, and the structure of prose.* Newark, DE: International Reading Association.

Chomsky, N. (1957). *Syntactic structures.* The Hague: Mouton.

Collins, A., Brown, J. S., & Larkin, K. M. (1980). Inference in text understanding. In R. J. Spiro, B. C. Bruce, and W. F. Brewer (Eds.), *Theoretical issues in reading comprehension.* Hillsdale, NJ: Erlbaum.

Crothers, E. J. (1972). Memory structure and the recall of discourse. In J. B. Carroll and R. O. Freedle (Eds.), *Language comprehension and the acquisition of knowledge.* Washington, DC: Winston.

Cummins, D. D., Kintsch, W., Reusser, K., & Weimer, R. (1988). The role of understanding in solving word problems. *Cognitive Psychology, 20,* 405–438.

Dale, E., & Chall, J. S. (1948). A formula for predicting readability. *Educational Research Bulletin* (Jan. 11–12 and Feb. 37–54).

Davidson, A., & Green, G. M. (1988). *Linguistic complexity and text comprehension: Readability issues reconsidered.* Hillsdale, NJ: Erlbaum.

Davidson, A., Wilson, P., & Herman, G. (1986). *Effects of syntactic connections and organizing cues on text comprehension..* Champaign, IL: Center for the Study of Reading.

Dee-Lucas, D., & Larkin, J. H. (1988). Attentional strategies for studying scientific texts. *Memory and Cognition, 16,* 469–479.

DeJong, D. E. (1979). *Skimming stories in real time.* Doctoral dissertation, Yale University.

Duffy, T. M. (1985). Readability formulas: What's the use? In T. M. Duffy & R. Waller (Eds.), *Designing usable texts.* New York: Academic Press.

Duffy, T. M., & Waller, R. (Eds.). (1985). *Designing usable texts.* New York: Academic Press.

Fillmore, C. J. (1968). The case for case. In E. Black & R. T. Harms (Eds.), *Universals of linguistic theory.* New York: Holt, Rinehart & Winston.

Flesch, R. F. (1948). A new readability yardstick. *Journal of Applied Psychology, 32,* 221–233.

Frederiksen, C. H. (1975). Acquisition of semantic information for discourse: Effects of repeated exposure. *Journal of Verbal Learning and Verbal Behavior, 14,* 158–169.

Frederiksen, C. H. (1977). Semantic processing units in understanding texts. In R. O. Freedle (Ed.), *Discourse production and comprehension*. Norwood, NJ: Ablex.

Frederiksen, C. H. (1979). Discourse comprehension and early reading. In L. B. Resnick & P. A. Weaver (Eds.), *Theory and practice of early reading*. Hillsdale, NJ: Erlbaum.

Freebody, P., & Anderson, R. C. (1983). Effects of vocabulary difficulty, text cohesion and schema availability on lexical access and reading comprehension. *Journal of Reading Research Quarterly 18*, 277–299.

Gardner, H. (1985). *The mind's new science*. New York: Basic Books.

Graesser, A. C. (1981). *Prose comprehension beyond the word*. New York: Springer-Verlag.

Gray, W. S., & Leary, B. E. (1935). *What makes a book readable?* Chicago: University of Chicago Press.

Huey, E. B. (1908). *The psychology and predagogy of reading*. New York: Macmillan.

Just, M. A., & Carpenter, P. A. (1980). A theory of reading: From eye fixations to comprehension. *Psychological Review, 87*, 329–354.

Keenan, J. M., MacWhinney, B., & Mayhew, D. (1977). Pragmatics in memory: A case study of natural conversation. *Journal of Verbal Learning and Verbal Behavior, 16*, 549–560.

Kieras, D. E. (1985a). *The potential for advanced computerized aids for comprehensible writing of technical documents* (Technical Report No. 17, TR-85/ONR-17). University of Michigan.

Kieras, D. E. (1985b). Thematic processing in the comprehension of technical prose. In B. Britton & J. Black (Eds.), *Understanding expository text*. Hillsdale, NJ: Erlbaum.

Kieras, D. E. (1985c). *Improving the comprehensibility of a simulated technical manual* (Technical Report No. 20, TR–85/ONR-20). University of Michigan.

Kieras, D. E., & Dechert, C. (1985). *Rules for comprehensible prose: A survey of the psycholinguistic literature* (Technical Report No. 21). University of Michigan.

Kintsch, E. (1990). Macroprocesses and microprocesses in the development of summarization skills. *Cognition and Instruction*.

Kintsch, W. (1974). The representation of meaning in memory. Hillsdale, NJ: Erlbaum.

Kintsch, W. (1982). Text representations. In W. Otto & S. White (Eds.), *Reading expository material* (pp. 87–102). New York: Academic Press.

Kintsch, W. (1988). The role of knowledge in discourse comprehension: A construction-integration model. *Psychological Review, 95*, 163–182.

Kintsch, W., & Greeno, J. G. (1985). Understanding and solving arithmetic word problems. *Psychological Review, 92*, 109–129.

Kintsch, W., & Keenan, J. M. (1973). Reading rate and retention as a function of the number of propositions in the base structure of sentences. *Cognitive Psychology, 5*, 257–279.

Kintsch, W., Kozminsky, E., Streby, W. J., McKoon, G., & Keenan, J. M. (1975). Comprehension and recall as a function of content variables. *Journal of Verbal Learning and Verbal Behavior, 14*, 196–214.

Kintsch, W., & van Dijk, T. A. (1978). Toward a model of discourse comprehension and production. *Psychological Review, 85*, 363–394.

Kintsch, W., & Vipond, D. (1979). Reading comprehension and readability in educational practice and psychological theory. In L. G. Nilsson (Ed.), *Perspectives of memory research*. Hillsdale, NJ: Erlbaum.

Kintsch, W., & Yarbrough, C. J. (1982). Role of rhetorical structure in text comprehension. *Journal of Educational Psychology, 74*, 828–834.

Klare, G. M. (1963). *The measurement of readability*. Ames: Iowa State University Press.

Klare, G. M. (1974/1975). Assessing readability. *Reading Research Quarterly, 10*, 62–102.

Klare, G. M. (1976). A second look at the validity of readability formulas. *Journal of Reading Behavior, 8*, 129–152.

Klare, G. M. (1984). Readability. In P. D. Pearson, R. Barr, M. L. Kamil, & P. Mosenthal (Eds.), *Handbook of reading research*, (Vol. 1). White Plains, NY: Longman.

McKoon, G., & Ratcliff, R. (1980). Priming in item recognition: The organization of propositions in memory for text. *Joutrnal of Verbal Learning and Verbal Behavior, 19*, 369–386.

Mannes, S., & Kintsch, W. (1987). Knowledge organization and text organization. *Cognition and Instruction, 4*, 91–115.

Meyer, B. J. F. (1975). *The organization of prose and its effect on memory*. Amsterdam: North-Holland.

Meyer, B. J. F. (1985). Prose analysis: Purposes, procedures, and problems. In B. K. Britton & J. B. Black (Eds.), *Understanding expository text* (pp. 269–304). Hillsdale, NJ: Erlbaum.

Meyer, B. J. F., & Rice, G. E. (1984). The structure of text. In P. D. Pearson, R. Barr, M. L. Kamil, & P. Mosenthal (Eds.), *Handbook of reading research*, (Vol. 1). White Plains, NY: Longman.

Miller, J. R., & Kintsch, W. (1980). Readability and recall for short passages: A theoretical analysis. *Journal of Experimental Psychology: Human Learning and Memory, 6*, 335–354.

Minsky, M. (1975). A framework for representing knowledge. In P. H. Winston (Ed.), *The psychology of computer vision*. New York: McGraw-Hill.

Norman, D. A., & Rumelhart, D. E. (1975). *Explorations in cognition*. San Francisco: Freeman.

Perfetti, C. A. (1985). *Reading ability*. New York: Oxford University Press.

Quantz, J. Q. (1897). Problems in the psychology of reading. *Psychology Monographs* (whole number 2).

Rosenblatt, L. M. (1978). *The reader, the text, the poem*. Carbondale: Southern Illinois University Press.

Rubin, A. (1984). What can readability formulas tell us about text? In J. Osborne, P. T. Wilson, & R. C. Anderson (Eds.), *Foundations for a literate America*. Lexington, MA: Lexington Books.

Sachs, J. S. (1967). Recognition memory for syntactic and semantic aspects of connected discourse. *Perception and Psychoanalysis, 2*, 437–442.

Schank, R. C. (1972). Conceptual dependency: A theory of natural language understanding. *Cognitive Psychology, 3*, 552–631.

Schank, R. C., & Abelson, R. (1977). *Scripts, plans, goals, and understanding*. Hillsdale, NJ: Erlbaum.

Spillich, G. J. (1983). Life-span components of text processing: Structural and procedural differences. *Journal of Verbal Learning and Verbal Behavior, 22*, 231–244.

Spillich, G. J., Vesonder, G. T., Chiesi, H. L., & Voss, J. F. (1979). Text processing of domain-related information for individuals with high- and low-domain knowledge. *Journal of Verbal Learning and Verbal Behavior, 18*, 275–290.

van Dijk, T. A. (1972). *Some aspects of text grammars*. The Hague, Netherlands: Mouton.

van Dijk, T. A. (1980). *Macrostructures*. The Hague: Mouton.

van Dijk, T. A., & Kintsch, W. (1983). *Strategies of discourse comprehension*. New York: Academic Press.

Vogel, M., & Washburne, C. (1928). An objective method of determining grade placement of children's reading material. *Elementary School Journal, 28*, 373–381.

11 RESEARCH ON THE READING-WRITING RELATIONSHIP: INTERACTIONS, TRANSACTIONS, AND OUTCOMES

Robert J. Tierney
and Timothy Shanahan

The goal of this paper is to discuss the state of research and theory on reading-writing relationships. To this end, the review divides research and theory into three interrelated topics:

What do reading and writing share?
How do readers and writers transact with one another?
What do readers and writers learn when reading and writing are connected?

The first topic addresses the nature of and extent to which reading and writing involve similar, shared, and overlapping linguistic, cognitive, or social resources. The second topic considers how readers and writers transact with one another as they negotiate the making of meaning. The third topic explores the thinking and learning that occurs as learners shift back and forth from reading to writing according to goals they pursue in different subject areas such as science, social studies, and literature.

WHAT DO READING AND WRITING SHARE?

Does development in reading go hand in hand with development in writing? If reading ability improves, should writing ability improve also? Do the same basic abilities and underlying processes govern reading and writing? Underlying a great deal of the curriculum development in reading and writing has been support for integrating the language arts. Traditionally, these developments or arguments have assumed that reading and writing together offer more than reading and writing apart. Such views often went hand in hand with the belief that reading involved reception and writing involved production. Tied to this notion was the assumption that undergirding reading and writing were similar prerequisite skills and abilities. That is, curricular developers (e.g., Durkin, 1988; Moffett & Wagner, 1983; Stauffer, 1980) have argued for the interrelationship of reading and writing based upon an assumption of underlying psychological identicality or unity. If the skills and abilities undergirding reading and writing knowledge and process are identical or highly similar, then the combination of reading and writing instruction could expedite literacy learning, or at least make instruction more efficient. There has even been debate over the need, at least at the elementary level, to teach *both* reading and writing if they share so much common knowledge (Graves, 1978); and it has been suggested that one reason for not including more writing instruction in the school curriculum has been the belief that it was unnecessary, given the great similarity of reading and writing (Shanahan, 1988). The strong belief in the underlying commonalities of reading and writing has been the basis for curricular innovations as diverse as the language experience approach, Fernald or V-A-K-T methods, strategies for phonics teaching, sentence combining, and integrated writing-based language arts programs.

Shared Knowledge and Process

Over the years, several studies have attempted to address the basic assumption of psychological sharing. Such studies usually have attempted to estimate the amount of psychological similarity in reading and writing, most often through correlational techniques. Initial efforts of this type attempted to relate two rather general measures of reading and writing ability. More recently, however, such studies have become increasingly sophisticated in their design and relatively more specific in their measurements. Such studies have begun to focus on process sharing as well, rather than being limited to simple comparisons or correlations of the products of reading and writing.

Performance-Based Correlational Studies

A large number of studies have correlated product- or performance-based measures of reading achievement and writing ability. Such measures examine compositions or specific reading outcomes (i.e., amount of comprehension for a set of passages) as external manifestations of literacy knowledge or process. Since such studies have been thoroughly reviewed elsewhere (Applebee, 1977; Galda, 1983; Shanahan, 1980, 1988; Stotsky, 1982; Stotsky, 1983), this chapter will examine some of the recent work in this area, and it will reexamine some of the more ambitious earlier efforts in light of recent theoretical and empirical developments.

One of the most notable examinations of the relationship between reading and writing abilities was completed by Loban (1963, 1964), who argued that the relationship between reading and writing was "so striking to be beyond question" (Loban, 1964, p. 212). Loban based this conclusion upon data collected in conjunction with an extensive longitudinal study of the reading and writing abilities of 220 students across 12 grade levels. Student performance was measured using the Stanford Achievement Test; and writing was scored using holistic assessment procedures applied to a single writing sample done in response to a picture prompt. As Figure 11.1 depicts for the sixth grade, Loban compared the reading level achieved by students at various grade levels with ratings of their writing. As illustrated in the data for other grade levels, there was a definite positive relationship between reading and writing—especially for students who performed very well or poorly. As he stated:

> *Every* child who writes at a superior level and the great majority who write at a high average level read above their reading age. On the other hand, *every* subject who writes at the illiterate level and virtually every subject who writes at the marginal level reads below his reading age. This is true for every year studied without exception. (Loban, 1964, p. 208)

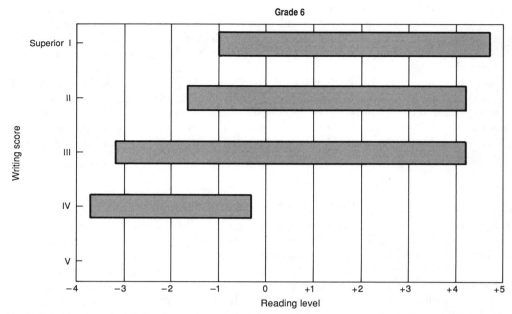

FIGURE 11.1   Loban's study: relation between reading and writing—written language scores compared to reading achievement above or below grade level. *Source:* From Relation between reading and writing, grade 6, by Walter Loban. In *The language of elementary school children.* Copyright © 1963 by the National Council of Teachers of English. Reprinted with permission.

Loban's study is most notable because of its large sample size, its emphasis on students across grade levels, its early emphasis on reading-writing relations, and its influential effect upon thinking in the field. The findings from Loban's study are probably overstated, however. First, among the average students there was considerable variation in reading and writing performance. The leveling of subjects that was used might have disguised real differences that existed. Second, across grade levels the correlations varied substantially, suggesting that the relationship was less consistent than was claimed. Third, the findings might have been an artifact of the measures examined—a group standardized test and a single writing sample represent a severely restricted sample of student work. Fourth, the findings may have been influenced by the instructional histories of the students. Loban omitted details as to the nature and amount of reading and writing instruction received by students in his study.

The results of some more recent research suggest that Loban's straightforward interpretation is probably misleading. Martin (1977), in a careful examination of case-study data from six Australian children (aged 12 years 9 months to 14 years 6 months), concluded that two subjects scored low on reading and writing mechanics and high on writing expression, a third child was a capable reader yet his writing was not of good quality, a fourth child was high on writing mechanics and low in reading and writing expression, and the final two subjects either did well or poorly in both reading and writing. "Despite the small numbers studied, the evidence suggests that reading and writing are intertwined, but in ways that are not easily predictable" (Martin, 1977, p. 52). Similarly, in a study that focused on process rather than performance, Tierney (1983) was able to identify students who were good readers-poor writers and poor readers-good writers. Frith (1980), in a study of word recognition-word production relations, was able to identify similarly disparate and, according to Loban's claims, unlikely samples.

Recently studies have attempted to be more explicit with regard to the types of knowledge that might be shared across reading and writing, and there has been a serious effort to describe how reading and writing relations might vary across proficiency and grade levels. Juel, Griffith, and Gough (1986) explored across grades one and two the relationship between word recognition, spelling, reading comprehension, and writing quality in a longitudinal study across grades one and two. Shanahan (1984) and Shanahan and Lomax (1986, 1988) examined the relationship between lexical, phonemic syntactic, and organizational-structural information, using second- and fifth-grade cohorts. Schewe and Froese (1987) examined the correlation between selected comprehension scores and writing measures for a small sample of fourth graders. Cox, Shanahan, and Sulzby (in press) have considered the relationship between the use of cohesive ties and cohesive harmony in the writing of narrative and expository text with reading comprehension performance. In all of these studies, reading and writing were significantly related on certain measures and not on others. Correlations varied by grade levels and correlations were maximized when reading and writing were viewed as interactive rather than unidirectional phenomena.

Shanahan (1984) and Shanahan and Lomax (1986, 1988), for example, examined 256 second and fifth graders in perhaps the most exhaustive analysis to date, finding that the correlation between reading and writing measures accounted for 43 percent of the variance. For beginning readers, phonics and spelling ability accounted for most of the total variance; as proficiency increased, however, writing measures such as vocabulary diversity and story structure (combined with a prose comprehension score) accounted for most of the variance. When alternative models of specific relationship patterns were tested against the data, an interactional view proved most tenable—that is, a model in which reading and writing relationships were defined as mutually interacting with each other rather than in a unidirectional fashion. Such a finding prompted Shanahan and Lomax (1986) to offer the following conclusion:

> The interactive model was robust with regard to its ability to summarize data collected from diverse samples of readers and writers. Reading influences writing, *and* writing influences reading; theories of literacy development need to emphasize both of these characteristics similarly. These findings suggest that reading and writing should be taught in ways that maximize the possibility of using information drawn from both reading and writing. (p. 208)

Such studies suggest that knowledge sharing in reading and writing is a likely phenomenon, though it is neither as simple nor as complete as was once assumed. Correlations between performance variables have been generally moderate, even in multivariate studies. Evidently reading and writing knowledge is either not identical or it is used or instantiated in strikingly different ways in reading and writing.

While correlational studies of the knowledge sharing between reading and writing have made a contribution to unraveling the precise nature of reading-writing relationships, some obvious cautions should be heeded as we extrapolate conclusions. First, correlational findings indicate the extent to which measures co-vary or change together. Such findings provide a necessary, but not a sufficient condition for confirming the actual knowledge sharing that takes place in literacy development. Second, these studies have relied entirely upon the examination of reading and writing products and have simply inferred sharing on the basis of connections between these products. Such evidence does not provide adequate proof of knowledge sharing. Third, correlational findings depend upon the measures employed to assess variables and the labels used to describe these variables. Poorly labeled variables and limited measures of certain abilities are in evidence in all such studies considered here or in those considered in previously published reviews. Fourth, although this is beginning to change, these studies have paid scant attention to the instructional conditions that may alter the pattern of knowledge sharing between reading and writing. Fifth, these studies have usually not matched the reading and writing tasks themselves. Students have almost never been asked even to read and write on the same topics in this type of study. Finally, the selection of some measures instead of others reflects theoretical decisions, usually implicit, that shape the possible outcomes. The inclusion of different variables or different measures of even these same variables might lead to different conclusions.

Future research needs to provide more precise and complete descriptions of the specific knowledge sharing in reading and writing. The sharing that does occur appears to be related to the literacy issues that are the major focus of attention at particular levels of development. Early on, the sharing seems to be more word related, but it becomes more global and substantive with development. Whether this is the result of some natural prioritization of literacy development, or simply the outcome of instructional emphasis, is unknown. Finally, these studies have shown that reading and writing knowledge is shared in both directions, suggesting the potential benefits of combining reading and writing instructionally. Fuller and more accurate descriptions of this knowledge sharing could help in the design of more mutually effective curricula.

Correlational studies of this type have considered knowledge sharing on the basis of performance or achievement variables. So far, such studies have considered the relations between such aspects of knowledge as vocabulary (Maloney, 1967; Vairo, 1976), print awareness and phonics (Chomsky, 1979; Tovey, 1978), orthography (Shanahan, 1984), word recognition (Juel, Griffith, & Gough, 1986), spelling (Clarke, 1988; Shanahan, 1984), sentence comprehension (Shanahan & Lomax, 1986), syntax (Zeman, 1969; Perron, 1977; Evanechko, Ollila, & Armstrong, 1974), cohesion and cohesive harmony (Cox, Shanahan, & Sulzby, in press; King & Rentel, 1979), text structure (Hiebert, Englert, & Brennan, 1983; King & Rental, 1979), creativity (Fishco, 1966), text format (Clay, 1967, 1976; Eckhoff, 1983), writing quality (Baden, 1981), and readability or prose complexity (Lazdowski, 1976). Future efforts need to continue to consider additional variables such as the role of content knowledge, expository text structure, use and interpretation of rhetorical devices and structures, and so on. On the one hand, future research would best add knowledge to the field through the estimation of relationships in a more comprehensive and theory-driven manner than has been typical up to now. Shanahan (1984) provided a more comprehensive analysis of several variables, but he failed to examine the relations within a well-established theoretical framework that would permit the fullest understanding of knowledge sharing. Other studies (Juel, Griffith, & Gough, 1986; Cox, Shanahan, & Sulzby, in press; Shanahan & Lomax, 1988) have worked from more substantial theoretical positions, although these studies were less comprehensive in variable selection or they used existing data, the collection of which was not determined by theory. Alternatively, studies are needed that pursue the relationship in a more open-ended fashion and that allow for theories to emerge.

Process-Based Correlational Studies

With the advent of constructivist thinking in reading comprehension and planned-based analysis of writers' protocols, a number of researchers and theorists have considered the parallels between the cognitive *processes* underlying reading and writing. Unlike the studies previously considered, these do not usually examine reading or writing products but instead collect information about cognitive processing through think-aloud protocols, interviews, and observations. The empirical efforts either have been formally correlational or have provided qualitative description of the corresponding similarities or differences in reading and writing.

Wittrock (1984) argues that reading and writing are generative cognitive processes in which readers and writers "create meanings by building relations between the text and what they know, believe, and experience" (p. 77). Likewise, Squire (1984) suggests that "both comprehending and composing seem basic reflections of the same cognitive processes" (p. 24). In a similar view, Tierney and Pearson (1983) have proposed a composing model of reading (see Figure 11.2) in which they suggest that reading and writing are acts of composing that share similar underlying processes: goal setting, knowledge mobilization, projection, perspective-taking, refinement, review, self-correction, and self-assessment.

Kucer (1985), from a slightly different perspective, suggests that readers and writers are involved in several strategies of "generating and integrating propositions through which the internal structure of meaning known as the text world is built" (p. 331). According to this view, to understand the relationship between reading and writing, each act should be recognized as an essentially separate instance of "text world production . . . drawing from a *common* pool of cognitive and linguistic operations." Kucer's model of text world production is depicted in Figure 11.3. It describes the role of context as well as strategies and procedures used by readers and writers in conjunction with accessing and transferring background knowledge.

Several recent research studies confirm and define the view of reading and writing advocated by these theorists: namely, that reading and writing can be defined in terms of the same general cognitive process (gathering ideas, questioning, hypothesizing, and so on). Where reading and writing appear to differ is in the extent to which these

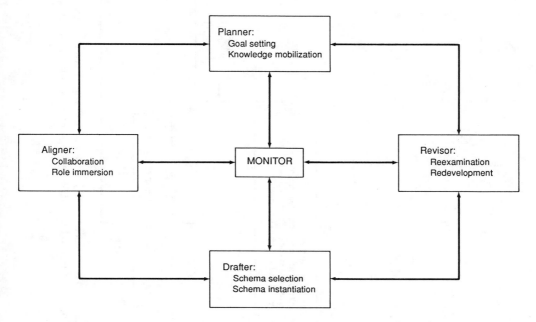

FIGURE 11.2   The Tierney and Pearson Composing Model of Reading *Source:* Toward a composing model of reading, by Robert J. Tierney and P. David Pearson. *Language Arts, 60,* May 1983.

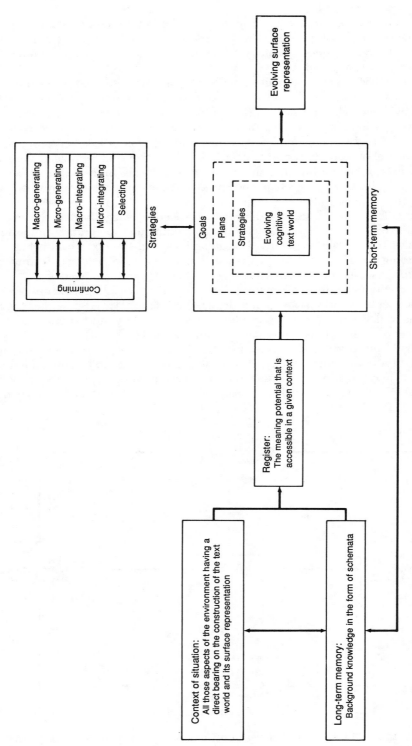

FIGURE 11.3 Model of text world production. *Source:* From Kucer, S. L, The making of meaning, *Written Communication,* 2(3). Copyright © 1985 by Sage Publications. Reprinted by permission of Sage Publications, Inc.

strategies are enlisted by students, or by what features of the reading or writing act lead them to instantiate a particular strategy. It should be noted that different students enlist different strategies in accordance with their idiosyncratic approach and overall abilities as readers or writers. For example, Ryan (1985) examined the verbal protocols of eight above-average readers/writers from a fifth-grade classroom as they read and wrote in both narrative and expository genres. She identified six thinking strategies common to reading and writing: reporting (reproducing and paraphrasing a message); conjecturing (hypothesizing, prediction of outcomes, and inferencing); contextualizing (relating to concepts and events through imagining, creating scenarios, and so on); structuring; monitoring; and revising. She also identified two response styles of readers and writers: reactive (or literally inclosed) and transactive (or more flexible). Ryan's findings with respect to genre revealed that although all strategies could be identified in response to both narrative and expository text, the balance of usage varied according to genre. "The strategies of reporting and structuring appeared to be more dominant in the expository protocols, while conjecturing, contextualizing, and monitoring appeared more frequently with narrative protocols" (p. 389).

Studies by Kirby (1986) and Martin (1987) yielded similar findings. For purposes of comparing student meaning-making strategies during reading and writing, Kirby (1986) videotaped five high-risk basic-level freshmen across four sessions involving reading and writing activities as well as retrospective interviews on the processes that were used. Subjects read realistic fiction and factual text and wrote and revised expressive and transactive text on topics paralleling those offered in the reading selections. Kirby found that subjects in her study "used more similar than different strategies in reading and writing" (p. 126). Across all of the tasks, regardless of whether or not they were involved in reading or writing, the students constantly related the texts (being read or written) to their personal experiences. Kirby also noted that shortcomings in strategy use during reading paralleled shortcomings in writing. Just as students did very little planning in writing, so they did little previewing or purpose-setting prior to reading. As Kirby suggested, limitations in the availability and implementation of strategies generalized across reading and writing.

Martin (1987) examined the think-aloud protocols, responses to interview questions, and the observable behaviors of seven senior high school seniors as they read abstract text and concrete text, and engaged in reflexive writing and extensive writing. Martin identified eight categories of meaning-making strategies: monitoring, phrasing content, using content prior knowledge, using text from knowledge, rereading, questioning, inferencing, and making connections to author/audience. (Table 11.1 includes a listing of the frequency of the different strategies by task.) While the extent to which certain strategies are enlisted varies with task and mode (reading or writing), the study shows that the same strategies emerge during reading and writing. In other words, the study supports the view that readers and writers enlist from the same pool of cognitive processes. These data also suggest that readers and writers might vary in the extent to which they employ certain strategies. In particular, during writing, students in Martin's study were more concerned about content knowledge; during reading, students were more concerned about paraphrasing content.

These findings are similar to those of Langer (1986a). Langer attempted to describe the knowledge sources, reasoning operations, specific strategies, and monitoring behaviors of 67 third-, sixth-, and ninth-grade children when they read and wrote stories and reports. The tasks that she used were similar in discourse type (stories or reports) and in terms of topic. Especially noteworthy were her analyses of the similarity between reasoning operations and strategies. Reasoning operations included questioning, hypothesizing, assuming, using schemata, making metacomments, citing

TABLE 11.1   Frequencies and Percentages of Strategies by Task

| TASK | READING | | WRITING | |
	ABSTRACT (%)	CONCRETE (%)	REFLEXIVE (%)	EXTENSIVE (%)
Monitoring	400 (37.9)	226 (27.6)	399 (53.3)	353 (54.1)
Phrasing content	430 (40.8)	447 (54.6)	172 (23.0)	151 (23.1)
Content knowledge	48 (4.5)	39 (4.8)	106 (14.2)	88 (13.5)
Text form	55 (5.2)	89 (10.9)	119 (15.9)	126 (19.3)
Rereading	179 (16.9)	72 (8.8)	171 (22.8)	142 (21.7)
Questioning	33 (3.1)	20 (2.4)	52 (6.9)	65 (10.0)
Inferencing	114 (10.8)	51 (6.2)	18 (2.4)	21 (3.2)
Making connections	71 (6.7)	37 (4.5)	9 (1.2)	10 (1.5)

evidence, and validating. Strategies included generating ideas, formulating meaning, evaluating, and revising. In general, her findings suggest that while reading and writing appear to pull from the same collection of cognitive processes, similarities and differences do exist in the pattern. In terms of commonalities, both readers and writers focus on meaning when formulating and refining ideas. Moreover, their behaviors vary in similar ways across time. In both reading and writing, the children's comments would focus on global units of text, on questioning and hypothesizing, on generating ideas and goal setting. After reading and writing, the comments showed a move to validating schemata together with the formulation and refinement of meaning. In terms of differences, readers generated more ideas when they read and formulated more ideas when they wrote. Readers tended to have more generalized concerns while writers exhibited a broad array of concerns. In reading they focused on garnering support for ideas; in writing they were more interested in the strategies they used to create meanings. Langer writes:

> The analysis of the varieties of behavior and approaches toward meaning lead me to conclude the following: (1) the behaviors are varied and complex, (2) they change with age and difficulty, and (3) they vary consistently between reading and writing.
>
> Further, the findings confirm the belief that children of all ages are concerned primarily with their developing ideas and the text world or envisionments they create, in both reading and writing (Langer, 1986a, p. 259).

The tendency for these processes, and their relations across reading and writing, to change as a result of development is supported by analogous findings in performance-based comparisons (Shanahan, 1984) and in earlier process-oriented analyses (Birnbaum, 1982; Tierney, 1983). The tendency of these processes to vary across reading and writing led Langer (1986b) to conclude that it may be, as she stated,

> oversimplistic to assume that reading and writing are similar activities. Though reading and writing share common language routines and reasoning strategies, they involve quite

different patterns of cognitive behaviors and different approaches to meaning-making, even when tasks and topics are parallel. (p. 25)

McGinley and Tierney (1989) suggest that the similarities and differences, which Langer's study highlights, may account for the advantages afforded when reading and writing work together. Drawing upon the work of Wittgenstein and Spiro, they argue that reading and writing offer ways to criss-cross explorations of topics involving often subtle but significant shifts in perspective.

There is a temptation in reviewing these process-oriented examinations of reading and writing to adopt a view of reading and writing as an activity that is merely schema activation and instantiation. Few process-oriented studies have considered notions of the transactional nature of reading and writing, of intertextuality, of how interpersonal factors influence meaning-making, and even of basic psycholinguistic decision making (i.e., staging, coherence). These omissions have occurred despite the emerging views (as evidenced in the writings of Shanklin [1981], Kucer [1985], Murray [1982b], and Smith [1984]) that suggest that meaning-making is related to what and how readers and writers negotiate with their inner selves and with others. These communicative, interpersonal, or transactional aspects of the literacy process will be considered in detail later.

So what should be concluded from attempts to describe the processes of reading and writing? Obviously, our understanding of the nature of reading and writing has been extended by the combined examination. Using reading as a metaphor for writing and writing as a metaphor for reading has proven to be a powerful vehicle for extending our understanding of literacy. Above all, they suggest a common model of human understanding and confirm a thesis originally offered by Petrosky (1982):

> One of the most interesting results of connecting reading, literary, and composition theory and pedagogy is that they yield similar explanations of human understanding as a process rooted in the individual's knowledge and feelings and characterized by the fundamental act of making meaning, whether it be through reading, responding, or writing. When we read, we comprehend by putting together impressions of the text with our personal, cultural, and contextual models of reality. When we write, we compose by making meaning from available information, our personal knowledge, and the cultural and contextual frames we happen to find ourselves in. Our theoretical understandings of these processes are convergent . . . around the central role of human understanding—be it of texts or the world—as a process of composing. (p. 34)

But how useful is such a model for actually understanding the specific nature of the cognitive sharing that takes place in reading and writing? Certainly these studies suffer from a number of limitations and flaws that temper specific conclusions that can be drawn. First, although in these studies variables were selected more on the basis of explicit theory than in performance-based studies, variable selection and description is still a problem. There seems to be little solid evidence that would differentiate the labels attributed to the behaviors and responses under analysis. Terms like inferencing, predicting, use of prior knowledge, conjecturing, and hypothesizing are used in similar, overlapping, and even different ways in various schemes. This, of course, limits the generalizability of the findings, and it is especially problematic in identifying processes *across* reading and writing. Is a behavior labeled as hypothesizing actually the same behavior in reading and writing?

Second, the measures and descriptions are often of questionable, or at least untested, reliability. Generally, researchers have done a reasonable job of showing that they were able to observe or examine the behaviors or protocols in a consistent fashion, but no study has yet demonstrated that the processing itself is reliable. Third, questions might be raised concerning the adequacy of introspective and retrospective think-alouds and interviews as a source of data. Certainly great care must be taken in drawing conclusions solely on the basis of such data.

Fourth, although these studies have provided a convincing demonstration that reading and writing employ similar, if not the same, cognitive processes, they have been less informative of the specific patterns of relationship. Although reading tasks will generally be more similar to each other than to analogous writing tasks, they themselves might be so different from each other that they would involve different patterns of behaviors. The same point can be made about writing tasks. The implications of the personal, motivational, informational, linguistic, pragmatic, and functional contexts of these tasks might prove to be so complex as to render the results, to date, limited in scope. Despite this possibility, the patterns, up to now, have been provocatively similar, suggesting a generalizability that might permit their use for instructional planning. Interestingly, in the late 1980s, curriculum developers in selected school districts proposed a set of objectives that include common goals for reading and writing. For example, curriculum developers in Fairfax County (Virginia) and Upper Arlington (Ohio) developed goals such as revising for meaning, organizing ideas, and planning for both reading and writing.

Fifth, sample sizes have been necessarily small because of the depth of analysis that has been required. Most of what we know in this area that has any generalizable or cumulative value has resulted from the amassing of data across studies. Analytical differences, however, render it especially important that researchers follow up such studies with replications and extensions.

Sixth, these studies, like the performance-based analyses, have usually neglected the instructional histories of the students examined. This makes it impossible to know whether the relations being described are natural psychological entities or whether they are learned features of written language behavior. Nevertheless, these studies have provided a good deal of insight and information about reading and writing in a very short span of time (less than a decade).

Experimental Efforts

Another approach to the issue of whether there is sharing of information or processes across reading and writing has been the experimental, or instructional, study. Typically such studies provide some type of writing instruction, and then the potential reading outcomes of this instruction are examined; or vice versa. These studies have sometimes been quite general, with very little specification of the type of cognitive sharing that should be apparent. For example, the landmark United States Office of Education Cooperative First Grade Studies (Bond & Dykstra, 1967) reported that, in general, programs that offered a writing component did better at instilling reading achievement than did those that had no such component. Maat (1977) was able to demonstrate improvements in reading comprehension as a result of a nine-week writing program in the high school. It seems reasonable to conclude, on the basis of such evidence, that reading and writing share some common core of knowledge or process. However, such studies often have not adequately described instructional conditions, and the outcome measures were far too general to allow the identification of the nature of the sharing that took place.

It should not be concluded that writing instruction automatically leads to reading improvement either. Obenchain (1971) provided an expository writing program to high school students, but no reading improvement resulted. Smith, Jensen, and Dillingofski (1971) found that writing activities led to no improvement on reading comprehension tests with elementary-grade students. It has even been shown that when reading is replaced with writing activity, reading achievement can improve, though not to the same degree that it would if additional reading instruction were provided (Heys, 1962). Such studies suggest that cognitive sharing can occur, at least under certain conditions, but they are less informative at specifying what types of sharing would result from reading or writing instruction.

Most often the experimental studies have focused on sharing from reading to writing than from writing to reading. This approach has usually been taken because researchers have generally assumed that the learning that took place in reading was fundamental to writing development (Smith, 1982), and that there would be no need for tests of such a self-evident hypothesis. There have been a few attempts to consider the influence of reading upon writing, nevertheless. One such study had students writing as a response to children's literature (Mills, 1974), and found improvements in standardized language achievement test scores. Bereiter and Scardamalia (1984) investigated the knowledge gained about genre features by students from exposure to single examples of literary types—suspense, fiction, restaurant review, and an invented fictional genre defined as "concrete fiction." Across all experiments, writing in conjunction with reading a single text proved to be a powerful vehicle for learning, even more powerful than direct instruction. Students who read demonstrated that they had gained a sense of genre features that was useful in writing.

Reading and writing instruction and activity can lead to the development of transferable knowledge or processes, though such sharing does not necessarily occur. But what kinds of sharing can take place as a result of integrated instruction? A number of recent studies have addressed this by using somewhat more specific types of training or outcome measures. For example, several investigations have examined the influence of writing on the word recognition ability of young children. In general, the results emerging from these studies are positive—especially for writing activities that allowed for invented spellings. For instance, Clarke (1988) demonstrated that a year-long writing program in which children were encouraged to use invented spelling was superior to a writing program that did not. These first-grade students not only wrote better when they had the freedom to spell without emphasis on standard forms, but their reading achievement and word recognition ability improved as a result of the activity. Similarly, in an investigation of IBM's "Write to Read" program (Educational Testing Service, 1984), it was found that computer composing using invented spelling had a positive impact on reading and writing. This study, however, did not control for the influence of time, and it provided the treatment groups with different types of phonics instruction, so it is impossible to attribute the reading gains specifically to the writing activities. In a third study, Mason, McDaniel, and Callaway (1974) randomly assigned 30 first-grade classes to treatment conditions and found that encouraging students to write, using words drawn from their basal curriculum, had a positive impact on their vocabulary knowledge and reading comprehension.

A number of studies have attempted to examine the influence of a highly constrained writing activity—sentence-combining—on reading comprehension. Although it has been found that such activities do enhance the complexity of sentence construction in writing, there is little convincing evidence that such increased complexity is implicated in qualitative improvements in writing performance (Hillocks, 1986). Nevertheless, sentence-combining activities have usually had a positive impact upon reading comprehension, but only when such measures emphasize sentence-level comprehension such as through the use of a cloze test (Straw & Schreiner, 1982).

Sentence-combining writing activities have not been found to improve reading comprehension when the measure has required the reading of relatively complete prose passages and the answering of questions.

The experimental manipulation of knowledge of text structure has also been examined in a number of studies. Taylor and Beach (1984) found that seventh graders' understanding of expository text structure was enhanced as a result of opportunities to write summaries, in contrast to merely responding to questions. Bean and Steenwyck (1984) had similar results with a summary-writing strategy taught to sixth graders. Even with narrative texts, writing instruction and activities designed to extend knowledge of story structure (Gordon & Braun, 1982) have been found to improve reading comprehension performance. In a different type of study, students were not asked to use reading to improve their writing or vice versa; instead, they were given direct instruction in the structural properties of expository text, and outcomes were measured in terms of both reading and writing. The expository text training was found to lead to significant improvements in both reading and writing achievement (Raphael, Englert, & Kirschner, 1986).

These studies have shown that writing led to improved reading achievement, reading led to better writing performance, and combined instruction led to improvements in both reading and writing. Such improvements are not always forthcoming. Overall group findings may overshadow individual achievements. Of note, Raphael, Kirschner, and Englert (1988) examined the success (or lack of success) associated with attempts to use writing as a means of enhancing students' understanding of the strategies used by authors of expository texts. She examined the processes of 15 students who made substantial gains in understanding and writing expository text with 15 students who were nongainers. Raphael et al. concluded that nongainers tended not to be able to relate new elements to an overall goal or framework in reading or writing. It seemed as if, according to Raphael et al., the students who accrued benefits from the procedure were those who tied together ideas.

Obviously, there is a need for more experimental studies of reading and writing relations. Like the correlational studies to which they are related, instructional studies need to examine a larger range of variables simultaneously. We still do not have a clear understanding of the shared knowledge development that might accrue from a comprehensive integrated reading and writing program. It is especially important that future studies examine process issues and not just product-based ones. Unlike most previous studies, future efforts should attempt to identify the specific conditions under which learning might be transferable. This can be done by providing much more detailed descriptions of instructional conditions than has usually been evident, or through the type of post-hoc analysis provided by Raphael and associates (1988). Studies have shown that instruction can have joint benefits for reading and writing achievement, but studies have generally lacked the detailed description necessary to allow such findings to be applied to instructional practice.

HOW READERS AND WRITERS TRANSACT
WITH ONE ANOTHER

In this article entitled "Learning to Read as a Writer," Frank Smith offered the following exultation:

> To read like a writer we engage with the author in what the author is writing. We anticipate what the author will say, so that the author is in effect writing on our behalf, not showing how something is done, but doing it with us. . . . (Smith, 1984, pap. 52–53.)

Issues of authorship and readership have prompted many theorists to conceive of reading and writing in terms similar to the relationship between speaker and listener in conversation, seeing the products of reading and writing as "situated accomplishments" (Cook, 1973). In accordance with this view, discourse is only meaningful in its context of situation; rather than simply a chain of utterances, discourse is understood according to who is speaking and why (Ohmann, 1971; Searle, 1969; Van Dijk, 1976). "To understand," Green (1980) explains, requires forming "a model of the speaker's plan in saying what he said such that this plan is the most plausible one consistent with the speaker's acts and the addressee's assumptions (or knowledge) about the speaker and the rest of the world" (p. 14). To read and write, as Augustine and Winterowd (1986); Beach and Liebman-Kleine (1986); Bruce (1980); Tierney, LaZansky, Raphael, and Cohen (1987); Pratt (1977); Pearson and Tierney (1984); and Shanklin (1981) have suggested, requires authors who expect meaning-making on the part of readers *and* readers who do the meaning-making. Writers, as they produce text, consider their readers—or at least the transactions in which readers are likely to engage. In other words, this view presupposes that writers try to address and satisfy what they project as the response of the reader to that speech act that underlies the surface structure of the communication. This activity occurs notwithstanding the fact that a writer might be his or her own reader. Readers, as they read text, respond to what they perceive writers are trying to get them to think of, as well as what readers themselves perceive they need to do. As Fillmore (1979) stated,

> A text induces the interpreter to construct an image or maybe a set of alternative images. The image the interpreter creates early in the text guides his interpretation of successive portions of the text and these in turn induce him to enrich or modify that image. While the image construction and image revision is going on, the interpreter is also trying to figure out what the creator of the text is doing—what the nature of the communication situation is. And that, too, may have an influence on the image-creating process." (p.4)

Or, as the Russian semiotician Bakhtin (1973) has argued, all text (spoken or written) needs to be viewed as "the product of the reciprocal relationship between speaker and listener, addresser and addressee . . ." (pp. 85–86). Or as he stated more fully,

> [T]he word is always oriented toward an addressee, toward who that addressee might be . . . each person's inner world, and thought has its stabilized *social audience* that comprises the environments in which reasons, motives, values, and so on are fashioned . . . the word is a two-sided act. It is determined equally by whose word it is and for whom it is meant. . . . Each and every word expresses the one relation to the other. I give myself verbal shape from another's point of view, ultimately from the point of view of the community to which I belong. A word is territory *shared* by both addresser and addressee, by the speaker and his interlocutor. (pp. 85–86)

In an effort to pull together these considerations, Nystrand (1986) argues that reading and writing should be viewed as a transaction between readers and writers; this involves a mutual awareness as well as shared expectations. Nystrand refers to these expectations as a reciprocal agreement. As he stated:

> This key assumption is the *Reciprocity Principle*, which is the foundation of all social acts, including discourse: *In any collaborative activity the participants orient their actions on certain standards which are taken for granted as rules of conduct by the social group to which they belong.* . . . The expectation for reciprocity in discourse is important because it means that the shape and conduct of discourse is determined not only by what the speaker or writer has to say (speaker/writer *meaning*) or accomplish (speaker/writer/*purpose*) but

also by the joining expectations of the conversants that they should understand one another (producer-receiver *contract*). Of these three forces that shape discourse, moreover, the contract is most fundamental: Without a contract between writer and reader, both meaning and purpose are unfathomable at best and untenable at worst. (p. 48)

How do these notions apply to the reality of classrooms? Several obvious questions emerge from the consideration of these accounts: To what extent do readers consider authorship? To what extent do writers consider audience? What happens to reading and writing when a sense of authorship or audience is enhanced?

To What Extent Do Readers Consider Authors?

Findings from several studies suggest (1) students at all ages have a sense of authorship, but younger and less proficient readers do not consider authorship either to the same degree or with as much breadth as older and more proficient readers; (2) oftentimes author intentionality is used by readers to resolve difficulties that they encounter as they pursue interpretations of text; and (3) similarly, the difficulties readers encounter are oftentimes due to a failure to appropriate an author's intentions in that text.

In the previously cited study by Martin (1987), making connections to authors was one of the eight categories that emerged from her study of high school seniors' self-reports during reading. Making connections to authors accounted for 6.7 percent of the comments offered in response to the abstract passage and 4.5 percent to the concrete. When probed further, most students revealed a rather vague sense of authorship. In a study by Flower (1987), a sense of authorship appeared to be both prevalent and important to meaning-making. Inferences she labelled as serving "to identify the rhetorical structure of the text . . . as a speech act or social transaction between Gould [the author] and his readers" were used 60 percent of the time as a means of resolving difficulties of interpretation.

In studies with younger children as well as adults, similar findings have emerged. For example, McGee (1983) conducted an extensive study with 108 subjects (36 second graders, 36 fifth graders, and 36 adults) in which individuals were interviewed after reading and summarizing two stories. Interview questions addressed why they thought the authors wrote the stories. Results indicated that adults compared with children did the following: (1) they gave more reasons why authors wrote, especially reasons related to communicating and interacting with readers; (2) they displayed a greater awareness of the author's intent to convey social information; and (3) they produced more information about the social nature of the discourse in their summaries than did second graders or fifth graders. Likewise, fifth graders displayed a greater awareness of the author's intent than did second graders and included more information dealing with social interactions. Second graders displayed little awareness that authors write to communicate, and their summaries contained very little social information.

What Happens When a Reader's
Sense of Author Is Enhanced?

A study by Tierney, LaZansky, Raphael, and Cohen (1987) suggested that a lack of sense of authorship may result in a failure to identify inconsistencies presented in certain text situations. By studying the responses of readers to inconsistent ideas inserted in nonfamiliar versus familiar text, as well as texts with and without dialogue, Tierney and associates found that better readers relied upon a consideration of an author's intent to unravel meanings, whereas poorer readers were not apt to consider authorial intent or negotiate their own meaning, especially in less-familiar text and text without dialogue.

The findings by Tierney and associates concur with Bruce's (1980) position: "Failure to understand the author's intention can cause problems for all levels of comprehension, from 'getting the idea' to subtle insights expected of skilled readers" (p. 380).

A number of educators suggest that enhancing a sense of authorship contributes to more critical thinking. With elementary-age students, Graves and Hansen (1983) as well as Calkins (1983) have claimed that students who write fluently and conference with others approach text with an awareness of authorship, a critical eye to an author's craft, and more flexibility in terms of the use of strategies. With college-level basic writers, Salvatori (1985) has demonstrated that a carefully developed sequence of writing experiences develops what might be termed a more transactional, "dialogical" attitude to reading. That is, after experiencing opportunities to write, Salvatori claims that students approach text written by others with a sense of their own purposes and a view to negotiating meaning that goes beyond acquiescing to text.

In ethnographically oriented studies of collaborative learning situations (Short, 1986a, 1986b; Rowe, 1986, 1987) findings that concur with these claims have surfaced; in classrooms where students were exposed to reading, writing, and conferencing opportunities, readers adopted more transactional stances and learning. As Short (1986b) comments:

> Children continually built off each other's texts but they always transformed the idea into their own construction. The idea never looked the same because it was intertextualized with their own ideas and because they always pulled their intertextual ties from such a variety of texts. Because of the collaborative learning environment established in the room, children collaborated with the texts of other authors, whether professional or classroom, rather than feeling that they had to try to transfer those authors' texts into their texts. (p. 345)

In more traditional studies of the effects of training students to consider an author's purpose (LaZansky & Tierney, 1985; Mosenthal, 1983), such effects were also apparent, but especially when students were dealing with more difficult text. Specifically, students who were directed to read with a sense of the author's purpose recalled more ideas from the more difficult text than did those who had not been so trained. Finally, text-based attempts to heighten author awareness have also yielded interesting results. In those situations when text seemed more personalized, students tended to recall more information and read it more critically. In one study (Tierney et al., 1987), college students who were asked to respond to the text most closely aligned with their experience recalled more and read more critically. In a second study (Crismore, 1985), metadiscourse inserted in hopes of personalizing text enhanced students' reading recall of these texts.

Gadamer (1986) once claimed that

> The understanding of a text has not begun at all as long as the text remains mute. But a text can begin to speak. . . . When it does begin to speak, however, it does not simply speak its word, always the same, in lifeless rigidity, but gives ever-new answers to the person who questions it and poses ever-new questions to him who answers it. To understand a text is to come to understand oneself in a kind of dialogue. This contention is confirmed by the fact that the concrete dealing with a text yields understanding only when what is said in the text begins to find expression in the interpreter's own language. Interpretation belongs to the essential unity of understanding. One must take up into himself what is said to him in such fashion that it speaks and finds an answer in the words of his own language. (p. 57)

Taken together, these findings suggest that a sense of authorship can be heightened; and once heightened, students tend to read more critically, more flexibly, and with a view to negotiating meanings for themselves. However, of all the areas of research examined in this chapter, this is probably the weakest. It has generated only a small set of research studies. Unlike other approaches to the relationship, no methods, measures, or paradigms have gained widespread use, and none has been explored in-depth across studies. This makes it very difficult to draw broad, educationally relevant conclusions from the findings.

Despite the claims of many experts, there are as yet no careful studies of the impact of extensive reading or writing programs on sense of authorship. It is certainly possible that a peer-conferencing-style program could exert an important influence on this aspect of literacy development, but findings up to this point are more provocative than substantive. Given the important differences that have been described in students' conferencing behaviors (DiPardo & Freedman, 1988), it is doubtful that all such approaches and interactions would lead to equivalent increases in authorship awareness.

Studies of authorship awareness have also been rather vague with regard to the theoretical dimensions of this construct. Issues such as reader's purposes, interactions of reader's and author's intentions, functions, and comprehension type have not been explored as of yet. Personalization is still weakly defined. No theory of reading provides an adequate description of the conditions under which a sense of authorship would be necessary, useful, or relevant; not surprisingly, these few studies have not yet adequately considered such issues.

Future work needs to consider sense of authorship as a basic outcome in a variety of reading and writing studies. Especially useful would be investigations that consider the writing, as well as the reading, outcomes of the authorship instruction. Research needs to consider the stability and generalizability of efforts to improve sense of authorship. It is one thing to find specific, short-term gains on experimenter-designed instruments; it is quite another to find generalizable outcomes that have long-lasting consequences. It is also important that researchers begin to consider alternative theoretical explanations for their findings. Does better alignment with the author lead to better comprehension because it causes a communications-oriented stance (an issue of transactional theory), or because of a simple knowledge-information alignment (a schema-theory issue)? How does alignment with the author interface with a reader's stance, including identification with story characters or perspective-taking? How does alignment with authors interface with a reader's consideration of a narrator? How does a sense of authorship relate to a sense of one's self as a reader?

To What Extent Do Writers Consider Their Audience?

Unlike sense of authorship, sense of audience has generated a substantial body of research. In conjunction with this extensive corpus of research dealing with writers' sensitivity to audience, there is substantial debate concerning the extent to which a concern for audience is pervasive.

The topic of audience yields a twofold problem: First, one question is whether, as Rubin (1984) argues, "writers are under all circumstances actively engaged in constructing representations of their readers" (p. 238); or, as Burleson and Rowan (1985, p. 41) contend, audience considerations underlie only those forms of discourse in which "audience knowledge" is centrally involved—that is, in writings such as persuasive, regulative, or communicative. The second problem is that it is difficult to know how or in what ways a sensitivity to audience manifests itself, assuming it does. As Kroll (1985) suggests, sensitivity to audience is apt to manifest itself in various and different ways for difficult discourses and their registers. Indeed, his research examining changes in the relationships between social cognitive complexity and holistic measures of written communication suggests that variation from one text to another should be expected, especially when one examines audience sensitivity for different texts in the same way. For example, in his study the correlation between holistic assessment of writing and social cognitive complexity varied from .25 to .04. Again, the problem remains, how does an awareness of audience manifest itself? The problem is to delineate the various dimensions along which a sensitivity to audience might manifest itself for different texts written for different audiences and different purposes.

Some inroads have been made as methodologies have emerged and measures have been explored. In particular, three methodologies have come to the forefront: one in which existing texts are analyzed for features that might reflect an awareness of audience, another in which writers are asked to develop a text for two or more audiences, and another in which individuals are required to redevelop a text for different audiences. In terms of measures, studies using these methodologies have tended to look at slightly different variables. Studies involving the first two methodologies have looked at syntactic complexity and sometimes rhetorical structuring or the extent to which writers have used reader-based prose such as elaborating, orienting information, and other stylistic features. Studies involving the third methodology have tended to consider rhetorical structuring as well as meaning changes, but not syntactic complexity.

A number of studies have asked writers to develop explanations for a game for an undetermined audience. For example, Kroll (1986) asked 24 students in grade five, 26 students in grade seven, 19 students in grade eleven, and 27 college freshman to generate written explanations following a videotaped introduction to the game. He found that fifth graders and seventh graders produced explanations that were less informative, leaving out such elements as general statements of the object of the game and orienting information, and they were less formal than college-level students.

Flower and Hayes (1981) had four proficient writers and four less proficient writers compose aloud as they wrote. Analyses of the transcripts revealed that the proficient writers generated new ideas in response to the rhetorical problem of communicating with others, while less proficient writers focused on just the ideas. A study by Crowhurst and Piché (1979) examined the effects of writing for different audiences upon the complexity of the writing of grade-six and grade-ten students, who wrote essays to audiences deemed different in age, intimacy, and authority. The audiences were teacher and best friend. Analyses revealed that the essays by the tenth graders were more complex when written for the teacher audience; in grade six there were no significant differences.

Rubin and Piché (1979) analyzed the persuasive essays produced by fourth, eighth, and twelfth graders and adults in response to a topic for gifted audiences of high, intermediate, and low intimacy. The results found correlations between age, audience, and syntactic complexity, which was consistent with previous research. The results of an analysis of the use of persuasive strategies suggested that older students tended to establish a broader context for the topic and adapted these strategies for different audiences. By examining the texts rewritten for different/younger audiences, Kroll (1985) explored the audience-adapted writing skills of students in grades five, seven, nine, and eleven. Analyses of student revisions to these texts suggested that younger students tended to focus on word-level vocabulary changes, whereas older students focused on more major changes that included retelling of stories, revamping of structure, addition of stylistic features, and redevelopment of the moral.

Roen and Willey (1988) assigned subjects to three experimental writing conditions. In one, audience was not discussed; in the second, audience was focused upon before and during drafting; and in the third, audience was discussed before and during revising. Both audience awareness conditions improved the quality of writing, but providing focus during drafting was not nearly as effective as it was during revision. Sense of audience operated differently across the writing process.

Taken together, the findings from these studies suggest that, at least for selected writing assignments, all students are sensitive to audience, but older and more proficient writers tend to adapt their texts differently to meet audience demands. Older students are apt to adapt for audiences by varying the syntax and structures, implementing other meaning-level changes (elaboration and structuring ideas rather than focusing upon word choice), and adopting a tenor to fit the intended purpose of the text and its audience. The influence of writing awareness varies across different parts of the writing process, and it probably varies with regard to many other aspects of writing situations. It is hoped that future studies will explore these issues in more detail and adopt a more open-ended orientation to how different writers might be cuing different readers. This may lead to a very different set of indices to those included in studies to date.

Can Sensitivity to Audience Be Enhanced and What Are the Effects of This Enhancement?

Audience awareness, at least insofar as it manifests itself in written products, seems quite susceptible to different contexts and instructional experiences. Several researchers, including Graves and Hansen (1983); Newkirk (1982); and Tierney, Leys, and Rogers (1986), have demonstrated the impact of collaborative learning experiences upon students' sense of audience. Students in classrooms that are collaborative and involve students in sharing their writing with others appear to be able to read their own writing with a great deal more objectivity, as well as an understanding of possible improvements, than are students in less-collaborative settings (Graves & Hansen, 1983; Newkirk, 1982; Tierney, Leys, & Rogers, 1986). In one study, Tierney, Leys, and Rogers (1986) compared sensitivity to audience of third graders who had been involved in a variety of collaborative experiences with third graders who were involved in more teacher-centered, teacher-directed activities. Students in the former setting identified the ability to affect audiences (what they saw, felt, and thought) as one of their goals, and they elaborated and staged their texts accordingly. Students in the teacher-centered setting offered comments about their audience that were vague and not manifest in their writing.

As Raforth (1985) and Scardamalia, Bereiter, and McDonald (1977) have demonstrated, a writer's sensitivity to audience can be enhanced if the writer is provided with information on the reader's viewpoint on a topic and related background of experience. Shriver (1986) and Swaney, Janik, Bond, and Hayes (1981) have been able to demonstrate that writers could become more sensitive to readers' problems if they were exposed to the types of problems readers encounter. Beach and Anson (1988), Loewenthal and Krostrevski (1973), and Wagner (1987) have demonstrated that role-playing situations (i.e., as the context for writing or as a follow-up activity) increase a writer's sensitivity to audience and lead to rhetorical restructuring and to writers' making substantial additions to the text. One particularly noteworthy study by Redd-Boyd and Slater (1989) comparing imaginary assigned reader with real assigned reader or no assigned reader found that whether or not a writer was assigned an audience had little impact upon scores of essays, but did affect the writer's interest, effort, and use of audience-based strategies. Furthermore, regardless of whether or not they were assigned an audience, students who said they wrote with someone in mind as an audience were twice as likely to persuade the reader.

While these studies indicate that a writer's sensitivity to audience can be enhanced, a number of issues remain unresolved. First, the research to date has not dealt with the issue of *transfer*. So far, very few studies have examined whether increased sensitivity to audience awareness transfers to tasks or contexts beyond those studied. Second, several issues pertaining to development have been slighted. One critical issue is how audience awareness changes over time. Does audience awareness develop in a linear fashion? In what ways might audience awareness be subsumed by a writer's interpretative community, which may or may not be the "intended" audience? Indeed, a number of theorists have argued that being overly concerned about audience may be problematic. Elbow (1981) suggests that perhaps the role an audience serves is to give writers that initial nudge. As he stated,

> A child cannot learn to speak unless he has other people around him (and it seems to work best if they are loving people). Yet after he has learned language he can speak and write in total solitude. There is a profound principle of learning here: we can learn to do alone what at first we could only do with others. (p. 190)

Third is an issue of definition. Audience awareness may manifest itself in ways that research to date has not addressed and in ways that are more subtle than analyses of written products or even think-alouds might uncover.

To close this section, what do we know about how authors and readers transact? There seems to be an imbalance between what has been suggested about what readers and writers do and what has been accounted for. Undoubtedly, readers read with a view to authorship, no matter what their own role as authors. Likewise, writers write with a view to readership in which they are their own audience, at least initially. In other words, successful writers not only consider the transactions their readers are likely to be engaged in, but they are also their own readers. What is lacking is a clear definition of the factors that intrude upon, or are part of, these transactions over time, and their contribution.

WHAT IS THE RESULT OF USING READING AND WRITING TOGETHER?

The studies discussed up to this point have treated reading and writing in terms of their shared cognitive features, or as a social act between people. However, another interesting approach to reading-writing relationships considers how reading and writing can be used together, and how using reading and writing in combination leads to different learning and thinking outcomes than would their separate uses. The basic research questions here are: How can reading and writing be used together? What do readers and writers learn and think when reading and writing are used together? The findings from several studies suggest that combined reading and writing engenders a more inquisitive attitude to learning, and that it facilitates the expansion and refinement of knowledge. In terms of reasoning, reading and writing support a complex and coordinated constellation of reasoning operations that varies in accordance with a learner's purposes, style, and uses of different reading and writing activities. For example, as a learner pulls together an analysis, he or she pursues various reading and writing activities (note taking, drafting, reviewing, reading, note taking again, and so on), driven by selected purposes (e.g., to pull together ideas), and accompanied by certain coordinated patterns or constellations of reasoning operations (generating ideas together with evaluating and so on).

There are a number of ways that reading and writing could be used together, probably as many ways as there are literacy functions (Goodman & Goodman, 1984; Halliday, 1973; Heath, 1980; Schmandt-Besserat, 1978; Scribner & Cole, 1981; Smith, 1982; Tierney, 1985). Reading and writing might be combined to accomplish some social interaction, or to enhance or engender some aesthetic appreciation. They might be combined toward the achievement of more powerful memory operations or to assist in reflection. However, no function has received more research attention than has academic learning, and none probably requires the use of as many of the reasoning operations inherently available in reading and writing. This section will focus on how reading and writing activities together influence learning and thinking.

How Reading and Writing
Contribute to Learning New Ideas

A thesis, well-accepted among psychologists, is that the more content is manipulated, the more likely it is understood and remembered. In accordance with this thesis, a number of researchers have hypothesized that writing will have an impact upon what is learned because it prompts learners to elaborate and manipulate ideas. In a study exploring this hypothesis directly, Hayes (1987) presented high school students with three different writing tasks (paraphrasing, formulating questions, developing a compare-and-contrast statement) to accompany the reading of selected passages on machines. Since the formulation of questions and compare-contrast statements appeared to involve more manipulation of ideas, he expected that students involved in those conditions would learn more from other passages on the same topic. As he had hypothesized, writing questions and compare-contrast statements resulted in greater amounts of new information in recalls from transfer passages. Also, writing questions resulted in the recall of proportionally more superordinate information. Hayes argued that the results reflected greater learner engagement and, in turn, greater learner orientation to significant information and the integration of text information with learner knowledge.

In a similar vein, Copeland (1987, in press) examined the effects of writing upon the ability of 120 sixth graders to learn from informational texts. Students were randomly assigned to a control group or one of three postreading treatment conditions directed at synthesizing major contexts (a writing activity, a multiple-choice question activity, or a directed reading activity); the control group was involved in vocabulary puzzles. Students' ability to learn from informational texts was assessed by having them apply the knowledge they had acquired during reading to interpreting a related text, as well as to answering multiple-choice questions directed at factual information. As was hypothesized, students who wrote more performed better on the transfer passage than did the other students. Copeland (in press) suggested that the writing groups seemed more able to apply what they had learned to new situations and attributed these differences to the writing activities that, unlike other activities, "required students to form relationships among ideas through the development of a unified response" (p. 25). It was not just that writing added to thinking time, but that the type of writing actually led students to treat the content in a qualitatively different, and more useful, manner.

The findings from the studies by Hayes (1987) and Copeland (1987, in press) suggest that writing may have an advantage over other learning adjuncts in terms of the extent to which learners integrate their ideas with those presented in the text and the extent to which learners will key on significant ideas. The results also suggest that the effects of reading together with writing for overall recall may vary. Hayes (1987) found no difference in overall recall; Copeland (1987, in press) did. Subsequent studies suggest that writing may contribute to better long-term recall, but offer little in the way of differences in immediate recall. Obviously, the nature of the writing task itself has an influence, and all the studies point to the need to examine outcomes in terms of the precise nature of the requirements of any particular writing assignment. For example, the differences in outcomes from the Hayes and Copeland studies may be due to the nature of the writing assignments.

A study by Penrose parallels the aforementioned investigations. Penrose (1988) was interested in the effects of writing upon reading from a 1,200-word academic text. To this end, 40 college freshman were assigned to a counterbalanced presentation of writing and studying activities. Her findings point to the limitations of measures of comprehension, the importance of protocol data to support interpretations of outcome measures, and the need to examine effects across time and across individuals. She found, for example, that studying appeared to have an advantage of immediate recall, but that this advantage was not sustained on delayed measures. On the other hand, protocol analyses suggested that the recalls may not have reflected the quality of thinking engaged in as a result of writing. As later studies support, writing prompted some students to think more critically and elaboratively. The disparities that emerged among individuals are noteworthy. Penrose indicated that writing had significant effects when writers took advantage of what writing had to offer. But, as she noted,

> not all writers recognize writing as an opportunity to engage in higher level learning and not all are able to take advantage of this opportunity. (p. 16)

As Penrose suggested, the effects of writing may be tied to the quality of thinking associated with learning, rather than to the number of ideas recalled.

A study by Newell (1984) has been quite influential in terms of directing researchers to incorporate measures of on-line thinking with outcome measures. In Newell's study, the effects of rotating eight eleventh graders through the use of note taking, study-guide questions, and essays for different topics were examined. Two major advantages emerged for essay writing. First, students involved in essay writing, especially those who had a limited knowledge of the topic, acquired more knowledge of key concepts than did students involved in note taking or responding to study-guide questions. Second, based on an analysis of students' think-aloud protocols when they were involved in these activities, essay writing prompted students to engage in a greater overall number of cognitive operations and proportionately more reasoning that went beyond the mere translation of ideas. In his conclusions from these findings, Newell argued that writing essays prompted more extensive and integrated thinking than more fragmentary written responses were apt to engender. As he stated,

> Essay writing . . . requires the writers, in the course of examining evidence and marshalling ideas, to integrate elements of the prose passage into their knowledge of the topic rather than leaving the information in isolated bits. (p. 282)

What emerges from these four studies is affirmation for the integrating effects that writing has upon long-term learning, especially of key issues related to a topic. What may be more important, however, are the provocative effects that writing has upon thinking. It is to those studies whose primary focus has been the impact of writing upon thinking that we now turn.

How Reading and Writing Contribute
to a More Thoughtful Consideration of Ideas

Using procedures to assess thought processes (e.g., think-aloud protocols, retrospective accounts), a number of researchers have directed their attention to the reasoning operations that learners pursue as they read and write. What has emerged from this research is a consistent finding: Writing prompts readers to engage in the thoughtful exploration of issues, whether it be in the context of studying science, social studies, or literature.

The effects that writing about literature has upon thinking and learning are explored in the work of Marshall (1987) and Salvatori (1985). Marshall (1987), for example, found that when students involved in personal and formal writing approached stories from a more diverse set of literary perspectives, they engaged in significantly more examination and deliberation of stories than did students who simply responded to study-guide questions. Salvatori (1985) demonstrated that writing prompted readers to be less passive and more reflective, evaluative, and enthused.

In a study with similar goals, Colvin-Murphy (1986) studied the effects of having 85 eighth graders complete one of the following: read poems followed by extended writing; read poems followed by worksheet activities; or just read. The extended writing activity was done in response to Bleich's (1975) heuristic: What did you see? What thoughts and associations come to mind? What other things does it lead you to think about? As with Marshall's and Salvatori's studies, writing prompted Colvin-Murphy's students to be deeply involved cognitively. Students engaged in writing not only remembered more content and were more sensitive to the author's craft, but Colvin-Murphy found that they were also more engaged in thinking about what they were reading.

Similar findings have been forthcoming in studying the effects of writing upon reading in science and social science. In the previously reported study by Newell, it was noted that writing essays prompted students to do more extensive thinking about a topic, including the examination of evidence, as well as marshalling ideas and reconstructing them. In a similar vein, the previously cited study by Penrose (1988) reported that writing was associated with greater engagement. As she stated, "The writing task seems to have provided some students an opportunity for critical reflection and elaboration" (p. 15).

A study by Tierney, Soter, O'Flahavan, and McGinley (1989) addressed the question of whether thoughtful engagement would be attributed to writing alone, reading alone, or the effects of reading and writing in conjunction. To this end, they examined the nature of thinking that over 120 students were engaged in as they either wrote a first draft, answered questions and then wrote a second draft, or wrote drafts but did not read, or just read, and so on. In addition, writing was compared to the effects of a background knowledge activation activity, and simply providing students with a brief introduction to the story. Analyses of the subjects' retrospective accounts of their thinking, together with detailed analyses of their revisions and other responses, suggested two major findings.

First, students who wrote prior to reading tended to read more critically than did students who were either involved in the background-knowledge activation task or were given simply an introduction to the story. Those students assigned to the latter groups tended to read to remember ideas. Second, writing, together with reading, prompted more thoughtful consideration of ideas than did writing alone, reading alone, or either writing or reading in combination with questions. This was apparent in terms of students' retrospective accounts of thought processes and in the types of revisions pursued by those students who wrote. Those students who wrote and read made substantial changes to their drafts (additions, deletions, point of view); those students who just wrote did not make substantial changes. In sum, the findings by Tierney and associates suggest that if cognitive engagement in a task is reflected in more comments about thinking, more evaluative thinking, or a greater willingness to revise one's position, then reading and writing in combination are more likely to induce learners to be more engaged.

Taken together, the aforementioned research provides substantial support for the thesis that writing in conjunction with reading prompts learners to be more thoughtfully engaged in learning. These studies, however, are not without limitations. All of these studies focused on the combination of reading and writing with proficient readers and writers; the increased thoughtfulness that was apparent might be less likely under other circumstances. Another important issue concerns the generalizability of these findings to different kinds of writing assignments and to various topics.

In an attempt to pin down some of these concerns, a study of Langer and Applebee (1986, 1987) addressed the effects of different kinds of writing across a range of topics. They conducted a three-year study that investigated the effects of different kinds of writing assignments upon thinking in high school science and social science classrooms. The study had two overriding goals: to provide support for the contribution that writing makes to learning by examining the thought processes and learning that results from various writing tasks; and to redirect teachers' assignments of student writing in various classroom settings toward tasks that required more application, analysis, and interpretation. In particular, Langer and Applebee explored the nature of the thinking and learning that result from various types of writing activities. Across three separate experiments, over 400 students from ninth to eleventh grade participated in a wide range of reading and/or writing tasks: read and study without writing, take notes after reading, answer study-guide questions, engage in supplemental reading, write a summary, or write an analytic essay.

These studies had three major outcomes. First, each of the writing activities contributed to better learning—especially of less familiar material—than when reading was done without some form of writing. If the content is familiar and relationships are straightforward, writing does not seem to make as much difference. Second, different kinds of writing tasks prompt different kinds of cognitive engagement. As they stated,

> different kinds of writing activities lead students to focus on different kinds of information, to think about that information in different ways, and in turn to take quantitatively and qualitatively different kinds of knowledge away from their writing experiences. (Langer & Applebee, 1987, p. 174)

In conjunction with examining the think-aloud protocols and those portions of the text to which learners attended, Applebee and Langer concluded that note taking, comprehension questions, and summarizing tasks focused the learners' attention rather loosely on a text; whereas essay writing prompted the learner to focus more deeply on specific sections. In terms of reasoning operations, essay writing prompted more comments, and these comments represented a greater variety of reasoning operations than either note taking or study guide questions.

A study of McGinley (1988) represents a noteworthy follow-up and extension to the work of Langer and Applebee (1986, 1987) and Tierney et al. (1989). McGinley pursued detailed analyses of the thinking and learning of seven university students involved in self-directed engagements in reading and writing. One of the characteristics of previous studies was that researchers prescribed the sequence of process by which students read, wrote, took notes, and so on. While McGinley specified the topic of the study and overall task, he did not prescribe the order of activities or process by which read, wrote, took notes, outlined, formulated questions, reread, revised drafts, and so on. Students could pursue these activities at different points in time as frequently as they desired. Think-aloud protocols and debriefing interviews were used as a major source of evidence in analyzing how students' thought processes and knowledge of the topic changed across time. The protocols and debriefing interviews were a source of information concerning the functions that different forms of reading and writing served; they also described the reasoning operations and basis for strategic decisions regarding shifting from one mode to another.

Two major findings emerged from this study. First, analyses of his think-alouds suggested that the reasoning associated with different writing activities was not as focused as Langer and Applebee's findings implied. In particular, McGinley found that reading and writing served complementary as well as unique ways to think about the topics. That is, McGinley found that the thinking associated with any task varied in accordance with the other activities with which it was immediately associated. For example, note taking during reading was associated with evaluating ideas, whereas note taking apart from reading was used primarily to generate new ideas. Using analyses of sequential dependencies, McGinley demonstrated the importance of studying patterns of thinking across time. Regardless of the mode, for example, students' reasoning typically involved self-questioning in the early stages of their work, whereas validating ideas dominated in the latter states.

A second aspect of McGinley's work involved a consideration of individual differences. Just as Penrose found that some students were not adept at using writing as a tool for learning, so McGinley found different levels of adeptness in shifting from one mode of discourse to another. More able learners seemed more aware of the reason for shifting from reading to writing to note taking, and so on, and seemed more aware of the type of thinking made possible by different forms of reading and writing. Less able students seemed to move from one mode to another for more arbitrary reasons. Individual learning styles or approaches to text that stemmed from a learner's past history and established goals.

Studying individual styles of using discourse modes was also the subject of work in the area of discourse syntheses by Spivey (1984), Spivey and King (1989) and in work on writing from sources (Ackerman, 1989; Greene, 1989; Kennedy, 1985; Nelson & Hayes, 1988). In her first study, Spivey (1984), examined the processes and products of young adults (able and less able comprehenders) who were given two texts to read on a single topic (armadillos) en route to writing a single essay. Based upon a detailed examination of each student's notes and final products, she found that less able and more able comprehenders varied in their ability to achieve effective syntheses. In particular, more able comprehenders incorporated more information, were better able to key on important ideas, and were more able to chunk ideas together in a more elaborated fashion. In a second study, Spivey and King (1989) examined the processes and products of accomplished and less accomplished readers in the sixth, eighth, and tenth grades who were given three source texts (encyclopedia articles on the rodeo) and asked to write a report. Spivey and King (1989) found that older students included more content, seemed more able to glean important ideas, and produced reports that were better connected. More accomplished readers were more likely to include information representing a range of levels of importance, they tended to produce more coherent reports, they appeared to expend more effort at the same time as they were more sensitive

In a similar vein, Kennedy (1985) compared the behaviors of three college students who were fluent readers with three college students who were not so fluent; the students were given three articles to read and were asked to write an objective essay.

Based upon an analysis of think-aloud protocols and observations over time, Kennedy discerned a number of differences between the fluent and not-so-fluent readers. Fluent readers did considerably more planning before starting their essays than not-so-fluent readers. Furthermore, they did considerably more rereading of sources and redevelopment of notes during what Kennedy labelled the prewriting-postreading phase.

In hopes of examining issues of task representation, Nelson and Hayes (1988) conducted two studies intent on examining the strategies various college-age students enlist as they pursue writing assignments involving the use of various sources. In the first study, Nelson and Hayes compared the strategies (via think-alouds) of eight freshmen and eight advanced students as they planned and searched sources in conjunction with developing an essay on the relationship between Latin America and the United States. A key difference between the sophisticated and less sophisticated students was their representation of the task and subsequent method for selecting and developing from sources. More sophisticated students appeared to be issue driven and were more focused and evaluative in the search for sources. Less sophisticated students appeared fact driven and tended to be less purposeful in their assembling of ideas. In the second study, they examined logs that college students kept as they pursued an extended assignment. Their examination over time revealed differences among the students, which they described as akin to high-investment and low-investment. Whereas high-investment students used elaborate combinations of reading and writing, low-investment students were minimally engaged, and, subsequently, little transformation in ideas or critical thinking occurred.

Along similar lines, Greene (1989) examined the impact of problem-based and content-based tasks upon the process and products of college students enrolled in an advanced course in history who were using six source texts to develop an essay on the European recovery after World War II. Students given the problem-based frame versus content-based frame tended to develop texts consistent with the assigned task (problem-solution versus collection). In addition, students given the problem-solution developed texts that were more integrated, incorporating into their arguments ideas from their resources together with ideas from their own ideas.

Finally, in an attempt to glean the impact of background knowledge, Ackerman (1989) pursued an examination of the processes and products of students' writing from different disciplines (business and psychology—topics related and unrelated to their academic areas). Ackerman found that background knowledge appeared to have an impact on what information from source texts was included, how the information was presented, and the writer's stance toward the topic and the audience. When students were writing in their academic discipline, they tended to adopt a more active orientation to their topic and seemed more conscious of the pragmatics of their situation.

Central to the pursuit of discourse synthesis studies and studies dealing with writing from multiple sources are notions of intertextuality or the relationships that are developed between texts (multiple source texts, interactions with others, and so on). It should not be surprising, therefore, that these aforementioned studies have much in common with those descriptions of classrooms found in studies detailing the early literacy experiences and reading and writing across the grades—all deal with issues of intertextuality (e.g., Allen, 1976; Atwell, 1987; Baghban, 1984; Bissex, 1980; Boutwell, 1983; Burton, 1985; Calkins, 1983; Clay, 1976; Durkin, 1966; Ferreiro, 1984; Ferreiro & Teberosky, 1982; Fulwiler & Young, 1982; Giacobe, 1982; Goodman, 1986; Goodman & Altwerger, 1981; Graves & Hansen, 1983; Harste, Woodward, & Burke, 1984; Hiebert, 1981; Janiuk & Shanahan, 1988; Martin, 1975; Snow, 1983; Sulzby, 1981, 1982, 1983a, 1983b, 1985a, 1985b, 1985c, 1986a, 1986b; Teale, 1986; Teale & Sulzby, in press; Tierney & Leys, 1986; Tierney, Leys, & Rogers, 1986; Tierney & O'Flahavan, 1989). For example, in conjunction with exploring the nature of literacy learning in a day-care environment for 3- and 4-year-olds, Rowe (1987) concluded that there are two general types of "intertextual" connections that are important. The first type is the *formation of shared meanings* through conversations and demonstrations so that these young literacy learners are members of a community that affords communication with others. The second type involves linking current literacy experiences to past experiences. As Rowe stated,

> . . . as children formed new communication goals, they flexibly combined various aspects of their existing knowledge . . . to construct situation-based hypotheses which met their communication goals. (p. 110)

Based upon her observations of first graders, Short (1986b) argues that the potential for learning and thinking are changed when the classroom environment facilitates intertextuality. A collaborative and meaning-centered learning environment engages learners more fully and actively in learning and encourages higher levels of thinking. Figure 11.4 is a diagram of the learning process that Short believed represented how learners pursue the construction of text, based upon their own experiences, interaction with others, and connections with other texts.

Along similar lines, Dyson (1983, 1985, 1986, 1988) has explored dimensions of literacy learning of preschool children in which she focused upon the interrelationships between texts (children's writings, drawings, talk, and so on). She argues that,

> children's major developmental challenge is not simply to create a unified text world but to move among multiple worlds, carrying out multiple roles and coordinating multiple space/ time structures. That is, to grow as writers of imaginary worlds and, by inference, other sorts of text worlds as well, children must differentiate, and work to resolve the tensions among, the varied symbolic and social worlds within which they write—worlds with differing dimensions of time and space. And it is our own differentiation of these competing worlds that will allow us as adults to understand the seemingly unstable worlds, the shifts of time frames and points of view, that children create. (1988, p. 356)

Also, Wells (1986) has argued from his longitudinal study of children from 15 months to elementary school, that it is the encouragement to be active meaning-makers, involved in meaningful and sustained interactions around texts that is crucial. As he stated, schools should try to provide environments for meaning-making—that is, "to try to make sense, to construct stories, to share them with others in speech and in writing" (p. 222).

Taken together, the studies dealing with discourse synthesis and how reading and writing might work together in classrooms, as well as in homes, reflect interesting tendencies. Discourse synthesis studies tend to examine reading and writing processes in detail and gloss over issues of context; descriptions of classrooms tend to describe larger issues including context dynamically, but gloss over details of reading and writing processes. Despite these limitations, both sets of studies do converge on similar findings—in particular, the importance of active meaning-making and the potency of an environment that facilitates transactions and tensions among texts.

To summarize the findings in this section: the previous research studies provide consistent support for viewing writing as a powerful tool for the enhancement of thinking and learning. Writing and reading together engage learners in a greater variety of reasoning operations than when writing or reading are apart *or* when students are given a variety of other tasks to go along with their reading. The nature of thinking

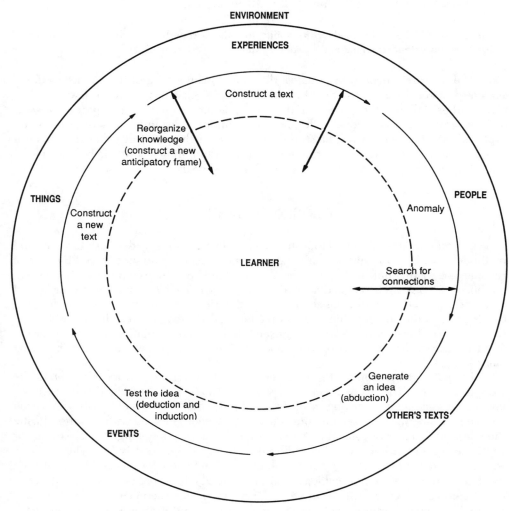

FIGURE 11.4   The learning process. *Source:* From Literacy as a *Collaborative Experience* (dissertation) by Kathy Short, Indiana University, 1984. Reprinted by permission.

associated with different types of writing tasks will vary, however, depending upon the nature of the writing task, the topic or problem being pursued, the purpose for which a writing task is enlisted at a particular time, and the individual approach of the learner. Writing extended essays seems apt to prompt a wider variety of reasoning operations than do writing tasks that require less integration and manipulation of ideas. But the nature of the reasoning operations associated with any writing tasks will vary across time. For example, whereas note taking may appear to be consumed with restating ideas at one point in time, it may involve hypothesizing and validating ideas at another. The finding that individuals may differ in their adeptness at negotiating meaning suggests a view of literacy learning as much concerned with the literacy journey as with the outcomes that are derived. As Mackie (1982) stated,

to be literate is not to have arrived at some predetermined destination, but to utilize reading, writing, and speaking skills so that our world is progressively enlarged. (p. 1)

Or as McGinley and Tierney (1988, 1989) argued,

> literacy should be understood as the ability to enlist a repertoire of discourse forms to explore and extend thinking and learning. (McGinley & Tierney, 1988, p. 13)

The research data substantiates this view, while suggesting an instructional agenda—especially an instructional research agenda—that has yet to be realized. Future studies will need to focus on the combination of reading and writing toward different goals, and individual differences in combining reading and writing must be explored. Most important will be studies that consider the possibility that students can be taught to use reading and writing together in an intentional strategic fashion, based upon the thinking operations required by learners' goals.

CLOSING REMARKS

Research on reading-writing relationships has made enormous strides both topically and methodologically. Topically, key assumptions about readers and writers and the role of reading and writing in learning have been subjected to careful examination. In terms of methodology, research on reading and writing has moved beyond comparing global measures of reading with global measures of writing to consider their underlying constructs and the ongoing thinking that readers and writers pursue. The researchers in the area of reading-writing relationships seem to have been willing to explore a variety of methodologies and measures in hopes of finding better windows for exploring emerging issues.

Despite such advances, the research on reading-writing relationships should be viewed as still in its infancy. Very few studies to date have examined the processes underlying reading and writing in those situations when reading and writing are used together. A number of developmental studies have been pursued with children during their first five years; beyond the age of 5 there exist very few longitudinal studies or studies exploring either individual differences or developmental issues. The research exploring instructional practice tends to highlight the benefits associated with selected practices, but these are more affidavits of the general effects rather than thick descriptions, comparisons, or explanations of effects. Those instructional studies that have pursued systematic examples of the effects of reading and writing upon learning have tended to adopt a regimented and somewhat prescriptive view of how reading and writing might work together. For example, most studies have involved assigning students to a predetermined sequence of activities, rather than affording them the opportunity to move back and forth between reading and writing in accordance with their own needs, self-determined purposes, and idiosyncratic, evolving understandings.

What is needed is research on literacy that explores reading and writing together with all the attendant complexity and does not retreat to exploring reading and writing simplistically or separately. What is needed most is a profound change of perspective in the field of literacy. Researchers should no longer be willing to choose between a reading or writing agenda. The Irish poet Seamus Heaney once wrote in another context,

> It was not a choice/Between, but of.

Likewise, for researchers in the field of literacy the focus of research should not be *between* reading and writing, but *of* reading and writing together. Historical and cross-cultural evidence suggests that literacy in a society might entail reading and writing as separate or related entities (Clifford, 1989). We believe strongly that in our society, at this point in history, reading and writing, to be understood and appreciated fully, should be viewed together, learned together, and used together.

REFERENCES

Ackerman, J. M. (1989). *Reading and writing in the academy.* Unpublished doctoral dissertation, Carnegie Mellon University, Pittsburgh, PA.

Allen, R. W. (1976). *Language experiences in communication.* Boston: Houghton Mifflin.

Applebee, A. N. (1977). Writing and reading. *Journal of Reading, 20,* 534–537.

Atwell, N. (1987). *In the middle.* Upper Montclair, NJ: Boynton/Cook.

Augustine, D., & Winterowd, N. R. (1986). Speech acts and the reader-writer transaction. In B. T. Peterson (Ed.), *Convergences: Transactions in reading and writing.* Urbana, IL: National Council of Teachers of English.

Baden, M. J. P. (1981). *A comparison of composition scores of third grade children with reading skills, prekindergarten verbal ability, self-concept, and sex.* Unpublished doctoral dissertation, University of Nebraska–Lincoln.

Baghban, M. J. M. (1984). *Our daughter learns to read and write: A case study from birth to three.* Newark, DE: International Reading Association.

Bakhtin, M. M. (1973). *Marxism and the philosophy of language.* Ladislav Matejka & I. R. Titunik (Trans.). New York: Seminar Press.

Beach, R., & Anson, C. M. (1988). The pragmatics of memo writing: Developmental differences in the use of rhetorical strategies. *Written Communication, 5*(2), 157–183.

Beach, R., & Liebman-Kleine, J. (1986). The writing/reading relationship: Becoming one's own best reader. In B. Peterson (Ed.), *Convergences: Transactions in reading and writing.* Urbana, IL: National Council of Teachers of English.

Bean, T. W., & Steenwyck, F. L. (1984). The effect of three forms of summarization instruction on sixth graders' summary writing and comprehension. *Journal of Reading Behavior, 16,* 297–306.

Bereiter, C., & Scardamalia, M. (1984). Learning about writing from reading. *Written Communication, 1*(2), 163–188.

Birnbaum, J. C. (1982). The reading and composing behavior of selected fourth- and seventh-grade students. *Research in the Teaching of English, 16,* 241–260.

Bissex, G. L. (1980). *GYNS AT WRK: A child learns to write and read.* Cambridge, MA: Harvard University Press.

Bleich, D. (1975). *Readings and feelings.* Urbana, IL: National Council of Teachers of English.

Bond, G. L., & Dykstra, R. (1967). The cooperative research program in first-grade reading instruction. *Reading Research Quarterly, 2,* 5–142.

Boutwell, M. (1983). Reading and writing process: A reciprocal agreement. *Language Arts, 60,* 723–730.

Bruce, B. C. (1980). Plans and social actions. In R. J. Spiro, B. C. Bruce, & W. F. Brewer (Eds.), *Theoretical issues in reading comprehension* (pp. 367–384). Hillsdale, NJ: Erlbaum.

Burleson, B. R., & Rowan, K. E. (1985). Are social-cognitive ability and narrative writing skill related? *Written Communication, 2*(1), 25–44.

Burton, F. (1985). *The reading-writing connection: A one-year study of third/fourth grade writers and their literacy experience.* Unpublished doctoral dissertation, The Ohio State University.

Calkins, L. (1983). *Lessons from a child.* Portsmouth Lake, NH: Heinemann.

Chomsky, C. (1979). Approaching reading through invented spelling. In L. B. Resnick & P. A. Weaver (Eds.), *Theory and practice of early reading* (Vol. 2). Hillsdale, NJ: Erlbaum.

Clarke, L. K. (1988). Invented versus traditional spelling in first graders' writings: Effects on learning to spell and read. *Research in the Teaching of English, 22,* 281–309.

Clay, M. M. (1967). The reading behavior of five-year-old children: A research report. *New Zealand Journal of Educational Studies, 2* 11–31.

Clay, M. M. (1976). *Young fluent readers.* London: Heinemann.

Clifford, G. J. (1989). A sisyphean task: Historical perspectives on writing and reading instruction. In A. H. Dyson (Ed.), *Collaboration through writing and reading.* Urbana, IL: National Council of Teachers of English.

Colvin-Murphy, C. (1986, December). *Enhancing critical comprehension of literary texts through writing.* Paper presented at the National Reading Conference, Austin, TX.

Cook, J. A. (1973). Language and socialization: A critical review. In B. Bernstein (Ed.), *Class codes and control* (pp. 293–341). London and Boston: Routledge & Kegan Paul.

Copeland, K. (in press). Writing as a means to learn from prose. *Research in the Teaching of English.*

Copeland, K. A. (1987). *Writing as a means to learn from prose.* Doctoral dissertation, University of Texas at Austin.

Cox, B. E., Shanahan, T., & Sulzby, E. (in press). Good and poor elementary readers' use of cohesion in writing. *Reading Research Quarterly.*

Crismore, A. (1985). *Metadiscourse as rhetorical act in social studies text: Its effect on student performance and attitude.* Unpublished doctoral dissertation, University of Illinois.

Crowhurst, M., & Piché, G. L. (1979). Audience and mode of discourse effects on syntactic complexity at two grade levels. *Research in the Teaching of English, 13,* 101–109.

DiPardo, A., & Freedman, S. W. (1988). Peer response groups in writing. *Review of Educational Research, 58,* 119–150.

Durkin, D. (1966). *Children who read early.* New York: Teachers College Press.

Durkin, D. (1988). *Teaching them to read* (5th ed.). Boston: Allyn & Bacon.

Dyson, A. (1988). Negotiations among multiple worlds: The space/time dimensions of young children's composing. *Research in the Teaching of English, 22*(4), 355–390.

Dyson, A. H. (1985). Individual differences in emerging writing. In M. Farr (Ed.), *Advances in writing research, Vol. I: Children's early writing development* (pp. 59–126). Norwood, NJ: Ablex.

Dyson, A. H. (1983). The role of oral language in early writing. *Research in the Teaching of English, 17,* 1–30.

Dyson, A. H. (1986). Children's early interpretations of writing: Expanding research perspectives. In D. B. Yaden and S. Templeton (Eds.), *Metalinguistic awareness and beginning literacy* (pp. 201–218). Portsmouth, NH: Heinemann.

Eckhoff, B. (1983). How reading affects children's writing. *Language Arts, 60,* 607–616.

Educational Testing Service. (1984). *The ETS evaluation of Writing to Read.* Princeton, NJ: ETS.

Elbow, P. (1981). *Writing with power.* New York: Oxford University Press.

Evanechcko, P., Ollila, L., & Armstrong, R. (1974). An investigation of the relationship between children's performance in written language and their reading ability. *Research in the Teaching of English, 8,* 315–326.

Ferreiro, E. (1984). The underlying logic of literacy development. In H. Goelman, A. Oberg, & F. Smith (Eds.), *Awakening to literacy* (pp. 154–173). Portsmouth Lake, NH: Heinemann.

Ferreiro, E., & Teberosky, A. (1982). *Literacy before schooling.* Translated from Spanish, 1979. Portsmouth Lake, NH: Heinemann.

Fillmore, C. (1979). Future of semantics. In C. Fillmore, G. Lakoff, & R. Lakoff (Eds.), *Berkeley studies in syntax and semantics.* Berkeley: University of California Press.

Fishco, D. T. (1966). *A study of the relationship between creativity in writing and comprehension in reading of selected seventh grade students.* Unpublished doctoral dissertation, Lehigh University.

Flower, L. (1987). Interpretative acts: Cognition and construction of discourse (Occasional Paper No. 1). Berkeley: Center for the Study of Writing, University of California.

Flower, L. S. & Hayes, J. R. (1981). The pregnant pause: An inquiry into the nature of planning. *Research in the Teaching of English, 15,* 229–243.

Frith, U. (1980). Unexpected spelling problems. In U. Frith (Ed.), *Cognitive processes in spelling.* London: Academic Press.

Fulwiler, T., & Young, A. (Eds). (1982). *Language connections: Writing and reading across the curriculum.* Urbana, IL: National Council of Teachers of English.

Gadamer, H. (1986). *Philosophical hemeneutics.* Berkeley: University of California Press.

Galda, L. (1983). The relations between reading and writing in young children. In R. Beach & L. S. Bridwell (Eds.), *New directions in composition research* (pp. 191–204). New York: Guilford Press.

Giacobbe, M. E. (1982). A writer reads, a reader writes. In T. Newkirk & N. Atwell (Eds.), *Understanding writing.* Chelmsford, MA: Northeast Regional Exchange.

Goodman, K. & Goodman, Y. (1984). Reading and writing relationships: Pragmatic functions. In J. Jensen (Ed.), *Composing and comprehending.* Urbana, IL: National Council of Teachers of English.

Goodman, Y. M. (1986). Children coming to know literacy. In W. H. Teale & E. Sulzby (Eds.), *Emergent literacy: Writing and reading* (pp. 1–14). Norwood, NJ: Ablex.

Goodman, Y. M., & Altwerger, B. (1981). *Print awareness in pre-school children: A study of the development of literacy in preschool children* (Occasional Paper No. 4). Tuscon: University of Arizona, Program in Language and Literacy, Arizona Center for Research and Development.

Gordon, C. J., & Braun, C. (1982). Story schemata: Metatextual aid to reading and writing. In J. A. Niles & L. A. Harris (Eds.), *New inquiries in reading research and instruction* (pp. 262–268). Thirty-first Yearbook of the National Reading Conference, Rochester, NY: National Reading Conference.

Graves, D. (1978). *Balance the basics: Let them write.* New York: Ford Foundation.

Graves, D., & Hansen, J. (1983). The author's chair. *Language Arts, 60,* 176–182.

Green, G. M. (1980). *Linguistics and the pragmatics of language use: What you know when you know languages . . . and what else you know.* (Technical Report No. 179; ERIC document No. 193666). Urbana: University of Illinois, Center for the Study of Reading.

Greene, S. (1989, November). *Intertextuality and moves to authority in writing from sources.* Paper presented at the National Reading Conference, Austin, TX.

Halliday, M. A. K. (1973). *Explorations in the functions of language.* London: Edward Arnold.

Harste, J. C., Woodward, V. A., & Burke, C. L. (1984). *Language stories and literacy lessons.* Portsmouth, NH: Heinemann.

Hayes, D. A. (1987) The potential for directing study in combined reading and writing activity. *Journal of Reading Behavior, 19*(4), 333–352.

Heath, S. B. (1980). The functions and uses of language. *Journal of Communication, 30,* 123–133.

Heys, F. (1962). The theme-a-week assumption: A report of an experiment. *English Journal, 51,* 320–322.

Hiebert, E. H. (1981). Developmental patterns and interrelationships of preschool children's print awareness. *Reading Research Quarterly, 16,* 236–260.

Hiebert, E. H., Englert, C. S., & Brennan, S. (1983). Awareness of text structure in recognition and production of expository discourse. *Journal of Reading Behavior, 15,* 63–79.

Hillocks, G., Jr. (1986). *Research on written composition: New directions for teaching.* Urbana, IL: ERIC Clearinghouse on Reading and Communication Skills.

Janiuk, D. M., & Shanahan, T. (1988). Applying adult literacy practices in primary grade instruction. *Reading Teacher, 41,* 880–887.

Juel, C., Griffith, P., & Gough, P. (1986). A longitudinal study of the changing relationships of word recognition, spelling, reading comprehension, and writing from first to second grade. *Journal of Educational Psychology, 78,* 243–255.

Kennedy, M. L. (1985). The composing processes of college students writing from sources. *Written Communication, 2,* 434–456.

King, M., & Rentel, V. (1979). Toward a theory of early writing development. *Research in the Teaching of English, 13,* 243–253.

Kirby, K. (1986). *Reading and writing processes of selected high-risk college freshman.* Unpublished doctoral dissertation, University of Georgia.

Kroll, B. M. (1985). Rewriting a complex story for a young reader: The development of audience-adapted writing skills. *Research in the Teaching of English, 19,* (2), 120–139.

Kroll, B. M. (1986). Explaining how to play a game: The development of informative writing skills. *Written Communication, 3*(2), 195–218.

Kucer, S. L. (1985). The making of meaning: Reading and writing as parallel processes. *Written Communication, 2*(3), 317–336.

Langer, J. A. (1986a). Reading, writing and understanding: An analysis of the construction of meaning. *Written Communication, 3*(2), 219–267.

Langer, J. A. (1986b). *Children reading and writing: Structures and strategies.* Norwood, NJ: Ablex.

Langer, J. A., & Applebee, A. N. (1986). *Writing and learning in the secondary school.* National Institute of Education Grant No. NIE-G-82-0027. School of Education, Stanford University.

Langer, J. A. & Applebee, A. N. (1987). *How writing shapes thinking.* Urbana, IL: National Council of Teachers of English.

LaZansky, J. & Tierney, R. J. (1985, December). *The themes generated by fourth-, fifth-, and sixth-graders in response to stories.* Paper presented at the National Reading Conference, San Diego.

Lazdowski, W. (1976). *Determining reading grade levels from analysis of written compositions.* Unpublished doctoral dissertation, New Mexico State University.

Loban, W. (1963). *The language of elementary school children.* Urbana, IL: National Council of Teachers of English.

Loban, W. (1964). *Language ability: Grades seven, eight, and nine.* Berkeley: University of California ERIC Ed 001275.

Loewenthal, K. & Krostrevski, B. (1973). The effects of training in written communication and verbal skills. *British Journal of Educational Psychology, 43,* 82–86.

Maat, D. (1977). *An inquiry into empirical relationships between reading and writing of exposition and argument.* Unpublished doctoral dissertation, State University of New York at Albany.

McGee, L. (1983). Perceptions of author's intentions: Effects on comprehension. In J. A. Niles & L. A. Harris (Eds.), *Searches for meaning in reading/language processing and instruction* (pp. 148–157). Rochester, NY: National Reading Conference Yearbook.

McGinley, W., & Tierney, R. J. (1988). Reading and writing as ways of knowing and learning (Technical Report No. 423). Champaign, IL: Center for the Study of Reading, University of Illinois.

McGinley, W. & Tierney, R. J. (1989). Traversing the topical landscape: Reading and writing as ways of knowing. *Written Communication, 6,* 243–269.

McGinley, W. (1988). *The role of reading and writing in the acquisition of knowledge: A study of college students' reading and writing engagements in the development of a persuasive argument.* Unpublished doctoral thesis, University of Illinois at Urbana–Champaign.

Mackie, R. (Ed.). (1982). *Literacy and revolution: The pedagogy of Paulo Freire.* New York: Continuum Publishing Corporation.

Maloney, H. G. (1967). *An identification of excellence in expository composition performance in a selected 9A population with an analysis of reasons for superior performance.* Unpublished doctoral dissertation, Columbia University.

Marshall, J. D. (1987). The effects of writing on students' understanding of literary text. *Research in the Teaching of English, 21,* 31–63.

Martin, N. (1975). *Writing across the curriculum.* London: Ward Lock.

Martin, P. (1977). A comparative analysis of reading and writing skills: Six case studies. *English in Australia, 40,* 51–53.

Martin, S. (1987, December). *The meaning-making strategies reported by provident readers and writers.*

Paper presented at the meeting of the National Reading Conference, St. Petersburg, FL.

Mason, G., McDaniel, H., & Callaway, B. (1974). Relating reading and spelling. A comparison of methods. *Elementary School Journal, 74,* 381–386.

Mills, E. (1974). Children's literature and teaching written composition. *Elementary English, 51,* 971–973.

Moffett, J., & Wagner, B. J. (1983). *Student-centered language arts and reading, K-13* (3rd ed.). Boston: Houghton Mifflin.

Mosenthal, J. (1983). *Instruction in the interpretation of a writer's argument: A training study.* Unpublished doctoral dissertation, University of Illinois

Murray, D. (1982b). Teaching the Other Self: The writer's first reader. *College Composition, 33,* 140–147.

Nelson, J. & Hayes, J. R. (1988). *How the writing context shapes college students' strategies for writing from sources* (Technical Report No. 16). Pittsburgh: Center for the Study of Reading.

Newell, G. (1984). Learning from writing in two content areas: A case study/protocol analysis. *Research in the Teaching of English, 18,* 205–287.

Newkirk, T. (1982). Young writers as critical readers. *Language Arts, 59*(5), 451–457.

Nystrand, M. (1986). *The structure of written communication.* New York: Academic Press.

Obenchain, A. (1971). *Effectiveness of the precise essay question in programming the sequential development of written composition skills and the simultaneous development of critical reading skills.* Unpublished master's thesis, George Washington University.

Ohmann, R. (1971). Speech acts and the definition of literature. *Philosophy and Rhetoric, 4,* 1–19.

Pearson, P. D. & Tierney, R. J. (1984). On becoming a thoughtful reader: Learning to read like a writer. In A. Purves & O. Niles (Eds.), *Becoming readers in a complex society.* Chicago: National Society for the Study of Education.

Penrose, A. M. (1988, April). *Examining the role of writing in learning factual versus abstract material.* Paper presented at the American Educational Research Association, New Orleans, LA.

Perron, J. (1977). *The impact of mode on written syntactic complexity: Part IV—Across the Grades' Differences and General Summary* (Studies in Language Education, Report No. 30). Athens, GA: Department of Language, University of Georgia.

Petrosky, A. (1982). From story to essay: Reading and writing. *College Composition and Communication, 33*(1), 19–35.

Pratt, M. L. (1977). *Toward a speech act theory of literary discourse.* Bloomington: Indiana University Press.

Raforth, B. A. (1985). Audience adaptation in the essays of proficient and nonproficient freshmen writers. *Research in the Teaching of English, 19*(3), 237–253.

Raphael, T. E., Englert, C. S., & Kirschner, B. W. (1986). *The impact of text structure instruction and school context on students' comprehension and production of expository text* (Research series no. 177.) East Lansing: Michigan State University for Research on Teaching.

Raphael, T. E., Kirschner, B. W., & Englert, C. S. (1988). Expository writing programs: Making connections between reading and writing. *Reading Teacher, 41*(8), 790–795.

Redd-Boyd, T. M. & Slater, W. H. (1989). The effects of audience specification on undergraduates' attitudes, strategies, and writing. *Research in the Teaching of English, 23*(1), 77–108.

Roen, D. H., & Willey, R. J. (1988). The effects of audience awareness on drafting and revising. *Research in the Teaching of English, 22,* 75–88.

Rowe, D. W. (1986). *Literacy in the child's world: Young children's exploration of alternative communication systems.* Unpublished doctoral dissertation, Indiana University.

Rowe, D. W. (1987). Literacy learning as an intertextual process. In J. E. Readence & R. Scott Baldwin (Eds.), *Research in literacy: Merging perspectives.* Rochester, NY: National Reading Conference.

Rubin, D. (1984). Social cognition and written communication. *Written Communication, 1*(2), 211–246.

Rubin, D. L., & Piché, G. L. (1979). Development in syntactic and strategic aspects of audience adaptation skills in written persuasive communication. *Research in the Teaching of English, 13,* 293–316.

Ryan, S. M. (1985). An examination of reading and writing strategies of selected fifth grade students. In J. Niles & R. Lalik (Eds.), *Issues in literacy: A research perspective* (pp. 386–390). Thirty-fourth Yearbook of the National Reading Conference, Rochester, NY: National Reading Conference.

Salvatori, Mariolina (1985). The dialogical nature of basic reading and writing. In D. Bartholomae & A. Petrosky (Eds.), *Facts, artifacts, and counterfacts* (pp. 137–166). NJ: Boynton/Cook Publishers.

Scardamalia, M. C., Bereiter, C., & McDonald, J. S. (1977, March). *Role-taking in written communication investigated by manipulating anticipatory knowledge.* Paper presented at Biennial Meeting of the Society for Research in Child Development, New Orleans, LA.

Schewe, A. & Froese, V. (1987). Relating reading and writing via comprehension, quality and structure. In J. E. Readence & R. Scott Baldwin (Eds.), *Research in literacy: Merging perspectives.* Rochester, NY: National Reading Conference.

Schmandt-Besserat, D. (1978). The earliest precursor of writing. *Scientific American, 238,* 50–59.

Scribner, S., & Cole, M. (1981). *The psychology of literacy.* Cambridge, MA: Harvard University Press.

Searle, J. (1969). *Speech acts.* New York and London: Cambridge University Press.

Shanahan, T. (1980). The impact of writing instruction on learning to read. *Reading World, 19,* 357–368.

Shanahan, T. (1984). Nature of the reading-writing relation: An exploratory multivariate analysis. *Journal of Educational Psychology, 76,* 466–477

Shanahan, T. (1988). The reading-writing relationship: Seven instructional principles. *The Reading Teacher*, *41*, 636–647.

Shanahan, T., & Lomax, R. (1986). An analysis and comparison of theoretical models of the reading-writing relationship. *Journal of Educational Psychology*, *78*, 116–123.

Shanahan, T., & Lomax, R. G. (1988). A developmental comparison of three theoretical models of the reading-writing relationship. *Research in the Teaching of English*, *22*(2), 196–212.

Shanklin, N. (1981). *Relating reading and writing: Developing a transactional theory of the writing process.* Monographs in teaching and learning, Indiana University.

Short, K. G. (1986a) Literacy as a collaborative experience: The role of intertextuality. In J. A. Niles & R. V. Lalik (Eds.), *Solving problems in literacy: Learners, teachers, and researchers* (pp. 227–232). Rochester, NY: National Reading Conference.

Short, K. G. (1986b). *Literacy as a collaborative experience.* Unpublished doctoral dissertation, Indiana University.

Schriver, K. A. (1986). *Teaching writers to predict readers' comprehension problems with text.* Paper presented at the American Educational Research Association, San Francisco.

Smith, F. (1982). *Writing and the writer.* New York: Holt, Rinehart & Winston.

Smith, F. (1984). Reading like a writer. In J. M. Jensen (Ed.), *Composing and comprehending.* Urbana, IL: National Council of Teachers of English.

Smith, R., Jensen, K., & Dillingofski, M. (1971). The effects of integrating reading and writing on four variables. *Research in the Teaching of English*, *5*, 179–189.

Snow, C. E. (1983). Literacy and language: Relationships during the preschool years. *Harvard Educational Review*, *53*, 165–189.

Spivey, N. N. & King, J. R. (1989). Readers as writers composing from sources. *Reading Research Quarterly*, *24*(1), 7–26.

Spivey, N. N. (1984). *Discourse synthesis: Constructing texts in reading and writing*, Newark, DE: International Reading Association.

Squire, R. J. (1984). Composing and comprehending: Two sides of the same basic processes. In J. M. Jensen (Ed.), *Composing and comprehending* (pp. 23–31). Urbana, IL: National Council of Teachers of English.

Stauffer, R. G. (1980). *The language-experience approach to the teaching of reading* (2nd ed.). New York: Harper & Row.

Stotsky, S. (1982). The role of writing in developmental reading. *Journal of Reading*, *25*, 330–340.

Stotsky, S. (1983). Research of reading/writing relationships: A synthesis and suggested directions. *Language Arts*, *60*, 568–580.

Straw, S. B., & Shreiner, R. (1982). The effect of sentence manipulation on subsequent measures of reading and listening. *Reading Research Quarterly*, *17*, 335–352.

Sulzby, E. (1981). *Kindergartners begin to read their own compositions: Beginning readers' developing knowledges about written language projects* (Final Report to the Research Committee of the National Council of Teachers of English). Evanston, IL: Northwestern University.

Sulzby, E. (1982). Oral and written mode adaptations in stories by kindergarten children. *Journal of Reading Behavior*, *14*, 51–59.

Sulzby, E. (1983a). *Beginning readers' developing knowledge about written language* (Final Report to the National Institute of Education, N.I.E.-80-0176). Evanston, IL: Northwestern University.

Sulzby, E. (1983b). *Children's emergent abilities to read a favorite storybook* (Final Report to the Spencer Foundation). Evanston, IL: Northwestern University.

Sulzby, E. (1985a). Kindergartners as writers and readers. In M. Farr (Ed.), *Children's early writing development.* Norwood, NJ: Ablex.

Sulzby, E. (1985b). Children's emergent reading of favorite storybooks: A developmental study. *Reading Research Quarterly*, *20*, 458–481.

Sulzby, E. (1985c). Kindergartners as writers and readers. In M. Farr (Ed.), *Advances in writing research, Vol. 1: Children's early writing development* (pp. 127–199). Norwood, NJ: Ablex.

Sulzby, E. (1986a). Writing and reading: Signs of oral and written language organization in the young child. In W. H. Teale & E. Sulzby (Eds.), *Emergent literacy: Writing and reading* (pp. 50–89). Norwood, NJ: Ablex.

Sulzby, E. (1986b). Young children's concepts for oral and written text. In K. Durkin (Ed.), *Language development during the school years* (pp. 95–116). London: Croom Helm.

Swaney, J. H., Janik, C. J., Bond, S. J., & Hayes, J. R. (1981). *Editing for comprehension: Improving the process through reading protocols.* Report for National Institute of Education. Contract 400-78-0043.

Taylor, B. M., & Beach, R. W. (1984). The effects of text structure instruction on middle-grade students' comprehension and production of expository text. *Reading Research Quarterly*, *19*(2), 134–146.

Teale, W. H. (1986). Home background and young children's literacy development. In W. H. Teale & E. Sulzby (Eds.), *Emergent literacy: Writing and reading* (pp. 173–206). Norwood, NJ: Ablex.

Teale, W. H., & Sulzby, E. (in press). Literacy acquisition in early childhood: The roles of access and meditation in storybook reading. In D. A. Wagner (Ed.), *The future of literacy in a changing world.* New York: Pergamon Press.

Tierney, R. J. (1983, December). *Analyzing composing behavior: Planning, aligning, revising.* Paper presented at the 33rd annual National Reading Conference, Austin, TX.

Tierney, R. J. (1985). Functionality of written literacy experiences. In M. Sampson (Ed.), *The pursuit of literacy.* Dubuque, IA: Kendall Hunt.

Tierney, R. J. & Leys, M. (1986). What is the value of connecting reading and writing? In B. T. Peterson (Ed.), *Convergences: transactions in reading and writing.* Urbana, IL: National Council of Teachers of English.

Tierney, R. J., & O'Flahavan, J. F. (1989). Literacy, learning, and students decision making: Establishing classrooms in which reading and writing work together. In D. Lapp & J. Flood (Eds.), *Using instructional strategies in high school classrooms.* Englewood Cliffs, NJ: Prentice-Hall.

Tierney, R. J., & Pearson, P. D. (1983). Toward a composing model of reading. *Language Arts, 60,* 568–580.

Tierney, R. J., LaZansky, J., Raphael, T., & Cohen, P. (1987). Author's intentions and reader's interpretations. In R. Tierney, P. Andes, & J. Mitchell (Eds.), *Understanding readers' understanding.* Hillsdale, NJ: Erlbaum.

Tierney, R. J., Leys, M., & Rogers, T. (1986). Comprehension, composition, and collaboration. In T. Raphael (Ed.), *The contexts of school-based literacy.* New York: Random House.

Tierney, R. J., Soter, A., O'Flahavan, J. F., & McGinley, W. (1989). The effects of reading and writing upon thinking critically. *Reading Research Quarterly, 24*(2), 134–173.

Tovey, D. (1978). Sound it out: A reasonable approach to spelling. *Reading World, 17,* 220–233.

Vairo, F. (1976). *Relationship between story writing skills and achievement in other selected language skills.* Unpublished doctoral dissertation, University of Pittsburgh.

van Dijk, T. A. (1976). *Pragmatics of language and literature.* Amsterdam: North Holland.

Wagner, B. J. (1987, April). *The effect of role playing on the written persuasion of fourth- and eighth-graders.* Paper presented at the American Educational Research Annual Meeting, Washington, DC.

Wells, G. (1986). *The meaning makers.* Portsmouth, NH: Heinemann.

Wittrock, M. C. (1984). Writing and the teaching of reading. In J. M. Jensen (Ed.), *Composing and comprehending* (pp. 77–83). Urbana, IL: National Council of Teachers of English.

Zeman, S. (1969). Reading comprehension and writing of second and third graders. *Reading Teacher, 23,* 144–150.

12 CLASSROOM ASSESSMENT OF READING

Robert Calfee and Elfrieda Hiebert

In his chapter on assessment in the first volume of the *Handbook of Reading Research*, Johnston (1984a) reviewed the history of standardized tests of reading. He pointed out the hazards of relying on any one method to the neglect of other approaches. Campbell (1975) argues that any given social indicator is likely to be compromised when the stakes are high. The use of standardized tests is nonetheless on the increase (Gallup & Elam, 1988). Plans are afoot to expand the National Assessment of Educational Progress (NAEP) to permit comparisons among states (Alexander, 1987). Alternatives to testing receive little attention. During the past decade, the *Summary of Investigations Relating to Reading* devoted 10 or more pages each year to assessment, virtually all on standardized tests. Of the handful of articles on teacher assessment, the primary topics were informal reading inventories and behavioral adjustment. The latest edition of *Educational Measurement* (Linn, 1988) highlights the technical issues of testing, with little treatment of the teacher's role in judging student achievement. An Educational Testing Service manual (1984) on classroom assessment directs teachers toward multiple-choice and short-answer questions, and away from essays and other methods requiring subjective judgment. In his study of classroom practices, Goodlad (1984, pp. 207 ff.) found much testing and little writing. On the positive side, "redirection of assessment" is being called for in some quarters (e.g., the April 1989 issue of *Educational Leadership*).

Johnston ends his chapter with a question: "What if . . . history had predisposed us to an individualized, descriptive, process-oriented assessment model instead of the standardized group silent-reading model?" (p. 168). We will pick up where Johnston left off, suggesting a stronger role for teacher-based classroom assessment of student performance in reading and writing, and exploring concepts and research relevant to that theme. The tension between externally mandated tests and internally generated assessments will frame our review. We have described elsewhere the role of teacher assessment for informing policy decisions outside the classroom (Calfee, 1988; Calfee & Hiebert, 1988; Hiebert & Calfee, 1989) and will comment briefly on that topic at the end of the chapter.

We will first review the distinctions between external and internal assessment and the tensions that these conflicting forces create for teachers. Next, we present models of the literacy curriculum and of classroom assessment that undergird our analysis. Throughout the chapter we will focus on literacy—reading and writing—in the elementary grades. Two succeeding sections examine in turn the nature and outcomes of external and internal assessment. The chapter concludes with thoughts about future directions for literacy assessment in research, practice, professional development, and policy.

Our primary audience is the community of educational researchers, and we assume familiarity with several topics covered elsewhere in these volumes. On the other hand, since the *Handbook* is also for graduate students and practitioners, we incorporate background material and practical examples along the way. We draw on the empirical literature where possible, but call on scholarship and practical experience where necessary.

TWO TIERS OF ASSESSMENT

The literate use of language is a primary outcome of the elementary grades of schooling. Two competing lenses provide information about the effectiveness of literacy instruction: (a) the evidence available to the teacher through daily exchanges with students, and (b) the various instruments based on the standardized test paradigm. The latter have become the primary source for the externally mandated assessments that serve local, state, and federal policy agencies. They generate the test scores that appear in local newspapers, informing the public about how well the schools are doing their job.

Today these instruments play an increasing role in classroom assessment, displacing informed teacher assessments as the basis for instructional decisions (Madaus, 1988). Although we will criticize the misuse of these instruments, it is worth remembering that one goal of objective tests was to reduce bias against individuals springing from subjective judgments (Sokal, 1987). They scarcely succeeded in attaining this goal, but they clearly served important roles, like informing the public agenda (e.g., the 1989 NAEP report, *American Education at the Crossroads*). Our aim is not the elimination of externally mandated standardized assessment, but a reasonable and appropriate balance in methods.

As Table 12.1 shows, policy makers and teachers differ in their needs for information about student achievement; these needs vary in purpose, criteria, and pragmatics (Calfee, 1984; Calfee & Drum, 1979; Cole, 1988). At the extremes, the gap between the two perspectives is substantial (Cole, 1988). For the teacher, the key issues are (or should be) *validity* (Does assessment match what I have taught and the way I have taught it?), *suitability* (Do the methods fit my purposes?), and *availability* (Will the information be there when I need it?). For the administrator and policy maker, the important facets are *reliability* (Does the evidence have scientific backing?), *efficiency* (How cheaply can we get it?), and *aggregability* (Can the information be reduced to a few numbers?).

External texts fall into two categories, *Norm-referenced tests* (NRTs) portray the relative standing of individuals and groups. Student performance is reduced to a few summative indices, usually statistical derivations of basic measures like percent correct. In the 1960s, *criterion-referenced tests* (CRTs) appeared as an alternative (Glaser, 1963, 1986) to measure mastery of specific objectives against an absolute performance level. Though different from NRTs in purpose and use, they are similar in format and content (e.g., Bloom, Hastings, & Madaus, 1971).

CRTs first saw widespread application by school districts to monitor centrally developed curriculum frameworks (Cooley & Bickel, 1986). They are now embedded in most published materials. In basal reading systems, for instance, end-of-unit tests serve as a check on student mastery. Typically group-administered and multiple-choice, these instruments steer teachers in setting the pace of instruction and placing students in reading groups. Current practice relies on piecemeal, short-term objectives (Fuchs & Fuchs, in press). Little evidence supports the reliability or validity of curriculum-embedded tests for instructional decision making (but see Tindal, Fuchs, Fuchs, Sinn, Deno, & Germann, 1985, who report the reliability and predictive validity for three

TABLE 12.1   Comparison between Assessment Instruments
Designed for Different Purposes

ASSESSMENT DESIGNED FOR INSTRUCTION	ASSESSMENT DESIGNED FOR EXTERNAL ACCOUNTABILITY
Purpose and Source	
Teacher-designed for classroom decisions	Designed by experts for policy makers
Combines several sources of information	Stand-alone, single index
Strong link to curriculum and instruction	Independent of curriculum and instruction
Criteria	
Valid for guiding instruction	Predictive validity
Profile reliability—strengths and weaknesses	Total test reliability
Sensitive to dynamic changes in performance	Stable over time and situations
Performance is often all-or-none	Normally distributed scores
Pragmatics	
Judgmental, quick turnaround, flexible	Objective, cost and time efficient, standardized
Performance-based, "real" task	Multiple-choice, recognition
Administer whenever needed	Once-a-year, sometimes twice

series). While psychometrics has made technical advances (e.g., sophisticated analysis techniques, computerization), most contemporary tests resemble Kelly's 1915 Silent Reading Test (Samuelson, 1987; also Farr & Carey, 1986).

Some scholars doubt that the external and internal approaches can be reconciled (Cole, 1988). We share that doubt but can imagine a scenario that connects the two extremes, where classroom-based assessment routinely enters into policy reviews and teachers find practical guidance from improved tests. Such a reform will have to be grounded in a vision of literacy that goes beyond the basic-skills conception that has prevailed for more than half a century. Equally important is a view of teachers as autonomous decision makers (Marshall, 1988; Myers, 1985). In the next section we present our concepts of critical literacy and of classroom assessment by teachers as informed professionals. The issues transcend the particulars of reading and writing, but need to be reasoned for specific curricula. In a sense, we have prepared a case study for the *Handbook*.

LITERACY AND ASSESSMENT: CONCEPTUAL FOUNDATIONS

Curriculum, instruction, and assessment are the essential core of education. *Curriculum* includes disciplinary concepts and methods (e.g., reading and writing, mathematics, social studies, science, and the arts). Curriculum may be represented by frameworks and materials, but its essence comprises a set of ideas. *Instruction* includes the pedagogical strategies for guiding student learning: direct instruction, small-group discussion, individual support, and so on. *Assessment* entails the collection and evaluation of evidence about student learning. Testing is part of the process, but so is the monitoring by which the teacher adjusts instruction to student needs. Curriculum is the driving force, hence our need to begin with a portrayal of the domain of literacy.

A Model of Critical Literacy

Today's public view of reading emphasizes the printed page. From this perspective, students become literate as they gain the capacity to decipher written text. The first task is to become a fluent decoder, after which other skills (e.g., vocabulary and comprehension) are acquired (Chall, 1983). The student must first learn to read, and then can read to learn. Literacy serves as handmaiden to more serious intellectual endeavors. Writing enters the picture only incidentally.

Recent theory and research suggest an alternative model, one grounded in a concept of *critical literacy* (Brown, 1987), the capacity to use language in all its forms as a tool for thinking, for problem-solving, and for communication (Brandt, 1989; Calfee, 1982a; Calfee & Drum, 1986; Heath, 1983; Horowitz & Samuels, 1987; Olson, 1977). This conception regards literacy not as a low-level skill serving a higher purpose, but as an intellectual achievement in its own right. Decoding and spelling aim toward an understanding of the historical and morphological structure of English orthography (Balmuth, 1982; Venezky, 1970), because otherwise the system seems senseless. Students acquire vocabulary concepts (McKeown & Curtis, 1987), story grammar (Stein & Glenn, 1979), and expository text structures (Chambliss & Calfee, 1989; Meyer, 1985) early in their school experience, because these structures allow them to work with ideas. The interplay of comprehension and composition is fostered in the primary grades, because comprehension is inherently reconstructive (Anderson & Pearson, 1984; Baker & Brown, 1984; Spivey, 1987; Squire, 1987). Active engagement replaces rote drill, because understanding requires monitoring and reflection (Palincsar & Brown, in press; Paris, 1987; Snow, 1980).

We think this alternative conception will displace the basic-skills approach in the next few years; some signs suggest that this move is already underway (Anderson, Hiebert, Scott, & Wilkinson, 1985; Reeves, 1986). The Grant Foundation survey (1988) shows that the breakpoint for tomorrow's generation is not a high school diploma but a college degree. A standard once reserved for the elite is now essential for all students, for the good of both the individual and society (Resnick & Resnick, 1985). The full shape of this revolution remains uncertain, but along with a reformation in curriculum and instructional practice, it will require novel methods for gauging student achievement.

A Model of Assessment

Educational assessment is best viewed not as an end in itself but as a form of applied social science research (Calfee & Hiebert, 1988; Cronbach, 1988; Messick, 1988; Shuell, 1988). Cronbach (1960) laid out this position when he identified three principal features of assessment: careful observations, a variety of methods and measures, and integration of information. The research perspective takes shape as a set of practical questions around the issues of *purpose* (What are the goals? What working hypotheses guide the activity?), *method* (How should the data be collected? How should the inquiry be designed?), and *interpretation and decision making* (Is the evidence reliable? Valid? What are the options for action?) (Hiebert & Calfee, in press).

In the next two sections, this model guides our review of classroom assessment practices, first under the rubric of externally mandated tests, and then for those driven by internal needs. We will focus on the teacher's role in negotiating the tension between these two endpoints.

INFLUENCES OF EXTERNALLY MANDATED
ASSESSMENTS ON CLASSROOM PRACTICE

In this section, we examine the external model, following the elements listed above. We then present research relevant to the impact of this model on teachers, curriculum, and instruction.

The External Model

Most elementary schools administer one or more standardized tests in reading and mathematics, often in response to district, state, and federal regulations or perceptions thereof (Dorr-Bremme & Herman, 1986; Madaus, 1985). For example, 45 of the 50 states administer standardized tests, 25 to determine promotion or graduation (Afflerbach, 1987; Educational Testing Service, 1988: Office of Educational Research and Improvement, 1988). The widespread use of tests has been debated in the national press and professional publications (Cannell, 1988; Houts, 1977; Resnick & Resnick, 1985; Samuelson, 1987; Tyler & White, 1979). The public function of testing is relatively new. While standardized achievement tests first appeared around 1910–1920, it was not until after World War II that schools began to employ this method for large-scale assessment (Anastasi, 1966; Greene & Gray, 1946; Haney, 1981; Henry, 1946; Smith & Tyler, 1942; Whipple, 1918). By the mid-1970s, in response to public concern about educational outcomes, state testing programs and the minimum competency movement proliferated (Airasian, 1987; Lerner, 1981). We now examine the standardized method from the perspective of the assessment model.

Purpose

The initial force behind standardized tests had two thrusts: First, they served as an accountability device for administrators of burgeoning urban schools after the turn of the century (Haertel & Calfee, 1983; Resnick & Resnick, 1985; Whipple, 1918). Second, they provided a check for those who doubted teachers' ability to judge student performance, and who suspected subjective bias (Sokal, 1987). Early tests resembled classroom examinations, but for reasons of bureaucratic efficiency moved to the recognition format (true-false, multiple-choice). Unlike public opinion surveys that rely on a carefully selected sample for information, educational assessments generally include every student, hence the need to minimize unit cost.

From the beginning, standardized tests found applications other than public reports. Grade-level scores provide an objective and numerical basis for selection and placement into classroom instructional groups and into special classes at both ends of the spectrum (Heller, Holtzman, & Messick, 1982: Martin, 1988). Test scores fused with readability measures to match students and materials. A student scoring at the 2.5 grade level was kept from more difficult texts because of the risk of frustration. The process is quantitative, and today can be totally automated (College Board, 1981; Dufflemeyer & Adamson, 1986; also cf. Carver, 1985). Such applications were at first ancillary to classroom instruction but now control many reading programs through worksheets and curriculum-embedded tests.

Methods

Externally mandated tests are grounded in the concepts and techniques of psychometrics and behavioral objectives. Exceptions occur (e.g., advanced placement), and the terminology of cognition and higher-order thinking appears on occasion (but see

Marzano & Costa, 1988). The approach divides a curriculum domain into small, testable pieces. Several test items are written for each objective. The collection is administered to a sample of students for statistical evaluation. Total test reliability is the primary yardstick (Calfee & Drum, 1979). If the reliability index is too low, troublesome items are revised or discarded. The technique guarantees that the test is unidimensional (Davis, 1968). Consequently, the instruments provide little information about strengths and weaknesses in student performance (Thorndike, 1973). The tests are highly correlated whether one compares subtests within or across a domain; reading and math tests are as closely related as comprehension and vocabulary subtests.

The reasons for unidimensionality are easily found; item difficulty depends more on idiosyncratic features of an item than on the labeled objective. Researchers (Drum, Calfee, & Cook, 1981; Hoopfer & Hunsberger, 1986; Johnston, 1983, 1984b; Langer, 1987) have analyzed the linguistic content of passages and questions, and found that format is often more important than substance. Langer (1987), after looking at the content of test passages and stem-choice relations, concluded that the materials often violated the structure and coherence rules of considerate text. Success depended on understanding the idiosyncrasies of the passage or question rather than the reading strategies employed with considerate text. Drum, et al. (1981) found a major predictor of item difficulty in comprehension tests to be the presence of a plausible alternative. For tests beyond the third grade, plausibility of an incorrect alternative had a powerful negative influence on performance, accounting for 20 percent to 50 percent of the item variance (a median of 44 percent).

These findings are for published tests. Less is known about the characteristics of curriculum-embedded tests. Teacher-made instruments, which account for a significant amount of classroom testing (Dorr-Bremme & Herman, 1986), appear to resemble standardized instruments (Stiggins, Conklin, Green, & Brody, 1986), a predictable outcome if teachers follow the advice that Calfee and Hiebert (1988) found in their analysis of the textbooks for educational psychology and measurement courses.

Interpretation and Decision Making

The meaning of standardized scores depends on the technique of analysis. Norm-referenced techniques yield transformed values like grade-level equivalents or percentiles. The result is an omnibus index that serves in the classroom for global decisions like group placement, retention, or assignment to a special program. Criterion-referenced methods indicate the student's performance mastery of a particular objective relative to a preestablished standard. An 80 percent criterion has become the standard. The earliest mention of this standard seems to be Bloom, Hastings, and Madaus (1971, pp. 129 ff.), who selected accuracy levels of 80 percent to 85 percent for a set of formative tests. They cautioned that the standard was arbitrary and should be adjusted to the task and instructional goals, but this advice is frequently disregarded.

In any event, interpretation is a largely mechanistic activity. Once a test is scored, the data are transformed into other indices that serve for interpretation. Preservice courses cover standardized testing methods, including the meaning of various indices, but textbooks handle interpretation rather poorly (Calfee & Hiebert, 1988). Teachers appear to have difficulty when asked to make sense of the information. Fraatz (1987) gives numerous examples of overreliance on statistically unsound profiles of test scores. Ruddell (1985) asked teachers to interpret changes in student achievement using scaled scores that did not differ reliably from one year to the next. In one scenario, for instance, Literal Comprehension dropped from 240 to 232, with a standard error of 20 points. Most teachers expressed concern about any decrease in scores. Only 10 percent of the teachers used the error of measurement for interpreting the profiles. Principals and district administrators reported they regularly scrutinized year-to-year changes to determine needed shifts in curriculum emphasis, with little regard for the reliability of the information (Cronbach & Furby, 1970).

The external mandate model of assessment leaves the teacher little responsibility for independent decision making. The main choices are retention and placement in ability groups. Curriculum-embedded tests also serve this purpose and play a significant role in the rate of progress through the curriculum (Barr & Dreeben, 1983). If a student fails to master a particular objective, the usual reaction is additional practice on supplemental worksheets for that objective. If an entire group performs badly, then the teacher slows the pace for all.

Effects on Teachers' Roles in Curriculum and Instruction

This section focuses on two questions. First, how does the intrusion of external assessment into classrooms influence teachers: the knowledge and skill required of them, the routines that they follow, the indicators that they rely on for feedback, and the working conditions of classroom and school (also see McClelland, 1988)? Second, what is the effect of the external model on curriculum and instruction—on what is taught and how it is taught?

We will organize our findings around three themes. First, external tests often serve incidentally to shape decisions about curriculum and instruction. Second, some advocates have recommended that tests directly define the curriculum. Third, several efforts are underway to enhance external assessments, either by improving multiple-choice procedures or through productive activities like writing.

Incidental Influences

Standardized tests, initially designed to serve policy makers, permeate today's classroom. Most instruments, whether NRTs or CRTs, provide both direction and support. Teachers receive profiles for the class and individual students on specific objectives, along with recommended instructional activities (Linn, 1986, p. 1156). Testing programs generally aggregate data at the school level; the focus is not on individual assessment but accountability. Even in this instance, school-wide decisions about curriculum priorities can be influenced by reports on specific objectives.

Teachers respect formal data for some purposes. Dorr-Bremme and Herman (1986) asked teachers to describe how they handled four decision points: the beginning of the school year, initial grouping or placement, changing assignments, and deciding grades. For every category, some type of standardized information was judged as crucial or important. Valencia (in press) found that teachers and principals agreed on several roles for external tests within the classroom: to assess student progress, to diagnose individual student problems and potential, and to group and place students. Principals valued these applications, but teachers were more concerned about instructional validity. "Tell me something I don't already know" and "Measure what I teach" were typical comments.

In follow-up interviews (Dorr-Bremme & Herman, 1986), teachers reported using standardized indices to judge students' capabilities. A teacher might use a test score, for example, to gauge whether a poorly performing student "has low ability" or "isn't working up to his ability level." Salmon-Cox (1981) describes how teachers reacted to discrepancies between their predictions and students' test results. If a student did less well than predicted, teachers discounted the test results. If a student scored above expectation, teachers wondered whether they had missed something. These teachers respected test scores but felt cautious about overuse of the information. An elementary teacher in the Dorr-Bremme and Herman (1986) survey captures the sentiment: "I feel good about [a test] if I can see where it is actually helping the child and you can put it in context. But when you pull it out of the context, out of the classroom teaching situation and the actual curriculum . . . , just to rate [a child] nationwide or whatever, that bugs me" (p. 69).

The teacher may be bothered because the information is not valuable. Several studies show that teachers can estimate standardized test scores reasonably well. Correlations between teacher rankings and students' total test scores range between .4 and .8, tending toward the upper end (Coladarci, 1986; Egan & Archer, 1985; Hoge & Butcher, 1984; Hopkins, George, & Williams, 1985; Perry, Guidubaldi, & Kehle, 1979). One interpretation is that the tests are valid because teachers, after countless hours with students, make similar judgments (Hoge, 1983). An alternative view is that teachers know test content and format.

Surveys also show that teachers place less emphasis on formal test results than on their own data (Dorr-Bremme & Herman, 1986; Ruddell, 1985; Stiggins et al., 1986; Thurlow & Ysseldyke, 1980; Valencia, in press). In addition, instructional decisions often appear to be -driven by neither data nor goals, but by activities and routines (Clark & Peterson, 1986; Clark & Yinger, 1977; Rudman et al., 1980). "Teacher planning begins with the content to be taught and the setting in which teaching will take place. The activity rather than the objective seems to be the unit of planning" (Clark & Yinger, 1977, p. 300).

Under these circumstances, externally mandated tests can provide a catalyst to disturb the routine and instigate thoughtful review. In the effective schools movement (Edmonds, 1985; Stedman, 1987), for instance, a focus on standardized tests may unite a staff. When Dorr-Bremme and Herman (1986) asked principals to judge the value of test results, the highest rating went to "informing the public," but next highest was "curriculum planning." In these situations, external tests are only one of several forces determining curriculum and instruction, but the influence appears significant.

Assessment as the Curriculum

Several theorists have proposed that tests should define educational goals. In the preceding section, schools and teachers were accountable to tests as external mandates; here the tests are the curriculum. The distinctions are sometimes subtle. In measurement-driven instruction (Popham, 1985, 1987a, 1987b), for instance, the criterial instruments may come from inside or outside a school. In criterion-referenced instruction (Cohen, 1987), the final assessment is the core of the curriculum. The important point is that education is defined by a set of CRTs. The aim is to assure efficient and effective instruction, regardless of the quality of the professional staff. As we will see below, studies of this approach generally show that, by directing teachers' and students' attention to test goals, test performance improves. We have found few reports of the effects of such mandates on classroom activities or curriculum changes. Most attention has focused on state initiatives; while we know about district programs, we have found few published reports (but see Cooley & Bickel, 1986, Case History 10; LeMahieu, 1984).

Popham (1985) reports favorable results from several states that have imposed high-stakes testing, mostly in the three Rs, and mostly for minimum competence.

When schools assign high priority to specific objectives as measured by standardized tests, test performance appears to improve by 10 to 15 percentage points, the largest increment occurring in the first year. Cohen (1987) describes four experiments (two on elementary reading) in which teaching the test produced effect sizes of one sigma or more.

In curriculum-based measurement, a variation employed with special-education classes, teachers monitor student growth on tasks directly related to curriculum goals (Fuchs, Fuchs, & Hamlett, 1989). The final goal is generally completion of a preset level in the reading series; the intermediate measures are more generic (e.g., recall of short stories; cloze tests). A computer program plots student progress. If a student performs below expectation, the teacher is encouraged to change instruction. Several studies have shown significant gains in student performance, usually as more rapid rates of progress.

These proposals appear to ensure *curriculum alignment*, the match between what is taught and what is tested (Crowell & Tissot, 1986; Leinhardt & Seewald, 1981; Wiley, 1988). The approach is sometimes little more than an accounting task, matching the frequency of objectives in textbooks and tests. If "main idea" appears on 20 percent of the test items, then it should appear equally often in text materials. If the numbers do not match, then some adjustment is required. An area like poetry, which appears in basal texts but seldom on tests (Flood & Lapp, 1986), is likely to lose out.

Critics of test-driven instruction have raised several concerns. Shepard (1988; also Airasian, 1988) argues that the critical flaw in these proposals is the questionable validity of the outcomes. A problem arises when not only content but also format is set by the assessment design (Mehrens & Kaminski, 1988). Tests are theoretically representative samples from a domain of skill and knowledge. When teacher and student both know that the primary criterion is a recognition test, the principle no longer works. By their nature, recognition tests call for inert knowledge; the student is not required to create or reconstruct the solution to a problem. High-level transfer (Perkins & Salomon, 1988) is not tapped under these conditions.

Bracey (1987) argues further that when curriculum and instruction are directed by test-based objectives, the result can be fragmentation and trivialization of education. Porter (1988) expands this point but also emphasizes the disengagement of teachers from the instructional process by the bureaucratization inherent in external indicators. The technical approach may achieve technical goals but will miss the opportunity to realize more significant educational goals.

Shepard (1988) has also questioned the empirical support for test-driven instruction. Reviewing test scores for Chapter I students in states that Popham held up as examples of the effectiveness of this approach, Shepard found small yearly changes, on the order of one or two percentile points. The gains were largely in lower-level domains, not in the higher levels of achievement (also see NAEP, 1989).

External intrusion can be counterproductive. Corbett and Wilson (1987) examined statewide testing in Maryland and Pennsylvania, states selected because the first had a high-stakes and the second a low-stakes testing program. During the study, the stakes increased in Pennsylvania, allowing examination of changes in curriculum and instruction. While the testing programs differed in several ways, raising the stakes had similar effects in the two states. Increased emphasis on the tests led to a concentration on strategies for increasing test scores. These strategies overrode existing efforts to improve curricula and, according to administrators, eroded the positive effects of testing. They felt that practices aimed at increasing test scores often conflicted with sound instructional practice.

Mathison's (1987) study of assessment practices in three school districts in a midwestern state reveals a similar pattern. In one district, for instance, a new superintendent announced that high test scores were the primary criterion for school effectiveness. The results were reduced staff morale and lowered student achievement.

NcNeill's (1986, 1988a, 1988b, 1988c) studies of magnet schools provides a third illustration of the negative effects of test-driven accountability. "The curriculum was criticized as lacking 'clarity'; in the words of the testing office, the goals and purposes needed to be made 'measurable. . . .' The magnet school teachers began to deliver 'double-entry' lessons. . . . They would put their 'real' lessons on hold for a few days to lecture about the proficiencies" (1988c, pp. 483–484). The results illustrate the vulnerability of teachers to demands for accountability; elementary teachers, who cannot fall back on subject matter expertise, are in an especially precarious position.

The evidence seems to show that externally mandated assessments may have a positive influence when they fill a vacuum. Where a faculty lacks a clear vision of curriculum goals, then tests give direction and purpose. The substantive impact on student achievement will depend on the character and quality of the assessment system. On the other hand, if a faculty already possesses a sense of purpose, then imposition of standardized testing can have a detrimental effect on teacher morale and may actually lower student achievement.

The arguments against the test-driven curriculum are significant. We doubt that high levels of literate thinking will be promoted by top-down methods of control; this approach seems limited even for tightly specified objectives (Elmore & McLaughlin, 1988). To be sure, schools cannot disregard external indices. College applicants need to be mindful of the SAT, and schools need to consider standardized tests. On the other hand, the high school that establishes the SAT as its primary curriculum goal is likely to fail its clients. Even if the graduates perform well on the SAT, they must ultimately face the challenge of college courses.

Enhancement of External Tests

Several efforts have been made in recent years to improve the quality of standardized assessments. One approach builds on the multiple-choice format by upgrading the content and the task demands. Moves in this direction have appeared in Illinois (Pearson & Valencia, 1987) and Michigan (Wixson & Peters, 1987). Comprehension passages are longer and more coherent. The choices tap more than basic literal and inferential knowledge, and ask students to identify the reasoning that supports an answer. It is too early to judge the effect of these initiatives, which have been accompanied by intensive staff development activities to inform teachers of the principles behind the test design (Anastasi, 1966, notes that at the first ETS Invitational Conference in 1936, participants voiced a concern that teachers might misuse tests because of lack of knowledge). The strategy is to change the content of the tests while retaining the efficient format and psychometric methodology.

During the past decade, writing has become a significant component of several state assessment programs (Chapman, 1988; Vickers, 1988). Program developers often consider one index of the success of these efforts to be changes in instruction that mirror the new requirements. When the test is reasonably well designed, evidence shows positive effects on student achievement. In North Carolina, for example, the statewide writing assessment requires students to compose clarification or description essays at grade six and point-of-view or persuasive essays at grade eight (Vickers, 1988). Evaluations have shown that the assessment program has prompted staff development and other efforts to strengthen writing curricula. Student ability to write coherently in different genres has improved steadily over five years (Vickers, 1988).

To be sure, these assessments differ significantly from what we know to be the best writing practice (Nystrand, 1987). Students typically have a fixed time in which to write on a commonplace topic, and the draft is holistically scored. As Bereiter and Scardamalia (1987) note, these features differ markedly from recommendations for effective writing instruction (Calkins, 1983; Graves, 1983). The writer usually plays a role in defining the topic, has time for planning and reflection, follows the first draft with one or more revisions, and does all this with support and feedback. Writing, like other productive aspects of literate performance (discussion, speech making, small-group participation), is an area in which the teacher can better render judgment about student achievement than is possible with existing externally mandated approaches.

INFLUENCE OF INTERNAL ASSESSMENT ON CLASSROOM PRACTICE

This section lays out a framework and reviews the research on the assessment of student performance based on teacher judgment. In designing the chapter, we had initial misgivings about this section. On the one hand, several lines of development point to the importance of this topic: the emphasis on critical literacy as opposed to basic skills, the move toward professionalization of teaching, and the emerging consensus that valid assessment requires multiple sources of information. On the other hand, our preliminary forays into the literature discouraged us about the prospect of finding sufficient substance for a review. As it turned out, the material is there but requires reframing the issues. Our task here is to convey these new perspectives in a coherent fashion.

We will follow a modified version of the previous framework. Where we could rely above on shared knowledge of the methodology of standardized tests, here we must construct a framework for methods of teacher assessment from the parts that are available. We have found the parts to be ample but poorly connected. We have accordingly included a section describing techniques for systematic teacher assessment of student achievement.

The Internal Model

In the ideal form that we imagine, classroom assessment is dynamic and adaptable to the shifting picture of student activities and instructional opportunities (Table 12.1). The goals may overlap those of external assessment, but the tactics and methods are different. The approach requires a high level of professional knowledge, skill, and flexibility—the teacher as applied social scientist (Hiebert & Calfee, in press).

In making this proposal, we are aware of skeptics' concerns. The proponents of measurement-driven instruction and variations thereon recommend a materials-based solution as easier to implement than selecting and supporting a cadre of expert teachers (e.g., Popham, 1987a, p. 679). As Johnston (in press) has noted, a "fundamental lack of trust in teachers" underlies many current policies. He disagrees with this distrust and supports the concept of professionalization, but doubts run deep (e.g., Mehan, Hert-weck, Combs, & Flynn, 1982). Our analyses and experiences lead us to be more optimistic, and so we press on. The assessment model sketched at the beginning of the paper provides a framework for examining the approach.

Purpose

The ultimate aim of assessment activities in the internal model is to guide instruction so that all students achieve a high level of critical literacy. Assessment at the classroom level has both summative and formative elements. That is, the teacher must keep in mind the ultimate goals for the year, but equally important are the day-to-day and even moment-to-moment events. Success on a given task is not simply a sign of mastery but must be joined to larger curricular goals. Momentary failure challenges the teacher to consider changes in the situation that reveal the causes of a problem, and to guide the student toward success.

Continual reflection on students' performance is the pivotal property of internal assessment that sets it apart from external assessment, and it is for this reason that we speak of this approach as *applied research*. As such, it demands an inquiring mind. The metaphor carries several significant implications. For instance, *what* a researcher does and *how* he or she does it are important, but more critical is the *why*. In some areas of science, theory provides a foundation, but research is also driven by hunches, hypotheses, and concepts. The activity cannot be mindless. Science, whether basic or applied, is driven by the need to understand.

Research also depends on explicitness. The scientist may work alone, but for a finding to be accepted it must be communicated, explained, and survive public review and criticism. A canon of science is replication; the work must be described clearly enough so that others can repeat it. Interpretation must be clearly reasoned so that others can follow it.

The teacher is in a unique position to apply the experimental method. When the connection between assessment and instruction is close, then initial observations lead to intervention, followed by the next round of observation. In this situation, the purpose of assessment is not only to determine student performance, but equally to guide the teacher's instructional decisions.

Methods

What sources of information suit the purposes sketched above? Tests and examinations are certainly part of the picture, but so are observations of actual performance. What principles can guide this inherently subjective task? In this section we will consider broad methodological issues and then review research on specific techniques of teacher assessment: questioning and discussion, interviews and inventories, observations, and performance assessment, including portfolios. Our neglect of pragmatic issues—contextualization, flexibility, and immediate feedback—is a result of limited space and not of a lack of importance.

The most fundamental principle for internal assessment is *construct validity*. External assessment relies on predictive validity, but where substantive instructional decisions depend on the findings, the methods must be true to the curriculum. Construct validity can be approached from two directions (Cronbach, 1988; Messick, 1988). The first is a clear image of the construct itself. As long as literacy is viewed as a complex and poorly defined concept, the direct method is difficult to apply. As noted at the beginning of the chapter, we think the model of critical literacy is both clear and parsimonious, and provides a sound foundation for classroom assessment. The second approach relies on the convergence of multiple sources of evidence. If several judgments of student literacy are highly correlated, then we have more confidence that the judgments intersect a core construct.

We see the two approaches as complementary. On the one hand, even the most clearly articulated educational construct is fuzzy in places, requiring empirical confirmation and revision. On the other hand, overreliance on statistical procedures (e.g., factor analysis) can yield results that are difficult to replicate or interpret. For instance, the evidence is solid for the convergence of standardized reading comprehension tests on a single underlying construct, but this construct may be better labeled test-taking than comprehension. Only as theory and evidence join do we gain confidence in the validity of a construct.

The balance today is toward empirical methods with less attention to the conceptual side. Archbald and Newmann (1988) address this issue under the rubric of *authenticity*, which they highlight under three headings. First, authentic assessments engage students in tasks that approximate those that experts perform. For instance, students may be asked to clarify and defend alternative interpretations of a piece of literature.

Second, students are required to join the pieces of a project into an integrated whole. In a typical test, the student might be asked to describe a story character. An authentic task, in contrast, asks the student to examine the character's motives in relation to others in the same book, in other narratives, or to other figures in society known to the student (friends, famous people, even cartoon characters).

Third, authentic assessments have utility beyond evaluation; they serve a function in addition to assessing student knowledge and skill. Consider the distinction between testing for school grades and tasks important in other contexts—arguing a point in a letter to an editor, or writing a news article for the school paper. These examples bring to mind functional literacy, but we have in mind more demanding and significant applications of critical literacy—beyond the reading of bus schedules or filling out of employment forms.

Interpretation and Decision Making

What do the data mean? For internal assessments, the answer is challenging in several respects. The data are typically qualitative and multifaceted. The teacher cannot look up a summary index in a prepared table. The job resembles narration far more than exposition. As noted in Table 12.1, the search is for a pattern rather than a scale reading. The emphasis is on relative strengths and weaknesses, on shifts in performance over time and conditions.

As with externally mandated tests, validity and reliability are important for interpretation but blend into a single entity. For validity, the issue is the convergence of multiple sources of evidence on a hypothesized construct (Messick, 1988). For reliability, the issue is consistency of the evidence over variations in time and situations. The teacher has numerous opportunities to observe performance in different contexts and different tasks. A performance estimate is trustworthy if several sources of evidence point to the same conclusion; for internal assessment, validity and reliability are judgments rather than correlations. How capable are classroom teachers in judging the validity of a given interpretation? This question is certainly amenable to investigation, but we have found little research other than studies that take standardized tests as the point of reference (Shavelson & Borko, 1979).

Translation of the findings from internal assessment into a course of action also differs from external assessment. Pacing and placement may be considerations, but equally plausible are decisions to gather additional information or to try out a brief instructional treatment. A group of fifth graders still struggles with the concept of *enterprise* at the end of a vocabulary lesson. Does it mean you do your chores? What if you don't get money for it? The answers are confused. Tomorrow the teacher may discuss *Where the Red Fern Grows*, a novel about a hard-working young boy; it evoked considerable interest last week. Or perhaps students' understanding will be illuminated by looking again at the thesaurus. The point is that the teacher has options other than announcing success or failure.

Techniques for Teacher-Directed Assessment

The literature on psychometrics and test theory is abundant both for method and practice. Classroom assessment is more fragmentary and scattered. Accordingly, in this section we will briefly review recent developments in this field. Our effort is partly to suggest a taxonomy for the field, but also to highlight and critique several innovative methodologies. In a sense, we are posing the question: If standardized tests were outlawed tomorrow, what might replace them?

Questioning and Discussion

The revival of interest in this domain is evidenced by a new journal (*Questioning Exchange*), research volumes (e.g., Dillon, 1988a; Graesser & Black, 1985), and practical texts (Alvermann, Dillon, & O'Brien, 1987; Dillon, 1988b; Foley and Bagley, 1988; Wilen, 1986; Hunkins, 1989). Earlier traditions focused either on the general effects of questioning or on microstructural issues. Significant factors included question types (typically, contrasts between factual and inferential question) or the placement of questions (i.e., before or after reading). The results on student learning were equivocal (e.g., Gage, 1978; Gall, 1984; Gall & Gall, 1976).

Recent work places more emphasis on instruction. The shift also lays a conceptual foundation for teachers to think about applications for assessment. Questioning becomes an integral part of the structures and functions of learning. Reciprocal teaching illustrates the technique (Palincsar, 1986; Palincsar & Brown, in press). Students learn techniques (predicting, questioning, summarizing, and clarifying) that allow them to analyze a text on their own. The goal of discussion is no longer to "guess the right answer" or "keep it going," but to treat the text as a problem to be solved. The instructional strategy has three facets: presentation of the techniques, modeling (including thinking aloud), and gradual release of control. The opportunities for teacher assessment of student progress receive little attention at present, although a connection exists with dynamic assessment, described below.

In a departure from the academic model, Graesser, Lang, and Horgan (1988) analyzed patterns of questioning from three situations: college students' queries about brief expository passages, adults' inquiries about a computer system, and dialogues from newspaper columns ("Ann Landers") and talk shows ("Dr. Ruth"). Their analysis led to a three-part taxonomy. The pragmatic facet reflects the purpose behind a question, which can range from bona fide requests for information to efforts at control. The semantic element covers the substance of an exchange. The communicative domain resembles the metalevel properties of reciprocal teaching.

The questions and answers in the preceding encounters differ markedly from the didactic and recitational methods that prevail in elementary instruction. We hesitate to make predictions from this brief survey, but we see promise in approaches that combine Socrates and "Dr. Ruth," which are principled and yet authentic. In retrospect, we suspect that this compromise may resemble the inductive teaching strategy proposed by Taba (1962).

Interviews and Inventories

Group interactions are a potential source of information about student achievement; different opportunities arise from one-on-one exchanges. Systematic research on individual assessment is scarce. We have found relatively few accounts of how elementary teachers talk with individual students about reading and writing. Some interesting material appears in studies of writing, but the connections to assessment are missing.

Three approaches warrant comment: informal reading inventories, miscue analysis, and dynamic assessment. Although all three techniques appear as published packages, each has promise as a basis for independent teacher judgment.

The *informal reading inventory* (IRI) is familiar to most elementary teachers. Gray (1920) recommended the method as an alternative to standardized tests in order to "professionalize" teachers. At the outset, however, the view of curriculum and assessment was limited. The Gray measure was "words per minute," taken from monthly oral reading samples. Subsequent reviews (Beldin, 1970; Johnson, Kress, & Pikulski, 1987; Jongsma & Jongsma, 1981; Pikulski & Shanahan, 1982; Schell & Hanna, 1982) show that a low-level conception of literacy still prevails. In commercial versions (e.g., Johns, 1988), the brief excerpts have the shortcomings of standardized test passages. Oral reading fluency is emphasized, and questions on vocabulary and comprehension are literal and factual.

Miscue analysis is a variation on the reading inventory (Goodman, Watson, & Burke, 1987). Although stressing the wholeness of language and the primacy of comprehension, current practice resembles other inventories. The focus is on oral reading errors, primarily at the word and sentence level. Students retell passages, but strategies for comprehension testing receive brief attention and are not linked to the rich conceptions from children's literature (Lukens, 1982) or the systematics of story grammar (Stein & Glenn, 1979).

A recent development, *dynamic assessment*, springs from the work of Feuerstein (1979; Lidz, 1987) with at-risk Israeli students. The aim is to assess learning rather than competence. "The examiner is an active intervener who monitors and modifies the interaction with the learner in order to induce successful learning" (Lidz, 1987, p. 3). Other researchers have explored variations on the concept (Heller et al., 1982, pp. 68 ff., on special populations; Lipson & Wixson, 1986; Paratore & Indrianso, 1987), and the origins are quite old. Although the basic concept mirrors the notion of teacher as applied researcher, present work is preliminary and has little connection to literacy.

Observations

From one perspective, observation is a natural activity for the teacher (Brown, 1987; Johnston, in press; Lucas, 1988; Moore, 1983). In most domains of science, however, learning to look is a significant task. We think the same is true for teaching. To the novice, the classroom is a buzzing confusion; the expert can see through the complexity to the underlying dynamics of instructional interactions.

Systematic classroom observation has a long history. Early concepts stressed qualitative methods grounded in the local context. In framing the Eight-Year Study around observational records, anecdotal records, questionnaires, interviews, checklists, records of activities, products, and the like, Smith and Tyler (1942) noted that "The responsibility for evaluating the school program belonged to the staff and clientele of the school" (p. 14). Today's methods range from highly formalized and quantitative approaches to qualitative narratives. At one end of the continuum is moment-by-moment tallying of behavioral events (Flanders, 1970); at the other is intuitive "kid watching" (Goodman, Goodman, & Hood, 1989). For the classroom teacher, a compromise may be ethnographic methods, where the participant-observer relies on "thick description" (Evertson & Green, 1986; Heath, 1990 [see this volume, ch. 1]; Newkirk & Atwell, 1982). Moffett and Wagner (1983) present a practical version for literacy instruction. "Ordinarily students don't do enough to provide the evaluator [teacher] something to see. But if students are constantly producing and receiving discourse in great volume and variety, and if the teacher is freed from emceeing to circulate and observe, then good evaluation becomes possible without resorting to special activities that detract from learning . . ." (p. 499). Their text includes numerous examples of the basic concept.

Performance Assessment, Writing, and Portfolios

At the core of this technique is the question, What is the ultimate outcome of the endeavor? The philosophy resembles measurement-based instruction in some ways; the difference is the emphasis on long-term and direct rather than short-term and indirect indicators. The student who passes a multiple-choice test is not assured success in college or on the job. Constructive activities that require analysis, problem solving, writing, and the completion of projects are preferred because they more closely match real-world demands. Below we sketch three areas of current activity: performance assessment, student writing, and portfolios.

The concept of *performance assessment* arose in reaction to standardized tests for certification and employment, and a call for face validity (Berk, 1986). In education, the major work has been by Stiggins and his colleagues (Stiggins, 1985, 1987; Stiggins, Conklin, Green, & Brody, 1986). The approach is in the early stages, with primary emphasis on staff development programs that foster teacher competence in conducting performance assessment. Issues of validity and reliability have also been a major consideration in the project. "No other single specification contributes more to the quality of your performance assessment than this one . . . . Place yourself in the hypothetical situation of giving feedback [instruction?] to someone who has performed poorly on the task" (p. 36).

The second touchstone is writing assessment. Writing and the integration of reading and writing have burgeoned in recent years as areas of theory, research, and practice. We will not review the entire field, but simply comment on the potential for teacher assessment of student achievement. Two points are worth particular mention. The first springs from the concept of an integrated language-literacy program mentioned earlier (Moffett & Wagner, 1983). The consolidation of reading and writing seems a sensible way to enhance opportunities for genuine assessment of the concept of literacy laid out in this chapter. To be sure, the concept is still more vision than reality, reflecting a long historical tension (Clifford, 1987). As things now stand, writing is not typically linked to reading in most classroom practice; the opportunities for assessment inherent in this connection are therefore lost.

The other point about writing assessment is the recent growth of research on valid methodology. Ruth and Murphy (1988), in their thorough review of the topic, find an emphasis on standardization, reflecting an external perspective. Lucas (1988) and Flitterman-King (1988), in contrast, connect writing with classroom practice. Unfortunately, they are less helpful with technical details. The focus in both examples is on writing as a holistic activity. For assessment purposes, writing provides the opportunity to determine how a student handles three distinctive facets: knowledge of topic, awareness of audience, and use of language as a formal system for communication (Applebee, 1982). Viewed from this perspective, writing is inherently constructive and requires active engagement. "Writing about reading" should therefore help the teacher lead students to a constructivist approach to comprehension (Squire, 1987; Rosenblatt, 1989), but this connection remains to be made.

The third topic is the *assessment portfolio*. At a practical level, teachers often rely on collections of student work as a basis for grading. The practice has received little attention by researchers except for studies of student journals, most often during process writing (see above; also Burnham, 1986). In the survey by Archbald and

Newmann (1988), the examples come from high schools, but they apply with equal force across the years of schooling. They describe several examples of classrooms in which student projects and portfolios are the primary means to support both instruction and assessment.

Valencia, McGinley, and Pearson (in press) present a conceptual framework for portfolio design in reading, in which they suggest a language for developing and criteria for evaluating portfolio procedures. The language comprises five continua: focus, structure, mode, locus of control, and intrusiveness. The criteria rate the degree to which a portfolio process is continuous, multifaceted, collaborative, conceptually grounded, and authentic. Valencia and associates employ this framework to examine five different assessment scenarios. The work is still in the early stages. Meanwhile, Vermont (Wilhelm, 1988) has decided to use locally generated samples of student writing to judge statewide achievement, a policy initiative ahead of research.

Effects on Teachers' Roles in Curriculum and Instruction

Our aim in this section is to review the impact on teachers when the techniques described above are the basis for instructional decision making. The section is organized around two questions. The first inquires into the extent and quality of teacher-based assessment. The available research shows that teachers rely on their own judgment for some purposes but not others, and that the basis for assessment is generally intuitive and implicit. The second question reviews research specific to the four techniques described above.

General Patterns of Teacher Assessment

While the model of teacher-as-researcher appears in an increasing number of studies (e.g., Goswami & Stillman, 1987; Heath, 1990), reality differs from the model. For reading, the prevailing trend is the basal manual, which provides the complete package for curriculum, instruction, and assessment. For writing, teachers have greater freedom, and the range of activities is much less circumscribed. We will consider the two areas separately.

As noted earlier in the chapter, basal reading systems generally hew to an external assessment model, with little need for teacher judgment. This pattern has developed over the past few decades. In the 1920s, reading teachers received support from a slim manual, a brief anthology of short stories, and advice to move quickly to good literature (Shannon, 1989; Smith, 1986; Venezky, 1987; Woodward, 1987; also Taylor, 1986, in British schools): "Children should read widely, think actively while reading, and refine habits . . ." (Woodward, 1987, from a 1937 teacher's manual). Standardized tests had emerged, but teacher assessment predominated (Whipple, 1925). This configuration contrasts with the assurance in a 1976 manual that "the all-inclusive Teachers Edition gives the teacher everything necessary to plan and provide instruction" (Woodward, 1987).

To be sure, teachers are encouraged in preservice training and workshops to collect information continuously and broadly (Anderson et al., 1985, pp. 100 ff.). Observational studies show that reading teachers rarely assess student readiness and check outcomes mainly through published materials (Clark & Peterson, 1986; Morine-Dershimer & Vallance, 1976; Peterson, Marx, & Clark, 1978; Taylor, 1970). The task is to cover materials and complete the routines. Fisher and associates (1978) found that less than 10 percent of classroom time fell into the category of "teacher monitoring." McDonald and Elias (1975) reported a similar pattern; teachers spent 10 percent and 15 percent of instructional time asking questions or checking answers, relying mostly on published materials.

The situation is quite different in writing. Partly as a result of state initiatives, writing has returned to a significant place in the elementary curriculum. The National Writing Project (Gray, 1986) promotes teacher autonomy and a student-centered curriculum, neither bound to external assessment. While centered on writing, the research also reveals opportunities for integrating oral and written literacy. The research relies on case studies, with rich portrayals of teacher-student interactions (Bissex & Bullock, 1987; Calkins, 1983; Genishi & Dyson, 1984; Graves, 1983). The teacher-as-researcher model also appears frequently in this literature.

This literature is extensive, and we will limit our comments to the implications for assessment. Our first observation is that the research does not yet realize its potential for informing assessment. A few authors address this issue directly; Genishi and Dyson (1984), for instance, remark on the opportunities for student assessment in a language-rich environment, with suggestions for documentation. Published studies provide stimulating excerpts of classroom discussion and student compositions, with insightful and provocative commentary. Missing from the investigations is an analysis of how the data might serve teachers for assessment.

The second point is that instructional exchanges around discussion and composition are more often employed for assistance than for assessment. We have found few instances of interactions or reflections where teachers use classroom exchanges to explore student understanding or to guide students in reflecting on their reasoning. More often the aim is completing a task or reaching a correct answer. The dialogues generally display a sound instructional style (e.g., Genishi & Dyson, 1984, p. 198), but the format is recitational (Corno & Snow, 1986, pp. 612 ff.) rather than reflective.

Our third observation is that studies of teacher-researchers seldom portray an image of research as a norm for classroom practice. Although the "inseparability of teaching and learning" is the expressed ideal (Bissex & Bullock, 1987, p. 207), the reality is that research is an add-on, often guided by collaboration with a university professor. The pattern resembles academic research more than the dynamic activity described earlier in this chapter. The titles in Bissex and Bullock (1987), for instance, could be dissertation topics: *Traci: A Learning-Disabled Child in a Writing-Process Classroom, Roles and Strategies in College Writing Conferences, The Effect of Poetry in a First-Grade Classroom*, and so on. This comment is not meant to downplay the importance of these exercises. They are significant contributions in their own right and also support the professionalization of teachers. The enthusiasm and engagement of teachers in these reports stand in sharp contrast to the despondency and inarticulateness of teachers reported by other investigators (e.g., Clark & Peterson, 1986; Fraatz, 1987). Our point is that none of the studies reveals the teacher acting routinely in a research mode.

Specific Effects

In this section we briefly comment on research in the four domains of methodology presented earlier. The focus will be on research informing the process by which teachers assess student achievement. First is the area of questioning and discussion. Here we have little to add to the previous discussion on methods. The potential of recent developments in these techniques remains to be explored in a systematic manner. Research on metacognitive instruction (Corno & Snow, 1986, pp. 623 ff.;

Palincsar, Stevens, & Gavelek, 1988) suggests that active and engaging discussion can enhance student learning, but we have been unable to locate research on the value for classroom assessment.

A promising line of research appears in ethnographic studies of classroom language. In her study of children from different socioeconomic levels, Heath (1980, 1983) found that middle-class students readily played the "school game," where the task was to answer literal questions with obvious answers. Black youngsters from poor backgrounds remained silent, but Heath tells how some students "found the voice" to express their confusion and frustration. As one parent put it, "My kid, he too scared to talk, 'cause nobody play by the rules he know. At home I can't shut him up. Miss Davis, she complain 'bout Ned not answerin' back. He say she asks dumb questions she already know 'bout" (p. 107). At home, these same children readily handled questions about complex topics. When Heath shared her findings with teachers and students, classroom discussion shifted from testlike questions to authentic conversations. Language use by all students became richer and more articulate. Sophisticated metaphor and extended story plots replaced the stilted language of the "school game."

The second domain includes interviews and inventories. Teachers spend considerable time thinking about students, but less time sharing these thoughts with youngsters. Clark and Peterson (1986) note that teachers' thoughts are reactive and puzzled: "You can't always tell with kids, you know, whether they're really inattentive or just mulling over what has been going on" (p. 269). Individual conversations with students are informal and personal (Fraatz, 1987). Elementary teachers lack a workable conceptual framework for communicating with students (Duffy, 1977), and so must rely on intuition.

Informal reading inventories (IRIs) provide a opportunity to investigate the effects of institutional influences on assessment practice. Preservice courses and textbooks urge teachers to be diagnostic, and the IRI is often recommended to implement this strategy. Harris and Lalik (1987) found that teachers were familiar with the IRI concept, but few actually used the instrument. They reported that children's reading status was determined by the basal level that they had completed the previous year, leaving little need for other measures. Those who used an IRI employed a commercial instrument for assigning students to groups early in the school year. Most often, other people (resource specialists and administrators) handled student assessment.

Research has also addressed the trustworthiness of IRI assessments. Can teachers employ interviews and inventories in a reliable and unbiased fashion? In the absence of solid conceptual grounding and practical experience, the answer appears to be "No." Allington (1978) and Page and Carolson (1975) found that reading specialists judging identical IRI results gave different recommendations for student placement. Other results (Lamberg, Rodriguez, & Tomas, 1978; Roe & Aiken, 1976) are more encouraging. Quality of preparation seems to matter (Pikulski & Shanahan, 1982). We suspect that the same is true for miscue analysis and dynamic assessment but have found no research on the effectiveness of teacher assessment with these methods.

In the third domain, surveys show that teachers often rely on their own observations to gauge student learning (Dorr-Bremme & Herman, 1986; Fraatz, 1987). These observations are generally informal and casual. Teachers keep few records and depend on memory. Amarel and Chittenden (1982) found that teachers maintained records when mandated by administrators, for bureaucratic rather than professional purposes. Richert (1988) reported that intern teachers varied in their recordkeeping practices, even when given time for reflection and encouragement to keep a journal. Teachers who did not keep journals were sure that they could remember events, but the data showed them to be overconfident. Those who kept records, often at a companion's urging, focused collegial discussions on student learning and achievement. Those who relied on memory were more likely to ruminate on philosophical and personal issues.

These findings probably depend on factors that remain to be systematically investigated. For instance, experience affects observational skills and practice. Berliner (1986) found that when experts, novices, and postulants (his term for non-teaching professionals) remarked on photographs of classroom events, novices' and postulants' observations remained at a surface level, while experts conjectured about explanatory principles. The novice saw "a room of students sitting at tables," while the expert described "students maybe doing small-group discussion on a project, because the seats are not in rows" (p. 10).

Systematic professional development probably matters more than random experience. In a series of studies, Michigan State researchers investigated the consistency of clinicians' diagnoses with their own and those of other clinicians (Gil, Polin, Visonhaler, & Van Roekel, 1980; Weinshank, 1979; Visonhaler, 1979). Reading clinicians, learning disability teachers, and classroom teachers made diagnostic judgments of simulated reading and learning difficulties. Correlations were in the low teens. After five weeks of training designed to improve judgmental consistency, however, diagnostic agreement among participants doubled (Visonhaler, Weinshank, Polin, & Wagner, 1983).

The final set of techniques covers the areas of performance assessment, writing, and portfolios. Except for writing, research in these domains remains nascent, with little empirical research available. As noted in the preceding section, writing in today's classrooms is embedded in a complex bundle of language activities, but systematic assessment does not emerge as a distinctive and explicit part of the package.

Performance assessment offers promise for enhancing current practice. Unlike observations, which must follow the twists and turns of classroom dynamics, performance assessment starts with a substantive task designed especially for evaluation, directed toward a summative accomplishment. The concept is that the teacher directs the design, the implementation, and the evaluation of the criterion task. An interesting lead for this process comes from the distinction between routine and adaptive expertise (Hatano, 1982; Brown & Campione, 1984). The routine expert is competent and fluent at performing the job, to the point that the activity is completely automated. The adaptive expert is equally facile but also possesses the capability to leave the automatic mode for a metalevel of analysis. For the teacher, this stance means moving from subject matter expertise to the student's perspective (Palincsar & Brown, in press). If performance assessment is to retain the dynamic quality in the present conception, then teacher expertise may lie in the capacity to become a novice while sustaining a metalevel view.

The teacher needs to develop a similar capacity in process-writing programs. As Brown (1986) argues, the goal is to develop "qualitative, not quantitative, objectivity" (p. 51). This challenge can be addressed in a couple of ways. The first harkens to the days of "grading papers" (e.g., Greenberg, Weiner, & Donovan, 1986), but with emphasis on the higher levels of discourse (topic, structure, audience) rather than mechanical details. White (1986) discusses the establishment of an interpretive community that can respond consistently to student writing, that can articulate the basis for judgments, and that sustains itself through collegial interactions. The second approach is the response journal (Flitterman-King, 1988), which joins the notion of comprehension as reconstruction with informal written responses to a text. The idea is not to create a book report but "triggers to get the mind working to provoke or impel a response, not to control it." The technique has promise for both instruction and assessment.

In our review, we have been struck by the sparseness of the literature (also see Madaus, 1988). Investigations focus on specific domains rather than a coordinated approach directed by curriculum goals. That is, we have found research on questioning, IRIs, writing, and so on, but *not* on convergent assessment of narrative or expository comprehension through a combination of methods. This concept is implicit in a few pieces (e.g., Genishi & Dyson, 1984) but remains to be clearly articulated.

NEXT STEPS

The main thesis of this chapter has been to contrast two approaches to assessment of student achievement, the first externally mandated for policy guidance, and the second internally driven for instructional direction. Although presented as categories, they are actually endpoints on a continuum. Most existing research and scholarship on this topic address externally mandated assessment and direct efforts to influence classroom instruction. Less work is available on internally driven assessment, where the teacher plays the major role. We have constructed a conceptual framework for this alternative and have compiled whatever information we could locate.

If we were to revise the chapter ten years hence, what would we hope to see beyond current offerings? The main need, of course, is a more extensive array of studies on the influence of informed teacher assessment of student literacy. In this crucial area of the school curriculum, assessment should be intense and continuing; teachers are best situated to meet these criteria. Achieving this goal requires significant change in the routines of teaching, and so the first item on our "wish list" covers staff development. While we think that our proposal is both practically and conceptually sound, it requires empirical verification, the second item on our list.

Staff Development

We have argued that, for assessment of literacy to move beyond today's routines, teachers must possess ideas and procedures of assessment as research. They also need to grasp the techniques of standardized assessment, for we are not suggesting the elimination of these procedures. Whatever the ultimate shape of our proposal, it clearly calls for major changes in classroom ambience. The teacher cannot talk and observe at the same time; Johnston (in press) notes that "For a child to be seen and heard, the child must show and tell."

Altering current patterns of classroom practice will require enhancements of preservice and in-service staff development as regards substance and style. Dorr-Bremme and Herman (1986) found that more than half the respondents had attended workshops presenting alternatives to tests for student assessment. They also said they still relied mostly on tests. This is not the place to examine alternatives to late-afternoon staff development, but current approaches are clearly not working. We imagine increased reliance on school-university consortiums for preservice education, along with demonstration-dissemination schools, where participants can see working models of integrated programs. Changes in assessment practices detached from overall school change are unlikely to have much impact.

Evaluation

Suppose that 10 years hence we could identify programs where teachers were responsible for assessment of student achievement. What evidence would best demonstrate the effectiveness of these programs? Standardized achievement tests would be inadequate, and so the question is not trivial. Solving the problem requires bootstrapping. That is, the evidence of effectiveness must build on teachers' judgments of students' work products and classroom performance. Researchers can then explore the consistency and validity of the judgments, and the conditions that foster effective assessment.

Such an effort does not have to start from scratch. Entire issues of *The Reading Teacher* (Squire, 1987) and *Topics in Language Disorders* (Calfee, 1982b) have been devoted to this topic, a sign of interest by researchers and practitioners. The Assessment Performance Unit (APU, 1987; Burstall, 1986) has conducted wide-scale national assessments in England and Wales that serve policy purposes but also act as a stimulant for staff development and a source of evaluation data.

The teaching profession is at a crossroads (Darling-Hammond, 1988). Elementary teachers in particular are described as semi-professionals. Their primary responsibility, helping youngsters become literate, presently takes shape as skills development driven by prescribed materials. The argument in this chapter points a direction for reprofessionalization. We propose that the concept of critical literacy, coupled with a view of informed teacher judgment as the key to effective assessment, provide the foundation for creating a significant agenda for theory, research, and practice during the next decade.

REFERENCES

Afflerbach, P. (1987). *The statewide assessment of reading.* Paper presented at the annual meeting of the American Educational Research Association, Washington, DC.

Airasian, P. W. (1987). State-mandated testing and educational reform: Context and consequences. *American Journal of Education, 95,* 393–412.

Airasian, P. W. (1988). MDI (management driven instruction): A closer look. *Education Measurement, 7* (4), 6–11.

Alexander, L. (1987). *The nation's report card: Improving the assessment of student achievement.* Cambridge, MA: National Academy of Education.

Allington, R. L. (1978). Teacher ability in recording oral reading performance. *Academic Therapy, 14,* 187–192.

Alvermann, D. E., Dillon, D. R., & O'Brien, D. G. (1987). *Using discussion to promote reading comprehension.* Newark, DE: International Reading Association.

Amarel, M., & Chittenden, E. A. (1982). *A conceptual study of knowledge use in schools.* Final report to the National Institute of Education.

Anastasi, A. (Ed.). (1966). *Testing problems in perspective: Twenty-fifth anniversary volume of topical readings from the invitational conference on testing problems.* Washington, DC: American Council on Education.

Anderson, R. C., Hiebert, E. H., Scott, J. A., & Wilkinson, I. A. G. (1985). *Becoming a nation of readers.* Washington, DC: National Institute of Education.

Anderson, R. C., & Pearson, P. D. (1984). The schema-theoretic view of basic processes in reading. In P. D. Pearson (Ed.), *Handbook of reading research* (Vol. 1). New York: Longman.

Applebee, A. (1982). *Tradition and reform in the teaching of English.* Urbana, IL: National Council of Teachers of English.

Applied Performance Unit (1987). *The assessment of reading.* London: NFER-Nelson.

Archbald, D. A., & Newmann, F. M. (1988). *Beyond standardized testing.* Reston, VA: NASSP.

Baker, L., & Brown, A. L. (1984). Cognitive monitoring in reading. In J. Flood (Ed.), *Understanding reading comprehension.* Newark, DE: International Reading Association.

Balmuth, M. (1982). *The roots of phonics: A historical introduction.* New York: McGraw-Hill.

Barr, R., & Dreeben, R., with Wiratchai, N. (1983). *How schools work.* Chicago: University of Chicago Press.

Beldin, H. D. (1970). Informal reading testing: Historical review and review of the research. In William K. Durr (Ed.), *Reading difficulties: Diagnosis, correction, and remediation.* Newark, DE: International Reading Association.

Bereiter, C., & Scardamalia, M. (1987). *The psychology of written composition.* Hillsdale, NJ: Erlbaum.

Berk, R. A. (Ed.) (1986). *Performance assessment: Methods and applications.* Baltimore, MD: Johns Hopkins Press.

Berliner, D. C. (1986). In pursuit of the expert pedagogue. *Educational Researcher, 15,* 5–13.

Bissex, G. L., & Bullock, R. H. (Eds.). (1987). *Seeing for ourselves: Case-study research by teachers of writing.* Portsmouth, NH: Heinemann.

Bloom, B. S., Hastings, J. T., & Madaus, G. F. (Eds.). (1971). *Handbook of formative and summative evaluation of student learning.* New York: McGraw-Hill.

Bracey, G. W. (1987). Measurement-driven instruction: Catchy phrase, dangerous practice. *Phi Delta Kappan, 69,* 683–686.

Brandt, R. (Ed.). (1989). Strategies for teaching and learning strategies. [Special issue]. *Educational Leadership, 46*(4).

Brown, R. (1986). A personal statement on writing assessment and education policy. In K. Greenberg, H. Weiner, & E. Donovan (Eds.), *Writing assessment: Issues and strategies.* White Plains, NY: Longman.

Brown, R. (1987). Who is accountable for thoughtfulness? *Phi Delta Kappan, 69*(1), 49–52.

Brown, A. L., & Campione, J. C. (1984). Three faces of transfer. In M. E. Lamb, A. L. Brown, & B. Rogoff (Eds.), *Advances in developmental psychology,* (Vol. 3). Hillsdale, NJ: Erlbaum.

Burnham, C. C. (1986). Portfolio evaluation: Room to breathe and grow. In C. Bridges (Ed.), *Training the teacher of college composition.* Urbana, IL: National Council of Teachers of English.

Burstall, C. (1986). Innovative forms of assessment: A UK perspective. *Educational Measurement, 5,* 17–22.

Calfee, R. C. (1982a). Literacy and illiteracy: Teaching the nonreader to survive in the modern world. *Annals of Dyslexia, 32,* 71–91. The Orton Dyslexia Society.

Calfee, R. C. (Ed.). (1982b). Assessment of formal school language: Reading, writing, and speaking. [Special issue]. *Topics in Language Disorders, 2.*

Calfee, R. C. (1984). The two faces of achievement tests: The Study of Stanford and the Schools. Stanford, CA: Stanford University.

Calfee, R. C. (1988). *Indicators of literacy: A monograph for the Center for Policy Research in Education.* Santa Monica, CA: RAND Corporation.

Calfee, R. C., & Drum, P. (1979). How the researcher can help the reading teacher with classroom assessment. In L. B. Resnick & P. A. Weaver (Eds.), *Theory and practice of early reading.* Hillsdale, NJ: Erlbaum.

Calfee, R. C., & Drum, P. A. (1986). Research on teaching reading. In M. C. Wittrock (Ed.), *Handbook of research on teaching* (3rd Ed). New York: Macmillan.

Calfee, R. C., & Hiebert, E. (1988). The teacher's role in using assessment to improve learning. In C. V. Bunderson (Ed.), *Assessment in the service of learning.* Princeton, NJ: Educational Testing Service.

Calkins, L. M. (1983). *Lessons from a child.* Portsmouth, NJ: Heinemann.

Campbell, D. T. (1975). Assessing the impact of planned social change. In *Social research and public policies: The Dartmouth/OECD conference.* Hanover, NH: Public Affairs Center, Dartmouth Center.

Cannell, J. J. (1988). The Lake Woebegon effect revisited. *Educational Measurement, 7*(4), 12–15.

Carver, R. P. (1985). Is the degrees of reading power test valid or invalid? *Journal of Reading, 29*(1), 34–41.

Chall, J. S. (1983). *Stages of reading development.* New York: McGraw-Hill.

Chambliss, M. J., & Calfee, R. C. (1989). Designing textbooks to enhance student understanding. *Educational Psychologist, 24*(3), 307–322.

Chapman, C. (1988). *Can writing assessment improve writing instruction?* Paper presented at the 18th Annual Assessment Conference. Boulder, CO: Educational Commission of the States.

Clark, C. M., & Peterson, P. L. (1986). In M. C. Wittrock (Ed.), *Handbook of research on teaching* (3rd ed.). New York: Macmillan.

Clark, C. M., & Yinger, R. J. (1977). Research on teacher thinking. *Curriculum Inquiry, 7*(4), 279–394.

Clifford, G. J. (1987). A Sisyphean task: Historical perspectives on the relationship between writing and reading instruction. To appear in A. J. Dyson (Ed.), *Writing and reading: Collaboration in the classroom.* Berkeley: University of California Press.

Cohen, S. A. (1987). Instructional alignment: Searching for a magic bullet. *Educational Researcher, 15,* 16–20.

Coladarci, T. (1986). Accuracy of teacher judgments of student responses to standardized test items. *Journal of Educational Psychology, 78,* 141–146.

Cole, N. S. (1988). A realist's appraisal of the prospects for unifying instruction and assessment. In C. V. Bunderson (Ed.), *Assessment in the service of learning.* Princeton, NJ: Educational Testing Service.

College Board (1981). *Degrees of reading power brings the student and the text together.* New York: College Board.

Cooley, W., & Bickel, W. (1986). *Decision-oriented educational research.* Boston: Kluver-Nijhoff Publishing.

Corbett, D., & Wilson, B. (1987). Abstract of technical report comparing effects of state minimum competency testing programs in Maryland and Pennsylvania.

Corno, L., & Snow, R. E. (1986). Adapting teaching to individual differences among learners. In M. C. Wittrock (Ed.), *Handbook of research on teaching* (3rd ed.). New York: Macmillan.

Cronbach, L. J. (1960). *Essentials of psychological testing* (3rd ed.). New York: Harper & Row.

Cronbach, L. J. (1988). Five perspectives on the validity argument. In H. Wainer & H. Braun (Eds.), *Test validity.* Hillsdale, NJ: Erlbaum.

Cronbach, L. J., & Furby, L. (1970). How should we measure "change"—or should we? *Psychological Bulletin, 74,* 68–80.

Crowell, R., & Tissot, R. (1986). *Curriculum alignment*. Elmhurst, IL: North Central Regional Educational Laboratory.

Darling-Hammond, L. (1988). The futures of teaching. *Educational Leadership, 46*(3), 4–10.

Davis, F. B. (1968). Research in comprehension in reading. *Reading Research Quarterly, 3*, 499–545.

Dillon, J. T. (1988a). *Questioning and teaching: A manual of practice*. New York: Teachers College Press, Columbia University.

Dillon, J. T. (1988b). *Questioning and discussion: A multidisciplinary study*. Norwood, NJ: Ablex.

Dorr-Bremme, D. W., & Herman, J. L. (1986). *Assessing student achievement: A profile of classroom practices* (CSE Monograph No. 11). Los Angeles: Center for the Study of Evaluation, UCLA.

Drum, P. A., Calfee, R. C., & Cook, L. K. (1981). The effects of surface structure variables on performance in reading comprehension tests. *Reading Research Quarterly, 16*, 486–514.

Dufflemeyer, F. A., & Adamson, S. (1986). Matching students with instructional level materials using the *Degrees of Reading Power* system. *Reading Research and Instruction. 25*, 192–200.

Duffy, G. (1977). *A study of teacher conceptions of reading*. Paper presented at the annual meeting of the National Reading Conference, New Orleans.

Edmonds, R. (1985). Characteristics of effective schools. In J. Osborn, P. T. Wilson, and R. C. Anderson (Eds.), *Reading education: Foundations for a literate America*. Lexington, MA: Lexington Books.

Educational Testing Service (1984). *Four keys to classroom testing*. Princeton, NJ: Educational Testing Service.

Educational Testing Service (1988). *State educational standards*. Princeton, NJ: Educational Testing Service.

Egan, O., & Archer, P. (1985). The accuracy of teachers' ratings of ability: A regression model. *American Educational Research Journal, 22*(1), 25–34.

Elmore, R. F., & McLaughlin, M. W. (1988). *Steady work*. Washington, DC: Rand Corporation.

Evertson, C. M., & Green, J. L. (1986). Observation as inquiry and method. In M. C. Wittrock, *Handbook of research on teaching* (3rd ed.). New York: Macmillan.

Farr, R., & Carey, R. F. (1986). *Reading: What can be measured?* (2nd ed.). Newark DE: International Reading Association.

Feuerstein, R. (1979). *The dynamic assessment of retarded performers: The learning potential assessment device, theory, instrument, and techniques*. Baltimore, MD: University Park Press.

Fisher, C. W., Filby, N. N., Marliave, R., Cahen, L. S., Dishaw, M. M., Moore, J. E., & Berlinger, D. C. (1978) *Teaching behaviors, academic learning time, and student achievement* (Technical Report V-1). San Francisco: Far West Regional Educational Laboratory.

Flanders, N. A. (1970). *Analyzing teacher behavior*. Reading, MA: Addison-Wesley.

Flitterman-King, S. (1988). The role of the response journal in active reading. *Quarterly of National Writing Project and Center for the Study of Writing, 10*(3), 4–11.

Flood, J., & Lapp, D. (1986). Types of texts: The match between what students read in basals and what they encounter in tests. *Reading Research Quarterly, 21*, 284–297.

Foley, J. P., & Bagley, M. T. (1988). *Suppose the wolf were an octopus? K to 2: A guide to creative questioning for primary grade literature*. Monroe, NY: Trillium Press.

Fraatz, J. M. B. (1987). *The politics of reading: Power, opportunity, and prospects for change in American public schools*. New York: Teachers College Press, Columbia University.

Fuchs, L. S., & Fuchs, D. (1989). Curriculum-based assessment. In C. Reynolds & R. R. Kamphaus (Eds.), *Handbook of psychological and educational assessment of children—Vol. 1: Intelligence and achievement*. New York: Guilford Press.

Fuchs, L. S., Fuchs, D., & Hamlett, C. L. (1989). Computer and curriculum-based measurement. *School Psychology Review, 18*, 112–125.

Gage, N. L. (1978). *The scientific basis of the art of teaching*. New York: Teachers College Press, Columbia University.

Gall, M. D. (1984). Synthesis of research on questioning. *Educational Leadership. 42*, 40–47.

Gall, M. D., & Gall, J. D. (1976). The discussion method. In N. L. Gage (Ed.), *The psychology of teaching methods: The Seventy-fifth yearbook of the NSSE, Part I* (pp. 166–216). Chicago: University of Chicago Press.

Gallup, A. M., & Elam, S. M. (1988). 20th national Gallup poll of public attitudes towards schools. *Phi Delta Kappan, 70*, 33–46.

Genishi, C., & Dyson, A. H. (1984). *Language assessment in the early years*. Norwood, NJ: Ablex.

Gil, D., Polin, R. M., Vinsonhaler, J. F., & Van Roekel, J. (1980). *The impact of training on diagnostic consistency* (Technical Report No. 67). East Lansing, MI: Institute for Research on Teaching.

Glaser, R. (1963). Instructional technology and the measurement of learning outcomes: Some questions. *American Psychologist, 18*, 519–521.

Glaser, R. (1986). The integration of instruction and testing. In *Proceedings of the 1985 ETS invitational conference: The redesign of testing for the 21st century*. Princeton, NJ: Educational Testing Service.

Goodlad, J. I. (1984). *A place called school*. New York: McGraw-Hill.

Goodman, K. S., Goodman, Y. M., & Hood, W. J. (Eds.). (1989). *The whole language evaluation book*. Portsmouth, NH: Heinemann.

Goodman, Y. M., Watson, D., & Burke, C. L. (1987). *Reading miscue analysis*. New York: R. C. Owen

Publishers.

Goswami, D., & Stillman, P. R. (Eds.). (1987). *Reclaiming the classroom: Teacher research as an agency for change*. Upper Montclair, NJ: Boynton Cook.

Graesser, A. C., & Black, J. B. (1985). *The psychology of questions*. Hillsdale, NJ: Erlbaum.

Graesser, A. C., Lang, K., & Horgan, D. (1988). A taxonomy for question generation. *Questioning Exchange*, 2, 3–15.

Grant Foundation. (1988). *The forgotten half: Pathways to success for America's youth and young families*. Washington, DC: William T. Grant Foundation Commission on Work, Family, and Citizenship.

Graves, D. (1983). *Writing, Teachers and children at work*. Portsmouth, NH: Heinemann.

Gray, J. (1986). University of California–Berkeley: Bay Area and National Writing Projects. In D. Fortune (Ed.), *School–college collaboration in English*. New York: Modern Language Association.

Gray, W. S. (1920). The value of informal tests of reading achievement. *Journal of Educational Research*, 1(2), 103–111.

Greenberg, K. L., Wiener, H. S., & Donovan, R. A. (Eds.). (1986). *Writing assessment: Issues and strategies*. White Plains, NY: Longman.

Greene, H. A., & Gray, W. S. (1946). The measurement of understanding in the language arts. In N. B. Henry (Ed.), *The forty-fifth yearbook of the National Society for the Study of Education*. Chicago, IL: University of Chicago Press.

Haertel, E., & Calfee, R. C. (1983). School achievement: Thinking about what to test. *Journal of Educational Measurement*, 20, 119–130.

Haney, W. (1981). Validity, vaudeville, and values: A short history of social concerns over standardized testing. *American Psychologist*, 36(10), 1021–1034.

Harris, L. A., & Lalik, R. M. (1987). Teachers' use of informal reading inventories: An example of school constraints. *Reading Teacher*, 40, 624–630.

Hatano, G. (1982). Cognitive consequences of practice in culture specific procedural skills. *Quarterly Newsletter of the Laboratory of Comparative Human Cognition*, 4(1), 15–18.

Heath, S. B. (1980). Questioning at home and at school: A comparative study. In G. Spindler (Ed.), *Doing the ethnography of schooling: Educational anthropology in action*. New York: Holt, Rinehart & Winston.

Heath, S. B. (1983). *Ways with words*. Cambridge, Eng.: Cambridge University Press.

Heath, S. B. (1990). The sense of being literate: Historical and cross-cultural features. See this volume, pp. 3–25.

Heller, K. A., Holtzman, W. H., & Messick, S. (Eds.). (1982). *Placing children in special education: A strategy for equity*. Washington, DC: National Academy Press.

Henry, N. B. (Ed.). (1946). *The forty-fifth yearbook of the National Society for the Study of Education. Part 1: The measurement of understanding*. Chicago, IL: University of Chicago Press.

Hiebert, E. H., Calfee, R. C. (1989). Advancing academic literacy through teachers' assessments. *Educational Leadership*, 46(7), 50–54.

Hiebert, E. H., & Calfee, R. C. (in press). What research has to say to the classroom teacher: Assessment. In A. Farstrup and S. J. Samuels (Eds.), *What research has to say about reading instruction*. Newark, DE: International Reading Association.

Hoge, R. D. (1983). Pyschometric properties of teacher-judgment measures of pupil aptitudes, classroom behaviors, and achievement levels. *Journal of Special Education*, 17(4), 401–429.

Hoge, R. D., & Butcher, R. (1984). Analysis of teacher judgments of pupil achievement levels. *Journal of Educational Psychology*, 76(5), 777–781.

Hoopfer, L., & Huntsberger, M. (1986). An ethnomethodological perspective on reading assessment. *Forum in Reading and Language Education*, 2, 103–123.

Hopkins, K. D., George, C. A., & Williams, D. D. (1985). The concurrent validity of standardized achievement tests by content area using teachers' ratings as criteria. *Journal of Educational Measurement*, 22(3), 177–182.

Horowitz, R., & Samuels, S. J. (Eds.). (1987). *Comprehending oral and written language*. New York: Academic Press.

Houts, P. L. (1977). *Myth of measurability*. New York: Hart Publishing Company.

Hunkins, F. P. (1989). *Teaching thinking through effective questioning*. Boston, MA: Christopher-Gordon.

Johns, J. L. (1988). *Basic reading inventory*. Dubuque, IA: Kendall Hunt Publishing.

Johnson, M. S., Kress, R. A., & Pikulski, J. J. (1987). *Informal reading inventories*, Newark, DE: International Reading Association.

Johnston, P. H. (1983). *Reading comprehension assessment: A cognitive basis*. Newark, DE: International Reading Association.

Johnston, P. H. (1984a). Assessment in reading. In P. D. Pearson, R. Barr, M. L. Kamil, & P. Mosenthal (Eds.), *Handbook of reading research*, (Vol. 1). White Plains, NY: Longman.

Johnston, P. H. (1984b). Prior knowledge and reading comprehension test bias. *Reading Research Quarterly*, 19, 219–239.

Johnston, P. H. (in press). Steps toward a more naturalistic approach to the assessment of the reading process. In J. Algina & S. Legg (Eds.), *Cognitive assessment of language and mathematics outcomes*. Norwood, NJ: Ablex.

Jongsma, K. S., & Jongsma, E. A. (1981). Test review: Commercial informal reading inventories. *Reading Teacher, 34*, 697–705.

Lamberg, W. J., Rodriguez, L., & Tomas, D. (1978). *Training in identifying oral reading departures from text which can be explained as Spanish-English phonological differences.* Paper presented at the annual meeting of the Southwest Educational Research Association, Austin, Texas.

Langer, J. A. (1987). The construction of meaning and the assessment of comprehension: An analysis of reader performance on standardized test items. In R. Q. Freedle & R. P. Duran (Eds.), *Cognitive and linguistic analyses of test performance.* Norwood, NJ: Ablex.

Leinhardt, F., & Seewald, A. M. (1981). Overlap: What's tested, what's taught. *Journal of Educational Measurement, 18*, 85–96.

LeMahieu, P. G. (1984). The effects on achievement and instructional content of a program of student monitoring through frequent testing. *Educational Evaluation and Policy Analysis. 6*, 175–187.

Lerner, B. (1981). The minimum competence testing movement: Social, scientific, and legal implications. *American Psychologist, 36*(10), 1057–1066.

Lidz, C. (Ed.). (1987). *Dynamic assessment: An interactional approach to evaluating learning potential.* New York: Guilford Press.

Linn, R. L. (1986). Educational testing and assessment: Research needs and policy issues. *American Psychologist, 41*, 1153–1160.

Linn, R. L. (Ed.). (1988). *Educational measurement* (3rd ed.). New York: Macmillan.

Lipson, M. Y., & Wixon, K. K. (1986). Reading disability research: An interactionist perspective. *Review of Education Research, 56*, 111–136.

Lucas, C. K. (1988). Toward ecological evaluation. *Quarterly of National Writing Project & Center for the Study of Writing, 10*, 1.

Lukens, R. J. (1982). *A critical handbook of children's literature* (2nd ed.). Oxford, OH: Scott, Foresman.

McClelland, M. C. (1988). Testing and reform. *Phi Delta Kappan, 69*(10), 768–772.

McDonald, F. J., & Elias, P. J. (1975). *The effects of teaching performances on pupil learning: Final report, Phase II BTES, Vol. I.* Princeton, NJ: Educational Testing Service.

McKeown, M. G., & Curtis, M. E. (Eds.). (1987). *The nature of vocabulary acquisition.* Hillsdale, NJ: Erlbaum.

McNeil, L. M. (1986). *Contradictions of control.* New York: Routledge & Kegan Paul.

NcNeil, L. M. (1988a). Contradictions of control, Part 1: Administrators and teachers. *Phi Delta Kappan, 69*, 333–339.

McNeil, L. M. (1988b). Contradictions of control, Part 2: Teachers, students, and curriculum. *Phi Delta Kappan. 69*, 433–438.

McNeil, L. M. (1988c). Contradictions of control, Part 3: Contradictions of reform. *Phi Delta Kappan, 69*, 478–485.

Madaus, G. F. (1985). Test scores as administrative mechanisms in education policy. *Phi Delta Kappan, 66*, 611–617.

Madaus, G. F. (1988). The influence of testing on the curriculum. In L. N. Tanner (Ed.), *Critical issues in the curriculum: Eighty-seventh yearbook of the National Society for the Study of Education.* Chicago, IL: University of Chicago Press.

Marshall, H. H. (1988). Work or learning: Implications of classroom metaphors. *Educational Researcher, 17*(9), 9–16.

Martin, A. (1988). Screening early intervention and remediation: Obscuring children's potential. *Harvard Educational Review, 58*, 488–501.

Marzano, R. J., & Costa, A. L. (1988). Question: Do standardized tests measure general cognitive skill? Answer: No. *Educational Leadership, 45*, 66–71.

Mathison, S. M. (1987). *The perceived effects of standardized testing on teaching and curriculum.* Unpublished dissertation, University of Illinois, Urbana–Champaign.

Mehan, H., Hertweck, A., Combs, S. E., & Flynn, P. J. (1982). Teachers' interpretations of students' behavior. In L. C. Wilkinson (Ed.), *Communicating in the classroom.* New York: Academic Press.

Mehrens, W. A., & Kaminski, J. (1988). *Using commercial test preparation materials for improving standardized test scores: Fruitful, fruitless, or fraudulent?* Paper presented at a symposium "Past presidents speak on the issues" at the annual meeting of the National Council of Measurement in Education, New Orleans.

Messick S. (1988). Meaning and values in test validation: The science and ethics of assessment. Paper presented at the annual meeting of AERA/NCME, New Orleans.

Meyer, B. J. F. (1985). Prose analysis: Purposes, procedures, and problems. In B. K. Britton & J. B. Black (Eds.), *Understanding expository text.* Hillsdale, NJ: Erlbaum.

Moffett, J., & Wagner, B. J. (1983). *Student-centered language arts and reading, K-13: A handbook for teachers* (3rd ed.). Boston, MA: Houghton Mifflin.

Moore, D. W. (1983). A case for naturalistic assessment of reading comprehension. *Language Arts, 60*, 957–969.

Morine-Dershimer, G., & Vallance, E. (1976). *Teacher planning* (Beginning Teacher Evaluation Study, Special Report C). San Francisco: Far West Laboratory.

Myers, M. (1985). *The teacher-researcher: How to study writing in the classroom.* Urbana, IL: ERIC Clearinghouse on Reading and Communication Skills and National Council of Teachers of English.

National Assessment of Educational Progress. (1989). *American education at the crossroads*. Princeton, NJ: Educational Testing Service.

Newkirk, T., & Atwell, N. (Eds.). (1982). *Understanding writing: Ways of observing, learning, and teaching*. Chelmsford, MA: Northeast Regional Exchange.

Nystrand, M. (1987). *Review of selected national tests of writing and reading*. Madison, WI: National Center on Effective Secondary Schools.

Office of Educational Research and Improvement (1988). *Creating responsible and responsive accountability systems*. Washington, DC: Department of Education.

Olson, D. R. (1977). From utterance to text: The bias of language in speech and writing. *Harvard Educational Review, 47*(3), 257–281.

Page, W. D., & Carlson, K. L. (1975). The process of observing oral reading scores. *Reading horizons, 15*, 147–150.

Palincsar, A. S. (1986). The role of dialogue in providing scaffolded instruction. *Educational Psychologist, 21*, 73–98.

Palincsar, A. S., & Brown, A. L. (in press). Classroom dialogues to promote self-regulated learning. In J. Brophy (Ed.), *Teaching for understanding and self-regulated learning* (Vol. 1). Greenwich, CT: JAI Press.

Palincsar, A. S., Stevens, D. D., & Gavelek, J. R. (1988). *Collaborating in the interest of collaborative learning*. New Orleans: AERA.

Paratore, J. R., & Indrisano, R. (1987). Intervention assessment of reading comprehension. *Reading Teacher, 40*(8), 778–783.

Paris, S. G. (Ed.). (1987). Current issues in reading comprehension [Special issue]. *Educational Psychologist, 22*(3–4).

Pearson, P. D., & Valencia, S. (1987). Assessment, accountability, and professional prerogative. In J. E. Readance & R. S. Baldwin (Eds.), *Research in Literacy: Merging Perspectives*. 36th Yearbook of the National Reading Conference. Rochester, NY: National Reading Conference.

Perkins, D. N., & Salomon, G. (1988). Teaching for transfer. *Educational Leadership, 45*, 22–32.

Perry, J. D., Guidubaldi, J., & Kehle, T. K. (1979). Kindergarten competencies as predictors of third-grade classroom behavior and achievement. *Journal of Educational Psychology, 71*(4), 443–450.

Peterson, P. L., Marx, R. W., & Clark, C. M. (1978). Teacher planning, teacher behavior, and student achievement. *American Educational Research Journal, 15*, 417–432.

Pikulski, J. J., & Shanahan, T. (Eds.). (1982). *Approaches to the informal evaluation of reading*. Newark, DE: IRA.

Popham, W. J. (1985). Measurement-driven instruction: It's on the road. *Phi Delta Kappan, 66*, 628–634.

Popham, W. J. (1987a). The merits of measurement-driven instruction. *Phi Delta Kappan, 68*, 679–682.

Popham, W. J. (1987b). Muddle-minded emotionalism. *Phi Delta Kappan. 68*, 687–689.

Porter, A. (1988). Indicators: Objective data or political tool? *Phi Delta Kappan, 69*, 503–508.

Reeves, M. S. (1986). Back to the beginning: Rethinking the elementary years. *Education Week, 69*, 16–19.

Resnick, D. P., & Resnick, L. B. (1985). Standards, curriculum, and performance: A historical and comparative perspective. *Educational Researcher, 14*, 5–20.

Richert, A. E. (1988). *Teaching teachers to reflect: A consideration of program structure*. Draft: Oakland, CA.

Roe, B. D., & Aiken, R. (1976). A CAI simulation program for teaching IRI techniques. *Journal of Computer Based Instruction, 2*, 52–56.

Rosenblatt, L. M. (1989). Writing and reading: The transactional theory. In J. M. Mason (Ed.), *Reading and writing connections*. Boston: Allyn & Bacon.

Ruddell, R. B. (1985). Knowledge and attitudes toward testing: Field educators and legislators. *Reading Teacher, 38*, 538–543.

Rudman, H. E., Keeley, J. L., Wanous, D. S., Mehrens, W. A., Clark, C. M., & Porter, A. C. (1980). *Integrating assessment with instruction: A review (1922–1980)* (Research Series No. 75). East Lansing, MI: Michigan State University, Institute for Research on Teaching. (ERIC Document Reproduction Service No. ED 189 136).

Ruth, L., & Murphy, S. (1988). *Designing writing tasks for the assessment of writing*. Norwood, NJ: Ablex.

Salmon-Cox, L. (1981). Teachers and standardized achievement tests: What's really happening? *Phi Delta Kappan, 62*, 631–634.

Samuelson, F. (1987). Was early mental testing: (a) racist inspired, (b) an objective science, (c) a technology for democracy, (d) the origin of multiple-choice exams, (e) none of the above? (mark the RIGHT answer). In M. M. Sokal (Ed.), *Psychological testing and American society, 1890–1930*. New Brunswick, NJ: Rutgers University Press.

Schell, L. M., & Hanna, G. S. (1982). Can informal reading inventories reveal strengths and weaknesses in comprehension subskills? *Reading Teacher, 35*, 263–268.

Shannon, P. (1989). *Broken promises: Reading instruction in twentieth-century America*. Westport, CT: Bergin & Garvey Publishers, Inc.

Shavelson, R. J., & Borko, H. (1979). Research on teachers' decisions in planning instruction. *Educational Horizons, 57*(4), 183–189.

Shepard, L. (1988). *Should instruction be measurement-driven?* Presented in debate on Measurement-Driven Instruction at the annual meeting of the American Educational Research Association, New Orleans.

Shuell, T. J. (1988). Teaching and learning as problem solving. In J. Brophy (Chair), *Metaphors of classroom research*. (Symposium conducted at the meeting of the American Educational Research Association, New Orleans).

Smith, E. R., & Tyler, R. W. (1942) *Appraising and recording student progress*. New York: Harper & Row.

Smith, N. B. (1986). *American reading instruction*. Newark, DE: International Reading Association.

Snow, R. E. (1980). Aptitude and achievement. In W. B. Schrader (Ed.), *Measuring achievement: Progress over a decade: New directions for testing and measurement* (No. 5). San Francisco: Jossey-Bass. (Proceedings of the 1979 ETS Invitational Conference).

Sokal, M. M. (Ed.). (1987). *Psychological testing and American society*. New Brunswick, NJ: Rutgers University Press.

Spivey, N. N. (1987). Constructing constructivism: Reading research in the U.S. *Poetics, 16*, 169–192.

Squire, J. (Ed.). (1987). The state of assessment in reading. [Special issue]. *Reading Teacher, 40*(8).

Stanley, J. C., & Hopkins, K. D. (1972). *Educational and psychological measurement and evaluation*. Englewood Cliffs, NJ: Prentice Hall.

Stedman, L. C. (1987) It's time we changed the effective schools formula. *Phi Delta Kappan, 69*, 215–224.

Stein, N. L., & Glenn, C. G. (1979). An analysis of story comprehension in elementary school children. In R. Freedle (Ed.), *New directions in discourse processing*. Norwood, NJ: Ablex.

Stiggins, R. J. (1985). Improving assessment where it means the most: In the classroom. *Educational Leadership, 43*, 69–74.

Stiggins, R. J. (1987). Design and development of performance assessments. *Educational Measurement, 6*, 33–42.

Stiggins, R. J., Conklin, N. F., Green, K. R., & Brody, C. (1986). *A feeling for the student: Understanding the art of classroom assessment*. Portland, OR: Northwest Regional Educational Laboratory.

Stiggins, R. J., Conklin, N. F., & Bridgeford, N. J. (1986). Classroom assessment: A key to effective education. *Educational Measurement: Issues and practices, 5*(2), 5–17.

Taba, H. (1962). *Curriculum development: Theory and practice*. New York: Harcourt, Brace, and World.

Taylor, P. H. (1970). *How teachers plan their courses*. Slough, Berkshire, Eng.: National Foundation for Education Research.

Taylor, P. H. (1986). *Expertise and the primary school teacher*. Windsor, Eng.: NFER-Nelson.

Thorndike, R. L. (1973). Dilemmas in diagnosis. In W. J. MacGinitie (Ed.), *Assessment problems in reading*. Newark, DE: International Reading Association.

Thurlow, M. L., & Ysseldyke, J. E. (1980). Current assessment and decision-making practices in model LD programs. *Learning Disability Quarterly, 2*, 15–24.

Tindal, G., Fuchs, L. S., Fuchs, D., Sinn, M. R., Deno, S. L., & Germann, G. (1985). Empirical validation of criterion-referenced tests. *Journal of Educational Research, 78*, 203–209.

Tyler, R. W., & White, S. J. (1979). *Testing, teaching, and learning: Report of a conference on research on testing*. Washington, DC: National Institute of Education, U.S. Department of Health, Education, and Welfare.

Valencia, S. W. (in press). National survey of the use of reading test data for educational decision-making. In P. Afflerbach (Ed.), *Issues in statewide reading assessment*. Washington, D. C.: American Institutes for Research.

Valencia, S. W., McGinley, W., & Pearson, P. D. (in press). Assessing reading and writing: Building a more complete picture. In G. Duffy (Ed.), *Reading in the middle school* (2nd ed.). Newark, DE: International Reading Association.

Venezky, R. L. (1970). *The structure of English orthography*. The Hague, Paris: Mouton.

Venezky, R. L. (1987). A history of the American reading textbook. *Elementary School Journal, 87*, 247–265.

Vickers, D. (1988). *Can writing assessment improve writing instruction?* Paper presented at the 18th Annual Assessment Conference. Boulder, CO: Educational Commission of the States.

Vinsonhaler, J. F. (1979). *The consistency of reading diagnosis* (Research Series No. 28). East Lansing: Institute for Research on Teaching, Michigan State University.

Visonhaler, J. F., Weinshank, A. B., Polin, R. M., & Wagner, C. C. (1983). *Improving diagnostic reliability in reading through training* (Research Series 176). East Lansing: Michigan State University, Institute for Research on Teaching. (ERIC Document Reproduction Service No. ED 237 934).

Weinshank, A. (1979, June). *An observational study of the relationship between diagnosis and remediation in reading* (Research Series No. 72). East Lansing: Institute for Research on Teaching, Michigan State University.

Whipple, G. M. (1918). *The seventeenth yearbook of the National Society for the Study of Education: Part II*. Bloomington, IL: Public School Publishing Company.

Whipple, G. M. (1925). *The twenty-fourth yearbook of the National Society for the Study of Education: Part I*. Bloomington, IL: Public School Publishing Company.

White, J. (1986). *The assessment of writing: Pupils aged 11 and 15*. Windsor, Eng.: NFER-Nelson.

Wilen, W. W. (1986). *Questioning skills for teachers* (2nd ed.). Washington, DC: National Education Association.

Wiley, D. E. (1988, April). *Alignment of test and curriculum: Some concepts and comments*. (Presented at symposium on "Issues in the alignment of curriculum and assessment" at the annual meeting of the American Educational Research Association, New Orleans).

Wilhelm, D. (1988). Vermonters eye student portfolios as tool in evaluating their schools. *Boston Globe*, Boston, MA (November 13).

Wixon, K. K., & Peters, C. W. (1987). Comprehension assessment: Implementing an interactive view of reading. *Educational Psychologist, 22,* 333–356.

Woodward, A. (1987). *From the professional teacher to activities manager: The changing role of the teacher in Reading Teachers' Guides, 1920–1985.* Paper presented at annual meeting of the American Educational Research Association, Washington, DC: April 20–24.

13 COMPUTERS IN READING AND WRITING

David Reinking
and Lillian Bridwell-Bowles

Historically, written language and technology have shared a parallel and complementary evolution. The invention of writing was itself an unprecedented technological advancement that led to the emergence of highly technological societies (see Ong, 1982). Successive technological developments such as the invention of the printing press have influenced considerably the nature of written communication. Consequently, technology has frequently played a dominant role in defining what reading and writing skills have been considered important, as well as how and to whom they were taught. A characteristic of the modern era has been an accelerated pace of technological development that has had notable effects on the form, substance, and purpose of written communication.

Computer technology is the latest page in the history of technology and written language. From our present vantage point it is difficult to argue conclusively that the new and unique effects of computer technology on written language will be pervasive and enduring, but there are indications that this may be the case. The use of computers for composing and disseminating textual information electronically is rapidly becoming a common experience. The proliferation of computers in schools, which began in the mid-1970s, when powerful and affordable microcomputers became available, has led to widespread interest in using computers for instruction in the language arts. Paralleling these trends has been the emergence of a prodigious literature concerning the use of computers for reading and writing. In its earliest stages speculative articles and reviews of instructional software dominated this literature (Nancarrow, Ross, & Bridwell, 1984), but gradually it has grown to include empirical studies and theoretical pieces.

Several factors complicate a review of this literature. One is the diversity of applications employing computer technology in reading and writing (cf. Balajthy, 1987; Blanchard, Mason, & Daniel, 1987; Bridwell, Nancarrow, & Ross, 1984; Kamil, 1987; Mason, 1980; Mason, Blanchard, & Daniel, 1983; Nacarrow, Ross, & Bridwell, 1984; Thompson, 1980). Existing research reflects this diversity, but as a result it lacks depth in several areas. It has also suffered from the conceptual and methodological shortcomings that are characteristic of pursuing new areas of inquiry. Another complication is that the rapid advances in computer technology and changes in the patterns of its use make the task of a reviewer akin to reading yesterday's newspapers. Also, despite the current trend towards merging the fields of reading and writing into a broader concern for literacy, there is a lack of symmetry in the way researchers have approached the use of computers in reading and writing.

We have addressed these complications by reviewing the literature that we believe is historically important, significant to our present knowledge base, or useful in

The authors wish to thank Ernest Balajthy for his reactions to a preliminary draft of this chapter.

setting a course for future research. Consistent with the intent of this volume we have approached our task primarily from the standpoint of researchers interested in data and theoretical positions that lead to testable hypotheses. Except when they are clearly pertinent to these goals, we have not reviewed publications that are predominantly speculative, evaluative, or technical. We also decided to omit reading and writing research in which the computer's role is not central to the purpose of the research. This category includes studies that use the computer to record and to analyze data (e.g., recording response latencies and eye movements) or that use a computer as a metaphor to create a model of language processing. We believe that the extent and importance of these applications are self-evident to anyone examining other reviews of reading and writing research such as those in this handbook; in addition, these applications have been discussed elsewhere (e.g., see Kamil, 1987).

Clearly in this review focused on computers, a comparison of reading research to writing research reveals two divergent emphases. Writing researchers have focused primarily on word processing, while reading researchers have explored a more diverse range of applications. Nonetheless, we have employed a single organizational structure to review both lines of research. This structure has two major sections: (1) the use of computers in reading and writing instruction, and (2) comparisons of electronic and conventional texts. A commentary discussing the strengths, weaknesses, and future directions of instructional research is included at the end of the first section. Although much of the research presented in the second section has implications for instruction, this research has been generated primarily by an interest in how reading and writing electronic text may differ from reading and writing conventional text. A discussion of theoretical perspectives that have emerged from this research follows this latter section.

COMPUTERS IN READING AND WRITING INSTRUCTION

Background

Among educators the most visible and widely discussed applications of computers in reading and writing have been related to instruction. Computers have been used to teach and to drill specific reading and writing skills, to keep records in order to manage students' progress, to motivate reluctant readers and writers, and to engage students in a variety of other computer-based activities that have been used to address the goals of language arts instruction (e.g., programming computers, using data bases, and writing with word-processing programs). Computers have also been integrated into teaching activities across the full spectrum of reading and writing instruction, including early literacy skills (e.g., Daiute, 1986; Schaudt, 1987), content area reading (e.g., Blanchard & Mason, 1985), college reading and writing skills (e.g., Alexander, 1984; Hawisher, 1987; Rosenthal, 1987), style analysis and correction (e.g., Kiefer & Smith, 1983); technical communication (Mikelonis & Gervicks, 1985); adult literacy (e.g., Young & Irwin, 1988), and teacher training (e.g., Alvermann, 1987; Vinsonhaler, Weinshank, Wagner, & Polin, 1983, 1987).

Several indicators suggest that computers are currently considered to be an important, ongoing factor in reading and writing instruction. For example, beginning in the mid-1980s, textbooks intended to prepare instructors to teach reading and writing have typically included separate chapters or major sections on the use of computers (e.g., Leu & Kinzer, 1987; Robinson & Good, 1987; Vacca, Vacca, & Gove, 1987). In addition, several books aimed at acquainting teachers with the use of computers in reading and writing instruction have been published (Balajthy, 1986; Daiute, 1985; Geoffrion & Geoffrion, 1983; Rodrigues & Rodrigues, 1986; Rude, 1986; Schwartz, 1985; Strickland, Feeley, & Wepner, 1987; Wresch, 1984). Major professional organizations like the International Reading Association and the National Council of Teachers of English have standing committees and special interest groups that monitor and disseminate information about the use of computers in reading and writing instruction. The computer in language arts instruction continues to be a topic addressed at professional conferences and in journal articles. Interest in computers for reading and writing instruction is also an international phenomenon. For example, more than 50 projects related to the use of computers for reading and writing have been initiated in Europe (Harrison, 1987; Potter, 1987).

Despite this widespread interest, data gathered since the early 1980s have indicated consistently that computer-based activities are not an integral part of the instructional program in most elementary and secondary schools. A study conducted by the Center for Social Organization in Schools (1983–1984) found that in the typical elementary school one or two teachers used the computer regularly for instruction and that the typical student used a computer for less than a half hour per week. Students in secondary schools used computers more often, but the dominant use was for programming. More recently a report by the Congressional Office of Technology Assessment (1988) estimated that U.S. schools spent approximately $2 billion on computer hardware between 1977 and 1987. In 1987, however, schools averaged only one computer for 30 students. The average student used the computer for one hour per week, a relatively small increase from the early 1980s, given that the number of schools equipped with computers for instructional uses increased from 18 percent to 95 percent between 1981 and 1987.

Other data also suggest that computers are not being used extensively for reading and writing instruction. The study conducted by the Center for Social Organization in Schools (1983–1984), for example, found that fewer than 7 percent of elementary and secondary schools with computers were using them regularly for writing, and that word-processing applications were frequently limited to business education classes. Data from a survey conducted as part of the National Assessment of Educational Progress (Martinez & Mead, 1988) suggest that computers are not being used regularly for instruction across a variety of school subjects. When asked if they had ever used a computer in reading or English classes, only about one-fourth of the third- and seventh-grade students and one-tenth of the eleventh-grade students responded affirmatively.

The use of computers for language arts instruction has also been influenced by the availability and characteristics of commercial software for reading instruction. Information concerning this software can be derived from a number of sources. Survey research conducted by the Technology Assisted Learning Market Information Service (see TALMIS, 1983) revealed that 43 percent of the commercial educational software packages marketed predominantly in the United States were classified by software publishers as designed for language arts instruction. The Educational Products and Information Exchange (EPIE) publishes reviews of educational software and maintains a large data base containing information about language arts software. There were 608 reading programs in this data base in 1984, a 500 percent increase from 1981 (see Haven, 1985, cited in Balajthy, 1987). Rubin (1983) classified the commercial language arts programs in a comprehensive catalog of educational software on the basis of their instructional emphasis. Of the 297 programs classified, only 21 required students to read and comprehend connected text; the remainder focused on individual letters, words, or sentences. Similar findings were reported by Day and Day (1984). They found that of 464 language arts software packages the majority were in the area of vocabulary, spelling, and grammar (51%); programs emphasizing comprehension accounted for only

7 percent of the programs. Reinking, Kling, and Harper (1985) tabulated the characteristics of commercial reading software reviewed in Resources in Computer Education (RICE), a data base containing detailed reviews of educational software. They concluded that typical reading software runs on the Apple II family of computers; employs a drill-and-practice format, often with elements of a game; is targeted for regular instruction in the middle grades; and focuses on reading skills that do not require reading connected texts.

Interpretations of the data from these summaries of commercial software are limited by the rapid changes in computer technology and its use in schools. Furthermore, these summaries omit public domain software as well as computer-based instructional activities that employ software not specifically aimed at language arts instruction (e.g., word-processing and data base programs). Reliable data about how computers are being used for instruction would be useful for characterizing their role in instruction, as would a mechanism for monitoring changes in patterns of their use.

Commercial language arts software has been the object of much criticism, predominantly because of its focus on low-level, isolated skills (see Smith, 1984); its frequent use of drill-and-practice formats (see Chall & Conrad, 1984); and its tendency to evaluate rather than guide students' responses (see Duin, 1987). Although there are a few notable exceptions (e.g., Balajthy, 1984; Siegel & Davis, 1987), much of the support for the use of computers in reading and writing instruction is focused on applications other than the drill and practice of specific skills. There are preliminary indications that publishers of commercial software are beginning to develop more diverse programs for language arts instruction and that they are becoming responsive to the concerns being expressed by educators (Reinking, 1989).

In summary, there is considerable interest in the use of computers for a wide range of applications in reading and writing instruction. This interest has not been linked consistently to commercial software, which although widely available, has been frequently criticized. The results of several national surveys indicate that computers are not being used extensively for instruction in most school subjects, including the language arts. No reliable data are available to indicate precisely how computers are being used for language arts instruction in schools.

Research on the Use of Computers in Reading and Writing Instruction

General Studies of Computer Effectiveness

Despite the lack of comprehensive studies of overall use, substantial research has examined the effects of using computers for particular kinds of instruction across a wide range of topics and age groups. In drawing conclusions about the use of computers for reading and writing instruction, previous reviewers have relied extensively on this research (cf. Balajthy, 1987, 1989; Kamil, 1982, 1987; Tanner, 1984). A general conclusion clearly supported by this research is that computer-based instruction increases student achievement at least as much as more conventional modes of instruction. This conclusion is supported by the results of a series of metanalyses conducted by Kulik (Kulik, Bangert, & Williams, 1983; Kulik, Kulik, & Bangert-Drowns, 1985; Kulik, Kulik, & Cohen, 1980). These analyses found an overall increase in student achievement across studies of computer-assisted instruction (CAI) that employed a variety of dependent measures; the average effect size was .47 and .32 standard deviation units for studies carried out in elementary and secondary schools, respectively. A more recent metanalysis by Roblyer, Castine, and King (1988) examined only studies conducted between 1980 and 1987. In addition, they compared the effectiveness of CAI in individual curricular areas. Although achievement increased in all the curricular areas studied, reading skills profited least. However, in some curricular areas conclusions were based on a relatively small number of studies.

Another consistent finding is that students have positive attitudes toward using computers and are motivated to use them for instructional activities (Clement, 1981), although extended instruction dispensed by a computer appears to decrease these effects (e.g., Saracho, 1982). Computers have also been found to be cost-effective when compared to other educational interventions. Levin (1986) found that CAI was more cost effective than employing adult tutors, increasing instructional time and reducing class size to 20 students. Of the interventions studied, only peer tutoring was more cost-effective for improving reading achievement (2.2 months of achievement gain for each $100 increase per student, compared to 1.9 months for CAI). Niemiec, Blackwell, and Walberg (1986) argued that Levin's procedures overestimated the effect of peer tutoring and underestimated CAI. Their analysis indicated that the cost-effectiveness of CAI for increasing reading achievement was double that of peer tutoring. Cumulatively, this research suggests that the computer is a viable medium of instruction across various school subjects, including the language arts.

Studies of Computer-Based Reading Curricula

A number of research studies have examined the effects of implementing computer-based reading curricula. To date, no comprehensive computer-based writing curricula have been developed, perhaps because educators considering the use of computers for writing have preferred to use them as an aid for writing as opposed to a management tool for moving students through a well-defined hierarchy of writing skills.

The development of computer-based reading curricula occurred primarily before the widespread availability of microcomputers in the late 1970s. Centrally located mainframe computers dispensed instructional lessons to individual terminals in various locations. The relative difficulty in developing and implementing educational applications dependent on mainframe computers encouraged developers to conceive of projects on a broad scale. Before the widespread availability of affordable microcomputers, it would not have been considered practical or cost effective to develop stand-alone programs aimed at a single reading skill. Thus, between the mid-1960s and the late 1970s, a number of projects, often supported by federal grants, developed around several comprehensive computer-based reading curricula (see Mason, Blanchard, & Daniel, 1983, for an extensive review of these projects).

Work on the first major computer-based reading curriculum was begun in 1964 under the direction of Richard Atkinson at Stanford University and was supported by a grant from the U.S. Office of Education. The result was a comprehensive first-grade reading curriculum, originally designed to eliminate the need for a classroom teacher (Atkinson, 1974). As was common in other early projects, the Stanford approach was to create an "integrated system" in which the computer provided computer-assisted instruction (CAI) and computer-managed instruction (CMI). That is, the computer introduced individual skills, accompanied by appropriate drill and practice (CAI), at the same time it recorded student performance and employed programmed algorithms to make decisions about a student's advancement through a hierarchy of skills (CMI). Atkinson and Hansen (1966) published a report of the Stanford project in the second volume of the *Reading Research Quarterly*. Foreshadowing dominant criticisms of CAI for reading instruction, Spache (1967) argued that the Stanford project ignored the central role of the reading teacher and it overemphasized the mastery of isolated skills in a drill-and-practice format.

Considering the number and scope of these early projects, they produced little research. Mason, Blanchard, and Daniel (1983) annotated 181 references related to more than a dozen major computer-based reading projects developed at various universities. Fewer than five of these citations can be considered published articles that report original research related to reading. The only article from this group that was published in a widely circulated peer-reviewed research journal was an evaluative study of the Stanford materials (Fletcher & Atkinson, 1972). In this study, 50 pairs of first-grade students were matched on the basis of reading readiness scores; one of the students in each pair worked 8 to 10 minutes daily on computer-based reading lessons from the Stanford project, while the other did not. Apparently both students in a pair participated in regular classroom reading instruction, and the control subjects were engaged in unspecified activities, while the experimental subjects worked at the computer. After five and one-half months, experimental subjects outperformed control subjects on a number of reading tests. Significant differences in favor of the experimental subjects included subtests requiring comprehension of connected texts, despite the fact that the Stanford curriculum stressed phonics skills.

More recently there have been fewer attempts to develop comprehensive, computer-based reading curricula, but there are a few notable exceptions. Several private firms have developed comprehensive reading curricula as commercial ventures. Some research, primarily evaluative studies, has focused on these curricula, but in most cases it has been conducted or sponsored by the firms marketing them. For example, several individuals who had directed work on the Stanford project founded the Computer Curriculum Corporation (CCC) and marketed a reading program based on that project. Between 1975 and 1977, CCC conducted a series of evaluative studies involving several thousand third- through sixth-grade students in schools across the United States. Although the summary report outlining the results of these studies (Poulson & Macken, 1978) does not indicate which differences are statistically significant, in general the results supported the earlier study by Fletcher and Atkinson (1972). That is, children who had regular 10-minute periods of computer-based reading instruction in addition to their regular classroom instruction outperformed those who had only classroom instruction.

WICAT Systems is another private firm that has developed integrated systems for computer-based reading instruction. Computer-based activities developed by WICAT range from beginning reading skills in the primary grades to comprehension monitoring strategies in the upper grades. The most extensively researched of WICAT's research and development projects was the Individual Reading and Instruction System (IRIS), supported by a grant from the U.S. Office of Education. Unlike most other integrated systems for reading instruction, the IRIS project focused on developing reading comprehension ability among students in the middle grades. In addition, computer-based activities proceeded from a well-defined theoretical position, namely schema theory. Instead of teaching and drilling specific comprehension skills, students working at a computer read texts and then completed five categories of activities: making inferences, deleting unnecessary sentences, interpreting graphic information, determining logical arguments, and practicing vocabulary. After several months, a formative evaluation of this program in several school systems indicated statistically significant gains in interpretive/critical and content reading as measured by a criterion-referenced test; but after two years there was no evidence of gains on a standardized achievement test (Schnitz, Maynes, & Revel, 1983).

Another commercial computer-based reading curriculum that has been evaluated empirically is the IBM Writing to Read program (Martin, 1984). Although a major component of this program is using the computer to teach children sound-symbol correspondences, off-line reading and writing are an integral part of the prescribed activities. IBM contracted Educational Testing Service to evaluate the effectiveness of the Writing to Read Program, and a report of findings (Murphy & Appel, 1984) indicated that the program resulted in higher reading achievement among kindergarten but not first-grade students in some schools using the program. Writing samples for students using the program were ranked higher than those for children not using the program. There was no direct evidence, however, concerning the role of the computer-based activities in effecting these increases because students using the Writing to Read program apparently read and wrote more than did students who did not use the program.

A few independent researchers have investigated the effects of commercial computer-based reading curricula. Saracho (1982), for example, investigated the effects of the CCC reading and mathematics curricula on the achievement of Spanish-speaking migrant children in the third through sixth grades. When compared to a control group that received only regular classroom reading instruction, the experimental group that completed the CCC curriculum, in addition to regular classroom instruction, demonstrated greater achievement gains. Norton and Resta (1986) compared the effects of having third- through sixth-grade remedial readers engage in conventional reading activities, problem-solving and simulation software, and one of three commercial computer-based reading curricula. After six weeks, they found statistically significant differences in reading achievement favoring the use of simulation and problem-solving software. However, their decision to group the three commercial programs together as a single treatment that preceded the other treatments precludes generalizing from the results of this experiment.

Most existing computer-based reading curricula have been aimed at children in elementary schools. Computer have also been employed, however, in programs for adults who have inadequate reading skills. For example, applications of computers to enhance literacy in the armed services have been described by Blanchard (1984). Some characteristics of computer-based reading instruction are advantageous for teaching adults. For example, individualized instruction with the aid of a computer can accommodate the flexible schedules of working adults and can also reduce the stigma that may be attached to attending courses that teach beginning reading and writing skills (see Turner, 1988).

Caldwell and Rizza (1979) have reported the results of several evaluative studies designed to determine the effectiveness of a computer-based system of reading instruction for adult nonreaders. The Basic Skills Learning System examined in these studies was developed by Control Data Corporation for the Programmed Logic for Automatic Teaching Operation (PLATO) system (first developed at the University of Illinois; see Obertino, 1974), and was aimed at adults whose reading skills were from the third- to eighth-grade level. Subjects were adults in several learning centers in three states. They found a statistically significant gain in reading achievement for adults using the computer-based program when compared to adults receiving traditional reading instruction. Adults in the Basic Skills groups averaged a gain of 1.12 grade levels in 13 hours of instruction, compared to negligible gains by those receiving traditional instruction for the same period of time. In addition, dropout rates that were as high as 50 percent for the traditional groups were less than 5 percent for the computer groups.

In summary, a consistent finding from investigations of reading curricula is that brief, but regular, computer-based reading lessons can enhance reading achievement. The results of these investigations, however, are based most often on the use of computer-based activities that supplement rather than replace conventional reading instruction. For the most part, the research has also been conducted by private firms with a commercial interest in the curriculum being investigated. Results have not been published in peer-reviewed journals, and thus this research remains outside the mainstream of academic scholarship. Among those who have developed these curricula, the rationale for using computers is frequently based on the belief that the computer offers a unique capability to match instructional content to the needs of an individual learner.

Research on Specific Instructional Applications

A third category of research includes studies that investigate applications of the computer to specific areas of reading and writing instruction (e.g., improving reading fluency or assisting writers as they develop topics for their writing). In general this research has been conducted more recently; and it has employed stand-alone microcomputers, as opposed to networked terminals serviced by larger, centrally located computers. The rationale that undergirds many of these studies is that a computer is a useful device for extending existing instructional activities. This rationale distinguishes these studies from other studies investigating applications that do not have readily identifiable analogs in existing pedagogical strategies. The latter category includes several studies that have instructional implications but that focus on the unique characteristics of texts displayed electronically and their effect on reading and writing processes. We discuss these studies in a subsequent section of this chapter.

Several studies have examined the use of computer-based activities to develop beginning reading skills. A study by Goodwin, Goodwin, Nansel, and Helm (1986) investigated the effects of using a variety of commercial reading readiness software with preschool children. Subjects were assigned to either an off-line control condition or to one of two on-line conditions that varied as to the type of adult assistance. They found no differences between these groups on a test of reading readiness. Their data, however, were collected during only three 20-minute sessions.

An emerging area of interest in beginning reading instruction is the use of computers equipped with devices that produce synthesized, digitized, or recorded speech. Olson and his colleagues (Olson & Wise, 1987; Olson, Foltz, & Wise, 1986) initiated a series of studies to determine if computer-generated speech feedback can improve decoding skills among disabled readers. The primary purpose of these studies was to compare three types of feedback that can be provided to a reader who identifies an unfamiliar word in text presented on a computer screen: syllable-by-syllable, subsyllable, or whole-word feedback. Preliminary findings indicated that readers' recognition of words pronounced by a synthetic speech device compared favorably with words pronounced by the experimenters (94.5 percent and 98.4 percent respectively). They also found that subjects requested help for approximately 65 percent of the words that they read incorrectly during oral reading. When comparing an on-line speech feedback condition to an on-line condition with no feedback, they found statistically significant differences in favor of the feedback condition for percent of oral errors targeted, postexperimental recognition of targeted and untargeted words, and percent of comprehension questions answered correctly. Although they found some advantage in whole-word feedback, the number of subjects in a pilot study was too small to generate sufficient statistical power.

Roth and Beck (1987) employed digitized speech in two microcomputer programs designed to improve word recognition and rates of decoding. In addition to assessing the effectiveness of the two programs, they employed several dependent measures to investigate how improvements in decoding might affect reading comprehension. In one program, children attempted to construct words when given an initial letter and several alternative endings. Digitized speech provided corrective feedback after errors. The second program required students to find a letter string that matched a word or "pseudoword" pronounced by the computer. Both activities were embedded in a gamelike format in which subjects accumulated points for accuracy and speed. Their results indicated that after using the programs for 20 weeks (three 20-minute sessions per week), fourth-grade subjects reading below grade level gained in their ability to recognize words and in their comprehension of sentences and propositions, but not of complete passages. However, both the experimental and control groups participated in regular classroom instruction during the experiment and the control group engaged in unspecified activities during the experimental treatment.

Reitsma (1988) compared the effects of three instructional activities designed to increase reading efficiency for beginning readers: oral reading guided by a teacher, reading while listening to a tape-recorded version of a text, and independent reading supported by student-selected pronunciations of unfamiliar words in a text mediated by a computer interfaced with a specially designed tape recorder. Six- and seven-year-old subjects in the three treatments and a control condition read five short stories, each containing 20 difficult target words. Results indicated that guided reading and independent reading with the support of the computer increased reading rate and reduced errors on the target words when compared to the reading-while-listening and control conditions.

An earlier study by McConkie (1983) supports these results. He found that adults who were poor readers made greater gains in reading achievement when they read with computer support that was similar to that used by Reitsma than did adults participating in a program of traditional reading instruction. In a related study Carver and Hoffman (1981) did not employ computer-generated speech but did investigate how a computer-based version of repeated reading (Samuels, 1979) would affect reading achievement. High school students who were poor readers read text displayed on a computer screen. Every fifth word in the text was replaced by a choice between the original word and an inappropriate distractor. Subjects repeatedly read each text until they achieved mastery. Data were gathered over a semester, during which subjects regularly engaged in this activity. They found statistically significant gains in reading fluency and also strong evidence that gains transferred to new materials requiring subjects to engage in the experimental task. Their findings were less robust, however, when subjects progressed to more difficult passages.

Another recent application of the computer to reading instruction is described in an investigation by MacGregor (1988). She developed a "computer-mediated text system" designed to encourage third-grade students to ask questions while reading texts displayed on a computer screen. Questions were either "clarification questions" concerning difficult vocabulary or "focus-of-attention questions" pertaining to literal information in the text. The computer program determined the appropriateness of the question and provided a response. Four treatment groups included two groups that had access to one of the computer-based questioning conditions, a group that had access to both types of questions, and a control group that read passages on the computer screen, but without questions. A comparison of subjects in the three experimental groups to subjects in the control group indicated a significant difference in favor of the experimental groups on measures of vocabulary knowledge and prediction of performance on the vocabulary measure. The performance of subjects having access to both types of questions was not significantly better than the groups having access to only one type of question; nor was there evidence that the experimental treatments had a greater effect on average readers when compared to good readers.

Two studies have compared the effects of off-line and on-line instructional activities in reading. Harper and Ewing (1986) compared junior high school special education students' comprehension after reading passages and answering questions either in a workbook or on a computer. Comprehension as measured by percent of questions answered correctly was greater on the computer, but the researchers did not report if the differences were statistically significant; nor did they report information about the relative difficulty of passages and questions in the treatment conditions. Balajthy (1988) had college students complete vocabulary-building activities, using either a worksheet, a computer video game, or a computer drill game. After using each format, subjects rated the effectiveness of the format. Based on their ratings, subjects were divided into high- and low-effectiveness groups that were compared on the basis of achievement, time on task, and interest in the activity. The clearest finding in this study was that performance on worksheets was better and faster regardless of the effectiveness rating, although all subjects rated the worksheets as the least interesting. This study highlights the importance of considering interactions between the medium of instruction, perceived effectiveness, interest, and performance.

When compared to the diverse applications of computers to reading instruction, the interest in using computers for writing instruction has been more narrowly focused. Although a variety of commercial software programs are available for writing instruction, word-processing applications predominate in the research literature. Much of this research has important implications for writing instruction, but it has focused primarily on comparing how writing differs when students write with and without the aid of a computer. Thus, we discuss this research in a subsequent section comparing electronic and conventional text. The research devoted to the use of computers in writing is also narrower in that the subjects tend to be college students or skilled writers (see Schwartz & Bridwell, 1984; Schwartz & Bridwell-Bowles, 1987). At least three factors may account for this characteristic of the writing research: (1) writing is often taught as a separate subject at the college level and subjects who typically have typing skills are readily available; (2) colleges and universities frequently make hardware and software for writing available to students; and (3) many writing researchers are affiliated with college or university departments that teach writing courses; thus they can conduct research in conjunction with their teaching responsibilities.

Despite researchers' emphasis on comparing word processing to conventional writing, a few studies have investigated the effects of using computers for specific applications in writing instruction. Alderman, Appel, and Murray (1978) conducted one of the earliest studies related to computers and writing. They analyzed the effectiveness of PLATO programs that provided drill and practice on mechanical aspects of writing. Although community college students reported positive attitudes toward using the computer programs, there was no evidence that the programs significantly improved their writing.

Burns (1984; Burns & Culp, 1980) developed and investigated a computer program that helped college-level writers develop topics prior to writing about them. The program generated open-ended questions based on heuristic models for developing topics (Aristotelian *topoi* and Burke's pentad) and also provided prompts based on an analysis of students' responses. For example, the program suggested that students wrote more when their responses were short. Subjects reported positive attitudes toward the heuristic models used by the program and toward the use of the computer to assist them in developing topics. They generated more topics for writing and their ideas were more sophisticated than in their invention without computers, but no studies of the actual text they produced were conducted. Gillis (1987) employed a computer program to encourage students in a basic writing course to gather more specific ideas before they wrote. Their responses were compared to students who had human tutors or traditional classroom instruction. The computer-based group outperformed the other groups on all measures (e.g., focus ratings and holistic ratings of essay quality) except fluency. Even though a pattern in favor of CAI was established, the findings were not statistically significant. No differences between the quantity of ideas generated or used in drafts were found when Strickland (1987) compared CAI that he designed (QUEST and FREE, see McDaniel, 1985) with traditional classroom methods. In addition, he examined a number of ideas generated with the CAI that the students used in their essays and found no significant differences between the CAI group and control groups; only those students who used a freewriting technique without the computer showed significant gains. Several writers have argued that the computer's potential for assisting writers as they develop topics before writing will not be realized until artificial intelligence evolves sufficiently to permit a more open-ended dialogue between the writer and the computer (see Kemp, 1987; Selfe, 1987).

Several studies suggest that positive attitudes towards writing increase when students collaborate with the aid of a computer. Duin, Jorn, and DeBower (in press) had college students use a campuswide computer network to assist in the writing of reports for a technical writing class. An analysis of the electronic messages sent during the writing of reports indicated that students used the network to plan, draft, revise, and format documents. They worked collaboratively, asking for and receiving feedback from other students and from the instructor. Students reported high levels of satisfaction in their use of the computer network for their writing. Eighty-five percent of the students indicated that the computer gave them more time to revise than traditional methods of writing, and 100 percent of them found that the file server, which provided telecommunication with the instructor, was especially helpful in sharing and receiving feedback. Similarly, Bruce and Rubin (1983) and Herrmann (1986) reported that junior high school students wrote more imaginatively and found more ways to improve their writing when they wrote collaboratively with the aid of a computer as opposed to traditional writing activities. Using a computer to communicate with other writers from a distance may also have a positive effect on writing performance, because the students sense the presence of an authentic reader. For example, Levin, Riel, Rowe, and Boruta (1985) found that elementary schoolchildren's writing improved when they used computer networks to communicate with other students.

An area of increasing interest is the use of computers to analyze characteristics of written materials, including instructional applications that provide feedback to writers about their own writing. Much of the development of applications in this area has been conducted at AT&T Bell Laboratories and has resulted in an array of programs collectively referred to as the Writer's Workbench (see Frase, 1987). Feedback in these programs ranges from the identification of mechanical errors and inappropriate constructions to the use of sophisticated algorithms that quantify stylistic features of a text. Although Frase (1987) has reported findings supporting the validity of analyses performed by various Writer's Workbench programs, little research has investigated the effects of using such programs as a means of improving writing. Studies by Kiefer and Smith (1983; Smith & Kiefer, 1982), however, did investigate the effects of using a modified version of Writer's Workbench in college composition courses. They found that although experimental subjects using the computer did not achieve higher holistic scores on their writing, they had positive attitudes toward using the program and scored higher on a postexperimental editing task. Ross and Bridwell (1985) argued that existing programs designed to analyze writing style have been limited to superficial features of writing. They suggested that the lack of adequate linguistic theories and computing power prevent these programs from inferring, interpolating, or connecting ideas at a level that approaches a human reader. Nonetheless, as the power of microcomputers increases, more sophisticated applications may be developed and research will be needed to study the effects of computer-based analyses of text.

Studies investigating specific applications of computers to reading and writing instruction are relatively disjointed, and cumulatively they lack the depth necessary to make generalizations. Preliminary evidence suggests, however, that computers, especially those equipped with devices that produce artificial speech, may provide an effective means for increasing decoding skills and reading fluency. In addition, a consistent finding in studies investigating the effects of computer-based writing activities is that these activities increase positive attitudes toward writing.

Commentary on Instructional Research

Existing research investigating the applications of computers to reading and writing instruction has been criticized for its methodological and conceptual shortcomings. Previous reviewers have detailed these shortcomings for reading (e.g., Balajthy, 1987) and for writing (e.g., Ross & Bridwell, 1985; Hawisher, 1986). The present commentary is limited to a discussion of those conceptual and methodological shortcomings that we believe are more serious and more pervasive. We also suggest ways that researchers might address these shortcomings in future research.

A major methodological limitation affecting existing research is the failure to investigate or to control fully the variables that might explain differences between experimental and control groups. For example, in studies investigating the effectiveness of computer-based instruction, experimental groups have typically completed instructional activities in addition to regular classroom instruction, while comparison groups have been exposed only to classroom instruction. This approach may provide useful information about the "additive" effects of supplementary computer-based instruction, but it does not distinguish the use of computers from other supplementary activities that may be equally effective for increasing achievement. A reasonable explanation for many of the studies that show improvement in reading and writing performance is that the subjects in these experiments have had additional instruction, frequently on those skills tested at the conclusion of the study.

Addressing this limitation leads to several practical problems for researchers who wish to investigate the effectiveness of computer-based reading and writing instruction in elementary and secondary schools. Administrators and teachers may not allow researchers to create treatment groups composed of subjects who are removed from regular classroom instruction for experimental computer-based activities. This issue is especially relevant in the elementary school, where reading instruction is often linked to carefully controlled progress through a basal reading series. In addition, it is difficult to control for effects that may result when subjects not allowed to use a computer during instructional time may feel disappointed. Likewise, the Hawthorne effect may be operating within experimental groups who view the opportunity to use the computer for reading instruction as a welcome novelty, although there is evidence that positive attitudes toward computer-based instruction decrease with increasing exposure to it (e.g., Saracho, 1982; Goodwin et al., 1986). Furthermore, there is evidence that the amount of training on the computer given to subjects prior to the collection of data in reading experiments may affect results (cf. Kunz, Schott, & Hovekamp, 1987; MacGregor, 1988; Reinking, 1988; Reinking & Schreiner, 1985).

Researchers may wish to consider several options for addressing these practical problems. First, selecting subjects that have considerable experience using computers for academic tasks reduces the likelihood that a Hawthorne or novelty effect will be confounded with other variables. Second, using training materials that provide ample time for subjects to become thoroughly familiar with a computer application before data are collected may also be important, although this usually adds considerably to the time and effort required to conduct experiments involving the computer. Finally, when it is not feasible to remove subjects from conventional instruction, comparison groups need to be selected carefully. One solution, for example, would be to have off-line comparison groups complete supplemental instructional activities related to the dependent measures while experimental groups work on the computer.

A major weakness in existing instructional research involving computers is that many researchers have failed to establish a well-defined conceptual and theoretical base for using computers for reading and writing instruction. Conceptual and theoretical issues play an important role in determining what questions need to be addressed, in making decisions about the design of experiments, and in interpreting results. For example, Clark's (1983) analysis of research comparing instructional media has clearly juxtaposed the fundamental issues that researchers must consider when investigating instructional media. In Clark's view, the selection of a medium for delivering instruction is inconsequential when compared to the selection of instructional content and the method for presenting it. He argues that results indicating advantages for computer-based instruction can be explained by a confounding of media differences with uncontrolled variation in content, method, and novelty effects. Given this premise, the important questions for media researchers to address are related to cost-effectiveness and the affective dimension of using computers for learning. Salomon (1979) has taken an opposing position. In his view, various instructional media have distinct attributes that define their potential to affect cognitive processing. The task of the researcher is to identify potentially important attributes of an instructional medium such as the computer and to study their effects on cognitive processing.

These opposing points of view suggest a common course for future research. In either view, global comparisons of computer-based and conventional instruction are not perceived as being productive except to determine cost-effectiveness. Instead, a profitable direction for future research would be to isolate variables that may account for the increased achievement found in previous studies and to determine which, if any, of these variables are directly related to the technological attributes of the computer. Such research will require researchers to develop underlying theoretical frameworks that include a clear rationale for using the computer for reading and writing instruction. Without a theoretical rationale it will be impossible to make generalizations beyond the conditions of a particular study, even if effects are strong.

These viewpoints also imply that researchers need to investigate a wider range of variables. In addition to achievement, independent and dependent variables might include time on task, motivation, and the social context of implementing computer-based instruction in schools (see McGee, 1987). Given the complex interactions among variables in instructional settings, qualitative studies would be a useful complement to quantitative studies (e.g., see Blackstock & Miller, 1988). Venezky (1983) included a qualitative component when he proposed that the following three types of research be included in attempts to evaluate a computer-based instructional program:

1. A standard pre- and posttest achievement-gains comparison, using standard instruments and control groups.
2. An affective-attitudinal survey of pupils, teachers, and parents, using questionnaires and interviews.
3. A participant-observer anthropological study, using *in situ* observers. (p. 35)

Another weakness in some existing studies is the failure to make a connection between the computer-based instructional activities under investigation and the relevant research and theory related to similar off-line activities. Reading and writing researchers investigating instructional applications of computers need to explain what benefits may be expected by using a computer to carry out conventional off-line activities and these explanations must be tied to prior research. For instance, Hague and Mason (1986) reported improvements in writing quality when students used computerized readability formulas to determine the average length of sentences and words in their writing. Teachers rated essays higher when they had longer sentences and more polysyllabic words, a finding reminiscent of the sentence-combining research conducted in the 1970s. Students can be taught to lengthen sentences using either method, but previous research suggests that changes are not always rhetorically appropriate (Kleine, 1983), and that, in general, manipulating isolated factors during composing is not likely to produce long-term improvement. In this case, there is little support for using the computer to duplicate an off-line instructional activity that is relatively easy to implement and that research has suggested is of questionable effectiveness.

Establishing Priorities for Instructional Research

As suggested by the latter example, another factor that limits research is the lack of clearly defined priorities for the development of computer-based instructional activities. At issue is the development of a rationale for distinguishing between what *can* be done instructionally with a computer and what *should* be done (Rubin, 1983). The development of such a rationale is framed by responses to basic questions about the nature of reading and writing, how literacy skills are best taught, and what attributes of the computer are most relevant for reading and writing instruction. Wilkinson (1983) has suggested that three criteria be used to set priorities for the development of computer-based instruction in reading and, by implication, in writing. Considering these criteria necessitates an explicit response to basic questions about reading and writing instruction. First, priority should be given to applications that employ the unique characteristics of the computer for displaying text. Second, applications should be based on accepted principles of reading and writing instruction. Finally, higher priority should be given to those applications that address problematic areas of instruction. We believe that instructional research in reading and writing that involves a computer would be improved if researchers would explicitly justify their research in terms of these three criteria.

Several writers have addressed issues related to these criteria. Lesgold (1983), for example, has outlined a specific rationale for using computers in beginning reading instruction. In his view, the computer has two important uses for instruction: providing practice in word recognition and diagnosing children's progress. The computer's advantage in providing practice is its capability to present sometimes tedious practice in game formats that children enjoy. Its advantage in diagnosis is in the prodigious ongoing data that can be used to make on-line instructional decisions. Reinking (1986) has argued that six fundamental advantages of computer-mediated texts should guide its use for reading and writing instruction:

1. Computers can enhance the ability of readers and writers to interact with text.
2. Computers permit the external control of written language processes.
3. Computers can lessen the drudgery associated with some aspects of reading and writing.
4. Computers can provide individualized help and guidance during independent reading and writing activities.
5. Computers can contribute to the development of purposeful communication in school, and thus they can bring together reading and writing activities.
6. Computers can facilitate the gathering of data concerning written texts and the processes of reading and writing.

Other than the many studies of word processing that are discussed in a subsequent section, relatively little research has been conducted on instructional applications of computers to writing; nonetheless, a number of writers have stressed the importance of developing applications that capitalize on the unique attributes of the computer (e.g., Bridwell, Nancarrow, & Ross, 1984) and that reflect current theories and research on writing (Beach & Bridwell, 1984). Miller and Burnett (1987) have also pointed out that the use of computers in the language arts classroom is inevitably affected by the long-standing debate between supporters of holistic as opposed to subskill approaches (Samuels, 1980). Similarly, discussions about priorities for research and development will hinge upon which view predominates.

COMPARISONS OF ELECTRONIC AND CONVENTIONAL TEXTS

Much research has compared electronic and conventional texts. Investigations have ranged from a consideration of inherent differences in displaying text on a cathode ray tube (CRT) to purposeful manipulations of the textual display made possible by computer technology. Underlying this research is the assumption that differences between electronic and conventional texts may affect basic reading and writing processes. Although this notion was initially ill-defined and intuitive, variables of potential significance are beginning to emerge and others are being dismissed as less important. Theoretical positions that relate these variables to current understandings of written language process have also begun to appear. We have grouped the research in this area into two categories: convergent studies that minimize differences between electronic and conventional texts, and divergent studies in which differences are heightened purposefully to improve reading or writing performance.

Convergent Studies

Convergent studies focus primarily on the inherent differences between displaying text either electronically or on printed pages. For example, unlike printed text, text displayed on a CRT is usually created by illuminating configurations of *pixels* (dots of light) against a dark background. A CRT screen may be analogous to a printed page, but it is distinguished by the fact that the visual presentation is more like a window to the contents of a computer's memory (Wilkinson, 1983; Yeaman, 1987). Researchers have been interested in whether these or similar differences affect factors like reading speed, comprehension, and visual fatigue. These studies are convergent in the sense that differences are typically minimized so that results can be attributed to differences inherent in the technologies used to display the text. For example, printed materials may be produced by a dot matrix printer, thus producing identical fonts on the page and on the CRT.

Even though writers must read what they write, minimal differences in textual displays are less relevant to writing; writing researchers have been more interested in word processing, a divergent application that capitalizes on the differences between the computer and conventional writing materials. Thus, this section includes primarily studies related to reading. Another characteristic of the investigations in this category is that many of them have been conducted by researchers in instructional technology, ergonomics, applied psychology, and related fields. The questions addressed and the methods employed in this research are reminiscent of the legibility studies conducted over several decades beginning in the 1930s (see Daniel & Reinking, 1987; Hulme, 1984, for a comparison of legibility factors related to printed and electronic texts).

Although findings are mixed, there is considerable evidence that under some conditions reading speed is slower for texts displayed on a CRT (Gould & Grischkowsky, 1983; Hansen, Doring, & Whitlock, 1978; Kruk & Muter, 1984; Muter, Latremouille, Treurniet, & Beam, 1982). In studies finding statistically significant differences, subjects have often read lengthy texts. For example, Muter and associates (1982) found that subjects reading text from a CRT were 28.5 percent slower than subjects reading the same text from a book, but subjects read continuously for two hours in each condition. Studies using passages of a few hundred words have not found statistically significant differences in reading speed (e.g., Fish & Feldman, 1987; Reinking, 1988).

A series of studies by Haas and Hayes (1985a, 1985b) suggests factors that may account for increased reading times. Consistent with earlier studies, they found that college students required more time to retrieve specific information from texts displayed on sequential computer screens than on printed pages. Differences were not significant, however, when each screen displayed more text or when text-editing functions were added (e.g., the capability to search the text for a particular word). Similarly, Wright and Lickorish (1983) found that proofreading was slower on a CRT, although accuracy was no different when the same text was proofread on printed pages. Based on the results of a subsequent study (Wright & Lickorish, 1984), they concluded that slowness on the CRT was due to the inability of subjects to annotate text on the screen, a clear example of the connection between reading and writing in the learning process.

Despite the frequently observed differences in reading time, there is no evidence that comprehension varies when comparing subjects who read minimally different presentations of printed and electronic texts. Studies finding variations in reading speed have typically not found concomitant variations in comprehension. Fish and Feldman (1987) looked specifically for comprehension differences between subjects reading comparable passages presented either on a computer screen or on printed pages. Controlling for subjects' reading ability, they found no significant differences on measures of comprehension for passages giving directions or providing information. Subjects in most of these studies have been mature readers; but a study by Gambrell, Bradley, and McLaughlin (1987) found no comprehension differences among third- and fifth-grade students reading stories from a basal reading series that were displayed either on printed pages or on the computer screen. One study contradicts these findings. Heppner, Anderson, Farstrup, and Weiderman (1985) found that adults performed more poorly on a standardized reading test when it was presented by a computer. They suggest, however, that poorer performance in the computer condition may have been due to the fact that the test was timed.

Some concern has been expressed about the physiological effects of prolonged reading from CRTs. A review of research by the National Research Council (1983) concluded that there was no cause for concern about radiation emitted by CRTs. There is some evidence that when compared to print, reading from a CRT screen can cause greater visual fatigue (Gunnarsson & Soderberg, 1983; Jelden, 1981; Mourant, Lakshmanan, & Chantadisai, 1981), but this difference may be eliminated as electronic textual displays are improved (Cushman, 1986).

Other studies have examined specific characteristics of electronic texts. These include scrolling versus "windowing" of texts (Bury, Boyle, Evey, & Neal, 1982); optimal screen size (Duchnicky & Kolers, 1983; Yeaman, 1987); computer-generated, fill-justified text (Trollip & Sales, 1986); all-capital versus regular mixed print (Henney, 1983); and automatic phrasing of texts (Jandreau, Muncer, & Bever, 1986). Reading speed has been affected by some of these factors, but there is no evidence that they have a significant effect on comprehension. Several writers (e.g., Merrill, 1985; Rubens & Krull, 1985) have attempted to translate these findings into general guidelines for the development of textual displays on computer screens. Using conceptual, linguistic, and visual aspects of these guidelines to develop well-designed and poorly designed writing software, Duin (1988) reported that college students performed more capably when using the well-designed software and preferred it over the poorly designed software.

A confounding factor that has been controlled in relatively few studies is subjects' experience in working with computers in general and reading electronic texts in particular. It is reasonable to expect some deterioration in reading performance when subjects who are novice users of a computer read texts presented by a computer. Even readers who have considerable experience in using computers have had considerably more experience in reading conventional printed material. On the other hand, a novelty effect may increase interest in materials presented electronically, and interest is known to affect reading performances (see Wigfield & Asher, 1984). The empirical evidence addressing these issues is conflicting. Heppner, et al. (1985) found that performance was poorer when a standardized test was administered by a computer, whether subjects were nonusers or regular users of computers. Gambrell, Bradley, and McLaughlin (1987) found no difference in comprehension, but elementary school students clearly preferred reading stories on a computer screen. There is some evidence that training and experience may affect results in studies examining the effects of reading electronic texts (cf. Reinking & Schreiner, 1985; Reinking, 1988). Apparently the effect of these factors on reading performance requires further study, and researchers may need to exercise caution in generalizing the results of computer studies that do not control for these factors.

Divergent Studies

In some studies the capabilities of the computer are employed to create electronic texts that are purposefully different from conventional printed texts. Differences are emphasized instead of minimized; therefore, we have categorized them as divergent. The goal of researchers in these studies has been to investigate the possibility that texts presented by a computer might be used to enhance reading and writing in ways that are not possible or feasible with conventional materials. Dependent variables are typically related to comprehension in the case of reading and to a variety of outcomes in the case of writing. Results are frequently discussed in terms of how texts displayed under the control of a computer might uniquely affect basic reading and writing processes.

The clearly dominant focus of writing researchers interested in computers has been on the effects that word-processing applications have on writing. A summary of this research is included in this section because the purpose of word-processing applications is to provide writers with a diverse range of computer-based writing capabilities that are either greatly enhanced by a computer or not feasible without one.

Divergent Studies in Reading

Divergent studies in reading have usually employed computer technology to expand or control readers' options for acquiring information from text. The earliest application to be researched in this category was a form of rapid reading developed by Forster (1970) called *rapid serial visual presentation* (RSVP). In RSVP, text is displayed rapidly one word at a time on a CRT, thus the need for strategic eye movements is eliminated, but so is the readers' control over what can be attended to during reading. Although first employed as a laboratory tool to investigate perceptual processes in reading, RSVP has been studied empirically as an alternative to the rapid reading of printed text. In their review of this research, Just and Carpenter (1987) concluded that in its usual form RSVP does not have any clear advantage over more conventional rapid reading. They speculate, however, that computer-based "intelligent" control of the presentation based on factors like word frequency and a determination of an individual reader's needs may increase the effectiveness of RSVP.

Another early study in this category investigated the effects of using a computer to adjust a textual presentation to the needs of poor readers. L'Allier (1980) programmed a computer to adjust a text's structure when readers had difficulty comprehending. The adjustment was based on a complex algorithm that took into account factors like reading time, response time for interspersed questions, and performance on comprehension probes. Poor high school readers reading under this condition comprehended texts as well as good readers reading the same texts on printed pages without assistance.

Blohm (1982) provided college students with optimal "computer-aided glosses" to assist them in comprehending two technical passages presented by the computer. Subjects having this option available recalled more idea units from the passages than did subjects reading the passages without glosses on the computer. In a later study (Blohm, 1987), he again had college students read passages presented by the computer, but one group could select among several "lookup aids" that included definitions, analogies, examples, and paraphrases. The number of idea units recalled was again greater for the group having access to assistance provided by the computer. The correlation between the number of lookups requested and the number of idea units recalled was not significant; neither was the difference in reading time between the two groups. Apparently, the subjects in this experiment were efficient in selecting appropriate options to increase recall. However, the design and procedures employed in this study limit generalizations. For example, there was no off-line comparison group and subjects were not permitted to look back to previous portions of the text once they had requested the next textual segment to be displayed on the computer screen.

Reinking and Schreiner (1985) studied the effects of using a computer to help good and poor intermediate-grade readers comprehend six expository passages that were classified as either easy or difficult. The computer was employed to provide definitions of difficult vocabulary, background information relevant to the topic of the passage, the main idea of each paragraph, and a less technical version of the passage. A group reading the passages displayed conventionally on printed pages was compared to three experimental groups reading passages on the computer. Experimental groups included subjects who read the passages with no assistance, with optional assistance, and with mandatory assistance. Findings indicated that comprehension increased for both good and poor readers when they were required to view the assistance provided by the computer and that subjects free to select options preferred the background knowledge option. The interpretation of their results was constrained, however, by an unanticipated interaction between passage difficulty and treatment.

In a related study, Tobias (1987) developed a computer program that required subjects to review relevant portions of text when they answered adjunct questions incorrectly. Subjects in this condition had higher scores on a postexperimental comprehension test than did subjects who could voluntarily review the same material. This finding was limited, however, to comprehension items related to the adjunct questions. In addition, he found no evidence of a relation between subjects' self-report of strategies used to read the passage and their actual use of options provided by the computer. Mandatory review also increased as subjects' anxiety increased. Noteworthy, however, is that text in this study was displayed one sentence at a time.

The cumulative record of research in this area suggests that using a computer to expand or control a reader's options for acquiring information from a text may increase reading comprehension. However, there are only preliminary indications of which variables may explain these increases. Reinking (1988) replicated his earlier study (Reinking & Schreiner, 1985) to investigate factors that may affect comprehension of computer-mediated texts. As in previous studies, he found increases in comprehension among subjects reading texts displayed by a computer that provided comprehension-related assistance. In addition, he found that when subjects received computer assistance they had significantly greater reading times, but their preference for texts and their estimation of their own learning did not vary significantly when reading texts off-line or in any of the three computer conditions. Original scores were then adjusted to control statistically for differences in reading time. After this adjustment, a strong effect for the treatment remained. Increases in comprehension apparently were not due to increased time on task. He concluded that increased comprehension may be due to deeper and more active processing of the text, which was stimulated by the computer-based assistance.

Other computer applications may be categorized as divergent, but they have not been included in this section for one of two reasons. Either they have not been investigated empirically or research has not addressed specifically how they differ from printed texts. For example, a range of computer applications currently grouped under the rubric *hypertext* have used computers to explore alternative ways of structuring textual information. Information in hypertext is not organized sequentially as in conventional texts, but instead is designed to encourage individual readers to explore flexibly the relations among interrelated textual segments (see Jonassen, 1986; and Weyer, 1982, for detailed explanations of hypertext, several representative applications, and a theoretical rationale for its use). Similarly, computer applications in reading developed by McConkie (1983) and MacGregor (1988) may be classified as divergent, but these applications have been examined primarily from the standpoint of their use for reading instruction. They were discussed, therefore, in a previous section of this review.

Divergent Studies Focusing on Word Processing

There has been much interest in, and some theoretical speculation about, how writing with computers may affect the development of writing ability in young children; but as has been noted in previous reviews (Daiute, 1983, 1985; Woodruff, Bereiter, & Scardamalia, 1981–1982), little empirical research has been conducted to explore these possibilities. One study conducted by Rosegrant (1984) indicated that for some young children writing may be easier with a computer keyboard than with pencils, but there is not enough research to indicate whether there are any substantive advantages for using word-processing activities with young children.

Studies comparing the effects of word processing and conventional writing activities with older school-aged children are mixed. Some studies indicate no significant differences (e.g., Schank, 1986, with fourth-grade students; Duling, 1986, with ninth-grade students), while others favor conventional writing (e.g., Philhower, 1986, with mildly handicapped secondary students). Butler-Nalin (1985), on the other hand, found that junior high school students revised more and reread their papers more often when they composed with a computer. Daiute (1986) reported that junior high school students corrected more errors in their writing with computers, but their revisions were no more extensive than when they composed without it. However, in this study the computer also prompted students to correct their errors.

Most of the research on the effects of word processing has been aimed at college students and accomplished writers, most likely for reasons noted earlier in this chapter (e.g., the availability of subjects with typing skills). Collier (1983) was one of the first to examine the effects of word processing on college-level writers. His case studies reported mixed results. Students wrote more, revised more, and reported more positive attitudes toward the computer; but difficulties with the word-processing program prevented him from determining whether students' writing improved. Echoing a consistent criticism of subsequent research, Pufahl (1984) faulted Collier's study for not including instruction in composing strategies that might have led students to use the computer more effectively. Using the computer as an enhanced typewriter, rather than a unique tool for composing, is not a valid indicator of how word processing may affect writing processes.

Other researchers have arrived at a similar conclusion. Hawisher (1987) analyzed the writing of advanced college freshmen to determine whether they revised more extensively and more successfully with computers than with their usual methods. After analyzing more than 4,000 revisions on 80 essays, she concluded that the computer alone did not affect the students' writing. Harris (1985) also noted that students revised less frequently and made fewer changes in a text's macrostructure when writing with the computer. These findings are counterintuitive because using a word processor makes revising easier. Harris concluded that unless students are given instruction on how to revise with a computer, they will not make good use of the technological advantages of a word-processing program.

Under similar conditions, however, other researchers have found that composing with the aid of a computer leads to improvements in overall writing quality. Etchison (1986), for example, found that essays written by college freshmen in a composition course were rated higher for overall quality when the students composed them with a word processor. Further analysis indicated that the essays composed at the computer had a greater number of words. Rosenthal (1987) also reported that college students composing with a word processor wrote longer essays with fewer mechanical and grammatical errors.

Bridwell, Sirc, and Brooke (1985) conducted case studies of advanced undergraduates who composed letters and memos in a business writing course. Data included (a) keystroke studies of composing processes (i.e., the computer recorded every key each student pressed while composing), (b) interviews based on "instant replays" of composing episodes using the keystroke data, and (c) analyses of revisions on and off the computer (see Sirc & Bridwell-Bowles, 1988, for a more detailed discussion of these methods). Some students were not as successful with the computer as they were with conventional methods of writing. They claimed that the speed of editing did not allow them to "mull things over." Some did not see the need to continue revising when the computer's printer turned their first effort into a neatly typed draft. For others, the polished look of their writing on the computer screen encouraged them to revise. The researchers concluded that the major effect of composing with the aid of a computer in this study was the increased attention paid to surface detail and the visual appearance of the writing, due perhaps to the emphasis placed on appearance in business writing. Also, the effects of the computer interacted with the students' conception of the task, their success in learning a particular word-processing system, and their writing ability.

Studies focusing on older, accomplished writers complement the findings from studies of college-level writers. Bridwell-Bowles, Johnson, and Brehe (1987) studied the effects of word-processing on Ph.D. candidates employed as professional writers. Subjects' writing strategies were studied both on and off the computer, and they were interviewed about their writing after each writing session over a period of several months. This study revealed unexpected patterns during an early period of adjustment to the computer. The degree of satisfaction with the computer hinged on subjects' existing "rituals" as writers and whether or not they could adapt these to the task of writing with a computer. Subjects characterized as global planners seemed most receptive to the computer during this phase, because the computer allowed them to execute a predesigned plan more easily than conventional methods. Those who wrote to discover what they had to say had more difficulty adjusting; they missed their stacks of paper, charts, and diagrams that helped them formulate their emerging ideas. Analysis of their keystrokes revealed, however, that all subjects steadily gained in speed and facility with the computer so that after several weeks they were as productive as they had been with conventional methods. The researchers argued that it is reasonable to conclude that novice writers, who may not yet have successful writing strategies, should be introduced to specific strategies for composing on computers.

Lutz (1987) asked experienced professional writers to revise their own and others' work on a computer as well as with pen and paper. She analyzed protocols from the writers at work to determine their cognitive strategies for improving writing. She found significant differences between revisions that subjects made on their own compared to others' writing. She concluded that little can be said conclusively about isolated variables such as revising behaviors without taking into account contextual variables like the writer's experience, the task, and the medium—a point that applies to writing without a computer as well.

The existing research on word processing leaves many questions unanswered (Gerrard, 1987), but tentative conclusions are supportable. Despite some promising new research (Bernherdt, Edwards, & Wojahn, 1989), little evidence can be found that word processing alone produces dramatic improvements in writing skill. It is more likely that word processing may contribute to improvements in writing when accompanied by appropriate preparatory and ongoing instructional activities, although there is a paucity of research that directly addresses this possibility or suggests what these activities might be. Under certain as yet ill-defined conditions, the use of computers for writing appears to affect factors like the overall length and quality of written work, the extent to which writers revise, and the attitudes writers have about their work. However, with the exception of the consistent finding that writers have positive attitudes about their writing on a word processor, the strength and direction of these findings have been decidedly mixed. More recent research has suggested that a wider range of variables may need to be considered in order to reconcile these contradictory findings. These factors include word-processing experience, reading ability, preferred writing style, contextual factors like the nature of the writing task, and the characteristics of individual word-processing programs.

The Movement toward Theoretical Frameworks

Theories enable researchers to generate hypotheses that guide experiments and that permit experimental findings to be generalized beyond the conditions of a single study. Much of the existing research that compares electronic and conventional text has not been guided by well-defined theoretical frameworks and thus, taken as whole, it is difficult to interpret. Nonetheless, several rudimentary theoretical positions have emerged recently, and these may be useful for interpreting past research as well as for planning new studies. The movement toward theoretical frameworks is an important development in the study of a phenomenon, and the emergence of theoretical speculation suggests that improvements in the research related to computers may be imminent (see Reinking, 1987). In this section we review theoretical issues related to comparisons of electronic and conventional texts, and we present several evolving theoretical positions.

Wright (1987) has argued that the development of adequate theories may be inhibited until more is known about the optimal formats for displaying electronic and printed texts. Comparing the performance of subjects reading a text displayed on a high-resolution color monitor to those reading it on a blurred photocopy does not lead to valid generalizations about either medium. Thus, investigating intra- as opposed to intermedia variables is a valid and perhaps more fruitful direction for research. An example of how this approach may prevent misleading generalizations is the comparison of reading speed for electronic and printed texts. The overall research evidence suggests that reading speed may be slower for electronic texts; but when Haas and Hayes (1985b) enhanced the textual display on the computer, reading speed increased to a level that was not significantly different from texts presented on printed pages. Similarly, it is difficult to interpret the results of studies using different word-processing programs when little is known about what characteristics separate good and poor programs.

Several researchers, consistent with their interest in divergent applications of computers to reading, have theorized about the differences between electronic and printed texts. Wilkinson (1983), for example, has argued that the fundamental differences between the computer and the printed page are related to framing, pacing, and control. With the aid of a computer, various units of texts ranging from individual letters to lengthy paragraphs can be presented as a single frame isolated from the remainder of a text. The rate at which these frames are presented to the reader can be controlled and that control can be allocated in varying degrees to either the computer or the reader. Daniel and Reinking (1987) have identified similar factors in a somewhat different framework. They use the label "static legibility" to refer to visual factors that have been associated with the legibility of printed texts and they discuss how these factors apply to electronic texts. They argue that unique factors associated with electronic texts go beyond static legibility to include "dynamic" and "interactive" legibility. *Dynamic legibility* refers to those factors that concern decisions about *when* to display text on a computer screen in addition to *where* it is to be displayed (these factors are similar to Wilkinson's notion of pacing). *Interactive legibility* refers to those factors associated with how a reader interacts with texts displayed via the computer (these factors subsume Wilkinson's notion of control).

Using Salomon's (1979) definition of an instructional medium, Reinking (1987) has argued that computer-mediated text and printed text may be considered separate media. In this view, a medium is defined by how its symbol systems and technological attributes affect cognitive processing. A particular medium requires a learner to employ a unique set of cognitive skills to derive meaning from that medium. Media can also be distinguished by the degree to which their technological attributes permit relevant cognitive skills to be modeled, practiced, or supplanted. He concluded that the technological attributes of computer-mediated text, when compared to printed text, vary considerably along these dimensions and that it may be useful to focus on these differences when developing and investigating computer-mediated text. For example, one way that computer-mediated text may affect cognitive processing during reading is that it can be used to instigate a literal interaction between a reader and a text (as opposed to the figurative interaction that is frequently referred to when discussing the comprehension of printed text).

Hypertext, for example, is an application that clearly illustrates how computers permit texts to respond to the needs of a particular reader. Likewise, the capability of computers to control interactions between a reader and a text (e.g., by limiting a reader's access to text) also illustrates how computer-mediated texts might be used to guide the development of metacognitive awareness and other comprehension skills. Reinking (Reinking & Schreiner, 1985; Reinking, 1988) employed this theoretical rationale to develop a computer-mediated text and to investigate its effect on reading comprehension. He argued that the results of these studies and others in which the technological attributes of the computer were used to expand or control readers' interactions with the text lend support to this theoretical position. Reader versus computer control has emerged as an important theoretical issue for those interested in studying computer-mediated text (see Reinking, 1986), and the prominence of this issue parallels the interest in learner control among those interested generally in computer-assisted instruction (see Carrier, 1984).

Duchastel (1986) has argued that the differences between text presented in books or by computers revolve around the central problem of how information is accessed. In his view, textual information can be either format structured (e.g., an airline schedule) or semantically structured (e.g., a chapter in a psychology text); and various means for accessing efficiently the information embedded in these structures have evolved over time. Semantically structured information presents a greater challenge for accessing information because it consists of a set of highly interrelated informational elements. A fundamental limitation of books is that they normally require semantically structured information to be presented in a single hierarchical sequence, and thus books do not permit a great degree of flexibility for accessing the information they convey. A computer, however, permits highly flexible and individualized approaches to structuring and to accessing information, but it also limits strategies like browsing to locate information (see Anderson-Inman, 1988). This flexibility implies that the structure of electronic texts may require readers to develop new strategies for locating and processing information. Designers of such texts must also develop methods to prevent readers from becoming disoriented while reading flexibly structured texts (Dede, 1988; Kerr, 1987; Yankelovich, Meyrowitz, & Van Dam, 1985). Like other writers, Duchastel (1986) also highlights the controlled access to information as a defining attribute of electronic texts.

Affective factors associated with instructional media have also been incorporated into theoretical models. Salomon (1984) has proposed such a model and he conducted an experiment to test its validity. Although he compared information presented via printed texts and a television program, the model and the experiment have implications for comparing printed and electronic texts. Simply stated, his model related learning to the amount of mental effort invested, which is mediated by the learner's perception of learning via a particular instructional medium. Subjects in the experiment believed learning from the text was more difficult than learning from television and therefore invested more mental effort while reading, which increased their learning. These results suggest that if readers perceive learning from printed and from electronic texts differently, their perceptions could influence comprehension.

As options for presenting texts electronically increase, theoretical positions must expand to accommodate them. For example, interactive video and other new video-based technologies have made it possible to integrate text, computer-generated graphics, and high-quality audio/video productions into highly flexible formats. Sherwood, Kinzer, Hasselbring, and Bransford (1986) found that using a computer to combine video and text led to greater comprehension. They developed a rationale for their findings, which was based on theories related to contextual learning, the role of environmental mediators, and semantically rich domains for problem solving. Similar theoretical speculation will be required as the display of electronic texts becomes more sophisticated.

The theoretical positions outlined in this section and the research to which they relate also have implications for using computers in reading instruction. For example, the capabilities of the computer to direct more actively a reader's processing of the text might lead to instructional activities designed to develop metacognitive skills.

EMERGING ISSUES AND TRENDS

The computer has been described as a machine that can become a machine (Ellis, 1974). This versatility has spawned increasingly widespread and diverse applications of computers to daily activities, including the ways in which people read and write. Several writers have chronicled the increasing use of computers for reading and writing and they have speculated about the implications of this trend for the future. Halpern and Liggett (1984) described the effects of new technologies like telecommunication, dictation systems, and word processing on writing in the workplace; and they have suggested changes that these technological developments imply for writing pedagogy. A collection of papers edited by Olson (1985) describes how technologies such as videodisc players, CAI in language learning, and mainframe computers affect writers in the humanities. Feldman and Norman (1987) have described how computer-based activities such as publishing, collecting and maintaining data bases, analyzing literature, and developing concordances change the nature of academic writing and how scholarly information is disseminated.

These and similar trends may make moot many of the practical questions addressed by current research. For example, the results of convergent studies comparing minimally different electronic and conventional texts may become more relevant for theory than for practice. Although it is unlikely that printed texts will disappear entirely, the increasingly widespread use of electronic media to compose and to display text is likely to continue. For the future it will be more important to know how to optimize reading performance when texts are displayed electronically. The challenge that this goal presents should not be underestimated. Decades of research devoted to optimizing the display of printed texts have not led to definitive recommendations (see Waller, ch. 14 in this volume). Despite some apparent limitations, the options for displaying texts electronically with the aid of a computer are infinitely greater than for printed texts. Researchers interested in electronic text, therefore, will need to address a more complex array of variables and a broader range of research questions.

The open-ended capabilities of the computer to monitor an individual's performance, to provide individual assistance, and to stimulate active processing of written language suggest that the computer will remain an important tool that significantly expands options for teaching reading and writing. For example, the increasing availability of computerized speech suggests interesting new possibilities for teaching sound-symbol correspondences as well as helping beginning readers decode words during independent reading. Likewise, improvements in computer programs that provide individualized feedback concerning students' writing will allow teachers to focus on more abstract components of the writing process.

Another current trend in instruction is the use of computer technology to develop authentic communicative contexts for reading and writing in schools (Reinking, 1986). For example, computer networks enable students to communicate with a wide variety of individuals beyond the walls of their classroom. This trend contributes significantly to the renewed interest in linking reading and writing activities in schools, and it is supported by the research indicating that writing for conventional school assignments is different from "free writing" outside of school (Kirby & Kirby, 1985). Similarly, due to computers, the often adversarial relationship between teachers and students in school-related writing activities is being replaced by a master-apprentice relationship. The computer has become a means for creating a sequence of temporary drafts that serve as a focus for ongoing student-teacher dialogues about the improvement of written work.

A related development is the increase in *desktop publishing*, the ability to create materials that are produced with widely available, relatively inexpensive, and easy-to-use microcomputers and printers. This development, coupled with the availability of electronic means for disseminating texts, may affect dramatically the current barriers to disseminating and accessing written information. One indication of this trend is the fact that the *New York Post* reports that half of its profits in 1986 were from selling rights to display the newspaper electronically (Anderson-Inmann, 1988). These developments augur important changes in the publishing industry—changes that will affect reading and writing in ways that are difficult to predict from our present vantage point.

Computers continue to have an expanding role in reading and writing research. In addition to using computers for data analyses, researchers are experimenting with new computer-based procedures to investigate internal cognitive processes. For example, by recording a reader's or a writer's use of a computer to interact with text, a researcher can make inferences about underlying processes (e.g., see Kunz, Schott, & Hovekamp, 1987; Wollen, Cone, Margres & Wollen, 1985). Such methods can corroborate findings derived from traditional methods such as recording physical data (e.g., eye movements) or verbal protocols. Advances in the use of computers to analyze the characteristics of a particular text also provide researchers with a new tool for characterizing and manipulating textual variables. Frase (1987), for example, conducted several experiments investigating writing styles based on computer-generated data concerning verb-adjective ratios and patterns of repetition for syllables and parts of speech.

We began this review by highlighting the historical link between technology and written language. We also suggested that the increasingly widespread use of computers to communicate information may prove to be a significant development in that history. One indication of this trend is that several writers have begun to discuss revising the definitions of literacy to include reading and writing electronically (e.g., Kamil, 1987; Calfee, 1985). The content of reading and writing instruction has begun to reflect these changes, most noticeably in the increasing use of word processors in writing instruction. As electronic texts become more prevalent, educators concerned with the teaching of reading and writing will need to confront these changes. Traditional skills like skimming and scanning printed texts, for example, will need to be reoriented because of the different contingencies associated with locating information from texts displayed by a computer on a CRT screen. The use of the card catalog as a reference source in libraries is quickly becoming obsolete. Students in the future will also need to learn how to search data bases and locate information stored via other electronic means.

These changes are likely to accelerate as new, hybrid forms of computer-mediated text appear. Hypertext, for example, will undoubtedly necessitate the development of new metacognitive strategies for locating and comprehending textual information. Writers of these texts will need new heuristics for approaching writing tasks. To meet the challenges implied by these emerging issues, researchers investigating applications of the computer to reading and writing must be equipped with a knowledge of existing research and an awareness of the critical questions that it defines. So equipped, researchers will be able to provide constructive guidance to our increasing dependence on computer technology for reading and writing.

REFERENCES

Alexander, C. (1984). *Microcomputers and teaching reading in college* (Research Monograph Series Report No. 8). New York: Instructional Resource Center, New York University.

Alderman, D. L., Appel, L. R., & Murray, R. T. (1978). PLATO and TICCIT: An evaluation of CAI in the community college. *Educational Technology, 18* (4), 40–44.

Anderson-Inman, L. (1988, May). *Problems in using computers to promote computers across the curriculum.* Paper presented at the meeting of International Reading Association, Toronto, Ontario.

Alvermann, D. (1987). Using computer-simulated instruction to study preservice teachers' thought processes. In D. Reinking (Ed.), *Reading and computers: Issues for theory and practice* (pp. 141–155). New York: Teachers College Press, Columbia University.

Atkinson, R. C. (1974). Teaching children to read with a computer. *American Psychologist, 29,* 169–178.

Atkinson, R. C., & Hansen, D. N. (1966). Computer-assisted instruction in initial reading: The Stanford project. *Reading Research Quarterly, 2,* 5–26.

Balajthy, E. (1984). Reinforcement and drilling by microcomputer. *Reading Teacher, 37,* 490–494.

Balajthy, E. (1986). *Microcomputers in reading and language arts.* Englewood Cliffs, NJ: Prentice-Hall.

Balajthy, E. (1987). What does research on computer-based instruction have to say to the reading teacher? *Reading Research and Instruction, 27* (1), 55–65.

Balajthy, E. (1988). An investigation of learner-control variables in vocabulary learning using traditional instruction and two forms of computer-based instruction. *Reading Research and Instruction. 27* (4), 15–24.

Balajthy, E. (1989). *Computers and reading: Lessons from the past and the technologies of the future.* Englewood Cliffs, NJ: Prentice-Hall.

Beach, R., & Bridwell, L. S. (Eds.). (1984). *New directions in composition research.* New York: Guilford Press.

Bernhardt, S. A., Edwards, P., & Wojahn, P. (1989). Teaching college composition with computers: A program evaluation study. *Written Communication, 6*(11), 108–133.

Blanchard, J. S. (1984). U.S. armed services computer-assisted literacy efforts. *Journal of Reading, 28,* 262–265.

Blanchard, J. S., & Mason, G. E., (1985). Using computers in content area reading instruction. *Journal of Reading, 29,* 112–117.

Blanchard, J. S., Mason, G. E., & Daniel, D. (1987). *Computer applications in reading* (3rd ed.). Newark, DE: International Reading Association.

Blackstock, J., & Miller, L. (1988). *Schools, computers, and learning: A longitudinal study of the mutual adaptation of new information technology and education* (Report No. 4). Toronto, Ontario: Ontario Ministry of Education.

Blohm, P. J. (1982). Computer-aided glossing and facilitated learning in prose recall. In J. A. Niles & L. A. Harris (Eds.), *New inquiries in reading research and instruction* (pp. 24–28). Thirty-first Yearbook of the National Reading Conference. Rochester, NY: National Reading Association.

Blohm, P. J. (1987). Effect on [sic] lookup aids on mature readers' recall of technical text. *Reading Research and Instruction, 26,* 77–88.

Bridwell, L. S., Nancarrow, P. R., & Ross, D. (1984). The writing process and the writing machine: Current research on word processors relevant to the teaching of composition. In R. Beach and L. S. Bridwell (Eds.), *New directions in composition research* (pp. 381–398). New York: Guilford Press.

Bridwell, L. S., Sirc, G., & Brooke, R. (1985). Revising and computing: Case studies of student writers. In S. Freedman (Ed.), *The acquisition of written language: Revision and response* (pp. 172–194). Norwood, NJ: Ablex.

Bridwell-Bowles, L. S., Johnson, P., & Brehe, S. (1987). Composing and computers: Case studies of experienced writers. In A. Matsuhashi (Ed.), *Writing in real time: Modelling production processes* (pp. 81–107). White Plains, NY: Longman.

Bruce, B., & Rubin, A. (1983). *Phase II report for the QUILL project.* Cambridge, MA: Bolt, Beranek, and Newman.

Burns, H. (1984) Recollections of first-generation computer-assisted prewriting. In W. Wresch (Ed.), *The computer in composition instruction* (pp. 15–33). Urbana, IL: National Council of Teachers of English.

Burns, H., & Culp, G. (1980). Stimulating invention in English composition through computer-assisted instruction. *Educational Technology, 20,* 5–10.

Bury, K. F., Boyle, J. M., Evey, R. J., & Neal, A. S. (1982). Windowing versus scrolling on a visual display terminal. *Human Factors, 24,* 385–394.

Butler-Nalin, K. (1985). *Process and product: How research methodologies and composing using a computer influence writing.* Unpublished doctoral dissertation, Stanford University.

Caldwell, R. M., & Rizza, P. J. (1979). A computer-based system of reading instruction for adult nonreaders. *AEDS Journal, 12,* 157–162.

Calfee, R. (1985). Computer literacy and book literacy: Parallels and contrasts. *Educational Researcher, 14* (5), 8–13.

Carrier, C. (1984). Do learners make good choices? *Instructional Innovator, 29,* 15–17.

Carver, R. P., & Hoffman, J. V. (1981). The effect of practice through repeated reading on gain in reading ability using a computer-based instructional system. *Reading Research Quarterly, 16,* 374–390.

Center for Social Organization of Schools. (1983–84). *School uses of microcomputers: Reports from a national survey* (Report Nos. 1–4). Baltimore, MD: Johns Hopkins University.

Chall, J., & Conrad, S. (1984). Resources and their use for reading instruction. In A. C. Penues & O. Niles (Eds.), *Becoming readers in a complex society.* Eighty-third Yearbook of the National Society for the Study of Education. Chicago, IL: University of Chicago Press.

Clark, R. E. (1983). Reconsidering research on learning from media. *Review of Educational Research, 53*, 445–459.

Clement, F. J. (1981). Affective considerations in computer-based education. *Educational Technology, 21* (4), 28–32.

Collier, R. M. (1983). The word processor and revision strategies. *College Composition and Communication, 34*, 149–155.

Congressional Office of Technology Assessment. (1988). *Power on: New tools for teaching* (Publication No. 052-003-01125-5). Washington, DC: U.S. Government Printing Office.

Cushman, W. H. (1986). Reading from microfiche, a VDT, and the printed page: Subjective fatigue and performance. *Human Factors, 28*, 63–73.

Daiute, C. (1983). The computer as stylus and audience. *College Composition and Communication, 34*, 134–145.

Daiute, C. (1985). *Writing & computers*. Reading, MA: Addison-Wesley.

Daiute, C. (1986). Physical and cognitive factors in revising: Insights from studies with computers. *Research in the Teaching of English, 20*, 141–159.

Daniel, D. B., & Reinking, D. (1987). The construct of legibility in electronic reading environments. In D. Reinking (Ed.), *Reading and computers: Issues for theory and practice* (pp. 24–39). New York: Teachers College Press, Columbia University.

Day, K. C., & Day, H. (1984). The availability of language arts software for the microcomputer. *Reading Improvement, 21*, 162–164.

Dede, C. (1988). *Emerging information technologies of significance for postsecondary occupational education*. Clear Lake, TX: University of Houston, Institute for Strategic Innovation.

Duchastel, P. (1986). Computer text access. *Computer Education, 10*, 403–409.

Duchnicky, R. L., & Kolers, P. A. (1983). Readability of text scrolled on visual display terminals as a function of window size. *Human Factors, 25*, 683–692.

Duin, A. H. (1987). Computer exercises to encourage rethinking and revision. *Computers and Composition, 4*, 66–105.

Duin, A. H. (1988). Computer-assisted instructional displays: Effects on students' computing behaviors, prewriting, and attitudes. *Journal of Computer-Based Instruction, 15*, 48–56.

Duin, A. H., Jorn, L., & DeBower, M. (in press). Collaborative writing—courseware and telecommunications. In M. Lay and W. Karis (Eds.), *Collaborative writing in industry*. Farmingdale, NY: Baywood.

Duling, R. A. (1986). Word processors and student writing: A study of their impact on revision, fluency, and quality of writing. *Dissertation Abstracts International, 46*, 1823-A.

Ellis, A. (1974). *The use and misuse of computers in education*. New York: McGraw-Hill.

Etchison, C. (1986). A comparative study of the quality and syntax of composition by first-year college students using handwriting and word processing. *Dissertation Abstracts International, 47*, 163-A.

Feldman, P. R., & Norman, B. (1987). *The wordworthy computer: Classroom and research applications in language and literature*, New York: Random House.

Fish, M. C., & Feldmann, S. C. (1987). A comparison of reading comprehension using print and microcomputer presentation. *Journal of Computer-Based Instruction, 14*, 57–61.

Fletcher, J. D., & Atkinson, R. C. (1972). Evaluation of the Stanford CAI program in initial reading. *Journal of Educational Psychology, 63*, 597–602.

Forster, K. I. (1970). Visual perception of rapidly presented word sequences of varying complexity. *Perception & Psychophysics, 8*, 215–221.

Frase, L. T. (1987). Computer analysis of written materials. In D. Reinking (Ed.), *Reading and computers: Issues for theory and practice* (pp. 76–96). New York: Teachers College Press, Columbia University.

Gambrell, L. B., Bradley, V. N., & McLaughlin, E. M. (1987). Young children's comprehension and recall of computer screen displayed text. *Journal of Research in Reading, 10*, 156–163.

Geoffrion, L. D., & Geoffrion, O. P. (1983). *Computers and reading instruction*. Reading, MA: Addison-Wesley.

Gerrard, L. (Ed.). (1987). *Writing at century's ends: Essays on computer-assisted composition*. New York: Random House.

Gillis, P. D. (1987). Using computer technology to teach and evaluate prewriting. *Computers and the Humanities, 21*, 3–19.

Goodwin, L. D., Goodwin, W. L., Nansel, A., & Helm, C. P. (1986). Cognitive and affective effects of various types of microcomputer use by preschoolers. *American Educational Research Journal, 23*, 348–356.

Gould, J. D., & Gischkowsky, N. (1983). Doing the same work with paper and cathode ray tube displays (CRT). *Human Factors, 24*, 329–338.

Gunnarsson, E., & Soderberg, I. (1983). Eye strain resulting from VDT work at the Swedish Telecommunications Administration. *Applied Ergonomics, 14*, 61–69.

Haas, C., & Hayes, J. (1985a). *Effects of text display variables on reading tasks: Computer screen vs. hard copy* (CDC Technical Report No. 3). Pittsburgh, PA: Carnegie-Mellon University, Communications Design Center.

Haas, C., & Hayes, J. (1985b). *Reading on the computer: A comparison of standard and advanced computer display and hard copy* (CDC Technical Report No. 7). Pittsburgh PA: Carnegie-Mellon University, Communications Design Center.

Hague, S. A., & Mason, G. E. (1986). Using the computer's readability measure to teach students to revise their writing. *Journal of Reading, 30,* 14–17.

Halpern, J. W., & Liggett, S. (1984). *Computers & composing: How the new technologies are changing writing.* Carbondale, IL: Southern Illinois University Press.

Hansen, W. J., Doring, R. R., & Whitlock, L. R. (1978). Why an examination was slower on-line than on paper. *International Journal of Man-Machine Studies, 10,* 507–519.

Harper, J. A., & Ewing, N. J. (1986). A comparison of the effectiveness of microcomputer and workbook instruction on reading comprehension performance of high-incidence handicapped children. *Educational Technology, 26* (5), 40–45.

Harris, J. (1985). Student writers and word processing: A preliminary evaluation. *College Composition and Communication, 36,* 323–330.

Harrison, C. (1987, December). *Computers and reading in the UK and Europe: A review of research.* Paper presented at the meeting of the National Reading Conference, St. Petersburg Beach, FL.

Hawisher, G. E. (1986). Studies in word processing. *Computers and Composition, 4* (1), 6–31.

Hawisher, G. E. (1987). The effects of word processing on the revision strategies of college freshmen. *Research in the Teaching of English, 21,* 145–159.

Henney, M. (1983). The effect of all-capital vs. regular mixed print, as presented on a computer screen, on reading rate and accuracy. *AEDS Journal, 16,* 205–217.

Heppner, F. H., Anderson, J. G. T., Farstrup, A. E., & Weidermann, N. H. (1985). Reading performance on a standardized test is better from print than from computer display. *Journal of Reading, 28,* 321–325.

Herrmann, A. (1986). An ethnographic study of a high school writing class using computers: Marginal, technically proficient, and productive learners. In L. Gerrard (Ed.), *Writing at century's end: Essays on computer-assisted composition* (pp. 79–91). New York: Random House.

Hulme, C. (1984). Reading: Extracting information from printed and electronic text. In A. Monk (Ed.), *Fundamentals of human-computer interaction.* London: Academic Press.

Jandreau, S. M., Muncer, S. J., & Bever, T. G. (1986). Improving readability of text with automatic phrase-sensitive formating. *British Journal of Educational Technology, 2,* 128–133.

Jelden, D. (1981). The microcomputer as a multiuser interactive instructional system. *AEDS Journal, 14,* 208–217.

Jonassen, D. H. (1986). Hypertext principles for text and courseware design. *Educational Psychologist, 21,* 269–292.

Just, M. A., & Carpenter, P. A. (1987). *The psychology of reading and language comprehension.* Boston, MA: Allyn and Bacon.

Kamil, M. L. (1982). Technology and reading: A review of research and instruction. In J. Niles & L. Harris (Eds.), *New inquiries in reading research and instruction* (pp. 251–260). Thirty-first Yearbook of the National Reading Conference. Rochester, NY: National Reading Conference.

Kamil, M. L. (1987). Computers and reading research. In D. Reinking (Ed.), *Reading and computers: Issues for theory and practice* (pp. 57–75). New York: Teachers College Press, Columbia University.

Kemp. F. (1987). The user-friendly fallacy. *College Composition and Communication, 38,* 32–39.

Kerr, S. T. (1987, February). *Finding one's way in electronic space: The relative importance of navigational cues and mental models.* Paper presented at the meeting of the Association for Educational Communication and Technology, Atlanta, GA.

Kiefer, K. E., & Smith, C. R. (1983). Textual analysis with computers: Tests of Bell Laboratories' computer software. *Research in the Teaching of English, 17,* 201–14.

Kirby, D. R., & Kirby, K. (1985). The reading-writing connection. In L. W. Searfoss & J. E. Readence (Eds.), *Helping children learn to read* (pp. 338–353). Englewood Cliffs, NJ: Prentice-Hall.

Kleine, M. (1983). *Syntactic choice and theory of discourse: Rethinking sentence combining.* Unpublished doctoral dissertation, University of Minnesota, Minneapolis, MN.

Kruk, R. S., & Muter, P. (1984). Reading continuous text on video screens. *Human Factors, 26,* 339–345.

Kulik, C. C., Kulik, J. A., & Cohen, P. A. (1980). Effectiveness of computer-based college teaching: A meta-analysis of findings. *Review of Educational Research, 50,* 524–535.

Kulik, J. A., Bangert, R. L., & Williams, G. W. (1983). Effects of computer-based teaching on secondary school students. *Journal of Educational Psychology, 75,* 19–26.

Kulik, J. A., Kulik, C. C., & Bangert-Drowns, R. L. (1985). Effectiveness of computer-based education in elementary schools. *Computers in Human Behavior, 1,* 59–74.

Kunz, G. C., Schott, F., & Hovekamp, D. (1987). *Analysis of self-regulation in learning from texts by means of the learner-controlled computer system CARLA* (Diskussionspapier No. 24). Giessen, West Germany: Universität Giessen, Fachbereich Psychologie, Arbeitsgruppe: Kognition und Instruktion.

L'Allier, J. J. (1980). *An evaluation study of a computer-based lesson that adjusts reading level by monitoring on task reader characteristics.* Unpublished doctoral dissertation, University of Minnesota, Minneapolis, MN.

Lesgold, A. M. (1983). A rationale for computer-based reading instruction. In A. C. Wilkinson (Ed.), *Classroom computers and cognitive science* (pp. 167–181). New York: Academic Press.

Leu, D. J., & Kinzer, C. K. (1987). *Effective reading instruction in the elementary grades.* Columbus, OH: Merrill.

Levin, H. M. (1986). Cost and cost effectiveness of computer-assisted instruction. In J. A. Culbertson & L. L.

Cunningham (Eds.), *Microcomputers and education*. Eighty-fifth Yearbook of the National Society for the Study of Education, Part I (pp. 156–174). Chicago, IL: University of Chicago Press.

Levin, J., Riel, M., Rowe, R., & Boruta, M. (1985). Muktuk meets jacuzzi: Computer networks and elementary school writers. In S. Freedman (Ed.), *The acquisition of written language: Revision and response*. New York: Ablex.

Lutz, J. A. (1987). A study of professional and experienced writers revising and editing at the computer and with pen and paper. *Research in the Teaching of English, 21*, 398–421.

MacGregor, S. K. (1988). Use of self-questioning with a computer-mediated text system and measures of reading performance. *Journal of Reading Behavior, 20*, 131–148.

Martin, J. (1984). An eclectic approach to reading. *School Administrator, 41* (2), 18–19.

Martinez, M. E., & Mead, N. A. (1988). *Computer competence: The first national assessment* (Research Rep. No. 17-CC-01). Princeton, NJ: Educational Testing Service.

Mason, G. E. (1980). Computerized reading instruction: A review. *Educational Technology, 20*, 18–22.

Mason, G. E., Blanchard, J. S., & Daniel, D. B. (1983). *Computer applications in reading* (2nd ed.). Newark, DE: International Reading Association.

McConkie, G. W. (1983, November/December). *Computer-aided reading: A help for illiterate adults*. Paper presented at the meeting of the National Reading Conference, Austin, TX.

McDaniel, E. (1985). *A bibliography of text analysis and writing instruction software*. Philadelphia: Temple University Working Papers in Composition.

McGee, G. W. (1987). Social context variables affecting the implementation of microcomputers. *Journal of Educational Computing Research, 3*, 189–206.

Merrill, P. F. (1985). Displaying text on microcomputers. In D. H. Jonassen (Ed.), *The technology of text* (Vol. 2) (pp. 401–414). Englewood Cliffs, NJ: Educational Technology Publications.

Mikelonis, V., & Gervicks, V. (1985). Using computers in the technical writing classroom: A selected bibliography, 1978–84. *Technical Writing Teacher, 12* (2), 161–176.

Miller, L., & Burnett, J. D. (1987). Using computers as an integral aspect of elementary language arts instruction: Paradoxes, problems, and promise. In D. Reinking (Ed.), *Reading and computers: Issues for theory and practice* (pp. 178–191). New York: Teachers College Press, Columbia University.

Mourant, R., Lakshmanan, R., & Chantadisai, R. (1981). Visual fatigue and cathode ray tube display terminals. *Human Factors, 23*, 529–540.

Murphy, R. T., & Appel, L. R. (1984). *Evaluation of the writing to read instructional system 1982–1984: A presentation from the second-year report*. Princeton, NJ: Educational Testing Service.

Muter, P., Latremouille, S., Treurniet, W., & Beam, P. (1982). Extended reading of continuous text on television screens. *Human Factors, 24*, 501–508.

Nancarrow, P. R., Ross, D., & Bridwell, L. S. (1984). *Word processing and the writing process: An annotated bibliography*. Westport, CT: Greenwood.

National Research Council. (1983). *Video displays, work, and vision*. Washington, DC: National Academy Press.

Niemiec, R. P., Blackwell, M. C., & Walberg, H. J. (1986). CAI can be doubly effective. *Phi Delta Kappan, 67*, 750–751.

Norton, P., & Resta, V. (1986). Investigating the impact of computer instruction on elementary students' reading achievement. *Educational Technology, 26* (3), 35–41.

Obertino, P. (1974). The PLATO reading project: An overview. *Educational Technology, 14* (2), 8–13.

Olson, R. K., Foltz, G., & Wise, B. (1986). Reading instruction and remediation with the aid of computer speech. *Behavior Research Methods, Instruments, and Computers, 18*, 93–99.

Olson, R. K., & Wise, B. (1987). Computer speech in reading instruction. In D. Reinking (Ed.), *Reading and computers: Issues for theory and practice* (pp. 156–177). New York: Teachers College Press, Columbia University.

Olson, S. (Ed.). (1985). *Computer-aided instruction in the humanities*. New York: Modern Language Association.

Ong, W. J. (1982). *Orality and literacy: The technologizing of the word*. New York: Methuen.

Philhower, S. C. (1986). The effects of the use of a word-processing program on the writing skills of mildly handicapped secondary students. *Dissertation Abstracts International, 47*, 867-A.

Potter, F. (1987). *New information technologies and literacy skills: Applications and implications for reading and writing* (Commission of the European Communities Grant No. 2438-86-11-NIT-UK). Ormskirk, U.K.: Edge Hill College of Higher Education.

Poulsen, G., & Macken, E. (1978). Evaluation studies of CCC elementary-school curriculums 1975–1977. *CCC Educational Studies, 1* (2), 1–68.

Pufahl, J. (1984). Response to Richard M. Collier, "The word processor and revision strategies." *College Composition and Communication, 34*, 91–93.

Reinking, D. (1986). Six advantages of computer-mediated text for reading and writing instruction. *Reading Instruction Journal, 29*, 8–16.

Reinking, D. (1987). Computers, reading, and a new technology of print. In D. Reinking (Ed.), *Reading and computers: Issues for theory and practice* (pp. 3–23). New York: Teachers College Press, Columbia University.

Reinking, D. (1988). Computer-mediated text and comprehension differences: The role of reading time, reader preference, and estimation of learning. *Reading Research Quarterly, 23*, 484–498.

Reinking, D. (1989). Misconceptions about reading that affect software development. *Computing Teacher, 16* (4), 27–29.

Reinking, D., & Schreiner, R. (1985). The effects of computer-mediated text on measures of reading comprehension and reading behavior. *Reading Research Quarterly, 20*, 536–552.

Reinking, D., Kling, M., & Harper, M. K. (1985). *Characteristics of computer software in reading: An empirical investigation.* Unpublished manuscript, New Brunswick, NJ: Graduate School of Education, Rutgers University.

Reitsma, P. (1988). Reading practice for beginners: Effects of guided reading, reading-while-listening, and independent reading with computer-based speech feedback. *Reading Research Quarterly, 23*, 219–235.

Robinson, R., & Good, T. L. (1987). *Becoming an effective reading teacher.* New York: Harper & Row.

Roblyer, M., Castine, W., & King, F. (1988). *The effectiveness of computer applications for instruction: A review and synthesis of recent research findings.* New York: Haworth Press.

Rodrigues, D., & Rodrigues, R. J. (1986). *Teaching writing with a word processor, grades 7–13.* Urbana, IL: National Council of Teachers of English.

Rosegrant, T. (1984). Fostering progress in literacy development: Technology and social development. *Seminars in Speech and Language, 5* (1), 47–57.

Rosenthal, J. W. (1987). Integrating word processing into freshman composition. *Computer-Assisted Composition Journal, 1*, 119–131.

Ross, D., Jr., & Bridwell, L. S. (1985). Computer-aided composing: Gaps in the software. In S. Olsen (Ed.), *Computer-aided instruction in the humanities* (pp. 103–115). New York: Modern Language Association.

Roth, S. F., & Beck, I. L. (1987). Theoretical and instructional implications of the assessment of two microcomputer word recognition programs. *Reading Research Quarterly, 22*, 197–218.

Rubens, P., & Krull, R. (1985). Application of research on document design to on-line displays. *Technical Communication, 32*, 29–34.

Rubin, A. (1983). The computer confronts the language arts: Cans and shoulds for education. In A. C. Wilkinson (Ed.), *Classroom computers and cognitive science* (pp. 201–217). New York: Academic Press.

Rude, R. T. (1986). *Teaching reading using microcomputers.* Englewood Cliffs, NJ: Prentice-Hall.

Salomon, G. (1979). *Interaction of media, cognition, and learning.* San Francisco, CA: Jossey-Bass.

Salomon, G. (1984). Television is "easy" and print is "tough": The differential investment of mental effort in learning as a function of perceptions and attributions. *Journal of Educational Psychology, 76*, 647–658.

Samuels, S. J. (1979). The method of repeated readings. *Reading Teacher, 32*, 403–408.

Samuels, S. J. (1980). The age-old controversy between holistic and subskill approaches to beginning reading instruction revisited. In C. M. McCullough (Ed.), *Inchworm, inchworm: Persistent problems in reading education* (pp. 202–221). Newark, DE: International Reading Association.

Saracho, O. N. (1982). The effects of a computer-assisted instruction program on basic skills achievement and attitudes toward instruction of Spanish-speaking migrant children. *American Educational Research Journal, 19*, 201–219.

Schank, E. T. (1986). *Word processor versus the pencil: Effects on writing.* Urbana, IL: ERIC Document Reproduction Service No. ED 270 291.

Schaudt, B. A. (1987). The use of computers in a direct instruction reading lesson. *Reading Psychology, 8*, 169–178.

Schnitz, J. E., Maynes, D., & Revel, L. (1983). *High technology and basic skills in reading* (Contract No. 300-80-0844). Washington, DC: U.S. Department of Education.

Schwartz, H. (1985). *Interactive writing: Composing with a word processor.* New York: Holt, Rinehart, & Winston.

Schwartz, H., & Bridwell, L. S. (1984). A selected bibliography on computers in composition. *College Composition and Communication, 35*, 71–77.

Schwartz, H., and Bridwell-Bowles, L. (1987). A selected bibliography on computers in composition: An update. *College Composition and Communication, 38*, 453–457.

Selfe, C. (1986). *Computer-assisted instruction in composition: Create your own.* Urbana, IL: NCTE.

Sherwood, R. D., Kinzer, C. K., Hasselbring, S., & Bransford, J. D. (1987). Macro-contexts for learning: Initial findings and issues. *Applied Cognitive Psychology, 1*, 93–108.

Siegel, M. A., & Davis, D. M. (1987). Redefining a basic CAI technique to teach reading comprehension. In D. Reinking (Ed.), *Reading and computers: Issues for theory and practice* (pp. 111–126). New York: Teachers College Press, Columbia University.

Sirc, G., & Bridwell-Bowles, L. (1988). A computer tool for analyzing the composing process. *Collegiate Microcomputer, 6* (2), 155–160.

Smith, C. R., & Kiefer, K. E. (1983). Using the Writer's Workbench programs at Colorado State University. In S. K. Burton & D. D. Short (Eds.), *Sixth International Conference on Computers and the Humanities* (pp. 672–684). Rockville, MD: Computer Science Press.

Smith, F. (1984). *The promise and threat of microcomputers in language education.* Victoria, British Columbia: Abel Press.

Spache, G. D. (1967). A reaction to "Computer-assisted instruction in initial reading: The Stanford project."

Reading Research Quarterly, 3, 101–109.

Strickland, D. S., Feeley, J. T., & Wepner, S. B. (1987). *Using computers in the teaching of reading.* New York: Teachers College Press, Columbia University.

Strickland, J. (1987). Computers, invention, and the power to change student writing. *Computers and Composition, 4,* 7–26.

TALMIS Education *Newsletter.* (1983, Spring). Software: Topics and types.

Tanner, D. E. (1984). Horses, carts, and computers in reading: A review of research. *Computers Reading and Language Arts, 2* (1), 35–38.

Thompson, B. J. (1980). Computers in reading: A review of applications and implications. *Educational Technology, 50,* 38–41.

Tobias, S. (1987). Mandatory text review and interaction with student characteristics. *Journal of Educational Psychology, 79,* 154–161.

Trollip, S. R., & Sales, G. (1986). Readability of computer-generated fill-justified text. *Human Factors, 28,* 159–163.

Turner, T. C. (1988). Using the computer for adult literacy instruction. *Journal of Reading, 31,* 643–647.

Vacca, J. L., Vacca, R. T., & Gove, M. K. (1987). *Reading and learning to read.* Boston: Little, Brown.

Venezky, R. L. (1983). Evaluating computer-assisted instruction on its own terms. In A. C. Wilkinson (Ed.), *Classroom computers and cognitive science* (pp. 31–49). New York: Academic Press.

Vinsonhaler, J. F., Weinshank, A. B., Wagner, C. C., & Polin, R. M. (1987). Computers, simulated cases, and the training of reading diagnosticians In D. Reinking (Ed.), *Reading and computers: Issues for theory and practice* (pp. 127–140). New York: Teachers College Press, Columbia University.

Weyer, S. A. (1982). The design of a dynamic book for information search. *International Journal of Man-Machine Studies, 17,* 87–107.

Wigfield, A., & Asher, S. R. (1984). Social and Motivational influences on reading. In P. D. Pearson (Ed.), *Handbook of reading research* (Vol. 1) (pp. 423–452). New York: Longman.

Wilkinson, A. C. (1983). Learning to read in real time. In A. C. Wilkinson (Ed.), *Classroom computers and cognitive science* (pp. 183–199). New York: Academic Press.

Wollen, K. A., Cone, R. S., Margres, M. G., & Wollen, B. P. (1985). Computer programs to facilitate detailed analysis of how people study text passages. *Behavior Research Methods, Instruments, and Computers, 17,* 371–378.

Woodruff, E., Bereiter, C., & Scardamalia, M. (1981–82). On the road to computer-assisted compositions. *Journal of Educational Technology Systems, 10,* 133–148.

Wresch, W. (Ed.) (1984). *The computer in composition instruction.* Urbana, IL: National Council of Teachers of English.

Wright, P. (1987). Reading and writing for electronic journals. In B. K. Britton & S. M. Glynn (Eds.), *Executive control processes in reading* (pp. 23–55). Hillsdale, NJ: Erlbaum.

Wright, P., & Lickorish, A. (1983). Proofreading texts on screen and paper. *Behaviour and Information Technology, 2,* 227–235.

Wright, P., & Lickorish, A. (1984). Ease of annotation in proofreading tasks. *Behaviour and Information Technology, 3,* 185–194.

Yankelovich, N., Meyrowitz, N., & Van Dam, A. (1985) Reading and writing the electronic book. *Computer, 18* (10), 15–30.

Yeaman, A. R. J. (1987, February). *Electronic text display: An experiment on page turning and window effect.* Paper presented at the meeting of the Association of Educational Communications and Technology, Atlanta, GA.

Young, D., & Irwin, M. (1988). Integrating computers in adult literacy programs. *Journal of Reading, 31,* 643–652.

14 TYPOGRAPHY AND DISCOURSE

Robert Waller

Typography is the design and arrangement of printed text (and, by extension, text that is displayed electronically). It is an important component of graphic design, which in recent years has become something of a growth industry as publishers and industrial corporations wake up to the commercial advantages of attractive and clear communications. And, although typography has traditionally been the domain of specialist typographers, graphic designers, and printers, the introduction of laser printers has confronted thousands of computer users with the need to choose typefaces and format pages. Interest in typography has probably never been so widespread.

Not surprisingly, a substantial literature has accumulated over the years. A problem facing the newly converted, though, is that it is widely dispersed. Much is in the form of practical handbooks and collections of award-winning designs. There is also a good deal that focuses on printing history and palaeography. Many studies can be found within the literature of applied psychology. But although many of the pioneer researchers of the reading process (reviewed by Pyke, 1926) investigated typography alongside other aspects of reading, it has achieved barely a mention in more recent theories of reading, language, and communication. However, there are signs that typographic research is in transition. This chapter aims to take stock of past achievements and problems and to review a current trend towards the integration of typographic factors into other approaches to the study of discourse.

APPLIED PSYCHOLOGISTS AND TYPOGRAPHIC RESEARCH

Over the years a great many studies have been published by psychologists (of various specialisms) who have examined the effect of typography on readers. The traditional distinction between the psychomotor, affective, and cognitive domains is reflected in the typographic research literature. Literacy involves the attainment of skills in all three domains, and all three have been addressed by typographic researchers using the methodologies of applied psychology.

Legibility: The Psychomotor Domain

Although Pyke lists instances of 18th- and early 19th-century work (e.g., by Babbage in 1827), Javal (1879) is generally credited as the first to apply the scientific method to typography; and a considerable number of studies of "reading hygiene," as the field was then called, were published in the first half of this century. The typographic variables listed by Legros (1922) typify the scope of much of the legibility research that still appears from time to time today:

All the figures used in this chapter are excerpted from *The Handbook of Sailing* by Bob Bond. London: Dorling Kindersley, 1980. Reprinted by permission.

size of character
thickness of strokes
white space between strokes
dissimilarity of characters
leading (i.e., line spacing)
line length
frequency of kerns (i.e., overlapping characters)
similarity of figures
width of figures
separation of lines from adjacent matter
unnecessary marks in or near characters
vulgar fractions
variations in type height
quality of paper
colour of paper
light-reflectance of paper
colour of ink
illumination
irradiation

Interestingly, typography was regarded as just one contribution to reading hygiene, alongside such things as lighting, paper colour, reflectance, the angle and curvature of the page, and even posture. With the introduction of electronic displays, similar factors have again become the focus of research attention.

The most prolific legibility researcher was Miles Tinker of the University of Minnesota, who with his colleague Donald Paterson published several dozen legibility experiments between 1929 and the publication of his books *The Legibility of Print* (1963) and *Bases for Effective Reading* (1965), now standard sources. They cover such variables as type size, type design, the colour of ink and paper, line length, and line spacing, but contain few surprises for those skilled in traditional printing practice. Reactions to Tinker differ, generally between those with practical experience in printing or typography and those without. Among the latter, Tinker's research is still widely cited. Spencer's (1969) review is a model of both clarity and discrimination and remains the most comprehensive, accessible, and reliable source of information about research findings to that date.

A number of general criticisms of legibility research were first voiced by Buckingham (1931). In particular he criticizes the univariate research model, in which experimenters try to vary a single factor while holding all others constant. Buckingham comments:

This is good experimental technique. It is an article of faith among investigators. Yet it won't work in the way it has been applied to typography unless one is prepared to go to very unusual lengths with it. (p. 104)

He goes on to note that (mostly paraphrased)

- "Several of those who have given out standards have simply used their imagination" (i.e., the recommendations do not always relate to the data).
- typographic variables interact: recommendations about line length, for example, "are valid only for the interlinear spacing employed, and the investigators do not tell us what that is. Widen the spacing and the probability is that a longer line may be employed to advantage."
- investigators often refer to, say, "10-pt type" without reporting the typeface used or the interline space.
- printers perceive the investigators' ignorance of typographical matters and ignore the results anyway.
- to do a full study of even a modest range of typefaces, sizes, line lengths, and line spacings would require more effort than anyone is prepared to put in (he outlines a simple study that would have required 1,792,000 returns).

In addition to Buckingham's criticisms, others have noted that

- technical research papers are ignored because they are difficult for printers and designers to understand (Rehe 1974).
- "the classical research literature in this field has concerned itself with molecular issues (i.e., with tiny details) rather than with molar ones (i.e., broad-scale issues)" (Hartley & Burnhill, 1977, p. 223).
- the research tends to be "divorced from the questions which are actually asked by practitioners when a choice of typeface has to be made" (Hartley and Burnhill, 1977, p. 224). Designers would like more details of the performance characteristics of individual typefaces: for example, can they be reduced or photocopied?

These problems, together with the fact that many experiments reveal only small differences, if any, have lead many typographic researchers to the opinion that it is not worth investing in traditional legibility research. Since the late 1960s, research on simple matters of legibility has tended to be undertaken only in special circumstances. New display technologies are of obvious interest, and ergonomists continue to publish numerous studies of the "human factors" of CRT displays (e.g., Reynolds, 1979; Bouma, 1980; Shurtleff, 1980). In addition, new type designs and page layouts are sometimes evaluated by their designers without the results being published.

An important trend in the post-Tinker era of typographic research has been the cooperation of psychologists with professional typographers. Burt (Burt, Cooper, & Martin, 1955; Burt, 1959/1974) consulted with the leading typographic pundits of the day, and a team at the Royal College of Art in London was perhaps the first to combine closely the skills of psychologists and designers, thus overcoming at least one of the criticisms of the earlier research. Although initially the emphasis was on legibility, they also looked at aspects of typographic and spatial signalling—for example, the layout of bibliographies (Spencer, Reynolds, & Coe, 1975). These studies had relatively modest and realistic goals. Essentially they were comparisons of a range of solutions to easily identified and frequently recurring psychomotor problems of scanning or searching. Searching for a name in an index or bibliography, for example, is an easily defined and common task. It is therefore valid to apply the findings directly to practical situations.

Developments at the Royal College of Art were paralleled by another prolific psychologist-typographer team, James Hartley and Peter Burnhill, who similarly moved from legibility research to structured information, including the design of academic journals (Hartley, Burnhill, & Fraser, 1974), textbooks (Burnhill and Hartley, 1975), indexes (Burnhill, Hartley, & Davies, 1977), and bibliographic references (Hartley, Trueman, and Burnhill, 1979).

Atmosphere Value: The Affective Domain

Typographers are often aware of the expressive properties of the typefaces they use. Following the lead of Berliner (1920), a number of psychologists have enquired whether this awareness is shared by readers. Early studies required subjects to choose typefaces appropriate for particular products (hers were fish, pancake flour, pork and beans, and marmalade). One of the most thorough series of studies of this kind was reported by Ovink (1938), whose subjects rated the suitability of typefaces for different text topics (literary styles, ideas, and commodities). Unfortunately, as with many typographic studies, his results were obtained with typefaces that are now mostly obsolete. More recent studies (reviewed by Rowe, 1982) attempt to overcome this problem by using the semantic differential technique. Typefaces are related to topics indirectly, via general dimensions such as "hard/soft," "active/passive," and so on. The suggestion is that a typeface with particular qualities could be used to imbue a message with those same qualities. Walker, Smith, and Livingstone (1986) have also published data demonstrating that typefaces considered by subjects to be suitable for advertising different professions turn out to have similar connotations to those professions when tested separately.

Zachrisson (1965) has noted about his own and other studies of atmosphere that researchers have failed to take account of the artistic or literary education of subjects—that is, their ability to discriminate between typefaces that, in the case of book faces, can look very similar. Moreover, descriptive terms thought up by experimenters may not be meaningful or relevant to subjects. Bartram (1982) tried to overcome this last objection by eliciting descriptive dimensions from subjects themselves. His purpose was also to provide designers with a means to test their intuitions against the perceptions of their audience (following Sless, 1980). He therefore supplied a procedure and a simple statistical technique for designers to conduct their own research when necessary. This goes some way towards meeting an objection raised by Spencer (1969):

> a review of press advertisements, in which typographic allusion is often a vital ingredient, published over the last half century suggests that findings on congeniality may have little temporal stability. (p. 29)

A reasonable assessment of this work is that, while studies of atmosphere value do not provide direct guidance about typeface choice, as some authors claim, they do substantiate the commonsense view that typographic style is noticed by readers and that their interpretations are not random. Although there is some disputed evidence that reader preferences affect reading speed (Burt, Cooper, & Martin, 1955), it is reasonable to suppose that anything about a text which is discernible to readers may affect their perception of the status of a document and consequently their expectations, critical stance, reading strategies, goals, and outcomes. It is hard to see applied psychologists going much beyond the present findings. Extremely subtle issues are involved—for example, how texts, through their use of stylistic nuances, may be seen to be "quoting" other texts.

Typographic Cuing: The Cognitive Domain

Some studies have looked at the effect of *typographic cuing* on learning (reviewed by Glynn, Britton, & Tillman, 1985). The term generally refers to the use of typography (bold or italic type, or underlining) to signal the important ideas in a text. In most studies, importance is assessed not by the author of the prose passage used, but by the experimenter or a group of independent judges. It is therefore a separate system of signalling overlayed onto the signalling already implicit in the author's prose structure (the presence of which has frequently been overlooked by researchers). In this respect typographic cuing is similar to other devices, sometimes known as *adjunct aids*, proposed and tested by educational researchers. These include advance organizers (Ausubel, 1963), behavioural objectives (cf. Davies, 1976), and inserted questions (Rothkopf, 1970), although these devices are more genuinely rooted in pedagogical theories.

There is little doubt that cuing does work in drawing attention to the cued material. The consensus is that people are more likely to remember cued ideas. Some researchers, though (e.g., Glynn & Di Vesta, 1979), have found that this is achieved at the expense of uncued ideas. It should also be noted that most studies of typographic cuing improve immediate recall but do not improve delayed recall. Quite apart from methodological objections raised by Hartley, Bartlett, and Branthwaite (1980), these conclusions are not altogether unexpected, since the cuing is effectively giving subjects advance warning of the recall questions. Indeed, Coles and Foster (1975, p. 105) suggest that the failure of typographic cuing to improve test scores in the first part of their own study might have been because "not having been informed that cued material would subsequently be tested, the students may have found cueing confusing or even distracting rather than helpful."

Innovative Formats

A number of studies have tested innovative and unusual typographic formats, some of which were published in a special issue of *Visible Language* by Hartley and Burnhill (1981). Jewett (1981) uses different levels of indentation to indicate hierarchical levels of argument, enabling the reader to scan the article while ignoring lower levels of the hierarchy. Shebilske and Rotondo (1981) distinguish between three kinds of "content": in addition to uncued text, bold type indicates "important" ideas, and square brackets indicate the "gist" of each idea. Once again, however, it seems to be forgotten that language already contains conventions for indicating structure. Shebilske and Rotondo's article uses parentheses to signal the gist of an idea—directly counter to their normal meaning, which is to interpolate unimportant (parenthetical, in fact) material. And, although Jewett claims that his format makes writing quicker by absolving the writer from the responsibility of verbalizing the hierarchical structure, it seems to have been impossible to shake off the habit: it is hard to avoid reference in higher-level paragraphs to information contained in the lower-level ones they follow. Researchers working within this tradition see themselves as extending a line of inquiry initiated by Klare, Mabry, and Gustafson (1955) and Hershberger and Terry (1965).

These studies of innovative typographic cuing reflect two wider trends in the typographic literature. First, researchers sometimes give an unfortunate impression of naïvety, both typographically and linguistically. Special functions are assigned to devices such as indention, bold type, line spaces, and parentheses as if they they have no preexisting function. Also ignored is the rich and diverse system of linguistic signalling that can be used by skilled readers to perceive the author's deployment of ideas. Writers and researchers outside educational psychology circles are not cited and probably not known about.

Second, they exemplify a tendency to want to reform a system that is seen as fundamentally irrational. With the exception of historians describing past practice, comparatively few people have attempted simple descriptions of typographic systems without prescriptive overtones. The reformist tendency is seen most clearly in studies of English spelling (cf. Venezky, 1970), suggestions to change the direction of writing or to present words in visual stacks (Huey, 1898; Andrews, 1949), and in attempts to design phonetic alphabets or simplify the existing one (reviewed by Spencer, 1969).

While they may be of limited practical value, the positive achievement of these studies is to have moved typographic research from the mundanities of "reading hygiene" towards the altogether trickier area of semantics. Here, the issue is how the appearance of printed material affects not just how much is understood, or how fast, but what is understood from it. However, questions like this cannot be answered in a vacuum. Unless we can describe the characteristics of a typographic display within some sort of descriptive framework, we cannot generalize from results obtained with it. To generalize from an applied psychologists' experiment to a problem in hand, we need to know what the two situations have in common. But whereas psychologists can experiment with sentence comprehension secure in the knowledge that the concepts such as "sentence" and "verb" will be generally understood (if not agreed upon by all linguistic scientists), no such agreement exists about variations in page layout. In other words, progress in typographic research awaits a better understanding of typography as a feature of language and discourse.

TYPOGRAPHY AND LINGUISTICS

The obvious place to investigate what Twyman (1982) called the "language element" underlying typography is linguistics, and some textbooks do indeed mention the terms "graphetics" and "graphology" in symmetrical opposition to "phonetics" and "phonology." However, these are largely empty categories since only a handful of linguists have investigated graphic aspects of language. Indeed, Crystal (1980) remarks in his dictionary entry for "graphetics":

> So far little analysis of texts in these terms has taken place, and the relationship between graphetics and graphology remains unclear. (p. 169)

Why have graphic factors received so little attention from modern linguists? Compared with other, weightier, matters that preoccupy the relatively young discipline of linguistics (such as "what is language?"), they are presumably seen as relatively trivial, although necessary to mention when the existence of writing is to be acknowledged. More than this, though, the exclusion of typography from mainstream linguistics can also be seen as a corollary of four major theoretical positions: the primacy of speech, the restriction to the sentence level (not many typographic events happen within the sentence), the arbitrariness of the linguistic sign, and the linearity of language.

The Primacy of Speech

Saussure, regarded by many as the founder of modern linguistics, placed writing firmly outside the linguistic domain:

> Language and writing are two distinct systems of signs; the second exists for the sole purpose of representing the first. (Saussure, 1916/1974,: p. 23)

Much of the debate concerning the status of writing in linguistics has been documented by Vachek (1973). In addition to Saussure, he cites the opposition of many of the most influential 20th-century linguists to the view that writing is something more than the transcription of speech. Bloomfield (1935, p. 21), for example, considered that "writing is not language, but merely a way of recording language by means of visible marks." Vachek quotes similar remarks from influential linguists from both earlier (e.g., Sapir, 1921) and later generations (e.g., Hockett, 1958).

The tone of the primacy of speech advocates is emphatic, even intemperate at times. Thus Saussure (1916/1974) speaks of the "tyranny of writing," of its "usurping" role, of "abuses," of the "annoying" tendency of grammarians who "never fail to draw attention to the written form." The title of one section of his *Course in General Linguistics*, though, may explain the tone: "Influence of writing; reasons for its ascendance over the spoken form." At the time (the *Course* is based on lectures given between 1906 and 1911), Saussure's purpose was to replace prescriptive grammars based on literary forms with a more fundamental description of natural language. Similarly, Bloomfield's remarks were made in the context of the development of techniques for the description of unwritten native American languages.

In contrast to the 20th-century attitude, Cohen (1977) remarks on the relatively detailed attention given to graphic factors by early linguists:

> The language texts of the period [1640–1785], reflecting an effort to represent the obvious sense of the written language, include sections on punctuation, capitalization, and often, handwriting and type styles. These sections are significantly prominent. (p. 50)

The Sentence Level

The preoccupation of Anglo-American linguistics with speech was accompanied for many years by Bloomfield's additional restriction of linguistic enquiry to the level of the sentence. Saussure had earlier made the important distinction between *langue* and *parole*, sometimes translated as "language system" and "language behaviour." A major task of linguistics has been to reveal the language system or grammar that underlies language behaviour. Since the sentence seems to be the highest level at which concepts of grammaticality are intuitively agreed by language users, the proper study of linguists is restricted to sentences. The construction of larger units, such as paragraphs, is seen as more a matter of rhetorical choice than the application of grammatical rules.

In view of this restriction, it is not surprising that graphic factors have featured so little in linguistics. Indeed, we may wonder why graphetics and graphology should ever have been posited by linguists in the first place. The sentence is a level at which few complex graphological events occur. Graphology becomes more interesting in non-sentences (such as bibliographic lists or equations) or in texts with headings, tables, footnotes, and other components that lie outside the scope of sentence grammar and that have received relatively little attention from linguists. It is noticeable that those linguists who have written about or acknowledged graphic factors (other than for the limited purpose of comparing writing systems) tend also to be those who have moved away from sentence-level linguistics. They include Vachek (1948/1967, 1959, 1973), Crystal and Davy (1969), Werlich (1976), and Bernhardt (1985).

Crystal and Davy's (1969) classic study of stylistics illustrates a problem that is typical of linguistic forays into graphic aspects of text: the lack of a technical linguistic metalanguage with which to handle graphic phenomena. They examine both spoken and written texts, ranging from sports commentary to sermons, newspapers to legal documents. Styles are clearly characterized not just by distinctive vocabulary and syntax but by prosodic and structural features: in the case of written texts these include their typographic format. There is a notable contrast, though, between Crystal and Davy's technical analysis of phonological matters and their nontechnical, ordinary language descriptions of graphological features. This may be due to the ease with which typography can be simply reproduced rather than transcribed, but it points to the lack of a common framework for theoretical discussion.

Werlich's text grammar (1976) provides another instance of a linguist who has clearly noticed graphic factors. It is a largely descriptive exercise, considering an unusually wide range of text—from advertisements to committee minutes—and describing their typical components and characteristics. Like Crystal and Davy whom he cites, Werlich is usually meticulous in his preservation of the typographic form of his examples, even where no special conclusion is drawn from it. For instance, examples that originated as newspaper articles are printed in narrow columns with rules between. Although Werlich is clearly aware of graphic and spatial factors in text, he presumably regards them as unproblematic or outside the scope of his grammar. There is no special section on typography, and it does not appear in the index. Where he does mention typography or layout, it is generally accorded the role of text type identifier. Thus we recognize a leading article by its conspicuous position and the newspaper's emblem at its head.

Vachek (1948/1967, 1959, 1973) is an old campaigner for the recognition of written language as autonomous from spoken. A member of the Prague School of linguists, he is a functionalist, maintaining that language features stem from the function of language in the community of language users. For example, a functionalist would argue that asking questions, making statements, and giving orders are universal uses for language, and therefore that grammarians can expect to find interrogative, declarative, and imperative forms in most languages. Vachek (1973) characterizes spoken language as immediate, dynamic, and relatively emotional, as distinct from the static, easily preservable and surveyable, and "purely communicative" nature of written language. There are obvious exceptions (ritualized and predictable spoken texts, dynamic and emotional posters), but this approach has the merit that it reserves a central role for the context and purpose of a text, and suggests that, since speech and writing are distinct in function as well as in mode, we should not expect to find exact parallels between phonology and graphology (as linguistics textbooks sometimes suggest).

Another Prague School concept is *binary opposites* (or marked pairs). Applied to lexical structure, for example, pairs of opposites such as "lion" and "lioness" are said to contain a marked and unmarked member (Lyons, 1977). In this example, "lion" is unmarked and "lioness" is marked. The marked can be distinguished from the unmarked not only by the formal addition of, in this case, the suffix "-ess," but also by their asymmetrical functions: thus the two terms can be defined as "male lion" and "female lion," but not as "male lioness" and "female lioness" (the one is contradictory, the other tautological). Vachek (1979) discusses typographic signalling in some detail, listing a range of functions for which marked sets of graphic symbols (e.g., italics) might be used to distinguish text features requiring emphasis or stylization from the unmarked norm (e.g., roman type).

A significant point that emerges from Vachek's discussion is that he appears to consider markedness to be a matter of distributional frequency within a linguistic community rather than just within a particular document. Referring to the practice of printing extended passages such as prefaces or abstracts in italics, he points out that in such circumstances printers have to reverse normal practice by using roman type, an unmarked form, for emphasis instead of italic. Although providing only anecdotal evidence, Vachek maintains that such signalling fails to convince the reader, and that such signalling in an italic context can only be achieved with some other marked set such as bold italic or small capitals. This is in contrast to a commonly held view, possibly originating with experiments on the psychology of perception, that figure-ground contrasts are largely a matter of proportion, and that therefore one might expect markedness to be relative to the proportion of two forms within a particular text.

What Vachek describes as "the inability of italics to figure as the unmarked member of the opposition "italic type/roman type" suggests that, as with "lion" and "lioness," italic type can be defined as "not roman type" but not vice versa. The significance of this line of argument is that it suggests that graphic conventions such as the italic-roman distinction can develop, through frequent usage or reasons of historical development, something approaching the comparatively immutable status of natural language (such a status being confined, as with natural language, to a particular language community at a particular time).

This brings us back to the debate about the linguistic status of written language. Although the primacy-of-speech advocates argued that spoken language is universal while written language is dispensable since it only exists in a proportion of language communities, Vachek's response is that "the goal to which language development has been directed in any community is the highest possible efficiency of lingual communication and the maximum development of its functional range," and furthermore that "language 'optimals' should not rank lower in importance than language universals" (1973, p. 17). The choice of an optimal language form is, of course, a pragmatic one, dependent on the communication context, the means available, and the purposes and limitations of both speaker/writer and listener/reader. Thus, theoretical advances in written language, and especially typography, are not to be expected from a view of language that is confined to explaining how words are combined into sentences.

Bernhardt (1985) writes in the context of Halliday and Hasan's systemic linguistics (1976). Their taxonomy of cohesive relationships lists a wide range of techniques used by writers to link text components (but no graphic ones). A question apparently not answered by Halliday and Hasan is, What leads a speaker or writer to choose a particular texture (their term for a set of cohesive techniques in actual use) over another? They point to social and contextual influences such as the nature of the audience and the purpose of the communication. Bernhardt set out to investigate this question by comparing four texts on the same subject written for different purposes. They are a research report, a legal statute, a brochure, and a "fact-sheet," each addressing the topic of a wetland area of the Great Lakes. Bernhardt comments that

> In an attempt to explain patterns of rhetorical strategy and the consequent realizations of cohesion with regard to context of situation, it soon became apparent that graphic design must figure prominently in the analysis of patterns of cohesive structuring. (p. 18)

Bernhardt proposes a continuum of visual organization (see Table 14.1) in which various kinds of text are ranged from the visually informative to the nonvisually informative. His choice of terms is interesting, since it enables him to confine his analysis to verbal language (i.e., to exclude pictures), while admitting spatial and graphic features. Through an analysis of examples, he arrives at a more elaborated schema that characterizes the poles of the continuum at various levels of *rhetorical control* (see Table 14.2).

Bernhardt's interest in graphic design arose out of an interest in rhetorical strategy and the influence of context, rather than primary message making. That is, graphic design in his schema is placed at a metalinguistic level, describing or structuring a message within a social framework rather than contributing to its propositional content. For Bernhardt, the presence of graphic structuring seems to represent a prediction by

TABLE 14.1   Bernhardt's Continuum
of Visual Organization

Visually informative
lists
forms
pamphlets
directions
legal texts
textbooks
articles
novels
Nonvisually informative

---

the writer about the need to attract readers and allow them a choice of pathways through the message.

Arbitrariness

For some linguists, Bernhardt's introduction of "visually informative" texts would be problematic, since *arbitrariness* has traditionally been one of the distinguishing features of language, as distinct from other sign systems (Saussure 1916/1974, p. 67). While an arbitrary sign bears a purely conventional or denotative relationship to its referent, an iconic one resembles or connotes it in some way. Being visually informative, a list (Bernhardt's example of a visually informative text) provides iconic information about the number, order, and grouping of its constituent parts.

Westcott (1971) disputes the arbitrariness criterion altogether, not only in relation to written language. For example, he cites numerous morphological examples ("longer" is longer than "long," and "longest" is longer than either; the argument breaks down, of course, if one considers "short," "shorter," "shortest"). He also uses syntactic examples (the normal subject-verb-object order represents the actual order of transitive events) and lists a range of different kinds of iconism in writing (Table 14.3). Similar examples are cited by other writers on this theme (e.g., Martin, 1972; Lotz, 1972).

Whereas iconicity and motivation, two terms used as the opposite to arbitrariness, are usually regarded as synonymous in relation to spoken language, Westcott's examples suggest that in written language it might be useful to distinguish between them. This is because ink offers the possibility of a much more literal iconicity than air. Written texts can contain not only traditionally defined motivated words (like "meow"), and motivated graphic effects like emboldening for emphasis, but also iconic displays (i.e., pictures or symbols) that are interpreted more or less directly, not via the (supposedly) phonetic writing system.

While it may be pedagogically convenient to use a working model of writing as a phonetic system, it is not wholly phonetic in practice, as Bolinger (1946) demonstrated in a paper entitled "Visual Morphemes." Since mature readers have little difficulty in distinguishing between differently spelled homophones, such as "meat" and "meet," it is obvious that it is not only symbols that are understood directly from the written surface without the need for phonological equivalence. Bradley (1919) also commented on the partly ideographic nature of writing, seeing evidence of the divergence of written and spoken language in the new "graphic" words that scientists (particularly chemists) construct from Greek or Latin roots with little regard to their pronunciation:

TABLE 14.2   Bernhardt's Continuum of Visual Organization
with Levels of Rhetorical Control

VISUALLY INFORMATIVE	RHETORICAL CONTROL	NONVISUALLY INFORMATIVE
Varied surface offers aesthetic possibilities; can attract or repel reader through the shape of the text; laws of equilibrium, good continuation, good figure, closure, similarity.	Visual Gestalt	Homogeneous surface offers little possibility of conveying information; dense, indistinguished block of print; every text presents the same face; formidable appearance assumes willing reader.
Localized: each section is its own locale with its own pattern of development; arrests reader's attention.	Development	Progressive: each section leads smoothly to the next; projects reader forward through discourse-level previewing and backwards through reviewing.
Iconic: spacing, headings reveal explicit, highly visible divisions; reader can jump around, process the text in a nonlinear fashion, access information easily, read selectively.	Partitioning	Integrated: indentations give some indication of boundaries, but sections frequently contain several paragraphs and sometimes divisions occur within paragraphs; reader must read or scan linearly to find divisions.
Emphasis controlled by visual stress of layout, type size, spacing, headings.	Emphasis	Emphasis controlled semantically through intensifiers, conjunctive ties; some emphasis achieved by placement of information in initial or final slots in sentences and paragraphs.
Subordinate relations signalled through type size, headings, indenting.	Subordinate Relations	Controlled semantically within linear sequence of paragraphs and sentences.
Signalled through listing structures, expanded sentences, parallel structures, enumerated or iconically signalled by spacing, bullets, or other graphic devices.	Coordinate Relations	Controlled semantically through juxtaposition, parallel structures, and cohesive ties, especially additive ties.
Linkage controlled visually; little or no use of semantic ties between sentences and sections; reliance on enumerative sequences or topicalization of a series.	Linking/ Transitional/ Intersentential Relations	Liberal use of cohesive ties, especially conjunctives and deictics; frequent interparagraph ties or transitional phrases.
Variety in mood and syntactic patterning; much use of Q/A sequences, imperatives; fragments and minor forms; phrases used in isolation.	Sentence Patterns	Complete sentences with little variation in mood; sentences typically declarative with full syntax.

Source: S. A. Bernhardt, Text structure and graphic design, In J. D. Benson & W. S. Greaves (Eds.), *Systematic prospective on discourse* (Vol. 2) 1985. Reprinted with the permission of Ablex Publishing Corporation.

TABLE 14.3   Categories of Iconic Symbols in the English Writing System
(adapted to table form from Westcott, 1971)

	pictogram ?
	ideogram
$	logogram
pp (meaning "pages")	morphogram (the second "p" only)
O in "IOU"	homophonic phonogram
&	syllabic phonogram (when it appears in "&c," meaning "etc.")
, (comma)	prosodic phonogram (when used to indicate a pause)

For these words the normal relation between alphabetic writing and speech is simply reversed: the group of letters is the real word, and the pronunciation merely its symbol. (p. 178)

That writing is treated as ideographic by readers is confirmed by psychologists, who have long debated whether written symbols need to be recorded into a phonological form before they can be understood. Reviewers (such as Massaro, 1979; Baddeley, 1979, 1984) have reported that subvocalization is not a necessary stage in the fluent reading of relatively easy sentences, although sometimes used for complex comprehension tasks. This, Baddeley argues, is because subvocalization helps retention in short-term memory by means of what he terms the "articulatory loop" (analogous to an audiotape loop that can be instantly replayed for checking). However, Baddeley and Lieberman (1980) also propose an equivalent subsystem for visual information: the "visuo-spatial sketch pad," and Kleiman (1975) suggested a model that contains both a visual and a phonological store. Although there is still some disagreement at the sentence level, there seems to be agreement at the word level that, although sometimes used by readers, phonological equivalence is not in itself a criterion for a readable symbol. The current view is fairly represented by Kolers (1985), who remarked

The linguist's view of reading as requiring phonological mediation might be said to imply that vision is dumb but hearing is smart. . . . This claim cannot be taken seriously any longer, and the wonder is that it was taken seriously for so long during the 1960s and 1970s. Are faces, scents, and music recognized by finding their surrogates in speech? (p. 410)

It is also worth noting that the concept of writing as a completely phonetic transcription of speech is a mistake that can only be made by users of alphabetic writing systems, such as our own. The inadequacy of that assumption must be obvious to the Chinese, whose own writing system is not phonetic, and who, having recently implemented major changes in the way their language is romanized, must be only too aware that alphabetic graphemes are but a crude approximation of phonemes.

It may be that the scope of the arbitrary/iconic distinction is relative to particular levels of linguistic analysis. Indeed, Westcott (1971) suggests that

iconism is a relative rather than an absolute characteristic of any communication system, language included. As regards iconism, then, the only realistic question we can ask about a given form is not "Is it iconic?" but rather "How iconic is it?" (p. 426)

If the existence of limited sets of highly iconic signs (such as pictograms) simply exploits the way we normally read, why should there be any problem in analysing a sentence that contains a pictogram instead of the word "telephone"? That pictograms are out of bounds is understandable only if we are looking for systematic relations between language components within the word (i.e., phonemes and morphemes). Above that level it seems irrelevant how particular words are graphically rendered, so long as they are comprehended in an equivalent way by readers. This is the view taken by Trager (1974), who, although somewhat uncompromising with regard to the primacy of speech, is prepared to accept symbols as writing if they constitute

a systematic representation of linguistic elements—specific morphological (words, phrases) or phonological (phonemes, syllables) items. (p. 380)

In practice, it should be added, there are limits to this. First, because there is a strictly limited vocabulary of symbols or formulaic pictures that we can rely on others to understand as reliably as if they were words; and, second, because many words contain grammatical as well as lexical information (i.e., "inflective" information about case, tense, and so on). In practice, pictograms can most reliably substitute for words in what Quirk, Greenbaum, Leech, and Svartvik (1985) call "block language"—single-word captions, headings, and labels—as distinct from sentenced language. For example, while some textbooks use the words "audiocassette" or "television" to draw attention to links between the main text and supplementary course components, others substitute directly equivalent icons of audiocassettes or televisions.

If pictograms can be treated as words, more elaborate iconic displays such as pictures might perhaps be viewed as linguistic components at a higher level of analysis: as equivalent to paragraphs or other verbal segments larger than the sentence. Indeed, Eco (1976) suggests that the verbal equivalent of an iconic sign

(except in rare cases of considerable schematization) is not a word but a phrase or indeed a whole story. (p. 215)

A picture of, say, a horse, is at a much greater level of particularization than the word "horse": it shows, for example, a black horse galloping or a white horse standing still.

In such cases, however, the image alone may be insufficient for its own interpretation. Indeed, Gombrich (1960) argues that no pictorial image gains the status of a "statement" unless an explicit reference is made to what it is supposed to represent. In the case of propaganda photographs of alleged war atrocities, for example, it is the false captions, not the photographs, that lie. Barthes (1977) uses the term "anchorage" to describe the relationship of pictures to captions or other accompanying verbal language: most pictures are capable of several interpretations until anchored to one by a caption. Eaton (1980) applies a conversational theory to picture interpretation, arguing that the communicative intention of pictures can be deduced from the context in which they appear, and by reference to conventions of normal depicting and asserting. Although these writers approach the question in markedly different ways and in terms of philosophical technicalities differ considerably, we may take it that iconic forms (or even iconic qualities of verbal forms—display typefaces with special associations, for example) need to be welded in to the context, or overall cohesive structure, of a particular text. This, of course, is no less true of verbal components of texts: words, and even sentences, however well-formed, are meaningless in isolation from a context.

Linearity

Saussure coupled arbitrariness with the linearity of the signifier (i.e., the language "surface") as fundamental principles of linguistic study. Most linguists are primarily concerned with "syntagmatic" relations between components: the relationship of each word to its predecessors and successors in the linear sequence. Those text linguists who take sentence linguistics as their model are similarly concerned with the relationship of sentences and paragraphs within the linear series. Linearity is fundamental for Saussure because it is the basis for one of his two fundamental categories of linguistic relations: syntagmatic (as distinct from associative, often referred to as paradigmatic). *Syntagmatic relations* are the relations that a word has with others in the linear string, or syntagm; *associative relations* are those that a word has with others that might take its place in the string.

Linearity is certainly implicit in unrecorded speech, bounded by time; but writing, with two dimensions available, can make large tracts of discourse instantly accessible to the searching eye. A table is perhaps the most obvious example of a two-dimensional text, but many other textual components also rely on spatial or graphic relations: footnotes, flowcharts, captions, lists, side notes, and heading hierarchies, for example. Many educational and nonfiction texts are now designed as doublespreads, integrating words and pictures in a series of self-contained "graphic arguments."

Linearity may be an obvious feature of language, but that is not to say that cognitively it is ideal. On the whole, it is not a great problem at the sentence level, where comprehension can be handled within working memory—the beginning of the sentence is still available for processing when the end is reached. In a lengthy text, though, readers may need to be explicitly reminded of earlier stages in the argument that must be retrieved from deeper levels of memory. Much of the work of text linguists is directed toward an account of the ways in which language users compensate for this constraint.

Linearity is a particular problem when the content or argument is nonlinear, as most arguments are. Besides the linguistic problem of cohesion, there is the semantic problem of coherence—of building up what Beaugrande calls a "text-world model" that must be both internally coherent and externally credible at all points in the argument—even before its linguistic exposition is complete. Although Westcott (1971) cites a number of examples of "iconic" syntax, in which word order reflects the order of the events described, such cases are rare, and the "fact structure" (as van Dijk, 1977, calls it) of the topic of discourse rarely corresponds to its linear sentence structure. With the exception of very simple narratives, with one participant and no overlapping episodes, most descriptive texts have to cope with information that is in some way nonlinear. Obvious examples are texts that describe complex structures such as machines, buildings, organizations, or political situations. In such cases, an essentially multidimensional "reality" must be sorted into a linear string in such a way that it can be reassembled by the reader. In any case, even where there is a simple linear fact structure, there may be rhetorical reasons for describing the facts in some other order.

Ivins (1953), comparing verbal language unfavorably with pictures, describes the linearity problem in this way:

The very linear order in which words have to be used results in a syntactical time order analysis of qualities that actually are simultaneous and so intermingled and interrelated that no quality can be removed from one of the bundles of qualities we call objects without changing both it and all the other qualities. . . . In a funny way words and their necessary linear syntactical order forbid us to describe objects and compel us to use very poor and inadequate lists of theoretical ingredients in the manner exemplified more concretely by the ordinary cook book recipes. (p. 63)

Grimes (1975) shows that even time-based narratives are subject to the constraints of linearity, since they often involve several participants who must be identified, and whose actions may be related by overlapping, cooperation, causality, and so on. Besides events and participants, most narratives contain "non-events," listed by Grimes as settings, background information, evaluations, and collateral information. While the linearity problem is at the heart of all text or discourse studies, few have directly addressed it as an issue. A recent exception is de Beaugrande's (1981, 1984) theory of linear action.

De Beaugrande identifies seven "linearity principles" listed in Table 14.4. They comprise a framework within which he is able to relate the various phases of cognitive processing involved in reading with the different rhetorical and linguistic forms used by writers (as well as the cognitive processes through which writers select and produce those forms). An examination of de Beaugrande's framework may offer some insight into the linearity of language, how it is overcome, and, perhaps, how typographic techniques might contribute in this respect.

The seven principles, de Beaugrande argues, govern the ways in which writers transcribe multidimensional ideas into a linear linguistic form. My "transcribe" telescopes de Beaugrande's fairly elaborate cognitive model of reading and writing into a single term, but it deserves a brief summary. De Beaugrande criticizes earlier serial models of writing that involve a series of discrete "black-boxed" stages. Ideas progress through pragmatic, semantic, syntactic, and lexical stages until they achieve surface expression as phonemes or graphemes. These reflect the structure of linguistics and are convenient for psychological experiments, but more recent "parallel interactive" models allow for the different levels to be activated simultaneously. In this context,

linearity reflects the organization of the language modalities of speech and writing, rather than one-by-one mental processes. (p. 104)

The psychological problem of how parallel processes are managed is not our present concern; but at some stage, although originating as nonlinear conceptual networks and processed at the deeper levels in nonlinear ways, ideas must eventually be linearized at the surface level. Hence the seven linearity principles.

De Beaugrande does recognize that linearity in writing is spatial, not temporal. But since his topic is the composition of continuous prose for fluent reading, it is perhaps not surprising that he restricts his view to the one-dimensional spatiality of the line, rather than the two-dimensional spatiality of the page. This one-dimensional view of language seems to be remarkably persistent among other scholars also. For example, Vachek (1948/1967) similarly observes the spatial dimension of writing, and similarly fails to develop the implications of that fact.

De Beaugrande also appears to miss or ignore a further important implication of

TABLE 14.4   Seven Linearity Principles (adapted to tabular form from de Beaugrande, 1984; the third column shows applications to typography by Waller)

PRINCIPLE	DE BEAUGRANDE'S EXPLANATION	EXAMPLES FROM TYPOGRAPHY
Core-and-adjunct	Distinguishes between core and peripheral entities	Typographic signalling of notes, glosses, etc.
Pause	Allows the on-line sequence to be retarded or suspended	Interpolated boxes, inserts, or footnotes
Look-back	Subsumes all consultations of the prior discourse	Regularity of layout pattern, tabular structure
Look-ahead	Subsumes all anticipations of the subsequent discourse	Regularity of layout pattern, tabular structure, headings
Heaviness	Concerns gradations of importance, emphasis, focus, length, salience, or novelty, in the sense that these all draw a "heavier" load on processing.	Typographic emphasis, spatial isolation
Disambiguation	Deals with excluding alternative patterns, both formal and conceptual	Use of layout to direct reading sequence or to group-related items; access structures
Listing	Handles the enumeration of comparable items in a sequence	"Bullets", numbering systems, tabular structure

the spatiality of writing, whether one- or two-dimensional. Because it is presented in space, not time, writing offers the reader the opportunity to physically look back, look forward, scan a list structure, and so on. Without this opportunity, long and complex arguments could neither be easily written nor critically read. However, de Beaugrande (1984) restricts this view to cognitive versions of those activities:

> The processor may routinely consult the mental representation of prior text and rescan the surface text only on strategic occasions, e.g., for revision. (p. 175)

However parallel the cognitive processes in de Beaugrande's model, then, the input is still assumed to be serial. But since one of the most significant aspects of writing is the release of the reader from the temporal linearity of speech, there seems no reason why the cognitive psychologist's perspective should not be extended. De Beaugrande attributes linearity principles to both writers and readers, so the implication is that "looks-back" among readers can be literal; that is, they can actually look back to an earlier point in the text rather than just their memory of it.

This suggests a crucial distinction. Still taking looks-back as an example, we might say that text features that are solely verbal "look back" to an earlier part of the linear text string in a metaphorical sense; the relationship is implicit in the language and must be cognitively apprehended by the reader. Text features that are graphic, or at least graphically signalled, transfer the responsibility for the look-back to the reader; the relationship is explicit in the graphic form of the text and can be perceptually apprehended by the reader—the look-back is real, not metaphorical.

Another way to express this is to say that the responsibility for the syntagm has shifted away from the writer towards the reader. (The syntagm is the linear series of language elements produced by a speaker or writer and encountered by a hearer or reader.) Given that readers of written text can move around it at will, it seems reasonable to propose a concept of reader-syntagm in contradistinction to the traditional syntagm, which is entirely controlled by the writer. There is a time dimension to reading, just as there is to speaking; so however nonlinear the text, the reader-syntagm still represents a linear input to the process of cognition. The order of that input, though, can be controlled by the reader, on the basis of a wide range of "relevance cues" (the term is from van Dijk, 1979, who lists graphical cues alongside a range of lexical and syntactic ones).

Texts clearly vary in the opportunities they offer for "syntagm control." Continuous prose, especially in the form of novels, offers few visible relevance cues to readers wishing to control their own pace. We are normally expected to read a novel from beginning to end; to do otherwise we need specially annotated study editions, or our own marginal notes and underlinings. A table, on the other hand, cannot sensibly be read in a linear order from top left to bottom right. In between these extremes lie dictionaries, reference manuals, textbooks, and the various examples proposed by Bernhardt (1985) in his continuum of visual informativeness.

GRAPHIC DESIGN AND TOPIC STRUCTURE

In the context of a view of text that allows an active role for readers, we may distinguish between two kinds of visual informativeness. The first, which I shall call *topic structure*, displays significant structures and boundaries within the writer's topic of discourse. The second, which I shall call *access structure*, provides visual clues to aid the reader in the use of the textual artefact as a learning resource.

Whatever their ultimate motives—to inform, educate, or persuade—authors of nonfiction texts are also trying to order their ideas, and graphic design is just one of a number of available tools. There may be cases where the topic has an inherent fact structure, and others where the writer may, for a particular rhetorical or pedagogic reason, prefer a different "argument structure." However, the term "topic structure" enables us to circumnavigate these distinctions altogether for the time being, since it simply refers to whatever the writer wishes to talk about. Following Grimes (1975, p. 337), the topic of a text may be defined as "that part of the surface form that represents the speaker's thematic choice"—whether that form represents a fact structure, an argument structure, or one of the other distinctions that arise in the literature of linguistics, psychology, and education—topic and comment, language and meta-language, for example. To talk of topic structure, then, enables us to avoid some of the trickier philosophical questions concerning the structure of knowledge and to confine our interest to those aspects of structure that can be made visible through typography, while still, following Grimes, concentrating on the writer's thematic choice. Texts seen as topic structures represent the writer's communication goals organized in the form of arguments, which in turn are expressed at the text surface through verbal language, pictures, and typographic layout.

The distinction between fact and argument structures might in any case be minimized by the abundance of visual and spatial metaphors in the literature of linguistics and semantics. For example, the literary critic Northrop Frye (1957) talked of the link between logic and rhetoric—or, we might say, a topic and the way it is addressed to an audience—as

. . . "doodle" or associative diagram, the expression of the conceptual by the spatial. . . . If a writer says "But on the other hand there is a further consideration to be brought forward in support of the opposing argument," he may be writing normal (if wordy) English, but he is also doing precisely what an armchair strategist does when he scrawls plans of battle on a tablecloth. Very often a "structure" or "system" of thought can be reduced to a diagrammatic pattern—in fact both words are to some extent synonyms of diagram. (p. 335)

Rather than advocating a literal expression of the conceptual by the spatial, Frye is actually addressing the function of metaphor in nonliterary prose. He is concerned that in the effort to "purify verbal communication from the emotional content of rhetoric," prose becomes, paradoxically, less clear, not more.

Analogy and metaphor allow us to discuss argument structures as if they were fact structures. Instances of spatial metaphor in the technical vocabulary of linguists suggest that it might be possible to identify graphic techniques that break away from the linear-hierarchical norm but that still correspond more or less directly to ways in which we are accustomed to organizing words and ideas.

Nash (1980), for example, suggests four kinds of "rhetorical design" that, he argues, are fundamental to all composition (although usually found in combination). Nash's categories—the step, the stack, the chain, and the balance—may all be interpreted as visual metaphors. The examples that follow are taken from an illustrated book on sailing that is typical of a recent genre of popular handbooks that use typography and illustration to display topic structures as single- or double-page spreads.

The *step* is the easiest one to identify in graphic form. A simple, if trivial, example of a stepped rhetorical design reflected in typographic layout can be seen in the section headed "Sail onto boom" in Figure 14.1

Awareness of the potential typographic reinforcement of rhetorical structures can sharpen our critical awareness of typographic layout. For example, we might puzzle over the inconsistent relationship between rhetorical and graphic design in Figure 14.2. Although the schematic drawing at the top right-hand corner of the page has "Shackling head to halyard" as step 4, preceding step 5, "Hoisting the jib," the layout seems to treat step 5 as a separate topic from steps 1–3, and step 4 as a comment on step 5.

In both Figure 14.2 and Figure 14.1 the clearly stepped design is diluted by the failure to repeat the enumeration of the steps in the subheadings; furthermore, the wording of the subheadings is not consistent with the steps as announced in the schematic summary drawings.

Nash's *stack design* is characterized by the announcement of a topic, followed by a series of amplifying or explanatory comments. Stacks are, in effect, lists of attributes or comments, and may be graphically treated as such. Figure 14.3 contains a small stack of ideas relating to the topic "rudder and tiller": "parts of the rudder," "fitting the rudder," and "tiller extension" (there seems no reason why this should not have a more prominent heading). Grimes (1975, pp. 245–246) discusses a similar rhetorical pattern, the star, whose name also suggests a graphic form. The star is a pattern of persuasive argument in which a number of independent points contribute to a central conclusion.

Of his four rhetorical designs, Nash's *chains* are the least amenable to graphic treatment since, as the metaphor suggests, they are essentially linearized. As he puts it,

Often the writer's procedures are less predictive than exploratory; he works through the expository maze, seeing no more than a sentence ahead, placing his trust in the clues afforded by syntactical or lexical connections. (1980, p. 14)

Rigging the mainsail

The sails are normally stored in the sailbag and must be rigged on the boat each time you go sailing. The way in which the mainsail is rigged will depend on the way the boat is designed but it is always first unrolled inside the boat, with the luff nearest the mast. If the sail has to be reefed (see pages 92–3), this should be done after the sail has been hoisted. The point at which the sail is fully hoisted depends on the launching conditions (see pages 74–85).

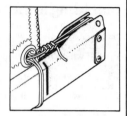

Order of rigging

The order of steps in rigging a mainsail is normally as shown left, but different classes of boat may have other requirements.

1 Sail onto boom
2 Battens into pockets
3 Head into track
4 Boom onto gooseneck
5 Hoist mainsail
6 Attach kicking strap

Sail onto boom

The sail is fitted into a track on the upper side of the boom. It is important to make sure that the sail is fully stretched when fitting it onto the boom. There is normally a marker at the end of the boom to indicate how far the sail should be pulled out. The sail must be fastened securely in position at both ends.

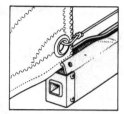

1 Slide clew of sail into mast end of boom, pulling it to marker at opposite end of boom.

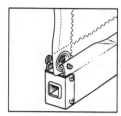

2 Secure tack of sail to mast end of boom by inserting tack pin through sail and boom.

3 Pull foot of sail taut and fasten clew outhaul to boom and secure.

Battens

The battens act as sail stiffeners so that the shaped edge of the sail does not curl over. Most sails have three battens slotted or tied into stitched pockets.

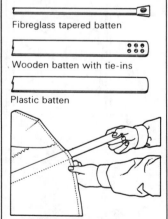

Fibreglass tapered batten

Wooden batten with tie-ins

Plastic batten

Fitting battens
Insert batten into pocket as far as possible and then push well down inside pocket to secure.

Sail onto mast

The mainsail is inserted into the mast track but normally only partially hoisted (right) while the boat is being rigged: a fully hoisted mainsail would flap out of control and should, therefore, only be hoisted at or after launching.

Headboard into track
Shackle the head of the sail to the main halyard (normally on the right hand side of the mast). Then thread the headboard into the mast track. Make sure that the main halyard is neither twisted nor fouling the rigging. Pull on the halyard at the base of the mast while feeding the luff of the sail into the mast track. Fasten halyard around cleat.

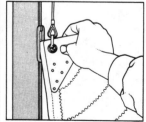

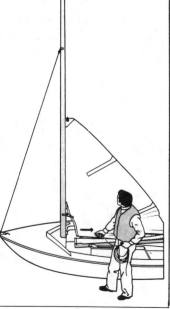

FIGURE 14.1 The three numbered procedures in the section entitled "Sail onto boom" are in a clear stepped relationship.

Rigging the jib

The jib is normally attached to the forestay with patent fastenings known as jib hanks. The jib itself is controlled by sheets attached to the clew of the sail. The sheets, which are controlled by the crew, lead around the mast, inside or outside the shrouds, to fairleads mounted on the side decks or tanks. The jib sheets are used to tension the jib correctly. Various modifications can be made to the position of the fairleads so that the angle of the jib can be altered to suit different requirements.

Order of rigging
The order of rigging the jib is usually as follows:

1 Shackle to bow
2 Fasten hanks
3 Fasten sheets
4 Shackle head to halyard
5 Hoist jib

Shackling to the bow

The tack of the jib should be fastened to the bow fitting. This has three eyes to which the forestay, the tack of the jib and the painter are attached. Normally the forestay is attached at (1), the tack of the jib at (2), and the painter at (3) but the position of each eye varies with the design of the boat.

Fastening the jib sheets

The jib sheets are fastened at the clew with a shackle or bowline knot (see page 331). They are led through fairleads and finished off with a stopping knot (see Knotting sheets, opposite). A jamming cleat holds the sheet in position, if required.

Fastening the hanks

Plastic or stainless steel hanks are used to fasten the jib to the forestay (shackles were formerly used). The hanks are fitted at right angles and then twisted to lock them onto the wire. The fastenings permit the jib to be raised or lowered quickly and neatly as required.

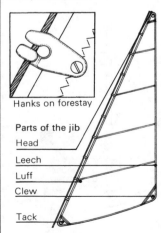

Hanks on forestay

Parts of the jib

Head

Leech

Luff

Clew

Tack

Hoisting the jib

Before hoisting the jib by pulling on the halyard, the head of the sail must be attached to the jib halyard. You should check first to make sure the jib halyard is not twisted. If the jib is not being hoisted straightaway, secure it to the forestay with a sheet. When the jib is hoisted, cleat the spare line.

Shackling the halyard
If the head of the sail is attached to the halyard with a D shackle, make sure the shackle pin is tightened properly so it does not loosen when the jib flaps.

FIGURE 14.2   The stepped relationship between the elements of this page is indicated by the schematic drawing (top right). However, it is not particularly well reflected in the layout.

Rudder and tiller

The rudder is one of the principal boat controls and has to be adjusted constantly by means of the tiller when the boat is being sailed. The rudder is effective only when the boat is moving and can be used either for steering, or as an accelerator or brake. It also helps to prevent sideways slip in the water and has to be able to withstand pressure.

The majority of sailing dinghies are fitted with a rudder which has a pivoting retractable blade to enable the boat to be sailed into and away from shallow water. The blade normally extends some 60 cm (2 ft) below the stern of the boat. The depth of the rudder is important as at least part of the rudder blade must remain in the water when the boat heels. During sailing, the blade is held down by means of a shock cord (or lanyard) which is cleated to the side or underside of the tiller.

Parts of the rudder

The rudder and tiller are fitted together at the hood (1). The rudder stock (2) is fitted with a blade which can be raised (3) or lowered (4). A shock cord (5) keeps the rudder in position.

Tiller extension
Most boats have an extension fitted to the tiller so that the helmsman can steer the boat when sitting well out. The extension is attached to the tiller by a universal joint (right) which permits movement in any direction (below).

Fitting the rudder

The rudder is attached to the centre line of the transom with two special hinges each comprising a metal rod (the pintle) which fits into an eye (the gudgeon). The rudder is best attached before the boat is afloat.

1 Align the pintles and gudgeons and drop the rudder into position.

2 Push the tiller into the rudder hood through the slot in the transom.

3 Secure the tiller in place with the split pin.

4 Fasten the shock cord or line to the side of the tiller to keep the blade in the down position.

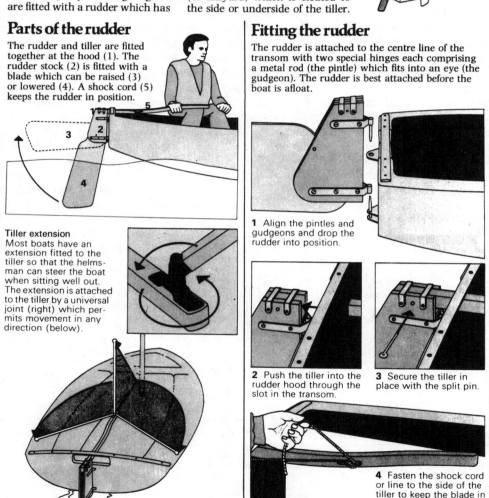

FIGURE 14.3 With the exception of the stepped sequence under "Fitting the rudder," most of this page consists of a stack of information about its topic.

So whereas each sentence in a stacked paragraph takes the same initial topic sentence as its point of departure, chained sentences simply relate to their immediate predecessors. Indeed, in view of this apparent lack of preplanning, it is hard to see why Nash includes chains as "designs" at all. Judging by his examples, chain structures are more characteristic of literary prose than expository or technical information.

Balanced rhetorical patterns present contrasting viewpoints—proposition and counterproposition. The balance would appear to be easily reflected in layout—the point-by-point comparison of two (or more) contrasting options can be easily made in a table, for example. Indeed, the bilateral symmetry implied by the term "balance" points to an advantage of graphic formats over prose—complex comparisons can be made in a considerably more orderly way.

In practice, the main provision for the typographic signalling of topic structures in most publishers' style guides is for hierarchical structures of headings and subheadings. A typical hierarchy might provide for chapter headings and three levels of subheadings, perhaps termed A, B, and C headings. In effect, a single graphic technique must serve for a variety of rhetorical purposes. Arguments may be represented as hierarchical structures, even when the "ideal" text-diagram might be rather different. Since topic structures do not always correspond to the structures implied by the hierarchical typographic arrangement enforced by the norms of book publishing (or to any simple, easily diagrammed structure, for that matter), the exact relationships between major points in an argument must usually be specified in some linguistic way. Interestingly, there is a noticeable similarity between Nash's fourfold classification of rhetorical designs and a distinction between four kinds of verbal conjunction made in Halliday and Hasan's (1976) influential account of linguistic cohesion in English texts (Table 14.5). So although Nash's categories simply seemed to be a useful starting point for this discussion because of their metaphorical names, confidence in them is enhanced by close parallels with other classifications suggested independently by scholars in related contexts. In another context still, the psychology of text comprehension, Meyer's categories of rhetorical structure are converging in a similar way. She has recently conflated her original eighteen categories (Meyer, 1975) into five categories, which, on examination, bear a close relationship to Halliday and Hasan's collection, description, causation, problem/solution, and comparison (Meyer, 1985).

Although conjunction is just one of Halliday and Hasan's five kinds of "cohesive tie," it is of special relevance to the present study. Whereas the other four—reference, substitution, ellipsis, and lexical cohesion—are embedded in the internal structure and wording of sentences, conjunction is normally achieved through separate, identifiable "adjuncts"—words and phrases. Halliday and Hasan (1976) explain that

> conjunctive relations are encoded not in the form of grammatical structures but in the looser, more pliable form of linkages between the components of a text. (p. 321)

TABLE 14.5   A Comparison of Nash's Rhetorical Designs and Halliday and Hasan's Conjunctive Relations

NASH'S RHETORICAL DESIGNS	HALLIDAY & HASAN'S CONJUNCTIVE RELATIONS	EXAMPLES OF CONJUNCTIVE ADJUNCTS
Step	temporal	first, then, next, finally
Stack	additive	and, furthermore, for instance
Chain	casual	so, because, consequently
Balance	adversative	but, however, on the other hand, rather

So if cohesive relations can be displayed through typography, itself a means of linking text components, they are most likely to be of the conjunctive kind. It should be remembered, of course, that Halliday and Hasan are for the most part interested in relatively short-range relations, typically between pairs of sentences, rather than the structure of extended arguments. Any extended prose passage will contain a variety of cohesive ties from many of their different categories and subcategories. But the sort of relations or structures found typographically signalled in the sailing handbook examples are usually less subtle than those in a typical page of prose. They relate to broad structures found (or imposed) with the page's topic.

Additive relations can be seen as inclusive of Nash's stacks (Figure 14.3). Figure 14.4 gives a further example. Temporal relations can be seen in terms of steps (Figure 14.1), although the latter may have causal links also. However, the apparent similarity between the Nash and the Halliday and Hasan schemes becomes rather more blurred when one examines the equivalence of chain and causal. From Nash's statement that each sentence in a chain takes its predecessor as a point of departure, we can see chain relations as being both causal and additive. Given our present interest in information rather than literary texts, "causal" is a rather more useful category than "chain," although it is no easier to show graphically. The equivalence of balance and adversative is also not straightforward, since Halliday and Hasan class balanced constructions as either adversative or additive, according to whether they refer to external contrasts (i.e., contrasts in the fact structure) or internal contrasts (in the linearized argument structure).

A problem emerges from this brief comparison of two categorical frameworks. Halliday and Hasan's four categories only correspond to Nash's if we select their external (fact structure) examples. But this is the opposite of what we might expect

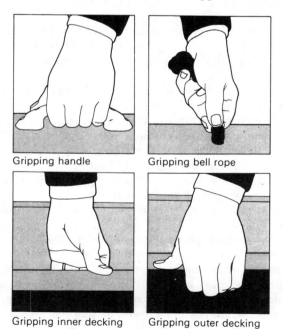

Gripping handle   Gripping bell rope

Gripping inner decking   Gripping outer decking

FIGURE 14.4   The identical frame size of these four methods of carrying a boat, and the absence of a linear sequence of their arrangement, is suggestive of "or" conjunctions—classed by Halliday and Hasan (1976) as an additive conjunctive relation (of the subcategory "alternative").

when we recall that Nash's purpose is to classify not fact structures but argument structures. The answer lies in the highly metaphorical character of Nash's categories: although he is describing argument structures, he uses the vocabulary of fact structures to do so.

If we look more closely at this vocabulary of fact structures in the context of semantics, once again we find a high degree of visual, or at least visualizable, metaphor. The lexical "sense relations" discussed by Lyons (1977) are listed below. Other textbooks (for example, Leech 1981) use similar terms.

Contrast

Binary Opposites

gradable (e.g., hot/cold)

non-gradable (e.g., male/female)

converse (e.g., husband/wife)

directional (e.g., North/South, up/down)

Non-binary set

Serially ordered

   gradable scales (e.g., poor . . . fair . . . excellent)

   non-gradable ranks (e.g., private, corporal . . . field marshal)

Cyclical (e.g., . . . spring, summer, autumn, winter, spring . . .)

Hierachy

Class inclusion (e.g., animal: cow, sheep, etc)

Part-whole relations (e.g., body: arms, legs, etc)

Many of these sense relations are suggestive of visual metaphor, and it is quite easy to find a number of them graphically displayed in the book used for the preceding examples. Figures 14.5 to 14.10 show examples of those compatible with the segmented character of typography.

Since the scope of all classifications is related to their purpose, it is understandable that some of Lyons's sense relations do not have a direct equivalent in graphic displays, and that some graphic conventions do not find a place in this list. And it is noticeable that some semantic relations work better than others within the rectilinear conventions of typographic layout. In particular, non-gradable sets (equivalent to Nash's steps and balances) are easily chunked and therefore tabulated or split into columns. Gradable sets, on the other hand, can be described in linear prose or by recourse to a separate diagram, but with difficulty through layout alone.

The linearity of language is rarely an obstacle to the connection of concepts at the sentence level. Halliday and Hasan's cohesive ties, for example, usually create links between sentences that are both physically close and available in short-term memory. But when a link is to be made across many pages rather than just a few sentences, language alone strains to compensate for its own linearity. Subtleties of sentence construction or inflection no longer suffice, and authors usually introduce *metalanguage*—whole sentences or paragraphs in which they step back from their argument and comment, seemingly objectively, on its progress. At this metalinguistic level some writers prefer to break out of the linear mode altogether and use graphic techniques. *Concept maps*—abstract diagrams showing the relationship between different aspects of a topic—are often used, particularly in textbooks, to help readers overview the author's argument.

Whether readers actually use or benefit from such diagrams is still an open question among educational psychologists. Jonassen and Hawk (1984) have tested

Heavy waterproof suit

A heavy duty two-piece waterproof suit gives the best protection for coastal cruising or ocean voyaging. You will be on the deck in all sorts of weather conditions and your clothes must be proof against wind, rain and breaking seas. The two-piece suit usually consists of a hooded jacket and chest-high trousers with a double-fold gusset and adjustable shoulder straps. It is designed and cut with the minimum number of seams. Insulating layers are worn underneath.

Wet suit

Most experienced dinghy sailors wear neoprene wet suits to combat loss of body heat in the water. The sleeveless "long John" type is the most popular as it does not restrict body movement. A hip-length jacket is usually worn over the top, and in cold weather, a hood, boots and gloves are worn.

Chest-high trousers

Jacket with hood

Double fold gusset

Hip-length jacket

Neoprene construction
Bonded outer fabric
Neoprene foam
Fleecy lining

Long John suit

FIGURE 14.5   Binary contrast, nongradable: The use of parallel columns is a typical way of showing an either/or relationship. The use of a different typeface for the main text vs. caption relationship could be seen as an example of a converse binary contrast.

"graphic organizers" and found advantages for immediate but not delayed recall. It is possible that training is needed to make use of such devices. Indeed, lack of familiarity with diagrams is suggested by Holliday (1976) as a possible explanation of his finding that where the information in the diagram was accompanied by the same information in prose form, readers preferred the familiar prose version. However, experiments that oblige readers to study in controlled conditions cannot measure how effective these devices are for less formal purposes such as browsing or revision. And in the absence of a basis for comparing the content, complexity, and style of diagrams, it is difficult to generalize from particular studies.

As Evans (1980) has shown, such diagrams have a long history. The medieval preoccupation with order and especially geometry made diagramming a particularly suitable medium for recording scholastic analysis. Evans describes the use of branching diagrams ("stemmata" is Evans' term), geometric diagrams, and visual metaphors such as trees, wheels, towers, and ladders. He includes the diagrammatic use of page layouts

Leaving

Before the boat's lines are cast off the skipper has to decide on his method of leaving. You need to check around first to see if there are any other boats in the process of leaving or arriving which may interfere with your proposed course of action. Not only should you consider the effects of wind and tide at the berth itself, but also on your path out of the marina. Your exit from the marina will probably be very slow and you need to be sure that you can control your craft properly.

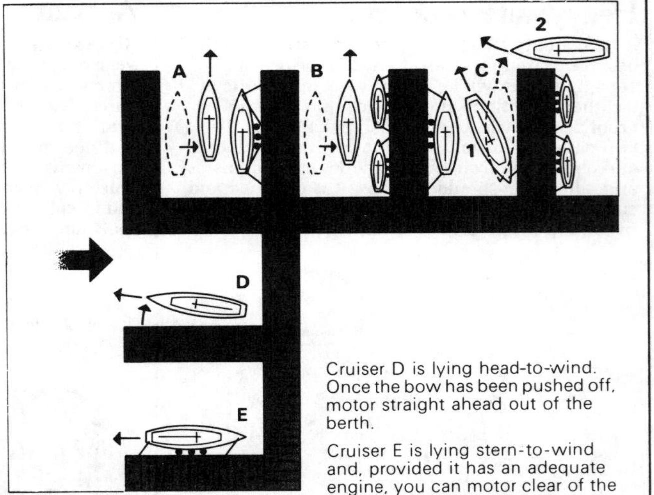

Cruiser D is lying head-to-wind. Once the bow has been pushed off, motor straight ahead out of the berth.

Cruiser E is lying stern-to-wind and, provided it has an adequate engine, you can motor clear of the berth in reverse, using prop walk (with a clockwise-rotating propeller) to take the stern clear of the pontoon. The crew could help you by walking the boat out using the stern line and aft spring, and climbing aboard as the boat passes the end of the pontoon.

Cruisers A and B have simple berths to leave from. Put the engine in neutral before the lines are cast off, then let the boat drift clear of the berth. Motor out into open water. If there is not enough wind to push the boat clear, push the bow off.

Cruiser C has a more difficult leaving situation, as it is berthed bow-on in a windward berth. Either spring off the stern (1) or warp the boat onto the end of the pontoon (2) so that it can leave with the bowlfacing into the wind.

Arriving

As a visitor, when planning to berth in a marina, you should first try and find out if there are special visitors' berths, or whether a visitor is expected to find his own berth. Usually, the pilot book for the harbour will give you the information you need. Before you come into the marina you should brief the crew. It is unlikely, however, you will know in advance which side of the boat will be alongside the berth and so the crew must be ready to rig the warps quickly as soon as the skipper himself knows the answer. If there are enough fenders to go around, hang them over both sides of the boat. The skipper should keep a watch for other boats entering or leaving the marina and control his own speed accordingly.

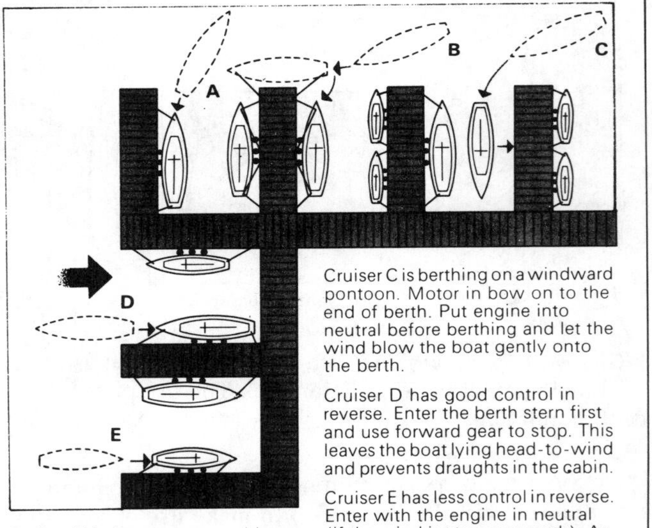

Cruiser A is berthing in a leeward berth. If your boat has good manoeuvrability and little prop walk on the engine, you can berth astern, allowing the stern to lie upwind slightly of the berth. Stop boat alongside and secure it.

Cruiser B is less manoeuvrable. Bring the boat alongside the end of the pontoon head-to-wind, and once the bow and stern lines have been secured, the crew can walk the boat into the berth.

Cruiser C is berthing on a windward pontoon. Motor in bow on to the end of berth. Put engine into neutral before berthing and let the wind blow the boat gently onto the berth.

Cruiser D has good control in reverse. Enter the berth stern first and use forward gear to stop. This leaves the boat lying head-to-wind and prevents draughts in the cabin.

Cruiser E has less control in reverse. Enter with the engine in neutral (if the wind is strong enough). As the boat arrives at the berth, the crew attaches the stern line and aft spring first to slow the boat down. (With good astern power, a final burst astern could be used instead.)

FIGURE 14.6 Binary contrast, directional: Here the order in which topics are presented reflects the directional or temporal order of topic—when taking a trip in a boat, you leave before you arrive back. In a different topic, it might have been more appropriate for arriving to precede leaving, the convention being to show temporal progression in terms of the norms of the writing system; in the case of the roman alphabet, from left to right, top to bottom. Other conceptual relationships are assigned directionality by metaphor: senior people thus rank above or before junior ones, and so on.

Sail onto boom

The sail is fitted into a track on the upper side of the boom. It is important to make sure that the sail is fully stretched when fitting it onto the boom. There is normally a marker at the end of the boom to indicate how far the sail should be pulled out. The sail must be fastened securely in position at both ends.

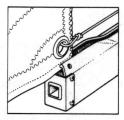

1 Slide clew of sail into mast end of boom, pulling it to marker at opposite end of boom.

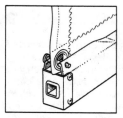

2 Secure tack of sail to mast end of boom by inserting tack pin through sail and boom.

3 Pull foot of sail taut and fasten clew outhaul to boom and secure.

FIGURE 14.7   Nonbinary sets, serially ordered nongradable. The numbered sequence is an obvious example.

in his account: "A different size of initial was used to begin book, chapter, and verse in the Bible; different grades of script were used to distinguish between text, commentary, and gloss" (p. 34).

Access Structures

The notion of topic structure focuses on the text as a vehicle for the author's expression. My second category of visual informativeness, *access structure*, reflects the role of text as a learning resource for selective readers. Many of the pedagogic devices commonly used by instructional designers—advance organisers, behavioural objectives, summaries, and so on—enhance the accessibility of a text by explicitly declaring its conceptual framework, goals, and structure (Waller 1982). But in addition to these "adjunct aids" (as they are sometimes known), accessibility can be further integrated into a text through the use of typographic signalling and layout.

The most basic access devices are regular numbering systems for pages or para-

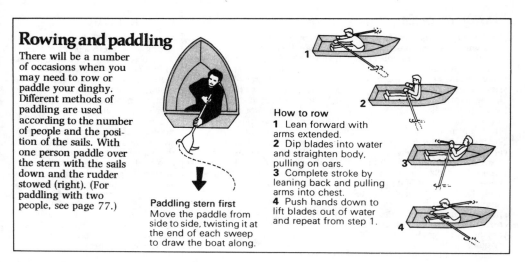

Rowing and paddling

There will be a number of occasions when you may need to row or paddle your dinghy. Different methods of paddling are used according to the number of people and the position of the sails. With one person paddle over the stern with the sails down and the rudder stowed (right). (For paddling with two people, see page 77.)

Paddling stern first
Move the paddle from side to side, twisting it at the end of each sweep to draw the boat along.

How to row
1 Lean forward with arms extended.
2 Dip blades into water and straighten body, pulling on oars.
3 Complete stroke by leaning back and pulling arms into chest.
4 Push hands down to lift blades out of water and repeat from step 1.

FIGURE 14.8   Nonbinary sets, cyclical: In this case the cycle is indicated by using the same illustration for step 4 as for step 1. An alternative might have been to arrange the steps into a circle, but this arrangement is particularly suited to the subject—the progress of the boat through the water.

Alternative forms of racing

Boat-for-boat racing in one-design and restricted development classes provides exciting racing, but there are other forms of racing which are equally popular and in some cases more common. Colleges, universities and many clubs often organize team racing, where the object is for the team rather than the individual competitor to win. This provides a quite different type of racing, involving an increased use of tactics and placing less emphasis on faster sailing. Many club races are organized on a handicap system so that several different types of boat may race together. This is popular with regatta committees who want to see as many boats competing as possible. The most individual form of racing is match racing, which is conducted between two boats. The America's Cup is probably the best known match racing event.

Team racing

Team racing, shown right, is usually organized between two teams of three or four boats in the same class. A match usually consists of two races, with the teams exchanging boats in between the races. The object is for the team, rather than the individuals, to win. Because of the scoring system, it is not necessary for a team to have first place to win the race. Thus the emphasis is less on individual prowess and boat speed and more on tactical ability. A good knowledge of the rules is vital and it is essential to be able to evaluate the overall position of your team at any time, as this will determine your tactics. For instance, if you are in second place with your team mates in fourth and fifth places, you will know that this is a losing combination and you will have to attack the opposition. The easiest way to improve your position is to try to slow down the boat in third place so that your team mates can pass him. This will give you second, third and fourth places – a winning combination. Team racing is, without doubt the best way to improve both your boat handling and knowledge of the rules.

Team racing in Enterprises. E19402 is helping a team mate to pass E19538 by allowing its jib to flap, thus disturbing the airflow reaching E19538.

Handicap racing

Handicap racing is common in clubs where no one class has enough boats to make single class racing worthwhile. But it is more usual for clubs to organize separate starts for their single class fleets and then to have a start for a handicap fleet to cater for those members who own boats other than those regularly raced. The most widely used handicapping system is based on "yardstick" numbers which are given to each class of dinghy. When a mixed fleet of dinghies races, the time each boat takes to complete the course is recorded and, by using a set of tables, a corrected time in relation to the yardstick numbers is worked out, giving the finishing positions. The yardstick numbers are corrected as evidence is built up from the information supplied by clubs to try to make the handicap system more accurate. In addition to handicapping classes of boat, some clubs handicap individual helmsmen. At the start of each season a helmsman with a proven consistent record is given the "scratch" rating. The other helmsmen are awarded handicaps around this level on the basis of their known ability. After each race the handicaps are adjusted.

Match racing

Match racing is a classic form of racing between two boats of the same class. It is often conducted in the form of a series of races between pairs of competitors making up a tournament. Each competitor must race against every other competitor and the overall winner is the one with the most wins. The match race really starts five or ten minutes before the actual start of the race as the two boats come together and attempt to get the best position for the start proper. The boat winning the start has a decided advantage and can control the other boat from ahead. However, as match racing is often very close, one bad tack can lose the race for the leading boat.

FIGURE 14.9 Hierarchy, class inclusion: The classic hierarchy, indicated by a hierarchy of headings of varying prominence.

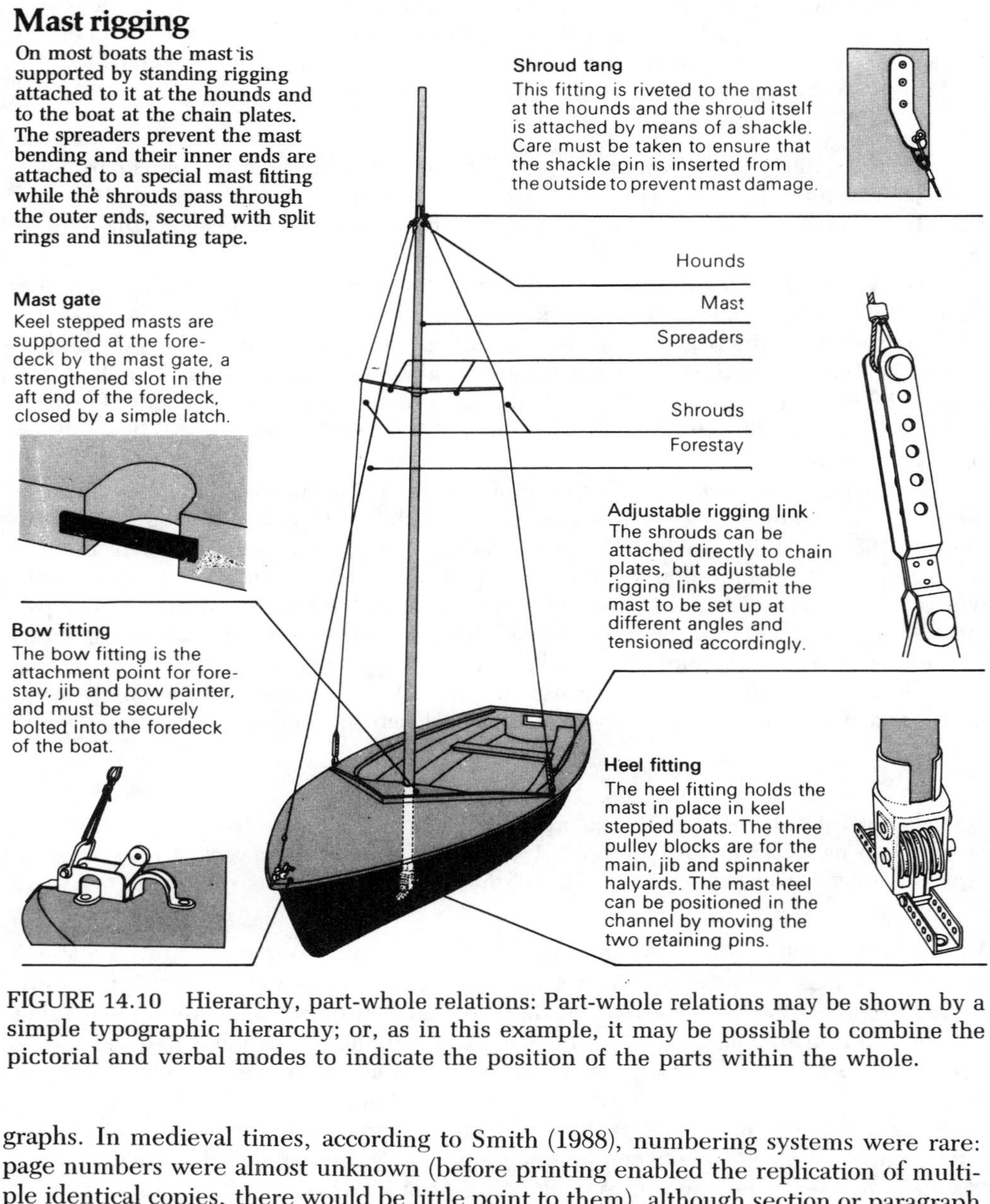

Mast rigging

On most boats the mast is supported by standing rigging attached to it at the hounds and to the boat at the chain plates. The spreaders prevent the mast bending and their inner ends are attached to a special mast fitting while the shrouds pass through the outer ends, secured with split rings and insulating tape.

Shroud tang

This fitting is riveted to the mast at the hounds and the shroud itself is attached by means of a shackle. Care must be taken to ensure that the shackle pin is inserted from the outside to prevent mast damage.

Mast gate

Keel stepped masts are supported at the fore-deck by the mast gate, a strengthened slot in the aft end of the foredeck, closed by a simple latch.

Bow fitting

The bow fitting is the attachment point for fore-stay, jib and bow painter, and must be securely bolted into the foredeck of the boat.

Hounds

Mast

Spreaders

Shrouds

Forestay

Adjustable rigging link

The shrouds can be attached directly to chain plates, but adjustable rigging links permit the mast to be set up at different angles and tensioned accordingly.

Heel fitting

The heel fitting holds the mast in place in keel stepped boats. The three pulley blocks are for the main, jib and spinnaker halyards. The mast heel can be positioned in the channel by moving the two retaining pins.

FIGURE 14.10   Hierarchy, part-whole relations: Part-whole relations may be shown by a simple typographic hierarchy; or, as in this example, it may be possible to combine the pictorial and verbal modes to indicate the position of the parts within the whole.

graphs. In medieval times, according to Smith (1988), numbering systems were rare: page numbers were almost unknown (before printing enabled the replication of multiple identical copies, there would be little point to them), although section or paragraph numbering was sometimes used. Even in the days when numbering systems were rare, of course, ideas always had a constant location within the copy each individual reader happened to have access to; and individuals would sometimes supply their own referencing systems. This stability of graphic layout, combined with the fact that books, being scarcer than today, were probably more intensively studied, might well have obviated the need for the elaborate access systems required by today's readers.

The Roman rhetorician Quintilian appears to have regarded the layout of pages (or wax tablets, rather) as a "more expeditious and efficacious" variation of the elaborate place-memory systems recommended by most rhetoric teachers of his era. He advises the student

. . . to learn by heart from the same tablets on which he has written; for he will pursue the remembrance of what he has composed by certain traces, and will look, as it were, with the eye of his mind, not only on the pages, but on almost every individual line, resembling, while he speaks, a person reading. (Book XI, Chapter II, p. 32)

Saenger (1982, p. 396) comments that "the new, readily available university texts of the later Middle Ages, replete with chapters, subdivisions, and distinct words, made possible a form of memorization based on the retention of the visual image of the written page."

Many people can supply anecdotal evidence that they are sometimes able to locate ideas in books, even if not in memory, simply from their location within the book—they remember whether the page is near the beginning or the end of the book, and whether the idea is at the top or the bottom of the page. Rothkopf (1971) tested this hypothesis in an experiment and reported evidence that seems to confirm such intuitions. Presumably the effect should be stronger where typographic layout is used to signal the author's topic structure.

This informal use of the appearance of a page for information retrieval is threatened by recent developments in electronic publishing. *Dynamic text*, or *hypertext* (Weyer, 1982; Conklin, 1986), offers the reader an interactive reading environment. Text is typically presented on a computer screen in a nested form—the reader points (with a mouse) to a heading (or to part of a diagram), and the relevant section "unwraps" onto the screen or cuts to a cross-referenced text. Hypertext systems can control large amounts of data in text, audio, and video form.

Electronically delivered text focuses us on features of books and reading that we mostly take for granted, especially their physical nature. Garland (1982, p. 5) comments:

> Whenever I rhapsodize about the opportunities presented by the electronic media, at the back of my mind I find myself thinking, "Yes, but a book is a book is a book. A reassuring, feel-the-weight, take-your-own-time kind of thing . . ."

And, as Kerr (1986) has pointed out, electronic text does not allow you to stick a finger between two pages while examining a third. Further problems with electronic text were noted by Waller (1987). The active reading strategies encouraged by educators assume that the text remains stable. Readers need to be able to build a mental map of the text as a physical object, in which headings, illustrations, and other graphic features act as landmarks. It must also be asked whether the amount of information to view at any one time has an effect on our ability to understand complex arguments. In the 25-line display typical of many current computers, there is a high probability that the beginning or end of the sentence you are reading will be out of sight.

These may be temporary problems; technical improvements will no doubt increase the resolution and size of screen displays, and writers and readers will develop new strategies. Indeed, history suggests that new communication techniques often require a transitional period in which they imitate the old, and in which new expressive and interpretative techniques can gradually develop. For example, early printed books imitated manuscripts, and early filmmakers used fixed cameras in imitation of the fixed viewpoint of the theatre audience. Hirsch (1967) suggests that "the transition from script to print was rarely dramatic. . . . [It] was continuous and broken, and I venture to say that all great discoveries, all so-called new movements, harbor the same contrasting elements, continuity and radical change" (pp. 1–2).

With this kind of consideration in mind, Benest and Morgan (1985) developed a prototype electronic text system that emulates traditional books, complete with realistically sized double-page spreads, with shadows imitative of the bulk of a real book.

TEXT AS ARTEFACT

Text is essentially and obviously an indirect medium in which writer and reader are separated in time and space. Moreover, the text seen by the reader has usually been mediated by a number of industrial processes that can influence its apparent structure. These processes include the application of professional editorial and design standards that smooth out the product of the writer's creative agony into an acceptable published document, and the constraints of printing processes. The most basic artefactual constraints of all are the need to break lines and pages.

A child learning to read must come to realise that while some breaks in the string of letters are meaningful, others are almost completely arbitrary. Spaces between letters indicate a word break, and in some early reading materials a new line indicates a new sentence and a new page announces a new topic. At some point, though, he or she learns that most line breaks have no significance—the end of the column has been reached.

Line breaks, page breaks, and, in the case of multi-column layouts, column breaks can be either arbitrary or meaningful. Table 14.6 suggests some of the semantic implications of meaningful breaks. At the line level, an arbitrary break is clearly just one of the conventions of the writing system that we take in our stride. Line breaks within paragraphs are generally not specified by authors, although they may object to awkward word breaks when they read their proofs. If a new sentence starts on an unforced new line, though, we regard it as the beginning of a new paragraph. If a succession of sentences, words, or phrases begin on new lines we are likely to regard them as forming a list.

In practice, meaningful line, column, or page breaks are often given extra coding to prevent ambiguity. Ambiguity is particularly acute when arbitrary line breaks occur in a list—where line endings would normally be seen as significant. In such cases a second coding—numbers, bullets, space between items, or indented turnovers—is normally added to clarify the structure. Paragraph breaks are almost always given a double coding—new line plus indention, or new line plus blank line—in view of the frequency with which sentence breaks within paragraphs happen to coincide with line breaks.

Unlike columns, which can vary in height and width as their content dictates, pages are invariable in size. There is therefore a trade-off between this inflexibility and the ability of page-organized texts to use two-dimensional diagramlike graphic effects to indicate topic structures. One point we may make in defence of the practice of writing and designing by spreads is that continuous prose is virtually the only format for

TABLE 14.6   Some Semantic Implications of Meaningful Breaks

| | | MEANINGFUL | |
	ARBITRARY	SINGLE BREAK	SUCCESSIVE BREAKS
Line	Prose	New paragraph	List
			Verse
Column	Prose	New topic	Table
			Parallel text
Page	Prose	New topic	Topic frame
		New chapter	

discourse that does not place limits on its length. Spoken addresses, such as speeches, lectures, and sermons, are ultimately bounded by the conventions of the occasion or the attention span of the audience. The fixed time of the school lesson is perhaps the most direct parallel to the treatment of a page or double-page spread as a topic frame. In the educational context, Duchastel (1982) has suggested larger page sizes for textbooks to enable them to make better use of graphic techniques—foldout posters that he terms "unbounded text."

Over the years a number of reformers have suggested changes to the practice of breaking lines at arbitrary points, suggesting that lines should only be broken at semantically or syntactically significant points. Indeed, a number of researchers have explored even more radical ideas for presenting text in small stacks of words or in spaced phrases (Andrews, 1949; North & Jenkins, 1951; Klare, Nichols, & Shuford, 1957; Carver, 1970; Wendt, 1979). The idea remains unproven, and for most purposes impractical.

Semantic or syntactic line breaks offer rather more hope of acceptance than the more radical proposals, since they do not look startlingly unusual. Coleman and Kim (1961), inspired by children's books that employed this system, did not obtain a significant result from their pilot study, but others seem to have been sufficiently encouraged to pursue the idea. Frase and Schwartz (1979) reported an impressively faster (14%-18%) response time for a task that required subjects to verify the answer to a question from the experimental text; this represents a typical use of a technical manual but does not resemble the reading of ordinary prose, where fluency is rather more important. In fact Raban (1982), who studied the effect of such line endings on childrens' reading, found that syntactic breaks were mistaken for the ends of sentences. It also seems strange to suggest that a particular punctuation technique (for that is what line breaks would become) should be distributed evenly throughout a text, and thus be determined by line length as well as sense. Hartley (1980) criticized Frase and Schwartz's methodology and failed to replicate their findings under different conditions.

A problem not addressed by the research literature is that rules for semantic line breaks would not be easy to determine. Moreover, such line breaks are normally associated with verse forms and may, paradoxically, draw attention to the form of language and away from its sense. Poets, of course, have long been aware of the typographic dimensions to language, which include the shape of stanzas (even to the extent of Herbert's shaped poems) and visual rhymes as well as line breaks.

COOPERATIVE AND UNCOOPERATIVE MEDIA

Early writing systems (in the evolution of the Roman alphabet) made few concessions to the busy reader. For example, word spaces, necessary for fluent silent reading, were not consistently used until the early Middle Ages. Over the centuries, other developments have included the codex format (the multileaf book), headings, title pages, contents lists, indexes, and so on. In effect, the introduction of greater accessibility has turned text from what Cherry (1966; p. 16) termed an uncooperative medium into a cooperative one.

A spoken conversation is the archetypal cooperative medium, since the participants must agree on the topic, when to interrupt or give way, and when to finish. An unsegmented written text, on the other hand, gives the reader little option but to start at the beginning and continue reading until the end is reached—or cope with the insecurity of random encounters. The greater the degree of segmentation of written language, and the greater the degree to which segments are labelled and indexed, the more cooperative the text becomes. The accessibility afforded by typographic structuring, and typographically structured adjuncts such as headings, contents lists, and so on, can be seen as the basis of a conversation between reader and text. The range of access devices in a typical textbook, for example, anticipates a range of reading purposes and enables the reader, in effect, to interrogate the text for the answers to a series of individually defined questions.

Conversational models of written text have been proposed by linguists (Gray, 1977; Winter, 1977; Widdowson, 1979; Hoey, 1983), semiologists (Eco, 1981), cognitive psychologists (Wright, 1978; Nystrand, 1986), and literary critics of the "reader-response" school (Tompkins, 1980). Not surprisingly, the detailed study of cooperation in discourse has mostly focused on spoken conversations. In fact, with a few exceptions, "discourse" is normally assumed by linguists, sociologists, and others involved in this interdisciplinary field to be spoken (for example, Gumperz, 1982; Coulthard, 1985). One of those who uses the term in relation to text, Hoey (1983), refers to the doctrine of the primacy of speech to justify his view of text as containing implicit dialogue:

> If dialogue has primacy over monologue, it is but a small step to seeing monologue as a specialized form of dialogue between the writer or speaker and the reader or listener. (p. 27)

Clearly we should be careful about applying concepts developed for one medium to the other. Telecommunications apart, spoken conversations involve the physical presence of both participants, who share a common situation: they share the place in which the conversation occurs, the physical presence of objects to which they may wish to refer, and the social setting. However, since discourse analysts ascribe many aspects of the management of conversations to prosody and paralanguage, and since typography and punctuation can be seen as the graphological equivalent of paralanguage (Crystal, 1971), it is worth reviewing the role of typography in the light of some recent studies of the pragmatics of discourse.

Two implications for typographers may be drawn from the conversational view of text. First, it suggests that textual units may not always be linked in the systematic way that a focus on topic structures alone might suggest. Headings, for example, might have no relationship, hierarchical or otherwise, with each other but only with their immediately preceding and following text. Such headings give prominence to an implied question that requires special emphasis or that constitutes a major transitional point in an argument, but have little meaning to the browsing reader. Editors and typographers have to take special care to coordinate this local role of headings with their global role as part of a hierarchy—to ensure that headings make sense not only in their local context as transitional devices but also when collected together in contents list.

Second, it is clear that that the context of a conversation affects both the relationship between participants and also what is said. Typography and layout can signal the text type or genre, and consequently may trigger different reader responses—in terms of both behaviour and critical stance. Moreover, each text implicitly signals to whom it is addressed—who is the "legitimate" reader, and who is cast in the role of observer or outsider. We may complement this with a similar link between conversational maxims and surface style that is made by Gumperz (1982):

> this channelling of interpretation is effected by conversational implicatures based on conventionalized co-occurrence expectations between content and surface style. (p. 131)

Large type and childish pictures suggest that children are being addressed: adults may choose such a book—as a gift for a child perhaps—and they may read it aloud to a child, or read it for some critical or evaluative purpose, but they do so as outsiders. The role of surface style becomes very obvious when new newspapers are launched: their choice of format (broadsheet or tabloid), the size of their banner headlines, and the busyness of their pages signals their desired readership as much as anything they say.

Widdowson (1984, p. 86) defines the achievement of accessibility as "an alignment of different states of knowledge so that a common frame of reference is created." Nystrand (1982) develops a similar concept of shared semantic space. In conversation this is negotiated—terms can be defined, language simplified, theories exemplified, and objections met on request. In text this can be achieved partly by the special adjuncts that have been developed to help readers navigate around complex texts. But it seems we must define access structure in broader terms also. By establishing and signalling the context—the genre—of written communication, typography indicates its relevance and scope and the social relations of its participants.

TYPOGRAPHY AND GENRES

Most documents are defined by genre or text type before they are actually written: on the whole, writers know whether they are writing for a textbook, a brochure, an advertisement, a catalogue, or a manual. That initial decision about genre normally represents an intuitive assessment of the context of the communication and of the relations between writer and reader. Elsewhere (Waller, 1987), I have developed the argument that genre conventions can be accounted for by particular combinations of the three underlying sources of structure discussed above: topic, artefact, and access structure, each of which corresponds to an aspect of the writer-text-reader relationship. However, although graphic formats can often be analyzed post hoc by reference to such concepts, they are rarely designed that way in practice.

As ordinary language categories, genres are intuitively and holistically understood. In practice, they are recognized not by their theoretical origins but by their more obvious and typical physical characteristics. These might be described or grouped in a number of ways. Concentrating on the most readily apparent graphic features, we might organize the typical features of typographic genres into four simple categories (illustrated in Table 14.7):

1. *Typical context of use*: Situations (industrial, domestic, educational, bureaucratic, etc.); products (books, periodicals, objects, packs, containers, etc.); in the case of historical examples, date of origination.
2. *Typical format and configuration*: Page (or field) size and shape, binding (where appropriate), paper or other surface material, frequency and use of colour, grid, boundary (line, box, column, page, book, container, etc.)
3. *Typical treatment of verbal language*: Composition system (letter fit, image quality, etc.), typographic style (atmosphere, associations), range of signalling (underlining, bold, italic, etc.), additional features (rules, tints, borders, etc.).
4. *Typical treatment of visual elements*: Pictorial syntax or style, proportion of visual to verbal language, how visual and verbal language are integrated.

By treating genres as basic categories, we may avoid the intellectual gymnastics that can result from attempts to generate usable categories from theoretical models. Ordinary-language genre labels are generated in response to real needs felt by communities of text producers and users; they thus have an empirical, perhaps an evolutionary, basis as social realities. This is precisely the view of the ordinary language philosophers, whose founding figure, J. L. Austin, justified it thus:

> Our common stock of words embodies all the distinctions men have found worth making, in the lifetimes of many generations: these surely are likely to be more numerous, more sound, since they have stood up to the long test of the survival of the fittest, and more

TABLE 14.7 Categories of Typical Features of Typographic Genres

	INSTRUCTIONS FOR DOMESTIC APPLIANCE	HOLIDAY BROCHURE	TRAFFIC SIGN
1. *Typical context of use*	Delivered with product.	In travel agencies or sent by post.	On posts or scaffolds near roads.
2. *Typical format and configuration*	Size may be restricted by container size; usually one or two colours; major division by language; minor division by operational task. Short examples may be on single sheets or concertina-folded, longer ones stitched.	Mostly designed to fit standard racks and envelopes. Some slimmer for timetable racks. Bright colour; cheap shiny paper; mostly saddle-stitched; short ones may be concertina-folded; long ones may have square backs.	Standard shapes; metal or backlit plastic; standard colours; Multiple signs stacked vertically.
3. *Typical treatment of verbal language*	Sans-serif type, multicolumn grid; blocked paragraphs; tables for technical info.; boxed or bold sections for warnings, etc.	Display type may have special atmosphere; tables, boxes, etc; small print at back; booking form on back page.	Standard bold sans-serif type (upper & lower case).
4. *Typical treatment of visual language*	Schematized diagram of product with parts identified on diagram; in multilingual examples, diagram folds out with parts identified by numbers: separate keys for each language.	Colour photographs; some of hotels, some symbolic of destination (Eiffel tower, etc.); May include drawings and decorative or atmospheric illustrations. Hotel illustrations are closely integrated with relevant prose and tabular info.	Heavy use of arrows & standard symbols, often used unaccompanied by words. Symbols & maps refer to immediate environment.

subtle, at least in all ordinary and reasonably practical matters, than any you or I are likely to think up in our arm-chairs of an afternoon—the most favoured alternative method. (Austin, 196, p. 182)

Among professional philosophers there seems to be considerable scepticism about Austin's faith in the survival of the fittest (Graham, 1977), but his ideas are widely cited by linguists and others interested in language and communication. Journalism can supply a simple example of the evolution of new descriptive terms to fit everyday linguistic categories. While book editors are usually content to see headings in terms of simple hierarchies (chapter heading, subheading, subsubheading; or A heading, B heading, C heading), journalists have coined words that reflect the way headings are used in newspapers: some terms are based on the location of headings (skyliner, double-decker), others on their purpose (kicker, screamer, teaser). Journalism textbooks such as Evans (1974) usually supply their own variations on such terminology.

The ordinary-language status of typographic genres may also facilitate their inclusion among the general skills of literacy. Within their own cultures, readers can develop a tacit knowledge of genres, even if they do not initially have the explicit technical knowledge needed to produce accurate examples themselves. In contrast, specialist linguistic or psychological terminology fits awkwardly into the context of typographic training—theoretical concepts like "schema" and "macrostructure" are hard to understand, and especially hard to apply to practical tasks, even by experts. On the other hand, their ordinary-language status means that descriptions of genres reflect the full complexity of human interaction rather than the symmetry of a theoretical model. It also means that new genres are constantly being developed as topic, artefact, and access structures change, or new combinations are required. Genres are therefore easier to instantiate than to classify—easier to recognize in retrospect than to specify in advance. The study of ordinary-language, or "de facto" genres, as they are termed by Miller (1984), is essentially ethnomethodological; in her words, "it seeks to explicate the knowledge that practice creates" (p. 155). New genres are probably recognised, and therefore named, by specialists before they percolate through to ordinary language use.

A further note of relativism and fuzziness is added when we recognize, firstly, that actual texts may belong to more than one genre, and, secondly, may contain components that belong to different genres. These problems were recognized by the sociologist Dell Hymes (1972, 1974), whose application of the concept of genre to spoken discourse has been influential among discourse analysts (cf. Brown & Yule, 1983; Coulthard, 1985). He tackles the first problem by distinguishing between a genre and its performance, suggesting the use of the term "speech act" to denote the latter. Actual speech acts need not necessarily fall neatly into a single genre category. He deals with the second problem by recognizing different levels of genres: elementary or minimal genres that in practice may be typically found grouped together in complex genres. Thus a religious service might constitute a complex genre, consisting of elementary genres such as hymns, prayers, sermon, and so on. Speech acts are instances of elementary genres, and Hymes uses the term "speech event" to describe instances of complex genres. Rather than propose a detailed hierarchy of genres in parallel to a hierarchy of speech acts (or text acts, documents, or whatever equivalent term one might choose), it would seem more realistic to recognize that any class of objects—not only linguistic ones—can be seen in terms of genres, kinds, types, or varieties, and that judgment about genre membership cannot be restricted to a single dimension. That is, we need not expect to find an exactly parallel relationship between categories of abstract entities (genres) and categories of real objects (texts). Campbell and Jamieson (1979) distinguish between a generic perspective and "a crusading search to find genres." They remark that "The generic perspective recognizes that while there may be few clearly distinguishable genres, all rhetoric is influenced by prior rhetoric, all rhetorical acts resemble other rhetorical acts" (p. 26).

CONCLUSION

To a large extent, the disillusionment that many publishing and design professionals feel about the typographic research literature reflects the fact that it was always somewhat removed from the broader issues surrounding the processes of writing and reading. Never really sure of its place in the linguistics and communications scenario, typography has become further left behind as discourse studies have progressed during the last decade. In this chapter I have explored some of the traditional barriers to the integration of typography with linguistics, and some of the ways in which it might be seen as part of the semantic (topic-centred) and communicative (reader-centred) armoury. I concluded by suggesting a generic perspective within which typographic research might be better contextualised and within which typographic practice might be better informed about reader expectations.

REFERENCES

Andrews, R. B. (1949). Reading power unlimited. *Texas Outlook*, *33*, 20–21.

Ausubel, D. P. (1963). *The psychology of meaningful verbal learning*. New York: Grune & Stratton.

Austin, J. L. (1961). *Philosophical papers*. London: Oxford University Press.

Baddeley, A. D. (1979). Working memory and reading. In R. Kolers, M. Wrolstad, & H. Bouma (Eds.), *Processing of visible language* Vol. 1. (pp. 355–370) New York: Plenum.

Baddeley, A. D. (1984). Reading and working memory. *Visible Language*, *4*, 311–322.

Baddeley, A. D., & Lieberman, K. (1980). Spatial working memory. In R. Nickerson (Ed.), *Attention and Performance*. Vol. VIII (pp. 521–539) Hillsdale, NJ: Erlbaum.

Barthes, R. (1977). The rhetoric of the image. In *Image, music, text* (S. Heath, Trans.). London: Fontana.

Bartram, D. (1982). The perception of semantic quality in type: Differences between designers and non-designers. *Information Design Journal*, *3*, 38–50.

Beaugrande, R. de (1981). The linearity of reading: Fact, fiction, frontier? In J. Flood (Ed.), *Issues in reading comprehension*. Newark, NJ: International Reading Association.

Beaugrande, R. de (1984). *Text production: Toward a science of composition*. Norwood, NJ: Ablex.

Benest, I. D., & Morgan, G. (1985). A humanized model for the electronic library. In *Paper versus screen: The human factor issues*, Digest No. 1985/80. London: Institution of Electrical Engineers.

Berliner, A. (1920). Atmospharenwert von Drucktypen. *Ztschf. angwandte Psychol.*, *17*, 165–172 (as cited by Ovink, 1938).

Bernhardt, S. A. (1985). Text structure and graphic design. In J. D. Benson & W. S. Greaves (Eds.), *Systematic perspectives on discourse* (Vol. 2). Norwood, NJ: Ablex.

Bloomfield, L. (1935). *Language* (rev. ed.) London: George Allen & Unwin.

Bolinger, D. L. (1946). Visual morphemes. *Language*, *22*, 333–340.

Bouma, H. (1980). Visual reading processes and the quality of text displays. In. E. Grandjean & E. Vigliani (Eds.), *Ergonomic aspects of visual display terminals*. London: Taylor & Francis.

Bradley, H. (1919). *Spoken and written English*. Oxford: Clarendon Press.

Brown, G., & Yule G. (1983). *Discourse analysis*. Cambridge, Eng.: Cambridge University Press.

Buckingham, B. R. (1931). New data on the typography of textbooks. *Yearbook of the National Society for the Study of Education*, *30*, 93–125.

Burnhill, P., & Hartley, J. (1975). The psychology of textbook design: A research critique. In J. Baggaley, G. H. Jamieson, & H. Marchant, *Aspects of educational technology*, Vol. VIII; Communication and Learning (pp. 65–78). London: Pitman.

Burnhill, P., Hartley, J., & Davies, L. (1977). Typographic decision making: The layout of indexes. *Applied Ergonomics*, *8*, 35–39.

Burnhill, P., Trueman, M., & Hartley, J. (1979). The role of special cues in the layout of journal references. *Applied Ergonomics*, *10*, 165–169.

Burt, C. (1959). *A psychological study of typography.* Cambridge, Eng.: Cambridge University Press. (Reprinted 1974 by Bowker.)

Burt, C., Cooper, W. F., & Martin, J. L. (1955). A psychological study of typography. *British Journal of Statistical Psychology, 8,* 29–57.

Campbell, K. K., & Jamieson, K. H. (Eds.). (1979). *Form and genre: Shaping rhetorical action.* Falls Church, VA: Speech Communication Association.

Carver, R. P. (1970). Effect of a "chunked" typography on reading rate and comprehension. *Journal of Applied Psychology, 54,* 288–296.

Cherry, C. (1966). *On human communication: A review, a survey and a criticism* (2nd ed.). Cambridge, MA: MIT Press.

Cohen, M. (1977). *Sensible words: Linguistic practice in England, 1640–1785.* Baltimore: John Hopkins University Press.

Coleman, E. B., & Kim, I. (1961). Comparison of several styles of typography. *Journal of Applied Psychology, 45,* 262–267.

Coles, P., & Foster, J. (1975). Typographic cueing as an aid to learning from typewritten text. *Programmed Learning & Educational Technology, 12,* 102–108.

Conklin, J. (1986). *A survey of hypertext* (Technical Report No. STP-356-86). Austin, TX: Microelectronics & Computer Technology Corporation.

Coulthard, M. (1985). *An introduction to discourse analysis* (2nd ed.). London: Longman.

Crystal, D. (1971). *Linguistics.* Harmondsworth, Eng.: Penguin.

Crystal, D. (1980). *A first dictionary of linguistics and phonetics.* London: Deutsch.

Crystal, D., & Davy, D. (1969). *Investigating English style.* London: Longman.

Davies, I. K. (1976). *Objectives in curriculum design.* London: McGraw-Hill.

Duchastel, P. (1982). Unbounded text. *Educational Technology, 22,* 19–21.

Eaton, M. (1980). Truth in pictures. *Journal of Aesthetics & Art Criticism, 39,* 15–26.

Eco, U. (1976). *A theory of semiotics,* Bloomington: Indiana University Press.

Eco, U. (1981). *The role of the reader,* London: Hutchinson.

Evans, H. (1974). *News headlines.* London: Heinemann.

Evans, M. (1980). The geometry of the mind. *Architectural Association Quarterly, 12,* 32–55.

Frase, L. T., & Schwartz, B. J. (1979). Typographical cues that facilitate comprehension. *Journal of Educational Psychology, 71,* 197–206.

Frye, N. (1957). *Anatomy of criticism.* Princeton, NJ: Princeton University Press.

Garland, K., & Associates. (1982). *Ken Garland and Associates: Designers—20 years work and play 1962–82.* London: Ken Garland & Associates.

Glynn, S. M., Britton, B. K., & Tillman, M. H. (1985). Typographic cues in text: Management of the reader's attention. In D. Jonassen (Ed.), *The technology of text* (Vol. 2) (pp. 192–209). Englewood Cliffs, NJ: Educational Technology Publications.

Glynn, S. M., & Di Vesta, F. J. (1979). Control of prose processing via instructional and typographical cues. *Journal of Educational Psychology, 71,* 595–603.

Gombrich, E. H. (1960). *Art and illusion: A study in the psychology of pictorial representation.* London: Phaidon.

Graham, K. (1977). *J. L. Austin: A critique of ordinary language philosophy.* Brighton, Eng.: Harvester Press.

Gray, B. (1977). *The grammatical foundations of rhetoric.* The Hague: Mouton.

Grimes, J. E.. (1975). *The thread of discourse.* The Hague: Mouton.

Gumperz, J. J. (1982). *Discourse strategies.* Cambridge, Eng.: Cambridge University Press.

Halliday, M. A. K., & Hasan, R. (1976). *Cohesion in English.* London: Longman.

Hartley, J. (1980). Spatial cues in text. *Visible Language, 14,* 62–79.

Hartley, J., Bartlett, S., & Branthwaite, A. (1980). Underlining can make a difference—sometimes. *Journal of Educational Research, 73,* 218–222.

Hartley, J., & Burnhill, P. (1977). Understanding instructional text: Typography, layout, and design. In. M. J. A. Howe (Ed.), *Adult Learning* (pp. 223–247). London: Wiley.

Hartley, J., & Burnhill, P. (Eds.). (1981). The spatial arrangement of text. *Visible Language, 15* (1) [special issue].

Hartley, J., Burnhill, P., & Fraser, S. (1974). Typographical problems of journal design. *Applied Ergonomics, 5,* 15–20.

Hartley, J., Trueman, M., & Burnhill, P. (1979). The role of spatial and typographic cues in the layout of journal references. *Applied Ergonomics, 10,* 165–169.

Hershberger, W. A., & Terry, D. F. (1965). Typographical cuing in conventional and programmed texts. *Journal of Applied Psychology, 40,* 55–60.

Hirsch, R. (1967). *Printing, selling and reading 1450–1550.* Wiesbaden: Otto Harrassowitz.

Hockett, C. F. (1958). *A course in modern linguistics.* New York: Macmillan.

Hoey, M. (1983). *On the surface of discourse.* London: George Allen & Unwin.

Holliday, W. G. (1976). Teaching verbal chains using flow diagrams and text. *AV Communication Review, 18,* 129–159.

Huey, E. B. (1898). Preliminary experiments in the physiology and psychology of reading. *American Journal of Psychology*, 9, 575–586.

Hymes, D. (1972). Models of the interaction of language and social life. In. J. J. Gumperz & D. Hymes (Eds.), *Directions in sociolinguistics* (pp. 35–71). New York: Holt, Rinehart & Winston.

Hymes, D. (1974). Ways of speaking. In R. Bauman & J. Sherzer (Eds.), *Explorations in the ethnography of speaking* (pp. 433–451). Cambridge, Eng.: Cambridge University Press.

Ivins, W. M., Jr. (1953). *Prints and visual communications*. Cambridge, MA: Harvard University Press.

Javal, E. (1878). Hygiène de la lecture. *Bulletin de la Société de Médecine Publique*, p. 569.

Javal, E. (1879). Essai sur le physiologie de la lecture. *Annales d'Oculistique*, 82, 242–253.

Jewett, D. L. (1981). Multi-level writing in theory and practice. *Visible Language*, 15, 32–40.

Jonassen, D., & Hawk, P. (1984). Using graphic organizers in instruction. *Information Design Journal*, 4, 58–68.

Kerr, S. T. (1986). Learning to use electronic text: An agenda for research in typography, graphics, and interpanel navigation. *Information Design Journal*, 4, 206–211.

Klare, G. R., Mabry, J. E., & Gustafson, L.M. (1955). The relationship of patterning (underlining) to immediate retention and to acceptability of technical material. *Journal of Applied Psychology*, 39, 40–42.

Klare, G. R., Nichols, W. H., & Shuford, E. H. (1957). The relationship of typographic arrangement to the learning of technical training material. *Journal of Applied Psychology*, 41, 41–45.

Kleiman, G. M. (1975). Speech recoding in reading. *Journal of Verbal Learning and Verbal Behavior*, 14, 323–339.

Kolers, P. A. (1985). Phonology in reading. In D. R. Olson, N. Torrance, & A. Hildyard (Eds.), *Literacy, language and learning* (pp. 404–411). Cambridge, Eng.: Cambridge University Press.

Leech, G. (1981). *Semantics: The study of meaning* (2nd ed.) Harmondsworth, Eng.: Pelican.

Legros, L. A. (1922). *A note on the legibility of printed matter*. London: HMSO.

Lotz, J. (1972). How language is conveyed by script. In J. F. Kavanagh & I. G. Mattingly (Eds.), *Language by ear and by eye* (pp. 117–24). Cambridge, MA: MIT Press.

Lyons, J. (1977). *Semantics* (2 vols.). Cambridge, Eng.: Cambridge University Press.

Martin, S. E. (1972). Nonalphabetic writing systems: Some observations. In J. F. Kavanagh & I. G. Mattingly (Eds.), *Language by ear and by eye* (pp. 81–102). Cambridge, MA: MIT Press.

Massaro, D. W. (1979). Reading and listening. In P. Kolers, M. Wrolstad, & H. Bouma (Eds.), *Processing of visible language* (Vol. 1, pp. 331–354). New York: Plenum.

Meyer, B. J. F. (1975). Identification of the structure of prose and its implications for the study of reading and memory. *Journal of Reading Behavior*, 7, 7–47.

Meyer, B. J. F. (1985). Prose analysis: Purposes, procedures, and problems. In B. K. Britton and J. B. Black (Eds.), *Understanding expository text* (pp. 11–64). Hillsdale, NJ: Erlbaum.

Miller, C. R. (1984). Genre as social action. *Quarterly Journal of Speech*, 70, 151–167.

Nash, W. (1980). *Designs in prose*. London: Longman.

North, A. J., & Jenkins, L. B. (1951). Reading speed and comprehension as a function of typography. *Journal of Applied Psychology*, 35, 225–228.

Nystrand, M. (1982). The structure of textual space. In M. Nystrand (Ed.), *What writers know: The language, process, and structure of written discourse* (pp. 75–86). New York: Academic Press.

Ovink, G. W. (1938). *Legibility, atmosphere-value, and forms of printing types*. Leyden, Neth.: A. W. Sijthoff.

Pyke, R. L. (1926). *The legibility of print*. London: HMSO.

Quintilian. (1870). *Institutes of oratory* (Trans. J. S. Watson) (Vol. II, Books VIII–XII). London: Bell & Daldy.

Quirk, R., Greenbaum, S., Leech, G., & Svartvik, J. (1985). *A comprehensive grammar of the English language*. London: Longman.

Raban, B. (1982). Text display effects on the fluency of young readers. *Journal of Research in Reading*. 5, 7–28.

Rehe, R. H. (1974). *Typography: How to make it legible*. Bloomington: Indiana University Press.

Reynolds, L. (1979). Teletext and viewdata—a new challenge for the designer. *Information Design Journal*, 1, 2–14.

Reynolds, L. (1984). The legibility of printed scientific and technical information. In. R. Easterby & H. Zwaga (Eds.), *Information design* (pp. 187–208). Chichester, Eng.: Wiley.

Rothkopf, E. Z. (1970). The concept of mathemagenic activities. *Review of Educational Research*, 40, 325–336.

Rothkopf, E. Z. (1971). Incidental memory for the location of information in text. *Journal of Verbal Learning & Verbal Behavior*, 10, 608–613.

Rowe, C. L. (1982). The connotative dimensions of selected display typefaces. *Information Design Journal*, 3, 30–37.

Saenger, P. (1982). Silent reading: Its impact on late medieval script and society. *Viator*, 13, 367–414.

Sapir, E. (1921). *Language*. New York: Harcourt Brace Jovanovich.

Saussure, F. de (1916/1974). *Course in general linguistics* (rev. ed.) (C. Bally & A. Sechehaye with A. Reidlinger, Eds.) (Trans. W. Baskin). London: Fontana. (originally published in 1916 as *Cours de linguistique générale*)

Shebilske, W. L., & Rotondo, J. A. (1981). Typographical and spatial cues that facilitate learning from textbooks. *Visible Language, 15,* 41–54.

Shurtleff, D. A. (1980). *How to make displays legible.* La Mirada, CA: Human Interface Design.

Sless, D. (1980). Image design and modification: An experimental project in transforming. *Information Design Journal, 1,* 17–80.

Smith, M. M. (1988). Printed foliation: Forerunner to printed page numbers. *Gutenberg Jahrbuch, 63,* 54–70.

Spencer, H. (1969). *The visible word* (2nd ed.) London: Lund Humphries.

Spencer, H., Reynolds, L., & Coe, B. (1975). Spatial and typographic coding with bibliographic entries. *Programmed Learning & Educational Technology, 12,* 95–101.

Tinker, M. A. (1963). *Legibility of print.* Ames: Iowa State University Press.

Tinker, M. A. (1965). *Bases for effective reading.* Minneapolis: University of Minnesota Press.

Tompkins, J. P. (Ed.). (1980). *Reader-response criticism.* Baltimore: John Hopkins University Press.

Trager, G. L. (1974). Writing and writing systems. In T. A. Sebeok (Ed.), *Current trends in linguistics: Vol. 12. Linguistics and adjacent arts and sciences* (pp. 373–496). The Hague: Mouton.

Twyman, M. L. (1982). The graphic presentation of language. *Information Design Journal, 3,* 2–22.

Vachek, J. (1948/1967). Written language and printed language. In *A Prague school reader in linguistics* (pp. 453–460). Bloomington: Indiana University Press. (Originally published in *Recueil Linguistique de Bratislavia,* 1948, 1, 67–75).

Vachek, J. (1959). Two chapters on written English. *Brno Studies in English, 1,* 7–38.

Vachek, J. (1973). *Written language: General problems and problems of English.* The Hague: Mouton.

Vachek, J. (1979). Some remarks on the stylistics of written language. In. D. J. Allerton, E. Carney, & D. Holdcroft (Eds.), *Function and context in linguistic analysis* (pp. 206–221). Cambridge, Eng.: Cambridge University Press.

van Dijk, T. A. (1977). *Text and context: Explorations in the semantics and pragmatics of discourse.* London: Longman.

van Dijk, T. A. (1979). Relevance assignment in discourse comprehension. *Discourse Processes, 2,* 113–126.

Venezky, R. L. (1970). *The structure of English orthography.* The Hague: Mouton.

Walker, P., Smith, S., & Livingston, A. (1986). Predicting the appropriateness of a typeface on the basis of its multi-modal features. *Information Design Journal, 5,* 29–42.

Waller, R. H. W. (1982). Text as diagram: Using typography to improve access and understanding. In D. Jonassen (Ed.), *The technology of text* (pp. 137–166). Englewood Cliffs, NJ: Educational Technology Publications.

Waller, R. H. W. (1987a). What electronic books will have to be better than. *Information Design Journal, 5,* 72–75.

Waller, R. H. W. (1987b). The typographic contribution to language. Ph.D. thesis, University of Reading.

Wendt, D. (1979). An experimental approach to the improvement of the typographic design of textbooks. *Visible Language, 13,* 108–133.

Werlich, E. (1976). *A text grammar of English.* Heidelberg: Quelle & Meyer.

Westcott, R. (1971). Linguistic iconism. *Language, 47,* 416–428.

Weyer, S. A. (1982). The design of a dynamic book for information search. *International Journal of Man-Machine Studies, 17,* 87–107.

Widdowson, H. G. (1979). *Explorations in applied linguistics.* Oxford, Eng.: Oxford University Press.

Widdowson, H. G. (1984). *Explorations in applied linguistics 2.* Oxford, Eng.: Oxford University Press.

Winter, E. O. (1977). A clause relational approach to English texts. *Instructional Science, 6,* 1–92.

Wright, P. (1978). Feeding the information eaters: Suggestions for integrating pure and applied research in language comprehension. *Instructional Science, 7,* 249–312.

Zachrisson, B. (1965). *Studies in the legibility of text.* Stockholm: Almqvist & Wiksell.

PART THREE

Constructs of
Reader Process

Section Editor: Peter B. Mosenthal

15 DEVELOPMENT OF THE ABILITY TO READ WORDS

Linnea C. Ehri

In learning to read English, beginners' eyes are confronted with three types of structural units that they use to make contact with their knowledge of language: letters, words, and sentences. During the course of learning to read, the eyes come to favor written words as units. The advantage of words over sentences is that words can be assimilated in one glance. The advantage of words over letters is that written words correspond more reliably to spoken words than letters correspond to phonemes. Many years ago, Cattell (1886), using a tachistoscope, found that readers can recognize a whole word as quickly as they can recognize a single letter, and in fact they can name a word faster than a letter. The intent of this chapter is to consider research and theory regarding how beginners develop the ability to read words so easily and efficiently.

Until recently, researchers have not been very analytic about how beginners read words. Only two ways were considered: by sight and by decoding (also referred to as *phonological recoding*).[1] *Decoding* meant applying letter-sound relations to transform printed words into pronunciations. *Sight word reading* meant the rote memorizing of connections between the visual forms of words and their meanings. These two ways to read words were assumed to arise from different methods of reading instruction. Decoding emerged from phonics-oriented programs. Sight word reading emerged from whole-word, look-say, meaning-emphasis programs.

In the 1970s, when reading researchers began to focus attention on word-reading processes, the traditional view was challenged. Findings indicated that as readers develop skill, they all become able to read words by sight regardless of the method of instruction. Also, they all learn to use letter-sound relations to read words. Moreover, sight word reading is not necessarily a rote memorization process that ignores letter-sound relations. Rather, there are multiple ways to read words by sight. Also, there are other ways to read words besides decoding and sight word reading. Words may be read by analogizing to known words, by orthographic structure, and by contextual guessing. Not only are there several ways to read words but also the particular ways used by readers change during the course of development. Instructional methods may influence which ways of word reading are used at the outset. However, other factors operate as well, such as the kinds of words that are read, the kinds of reading and writing activities that are practiced, and the cognitive maturation of the reader (Juel, 1984).

In this chapter, we examine the development of word-reading processes. Our focus is on concepts, theories, and evidence to explain how beginners attain competence at processing the written forms of words. Our review is selective rather than exhaustive. Studies that investigate normal readers rather than poor readers are emphasized. We agree with Byrne (in press) that by developing an explanation of reading success, we are in a better position to study reading failure.

First, the various ways to read words are described. Then how these processes develop is examined. The course of development is portrayed in three phases—logographic, alphabetic, and orthographic—to reflect the types of information used in reading words (Frith, 1985). The concept of phases is preferred to that of stages to limit presumptions about developmental relationships among the phases.

VARIOUS WAYS TO READ WORDS

Speakers of a language possess a *lexicon*—that is, a store of words held in memory. When people read words by sight or lexical access, they utilize information that is remembered about the words from previous experiences reading those words. Upon seeing the spellings, readers access the identities of the words in memory. These identities include the word's pronunciation, its meaning, its syntactic identity (i.e., its typical grammatical role in sentences), and its orthographic identity (i.e., information remembered about its conventional spelling) (Ehri, 1978, 1980).

Theorists disagree about the nature of the retrieval routes that are formed to access words in memory from their written forms (Barron, 1986; Ehri, in press). According to *dual-route theory*, readers form connections between the visual configuration of written words and their meanings in memory. The connections are learned by rote and require much practice (Baron, 1977, 1979; Coltheart, Davellar, Johassen, & Besner, 1977; Frith, 1980). According to Ehri (1978, 1980, 1984, 1987, in press), readers who know about letter-sound correspondences form connections between letters in spellings and phonemes in the pronunciations of specific words.

Dual-route theory reflects the traditional nonphonological view of sight word reading. The problem with this view is that it ignores the matter of *access*—that is, how readers *find* one particular word in memory when they look at its spelling. Readers need an access route that is reliable, memorable, and easily learned. In English, spellings symbolize pronunciations of words, so the most effective access routes are ones that capitalize on this relationship and that do it systematically.[2]

For example, readers of English who are told that LFT symbolizes *elephant* can establish a memorable access route easily, using their knowledge of letter name/sound correspondences to link L and F to the first two syllables and T to the final phoneme. In contrast, readers who are told that LFT symbolizes *monkey* must rote memorize an arbitrary access route. They may be able to do it for one word; but if they have to form arbitrary access routes for very many words, they will have trouble.

Although the LFT-elephant access route is memorable, it is not completely reliable, because LFT might also be an access route for *lift* or *left*. A highly reliable access route can be formed out of ELEPHANT if every letter or digraph is linked to a phoneme in the word's pronunciation.

The problem of access has been neglected by dual-route theorists. As a result they have overlooked the contribution that knowledge of letter-sound correspondences makes to the learning of sight words. This turns out to be a fundamental process that emerges during development and explains how beginners achieve competence at reading words by sight.

Words that occur frequently in text are more apt to be read by sight than words appearing infrequently because the former are more likely to be encountered and practiced. Several behaviors may indicate sight word reading: when words are read as whole units without any pauses between phonemes or syllables; when words are read rapidly, faster than the reader can read nonsense words having the same spelling patterns; when the correct spellings of words can be distinguished from homophonous spellings (e.g., *rain* vs. *rane*; *sword* vs. *sord*) (Olson, 1985); when irregularly spelled words are pronounced correctly rather than phonetically as they are spelled (e.g., reading *recipe* as /rĕ-sə-pē/ rather than /rē-sīp/).[3]

Adams and Huggins (1985) developed a sight vocabulary test which consisted of 50 words having irregular spellings that are graduated in frequency from high to low (e.g., *ocean, rhythm, recipe, bouquet*). In analyzing the readings of students (second through fifth graders) as they progressed through the list, Adams and Huggins detected three phases that reflected a shift from reading familiar words by sight to reading unfamiliar words by phonological recoding. Readers read words at the beginning of the list quickly and accurately. Eventually a point was reached where their readings became hesitant and occasionally incorrect. This lasted for a span of from five to ten words. After that, all readings became incorrect, and words were pronounced according to grapheme-phoneme correspondence rules.

The second way of reading words, by phonological recoding, is a slower process than that of reading words by sight. *Phonological recoding* involves transforming spellings of words into pronunciations via the application of grapheme-phoneme rules and then searching the lexicon of spoken words to find a meaningful word that matches the pronunciation just generated. In phonologically recoding polysyllabic words, readers need to distinguish constituent syllables and be skilled at recoding them. In descriptions of the transformation process, the operations of sounding out and blending are often cited. However, these operations are not usually visible except perhaps in beginning readers who receive explicit phonics instruction (Beck, 1981; Monaghan, 1983).

Because the English spelling system is not perfectly phonemic, some experimentation with alternative pronunciations may be necessary to derive a recognizable word. As evident in the study by Adams and Huggins (1985), this approach is adopted when readers are confronted with unfamiliar words that have not achieved sight status. The success of this approach in reading particular words depends upon the regularity of the spellings of the words—that is, whether the letter-sound correspondences conform to the conventional system and hence can be generated correctly, and also upon the extent of the reader's knowledge of this system. The most common means to assess readers' phonological recoding skill is to have them read nonsense words that are presumed to be unfamiliar and hence not known by sight.

There are two other ways to read unfamiliar words besides phonological recoding, however. Readers might read the words by analogizing to known sight words or by detecting and pronouncing orthographic patterns. These two processes are similar in that both utilize parts of word spellings stored in lexical memory. However, they are not identical. Baron (1979) distinguishes between a true analogy-based process in which readers search memory for *specific* words having parts like those in the words being read (e.g., reading *yave* by analogy to *gave* or *have*), and a process in which spelling patterns are applied that have been generalized from several known words (e.g., reading *yave* by recognizing its stem *-ave* as a general pattern pronounced /ăv/ or /āv). For example, if readers see *tashion*, are reminded of the known word *fashion*, and substitute /t/ for /f/ in the pronunciation, they are analogizing. If they recognize *tashion* as containing the common stem *-ash* and suffix *-ion* and put these parts together to read the word, they are using orthographic patterns. Readers might also read unfamiliar words by recognizing smaller familiar words in spellings—for example, the three small words in *investor*, or *ring* in *bring*.

A conflict test has been used to distinguish analogizing from phonological recoding (Marsh, Friedman, Welch, & Desberg, 1981b). In such a test, readers are given nonwords—for example, *pednesday*. If they say /pĕd-nəs-dāy/, they are assumed to be phonologically recoding the word. If they read it as rhyming with *Wednesday*, they are analogizing.

The method of using generalized orthographic patterns to read words requires having the spellings of several words stored in memory and organized by spelling patterns. The activation-synthesis model proposed by Glushko (1979, 1981) portrays how this process works to read a word. "As letters in a word are identified, an entire neighborhood of words that share orthographic features is activated in memory, and the pronunciation emerges through the coordination and synthesis of many partially activated phonological representations" (p. 62). The orthographic features shared by neighborhoods of words might involve various kinds of spelling similarities in initial, medial, or final positions of words. However, Glushko's (1981) findings indicate that identical stems may be the most salient basis for a neighborhood. Also Treiman's (1985, 1986) research indicates that dividing syllables into their onsets (initial consonants) and rimes (remaining vowel stems) is easier and more psychologically natural than dividing at other points in the syllable.

Glushko (1979, 1981) argues that reading words by analysis and synthesis of orthographic patterns more accurately portrays how mature readers operate than reading words by phonological recoding. In one of his studies, he presented readers with two types of nonwords. Both types had phonemically regular spellings, but one type involved spelling patterns that were pronounced consistently across many real words (e.g., *bink* pronounced like *pink*, *sink*, and so on), and the other type consisted of patterns that were pronounced inconsistently across real words (e.g., *bint* pronounced like either *lint* or *pint*). He found that readers read consistent words faster than inconsistent words, despite the fact that both contained regular grapheme-phoneme correspondences. His explanation is that in the inconsistent case two competing pronunciations were activated by the orthographic patterns and slowed down processing.

The final way to read words is by processing contextual cues that enable readers to form expectations about words and, on this basis, to guess what they are or at least to narrow the possibilities. In the analysis of miscues produced during the oral reading of text, Biemiller (1970), Goodman (1965), Weber (1970), and others have observed that young readers substitute words that are semantically and syntactically consistent with the text read up to that point, indicating that expectations are operating. Other studies have indicated that contextual guessing is used mainly to read unfamiliar words, when readers lack the phonological recoding skill to figure them out (Carnine, Carnine, & Gersten, 1984). If the words being read are well established in readers' sight vocabularies, they are recognized so quickly and automatically that contextual expectations do not have time to facilitate this process (Perfetti, 1985; Stanovich, 1980, 1986).

Contextual guessing cannot account for the way that most words are read by skilled readers. In order to guess words effectively, the surrounding words must be known for certain. To read surrounding words accurately, processes other than contextual guessing are required, processes that utilize graphic information. Thus, the key to reading words successfully in text is being able to read words using the other methods we have described above (Stanovich, 1980). Because of this, and also because our focus is upon how readers develop skill at processing graphic information, we do not review studies on contextual guessing here.

There is another aspect to development besides learning to read words in various ways. Readers also learn to execute these processes more readily. LaBerge and Samuels (1974) distinguish three levels of achievement: (1) being able to read words accurately and consistently when the same words recur; (2) being able to read words automatically without attention and without deliberate processing of component parts; and (3) being able to read words at maximum speed, indicating unitization of the various identities of the words in memory (Ehri & Wilce, 1979, 1983). The ability to read words rapidly is thought to be highly important for text comprehension, the explanation being that the faster and more automatically that words can be recognized, the more space in memory is made available for the execution of higher-level comprehension processes (Perfetti, 1985). Although these aspects of word reading are highly important, the focus of this chapter is not upon developing automaticity or speed but rather upon developing accuracy in using the various ways to read words.

PHASES OF DEVELOPMENT
IN LEARNING TO READ WORDS

Various developmental schemes have been proposed to explain how beginners function at successive growth points in learning to read words. We attempt to integrate these schemes in order to fashion a coherent view of development. The terms selected by Frith (1985) in her three-phase scheme are adopted here: logographic, alphabetic, orthographic. *Logographic* refers to the use of graphic features to read words, as is done in reading Chinese orthography. *Alphabetic* refers to the use of grapheme-phoneme relations to read words. *Orthographic* refers to the use of spelling patterns.

First we describe the logographic phase when sight word reading first emerges. Then we consider a different kind of sight word reading that involves rudimentary letter-sound cues rather than strictly visual cues. This form of sight word reading signals the beginning of the alphabetic phase. Developing later during the alphabetic phase is phonological recoding skill. This skill not only enables readers to decode unfamiliar words but also makes possible a kind of sight word reading in which the full set of grapheme-phoneme correspondences in a word is used to form its access route into memory. The orthographic phase is the final phase to develop. Reading words by analogy is considered to be part of this phase, although evidence suggests that analogizing begins earlier during the alphabetic phase.

Logographic Phase

In logographic writing systems such as Chinese, visual symbols are used to represent units of language at the level of words or morphemes, not at the level of phonemes as is done in alphabetic writing systems. The term logographic is used to characterize the first phase of word reading because it denotes the fact that beginners use strictly visual characteristics rather than letter-sound correspondences to read words. However, unlike Chinese readers, who process logographic symbols globally as wholes or Gestalts, beginning readers do not process words as visual Gestalts (Gough, Juel, & Griffith, in press). Rather they select only a limited portion of the visual array, a salient graphic cue, and associate this with the word in memory.

Logographic-phase readers might learn to read a word by remembering the shape of a letter, or a logo accompanying it (e.g., the golden arches behind "McDonalds"), or a thumbprint appearing next to it (Gough & Hillinger, 1980). Other graphic cues such as the remaining letters and their order are ignored. If readers select letters as cues, they do so because their shapes are visually salient, not because the letters have anything to do with sounds in the word. A visual cue that is selected and remembered because it is related to the word's meaning might be found, such as two eyes in the middle of *look*, or the humps in the middle of *camel*. Such semantic cues provide memorable access routes for retrieving words, but it is hard to find meaning-bearing cues in most spellings.

Gough refers to logographic word reading as code reading (Gough & Hillinger, 1980; Gough, Juel & Roper/Schneider, 1983). Because of the confusion between their term and the word decoding, which denotes a different way of reading words, Ehri has renamed this *visual cue reading* (Ehri, 1987; Ehri & Wilce, 1985, 1987a, 1987b). *Paired-associate learning* is the process that portrays how logographic readers learn to read words using visual cues (Gough & Hillinger, 1980). Readers form an association between a written word and its identity in memory by selecting some attribute of the written form that distinguishes it from its competitors. The next time that attribute is seen either in the same or another word, the response word associated with that attribute is retrieved from memory.

Gough, Juel, and Griffith (in press) present evidence that logographic readers select salient visual cues rather than process words as Gestalts. In one study, they taught 4- and 5-year-olds to read four words, one of which had a thumbprint next to it. Children learned to read the thumbprint word the fastest. When the thumbprint was removed, children did not recognize the word. However, when only the thumbprint was shown, nearly all identified the word that had accompanied it.

In another study by the same researchers, after preschoolers had learned to read four words, they were asked to recognize the words by looking only at the first or last half of the word. Consistent with the idea that logographic readers select only single cues, children who could not recognize the word from its first half were twice as likely to recognize it from its second half, and vice versa.

The logographic approach to reading alphabetically written words carries several difficulties for readers. The associations formed between visual cues and words are hard to remember unless practiced frequently because they are unsystematic and arbitrary. Visually similar words are mistaken for each other because the visual cues selected are not unique to individual words. As more words are learned, it becomes increasingly difficult to find attributes that distinguish among the words because different words contain the same visual cues. Rather than reading the exact word symbolized in print, logographic readers may produce synonyms or semantic associates of written words because the visual cues selected do not systematically target a particular pronunciation in memory as they do when letters are analyzed alphabetically as symbols for pronunciations.

Various studies provide evidence regarding the difficulties of logographic word reading. In a longitudinal study with preschoolers, Mason (1980) distinguished three developmental levels of word reading. The least mature level was called *context dependency* and corresponds to the logographic phase. Logographic readers were able to read only a few words: their own name; the words *stop, milk, exit*; food labels such as cereal names and soft drinks; and names of stores. When these children were shown a list of easy three-letter words to read, they either refused to read them or guessed at the words by offering totally unrelated words. This is not surprising because logographic readers lack any way to read unfamiliar words except by using context to guess or by mistaking the words for familiar sight words.

Mason (1980) gave the children practice reading a 10-item word list. The logographic readers were able to learn only three to four words, and they forgot most of the words after 15 minutes. This reveals how hard it is for logographic readers to learn to read words out of context.

Mason (1980) also taught the children to read several words that were printed either in lower case or in upper case. After four learning trials, children were shown the same words but with their cases changed. Few if any children remained able to read the words, indicating that they were not using letter cues, even though they could identify many upper- and lower-case letters.

Other studies corroborate logographic readers' use of visual contextual cues rather than alphabetic cues to read labels and signs in their environment (DeWittz & Stammer, 1980; Goodman & Altwerger, 1981; Harste, Burke, & Woodward, 1982; Hiebert, 1978; Masonheimer, Drum, & Ehri, 1984; Ylisto, 1967). In a study by Masonheimer et al. (1984), preschoolers were selected for their expertise at reading environmental signs. When the children were shown the same signs without any environmental cues, most of the experts could no longer read the signs. When letters were altered in the signs accompanied by their logos (e.g., *Pepsi* changed to *Xepsi*), most children "read" the logo and did not even notice the changes in its letters, even when they were asked whether there might be a mistake in the label.

One reason why logographic readers do not remember letters in words is that they have not mastered letter names or sounds. In Masonheimer et al.'s (1984) study, most of the environmental print experts were unable to read any preprimer words in isolation, and they knew names of only 62 percent of the letters. Other studies have found this as well (Ehri & Wilce, 1985; Mason, 1980). Of course, environmental signs contain other more salient visual cues than letters, so there is little reason to focus on letters for discriminating among environmental signs.

It is not the case that logographic readers are insensitive to letters when they are shown signs and labels. McGee, Lomax, and Head (1988) asked prereaders to read various types of environmental print. Although they did not read the words, several subjects responded by naming letters seen in the words. This indicates that logographic readers may notice letters in printed language. What they lack is the ability to use the letters they recognize in remembering how to read words.

Ehri and Wilce (1985) studied the kinds of cues that logographic readers find most useful in learning to read words. Preschoolers and kindergartners were grouped according to their isolated word-reading ability into prereaders (no words read), novices (a few words read), and veterans (several words read). Subjects were given several practice trials to learn to read two different kinds of word spellings: those with letters that were visually distinctive but lacked any relation to sounds in the words (e.g., *yMp* for *turtle*), and those with letters that corresponded to some sounds in the words (e.g., *JRF* for *giraffe*).

Results showed that the prereaders read words logographically. They learned to read the visually distinctive spellings more readily than the phonetic spellings, indicating that they were learning to read the words by forming associations out of salient graphic cues. In contrast, the novices and veterans learned to read the phonetic spellings more readily than the visual spellings, indicating that they were reading the words alphabetically. It was harder for logographic readers to learn to read all six words on the list than for alphabetic readers, indicating that strictly visual associations are less powerful mnemonically than letter-sound associations. Poor performance on a spelling memory task given after the word-learning trials confirmed that logographic readers were not storing letter cues in memory to read words.

In other environmental print studies (Goodman & Altwerger, 1981; Harste, Burke, & Woodward, 1982), researchers have observed logographic readers to produce variable rather than exact wordings when they read signs and labels. For example, they might read CREST as *brush teeth* or *toothpaste*, DYNAMINTS as *fresh-a-mints*. This lack of correspondence at the phonological level but equivalence at the semantic level indicates that the associations formed in lexical memory are between salient visual cues and meanings of words. This contrasts with later phases of word reading where the involvement of letter-sound associations restricts the word accessed in memory to a single pronunciation tied to the word's spelling.

Byrne (in press) performed several studies to examine what it takes to get children in the logographic phase to become analytic about the letter-sound structure of words that they are taught to read. His approach was to select preliterate preschoolers, teach them to read two words (e.g., *fat*, *bat*) in which the initial letters distinguished the two words, show them new words structured like the old words (e.g., *fun, bun, fig, big, fell, bell*), and then ask them about the identity of each new symbol (e.g., Is this *fun* or *bun*?). The purpose of his transfer task was to find out whether, in learning to read the two words, children had spontaneously deduced the relationship between letters and initial sounds. He found that children had not, that their performance on the transfer task was no better than chance.

In additional studies, he made various changes in the initial learning phase: teaching letter-sound associations along with the words (e.g., F = /f/, B = /b/, AT = /at/ as well as *fat* and *bat*), teaching four rather than two words (e.g., *fat, bat, fin, bin*), using geometric shapes rather than letters, using more easily distinguished initial sounds (e.g., /s/ and /m/), varying the stem and holding the initial sound constant (e.g., *hug, hot*). He found that the logographic readers still remained unanalytic on the forced-choice transfer task. When the units symbolized in print were changed from phonemes to words (e.g., *clean chair, dirty chair*), children were successful in processing the first symbol to distinguish between transfer items (e.g., *clean plate, dirty plate*), indicating that they were capable of being analytic when meaningful words were the printed units.

Byrne (in press) suggests that children possess a natural tendency to build associations between print and speech at the level of words but not at the level of phonemes. When exposed to orthography, they adopt this "unbiased acquisition procedure." Biasing influences such as instruction in phonemic awareness, reading, or spelling are required to shift their attention from the lexical to the phonemic level of language.

To summarize, logographic readers are limited to reading words by sight. They do this by selecting distinctive visual characteristics and associating these with the meanings of words in memory. However, because the associations are arbitrary, logographic readers have trouble remembering how to read words, particularly in isolation.

Transitional Phase: Logographic or Rudimentary Alphabetic?

When readers begin to read words by processing letter-sound relations, they move into the *alphabetic phase*. However, researchers differ in their views about when the logographic phase ends and the alphabetic phase begins. Some regard the acquisition of phonological recoding skill as marking the shift (Gough & Hillinger, 1980; Seymour & Elder, 1986; Frith, 1985; Lundberg, in press). Other researchers see more rudimentary letter-sound processes marking the beginning of the alphabetic phase (Ehri, 1987, 1989a; Ehri & Wilce, 1985, 1987a, 1987b). One reason for the disagreement is that it has not been clear how to interpret novice readers' behavior when they process only some of the letters in reading words by sight (e.g., the first letter or the boundary letters). Are they processing these letters as strictly visual logographic cues or as visual alphabetic cues linked to sounds in words?

Huba (1984) provides some suggestive correlational data. She conducted a study with kindergartners who knew some letter-sound relations but could not phonologically recode nonsense words. She measured subjects' phonological awareness and also their ability to learn to read a set of words by sight. Because her subjects were nondecoders, she expected them to learn to read the sight words logographically, and she did not expect her phonemic awareness measure to predict success on the sight word task. However, she was wrong. Significant correlations were found between phonemic awareness and sight word learning, indicating that phonological processes may have been involved.

In her developmental scheme, Mason (1980) labeled readers at the second level of word reading *visual recognition readers*. These were children who read labels and signs, and in contrast to readers at the first contextual dependency level, were able to read a few "book" words such as *dog, cat, mom, dad, yes, no, go, in, out,* and *the*. They had mastered letter names and alphabet recitation. They could print most letters and they were interested in trying to spell words. In the word-learning task, they learned to read several words and were able to remember them after 15 minutes. They often correctly preserved the beginning consonant in words they misread (e.g., *key* for *kit, me* for *man, cat* for *cut*).

These observations indicate that visual recognition readers had analyzed words into their letters. Did their analyses involve letter sounds as well? Two of Mason's (1980) findings favor this possibility: children made attempts to spell words by analyzing sounds and picking letters for those sounds, and they preserved the sounds of first letters in their misreadings.

Ehri has described a rudimentary form of alphabetic reading called *phonetic cue reading* that contrasts with logographic, or visual cue, reading and that explains how beginners are able to use alphabetic cues in reading words by sight (Ehri, 1987; 1989a; in press; Ehri & Wilce, 1985, 1987a, 1987b). Beginners read words by forming access routes out of partial letter-sound correspondences. That is, they associate only some of the letters seen in spellings to sounds detected in pronunciations. Perhaps only the initial letter or the initial and final letters form the access routes. The letters may be linked to various types of phonetic units in pronunciations—for example, sounds such as /d/ in *dog* or letter names such as /be/ in *beak* or *beaver*.

Whereas logographic access routes are arbitrary, rudimentary alphabetic access routes are systematic because they make use of letter-sound correspondences that beginners already know. To illustrate the difference, logographic readers might remember how to read *yellow* by the "two-sticks" in the middle (Seymour & Elder, 1986). In contrast, phonetic cue readers might see the two l's in *yellow*, hear their name in the pronunciation, and use this information to connect the spelling to the word in memory. Research on paired-associate learning has shown that having such a mnemonic that is systematic rather than arbitrary makes it much easier to remember the association and hence to read the word when it recurs.

Ehri and Wilce (1985) have found that as soon as children master letters and exhibit the ability to read a few words in isolation, they are capable of operating alphabetically rather than logographically and of using letter-sound relations to read sight words. In the study described above in which prereaders, novices, and veterans were taught to read visual and phonetic spellings of words, the novices contrasted with the logographic prereaders in learning to read the simplified phonetic spellings more readily than the visually distinctive but nonphonetic spellings. The phonetic spellings they learned were partial, having three or four letters that corresponded to only some sounds (e.g., *JRF* for *giraffe*) and that had names containing the relevant sounds (e.g., *J* named *jay* containing /j/). Ehri and Wilce (1985) suggest that novices use this same kind of phonetic cue to read their core of sight words.

Scott and Ehri (in press) suggest that letter knowledge may be the factor that enables children to read words alphabetically rather than logographically. They selected preschoolers and kindergartners who could read few if any preprimer-level words but who could name all the target letters that were used in the word-learning task. Children practiced reading either six simplified phonetic spellings or six visually distinctive spellings for several trials. The procedures were similar to those used in the previous study (Ehri & Wilce, 1985), except that subjects' attention was drawn to letters by having them name or count the letters as they practiced reading the words.

These prereaders learned to read the simplified phonetic spellings more readily than the visually distinctive spellings. This contrasts with prereaders in the earlier study who did not know all the letters and who had more trouble learning phonetic spellings than visual spellings. These findings indicate that when beginners know the names or sounds of letters in words, when these letters correspond to sounds in pronunciations, and when readers' attention is drawn to the letters, they are capable of learning to read the words using phonetic cues.

Results of this study contrast with results of Byrne's (in press) studies mentioned above in which he was unable to get prereaders to attend to letter-sound relations in learning to read words. It may be that the difference in tasks accounts for the discrepancy. Whereas Scott and Ehri (in press) gave subjects several trials to learn to read words, Byrne gave subjects one trial to select correct words in a forced-choice recognition task. Success in the latter task may have required more conscious awareness of letter-sound units and how they function in words than success in Scott and Ehri's task.

In two other studies, Ehri and Wilce (1987a, 1987b) explored phonetic cue reading experimentally. Kindergartners who had mastered letters and could read a few words in isolation were taught either to spell words phonetically (the experimental group) or to associate isolated sounds with letters (the control group). Then subjects were given several trials to learn to read 12 similarly spelled words, not words studied during training. Spelling-trained subjects learned to read more words than control subjects.

Various aspects of their performance indicated that both groups used partial letter-sound cues rather than strictly visual cues to read the words by sight. When subjects misread words, they included sounds corresponding to some of the letters in spellings. Experimentals exceeded controls in this respect. In misreading words, subjects often substituted other words from the list. The proportion of letters shared by each word with the other words was highly correlated with subjects' difficulty in reading the words, more so among experimentals ($r = .91$) than among controls ($r = .60$). This indicates that partial letter cues were influencing the word-learning performance of both groups, with the impact much greater on spelling-trained subjects than on letter-sound-trained subjects.

Words on the list learned by subjects differed in their meaningfulness (e.g., *snake* is more meaningful than *soles*). Meaningfulness ratings of the words were found to be significantly correlated with the ease of learning to read the words among control subjects but not among experimentals. These findings indicate that as readers become better at phonetic cue reading, they make greater use of letter-sound associations to read words by sight and make less use of semantic associations. This is not to say that word meanings are not processed by the better readers but only that meanings do not provide the access routes linking spellings to words in memory. This is not surprising since letter-sound routes provide more systematic, easily remembered links to words in memory than do semantic routes.

One other characteristic of phonetic cue readers observed in this study was their inconsistency in reading the same words correctly over trials. Subjects read only 30 percent to 31 percent of the words correctly on subsequent trials that they had read correctly on an earlier trial. One reason was that subjects used the same letter cues for several words and got them mixed up. This illustrates one of the drawbacks of phonetic cue reading. Partial letter-sound cues are not completely reliable for signaling one word and excluding all others.

In this study, neither group was able to read words by phonological recoding. This was evidenced by their difficulty in blending sounds to form words, which is not surprising since spelling training does not teach blending but only phonemic segmentation.

In another study, Ehri & Wilce (1987b) compared word-learning processes in phonetic cue readers and readers who could phonologically recode words, referred to as *cipher readers* (Gough & Hillinger, 1980). The two kinds of readers were created experimentally by training the former in single letter-sound associations and the latter in phonological recoding. After training, subjects were given several trials to learn to read 15 similarly spelled words. Most cipher readers mastered the words, whereas cue readers never did. Cue readers read words more inconsistently over trials than did cipher readers, indicating that cue readers were forgetting or mixing up the words. It was apparent that cue readers were processing partial letter-sound cues rather than strictly visual cues. Most of their misreadings contained some of the letter-sounds appearing in print. For example, LAP was misread as *lamp*, and STAB was misread as *stamp*.

Subjects were asked to recall the spellings of words after they practiced reading them. Cipher readers were more accurate than cue readers, not surprisingly since they learned to read more words. Although cue readers' memory for medial letters was weak, they did remember most initial and final consonants (M = 79%), indicating that boundary letters may have been the phonetic cues that they used to remember how to read the words.

Seymour and Elder's (1986) longitudinal study is commonly cited as evidence for logographic reading. However, phonetic cue reading may better explain how beginners were processing words. Seymour and Elder (1986) studied first graders who were receiving whole-word reading instruction. They inferred that the students were reading words logographically without any phonology because the reading program did not teach letter-sound relations or phonological recoding, and because most students did not attempt to sound out and blend unfamiliar words. However, examination of subjects' performances indicates that they may have been transitional alphabetic readers rather than logographic readers. Students did receive *spelling* instruction that introduced letter-sound associations through writing exercises early in the year, so they were not unfamiliar with phonics concepts. Let us look at this study to see which interpretation is favored.

Seymour and Elder (1986) tested 24 students at various times throughout first grade. At the start of school, the teacher reported that none of the students was able to read, none knew any letter-sound correspondences, and only a few were familiar with one or two letter names. Students were taught between 82 and 118 sight words during the year. On isolated word-reading tests tailored to their experiences, students were able to read many of the words they had been taught (M = 59%), but very few of those they were not taught (M = 2%), indicating that students were building up sight vocabularies but lacked any strategy for decoding unfamiliar words.

When students misread words, they drew their responses from the set of words they had been taught to read rather than from untaught words or nonsense words, a sign that they were not phonologically recoding unfamiliar words. Their misreadings were usually words that were similar in length to target words and that shared salient letters, indicating that length and partial letters were the primary cues used to remember how to read words and to distinguish among them. Longer words were not read more slowly than shorter words, indicating that readers were not analyzing the spellings serially letter by letter but rather were processing cues in the words in parallel.

In an auditory recognition task with no spellings present, students were very accurate at telling the experimenter which words they could read and which words they could not read, indicating that words they could read were represented differently in their lexicons.

To determine whether word shape played an important role in word recognition, subjects were shown familiar words whose letters were lined up horizontally in normal format, or were printed in zigzag horizontal format, or in vertical format that destroyed shape. Many of the children were still able to read distorted words correctly, indicating that they were not using shape or unanalyzed Gestalts to recognize the words but rather were using letter identities that remained unchanged. This contrasts with logographic reading, where letters are not the cues remembered about words.

Although semantic misreadings occurred (e.g., misreading *room* as *house*), these were infrequent, indicating that access routes into memory were not primarily semantic. This contrasts with the frequent occurrence of semantically equivalent readings that characterize logographic readers.

Three-quarters into the school year, the children were given six unfamiliar CVC (consonant, vowel, consonant) words to spell. All but two of the children spelled at least one initial sound correctly, several spelled a number of sounds correctly, and half spelled at least one nonword correctly. These findings indicate that most students were capable of processing phonetic cues in words.

Seymour and Elder (1986) infer that beginners were reading words logographically by a process of feature discrimination that includes length, shapes of salient letters, and salient feature position. "A vocabulary of a hundred or so words could be discriminated using perhaps three values of length (short, medium, long), three positions (left, central, right), and a dozen or so salient shapes" (Seymour & Elder, 1986, p. 29).

One problem with this explanation, however, is that logographic access routes are completely arbitrary and thus difficult to remember. Other studies have found that logographic readers have much trouble remembering how to read words in isolation. It is likely that something with more mnemonic power than arbitrary visual cues served to link spellings to pronunciations in memory, particularly for those readers with larger lexicons of printed words. The more associations that are formed in reading words by sight, the bigger the advantage in having a system that secures the associations in memory. The novices in Seymour and Elder's study knew letter names and sounds from their writing instruction. From other studies we know that children who know letters are capable of using this information to read words by forming access routes out of partial letter-sound cues.

In sum, our analysis indicates that Seymour and Elder's (1986) readers bore a greater resemblance to rudimentary alphabetic readers than to logographic readers. It may be that readers combined phonetic cues with logographic cues such as word length. Arbitrary cues may be easier to store in memory when these cues accompany letter-sound cues that are systematic and provide the access route into memory. This possibility awaits study.

What factors influence the partial cues that are selected by rudimentary alphabetic readers when they learn to read a set of words? According to Gough and Hillinger (1980), readers select the minimum cues needed to distinguish among the set of words being read. The more similar the words, the more cues they need to remember, and the longer it takes them to learn to read the words.

Several studies provide evidence that children who practice reading similarly spelled words (i.e., *pots, post, spot, stop*) take longer to learn to read the words than children who practice reading dissimilar words (i.e., *play, fire, bugs, honk*). Moreover, these studies indicate that on a transfer task consisting of new words that share letters with the old words, dissimilar-word-reading subjects mistake more of the new words as old words than similar-word-reading subjects. The explanation is that because the dissimilar group attended to fewer letter cues in learning to read the old words, they had more trouble discriminating between the old and new words than the similar group (Gilbert, Spring & Sassenrath, 1977; McCutcheon & McDowell, 1969; Otto & Pizillo, 1970; Samuels & Jeffrey, 1966; Spring, Gilbert, & Sassenrath, 1979).

An alternative explanation, however, is that what readers remember about the cues in words is a function of the amount of practice they receive reading the words. In the above studies, subjects reading dissimilar words received less practice than subjects reading similar words since the former subjects reached criterion sooner. To test this hypothesis, Spring et al. (1979) included a third group that learned to read dissimilar words but received additional practice comparable to that received by subjects reading similar words. They found that this third group achieved transfer scores equal to those of the group learning similar words and superior to those of the dissimilar-word group, providing support for the practice hypothesis.

These results indicate that the cues that beginners use to read words are not strictly a function of the cues present in other words that require discrimination. One reason that additional cues not needed for discrimination might be stored is that phonetic cue readers may spontaneously use their letter-sound knowledge to detect and store additional associations between letters in spellings and sounds in pronunciations.

Morris (1989) discusses one way that phonetic cue reading might emerge and develop in a meaning-emphasis program such as language experience. He proposes that once readers learn to distinguish initial consonants in words, and once they know letters for these sounds, they can learn to track by finger pointing the correspondences between printed and spoken words as they read lines of a predictable text. They can recognize which printed words correspond to which spoken words, and they can detect mismatches and self-correct by paying attention to initial letter-sound correspondences in words. Morris refers to this as developing a *concept of word*. During the course of practicing this type of reading, students begin to detect correspondences between final as well as initial consonant letters and sounds in pronunciations. This advances the child's awareness of phonemic segments in words, which in turn facilitates his or her growth of a sight vocabulary by enriching the number of letter-sound connections he or she is able to include in an access route. Morris provides cross-lag correlational evidence that these skills—initial consonants, concept of word, phonemic segmentation, and sight word reading—develop in this sequence rather than in alternative sequences during the kindergarten year. More research is needed to confirm the causal nature of these relationships, for they appear intriguing and promising.

To summarize, rudimentary alphabetic readers, like logographic readers, are limited to reading words by sight because they lack any means of decoding unfamiliar words. However, they differ from logographic readers in being able to use letter identity information to remember how to read sight words. Letters are connected to words in memory by associating them with sounds in their pronunciations.

Alphabetic Phase

Although there is disagreement about when the alphabetic phase begins, it is definitely underway when readers become able to phonologically recode spellings into pronunciations according to grapheme-phoneme correspondence rules. One advantage of phonological recoding over logographic reading and phonetic cue reading is that readers have a means of reading unfamiliar written words accurately. Another advantage is that readers are enabled to read sight words with greatly increased accuracy.

Phonological Recoding

Most theories of the development of reading skill regard phonological recoding as a central achievement. Preferring the language of cryptography, Gough and Hillinger (1980) refer to this as *cipher reading*, which they see as involving mastery of the system of rules by which letters and letter sequences map onto phonological forms. Marsh et al. (1981b) analyze phonological recoding skill into two types: sequential decoding, which develops first; and hierarchical decoding, which follows. Whereas sequential decoders use a simple sequential strategy based on one-to-one correspondence rules, hierarchical decoders use conditional rules and take account of letter combinations in which one letter signals the phoneme symbolized by another letter. For example, final *e* in *college* and *peace* marks the preceding *g* and *c* as /j/ and /s/, respectively; *i* in *city* and *e* in *cell* mark the *c* as /s/; final *e* in *make* marks the *a* as tense, or long. Many of the rules proposed by Venezky (1970) are thought to be used to decode sequentially and hierarchically.

Venezky and Johnson (1973) studied first- second-, and third-grade readers' knowledge of sequential and conditional rules in a nonsense word decoding task. By the end of first grade, most sequential rules were known—for example, pronouncing *c* correctly as /k/. Hierarchical rules were later to emerge. By the end of third grade, most subjects correctly varied their pronunciation of short and long vowels to reflect the presence of a final *e* marker. By the end of second grade, most subjects pronounced final *-ce* as /s/. However, even by the end of third grade, only a minority of subjects (40%) was pronouncing initial *c* as /s/ (i.e., *cipe*). Apparently, this is a more difficult conditional rule to acquire. One reason may be that few words in beginning reading texts exhibit this pattern.

In a study by Taylor and Ehri (1984), the kinds of errors that beginners exhibited revealed that they were applying letter-sound correspondence rules to read short and long vowels in nonwords. Taylor and Ehri (1984) selected first and second graders receiving phonics instruction, grouped them according to their reading maturity based on Slosson word-reading scores, and had them read a list of nonsense words containing short- and long-vowel spellings. The least mature readers who knew how to read short but not long vowels overgeneralized short-vowel rules to long-vowel forms—for example, misreading *rife* as /rĭf/ or /rĭ - fĕ/. More mature readers who were learning long vowels sometimes overgeneralized long-vowel pronunciations to short-vowel spellings—for example, misreading *vak* as /vāk/. In fact, this tendency interfered and caused their short-vowel reading accuracy to drop significantly below that of the least and most mature readers on the nonsense word task. These misreadings were not a result of analogizing, because few if any real words have spellings and pronunciations that are analogous.

This evidence indicates that when knowledge of the long-vowel decoding rule is acquired, it temporarily disrupts short-vowel decoding while it is being mastered and integrated with knowledge of other regularities. Mason (1976) also observed long-vowel overgeneralization errors in beginners. The phenomenon of *overgeneralization* is especially interesting because it constitutes a case where regression signals developmental progress, where the replacement of correct performance by errors is a good sign indicating that new structural knowledge is emerging.

Monaghan (1983) identified several stages in the emergence of recoding skill in children trained in a synthetic phonics program. She observed these children read a list of nonwords (dubbed "fake words" by one subject) at the end of first grade. Children at the least mature stage knew several letter-sound correspondences and could sound out, but they were unable to blend the sounds into words. At the next stage were children who could sound out and blend but were quite slow. Differential progress was evident among them. Whereas the slowest decoders sounded out and blended overtly, the fastest of these slow decoders were very quiet (sotto voce) or soundless and moved their lips rapidly before pronouncing words aloud. At the next stage were subjects who read the words much more rapidly and pronounced them as units without sounding them out either aloud or subvocally. The slowest reader at this stage was 50 seconds faster than the speediest subject at the previous stage. These observations suggest that during development phonological recoding progresses from a slow overt process to a covert process that is executed rapidly and automatically.

Jeffrey and Samuels (1967) and Carnine (1977) showed that beginners who can phonologically recode print have a big advantage in reading unfamiliar words that conform to the rules they have learned. In Carnine's (1977) study, preschoolers who were prereaders received either phonics training or whole-word training. The phonics group learned eight letter-sound correspondences, then was taught to sound out and blend letters to form 18 CVC words, and then practiced reading the 18 words to criterion. The whole-word group was simply taught to read the 18 words to criterion. On a transfer task, subjects read six new words comprising the same letter-sound relations and six words with irregular letter-sound relations. Phonics subjects read 92 percent of the regularly spelled words correctly, whereas word-practice subjects read only 28 percent. Few if any irregularly spelled words were read by either group. These results verify the advantage of phonological recoding skill for reading unfamiliar words that conform to spelling rules. They indicate that readers do not pick up phonological recoding skill simply by learning to read 18 words exhibiting systematic letter-sound relations, at least not in a short-term experiment.

Fox and Routh (1984) performed a similar study but with different control groups. One control group received letter-sound training prior to the word-reading transfer task. Another control group received letter-sound training and phonemic segmentation training. The experimental group was taught all of this as well as blending. Only the experimental group learned to read the transfer words to criterion. Controls never learned the list even after 40 trials of practice. In two other studies, Yopp (1985) and Fox and Routh (1976) found that blending instruction was not very effective at enabling beginners to read unfamiliar transfer words if the readers were not also strong at phonemic segmentation. These results indicate that acquisition of phonological recoding skill entails learning to blend as well as learning letter-sound relations and phonemic segmentation.

The kinds of errors that beginners produce as they read words reflect the acquisition of phonological recoding skill. Cohen (1974–1975) studied the oral text-reading errors of first graders during their first year of phonics instruction. She observed that errors changed over the course of the year as sequential decoding skill developed. At the outset, no-response errors were common. Children halted on a word because they were unable to recode it and unable to guess a word that resembled the letters of the printed word. This type of error predominated until the second half of the year, when nonsense word errors and word substitutions became as frequent as no-response errors. Nonsense words resulted from recoding attempts that failed to yield recognizable words. By midyear, at least half of the nonword and word substitution errors resembled the printed words closely, sharing at least half of their letters, indicating that subjects were attempting to recode the letters.

Among the good readers, no-response errors peaked in November and then declined. Nonsense errors peaked in January and then declined. Word substitutions continued to rise gradually throughout the year, with a high proportion sharing at least half of the letters with the words in print.

Barr (1972) compared the reading errors of beginners given short-term training either in a phonics program or in a whole-word program. In analyzing their word substitutions, she found that the whole-word readers produced mainly words from the same list, whereas phonics-trained readers produced a greater proportion of previously taught words, untaught words, and nonsense words. Others have reported similar findings (Biemiller, 1970; Elder, 1971; DeLawter, 1970). This indicates that when readers are taught to sequentially decode words, they do not limit themselves to the set of words they are learning to read or know how to read already. Rather, a decoding strategy elicits responses that are open ended; and as a result, the readings bear a greater resemblance to the printed word, even though they may be nonwords. As evident in Cohen's (1974–1975) study, nonsense words are a temporary phenomenon and decline in frequency as readers' phonological recoding skill improves.

To summarize, phonological recoding skill enables readers to read words by applying grapheme-phoneme correspondence rules. At first, sounding out and blending operations are performed slowly and overtly, but with practice they become rapid covert processes. The kinds of reading errors that are produced by phonics-trained beginners change as readers acquire more skill, from no-response errors to nonsense word errors to word substitution errors. Sequential decoding emerges before hierarchical decoding because the latter involves more complex conditional rules. As students practice applying new rules, overgeneralization errors may temporarily disrupt previous learning.

Phonics Instruction

According to Gough and Hillinger (1980), phonics instruction promotes acquisition of cipher reading, but the rules taught as part of phonics instruction "bear only a superficial resemblance to the rules which the fluent reader has internalized" (p. 187). Rules of phonics are taught as conscious, explicit statements, whereas the rules that readers use are unconscious and implicit. To illustrate, many readers can decode *cibe* and *cabe* correctly /sīb/ and /kāb/, respectively, but are unable to explain the rule. The important capability to be learned for recoding is to look at letters and generate their pronunciations, not to vocalize rules. Beck (1981) states that she "has witnessed many children who enter remedial reading clinics with the ability to recite such rules, but who are unable to apply them to unlock the pronunciation of a new word" (p. 72).

One problem with rules is that they are partly inaccurate. For example, children may be taught that *b* stands for *buh* whereas in reality *b* stands for a phoneme /b/ that cannot be pronounced in isolation. Another problem is that many rules taught as part of phonics instruction have only limited utility (Clymer, 1963). For example, the following rule accounts for only 45 percent of the spellings to which it applies: "When there are two vowels side by side, the long sound of the first one is heard and the second is usually silent." One further problem is that the process is executed much too rapidly by those who are skilled at phonological recoding to be mediated by the conscious access and application of letter-sound rules.

Gough and Hillinger (1980) conclude that the cipher knowledge used by readers is not the same as that taught in phonics programs. Nonetheless, they see phonics instruction as helpful. Although the rules taught are artificial, if learners apply these rules when they process printed word–spoken word pairs, they may be aided in discovering the real rules.

The existence of a disparity between the operations that learners are taught and those that skilled performers use is not unique to reading instruction. There are theories of knowledge acquisition in other domains that assign importance to such a disparity. In discussing the acquisition of mathematical competence, Resnick (1980) proposes stages of competence to distinguish between ways that novices organize information for learning and ways that experts do it. Glaser (1984) proposes the value of *temporary* models of knowledge structures created by teachers (he calls these *pedagogical theories*). These temporary models resemble but differ from the knowledge structures actually acquired by learners. The models are taught in order to provoke learners to restructure and further develop their own knowledge. It may be advantageous and perhaps even essential for learners to *deviate* from expert performance during the course of acquiring knowledge in order to attain expertise.

The use of artificial devices that get processes underway initially but are abandoned as those processes develop may portray what happens in learning to sound out and blend. Although learners are told that *buh* is the sound made by *b* to be blended with other sounds, as soon as they practice blending and get the idea, they quickly figure out that it is not really the syllable *buh* but rather the phoneme /b/ in the syllable that is critical. Learning to ignore the schwa vowel is made easier by the fact that the schwa vowel recurs in other sounds as well, *puh, duh*, and so on, making it apparent that *uh* is irrelevant. Thus, although explicit phonics instruction teaches operations that are not part of skilled decoding, this may be the most direct way of initiating development of this skill.

Implicit (or analytic) phonics contrasts with explicit synthetic phonics instruction in not teaching students to pronounce and blend isolated sounds. Implicit phonics has been found to be less effective for teaching recoding skill (Johnson & Baumann, 1984). One reason may be that implanting phonological recoding processes in students may be much harder without an artificial teaching device. In fact, Durkin (1984) observed that teachers using implicit phonics programs often deviated from their manuals and produced isolated sounds for students because they believed this was necessary to help students hear the separate sounds in words. Studies examining beginning readers' phonemic segmentation skill verify that dividing words into constituent sounds is very difficult and that teaching students to do this helps them learn to read (Bradley & Bryant, 1985; Ehri, 1979; Juel, Griffith, & Gough, 1986; Lundberg, Frost, & Petersen, 1988; Stanovich, 1988; Williams, 1980). Thus, there appears to be little harm and much value in explicit phonics instruction (Anderson, Hiebert, Scott & Wilkinson, 1985).

Gough and Hillinger (1980) and Marsh et al. (1981b) draw a distinction between the strategies used by beginners to read words (i.e., by sight, by decoding) and the method of instruction they receive (i.e., phonics vs. whole word). Readers may receive one type of instruction, but whether or not they use the instructed approach in their reading is influenced by other factors as well.

Barr (1974–1975) addressed the question of whether instructional method determines strategy use in a study examining the word-reading responses of first graders. Half of the subjects were taught by a phonics method, the other half by a whole-word method. Inferences regarding subjects' use of a recoding strategy or a sight word strategy were based on two aspects of their word-reading errors. A recoding strategy was inferred if subjects produced nonwords and word substitutions that did not come from their reading vocabularies. A sight word strategy was inferred if subjects substituted only real words, at least 75 percent of which came from their reading vocabularies.

Barr (1974–1975) found that midway through the year, 63 percent of the phonics students were exhibiting a recoding strategy, while the remainder were using a sight word strategy. However, by the end of the year, most had shifted to a recoding strategy. In contrast, most whole-word students (94%) exhibited a sight word strategy midway into the year, and most stuck to this strategy throughout the year. Only two whole-word subjects showed some signs of recoding by the end of the year, and these were among the best readers. These results indicate that instructional method influences the way words are read, particularly as experience with a method grows and particularly in the case of recoding. Also, they indicate that reading words by sight emerges earlier and is an easier way for beginners to read words than reading words by recoding, even for students receiving phonics instruction.

Barr's (1974–1975) study has two limitations that preclude inferences about the development of phonological recoding skill in whole-word students and the development of sight word reading in phonics-trained students. One is that children were not observed beyond first grade. It may be that whole-word students do not acquire sufficient knowledge of the spelling system to develop a recoding strategy until after they have acquired an extensive sight vocabulary. The fact that the two students exhibiting recoding skill were better readers is consistent with this possibility.

Thompson (1986) provides evidence that whole-word-trained readers do develop phonological recoding skill after a longer period of instruction. He studied a very large sample of New Zealand students who had received "book experience" instruction for at least 12 months (Clay, 1979). Readers were given a list of words graded in difficulty to read. Thirteen percent of their errors were nonwords, indicating use of a recoding strategy. Thirty-four percent were real-word substitutions. Nonword errors were highly correlated with word reading success ($r = .63$), while lexical substitutions were negatively correlated ($r = -.12$), indicating that better readers were the ones producing nonword errors. Inspection of nonword errors revealed that they were not mispronunciations of words but rather were recoding flaws (e.g., /bē-līf/ for belief, /tĭn-jē/ for tongue). These results suggest that readers, regardless of instructional program, reach a point during acquisition when they become sufficiently proficient at reading to generate nonwords. Recoding skill in whole-word students may result from implicit learning of letter-sound relations and blending acquired from reading experiences, or it may be facilitated by spelling instruction (Uhry, 1989). This matter needs further study.

Another limitation of Barr's (1974–1975) study is that use of a sight word-reading strategy was inferred when students produced real-word substitutions drawn from their reading vocabularies. These criteria may not be appropriate for assessing sight word reading in phonics-trained readers. As will be discussed shortly, readers with recoding skill who read words by sight make very few errors. Moreover, it becomes difficult to keep track of their "reading vocabularies" because they grow rapidly with only a few exposures to new words (Reitsma, 1983).

The development of recoding skill in English is influenced not only by the kind of instruction received but also by the kinds of words that learners practice reading. This is because the spelling patterns of English words exhibit some variability and irregularity. Surber and Mason (1977) selected preschoolers who knew letters. On each of four days, subjects were drilled on a rule (e.g., if a is in the middle and e at the end, a says its name and e is silent), and then they practiced reading words that either conformed to the rule (e.g., *snake, cage, later*) or lacked consistency with the rule (e.g., *was, large*). A week later, both groups were able to read the same number of training words correctly. However, subjects who learned to read consistent exemplars applied the rule in reading transfer nonwords, whereas subjects who learned inconsistent exemplars did not. This indicates that if beginners do not practice reading words that conform to rules they are taught, the rules will not become operational and influence their reading of unfamiliar words. Juel and Roper/Schneider (1985) report similar findings in a classroom study.

To summarize, although phonics instruction teaches beginners rules and operations that are inaccurate and not used by mature phonological recoders, such artificial devices may have pedagogical value in getting readers to attend to and do the things that enable them to become skilled recoders. This may be why explicit phonics instruction is more effective than implicit phonics instruction. Whether or not beginners exhibit signs of phonological recoding during their first year of instruction is influenced by the way they are taught to read as well as by the spelling regularity of the words they practice reading. However, even whole-word-trained readers appear to acquire recoding skill eventually, at least those who make progress in learning to read.

Sight Word Reading

Phonological recoding skill is regarded as the key ingredient for learning to read words. However, studies of mature readers show that they do not read most words by phonological recoding (Gough, 1984). In fact, children as young as first grade read familiar words without recoding them. In one study, Barron and Baron (1977) showed children in grades one through eight several picture-word pairs and had them decide whether each was either similar in meaning (e.g., *pants-shirt*) or similar in sound (e.g., *plane-rain*). Repeating the word *double* concurrently while making the decisions interfered with the sound task but not with the meaning task across all grades. Lack of interference in the meaning task was interpreted to indicate that readers were not phonologically recoding the words but rather were reading the words by sight.

If readers who are capable of phonologically recoding words do not use this approach but rather read words by sight, then why is phonological recoding thought to be so necessary for mature reading? Jorm and Share (1983) offer one explanation for the value of phonological recoding. They suggest that being able to recode words enables beginners to read unfamiliar words successfully *on their own*, thereby insuring many "positive learning trials" that establish the words as sight words in memory. This part of their theory makes sense. However, one other part does not. Jorm and Share's (1983) view of sight word memory comes from dual-route theory, which regards the process as logographic, consisting of the creation of access routes that are arbitrary, nonphonological, and learned by rote.

The main problem with this proposal is that phonological recoding is not regarded as a necessity for sight word learning but merely as a facilitator. Poor phonological recoders are seen as forming the same kind of retrieval routes to establish sight words in memory as good phonological recoders. Poor recoders' only handicap is that they must depend upon external aids for identifying new words, either a literate tutor to tell them the words or an informative context to enable guessing the unfamiliar words. (For a more extensive critique of dual-route theory and its difficulties in accounting for the development of word reading skill, see Barron, 1986.)

However, evidence shows that children who cannot phonologically recode do not become good readers (Gough & Tunmer, 1986). Dyslexics are uniformly deficient in phonological recoding skill (Firth, 1972; Vellutino, 1979) and also in spelling skill, which

is a related kind of phonological knowledge (Ehri, 1986, 1989b). Phonological awareness, along with letter knowledge, are the strongest predictors of beginning reading
achievement (r = .58 to .68), stronger even than intelligence (r = .39 to .41) (Share,
Jorm, Maclean, & Matthews, 1984). This evidence suggests that phonological recoding
skill is not a mere facilitator but a necessity for reading words by sight.

Ehri (1980, 1984, 1987, in press) proposes an alternative conception of the process
of learning to read words by sight, a conception that regards phonological recoding skill
as essential. According to this view, when readers practice reading specific words by
phonologically recoding the words, they form access routes for those words into memory. These access routes are built using knowledge of grapheme-phoneme correspondences that connect letters in spellings to phonemes in pronunciations of the words.
The letters are processed as visual symbols for the phonemes; and the sequence of
letters is retained in memory as an alphabetic, phonological representation of the word.
The first time an unfamiliar word is seen, it is read by phonological recoding. This
initiates an access route into memory. Subsequent readings of the word strengthen the
access route until the connections between letters and phonemes are fully formed and
the spelling is represented in memory.

Reading words by sight in this way is different from phonologically recoding the
words because, once the access route is established in memory, phonological rules are
no longer applied to convert the word to a pronunciation before accessing its meaning.
The middle steps drop out. Seeing the spelling of the word activates connections that
lead directly to the pronunciation of that word in memory, where its meaning is also
found.

What evidence is there to show that sight word reading involves establishing
visual-phonological access routes rather than strictly visual, logographic routes into
lexical memory? Most studies used to support dual-route theory's view of sight word
reading are not very informative on this question, because the words used to examine
logographic processing are not devoid of phonological information. *Irregular* spellings
have been used, yet most of the letters in irregular spellings correspond to sounds in
pronunciations (e.g., italicized letters in *sword*). Dual-route theorists reason that because irregular spellings cannot be read accurately by phonological recoding, these
words must be read logographically by sight.

To support their claim, dual-route theorists Baron (1977) and Treiman (1984)
showed that correlations between reading irregularly spelled words (presumed to be
read logographically) and reading nonsense words (i.e., a measure of recoding skill)
were significantly lower than correlations between reading nonsense words and reading
regularly spelled words. However, this does not constitute evidence that readers use a
logographic route to read irregularly spelled words and a phonological recoding route to
read regularly spelled words. There are other explanations for how irregularly spelled
words are read besides a logographic one. Moreover, the fact that the correlation
between irregular word reading and nonsense word reading was far above zero (i.e., r
= .55 in Treiman, 1984; r = .71 in Freebody & Byrne, 1988) indicates that the
processes used to read irregularly spelled words may have a lot to do with processes
used to phonologically recode nonsense words. Ehri's (in press) explanation for the
relationship is that irregularly spelled words are established as sight words in memory
by forming access routes out of those letters that symbolize phonemes in the words.

A few studies have examined whether readers use the same or different processes
to read phonological and nonphonological (logographic) spellings (e.g., *CHR* vs. *XND* to
spell *chair*). In one study, Brooks (1977) gave adults 400 trials to learn to read two types
of spellings written in artificial orthography, one with letters corresponding to sounds,
and one with letters arbitrarily related to words. If dual-route theory is correct, that all

sight words are read by a nonphonological visual route, then one would expect readers to learn to read both types of words with equal skill following lots of practice when the words acquire sight status. However, this did not happen. During the first 200 trials, phonological spellings were read more slowly than logographic spellings; whereas during the second 200 trials, the pattern reversed and phonological spellings were read more rapidly than logographic spellings. Spring (1978) obtained similar results.

These findings indicate that logographic and phonological spellings are not processed similarly when they become sight words. Ehri's (in press) explanation is that access is faster for phonological spellings because they are linked directly and systematically to the phonemic units involved in pronouncing the words to read them, whereas logographic spellings are linked to pronunciations through connections that are arbitrary and that lack any system for activating that word and excluding other words.

The foregoing studies indicate that reading sight words via a logographic route is a different process from reading sight words via an alphabetic route. Other studies indicate that the alphabetic way of reading words by sight is also different from phonologically recoding the words. The main difference is that a *word-specific memory trace* is used in the former but not the latter case. That is, when words are read alphabetically by sight, they are accessed in memory as soon as the visual letter cues are seen. In contrast, when words are recoded, they are not accessed in memory until after recoding rules have transformed visual cues into recognizable pronunciations.

If this distinction is correct, one would expect readers to be able to read recodable spellings that have become sight words faster than they can read recodable spellings that have not been seen before, even when the two types of spellings are phonologically identical. For example, once the word *seed* is set up in memory, readers should be able to read it faster than they can read *ceed or sead* or *cead*, which they have never seen. This is because the former word is read by accessing word-specific visual-phonological connections in memory whereas the latter words are read by applying a phonological recoding routine.

Reitsma (1983) conducted a study providing supportive evidence. Second-grade Dutch readers were familiarized with the pronunciations of 20 pseudowords. Then they practiced reading 10 of the words. Then their ability to read these 10 words plus 10 alternative unseen spellings of the same words (homophonic spellings) plus 10 control words was tested. Analysis of readers' latencies revealed that practiced spellings were read faster than homophonic and control spellings, indicating that readers learned to recognize the specific patterns of letters constituting the words they read.

Reitsma (1983) showed that the difference was not due to subjects' hearing the words that were read more times. Also, he found that only a few exposures to the spellings were necessary to make a difference, as few as four exposures in one experiment.

Ehri and Wilce (1983) performed a study showing that recodable words that are familiar are read more like single digits than like recodable nonsense words. They measured beginning readers' speed to read familiar real words (e.g., *cat, book, see, stop, jump, red*), nonsense words (e.g., *nel, jad, mig, fup*), and to name single digits. The subjects were skilled and less-skilled readers in first, second, and fourth grades. It was reasoned that if readers read familiar real words by sight rather than by recoding, they ought to read the real words faster than the nonsense words. If they are reading the words as single holistic units, then they ought to read the words as fast as they can name single digits. Being able to read words as units is thought to become possible when the spellings of sight words are fully connected phonemically to pronunciations in memory.

Results revealed that both skilled and less-skilled readers at all grade levels read familiar words much faster than nonsense words, indicating that they were not recoding the words but rather were reading them by sight. All of the skilled readers, but only the oldest less-skilled readers, were able to read the words as fast as they could name the digits, indicating that only the better readers had formed complete connections in memory between spellings and pronunciations.

In a second experiment, skilled and less-skilled first- and second-grade readers were given several practice trials to read real and nonsense words. This practice enabled skilled readers to read the nonsense words as fast as the real words and digits, indicating that the nonsense words had become completely connected sight words. However, even 18 practice trials did not enable poor readers to read nonsense words as fast as real words and real words as fast as digits. Ehri and Wilce's (1983) explanation is that less-skilled readers lacked the phonological recoding skill to form complete connections between spellings and pronunciations when they set up access routes for the sight words in memory.

Ehri (1980) performed another study to show that when beginners learn to read words, the particular spellings they see are stored in memory. Second graders practiced reading eight pseudowords spelled in one of two ways. For example, half of the subjects read *bistion* and half read *bischun*, both pronounced identically. Then they wrote out the words from memory. Subjects were observed to remember particular letters in the spellings they saw rather than phonologically equivalent letters, indicating that they were not simply recoding the words when they read them but were storing letter-sound connections in memory. Every subject who saw *bistion* and misspelled it included *-st-* but never *-ch-* in her misspelling, whereas every subject who saw *bischun* and misspelled it included *-ch-* but never *-st-*.

Another type of evidence is interpreted to support Ehri's (1987) claim that phonological recoding underlies the storage of sight words in memory. These studies show that the process of learning to read words influences readers' conception of phonemes in the words, particularly when the phonemes are ambiguous (Ehri, 1984, 1985, 1987; Ehri & Wilce, 1980b, 1986; Ehri, Wilce, & Taylor, 1987). For example, letters in the spelling of *pitch* identify four sounds, /p/-/i/-/t/-/ch/, each of which can be found in the word's pronunciation, whereas letters in the spelling of *rich* distinguish only three sounds, /r/-/i/-/ch/ with no /t/. Spellings such as these were found to influence children's judgments about sounds in words. Ehri and Wilce (1980b) gave fourth graders a phonemic segmentation task requiring them to divide the pronunciations of words into sounds, to pronounce each sound, and to mark it with a token. The children were observed to analyze words like *pitch* and *rich* into segments suggested by the spellings.

In a second study, Ehri and Wilce (1980b) verified experimentally that it was the spellings that shaped subjects' conceptualization of the phonemic structure of the words. Subjects learned to read two types of nonsense-word spellings, one with a letter suggesting an extra sound and one without the extra letter—for example, *tadge* vs. *taj*. Then subjects segmented the words. As expected, subjects found more segments in the words with extra letters than in those without, four segments in *tadge* with /d/ and /g/ separated as opposed to three in *taj*.

It was not the case that subjects were simply marking remembered letters rather than sounds (Tunmer & Nesdale, 1982). In the segmentation task, subjects were required to pronounce each sound segment as they marked it, and they were not observed to create separate segments for letters in digraphs such as *ch* and for final silent *e*. This study and others (Ehri, 1984, 1985, 1987; Ehri & Wilce, 1980b, 1986; Ehri et al., 1987) are interpreted to indicate that learning the spellings of words influences people's conception of sounds in the words, because readers with phonological recoding skill interpret spellings as symbols for pronunciations and they store the words in memory this way.

In summary, findings of various studies indicate that phonological recoding skill is necessary for proficient sight word reading. Sight words are stored in memory by forming access routes linking spellings to the phonological structure of words in memory. This type of sight word reading is qualitatively different from logographic sight word reading, which characterizes how immature readers read words.

Orthographic Phase

According to Frith (1985),

> *Orthographic skills* refer to the instant analysis of words into orthographic units without phonological conversion. The orthographic units ideally coincide with morphemes. They are internally represented as abstract letter-by-letter strings. These units make up a limited set that—in loose analogy to a syllabary—can be used to create by recombination an almost unlimited number of words. The orthographic strategy is distinguished from the logographic one by being analytic in a systematic way and by being nonvisual. It is distinguished from the alphabetic one by operating in bigger units and by being nonphonological. (p. 306)

The orthographic phase begins when children accumulate sufficient knowledge of spelling patterns that recur across words to use this knowledge in reading and in remembering how to read words. Orthographic knowledge accumulates as readers phonologically recode different words sharing the same patterns, as their phonological recoding of letter sequences becomes automatic, and as they learn to read similarly spelled sight words by storing alphabetic information about the words in memory. When readers gain sufficient experience with the spellings of different English words, they begin to recognize letter patterns that recur across words. These patterns become part of their generalized knowledge of the spelling system. For example, readers are able to read the following patterns as wholes— *-ing, -ment, -tion*—without having to phonologically recode constituent letters.

From this description, it is apparent that readers must acquire skill at alphabetic-phase reading to become proficient at orthographic reading. If readers process letters in words only partially, as in phonetic cue reading, or not at all as in logographic reading, they will not learn what they need to know about letter sequences for orthographic-phase reading.

The value of orthographic knowledge for word reading is thought to be threefold: (1) it facilitates the decoding of unfamiliar words, particularly multisyllabic words that would be hard to phonemically recode because of the large number of letters needing conversion—for example, blending the 10 letter-sounds in *consignment*; (2) it enables readers to set up access routes in memory for reading words by sight, the access routes consisting of spelling patterns symbolizing multiphoneme segments in pronunciations (Ehri, 1986); and (3) it speeds up the process of accessing sight words by facilitating letter identification when the letters conform to familiar patterns (Juel, 1983; Venezky & Massaro, 1979).

What sorts of spelling patterns might be detected by readers? Various descriptions have been proposed. Becker, Dixon, and Anderson-Inman (1980) analyzed English word into root word and morphographs, defined as irreducible units of meaning in written English. In analyzing 26,000 high-frequency words, they detected about 8,100 different root words and about 800 different morphographs (e.g., *-ed, -ing, -ible, -ate, -ment*) that occurred in at least 10 different words.

Glushko (1979, 1981) proposed the concept of orthographic neighborhoods to depict sets of words that share letter sequences—for example, words having common stems such as *-eak, -ave, -ost, -ade*. Words in the same neighborhood may symbolize consistent pronunciations (e.g., *made, wade, fade*) or inconsistent pronunciations (e.g., *steak-creak, wave-have, most-cost*).

Also, English word spellings have been analyzed to determine letter cooccurrence patterns and positional frequencies of letters and combinations of letters. Analyses have been performed to reflect the number of times readers see different letter patterns in running text as well as the number of different words sharing those patterns (Solso & Juel, 1980; Venezky & Massaro, 1979).

In a study with adults, Massaro et al. (1979, 1980, 1981) examined the psychological reality of two kinds of orthographic structure: *statistical redundancy*, which takes account of the frequency of occurrence of letters and letter sequences within words in written text[4]; and *rule-governed regularity*, which takes account of phonological constraints in English and scribal conventions for sequencing letters in words. Adults performed forced-choice and ratings tasks on nonsense words (e.g., *rodipe, dripoe, prdioe, dpireo*) to indicate which sequences they regarded as bearing greater resemblance to English words. Subjects were found to be more sensitive to rule-governed regularity than to statistical redundancy. The greater importance of rule-governed regularity is consistent with the idea that knowledge of orthographic structure emerges from a background of competence in alphabetic-phase reading.

Various studies have examined when children become able to distinguish legal from illegal letter sequences. Results indicate that this develops during second grade. In a study by Golinkoff (cited in Gibson & Levin, 1975), end-of-the-year first and second graders were shown legal and illegal nonwords having the same letters (e.g., *nar* vs. *rna*) and were asked to select the one that was more like a real word. Whereas first graders performed only slightly better than chance, second graders performed significantly better than chance (82.5% correct). Performance on this task was correlated with scores on a reading achievement test ($r = .50$). Other studies have confirmed these findings and have indicated that reading ability is more highly correlated with orthographic judgments than grade level is (Allington, 1978; Leslie & Thimke, 1986; Massaro & Hestand, 1983). These results are consistent with the idea that knowledge of orthographic patterns emerges as readers become more practiced at phonological recoding and as their lexicon of printed words grows larger.

In order to determine whether beginning readers use their knowledge of orthographic structure in reading, researchers have devised search tasks in which readers read through lists of words and nonwords to find target words. It is reasoned that if readers are sensitive to orthographic structure, then they should search through illegally spelled nonwords faster than legally spelled nonwords and words, because the latter are more similarly structured to the targets than the former. However, if readers are sensitive only to the difference between familiar and unfamiliar sight words, then they should not search through illegally spelled nonwords any differently from legally spelled nonwords, because both legal and illegal nonwords are unfamiliar.

Leslie and Thimke (1986) had first and second graders search through lists of real words, legally spelled nonwords, and illegally spelled nonwords for words that named animals and were in the children's reading vocabularies. They grouped children according to the size of their reading vocabularies into first- and second-grade readers. They found that first-grade readers searched through the two kinds of nonwords equally fast and faster than the words, whereas second-grade readers searched through illegal nonwords faster than legal nonwords, which did not differ from real words. Thus, only the second-grade readers used orthographic structure in their searches, not the first-grade readers. These findings and those in other similar studies (Juola, Schadler, Chabot, & McCaughey, 1978; Leslie & Shannon, 1981) indicate that second grade is the time when children acquire sufficient experience reading words to recognize standard English spelling patterns.[5]

Juel (1983) showed that knowledge of orthographic structure enables readers to read familiar words more rapidly. She measured second and fifth graders' reaction times to read 64 target words varying in word frequency, decodability, and two types of orthographic regularity (i.e., frequency of two-letter patterns in specific positions of words in running text; and frequency of two-letter patterns in specific positions across different words). She found that only the latter type of regularity proved important. Orthographic regularity across different words exerted an impact on fifth graders but not on second graders. That is, fifth graders read words that shared letter positions with many other words more rapidly than words having less-common letters. This factor made little difference to second graders, who were influenced primarily by the decodability of the words. These findings indicate that word-reading speed is facilitated by orthographic structure sometime after second grade. Also, findings are consistent with the idea that knowledge of orthographic regularity is derived from readers' knowledge of different words, perhaps those stored in lexical memory, rather than from sheer exposure rates to words.

It is interesting to note that letter overlap among words has the opposite effect upon beginning readers, who have a harder time reading words that share letters with other words. This is because they use partial letter cues to read words, and these cues do not make similarly spelled words unique. In contrast, orthographic readers have an easier time reading words with similar patterns. This is because their orthographic knowledge helps them recognize which letters are in the words, and they are able to process all of the letters easily to distinguish between words.

In reading unfamiliar words, orthographic-phase readers are thought to divide letter strings into root words and affixes or into syllables, convert these to pronunciations, and then blend them to derive a recognizable word. However, in their review Johnson and Bauman (1984) found few if any studies showing that students trained in syllabication were able to read unfamiliar words better than control groups. According to these authors, the flaw in expecting syllabication instruction to be effective for pronouncing unfamiliar words is that in order to know how to apply traditional syllabication rules, one needs to know how to pronounce the word, which is the goal of syllabication.

However, a recent study appears more promising. Henry (1988) developed an effective series of lessons to teach orthographic patterns that included more than syllabication instruction. She taught upper-grade elementary students to distinguish words in terms of their word origin—Anglo-Saxon, Romance, or Greek—and then to identify letter-sound correspondences, syllable patterns, and morpheme patterns for each origin type (Calfee & Drum, 1986). Also she taught them the technical vocabulary for discussing decoding concepts. She observed significant pre- to posttest gains on word reading as well as on spelling measures and superior performance compared to control subjects.

Because Henry's (1988) instructional program included many components, it is not clear what made the difference. However, she points out that words of Latin origin are highly regular and easy to decode once the root words and affixes are known. Examples of words derived from Latin are *reconstruction, disruptive, admission*. She attributes the success of her instruction to the fact that students knew which rules to apply to which words because they were taught to distinguish the origins of the words.

Most studies have examined whether instruction in orthographic patterns affects the ability to read unfamiliar words. Few have examined whether it enables readers to learn to read words more effectively by sight. According to Ehri's (1986) view, knowledge of orthographic structures should enhance readers' ability to store the spellings of sight words in memory by enabling them to process and remember chunks of letter sequences as symbols for segments of pronunciations. This possibility awaits investigation.

In summary, the orthographic phase of word reading emerges after competence with alphabetic-phase reading has been achieved. In reading words, orthographic-phase readers process familiar sequences of letters as units. Sensitivity to orthographic structure emerges in second grade. Use of orthographic structure to speed up word reading emerges between second and fifth grades.

Reading Words by Analogy

In their stage theory, Marsh et al. (1981b) regard reading by analogy to be a more advanced form of word reading than reading by sequential decoding because of the complexity of knowledge presumably needed to analogize. They speculate that as readers internalize and remember the visual alphabetic forms of words, as they learn to process hierarchical regularities spanning the entire spelling of a word (e.g., *cīme* in which *i* influences the sound of *c*, and *e* influences the sound of *i*), and as they learn lexically based patterns that are not phonemically regular but that recur across words (e.g., *could, would, should; night, fight, sight*), they shift from phonemically recoding individual letters in words to reading them according to the similarity of their letter patterns to known words stored in lexical memory.

To assess whether second-grade, fifth-grade, and college students would employ an analogy strategy, Marsh et al. (1981b) presented them with nonsense words that, pronounced one way, would indicate a decoding strategy and, pronounced another way, would indicate an analogy strategy. For example, the word *faugh*, if pronounced *faw* would indicate decoding; if pronounced *faff*, rhyming with *laugh*, would indicate use of an analogy. The percentages of subjects reading by analogy were: 14 percent (second graders), 34 percent (fifth graders), 38 percent (college students). These results indicate that reading words by analogy is more common among more advanced readers.

Manis, Szeszulski, Howell, and Horn (1986) found that second and third graders read some nonsense words by analogy, although they read the majority by following decoding rules. Subjects were more apt to read nonwords by analogy if the analogs were high-frequency rather than low-frequency words. Older dyslexics reading at the same level as the second and third graders were found to produce fewer analogous readings of the nonwords, even though both groups were able to read the real-word analogs equally well. Frith (1980) reports similar findings. One explanation may be that dyslexics' knowledge of the spellings of real-word analogs is only partial and insufficiently analyzed into letter sequences as a result of their weak phonological recoding skill.

In support of Marsh et al.'s (1981b) claim that reading words by analogy develops later during the orthographic phase, Zinna, Liberman, and Shankweiler (1986) found that third and fifth graders were influenced by orthographic neighborhoods as well as word frequency in reading words, whereas first graders were influenced only by word frequency. In this study, they had subjects read high- and low-frequency words containing vowel digraph units having invariant or variant pronunciations. Variant pronunciations were of two sorts: digraphs embedded in consonant stems coming from consistent neighborhoods (e.g., *-ean* as in *clean* and *dean*); and those coming from inconsistent neighborhoods (e.g., *-eak* pronounced two ways as in *speak* and *steak*). Third and fifth graders read low-frequency words from consistent neighborhoods as accurately as high-frequency words and more accurately than low-frequency words from inconsistent neighborhoods. In contrast, first graders were not affected by neighborhood consistency but only by frequency in their readings. The explanation is that only the older readers possessed generalized knowledge of orthographic patterns, not the younger readers.

Marsh et al (1981b) interpret their findings to indicate that the analogy strategy does not become prominent until later, during the orthographic phase of reading development. However, Goswami (1986) has criticized these studies for failing to use spelling patterns that were sufficiently familiar to the younger readers and for failing to verify that younger subjects could read the analogs. Lack of familiarity may be why first and second graders did not analogize.

Actually Marsh, Friedman, Desberg, and Saterdahl (1981a) provide some evidence that younger readers are capable of reading words by analogy. In this study, second graders read a list of the real-word analogs before they read nonsense words, and they were told that the nonsense words were spelled like the real words. They found that 78 percent of the second graders' responses were analogies.

Goswami (1986, 1987, 1988a, 1988b, 1989) has performed several experiments that indicate that reading words by analogy develops earlier than reading words by sequential decoding. In the first study, she presented beginning readers with a clue word (e.g., *beak*) and then asked them to read several other words and nonwords, some of which were analogs of the clue word and others of which were not analogous but were equally easy to recode (e.g., *bean, beal, peak, neak, lake, pake*). Clue words were printed above test words and were pronounced before the child read each test word. She found that first-grade-level readers read more analogs correctly than control words. Analogs sharing the same stem (rime) were correct more often than analogs sharing beginning letters. Even nonreaders—that is, children who read no words on the Schonell word-reading test (Schonell & Goodacre, 1971)—were observed to read some analogies between the stems of words correctly (Goswami, 1986, 1988a).

Several alternative explanations were ruled out (Goswami, 1986, 1988a), particularly the number of letters shared by clue words and analogs; and the visual similarity between clue words and analogs. She found that whether or not clue words and analogs contained letters printed in the same or different upper- and lower-case letters made little difference to performance. Also, she found that words were less apt to be read by analogy when the words rhymed but the spellings were different (e.g., *most-toast*) (Goswami, 1989). These results indicate that the identities of letters rather than the visual configuration of words or sound similarities between words provide the basis for analogizing.

Goswami (1987) found that children's ability to detect rhyming words in a sequence was strongly predictive of their analogical reading performance, stronger than other phonological skills (Goswami, 1987). This suggests that the ability to divide words into onset and rime subunits may be important for being able to read words by analogy. Sensitivity to rime units may aid beginning readers in recognizing common spelling patterns present in the stems of different words and hence in reading the words, particularly words with letter-sound irregularities (e.g., *light, night, fight*) that cannot be recoded according to letter-sound rules.

Goswami has interpreted her findings to challenge the claims of Frith (1980) and Marsh et al. (1981b) that the use of analogy to read words develops later during the orthographic phase. Rather, she argues that orthographic processing can be performed even by the least mature beginning readers, before they learn sequential decoding.

One might argue that Goswami made it very easy for readers to reveal an analogy strategy and in fact prompted this response by keeping clue words in full view of subjects. However, in some of her studies the clue words were not in view when subjects read the target words (Goswami, 1988a). Another criticism is that Goswami (1986) made decoding control words more difficult by the use of more complex spelling patterns containing consonant blends or long vowels (e.g., *lake, real, cast*). Many beginning readers do not learn to decode long vowels and consonant clusters until they have learned short vowels and CVCs. Thus, because her measure may not have detected beginning recoding skill, her claim that analogizing emerges before sequential decoding may pertain only to the kinds of spellings being tested, not to the reading skill of the subjects.

Ehri and Robbins (1989) took a closer look at the reading skills of beginners who were able to read words by analogy. Kindergartners and first graders' word and nonword reading skills were assessed. In the analogy task, they were taught to read five words to criterion (e.g., *KAAV, FEEL, MiiN, ROOP*, and *BUUT*, symbolizing the words *cave, feel, mine, rope*, and *boot*, respectively) and then were shown five transfer words sharing stems with the original words, which were not in view (e.g., *SAAV, SEEL, SiiN, SOOP*, and *SUUT* symbolizing the words *save, seal, sign, soap*, and *suit*, respectively). Control subjects learned to read a different list of original words containing the same letter-sound correspondences (e.g., *RAAN, KEEP, FiiT, BOOL*, and *MUUV*, symbolizing the words *rain, keep, fight, bowl*, and *move*, respectively), but they were shown the same transfer words. More transfer words were read by analogy subjects than by control subjects, but only among those who could recode at least a few CVC nonwords. Subjects who lacked recoding skill did not display this difference. In fact, they read few if any transfer words at all.

Prereaders who read neither real words nor nonwords had trouble learning to read the five base words to criterion, and those who did learn the words did not read transfer analogs correctly. Rather, they sometimes misread the transfer words as the original words, indicating that they were responding to partial cues. These results indicate that in order for beginning readers to process words by analogy to known words, they must have some alphabetic skill so that they can process the correspondences between letters in spellings and sounds in pronunciations.

Although Ehri and Robbins' (1989) findings challenge the claim that reading words by analogy develops before reading words by sequential decoding, the study may be open to criticism for its use of somewhat novel orthography. Although the representation of vowels was explained (i.e., "there are two letters saying their own names and marked with a bar"), it may be that recoding skill was required to recognize how this system worked.

Effective instructional programs have been developed to teach students to read unfamiliar words by detecting known words and word parts in the unfamiliar spellings. In Cunningham's (1975–1976, 1979) program, training includes, but is not limited to, reading words by analogy. In her study, second graders who could read many common words but were weak at reading unfamiliar words received this training while control subjects rested. On a posttest consisting of novel words, experimentals significantly outperformed controls. This indicates the value of teaching students to read unfamiliar words by looking for familiar parts. However, as indicated in Goswami's studies, students must have the identities of letters in known words stored in memory in order to succeed in such a program.

In summary, older readers are more likely to read words by analogy to known words than younger readers. It appears that in order for younger readers to use this strategy, they need to (1) have the analog and its constituent letters stored in memory, (2) be able to segment words into onset and rime, and (3) have some phonological recoding skill. Reading unfamiliar words by recoding is more frequently used than reading by analogy. However, the reason may be that beginners are usually not taught to analogize. With instruction, the strategy might become more common.

CONCLUDING COMMENTS

Although the concept of sight reading implies one way to read words, it is apparent from our developmental view that different processes may be involved, depending upon the phase of development. At the logographic phase, sight words are read using strictly visual cues to form access routes into memory. At the transitional alphabetic phase, partial letter-sound cues form the associations. At the mature alphabetic phase, complete connections between spellings and the phonemic structure of words are formed. Thus, sight word reading is not a unitary process. Nor it is a way of reading words that is limited to students who receive sight word instruction. All students learn to read words by sight, with mature readers reading sight words more effectively than immature readers.

Although three phases of word-reading development have been described, all phases may not be equally essential in learning to read. The logographic phase reflects children's natural unanalytic approach in attempting to read words. There appears to be no reason why word-reading experiences at this phase are required in order for beginners to make progress learning to read alphabetically. In contrast, achieving proficiency at the alphabetic phase is thought to be critical for success at the orthographic phase.

The alphabetic and orthographic phases of word reading can be analyzed as having an onset and a culmination, with the onset rooted in processes happening during the earlier phase. The onset of the alphabetic phase lies in phonetic cue reading, which may begin as soon as logographic readers learn letter names or sounds and recognize their relationship to words. This is illustrated by an environmental print expert whose accurate reading of *emporium* was disrupted by letter learning. The Emporium is a San Francisco department store whose stylized spelling is dominated by a very large initial E. On one of this child's frequent visits to the store, she looked at its name and commented in surprise, "Mom! That doesn't say *emporium* [i.e., *m-porium*]. That says *e-porium!*" The earliest form of phonetic cue reading involves paying attention to initial letters as they correspond to sounds in pronunciations of words.

Likewise, the onset of the orthographic phase may lie in reading words by analogy, which emerges during the alphabetic phase. Once children become analytic about the spelling of words, they may begin to notice letter patterns that recur across words. The orthographic processing of words may not culminate until after readers have acquired phonological recoding skill and after they have used it to store the spellings of many words with similar patterns in memory. Patterns may not be generalized until several specific words are known.

The developmental phase theory of word reading reviewed here carries implications for research on beginning reading processes. It is important for researchers to consider the processes that readers are using to read words at the point of development that is being studied. Giving this matter some attention helps to insure that the tasks administered to readers hold promise of revealing important information about their reading development. For example, if the aim is to assess the word-reading ability of logographic or rudimentary alphabetic readers, it would be informative to present them with words that they had read before, or to observe how easily they learn to read a set of words. It would be uninformative to have them read unfamiliar words, because they lack any means of recoding novel print. A case in point is a study by McGee et al. (1988), in which logographic and rudimentary alphabetic readers were given environmental print such as a telephone directory and a newspaper to read. Not surprisingly, they failed even though they knew many letters.

In studying beginning readers, researchers can no longer overlook the reading-related skills of the subjects they are treating and testing. In our work, we have found that children similar in age within the same preschool, kindergarten, or first-grade classroom, may vary markedly in their reading-related skills, ranging from logographic phase readers with little knowledge of the alphabet to orthographic phase readers with extensive print lexicons. The extent of their reading ability is dependent not only on classroom instruction but also upon their experiences at home and in preschools. These sources create great variability among beginners and influence strongly their performance on any reading-related tasks they are given. In this chapter, we have outlined several ways that words might be read during development and important skills and experiences needed to read words in these ways. It is hoped that this developmental scheme will prove valuable to researchers by enabling them to gauge just how far along individual subjects in their samples are in learning to read words.

To distinguish among beginners in terms of their reading knowledge, one might assess their ability to name alphabet letters, to read isolated words varying in difficulty from the easiest preprimer-level to second- and third-level words, and to read nonsense words. According to our developmental scheme, the following groups might be distinguished: (1) logographic readers or prereaders who read few if any words in isolation; words that they might read are *no* or *stop*; (2) rudimentary alphabetic readers, also called phonetic cue readers, who can read some real words but not any nonsense words; almost always they can name most upper-case alphabet letters; (3) alphabetic readers, or phonological recoders, who can read several real words and also can phonologically recode nonwords. Other tests might be added to clarify subjects' ability to divide pronunciations of words into onset and rime as well as into phonemic segments, their ability to generate phonetically accurate spellings of words, their ability to distinguish orthographically legal from illegal letter sequences.

We expect that if researchers obtain such information about their subjects and then group them accordingly, they will be in a much better position to account for variance and to make new discoveries in their investigations of beginning reading processes. If subjects are grouped only according to grade or chronological age, then reading ability differences may mask effects of the independent variables. Grouping subjects by "reading age" is better, but numerical values such as these are still not informative about what readings skills the subject actually possess.

The developmental phase theory of word reading reviewed here has consequences bearing on reading instruction. One is to show that, regardless of how students are taught to read, by a phonics approach or by a whole-word approach, those who make progress in learning to read acquire the ability to phonologically recode and also to read words as wholes by sight. Moreover, proficient sight word reading appears to depend upon knowing how the spelling system symbolizes phonemes in speech. This suggests that a method of learning to read that does not make provision for fostering the various ways of reading words is not going to be completely successful in promoting the development of reading skill. During the alphabetic phase, students need to learn how to phonologically recode unfamiliar spellings. Also they need sufficient practice phonologically recoding the same spellings so that the words become familiar forms with reliable access routes established in memory. Very likely words also need to be practiced in a meaningful context so that the associations formed include correct meanings for pronunciations. This is particularly important in the case of words with ambiguous pronunciations (e.g., *their* vs. *there* vs. *they're*) and words that depend upon contexts to be meaningful (i.e., function words such as *of, and, was*) (Ehri & Roberts, 1979; Ehri & Wilce, 1980a). Likewise, instruction is needed to develop competence at the orthographic phase of word reading. How to do this is less clear and requires more research.

NOTES

1. The word *decoding* is ambiguous. To some researchers, it refers specifically to the process of phonologically recoding words, while to others it simply means word identification and covers sight word reading as well as phonological recoding. In this chapter, we will use decoding interchangeably with phonological recoding in the specific sense.
2. In nonalphabetic written languages such as Chinese, orthographic characters symbolize concepts rather than pronunciations, so establishing systematic phonological access routes is not possible. Access routes link symbols to meanings. Interestingly, speakers of Mandarin and Cantonese can communicate in writing because they have established the same access routes between written characters and their meanings. However, they cannot talk to each other because their pronunciations for the symbols are different.
3. In this chapter, symbols marking phonetic and phonemic transcriptions are placed between slashes. To represent short and long vowels, symbols employed in dictionaries rather than phonemic symbols are used because these are better known by nonlinguists. Short vowels are marked as they are in the following words: *băt, bĕt, bĭt, tŏp, bŭt*. Long vowels are marked as follows: *bāke, bēet, bīte, pōke, dūke*. The symbol for schwa, the vowel in unstressed syllables, is ə. Although linguists distinguish between the terms *phonetic* and *phonemic*, we use them synonymously here.
4. Statistical orthographic redundancy involves counts of how often letters occur within words in running text. Spelling patterns of frequently occurring words such as *the* contribute much more to these counts than less frequently occurring words. As a result, letters such as *th* in initial position are regarded as common patterns, even though relatively few different words begin with *th*.
5. One might wonder whether superior performance with legal patterns in these tasks reflects readers' knowledge of orthographic structure or phonological recoding ability, since the two variables are confounded. However, the confounding is unavoidable since orthographic structure is derived from phonological regularities (Massaro et al., 1979, 1980, 1981).

REFERENCES

Adams, M. J., & Huggins, A. W. F. (1985). The growth of children's sight vocabulary: A quick test with educational and theoretical implications. *Reading Research Quarterly, 20*, 262–281.

Allington, R. L. (1978). Sensitivity to orthographic structure as a function of grade and reading ability. *Journal of Reading Behavior, 10*, 437–439.

Anderson, R. C., Hiebert, E. H., Scott, J. A., & Wilkinson, I. A. G. (1985). *Becoming a nation of readers.* Washington, DC: National Institute of Education.

Baron, J. (1977). Mechanisms for pronouncing printed words: Use and acquisition. In D. LaBerge & S. J. Samuels (Eds.), *Basic processes in reading: Perception and comprehension* (pp. 175–216). Hillsdale, NJ: Erlbaum.

Baron, J. (1979). Orthographic and word specific mechanisms in children's reading of words. *Child Development, 50*, 587–594.

Barr, R. C. (1972). The influence of instructional conditions on word recognition errors. *Reading Research Quarterly, 7*, 509–529.

Barr, R. C. (1974–1975). The effect of instruction on pupil reading strategies. *Reading Research Quarterly, 10*, 555–582.

Barron, R. W. (1986). Word recognition in early reading: A review of the direct and indirect access hypotheses. *Cognition, 24*, 93–119.

Barron, R. W., & Baron, J. (1977). How children get meaning from printed words. *Child Development, 48*, 587–594.

Beck, I. L. (1981). Reading problems and instructional practices. In G. E. Mackinnon & T. G. Waller (Eds.), *Reading research: Advances in theory and practice* (Vol. 2, pp. 55–95). New York: Academic Press.

Becker, W. C., Dixon, R., & Anderson-Inman, L. (1980). *Morphographic and root word analysis of 26,000 high-frequency words*. Eugene, OR: University of Oregon College of Education.

Biemiller, A. (1970). The development of the use of graphic and contextual information as children learn to read. *Reading Research Quarterly, 6*, 75–96.

Bradley, L., & Bryant, P. E. (1985). *Rhyme and reason in reading and spelling*. Ann Arbor: University of Michigan Press.

Brooks, L. R. (1977). Visual pattern in fluent word identification. In A. S. Reber & D. L. Scarborough (Eds.), *Toward a psychology of reading* (pp. 143–181). Hillsdale, NJ: Erlbaum.

Byrne, B. (in press). Studies in the unbiased acquisition procedure for reading: Rationale, hypotheses, and data. In P. B. Gough (Ed.), *Reading acquisition*. Hillsdale, NJ: Erlbaum.

Calfee, R., & Drum, P. (1986). Research on teaching reading. In M. Wittrock (Ed.), *Handbook of research on teaching* (pp. 804–849). New York: Macmillan.

Carnine, D. W. (1977). Phonics versus look-say: Transfer to new words. *Reading Teacher, 30*, 636–640.

Carnine, L., Carnine, D., & Gersten, R. (1984). Analysis of oral reading errors made by economically disadvantaged students taught with a synthetic-phonics approach. *Reading Research Quarterly, 19*, 343–356.

Cattell, J. M. (1886). The time it takes to see and name objects. *Mind, 11*, 63–65.

Clay, M. M. (1979). Theoretical research and instructional change: A case study. In L. B. Resnick & P. A. Weaver (Eds.), *Theory and practice of early reading* (Vol. 2, pp. 149–171). Hillsdale, NJ: Erlbaum.

Clymer, T. (1963). The utility of phonic generalizations in the primary grades. *Reading Teacher, 16*, 252–258.

Cohen, A. S. (1974–1975). Oral reading errors of first-grade children taught by a code-emphasis approach. *Reading Research Quarterly, 10*, 616–650.

Coltheart, M., Davelaar, E., Jonassen, J. T., & Besner, D. (1977). Access to the internal lexicon. In S. Dornic (Ed.), *Attention and performance* (Vol. 6). Hillsdale, NJ: Erlbaum.

Cunningham, P. M. (1975–1976). Investigating a synthesized theory of mediated word identification. *Reading Research Quarterly, 11*, 127–143.

Cunningham, P. M. (1979). Mediated word identification: A compare/contrast approach. In J. E. Button, T. C. Lovitt, & T. D. Rowland (Eds.), *Communications research in learning disabilities and mental retardation*. Baltimore, MD: University Park Press.

Delawter, J. (1970). *Oral reading errors of second-grade children exposed to two different reading approaches*. Unpublished Ph.D. dissertation, Teachers College, Columbia University.

Dewitz, P., & Stammer, J. (1980). *The development of linguistic awareness in young children from label reading to word recognition*. Paper presented at the National Reading Conference, San Diego, CA.

Durkin, D. (1984). Is there a match between what elementary teachers do and what basal reader manuals recommend? *Reading Teacher, 37*, 734–744.

Ehri, L. C. (1978). Beginning reading from a psycholinguistic perspective: Amalgamation of word identities. In F. B. Murray (Ed.), *Development of the reading process* (IRA Monograph No. 3). Newark, DE: International Reading Assoc.

Ehri, L. C. (1979). Linguistic insight: Threshold of reading acquisition. In T. G. Waller & G. E. MacKinnon (Eds.), *Reading research: Advances in theory and practice* (Vol. 1, pp. 63–114). New York: Academic Press.

Ehri, L. C. (1980). The development of orthographic images. In U. Frith (Ed.), *Cognitive processes in spelling* (pp. 311–338). London: Academic Press.

Ehri, L. C. (1984). How orthography alters spoken language competencies in children learning to read and spell. In J. Downing & R. Valtin (Eds.), *Language awareness and learning to read* (pp. 119–147). New York: Springer Verlag.

Ehri, L. C. (1985). Effects of printed language acquisition on speech. In D. R. Olson, N. Torrance, & A. Hildyard (Eds.), *Literacy, language, and learning: The nature and consequences of reading and writing* (pp. 333–367). Cambridge, Eng.: Cambridge University Press.

Ehri, L. C. (1986). Sources of difficulty in learning to spell and read. In M. L. Wolraich & D. Routh (Eds.), *Advances in developmental and behavioral pediatrics* (pp. 121–195). Greenwich, CT: Jai Press.

Ehri, L. C. (1987). Learning to read and spell words. *Journal of Reading Behavior, 19*, 5–31.

Ehri, L. C. (1989a). Movement into word reading and spelling: How spelling contributes to reading. In J. Mason (Ed.), *Reading and writing connections* (pp. 65–81). Boston, MA: Allyn & Bacon.

Ehri, L. C. (1989b). The development of spelling knowledge and its role in reading acquisition and reading disability. *Journal of Learning Disabilities, 22*, 356–365.

Ehri, L. C. (in press). Reconceptualizing the development of sight word reading and its relationship to recoding. In P. B. Gough (Ed.), *Reading acquisition*. Hillsdale, NJ: Erlbaum.

Ehri, L. C., & Robbins, C. (1989, April). *What reading skills are needed to read words by analogy?* Paper presented at the meeting of the American Educational Research Association, San Francisco, CA.

Ehri, L. C., & Roberts, K. T. (1979). Do beginners learn printed words better in contexts or in isolation? *Child Development, 50*, 675–685.

Ehri, L. C., & Wilce, L. S. (1979). Does word training increase or decrease interference in a Stroop task? *Journal of Experimental Child Psychology, 27*, 352–364.

Ehri, L. C., & Wilce, L. S. (1980a). Do beginners learn to read function words better in sentences or in lists? *Reading Research Quarterly, 15*, 451–476.

Ehri, L. C., & Wilce, L. S. (1980b). The influence of orthography on readers' conceptualization of the phonemic structure of words. *Applied Psycholinguistics, 1,* 371–385.

Ehri, L. C., & Wilce, L. S. (1983). Development of word identification speed in skilled and less-skilled beginning readers. *Journal of Educational Psychology, 75,* 3–18.

Ehri, L. C., & Wilce, L. S. (1985). Movement into reading: Is the first stage of printed word learning visual or phonetic? *Reading Research Quarterly, 20,* 163–179.

Ehri, L. C., & Wilce, L. S. (1986). The influence of spellings on speech: Are alveolar flaps /d/ or /t/? In D. Yaden & S. Templeton (Eds.), *Metalinguistic awareness and beginning literacy* (pp. 101–114). Exeter: NH: Heinemann.

Ehri, L. C., & Wilce, L. S. (1987a). Does learning to spell help beginners learn to read words? *Reading Research Quarterly, 18,* 47–65.

Ehri, L. C., & Wilce, L. S. (1987b). Cipher versus cue reading: An experiment in decoding acquisition. *Journal of Educational Psychology, 79,* 3–13.

Ehri, L. C., & Wilce, L. S., & Taylor, B. B. (1987). Children's categorization of short vowels in words and the influence of spellings. *Merrill Palmer Quarterly, 33,* 393–421.

Elder, R. D. (1971). Oral reading achievement of Scottish and American children. *Elementary School Journal, 71,* 216–230.

Firth, I. (1972). *Components of reading disability.* Ph.D. Thesis, University of New South Wales.

Fox, B., & Routh, D. K. (1976). Phonemic analysis and synthesis as word-attack skills. *Journal of Educational Psychology, 68,* 70–74.

Fox, B., & Routh, K. D. (1984). Phonemic analysis and synthesis as word-attack skills: Revisited. *Journal of Educational Psychology, 76,* 1059–1064.

Freebody, P., & Byrne, B. (1988). Word-reading strategies in elementary school children: Relations to comprehension, reading time, and phonemic awareness. *Reading Research Quarterly, 23,* 441–453.

Frith, U. (1980). Unexpected spelling problems. In U. Frith (Ed.), *Cognitive processes in spelling.* London: Academic Press.

Frith, U. (1985). Beneath the surface of developmental dyslexia. In K. E. Patterson, J. C. Marshall, & M. Coltheart (Eds.), *Surface dyslexia* (pp. 301–330). London: Erlbaum.

Gibson, E. J., & Levin, H. (1975). *The psychology of reading.* Cambridge, MA: MIT Press.

Gilbert, N., Spring, C., & Sassenrath, J. (1977). Effects of overlearning and similarity on transfer in word recognition. *Perceptual and Motor Skills, 44,* 591–598.

Glaser, R. (1984). Education and thinking: The role of knowledge. *American Psychologist, 39,* 93–104.

Glushko, R. J. (1979). The organization and activation of orthographic knowledge in reading aloud. *Journal of Experimental Psychology: Human Perception and Performance, 5,* 674–691.

Glushko, R. J. (1981). Principles for pronouncing print: The psychology of phonography. In A. M. Lesgold & C. A. Perfetti (Eds.), *Interactive processes in reading* (pp. 61–84). Hillsdale, NJ: Erlbaum.

Goodman, K. S. (1965). A linguistic study of cues and miscues in reading. *Elementary English, 42,* 639–643.

Goodman, Y. M., & Altwerger, B. (1981). *Print awareness in preschool children: A working paper. A study of the development of literacy in preschool children.* (Occasional Paper No. 4, Program in Language and Literacy, University of Arizona.)

Goswami, U. (1986). Children's use of analogy in learning to read: A developmental study. *Journal of Experimental Child Psychology, 42,* 73–83.

Goswami, U. (1987). *Annotation: A special link between rhyming skill and the use of orthographic analogies by beginning readers.* Manuscript submitted for publication.

Goswami, U. (1988a). Orthographic analogies and reading development. *Quarterly Journal of Experimental Psychology, 40,* 239–268.

Goswami, U. (1988b). *Orthographic skills and reading development.* Manuscript submitted for publication.

Goswami, U. (1989). *Phonological priming and orthographic analogies in reading.* Manuscript submitted for publication.

Gough, P. B. (1984). Word recognition. In P. D. Pearson (Ed.), *Handbook of reading research* (Vol. 1, pp. 225–253). New York: Longman.

Gough, P. B., & Hillinger, M. L. (1980). Learning to read: An unnatural act. *Bulletin of the Orton Society, 30,* 180–196.

Gough, P. B., Juel, C., & Griffith, P. L. (in press). Reading, spelling, and the orthographic cipher. In P. B. Gough (Ed.), *Reading acquisition.* Hillsdale, NJ: Erlbaum.

Gough, P. B., Juel, C., & Roper/Schneider, D. (1983). Code and cipher: A two-stage conception of initial reading acquisition. In J. A. Niles & L. A. Harris (Eds.), *Searches for meaning in reading/language processing and instruction. Thirty-second yearbook of the National Reading Conference* (pp. 207–211). Rochester, NY: National Reading Conference.

Gough, P. B., & Tunmer, W. E. (1986). Decoding, reading, and reading disability. *Remedial and Special Education, 7,* 6–10.

Harste, J. C., Burke, C. L., & Woodward, V. A. (1982). Children's language and world: Initial encounters with print. In J. Langer & M. Smith-Burke (Eds.), *Bridging the gap: Reader meets author* (pp. 105–131). Newark, DE: International Reading Association.

Henry, M. K. (1988). *Understanding English orthography: Assessment and instruction for decoding and spelling.* Unpublished doctoral dissertation, Stanford University, Stanford, CA.

Hiebert, E. (1978). Preschool children's understanding of written language. *Child Development, 49*, 1231–1234.

Huba, M. E. (1984). The relationship between linguistic awareness in prereaders and two types of experimental instruction. *Reading World, 23*, 347–363.

Jeffrey, W. E., & Samuels, S. J. (1967). Effect of method of reading training on initial learning and transfer. *Journal of Verbal Learning and Verbal Behavior, 6*, 354–358.

Johnson, D. D., & Baumann, J. F. (1984). Word identification. In P. D. Pearson (Ed.), *Handbook of reading research* (Vol. 1, pp. 583–608). New York: Longman.

Jorm, A. F., & Share, D. L. (1983). An invited article: Phonological recoding and reading acquisition. *Applied Psycholinguistics, 4*, 103–147.

Juel, C. (1983). The development and use of mediated word identification. *Reading Research Quarterly, 18*, 306–327.

Juel, C. (1984). An evolving model of reading acquisition. In J. A. Niles (Ed.), *Changing perspectives on research in reading/language processing and instruction. Thirty-third yearbook of the National Reading Conference* (pp. 294–297). Rochester, NY: National Reading Conference.

Juel, C., Griffith, P. L., & Gough, P. B. (1986). Acquisition of literacy: A longitudinal study of children in first and second grade. *Journal of Educational Psychology, 78*, 243–255.

Juel, C., & Roper/Schneider, D. (1985). The influence of basal readers on first-grade reading. *Reading Research Quarterly, 20*, 134–152.

Juola, J. F., Schadler, M., Chabot, R., & McCaughey, M. (1978). The development of visual information-processing skills related to reading. *Journal of Experimental Child Psychology, 25*, 459–476.

LaBerge, D., & Samuels, S. J. (1974). Toward a theory of automatic information processing in reading. *Cognitive Psychology, 6*, 293–323.

Leslie, L., & Shannon, A. J. (1981). Recognition of orthographic structure during beginning reading. *Journal of Reading Behavior, 13*, 313–324.

Leslie, L., & Thimke, B. (1986). The use of orthographic knowledge in beginning reading. *Journal of Reading Behavior, 18*, 229–241.

Lundberg, I., Frost, J., & Peterson, O. (1988). Effects of an extensive program for stimulating phonological awareness in preschool children. *Reading Research Quarterly, 23*, 263–284.

Lundberg, I. (in press). Two dimensions of decontextualization in reading acquisition. In P. B. Gough (Ed.), *Reading acquisition*. Hillsdale, NJ: Erlbaum.

Manis, F. R., Szeszulski, P. A., Howell, M. J., & Horn, C. C. (1986). A comparison of analogy- and rule-based decoding strategies in normal and dyslexic children. *Journal of Reading Behavior, 18*, 203–218.

Marsh, G., Friedman, M., Desberg, P., & Saterdahl, K. (1981a). Comparison of reading and spelling strategies in normal and reading-disabled children. In M. P. Friedman, J. P. Das, & N. O'Connor (Eds.), *Intelligence and learning* (pp. 363–367). New York: Plenum.

Marsh, G., Friedman, M., Welch, V., & Desberg, P. (1981b). A cognitive-developmental theory of reading acquisition. In G. E. Mackinnon & T. G. Waller (Eds.), *Reading research: Advances in theory and practice* (Vol. 3, pp. 199–221). New York: Academic Press.

Mason, J. M. (1976). Overgeneralization in learning to read. *Journal of Reading Behavior, 8*, 173–182.

Mason, J. (1980). When *do* children begin to read: An exploration of four-year-old children's letter and word reading competencies. *Reading Research Quarterly, 15*, 203–227.

Masonheimer, P. E., Drum, P. A., & Ehri, L. C. (1984). Does environmental print identification lead children into word reading? *Journal of Reading Behavior, 16*, 257–271.

Massaro, D. W., Jastrzembski, J. E., & Lucas, P. A. (1981). Frequency, orthographic regularity, and lexical status in letter and word perception. In G. A. Bower (Ed.), *The psychology of learning and motivation* (Vol. 15, pp. 163–200). New York: Academic Press.

Massaro, D. W., Venezky, R. L., & Taylor, G. A. (1979). Orthographic regularity, positional frequency, and visual processing of letter strings. *Journal of Experimental Psychology: General, 108*, 107–124.

Massaro, D. W., Taylor, G. A., Venezky, R. L., Jastrzembski, J. E., & Lucas, P. A. (1980). *Letter and word perception: Orthographic structure and visual processing in reading*. Amsterdam: North-Holland.

Massaro, D. W., & Hestand, J. (1983). Developmental relations between reading ability and knowledge of orthographic structure. *Contemporary Educational Psychology, 8*, 174–180.

McCutcheon, B. A., & McDowell, E. E. (1969). Intralist similarity and acquisition and generalization of word recognition. *Reading Teacher, 23*, 103–107.

McGee, L. M., Lomax, R. G., & Head, M. H. (1988). Young children's written language knowledge: What environmental and functional print reading reveals. *Journal of Reading Behavior, 20*, 99–118.

Monaghan, E. J. (1983, April). *A four-year study of the acquisition of letter-sound correspondences*. Paper presented at the meeting of the American Educational Research Association, Montreal, Quebec.

Morris, D. (1989). *The relationship between word awareness and phoneme awareness in learning to read: A longitudinal study in kindergarten*. Paper submitted for publication.

Olson, R. K. (1985). Disabled reading processes and cognitive profiles. In D. Gray & J. Kavanagh (Eds.), *Behavioral measures of dyslexia* (pp. 215–267). Parkton, MD: York Press.

Otto, W., & Pizillo, C. (1970). Effect of intralist similarity on kindergarten pupils' rate of word acquisition and transfer. *Journal of Reading Behavior, 3*, 14–19.

Perfetti, C. A. (1985). *Reading ability*. New York: Oxford University Press.

Reitsma, P. (1983). Printed word learning in beginning readers. *Journal of Experimental Child Psychology, 36*, 321–339.

Resnick, L. B. (1980). The role of invention in the development of mathematical competence. In R. W. Kluwe & H. Spada (Eds.), *Developmental models of thinking* (pp. 213–244). New York: Academic Press.

Samuels, S. J., & Jeffrey, W. E. (1966). Discriminability of words and letter cues used in learning to read. *Journal of Educational Psychology, 57*, 337–340.

Schonell, F., & Goodacre, E. (1971). *The psychology and teaching of reading* (5th ed.). London: Oliver & Boyd.

Scott, J. A., & Ehri, L. C. (in press). Sight word reading in prereaders: Use of logographic vs. alphabetic access routes. *Journal of Reading Behavior*.

Seymour, P. H. K., & Elder, L. (1986). Beginning reading without phonology. *Cognitive Neuropsychology, 3* 1–36.

Share, D. L., Jorm, A. F., Maclean, R., & Matthews, R. (1984). Sources of individual differences in reading acquisition. *Journal of Educational Psychology, 76*, 466–477.

Solso, R. L., & Juel, C. L. (1980). Positional frequency and versatility of bigrams for two through nine-letter English words. *Behavior Research Methods and Instrumentation, 12*, 297–343.

Spring, C. (1978). Automaticity of word recognition under phonics and whole-word instruction. *Journal of Educational Psychology, 70*, 445–450.

Spring, C., Gilbert, N., & Sassenrath, J. (1979). Learning to read words: Effects of overlearning and similarity on stimulus selection. *Journal of Reading Behavior, 11*, 69–71.

Stanovich, K. E. (1980). Toward an interactive compensatory model of individual differences in the development of reading fluency. *Reading Research Quarterly, 16*, 32–71.

Stanovich, K. E. (1986). Matthew effects in reading: Some consequences of individual differences in the acquisition of literacy. *Reading Research Quarterly, 21*, 360–406.

Stanovich, K. E. (1988). *Children's reading and the development of phonological awareness*. Detroit, MI: Wayne State University Press.

Surber, J. R., & Mason, J. M. (1977). Effects of rule-consistent examples in learning letter-sound correspondences. *Journal of Reading Behavior, 9*, 400–404.

Taylor, B. B., & Ehri, L. C. (1984). *Acquisition of short- and long-vowel knowledge in beginning readers*. Unpublished manuscript.

Thompson, G. B. (1986). When nonsense is better than sense: Nonlexical errors to word reading tests. *British Journal of Educational Psychology, 56*, 216–219.

Treiman, R. (1984). Individual differences among children in spelling and reading styles. *Journal of Experimental Child Psychology, 37*, 463–477.

Treiman, R. (1985). Onsets and rimes as units of spoken syllables: Evidence from children. *Journal of Experimental Child Psychology, 39*, 161–181.

Treiman, R. (1986). The division between onsets and rimes in English syllables. *Journal of Memory and Language, 25*, 476–491.

Tunmer, W. E., & Nesdale, A. R. (1982). The effects of digraphs and pseudowords on phonemic segmentation in young children. *Applied Psycholinguistics, 3*, 299–311.

Uhry, J. (1989). *The effect of spelling instruction on the acquisition of beginning reading strategies*. Unpublished doctoral dissertation, Teachers College, Columbia University, New York.

Vellutino, F. R. (1979). *Dyslexia: Theory and research*. Cambridge, MA: MIT Press.

Venezky, R. (1970). *The structure of English orthography*. The Hague: Mouton.

Venezky, R. L., & Johnson, D. (1973). Development of two letter-sound patterns in grades one through three. *Journal of Educational Psychology, 64*, 109–115.

Venezky, R. L., & Massaro, D. W. (1979). The role of orthographic regularity in word recognition. In L. Resnick & P. Weaver (Eds.), *Theory and practice of early reading* (pp. 85–107). Hillsdale, N.J.: Erlbaum.

Weber, R. M. (1970). A linguistic analysis of first-grade reading errors. *Reading Research Quarterly, 5*, 427–451.

Williams, J. P. (1980). Teaching decoding with an emphasis on phoneme analysis and phoneme blending. *Journal of Educational Psychology, 72*, 1–15.

Ylisto, I. (1967). *An empirical investigation of early reading responses in young children*. Unpublished doctoral dissertation, University of Michigan, Ann Arbor.

Yopp, H. K. (1985). Phoneme segmentation ability: A prerequisite for phonic and sight word achievement in beginning reading? In J. A. Niles & R. V. Lalik (Eds.), *Issues in literacy: A research perspective. Thirty-fourth yearbook of the National Reading Conference* (pp. 330–336). Rochester, NY: National Reading Conference.

Zinna, D. R., Liberman, I. Y., & Shankweiler, D. (1986). Children's sensitivity to factors influencing vowel reading. *Reading Research Quarterly, 21*, 465–480.

16 WORD RECOGNITION: CHANGING PERSPECTIVES

Keith E. Stanovich

Gough (1984) began his review of word recognition in the first volume of the *Handbook of Reading Research* by noting that "Word recognition is the foundation of the reading process" (p. 225). It would indeed be surprising if such a fundamental conclusion were no longer true. Fortunately, no such surprise is in store. Research continues to indicate that word recognition is the foundational process of reading.

Importantly, the context for the statement that word recognition is the foundational process of reading is becoming more widely understood. It is now generally acknowledged that to emphasize the centrality of word recognition is not to deny that the ultimate purpose of reading is comprehension (Daneman, Chapter 19 of this volume; Juel, Chapter 27 of this volume). Neither does an emphasis on the fundamental role of word recognition in models of reading necessarily translate into particular instructional practices. The interface between models of reading and instructional practices is so complex that instructional prescriptions cannot be assumed simply from a knowledge of which processes receive emphasis in a particular model of reading.

Nevertheless, skill at word recognition is so central to the total reading process that it can serve as a proxy diagnostic for instructional methods. That is, while it is possible for adequate word recognition skill to be accompanied by poor comprehension abilities, the converse virtually never occurs. It has never been empirically demonstrated, nor is it theoretically expected, that some instructional innovation could result in good reading comprehension without the presence of at least adequate word recognition ability. Since word recognition skill will be a by-product of any successful approach to developing reading ability—whether or not the approach specifically targets word recognition—lack of skill at recognizing words is always a reasonable predictor of difficulties in developing reading comprehension ability.

THE CENTRALITY OF WORD RECOGNITION: INDIVIDUAL DIFFERENCES

It has been amply documented that skill at recognizing words is strongly related to the speed of initial reading acquisition (Bertelson, 1986; Biemiller, 1977–1978; Curtis, 1980; Gough & Hillinger, 1980; Juel, this volume; Juel, Griffith, & Gough, 1986; Liberman, 1982; Perfetti, 1985; Rayner & Pollatsek, 1989; Stanovich, 1982, 1985, 1986b; Stanovich, Cunningham, & Feeman, 1984a). Additionally, there is evidence that this relationship is causal—that the development of word recognition skill leads to increases in reading comprehension ability (Biemiller, 1970; Blanchard, 1980; Chall, 1989; Herman, 1985; Lesgold, Resnick, & Hammond, 1985; Lomax, 1983; Stanovich, 1985); although the situation is undoubtedly characterized by reciprocal causation (Stanovich, 1986b). It is true, however, that as the general level of reading ability increases, the proportion of variance in reading ability accounted for by word recognition decreases and the proportion of variance in reading linked to listening comprehension abilities increases (Chall, 1983; Curtis, 1980; Daneman & Carpenter, 1980; Jackson & McClelland, 1979; Palmer, MacLeod, Hunt & Davidson, 1985; Stanovich, Cunningham, & Feeman, 1984a; Sticht & James, 1984).

Despite the fact that, at the more advanced levels of adult reading skill, comprehension ability becomes strongly related to listening abilities, even among adults, word recognition efficiency accounts for a sizable amount of variance in reading ability (Briggs & Underwood, 1982; Butler & Haines, 1979; Frederiksen, 1978; Liberman, Rubin, Duques, & Carlisle, 1985; Mason, 1978; Perfetti, 1985; Read & Ruyter, 1985; Scarborough, 1984). It is simply not accurate to imply that reading ability in adults is independent of word recognition skill, as does, for example, Thorndike (1973–1974), who argues, "At age 13 . . . reading is no longer—to any substantial degree—a decoding problem. . . . It is a thinking problem" (p. 145). This statement implies that, in adult readers, variance in reading ability cannot be linked to decoding skill, and it is empirically inaccurate.

Not only does word recognition skill correlate with reading comprehension ability in adults (Perfetti, 1985; Scarborough, 1984), it is actually an independent predictor. That is, word recognition skill predicts reading comprehension ability in adults even after variance due to listening comprehension ability has been partialled out. For example, Cunningham, Stanovich, and Wilson (in press) demonstrated that word-decoding skill accounted for significant additional variance in the reading comprehension ability of adult college readers even after measures of general intelligence, listening comprehension, sentence memory, and vocabulary were entered into a regression equation.

Efficient word recognition seems to be a necessary but not sufficient condition for good comprehension in adults, just as it is in children. While it is quite possible for an adult to have poor reading comprehension ability despite adequate word-decoding skills—probably due to deficient general listening comprehension skills—it is highly unlikely that excellent reading comprehension will be observed in the face of deficient word recognition skills. The reason for the dependence of comprehension processes on word recognition efficiency can be illustrated by looking at recent global models of the reading process, virtually all of which embody some type of hierarchical structure whereby the meanings activated by the successful recognition of words (the process of *lexical access*) are the building blocks for subsequent comprehension processes.

WORD RECOGNITION IN CONTEMPORARY MODELS OF READING

Recent models of the reading process diverge from the earlier "classic" bottom-up and top-down models in several ways. First, the newer conceptualizations are more data based than earlier frameworks. The latter were naturally more apt to be influenced by nonempirical philosophical preferences because they were developed in an era when there were far fewer empirical constraints on possible models (Gough, 1985; Stanovich, 1986b). Second, these more recent models have relaxed some of the more objectionably strong assumptions of the early top-down and bottom-up models.

For example, most current models more severely restrict where in the processing hierarchy expectancy-based, top-down processing can occur. Current models do not allow expectancy-based processing to influence feature extraction from words. Indeed, most current models largely restrict expectancy-based processing and hypothesis-testing mechanisms to the postlexical level (Henderson, 1982; Kintsch & Mross, 1985; Rayner & Pollatsek, 1989; Seidenberg, 1985b, 1985c; Stanovich, 1986b; Stanovich &

West, 1983a; Till, Mross, & Kintsch, 1988). Additionally, however, several long-standing assumptions contained in bottom-up views have been modified. The idea of strict sequentiality of processing stages—the assumption that a later stage could not begin to execute until earlier stages had run to completion—has been abandoned. Most models now assume a cascadelike (see McClelland, 1979) processing structure, where later stages may begin their computations before earlier stages have completed processing.

Two exemplary recent models—Just and Carpenter's (1980, 1987) production system model, READER; and Rayner and Pollatsek's (1989) model—are both notable for relying heavily on the empirical constraints derived from recent research on information processing during reading. The general architecture of the Just and Carpenter (1980, 1987) model is illustrated in Figure 16.1, although it has considerably more processing complications than can be captured in a schematic flow diagram (see Just & Carpenter, 1987). The heart of the model is a production system, which is a set of condition-action rules that operate on the contents of working memory. A particular production rule fires when it recognizes critical elements present in working memory. The production then carries out its particular operations, which could involve aspects of building a text structure or inserting new elements into working memory. Productions are executed in recognize-act cycles. During one such cycle the contents of working memory are simultaneously assessed by all the productions; and those productions, having their conditions satisfied, then simultaneously execute their functions. Executing productions alter the contents of various memory systems, thus readying the system for the next recognize-act cycle.

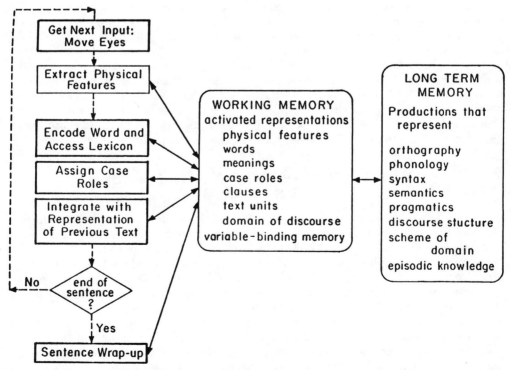

FIGURE 16.1   The Just and Carpenter (1987) model of reading. *Source:* From *The psychology of reading and language comprehension* by Marcel Just and Patricia Carpenter. Copyright © 1987 by Allyn & Bacon. Reprinted by permission.

While it is clear that the Just and Carpenter model incorporates substantial parallel processing and that the strict seriality of earlier bottom-up models (e.g., Gough, 1972) is violated, the architecture in Figure 16.1 does share certain features of bottom-up frameworks. Specifically, a stage of lexical access (the extraction of word meaning from the visual features) is demarcated, and later stages of case role assignment and text integration are dependent on the output from the lexical access stage because the processes of lexical access are inserting into working memory the results of their computations. This dependency explains why, in analyses of individual differences, efficiency of word recognition is a necessary but not sufficient condition for good comprehension.

A similar processing hierarchy is present in the model that Rayner and Pollatsek (1989) have developed, based on their extensive data using an eye-movement display technology where a computer manipulates the text contingent upon where the subject happens to be fixated. Unlike Just and Carpenter's model, which is a running computer simulation, Rayner and Pollatsek's model is summarized in a standard flow diagram (reproduced in Figure 16.2). To understand exactly how the model works, one must consult the extensive set of research findings contained in their excellent book. Nevertheless, the general framework is apparent from Figure 16.2. The model shares one key feature with the architecture of the Just and Carpenter (1987) model: the thematic processor is dependent on the outputs of the processes of lexical access. As in the Just and Carpenter model, individual differences in the efficiency of lexical access become reflected in differences in the outcomes of comprehension processes.

The empirical results that led theorists like Just and Carpenter (1987) and Rayner and Pollatsek (1989) to base their models on these types of processing architectures are varied, but most important were results from eye-movement experiments. One important result that is relevant to how we view the role of word recognition in reading is the finding that text is sampled in a fairly dense manner during reading. Research using various eye-movement methodologies is consistent in indicating that the vast majority of content words in text receive a direct visual fixation (Balota, Pollatsek, & Rayner, 1985; Hogaboam, 1983; Just & Carpenter, 1980, 1987; Pollatsek, Rayner, & Balota, 1986; Rayner & Pollatsek, 1989). Short function words and highly predictable words are more likely to be skipped, but even many of these are fixated. Additionally, research has indicated that nonfixated words may be processed to a certain extent in parafoveal vision (Rayner & Pollatsek, 1989). In short, the sampling of visual information in reading, as indicated by fixation points, is relatively dense. Readers do not engage in the wholesale skipping of words during reading. One reason for the dense sampling of visual information in reading is that the span of effective visual information during a fixation is quite small—contrary to the bogus claims of the advocates of many "speed-reading" courses.

The study of the processing of visual information within a fixation has indicated that the visual array is rather completely processed during each fixation. This appears to be true even when the word is highly predictable (Ehrlich & Rayner, 1981; McConkie & Zola, 1981; Balota, et al., 1985; Zola, 1984). Summarizing their experiments on the processing of words varying in predictability, Balota et al. (1985) stated:

> There is little doubt (as indicated by the present production task norms) that subjects could have guessed the next word in our example sentence to be *cake* based on relatively ambiguous parafoveal information (*cahc*). However, because of the dynamics of the eye-movement system in reading, the subjects usually waited until their eyes directly fixated the target to identify it. . . . It appears that subjects were not likely to make a strong commitment about ambiguous parafoveal information even when the target words were highly predictable from the sentence context. . . . Thus, the data contradict a view of reading wherein expectations and predictions about forthcoming information are primary and visual information is there merely for confirmation. (pp. 387–388)

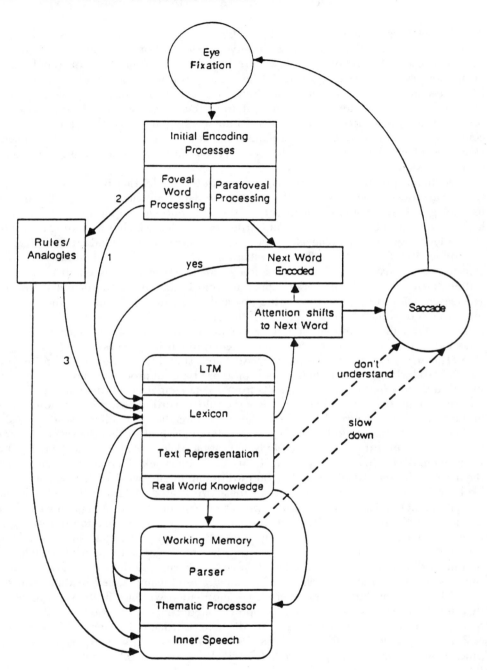

FIGURE 16.2   The Rayner and Pollatsek (1989) model of reading. *Source:* From *The psychology of reading* by K. Rayner and A. Pollatsek, p. 473. Copyright © 1989 by Prentice-Hall, Englewood Cliffs, NJ. Reprinted by permission of Prentice-Hall, Inc.

An important study by Rayner and Bertera (1979) demonstrated that efficient reading is dependent on a detailed sampling of the visual information in the text. Using the contingent display possibilities afforded by modern computer technology, they had subjects read text while a computer masked one letter in their foveal vision on each fixation. The loss of this *single letter* reduced reading speed by 50 percent. Clearly, efficient reading depended on the visual information contained in each of the individual letters that were within foveal vision. Based on the results from a related experiment, Zola (1984) concluded, "Readers apparently notice small distinctions among letters within the region of text falling on the fovea, even from words that are almost completely predictable from the preceding context. . . . Readers notice specific letter information, down to small distinctions among letters" (p. 281).

These research findings indicate that the often-repeated conjecture that the visual information in text is almost of secondary importance (e.g., "it is clear that the better reader barely looks at the individual words on the page," Smith, 1973, p. 190) is quite patently false. Consistent with the outcome of studies of individual differences in reading comprehension, information-processing analyses of the reading process and eye-movement studies have indicated that word recognition is a fundamental component of reading comprehension.

Finally, although it is sometimes asserted that word recognition commonly occurs without necessarily accessing meaning, in fact, there is no research evidence indicating that activating a word's phonological or orthographic code often takes place without meaning extraction, even in poor readers. To the contrary, a substantial body of evidence indicates that, even for young children, word decoding automatically leads to semantic activation (Bentin & Katz, 1984; Ehri, 1977; Guttentag, 1984; Guttentag & Haith, 1978, 1980; Goodman, Haith, Guttentag, & Rao, 1985; Kraut & Smothergill, 1980; Parkin, 1984; Rosinski, 1977)—*provided*, of course, that the meaning of the word is adequately established in memory. Forgetting the latter stricture is, of course, what has led to the misconstrued discussions of the so-called phenomenon of "word calling" that still plague the literature on reading acquisition (see Stanovich, 1986b, for a complete discussion of this issue).

Having outlined the reasons why reading theorists have given processes of word recognition a central role in their models, we will now turn to some of the fundamental questions that have motivated research. Three such questions have been central to research on word recognition since the beginning of empirical investigations into reading: (1) Is word recognition an automatic process in fluent adult readers? (2) What is the role of context in word recognition during reading? and (3) To what extent is phonological coding implicated in word recognition? These questions remain the focus of intense research effort, although the theoretical frameworks for viewing the questions have been shifting somewhat in recent years. As will be discussed, we now have not only more accurate empirical evidence on these issues, but also better ways to phrase the questions.

IS WORD RECOGNITION AUTOMATIC?

Most major concepts that are used in current reading theory can be traced back to Huey's (1908/1968) classic work (see Henderson, 1987), and the concept of *automaticity* is no exception:

> Perceiving being an act, it is, like all other things that we do, performed more easily with each repetition of the act. To perceive an entirely new word or other combination of strokes requires considerable time, close attention, and it is likely to be imperfectly done, just as when we attempt some new combination of movements, some new trick in the gymnasium or new "serve" at tennis. In either case, repetition progressively frees the mind from attention to details, makes facile the total act, shortens the time, and reduces the extent to which consciousness must concern itself with the process. (p. 104)

As many histories of the study of reading have noted (Venezky, 1977), after Huey there was darkness—the behaviorist era led to a decrease in the type of cognitive theorizing about the reading process evident throughout Huey's work. The concept of automaticity was resurrected after the cognitive revolution, largely due to a paper by LaBerge and Samuels (1974) that reintroduced the concept into reading theory. At the very beginning of their paper, LaBerge and Samuels (1974) outlined the basic limited-capacity argument for the importance of automaticity that was accepted, either explicitly or implicitly, by reading researchers throughout most of the subsequent decade:

> During the execution of a complex skill, it is necessary to coordinate many component processes within a very short period of time. If each component process requires attention, performance of the complex skill will be impossible, because the capacity of attention will be exceeded. But if enough of the components and their coordinations can be processed automatically, then the loads on attention will be within tolerable limits and the skill can be successfully performed. Therefore, one of the prime issues in the study of a complex skill such as reading is to determine how the processing of component subskills becomes automatic. (p. 293)

Several assumptions in LaBerge and Samuels' treatment became canonical for many reading researchers. First, their theory assumed a strong demarcation between word recognition processes and all postlexical processing, because it was assumed that most, if not all, postlexical comprehension processes would be resource-demanding and probably would not be good candidates for the development of acquired automaticity (in general—see Perfetti, 1985, pp. 102–106; Perfetti & Curtis, 1986). Most demonstrations of acquired automaticity thus focused on prelexical processes such as feature extraction, orthographic segmentation, and phonological coding. The examples in the classic LaBerge and Samuels paper were all of this type. Few assumptions about how capacity was allocated postlexically were made. Instead, it was merely assumed that whatever the distribution of postlexical capacity allocation, the key to optimal processing at this level was the reallocation of unneeded capacity from lower levels via the acquired automaticity of lexical access.

Interestingly, however, when LaBerge and Samuels (1974) attempted to operationalize their concept of automatic processing, they chose not to tackle directly the measurement problems inherent in assessing resource-free processing. Instead, they chose a correlated characteristic of capacity-free processing: *obligatory execution*, the tendency for an automatized process to execute regardless of where the conscious attention of the subject is directed. Specifically, they argued: "Our criterion for deciding when a skill or subskill is automatic is that it can complete its processing while attention is directed elsewhere" (p. 295).

This particular choice was to have important consequences for the subsequent history of the automaticity concept in reading theory. LaBerge and Samuels had implicitly equated the obligatory nature of an automatic process—its unconscious triggering and ballistic execution—with capacity-free processing. In addition, the use of processing resources was conflated with the idea of conscious attention and, conversely, lack of conscious attention was viewed as synonymous with resource-free processing. Only later was the necessity of theoretically separating the issues of obligatory execution, resource use, and conscious attention fully recognized (Humphreys, 1985; Logan, 1985; Paap & Ogden, 1981; Stanovich, in press).

LaBerge and Samuels' original paper relied heavily on the *catch-trial technique* to demonstrate the properties of an automatic process. Generically, this methodology involves surprising the subjects with a few "catch trials" interspersed randomly within a sequence of trials that have oriented the subject's attention to some other stimulus. When the catch-trial stimulus appears, the subject has to reorient attention to that stimulus and remember precisely what he/she had been instructed to do with it. This attentional reorientation presumably takes some finite amount of time. The key manipulation concerns the prior familiarity with the catch-trial stimuli. The assumption is that only if the catch-trial stimulus was automatized would processing take place during the attentional shift. Nonautomatized stimuli, in contrast, would have to wait for the attentional shift to be complete before processing of them could begin. LaBerge and Samuels (1974) presented several examples of different sets of stimuli that were processed equivalently when given direct attention, but that resulted in differential performance (in favor of the familiar stimuli) when the attentional reorientation of the catch-trial procedure was required. Additionally, LaBerge and Samuels demonstrated that the performance difference between such stimulus sets decreased as the non-automatized set received more practice.

Another paradigm that has been employed extensively as an index of automaticity is the Stroop paradigm, which seems to straightforwardly operationalize the idea of stimulus processing while attention is directed elsewhere. In the generic Stroop paradigm (see Dyer, 1973; La Heij, 1988) the subject must respond by naming a simple property of a stimulus (naming the color of a patch, the name of a line drawing, or the number of items in an array), while in close proximity is a verbal stimulus (e.g., written word) that conflicts with the required response (e.g., the word *blue* written on a red patch to which the subject must respond by saying *red*). Automatic word recognition is inferred by the lengthened response time in the conflict situation compared to the baseline situation, where there is no conflicting verbal stimulus. The interference caused by the conflicting written word becomes an index of automaticity via the argument that the Stroop task reflects the obligatory (indeed, unwanted) processing of the word even though the subject's attention is directed elsewhere. Actually, the Stroop task seems to be an extreme case of the "processing while attention is directed elsewhere" logic, because after several trials, most subjects are actively attempting (unsuccessfully) to *ignore* the written word.

By the early 1980s, however, experiments that had employed variants of the Stroop task and that had examined developmental and reading-skill trends had uncovered a puzzling theoretical problem. Numerous studies (e.g., Ehri & Wilce, 1979; Guttentag & Haith, 1978, 1980; Posnansky & Rayner, 1977; Schadler & Thissen, 1981; Stanovich, Cunningham, & West, 1981; West & Stanovich, 1978, 1979) had indicated that automatic word recognition developed remarkably early. At least for words of moderate to high frequency (most current accounts emphasize that it is stimuli, not processes, that become automatized; see Logan, 1988; Perfetti, in press), robust indications of automaticity were present by the middle of the first-grade year, and by second or third grade many Stroop indicators of automaticity were at asymptote. This finding was at odds with the general (although mainly untested) assumption that the development of automatic word recognition skills was a mechanism that fueled comprehension increases for a long period of fluency acquisition.

Differentiating Components of Automaticity

What the puzzling developmental findings actually indicated was that the idea of obligatory/intentionless processing and that of resource-free processing had been too readily conflated in discussions of the automaticity concept. Direct experimental evidence supporting such a criticism was contained in the work of Paap and Ogden (1981; Ogden, Martin, & Paap, 1980). These investigators employed the dual-task methodology that had been used by experimental psychologists to index the differential capacity used by various cognitive processes. Posner and Boies (1971) did some of the seminal work that demonstrated the utility of the technique. The methodology involves defining a primary task, the cognitive components of which are to be assessed for capacity usage. Subjects become practiced at completing the primary task, while sometimes responding to a probe (or secondary task) that occurs on random trials during the execution of the primary task. The probe is usually something like a white-noise tone to which the subject makes a single predetermined response, usually a button press. The reaction time to the probe becomes an index of the relative capacity usage of the primary-task processes occurring at the time of probe onset. The slower the reaction time to the probe (compared to a baseline where only the secondary task is being performed), the more cognitive capacity the overlapping process in the primary task is assumed to draw.

Paap and Ogden (1981) superimposed a probe task on a letter-matching task and found that basic letter-encoding processes were not entirely free from capacity utilization, even though they displayed the characteristic of obligatory processing. Paap and Ogden (1981) concluded, "With respect to letter encoding, an automatic process is usually defined as a process that occurs without intention and without interfering with a concurrent secondary task. . . . The most significant general conclusion that can be drawn from these experiments is that the criteria of obligatory processing and interference-free processing should be disassociated" (p. 518). Subsequent studies with the dual-task methodology have extended Paap and Ogden's (1981) conclusion from letters to words. It appears that although word recognition is an obligatory process (Bentin & Katz, 1984), it nevertheless seems to demand some attentional capacity (Herdman & Dobbs, 1989). Also, low-frequency words seem to require more attentional capacity than high-frequency words (Becker, 1976; Herdman & Dobbs, 1989), even though both are recognized on an obligatory basis.

Results like those of Paap and Ogden (1981) made researchers reconsider the linkages assumed in the automaticity framework that had been outlined by LaBerge and Samuels. Subsequent work has reinforced the conclusion that the standard criteria for automaticity do not completely converge (Humphreys, 1985; Kahneman & Chajcyzk, 1983; Kahneman & Treisman, 1984; Logan, 1985; Zbrodoff & Logan, 1986). In particular, processes that are obligatory—in that they are executed in the presence of the appropriate stimulus, regardless of the direction of attention or of conscious intent—may still utilize cognitive resources. Thus, it cannot be assumed that measures of obligatory processing—such as the Stroop task—are direct indicators of capacity usage.

The dissociation between automaticity criteria demonstrated in the Paap and Ogden (1981) work dissolves the seeming paradox in the developmental studies employing the Stroop task. It appears that obligatory execution of word recognition processes develops quite rapidly, but that the speed and efficiency of execution, in terms of decreasing resource use, continue to develop even after recognition has become obligatory (Herdman & Dobbs, 1989). Early theorists had described automatic processes as being fast, unconscious, obligatory, and effortless and had implied that these properties were almost totally redundant. More recent theorizing has favored the position expressed by Zbrodoff and Logan (1986): "There are no strong theoretical reasons to believe in the unity of automaticity. The idea that the various properties should co-occur has not been deduced from established theoretical principles, although a number of theorists . . . have asserted it as if it were fact" (p. 118).

Developmental work has confirmed the finding that speed, obligatory processing, and capacity usage are at least partially dissociable. For example, it is clear that children's word recognition speed continues to decrease even after Stroop indices of obligatory processing are at asymptote (Ehri & Wilce, 1979; Stanovich, Cunningham, & West, 1981). In addition, Manis and colleagues (Horn & Manis, 1987; Manis, Keating, & Morrison, 1980) have extended the use of the dual-task probe technique to children and found that this index of capacity usage does not track either the development of speed or the development of obligatory processing. Horn and Manis (1987) extended the work of Paap and Ogden (1981) by employing words as stimuli and testing first, second, third, and fifth graders. They argued that word recognition was obligatory but also capacity demanding, and they concluded, "there may be a developmental asynchrony between automaticity in the sense of obligatory processing (Stroop-type test) and automaticity in the sense of limited attentional allocation" (p. 106).

Most recent research has thus focused on individual components of the several dissociable properties once lumped together under the automaticity rubric. The issue of resource usage has separated from issues of speed and obligatory execution. The moral of the experimental work with adults (Herdman & Dobbs, 1989; Humphreys, 1985; Logan, 1985; Paap & Ogden, 1981; Zbrodoff & Logan, 1986) and with children (Ehri & Wilce, 1979; Horn & Manis, 1987; Manis et al., 1980; Stanovich, Cunningham, & West, 1981) is that Stroop interference cannot safely be used as a proxy measure of resource use because it is tapping a partially dissociable aspect of automaticity. Similarly, speed of execution is not synonymous with either obligatory execution or capacity usage. Although we would surely expect some intercorrelations among these properties, each must be theoretically differentiated and measured with separate techniques. For example, while the capacity used by word recognition appears to decrease as reading skill increases, even the word recognition processes of fluent adults do seem to utilize some capacity, even though they execute in an obligatory fashion.

The Question Reframed: The Concept of Modularity

The result of the more refined theoretical differentiation of the automaticity concept was that after almost 10 years of popularity, resource-based theories of reading—to which the automaticity concept is tied—became less the focus of research interest. The assumption that relative resource use is the most important dimension of the generic automaticity concept has been questioned. Recent theory has focused on an alternative (but related) construct that reframes the traditional questions about automaticity somewhat

This shift in theoretical emphasis is reflected in the considerable influence that Fodor's (1983) concept of modularity has had on reading theory. The enormous attention garnered by Fodor's book, *The Modularity of Mind*, contributed to a trend already discernible in theories about individual differences in reading skill: a shift from cognitive resource use to knowledge representation.

Fodor's concept of modularity, like the related concept of automaticity, is a complex construct that conjoins a number of separate properties (Forster, 1979; Humphreys, 1985; Logan, 1985; Stanovich, 1990). The key property distinguishing modular processes from central, nonmodular ones is whether a particular process is directed by expectancies based on prior knowledge structures stored in long-term memory. The situation where previously stored world knowledge does not influence the process in question has been termed *information encapsulation* by Fodor. It is the defining feature of the modular process, according to his view. In Fodor's conceptualization, other properties—such as fast execution, domain specificity, and obligatory execution—tend to concur with information encapsulation. Central processes, according to Fodor (1983), have the converse set of properties. They are slow acting, domain general, under strategic control, and, most importantly, informationally unencapsulated.

The reader should be warned that, in recent theoretical writings in cognitive science, the property of information encapsulation has travelled under a variety of different names. Humphreys (1985) mentions some of these in his discussion of encapsulation:

> If word processing does proceed involuntarily on at least some occasions, there are some interesting implications concerning the control of such operations. For instance, one possibility is that control operates locally so that once a set of word-processing procedures is activated, it runs to completion and cannot be amended by other higher order processes (i.e., it is "cognitively impenetrable"; see Pylyshyn, 1981). Such processes may be termed functionally autonomous (Forster, 1979). An implication of this is that word processing cannot be benefited by other ongoing processes (e.g., see Fodor, 1983). This is a different prediction from that which holds that the effects of word processing cannot be prevented (cf. the argument that processing is involuntary), since it is feasible that subjects are unable to prevent a particular process but they may still supplement it when required. (pp. 292–293)

Thus, informational encapsulation (or the synonymous terms "functional autonomy" and "cognitive impenetrability") means that the operation of a processing module is not controlled by higher-level operations or supplemented by information from knowledge structures not contained in the module itself. Importantly, low resource use is not a defining feature of a modular process, as it was in early theorizing about automaticity. Fodor (1985) is at pains to point out that his modern version of a "vertical faculty psychology" does not share Gall's definition of lack of competition for horizontal resources: "I take the essential fact about modularity to be *informational* (not resource) encapsulation" (p. 37). Instead, it is the property of information encapsulation that is the defining feature of a modular process. According to Fodor, "The claim that input systems are informationally encapsulated is equivalent to the claim that the data that can bear on the confirmation of perceptual hypotheses include . . . considerably less than the organism may know. That is, the confirmation function for input systems does not have access to all of the information that the organism internally represents; there are restrictions upon the allocation of internally represented information to input processes" (1983, p. 69). Seidenberg (1985a, 1985c) has emphasized how modularity acts as a constraint on the interactivity of processing (see also Navon, in press) and how the more encapsulation that is built into an interactive model the more falsifiable it will be, a desirable feature in a reading model since almost all of our theoretical formalisms are too powerful (Tanenhaus, Dell, & Carlson, 1987).

Fodor (1983) views processes such as basic speech perception and fact perception as candidates for modular input systems and in his book cites numerous instances of where, in these domains, "at least *some* of the background information at the subject's disposal is inaccessible to at least some of his perceptual mechanisms" (p. 66). Although Fodor rejects the idea of acquired modularity and equivocates in applying the modularity concept to reading, many other cognitive scientists have endorsed the idea of acquired modularity as theoretically coherent (Forster, 1979; Humphreys, 1985; Logan, 1985; McLeod, McLaughlin, & Nimmo-Smith, 1985; Perfetti & McCutchen, 1987; Seidenberg, 1985b, 1985c; Sternberg, 1985). Others have applied the modularity concept to the process of word recognition and its development (Forster, 1979; Kintsch & Mross, 1985; Perfetti, in press; Perfetti & McCutchen, 1987; Stanovich, 1986b, 1987, 1988b; Stanovich, Nathan, West, & Vala-Rossi, 1985; Stanovich & West, 1983a; West & Stanovich, 1988). Interestingly, perhaps more actual empirical work has been done in the acquired domain of visual word recognition than in some of the other hypothesized modular domains that Fodor (1983) originally championed. In addition, it should also be noted that the theoretical claims in the area of visual word recognition have been more restricted to questions of the nature of information encapsulation (Seidenberg, 1985b, 1985c; Stanovich & West, 1983a) and have not generally included the more far-reaching and tenuous claims that Fodor makes in his conceptualization of modularity (e.g., innateness, hard-wiring, specific ontogenic sequencing).

Why Modularity?

If informational encapsulation, as much as the issue of resource allocation, has become the focus of current theories of reading ability, then we must address the issue of how encapsulation facilitates the process of reading. In short, we may ask the question of why information encapsulation is a benefit to a processing system engaged in a task like reading.

Discussing the computer analogy to human information processing that is popular in some domains of cognitive science, Fodor (1983) argues that researchers have inappropriately deemphasized the importance of making contact with the environment and have overly focused on self-contained computational systems. In his words, "the sole determinants of their computations are the current machine state, the tape configuration, and the program, the rest of the world being quite irrelevant to the character of their performance; whereas, of course, organisms are forever exchanging information with their environments" (p. 39). What follows, according to Fodor, is "What perception must do . . . to so represent the world . . . as to make it available to thought" (p. 40). In short, higher-level processing operations and inference-making processes will work more efficiently when perceptual processes deliver to them accurate representations of the world. The types of perceptual processes that do this best are modular ones—input systems that fire without accessing all of the organism's background information and beliefs. Modular cognitive processes are like reflexes in that "they go off largely without regard to the beliefs and utilities of the behaving organism" (Fodor, 1985, p. 2).

Modular processes are thus isolated from background knowledge, belief, and set. This confers two great advantages. One is the veridicality that results from the organism's ability to code—at least at some level—the features of the environment without distortion. As Fodor, in his inimitable style, points out: "The ecological good sense of this arrangement is surely self-evident. Prejudiced and wishful seeing makes for dead animals" (1985, p. 2). The second advantage—that of speed—follows along these same lines: "Automatic processes are, in a certain sense, deeply unintelligent; of the whole range of computational . . . options available to the organism, only a stereotyped subset is brought into play. But what you save by this sort of stupidity is *not having to make up your mind*, and making your mind up takes time" (1983, p. 64).

Referring to Ogden Nash's "If you're called by a panther/don't anther," Fodor argues that what the organism needs is a panther identification mechanism that is fast and that errs only on the side of false positives. Thus, "we do not want to have to access panther-identification information from the (presumably very large) central storage . . . on the assumption that large memories are searched slowly" (p. 70). In fact, even if such access were fast, it would not be efficacious because "the property of being 'about panthers' is not one that can be surefootedly relied upon. Given enough context, practically everything I know can be construed as panther related; and I do not want to have to consider everything I know in the course of perceptual panther identification. . . . The primary point is to so restrict the number of confirmation relations that need to be estimated as to make perceptual identifications fast" (p. 71). . . . "Feedback is effective only to the extent that, *prior* to the analysis of the stimulus, the perceiver knows quite a lot about what the stimulus is going to be like. Whereas, the point of perception is surely that it lets us find out how the world is even when the world is some way that we don't expect it to be" (p. 67).

In short, an advantage accrues to encapsulation *when the specificity and efficiency of stimulus-analyzing mechanisms is great relative to the diagnosticity of the background information that might potentially be recruited to aid recognition.* This is a point that has fundamental importance for reading theory, as we will now outline.

THE ROLE OF CONTEXT
IN WORD RECOGNITION

The debate in the cognitive science literature regarding the benefits of encapsulation finds immediate correspondence with issues in the reading literature. One of Fodor's (1983, 1985) recurring themes was that "poverty of the stimulus" arguments inherited from the "New Look" period of perceptual research had led cognitive psychology astray. An analogous trend has characterized reading theory during the last two decades (see Kintsch, 1988).

Models of reading acquisition and individual differences in reading ability were dominated for a considerable time by top-down conceptualizations (e.g., Smith, 1971) that borrowed heavily from the New Look movement in perceptual research (Henderson, 1987). These models strongly emphasized the contribution of expectancies and contextual information. According to such models, the word recognition process was heavily penetrated by background knowledge and higher-level cognitive expectancies. However, it appears that reading theory—at least regarding word recognition—went wrong in exactly the same ways as did perceptual theory in cognitive psychology.

First, "poverty of the stimulus" arguments were overgeneralized. Reading theorists were considerably influenced by analysis-by-synthesis models of speech perception, and interactive models of recognition that derived from artificial intelligence work in speech perception (Rumelhart, 1977). The problem here is that the analogy to written language is not apt. The ambiguity in decontextualized speech is well known. For example, excised words from normal conversation are often not recognized out of context. This does not hold for written language, obviously. A fluent reader can identify written words with near-perfect accuracy out of context. In short, the physical stimulus alone completely specifies the lexical representation in writing, whereas this is not always true in speech. The greater diagnosticity of the external stimulus in reading, as opposed to listening, puts a greater premium on an input system that can deliver a complete representation of the stimulus to higher-level cognitive systems.

Another problem concerns the assumptions that have been made about the properties of contextual information. Laboratory demonstrations of contextual priming effects have often led to an overestimation of the magnitude of facilitation to be expected from contextual information (see below), because these studies—often for sound theoretical reasons—employed stimulus materials that had strong semantic associations and that were vastly more predictable on a word-by-word basis than in natural text (Gough, 1983; Stanovich & West, 1983b). Also, it is often incorrectly assumed that predicting upcoming words in sentences is a relatively easy and highly accurate activity. Actually, many different empirical studies have indicated that naturalistic text is not all that predictable. Alford (1980) found that for a set of SAT-type passages, subjects needed an average of more than four guesses to correctly anticipate upcoming words in the passage (the method of scoring actually makes this a considerable underestimate). Across a variety of subject populations and texts, a reader's probability of predicting the next word in a passage is usually between .20 and .35 (Aborn, Rubenstein, & Sterling, 1959; Gough, 1983; Miller & Coleman, 1967; Perfetti, Goldman, & Hogaboam, 1979; Rubenstein & Aborn, 1958). Indeed, as Gough (1983) has shown, this figure is highest for function words and is often quite low for the very words in the passage that carry the most information content.

Thus, we have in reading precisely the situation where an enormous advantage accrues to encapsulation: the potential specificity of stimulus-analyzing mechanisms is great relative to the diagnosticity of the background information that might potentially be recruited to aid recognition. In short, a consideration of the stimulus ecology of the reading task has led an increasing number of investigators to endorse the idea of the acquired modularity of the word recognition module. But what does empirical evidence show?

Empirical Studies of Context Effects

Before reviewing the research evidence, however, it is imperative to highlight the issue of levels of processing, because failure to emphasize this principle has confused the literature on the effects of context for so long. For example, there *is* considerable evidence that better readers are better able to use contextual information to facilitate their comprehension processes (Baker & Brown, 1984; Stanovich & Cunningham, in press). However, research in recent years has shown that hypotheses about context use as an individual difference variable were inappropriately generalized to the *word recognition* level. That is, the hypothesis that the superior word recognition skills of the better reader were due to their superior context-use skills—a hypothesis that once had great popularity in the reading literature—is now known to be false. This is not the explanation for the more efficient word recognition of the better reader.

In understanding how context-use skills operate in reading, it is absolutely essential to differentiate levels in the processing system (Schustack, Ehrlich, & Rayner, 1987). Otherwise, we will be prone to mistaken inferences and theoretical confusion. Failure to observe this stricture is precisely why the reading literature on context use remained confused for so long. It turns out that contextual abilities are a potent source of differences in comprehension skills among children, but they are not—as implied in many of the top-down models of reading—a potent source of the individual differences observed in word recognition skills.

Studies employing a wide variety of paradigms have failed to find that good readers rely more on context for word recognition than poorer readers. Many discrete-trial reaction-time studies of context effects have been conducted to investigate this question. Most of these studies have used priming paradigms where a context (sometimes a word, sometimes a sentence, and sometimes several sentences or paragraphs) precedes a target word to which the subject must make a naming or lexical decision response. Although this paradigm does not completely isolate the word recognition level of processing (Balota & Chumbley, 1985; Seidenberg, Waters, Sanders, & Langer, 1984; West & Stanovich, 1982, 1986), it does so more than most other methodologies that have been used. The finding has consistently been that not only do the poorer readers in these studies use context, but they often show somewhat larger contextual effects than do the better readers (Becker, 1985; Briggs, Austin, & Underwood, 1984; Perfetti, 1985; Pring & Snowling, 1986; Schvaneveldt, Ackerman, & Semlear, 1977; Schwantes, 1985; Simpson & Foster, 1986; Simpson, Lorsbach, & Whitehouse, 1983; Stanovich, 1980, 1986b; Stanovich, et al., 1985; Stanovich, West & Feeman, 1981; West & Stanovich, 1978).

Some investigators have employed oral reading error analyses in order to examine individual differences in the use of context to facilitate word recognition. However, the use of the technique for this purpose is problematic because oral reading errors often implicate levels of processing beyond word recognition (Bowey, 1985; Kibby, 1979; Leu, 1982; Wixson, 1979). For example, self-corrections, in part, reflect comprehension monitoring. Nevertheless, analyses of initial substitution errors have been used to throw light on the issue of the facilitation of word recognition by context, and it is likely that these errors do partially implicate processes operating at the word recognition level. Fortunately, the results of oral reading error studies largely converge with those of reaction-time studies. When skilled and less-skilled readers are in materials of comparable difficulty (an important control, see Stanovich, 1986b), the reliance on contextual information relative to graphic information is just as great—in many cases greater—for the less-skilled readers (Allington & Fleming, 1978; Biemiller, 1970, 1979; Harding, 1984; Juel, 1980; Lesgold, Resnick, & Hammond, 1985; Leu, DeGroff, & Simons, 1986; Nicholson & Hill, 1985; Nicholson, Lillas, & Rzoska, 1988; Perfetti & Roth, 1981; Richardson, DiBenedetto, & Adler, 1982; Simons & Leu, 1987; Whaley & Kibby, 1981). The results from studies of text disruption effects, timed text reading, and a variety of other paradigms also display a similar pattern (Allington & Strange, 1977; Biemiller, 1977–1978; Ehrlich, 1981; Lovett, 1986; Schwartz & Stanovich, 1981; Stanovich, Cunningham, & Feeman, 1984b; Strange, 1979). Thus, the results from a variety of different paradigms indicate that the effects of background knowledge and contextual information attenuate as the efficiency of word recognition processes increases.

The consistent trend indicating that contextual effects on word recognition decrease as reading skill increases has led several theorists to conceptualize the logic of contextual facilitation on word recognition as compensatory in nature (Durgunoglu, 1988; Perfetti, 1985; Perfetti & Roth, 1981; Stanovich, 1980, 1986b). It is hypothesized that the information-processing system is arranged in such a way that when the bottom-up stimulus analysis processes that result in word recognition are deficient, the system compensates by relying more heavily on other knowledge sources (e.g., contextual information). In terms of Fodor's (1983) conceptualization, data on developmental trends and individual differences seem to indicate that the word recognition module becomes more encapsulated—able to execute without recruiting background knowledge or employing expectancy-based processing—at the higher levels of reading skill.

We will see that this conclusion from work on individual differences in word recognition and context use meshes nicely with the research findings generated by investigators who have focused on the word recognition performance of fluent adult readers. For example, early experiments employing reaction-time priming paradigms seemed to indicate that the magnitude of semantic context effects on word recognition was quite large (Becker & Killion, 1977; Fischler, 1977; Meyer, Schvaneveldt, & Ruddy, 1975; Neely, 1977; Schuberth & Eimas, 1977; Stanovich & West, 1979, 1981; West & Stanovich, 1978). However, subsequent investigators (e.g., Gough, 1983; Stanovich & West, 1983b) emphasized that—often for sound reasons following from theory—many of these studies employed materials that were highly predictable and loaded with semantic associates. While the nature of these stimulus materials followed logically from the particular aspects of the cognitive models being tested, the magnitude of the context effects observed in such experiments should not be extrapolated into estimates of the actual magnitude of contextual effects in the reading of normal text. Indeed, experiments that have employed materials more representative of the text read by fluent adults have indicated that the actual magnitude of the context effect on the average word in text is extremely small, a matter of a few milliseconds (Forster, 1981; Gough, Alford, & Holley-Wilcox, 1981; Henderson, 1982; Mitchell, 1982; Mitchell & Green, 1978; Stanovich & West, 1983b).

Similarly, it has been argued that many of the early experiments on context effects employed paradigms that introduced fairly long time intervals between the reading of the context and the response to the target word (Mitchell, 1982; Mitchell & Green, 1978; Stanovich, 1981; Stanovich & West, 1983b). These unusually long intervals may allow the subject to employ conscious prediction strategies that would be precluded during normal reading due to the speed of ongoing word recognition. Experiments that have eliminated these unusually long intervals have observed results indicating that context effects on word recognition are markedly reduced (Ehrlich & Rayner, 1981; Mitchell, 1982; Mitchell & Green, 1978; Rayner & Pollatsek, 1989; Stanovich, 1981; Zola, 1984).

The result of these and many other experiments (Foss, 1988; Henderson, 1982; Mitchell, 1982; Rayner & Pollatsek, 1989; Schustack, Ehrlich, & Rayner, 1987; Stanovich et al., 1985; Stanovich & West, 1983a; Till et al., 1988) have led most current theorists to deemphasize the importance of context effects on the ongoing word recognition processes of fluent adult readers. The small effects of context that are observed appear to be largely due to automatic spreading activation in semantic memory, rather than conscious predictive expectancies. Spreading activation based on associative connections is a within-module effect and does not violate the notion of encapsulation (Fodor, 1983; Masson, in press; Seidenberg, 1985b; Tanenhaus & Lucas, 1987). It appears that conscious strategies of contextual prediction do not normally guide lexical access in the fluent reader. Spreading activation from closely associated words can briefly facilitate recognition via spreading activation, but situations where such associates occur close enough together are rare in actual text (Forster, 1979, 1981; Henderson, 1982).

The results of studies like those just reviewed led Foss (1988) to conclude his review of this literature in the *Annual Review of Psychology* by stating, "Results also suggest that there are strong limits on the usefulness of the priming phenomena when interpreted as an aid to lexical access" (p. 314). . . . "The bulk of the evidence suggests that there can be facilitation from one lexical item to associated items, but that at normal rates of listening and reading there is little if any contextual influence on lexical access" (p. 316). Foss (1988) thus joins many other recent theorists who emphasize the considerable extent to which the word recognition processes of fluent adults display acquired modularity (Gough, 1983; Henderson, 1982; Kintsch & Mross, 1985; Masson, 1988; Seidenberg, 1985b; Stanovich, 1986b, 1988b; Stanovich et al., 1985; Stanovich & West, 1983a; see, however, Schwanenflugel & LaCount, 1988; Simpson, Peterson, Casteel, & Burgess, 1989).

Of course, compensatory processing guarantees quite a different situation for novice readers. For them, background knowledge and expectancies are much more likely to penetrate the word recognition module during lexical access. Finally, although Foss's (1988) conclusion about the relative modularity of the word recognition module appears to be correct, it should be emphasized that there is evidence that context can have very early occurring *postlexical* effects (Kutas & Hillyard, 1980, 1983, 1984; Masson, 1986; Schustack et al., 1987; Van Petten & Kutas, 1987), because lexical access in the fluent adult can be complete within 100 to 200 milliseconds after fixation on a word (Gough & Cosky, 1977; Kramer & Donchin, 1987; Rayner & Pollatsek, 1989; Sabol & DeRosa, 1976).

In summary, current theories of fluent reading are quite interestingly bifurcated. The idea that background knowledge should saturate central processes of text inferencing, comprehension monitoring, and global interpretation is now widely accepted (Anderson & Pearson, 1984; Paris, 1987; Paris, Lipson, & Wixson, 1983; Spiro, Bruce, & Brewer, 1980; Wixson & Peters, 1987). At the same time the advantage of modularly organized word recognition processes is acknowledged. Indeed, the dangers of cognitive penetrability at too low a level have become apparent in discussions of nonaccommodating reading styles (Kimmel & MacGinitie, 1984; Maria & MacGinitie, 1982; Stanovich & Cunningham, in press). As Evans and Carr (1985) point out:

> If print-specific encoding mechanisms send incomplete or erroneous data to the language comprehension processes, what could result but an incomplete or erroneous understanding of the text? In addition, the more powerful the language skills that are applied to the erroneous data, the greater the chance that a seemingly acceptable interpretation can be constructed. (p. 342)

Of course, there is an analogy here to Fodor's "panther detector." The organism is much better off with a correct rendition of the stimulus as opposed to a sloppy stimulus representation and a geometric explosion of "panther-related" general information. Similarly, the reader is better off having the proper lexical entry activated.

PROCESSING WITHIN THE WORD RECOGNITION MODULE: PHONOLOGICAL CODING

The issue of information encapsulation concerns how enclosed and isolated the word recognition module is from other information that could possibly be used to aid recognition. The issue of whether phonological processing mediates lexical access concerns the internal structure of the word recognition module itself.

Although this issue again dates back to Huey's (1908/1968) time and before, it was revived in modern form in a seminal paper by Rubenstein, Lewis, and Rubenstein (1971), in which they introduced what was termed the *phonological recoding hypothesis*. As phrased by Gough (1984), "The phonological recoding hypothesis holds that the recognition of a printed word is mediated by its phonological form" (p. 235). There is an enormous literature on this issue, and several reviews containing references to hundreds of papers have been published (Barron, 1986; Henderson, 1982, 1985; Humphreys & Evett, 1985; McCusker, Hillinger, & Bias, 1981; Patterson & Coltheart, 1987; Van Orden, Pennington, & Stone, 1988). Our purpose is not to exhaustively review this extensive literature but instead to focus on how the phonological recoding hypothesis has been reframed in recent years.

It is important that we reiterate the same caution we gave in our discussion of context effects. In understanding the role of phonological processes in reading, it is important to differentiate levels of processing. Virtually all theorists agree that phonological codes in working memory play some role in supporting comprehension processes (e.g., Baddeley, 1986; Patterson & Coltheart, 1987; Perfetti, 1985; Rayner & Pollatsek, 1989). The major dispute has centered around the role of phonological processes in *word recognition*—in short, whether phonological coding is implicated in lexical access. Finally, it is also important to realize that the more contentious disputes surround the role of phonological coding in the word recognition processes of the fluent adult reader. A vast array of evidence points to the importance of phonological processes in early reading acquisition (Bradley & Bryant, 1985; Gough & Tunmer, 1986; Juel, ch. 27, this volume; Juel et al., 1986; Kamhi & Catts, 1989; Liberman & Shankweiler, 1985; Lundberg, Frost, & Peterson, 1988; Mann, 1986; Stanovich, 1986a, 1986b, 1988a, 1988b; Vellutino & Scanlon, 1987; Wagner, 1988; Wagner & Torgesen, 1987; Williams, 1986).

In the decade subsequent to the reintroduction of the phonological coding issue into reading theory by Rubenstein, Lewis, and Rubenstein (1971; see Gough's [1984] discussion of their seminal work), it was not difficult to generate data that seemingly indicated the influence of phonological factors on the two tasks most often taken to be measures of lexical access: naming and lexical decision (Baron & Strawson, 1976; Bauer & Stanovich, 1980; Gough & Cosky, 1977; McCusker et al., 1981; Stanovich & Bauer, 1978). However, in the early 1980s it became apparent that the simplifying assumption that only prelexical processes were tapped by these tasks was incorrect (Balota & Chumbley, 1984, 1985; Chumbley & Balota, 1984; deGroot, 1985; Forster, 1979; Lorch, Balota, & Stamm, 1986; Monsell, Doyle, & Haggard, 1989; Seidenberg, Waters, Sanders, & Langer, 1984; Stanovich & West, 1983a; Wagner & Rashotte, 1989; West & Stanovich, 1982). Since the postlexical effects of phonological variables are not a matter of dispute, observing an effect without being able to locate it at a prelexical stage rendered many of the earlier experiments less diagnostic than previously thought.

Nevertheless, a strong form of the phonological recoding hypothesis—that phonological codes were always computed prior to lexical access for all words (Gough, 1972; Rubenstein et al., 1971)—was quickly abandoned, based on the outcomes of early research (Banks, Oka, & Shugarman, 1981; Carr & Pollatsek, 1985; McCusker et al., 1981; Perfetti & McCutchen, 1982; Vellutino, 1982). Much attention was then focused on developing versions of what came to be called *dual-route models* (Coltheart, 1978; Forster & Chambers, 1973; Meyer, Schvaneveldt, & Ruddy, 1974). This class of model posits two alternate recognition pathways to the lexicon: a direct visual access route that does not involve phonological mediation and an indirect route through phonology that utilizes stored spelling-to-sound correspondences. The size of the spelling-to-sound correspondences that make up the phonological route differ from model to model. Versions of dual-route models also differ in assumptions about the various speeds of the two access mechanisms involved and how conflicting information is resolved. Excellent discussions of the many variants of this type of model are contained in several recent publications (see Carr & Pollatsek, 1985; Henderson, 1982, 1985; Humphreys & Evett, 1985; Patterson & Coltheart, 1987; Patterson & Morton, 1985; Rayner & Pollatsek, 1989).

In all such views, the phonological route becomes a processing option (although not one necessarily under conscious control) that may or may not become implicated in performance depending upon the status of the other route (Patterson, Marshall, & Coltheart, 1985) and upon the nature of the words being read. Two important factors in the latter class are the frequency and the spelling-to-sound regularity of the words used as stimuli. Indeed, studies of the spelling-sound regularity effect in word recognition have become a major source of data for addressing questions about the role of phonological coding in word recognition.

Spelling-sound regularity refers to the consistency of the mapping between the letters in the word and the sounds in its pronunciation. *Regular words* are those whose pronunciations reflect common spelling-sound correspondences (e.g., *made, rope*); *irregular words* are those whose pronunciations reflect atypical correspondences (e.g., *sword, pint, have, aisle*). Two important caveats must always be emphasized, however. First, although terms like regular versus irregular or regular versus exception appear often in the literature, regularity is a continuous variable, not a discrete category (Barber & Millar, 1982; Glushko, 1979; Patterson & Coltheart, 1987; Patterson & Morton, 1985; Rosson, 1985; Seidenberg, in press; Seidenberg & McClelland, in press; Venezky & Massaro, 1987). Secondly, the issue of how best to define regularity is maddingly complex and contentious (Brown, 1987b; Henderson, 1982, 1985; Humphreys & Evett, 1985; Kay & Bishop, 1987; Patterson, Marshall, & Coltheart, 1985; Rosson, 1985; Venezky & Massaro, 1987). Two investigators in the area have referred to the complexities surrounding the concept of spelling-sound regularity as a "psycholinguistic hornet's nest" (Prior & McCorriston, 1985, p. 70). The extensive discussions of these complexities in the literatures of psycholinguistics and cognitive psychology stand in stark contrast to the glib statements about the alleged "irregularity" or "regularity" of English that are often tossed about in educational debates about the teaching of reading.

Disagreement about how to classify words in terms of spelling-sound regularity is common because the degree of regularity assigned depends greatly on the size of the coding unit that is assumed for spelling-sound correspondences (Kay & Bishop, 1987). Simply put, many more words are regular when large-unit mappings are employed (Henderson, 1982; Mason, 1977; Ryder & Pearson, 1980; Treiman & Zukowsky, in press; Venezky, 1970). For example, the *gh* (and *i*) of *light* seems irregular when considered as an isolated unit, because it has several different correspondences (*ghost, tough, light*), but in the *i--t* context, it is regular. That is, *ight*, considered as a unit, maps regularly to /ayt/ (e.g., *light, fight, right, might*). The large-scale unit is actually quite regular. However, researchers often cannot agree on the size of the units that are used as access codes. Fortunately, most of our discussion here does not depend on the resolution of this dispute.

The results from early studies of the regularity effect were hard to integrate because a variety of different data patterns were obtained (Andrews, 1982; Bauer & Stanovich, 1980; Coltheart, Besner, Jonasson, & Davelaar, 1979; Parkin, 1982; Parkin & Underwood, 1983). Effects of regularity occurred in some experiments but not others; occurred in some types of tasks but not others; and varied in magnitude even when they did consistently occur. However, a series of experiments by Seidenberg and colleagues (Seidenberg, Waters, Barnes, & Tanenhaus, 1984; Waters & Seidenberg, 1985) and a theoretical review by Seidenberg (1985c) helped greatly to clarify the situation. Seidenberg and colleagues confirmed the existence of an interaction between spelling-sound regularity and word frequency. Regularity effects are minimal or nonexistent for high-frequency words and increase in magnitude as word frequency decreases. The existence of this interaction accounts for some of the inconsistencies across experiments because, in many cases, frequency varied from study to study in an uncontrolled fashion.

Additionally, Seidenberg (1985c) provided a principled explanation of why the observation of regularity effects may vary across tasks—specifically, of why regularity effects are more variable in lexical decision tasks than in naming tasks. Previous research had shown lexical decision tasks to be less valid indicators of word recognition processes because they were prone to reflect criterion effects, stimulus composition effects, and postlexical response bias effects (Balota & Chumbley, 1984; Forster, 1979; Seidenberg, Waters, Sanders, & Langer, 1984; Stanovich & West, 1983a; West & Stanovich, 1982). Seidenberg (1985c) gave principled explanations of how such response bias and stimulus composition effects accounted for the variation in the regularity effect across different lexical decision experiments.

In summary, Seidenberg's (1985c) theoretical and empirical synthesis seemed to establish that phonological coding is implicated prior to lexical access, at least for low-frequency words—although disputes about the mechanism that mediated the phonological effects continued to fuel research (Patterson & Coltheart, 1987). For example, an influential set of experiments was conducted by Glushko (1979, 1981; see also Bauer & Stanovich, 1980), in which he found that regular words such as *gave* that had irregular neighbors (in this case, *have*) took longer to pronounce than regular words without irregular neighbors (e.g., *coat*). Similarly, nonwords such as *bint* that have word neighbors that are inconsistent in pronunciation (*pint, mint*) took longer to pronounce than nonwords without inconsistent word neighbors (e.g., *tade*). These findings seemed to indicate that word naming was affected by nearby lexical entries, and they motivated several investigators to explore models of word processing that involved only lexical entries and that did not accomplish phonological coding by employing small-unit, grapheme-phoneme correspondence rules.

One such lexical-analogy model (see Carr & Pollatsek, 1985; Henderson, 1982) was Glushko's *activation-synthesis model* (1979, 1981), which he used to explain the aforementioned findings. In this model, visual letter strings activate orthographic codes at the word level based on letter similarity between the stimulus and the abstract letter codes of the orthographic representations. The resulting activated orthographic entries activate phonological representations. The set of activated orthographic and phonological representations are integrated and synthesized and then sent to processes capable of executing naming and lexical decision responses. The synthesis process for words with inconsistently pronounced lexical neighbors will be slowed. The key aspect of the model is that the architecture contains no separable phonological coding mechanism, as in the dual-route models. There is no set of stored grapheme-phoneme rules. Instead, phonological coding in the activation-synthesis model is accomplished by the use of previously stored lexical entries.

Glushko's model, in conjunction with the seminal work of McClelland and Rumelhart (1981; Rumelhart & McClelland, 1982; see also Paap, Newsome, McDonald, & Schvaneveldt, 1982), anticipated the popularity of the distributed processing models in the subsequent decade of work on word recognition. The development of the lexical-analogy models such as the activation-synthesis model and its derivatives began a period during which the phonological coding hypothesis was reformulated somewhat. The classic form of the hypothesis—stated in terms of whether phonological codes are activated prior to or subsequent to lexical access—has been altered as researchers moved toward modeling regularity and consistency effects with distributed, connectionist networks that blur the distinction between phonological coding prior to lexical access and postaccess phonological activation (Henderson, 1987).

Perfetti (1985; Perfetti & McCutchen, 1982) constructed one such distributed network model of automatic speech activation by borrowing from and extending the interactive activation model of McClelland and Rumelhart (1981; Rumelhart & McClelland, 1982). The part of the model most relevant to issues in word recognition is displayed in Figure 16.3. Letter, phoneme, and word codes all simultaneously activate each other within the word recognition module. When letter codes become activated, phonological information is automatically activated and in turn begins to activate word

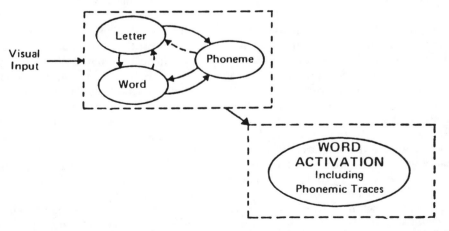

FIGURE 16.3   A portion of Perfetti's (1985) automatic speech activation model.

codes. Perfetti (1985) emphasizes that in his model of automatic speech activation within a connectionist network:

> The question of speech recoding becomes irrelevant. Phonetic activation is not a first step to lexical access; rather, it is part of the access, sometimes reaching a high level prior to the completion of access and sometimes not. The former would look like "recoding" and the latter would not. (p. 59)

Thus, the old issue of whether phonological recoding takes place prior to lexical access or not has become recast. The older question was phrased in a very discrete manner. Phonological information was activated either before lexical access *or* subsequent to it. Such a conceptualization fails to capture the continuous and distributed nature of phonological processing within the word recognition module. Activation of phonological codes by visual letter codes appears to take place almost immediately after stimulus onset, and these phonological codes immediately begin activating word codes, thus contributing to the ongoing word recognition process (see Perfetti, Bell, & Delaney, 1988; Van Orden, 1987). How much phonological codes contribute is determined by how long it takes to bring the activation in a word detector to threshold: "If the activation process is slow, the phoneme level gets a lot of activation from the letter level before a word decision is made. In this case, word identification will be affected by phoneme activation. If the word is identified fairly rapidly, then phoneme activation will lag behind" (Perfetti, 1985, p. 59).

Seidenberg (1985c) has developed a *time course model* of phonological activation during word recognition that embodies assumptions similar to Perfetti's (1985). Like Perfetti's (1985) model, Seidenberg's (1985c) time course model employs a distributed network conceptualization (Feldman & Ballard, 1982) in place of the dual-route framework with separate pathways and turns the discrete phonological recoding hypothesis into a question about the magnitude of activation on a continuous function:

> Rather than postulating separate orthographic and phonological processes operating in parallel, the time course model emphasizes a single interactive process with differences in the availability of orthographic and phonological information over time. Whether direct or mediated access occurs simply falls out from the facts about the time course of code activation. "Direct access" results when sufficient orthographic information is extracted from the input to permit recognition prior to the access of phonology. (p. 227)

Thus, as in Perfetti's (1985) model, but in contrast to earlier formulations of the phonological recoding hypothesis, the question of prelexical versus postlexical activation is replaced by the question of how *much* phonological mediation.

Seidenberg's (1985c) time course model nicely accounts for the empirical finding of an interaction between word frequency and spelling-to-sound regularity. Phonological activation should have more of an opportunity to build up—and thus affect word recognition via interactive activation—when word recognition is slow, as in the case of low-frequency words. In contrast, high-frequency words are recognized before substantial phonological activation has time to build up and to influence the recognition process substantially. Interestingly, Seidenberg (1985c) has shown that word recognition skill mimics the effects of word frequency. Specifically, skilled readers, who recognized words rapidly, did not display spelling-sound regularity effects, whereas less-skilled readers, who recognized words more slowly, displayed significant regularity effects. This interchangeability of word recognition skill and stimulus variables that affect word recognition time is similar to that observed in experiments on sentence context effects on word recognition (Perfetti, 1985; Stanovich, 1980, 1986b; Stanovich & West, 1983a).

Although Seidenberg's (1985c) time course model and Perfetti's (1985) automatic speech activation model helped to demonstrate how ideas about parallel distributed processing might alter the nature of our questions about the role of phonological coding in word recognition, both of these models in actuality were relatively unconstrained verbal accounts of word processing. Recently, however, several theorists have attempted to develop more explicit computational accounts of the operation of the word recognition module (see Brown, 1987b; Seidenberg & McClelland, 1989; Sejnowski & Rosenberg, 1986, 1988; Van Orden, Pennington, & Stone, 1988). Seidenberg and McClelland (in press) have developed a particularly impressive computer simulation of processing within the word recognition module by employing connectionist distributed processing architectures and assumptions.

Connectionist distributed processing models have had a decided impact on theorizing in cognitive psychology during the last decade (Besner, 1984; MacWhinney, Leinbach, Taraban, & McDonald, 1989; Massaro, 1988; McClelland, 1988; McClelland & Rumelhart, 1986; Nadel, Cooper, Culicover, & Harnish, 1989; Navon, in press; Schneider, 1987; Smolensky, 1988; Tanenhaus, Dell, & Carlson, 1987). These models simulate behavioral patterns by adjusting connections among networks of simple processing units based on feedback about the adequacy of the output from response units. Such models, although they are not preprogrammed with rules as in more traditional simulation models in cognitive science, have displayed the capability to emit "rulelike" behavior. For example, in the domain of word recognition, these connectionist models—after training—take longer to recognize words that depart from spelling-to-sound correspondence "rules" even though no such rules were used a priori to structure the networks (Sejnowski & Rosenberg, 1986, 1988; Seidenberg & McClelland, 1989).

The model developed by Seidenberg and McClelland (1989) departs from parallel activation models like that of Perfetti (1985) and Glushko (1979, 1981) in that the network contains no word-level representations; there is no lexicon built into the network (Seidenberg, in press). Obviously, models such as this provide an extreme example of how the question of whether phonological activation is pre- or postlexical can be dissolved, given the appropriate model (however, see Besner, in press).

The general connectionist architecture that provided their framework is illustrated on the left of Figure 16.4 (the unlabeled ovals represent so-called "hidden units," which mediate between representational levels and which increase the computational power of the network), and the smaller piece of the architecture that they actually simulate is shown on the right. Visually presented words activate orthographic units, which in turn activate a set of hidden units, which activate phonological units. The hidden units feed

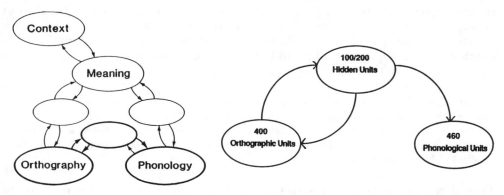

FIGURE 16.4   The general architecture of Seidenberg and McClelland's (1989) parallel distributed processing model.

back activation to orthographic units. In addition to the connections displayed in Figure 16.4, the output of the 460 phonological units is interfaced with a system that constructs an articulatory-motor program, which is then executed by a motor system, thus enabling pronunciation. The 400 orthographic units are interfaced to response decision processes that play a role in tasks like lexical decision. A learning algorithm adjusts the weights of units based on the accuracy of the system's output via a process that is beyond our scope here (Rumelhart, Hinton, & Williams, 1986; Seidenberg & McClelland, 1989).

Seidenberg and McClelland (1989) demonstrate that such a connectionist model can predict the word frequency by regularity interaction for exactly the set of words employed in the experiments that have observed the interaction. Other even more subtle effects involving the consistency of the spelling-sound correspondences in a word's orthographic neighborhood are predicted. Developmental data on children of various skill levels and ages naming words that vary in regularity (Backman, Bruck, Hebert, & Seidenberg, 1984) are also predicted by the model. Seidenberg and McClelland (1989) emphasize the unusual features of the model by stressing that there is no separate phonological route in such a model—as in traditional dual-route conceptualizations—and neither is there a separate lexicon as in most dual-route theories and as in some parallel activation conceptualizations:

> Our model departs from these precursors in a fundamental way: lexical memory does not consist of entries for individual words; there are no logogens. Knowledge of words is embedded in a set of weights on connections between processing units encoding letters, phonemes, and the correlations between them. . . . Thus, the notion of lexical access does not play a central role in our model because it is not congruent with the model's representational and processing assumptions. (p. 36)

Irrespective of whether any version of a parallel activation model becomes the standard way of conceiving the internal structure of the word recognition module, parallel activation models such as those of Perfetti (1985) and Seidenberg and McClelland (1989) are consistent in emphasizing that phonological information is accessed rapidly and is an obligatory consequence of orthographic activation. Consistent with this assumption, some studies by Perfetti, Bell, and Delaney (1988) have indicated that phonological activation occurs almost immediately in word recognition. They employed a tachistoscopic recognition paradigm in which words were masked by pseudowords. They found that, compared to control masks, pseudoword masks that were graphemically similar (but of different case) to the target word (*BRANT* as a mask for *brain*) resulted in superior word recognition performance. This finding indicated that abstract graphemic codes were activated early in the word recognition process. More interestingly, however, pseudoword masks that had equal graphemic similarity to the target but that were homophonic with it (*BRANE* as a mask for *brain*) resulted in even better performance. Perfetti et al. (1988) argued:

> The mask reduction effect for a homophone mask reflects the reinstatement of phonetic codes already activated by the incomplete identification of the target. . . . The backwards effect of the mask, we assume, is on an identification process not yet completed at the onset of the mask. It is phonetic information activated during this incomplete process that is affected by the mask. (pp. 66–67)

Thus, they endorse the idea of the activation of phonetic codes during the very earliest stages of the word identification process.

Van Orden (1987; Van Orden, Johnston, & Hale, 1988) has similarly argued for the idea that phonological information is immediately activated during the course of recognition and that its activation is obligatory. He found that in a categorization task subjects made more false positives to word homophonic foils (e.g., responding affirmatively that *hare* is "A part of the body") and to nonword homophonic foils (e.g., responding affirmatively that *sute* is "an article of clothing") than to spelling controls. Van Orden (1987; Van Orden et al., 1988) demonstrated that the phenomenon obtained under conditions of patterned masking and subsequent experiments ruled out various alternative explanations based on late-occurring processes.

Based on these results and on a reinterpretation of some previous outcomes, Van Orden (1987; Van Orden et al., 1988) advanced the position that the computation of phonological codes was a routine and earlier-occurring aspect of word recognition during normal reading for meaning. The lack of a spelling-sound regularity effect for high-frequency words (Seidenberg et al., 1984) is not evidence against this view since it may simply result from the asymptotic efficiency with which orthographic strings—even irregular ones—activate phonology once the string patterns have received enough exposures (Brown, 1987b). Connectionist models with obligatory phonological code activation can predict this finding (Seidenberg & McClelland, 1989). The activation of phonological codes during the recognition of words in English may also be expected since even in most exception words the majority of spelling-sound correspondences are regular (e.g., the *p-nt* part of *pint* is quite regular).

The results of Perfetti et al. (1988) and Van Orden (1987; see also Frost & Katz, 1989) are somewhat at odds with the prevailing assumptions of most dual-route theories—and those of some time course parallel activation theories—that direct visual access predominates in the word recognition of fluent adult readers (Ehri, 1985; Ellis, 1984; Henderson, 1982; Juel, 1983; McCusker et al., 1981; Reitsma, 1984; Waters, Seidenberg, & Bruck, 1984). However, the whole notion of "direct visual access" becomes much less clear within some types of connectionist distributed processing models without lexicons (Seidenberg, in press). Finally, Van Orden (1987; Van Orden, Pennington, & Stone, 1988) argues that there exists no real evidence for the existence of an independent direct access route, and argues for a version of a distributed processing model.

One major source of evidence that has led researchers to cling to the dual-route notion has been the existence of the acquired dyslexia syndromes, whereby there seems to be a dissociation of various processing "pathways" (Carr & Pollatsek, 1985; Coltheart, Patterson, & Marshall, 1980; Humphreys & Evett, 1985; Patterson, Marshall, & Coltheart, 1985; Rayner & Pollatsek, 1989). Certain types of brain damage have resulted in reading disorders whereby subjects can read words that were learned prior to the acquired dyslexia but have inordinate difficulty with nonwords. Other subjects have displayed acquired dyslexia syndromes where they can name pseudowords and regular words but have inordinate difficulty with irregular words and in differentiating homophones. Such findings have seemed to support the idea of selective damage to a grapheme-phoneme recoding "route" and a direct visual access "route," respectively (however, see Brown, 1987a; Henderson, 1981; Monsell, Doyle, & Haggard, 1989; Seidenberg, 1988). Thus, while the research reviewed above has led many investigators to endorse distributed processing models that do away with the notion of independent access paths, evidence from the acquired dyslexias would seem to present an obstacle to further theoretical developments of this nature.

There are two ways out of this dilemma for connectionist modelers. One would be to provide convincing demonstrations that such parallel distributed models can actually mimic the performance patterns of the various acquired dyslexias when they are suitably lesioned or degraded by reducing the proportion of hidden units (Patterson, Seidenberg, & McClelland, 1989; Seidenberg, 1988; Seidenberg & McClelland, 1989). Alternatively, connectionist architectures that embody some modular properties might be explored. Seidenberg (1985c) has noted in the context of discussing the purposes served by a word recognition module encapsulated from background knowledge:

> Developing an explanatory theory within the parallel activation framework will require the discovery of principled constraints on its basic computational mechanisms. . . . The modularity hypothesis represents a first step in this direction. It postulates a basic constraint on the scope of interactive processes. (p. 245)

Such constraints on models are good because they decrease computational power, thus making them more falsifiable (Tanenhaus, Dell, & Carlson, 1987). There is no reason why we could not conceive of at least some limited degree of encapsulation within the word recognition module itself. That is, it might not be a totally uniform network. For example, we might conceive of the connections involving large-unit spelling-sound correspondences as being distributed somewhat separately from those involving small-unit spelling-sound correspondences (Brown, 1987b; Carr & Pollatsek, 1985). Such a structure might be able to mimic the acquired dyslexic syndromes if a totally uniform connectionist architecture could not.

CONCLUSIONS AND SUMMARY

Word recognition remains the central subprocess of the complex act of reading. This statement in no way denies that the goal of reading is to extract and construct meaning from textual material. It only serves to emphasize that developing skill at recognizing words is the major determinant of reading ability in the early grades (Curtis, 1980; Juel, 1988; Juel et al., 1986; Perfetti, 1985; Stanovich, 1985, 1986b; Stanovich & Cunningham, in press; Stanovich, Cunningham, & Feeman, 1984a) and is a substantial contributor to variance in reading ability among adults (Cunningham et al., in press; Perfetti, 1985).

Beyond the issue of individual differences, there are sound theoretical reasons for expecting word recognition to be a fundamental component of the reading process. Lexical access results in the activation of the information associated with the word's orthographic representation, including the word's meanings and its phonological representation. The phonological representation serves as an access code in working memory for text integration processes that construct meaning. If processes of word recognition do not quickly activate the appropriate lexical entry and produce a phonological representation of sufficient quality to sustain the identified word in working memory, then comprehension processes do not have the raw materials to operate efficiently and understanding of the text will be impaired (Just & Carpenter, 1987; Perfetti, 1985; Rayner & Pollatsek, 1989). Thus, both as an individual difference variable and as a mechanism in general theories of reading, word recognition is a central process.

Several recurring questions have motivated research on the word recognition process. In considering several of these, we observed how steady progress has been made on some of them and how others have been dissolved or reformulated by theoretical developments. Many of these reformulations are due to the impact of concepts imported into reading research from cognitive science in the last decade. For example, the classic question of whether phonological recoding mediates lexical access in reading, or is a postlexical process, seems to have been tied to an outmoded theoretical conceptualization of reading as a strict sequential stage process (e.g., Sternberg, 1969) that precluded both parallel processing and cascaded processing (e.g., McClelland, 1979), whereby the operations of later stages can begin prior to the completion of earlier stages. The parallel distributed models of reading subprocesses that are now popular dissolve the phonological recoding question in its either/or form and replace it with questions about a continuous activation function. Recent research indicates that phonological coding is not an optional strategy in adult readers. Instead, the activation of phonological information in word recognition is an obligatory process that initiates very soon after visual information is extracted from the word under fixation.

The question of whether fluent word recognition is an automatic process has also been reformulated somewhat. Research in the last 10 years has "unpacked" the concept of automaticity—revealing that it is really a complex construct conjoining many different properties. The question of whether word recognition is automatic is thus not a good one because it conflates many important properties of word recognition that are theoretically and empirically differentiable: speed, capacity usage, conscious control, obligatory execution, and encapsulation. It has been found that the developmental growth curves and/or practice functions of these properties may not coincide. In the sense of using less cognitive capacity, the word recognition process does become more automatic as skill develops. The identification of words becomes less capacity demanding as experience with words increases. However, word recognition, even in adult readers, is probably not completely free of capacity demands, as some earlier views had suggested.

In recent years, the issue of capacity usage has been superseded in reading theory by the issue of information encapsulation: the question of whether word recognition can occur without recruiting outside knowledge sources such as local textual expectations or general world knowledge. The concept of modularity, imported into reading theory from cognitive science, has as its defining feature the idea of informational encapsulation. The classic issue of the role of context in word recognition is thus highly relevant to theories of modularity in cognitive science (Tanenhaus et al., 1987). Gough's (1983, 1984) previous summary of the evidence here has stood the test of time: word recognition is less affected by context as reading skill develops; or, to use the more contemporary terminology, word recognition becomes increasingly encapsulated with skill development. Thus, the structure of processing becomes more modularized at the higher levels of reading ability. There are sound theoretical reasons—again, principles not unique to reading but that have been invoked in other areas of cognitive science—why a modular input system is often advantageous and why in reading specifically, a modular word recognition system is adaptive. For example, an advantage accrues to encapsulation when the specificity and efficiency of stimulus-analyzing mechanisms are great relative to those of the other information sources that might be used to aid recognition— precisely the situation that obtains in fluent adult reading.

The most accurate model of the processing taking place within the word recognition module itself is, however, still a matter of serious dispute. The classic dual-route models of lexical access that proposed separate phonological and orthographic access routes (e.g., Coltheart, 1978) have come in for substantial criticism in recent years (Humphreys & Evett, 1985). Considerable research and theoretical effort has been expended in examining whether distributed network models could produce a more accurate and parsimonious account of the extant data patterns than dual-route models. This effort has largely been successful, as most of the important data on lexical access can be modeled more accurately and parsimoniously with connectionist models. Only the case study data from the investigation of the acquired dyslexias has seemed to elude such accounts. Future theoretical work will no doubt be directed at the accommodation of these findings. It was speculated that a structure that may give an account of this evidence, while maintaining falsifiability, will introduce some limited encapsulation within a connectionist model that represents processing units of varying size.

Theory in the area of word recognition has certainly evolved in recent years—but has it progressed? The answer is, very clearly—yes. A relevant framework is, I believe, provided in the work of Imre Lakatos (1970), a philosopher of science who partitions scientific developments into what he terms progressive versus degenerating research programs. In order to differentiate the two, one must examine what happens to explanatory mechanisms when problem shifts occur within a scientific subarea. Content-reducing problem shifts are a sure sign of a degenerating research program. Content-increasing problem shifts signal progressive research programs. One only has to examine in detail the refined predictions made by the connectionist models of Seidenberg and McClelland (1989) and Brown (1987b) to realize that the scope and content of theoretical shifts in word recognition models are of a progressive nature. Although many questions remain, word recognition continues to be an area of reading research characterized by steady scientific progress.

REFERENCES

Aborn, M., Rubenstein, H., & Sterling, T.D. (1959). Sources of contextual constraint upon words in sentences. *Journal of Experimental Psychology, 57,* 171–180.

Alford, J. (1980, May). *Predicting predictability: Identification of sources of contextual constraint on words in text.* Paper presented at the meeting of the Midwestern Psychological Association, St. Louis.

Allington, R. L., & Fleming, J. T. (1978). The misreading of high-frequency words. *Journal of Special Education, 12,* 417–421.

Allington, R. L., & Strange, M. (1977). Effects of grapheme substitutions in connected text upon reading behaviors. *Visible Language, 11,* 285–297.

Anderson, R. C., & Pearson, P. D. (1984). A schema-theoretic view of basic processes in reading comprehension. In P. D. Pearson (Ed.), *Handbook of reading research* (Vol. 1, pp. 255–291). New York: Longman.

Andrews, S. (1982). Phonological recoding: Is the regularity effect consistent? *Memory & Cognition, 10,* 565–575.

Backman, J., Bruck, M., Hebert, M., & Siedenberg, M. (1984). Acquisition and use of spelling-sound correspondences in reading. *Journal of Experimental Child Psychology, 38,* 114–133.

Baddeley, A. D. (1986). *Working memory.* New York: Oxford University Press.

Baker, L., & Brown, A. L. (1984). Metacognitive skills and reading. In P. D. Pearson, R. Barr, M. L. Kamil, & P. Mosenthal (Eds.), *Handbook of reading research,* (Vol. 1). White Plains, NY: Longman.

Balota, D., & Chumbley, J. I. (1984). Are lexical decisions a good measure of lexical access? The role of word frequency in the neglected decision stage. *Journal of Experimental Psychology: Human Perception and Performance, 10,* 340–357.

Balota, D., & Chumbley, J. I. (1985). The locus of word-frequency effects in the pronunciation task: Lexical access and/or production? *Journal of Memory and Language, 24,* 89–106.

Balota, D., Pollatsek, A., & Rayner, K. (1985). The interaction of contextual constraints and parafoveal visual information in reading. *Cognitive Psychology, 17,* 364–390.

Banks, W. P., Oka, E., & Shugarman, S. (1981). Recoding of printed words to internal speech: Does recoding come before lexical access? In O. Tzeng & H. Singer (Eds.), *Perception of print* (pp. 137–170). Hillsdale, NJ: Erlbaum.

Barber, P. J., & Millar, D. G. (1982). Subjective judgments of spelling-sound correspondences: Effects of word regularity and word frequency. *Memory & Cognition, 10,* 457–464.

Baron, J., & Strawson, C. (1976). Use of orthographic and word-specific knowledge in reading words aloud. *Journal of Experimental Psychology: Human Perception and Performance, 2,* 386–393.

Barron, R. (1986). Word recognition in early reading: A review of the direct and indirect access hypothesis. *Cognition, 24,* 93–119.

Bauer, D. W., & Stanovich, K. E. (1980). Lexical access and the spelling-to-sound regularity effect. *Memory & Cognition, 8,* 424–432.

Becker, C. A. (1976). Allocation of attention during visual word recognition. *Journal of Experimental Psychology: Human Perception and Performance, 2,* 556–566.

Becker, C. A. (1985). What do we really know about semantic context effects during reading? In D. Besner, T. Waller, & G. MacKinnon (Eds.), *Reading research: Advances in theory and practice* (Vol. 5, pp. 125–166). New York: Academic Press.

Becker, C. A., & Killion, T. H. (1977). Interaction of visual and cognitive effects in word recognition. *Journal of Experimental Psychology: Human Perception and Performance, 3,* 389–401.

Bentin, S., & Katz, L. (1984). Semantic awareness in a nonlexical task. *Bulletin of the Psychonomic Society, 22,* 381–384.

Bertelson, P. (1986). The onset of literacy: Liminal remarks. *Cognition, 24,* 1–30.

Besner, D. (1984). Specialized processors subserving visual word recognition: Evidence for local control. *Canadian Journal of Psychology, 38,* 94–101.

Besner, D. (in press). Does the reading system need a lexicon? In D. Balota, G. Flores d'Arcais, & K. Rayner (Eds.), *Comprehension processes in reading.* Hillsdale, NJ: Erlbaum.

Biemiller, A. (1970). The development of the use of graphic and contextual information as children learn to read. *Reading Research Quarterly, 6,* 76–96.

Biemiller, A. (1977–1978). Relationships between oral reading rates for letters, words, and simple text in the development of reading achievement. *Reading Research Quarterly, 13,* 223–253.

Biemiller, A. (1979). Changes in the use of graphic and contextual information as functions of passage difficulty and reading achievement level. *Journal of Reading Behavior, 11,* 307–319.

Blanchard, J. (1980). Preliminary investigation of transfer between single-word decoding ability and contextual reading comprehension by poor readers in grade six. *Perceptual and Motor Skills, 51,* 1271–1281.

Bowey, J. A. (1985). Contextual facilitation in children's oral reading in relation to grade and decoding skill. *Journal of Experimental Child Psychology, 40,* 23–48.

Bradley, L., & Bryant, P. E. (1985). *Rhyme and reason in reading and spelling.* Ann Arbor: University of Michigan Press.

Briggs, P., Austin, S., & Underwood, G. (1984). The effects of sentence context in good and poor readers: A test of Stanovich's interactive-compensatory model. *Reading Research Quarterly, 20,* 54–61.

Briggs, P., & Underwood, G. (1982). Phonological coding in good and poor readers. *Journal of Experimental Child Psychology, 34,* 93–112.

Brown, G. (1987a). Constraining interactivity: Evidence from acquired dyslexia. *Proceedings of the Annual Conference of the Cognitive Science Society, 9,* 779–793.

Brown, G. (1987b). Resolving inconsistency: A computational model of word naming. *Journal of Memory and Language, 26,* 1–23.

Butler, B., & Hains, S. (1979). Individual differences in word recognition latency. *Memory & Cognition, 7,* 68–76.

Carr, T. H., & Pollatsek, A. (1985). Recognizing printed words: A look at current models. In D. Besner, T. G. Waller, & G. E. MacKinnon (Eds.), *Reading Research: Advances in theory and practice* (Vol. 5, pp. 1–82). Orlando, FL: Academic Press.

Chall, J. S. (1983). *Stages of reading development.* New York: McGraw-Hill.

Chall, J. S. (1989). Learning to read: The great debate 20 years later. *Phi Delta Kappan, 70*(7), 521–538.

Chumbley, J. I., & Balota, D. A. (1984). A word's meaning affects the decision in lexical decision. *Memory & Cognition, 12,* 590–606.

Coltheart, M. (1978). Lexical access in simple reading tasks. In G. Underwood (Ed.), *Strategies of information processing* (pp. 151–216). London: Academic Press.

Coltheart, M., Besner, D., Jonasson, J. T., & Davelaar, E. (1979). Phonological encoding in the lexical decision task. *Quarterly Journal of Experimental Psychology, 31,* 489–508.

Coltheart, M., Patterson, K., & Marshall, J. C. (1980). *Deep dyslexia.* London: Routledge & Kegan Paul.

Cunningham, A. E., Stanovich, K. E., & Wilson, M. R. (in press). Cognitive variation in adult students differing in reading ability. In T. Carr & B. A. Levy (Eds.), *Reading and development: Component skills approaches.* New York: Academic Press.

Curtis, M. (1980). Development of components of reading skill. *Journal of Educational Psychology, 72,* 656–669.

Daneman, M., & Carpenter, P. A. (1980). Individual differences in working memory and reading. *Journal of Verbal Learning and Verbal Behavior, 19,* 450–466.

de Groot, A. M. B. (1985). Word-context effects in word naming and lexical decision. *Quarterly Journal of Experimental Psychology, 37A,* 281–297.

Durgunoglu, A. Y. (1988). Repetition, semantic priming, and stimulus quality: Implications for the interactive-compensatory model. *Journal of Experimental Psychology: Learning, Memory, and Cognition, 14,* 590–603.

Dyer, F. N. (1973). The Stroop phenomenon and its use in the study of perceptual, cognitive, and response processes. *Memory & Cognition, 1,* 106–120.

Ehri, L. C. (1977). Do adjectives and functors interfere as much as nouns in naming pictures? *Child Development, 48,* 697–701.

Ehri, L. C. (1985). Effects of printed language acquisition on speech. In D. Olson, N. Torrance, & A. Hildyard (Eds.), *Literacy, language, and learning* (pp. 333–367). Cambridge, Eng.: Cambridge University Press.

Ehri, L. C., & Wilce, L. S. (1979). Does word training increase or decrease interference in a Stroop task? *Journal of Experimental Child Psychology, 27*, 352–364.

Ehrlich, S. (1981). Children's word recognition in prose context. *Visible Language, 15*, 219–244.

Ehrlich, S., & Rayner, K. (1981). Contextual effects on word perception and eye movements during reading. *Journal of Verbal Learning and Verbal Behavior, 20*, 641–655.

Ellis, A. W. (1984). *Reading, writing, and dyslexia: A cognitive analysis.* Hillsdale, NJ: Erlbaum.

Evans, M. A., & Carr, T. H. (1985). Cognitive abilities, conditions of learning, and the early development of reading skill. *Reading Research Quarterly, 20*, 327–350.

Feldman, J. A., & Ballard, D. H. (1982). Connectionist models and their properties. *Cognitive Science, 6*, 205–254.

Fischler, I. (1977). Semantic facilitation without association in a lexical decision task. *Memory & Cognition, 5*, 335–339.

Fodor, J. A. (1983). *Modularity of mind.* Cambridge, MA: MIT Press.

Fodor, J. A. (1985). Precis of *The modularity of mind. Behavioral and Brain Sciences, 8*, 1–42.

Forster, K. I. (1979). Levels of processing and the structure of the language processor. In W. E. Cooper & E. Walker (Eds.), *Sentence processing: Psycholinguistic studies presented to Merrill Garrett* (pp. 27–85). Hillsdale, NJ: Erlbaum.

Forster, K. I. (1981). Priming and the effects of sentence and lexical contexts on naming time: Evidence for autonomous lexical processing. *Quarterly Journal of Experimental Psychology, 33A*, 465–495.

Forster, K. I., & Chambers, S. (1973). Lexical access and naming time. *Journal of Verbal Learning and Verbal Behavior, 12*, 627–635.

Foss, D. J. (1988). Experimental psycholinguistics. *Annual Review of Psychology, 39*, 301–348.

Frederiksen, J. R. (1978). Assessment of perceptual, decoding, and lexical skills and their relation to reading proficiency. In A. Lesgold, J. Pellegrino, S. Fokkema, & R. Glaser (Eds.), *Cognitive psychology and instruction* (pp. 153–169). New York: Plenum.

Frost, R., & Katz, L. (1989). Orthographic depth and the interaction of visual and auditory processing in word recognition. *Memory & Cognition, 17*, 302–310.

Glushko, R. J. (1979). The organization and activation of orthographic knowledge in reading aloud. *Journal of Experimental Psychology: Human Perception and Performance, 5*, 674–691.

Glushko, R. J. (1981). Principles for pronouncing print: The psychology of phonography. In A. Lesgold & C. Perfetti (Eds.), *Interactive processes in reading* (pp. 61–84). Hillsdale, NJ: Erlbaum.

Goodman, G. S., Haith, M. M., Guttentag, R. E., & Rao, S. (1985). Automatic processing of word meaning: Intralingual and interlingual interference. *Child Development, 56*, 103–118.

Gough, P. B. (1972). One second of reading. In J. Kavanagh & I. Mattingly (Eds.), *Language by ear and eye* (pp. 331–358). Cambridge, MA: MIT Press.

Gough, P. B. (1983). Context, form, and interaction. In K. Rayner (Ed.), *Eye movements in reading* (pp. 203–211). New York: Academic Press.

Gough, P. B. (1984). Word recognition. In P. D. Pearson (Ed.), *Handbook of reading research* (Vol. 1, pp. 225–253). New York: Longman.

Gough, P. B. (1985). One second of reading: Postscript. In H. Singer & R. Ruddell (Eds.), *Theoretical models and processes of reading* (3rd ed., pp. 687–688). Newark, DE: International Reading Association.

Gough, P. B., Alford, J., & Holley-Wilcox, P. (1981). Words and contexts. In O. Tzeng & H. Singer (Eds.), *Perception of print: Reading research in experimental psychology* (pp. 100–120). Hillsdale, NJ: Erlbaum.

Gough, P. B., & Cosky, M. J. (1977). One second of reading again. In N. J. Castellan, D. B. Pisoni, & G. R. Potts (Eds.), *Cognitive theory* (Vol. 2, pp. 271–286). Hillsdale, NJ: Erlbaum.

Gough, P. B., & Hillinger, M. L. (1980). Learning to read: An unnatural act. *Bulletin of the Orton Society, 30*, 171–176.

Gough, P. B., & Tunmer, W. E. (1986). Decoding, reading, and reading disability. *Remedial and Special Education, 7*, 6–10.

Guttentag, R. E. (1984). Semantic memory organization in second graders and adults. *Journal of General Psychology, 110*, 81–86.

Guttentag, R. E., & Haith, M. M. (1978). Automatic processing as a function of age and reading ability. *Child Development, 49*, 707–716.

Guttentag, R. E., & Haith, M. M. (1980). A longitudinal study of word processing by first-grade children. *Journal of Educational Psychology, 72*, 701–705.

Harding, L. M. (1984). Reading errors and style in children with a specific reading disability. *Journal of Research in Reading, 7*, 103–112.

Henderson, L. (1981). Information-processing approaches to acquired dyslexia. *Quarterly Journal of Experimental Psychology, 33A*, 507–522.

Henderson, L. (1982). *Orthography and word recognition in reading.* London: Academic Press.

Henderson, L. (1985). Issues in the modelling of pronunciation assembly in normal reading. In K. E. Patterson, J. C. Marshall, & M. Coltheart (Eds.), *Surface dyslexia* (pp. 459–508). London: Erlbaum.

Henderson, L. (1987). Word recognition: A tutorial review. In M. Coltheart (Ed.), *Attention and performance* (Vol. 12, pp. 171–200). London: Erlbaum.

Herdman, C., & Dobbs, A. (1989). Attentional demands of visual word recognition. *Journal of Experimental Psychology: Human Perception and Performance, 15*, 124–132.

Herman, P. A. (1985). The effect of repeated readings on reading rate, speech pauses, and word recognition accuracy. *Reading Research Quarterly, 20,* 553–565.

Hogaboam, T. W. (1983). Reading patterns in eye-movement data. In K.. Rayner (Ed.), *Eye movements in reading: Perceptual and language processes* (pp. 309–332). New York: Academic Press.

Horn, C. C., & Manis, F. R. (1987). Development of automatic and speeded reading of printed words. *Journal of Experimental Child Psychology, 44,* 92–108.

Huey, E. B. (1908/1968). *The psychology and pedagogy of reading.* Cambridge, MA: MIT Press.

Humphreys, G. W. (1985). Attention, automaticity, and autonomy in visual word processing. In D. Besner, T. Waller, & G. MacKinnon (Eds.), *Reading research: Advances in theory and practice* (Vol. 5, pp. 253–309). New York: Academic Press.

Humphreys, G. W., & Evett, L. J. (1985). Are there independent lexical and nonlexical routes in word processing? An evaluation of the dual-route theory of reading. *Behavioral and Brain Sciences, 8,* 689–740.

Jackson, M., & McClelland, J. (1979). Processing determinants of reading speed. *Journal of Experimental Psychology: General, 108,* 151–181.

Juel, C. (1980). Comparison of word identification strategies with varying context, word type, and reader skill. *Reading Research Quarterly, 15,* 358–376.

Juel, C. (1983). The development and use of mediated word identification. *Reading Research Quarterly, 18,* 306–327.

Juel, C. (1988). Learning to read and write: A longitudinal study of 54 children from first through fourth grades. *Journal of Educational Psychology, 80,* 437–447.

Juel, C., Griffith, P. L., & Gough, P. B. (1986). Acquisition of literacy: A longitudinal study of children in first and second grade. *Journal of Educational Psychology, 78,* 243–255.

Just, M. A., & Carpenter, P. A. (1980). A theory of reading: From eye fixations to comprehension. *Psychological Review, 4,* 329–354.

Just, M. A., & Carpenter, P. A. (1987). *The psychology of reading and language comprehension.* Boston: Allyn & Bacon.

Kahneman, D., & Chajczyk, D. (1983). Tests of the automaticity of reading: Dilution of Stroop effects by color-irrelevant stimuli. *Journal of Experimental Psychology: Human Perception and Performance, 9,* 497–509.

Kahneman, D., & Treisman, A. (1984). Changing views of attention and automaticity. In R. Parasuraman & R. Davies (Eds.), *Varieties of attention* (pp. 29–61). New York: Academic Press.

Kamhi, A., & Catts, H. (1989). *Reading disabilities: A developmental language perspective.* Boston: College-Hill Press.

Kay, J., & Bishop, D. (1987). Anatomical differences between nose, palm, and foot, or, the body in question: Further dissection of the processes of sublexical spelling-sound translation. In M. Coltheart (Ed.), *Attention and performance* (Vol. 12, pp. 449–469). London: Erlbaum.

Kibby, M. W. (1979). Passage readability affects the oral reading strategies of disabled readers. *Reading Teacher, 32,* 390–396.

Kimmel, S., & MacGinitie, W. H. (1984). Identifying children who use a perseverative text-processing strategy. *Reading Research Quarterly, 19,* 162–172.

Kintsch, W. (1988). The role of knowledge in discourse comprehension: A construction-integration model. *Psychological Review, 95,* 163–182.

Kintsch, W., & Mross, E. (1985). Context effects in word identification. *Journal of Memory and Language, 24,* 336–349.

Kramer, A. F., & Donchin, E. (1987). Brain potentials as indices of orthographic and phonological interaction during word matching. *Journal of Experimental Psychology: Learning, Memory, and Cognition, 13,* 76–86.

Kraut, A. G., & Smothergill, D. W. (1980). New method for studying semantic encoding in children. *Developmental Psychology, 16,* 149–150.

Kutas, M., & Hillyard, S. A. (1980). Reading senseless sentences: Brain potentials reflect semantic incongruity. *Science, 207,* 203–205.

Kutas, M., & Hillyard, S. A. (1983). Event-related brain potentials to grammatical errors and semantic anomalies. *Memory & Cognition, 11,* 539–550.

Kutas, M., & Hillyard, S. A. (1984). Brain potentials during reading reflect word expectancy and semantic association. *Nature, 307,* 161–163.

LaBerge, D., & Samuels, S. (1974). Toward a theory of automatic information processing in reading. *Cognitive Psychology, 6,* 293–323.

La Heij, W. L. (1988). Components of Stroop-like interference in picture naming. *Memory & Cognition, 16,* 400–410.

Lakatos, I. (1970). Falsification and the methodology of scientific research programmes. In I. Lakatos & A. Musgrave (Eds.), *Criticism and the growth of knowledge* (pp. 91–196). Cambridge, Eng.: Cambridge University Press.

Lesgold, A., Resnick, L., & Hammond, K. (1985). Learning to read: A longitudinal study of word skill development in two curricula. In G. MacKinnon & T. Waller (Eds.), *Reading research: Advances in theory and practice* (Vol. 4, pp. 107–138). London: Academic Press.

Leu, D. (1982). Oral reading error analysis: A critical review of research and application. *Reading Research Quarterly, 17*, 420–437.

Leu, D. J., DeGroff, L., & Simons, H. D. (1986). Predictable texts and interactive-compensatory hypotheses: Evaluating individual differences in reading ability, context use, and comprehension. *Journal of Educational Psychology, 78*, 347–352.

Liberman, I. (1982). A language-oriented view of reading and its disabilities. In H. Mykelbust (Ed.), *Progress in learning disabilities* (Vol. 5, pp. 81–101). New York: Grune & Stratton.

Liberman, I. Y., & Shankweiler, D. (1985). Phonology and the problems of learning to read and write. *Remedial and Special Education, 6*, 8–17.

Liberman, I. Y., Rubin, H., Duques, S., & Carlisle, J. (1985). Linguistic abilities and spelling proficiency in kindergarteners and adult poor spellers. In D. Gray & J. Kavanagh (Eds.), *Biobehavioral measures of dyslexia* (pp. 163–175). Parkton, MD: York Press.

Logan, G. D. (1985). Skill and automaticity: Relations, implications, and future directions. *Canadian Journal of Psychology, 39*, 367–386.

Logan, G. D. (1988). Toward an instance theory of automatization. *Psychological Review, 95*, 492–527.

Lomax, R. (1983). Applying structural modeling to some component processes of reading comprehension development. *Journal of Experimental Education, 52*, 33–40.

Lorch, R. F., Balota, D. A., & Stamm, E. G. (1986). Locus of inhibition effects in the priming of lexical decisions: Pre- or postlexical access? *Memory & Cognition, 14*, 95–103.

Lovett, M. W. (1986). Sentential structure and the perceptual spans of two samples of disabled readers. *Journal of Psycholinguistic Research, 15*, 153–175.

Lundberg, I., Frost, J., & Peterson, O. (1988). Effects of an extensive program for stimulating phonological awareness in preschool children. *Reading Research Quarterly, 23*, 263–284.

McClelland, J. L. (1979). On the time relations of mental processes: An examination of systems of processes in cascade. *Psychological Review, 86*, 287–330.

McClelland, J. L. (1988). Connectionist models and psychological evidence. *Journal of Memory and Language, 27*, 107–123.

McClelland, J. L., & Rumelhart, D. E. (1981). An interactive activation model of context effects in letter perception: Part 1. An account of basic findings. *Psychological Review, 88*, 375–407.

McClelland, J. L., & Rumelhart, D. E. (1986). *Parallel distributed processing: Explorations in the microstructure of cognition* (Vol. 2). Cambridge, MA: MIT Press.

McConkie, G. W., & Zola, D. (1981). Language constraints and the functional stimulus in reading. In A. M.. Lesgold & C. A. Perfetti (Eds.), *Interactive processes in reading* (pp. 155–175). Hillsdale, NJ: Erlbaum.

McCusker, L. X., Hillinger, M. L., & Bias, R. G. (1981). Phonological recoding and reading. *Psychological Bulletin, 89*, 217–245.

McLeod, P., McLaughlin, C., & Nimmo-Smith, I. (1985). Information encapsulation and automaticity: Evidence from the visual control of finely timed actions. In M. Posner & O. Marin (Eds.), *Attention and performance* (Vol. 11, pp. 391–406). Hillsdale, NJ: Erlbaum.

MacWhinney, B., Leinbach, J., Taraban, R., & McDonald, J. (1989). Language learning: Cues or rules? *Journal of Memory and Language, 28*, 255–277.

Manis, F. R., Keating, D. P., & Morrison, F. J. (1980). Developmental differences in the allocation of processing capacity. *Journal of Experimental Child Psychology, 29*, 156–169.

Mann, V. (1986). Why some children encounter reading problems. In J. Torgesen & B. Wong (Eds.), *Psychological and educational perspectives on learning disabilities* (pp. 133–159). New York: Academic Press.

Maria, K., & MacGinitie, W. H. (1982). Reading comprehension disabilities: Knowledge structures and nonaccommodating text-processing strategies. *Annals of Dyslexia, 32*, 33–59.

Mason, J. M. (1977). Refining phonics for teaching beginning reading. *Reading Teacher, 30*, 179–184.

Mason, J. M. (1978). From print to sound in mature readers as a function of reader ability and two forms of orthographic regularity. *Memory & Cognition, 6*, 568–581.

Massaro, D. W. (1988). Some criticisms of connectionist models of human performance. *Journal of Memory and Language, 27*, 213–234.

Masson, M. (1986). Comprehension of rapidly presented sentences: The mind is quicker than the eye. *Journal of Memory and Language, 25*, 588–604.

Masson, M. (1988). The interaction of sentence context and perceptual analysis in word identification. *Memory & Cognition, 16*, 489–496.

Masson, M. (in press). A distributed memory model of context effects in word identification. In D. Besner & G. W. Humphreys (Eds.), *Basic processes in reading: Visual word recognition*. Hillsdale, NJ: Erlbaum.

Meyer, D. E., Schvaneveldt, R. W., & Ruddy, M. G. (1974). Functions of graphemic and phonemic codes in visual word recognition. *Memory & Cognition, 2*, 309–321.

Meyer, D. E., Schvaneveldt, R. W., & Ruddy, M. G. (1975). Loci of contextual effects on word recognition. In P. M. A. Rabbitt & S. Dornic (Eds.), *Attention and performance* (Vol. 5, pp. 98–118). New York: Academic Press.

Miller, G. R., & Coleman, E. B. (1967). A set of thirty-six prose passages calibrated for complexity. *Journal of Verbal Learning and Verbal Behavior, 6*, 851–854.

Mitchell, D. (1982). *The process of reading: A cognitive analysis of fluent reading and learning to read.* Chichester, Eng.: John Wiley.

Mitchell, D., & Green, D. W. (1978). The effects of context and content on immediate processing in reading. *Quarterly Journal of Experimental Psychology, 30,* 609–636.

Monsell, S., Doyle, M., & Haggard, P. (1989). Effects of frequency on visual word recognition tasks: Where are they? *Journal of Experimental Psychology: General, 118,* 43–71.

Nadel, L., Cooper, L. A., Culicover, P., & Harnish, P. M. (Eds.). (1989). *Neural connections, mental computation.* Cambridge, MA: MIT Press.

Navon, D. (in press). The importance of being visible: On the role of attention in a mind viewed as an anarchic intelligence system. *European Journal of Cognitive Psychology.*

Neely, J. H. (1977). Semantic priming and retrieval from lexical memory: Roles of inhibitionless spreading activation and limited-capacity attention. *Journal of Experimental Psychology: General, 106,* 226–254.

Nicholson, T., & Hill, D. (1985). Good readers don't guess—Taking another look at the issue of whether children read words better in context or in isolation. *Reading Psychology, 6,* 181–198.

Nicholson, T., Lillas, C., & Rzoska, M. (1988). Have we been misled by miscues? *Reading Teacher, 42*(1), 6–10.

Ogden, W. C., Martin, D. W., & Paap, K. R. (1980). Processing demands of encoding: What does secondary task performance reflect? *Journal of Experimental Psychology: Human Perception and Performance, 6,* 355–367.

Paap, K. R., Newsome, S. L., McDonald, J. E., & Schvaneveldt, R. W. (1983). An activation-verification model for letter and word recognition: The word superiority effect. *Psychological Review, 89,* 573–594.

Paap, K. R., & Ogden, W. C. (1981). Letter encoding is an obligatory but capacity-demanding operation. *Journal of Experimental Psychology: Human Perception and Performance, 7,* 518–527.

Palmer, J., MacLeod, C. M., Hunt, E., & Davidson, J. E. (1985). Information-processing correlates of reading. *Journal of Memory and Language, 24,* 59–88.

Paris, S. G. (1987). Introduction to current issues in reading comprehension. *Educational Psychologist, 22,* 209–212.

Paris, S. G., Lipson, M. Y., & Wixson, K. K. (1983). Becoming a strategic reader. *Contemporary Educational Psychology, 8,* 293–316.

Parkin, A. G. (1982). Phonological recoding in lexical decision: Effects of spelling-to-sound regularity depend on how regularity is defined. *Memory & Cognition, 10,* 43–53.

Parkin, A. G. (1984). Levels of processing, context, and the facilitation of pronunciation. *Acta Psychologica, 55,* 19–29.

Parkin, A. G., & Underwood, G. (1983). Orthographic vs. phonological irregularity in lexical decision. *Memory & Cognition, 11,* 351–355.

Patterson, K. E., & Coltheart, V. (1987). Phonological processes in reading: A tutorial review. In M. Coltheart (Ed.), *Attention and performance* (Vol. 12, pp. 421–447). London: Erlbaum.

Patterson, K. E., Marshall, J., & Coltheart, M. (Eds.). (1985). *Surface dyslexia.* London: Erlbaum.

Patterson, K. E., & Morton, J. (1985). From orthography to phonology: An attempt at an old interpretation. In K. E. Patterson, J. C. Marshall, & M. Coltheart (Eds.), *Surface dyslexia* (pp. 335–359). London: Erlbaum.

Patterson, K. E., Seidenberg, M. S., & McClelland, J. (1989). Connections and disconnections: Acquired dyslexia in a computational model of reading processes. In P. Morris (Ed.), *Parallel distributed processing: Implications for psychology and neuroscience* (pp. 131–181). Oxford, Eng.: Oxford University Press.

Perfetti, C. A. (1985). *Reading ability.* New York: Oxford University Press.

Perfetti, C. A. (in press). The representation problem in reading acquisition. In P. Gough (Ed.), *Reading acquisition.* Hillsdale, NJ: Erlbaum.

Perfetti, C. A., Bell, L. C., & Delaney, S. M. (1988). Automatic (prelexical) phonetic activation in silent word reading: Evidence from backward masking. *Journal of Memory and Language, 27,* 59–70.

Perfetti, C. A., & Curtis, M. E. (1986). Reading. In R. F. Dillon & R. J. Sternberg (Eds.), *Cognition and instruction* (pp. 13–57). New York: Academic Press.

Perfetti, C. A., Goldman, S., & Hogaboam, T. (1979). Reading skill and the identification of words in discourse context. *Memory & Cognition, 7,* 273–282.

Perfetti, C., & McCutchen, D. (1982). Speech processes in reading. In N. Lass (Ed.). *Speech and language: Advances in Basic Research and Practice* (Vol. 7, pp. 237–269). New York: Academic Press.

Perfetti, C. A., & McCutchen, D. (1987). Schooled language competence: Linguistic abilities in reading and writing. In S. Rosenberg (Ed.), *Advances in applied psycholinguistics* (Vol. 2, pp. 105–141). Cambridge, Eng.: Cambridge University Press.

Perfetti, C. A., & Roth, S. (1981). Some of the interactive processes in reading and their role in reading skill. In A. Lesgold & C. Perfetti (Eds.), *Interactive processes in reading* (pp. 269–297). Hillsdale, NJ: Erlbaum.

Pollatsek, A., Rayner, K., & Balota, D. A. (1986). Inferences about eye-movement control from the perceptual span in reading. *Perception & psychophysics, 40,* 123–130.

Posnansky, C. J., & Rayner, K. (1977). Visual-feature and response components in a picture-word interference task with beginning and skilled readers. *Journal of Experimental Child Psychology, 24,* 440–460.

Posner, M. I., & Boies, S. J. (1971). Components of attention. *Psychological Review, 78,* 391–408.

Pring, L., & Snowling, M. (1986). Developmental changes in word recognition: An information-processing account. *Quarterly Journal of Experimental Psychology, 38A,* 395–418.

Prior, M., & McCorriston, M. (1985). Surface dyslexia: A regression effect? *Brain and Language, 25,* 52–71.

Rayner, K., & Bertera, J. H. (1979). Reading without a fovea. *Science, 206,* 468–469.

Rayner, K., & Pollatsek, A. (1989). *The psychology of reading.* Englewood Cliffs, NJ: Prentice-Hall.

Read, C., & Ruyter, L. (1985). Reading and spelling skills in adults of low literacy. *Remedial and Special Education, 6,* 43–52.

Reitsma, P. (1984). Sound priming in beginning readers. *Child Development, 55,* 406–423.

Richardson, E., DiBenedetto, B., & Adler, A. (1982). Use of the decoding skills test to study differences between good and poor readers. In K. Gadow & I. Bialer (Eds.), *Advances in learning and behavior disabilities* (Vol. 1, pp. 25–74). Greenwich, CT: JAI Press.

Rosinski, R. (1977). Picture-word interference is semantically based. *Child Development, 48,* 643–647.

Rosson, M. B. (1985). The interaction of pronunciation rules and lexical representations in reading aloud. *Memory & Cognition, 13,* 90–99.

Rubenstein, H., & Aborn, M. (1958). Learning, prediction, and readability. *Journal of Applied Psychology, 42,* 28–32.

Rubenstein, H., Lewis, S. S., & Rubenstein, M. (1971). Evidence for phonemic recoding in visual word recognition. *Journal of Verbal Learning and Verbal Behavior, 10,* 645–657.

Rumelhart, D. E. (1977). Toward an interactive model of reading. In S. Dornic (Ed.), *Attention and performance* (Vol. 6, pp. 573–603). New York: Academic Press.

Rumelhart, D. E., & McClelland, J. L. (1982). An interactive activation model of context effects in letter perception: Part 2. The contextual enhancement effect and some tests and extensions of the model. *Psychological Review, 89,* 60–94.

Rumelhart, D. E., Hinton, G. E., & Williams, R. J. (1986). Learning internal representations by error propagation. In Rumelhart, D. E., & McClelland, J. L. (Eds.), *Parallel distributed processing: Explorations in the microstructure of cognition* (Vol. 1, pp. 318–362). Cambridge, MA: MIT Press.

Ryder, R., & Pearson, P. D. (1980). Influence of type-token frequencies and final consonants on adults' internalization of vowel digraphs. *Journal of Educational Psychology, 72,* 618–624.

Sabol, M. A., & DeRosa, D. V. (1976). Semantic encoding of isolated words. *Journal of Experimental Psychology: Human Learning and Memory, 2,* 58–68.

Scarborough, H. S. (1984). Continuity between childhood dyslexia and adult reading. *British Journal of Psychology, 75,* 329–348.

Schadler, M., & Thissen, D. M. (1981). The development of automatic word recognition and reading skill. *Memory & Cognition, 9,* 132–141.

Schneider, W. (1987). Connectionism: Is it a paradigm shift for psychology? *Behavior Research Methods, Instruments, & Computers, 19,* 73–83.

Schuberth, R. E., & Eimas, P. D. (1977). Effects of context on the classification of words and nonwords. *Journal of Experimental Psychology: Human Perception and Performance, 3,* 27–36.

Schustack, M. W., Ehrlich, S. F., & Rayner, K. (1987). Local and global sources of contextual facilitation in reading. *Journal of Memory and Language, 26,* 322–340.

Schvaneveldt, R., Ackerman, B., & Semlear, T. (1977). The effect of semantic context on children's word recognition. *Child Development, 48,* 612–616.

Schwanenflugel, P., & LaCount, K. (1988). Semantic relatedness and the scope of facilitation for upcoming words in sentences. *Journal of Experimental Psychology: Learning, Memory, and Cognition, 14,* 344–354.

Schwantes, F. M. (1985). Expectancy, integration, and interactional processes: Age differences in the nature of words affected by sentence context. *Journal of Experimental Child Psychology, 39,* 212–229.

Schwartz, R. M., & Stanovich, K. E. (198). Flexibility in the use of graphic and contextual information by good and poor readers. *Journal of Reading Behavior, 13,* 263–269.

Seidenberg, M. S. (1985a). Lexicon as module. *Behavioral and Brain Sciences, 8,* 31–32.

Seidenberg, M. S. (1985b). The time course of information activation and utilization in visual word recognition. In D. Besner, T. Waller, & G. MacKinnon (Eds.), *Reading research: Advances in theory and practice* (Vol. 5, pp. 199–252). New York: Academic Press.

Seidenberg, M. S. (1985c). Constraining models of word recognition. *Cognition, 20,* 169–190.

Seidenberg, M. S. (1988). Cognitive neuropsychology and language: The state of the art. *Cognitive Neuropsychology, 5,* 403–426.

Seidenberg, M. S. (in press). Lexical access: Another theoretical soupstone? In D. Balota, G. Flores d'Arcais, & K. Rayner (Eds.), *Comprehension processes in reading.* Hillsdale, NJ: Erlbaum.

Seidenberg, M. S., & McClelland, J. L. (1989). A distributed, developmental model of word recognition and naming. *Psychological Review, 96,* 523–568.

Seidenberg, M. S., Waters, G. S., Barnes, M. A., & Tanenhaus, M. K. (1984). When does irregular spelling or pronunciation influence word recognition? *Journal of Verbal Learning and Verbal Behavior, 23,* 383–404.

Seidenberg, M. S., Waters, G. S., Sanders, M., & Langer, P. (1984). Pre- and post-lexical loci of contextual effects on word recognition. *Memory & Cognition, 12,* 315–328.

Sejnowski, T. J., & Rosenberg, C. R. (1986). *NETtalk: A parallel network that learns to read aloud.* (Tech. Rep. No. JHU/EECS-86/01). Department of Electrical Engineering and Computer Science, Johns Hopkins University, Baltimore, MD.

Sejnowski, T. J., & Rosenberg, C. R. (1988). Learning and representation in connectionist models. In M. S. Gazzaniga (Ed.), *Perspectives in memory research* (pp. 135–178). Cambridge, MA: MIT Press.

Simons, H. D., & Leu, D. J. (1987). The use of contextual and graphic information in word recognition by second-, fourth-, and sixth-grade readers. *Journal of Reading Behavior, 19*, 33–47.

Simpson, G. B., & Foster, M. R. (1986). Lexical ambiguity and children's word recognition. *Developmental Psychology, 22*, 147–154.

Simpson, G. B., Lorsbach, T., & Whitehouse, D. (1983). Encoding and contextual components of word recognition in good and poor readers. *Journal of Experimental Child Psychology, 35*, 161–171.

Simpson, G. B., Peterson, R. R., Casteel, M. A., & Burgess, C. (1989). Lexical and sentence context effects in word recognition. *Journal of Experimental Psychology: Learning, Memory, and Cognition, 15*, 88–97.

Smith, F. (1971). *Understanding reading*. New York: Holt, Rinehart & Winston.

Smith, F. (1973). *Psycholinguistics and reading*. New York: Holt, Rinehart & Winston.

Smolensky, P. (1988). On the proper treatment of connectionism. *Behavioral and Brain Sciences, 11*, 1–74.

Spiro, R. J., Bruce, B. C., & Brewer, W. F. (Eds.). (1980). *Theoretical issues in reading comprehension*. Hillsdale, NJ: Erlbaum.

Stanovich, K. E. (1980). Toward an interactive-compensatory model of individual differences in the development of reading fluency. *Reading Research Quarterly, 16*, 32–71.

Stanovich, K. E. (1981). Attentional and automatic context effects in reading. In A. Lesgold & C. Perfetti (Eds.), *Interactive processes in reading* (pp. 241–267). Hillsdale, NJ: Erlbaum.

Stanovich, K. (1982). Individual differences in the cognitive processes of reading I: Word decoding. *Journal of Learning Disabilities, 15*, 485–493.

Stanovich, K. E. (1985). Explaining the variance in reading ability in terms of psychological processes: What have we learned? *Annals of Dyslexia, 35*, 67–96.

Stanovich, K. E. (1986a). Cognitive processes and the reading problems of learning disabled children: Evaluating the assumption of specificity. In J. Torgesen & B. Wong (Eds.), *Psychological and educational perspectives on learning disabilities* (pp. 87–131). New York: Academic Press.

Stanovich, K. E. (1986b). Matthew effects in reading: Some consequences of individual differences in the acquisition of literacy. *Reading Research Quarterly, 21*, 360–407.

Stanovich, K. E. (1987). Perspectives on segmental analysis and alphabetic literacy. *Cahiers Psychologie Cognitive, 7*, 514–519.

Stanovich, K. E. (Ed.). (1988a). *Children's reading and the development of phonological awareness*. Detroit, MI: Wayne State University Press.

Stanovich, K. E. (1988b). The right and wrong places to look for the cognitive locus of reading disability. *Annals of Dyslexia, 38*, 154–177.

Stanovich, K. E. (1990). Concepts in developmental theories of reading skill: Cognitive resources, automaticity, and modularity. *Developmental Review, 10*, 1–29.

Stanovich, K. E., & Bauer, D. W. (1978). Experiments on the spelling-to-sound regularity effect in word recognition. *Memory & Cognition, 6*, 410–415.

Stanovich, K. E., & Cunningham, A. E. (in press). Reading as constrained reasoning. In S. Sternberg & P. Frensch (Eds.), *Complex problem solving: Principles and mechanisms*. Hillsdale, NJ: Erlbaum.

Stanovich, K. E., Cunningham, A. E., & Feeman, D. J. (1984a). Intelligence, cognitive skills, and early reading progress. *Reading Research Quarterly, 19*, 278–303.

Stanovich, K. E., Cunningham, A. E., & Feeman, D. J. (1984b). Relation between early reading acquisition and word decoding with and without context: A longitudinal study of first-grade children. *Journal of Educational Psychology, 76*, 668–677.

Stanovich, K. E., Cunningham, A. E., & West, R. F. (1981). A longitudinal study of the development of automatic recognition skills in first graders. *Journal of Reading Behavior, 13*, 57–74.

Stanovich, K. E., Nathan, R. G., West, R. F., & Vala-Rossi, M. (1985). Children's word recognition in context: Spreading activation, expectancy, and modularity. *Child Development, 56*, 1418–1429.

Stanovich, K. E., & West, R. F. (1979). Mechanisms of sentence context effects in reading: Automatic activation and conscious attention. *Memory & Cognition, 7*, 77–85.

Stanovich, K. E., & West, R. F. (1981). The effect of sentence context on ongoing word recognition: Tests of a two-process theory. *Journal of Experimental Psychology: Human Perception and Performance, 7*, 658–672.

Stanovich, K. E., & West, R. F. (1983a). On priming by a sentence context. *Journal of Experimental Psychology: General, 112*, 1–36.

Stanovich, K. E., & West, R. F. (1983b). The generalizability of context effects on word recognition: A reconsideration of the roles of parafoveal priming and sentence context. *Memory & Cognition, 11*, 49–58.

Stanovich, K. E., West, R. F., & Feeman, D. J. (1981). A longitudinal study of sentence context effects in second-grade children: Tests of an interactive-compensatory model. *Journal of Experimental Child Psychology, 32*, 185–199.

Sternberg, R. J. (1985). Controlled versus automatic processing. *Behavioral and Brain Sciences, 8*, 32–33.

Sternberg, S. (1969). The discovery of processing stages: Extensions of Donders' method. In W. Koster (Ed.), *Attention and Performance* (Vol. 2, pp. 276–315). Amsterdam: North-Holland.

Sticht, T. G., & James, J. H. (1984). Listening and reading. In P. D. Pearson, R. Barr, M. L. Kamil, & P. Mosenthal (Eds.), *Handbook of reading research*, (Vol. 1). White Plains, NY: Longman.

Strange, M. (1979). The effect of orthographic anomalies upon reading behavior. *Journal of Reading Behavior, 11,* 153–161.

Tanenhaus, M. K., Dell, G. S., & Carlson, G. (1987). Context effects in lexical processing: A connectionist approach to modularity. In J. Garfield (Ed.), *Modularity in knowledge representation and natural language understanding* (pp. 160–187). Cambridge, MA: MIT Press.

Tanenhaus, M. K., & Lucas, M. M. (1987). Context effects in lexical processing. *Cognition, 25,* 213–234.

Thorndike, R. L. (1973–1974). Reading as reasoning. *Reading Research Quarterly, 9,* 135–147.

Till, R. E., Mross, E. F., & Kintsch, W. (1988). Time course of priming for associate and inference words in a discourse context. *Memory & Cognition, 16,* 283–298.

Treiman, R., & Zukowsky, A. (in press). Levels of phonological awareness. In S. Brady & D. Shankweiler (Eds.), *Phonological processes in literacy.* Hillsdale, NJ: Erlbaum.

Van Orden, G. (1987). A ROWS is a ROSE: Spelling, sound, and reading. *Memory & Cognition, 15,* 181–198.

Van Orden, G., Johnston, J., & Hale, B. (1988). Word identification in reading proceeds from spelling to sound to meaning. *Journal of Experimental Psychology: Learning, Memory, and Cognition, 14,* 371–386.

Van Orden, G., Pennington, B., & Stone, G. (1988). Word identification in reading and the promise of subsymbolic psycholinguistics. Unpublished manuscript.

Van Petten, C., & Kutas, M. (1987). Ambiguous words in context: An event-related potential analysis of the time course of meaning activation. *Journal of Memory and Language, 26,* 188–208.

Vellutino, F. R. (1982). Theoretical issues in the study of word recognition: The unit of perception controversy reexamined. In S. Rosenberg (Ed.), *Handbook of applied psycholinguistics* (pp. 13–197). Hillsdale, NJ: Erlbaum.

Vellutino, F. R., & Scanlon, D. (1987). Phonological coding, phonological awareness, and reading ability: Evidence from a longitudinal and experimental study. *Merrill-Palmer Quarterly, 33,* 321–363.

Venezky, R. L. (1970). *The structure of English orthography.* The Hague: Mouton.

Venezky, R. L. (1977). Research on reading processes: A historical perspective. *American Psychologist, 32,* 339–345.

Venezky, R. L., & Massaro, D. W. (1987). Orthographic structure and spelling-sound regularity in reading English words. In A. Allport, D. MacKay, W. Prinz, & E. Scheerer (Eds.), *Language perception and production* (pp. 159–179). London: Academic Press.

Wagner, R. K. (1988). Causal relations between the development of phonological processing abilities and the acquisition of reading skills: A meta-analysis. *Merrill-Palmer Quarterly, 34,* 261–279.

Wagner, R. K., & Rashotte, C. A. (1989). Word frequency and consistency in word recognition: Pre-lexical effects or post-lexical artifacts? Unpublished manuscript.

Wagner, R. K., & Torgesen, J. K. (1987). The nature of phonological processing and its causal role in the acquisition of reading skills. *Psychological Bulletin, 101,* 192–212.

Waters, G., & Seidenberg, M. (1985). Spelling-sound effects in reading: Time-course and decision criteria. *Memory & Cognition, 13,* 557–572.

Waters, G., Seidenberg, M., & Bruck, M. (1984). Children's and adults' use of spelling-sound information in three reading tasks. *Memory & Cognition, 12,* 293–305.

West, R. F., & Stanovich, K. E. (1978). Automatic contextual facilitation in readers of three ages. *Child Development, 49,* 717–727.

West, R. F., & Stanovich, K. E. (1979). The development of automatic word recognition skills. *Journal of Reading Behavior, 11,* 211–219.

West, R. F., & Stanovich, K. E. (1982). Sources of inhibition in experiments on the effect of sentence context on word recognition. *Journal of Experimental Psychology: Learning, Memory, and Cognition, 8,* 385–399.

West, R. F., & Stanovich, K. E. (1986). Robust effects of syntactic structure on visual word processing. *Memory & Cognition, 14,* 104–112.

West, R. F., & Stanovich, K. E. (1988). How much of sentence priming is word priming? *Bulletin of the Psychonomic Society, 26,* 1–4.

Whaley, J., & Kibby, M. (1981). The relative importance of reliance on intraword characteristics and interword constraints for beginning reading achievement. *Journal of Educational Research, 74,* 315–320.

Williams, J. P. (1986). The role of phonemic analysis in reading. In J. Torgesen & B. Wong (Eds.), *Psychological and educational perspectives on learning disabilities* (pp. 399–416). New York: Academic Press.

Wixson, K. K. (1979). Miscue analysis: A critical review. *Journal of Reading Behavior, 11,* 163–175.

Wixson, K. K., & Peters, C. W. (1987). Comprehension assessment: Implementing an interactive view of reading. *Educational Psychologist, 22,* 333–356.

Zbrodoff, N. J., & Logan, G. D. (1986). On the autonomy of mental processes: A case study of arithmetic. *Journal of Experimental Psychology: General, 115,* 118–130.

Zola, D. (1984). Redundancy and word perception during reading. *Perception & Psychophysics, 36,* 277–284.

17 RESEARCH ON RESPONSE TO LITERATURE

Richard Beach and Susan Hynds

In his, book, *The Reflective Practitioner*, Donald Schön (1983) describes a typical public school, where "[t]he curriculum is conceived as a menu of information and skills, each lesson plan is a serving, and the entire process is treated as a cumulative, progressive development" (p. 329). Research, evaluation, and teaching based on what Schon calls a "bureaucratic efficiency" model is aimed at providing a normative, uniform curriculum for the majority of students.

Many of the chapters in this volume appear to reflect this normative orientation. Reading research has largely focused on *referential meaning* (as measured by recalls, think-alouds, cloze tests, or multiple-choice items). Since referential meaning can be easily measured, reading researchers are able to assess, through standardized tests, how well readers approximate an ideal or appropriate response (Applebee, Langer, & Mullis, 1987; Educational Commission of the States, 1981; Ravitch & Finn, 1987). Instructional approaches based on schema theoretic and text grammar models of reading have been designed to help the majority of readers develop cognitive frameworks for dealing with school-based texts. While it could be argued that such reading assessments yield valuable information, they can also be criticized for their limitations in approximating nonacademic reading situations and their insensitivity to differences among readers (Tierney, in press).

In contrast to a normative, skills-based model, Schön proposes a curriculum based on

> an inventory of *themes* of understanding and skill to be addressed rather than a set of materials to be learned. Different students present different phenomena for understanding and action. Each student makes up a universe of one, whose potentials, problems, and pace of work must be appreciated as the teacher reflects-in-action on the design of her work. (p. 333)

In contrast to much reading research, researchers in literary response have tended to conceptualize each reader as "a universe of one," thus challenging the notion of the normative response to literary texts. Many studies in literary response have explored reader characteristics such as gender, personality orientation, and attitudes, as well as a variety of text characteristics as related to readers' response processes.

It should be noted, though, that while the field of literary response research *as a whole* is based on the notion that readers' responses are individual and multifaceted, *individual* studies of literary response may appear somewhat fragmented in limiting the cause of individual differences to isolated reader attributes. In studying gender and reading, for example, one might argue that the responses of white college-educated women in a classroom setting may reveal far different response patterns than responses of noneducated racially and ethnically mixed populations of women in a workplace environment. Thus, studies that isolate "gender" in literary response are limited in explaining how this factor interacts with other variables in the literary experience.

Recently, literary response theorists have also begun to ask, "How individual is the 'individual' reader's response?" arguing that people read within a variety of social contexts and interpretive communities (Culler, 1980; Fish, 1980; Mailloux, 1982). Readers themselves are defined by their membership in particular discourse communities. For example, students may learn to conceive of themselves as "literary critics," "mystery buffs," and so on through participation in *discourse practices* (Cooper, in press) within particular interpretive environments. Thus, it is problematic to speak of global reader "attributes" apart from a consideration of contextual factors. While each reader is unique, each also shares particular cultural, social, and interpretive experiences with other readers.

Some recent studies have responded to this complexity by attempting to study reading processes within, and not apart from, the contexts of home and school (Harste, Woodward & Burke, 1984; Heath, 1985, Marshall, 1987). Studying these processes in context has the obvious advantage of exploring readers' responses in natural settings. However, considering the fact that literary response processes are often implicit, rather than explicit, researchers must invariably impose some artificial constraints such as think-aloud or interview procedures on informants.

Furthermore, when a researcher is interested in one particular factor such as gender, age, or previous experience with reading, it is often difficult to find narrowly defined populations of readers within "natural contexts." Although particular reader attributes can be isolated through quasi-experimental procedures, it is important to remember that in real reading situations, reader attributes do not operate independently of each other.

Thus, researchers often choose to isolate particular reader variables, while recognizing that such neat distinctions do not exist among real readers. When viewed in isolation, then, the range of individual differences defined by particular studies in this review is not very large, nor are the contributing factors. However, when considered as a whole, such studies begin to paint a composite picture of the ways that individuals respond to texts and the factors that influence their responses.

Researchers in literary response are interested in several questions: What different processes operate during reading? What types of responses are readers likely to make? What stances or orientations do readers bring to literary texts? How have their knowledge of textual and social conventions and their reading experiences in the home and school influenced their responses? What types of strategies do they use in responding to literature? What is the influence of their knowledge, ability, attitude, interest, personality, or purpose on their responses?

The purpose of this review is to address these issues in both broad and narrow strokes. Broadly, the chapter will discuss theoretical and research perspectives underlying recent work in literary response, as well as methodological considerations relevant to researchers. More narrowly, it will present the results of recent studies that focus on response processes as influenced by factors in the reader, the text, and the instructional context. We begin by discussing some theoretical underpinnings of response research.

PERSPECTIVES ON LITERARY RESPONSE

Although theorists and researchers in literary response ascribe varying degrees of importance to reader and text in the creation of meaning, most view the process as somewhat "transactional" in nature (for reviews of different theories, see de Beaugrande, 1988; Eagleton, 1983; Freund, 1987; and Ray, 1984). In his seminal study of Cambridge undergraduates, Richards (1929) discovered a variety of readings, or "misreadings," in students' responses to poetry. While the New Critics were later to focus on the sources of those misreadings, the reader response critics, beginning with Louise

Rosenblatt (1983), focused on the variety of possible interpretations within any group of readers. In contrast to the New Critical view that all meaning resides in the text, several scholars (Britton, 1984; Harste, 1985; Rosenblatt, 1978, 1983) have argued that meaning emerges in the *transaction* between reader and text. According to this transactional view, Louise Rosenblatt observed that ". . . the human being is not seen as a separate entity, acting upon the environment, nor the environment as acting on the organism, but both as parts or aspects of a total event" (1978, p. 98).

While reading researchers often consider the unique contributions of reader and text to the total reading experience, their perspective is characterized by Rosenblatt as "an interactional view in which the text, on the one hand, and the personality of the reader, on the other, can be separately analyzed" (1985, p. 100). Rosenblatt calls for sharper distinctions between "interactive" and "transactive" views of reading when she says:

> Both the "bottom-up" and "top-down" approaches to the reading process need a thorough critical rethinking in the light of the transactional theory of reading which sees both reader and text as active, but in an organic, rather than a linear mechanical way. "Inferring" is not something that is simply to be added on to "decoding," for example. (1985, p. 101)

Thus, readers both transform and are transformed by literary works. By this notion, the reading experience is influenced by the stances readers take toward texts (Britton, 1968, 1984; Dillon, 1978, 1982; Harding, 1962; Hunt & Vipond, 1985, 1986b); Rosenblatt, 1978, 1983, 1985; as well as the cognitive and psychological processes they bring to the reading process (Applebee, 1978; Bleich, 1978, 1980, 1986a; Holland, 1973, 1975, 1985b; Petrosky, 1977b). However, while interpretations presumably differ from one reader to the next, commonalities or "recurrences" of meaning within any community of readers emerge as readers share common backgrounds, psychological predispositions, and interpretive strategies (Beach & Brown, 1987; Bleich, 1986a; Flynn, 1983; Petrosky, 1981).

Within this transactional perspective shared by most response theorists, there is considerable disagreement as to the degree to which the reader and/or the text contributes to meaning and how meaning is constituted. Moreover, researchers come to the study of response from a variety of theoretical perspectives—cognitive psychology, literary theory, psychoanalytic theory, and rhetoric—resulting in different explanations of readers' responses. For example, researchers from cognitive psychological orientations explain a reader's understanding in terms of applying appropriate cognitive structures (Bruce & Rubin, 1984; Collins, Brown, & Larkin, 1980), while researchers from a psychoanalytic orientation explain response in terms of readers' fantasies, identity themes, or other psychological predispositions (Bleich, 1978; Holland, 1973, 1975). Such theoretical distinctions among researchers in literary response strongly influence research methodologies, as well as the nature and validity of elicited responses. The following section describes several frameworks for conceptualizing readers' responses.

RESEARCH ON RESPONSE CATEGORIES, LEVELS, AND PROCESSES

In this section we explore the category systems that have been used to describe the types and levels of readers' responses. We then review current research on specific response processes. This review of research on response to literature leans more towards recent theory and research. For other reviews of research, refer to Applebee, 1977; Beach and Hynds, 1989; Cooper, 1976; Hauptmeier, Neutsh, & Viehoff (1989); Klemenz-Belgardt, 1981; Monson and Petola, 1976; Petrosky, 1977a; Purves and Beach, 1972; and Schmidt, 1985.

Response Category Systems

The analytical frameworks emanating from content analyses of written and oral protocols are typically used to illustrate types, levels, or quality of responses. Table 17.1 summarizes the major category systems employed in previous studies of literary response. Readers, for example, may respond to texts by describing, evaluating certain aspects, engaging personally, analyzing, or in a host of other ways.

In a critique of the Squire (1964), Purves and Rippere (1968), and Purves and Beach (1972) categories, Applebee (1977) questions whether such systems are valid and reliable taxonomies, in that they may fail to capture the complexities of the response process of readers' underlying intentions. As with any content analysis category system, an investigator cannot intuit the underlying purpose of a statement. For example, while on the surface, readers may be employing an "engagement response," they may have intended the overall response to be judgmental.

Analyzing specific "statements," or T-units, may also fail to capture readers' overall preferred response mode. Cooper and Michalak's (1981) analyses of inconsistencies in students' responses, using the Purves and Rippere (1968) system, reveal that analyses of percentages of separate response statements employed were inconsistent with readers' overall response orientations within the essay response. For example, readers may employ a high percentage of judging or engaging statements, but their overall orientation may actually be "interpretation."

More recently, researchers have revised the Purves categories to determine the reader's focus on specific aspects of texts (Galda, 1983a; Nissel, 1987), or the degree to which responses are text or reader based (Galda, 1983b; MacLean, 1986). In a study of fourth-grade female response to both fantasy and realistic stories, Nissel (1987) generated a category system based on readers' focus on "characters," "themes," and "events." Thus, researchers have begun to move beyond simple descriptions of response types to consider the underlying purposes or focus of response.

While studies of response types have yielded valuable information about global ways that readers interpret texts, more recent research has begun to investigate how readers use various combinations of responses in the process of reading. Some interesting studies have examined how readers systematically employ *frameworks*, or *heuristics*, for exploring meaning (Odell & Cooper, 1976). For example, based on Bleich's (1975) three-stage heuristic ("describe," "autobiographical," and "interpret"), Petrosky (1981) examined writers' uses of text perceptions to evoke autobiographical recollections, instrumental in interpreting the text.

Researchers using a *clustering technique* (Beach 1983, 1985; Beach & Wendler, 1987) have focused on categories of readers' inferences (e.g., the degree to which a group of readers inferred that Willy Loman in *Death of a Salesman* was "tragic" or merely "pathetic"). For example, in Beach and Wendler (1987), judges clustered answers to questions about a specific character's acts, beliefs, and goals, resulting in three to five composite categories for each answer. Similarly, Radway (1984) clustered reasons that women readers cited for liking romance novels (e.g., "happy ending"). Determining these categories provides some understanding of the range of different perceptions of the same phenomenon.

Analyses of Levels of Response

Beyond content analysis systems for describing responses, some investigators have attempted to judge the quality, or *level*, of response according to the criteria cited in Table 17.2. While most researchers in literary response are careful not to specify an *ideal* response, some category systems appear to differentiate more complex from less

TABLE 17.1   Category Systems Describing Types of Response

INVESTIGATOR	CATEGORIES
Richards (1929)	"making sense," "sensuous apprehension," "visualizing," "imagery," "mnemonic irrelevancies," "stock responses," "oversentimentality," "inhibition," "doctrinal adhesions," "technical presuppositions," "critical preconceptions about literature"
Squire (1964)	"associational," "prescriptive judgment," "self-involvement," "narrational reaction," "interpretation," "evaluation," "miscellaneous"
Purves & Rippere (1968)	"engagement," "perception," "interpretation," "evaluation," "miscellaneous"
Johnson (1975)	"decoding," "valuing," "situating literary context," "interpreting," "inferring social conjectures," "adducing private associations"
Odell & Cooper (1976)	"contrast," "classification," "causality," "physical context," "temporal sequence"
Applebee (1978)	"narration," "summarization," "analysis," "generalization"
NAEP (1981)	"egocentric," "personal-analytic," "personal-global," "emotional," "retelling," "inferencing," "generalization," "analysis-superficial," "analysis-elaborated," "other works—general," "other works—specific," "evaluation"
Lytle (1982)	*think-aloud protocols:* "monitoring," "signaling," "analyzing," "elaborating," "judging," "reasoning"
Kintgen (1983)	*poetry responses:* "comment," "narrate," "read," "select," "locate," "word," "phonology," "syntax," "paraphrase," "form," "deduce," "generalize," "connect poem: nature, history, literature," "test," "justify," "qualify," "specify," "interpret."
Vipond & Hunt (1984)	*orientation:* "information-driven," "story-driven," "point-driven"
de Beaugrande (1985)	"staging," "hedging," "citing," "key-word;" "associations," "paraphrasing," "normalizing," "generalizing"
Dias (1987); Dias & Hayhoe (1988)	*poetry responses:* "paraphrasing," "thematicizing," "allegorizing," "problem-solving"
Hynds (1987)	*text-invoked:* "literal/descriptive" (work, characters, context); "interpretive/inferential (story, character) *reader-invoked:* "personal evaluations," "engagement," "disengagement"
Nissel (1987)	*characters:* "evaluation" vs. "inferences" *events:* "evaluation" vs. "inferences" *themes:* "isolated" vs. "integrated"
Langer (1989)	*stances:* "being out and stepping into," "being in and moving through," "stepping back and rethinking what one knows," "stepping out and objectifying the experience"

TABLE 17.2   Category Systems Describing Levels of Response

INVESTIGATOR	CATEGORIES
NAEP (1981)	*Analysis of characters:* "Unable to identify traits," "traits identified," "no" vs. "minimal" vs. "extensive substantiation"
	Analysis of poetry themes: "synopsis," "state theme," "no analysis," "minimal analysis," "integrated analysis"
	Citing criteria for judgments: "unelaborated vs. two or more unelaborated vs. elaborated criteria," "two elaborated criteria"
Svensson (1985)	"literal description," "literal interpretation," "mixed literal-thematic," "thematic," "mixed literal-symbolic," "symbolic"
Hillocks & Ludlow (1984)	*Identifying:* "basic stated information," "key detail," "stated relationship"
	Inferring: "simple implied relationship," "complex implied relationship," "author's generalization," "structural generalization"
Marshall (1987)	*Levels of interpretation:* (1) "brief, shallow answer; little effort"; (2) "summarizes narrative; low-level inferences"; (3) "one or more inferences; little specific support"; (4) "one or more, but incomplete inferences with some specific support"; (5) "reports and associates details with inferences"; (6) "one or more elaborated inferences with specific support from text"
Thompson (1987)	"unreflective interest in action," "empathizing," "analogizing," "reflecting on significance of events and behavior," "reviewing the work as the author's creation," "defining one's own and the author's ideology"

complex response processes. Researchers, for example, may distinguish between readers who are more and less able to identify character traits and psychological states, or readers who exhibit more or less elaborated analyses of texts.

It is tempting to conclude that such category systems appear to represent a normative, or standardized, view of response. However, despite the fact that some studies deal with different levels of response, few would argue that such responses are the *only* acceptable responses within every reading context. In particular instructional settings, for instance (i.e., when teachers ask for elaborated inferences about characters or meanings), readers need to develop a repertoire of skills for producing sophisticated analyses of texts. However, some reading situations (i.e., reading for pleasure) do not demand such complex processes. In fact, one might argue that, in the context of "light reading," engagement-involvement responses might be more appropriate than analytic responses, just as a "story-driven" orientation (Vipond & Hunt, 1984) might be more appropriate than a "point-driven" orientation.

As Rosenblatt (1985) has argued, "Since much of our linguistic activity hovers near the middle of the 'efferent-aesthetic' continuum, it becomes essential that in any particular speaking/listening/writing/reading event we adopt the predominant stance appropriate to our purpose" (p. 102). Similarly, Hunt, Vipond, Reither, and Jewett (in press) make the point that

> No one mode [of response] is best, but we do suggest that full reading capacity requires that the reader be able to use, flexibly, whichever mode or modes is most appropriate to the specific conjunction of text, purpose, and situation. Given that texts and situations vary, readers who are able to move freely in and out of any of the modes . . . would, by most external criteria, be judged more "successful" than those readers restricted to one or two modes. (p. 34).

Thus, while most researchers in response to literature are careful to avoid defining "good" reading in terms of specific *types* of response, an underlying assumption seems to be that developing a sophisticated *repertoire* of response options to use in a variety of reading situations should be a major goal of literature instruction. In light of this definition of good response, it is important to be aware of the value assumptions underlying any analysis of response levels. For example, the National Assessment of Educational Progress (NAEP) criteria (Educational Commission of the States, 1981) measure the degree of evidence that students use to support a thesis from a text. Such underlying criteria seem to represent a conflation of logical ability, insightfulness, and knowing the proper discourse form for the typical literary essay. Criteria from standardized tests should also be viewed cautiously, in that these criteria are useful for defining success within a particular examination setting, and not within every reading context.

Research on Response Processes

While readers' responses can be categorized according to some global response types or levels, many recent studies have attempted to define the *processes* that readers engage in during reading. In this section, we review studies focusing on such processes as engaging, conceiving, connecting, problem solving, explaining, interpreting, and judging. This discussion will set the stage for the subsequent exploration of how such strategies are influenced by factors in the reader, the text, and the instructional context.

Engaging. Readers' emotional experiences are central to their literary experience. Bruner (1986) argues that literature "subjunctivizes" experience or "makes strange, renders the obvious less so, the unknowable less so as well" (p. 59). Drawing on Todorov's analysis of transformations of uses of verbs from a static to an ongoing subjunctive mode, he found that a reader's own delayed recall of a Joyce story contained similar subjunctive transformations employed in the Joyce story. This suggested to Bruner that the subjunctive mood intentionally created in the story is preserved in the reader's response.

Other studies have similarly concluded that emotional content in stories is reflected in readers' responses. Based on readers' responses to 58 "perception-appraisal" and 21 "stimulus-specific" feeling scales, Hansen (1986) found, not surprisingly, that readers responded more positively to an optimistic, upbeat poem than to a "negative" poem. Also, not surprisingly, readers' emotional states are influenced by the emotional content of literature; readers who were unhappy before reading a relatively gloomy poem became even more unhappy after reading the poem (Hansen, 1986).

Becoming engaged or involved in the fictional world of a text requires readers to suspend disbelief and accept the fictional world as distinct from their own (Britton,

1970; Galda, 1983a; Petrosky, 1977b). Several studies indicate that readers often have difficulty suspending disbelief and adopting characters' perspectives (Benton, 1983; Britton, 1984; Jacobsen, 1982; Landry, Kelly, & Gardner, 1982). These "reality-bound" readers react negatively to texts that do not conform to their sense of reality (Culp, 1977, 1985; Hunt & Vipond, 1985).

Other researchers have concluded that story liking is related to readers' willingness to seek out texts and judge characters positively (Stout, 1964; Thomson, 1987), as well as their expectations about story structure (Jose & Brewer, 1984). Readers who have positive attitudes toward texts have a higher degree of engagement than do readers with negative attitudes (Shedd, 1976). *Literary transfer*, or the tendency to apply literature to life, has been related to the tendency among readers to select questions about literature focused on the relationships between characters' acts and real life, as well as the emotional effect of the text and the reader's involvement (Purves, 1981). Readers who derive a high degree of pleasure from reading are more likely to vary their reading rates in order to "savor" certain passages and to enter into a dreamlike trance while reading (Nell, 1988).

As could be expected, young children tend to like stories with characters whom they perceive as similar to themselves and identify with, as well as outcomes that adhere to a "just world" motif (good characters receive good outcomes and bad characters receive bad outcomes) (Jose & Brewer, 1984). Such a finding is similar to Squire's (1964) concept of "happiness-binding," or adolescents' expectations that stories should end positively.

Researchers have examined how engagement is related to story understanding and liking (Jose & Brewer, 1984; Black & Seifert, 1985; Golden & Guthrie, 1986; Mosenthal, 1987). Golden and Guthrie (1986) found a significant relationship between high school students' empathy for a story character and understanding of the story conflict. By empathizing with a certain character, students were more likely to select a conflict option involving that character. As readers empathize with characters' failures to achieve certain goals, they attempt to explain those failures by applying knowledge of certain themes (Black & Seifert, 1985). For example, readers familiar with the theme, "Don't count your chickens before they hatch," may empathize with a character who prematurely believed that he or she would achieve a goal. Similarly, readers who are attuned to suspense-creating linguistic devices dramatizing conflict develop an engagement with the text (Mosenthal, 1987).

The degree to which readers like a text has been related to their tendencies to infer its emotional and intellectual implications (Purves, 1981). Such findings regarding the importance of engaging are interesting, in light of analyses of sixth-grade basal manuals that indicated a predominance of cognitive as opposed to affective activities (Shapiro, 1985).

Conceiving.   Research that focuses on conceiving explores readers' descriptions or conceptions of texts, which function as necessary prerequisites for further explanation and interpretation (Hillocks & Ludlow, 1984). While much research has focused on individual differences among readers, many studies have discovered highly similar perceptions of the same text among groups of readers (e.g., Hansson, 1973, 1985). Researchers have begun to explore how readers use personal constructs (Kelly, 1955) in responding to literature. For example, Miall (1985) found that readers apply certain sets of constructs (i.e., "ignorance/knowledge," "enduring/not enduring") to interpret poetry. Readers who had difficulty defining their initial emotional reactions had difficulty generating and defining these constructs. In another study of personal constructs and responses to literature, adolescents applied their constructs for death to their responses to novels (Mauro, 1983). Thus, personal constructs formed from experiences in the real world shape readers' responses in the fictional world.

Readers also differ in their conceptions of literary characters. For example, as readers shifted focus from story development to character relationships in response to *The Tempest*, their perceptions and judgments of characters became increasingly more complex (DeVries, 1973). College students were significantly more likely than high school students to conceive of characters' acts in terms of social and psychological phenomena (as opposed to physical behaviors) and characters' goals in terms of long-range (as opposed to short-term) consequences (Beach & Wendler, 1987). Readers with a large interpersonal construct repertoire tended toward more elaborate and complex interpretations of the actions and behaviors of literary characters than readers with a smaller construct repertoire (Hynds, 1985).

Connecting experiences, attitudes, and knowledge to texts.   Some studies have focused on the ways in which readers apply autobiographical experiences (Beach, 1983; Shedd, 1976), cultural attitudes (Lipson, 1983), and knowledge of other texts (Agee, 1983; Beach, Appleman, & Dorsay, in press; Black, Wilkes-Gibbs, & Gibbs, 1981; Svensson, 1985) to their literary responses (for a review, see Beach, 1980; Heine, 1985; Lipson, 1983; Ortony, Turner, & Larson-Shapiro, 1985; Reynolds, Taylor, Steffeusen, Shirley, & Anderson, 1982). Studies of college students' responses in journals (Beach, 1987; Harste, 1986) reported that a relatively high percentage of readers connect literary works with related experiences, other texts, literary prototypes, and personal attitudes. Readers who are more able to elaborate on their own experiences are also better able to define the point of those experiences, and consequently better able to interpret literary texts (Beach, in press; Petrosky, 1981). Some researchers have argued that one of the major gaps in response research is in understanding how "intertextual" references to other works serve to evoke knowledge of literary prototypes that may be used to understand the current text (Lehr, 1988; Wolf, 1988).

Problem solving/question asking.   Few studies have explored the role of problem-solving strategies or question asking in understanding literature (Black & Bower, 1980; Bruce & Rubin, 1984; Newkirk, 1984; Young, 1986). Singer and Donlan (1982) found that readers taught to pose their own questions about stories achieved better story understanding than readers who were not taught to do so. Newkirk (1984) found that when readers were able to articulate difficulties in understanding texts, they were better able to apply problem-solving strategies to cope with those difficulties. Less able readers applied problem-solving strategies with less flexibility than better readers (Olshavsky, 1976). Secondary students were more likely to define problems in terms of understanding characters and their actions, while college students were more likely to define problems in terms of understanding thematic meanings (Beach & Saxton, 1982). In an analysis of secondary students' revisions of responses across re-readings of poems, Teasey (1988) found that students used question asking to define consistent patterns linking similar images and concepts in the poems.

Explaining.   The National Assessment of Educational Progress examined 13- and 17-year-olds' ability to write essays explaining inferences about a character or mood or their overall feelings about a text (Educational Commission of the States, 1981). Only one-fourth of 13-year-olds and two-fifths of 17-year-olds were able to provide an explanation of inferences judged to be "adequate" by the raters. The majority of students provided little or no evidence to support their inferences. Students were better able to explain feelings than interpretations about characters or mood, but even essays explaining feeling lacked any systematic approach. The poor performance of disadvantaged and minority students, as well as the lower overall performance of students when compared with students a decade earlier, suggested to NAEP investigators that students lacked systematic heuristic strategies for citing textual evidence to support their explanations.

Other researchers have found that attitudes toward reading or information about characters' act, belief, and goal relationships provided in particular texts influenced readers' abilities to infer and explain characters' actions (see Black & Seifert, 1985, for a review). Bruce (1984) discovered that the tendency of modern literary textbooks to delete beliefs and motives of characters in their story "revisions" may contribute to students' difficulty in explaining characters' acts.

Interpreting.   Unfortunately, few studies in the area of literary response describe the specific processes contributing to symbolic or thematic interpretation. Some studies from a reading perspective have concluded that readers construct models (Collins, Brown, & Larkin, 1980) or interpretive hypotheses (Bruce & Rubin, 1984) designed to extract the point or theme of a story (Labov, 1972; Schank, 1982). However, only a few researchers have begun to explore how this interpretive process is influenced by such factors as readers' stances toward texts, their cognitive development, the tasks they are asked to perform, and their previous experience with literature.

Hunt and Vipond (1985, 1986a) demonstrated that the majority of adolescents and young adults studied lacked the "point-driven" orientation, which predisposed them to interpret the author's intention in literary texts. The majority of students were either "information driven" or "story driven" in orientation. Hunt and Vipond's findings are consistent with much of the developmental research, which indicates that prior to high school, few readers focus their response predominately on interpretation (Applebee, 1978; Educational Commission of the States, 1981; Purves, 1981).

In a study of 9-, 13- and 17-year-old students' interpretations of poems, Svensson (1985) found that few 11-year-olds, some 14-year-olds, and most 17-year-olds could infer symbolic or thematic significance in poems. Svensson further concluded that students with more exposure to literature at school and in the home were more likely to make such interpretations.

Conclusions drawn from the NAEP report (Educational Commission of the States, 1981) indicate that both 13- and 17-year-old students were less likely to generalize or analyze texts than to employ retelling, engaging, evaluation, or specific inferences in their responses. The NAEP data did reveal, however, that students were more likely to analyze stories with familiar than with unfamiliar story content.

Readers' interpretations of literature are also influenced by their background experiences with literature (Black & Seifert, 1985; Heath, 1985). In a case-study analysis of preschoolers, Martinez (1983) found that parent-child interactions about children's literature fostered inferences, and that the child's response profile matched that of the parent. Thus, Martinez concluded that children undergo early socialization in literary interpretation processes. Svennson (1985) has argued that conclusions about cognitive development are limited because of the pervasive influence of cultural background or exposure to reading in the school and home. Thus, it is difficult to tease out issues of development in interpretation from issues of what Svennson calls "cultural socialization," or the ways in which reading is presented within a reader's home and school culture.

Judging.   Research on judging has examined the personal and intellectual criteria that contribute to readers' evaluations of the form and content of literary texts (Purves & Beach, 1972). As readers acquire knowledge of literature, they are more likely to base judgments on the complexity and depth of form of literary works, as opposed to the story content (Britton, 1984). Given the tendency of younger readers to focus on content rather than form, they are more likely than older readers to judge texts they do not understand negatively (Squire, 1964).

Binkney (1986) found significant differences between adults and secondary students in judgments of adolescent novels on criteria of subject matter, critical recommendation, and appearance. Thus, there may be little relationship between what adults approve of and what adolescents prefer to read.

Reading interest and cognitive maturity have also been found to be related to aesthetic judgment. Adult readers who read voraciously perceived literary quality or merit as inversely related to pleasure, a finding attributed to the Protestant ethic of hard work as opposed to "simple pleasures" (Nell, 1988). College students' levels of aesthetic judgment were correlated with levels of cognitive maturity (Parnell, 1984). High school students with a high interest in literature were more likely to prefer responses involving critical analyses of texts than were low-interest students (Purves, 1981). It is difficult to make generalizations about discrete response types, since responses such as explaining or describing are often embedded in superordinate strategies such as judging or interpreting. Large-scale evaluations that attempt to define reading "ability" according to criteria, such as supporting a thesis about a text, may fail to tease out the variety of subprocesses that contribute to "competence" (i.e., knowledge of discourse conventions, knowledge of what constitutes evidence, and affective factors such as the will or the predisposition to read analytically). Thus, curricula based solely on skill or competence building may often be ineffective in promoting the very competencies they are designed to foster. In addition to exploring response processes and strategies, many studies have explored factors in the reader, the text, and the institutional context that influence readers' responses.

THE READER

While the preceding discussion focused on categories, levels, and processes of response, this section focuses on the *reader*. Previous research has found that readers differ according to their stances toward texts and reading, social and cultural attitudes, personality, cognitive and social-cognitive attributes, and knowledge of social and discourse conventions. This brief review of the various conceptions of the reader in research and theory on literary response will set the stage for the discussion of textual and contextual influences to follow.

Stances, Orientations, and Attitudes

Stances toward texts and reading. Readers' stances toward literature, or their degree of interest in particular texts, influence the amount of reading and literature achievement, which, in turn, affect response preference (Purves, Foshay, & Hanson, 1973; Purves, 1981). Readers also differ in terms of their purpose or goals for reading—differences that shape their orientations or stances toward the text (Dillon, 1978; Vipond & Hunt, 1984). Based on a series of studies, Hunt and Vipond (1985) and Vipond and Hunt (1984) distinguished between "information-driven," story-driven," and "point-driven" orientations. In adapting an *information-driven orientation*, a reader simply reads for information in the text. This is similar to what Rosenblatt (1978) termed an "efferent" stance (i.e., reading that focuses on extracting information, as opposed to "aesthetic reading," which focuses on the immediate experience of reading itself). In adopting a *story-driven orientation*, a reader is primarily reading for the enjoyment of the text and is therefore simply focusing on understanding what happened. In contrast, a reader who adopts a *point-driven orientation* is inferring the author's point or theme. An analysis of secondary students' group responses to poetry (Hurst, 1988) indicated that students applied three different "frames" to the poems—text as "story," "product of the poet," and "form" (p. 176). Students' initial responses, often based on a "story" frame, served to build towards responses based on the "poet" and "form" frames.

Dillon (1978, 1982) defined three basic styles in the reading process. His CAM (Character-Action-Moral) orientation toward reading treats the world of the text as similar to the reader's own world. This process of immersion differs from the critical distance associated with Dillon's other two styles: the "digger for secrets," who searches for the underlying hidden meanings behind events in the story; and the "anthropologist," who searches for the cultural norms and values behind characters' actions.

Flynn's (1986) case study of male and female college students yielded three different stances: "dominant," in which readers control the text by imposing their own assumptions and attitudes onto the text; "submissive," in which readers are controlled by the text, failing to articulate their own perspectives; and "integrated," in which readers neither dominate nor submit to the text, but engage in meaningful transactions.

Readers' stances toward literature and reading in general have been found to influence the elaboration and quality of their responses (Evans, 1969; Golden & Guthrie, 1986; Purves, 1981; Tutton, 1979). For example, Hynds (1989) demonstrated that readers with negative attitudes toward reading, English classes, or particular texts were often reluctant to bring the full range of their interpersonal knowledge to literature. (For a review of methods for analyzing attitudes towards literature, see Chester & Dulin, 1977.)

Social and cultural attitudes.   Readers may respond positively or negatively to texts, depending on the extent to which their attitudes toward interpersonal or social phenomena are reinforced or threatened. For instance, education majors, who held more "liberal" attitudes regarding the teaching of literature, judged a teacher character employing "traditional" teaching methods more negatively than did high school students (Beach, 1983). Similarly, readers with more positive attitudes toward police authority judged a policeman character more positively than did readers with more negative attitudes (Beach & de Beaugrande, 1987).

Readers' attitudes toward social phenomena may also relate to their liking of story characters and resolutions. Younger elementary age readers responded more positively to just-world endings, positive outcomes for good characters and negative outcomes for bad characters (Jose & Brewer, 1984). Dorfman (1985) investigated the idea that when perceptions of character and outcome are consistent with reader beliefs, readers are better able to infer the point of the story. Adult readers in Dorfman's study were better able to infer the point of stories with consistent character/outcome relationships than when character/outcome relationships were inconsistent. That is, when positive characters achieved positive outcomes and negative characters achieved negative outcomes, readers were better able to understand the stories.

The socialization process that occurs in school also shapes readers' responses. A reader may respond publicly as "student," "critic," "psychologist," "teacher," "feminist," and so forth. These roles (Fish, 1980) are influenced by the academic norms associated with schools of literary analysis (Bartholomae, 1985). Students in particular groups are sometimes socialized through instruction to respond differently, with higher SES students responding on a more abstract level than low SES students (Barnes, Barnes, & Clarke, 1984; Purves, 1986).

Students in academic contexts often respond according to what they believe are appropriate, sanctioned responses in a classroom (Harste, 1986), or in terms of creating a social network in the classroom (Hickman, 1983; McClure, 1985). Responses therefore reflect readers' perceptions of their roles as constituted by social, rhetorical, and cultural conventions, so that the social function of responding becomes a means of publicly defining and verifying one's perceptions and attitudes with others.

Personality Characteristics and Attributes

Some theorists conceive of the reader in terms of unique personality attributes or concerns. Through the process of empathizing or engaging with the fantasy or psychological themes in a text, a reader's identity is clarified or transformed on a subconscious, and often later on a conscious, level (Alcorn & Bracher, 1985; Bleich, 1978, 1980; Holland 1973, 1985a, 1985b).

Studies of psychological and personality factors have concluded that readers read in accordance with certain personal "identity themes" (Bleich, 1980; Holland 1973, 1975, 1985a, 1985b; Petrosky, 1977b), and that they recreate literary works in accordance with their own psychological predispositions. For example, such factors as tolerance for ambiguity (Peters & Blues, 1978), assertiveness, ego strength, aggressiveness (Bleich, 1986b), ego development (Trimble, 1984), and self-actualization (Ebersole & DeVogler-Ebersole, 1984) have been related to readers' responses.

In a study using the Myers-Briggs personality inventory, Hynd and Chase (1986) found that college students classified as "feeling types" (those who base judgments on strongly held personal attitudes or values) were more likely to make evaluative, judgmental responses to literature than were "thinking types" (those who make judgments according to logical, objective criteria).

Using an Adjective Check List, Beach and Brunetti (1976) found that high school students were more likely to impose their own personality attributes onto characters than were college students, who tended to view themselves as different from their character in their ability to accept themselves and establish relationships with others. Wheeler (1983) found that "field-dependent" college students (who relied on one structured approach) employed more engagement and perception responses, while "field-independent" students (who transcended one approach) employed more interpretation and evaluation responses.

Cognitive and Social Cognitive Factors

Cognitive and moral development.   Developmental studies of response to literature have demonstrated that as readers enter the formal operations stage, they become increasingly able to think abstractly about literature (Applebee, 1978; Fusco, 1983; Parnell, 1984), while readers in the early formal operations stage tend to respond in terms of surface physical behaviors (Petrosky, 1977b). For example, readers demonstrated a steady increase from ages 7 to 9 to 11 in inferential, as opposed to literal-level, responses (Bunbury, 1985).

In response to two novels, fourth graders responded primarily in terms of retelling and inferring simplistic messages, sixth graders in terms of some symbolic meanings and themes, and eighth graders in terms of multiple meanings and implications for their own lives (Cullinan, Harwood, & Galda, 1983). Similarly, comparisons of eighth graders, eleventh graders, college freshmen, and college seniors have revealed that secondary students were more likely than college students to conceive of characters' acts in terms of physical behaviors as opposed to social or psychological phenomena, characters' perceptions in terms of feelings rather than beliefs, and characters' goals in terms of immediate needs as opposed to long-range strategies (Beach & Wendler, 1987).

A number of studies point to a relationship between readers' levels of moral reasoning and their literary responses (Bennett, 1979; Christensen, 1983; Galda, 1983a; Parnell, 1984; Perine, 1978; Pillar, 1983). For example, Bennett (1979) found that high school males who operated at the principled level of reasoning were more likely to prefer an interpretive mode of response than were students operating at the conventional level. Research using the Defining Issues Test (Rest, 1979) indicates that junior high school students typically reason at stage three ("approval seeking") and stage four ("rule orientation"), while high school students reason more at stage four and stage five ("social utility") (Pierce, 1985).

Social-cognitive aspects of response.   Studies of social cognition in response to literature have begun to explore the ways in which readers use their knowledge of social phenomena in interpreting stories. Studies of story recall and understanding have moved beyond purely cognitive concerns to focus on the psychosocial dimensions of discourse processing (Freedle, 1975; Freedle, Naus, & Schwartz, 1977). For example, Gruenich and Trabasso (1981) reviewed several studies that focused on the attribution of characters' intentions and consequences in stories, and concluded that as readers grow older, a focus on the consequences of characters' behavior declines in favor of a focus on the intentions behind behavior.

Consistent with Piagetian notions of egocentrism and perspectivism, research on adolescent and young adult readers has demonstrated a greater tendency among younger than older readers to project their own self-concepts onto their perceptions of characters (Beach & Brunetti, 1976). Jose and Brewer (1984) studied children in grades two through six, and reported increasingly stronger relationships with age between perceived similarity to story characters and other factors of reader identification and story liking. Readers appear to move from a strong need for character identification to greater recognition of and tolerance for multiple interpersonal perspectives.

Based on the work of Kelly (1955) and Crockett (1965), researchers have found relationships between "interpersonal cognitive complexity," or numbers of interpersonal constructs, for peers and story characters (Hynds, 1985, 1989, in press; Scarlett, Press, & Crocket, 1971). Further research has revealed that cognitive complexity is related to college readers' character interpretation responses, but not to their engagement, evaluation, or literal text-centered responses (Hynds, 1987).

Interestingly, readers are not always predisposed to bring the full range of their interpersonal constructs to particular texts (Hynds, 1985, 1989). Readers who read large numbers of books for pleasure are those with strong tendencies to utilize personal constructs in their character impressions (Hynds, 1985). Such factors as attitudes toward reading and English classes, social support for reading, and liking of particular texts influence the likelihood that readers will use social cognitive processes in interpreting literature (Hynds, 1989).

Thus, an understanding of characters' motives and underlying psychological states is related to social cognitive knowledge formed through interactions in the social world. As readers develop interpersonal knowledge through their relationships with others, they learn to make attributions about the psychological states and behaviors of literary characters. Similarly, as they use social cognitive processes in reading, they develop social knowledge useful in everyday life. The degree to which readers are likely to bring such knowledge to texts, however, is strongly influenced by the academic and social contexts within which they read.

Reader Knowledge

Knowledge of social and discourse conventions.   Previous work has shown that readers' background experiences with certain discourse or literary forms influence their responses. Children who frequently engaged in "sounding" or "playing the dozens" comprehended figurative language better than those who did not (Ortony, Turner, & Larson-Shapiro, 1985). Sixth graders supplied more missing information about character motives in a fairy tale than did third or first graders (Rubin & Gardner, 1985). Similarly, seventh graders demonstrated more critical understanding of satire than did fourth graders (McNamara, 1981). These findings suggest that the older readers were applying knowledge of fairy tale and satire frames or scripts.

In responding to texts, readers learn to adopt certain reader roles involving certain discourse strategies or conventions (Mailloux, 1982; Rabinowitz, 1983, 1985, 1987). For example, a reader who reads mystery stories may acquire a set of conventions constituting the role of "mystery buff" (Rabinowitz, 1985). Readers also acquire knowledge of interpretive strategies associated with "literary competence" (Culler, 1980), or a knowledge of literary conventions such as the notion that "everything counts" in a text.

Other researchers analyzing developmental differences in children's writing have found complexity of character and story interpretations related to their increasing knowledge of literary conventions (Denise, 1986; Pleasnick, 1983; Vardell, 1982). Dressel (1986) studied the effects of reading detective stories aloud in elementary students' story writing and found the greatest improvement in the use of prototypical detective genre characteristics for the high-ability readers.

Readers use this knowledge of literary conventions as well as knowledge of social and cultural conventions (Beach & Brown, 1987; Meustch, 1986; Meutsch & Schmidt, 1985; Viehoff, 1986) to recognize narrators' or speakers' deliberate use of storytelling techniques, as well as characters' violation of social conventions that dramatize the unusual, the extraordinary, or the "tellability" of narratives (Labov, 1972; Pratt, 1976).

Knowledge of literature.   Large-scale assessments of literary knowledge have focused on factual information about texts and authors (Applebee, Langer, & Mullis, 1987; Hirsch, 1987; Ravitch & Finn, 1987). In an analysis of the 1986 NAEP study of 8,000 eleventh graders, Ravitch and Finn (1987) reported that 48 percent of the students answered questions about authors, texts, and literary periods incorrectly. Successful performance on the test was directly related to the amount of instruction and homework students received, as well as their degree of leisure reading. One of three students in the top quarter of performance read for pleasure, while only one of eight in the bottom quarter did so. Fewer than half of all students read for their own purposes or pleasure once a week. It seems plausible that students acquire more knowledge about literature from additional reading. Further research is needed, however, to explore how reading for pleasure relates to a more positive attitude towards literature achievement (Purves, 1981).

Gender

Recent research exploring gender differences in response points to distinctly different response orientations (for a review of research, see Crawford & Chaffin, 1986). Flynn (1986) found that males tended either to distance themselves from the text, attempting to dominate it, or to become exclusively focused on their own personal perceptions and attitudes. In detaching themselves from the emotional content of the text, or in becoming overly conscious of their own perspectives, the male students often failed to understand the complexities of the characters' dilemmas. Females, on the other hand, were more able to achieve a balanced relationship between distance and immersion in the text. However, when texts portray women's traditional sex roles, women readers have been found to distance themselves, "resisting" the implied values (Fetterly, 1979; Kaivola, 1987). Gender has been found to influence not only readers' stances toward texts, but their story liking as well. Twelfth graders who favored changes in women's roles responded more positively to portrayals of women in "liberated roles" than did readers who did not favor change (Shedd, 1976). On the other hand, fourth-, seventh-, and twelfth-grade females responded more positively to narratives about "traditional" than "nontraditional" females (Scott, 1986).

A study of children's book preferences in grades four to ten revealed that the importance of male protagonists decreases for males and increases for females, while the importance of female protagonists increases for males, but not for females (Johnson, Peer, & Baldwin, 1984). Hansen (1986) found that males responded to more formal aspects of poems about war and death than did females, who responded more to the poems' issues or messages. These differences were attributed to males' tendency to distance themselves emotionally from the text and to female readers' concern about issues of death and war portrayed in the poems. Similarly, in Bleich's (1986b) study, adult males distanced themselves more from stories than did females.

High-SES females have demonstrated higher academic achievement in literature and a concern with hidden and thematic meanings when compared to males (Purves, 1981). Other gender differences have been found in cultural attitudes and basic modes of thinking (Belencky, Clinchy, Goldberger, & Tarale, 1986; Person, 1988). In her related research on sex-role differences in moral reasoning, Gilligan (1982) found that while both girls and boys recognized feelings in others, girls were more likely to experience and share those feelings, while boys focused more on defining persons' acts and plans. Thus, readers' personality characteristics, stances, and attitudes toward reading, knowledge of social and literary conventions, and experiences in social and institutional contexts influence their responses to literature. Such reader attributes exist in relationship to a variety of text factors in the transaction between reader and text.

THE TEXT

Studies focused on text factors have explored specific aspects of texts influencing response and the degree of influence texts exert upon readers.

Aspects of Texts Influencing Response

Consistent with a transactional model of response, the meaning of particular text aspects varies with differences in readers' ability, needs, attitudes, and knowledge. According to narrative theory (Labov, 1972; Pratt, 1976), readers' knowledge of social and literary conventions, as evidenced in retelling (Mosenthal, 1987), shapes their ability to attend to textual cues implying violations of expectations.

It may be the case that aspects of texts invoke or trigger expectations, "envision-ments" (Fillmore, 1981; Langer, 1986, 1989), or knowledge (Fish, 1970; McCormick, 1985). Readers who are knowledgeable about narrative or social conventions attend to text aspects that cue or signal these conventions (i.e., "Once upon a time") (Beach & Brown, 1987). These cues often consist of "evaluative" comments (Labov, 1972), narra-tors' asides (i.e., "you won't believe what happened next . . ."), or comments that signal something extraordinary is occurring. Hunt and Vipond (1986a) defined three types of evaluations: "discourse" (stylistic patterns, diction, or rhetorical figures that are incon-gruous with discourse norms), "story" (story events that violate text, social, or cultural norms), and "telling" (narrator comments or asides about the act of narrating).

However, readers may vary in their ability to attend to these cues, depending on their orientation (Hunt & Vipond, 1986a). Information- or story-driven readers may treat these evaluations as facts, while point-driven readers may treat them as signalling deliberate, consistent divergences from norms, designed to convey the point of a story.

The degree of explicitness of information about characters' actions in texts is another factor influencing readers' responses. For example, readers take more time to make inferences about stories in which information about characters' plans, goals, and states is deleted (Seifert, Robinson, & Black, 1982). Thus, abbreviated versions of stories for basal series that often delete characters' motives (Bruce, 1984) may provide difficulties for low-ability readers who cannot impute such information.

Cultural aspects of texts also influence readers' responses (Lee, 1985; Noda, 1981; Ross, 1978). For example, Canadian high school students responded with more inter-pretation to Canadian poems than did New Zealand students, who, in turn, responded with more interpretation to New Zealand poems (Ross, 1978).

Influence of Texts on Readers

Some theorists and researchers, applying a rhetorical analysis of the response process, argue for the need to examine readers' cultural attitudes and beliefs as shaped by attitudes and beliefs portrayed in texts (Booth, 1989; Eagleton, 1983; Radway, 1984; Ray, 1984; Scholes, 1985). Despite claims for the value of literature in shaping students' attitudes, behaviors, and self-concepts, results of research have been mixed (for a review of the research, see Edwards & Simpson, 1986).

In addition to examining how readers attend to certain aspects of texts, it is also useful to examine the ways in which differences in character types, conflict, and story resolutions serve to reinforce or challenge readers' attitudes and values (Culp, 1977, 1985). Radway's (1984) analysis of readers' responses to aspects of romance novels demonstrated that such features as happy endings, the gradual and consistent develop-ment of love, and detailed descriptions about the hero and heroine were ranked as most appealing. Unhappy endings and portrayals of torture, rape, or violence were ranked as least appealing. Radway (1984) concluded that the typical plot development of romance (in which a heroine transforms the often reluctant, impersonal hero through her nurturing side) reinforces women's nurturing role as housewives. A replication of Radway's study using seventh graders yielded similar results (Willinsky & Hunniford, 1986). Similarly, content analyses of transcripts taken from Texas textbook review hearings demonstrated that readers' objections focused on aspects of texts that threat-ened white Protestant "traditional" values (Last, 1984). Thus, readers' social roles and other social/cultural factors often drive their responses to plot development.

Some studies have demonstrated that nonprint aspects of texts such as illustrations influence comprehension and response, particularly among children (Kiefer, 1982; Monson, 1978; Sheldon, 1986). In addition, peripheral aspects of texts, such as ques-tions, shape readers' responses. For example, Ambrulevich's (1986) analysis of questions in 15 commonly used eighth-, ninth-, and tenth-grade textbooks, according to Bloom's taxonomy, revealed that low-level "comprehension" and "knowledge" questions predominated. The fewest questions were posed on the highest levels of "application" and "synthesis." Thus, both the content and the form of literary texts have been shown to influence response. It is important to understand, however, that this literary transaction occurs within, and is greatly influenced by, the context in which the literature is encountered.

THE INSTRUCTIONAL CONTEXT

Rather than a review of the research on literature instruction, we limit this review to those specific instructional factors influencing response (see Beach & Hynds, 1988; Purves & Beach, 1972; Travers, 1984; Webb, 1985, for reviews on literature instruction). Much of this research examines aspects of curriculum and teaching which influence readers' responses.

Curricular Influences on Response

The International Education Association (IEA) studies of cultural influences on response (Purves, 1975) demonstrated that the curriculum of particular countries strongly influenced response preference among students. Much of the research on literature discussion paints a composite picture predominated by what Barnes, Barnes, and Clarke (1984) defined as *transmission*, or instruction lacking the internalization of competing perspectives (Bruner, 1986) necessary for interpretation. In their extensive observations of British classrooms, Barnes, Barnes, and Clarke (1984) found that discussions were typically teacher dominated, inhibiting students' expression of their own responses. In addition, more time was devoted to literature instruction in the high track than the lower tracks. This finding is similar to Purves's (1981) conclusion that in working with less able students, American teachers relied more on seatwork and drills than on instructional strategies focused on literary response and interpretation. Further, the textbooks employed in secondary schools typically contain questions at the lower end of the Bloom taxonomy (Ambrulevich, 1986).

Studies of group discussion in literature instruction have revealed that high school students perceived little opportunity to express or reflect on private responses in larger group discussions (Gross, 1984). By contrast, college students were likely to express private responses in small-group discussions, depending on their perceptions of the group (Beach, 1972). Graup (1985) found that students in discussion groups evidenced better comprehension than did individuals. Secondary students in group discussions of poetry had significantly higher posttest scores on a poetry comprehension test than did students in traditional large-group discussions (Dias, 1979); a replication of this study found the same results (Bryant, 1984).

Teacher Influences on Response

Several studies have examined the influence of teacher direction or structure on response (see Hickman, 1981, for a review). Teachers who fostered genuine sharing of student ideas enhanced the quality of student responses to poetry (McClure, 1985). High school students engaged in student-directed discussion groups were more likely to employ a point-driven orientation than students in a teacher-led discussion (Straw, 1986). Unstructured small groups of tenth graders meeting over a period of time generated responses more similar to adult responses than those produced in more structured groups (Fisher, 1985). Doerr (1980) found that college students in unstructured groups made greater gains in self-esteem than students taught to apply the Purves categories to their responses. However, no significant difference emerged in quality or elaboration of responses. Harris (1982) found no differences in responses between students in teacher-led, small-group, or creative dramatics instruction.

A few studies have shown that students may benefit from teacher modeling of responses (Kirkpatrick, 1972; Bell, 1988). On the other hand, students may simply mimic teachers' responses (Michalak, 1977) or may show little benefit from teacher-directed instruction.

Using both descriptive/observational and experimental methods, Webb (1980, 1985) examined the influence of response-based versus traditional approaches to literature instruction. She found that the response-based approach had no significant effect on literature achievement or cognitive maturity, but it did have a significant positive effect on students' attitudes toward literature. She noted that although response-based teaching increased during the semester, the teachers reverted to the more traditional approach as they began to prepare students for the New York State Regents examination. College freshmen receiving response-based instruction produced poetry interpretations of higher quality than students receiving more traditional instruction (Price, 1986).

Yarbrough's (1984) observational analysis of one teacher indicated that effective literature teaching involves a number of strategies: "acclimating," "evoking," "establishing rapport," "staging," "elucidating," and "expressing purpose." Young (1986) demonstrated that students' articulation of responses often evolves within a framework of six elements: the unstructured encounter, the initial journal entry, the reflective reading, group discussion, the instructed encounter, and the public written response. However, there is some evidence that teachers' own unique styles carry more weight than the methods they employ (Wade-Maltais, 1981; Travers, 1984). Differences between teachers' intellectual disposition, for example, influence their classroom behavior (Peters & Blues, 1978).

Thus, the literary response process operates within a variety of social, institutional, and rhetorical contexts. Readers bring particular orientations and attributes to literature. In turn, their experiences with literature in schools, as well as a variety of textual factors, shape these orientations and attitudes. Researchers in literary response must account for such complexities in the design and implementation of studies.

METHODOLOGICAL CONSIDERATIONS IN LITERARY RESPONSE RESEARCH

Design

Literary response researchers vacillate precariously between two competing perspectives or worlds: the alleged "science" of psychological and cognitive research, and the humanist perspective of literary studies. Bruner contrasts these two perspectives: "Science attempts to make a world that remains invariant across human intentions and human plights . . . the humanist deals principally with the world as it changes with the position and stance of the viewer" (1986, p. 50). In attempting to explain readers' responses and to test hypotheses, response researchers seek certain consistent patterns in readers' responses. On the other hand, they are sensitive to the uniqueness of individual readers' perspectives and the biases inherent in their own orientations. Thus, there is considerable debate between researchers regarding the assumptions shaping the validity of their methods.

On the one hand, some argue for the sanctity of the unique, individual reader (Holland, 1985a, 1985b; Bleich, 1980), while others argue for the establishment of certain levels of "competent reading," as evident in groups of readers (Culler, 1975; Scholes, 1985). Thus, some argue that the case-study method focusing on individual readers (Bleich, 1980; Galda, 1983a; Sims, 1983) is the most valid method, and that analysis of "composite" responses generated by a group of readers masks the uniquely personal nature of response (Bleich, 1980). On the other hand, because case-study methods preclude many generalizations about readers, it is often necessary to study groups of readers in order to make generalizations.

Those in the middle of the two extremes argue that it is possible to generalize from individual readers by selecting readers as representative of types, levels, or extremes of different factors: gender, cognitive level, attitudes, background knowledge, and so forth (Purves, 1985). By this argument, researchers could determine the degree to which readers with common background knowledge share similar responses to texts.

Literary response researchers typically opt for more descriptive, nonexperimental, and quasi-experimental designs, given the futility in trying to control for all of the variables that might shape a reader's response. Moreover, by allowing unpredicted influences to emerge, researchers remain open to a range of explanations for differences in elicited response.

Methods of Eliciting Response

In addition to considerations of design, several other methodological issues must be considered, including how responses are elicited, how many readings or texts readers encounter, and the types of prompts used in eliciting response. This section will discuss some of these considerations.

Open-ended versus closed-ended responses.   The most frequent method for eliciting response has been the retrospective essay or interview (Applebee, 1978; Dixon & Brown, 1984, 1985; Educational Commission of the States, 1981; Holland, 1973, 1975) in which students respond to questions or prompts. An increasingly popular technique for research on comprehension as well as response has been the use of *think-alouds* during the reading process (Afflerbach & Johnston, 1984; Dias, 1985, 1987; Dias & Hayhoe, 1988; Lytle, 1983; Olshavsky, 1976; Olson, Duffy, & Mack, 1984; Viehoff, 1986). In the think-aloud procedure, readers are asked to explicate their thought processes as they are reading a text (Crowhurst & Koog, 1986). Other open-ended responses involve written protocols or journal entries, which are later analyzed for distinguishing features (Beach, in press; de Beaugrande, 1985; Kintgen, 1983).

Some studies determine "response preference" by asking readers to select from a variety of optional responses that might relate to a literary work (Golden & Guthrie, 1986; Purves, 1981; Zaharias & Mertz, 1983) or by using semantic differentials (De-Vries, 1973; Hansson, 1973, 1985), "repertory grid" ratings (Applebee, 1978; Miall, 1985), or Q-sort methods (Stevenson, 1985). In other studies, readers have been asked to select a sample of questions representing their preferred response orientation from among several that might be asked about a literary work (Purves, Foshay & Hansson, 1973; Purves, 1981; Zaharias & Mertz, 1983).

One problem with such closed-ended methods is that an uneven distribution of items may provide a limited or invalid representation of options, and consequently might fail to reflect readers' actual response preferences or proclivities (Cooper &

Michalak, 1981; Zaharias & Mertz, 1983). As an alternative to preselecting categories of response, Zaharias and Mertz (1983) factor-analyzed Likert Scale responses to several items and found four independent factors similar to the Purves and Rippere (1968) categories of engagement (readers' emotional involvement or experience), perception (descriptions of characters or events), interpretation (inferences about symbolic or thematic meaning), and evaluation (judgment of aesthetic quality).

One obvious advantage of closed-ended approaches, particularly with large samples (Purves, Foshay, & Hansson, 1973; Purves, 1981) is the saving in time and effort to train judges and establish interjudge reliability associated with open-ended measures. Moreover, because the same response options exist within and between texts, comparisons can be made, enhancing reliability. Closed-ended responses are also less likely to be confounded by differences in readers' abilities to articulate responses (Jordan, 1986), or influences in the rhetorical context. However, an obvious limitation of using preformulated response or rating scales is that readers are selecting from options provided by the investigator, rather than those they might have generated themselves (Cooper & Michalak, 1981). Hence, while reliability may be enhanced, validity may suffer.

Immediate versus retrospective accounts.   Much has been written about the use of immediate oral think-alouds in composition research. Proponents of the method in writing research (Flower & Hayes, 1983; Steinberg, 1986) argue that think-alouds provide insights into thinking processes; critics argue that the underlying problem-solving model shaping the protocol is limited to conscious processes (Dobrin, 1986) and ignores the influence of social context. A commonly cited limitation of think-alouds in literary response research is that, given the immediacy and intrusiveness of "on-line" responding, readers may not provide as elaborated or reflective responses as they might in retrospective accounts.

While oral or written retrospective responses to literature allow readers the chance to "digest" and reflect on a particular reading, they are limited in other ways. Individual retrospective accounts may not represent immediate response processes (Applebee, 1977; Dias, 1985) and may be influenced by differences in memory, reasoning ability, or writing ability. Further, one-on-one oral interviews are sometimes unsuccessful with shy or reticent readers (Hynds, 1989).

Although research employing formal essay response provides useful information about readers' abilities to logically organize response or persuasively argue a position (Educational Commission of the States, 1981), studies using formal essays do not provide information about how students might respond in a less formal context. For instance, informal journal or free-association responses have been found to generate a relatively high degree of engagement and autobiographical response (Beach, 1972, in press; Harste, 1986; Monseau, 1986).

In retrospective group interviews, investigators must realize the influence of group context on response (Bleich, 1986a, 1986b; Marshall, 1988; Morris, 1971). Research comparing "private," self-initiated response and "public" group response (Beach, 1972; Ericson, 1984; Gross, 1984; Nissel, 1987) suggests that participation in group discussion influences and enhances the quality of readers' responses, in that the responses and questions of others stimulate additional responses. Further, reliance on groups requires an investigator to account for the influence of a group's response agenda, degree of facilitation, or purpose, which might shape individual readers' responses (Golden, 1987; Kintgen & Holland, 1984; Taylor, 1986).

Assessing procedural knowledge.   While it is relatively simple to assess readers' knowledge about literary works, periods, and terminology, researchers in literary response must often indirectly assess the degree to which readers utilize their knowledge of social, cultural, and literary conventions in reading. Because knowledge of literary conventions, to use Gilbert Ryle's (1949) distinction, is procedural ("knowing-how") rather than declarative ("knowing-that") knowledge, in order to infer readers' procedural knowledge, researchers must often rely on inferences drawn from content analyses of readers' responses (Beach, 1985; Beach & Wendler, 1987; Hynds, 1985).

Some researchers have asked readers to invent stories, which may reflect differences in knowledge of narrative literary conventions (Sutton-Smith, 1981; Vardell, 1982). However, even with this method, differences in narrative complexity could be influenced by readers' motivation and sense of purpose, as well as by their knowledge of literary conventions. Another option has been to provide children with a skeletal version of a genre story in order to determine their knowledge of the conventions constituting that genre (Gardner & Gardner, 1971; Rubin & Gardner, 1985; Scarlett & Wolf, 1979).

Thus, readers' responses may be influenced by whether they are elicited during or after reading, or through open-ended versus closed-ended methods. Researchers should carefully consider these limitations, as well as limitations of inferences about procedural knowledge drawn from content analyses of expressed responses.

Single versus Multiple Readings and Texts

Investigators need to recognize that readers are often encountering a text for the first time—a "primary" exposure—while an investigator may have had many "secondary" exposures. While researchers should not rely solely on primary readings, particularly with shorter texts, they do need to consider the influence of the nature and number of rereadings on responses. Initial readings may focus more on engagement or comprehension processes, leading up to subsequent interpretive or judgmental responses on later readings (Beach, 1972). On the other hand, while readers do reread favorite books (Smith, 1984), responses to extensive rereadings may not represent a valid measure of what readers normally do, particularly with longer texts.

Investigators must also consider whether to use more than one text in order to obtain a reliable picture of readers' responses. Research on the effects of particular texts on response has yielded mixed results. Purves (1981) found that across five different stories, secondary students consistently selected the same strategies: inferring hidden meaning, a lesson, messages about people or ideas, organization, and emotional arousal, in that order. Similarly, Bunbury (1985), in interviews with 7-, 9-, and 11-year-olds, found that "literal" responses declined and "inferential" responses increased with age, regardless of differences in genre (i.e., poetry, folktales, and short stories).

However, other researchers have found that responses vary according to differences among texts (Educational Commission of the States, 1981; Golden & Guthrie, 1986; Svensson, 1985). For instance, Zaharias (1986), investigating the influence of genre on response, found that college students responded more descriptively to three poems and more personally to three short stories. Thus, readers' responses may be influenced by the number of readings and the texts they encounter.

Influences of Prompts on Response

The prompts or questions employed in eliciting response may also influence or bias response. Marshall (1987) found that high school students had lower mean quality ratings for level of interpretation on short-answer essay questions about literature than they did in response to formal essay questions. Beach (1972) found that oral taped free-association responses generated more engagement responses than did written free-association responses, which generated more interpretive responses. Assignments with "prewriting" question-listing activities resulted in essays of higher quality than did no-prewriting assignments (Appleman, 1986; Kern, 1983; Reilly, Beach, & Crabtree, 1986).

Across two different stories, an essay prompt referring to the student as "you" resulted in a significantly higher quality of essay response than did a more impersonal prompt (Newell, Suszynaski, & Weingart, 1989). As part of their assessment of British students' written essay responses, Dixon and Stratta (1985) demonstrated that prompts inviting students to define their own relationship with a text, as opposed to more impersonal prompts, precipitated a more personal rather than impersonal stance, a more informal rather than formal relationship with audience, and a more tentative rather than authoritative voice in sample essays.

Applebee (1985) found that despite high school teachers' emphasis on the composing process, students lacked a sense of purpose when writing literary analysis papers designed to influence an audience. Similarly, elementary students' self-initiated letters to an author contained more interpretation responses than did their assigned letters (Rapport, 1982). Thus, studies of "response" are necessarily limited by the methods of eliciting response.

EXAMINING ASSUMPTIONS FROM A LITERARY RESPONSE PERSPECTIVE

In this chapter we have attempted to (1) explore the ways in which readers' responses have traditionally been conceptualized; (2) discuss how reader, text, and contextual factors influence response; and (3) explicate the methodological decisions relevant to researchers in literary response. As we noted at the outset, much of this research calls into question some of the assumptions shaping a "normative" orientation in reading comprehension research. To conclude this review, we discuss some of these assumptions and then propose some new directions for research in literary response.

Examining Assumptions about Reading

1. Reading as "decontextualized" versus "transactive."   Researchers in literary response have a vast array of options for investigating response. For instance, a researcher may be interested in the different types of responses expressed (i.e., engagement, interpretation), the overall focus or level of response (i.e., text-centered, reader-centered), or the response strategies readers use (i.e., connecting, judging).

However, it is important to realize that the types, levels, or purposes of response are influenced by qualities in the text, the reader, and the reading context. The author's suspense-creating devices and unusual format, as well as readers' attitudes, expectations, cognitive maturity, and the context of reading all play a part in the literary response process. Thus, research in literary response should consider these factors in a transactional relationship with one another, rather than as isolated entities in the reading process. As Rosenblatt (1985) has argued, "Not only what the reader brings to the transaction from past experience with life and language, but also the socially molded circumstances and purpose of the reading provide the setting for the act of symbolization. The reading event should be seen in its total matrix" (p. 104).

2. Meaning as "static" versus "evolving."   Much reading research assumes that the construal of "meaning" occurs at defined "snapshot" moments at the completion of a text or at the time of a "delayed recall." However, response research suggests that meaning gradually emerges or evolves over time as a reader discovers new meanings through articulation, reflection, and application of related experiences or texts (Beach, in press; Marshall, 1987; Rogers, 1988).

As think-aloud research (Langer, 1986; Lytle, 1982; Viehoff, 1986) indicates, readers move recursively through certain phases of response, often beginning with "engagement" or "conceiving" responses, which lead to "connecting," "interpreting," or "judging" responses (Beach, 1987). Langer (1986, 1989), for instance, argues that readers develop "envisionments," or on-line representations, which are "subject to change well after the pages have been removed from sight" (p. 2).

Rather than assuming a static conception of meaning, further research needs to focus on the developing responses of readers as they read texts. For instance, researchers might examine the on-line processes by which readers extend, elaborate, and reflect on their interpretations. In some cases, for instance, readers extend their responses as they proceed through a text by employing certain heuristics such as the "describe/autobiographical/interpret" heuristic (Bleich, 1975; Petrosky, 1981).

Since literary responses occur not only at the moment of reading but before and after an actual encounter with text, the surrounding activities in the literature classroom can be studied as a dimension of readers' responses. For example, some research suggests that writing in an informal, tentative mode, as opposed to the formal essays typically assigned in schools, encourages students to explore the meaning and significance of text elements. As Newell, Suszynski, and Weingart (1989) have shown, the personal essays of tenth-grade students reflected a combination of their own experiences as well as text elements, while their formal essays were focused entirely on text elements. Furthermore, students writing in the personal mode produced essays judged to be significantly higher in level of interpretation than students writing in the formal mode.

Further research needs to examine how certain instructional techniques (i.e., journal responses, formal papers, discussions, etc.) serve to foster elaboration of response and interpretation at various points in the process. Studies of literary response should attempt to combine methods, as well as a variety of texts, prompts, and response modes, in order to strengthen reliability and validity. Studies should move beyond simple descriptions of the global "types" of readers' responses, to consider the purposes underlying various response types.

For example, do readers engage with texts as a way of understanding their personal experiences or escaping them? Are story interpretations used to probe the complex motivations behind human behavior, or to demonstrate competence in a literary analysis paper? Do information-driven readers seek information in order to compare writers' accounts of the same event, or to remember facts useful in passing a test? By focusing on readers' purposes, researchers can then begin to explain how responses are shaped by those purposes.

3. Emotional response as unrelated to understanding.   A normative orientation, drawing on the New Critical tenet of the "affective fallacy," often assumes that a reader's emotional response is irrelevant to understanding a text. However, building on interest in affective aspects of comprehension (Mosenthal, 1987), researchers are finding that readers' inferences are facilitated by the recollection of familiar emotions such as desire, envy, sorrow, fear, jealousy, and so forth. (Golden & Guthrie, 1986; Nell, 1988; Sadoski & Goetz, 1985; Sadoski, Goetz, & Kangiser, 1988). Readers' emotional reactions also make them more aware of a narrator's or speaker's "evaluations," which indicate violations of social norms (i.e., asides, comments, or syntactical deviations, signaling the significance or point of an event) (Labov, 1972; Hunt & Vipond, 1986a). This awareness makes them more able to adopt a point-driven orientation toward literature (Vipond & Hunt, 1984). Similarly, drawing on Bruner's (1986) theory of subjunctification, Hade (1988) found that children resonated emotionally with stories, to the extent that they incorporated the story's language into their own language.

Further research needs to examine how responding itself recaptures and extends these emotional experiences, as well as how such emotional reactions enable readers to interpret literary texts.

Examining Assumptions about Readers

1. Prior knowledge as independent of reader beliefs and attitudes.   Much comprehension research assumes that readers' prior knowledge consists of shared, predetermined *schema*, such as cognitive scripts, concepts, or story grammars. From a normative perspective, such schema are presumed to operate independently of readers' beliefs and attitudes. However, as just-ending story research indicates (Dorfman, 1985; Jose & Brewer, 1984), readers apply their own unique beliefs about the world in judging story outcomes and characters positively or negatively. In a similar vein, Radway (1984) found that women readers responded positively to "nurturing" heroine roles because such roles reinforced their own culturally constituted roles. Further research needs to examine the processes by which readers' attitudes interact with story schema, and the processes by which readers change their own attitudes and beliefs through responding to texts.

2. Readers' responses as independent of stance and orientation.   Reading research often assumes that readers can be described in terms of abstract, stable categories (i.e., "high" versus "low" ability or knowledge). In contrast to this assumption, research in literary response often assumes that readers are constantly shifting orientations, perspectives, goals, strategies, and roles due to differences in texts, social contexts, reader interest, and motivation (Hynds, 1989; Langer, 1986; Purves, 1981; Zaharias, 1986).

For example, readers can enter into a "dialogic" relationship with a text, aligning, empathizing, or distancing themselves, depending upon their perception of an author's or speaker's purpose or motives (Vipond, Hunt, Jewett, & Reither, in press). Readers' responses also exist within a system of "social practice" (Gee, 1988). That is, readers learn to adopt certain roles, goals, strategies, or stances as appropriate for certain texts or social contexts. Further research needs to examine the ways in which such shifting orientations, perceptions, goals, strategies, and roles influence response, as well as the ways in which such orientations are developed among readers. Few longitudinal or long-range studies of readers' orientations exist. More research is needed to explore readers' shifting orientations, stances, and attitudes over time and across texts.

3. Development in reading as independent of context.   Cognitive-stage models of response development are limited, in that differences may be due less to cognitive ability than to differences in social and cultural experience, or difficulties in responding to "developmental tasks" (Bruner, 1986; Donaldson, 1978). For example, readers' abilities to interpret texts may be related to prior literature instruction and exposure to literature in the home. Thus, stage models of aesthetic development may fail to account for differences in "social culturalization" (Svennson, 1985).

Response preference may also vary according to the curricular emphasis in a student's country. For example, American students' preference for interpretation and the concern of high-ability students for morals and theme appears to reflect a learned strategy consistent with an emphasis on writing literary critical essays (Purves, 1981), rather than a purely developmental phenomenon.

Another problem with so-called developmental studies of response is that it may be difficult to distinguish between development of response and development of the ability to adequately express response (Hansson, 1985). The articulation of readers' responses may be confounded by their perceptions of the surrounding rhetorical context. Thus, researchers in literary response must be careful about drawing conclusions concerning development, considering the pervasive influence of schooling, surroundings, environment, and research methodologies.

It is difficult, then, to talk about "the reader" as an abstract or stable entity. Readers are defined by changing personality characteristics, orientations toward reading, knowledge of textual and cultural conventions, and membership in social communities. One reader may appreciate a text for its formal features; another may focus on personal or autobiographical associations.

Examining Assumptions about Texts

1. Meaning as "text-bound" versus "intertextual."   Much reading research assumes that readers experience texts as discrete, separate entities. However, reader response research suggests that readers understand texts in terms of other texts. Such *intertextual responses* evoke and develop readers' social and literary knowledge (Beach, Appleman, & Dorsey, in press; Lehr, 1988; Rogers, 1988), as readers learn to "read resonantly" (Wolf, 1988). Further research needs to examine the processes by which readers use intertextual links to interpret literary texts, and the ways in which autobiographical and intertextual responses interact.

For example, by conceiving of texts as genre types (e.g., as poems, allegories, mysteries, and so on), or text aspects in terms of prototypical concepts (e.g., villain, happy ending, foreboding event, and so on), readers evoke knowledge of related literary or autobiographical experiences. As is the case with analogical reasoning (Shank, 1982), the more readers elaborate on their evoked knowledge or experience, the more likely they are to define specific aspects or attitudes related to thematic meanings that can be used to illuminate the current text (Beach, in press). Thus, intertextual knowledge enables readers to transcend the current text and create potentially richer interpretations through evoked recollections of other texts.

In a discussion, readers may collaboratively evoke intertextual links, associating current and past texts by genre, topics, or related emotional experience (Cox, Beach, & Many, in preparation). In cases where texts deviate from readers' current social and literary knowledge, readers need to develop a tolerance for dissonance and the openness to continually revise such knowledge. Further developmental or longitudinal research needs to examine how readers develop the capacity to make intertextual connections through reading experiences in the home and cumulative experiences with the school literature curriculum.

2. Text structures as independent of reader attitudes and beliefs.   Schema theoretic and text grammar models of reading tend to operate on the premise that "good reading" occurs as readers' cognitive schemata are isomorphic with certain text structures. However, recent research has revealed that structural properties of texts are interactive with readers' affective states (Jose & Brewer, 1984) and values (Lester, 1982).

Researchers interested in textual influences on response may wish to further explore specific ways in which the values portrayed in texts serve to reassure or violate or confirm readers' values, needs, and expectations (Kumer, 1982). Further research is also needed to examine the influence of questions, activities, and illustrations in literature textbooks on readers' responses (Morrison, 1987). Finally, comparisons of responses to films and literature (Cox, 1975, 1978; Lewis, 1972; Worthington, 1978) may provide some understanding of how immersion in the "media culture" affects readers' expectations about literary texts.

Examining Assumptions
about Curriculum and Evaluation

1. Equating test taking with understanding.   Reading research based on standardized measures such as multiple-choice tests assumes that these texts can be equated with "understanding." It further assumes that such tests measure real-world reading processes, rather than test-taking abilities. Even the use of open-ended written tasks on literature assessments is subject to many of the same criticisms, as is the use of writing assessments (Appleman, 1986). As an alternative to such normative approaches, "portfolio" systems have been designed, which allow evaluators access to readers' responses collected over a period of time—often several years. Further research needs to explore methods for evaluating readers' responses, drawing perhaps on criteria employed in recent research on using writing in the context of literature (Marshall, 1987; Newell, Suszynski, & Weingart, 1989).

2. Equating "knowledge" and "achievement."   In a global sense, we know that literature achievement relates to certain patterns of response. For instance, high achievers are more apt to analyze literary elements than low achievers (Purves, 1981). We still know little about the relationships between factual knowledge about literature and the depth or quality of readers' responses. Furthermore, research is needed to examine how readers develop, organize, and evoke their knowledge of literature in order to understand texts. We might ask whether knowledge of literary conventions and reading ability alone guarantee a sophisticated response. Researchers might also investigate just what sort of "knowledge" reading competency tests are measuring, and whether such tests actually predict success in reading outside of the examination situation.

3. Normative versus individualized views of teaching and evaluation.   Large-scale assessments of reading and curricular decisions based upon a normative, standardized, "correct response" view of reading often fail to recognize the incredible range, diversity, and complexity of readers' responses. Whether reading ability is measured by recall and mastery of textual information, knowledge of literary terminology, or ability to construct logical arguments about literature, the individual student is often lost in the attempt to provide the best instruction and evaluation for the majority of readers.

Future research on instructional influences should employ a combination of methods, including observation, elicitation of student and teacher perceptions and attitudes, and measures of change or learning (Travers, 1984). Little is still known about teacher assumptions shaping decisions involved in devising and sequencing response activities, or about the influence of prior training on the methodological decisions and orientations of teachers (Reed & Bontempo, 1987). Researchers also need to examine the complex social perceptions that operate in the literature classroom, involving student and teacher conceptions of the purpose, value, and social agendas of classroom interaction (Hynds, 1989, in press).

SUMMARY AND IMPLICATIONS

Over the past several years, reader response criticism and scholarship have moved from global descriptions of response types to analyses of the focus and purpose of response, as well as an understanding of the meaning-making processes in which readers engage. Researchers have demonstrated that readers differ not only in cognitive abilities but also in their stances toward reading, personality orientations, social-cognitive capacities, knowledge of literature, and language conventions.

Such reader attributes cannot be understood in isolation but must be viewed in a transactional relationship to a variety of text aspects such as literary devices, narrative evaluations (Hunt & Vipond, 1986a), textual portrayal of social events and cultural attitudes, as well as a variety of other structural and nonprint factors. Furthermore, the literary transaction cannot be understood apart from surrounding contextual influences in the home, school, and the larger culture.

Thus, literary reading should not be taught, tested, or studied according to a purely normative orientation, based on a model of bureaucratic efficiency. The problem is in recognizing and preserving the integrity of each student's response within a highly technological and bureaucratic culture that demands standardization and accountability. This dilemma is voiced by Schon (1983), when he says, "Within highly specialized, technically administered systems of bureaucratic control, how can professionals . . . strive to achieve the standards of professional excellence, cultivate artistry, and concern themselves with the unique features of a particular case?" (p. 337).

We argue that an individualized view of reading should not sacrifice intellectual rigor in literature instruction, or the value of formal evaluation. On the contrary, we suggest the need for greater awareness and acknowledgement of what is being "measured" by researchers, teachers, and evaluators when they elicit readers' responses within particular discourse modes and institutional contexts. Assessments that provide a variety of prompts, response modes, and contexts for responding to literary texts, and that are congruent with instructional goals will allow for the most reliable evaluation of readers.

Similarly, teachers and curriculum planners should direct their energies to broadening, rather than narrowing, the range of readers' responses and developing a repertoire of strategies to be evoked in response to particular readings, rather than a set of generic skills. In this way, we can promote competence in literary reading, while preserving the individual integrity and uniqueness of each reader's response.

REFERENCES

Afflerbach, P., & Johnston, P. (1984). Research methodology on the use of verbal reports in reading research. *Journal of Reading Behavior, 16*, 307–322.

Agee, H. (1983). Literary allusion and reader response: Possibilities for research. *Journal of Research and Development in Education, 16*, 55–59.

Alcorn, M., & Bracher, M. (1985). Literature, psychoanalysis, and the re-formation of the self. *PMLA*, *100*, 342–354.

Ambrulevich, A. K. (1986). An analysis of the levels of thinking required by questions in selected literature anthologies for grades eight, nine, and ten (Doctoral dissertation, University of Bridgeport). *Dissertation Abstracts International*, *47*, 769A.

Applebee, A. (1977). The elements of response to a literary work: What we have learned. *Research in the Teaching of English*, *11*, 255–271.

Applebee, A. (1978). *The child's concept of story*. Chicago: University of Chicago Press.

Applebee, A. (1985). *Contexts for learning to write*. Norwood, NJ: Ablex.

Applebee, A., Langer, J., & Mullis, I. V. S. (1987). *Learning to be literate in America: Reading, writing and reasoning*. National Assessment of Educational Progress. Princeton, NJ: Educational Testing Service.

Appleman, D. (1986). The effects of heuristically based assignments on adolescents' responses to literature (Doctoral dissertation, University of Minnesota). *Dissertation Abstracts International*, *47*, 11A.

Barnes, D., Barnes, D., & Clarke, S. (1984). *Versions of English*. London: Heinemann.

Bartholomae, D. (1985). Inventing the university. In M. Rose (Ed.), *When a writer can't write: Studies in writer's block and other composing process problems* (pp. 134–165). New York: Guilford.

Beach, R. (1972). The literary response process of college students while reading and discussing three poems (Doctoral dissertation, University of Illinois). *Dissertation Abstracts International*, *34*, 656A.

Beach, R. (1980). Studying the relationship between prior knowledge and response to literature. *English Journal*, *69* (9), 93–96.

Beach, R. (1983). Attitudes, social conventions, and response to literature. *Journal of Research and Development in Education*, *16*, 47–54.

Beach, R. (1985). Discourse conventions and researching response to literary dialogue. In C. Cooper (Ed.), *Researching response to literature and the teaching of literature* (pp. 103–127). Norwood, NJ: Ablex.

Beach, R. (1987). Literature teaching. In B. Jones, D. Ogle, A. Palincsor, & E. Carr (Eds.), *Strategic teaching and learning* (pp. 135–159). Alexandria, VA: ASCD.

Beach, R. (in press). The creative development of meaning: Using autobiographical experiences to interpret literature. In S. Straw & D. Bogdon (Eds.), *Beyond communication: Reading comprehension and criticism*. Portsmouth, NH: Boynton Cook.

Beach, R., Appleman, D., & Dorsey, S. (in press). Developing literary knowledge through intertextual links. In R. Beach & S. Hynds (Eds.), *Developing discourse practices in adolescence and adulthood*. Norwood, NJ: Ablex.

Beach, R., & Brown, R. (1987). Discourse conventions and literary inferences. In R. Tierney, P. Anders, & J. Mitchell (Eds.), *Understanding readers' understanding* (pp. 147–174). Hillsdale, NJ: Erlbaum.

Beach, R., & Brunetti, G. (1976). Differences between high school and university students in their conceptions of literary characters. *Research in the Teaching of English*, *10*, 259–268.

Beach, R., & de Beaugrande, R. (1987). Authority attitudes in response to literature. *Pszichologia*, *7*, 67–92.

Beach, R., & Hynds, S. (1988). *Research on the learning and teaching of literature: A selected bibliography*. Albany, NY: Center for Research on the Learning and Teaching of Literature.

Beach, R., & Saxton, C. (1982). Developmental differences in readers' problem-solving strategies. Paper presented at the National Council of Teachers of English, Minneapolis.

Beach, R., & Wendler, L. (1987). Developmental differences in response to a short story. *Research in the Teaching of English*, *21*, 286–298.

Belencky, M., Clinchy, B., Goldberger, N., & Tarale, J. (1986). *Women's ways of knowing: The development of self, voice, and mind*. New York: Basic Books.

Bell, R. (1988). Four readers reading. In M. Benton, J. Teasey, R. Bell, & K. Hurst. *Young readers responding to poems* (pp. 88–156). New York: Routledge.

Bennett, S. (1979). The relationship between adolescents' levels of moral development and their responses to short stories (Doctoral dissertation). *Dissertation Abstracts International*, *40*, 34A.

Benton, M. (1983). Secondary worlds. *Journal of Research and Development in Education*, *16*, 68–75.

Binkney, R. H. (1986). A study of the criteria adolescents use in the selection of novels (Doctoral dissertation, Georgia State University). *Dissertation Abstracts International*, *47*, 04A.

Black, J., & Bower, G. (1980). Story understanding as problem solving. *Poetics*, *9*, 223–250.

Black, J., & Seifert, C. (1985). The psychological study of story understanding. In C. Cooper (Ed.), *Research response to literature and the teaching of literature* (pp. 190–211). Norwood, NJ: Ablex.

Black, J., Wilkes-Gibbs, D., & Gibbs. R. (1981). What writers need to know that they don't know they need to know. In M. Nystrand (Ed.), *What writers know* (pp. 325–344). New York: Academic Press.

Bleich, D. (1975). *Readings and feelings: An introduction to subjective criticism*. Urbana, IL: National Council of Teachers of English.

Bleich, D. (1978). *Subjective criticism*. Baltimore: Johns Hopkins University Press.

Bleich, D. (1980). The identity of pedagogy and research in the study of response to literature. *College English*, *42*, 350–366.

Bleich, D. (1986a) Cognitive stereoscopy and the study of language and literature. In B. Peterson (Ed.), *Convergences* (pp. 99–114). Urbana, IL: National Council of Teachers of English.

Bleich, D. (1986b). Gender interests in reading and language. In E. Flynn & P. Schweickert (Eds), *Gender and reading* (pp. 213–238). Baltimore: Johns Hopkins University Press.

Booth, W. (1989). *The company we keep: An ethics of fiction.* Berkeley: University of California Press.

Britton, J. (1968). Response to literature. In J. Squire (Ed.), *Response to literature* (pp. 3–10). Urbana, IL: National Council of Teachers of English.

Britton, J. (1970). *Language and learning.* Harmondsworth, Eng.: Penguin.

Britton, J. (1984). Viewpoints: The distinction between participant and spectator role language in research and pratice. *Research in the Teaching of English, 18,* 320–331.

Bruce, B. (1984). Stories in readers and tradebooks. In J. Osborn, P. Wilson, & R. Anderson (Eds.), *Reading education: Foundations for a literate America* (pp. 204–232). New York: Lexington Books.

Bruce, B. & Rubin, A. (1984). Strategies for controlling hypothesis formation in reading. In J. Flood (Ed.), *Promoting reading comprehension* (pp. 97–112). Newark, DE: International Reading Association.

Bruner, J. (1986). *Actual minds, possible worlds.* Cambridge, MA: Harvard University Press.

Bryant, C. (1984). Teaching students to read poetry independently: An experiment in bringing together research and the teacher. *English Quarterly, 17,* 48–57.

Bunbury, R. (1985). Levels of response to literature. *Australian Journal of Reading, 8,* 220–228.

Chester, R. D., & K. L. Dulin (1977). Three approaches to the measurement of secondary school student's attitudes towards books and reading. *Research in the Teaching of English, 11,* 193–200.

Christensen, S. (1983). An application of Kohlberg's cognitive-developmental theory of moralization to ninth-grade student response to the novel (Doctoral dissertation, University of Massachusetts). *Dissertation Abstracts International, 43,* 2601A.

Collins, A., Brown, J., & Larkin, K. (1980). Inference in text understanding. In R. Spiro, B. Bruce, & W. Brewer (Eds.), *Theoretical issues in reading comprehension* (pp. 385–410). Hillside, NJ: Erlbaum.

Cooper, C. (1976). Empirical studies of response to literature. *Journal of Aesthetic Education, 10,* 77–93.

Cooper, C., & Michalak, D. (1981). A note on determining response styles in research on response to literature. *Research in the Teaching of English, 15,* 163–169.

Cooper, M. (in press). The answers are not in the back of the book: Developing discourse practices. In R. Beach & S. Hynds (Eds.), *Developing discourse practices in adolescence and adulthood.* Norwood, NJ: Ablex.

Cox, C. (1975). Film preference patterns of fourth- and fifth-grade children (Doctoral dissertation, University of Minnesota).

Cox, C. (1978). Films children like and dislike. *Language Arts, 7,* 334–338.

Cox, C., Beach, R., & Many, J. (in preparation). *Children's intertextual links.*

Crawford, M., & Chaffin, R. (1986). The reader's construction of meaning: Cognitive research on gender and comprehension. In E. Flynn & P. Patriocinio (Eds.), *Gender and reading* (pp. 3–30). Baltimore: Johns Hopkins University Press.

Crockett, W. H. (1965). Cognitive complexity in impression formation. In B. Maher (Ed.), *Progress in experimental personality research* (Vol. 2, pp. 47–90). New York: Academic Press.

Crowhurst, M., & Kooy, M. (1986). The use of response journals in teaching the novel. *Reading-Canada-Lecture, 3,* 256–266.

Culler, J. (1980). Literary competence. In J. Tompkins (Ed.), *Reader-response criticism* (pp. 101–117). Baltimore: Johns Hopkins University Press.

Cullinan, R., Harwood, K., & Galda, L. (1983). The reader and the story: Comprehension and response. *Journal of Research and Development in Education, 16,* 29–38.

Culp, M. (1977). Case studies of the influence of literature on the attitudes, values, and behavior of adolescents. *Research in the Teaching of English, 11,* 245–253.

Culp, M. (1985). Literature's influence on young adult attitudes, values, and behavior, 1975 and 1984. *English Journal, 74* (8), 31–35.

de Beaugrande, R. (1985). Poetry and the ordinary reader: A study of immediate responses. *Empirical Studies of the Arts, 3,* 1–21.

de Beaugrande, R. (1988). *Critical discourse: A survey of literary theorists.* Norwood, NJ: Ablex.

Denise, S. A. (1986). A study of the relationship between children's literature and student writing in an intermediate grade classroom (Doctoral dissertation, Columbia University). *Dissertation Abstracts International, 47,* 815A.

DeVries, J. (1973). A statistical analysis of undergraduate readers' responses to selected characters in Shakespeare's "The Tempest" (Doctoral dissertation, University of Illinois).

Dias, P. (1979). Developing independent readers of poetry: An approach in the high school. *McGill Journal of Education, 14,* 199–214.

Dias, P. (1985). Researching response to poetry—Part I: A case for responding-aloud protocols. *English Quarterly, 18,* 104–118.

Dias, P. (1987). *Making sense of poetry: Patterns in the process.* Ottawa: Canadian Council of Teachers of English.

Dias, P., & Hayhoe, M. (1988). *Developing response to poetry.* Philadelphia: Open University Press.

Dillon, G. (1978). *Language processing and the reading of literature.* Bloomington, IN: Indiana University Press.

Dillon, G. (1982). Styles of reading. *Poetics Today, 5*, 77–88.

Dixon, J., & Brown, J. (1984, 1985). *Responses to literature: What is being assessed?* Parts I, II, and III. London: Schools Council Publication.

Dixon, J., & Stratta, L. (1986). *Writing narrative and beyond.* Ottawa: Canadian Council of Teachers of English.

Dobrin, D. (1986). Protocols once more. *College English, 48*, 713–725.

Doerr, D. (1980). A study of two teaching methods emphasizing the responses to literature of junior college students (Doctoral dissertation, University of Pittsburgh). *Dissertation Abstracts International, 40*, 4451A.

Donaldson, M. (1978). *Children's minds.* New York: Norton.

Dorfman, M. (1985). A model for understanding the points of stories: Evidence from adult and child readers. Paper presented at the Seventh Annual Conference of the Cognitive Science Society, Irvine, CA.

Dressel, J. (1986). Listening to children's literature read aloud: Its effect on selected aspects of the narrative writing of fifth-grade students (Doctoral dissertation, Michigan State University). *Dissertation Abstracts International, 47*, 3307A.

Eagleton, T. (1983). *Literary theory.* Minneapolis: University of Minnesota Press.

Ebersole, P., & DeVogler-Ebersole, K. (1984). Depth of meaning in life and literary preference. *Psychology, 22* (3–4), 28–30.

Educational Commission of the States (1981). *Reading, thinking and writing: Results for the 1979–80 National Assessment of Reading and Literature.* Denver: Education Commission of the States.

Edwards, P., & Simpson, L. (1986). Bibliography: A strategy for communication between parents and their children. *Journal of Reading, 30*, 110–118.

Ericson, B. O. (1984). A descriptive study of the individual and group responses of three tenth-grade readers to two short stories and two textbook selections (Doctoral dissertation, Syracuse University). *Dissertation Abstracts International, 46*, 388A.

Evans, J. L. (1969). Two aspects of literary appreciation among high school students: Judgment of prose quality and emotional responses to literature, and selected aspects of their reading interests (Doctoral dissertation, University of Minnesota). *Dissertation Abstracts International, 30*, 617A.

Fish, S. (1970). Literature in the reader: Affective stylistics. *New Literary History, 2*, 123–162.

Fish, S. (1980). *Is there a text in this class? The authority of interpretative communities.* Cambridge, MA: Harvard University Press.

Fisher, R. (1985). A comparison of 10th-grade students' small-group discussions to adults' small-group discussions in response to literature (Doctoral dissertation, Virginia Polytechnic Institute). *Dissertation Abstracts International, 47*, 2062A.

Fetterly, J. (1979). *The resisting reader: A feminist approach to American fiction.* Bloomington: Indiana University Press.

Fillmore, C. (1981). Ideal readers and real readers. *Proceedings of the Georgetown University Roundtable Conference.* Washington, DC: Georgetown University.

Flower, L., & Hayes, J. R. (1983). Uncovering cognitive processes in writing: An introduction to protocol analysis. In P. Mosenthal, L. Tamor, & S. Walmsley (Eds.), *Research on written language: Principles and methods* (pp. 206–219). New York: Guilford Press.

Flynn, E. (1983). Composing responses to literary texts: A process approach. *College Composition and Communication, 39*, 342–348.

Flynn, E. (1986). Gender and reading. In E. Flynn, & P. Schweichart (Eds.), *Gender and reading* (pp. 267–289). Baltimore: Johns Hopkins University Press.

Freedle, R. (1975). Dialogue and inquiry systems: The development of a social logic. *Human Development, 18*, 97–118.

Freedle, R., Naus, M., & Schwartz, L. (1977). Prose processing from a psychosocial perspective. In R. Freedle (Ed.), *Discourse processes: Advances in research and theory* (Vol. 1, pp. 175–192). Norwood, NJ: Ablex.

Freund, E. (1987). *The return of the reader: Reader response criticism.* London: Methuen.

Fusco, E. (1983). The relationship between children's cognitive level of development and their response to literature (Doctoral dissertation, Hofstra University). *Dissertation Abstracts International, 45*, 5A. (University Microfilms No. 84–10, 959)

Galda, L. (1983a). Assuming the spectator stance: An examination of the responses of three young readers. *Research in the Teaching of English, 16*, 1–20.

Galda, L. (1983b). Research in response to literature. *Journal of Research and Development in Education, 16*, 1–7.

Gardner, H., & Gardner, J. (1971). Children's literacy skills. *Journal of Experimental Education, 39*, 42–46.

Gee, J. P. (1988). The legacies of literacy: From Plato to Freire through Harvey Graff. *Harvard Educational Review, 58*, 195–212.

Gilligan, C. (1982). *In a different voice.* Cambridge, MA: Harvard University Press.

Golden, J. (1987). An exploration of reader-text interaction in a small-group discussion. In D. Bloom (Ed.), *Literacy, language, and schooling* (pp. 169–192). Norwood, NJ: Ablex.

Golden, J., & Guthrie, J. (1986). Convergence and divergence in reader response to literature. *Reading Research Quarterly, 21,* 408–421.

Graup, L., (1985). Response to literature: Student-generated questions and collaborative learning as related to comprehension (Doctoral dissertation, Hofstra University). *Dissertation Abstracts International, 47,* 482A.

Gross, B. (1984). Private response and public discussion: Dimensions of individual and classroom responses to literature (Doctoral dissertation, Rutgers University). *Dissertation Abstracts International, 45,* 03A.

Gruenich, R., & Trabasso, T. (1981). The story as social environment: Children's comprehension and evaluation of intentions and consequences. In J. Harvey (Ed.), *Cognition, social behavior, and the environment* (pp. 265–287). Hillsdale, NJ: Erlbaum.

Hade, D. (1988). Children, stories, and narrative transformations. *Research in the teaching of English, 22,* 310–325.

Hansen, E. (1986). *Emotional processes engendered by poetry and prose reading.* Stockholm: Almquist & Wiksell.

Hansson, G. (1973). Some types of research on response to literature. *Research in the Teaching of English, 7,* 260–284.

Hansson, G. (1985). Verbal scales in research on response to literature. In C. Cooper (Ed.), *Researching response to literature and the teaching of literature* (pp. 212–232). Norwood, NJ: Ablex.

Harding, D. W. (1962). Psychological processes in the reading of fiction. *British Journal of Aesthetics, 2,* 133–137.

Harris, L. (1982). A description of the extent to which affective engagment with literature takes place using three different classroom strategies: Teacher-directed lecture-discussion, self-directed small-group, and creative drama exercises (Doctoral dissertation, Rutgers University). *Dissertation Abstracts International, 44* (1983), 411A.

Harste, J. C. (1986). What it means to be strategic: Good readers as informants. Paper presented at the National Reading Conference, Austin, TX.

Harste, J. C., Woodward, V. A., & Burke, C. L. (1984). Examining our assumptions: A transactional view of literacy and learning. *Research in the Teaching of English, 18,* 84–108.

Harste, N. (1985). Portrait of a new paradigm: Reading comprehension research. In A. Crismore (Ed.), *Landscapes: A state-of-the-art assessment of reading comprehension research, 1974–1984* (pp. 12:1–24). Bloomington: Center for Reading and Language Studies, University of Indiana.

Hauptmeir, H., Meutsch, D., & Viehoff, R. (1989). Empirical research on understanding literature. *Poetics Today, 10,* 563–564.

Heath, S. (1985). Being literate in America: A sociohistorical perspective. In J. Niles & R. Lalik (Eds.), *Issues in literacy: A research perspective* (pp. 1–18). Rochester, NY: National Reading Conference.

Heine, D. (1985). Readers as explorers: Using background knowledge. In A. Crismore (Ed.), *Landscapes: A state-of-the-art assessment of reading comprehension research, 1974–1984* (pp. 9:1–24). Bloomington: Center for Reading and Language Studies, University of Indiana.

Hickman, J. (1981). A new perspective on response to literature: Research in an elementary school setting. *Research in the Teaching of English, 15,* 343–354.

Hickman, J. (1983). Everything considered: Response to literature in an elementary school setting. *Journal of Research and Development in Education, 16* (3), 8–13.

Hillocks, G., & Ludlow, L. (1984). A taxonomy of skills in reading and interpreting fiction. *American Educational Research Journal, 21,* 7–24.

Hirsch, E. D. (1987). *Cultural literacy: What every American needs to know.* Boston: Houghton Mifflin.

Holland, N. (1973). *Poems in persons.* New York: Norton.

Holland, N. (1975). *Five readers reading.* New Haven, CT: Yale University Press.

Holland, N. (1985a). Reading readers reading. In C. Cooper (Ed.), *Researching response to literature and the teaching of literature* (pp. 3–21). Norwood, NJ: Ablex.

Holland, N. (1985b). *I,* New Haven, CT: Yale University Press.

Hunt, R., & Vipond, D. (1985). Crash-testing a transactional model of literary learning. *Reader, 14,* 23–39.

Hunt, R., Vipond, D., Jewett, T., & Reither, J. (in press). The social dimensions of reading. In R. Beach & S. Hynds (Eds.) *Developing discourse practices in adolescence and adulthood.* Norwood, NJ: Ablex.

Hunt, R., & Vipond, D. (1986a). Evaluations in literary reading. *Text, 6,* 53–71.

Hunt, R., & Vipond, D. (1986b). *The reader, the text, and the situation: Blocks and affordances in literary reading.* Unpublished paper, Department of Psychology, St. Thomas University, Fredericton, New Brunswick, Canada.

Hurst, K. (1988). Group discussions of poetry. In M. Benton, J. Teasey, R. Bell, & K. Hurst. *Young readers responding to poems* (pp. 157–201). New York: Routledge.

Hynd, C., & Chase, N. (1986). *The responses of college freshman to expository and narrative text.* Paper presented at the National Reading Conference, Austin, TX.

Hynds, S. (1985). Interpersonal cognitive complexity and the literary response processes of adolescent readers. *Research in the Teaching of English, 19,* 386–404.

Hynds, S. (1989). Bringing life to literature and literature to life: Social constructs and contexts of four adolescent readers. *Research in the Teaching of English, 23,* 30–61.

Hynds, S. (in press). Reading as a social event: Comprehension and response in the classroom, text, and world. In S. Straw & D. Bogdan (Eds.), *Beyond communication: Reading comprehension and criticism.* Portsmouth, NH: Boynton Cook.

Jacobsen, M. (1982). Looking for literary space: The willing suspension of disbelief. *Research in the Teaching of English, 16,* 21–38.

Johnson, D., Peer, G., & Baldwin, R. S. (1984). Protagonist preferences among juvenile and adolescent readers. *Journal of Educational Research, 77,* 147–150.

Johnson, P. (1975). Getting acquainted with a poem. *College English, 37,* 358–367.

Jordan, E. (1986). The comprehending and composing processes of good writers who are good readers. (Doctoral dissertation, Temple University). *Dissertation Abstracts International, 47,* 2972A.

Jose, P., & Brewer, S. (1984). Development of story liking: Character identification, suspense, and outcome resolution. *Developmental Psychology, 20,* 911–924.

Jose, P., & Brewer, W. (1983). The development of story liking: Character identification, suspense, and outcome resolution (Technical Report No. 291). Champaign: Center for the Study of Reading, University of Illinois.

Kaivola, K. (1987). Becoming woman; Identification and desire in *The Sound and the Fury. Reader, 17,* 29–43.

Kelly, G. (1955). *The psychology of personal constructs.* New York: Norton.

Kern, S. (1983). The effects of introductory activities upon reading comprehension. Master's thesis, University of Chicago.

Kiefer, B. (1982). *Response of primary children to picture books.* Unpublished doctoral dissertation, Ohio State University.

Kintgen, E. (1983). *The perception of poetry.* Bloomington: Indiana University Press.

Kintgen, E., & Holland, N. (1984). Carlos reads a poem. *College English, 44,* 459–486.

Kirkpatrick, C. G. (1972). The college literature class: Observations and descriptions of class sessions of *The Scarlet Letter.* (ERIC No. ED 070 098.)

Klemenz-Belgardt, E. (1981). American research on response to literature: The empirical studies. *Poetics, 10,* 357–380.

Kumer, K. (1982). Literature in the reading textbook: A comparative study from a sociological perspective. *Research in the Teaching of English, 16,* 301–319.

Labov, W. (1972). *Language of the inner city.* Philadelphia: University of Pennsylvania Press.

Landry, M., Kelly, H., & Gardner, H. (1982). Reality-fantasy discriminations in literature: A developmental story. *Research in the Teaching of English, 16,* 39–54.

Langer, J. A. (1986). *Children reading and writing: Structures and strategies.* Norwood, NJ: Ablex.

Langer, J. A. (1989). *The process of understanding literature.* Technical Report. Center for the Learning and Teaching of literature, Albany, New York.

Last, E. (1984). Textbook selection or censorship: An analysis of the complaints filed in relation to three major literature series proposed for adoption in Texas in 1978 (Doctoral dissertation, University of Texas). *Dissertation Abstracts International, 45,* 2174A.

Lee, S., (1985). Comparative responses to literature by Korean and American college students (Doctoral dissertation, University of Pittsburgh). *Dissertation Abstracts International, 47,* 1635A.

Lehr, S. (1988). The child's developing sense of theme as a response to literature. *Reading Research Quarterly, 23,* 337–357.

Lester, N. (1982). A system for analyzing characters' values in literary texts. *Research in the Teaching of English, 16,* 321–338.

Lewis, W. J. (1972). A comparison of responses of adolescents to narrative and lyric literature and film (Doctoral dissertation, Florida State University). *Dissertation Abstracts International, 33,* 22,1A.

Lipson, M. (1983). The influence of religious affiliation on children's memory for text information. *Reading Research Quarterly, 18,* 448–457.

Lytle, S. (1982). Exploring comprehension style: A study of twelfth-grade readers' transactions with text (Doctoral dissertation, Stanford University).

McClure, A. A., (1985). Children's responses to poetry in a supportive literary context (Doctoral dissertation, Ohio State University). *Dissertation Abstracts International, 46* (1986), 2603A.

McCormick, K. (1985). Psychological realism: A new epistemology for reader-response criticism. *Reader, 14,* 40–53.

MacLean, M. (1986). A framework for analyzing reader-text interactions. *Journal of Research and Development in Education, 19,* 17–21.

McNamara, S. (1981). Responses of fourth- and seventh-grade students to satire as reflected in selected contemporary picture books (Doctoral dissertation, Michigan State University). *Dissertation Abstracts International, 41,* 2978A–2979A.

Mailloux, S. (1982). *Interpretive conventions: The reader in the study of American fiction.* Ithaca, NY: Cornell University Press.

Mailloux, S. (1985, June). Rhetorical hermeneutics. *Critical Inquiry.*

Marshall, J. (1987). The effects of writing on students' understanding of literary texts. *Research in the Teaching of English, 21,* 30–63.

Marshall, J. (1988). Classroom discourse and literary response. In B. Nelms (Ed.), *The 1987 Yearbook of the National Council of Teachers of English* (pp. 45–57). Urbana, IL: National Council of Teachers of English.

Martinez, M. F. (1983). Young children's verbal responses to literature in parent-child storytime interactions (Doctoral dissertation, University of Texas at Austin). *Dissertation Abstracts International, 44*, 1044A.

Mauro, L. (1983). Personal constructs and response to literature: Case studies of adolescents reading about death (Doctoral dissertation, Rutgers University). *Dissertation Abstracts International, 44*, 2072A.

Meutsch, D. (1986). Mental models in literary discourse. *Poetics, 15*, 307–331.

Meutsch, D., & Schmidt, S. (1985). On the role of conventions in understanding literary texts. *Poetics, 14*, 551–574.

Meutsch, D., & Viehoff, R. (Eds.). (1986). *Comprehension of literary discourse*. Berlin: de Gruytor.

Miall, D. (1985). The structure of response: A repertory grid study of a poem. *Research in the Teaching of Literature, 19*, 254–268.

Michalak, D. A. (1977). The effect of instruction in literature on high school students' preferred way of responding (Doctoral dissertation, State University of New York at Buffalo). *Dissertation Abstracts International, 37*, 4829A.

Monseau, V. (1986). Young adult literature and reader response: A descriptive study (Doctoral dissertation, University of Michigan). *Dissertation Abstracts International, 47*, 404A.

Monson, D. (1978, August). A look at humor in literature and children's responses to humor. Paper presented at the 7th International Reading Association World Congress on Reading, Hamburg, West Germany.

Monson, D., & Petola, B. (1976). *Research in children's literature: An annotated bibliography*. Newark, NJ: International Reading Association.

Morris, W. P. (1971). Unstructured oral responses of experienced readers reacting to a given poem (Doctoral dissertation, Indiana University). *Dissertation Abstracts International, 31*, 5673A.

Morrison, T. G. (1987). Question types and fates of student responses in second- and fourth-grade basal reading (Doctoral dissertation, University of Illinois at Urbana-Champaign). *Dissertation Abstracts International, 47*, 3383A.

Mosenthal, J. (1987). The reader's affective response to narrative text. In R. Tierney, P. Anders, & J. Mitchell (Eds.), *Understanding readers' understanding* (pp. 95–105). Hillsdale, NJ: Erlbaum.

National Assessment of Educational Progress. (1981). *Reading, thinking and writing: Results From the 1979–1980 National Assessment of Reading and Literature*. Denver, Co.: National Assessment of Educational Progress.

Nell, V. (1988). The psychology of reading for pleasure: Needs and gratifications. *Reading Research Quarterly, 23*, 6–50.

Newell, G., Suszynski, K., & Weingart, R. (1989). The effects of writing in a reader-based and text-based mode on students' understanding of two short stories. *Journal of Reading Behavior, 21*, 37–58.

Newkirk, T. (1984). Looking for trouble: A way to unmask our readings. *College English, 46*, 756–766.

Nissel, M. (1987). The oral responses of three fourth graders to realistic fiction and fantasy (Doctoral dissertation, Fordham University). *Dissertation Abstracts International, 48*, 4A.

Noda, L. A. (1981). Literature and culture: Japanese and American reader responses to modern Japanese short stories (Doctoral dissertation, New York University). *Dissertation Abstracts International, 41*, 4894A.

Odell, L., & Cooper, C. (1976). Describing responses to works of fiction. *Research in the Teaching of English, 10*, 203–225.

Olshavsky, J. (1976). Reading as problem solving: An investigation of strategies. *Reading Research Quarterly, 12*, 654–674.

Olson, G., Duffy, S., & Mack, R. (1984). Thinking-out-loud as a method for studying real-time comprehension processes. In D. Kieras & M. Just (Eds.), *New methods in reading comprehension research* (pp. 253–286). Hillsdale, NJ: Erlbaum.

Ortony, A., Turner, T., & N. Larson-Shapiro (1985). Cultural and instructional influences on figurative language comprehension by inner city children. *Research in the Teaching of English, 19*, 25–36.

Parnell, G. (1984). Levels of aesthetic experience with literature (Doctoral dissertation, Brigham Young University). *Dissertation Abstracts International, 45*, 06A.

Perine, M. H. (1978). The response of sixth-grade readers to selected children's literature with special reference to moral judgment (Doctoral dissertation, Columbia University). *Dissertation Abstracts International, 39*, 2729A.

Person, E. (1988). *Dreams of love and fateful encounters*. New York: Norton.

Peters, W., & Blues, A. (1978). Teacher intellectual disposition as it relates to student openness in written response to literature. *Research in the Teaching of English, 12*, 12–136.

Petrosky, A. R. (1977a). Response to literature: Research roundup. *English Journal, 66*, 86–88.

Petrosky, A. R. (1977b). Genetic epistemology and psychoanalytic ego psychology: Clinical support for the study of response to literature. *Research in the Teaching of English, 11*, 28–38.

Petrosky, A. R. (1981). From story to essay: Reading and writing. *College Composition and Communication, 33*, 19–36.

Pierce, R. (1985). The effect of moral judgment development on the responses of eight adolescent readers to two short stories. Master's thesis, University of Minnesota.

Pillar, A. (1983). Aspects of moral judgment in response to fables. *Journal of Research and Development in Education, 16*, 39–46.

Pleasnick, W. (1983). An investigation of first graders' original narratives as a reflection of schema for story and of the relationships between schema for story and reading readiness and reading achievement (Doctoral dissertation, Georgia State University). *Dissertation Abstracts International, 44*, 11A.

Pratt, M. L. (1976). *A speech act theory of literary discourse.* Bloomington: Indiana University Press.

Price, M. (1986). Reader-response criticism: A test of its usefulness in a first-year college course in writing about literature (Doctoral dissertation, Florida State University). *Dissertation Abstracts International, 47*, 1637A.

Purves, A. (1975). *International studies in evaluation VIII: An empirical study of education in twenty-one countries.* Stockholm: Almqvist and Wiksell.

Purves, A. (1981). *Reading and literature: American achievement in international perspective.* Urbana, IL: National Council of Teachers of English.

Purves, A. (1985). That sunny dome: Those caves of ice. In C. Cooper (Ed.), *Researching response to literature and the teaching of literature* (pp. 54–69). Norwood, NJ: Ablex.

Purves, A. (1986). Cultural literacy and response to literature. Paper presented at the meeting of the NCTE Assembly on Research, Chicago.

Purves, A., & Beach, R. (1972). *Literature and the reader: Research on response to literature, reading interests, and teaching of literature.* Urbana, IL: National Council of Teachers of English.

Purves, A., Foshay, A., & Hansson, G. (1973). *Literature education in ten countries.* New York: John Wiley.

Purves, A., & Rippere, V. (1968). *Elements of writing about a literary work: A study of response to literature.* Urbana, IL: National Council of Teachers of English.

Rabinowitz, P. (1983). Assertion and assumption: Fictional patterns and the external world. *PMLA, 96*, 408–419.

Rabinowitz, P. (1985). The turn of the glass key: Popular fiction as reading strategy. *Critical Inquiry, 11*, 418–430.

Rabinowitz, P. (1987). *Before reading.* Ithaca, NY: Cornell University Press.

Radway, J. (1984). *Reading the romance: Women, patriarchy, and popular literature.* Chapel Hill: University of North Carolina Press.

Rapport, R. (1982). Reader-initiated response to self-elected literature compared with teacher-selected literature. (Doctoral dissertation, University of Michigan). Dissertation *Abstracts International, 44*, 413a.

Ravitch, D., & Finn, C. E. (1987). *What do our 17-year-olds know?* New York: Harper & Row.

Ray, W. (1984). *Literary meaning.* New York: Blackwell.

Reed, M., & Bontempo, B. (1987, November). The effect of how prospective teachers were taught literature and how they plan to teach literature. Paper presented at the meeting of the National Council of Teachers, Los Angeles.

Reilly, S., Beach, R., & Crabtree, L. (1986, April). The effects of guided prewriting activities on students' literary responses to short stories. Paper presented at the meeting of the American Educational Research Association, San Francisco.

Rest, J. (1979). *The defining issues test.* Minneapolis: University of Minnesota Press.

Reynolds, R., Taylor, M., Steffeusen, M., Shirley, L., & Anderson, R. (1982). Cultural schemata and reading comprehension. *Reading Research Quarterly, 17*, 353–366.

Richards, I. A. (1929). *Practical Criticism.* New York: Harcourt, Brace, & World.

Rogers, T. (1988). *Students as literary critics: The interpretive theories, processes, and experiences of ninth-grade students* (Unpublished doctoral dissertation, University of Illinois, Champaign/Urbana).

Rosenblatt, L. (1978). *The reader, the text, the poem.* Carbondale: Southern Illinois University Press.

Rosenblatt, L. (1983). *Literature as exploration.* New York: Modern Language Association.

Rosenblatt, L. (1985). Viewpoints: Transaction versus interaction—A terminological rescue operation. *Research in the Teaching of English, 19*, 96–107.

Ross, C. (1978). A comparative story of the responses made by grade 11 Vancouver students to Canadian and New Zealand poems. *Research in the Teaching of English, 12*, 297–306.

Rubin, S., & Gardner, H. (1985). Once upon a time: The development of sensitivity to story structure. In C. Cooper (Ed.), *Researching response to literature and the teaching of literature* (pp. 169–189). Norwood, NJ: Ablex.

Ryle, G. (1949). *The concept of mind.* New York: Barnes.

Sadoski, M., & Goetz, E. (1985). Relationships between affect, imagery, and importance ratings for segments of a story. In J. Niles & R. Colik (Eds.), *Issues in literacy: A research perspective. 34th yearbook of the National Conference on Reading* (pp. 180–185). Rochester, NY: National Conference on Reading.

Sadoski, M., Goetz, E., & Kangiser, S. (1988). Imagination in story response: Relationships between imagery, affect, and structural importance. *Reading Research Quarterly, 23*, 320–336.

Scarlett, G., & Wolf, D. (1979). When it's only make-believe. *Directions in Child Development, 6*, 29–40.

Scarlett, H. H., Press, A. N., & Crockett, W. H. (1971). Children's descriptions of peers: A Wernerian developmental analysis. *Child Development, 44,* 439–453.

Schmidt, S. (1985). Foundations of a constructivist empirical study of literature. *Reader, 14,* 5–22.

Scholes, R. (1985). *Textual power.* New Haven, CT: Yale University Press.

Schon, D. (1983). *The reflective practitioner: How professionals think in action.* New York: Basic Books.

Scott, K. (1986). Effects of sex-fair reading materials on pupils' attitudes, comprehension, and interest. *American Educational Research Journal, 23,* 105–116.

Shapiro, S. (1985). An analysis of poetry teaching procedures in sixth-grade basal manuals. *Reading Research Quarterly, 20,* 368–381.

Shank, R. (1982). *Dynamic memory: A theory of reminding and learning in computers and people.* New York: Cambridge University Press.

Shedd, P. (1976). The relationship between attitude of the reader towards women's changing role and response to literature which illuminates women's role. (ERIC Document No. ED 142 956)

Sheldon, A. (1986). The influence of illustration on fifth graders' response to the illustrated poem. *Dissertation Abstracts International, 47,* 07A. (University Microfilms No. 86–25, 289)

Siefert, C., Robertson, S., & Black, J. (1982). *On-line processing of pragmatic inferences.* Cognitive Science Technical Report No. 15. New Haven, CT: Yale University Press.

Sims, R. (1983). Strong black girls: A ten-year-old responds to fiction about Afro-Americans. *Journal of Research and Development, 16,* 21–28.

Singer, H., & Donlan, D. (1982). Active comprehension: Problem-solving schema with question generation for comprehension of complex short stories. *Reading Research Quarterly, 17,* 166–185.

Smith, L. (1984). Rereading: A response to literature (Doctoral dissertation, University of Minnesota). *Dissertation Abstracts International, 45,* 2382A.

Squire, J. (1964). *The responses of adolescents while reading four short stories.* Urbana, IL.: National Council of Teachers of English.

Steinberg, E. (1986). Protocols, retrospective reports, and the stream of consciousness. *College English, 48,* 697–712.

Stout, D. A. (1964). The responses of college freshman to characters in four short stories (Doctoral dissertation, University of California at Berkeley). *Dissertation Abstracts International, 25,* 1794.

Straw, S. (1986, November). Learning about poetry in small groups. Paper presented at the meeting of the National Council of Teachers of English, San Antonio, TX.

Sutton-Smith, B. (1981). *The folk-stories of children.* Philadelphia: University of Pennsylvania Press.

Svensson, C. (1985). *The construction of poetic meaning: A cultural-developmental study of symbolic and nonsymbolic strategies in the interpretation of contemporary poetry.* Lund, Sweden: Liber Forlag.

Taylor, E. A. (1986). Young children's verbal responses to literature: An analysis of group and individual differences (Doctoral dissertation, University of Texas at Austin). *Dissertation Abstracts International, 47,* 1599A.

Teasey, J. (1988). Four readers reading. In M. Benton, J. Teasey, R. Bell, & K. Hurst. *Young readers responding to poems* (pp. 36–87.) New York: Routledge.

Thomson, N. (1987). *Understanding teenagers' reading.* New York: Nichols.

Tierney, R. (in press). New vistas for reading comprehension, research, and practice. In R. Beach & S. Hynds (Eds.), *Developing discourse practices in adolescence and adulthood.* Norwood, NJ: Ablex.

Travers, D. (1984). The poetry teacher: Behaviors and attitudes. *Research in the Teaching of English, 18,* 367–384.

Trimble, C. (1984). The relationship among fairy tales, ego development, grade level, and sex (Doctoral dissertation, University of Alabama). *Dissertation Abstracts International, 46,* 04A.

Tutton, B. (1979). Response to short stories as related to interest among community college students (Doctoral dissertation, University of Minnesota).

Vardell, S. (1982). The development in use and understanding of literary conventions in children's reading and writing of stories (Doctoral dissertation, University of Minnesota). *Dissertation Abstracts International, 44,* 414A.

Viehoff, R. (1986). How to construct a literary poem? *Poetics, 15,* 287–306.

Vipond, D., & Hunt, R., (1984). Point-driven understanding: Pragmatic and cognitive dimensions of literary reading. *Poetics, 13,* 261–277.

Vipond, D., Hunt, R., Jewett, J., & Reither, J. (in press). Making sense of reading. In R. Beach & S. Hynds (Eds.), *Developing discourse practices in adolescence and adulthood.* Norwood, NJ: Ablex.

Wade-Maltais, J. (1981). Responses of community college readers to a short story when audience interpretations are not known (Doctoral dissertation, University of California, Riverside). *Dissertation Abstracts International, 43,* 1A.

Webb, A. J. (1980). Introducing the transactive paradigm for literary response into the high school literature program: A study of effects on curriculum, teaching, and students (Doctoral dissertation, State University of New York at Buffalo). *Dissertation Abstracts International, 41,* 929A.

Webb, A. J. (1985). Studying the effects of literature instruction in classrooms: Collaborative research in schools. In C. Cooper (Ed.), *Researching response to literature and teaching of literature* (pp. 273–286). Norwood, NJ: Ablex.

Wheeler, V. (1983). Field orientation as a predictor of reader response to literature (Doctoral dissertation, Illinois State University). *Dissertation Abstracts International, 44,* 2756A.

Willinsky, J., & Hunniford, R. M. (1986). Reading the romance younger: The mirrors and fears of a preparatory literature. *Reading-Canada-Lecture, 4,* 16–31.

Wolf, D. (1988). *Reading reconsidered: Students, teachers, and literature.* Cambridge, MA: Harvard Graduate School of Education.

Worthington, J. (1978). A comparison of responses of selected eleventh graders to written and filmed versions of selected short stories (Doctoral dissertation). *Dissertation Abstracts International, 38,* 7192A.

Yarbrough, J. (1984). A grounded theory of the social psychological process of involving college students in a course on adolescent literature (Doctoral dissertation, University of Florida). *Dissertation Abstracts International, 45,* 2019A.

Young, A. E. (1986). Fostering response to literature in the college English classroom (Doctoral dissertation, University of Pennsylvania). *Dissertation Abstracts International, 47,* 1268A.

Zaharias, J. (1986). The effects of genre and tone on undergraduate students' preferred patterns of response to two short stories and two poems. *Research in the Teaching of English, 20,* 56–68.

Zaharias, J., & Maertz, M. (1983). Identifying and validating the constituents of literary response through a modification of the response preference measure. *Research in the Teaching of English, 17,* 231–241.

18 MENTAL MODELS AND READING COMPREHENSION

Timothy P. McNamara, Diana L. Miller, and John D. Bransford

The year 1987 marked the thirtieth anniversary of the publication of Noam Chomsky's *Syntactic Structures*. This work was extremely influential in psychology for many reasons, not the least of which was Chomsky's introduction of the concept of transformations. These rules mapped underlying forms of sentences onto their observed forms. Psychologists seized on these ideas and, in spite of Chomsky's resistance, interpreted them as a psychological theory of language production and comprehension. Although it is a dangerous business pegging the birthday of an intellectual enterprise, one would not be too far off in claiming that 1957 marked the beginning of modern psycholinguistics.

So what have we learned in 32 years? Quite a lot, we think. The psychology of language comprehension, in general, and the psychology of reading, in particular, have advanced tremendously. Several major changes in theory and methodology have occurred in the past 32 years.

First, researchers have moved from a primary focus on memory for lists of words; to comprehension of, and memory for, meaningful sentences; and, finally, to the mental processes involved in understanding and remembering sets of sentences that form coherent texts.

Second, it has become clear that language comprehension requires knowledge of the world as well as knowledge of the language. Theoretical approaches have emerged that focus on the knowledge that readers and listeners bring to comprehension. Schema theory is one such approach, and there is little doubt that this perspective provides insights into the process of comprehension. By the same token, people are able to understand novel information that does not fit neatly into previously acquired schemata; hence, something beyond schema theory is required. The concept of mental models offers a useful way of thinking about how readers and listeners *construct* meaningful interpretations of language.

Third, experimental methods have been developed that permit relatively precise assessments of the degree to which various language processes—making inferences, for example—occur automatically at the time of comprehension, as opposed to strategically, when particular types of test questions are asked. These methods have contributed greatly to our understanding of how texts are mentally represented and how these representations are constructed.

This chapter is organized around these three advancements. We begin with an overview of the movement from a focus on words to a focus on paragraphs. We also look briefly at schemata and the role of prior knowledge in comprehension. In the second section, we turn to the primary topics of this chapter—the concept of mental models and the research that this theoretical framework has generated. Throughout this discussion we consider some of the methodological refinements that have allowed researchers to determine when and how mental processes occur. We conclude by discussing some possible directions for future research.

BACKGROUND

From Words to Sentences

In the mid-1950s, most research involving language used lists of words as stimuli (Baars, 1987). It was easy to assess what people remembered; the words presented during acquisition either were or were not recalled (or recognized) at the time of test. In contrast, using sentences as stimuli was much harder. How did one account for the fact that various types of paraphrase seemed to preserve meaning despite major changes in wording?

Chomsky's work in linguistics furnished psychologists with the theoretical tools needed to handle this problem. His arguments for the need to analyze the structure of sentences at two levels—which came to be known as surface structure and deep structure (Chomsky, 1965)—were particularly useful in going beyond the notion that memory of a sentence was equivalent to a list of the words that the sentence contained.

A number of attempts to create psychological theory from Chomsky's linguistic theory met with failure, however. The most famous of these theories was probably the *Derivational Theory of Complexity* (DTC). The hypothesis was that the difficulty of understanding a sentence was directly related to its transformational history: Sentences requiring more, or more complex, transformations should be more difficult to understand than sentences requiring fewer, or less complex, transformations.

Although there was some early support for DTC, later research and astute reexaminations of the earlier work did not support the theory (see Fodor, Bever, & Garrett, 1974, for a review). A positive outcome of this research was an appreciation of the importance of sentence clauses to comprehension (e.g., Bever, Lackner, & Kirk, 1969; Caplan, 1972). This work supplied a conceptual foundation for the view that propositions might be the functional units in language comprehension.

From Sentences to Texts

Kintsch and his colleagues (1974; Kintsch & van Dijk, 1978) played a major role in developing a theory of reading based on propositions (see Meyer & Rice, 1984, for a review). *Propositions* are the smallest units of knowledge that can stand as separate assertions; the smallest units that can be true or false. Consider, for example, the sentence:

1. Reagan gave a beautiful Bible to Khomeini, who was the leader of Iran.

This sentence contains three propositions:

2. Reagan gave a Bible to Khomeini.
3. The Bible was beautiful.
4. Khomeini was the leader of Iran.

Propositions are ideas that can be expressed in words, not the words themselves. Kintsch's (1974) notation, though somewhat cumbersome, is useful in this regard:

5. (give, Reagan, Bible, Khomeini, past)
6. (beautiful, Bible, past)
7. (leader-of, Khomeini, Iran, past)

One of the advantages of propositional theories is that they can be extended to account for sets of sentences that form coherent texts. The results of several research studies conducted in the early 1970s suggested that, just as sentence comprehension involved more than memory for words in the sentence, text comprehension involved more than memory for the individual sentences that formed the text (Bransford & Franks, 1971; Pearson, 1974).

There is little doubt that propositions are functional in language comprehension. Kintsch and Keenan (1973) demonstrated that reading times correlated very highly with numbers of propositions but not at all with numbers of words in sentences. Ratcliff and McKoon (1978; McKoon & Ratcliff, 1980) have reported compelling evidence of the priority of propositions in memory for discourse. In one of their experiments, subjects read sets of sentences like those in entries 8–10:

8. The host mixed a cocktail but the guest wanted coffee.
9. The driver bruised a hip and the passenger strained a knee.
10. A gust crushed the umbrella and rain soaked the man.

After reading the sentences, subjects received a recognition test for words in the sentences. Words were displayed one at a time on a computer display; the subjects' task was simply to decide whether or not each word had appeared in any of the sentences. Ratcliff and McKoon found that responses to a word were faster and more accurate when it was immediately preceded in the test list (i.e., primed) by a word from the same proposition as opposed to a different proposition. For example, subjects recognized "cocktail" faster when it was primed by "host" than when it was primed by "guest." (A propositional analysis of sentence 8 is [mix, host, cocktail] & [want, guest, coffee].) Importantly, the number of words between the prime and the target was the same in both cases. This facilitation in responding has been shown to be "automatic"; that is, it is unconscious and not influenced by retrieval strategies (Ratcliff & McKoon, 1981; for additional discussion of automatic and strategic processes, see below). Thus, these data are informative about how sentences are actually represented in memory.

The Role of Knowledge in Comprehension

A problem with propositional representations is that they are often more representative of the structure of the text than they are of the structure of memory for the text. We know, for example, that normal language understanding relies heavily on context (e.g., Bransford & Johnson, 1972; Dooling & Lachman, 1971). Moreover, there has been a plethora of demonstrations of the importance of prior knowledge, such as scripts or schemata, in reading comprehension (see R. C. Anderson & Pearson, 1984, for a review). When readers know something about restaurants, for example, they are able to understand the following passage, even though the passage itself is vastly underdetermined:

John was hungry and decided to order a large meal. He was pleased that the waitress was attentive and prompt. After he finished the meal, he paid his bill and left an extra five dollars under his plate.

According to schema-based models, the activation of a restaurant script allows the reader to infer that John ordered his meal from the waitress, received his meal from the waitress, and left the five dollars as a tip for the waitress. Understanding the passage requires understanding these relationships, and it is difficult to see how readers could understand these relationships without referring to schematic knowledge about restaurants.

There is no doubt that readers use schemata in comprehension. It is not clear, however, what readers actually do with schemata. Schema theorists have proposed that comprehension simply involves the instantiation of schemata: Readers activate a schema and fill in generic "slots" (e.g., customer) with the right text-specific information (e.g., John). But schema instantiation does not explain how or why readers understand texts about unfamiliar objects and events (Johnson-Laird, 1983). A more general approach— one that can handle scripted and unscripted activities—is to view comprehension as a process of building and maintaining a model of situations and events described in a text. We turn to this approach now.

MENTAL MODELS

Comprehension theories that involve the representation of situations described by the text have been termed *mental model theories*. According to these theories (Johnson-Laird, 1983; Sanford & Garrod, 1981; van Dijk & Kintsch, 1983), readers not only process a text at a propositional level, they also construct a mental model that is analogous in structure to the events, situations, or layouts described by the text. Differences between propositional representations and mental models can be illustrated with the following example (adapted from Glenberg, Meyer & Lindem, 1987).

Bransford, Barclay, and Franks (1972) showed that subjects who memorized sentence 11 later had difficulty deciding whether they had learned that sentence or a similar sentence, sentence 12:

11.   Three turtles rested on a floating log, and a fish swam beneath them.
12.   Three turtles rested on a floating log, and a fish swam beneath it.

According to a propositional analysis, these sentences differ by a single proposition; namely, the proposition that specifies whether the fish swam under the turtles or under the log. Given that the sentences differ by a single proposition, the memory confusions are not very surprising.

However, subjects who memorized sentence 13 did not confuse it with sentence 14:

13.   Three turtles rested beside a floating log, and a fish swam beneath them.
14.   Three turtles rested beside a floating log, and a fish swam beneath it.

Note that these sentences differ by the same proposition that distinguishes 11 and 12. According to a propositional analysis, then, sentences 13 and 14 should be just as confusable as sentences 11 and 12.

The difference between these pairs of sentences lies in the situations they describe. Sentences 11 and 12 describe the same event in the world: A fish swam beneath some turtles on a log. Sentences 13 and 14, however, describe different events. According to sentence 13, a fish swam beneath some turtles but not necessarily a log; whereas according to sentence 14, a fish swam beneath a log but not necessarily some turtles. If subjects mentally represented the sentences as models of the situations, then the memory confusions observed by Bransford and associates (1972) make sense. Mental models of sentences 11 and 12 would be identical, but mental models of sentences 13 and 14 would be quite different.

Structure and Function

A mental model consists of mental tokens arranged in a structure that depicts the situation described by a text.[1] *Mental tokens* are symbols representing objects or characters in a narrative. A mental model of sentence 14, above, would include three tokens representing the turtles. These turtle tokens would be represented as beside a token log, which in turn would be represented as being above a token fish. The mental model can give rise to images, although mental models can also contain nonperceptual information, such as goals and causal relationships.

Whether the reader places more emphasis on the construction of a mental model or the encoding of a propositional description seems to be governed by the nature of the text material and the nature of the reader's task. Mani and Johnson-Laird (1982) found that subjects used different encoding strategies, depending on whether they were reading a spatially determinate description or a spatially indeterminate description. The former described a set of objects that could be in one, and only one, spatial arrangement; whereas the latter described a set of objects that could be in at least two different spatial arrangements (see Table 18.1).

Subjects in these experiments read verbal descriptions and had to verify whether or not pictures were true of them. Afterwards, subjects were given an unexpected test in which they had to rank-order sets of verbal descriptions according to how well each description matched their memory of a description presented in the first phase of the experiment. Each set of alternative descriptions contained: (1) the original, previously presented verbal description; (2) a consistent but nonidentical description; and (3) two foil descriptions that were not consistent with the original description. For example, if the original description contained the sentence, "The chair is in front of the table," then the consistent description might contain the sentence, "The table is behind the chair."

TABLE 18.1   Determinate and Indeterminate Spatial Descriptions Used
by Mani and Johnson-Laird (1982)

TYPE	VERBAL DESCRIPTION	PICTORIAL LAYOUT		
Determinate	The bed is behind the bookshelf. The bed is to the left of the table. The chair is to the right of the table.	bed bookshelf	table	chair
Indeterminate	The bed is behind the bookshelf. The bed is to the left of the table. The chair is to the right of the bed.	bed bookshelf or bed bookshelf	table chair	chair table

(*Foil descriptions* contained inconsistent sentences like "The table is in front of the chair.")

Mani and Johnson-Laird (1982) concluded that subjects formed mental models of determinate descriptions but encoded propositional representations for the indeterminate descriptions. Mental models are easier to remember than propositional representations (Johnson-Laird, 1983), and subjects were correspondingly better at remembering the gist of determinate than indeterminate descriptions. Subjects correctly rank-ordered the foil descriptions lower than the original and the consistent descriptions for 70 percent of the spatially determinate descriptions but for only 39 percent of the spatially indeterminate descriptions. But because mental models do not preserve verbatim detail, subjects confused the consistent descriptions with the original, spatially determinate descriptions. Subjects were no better than chance at rank-ordering the original description higher than the consistent description for the spatially determinate descriptions, but they were significantly better than chance at doing so for the indeterminate descriptions. Evidently, the encoding of indeterminate descriptions as propositional representations—which closely correspond to text structure—enabled subjects to distinguish between the original and the consistent descriptions, even though overall memory for the indeterminate descriptions was poor.

Garnham (1981) also provided evidence that people can choose whether to emphasize propositional or mental model processing. When subjects in Garnham's experiments were not warned about a memory test following the readings, they seemed to encode texts as mental models. Subjects had difficulty recalling exact sentence structure and could not distinguish between sentences that had been presented and sentences that had not been presented but were consistent with the mental model. For example, subjects heard one narration that contained the sentences, "By the window was a man with a martini" and "The man standing by the window shouted to the host." Subjects were later unable to remember whether they heard the latter sentence or the coreferential sentence, "The man with the martini shouted to the host." Subjects who were warned about the upcoming memory test, however, were apparently unable to use propositional encoding during comprehension. These subjects had no trouble with the memory test, which suggests that their test representations were similar to the actual text structure (see also Schmalhofer & Glavanov, 1986).

In summary, readers are able to process a text either as a set of propositions or as a mental model. Depending upon the reading material and the task, people can select one of these processing modes over the other. Readers emphasize propositional encoding, retaining text structure when they want to remember the text material verbatim. They also use propositional encoding when the indeterminate nature of the text makes mental model construction difficult. However, when the text material is conducive to mental model processing, as in task instructions, narrations, or spatially determinate descriptions, people avail themselves of its benefits. Mental models do not retain text structure but can support better recall of events described by a text.

Processing Evidence

The research described above offers a general picture of what mental models are like and when they are used. The rich complexity of mental models is even better revealed in recent studies of the mental processes that occur during reading.

Glenberg, Meyer, and Lindem (1987) investigated how readers update their mental models as a story unfolds. They gave subjects paragraphs to read, on a computer screen, in which a character either spatially associated him- or herself with an object or spatially dissociated him- or herself from an object. For the object "flower," for example, subjects read, "He put the last flower in his buttonhole, then left the house to go shopping for groceries" (spatially associated); or, alternatively, "He put the last flower in the vase, then left the house to go shopping for groceries" (spatially dissociated). Later in the paragraph subjects were given an item recognition test, in which the target object name ("flower") or a foil was flashed on the screen. Subjects had to decide whether the object noun had or had not previously appeared in the paragraph.

Response times were faster for spatially associated targets than for spatially dissociated targets. The results could not be explained by appealing to the idea that spatial association made the object more "important." In some paragraphs, the dissociation actually made the object more important (e.g., a child wandering away from the main character). In addition, there was no difference in response times for tests presented immediately following the critical sentence. If more attention had been allotted to the spatially associated targets, then a difference should also have been found there, as well as later in the paragraph.

The facilitation for spatially associated objects suggests that readers keep only a portion of the information that they have read in a highly accessible *foreground*. This foreground corresponds to an updated situational model reflecting the current status of objects or events described by the text. The foreground can be thought of as a working mental model, containing information about the situation that is likely to be needed for processing subsequent sentences. In the study by Glenberg and colleagues (1987), information was relevant if it corresponded to the current status of the main character. When the main character left the house to go shopping, objects remaining in the house, such as a flower placed in a vase, were not as relevant as objects that were in the grocery store with the main character, such as a flower placed in his buttonhole.

Morrow (1985) also demonstrated that readers construct working mental models to reflect information relevant to the prominent character. Morrow was particularly interested in the comprehension of texts that included two or more characters, with shifts in character prominence. Subjects in his experiments tended to construct mental models according to the protagonist's perspective; however, they could change the mental model to make the nonprotagonist prominent when the text specified that the nonprotagonist was to be foregrounded.

The chief method of foregrounding a nonprotagonist was through verb tense. For example, one of Morrow's (1985) paragraphs introduced Tom as the protagonist and later introduced Harry, Tom's friend. The paragraph said that Tom and Harry were at a fair, and that they decided to split up for a while. The paragraph then stated, "After Tom had gone into the hall, Harry walked toward the ferris wheel. He saw a friend and said 'Hello'." Readers tended to choose Harry, the nonprotagonist, as the referent of the pronoun "he," indicating that Harry was now in the foreground. The simple past tense verb "walked," acted as a situational cue, placing Harry in the foreground. The past perfect verb "had gone" placed Tom in the background.

This effect occurred regardless of whether the sentence mentioned the "Tom" clause or the "Harry" clause first. Order of mention was used by subjects only in sentences that did not contain clear situational cues (i.e., did not use past tense vs. past perfect verbs) about foreground and background events. When paragraphs contained clear situational cues about the characters and the events, readers relied solely on these cues, suggesting that they were updating a situational model of the text.

Readers, therefore, appear to focus on information relevant to the prominent character in a narrative. Readers can update their mental models to reflect a new situation for the prominent character (Glenberg et al., 1987) or to shift to another character's perspective (Morrow, 1985).

While updating mental models to contain information relevant to the prominent character, readers may need to draw upon previously learned information. Morrow, Greenspan, and Bower (1987) examined the incorporation of previously learned information into mental models. These researchers had subjects learn the spatial layout of a building before reading a narrative that described a character moving through the building. As subjects read the text, pairs of target words appeared. The targets were two objects from the building layout. Subjects had to decide whether the objects were from the same room or from different rooms.

The results showed that, after reading a sentence such as, "Wilbur walked from the library into the conference room," subjects could decide that two objects were in the conference room faster than they could decide that two objects were in the library. This difference in accessibility suggests that the readers had updated their mental model to include the now-relevant objects in the conference room and to exclude the now-irrelevant objects in the library. Subjects were not using order-of-mention cues, since the same effect was found for the sentence, "Wilbur walked into the conference room from the library."

Readers also seemed capable of keeping objects from more than one room in the mental model when both rooms were relevant. In the sentence, "While Wilbur was walking through the conference room toward the library, he looked under the table," both the library and the conference room are relevant to the action in the sentence. Readers correspondingly showed high accessibility for target objects in both rooms.

In summary, several experiments have assessed comprehension while a person is actively engaged in reading. These experiments indicate that readers maintain a remarkably complex working mental model. Readers seem to focus on information relevant to the main character in a narrative, recording and updating spatial relations between the protagonist and objects with which he or she interacts. Readers also make perspective shifts from one character to another as the situation requires. While updating mental models, readers often must retrieve previously learned information. Available data indicate that readers can retrieve episodically learned information (e.g., spatial relations depicted in a map) if it aids in understanding the situation described by a narrative. Past research on schemata (e.g., R. C. Anderson & Pearson, 1984) has already demonstrated the functional role of scripted, semantic knowledge in reading comprehension.

Specification

Constructing a mental model using previously learned or schematic knowledge requires the reader to make inferences about the situations in the text. The number of inferences that could be made is potentially infinite, so readers must place some limits on how completely and specifically they construct the situational model. Evidently, these limits are fairly severe. Based on a review of the literature, Alba and Hasher (1983) concluded that there was little empirical support for schema theories that predicted large numbers of inferences.

In this section of the chapter, we review evidence on four types of specification inferences: case-filling, instantiation, predictable-event, and property. Many studies on inferencing have been criticized because they cannot determine whether an inference was made during encoding or at the time of the memory test (Tulving, 1976). We limit our review to studies for which the argument can be made that inferences occurred during comprehension, not at the time memory was probed.

Case-Filling Inferences

Case-filling, or instrumental, inferences occur when the reader infers that an action (e.g., digging a hole) was performed with a specific tool (e.g., a shovel). McKoon and Ratcliff (1981) found that readers make case-filling inferences in some circumstances. In one experiment, subjects read paragraphs, such as the one in Table 18.2, and then received a recognition test. Some of the test words were instruments mentioned in the beginning of the paragraph (e.g., hammer). Subjects were faster at indicating that the instrument had appeared in the paragraph when the last sentence suggested that the instrument was used ("Bobby pounded the boards together with nails") than when it suggested that the instrument was not used ("Bobby stuck the boards together with glue"). This difference in reaction time indicates that subjects made the inference that the instrument (hammer) was used for the appropriate action (pounding the boards).

Another experiment showed that this effect was not simply due to semantic activation. Subjects who read a modified paragraph, shown in Table 18.3, did not show facilitation on "hammer," even when the last sentence read "Bobby pounded the boards together with nails." (Subjects who read these paragraphs were not tested on "mallet.")

Subjects appeared to make instrumental inferences only for highly typical instruments. When the word "hammer" was replaced by "mallet" (see Table 18.4), subjects did not seem to make the inference that a mallet was used to perform the final action. That is, responses to "mallet" were not facilitated after reading a paragraph that mentioned mallets but not hammers. It is possible, however, that readers initially processed "mallet" as equivalent to the more familiar "hammer." Unfortunately, subjects who read the paragraph in Table 18.4 were not tested on "hammer."

Another interpretation of these results is based on the relative costs and benefits of inferencing. Subjects might not have made the "mallet" inference after reading a paragraph like the one in Table 18.4 because the cost of processing outweighed the usefulness of the inference. Inferences about atypical instruments may require more processing energy than inferences about typical instruments, which are frequently associated with the event in the paragraph. In order to maintain efficient processing, the language system may only specify atypical instruments in cases where the use of the instrument is important, or highly focused. McKoon and Ratcliff (1981) suggested that their "hammer" and "mallet" paragraphs (Tables 18.2 and 18.4) did not highlight the use of the instrument very strongly; the reader only needs to know that some boards were joined together. Typical instruments, on the other hand, presumably have lower

TABLE 18.2   A Test Paragraph Used by McKoon and Ratcliff (1981)
to Assess Typical Case-Filling Inferences

Bobby got a saw, hammer, screwdriver, and square from his toolbox. He had already selected an oak tree as the site for the birdhouse. He had drawn a detailed blueprint and measured carefully. He marked the boards and cut them out.

Final sentence (biasing): Then Bobby pounded the boards together with nails.

Final sentence (nonbiasing): Then Bobby stuck the boards together with glue.

Test word: hammer

TABLE 18.3   A Modified Test Paragraph Used by McKoon and Ratcliff (1981)

Bobby opened his toolbox and pulled out a mallet, a hammer which had been broken earlier that week, and a screwdriver. He also collected the lumber and paint he had bought. He had already selected an oak tree as the site for the birdhouse. He had drawn a detailed blueprint and measured carefully. He marked the boards and cut them out.

Final sentence (biasing): Then Bobby pounded the boards together with nails.

Final sentence (nonbiasing): Then Bobby stuck the boards together with glue.

Test word: hammer

processing costs; and thus the benefits of making the inference are relatively greater.

These observations could explain why atypical inferencing was not observed for paragraphs like the one in Table 18.4 but typical inferencing was observed for paragraphs like the one in Table 18.2. The question remains whether or not atypical inferencing occurs for paragraphs that highlight the atypical instrument, such as the one in Table 18.3. When reading this paragraph, subjects did not infer that a hammer was used but they might very well have inferred that a mallet was used.

In summary, the experiments reported by McKoon and Ratcliff (1981) clearly indicate that subjects make case-filling inferences for typical instruments, but they do not indicate whether readers make case-filling inferences for atypical instruments if the instruments are clearly distinguished from typical ones, are strongly highlighted by the text, or both.

Another widely cited study on instrumental inferencing was conducted by Dosher and Corbett (1982). In these experiments, a simple sentence (e.g., "The man swept the floor") was presented for subjects to read. The sentence was replaced by a target word, which could be a typical instrument (e.g., broom) or an atypical instrument (e.g., mop). The subjects' task was to name the color of the ink used to print the target word (Stroop, 1935). There was no evidence of Stroop interference on implied instrument test words, regardless of their typicality. In contrast to McKoon and Ratcliff (1981), Dosher and Corbett concluded that readers do not normally make case-filling inferences, especially for short sentences that do not require integrating much information.

This conclusion may be too strong, however. The Stroop test, unlike recognition, does not require subjects to refer to the text representation; it may only measure activation in the lexicon, not presence or absence within the text representation. In Dosher and Corbett's experiments, subjects did not see the test words until after the sentences had remained in view for 2.5 seconds. The sentences were only four to six words in length, so subjects probably experienced at least a 1.5-second delay between

TABLE 18.4   A Test Paragraph Used by McKoon and Ratcliff (1981)
to Assess Atypical Case-Filling Inferences

Bobby got a saw, mallet, screwdriver, and square from his toolbox. He had already selected an oak tree as the site for the birdhouse. He had drawn a detailed blueprint and measured carefully. He marked the boards and cut them out.

Final sentence (biasing): Then Bobby pounded the boards together with nails.

Final sentence (nonbiasing): Then Bobby stuck the boards together with glue.

Test word: mallet

reading and test. After such a delay, activation in the lexicon from making the inference "broom" could have diminished to unmeasurable levels. This potential effect of delay is especially suspect because Dosher and Corbett also tested for inferences about body parts (e.g., the inference "teeth" for the sentence, "He bit the apple") and found no Stroop interference. In contrast, other studies using shorter delays (Whitney, McKay, Kellas, & Emerson, 1985; Merrill, Sperber, & McCauley, 1981) have found Stroop interference for these types of inferences. In sum, Dosher and Corbett's studies may have little to say about instrumental inferencing.

Instantiation Inferences

Instantiation inferences occur when the reader infers that an object in a general category (e.g., fish) is more specific than stated (e.g., shark). Whitney and Kellas (1984) used the Stroop paradigm to test for the instantiation of typical and atypical exemplars (see, e.g., R. C. Anderson et al., 1976). Whitney and Kellas used as stimuli sentences like, "The guest saw the bird that roasted on the grill." Here, the sentence biases "chicken," an atypical exemplar of "bird," rather than "robin," a typical exemplar of "bird." Stroop interference occurred only for typical exemplars, even when sentences biased atypical exemplars. Whitney and Kellas concluded that the Stroop effects were simply due to semantic relatedness, not to instantiation.

Whitney (1986) reasoned that readers may require more focusing of a category term before they will instantiate it. He had subjects read paragraphs (one or two sentences in length) that strongly biased either typical or atypical exemplars. For example, the atypical exemplar "helicopter" was biased in the paragraph, "The reporter in the vehicle looked down on the parade. While she was up in it, she could see all the people." The typical exemplar "car" was biased by changing the paragraph to read, "The reporter went to the vehicle to look for the papers. She hoped they were in it as she had left them." After reading a paragraph or a sentence, subjects had to name the color of the ink used to print target words, which could be typical or atypical exemplars.

Whitney (1986) found evidence of typical and atypical instantiation inferences. However, his results also suggested that the type of inference depended on typicality. Typical exemplars showed Stroop facilitation (i.e., color-naming responses were facilitated when the target was a typical exemplar—e.g., "car" for "vehicle"), whereas atypical exemplars showed Stroop inhibition (i.e., color-naming responses were inhibited when the target was an atypical exemplar—e.g., "helicopter" for "vehicle"). One of Whitney's experiments indicated that facilitation was observed because subjects consciously generated typical exemplars while reading the paragraphs (see also Dosher & Corbett, 1982). Inhibition occurred, he argued, when concepts were activated in memory but not consciously generated. In other words, the hypothesis was that instantiation inferences were more complete for typical than for atypical exemplars. This interpretation may or may not be the correct one. Nevertheless, his experiments clearly demonstrate that instantiations for typical and atypical exemplars differ.

Predictable-Event Inferences

Inferences about predictable events are those that are made when the occurrence of an event is strongly implied but not explicitly stated. For example, after reading the following sentence, we might expect readers to infer that the bees stung Joan:

15.   The angry swarm of bees flew out of the hive and landed on Joan's hand.

In fact, available evidence suggests that inferences of this kind are made in a partial or incomplete fashion, if at all.

McKoon and Ratcliff (1986) used several methods, including priming in recognition, to examine whether or not inferences were made about predictable events. In the most informative study (Experiment 4), subjects read paragraphs containing a sentence that either predicted or did not predict some event. An example of the former was 15 and an example of the latter was 16:

16.   Angry, Joan complained that the bees had not been moved to their new hive.

After reading a paragraph, subjects received a recognition test. On each trial, a prime word was displayed for 200 milliseconds (ms) and then followed by a target word. The subjects' task was to decide whether or not the target had been in the paragraph. A deadline procedure was used to force subjects to respond as quickly as possible. That is, a short period (250 ms) after the target had been displayed, a signal was given for the subject to respond. Subjects were told to respond within 300 ms of the appearance of the signal. Using this procedure, McKoon and Ratcliff hoped to eliminate strategic processing of the prime (see below). The critical dependent measure in this experiment was error rate. Response latencies were rendered useless by the deadline procedure.

The results of primary interest were error rates on targets in the neutral-priming condition ("sting" preceded by the neutral prime "READY") as a function of the preceding paragraph. Error rates were 36 percent for predicting versions and 27 percent for control versions. In other words, there was a greater tendency for subjects to think that "'sting" had occurred in the predicting paragraph 15 than to think that "sting" had occurred in the control paragraph 16. This effect, however, was rather weak ($p < .05$, one-tailed). McKoon and Ratcliff concluded:

> . . . the event represented by the predicted word is encoded only minimally during reading. For example, the encoding of the predicted event for "falling off the 14th story" might be "something bad happened." (p. 87).

We think this conclusion may be too conservative, and our concern is based solely on the power of their experiment: only 16 subjects were tested. The reliability of the effect may be more pronounced with greater power. But in the absence of additional work on this topic, a fair conclusion is that predictable-event inferences are made, but only partially or only in a relatively small number of cases.

Property Inferences

It has been argued elsewhere (McNamara & Miller, 1989) that, when readers understand a word, they are immediately provided with a set of properties corresponding to the concept evoked by the word. This set of property inferences then can be modified by the context surrounding the word. According to this view, for example, reading "dog" results in the immediate specification of certain properties, such as "has fur" or "has four legs." These properties can be respecified within the mental model if, for instance, the reader finds out that the dog in question is a three-legged Mexican hairless.

Whitney, McKay, Kellas, and Emerson (1985; see also Greenspan, 1986) have reported evidence consistent with these kinds of property specifications and context effects. Using Stroop tests, they tested for activation of salient properties and nonsalient properties. Whitney et al. had subjects listen to sentences that emphasized salient or nonsalient properties of objects referred to in the sentences. For example, the sentence "The father called the dog" emphasized a salient property of dogs (ears), whereas the sentence "The father was scratched by the dog" emphasized a less-salient property of dogs (claws). Each sentence was followed by a salient or nonsalient property after a 0-, 300-, or 600- ms delay (interstimulus interval, or ISI). The subjects' task, again, was to name the color of the ink used to print the property. The dependent measure was naming latency—in particular, inhibition in naming responses as a function of (1) the relation between the sentence and the target property and (2) ISI.

The important results were the relative levels of performance on salient and nonsalient properties for appropriate, inappropriate, and neutral contexts, within each ISI. At the 0-ms delay, subjects' naming responses were inhibited for both salient and nonsalient properties (relative to the control condition), regardless of whether the sentential context was appropriate or inappropriate. That is, naming responses to "ears" and "claws" were equally inhibited, regardless of whether they were preceded by "called the dog" or by "scratched by the dog." At the 300- and 600- ms ISIs, the patterns changed dramatically. For these ISIs, responses to salient properties were always inhibited, regardless of sentential context; but responses to nonsalient properties were inhibited only when sentences emphasized a nonsalient property.

These results indicate that readers activate a certain set of property inferences (both salient and nonsalient) upon reading a word. Only salient and contextually relevant nonsalient properties, however, are integrated with the text information and specified within the mental model. These are the only properties that remain active after a delay. Barsalou (1982) has shown that properties unlikely to be activated upon the initial reading of a word (e.g., the property "floats" for "basketball") can nonetheless become activated in memory during specialized, biasing contexts; and it seems likely that these unusual but relevant property inferences are specified within the mental model as well.

Although the studies reported by Whitney et al. (1985) are provocative, they are limited in several ways. First, there is no guarantee that inhibition was caused by the semantic relation between the concept and its property; inhibition might appear for any associate of the concept, including syntagmatic ones (e.g., mother-love). Second, the experimental procedures might have encouraged subjects to employ strategies not normally used in reading. Subjects were always presented with the word in the Stroop task immediately or soon after the last word in the sentence. The sentences were simple subject-verb-object sentences. Subjects could have easily determined when they had encountered the final word and predicted when the test word was going to appear. Although two-thirds of the test words were not properties of the terminal noun, subjects might still have generated properties in anticipation of being tested. Hence, the finding that salient and nonsalient properties were retrieved initially might have been an artifact of the design, rather than a general retrieval process.

This hypothesis has been supported by the results of recent studies of inferencing during reading (Miller & McNamara, 1989). In these experiments, subjects read short vignettes, which were displayed one word at a time at a fixed position (the "text window") on a computer terminal screen. The rate of presentation was adjusted to approximate leisurely reading. This method of presentation is called *rapid serial visual presentation*, or RSVP. Research has shown that comprehension in RSVP conditions is as good as, if not better than, comprehension during normal reading (Juola, Haugh, Trast, Ferraro, & Liebhaber, in press; Juola, Ward, & McNamara, 1982).

At critical points during the presentation of a paragraph, a test word was displayed above the text window. (A subject was tested only twice in a three-sentence paragraph, so the procedure was not very disruptive.) Test words were salient and nonsalient properties of nouns in the sentence, as well as "neutral" words unrelated to any of the concepts in the paragraph. The subjects' task was to decide whether or not the test word had appeared so far in the paragraph. The dependent variables were response latencies and error rates for "no" responses.

Consider, for example, the following sentence (ignore the numerals for the moment):

1   2   3   4   5   6

17.   The spider on the road spotted a hiding place and raced under the rock.

The test word "legs" might appear immediately after "spider." The correct answer would be "no." To the extent that a concept is active in memory, responses to these words should be inhibited: Response latencies should be long and error rates should be high. However, if a concept is not active in memory, which should be the case for a control word such as "wool," responses should not be inhibited. Thus, we used inhibition in "no" responses to assess the extent to which properties were active in memory.

Subjects were tested at one of six test points indicated by the numerals in the sentence above: (1) immediately after the target noun; (2) two words after the target noun; (3) immediately after a "biasing" verb (the verb "spotted" implicitly emphasizes that spiders have eyes); (4) two words after the first biasing verb; (5) immediately after another biasing verb (the verb "raced" implicitly emphasizes that spiders have legs); and (6) two words after the second biasing verb. Biasing verbs were selected on the basis of pilot work so that they emphasized a property of a noun but did not have sufficiently strong associations with that property to produce inhibition. Our goal was to trace the activation levels of salient (legs) and nonsalient (eyes) properties as a function of context and of individual differences in reading comprehension ability.

Results indicated that initial retrieval of a concept's meaning might not be as exhaustive as suggested by Whitney et al. (1985). In particular, our data suggested that the probability of retrieving a property increased with salience, inasmuch as inhibition in responding was greater for salient than for nonsalient properties. Equally interesting was the finding that once a property had been retrieved, it stayed active in the mental model throughout comprehension of the sentence, even if it was not contextually relevant. At this point, we do not have enough data to examine individual differences in patterns of results and how these patterns relate to reading comprehension ability.

Our interest in individual differences in specification was motivated in part by an experiment conducted by Merrill, Sperber, and McCauley (1981). Using a task similar to the one used by Whitney et al. (1985), Merrill et al. (1981) found that after a one-second delay, poor readers showed inhibition on both contextually relevant and contextually irrelevant properties. Good readers, on the other hand, showed inhibition only on contextually relevant properties. Poor readers might have unintentionally allocated processing resources to the specification of irrelevant properties, thereby reducing resources needed for other reading processes. This overspecification could also make it difficult to highlight vital relationships between concepts in the text. Using context to reduce unnecessary specification may be an essential step for achieving efficient, skilled reading.

In summary, readers must limit specification of the mental model. A principal constraint on specification is context. When context does not highlight the information that could be provided by atypical case-filling inferences (e.g., "mallet" for "pounded the boards"), instantiation inferences (e.g., "shark" for "fish"), and nonsalient property inferences (e.g., "has claws" for "dog"), the mental model will not specify this information. These inferences seem to be specified only when context focuses on them. These specifications may have high processing costs, rendering them inefficient unless they are highly focused and especially relevant to the context.

Other types of inferencing seem to take place without such a strong reliance on context. Specification of typical instruments (e.g., "hammer" for "pounded the boards") and salient properties (e.g., "ears" for "dog") seems to occur readily. These types of inferences are probably easy to make because of the frequency with which they are related to the types of objects and events described by the text.

Knowledge Integration

An implicit assumption of mental model theories is that people can construct integrated mental representations of spatial and nonspatial information. In a recent series of experiments, these assumptions have been tested and confirmed (McNamara, Halpin & Hardy, 1989).

In one of these experiments, students at Vanderbilt University learned facts about buildings on their campus. Buildings could be divided into critical triads, in which two buildings, such as Neely and Alumni Hall, were close together, and a third, such as Wesley Hall, was far from each of the others. Subjects learned, for example, that Neely contained a dramatic theater, that Alumni Hall was named for alumni who died in World War I, and that Wesley Hall had a swimming pool in the basement. The question of interest was whether or not the nonspatial facts were integrated in memory with the knowledge of the buildings' locations.

After learning the facts, subjects took part in a primed classification task. On each trial, a prime and a target were displayed. The primes were content words from the facts, such as "World War I." The targets were building names. Subjects were instructed to read the prime and the target, and then to decide whether the target building was in one part of the campus or another (subjects made no response to the prime). The critical dependent measure was response time.

To test knowledge integration, classification times in two conditions were compared: (1) when a building was primed by a fact about a neighboring building (e.g., World War I—Neely); and (2) when a building was primed by a fact about a distant building (e.g., Swimming Pool—Neely). If the spatial and the factual knowledge were integrated in memory, then a distance effect should appear in the classification times: Responses to Neely should be faster when primed by "World War I" than when primed by "Swimming Pool." In fact, exactly that pattern emerged. Mean latencies were 951 ms in the "close" condition and 990 ms in the "far" condition.

This study indicates that people can integrate spatial and nonspatial knowledge and that they can draw upon both "semantic" and "episodic" sources. Although this research does not address reading comprehension directly, it vindicates a cardinal assumption of mental model theories of comprehension—namely, that spatial and nonspatial information can be encoded in a common memory representation.

Automatic and Strategic Processing

An extremely important issue that we have glossed over so far is the role of automatic and strategic processing in reading comprehension. The idea that some mental events are automatic, effortless, and unconscious, and that other mental events are strategic, effortful, and conscious, goes back at least to William James (1890), if not further. This distinction is crucial for at least two reasons: First, it is important methodologically because the conclusions one can reach about structure and process are necessarily constrained by the relative contributions of automatic and strategic processes to the tasks used to measure reading comprehension. Second, the distinction is important theoretically because the relative automaticity of comprehension processes may be informative about their ontogenesis and the extent to which they can be trained.

Psychologists have examined automatic and strategic processing for some time, and there are now several theories of automaticity in the literature (see, in particular, Hasher & Zacks, 1979; Schneider & Shiffrin, 1977; Shiffrin & Schneider, 1977; Posner & Snyder, 1975a, 1975b). A comprehensive review of these theories is beyond the scope of this chapter, but we can summarize characteristics of automatic and strategic processes that are common to the various theories.

Six variables can be used to distinguish strategic from automatic processes. These include speed, sensitivity to conscious expectations, costs and benefits, intentionality, capacity limitations, and trainability. These characteristics probably form continua, but for pedagogical purposes we treat them as dichotomous.

Strategic processes are slow, are sensitive to conscious expectations, produce both costs and benefits, are intentional, require mental resources, and improve with training. The neophyte reader, for example, uses many strategic processes, such as identifying individual letters and then assembling them into a whole word. There also seems to be a strategic component in priming in lexical (word vs. nonword) decisions, because the size of the priming effect depends on the relative mix of related items (e.g., nurse-doctor) and unrelated items (e.g., butter-doctor) in the test lists (Neely, Keefe, & Ross 1989; Tweedy, Lapinski & Schavaneveldt, 1977). Moreover, priming in lexical decisions shows both benefits and costs (e.g., Balota & Chumbley, 1984; Becker, 1980; Seidenberg, Waters, Sanders, & Langer, 1984). That is, when the prime is related to the target (e.g., nurse-doctor), responses to the target are fast relative to a neutral baseline (e.g., READY-doctor); but when the prime is unrelated to the target (e.g., bread-doctor), responses to the target are, under certain conditions, slow relative to the same neutral baseline. There is evidence that subjects can use the prime to make predictions about the target (Becker, 1980). When these predictions are correct, responses are fast; but when they are incorrect, responses are slow.

Automatic processes, on the other hand, are fast, not sensitive to conscious expectations, produce benefits but few costs, are unintentional, require few mental resources, and (although trainable) do not benefit from further training. The "expert" reader, for example, can recognize words with little or no effort; in fact, there is evidence that the practiced reader can recognize a word without identifying all of its constituent letters (e.g., Healy, 1976, 1980). At the methodological end, there is evidence that priming in item recognition has a very fast onset (about 50 ms), is not sensitive to the relative mix of "related" and "unrelated" items, and produces benefits but few costs (Ratcliff & McKoon, 1981). In short, priming in item recognition seems to be an automatic process.

Mental model theories of reading comprehension have as a principal goal the description of mental representations of text. But psychologists have known for some time that behavior is not constrained by structure alone. Different structural theories can make identical behavioral predictions if they are coupled with appropriate processing assumptions (see, e.g., J. R. Anderson, 1978; Pylyshyn, 1979). This indeterminacy has engendered in many psychologists a sense of doubt about the ability of behavioral data to distinguish among alternative theories of internal representation (J. R. Anderson, 1978). Such pessimism is unwarranted (see, in particular, Pylyshyn, 1979). Skeptics have ignored, among other things, that (1) the requisite processing assumptions may be components of theories in other domains and, therefore, have explanatory roles outside the confines of particular experiments, and (2) these assumptions may be subject to independent verification, either directly or through converging operations (Garner, Hake, & Eriksen, 1956).

In particular, if it can be shown that processing in a particular task is primarily automatic, and consequently not influenced by retrieval strategies (Tulving, 1976), then that task may be informative about how information is actually encoded in memory. This criterion is satisfied by priming in item recognition, priming in lexical decisions (under appropriate conditions), and Stroop interference.[2] Hence, one can be reasonably confident that many of the studies on foregrounding, specification inferences, and knowledge integration (reviewed above) are informative about the structure of the mental model. Studies using other tasks also may be informative, but because less is known about strategic contributions to these tasks, a more cautious attitude is called for.

Theoretical explanations of comprehension processes also seem to require a distinction between strategic and automatic processes. For example, Garnham's (1981) finding that subjects could "choose" whether to encode a text as a mental model or as a propositional description clearly implicates the role of strategic processes in reading. On the other hand, the results from a number of studies (Greenspan, 1986; Miller & McNamara, 1989; Whitney et al., 1985) indicate that comprehension of a concept initially requires retrieval, or activation, of salient semantic properties. This initial retrieval is rapid and context independent, and thus is probably an automatic process.

Automatic processes are revealed in other kinds of reading processes, such as syntactic processing. Ferreira and Clifton (1986) found that the mental syntactic parser automatically makes certain types of grammatical assignments. When people read a sentence beginning with "The person examined . . . ," they automatically assign an active sentence structure. Readers then revise this structure if the sentence turns out to be passive, as in "The person examined by the lawyer was convincing." Surprisingly, this automatic assignment of active structure occurs in the face of counterindicating contextual information, which appears in the fragment, "The evidence examined . . ." Even though evidence cannot examine anything, people still seem to assign an active subject-object interpretation (Ferreira & Clifton, 1986). This initial assignment is not corrected until it must be, which happens in the sentence "The evidence examined by the lawyer was convincing."

The advantage of automatic assignment lies in the efficiency it provides. Active grammatical structures are more common than passive ones (at least in spoken language) and, moreover, usually have simpler structural descriptions. Automatic assignment of simple active structural descriptions guarantees minimal processing costs in the majority of instances. The down side, of course, is that, on occasion, the syntactic parser is led astray and forced to recompute the structural description.

Similarly, automatic retrieval of certain properties provides the understander with features that are frequently associated with the use of a concept. These features are likely to be relevant to the context because they are frequent and salient. The language processor is spared the extra processing that would be required if conceptual entries were always searched for relevant properties. These savings in cognitive resources can be applied to building and restructuring the mental model, anticipating events in the story, and the like. Only rarely does the language system need infrequent properties; and when they are needed, they can be retrieved from other levels of the conceptual entry.

Representing Multiple Situations:
The Passage Mental Model

The research that we have discussed so far has examined mental models as they function in the representation of ongoing events in the text. We call this structure the *working mental model*. This working model contains information that is relevant to and descriptive of the current situation, and is updated with new information as episodes develop and situations change.

After reading a story or a passage, however, readers are not simply left with the information that was activated in the working mental model at the end of the passage. They also retain knowledge of the entire passage. We shall refer to this representation as the *passage mental model*. This section of the chapter concentrates on the notion of a passage mental model and the evidence for specific types of passage representations.

Johnson-Laird (1983) discussed various types of mental models consistent with the concept of a passage mental model. Among these types were kinematic and dynamic models. The kinematic model represents changes and movements via a sequence of frames. For example, a kinematic model of the sentence, "I sold my car to Alex for two hundred dollars," would contain a first frame in which the speaker is the owner of the car and Alex is the owner of two hundred dollars. The next frame would represent a later time and show the exchange of the two entities, so that the speaker now possessed the two hundred dollars and Alex possessed the car. The kinematic model becomes a dynamic model when the causal relations between events in different frames are represented.

Recent research on people's memory for stories has highlighted the existence of causal connections between story events within the passage representation. Trabasso and his colleagues (Trabasso & Sperry, 1985; Trabasso & van den Broek, 1985) have developed a causal structure for representing narratives. In this analysis, stories are first divided into idea units (Johnson, 1970), which are similar to propositions. Then, units with direct causal relations are connected (rules for determining what constitutes a direct cause are described in Trabasso & Sperry, 1985).

For example, in a story about a father's and son's journey to town to sell a donkey, the proposition expressing the idea of taking the donkey to town would be connected to the proposition expressing their movement over a bridge. If the characters were not going to town, then they would not have gone over the bridge; the goal of going to town "caused" them to go over the bridge.

Trabasso and van den Broek (1985) found that properties of causal representations were more effective than properties of traditional propositional representations (Kintsch & van Dijk, 1978) in predicting story recall, summarization, and judged importance of events. Whether or not a proposition was remembered, included in a summary, or judged as important seemed to depend largely on the number of causal connections it shared with other propositions, as well as whether it was on or off the causal chain. The recall, summarization, and importance-judgment data were not predicted by serial position, argument overlap, or concreteness.

The validity of causal representations was further shown by O'Brien and Myers (1987). Subjects read a paragraph and immediately answered questions concerning target objects. Retrieval times were predicted by properties of the causal network but not by properties of Kintsch and van Dijk's (1978) propositional model. Moreover, retrieval times for targets did not depend on whether the target object appeared early or late in the paragraph.

SUMMARY AND PROSPECTUS

There is ample evidence that reading is a much richer activity than propositional models alone would predict. People can encode a text in terms of propositions, but they also can build a mental representation of the situations described in the text. Readers are able to stress one processing mode over the other, depending on task constraints and on the type of text being read (Mani & Johnson-Laird, 1982; Garnham, 1981; Schmalhofer & Glavanov, 1986). Mental model processing appears to be most predominant for spatial descriptions, instructions for completing a task, and narrations.

Most of the research on mental models has looked at comprehension of narrative material. During narrative comprehension, a working mental model is constantly updated to contain information relevant to the situation currently being described (Glenberg et al, 1987; Morrow, 1985; Morrow et al., 1987). Readers also can draw upon schemata and more localized knowledge structures to specify information about the situation that is not explicitly stated in the text (Morrow et al., 1987).

The working mental model does not completely specify everything about a situation. The model appears to contain some highly focused, fine-grain specifications and other fuzzy, coarse-grain specifications. Readers appear to have some of these specification processes automatized (Greenspan, 1986; McKoon & Ratcliff, 1981, 1986; Miller & McNamara, 1989; Sanford, 1987; Whitney et al., 1985). In many cases, the automaticity of these processes saves mental resources; but in certain unusual contexts, readers will have to use strategic processing in order to add specifications or to revise specifications that have turned out to be inappropriate.

In order to represent a whole passage, people need to combine information that was relevant at the beginning of the text with information that has become relevant as the text has progressed. It has been proposed that this passage mental model consists of a kinematic sequence of frames with causal links between events in different frames (Johnson-Laird, 1983). The significance of causal links is evident in the ability of causal network models to predict recall, summarizations, importance judgments, and retrieval times for narrative passages (Trabasso & van den Broek, 1985; O'Brien & Myers, 1987).

Several other interesting issues concerning mental models remain to be explored. One issue concerns the processing-time properties of kinematic models. Having a kinematic sequence of frames that can be "run" (Johnson-Laird, 1983) suggests that readers would take longer to encode or decode greater amounts of change than smaller amounts of change. For example, a movie sequence of a man circling a podium twice will take longer to run than a sequence of him circling the podium once. Will people take longer to read "John circled the podium twice" than to read "John circled the podium once"?

Johnson-Laird (1983) has already pointed out that processing limitations require some integration of propositional information with mental models. For example, it seems doubtful that readers would encode "John circled the podium a thousand times" by processing a thousand frames of John and the podium. Similarly, when reading "Two hundred men are driving cars," the reader cannot possibly place two hundred tokens within a representation of the situation. Johnson-Laird suggests several potential processing strategies for these situations, and these strategies should be tested empirically.

A final research question concerns the relationship between individual differences in mental model construction and individual differences in overall reading ability. Johnson-Laird (1983) has argued that inadequate construction of a mental model causes errors in syllogistic reasoning. And it was noted earlier that overspecification of irrelevant information within a model seems to be a characteristic of poor readers. Since a large part of comprehension ability seems to rest on the ability to construct appropriate mental models, we need to find ways of teaching reading that will focus on meaning construction. One approach may be to combine visual information with texts in ways that help readers to experience the construction of precise mental models and to acquire knowledge that can be used in future constructions (e.g., Bransford, Sherwood, & Hasselbring, 1988; Bransford, Vye, Kinzer, & Risko, in press). In general, reading needs to be seen as an engineering problem: using available resources to build a model of meaning that is well suited for the job, cost effective, and structurally sound.

NOTES

1. The view of mental models expressed here differs in certain respects from versions discussed elsewhere (e.g., Kintsch, 1988).
2. There is a paradox here: Automatic processes do not produce inhibition and yet Stroop interference is claimed to be automatic. The paradox is resolved by examining the hypothesized underlying mechanisms. The argument is that salient properties, for example, are automatically specified, which means they are active in memory. The elevated activation level increases the tendency for the subject to name the property rather than the color, thus producing inflated color-naming latencies.

REFERENCES

Alba, J. W., & Hasher, L. (1983). Is memory schematic? *Psychological Bulletin, 93*, 203–231.

Anderson, J. R. (1978). Arguments concerning representations for mental imagery. *Psychological Review, 85*, 249–277.

Anderson, R. C., & Pearson, P. D. (1984). A schema-theoretic view of basic processes in reading comprehension. In P. D. Pearson, R. Barr, M. L. Kamil, & P. Mosenthal (Eds.), *Handbook of reading research* (Vol. 1, pp. 225–253). New York: Longman.

Anderson, R. C., Pichert, J. W., Goetz, E. T., Shallert, D. L., Stevens, K. W., & Trollip, S. R. (1976). Instantiation of general terms. *Journal of Verbal Learning and Verbal Behavior, 15*, 667–679.

Baars, B. J. (1987). *The cognitive revolution in psychology*. New York: Guilford.

Balota, D. A., & Chumbley, J. I. (1984). Are lexical decisions a good measure of lexical access? The role of word frequency in the neglected decision stage. *Journal of Experimental Psychology: Human Perception and Performance, 10*, 340–357.

Barsalou, L. W. (1982). Context-independent and context-dependent information in concepts. *Memory & Cognition, 10*, 82–93.

Becker, C. A. (1980). Semantic context effects in visual word recognition: An analysis of semantic strategies. *Memory & Cognition, 8*, 493–512.

Bever, T. G., Lackner, J. R., & Kirk, R. (1969). The underlying structures of sentences are the primary units of understanding. *Perception and Psychophysics, 5*, 225–234.

Bransford, J. D., Barclay, J. R., & Franks, J. J. (1972). Sentence memory: A constructive versus interpretive approach. *Cognitive Psychology, 3*, 193–209.

Bransford, J. D., & Franks, J. J. (1971). The abstraction of linguistic ideas. *Cognitive Psychology, 2*, 331–350.

Bransford, J. D., & Johnson, M. K. (1972). Contextual prerequisites for understanding: Some investigations of comprehension and recall. *Journal of Verbal Learning and Verbal Behavior, 11*, 717–726.

Bransford, J. D., Sherwood, R., & Hasselbring, T. (1988). Effects of the video revolution on cognitive development: Some initial thoughts. In G. Foreman & P. Pufall (Eds.), *Contructivism in the computer age* (pp 173–220). Hillsdale, NJ: Erlbaum.

Bransford, J. D., Vye N., Kinzer, C., & Risko, V. (in press). Teaching thinking and content knowledge: Toward an integrated approach. In B. Jones & L. Idol (Eds.), *Dimensions of thinking and cognitive instruction*. Hillsdale, NJ: Erlbaum.

Caplan, D. (1972). Clause boundaries and recognition latencies for words in sentences. *Perception & Psychophysics, 12*, 73–76.

Chomsky, N. (1957). *Syntactic structures*. The Hague: Mouton.

Chomsky, N. (1965). *Aspects of the theory of syntax*. Cambridge, MA: MIT Press.

Dooling, D. J., & Lachman, R. (1971). Effects of comprehension on retention of prose. *Journal of Experimental Psychology, 88*, 216–222.

Dosher, B. A., & Corbett, A. T. (1982). Instrument inferences and verb schemata. *Memory & Cognition, 10*, 531–539.

Ferreira, F., & Clifton, C., Jr. (1986). The independence of syntactic processing. *Journal of Memory and Language, 25*, 348–368.

Fodor, J. A., Bever, T. G., & Garrett, M. F. (1974). *The psychology of language*. New York: McGraw-Hill.

Garner, W. R., Hake, H. W., & Eriksen, C. W. (1956). Operationism and the concept of perception. *Psychological Review, 63*, 149–159.

Garnham, A. (1981). *Mental models as representations of discourse and text*. Unpublished doctoral thesis, Sussex University.

Glenberg, A. M., Meyer, M., & Lindem, K. (1987). Mental models contribute to foregrounding during text comprehension. *Journal of Memory and Language, 26*, 69–83.

Greenspan, S. L. (1986). Semantic flexibility and referential specificity of concrete nouns. *Journal of Memory and Language, 25*, 539–557.

Hasher, L., & Zacks, R. T. (1979). Automatic and effortful processes in memory. *Journal of Experimental Psychology: General, 108*, 356–388.

Healy, A. F. (1976). Detection errors on the word *the*: Evidence for reading units larger than letters. *Journal of Experimental Psychology: Human Perception and Performance, 2*, 235–242.

Healy, A. F. (1980). Proofreading errors on the word *the*: New evidence on reading units. *Journal of Experimental Psychology: Human Perception and Performance, 6*, 45–57.

James, W. (1890). *Principles of Psychology*. New York: Holt.

Johnson, R. E. (1970). Recall of prose as a function of structural importance of the linguistic unit. *Journal of Verbal Learning and Verbal Behavior, 9*, 12–20.

Johnson-Laird, P. N. (1983). *Mental models*. Cambridge, MA: Harvard University Press.

Juola, J. F., Haugh, D., Trast, S., Ferraro, F. R., & Liebhaber, M. (in press). Reading with and without eye movements. In J. K. O'Regan and A. Levy-Schoen (Eds.), *Eye movements: From physiology to cognition*. Amsterdam: Elsevier-North Holland.

Juola, J. F., Ward, N. J., & McNamara, T. P. (1982). Visual search and reading of rapid serial presentations of letter strings, words, and text. *Journal of Experimental Psychology: General, 111*, 208–227.

Kintsch, W. (1974). *The mental representation of meaning*. Hillsdale, NJ: Erlbaum.

Kintsch, W. (1988). The role of knowledge in discourse comprehension: A construction-integration model. *Psychological Review, 95*, 163–182.

Kintsch, W., & Keenan, J. M. (1973). Reading rate as a function of the number of propositions in the base structure of sentences. *Cognitive Psychology, 5*, 257–274.

Kintsch, W., & van Dijk, T. A. (1978). Toward a model of text comprehension and production. *Psychological Review, 85*, 363–394.

McKoon, G., & Ratcliff, R. (1980). Priming in item recognition: The organization of propositions in memory for text. *Journal of Verbal Learning and Verbal Behavior, 19*, 369–386.

McKoon, G., & Ratcliff, R. (1981). The comprehension processes and memory structures involved in instrumental inference. *Journal of Verbal Learning and Verbal Behavior, 20*, 671–682.

McKoon, G., & Ratcliff, R. (1986). Inferences about predictable events. *Journal of Experimental Psychology: Learning, Memory, and Cognition, 12*, 82–91.

McNamara, T. P., Halpin, J. A., & Hardy, J. K. (1989). *The representation and integration in memory of spatial and nonspatial information*. Manuscript submitted for publication.

McNamara, T. P., & Miller, D. L. (1989). Attributes of theories of meaning. *Psychological Bulletin, 106*, 355–376.

Mani, K., & Johnson-Laird, P. N. (1982). The mental representation of spatial descriptions. *Memory & Cognition, 10*, 181–187.

Merrill, E. C., Sperber, R. D., & McCauley, C. (1981). Differences in semantic encoding as a function of reading comprehension skill. *Memory & Cognition, 9*, 225–236.

Meyer, B. J. F., & Rice, G. E. (1984). The structure of text. In P. D. Pearson, R. Barr, M. L. Kamil, & P. Mosenthal (Eds.), *Handbook of Reading Research*, (Vol. 1, pp. 319–351). New York: Longman.

Miller, D. L., & McNamara, T. P. (1989). Research in progress.

Morrow, D. G. (1985). Prominent characters and events organize narrative understanding. *Journal of Memory and Language, 24*, 304–319.

Morrow, D. G., Greenspan, S. L., & Bower, G. H. (1987). Accessibility and situation models in narrative comprehension. *Journal of Memory and Language, 26*, 165–187.

Neely, J. H., Keefe, D. E., & Ross, K. L. (1989). Semantic priming in the lexical decision task: Roles of prospective prime-generated expectancies and retrospective semantic matching. *Journal of Experimental Psychology: Learning, Memory and Cognition, 15*, 1003–1019.

O'Brien, E. J., & Myers, J. L. (1987). The role of causal connections in the retrieval of text. *Memory & Cognition, 15*, 419–427.

Pearson, P. D. (1974). The effects of grammatical complexity on children's comprehension, recall, and conception of certain semantic relations. *Reading Research Quarterly, 10*, 155–192.

Posner, M. I., & Snyder, C. R. (1975a). Attention and cognitive control. In R. L. Solso (Ed.), *Information processing and cognition* (pp. 55–85). Hillsdale, NJ: Erlbaum.

Posner, M. I., & Snyder, C. R. (1975b). Facilitation and inhibition in the processing of signals. In P. M. A. Rabbitt (Ed.), *Attention and performance* (Vol. 5, pp. 669–682). London: Academic Press.

Pylyshyn, Z. W. (1979). Validating computational models: A critique of Anderson's indeterminacy of representation claim. *Psychological Review, 86*, 383–394.

Ratcliff, R., & McKoon, G. (1978). Priming in item recognition: Evidence for the propositional structure of sentences. *Journal of Verbal Learning and Verbal Behavior, 17,* 403–417.

Ratcliff, R., & McKoon, G. (1981). Automatic and strategic priming in recognition. *Journal of Verbal Learning and Verbal Behavior, 20,* 204–215.

Sanford, A. J. (1987). *The mind of man: Models of human understanding.* Sussex, Eng.: Harvester Press Limited.

Sanford, A. J., & Garrod, S. C. (1981). *Understanding written language.* New York: Wiley.

Schmalhofer, F., & Glavanov, D. (1986). Three components of understanding a programmer's manual: Verbatim, propositional, and situational representations. *Journal of Memory and Language, 25,* 279–294.

Schneider, W., & Shiffrin, R. M. (1977). Controlled and automatic human information processing: I. Detection, search, and attention. *Psychological Review, 84,* 1–66.

Seidenberg, M. S., Waters, G. S., Sanders, M., & Langer, P. (1984). Pre- and postlexical loci of contextual effects on word recognition. *Memory & Cognition, 12,* 315–328.

Shiffrin, R. M., & Schneider, W. (1977). Controlled and automatic human information processing: II. Perceptual learning, automatic attending, and a general theory. *Psychological Review, 84,* 127–190.

Stroop, J. R. (1935). Studies of interference in serial verbal reactions. *Journal of Experimental Psychology, 18,* 643–662.

Trabasso, T., & Sperry, L. L. (1985). Causal relatedness and importance of story events. *Journal of Memory and Language, 24,* 595–611.

Trabasso, T., & van den Broek, P. (1985). Causal thinking and the representation of narrative events. *Journal of Memory and Language, 24,* 612–630.

Tulving, E. (1976). Ecphoric processes in recall and recognition. In J. Brown (Ed.), *Recall and recognition.* (pp. 37–73). London: Wiley.

Tweedy, J. R., Lapinski, R. H., & Schvaneveldt, R. W. (1977). Semantic-context effects on word recognition: Influence of varying the proportion of items presented in an appropriate context. *Memory & Cognition, 5,* 84–89.

van Dijk, T. A., & Kintsch, W. (1983). *Strategies of discourse comprehension.* New York: Academic Press.

Whitney, P. (1986). Processing category terms in context: Instantiations as inferences. *Memory & Cognition, 14,* 39–48.

Whitney, P., & Kellas, G. (1984). Processing category terms in context: Instantiation and the structure of semantic categories. *Journal of Experimental Psychology: Learning, Memory, and Cognition, 10,* 95–103.

Whitney, P., McKay, T., Kellas, G., & Emerson, W. A., Jr. (1985). Semantic activation of noun concepts in context. *Journal of Experimental Psychology: Learning, Memory, and Cognition, 11,* 126–135.

19 INDIVIDUAL DIFFERENCES IN READING SKILLS

Meredyth Daneman

According to an old Italian proverb, "There is no worse robber than a bad book." As fluent readers of English, we have likely all had the occasion to feel robbed by a book that proved less entertaining or less informative than we would have liked. Imagine how the more robbed we might feel if our reading skills were so deficient and effortful that the information in any book (good or bad) was not readily accessible to us.

People who are unskilled at reading are indeed robbed of, or at least severely handicapped in, their ability to acquire information from written text. Nowhere is their handicap more evident than in academic settings, where reading is the major medium for acquiring knowledge and skills. Individuals with low reading achievement have lower academic achievement too. It is not uncommon to find that reading comprehension ability is highly correlated with school performance in subjects as diverse as literature and science (Bloom, 1976; Perfetti, 1976). The correlation coefficients are typically 0.60 or larger. Moreover, reading comprehension seems to account in large part for the high correlations in performance on different school subject areas. For example, the 0.40 correlation between achievement in science and literature approaches zero when the effects of reading comprehension are partialled out (Bloom, 1976). In other words, reading comprehension seems to be the major common denominator in most of school learning.

What is particularly striking is that schooling does not reduce the differences among individuals in their reading ability (see Just & Carpenter, 1987). On the contrary, individual differences are pervasive and persistent and, if anything, become more pronounced with more years of schooling. For example, the differences among the reading achievement levels of twelfth graders are much larger than the differences among first graders (see Just & Carpenter, 1987), and there are still large individual differences in the reading skills of college students (Palmer, MacLeod, Hunt, & Davidson, 1985; Perfetti, 1985). As Perfetti (1985) points out, there are college students who read about 150 words a minute and others who can read 400 words a minute. Differences in comprehension ability can be just as large. Good readers not only understand the literal facts in a passage, but they abstract the passage's main point, make the inferences intended by the author, analyze the passage's organization, and recognize the author's tone and style. By contrast, less-skilled readers may read an entire passage without understanding or retaining even the main point (Just & Carpenter, 1987). What accounts for the enormous differences in how fast and how accurately people can read? These are the questions addressed in this chapter.

The chapter will not attempt an exhaustive review of potential loci of individual differences in reading ability. Two considerations delimit its scope. First, the chapter is concerned only with accounting for the range of individual differences that might be encountered in a typical school or university classroom. Most of the research that will be discussed does not deal with beginning readers or severely disabled readers (dyslexics), topics covered in detail elsewhere in this volume. While many of the findings and conclusions covered in this chapter may be generalizable to other populations of readers, not all will be.

Second, the chapter is concerned with sources of difference that are interesting from an information-processing standpoint. In other words, although there are likely a multiplicity of noncognitive factors that affect reading achievement—factors such as motivation, home and school background, and so on—the purpose of this chapter is to account for differences in reading skill in terms of the cognitive structures and processes presumed to underlie reading.

The chapter is divided into two main sections. The first section provides a brief information-processing analysis of the reading task in order to isolate the cognitive components of reading and highlight potential sources of individual differences in these components. The second section considers which of the cognitive components actually do contribute to individual differences in reading ability.

COGNITIVE COMPONENTS OF READING

Reading is a complex cognitive skill, consisting of the coordinated execution of a collection of oculomotor, perceptual, and comprehension processes. These include processes that direct the eye from location to location, word-level processes that encode the visual pattern of a word and access its meaning from memory, and text-level processes that compute the semantic, syntactic, and referential relationships among successive words, phrases, and sentences in a text.

The components entailed in reading are best illustrated by considering how we read the following short prose passage:

> Clyde did not want to arouse suspicion. So he sat down in the waiting room with his hand over his holster and smiled politely at the other occupants of the room. He thumbed disinterestedly through the heaps of reading matter on the table until he spotted the latest *Newsweek*. He opened the magazine and then carefully counted the number of bullets it held, waiting to be fired. When the office door opened, Clyde was poised and ready.

As skilled readers most of us have the subjective impression that we can read words in chunks. We even have the impression that we selectively skip over words, directly fixating only one out of every three or four. Both impressions are wrong. We process most words one at a time and very few words are skipped. If our eye movements were monitored while we read the above passage, the record would show that our eye paused on, or *fixated*, a large proportion (over 80 percent) of the content words such as the nouns, verbs, adjectives, and adverbs. Our eyes probably fixated a somewhat smaller proportion of the function words such as the articles (*the* and *a*) and the prepositions, producing an overall average of 65 percent of the words being fixated. Had the text been more difficult to comprehend, we would have fixated an even larger proportion of the words!

One reason why more words are fixated is that our perceptual span is restricted to a very small window around the point of fixation (McConkie & Rayner, 1975; Rayner,

1975; Rayner & Pollatsek, 1987). The kind of detailed information needed to make semantic decisions can only be picked up at most six printed characters in advance of the point at which we are fixating (Rayner, 1975). As a consequence, we typically only identify and process the word we are fixating unless we happen to fixate immediately to the left of a short, familiar function word.

Now, although we fixated many of the words in the passage about Clyde, we did not fixate all for the same amount of time. For example, we would likely have spent more time fixating the word *smiled* than the word *sat* because *smiled* has six letters whereas *sat* has only three. Moreover, even though *holster* and *waiting* are of equivalent length, we would likely have spent more time fixating *holster* than *waiting* because it is a word that we will have encountered less frequently in the past. How long we spent on any given word in the passage would have depended in part on how long it took to recognize that word. Word recognition involves a combination of two processes: (1) encoding the visual pattern of a printed word (*word encoding*), and (2) accessing its meaning in a mental dictionary or lexicon (*lexical access*) (Just & Carpenter, 1987). The length of a word is assumed to affect the speed with which the reader can encode the word as a visual percept; the frequency of the word is assumed to affect the ease with which the reader can access its meaning (Just & Carpenter, 1987).

Not only do properties such as the length and frequency of a word affect the ease or speed with which it will be recognized, the context in which it is encountered will also (Carpenter & Daneman, 1981). For example, we were probably all quick to read the word *magazine* and access the "reading periodical" meaning for it because the immediately preceding text described Clyde thumbing through reading matter in the waiting room and spotting the latest *Newsweek*. In this example, the word *magazine* has more than one meaning, so the preceding context did not only affect the speed of the lexical access process, but the outcome too. It is unlikely that any of us would have initially interpreted *magazine* to mean "revolver chamber," the interpretation that must ultimately be selected. Theories of word recognition differ in the extent to which they incorporate context effects into the word recognition process. Some theories view word recognition as a strictly bottom-up or stimulus-driven process; others view word recognition as an interactive process in which information from semantic and syntactic sources combines with information from the word itself (e.g., see Gough, 1972; Henderson, 1982; Rumelhart & McClelland, 1982).

Theories of word recognition also differ in the role they assign to phonological recoding, the process of converting the visually based representation into its corresponding phonological code. Some theories propose that fluent readers access word meanings directly from the visual representation (Smith, 1971; Thibadeau, Just, & Carpenter, 1982); others argue for phonological recoding (Massaro, 1975; van Orden, 1987); and others for a dual route, with the visual route being faster and used for familiar words while the phonological route is slower and used for unfamiliar words (Coltheart, Davelaar, Jonasson, & Besner, 1977; McCusker, Hillinger, & Bias, 1981). As will become evident in this review, individual differences in reading ability have been attributed to differences in the reliance on contextual and phonological processes in word recognition.

To have understood the Clyde passage, we had to do more than just recognize and comprehend the individual words. We also had to compute the relationships among the successive words, phrases, and sentences, thereby constructing a coherent and meaningful representation of the passage as a whole. These higher-level comprehension and integration processes involved a number of component processes at the sentence and text levels.

At the sentence level, we had to extract the *underlying propositions*—that is, the elementary units of meaning that described a state or action and the participants in that state or action (Kintsch, 1974). For the sentence fragment, "He opened the magazine . . . ," the underlying proposition consists of the action *open* with the participants *he* and *magazine*; *he* is the agent of the action, *magazine* the object. Semantic and syntactic processes are assumed to collaborate in the task of extracting or assembling the underlying propositions (Just & Carpenter, 1987).

The text itself can be conceptualized as a list of interrelated propositions. At the text level, then, we had to *integrate* each newly assembled proposition with ones assembled in previous portions of the text. One mechanism for this integration is the recurrence of an element in different propositions ("argument overlap" in the Kintsch & van Dijk, 1978, model); for example, the same noun could appear in two different propositions or there could be a pronoun that has an anaphoric connection to an antecedent noun. Thus, the proposition underlying "He opened the magazine" can be integrated with any of the propositions from preceding sentences that share the pronoun *he* or its antecedent referent noun, *Clyde*.

Integration also depends on computing the semantic relationships among successive propositions. Having assembled the propositions underlying "the number of bullets it held, waiting to be fired," we likely all encountered difficulty integrating them with the proposition represented by the preceding clause, "He opened the magazine." Our difficulty did not arise because of a lack of argument overlap; on the contrary, we could infer that the pronoun *it* was coreferential with *magazine*. But this left us with a semantic inconsistency because "reading periodical," the meaning we had accessed for *magazine*, is semantically incompatible with the idea of a receptacle for bullets.

Successful integration would have required sophisticated error recovery heuristics (Carpenter & Daneman, 1981; Frazier & Rayner, 1982) that identified *magazine* as the source of the error and selected its alternate meaning, "revolver chamber." Like the processes for word recognition, these higher-level integration processes are also reflected in the duration of the eye fixations. So for example, the processes involved in detecting and repairing the inconsistency would have resulted in fixations on the inconsistent portion of the text, "held, waiting to be fired" that were longer in duration than would be predicted based on the lengths and frequencies of the individual words alone. For some of us, error recovery may have even involved additional regressive eye fixations—that is, fixations to previously read parts of the text such as "He opened the magazine." As we will see, readers differ in their ability to integrate successively encountered ideas into a coherent representation.

Since readers do not engage in a large amount of backtracking, integration often depends on the reader's ability to store recently processed information at least temporarily. Some theorists have invoked the construct of *working memory* to account for temporary storage during reading, and the construct of *working memory capacity* to account for individual differences in temporary storage during reading.

To have understood the Clyde passage, we had to do more than assemble and integrate the successively encountered propositions in a text. For a start, some of the propositions we encoded into our representation of the passage were not explicitly mentioned in the text at all; however, they were semantically or logically implied. For example, if we finally interpreted the *magazine* sentence to mean that Clyde opened the chamber of his gun and counted the bullets inside it, we will have had to have added to our representation the following propositions: *his holster contained a gun, he took his hand off the holster, he removed the gun.* We filled in these propositions by making inferences based on our knowledge of the world. In building an overall representation for the passage, we probably made the following kinds of knowledge-based inferences too: *Clyde wanted to murder the occupant of the office, the office belonged to a doctor, or perhaps a lawyer.* These inferences were not semantically or logically implied by the text, but were psychologically plausible nonetheless, given our knowledge about why people carry loaded guns, what kinds of people have offices with waiting rooms, and so on. The terms *schema* (Anderson, Spiro, & Anderson, 1978; Bartlett, 1932; Rumelhart & Ortony, 1977) and *script* (Owens, Bower, & Black, 1979) have been used to refer to organized knowledge about concepts and events that readers use, in combination with what the text explicitly "says," to construct the larger text meaning. As we will see, some theorists have appealed to differences in knowledge and knowledge application to account for individual differences in reading ability.

In summary, reading is a complex skill that draws on many component processes and resources. Any of the component processes of reading has the potential for being a source of individual differences in reading ability. Many—but not all—are. The next section reviews the evidence on individual differences in the cognitive components of reading.

INDIVIDUAL DIFFERENCES IN THE COGNITIVE COMPONENTS

This section is divided into six parts. Each of the first four parts focuses on one particular group of reading processes, evaluating their role in accounting for individual differences among readers. The first examines the role of *eye movements* in explaining differences between good and poor readers. The second examines individual differences in *word recognition processes*, and the third individual differences in *word knowledge*. The fourth part focuses on *language comprehension processes*—that is, on the comprehension processes that extend beyond the individual word. Individual differences in reading skill could be due not only to a specific process but also to resources shared by many component processes. The remaining two parts focus on the role of two such resources: *working memory capacity* and *knowledge*.

Eye Movements

Two hypotheses have been considered concerning the role eye movements might play in determining reading skill. One is that good readers might be distinguished from poor readers in the extent to which they have control over the movement and placement of the eye during reading. Another is that good readers might differ from poor readers in the amount of visual information they can extract during a single eye fixation. These possibilities are discussed below.

Eye-Movement Control

Eye-movement control is one component of reading that does *not* appear to account for individual differences in reading skill. It is not that poor readers display the same pattern of eye movements and fixations as good readers. On the contrary; they differ on just about any index of eye-movement behavior. Early on, reading researchers noted that poor readers make more and longer fixations than good readers, as well as many more regressions (Buswell, 1937). However, the correlation between eye-movement behavior and reading skill has not always been interpreted to mean that poor eye-movement control is a manifestation of underlying cognitive and linguistic problems. Indeed, some researchers argued the exact opposite—that is, that erratic and inefficient eye movements are the source of poor reading comprehension. Based on this reasoning, attempts were made to improve the reading comprehension performance of poor readers by training them to make the same pattern of eye movements as good readers—namely, shorter fixations and fewer regressive fixations.

Although there are still some researchers who propose that poor movement and placement of the eye is the source of reading problems (Nodine & Lang, 1971; Nodine & Simmons, 1974; Pavlidis, 1981), the majority now believe that it is simply a reflection of the reading problems (Just & Carpenter, 1980, 1987; Rayner & Duffy, 1988). This conclusion is based on evidence that the oculomotor training studies were sometimes able to alter readers' eye movements but never to improve their comprehension performance (Tinker, 1958), and on observations that poor readers' immature eye movements did not generalize to non-reading scanning tasks like picture scanning (Stanley, 1978). Pavlidis (1981), who is the most recent person to have revived the eye-movement argument, claims to have shown that dyslexic children are deficient at tracking nonverbal stimuli. Nevertheless, the generality of his results has been called into question because at least three independent laboratories have failed to replicate them (Brown et al., 1983; Olson, Kliegl, & Davidson, 1983; Stanley, Smith, & Howell, 1983). At best, the incidence of eye-movement problems among severely disabled readers must be very low; and presumably, the incidence among the kinds of non-disabled poor readers we are concerned with here, must be even lower.

Perceptual Span

Even if reading problems originating from the neuromotor control of eye fixations are rare, it could be that reading problems arise out of differences in the low-level visual-perceptual processes that extract information during a fixation. For example, it has been claimed that good readers can extract and identify more letters and words during a single fixation (Gibson, 1965; Smith, 1971). If good readers can extract information from a larger region during a fixation, this would account for the fact that they make approximately one-third to one-half the number of fixations that poor readers do.

Empirical support for this claim rests on evidence from two kinds of techniques used to determine the size of the perceptual span (see Underwood & Zola, 1986, for a more extensive review of these and other techniques). The first technique attempts to simulate a single fixation by presenting verbal materials (random letter strings, words, phrases) for up to 250 milliseconds via a tachistoscope, and having subjects report as much of the display as they can. Using this technique, Marcel (1974) found that poor readers were able to report less from the tachistoscopic displays than good readers. However, as Sperling (1960) has demonstrated, this technique may underestimate the amount of information actually seen during a fixation, since subjects can see more than they can store and report. The fact that poor readers report less may reflect limitations in their ability to store or report rather than limitations in what they see.

The second technique used to estimate the size of the perceptual span tries to estimate how far from the center of fixation individually presented letters and words can be identified (Bouma, 1973). Using this technique with 10- to 14-year-olds, Bouma and Legein (1977) found that dyslexic readers were less able to identify peripherally presented words or letters flanked by X's than were average readers. Apart from the fact that the deficit may not generalize to nondyslexic poor readers, it is difficult to interpret the individual-differences results because of two problems with the technique itself. The first problem is that the technique may give some indication of the range over which information can *potentially* be used during reading, but says nothing about the range over which information is *actually* used during reading. After all, there is no reason to assume that readers always use all the information available to them. Thus, the technique may be overestimating the perceptual span during normal reading. The second problem is that language constraints can facilitate the identification of letters and words (Zola, 1984), which means that this technique would be underestimating the region of text within which identification occurs during normal reading of connected text. All in all, these criticisms point to the need to compare good and poor readers on a task that measures the effective perceptual span while reading naturalistic text.

One recent study does just this. Underwood and Zola (1986) used a modified version of the McConkie and Rayner (1975) paradigm to investigate the span of letter recognition for good and poor fifth-grade readers during a reading task. In the McConkie and Rayner (1975) paradigm, the subject reads a text displayed on a computer-controlled screen. The computer that displays the text also tracks the reader's eye fixations and can make display changes contingent on where the reader is fixating at any moment in time. With this technology it is possible to investigate what aspects of the text are picked up at different distances from the center of fixation. The computer is programmed so that at any particular time a segment of the original text is displayed in the immediate vicinity of the reader's fixation point and the rest of the text is mutilated (that is, replaced by X's or letters visually confusable with the original ones). This manipulation produces a "window" of normal text around the point of fixation. When the reader makes an eye movement, the text in the window area is mutilated and a new window of normal text is created at the location of the next fixation. Thus, wherever the reader pauses there is normal text to read. The computer is also programmed to vary the size of the window and the nature of the visual pattern outside the window. This enables the researchers to determine how far into the periphery various types of visual information (e.g., specific letters, word shape, word length) could be processed during a fixation by determining how small the window could be made without causing a disruption in reading performance. Variations of this paradigm have been used frequently with relatively skilled adult readers (Denbuurman, Boersema, & Gerrisen, 1981; Ikeda & Saida, 1978; McConkie & Rayner, 1975; Rayner, 1975) and have typically shown the effective span for letter and word identification to be very small; it is limited to a region extending from the beginning of the currently fixated word (but no more than three or four characters to the left of fixation) to roughly six to eight character spaces to the right of fixation (Rayner & Duffy, 1988).

But what about the question of whether perceptual span differentiates good from poor readers? The Underwood and Zola (1986) study suggests that the answer is *no*. Not only does their study show that the span of letter recognition in children is the same for good and poor readers (a span extending from two letters to the left of fixation point to six or seven letters to the right), but this span is remarkably similar to the one that has been described for adult skilled readers. Underwood and Zola's result is also consistent with a report by Samuels, LaBerge, and Bremer (1978) that the processing units of fourth-grade readers are very similar to those of sixth-grade and adult readers. There is always the possibility that developmental differences would be found if even younger readers were included in the study. However, the current data strongly suggest that the size of the perceptual span during reading is not a major determinant of developmental or individual differences in reading ability.

In summary, reading problems are not due to deficits in the neuromotor control of eye fixations nor are they due to deficits in the size of the perceptual span during a fixation. Almost all reading problems are due to difficulties in recognizing words and comprehending language. These are the components that will be explored next.

Word Recognition

Numerous researchers have proposed that word recognition processes are an important, if not the most important, determinant of reading skill (LaBerge & Samuels, 1974; Perfetti & Lesgold, 1977; Stanovich, 1986). It is obvious that slow and effortful word recognition processes will lead to slow, nonfluent reading. However, these researchers argue that a bottleneck in word recognition not only causes slow reading but qualitatively poorer comprehension as well. The reasoning is that slow and effortful word recognition processes will consume so much of the reader's limited attentional resources that there may not be sufficient resources left to execute the high-level comprehension processes (Perfetti, 1985). This section reviews evidence for the theory. As we will see, the theory needs some qualification based on the age of the reader and the kind of reading skill under consideration.

The evidence for the role of word recognition in determining reading skill is largely correlational. A consistent finding among elementary school children is that poor reading comprehenders are slower to recognize words than good reading comprehenders, even when differences in word recognition accuracy are controlled (Hogaboam & Perfetti, 1978; Perfetti, Finger, & Hogaboam, 1978; Perfetti & Hogaboam, 1975; Stanovich, Cunningham, & Feeman, 1984). The correlations are typically in the 0.50 to 0.80 range (Stanovich et al., 1984). Some researchers have even reported a correlation between word recognition speed and reading comprehension within relatively restricted ranges of fluent adult readers (Briggs & Underwood, 1982; Frederiksen, 1978).

In contrast, other researchers have found that word recognition speed plays only a minor role in distinguishing skilled from less-skilled adult readers, and tends to be more closely related to measures of reading speed than to measures of reading comprehension (Chabot, Zehr, Prinzo, & Petros, 1984; Jackson & McClelland, 1979; Palmer et al., 1985).

Since word recognition is itself a complex skill, consisting of word encoding, lexical access, and possibly phonological and contextual processes too, it is important to examine which of its component processes are associated with individual differences in reading comprehension and reading speed.

Word Encoding

Word encoding, the process of forming a representation of the perceptual form of a word, is mediated by letter recognition (Just & Carpenter, 1987; Perfetti, 1983). In the section on eye fixations we saw that poor readers can acquire letter information from the same-size region of text during a fixation as can good readers. But are they slower or less accurate in perceiving the individual letters? Again it appears that the answer is *no*. Research has shown that poor readers perceive letters as well as good readers (Frederiksen, 1978; Jackson & McClelland, 1979). Reading ability is not related to performance on simple letter identification, measured either by single-letter report thresholds or double-letter ("letter separation") report accuracy (Jackson & McClelland, 1975, 1979). Differences between good and poor readers become apparent only when some verbal or linguistic coding operation is involved, as in the accessing in memory of name codes or meaning codes associated with the visual input. These are the processes central to lexical access, to be discussed next.

It is not surprising that simple perceptual processes do not account for the ability differences found in a typical school or college population. Recent evidence suggests that simple perceptual processes do not account for ability differences even when the extreme low end of the reading ability continuum is included (Perfetti, 1985; Stanovich,

1986). Whereas deficits in simple perceptual processes such as shape and form perception once dominated theories of dyslexia (Orton, 1925), they have given way to the better-substantiated verbal deficit theories (Fischer, Liberman, & Shankweiler, 1978; Vellutino, 1979).

Lexical Access

During *lexical access*, the reader accesses or retrieves information about the word from memory, information about the meaning and pronunciation of the word. Numerous researchers suggest that the speed or efficiency of retrieving verbal information during lexical access is an important determinant of individual differences in reading ability (Baddeley, Logie, Nimmo-Smith, & Brereton, 1985; Ellis & Miles, 1978; Hunt, Lunneborg, & Lewis, 1975; Jackson & McClelland, 1979; Palmer et al., 1985).

The most commonly used task to study the speed of retrieving verbal information compares the time to retrieve and match letter or name codes from memory with the time to match physical or visual codes (Posner, Boies, Eichelman, & Taylor, 1969). In this task, subjects are timed while they compare two visually presented letters (like *A-A*; *A-a*; *A-b*). In one condition, they must judge whether the letters are physically identical. In a second condition, they must judge whether the letters have the same name. To judge whether two letters are physically identical (like *A-A*), the subject need only encode and compare two visual symbols. To judge whether two letters that are physically different have the same name (like *A-a*), the subject must also access their names from memory. The difference in time to say that two letters have the same name (*A-a*) versus the time to say that two letters have the same physical form (*A-A*) provides an estimate of the time to retrieve the name code from memory. This difference is greater for college students who score low on verbal ability tests (Hunt et al., 1975) and on reading speed and reading comprehension tests (Jackson & McClelland, 1979). Jackson and McClelland (1979) found that poor college readers are also slower at other semantic matching tasks such as responding "same" if two words are synonyms (e.g., *large-great*) or homonyms (e.g., *read-reed*). However, poor readers are not slower at matching dot patterns, suggesting that the processing-speed deficit is localized to visual displays with verbal content.

Although the correlation between reading ability and retrieving overlearned word or letter-name codes has been replicated many times, it always tends to be around 0.30, particularly for adult readers. Given the low correlation, it is unlikely that speed of lexical access is a very large determinant of reading ability. Moreover, as recent studies (e.g., Chabot et al. 1984; Palmer et al., 1985) have pointed out, at least with respect to adult readers, the speed of retrieving letter- and word-name codes may be more related to measures of reading *speed* than to measures of reading *comprehension* ability (see also Jackson & McClelland, 1979, p. 168). For these reasons, some researchers have argued for the implication of high-level processes in accounting for individual differences in reading comprehension ability (Daneman, 1984; Palmer et al., 1985). Of course there is also the question of whether a causal inference is justified, since the evidence linking lexical access and reading ability is supported largely by correlational data only. This point will be taken up in more detail at the end of the section on word recognition.

Phonological Recoding

Considerable attention has been focused on the role of phonological processes in accounting for developmental and individual differences in reading ability. It is generally assumed that there are two ways to generate the phonological representation of a word. One way is to generate the code directly from the print, using spelling-to-sound or grapheme-to-phoneme rules. For example, the letters *c-a-t* are mentally converted or "phonologically recoded" into their corresponding phonemes /k/, /ae/, /t/. It is this pathway that is used to sound out unfamiliar words, and the resulting phonological code could then be used to access the word's meaning. Because such a code is generated piece by piece independently of lexical access and probably before lexical access, it has been referred to as an *assembled code* (Patterson & Coltheart, 1987) and a *prelexical code* (Jorm & Share, 1983). Such codes may be particularly important for beginning readers and unskilled readers, but not all researchers agree on whether they are generated by skilled readers (Patterson & Coltheart, 1987). The second way in which a phonological code is generated is as a result of lexical access. Information about a word's pronunciation is presumably stored in the lexical entry for that word, along with information about the word's meaning, syntactic properties, and so on. When a word is lexically accessed, its phonological code is too (Perfetti & McCutchen, 1982). Because such a code is stored in a preassembled form and is a product of lexical access, it has been referred to as an *addressed code* (Patterson & Coltheart, 1987) and as a *postlexical code* (Jorm & Share, 1983).

First, let us consider individual differences in prelexical phonological processes because they are assumed to mediate lexical access and, hence, word recognition. It is obvious that prelexical phonological recoding is critical in the acquisition of reading skill; children must at some point acquire skill at "cracking" the spelling-to-sound code (Gough & Hillinger, 1980; LaBerge & Samuels, 1974; Liberman, 1982); and there is evidence that phonological recoding ability is related to early reading success (Jorm & Share, 1983; Stanovich, 1986). However, do differences in this kind of phonological recoding account for individual differences in reading ability beyond the beginning stages? The answer appears to be *yes*, even for readers of high school age. This conclusion is based on the finding that the task that most clearly and consistently differentiates good and poor readers is the speed and accuracy with which they can name pseudowords—that is, pronounceable nonwords like *troom* and *flim* (Jorm & Share, 1983). The ability to read simple nonwords has been used as a measure of phonological recoding skill because nonwords do not have representations in the lexicon, so it is assumed that their pronunciations must be assembled through the application of grapheme-to-phoneme (phonological recoding) rules.

The finding that poor readers are less good at reading pronounceable nonwords has been observed for children in grades one through six (Firth, 1972; Hogaboam & Perfetti, 1978; Jorm, 1981; Perfetti & Hogaboam, 1975; Seymour & Porpodas, 1980) and in high school students (Frederiksen, 1982). For example, Frederiksen (1982) showed that speed of pronouncing pseudowords correlated 0.68 with high school students' reading comprehension scores and 0.48 with reading speed. The correlations do not depend on overt pronunciation. For example, Snowling (1980) used a procedure in which children were shown a printed pseudoword and then supplied a pronunciation for it. Their task was simply to judge whether or not the pronunciation corresponded to the printed nonword. Even though no overt pronunciation was required, Snowling (1980) found that poor readers still had problems reading the nonwords. In summary, the data suggest that skill at phonological recoding is strongly related to overall reading skill.

Many researchers now believe that skill at phonological processes (whether prelexically assembled or postlexically addressed) has its effects beyond the level of word recognition. During reading, sequences of words must be held in a temporary storage buffer while the comprehension processes integrate them into a meaningful conceptual structure that can be stored in long-term memory. It has been argued that the most stable short-term memory code is a sound-based one (Baddeley, 1966; Conrad, 1964).

Readers who are able to generate high-quality phonological codes as a part of lexical access are at an advantage because such codes are less vulnerable to memory loss, allowing readers to keep track of exact words rather than rough meanings. Theoretically then, phonological representations could assist comprehension by virtue of their compatibility with short-term memory (Patterson & Coltheart, 1987).

The hypothesis that good readers rely on phonological codes in short-term memory more than do poor readers has received some empirical support. These studies have examined the effects of phonological confusability on short-term recall. For example, Liberman, Shankweiler, Liberman, Fowler, and Fischer (1977) tested short-term recall for visually presented letter strings that consisted of either phonologically confusable (rhyming) letters (e.g., P, C, D) or phonologically nonconfusable ones (e.g., K, M, W). They found that good second-grade readers recalled fewer of the phonologically confusable items compared to the nonconfusable ones. In contrast, poor second-grade readers were less disadvantaged by the phonologically confusable items. The finding that good readers are more prone to errors in remembering rhyme materials has been replicated with word strings and sentences (Mann, Liberman, & Shankweiler, 1980). Nevertheless, there have been some recent discrepant results (e.g., Hall, Wilson, Humphreys, Tinzmann, & Bowyer, 1983; Johnston, 1982) and criticisms that the Liberman findings are an artifactual consequence of marked differences in overall task difficulty for the reading groups being compared (Hall et al., 1983). Until further research clarifies the issues, the results are at best suggestive of the idea that phonological codes might aid comprehension processes in short-term memory.

There is also the suggestion that good readers rely on phonological codes in long-term memory (Byrne & Shea, 1979; Mark, Shankweiler, Liberman, & Fowler, 1977). Mark et al. (1977) gave children a list of easy words (e.g., know, good) to read aloud and then surprised them with a recognition test in which half the distractor words were phonologically similar to target words (e.g., go for know; could for good), and half were phonologically dissimilar. They found that good readers made more false positive responses to phonologically similar distractors than to dissimilar ones; poor readers produced similar rates of false positives for both sorts of distractors. Byrne and Shea (1979) used a continuous recognition task in which children were presented with spoken words and had to indicate whether each word had or had not been presented previously. Some of the distractors were phonologically similar to words presented earlier (e.g., comb for home) and others were semantically similar (e.g., house for home). Again, poor readers were found to make fewer false alarms to phonologically similar distractors. Poor readers tended to false alarm more to semantic distractors although the effect was not significant.

It is not immediately obvious why it would be advantageous for readers to encode phonological information in long-term memory, because long-term memory is generally assumed to be specialized for holding information in an abstract semantic code rather than in a phonological or visual code. One possibility is that phonological codes allow readers to maintain precise lexical information that may be useful for certain kinds of comprehension processes, such as maintaining thematic information, resolving anaphoric references, and constructing inferences (Glanzer, Fischer, & Dorfman, 1984). Ever since Sachs (1967) showed that memory for surface or stylistic information is poor whereas memory for gist is good, researchers have tended to downplay the importance of a verbatim representation in long-term memory, favoring instead a more abstract propositional representation that excludes specific lexical information (cf. Miller, 1972; Schank, 1972). Although it is indeed unlikely that even the best of readers maintain certain aspects of the verbatim information (e.g., the precise word order), Hayes-Roth and Hayes-Roth (1977) have shown rather convincingly that people do have memory for verbatim *lexical* information. Skill at encoding and maintaining lexical information may turn out to be an important individual-differences parameter, and one that is closely linked to reading comprehension skill.

The Use of Context

Many researchers have argued that good and poor readers can be differentiated on the basis of how they use context to facilitate word recognition. However, these researchers have represented two radically different views on the extent to which context influences word recognition as well as on the nature of the relationship between context use and reading ability. One camp argues that context is an important part of word recognition; hence, it is the good readers who might be using context more. The other camp deemphasizes the role of context in favor of fluent and automatic word encoding and lexical access; hence, it is the poor readers who might be resorting to context more.

Several influential models of reading developed in the 1960s and 1970s argued that readers use context to guess the upcoming words in a text (Goodman, 1965, 1976; Levin & Kaplan, 1970; Smith, 1971). The implication of these models was that the advantage of good readers lay in their sensitivity to the semantic and syntactic cues afforded by previously processed text, rather than in their skill at the bottom-up processes of word encoding and lexical access. However, recent research has overwhelmingly disproved the hypothesis and its implications. First of all, good readers are better than poor readers at word recognition, both in and out of context (Perfetti, Goldman, & Hogaboam, 1979; Stanovich, 1980; Stanovich & West, 1981). Their superior recognition skills for words out of context suggests that good readers are better at the bottom-up word recognition processes. But more important is the finding that the word recognition differences between good and poor readers are smaller when the words are in context (Perfetti et al., 1979). This suggests that context helps poor readers recognize a word more than it helps good readers; or put the other way, poor readers make more use of context for word recognition than do good readers. To say that poor readers use context more is not to say that they are better at using context, better at playing "the psycholinguistic guessing game" (Goodman, 1976). On the contrary, Perfetti et al. (1979) have shown that good readers are superior at a clozelike prediction task. It is just that poor readers have to *rely* more on context to support their slow bottom-up word recognition processes (Stanovich, West, & Freeman, 1981). If good readers' word encoding and lexical access processes are slowed down artificially—for example, by degrading the words so that they are difficult to perceive—then context also has a large influence on the good readers' word recognition time (Perfetti & Roth, 1981; Stanovich & West, 1981; West & Stanovich, 1978). Thus, it appears that poor readers are helped more by the context only because they typically take longer than good readers to encode and access words. These results suggest that the contextual influences on the speed of word recognition are not a primary source of individual differences; rather, such effects are due to differences in the speed of the bottom-up aspects of word recognition discussed earlier.

Summary of Findings on Word Recognition Processes

In general, there appears to be relatively strong evidence that individual differences in word recognition processes are related to individual differences in reading skill. However, the relationship is greatest for young readers. For adults, for example, speed of lexical access accounts for only about 10 percent of the variance in reading ability. Moreover, speed of lexical access may be more related to reading fluency than to reading comprehension ability. This finding suggests that the construct of reading skill might best be construed as two separate and partially independent skills: reading speed and reading comprehension. Such a conclusion receives additional support when we consider individual differences in high-level processes.

Because the evidence relating word recognition processes to reading ability is largely correlational, we have to be cautious in imputing a causal link. While skill at word recognition processes could cause increases in reading comprehension ability, it is possible that good readers are exposed to more text and, as a consequence, become better at recognizing words. There have been a number of training studies aimed at investigating the causal relationship. These training studies succeeded in improving the word recognition speed of poor readers but did not find commensurate improvements in their reading comprehension levels (Fleisher, Jenkins, & Pany, 1979; Samuels, Dahl, & Archwamety, 1974). For example, Fleisher et al. (1979) trained poor fourth- and fifth-grade readers to recognize individual words and phrases until their speed was comparable to that of good readers. However, subsequent tests of reading comprehension showed that the poor readers' comprehension scores were no higher after training than before.

These results can be interpreted in two ways. First, they could demonstrate that rapid word recognition is necessary but not sufficient for good comprehension (Just & Carpenter, 1987). Perhaps the same readers who are experiencing difficulty with word recognition may have not had sufficient practice in high-level comprehension processes, such as making inferences or abstracting the main theme. Since reading involves the coordination of a complex number of processes, it is unlikely that efficient word recognition would be sufficient to allow these other processes to function normally. Poor readers may have needed practice or training in the higher-level processes too. A second conclusion is that word recognition speed is neither necessary nor sufficient for good comprehension; rather, the observed correlations are based on the fact that good readers are exposed to more text and consequently become more skilled at recognizing lots of words.

Although more evidence is needed, Stanovich (1986) provides a few reasons for suspecting that word recognition *does* influence comprehension. One is that the word recognition deficits of the poorer reader persist even when the possibility of differential exposure to and practice with text is eliminated (Guthrie & Tyler, 1976). Another is that the relationship between word recognition and comprehension is apparent at the very early stages of reading acquisition (Biemiller, 1970; Groff, 1978), making it unlikely that word recognition skill is an incidental correlate of the reading experience of good readers. A recent interesting longitudinal study by Lesgold and Resnick (1982) also supports this conclusion. They presented evidence from a cross-lag panel design indicating that increased word recognition speed leads to improved reading comprehension ability, rather than the reverse.

Word Knowledge

Numerous researchers have noted that poor readers have smaller vocabularies than good readers. Indeed, vocabulary knowledge is one of the best single predictors of reading comprehension performance (e.g., Davis, 1968; Thorndike, 1973). For example, Thorndike collected data from over 100,000 students in three age groups from 15 countries and found median correlations between vocabulary knowledge and reading comprehension of 0.71 (10-year-olds), 0.75 (14-year-olds), and 0.66 (18-year-olds). Thorndike concluded that reading performance is "completely . . . determined by word knowledge" (1973, p. 62). Some researchers have reported that the correlation between vocabulary and reading comprehension is almost as high as the correlation between alternate forms of a reading comprehension test (see Just & Carpenter, 1987).

One interpretation of the high correlations is that there is a direct causal connection between vocabulary knowledge and reading ability. Students who know fewer words will have more difficulty constructing an overall meaning for any given text because they are more likely to encounter unknown words in that text; that is, words for which they have no stored meaning representation in memory. Unknown words would create gaps in the meaning of the text and hinder or prevent the construction of a coherent representation for it.

However, numerous training studies have failed to establish this direct relationship (e.g., Jenkins, Pany, & Schreck, 1978; Tuinman & Brady, 1974). For example, Tuinman and Brady (1974) found that pretraining on vocabulary items from passages to be read did not increase elementary school children's comprehension scores for those passages. Although knowledge of the word meanings of a text may be a necessary condition for comprehending that text, it may not be sufficient to improve comprehension. The reader must be able to interrelate the underlying conceptual structures after the individual word meanings are retrieved. This additional step is central to Sternberg and Powell's (1983) learning-from-context theory of the relationship between vocabulary and reading ability.

According to the *learning-from-context hypothesis*, vocabulary and comprehension are correlated because both reflect the individuals' ability to learn or acquire new information from context. While some word meanings may be acquired through explicit reference (asking mother or teacher, or looking up the definition in a dictionary), many word meanings are learned through implicit or contextual reference (inferring the meaning from cues in the verbal context in which the word is encountered). According to Sternberg and Powell (1983), the ability to infer meaning from spoken or written contexts is an important component of vocabulary acquisition (see also Werner & Kaplan, 1952); and the net products of this ability are reflected in the extent of an individual's vocabulary knowledge. People with large current vocabularies are the people who have been successful at inferring word meanings from reading and listening. In other words, vocabulary knowledge is partially a product of reading comprehension skill. The same types of semantic, syntactic, and integration processes that are used to comprehend a text with known words also help a reader infer the meanings of unknown words. If these processes are functioning well, the reader will acquire a large vocabulary over his or her many years of reading. Sternberg and Powell (1983) showed that the ability of high school readers to infer the meanings of unknown words from context was indeed significantly correlated with reading comprehension ($r = 0.65$) as well as with other tests of vocabulary knowledge ($r = 0.56$). Thus, vocabulary tests can be seen as a measure of vocabulary acquisition skill and, in particular, as a measure of the reader's ability to learn from context. According to this view, then, differences in vocabulary knowledge are a result of differences in reading skill rather than a primary cause of such differences. Support for this interpretation of the correlation comes from the finding that the successful vocabulary-training programs are the ones that teach readers to make plausible inferences about the meaning of a new word as they encounter the word in a variety of contexts (e.g., Beck, McKeown, & Omanson, 1984; Beck, Perfetti, & McKeown, 1982).

Language Comprehension Processes

This section examines the role played by the comprehension processes beyond the level of the word. These include sentence-level and text-level processes. The section is divided into two parts. The first discusses the relationship between reading comprehension ability and listening comprehension ability. The second discusses individual differences in some comprehension processes, particularly the processes that integrate successive words and sentences in a text.

The Relationship between Reading and Listening Comprehension

One clue that visual word recognition processes cannot account for all the variance in reading ability is the finding that good readers tend to be good listeners and, conversely, poor readers tend to be poor listeners. This is particularly true at the more advanced levels of reading acquisition. For example, almost all studies of readers beyond the elementary grades report significant correlations between reading comprehension and listening comprehension skill. The relationship is very strong in adults (Daneman & Carpenter, 1980; Jackson & McClelland, 1979; Sticht & James, 1984), moderately strong in the middle grades, and weak but still significant in the early elementary grades (Stanovich et al., 1984; Chall, 1983; Curtis, 1980). Of course, the absolute size of the correlation depends on many factors, including the range of reading and listening skills in the sample. It is quite typical, however, to find correlations between 0.60 and 0.80 for high school and college students (Sticht & James, 1984). Among college students, reading skill is correlated with listening skill more than with measures of simpler processes, such as speed of lexical access (Jackson & McClelland, 1979; Palmer et al., 1985). For example, Jackson and McClelland (1979) found that listening comprehension accounted for 50 percent of the variance in reading skill, whereas the Posner name-letter matching task accounted for only 10 percent. And Palmer et al. concluded that "reading comprehension ability is indistinguishable from listening comprehension ability" (1986, p. 59).

Together, the data indicate that as the absolute level of reading performance increases, so the proportion of reading variance accounted for by listening comprehension ability also increases. Reading seems to depend on a set of language processes that are common to both reading and listening. Word-encoding and lexical access skills may account for relatively little of the variance once readers get beyond the beginning stages of reading. After that, general language comprehension skills seem to be a larger source of individual differences.

Integration Processes

Relatively few studies have examined exactly which of the high-level processes shared by reading and listening are responsible for the individual differences. However, from the little evidence we do have, a consistent picture seems to emerge. Poor readers are at a particular disadvantage when they have to execute a process that requires them to integrate newly encountered information with information encountered earlier in the text or retrieved from semantic memory. So, for example, poor readers have problems

interrelating successive topics (Lorch, Lorch, & Morgan, 1987) and integrating informa-
tion to derive the overall gist or main theme of a passage (Daneman & Carpenter, 1980;
Oakhill, 1982; Palincsar & Brown, 1984; Smiley, Oakley, Worthen, Campione, &
Brown, 1977). They have more difficulty making inferences (Masson & Miller, 1983;
Oakhill & Yuill, 1986) and tend to make fewer of them during text comprehension
(Oakhill, 1982). Poor readers also have more difficulty computing the referent for a
pronoun (Daneman & Carpenter, 1980; Oakhill & Yuill, 1986). In their study, Oakhill
and Yuill (1986) had good and poor elementary school children read sentences such as
the following: "Peter lent ten pence to Max because he was very poor," and then asked
them "Who was very poor, Peter or Max?" Poor readers were less able to compute the
pronoun's referent even if gender cues to the referent were available as in "Peter lent
ten pence to Liz because she was very poor." Other researchers have found that poor
readers do not demand informational coherence and consistency in a text, and often fail
to detect, let alone repair, semantic inconsistencies (Garner, 1980).

Two main mechanisms have been proposed to account for the integration difficulties of poor readers and indeed for poor reading ability in general. One is working
memory capacity. The second is use of background knowledge. What makes them
attractive candidates to account for individual differences in general reading ability is
that they are not localized to a single process but are resources shared by many of the
component processes.

Working Memory Capacity

The term *working memory* refers to a conception of short-term memory that includes
both storage and processing functions. Many theories of reading assume that short-term
memory plays an important role in reading; in the section on phonological processes, for
example, we saw how theorists assume that readers have to buffer several words or
phrases in order to assemble and integrate the underlying propositions. However,
measures of short-term memory span, such as the ability to recall a list of random digits or
unrelated words, are not significantly correlated with reading comprehension (Perfetti
& Lesgold, 1977), unless severely retarded readers are included in the sample. A
possible explanation for the low correlation may be that traditional span measures are
primarily measures of passive storage capacity. For example, in a digit span test, the
subject must simply encode the string of digits and try to maintain some record of their
order of occurrence. By contrast, working memory reflects a conception of a more active
short-term memory, a short-term memory that has processing functions too. Moreover,
because working memory has a limited pool of resources, the processing and storage
functions trade off against each other (Baddeley & Hitch, 1974). A computationally
demanding task will consume more of the available capacity, leaving less capacity for
storing information. If the digit span test required subjects to report the digits in
reverse order, subjects would be able to store fewer digits because of the additional
computational demands of the reversal operation. This conception of working memory
can be applied to differences in reading skill.

Daneman and Carpenter (1980) hypothesized that skilled readers have larger
functional working memory capacities than less-skilled readers. The greater capacity for
both processing and storing information may arise from several sources. Skilled readers
may be faster and more automatic at many of the component processes of reading,
including encoding, lexical access, and higher-level semantic and syntactic processing.
Readers who are efficient at many or all of these processes will have a larger functional

capacity for temporary storage in working memory because less capacity will be consumed in the execution of the processes (see also Perfetti, 1985).

This hypothesis was explored by constructing a test that required the simultaneous processing and storage of information in working memory (Daneman & Carpenter, 1980). The test, called the *reading span test*, required subjects to read aloud a set of unrelated sentences and, at the end of the set, recall the final word of each sentence. For example, consider the following set of two sentences: (1) "He had an odd elongated skull which sat on his shoulders like a pear on a dish," and (2) "The products of digital electronics will play an important role in your future." After reading these two sentences, the subject was to recall the words *dish* and *future*. A reader was presented with sets containing two to six sentences to determine the largest set size from which he or she could reliably recall all of the sentence-final words. The largest such set size was defined as the subject's span. The rationale behind the test was that the comprehension processes used in reading the sentences would consume less of the working memory resources of the better readers; consequently, they should have more residual capacity to store the sentence-final words.

The findings were very encouraging. Reading span predicted reading comprehension performance in cases where traditional digit span and word span tests failed (Daneman & Carpenter, 1980). Individuals with reading spans of only two or three sentence-final words performed more poorly than individuals with reading spans of four or five sentence-final words on a global test of reading comprehension and also on more specific tests of integration. The findings have since been replicated across a fairly wide range of ages and comprehension tasks (e.g., Baddeley et al., 1985; Baker, 1985; Daneman & Carpenter, 1983; Daneman & Green, 1986; Masson & Miller, 1983). The correlations between reading span and reading comprehension have been quite impressive. They range between 0.42 and 0.90, and with a modal correlation of 0.55 tend to be well above the 0.30 barrier that typically plagues individual-differences researchers (Hunt, 1980).

Working memory seems to play a particularly important role in the processes that integrate successive ideas in a text. The reading span measure correlated quite highly with tasks that require readers to retrieve information mentioned earlier in the passage and relate it to the information they are currently reading. These are precisely the kinds of sentence- and text-level processes that were shown to be related to reading comprehension ability. Let us examine some of these in more detail.

One process requiring integration is computing the antecedent referent for a pronoun. Daneman and Carpenter (1980) assessed this by interrogating readers about a pronoun mentioned in the last sentence of a passage just read. So for example, one passage about famous men and their wives ended in the following manner:

> And then there's the poet Milton, author of *Paradise Lost*, and his wife. It's hard to believe that Mary had nothing to do with Milton's career. After being married for a while, Milton wrote a pamphlet in favor of divorce. She is best known for this insignificant and deprecating fact.

The pronoun question at the end was "Who is best known for this insignificant and deprecating fact?" Readers would have to know that *she* referred back to Mary Milton and not to Napoleon's wife Josephine, or Socrates' wife Xanthippe, both of whom had been mentioned earlier in the passage. Readers with small spans were less accurate at computing pronominal reference (Daneman & Carpenter, 1980). Moreover, readers with small spans were less likely to compute a pronoun's referent when six or seven sentences intervened between pronoun and referent. By contrast, large span readers could always compute the referent, even at these longer distances. The theory is that the process of associating a pronoun with its referent noun is easier if the referent noun is more active in working memory and the duration that a piece of information remains active will vary as a function of the individual's working memory capacity. A writer uses a pronoun rather than a noun when he or she assumes that the referential concept is active, or *foregrounded* (Chafe, 1972). Chafe suggested that the foregrounding is attenuated after two sentence boundaries, although he admitted that this criterion is arbitrary and that he was unable to formalize the upper limit. This working memory analysis suggests that the boundary might vary for different readers, with large span readers able to keep a concept foregrounded for a longer period of time.

Monitoring and revising one's comprehension errors is another skill that involves the integration of successive ideas in a text. Daneman and Carpenter (1983) examined such integration skills by assessing the reader's ability to detect and recover from apparent inconsistencies, as in "He opened the magazine and then carefully counted the number of bullets it held, waiting to be fired." When probed after reading garden path passages such as the *Clyde* one, small span readers were much less accurate in answering questions like "What did Clyde open?" Small span readers would frequently say, "He opened the *Newsweek*," indicating that they had not resolved the inconsistency. By contrast, large span readers would more often say, "He opened up the bullet compartment of his gun," indicating that they had detected the inconsistency and recovered the correct interpretation. Presumably recovery of the correct interpretation was harder for small span readers because they were less likely to have in working memory some representation of the orthographic or phonological properties of the misinterpreted word. Since the orthographic and phonological information for *magazine* is the only property shared by the two meanings, "reading periodical" and "revolver chamber," without such information small span readers would be lacking a useful retrieval route to the alternative meaning. Readers with small spans may have devoted so much capacity to the processes of reading that they would be less likely to have accessible in working memory a verbatim representation of the earlier phrase containing the ambiguous word.

Recovery from an inconsistency also depends on whether the verbatim wording has been purged from working memory by an intervening sentence boundary. Daneman and Carpenter (1983) demonstrated this by contrasting the following two versions of the *magazine* passage:

1. He opened the magazine and then carefully counted the number of bullets it held, waiting to be fired.
2. He opened the magazine. He then carefully counted the number of bullets it held, waiting to be fired.

In case 2, a sentence boundary intervened between the ambiguous word and the disambiguating phrase. Readers with small spans were less able to integrate information across a sentence boundary. By contrast, readers with large spans answered as many questions correctly when a sentence boundary intervened as when it did not (Daneman & Carpenter, 1983). These results were explained in terms of the accessibility of the earlier-read verbatim wording. A sentence boundary causes a marked decline in verbatim memory for recently comprehended text (Jarvella, 1971). Eye-fixation and reading time studies have shown that readers pause at the ends of sentences, possibly to do additional integration processes (Just & Carpenter, 1980). These additional processes may stress the limits of working memory capacity and contribute to the purging of verbatim wording. Presumably, readers with small working memory capacities are more prone to losing the verbatim wording at sentence boundaries and this is why they were less able to recover from inconsistencies when the text required the integration of information across a sentence boundary.

In the above examples, it was assumed that readers know both meanings of *magazine*. What if they don't? They could try to infer the meaning of *magazine* from the contextual cues. The acquisition of new word meanings from context also requires sophisticated integration skills. Daneman and Green (1986) found that readers with small working memory capacities had more difficulty piecing together cues in the context to infer the meaning of a previously unknown word.

In summary, there is considerable evidence that working memory capacity is highly correlated with expertise at the integration skills of reading comprehension.

Knowledge

Integration involves relating newly encountered information to information encountered earlier in the text or retrieved from long-term memory. As we have seen, the working memory view focuses on the earlier information, and proposes that skill at integration depends on keeping that relevant earlier information active in temporary storage. In contrast, the *knowledge view* focuses on retrieving information stored in long-term memory, and proposes that skill at integration depends on having the knowledge and using it to make inferences about the relationships between successive ideas in a text.

According to the knowledge view, a reader understands what he or she is reading only in relationship to what he or she already knows. This was nicely demonstrated by Anderson, Reynolds, Schallert, and Goetz (1977), who presented readers with the following passage about Rocky:

> Rocky slowly got up from the mat and planned his escape. He hesitated a moment and thought. Things were not going well. What bothered him the most was being held, especially since the charge against him had been weak. He considered his present situation. The lock that held him was strong but he thought he could break it. He knew, however, that his timing had to be perfect. Rocky was aware that it was because of his early roughness that he had been penalized so severely—much too severely from his point of view. The situation was becoming frustrating; the pressure had been grinding on him far too long. He was being ridden unmercifully. Rocky was getting angry now. He felt he was ready to make his move. He knew that his success or failure depended on what he did in the next few seconds. (p. 372)

Notice that the passage has been phrased vaguely so that two interpretations are possible: Rocky in the midst of a prison escape or a wrestling match. Anderson et al. (1977) found that students in an educational psychology class tended to give the passage the prison escape interpretation, while students in a weight-lifting class tended to give it the wrestling interpretation. Thus, readers will interpret the same passage in different ways, depending on their background knowledge and interests.

The work of Voss and colleagues provides a more direct demonstration that background knowledge about a topic can affect the level of comprehension attained (Chiesi, Spilich, & Voss, 1979; Spilich, Vesonder, Chiesi, & Voss, 1979; Voss, Fincher-Kiefer, Greene, & Post, 1985). In these experiments, subjects differed in their knowledge of baseball but not in their general reading comprehension level. Knowledge of baseball helped the baseball experts to comprehend and recall a text about a fictitious baseball game by allowing them to draw the appropriate inferences when relations among facts were left implicit, and by allowing them to integrate and organize the facts around their knowledge of the game's goal structure.

Research such as this does indeed suggest that comprehension depends on knowledge; that schemata help readers organize information, interrelate it, draw the appropriate inferences, and develop a retrieval structure to aid later recall. However, so far there are no data on the question of interest here: "What role does knowledge play in accounting for individual differences in *general* reading skill?" Indeed, in the baseball studies, subjects in the high- and low-knowledge groups were equated on general reading ability. What has been demonstrated so far is that individual differences in specific knowledge lead to individual differences in comprehending knowledge-related texts. For schema theory to be a theory of general reading ability, it would have to assume that individuals who are high in general reading ability have more useful knowledge on many topics than do individuals of low ability (see also Perfetti, 1988). Otherwise, there would be no such phenomenon as general reading ability, merely differences in reading performance, depending on the match between a text and a reader. Some individuals would be better at reading about baseball, others about football, and yet others about Oriental carpets or murder mysteries. To the extent that there is such a thing as general reading comprehension skill, the question is "Do good readers have more general knowledge than poor readers?" While there are no direct answers, the thesis seems quite plausible, given that good readers are likely to read more and acquire more information from text. Of course, critics would complain that the reasoning has become circular: Individuals are good reading comprehenders because they have a lot of knowledge, and they have a lot of knowledge because they are good readers. Ultimately, any knowledge-based theory of reading skill needs to tackle the question of how individual differences in knowledge arise in the first place. Learning-from-context (Sternberg & Powell, 1983) or working memory capacity (Daneman, 1988; Daneman & Green, 1986) are attractive candidates to account for knowledge acquisition from verbal contexts.

Of course, acquiring the relevant knowledge structure is not sufficient for comprehension; the reader needs to know when to apply it. In the baseball experiments, the relevant schema was transparent. In the case of complex text, the relevant schema is not necessarily obvious, not necessarily signaled explicitly in the text. It is the notion of *schema selection* (Spiro, 1980) that may be most relevant to a theory of individual differences in general reading ability. Poor readers may possess as much relevant knowledge on a given topic as good readers, but they may be less knowledgeable about when to evoke it. So far, however, there has been no demonstration of a relationship between appropriate schema selection and reading ability (Perfetti, 1988). And even if a relationship were shown, it could be a result of a problem elsewhere in the reading process, such as inefficient word recognition skills that leave too little capacity for effectively evoking knowledge-based processing.

Whereas a schema selection deficit may lead to underutilization of preexisting knowledge, a *schema instantiation* problem (failure to accommodate one's schema to specific text information) or a *schema refinement* problem (failure to switch schemata when the text demands it) would lead to overutilization (Spiro, 1980). Readers with schema instantiation or refinement problems could be characterized as too "top-down," because they would fail to incorporate any information that deviated from their selected schema. Again, there is no empirical evidence on the relationship between schema flexibility and reading ability. And even if the relationship were demonstrated, the overreliance on knowledge-based processes could again be the result of poor word recognition skills (as in the interactive-compensatory theory of Stanovich and colleagues discussed in the earlier section on context effects in word recognition).

One final kind of knowledge difference that may give rise to general reading ability differences is knowledge about knowledge, the kind of knowledge usually referred to as *metacognition*. Individuals do differ in their ability to assess their own knowledge. For example, children often fail on different problem-solving tasks because they fail to assess their progress on the task; they may fail to plan ahead, monitor the outcomes of their processes, or recognize increases in difficulty level (Brown, 1978). In theory, a similar metacognitive deficit could be responsible for poor ability in reading (Perfetti, 1985). A case can be made for metacognitive abilities contributing to the development of reading skill as children learn strategies for comprehension (Brown, 1980). Whether they account for reading ability differences among older readers and adults remains to be seen. For example, there is some conflicting evidence as to whether good and poor readers differ in their ability to know what is important in a text (Perfetti, 1985; Smiley et al., 1977). It appears that even poor readers can differentiate central content from supportive detail, but may be less sophisticated when it comes to distinguishing more than two levels of importance.

In summary, the application of knowledge may be a critical factor in accounting for individual differences in general reading ability. More empirical work is needed to establish the relationship.

CONCLUDING REMARKS

Sir William Osler, the medical educator and philosopher known for his wit and his wisdom, once remarked that "it is easier to buy books than to read them and easier to read them than to absorb them." These insights, made at the turn of the century, capture quite succinctly a number of themes that emerge from the recent flurry of research on reading ability.

Reading consists of a collection of processes, ranging from the lower-level processes that recognize the printed words and encode contextually appropriate meanings for them to the higher-level processes that assemble and integrate the underlying propositions and relate them to previously acquired knowledge. Not only are deeper levels of understanding less easy to achieve, but readers differ in the ease with which they can achieve them. One general conclusion that emerges from the literature is that word recognition ability alone cannot account for why some readers are better than others; the processes involved in comprehending and "absorbing" the text meaning are important determinants of reading success, too.

Although such a conclusion may seem obvious now, it has not always been widely endorsed. Indeed, there have been researchers who have tried to keep comprehension outside the scope of general reading research on the grounds that the psychology of reading has no particular claim on comprehension because the mechanisms underlying reading comprehension are identical to those underlying oral language comprehension (e.g., Crowder, 1982). And even if reading is defined to include comprehension as well as written-word identification, there have been researchers who have tried to keep comprehension differences out of their explanations of individual differences in reading ability (Carr, 1981). By differentiating between *reading* books and *absorbing* them, Osler reminds us that comprehension is the single most important goal of reading. Any complete theory of reading ability will have to account for individual differences both in terms of the ability to recognize words from print, and the ability to comprehend and absorb the underlying message. It is unlikely that all the variance in performance on a task as complex as reading can be accounted for by differences in the lower-level processes alone.

Whereas there is now considerable agreement that both word recognition processes and higher-level comprehension processes contribute to individual differences in reading achievement, there is probably less consensus concerning their relative contributions. More than likely the answer depends on the age level of the readers being considered, with word identification skills carrying less weight as reading experience and reading performance increase (Jackson & McClelland, 1979; Palmer et al., 1985). Clearly though, there is a need for more multivariate studies that determine the relative amounts of variance in reading ability uniquely associated with each of the component processes discussed in this chapter.

Also needed are studies that establish the causal links between the various cognitive components and reading ability. An obvious limitation of most individual-differences research is that it is inherently correlational by virtue of the fact that many interesting individual-differences parameters (e.g., working memory capacity) cannot be manipulated readily in the laboratory. We have seen several examples in this chapter of the dangers of deciding which side of the correlational equation is cause and which result. The most dramatic example of this concerned the well-established correlation between eye-movement patterns and reading ability. Whereas erratic eye movements were once taken to be the cause of reading problems, they are now widely believed to be the result of the reading comprehension problems. If it is at all possible to manipulate a candidate individual-differences parameter through training studies, this should be encouraged. Otherwise, more use should be made of statistical techniques that allow researchers to make inferences about causality (cf. Kenny, 1979).

Although the recent trend has generally been in the direction of replacing single-component theories of reading ability differences with multiple-component theories (Carr, 1981), there are, paradoxically, some signs of the opposite trend too. As more and more component skills have been shown to correlate with overall reading comprehension achievement, so there have been efforts to find a common underlying mechanism to account for these differences. The working memory and knowledge approaches are examples of this trend. There is even a recent study that proposes working memory to be the mechanism mediating the positive effect that background knowledge has upon the comprehension and recall of prose (Fincher-Kiefer, Post, Greene, & Voss, 1988). While the construct of working memory may prove very useful in the construction of theories for why individuals differ in their ability to perform complex cognitive tasks such as reading, there is the danger of its becoming a "vacuous catch-all concept" (Baddeley, 1981, p. 18) if it is used indiscriminately as a label for all performance differences.

Although this chapter has been cast from the perspective of accounting for individual differences in reading skill, the research discussed has relevance for constructing and testing our nomothetic or general theories of reading too. Indeed, one of the most fruitful approaches to developing a general theory of reading is to capitalize on the fact that individuals are likely to differ on most important cognitive dimensions and processes, and use any systematic sources of individual differences we discover as clues to what component structures and processes should be built into our general theories of reading. Similarly, even if our interest is in modeling general or mean reading performance, many of the processes we postulate imply the existence of certain patterns of individual differences, and so their validity can be tested within an individual-differences framework. Of course, for individual differences to be central to the construction of a general theory of reading, the individual-differences variables cannot simply be age, grade, sex, and social status; rather, the variables must be the kinds of cognitive processes and structures considered in this chapter.

REFERENCES

Anderson, R. C., Reynolds, R. E., Schallert, D. L., & Goetz, E. T. (1977). Frameworks for comprehending discourse. *American Educational Research Journal, 14*, 367–381.

Anderson R. C., Spiro, R. J., & Anderson, M. C. (1978). Schemata as scaffolding for the representation of information in discourse. *American Educational Research Journal, 15*, 433–440.

Baddeley, A. D. (1966). Short-term memory for word sequences as a function of acoustic, semantic, and formal similarity. *Quarterly Journal of Experimental Psychology, 18*, 362–365.

Baddeley, A. D. (1981). The concept of working memory: A view of its current state and probable future development. *Cognition, 10*, 17–23.

Baddeley, A. D., & Hitch, G. J. (1974). Working memory. In G. A. Bower (Ed.), *The psychology of learning and motivation*, (Vol. 8, pp. 47–89). New York: Academic Press.

Baddeley, A. D., Logie, R., Nimmo-Smith, I., & Brereton, N. (1985). Components of fluent reading. *Journal of Memory and Language, 24*, 119–131.

Baker, L. (1985). Working memory and comprehension: A replication. *Bulletin of the Psychonomic Society, 23*, 28–30.

Bartlett, F. C. (1932). *Remembering.* Cambridge, Eng.: Cambridge University Press.

Beck, I. L., McKeown, M. G., & Omanson, R. C. (1984). The fertility of some types of vocabulary instruction. In R. Glaser (Chair), *What is the role of instruction in learning and using vocabulary?* Symposium conducted at the meeting of the American Educational Research Association, New Orleans, LA.

Beck, I. L., Perfetti, C. A., & McKeown, M. G. (1982). The effects of long-term vocabulary instruction on lexical access and reading comprehension. *Journal of Educational Psychology, 74*, 506–521.

Biemiller, A. (1970). The development of the use of graphic and contextual information as children learn to read. *Reading Research Quarterly, 6*, 75–96.

Bloom, B. S. (1976). *Human characteristics and school learning.* New York: McGraw-Hill.

Bouma, H. (1973). Visual interference in the parafoveal recognition of initial and final letters of words. *Vision Research, 13*, 767–782.

Bouma, H., & Legein, C. P. (1977). Foveal and parafoveal recognition of letters and words by dyslexics and by average readers. *Neuropsychologia, 15*, 69–80.

Briggs, P., & Underwood, G. (1982). Phonological coding in good and poor readers. *Journal of Experimental Child Psychology, 34*, 93–112.

Brown, A. L. (1978). Knowing when, where, and how to remember: A problem of metacognition. In R. Glaser (Ed.), *Advances in instructional psychology* (pp. 77–165). Hillsdale, NJ: Erlbaum.

Brown, A. L. (1980). Metacognitive development and reading. In R. J. Spiro, B. C. Bruce, & W. F. Brewer (Eds.), *Theoretical issues in reading comprehension* (pp. 453–481). Hillsdale, NJ: Erlbaum.

Brown, B., Haegerstrom-Portnoy, G., Adams, A., Yingling, C., Galin, D., Herron, J., & Marcus, M. (1983). Predictive eye movements do not discriminate between dyslexic and control children. *Neuropsychologia, 21*, 121–128.

Buswell, G. T. (1937). *How adults read.* Chicago: University of Chicago Press.

Byrne, B., & Shea, P. (1979). Semantic and phonetic memory codes in beginning readers. *Memory & Cognition. 7*, 333–338.

Carpenter, P. A., & Daneman, M. (1981). Lexical retrieval and error recovery in reading: A model based on eye fixations. *Journal of Verbal Learning and Verbal Behavior. 20*, 137–160.

Carr, T. H. (1981). Building theories of reading ability: On the relation between individual differences in cognitive skills and reading comprehension. *Cognition, 9*, 73–114.

Chabot, R. J., Zehr, H. D., Prinzo, O. V., & Petros, T. V. (1984). The speed of word recognition subprocesses and reading achievement in college students. *Reading Research Quarterly, 19*, 147–161.

Chafe, W. L. (1972). Discourse structure and human knowledge. In R. O. Freedle & J. B. Carroll (Eds.), *Language comprehension and the acquisition of knowledge* (pp. 41–69). Washington, DC: Winston.

Chall, J. (1983). *Stages of reading development.* New York: McGraw-Hill.

Chiesi, H. L., Spilich, G. J., & Voss, J. F. (1979). Acquisition of domain-related information in relation to high- and low-domain knowledge. *Journal of Verbal Learning and Verbal Behavior, 18*, 257–274.

Coltheart, M., Davelaar, E., Jonasson, J. T., & Besner, D. (1977). Access to the internal lexicon. In S. Dornic (Ed.), *Attention and performance* (Vol. 6, pp. 535–555). New York: Academic Press.

Conrad, R. (1964). Acoustic confusions in immediate memory. *British Journal of Psychology, 55*, 75–84.

Crowder, R. G. (1982). *The psychology of reading.* New York: Oxford University Press.

Curtis, M. (1980). Development of components of reading skill. *Journal of Educational Psychology, 72*, 656–669.

Daneman, M. (1984). Why some readers are better than others: A process and storage account. In R. J. Sternberg (Ed.), *Advances in the theory of intelligence* (Vol. 2, pp. 367–384). Hillsdale, NJ: Erlbaum.

Daneman, M. (1988). Word knowledge and reading skill. In M. Daneman, G. E. MacKinnon, & T. G. Waller (Eds.), *Reading research: Advances in theory and practice* (Vol. 6, pp. 145–175). New York: Academic Press.

Daneman, M., & Carpenter, P. A. (1980). Individual differences in working memory and reading. *Journal of Verbal Learning and Verbal Behavior, 19*, 450–466.

Daneman, M., & Carpenter, P. A. (1983). Individual differences in integrating information between and within sentences. *Journal of Experimental Psychology: Learning, Memory, and Cognition, 9*, 561–583.

Daneman, M., & Green, I. (1986). Individual differences in comprehending and producing words in context. *Journal of Memory and Language, 25*, 1–18.

Davis, F. B. (1968). Research in comprehension in reading. *Reading Research Quarterly, 3*, 499–545.

Denbuurman, R., Boersema, T., & Gerrisen, J. F. (1981). Eye movements and the perceptual span in reading. *Reading Research Quarterly, 16*, 227–235.

Ellis, N. C., & Miles, T. R. (1978). Visual information processing in dyslexic children. In M. M. Gruneberg, P. E. Morris, & R. N. Sykes (Eds.), *Practical aspects of memory* (pp. 561–569). London: Academic Press.

Fincher-Kiefer, R., Post, T. A., Greene, T. R., & Voss, J. F. (1988). On the role of prior knowledge and task demands in the processing of text. *Journal of Memory and Language, 27*, 416–428.

Firth, I. (1972). *Components of reading disability.* Unpublished doctoral dissertation, University of New South Wales, Australia.

Fischer, F., Liberman, I., & Shankweiler, D. (1978). Reading reversals and developmental dyslexia: A further study. *Cortex, 14*, 496–510.

Fleisher, L. S., Jenkins, J. R. & Pany, D. (1979). Effects on poor readers' comprehension of training in rapid decoding. *Reading Research Quarterly, 15*, 30–48.

Frazier, L., & Rayner, K. (1982). Making and correcting errors during sentence comprehension: Eye movements in the analysis of structurally ambiguous sentences. *Cognitive Psychology, 14*, 178–210.

Frederiksen, J. (1978). Assessment of perceptual, decoding, and lexical skills and their relation to reading proficiency. *Technical Report No. 1.* Cambridge, MA: Bolt, Beranek, & Newman.

Frederiksen, J. R. (1982). A componential theory of reading skills and their interactions. In R. J. Sternberg (Ed.), *Advances in the psychology of human intelligence* (Vol. 1, pp. 125–180). Hillsdale, NJ: Erlbaum.

Garner, R. (1980). Monitoring of understanding: An investigation of good and poor readers' awareness of induced miscomprehension of text. *Journal of Reading Behavior, 12*, 55–64.

Gibson, E. J. (1965). Learning to read. *Science, 148*, 1066–1072.

Glanzer, M., Fischer, B., & Dorfman, P. (1984). Short-term storage in reading. *Journal of Verbal Learning and Verbal Behavior, 23*, 467–486.

Goodman, K. (1965). A linguistic study of cues and miscues in reading. *Elementary English, 42*, 639–643.

Goodman, K. (1976). Reading: A psycholinguistic guessing game. In H. Singer, & R. Ruddell (Eds.), *Theoretical models and processes of reading* (pp. 497–508). Newark, DE: International Reading Association.

Gough, P. (1972). One second of reading. In J. K. Kavanaugh & I.G. Mattingly (Eds.), *Language by ear and by eye* (pp. 331–358). Cambridge, MA: MIT Press.

Gough, P. B., & Hillinger, M. (1980). Learning to read: An unnatural act. *Bulletin of the Orton Society, 30*, 171–196.

Groff, P. (1978). Should children learn to read words? *Reading World, 17*, 256–264.

Guthrie, J., & Tyler, S. (1976). Psycholinguistic processing in reading and listening among good and poor readers. *Journal of Reading Behavior, 8*, 415–426.

Hall, J., Wilson, K., Humphreys, M., Tinzmann, M., & Bowyer, P. (1983). Phonemic-similarity effects in good vs. poor readers. *Memory & Cognition, 11*, 520–527.

Hayes-Roth, B., & Hayes-Roth, F. (1977). The prominence of lexical information in memory representations of meaning. *Journal of Verbal Learning and Verbal Behavior, 16*, 119–136.

Henderson, L. (1982). *Orthography and word recognition in reading.* New York: Academic Press.

Hogaboam, T., & Perfetti, C. A. (1978). Reading skill and the role of verbal experience in decoding. *Journal of Verbal Learning and Verbal Behavior, 70*, 717–729.

Hunt, E. B. (1980). Intelligence as an information-processing concept. *British Journal of Psychology, 71*, 449–474.

Hunt, E. B., Lunneborg, C., & Lewis, J. (1975). What does it mean to be high verbal? *Cognitive Psychology, 2*, 194–227.

Ikeda, M., & Saida, S. (1978). Span of recognition in reading. *Vision Research, 18*, 83–88.

Jackson, M. D., & McClelland, J. L. (1975). Sensory and cognitive determinants of reading speed. *Journal of Verbal Learning and Verbal Behavior, 14*, 565-574.

Jackson, M. D., & McClelland, J. L. (1979). Processing determinants of reading speed. *Journal of Experimental Psychology: General, 108*, 151–181.

Jarvella, R. J. (1971). Syntactic processing of connected speech. *Journal of Verbal Learning and Verbal Behavior, 10*, 409–416.

Jenkins, J. R., Pany, D., & Schreck, J. (1978). Vocabulary and reading comprehension: Instructional effects. *Tech. Rep. No. 100.* Urbana-Champaign, IL: Center for the Study of Reading.

Johnston, R. (1982). Phonological coding in dyslexic readers, *British Journal of Psychology, 73*, 455–460.

Jorm, A. F. (1981). Children with reading and spelling retardation: Functioning of whole-word and correspondence-rule mechanisms. *Journal of Child Psychology and Psychiatry, 22*, 171–178.

Jorm, A. F., & Share, D. L. (1983). Phonological recoding and reading acquisition. *Applied Psycholinguistics*, 4, 103–147.

Just, M. A., & Carpenter, P. A. (1980). A theory of reading: From eye fixations to comprehension. *Psychological Review*, 87, 329–354.

Just, M. A., & Carpenter, P. A. (1987). *The psychology of reading and language comprehension*. Boston: Allyn & Bacon.

Kenny, D. A. (1979). *Correlations and causality*. New York: Wiley.

Kintsch, W. (1974). *The representation of meaning in memory*. Hillsdale, NJ: Erlbaum.

Kintsch, W., & van Dijk, T. A. (1978). Toward a model of text comprehension and production. *Psychological Review*, 85, 363–394.

LaBerge, D., & Samuels, S. J. (1974). Toward a theory of automatic information processing in reading. *Cognitive Psychology*, 6, 293–323.

Lesgold, A., & Resnick, L. (1982). How reading difficulties develop: Perspectives from a longitudinal study. In J. Das, R. Mulcahey, & A. Wall (Eds.), *Theory and research in learning disabilities* (pp. 155–187). New York: Plenum.

Levin, H., & Kaplan, E. L. (1970). Grammatical structure and reading. In H. Levin & J. P. Williams (Eds.), *Basic studies on reading*. New York: Basic Books.

Liberman I. (1982). A language-oriented view of reading and its disabilities. In H. Myklebust (Ed.), *Progress in learning disabilities* (Vol. 5, pp. 81–101). New York: Grune and Stratton.

Liberman, I. Y., Shankweiler, D., Liberman, A. M., Fowler, C., & Fischer, F. W. (1977). Phonetic segmentation and recoding in the beginning reader. In A. S. Reber & D. Scarborough (Eds.), *Toward a psychology of reading: The proceedings of the CUNY conference* (pp. 207–225). Hillsdale, NJ: Erlbaum.

Lorch, R. F., Lorch, E. P., & Morgan, A. M. (1987). Task effects and individual differences in on-line processing of the topic structure of a text. *Discourse Processes*, 10, 63–80.

McConkie, G. W., & Rayner, K. (1975). The span of the effective stimulus during a fixation in reading. *Perception & Psychophysics*, 17, 578–586.

McCusker, L. X., Hillinger, M., & Bias, R. G. (1981). Phonological recoding and reading. *Psychological Bulletin*, 89, 217–245.

Mann, V. A., Liberman, I. Y., & Shankweiler, D. (1980). Children's memory for sentences and word strings in relation to reading ability. *Memory & Cognition*, 8, 329–335.

Marcel, T. (1974). The effective visual field and the use of context in fast and slow readers of two ages. *British Journal of Psychology*, 65, 479–492.

Mark, L. S., Shankweiler, D., Liberman, I. Y., & Fowler, C. A. (1977). Phonetic recoding and reading difficulty in beginning readers. *Memory & Cognition*, 5, 623–629.

Massaro, W. (1975). *Understanding language: An information-processing analysis of speech perception, reading, and psycholinguistics*. New York: Academic Press.

Masson, M., & Miller, J. A. (1983). Working memory and individual differences in comprehension and memory of text. *Journal of Educational Psychology*, 75, 314–318.

Miller, G. A. (1972). English verbs of motion: A case study in semantics and lexical memory. In A. W. Melton & E. Martin (Eds.), *Coding processes in human memory*, (pp. 335–372). New York: Wiley.

Nodine, C. F., & Lang, N. J. (1971). The development of visual scanning strategies for differentiating words. *Developmental Psychology*, 5, 221–232.

Nodine, C. F., & Simmons, F. G. (1974). Processing distinctive features in the differentiation of letterlike symbols. *Journal of Experimental Psychology*, 103, 21–28.

Oakhill, J. (1982). Constructive processes in skilled and less-skilled comprehenders' memory for sentences. *British Journal of Psychology*, 73, 13–20.

Oakhill, J., & Yuill, N. (1986). Pronoun resolution in skilled and less-skilled comprehenders: Effects of memory load and inferential complexity. *Language and Speech*, 29, 25–37.

Olson, R., Kliegl, R., & Davidson, B. (1983). Dyslexic and normal readers' eye movements. *Journal of Experimental Psychology: Human Perception and Performance*, 9, 816–825.

Orton, S. T. (1925). "Word-blindness" in school children. *Archives of Neurology and Psychiatry*, 14, 581–615.

Owens, J., Bower, G. H., & Black, J. B. (1979). The "soap opera" effect in story recall. *Memory & Cognition*, 7, 185–191.

Palincsar, A. S., & Brown, A. L. (1984). Reciprocal teaching of comprehension-fostering and comprehension-monitoring activities. *Cognition and Instruction*, 1, 117–175.

Palmer, J., MacCleod, C. M., Hunt, E., & Davidson, J. E. (1985). Information-processing correlates of reading. *Journal of Memory and Language*, 24, 59–88.

Patterson, K., & Coltheart, V. (1987). Phonological processes in reading: A tutorial review. In M. Coltheart (Ed.), *Attention and performance: The psychology of reading*. (Vol. 12, pp. 421–447). Hillsdale, NJ: Erlbaum.

Pavlidis, G. (1981). Sequencing, eye movements, and the early objective diagnosis of dyslexia. In G. Pavlidis & T. Miles (Eds.), *Dyslexia research and its applications to education*. Chichester: Wiley.

Perfetti, C. A. (1976). Language comprehension and the deverbalization of intelligence. In L. B. Resnick (Ed.), *The nature of intelligence* (pp. 283–292). Hillsdale, NJ: Erlbaum.

Perfetti, C. A. (1983). Individual differences in verbal processes. In R. Dillon & R. R. Schmeck (Eds.)., *Individual differences in cognition* (pp. 65–104). New York: Academic Press.

Perfetti, C. A. (1985). *Reading ability.* New York: Oxford University Press.

Perfetti, C. A. (1988). Verbal efficiency in reading ability. In M. Daneman, G. E. MacKinnon, & T. G. Waller (Eds.), *Reading research: Advances in theory and practice* (Vol 6, pp. 109–143). New York: Academic Press.

Perfetti, C. A., Finger, E., & Hogaboam, T. (1978). Sources of vocalization latency differences between skilled and less-skilled young readers. *Journal of Educational Psychology, 70,* 730–739.

Perfetti, C. A., Goldman, S., & Hogaboam, T. (1979). Reading skill and the identification of words in discourse context. *Memory & Cognition, 7,* 273–282.

Perfetti, C. A. & Hogaboam, T. (1975). The relationship between single-word decoding and reading comprehension skill. *Journal of Educational Psychology, 67,* 461–469.

Perfetti, C. A., & Lesgold, A. M. (1977). Discourse comprehension and sources of individual differences. In M. A. Just & P. A. Carpenter (Eds.), *Cognitive processes in comprehension* (pp. 141–183). Hillsdale, NJ: Erlbaum.

Perfetti, C. A., & McCutchen, D. (1982). Speech processes in reading. In N. Lass (Ed.), *Speech and language: Advances in basic research and practice* (Vol. 7, pp. 237–269). New York: Academic Press.

Perfetti, C. A. & Roth, S. (1981). Some of the interactive processes in reading and their role in reading skill. In A. M. Lesgold & C. A. Perfetti (Eds.), *Interactive processes in reading* (pp. 269–297). Hillsdale, NJ: Erlbaum.

Posner, M. I., Boies, S., Eichelman, W., & Taylor, R. (1969). Retention of visual and name codes of single letters. *Journal of Experimental Psychology Monographs, 79* (1, Part 2).

Rayner, K., (1975). The perceptual span and peripheral cues in reading. *Cognitive Psychology, 7,* 65–81.

Rayner, K., & Duffy, S. A. (1988). On-line comprehension processes and eye movements during reading. In M. Daneman, G. E. MacKinnon, and T. G. Waller (Eds.), *Reading research: Advances in theory and practice* (Vol. 6, pp. 13–56). New York: Academic Press.

Rayner, K., & Pollatsek, A. (1987). Eye movements in reading: A tutorial review. In M. Coltheart (Ed.), *Attention and performance: The psychology of reading* (Vol. 12, pp. 327–362). Hillsdale, NJ: Erlbaum.

Rumelhart, D. E., & McClelland, J. L. (1982). An interactive activation model of context in letter perception (Part 2): The contextual enhancement effect and some tests and extensions of the model. *Psychological Review, 89,* 60–94.

Rumelhart, D. E., & Ortony, A. (1977). The representation of knowledge in memory. In R. C. Anderson, R. J. Spiro, & W. E. Montague (Eds.), *Schooling and the acquisition of knowledge* (pp. 99–136). Hillsdale, NJ: Erlbaum.

Sachs, J. S. (1967). Recognition memory for syntactic and semantic aspects of connected discourse. *Perception & Psychophysics 2,* 437–442.

Samuels, S. J., Dahl, P., & Archwamety, T. (1974). Effect of hypothesis/test training on reading skill. *Journal of Educational Psychology, 66,* 835–844.

Samuels, S. J., LaBerge, D., & Bremer, C. D. (1978). Units of word recognition: Evidence for developmental changes. *Journal of Verbal Learning and Verbal Behavior, 17,* 715–720.

Schank, R. C. (1972). Conceptual dependency: A theory of natural language understanding. *Cognitive Psychology, 3,* 552–631.

Seymour, P. H., & Porpodas, C. D. (1980). Lexical and nonlexical processing of spelling in dyslexia. In U. Frith (Ed.), *Cognitive processes in spelling* (pp. 443–473). London: Academic Press.

Smiley, S. S., Oakley, D. D., Warthen, D., Campione, J. C., & Brown, A. L. (1977). Recall of thematically relevant material by adolescent good and poor readers as a function of written and oral presentation. *Journal of Educational Psychology, 69,* 881–887.

Smith, F. (1971). *Understanding reading.* New York: Holt, Rinehart & Winston.

Snowling, M. (1980). The development of grapheme-phoneme correspondence in normal and dyslexic readers. *Journal of Experimental Child Psychology, 29,* 294–305.

Sperling, G. (1960). The information available in brief visual presentation. *Psychological Monographs, 43,* 93–120.

Spilich, G. J., Vesonder, G. T., Chiesi, H. L., & Voss, J. F. (1979). Text processing of domain-related information for individuals with high- and low-domain knowledge. *Journal of Verbal Learning and Verbal Behavior, 18,* 275–290.

Spiro, R. J. (1980). Constructive processes in prose comprehension and recall. In R. J. Spiro, B. C. Bruce, & W. F. Brewer (Eds.), *Theoretical issues in reading comprehension* (pp. 245–278). Hillsdale, NJ: Erlbaum.

Stanley, G. (1978). Eye movements in dyslexic children. In G. Stanley & K. W., Walsh (Eds.), *Brain impairment: Proceedings of the 1977 Brain Impairment Workshop,* Victoria, BC: Dominion Press.

Stanley, G., Smith, G., & Howell, E. (1983). Eye movements and sequential tracking in dyslexic and control children. *British Journal of Psychology, 74,* 181–187.

Stanovich, K. E. (1980). Toward an interactive-compensatory model of individual differences in the development of reading fluency. *Reading Research Quarterly, 16,* 32–71.

Stanovich, K. E. (1986). Explaining the variance in reading ability in terms of psychological processes: What have we learned? *Annals of Dyslexia*, *67*, 67–96.

Stanovich, K. E., Cunningham, A., & Feeman, D. J. (1984). Intelligence, cognitive skills, and early reading progress. *Reading Research Quarterly*, *19*, 278–303.

Stanovich, K. E., & West, R. F. (1981). The effect of sentence context on ongoing word recognition: Tests of a two-process theory. *Journal of Experimental Psychology: Human Perception and Performance*, *7*, 658–672.

Stanovich, K. E., West, R. F., & Feeman, D. J. (1981). A longitudinal study of sentence context effects in second-grade children: Tests of an interactive-compensatory model. *Journal of Experimental Child Psychology*, *32*, 185–199.

Sternberg, R. J., & Powell, J. S. (1983). Comprehending verbal comprehension. *American Psychologist*, *38*, 878–893.

Sticht, T. G., & James, J. H. (1984). Listening and reading. In P. D. Pearson, R. Barr, M. L. Kamil, & P. Mosenthal (Eds.), *Handbook of reading research* (Vol 1, pp. 293–317). White Plains, NY: Longman.

Thibadeau, R., Just, M. A., & Carpenter, P. A. (1982). A model of the time course and content of reading. *Cognitive Science*, *6*, 157–203.

Thorndike, R. L. (1973). *Reading comprehension education in fifteen countries*. New York: Wiley.

Tinker, M. A. (1958). Recent studies of eye movements in reading. *Psychological Bulletin*, *55*, 215–231.

Tuinman, J. J., & Brady, M. E. (1974). How does vocabulary account for variance on reading comprehension tests? A preliminary instructional analysis. In P. L. Nacke (Ed.), *Interaction: Research and practice for college-adult reading. Twenty-third yearbook of the National Reading Conference*. Clemson, SC: National Reading Conference.

Underwood, N. R., & Zola, D. (1986). The span of letter recognition of good and poor readers. *Reading Research Quarterly*, *22*, 6–19.

Van Orden, G. C. (1987). A ROWS is a ROSE: Spelling, sound, and reading. *Memory & Cognition 15*, 181–198.

Vellutino, F. R. (1979). *Dyslexia: Theory and research*. Cambridge, MA: MIT Press.

Voss, J. F., Fincher-Kiefer, R. H., Greene, T. R., & Post, T. A. (1985). Individual differences in performance: The contrast approach to knowledge. In R. J. Sternberg (Ed.), *Advances in the psychology of human intelligence* (Vol 3, pp. 297–334). Hillsdale, NJ: Erlbaum.

Werner, H., & Kaplan, E. (1952). The acquisition of word meanings: A developmental study. *Monographs of the Society for Research in Child Development*, *15*, 190–200.

West, R. F., & Stanovich, K. E. (1978). Automatic contextual facilitation in readers of three ages. *Child Development*, *49*, 717–727.

Zola, D. (1984). Redundancy and word perception during reading. *Perception & Psychophysics*, *36*, 277–284.

20 PERSPECTIVES ON READING DISABILITY RESEARCH

Karen K. Wixson
and Marjorie Youmans Lipson

D espite many years of research on reading disability, there is still no unified understanding of its causes and/or treatments. One reason for this is the diversity of research on reading disability that results from the variety of perspectives from which investigations have been conducted. For example, physicians study brain-behavior relations, psychologists study cognitive processes, sociolinguists study the culture of educational systems, and educators study methods of assessment and instruction. The variety of perspectives from which research on reading disability has been conducted accounts, in large part, for the diversity of findings and the lack of agreement regarding the basic issues in the area of reading disability.

This review is organized around the various major perspectives that have been used to guide research in the area of reading disability since the turn of the century. Definitional and historical influences are examined in the background segment of the chapter, which reviews research associated with long-standing medical and psycho-educational perspectives on reading disability. Next, the research contributions of current information-processing and social perspectives are discussed. Finally, an emerging interactive perspective is introduced, suggesting a research agenda for the future. Examination of the research on disability in this way demonstrates how research has been shaped by the perspective from which it is conducted. In the conclusion to this review, it is argued that continued progress in understanding reading disability can occur only if future research evolves from a more unified perspective.

BACKGROUND

This section is primarily a review of the influences of two early views on reading disability: medical and psychoeducational perspectives. The discussion is not, however, exclusively historical since research within these perspectives is still ongoing today. In addition, it is necessary in this section to provide background regarding definitional issues, the development of research paradigms, and the emergence of assumptions about reading disability that have profoundly influenced current research in the area.

Medical Perspectives

The earliest studies of reading disability were reported by professionals in the field of medicine (e.g., Morgan, 1896; Hinshelwood, 1917). In 1896, Morgan published one of the first accounts of an individual who had failed to learn to read. About the same time,

Hinshelwood (1917) initiated a series of clinical studies that examined the role of the brain in dyslexia and culminated in the publication of his book *Congenital Word-Blindness.*

These clinical case studies gave rise to a view of reading disability that is still in existence today and is commonly referred to as the *medical model.* The medical model encompasses many perspectives on the origins of reading disability, including those that emphasize developmental lag, brain damage, minimal brain dysfunction, hemispheric imbalance, and pathological brain-behavior relations. What all of these perspectives have in common is the assumption of neurological involvement in reading disability. In the case of the early clinical studies, for example, the assumption was that the condition of severe reading failure was related to visual-perceptual problems of neurological origin. What is less clear, however, are the theories or conceptualizations of reading that underlie neurologically oriented research on reading disability.

Before discussing the research that emanates from these early efforts, it is important to clarify the concept of dyslexia because of the prominent role it plays in a medical view of reading disability. For many years, investigators have offered various definitions of dyslexia, each viewing it from their own perspective and each suggesting different etiologies. The resulting confusion has led many to define dyslexia in an exclusionary manner. Perhaps the best-known exclusionary definition is the one provided in the U.S. Education for All Handicapped Children Act, or Public Law 94–142. Learning disabilities, which specifically include dyslexia as a typology, is defined as

> a disorder in one or more of the basic psychological processes involved in understanding or in using language, spoken or written, which may manifest itself in the imperfect ability to listen, think, read, write, spell, or do mathematical calculations. . . . The term does not include children who have learning problems which are primarily the result of visual, hearing, or motor handicaps, of mental retardation, emotional disturbance, or environmental, cultural, or economic disadvantage (*Federal Register*, 42, 1977, p. 65083).

Although this definition represents the first official recognition of dyslexia as a diagnosable condition requiring special educational placement, many are dissatisfied with its imprecise nature. This dissatisfaction led to the formation of the National Joint Committee for Learning Disabilities, which comprises of various professional organizations concerned with the education of individuals with learning disabilities.

The definition proposed by the National Joint Committee states that learning disabilities (of which dyslexia is a part) are intrinsic to the individual and presumed to be due to central nervous system dysfunction, the evidence for which may or may not be elicited in the course of a neurological examination (Hammill, Leigh, McNutt, & Larsen, 1981). A similar move away from exclusionary definitions is evident in the International Reading Association's *Dictionary of Reading and Related Terms*, which states that "dyslexia is a rare but definable and diagnosable form of primary reading retardation with some form of central nervous system dysfunction" (Harris & Hodges, 1981, p. 95). Consistent with this trend, dyslexia is used in this discussion to refer to conceptualizations of reading disability that assume neurological involvement. However, not all the research conducted within the medical model assumes a dyslexia definition of reading disability.

The early case studies provided the foundation for the study of reading disability and this methodology continues to be a productive approach to medical research in this area today. For example, autopsy studies by Galaburda and colleagues have revealed abnormalities in the regions of the brain known to be important for reading in reading-disabled individuals (e.g., Galaburda & Eidelberg, 1982; Galaburda & Kemper, 1979). According to Hynd and Hynd (1984), the results of this type of research suggest that each individual probably has a unique distribution of neurodevelopmental anomalies contributing to their reading failure, and that this may be the reason that so many varied subtypes have been identified. Indeed, subtype research represents another whole area of inquiry in the field of reading disability that will be discussed more fully in a subsequent section.

Another important line of research conducted from a medical perspective is the body of work known as *laterality studies*. The term "laterality" refers to the specialization and the reciprocal relationship of the left and right hemispheres of the brain for different psychological functions (Leong, 1982). The view that hemispheric imbalance causes dyslexic children to process a reversed image of the word was first popularized by Orton in 1925. Although Orton's work has been viewed with skepticism by some and as outdated by others, he has become recognized by neurologists for his foresight in conceptualizing reading disorder as part of speech and language disability and for his attempts to relate reading disability to the functional organization of the cerebral hemispheres (Downing & Leong, 1982).

Orton's theoretical formulation is both detailed and testable (Benton, 1975). However, it was not subjected to direct, empirical testing until the early 1960s with the advent of the dichotic listening technique in audition, and the visual hemifield technique in vision. Findings in the 1960s regarding the specialization on the left hemisphere for processing written and spoken language and of the right hemisphere for visuospatial stimuli served as the basis for investigations of laterality-reading relations. These studies are characterized by specific hemispheric stimulation with individuals known to have serious reading problems.

In general, the results of these studies have been disappointing (see Benton, 1975; Kinsbourne & Hiscock, 1978). However, Downing and Leong (1982) described several lines of promising research that relate reading strategies and processes to hemispheric functions. For example, research by Bakker and colleagues (Bakker, 1973; Bakker, Teunissen, & Bosch, 1976; Bakker, 1979) suggests that proficient early reading, which relies heavily on perceptual processes, may go with left or right cerebral laterality, and later-stage fluent reading, which depends more on linguistic processes, may go more with left hemisphere laterality. A similar, process-oriented approach has led researchers such as Pirozzolo and Rayner (1977) to consider word recognition as a multistage process involving feature analysis by the right hemisphere and decoding and naming by the left hemisphere. Their research suggests that successful word perception involves a reciprocal contribution from both the right and left hemispheres in varying degrees and for varying individuals at varying stages of reading.

Additional efforts to examine the relationship between specific brain functions and reading activities are evident in the recent work of Duffy, Denckla, Bartels, Sandini, and Kiessling (1980) and Duffy, Denckla, Bartels, & Sandini (1980). These researchers have developed a computerized program to investigate electrical activity and provide "maps" of regional electrical activity in the brain between normal and severely disabled readers during reading activities. Their research suggests that there are differences in the electrical activity of normal and disabled readers during reading and listening in the regions of the brain known to be important in reading that do not occur during "rest."

Developmental studies using cross-sectional and longitudinal designs have also been used to examine reading disability from a neurological perspective. A well-known example of this type of research is the work of Satz and his colleagues, who proposed a functional maturational lag postulate to explain severe reading disability (Satz & van Nostrand, 1973). The essence of this view is that specific reading disability reflects a lag in the maturation of the brain that delays differentially those skills that mature or are of primary importance at different chronological ages.

This *maturational lag hypothesis* predicts that kindergarten children who are delayed developmentally in the perceptual-motor skills that are of primary importance at this stage will eventually fail in acquiring reading proficiency. Although such children will eventually catch up on these earlier developing skills, they will then lag on the cognitive-linguistic skills essential to reading proficiency that have a slower and later development. If the dyslexic child fails to catch up on these cognitive-language skills that develop later when the brain is reaching full maturation, then more permanent delays in language and reading skills are predicted. Therefore, dyslexia is seen as a disorder in central processing, the nature of which varies with the chronological age of the child.

Satz and his colleagues have studied this maturational lag hypothesis for a period of more than 10 years in a series of longitudinal, follow-up, and cross-validation studies (e.g., Satz, Taylor, Friel, & Fletcher, 1978). Analyses indicated that performance in kindergarten on a small number of tests representing perceptual-motor skills, believed crucial to the early phases of reading, accurately predicted reading-group membership in later grades for children at both extreme ends (severe and superior) of the reading distribution. Although Satz remains cautious in his interpretation of the maturational lag postulate, he suggests that the predictive power of psycholinguistic variables may be secondary to the preconceptual sensory-motor and perceptual skills that have been shown to develop earlier between the ages of 5 to 7 (Satz et al., 1978).

Summary

From the earliest to the most recent studies, research conducted from medical or neurological perspectives has provided valuable information regarding the relations between various activities of the brain and reading ability. The importance of this area of research is underscored by the publication of the first NSSE (National Society for the Study of Education) yearbook, *Education and the Brain*, in 1978 (Chall & Mirsky). A major theme of this book is the importance of cerebral mechanisms for cognition and learning and the interpretation of these mechanisms in terms of information-processing strategies for both learning and teaching. Although medically oriented research has not yet advanced to the point where it can provide clear educational applications in reading assessment and instruction, recent advances in neuropsychological measures suggest that these applications may not be too far away.

Meanwhile, it is important to exercise caution in interpreting the findings of this research for educational purposes. The problems associated with research in this area noted by Valtin (1978–1979), include the varying criteria for dyslexia used in sample selection that may alter and/or distort results. She also noted that the failure to base research on a theoretical model of the reading process leads to an emphasis on psycho-physical functions with no demonstrable causal relationship to reading.

Although there is little doubt that neurological dysfunction plays a role in certain cases of reading disability, the percentage of cases accounted for by a medical model appears to be extremely small (Chall, 1983; Downing & Leong, 1982; Hynd & Hynd, 1984). The majority of individuals who have difficulties in reading are not likely to be included in the categories of disability described by this model. The large number of individuals who appear to have reading problems that are not rooted in neurological impairment are the focus of the next section on the psychoeducational perspective.

Psychoeducational Perspectives

A major result of the scientific movement in education around the turn of the century was the development of instruments to be used for educational measurement. As instruments were developed and used for the measurement of reading, it became evident to educators that many students were either failing to learn to read or were performing far below expected levels. The advent of norm-referenced group tests of silent reading (e.g., Thorndike, 1914) and individual tests of oral reading (e.g., Gray, 1915) opened the door to investigations of reading disability. Thus, reading "deficiencies" became the domain of educators and psychologists as well as medical professionals. This resulted in an account of reading disability in which a variety of physical, social, psychological, emotional, linguistic, and educational factors were seen as sources of reading difficulties. What distinguished this *psychoeducational view* from the existing medical models was that neurological impairment was not assumed to be the primary source of the problem. Although neurological factors might be considered as one possible source of difficulty, the emphasis clearly was on nonneurological factors.

The focus of early studies was on the establishment of diagnostic procedures, and the identification of sources of reading difficulties and appropriate procedures for remediation and/or prevention (e.g., Uhl, 1916; Zirbes, 1918). Rather than being grounded in explicit theories of reading, these investigations were based on the assumption of multiple underlying causes suggested by the growing evidence of relationships between reading disability and a multitude of physical, social, psychological, and educational factors.

Arthur Gates was a pioneer in the development of diagnostic-prescriptive techniques whose research in this area culminated in the publication of *The Improvement of Reading* in 1927. This book described procedures developed in studies with over 13,000 students and summarized the diagnoses of 411 "backward" readers. The clear emphasis on psychoeducational factors was evident from the introduction:

> The diagnostic instruments and techniques to be reported in this book were designed to appraise habits, skills, or acquired functions on the one hand and fundamental capacities or machinery on the other. So far as they are to be utilized by the classroom teacher, the former are more useful and important. (p. 8)

Gates's summary of the diagnoses of backward readers was based on a sample of students with IQs of 85 or above who had attended school for at least two years and were retarded in reading age 50 percent or more of the number of years they had attended school. He concluded that the majority of problems resulted from "the failure to acquire essential techniques or as the result of acquiring inappropriate techniques or both" (p. 351). He also noted the almost universal appearance of difficulties in the techniques of analyzing, studying, and perceiving of word forms among the skill deficiencies that characterized the poor readers. Finally, he indicated that all combinations of the mainly organic and the mainly acquired defects were to be expected, but that knowledge of acquired defects was likely to be more important for the purposes of remediation.

A landmark investigation conducted from a psychoeducational perspective was Monroe's 1932 study entitled *Children Who Cannot Read*. This study focused clearly on the "atypical children who do not learn to read so well as would be expected from their other intellectual abilities" and posited that these children "may be regarded as having a special defect" (p. 1). Monroe maintained that learning to read was a complex process that extended over several years and was subject to the influence of methods, attitudes, interests, motivations, distributions of time and effort, and almost all factors that influence learning.

Monroe studied 415 children who had special reading defects and compared them with a control group of 101 children in an average school population. A notable feature of Monroe's study was the development of a *reading index* to determine the extent of each student's reading defect. This concept of underachievement and the reading index have had considerable effect on the identification of children with reading difficulties even to the present day, although not without controversy (cf. Thorndike, 1963).

In addition to determining the extent of reading retardation, extensive analyses of students' oral reading errors were undertaken to determine the nature of their difficulties for the purpose of instructional planning. In summarizing the results of the evaluations, Monroe provided a list of all the visual, auditory, motor, conceptual, methodological, environmental, and emotional factors observed to be associated with reading disability, "although only a few aspects of some of them were quantitatively measured" (p. 105). She concluded this portion of her study with the following findings: no one factor was present in all cases; a number of factors showed statistically significant differences between the reading-defect cases and the controls; each differentiating factor showed an overlap between the groups of reading-defect cases and controls; factors that were not statistically significant in differentiating the groups seemed to be definitely impeding factors in individual cases; it is probable that the reading defects were caused by a constellation of factors rather than one isolated factor (p. 110).

In the second part of Monroe's study, 235 students who received remedial instruction in one of two groups—close supervision or classroom instruction—were compared to 50 others who did not receive remedial instruction. The results indicated that the remedial work was successful in 93 percent of the cases in the intensive group and 52 percent of cases in the classroom group, as judged by a criterion of more than one month's progress for one month's training. Subjects in the control group failed to achieve this criterion for accelerated progress. Monroe concluded that children who have difficulty in learning to read do not usually overcome the difficulty under ordinary school instruction, but are able to make normal and accelerated progress under special methods adapted to their difficulties.

During this same time period, the emphasis in disability research began to change from instruction to causation (e.g., Bennett, 1938). The search for causes led to a series of studies conducted by Gray and his colleagues at the University of Chicago and published by Robinson in 1946. These studies examined 30 cases of reading disability over a five-year period. The students' chronological ages ranged from 6 years 9 months to 15 years 3 months, with reading retardation varying from 9 months to 75 months. A primary purpose of this research was to study the various causal factors contributing to severe cases of reading disability by considering the variety of causes that operate in each case rather than by studying each factor in isolation. An important feature of this research was the operational definition of cause as a factor that is found to be responsible for part or all of the reading deficiency such that, when the factor is eliminated or compensated for, improvement occurs.

Each student was examined by the following specialists: a social worker, a psychiatrist, a pediatrician, a neurologist, three ophthalmologists, a speech-correction specialist, an otolaryngologist, an endocrinologist, a reading specialist, and the investigator, who acted as psychologist and reading technician. The specialists then met to evaluate each separate finding in light of the total picture and to identify possible causes of reading retardation operating in each case, and an intensive remedial program was undertaken for 22 of the 30 cases to secure evidence of the potency of each of these possible causes.

The results of this research indicated that the cases presented different patterns of anomalies, with the 10 students who were most seriously retarded in reading exhibiting a greater number of anomalies (i.e., 39) than the 10 least seriously retarded cases (i.e., 26). The evidence also indicated that certain types of anomalies operated as causes more frequently than others. Social, visual, and emotional difficulties appeared most frequently as causes of reading problems. Inappropriate school methods, neurological difficulties, and speech or functional auditory difficulties appeared less frequently; and endocrine disturbances, general physical difficulties, and insufficient auditory acuity appeared to be least important as causes of deficient reading.

Importantly, it was also determined that certain of the anomalies had no direct relationship to the reading deficiency. In addition, a number of the deficiencies identified by the specialists were not proven to be causes of reading failure after remedial treatment had been given. Foretelling the results of several decades of subsequent research, Robinson concluded that the mere presence of anomalies did not justify the conclusion that they were causes of reading failure.

In addition to the various types of large-scale studies, the psychoeducational perspective is characterized by a host of descriptive research studies on *single-factor causes* of reading disability that examine the relation between able and disabled readers on some specified factor believed to correlate with reading ability. The views underlying these single-factor studies imply that reading and reading disability can be defined in large measure by the factor under investigation. Although a comprehensive review of this literature is beyond the scope of this chapter, the reader should be aware of the massive literature (e.g., see Bond & Tinker, 1967; Harris & Sipay, 1985) that exists on various psychoeducational correlates of reading disability, including visual and auditory defects, intelligence, emotional and personality problems, and environmental and social factors.

Among the most thoroughly researched correlates of reading disability are the factors that fall under the heading of *visual and/or auditory defects*. The earliest studies of visual defects focused on eye-movement behavior during the process of reading (e.g., Judd, 1907; Buswell, 1922), which were followed closely by studies of characteristic eye-movement patterns associated with good and poor reading (e.g., Tinker, 1933). In addition, there were numerous studies of various visual defects associated with reading difficulties including acuity, refractive errors, and binocular coordination (e.g., Betts, 1934; Dearborn & Anderson, 1938; Witty & Kopel, 1936). Early studies of auditory, speech, and language functions focused on factors such as auditory acuity, discrimination memory, speaking vocabulary, and articulatory disorders (e.g., Bennett, 1938; Bond, 1935; Gates & Bond, 1936).

The emphasis of studies on visual and auditory factors gradually changed from specific defects to perceptual processing based on various theories and models of learning and language development. For example, Myklebust (1964) concentrated on a model of normal language development as a means of understanding language disturbances. By expanding normal language development theory to include reading and writing, he linked language disorders and learning disabilities. Myklebust viewed reading as the superimposing of the read word onto a known auditory word. Writing was superimposed on all earlier acquired language functions, and was considered to be the highest level of language attainment (Myklebust, 1965). He suggested that, in normal development, children could not express themselves in writing until they comprehended the written word through reading, and formulated vocabulary and grammar. An impairment at any lower level could disrupt all higher levels of development.

A related example is provided by Kirk's development of the *Illinois Test of Psycholinguistic Ability* (ITPA) (Kirk, McCarthy, & Kirk, 1968), based on Osgood's

(1957) model of communication. Osgood suggested that there were two stages to all behaviors: *decoding*, or interpreting the significance of signals received from the environment; and *encoding*, or expressing intentions through overt acts. The ITPA is a battery of 12 subtests intended to sample reception of information, central processing, and response at rote and meaningful levels. This test has figured prominently in research on reading disability, as evidenced by Newcomer and Hammill's (1975) analysis of 28 studies reporting correlations between ITPA subtests and reading. Although the theoretical validity of the models, tests, and remedial practices related to these and other related views of language and learning have been criticized (cf. Hammill & Larsen, 1974), this body of work did make visible the critical relationship between language and learning disorders in children. Studies in this area were the precursors of the cognitive information-processing research on reading disability discussed in the following section.

Summary

This brief background review suggests that there were at least two related research perspectives on reading disability that could be identified by 1930: the medical view and the psychoeducational view. The research conducted from medical perspectives remains highly visible today and promises to advance our understanding of those individuals for whom neuropsychological dysfunction is clearly implicated in reading disability. These individuals are few, however, and psychoeducational views of reading disability have dominated the reading disability field for the past four decades. During this time, psychoeducational perspectives have taken a number of different forms, including those that emphasize developmental factors and those that stress weaknesses in various subskills. What all of these approaches have in common is the search for causative factors of reading disability within the reader. Thus, educators and researchers have continued to focus on the identification of reader deficits, and little attention has been given to the role of instructional contexts.

CURRENT PERSPECTIVES

As noted in the previous section, early investigations of reading disability were largely atheoretical. Although it is important to acknowledge the rich foundation laid by this earlier work, it is probably fair to say that no real attempts at building models of reading existed much before 1953 (Holmes, 1953; Samuels & Kamil, 1984). However, this situation changed in the late 1960s and early 1970s, when researchers were simultaneously investigating aspects of cognitive development, and conducting more field-based research in classrooms.

In this section, two types of perspectives on reading disability are examined: information-processing perspectives and social perspectives. The theoretical orientation of each is quite different. Information-processing research is driven by theories of reading as a cognitive process, whereas social perspectives generate research from within theories of reading as a social phenomenon.

Information-Processing Perspective

Philip Gough published his seminal (and controversial) work "One Second of Reading" in 1972, proposing a model of reading with a strong information-processing perspective. Other models quickly followed, each focusing on different aspects of the reading process

(LaBerge & Samuels, 1974; Rumelhart, 1977). With the publication of Guthrie's (1973) investigation of the "assembly" versus the "system" models of reading, the information-processing perspective was well established for the study of both reading ability and disability.

An *information-processing model* of learning/reading is characterized by a focus on the psychological processes that underlie cognitive ability (see Shuell, 1986, for an excellent review). Research driven by an information-processing model of reading attempts to describe both how information is processed and what mental representations are formed (Just & Carpenter, 1987). This has involved efforts to identify the skills, abilities, and knowledge structures that are critical for performing complex cognitive tasks—to build a model of cognition. For example, one area of information-processing research, artificial intelligence, has attempted to develop systems that organize and process information in ways that parallel skilled human behavior (Schank, 1975). A program is considered successful, and critical aspects of the information-processing system identified, when the artificial system imitates skilled performance.

Information-processing perspectives on reading disability have provided a rich testing ground for researchers and practitioners in both the medical and psychoeducational communities. As Samuels (1987) has pointed out

> An information-processing perspective uses a computer analog to explain how the human mind works. Assuming that the computer operator is competent, if a computer malfunctions, the problem may be traced either to its hardware or software system. The difficulty the student experiences learning to read may be identified with some physiological factor, which would be similar to a computer hardware problem, or the difficulty may be identified with failure to learn the skills and strategies necessary for reading, which would be similar to a software problem. (p. 18).

Massaro (1984) has made this same distinction, adding that a psychological model may have more applicability than a physiological model for the educational community because "its level of description may be more appropriate for assessment, intervention, and control" (p. 112). Although the discussion that follows is based largely on a software perspective, it is also consistent with Massaro's (1984) view that hardware can constrain certain aspects of processing, even in the "normal" population. For a richer discussion of the neuropsychological aspects of reading, the interested reader should refer to Chapter 21 by Vellutino and Denckla.

Under the rubric of information processing, researchers have examined an enormous array of phenomena (see Roediger, 1980). A thorough examination of this issue is not possible here. However, it is important to understand that the unifying theme for the research from this perspective is the assumption that various cognitive processes underlie successful reading achievement. This focus on a search for underlying processes has profoundly influenced the construct of reading disability. Indeed, information-processing perspectives on *reading* are often so intertwined with perspectives on *reading disability* that the two are difficult to separate. Working from this perspective, researchers typically compare the skills or products of skilled readers with those of less-skilled readers. When differences in some component have been observed, that component is presumed to represent a key processing element.

Fueled by a burgeoning research literature, the information-processing view of reading disabilities has evolved substantially over the past two decades. In the brief review to follow, this development is discussed within the framework of three related, but distinct, views. Information-processing perspectives have evolved from purely cognitive into more metacognitive views. Information-processing perspectives of the 1980s often imply that skilled reading entails the acquisition of both basic information-processing mechanisms *and* mechanisms for controlling and monitoring cognitive activity. The evolution of information-processing accounts of disability permits a distinction here; and thus, the cognitive view and the metacognitive view will be discussed in turn.

Research in the area of information processing has also highlighted the complexity of the reading process. Although early information-processing research on disability was wedded to a search for a single etiology, more recent research has suggested that there may be multiple and interacting paths to poor reading achievement. This has resulted in a melding of cognitive and affective accounts of disability, with motivation increasingly added to the factors under consideration. Thus, a description of research generated from a *motivational view* is also provided.

A Cognitive View

Much of the early information-processing research on reading disability involved a series of unitary trait studies, each proposing a single factor as the cause of disability (Carr, 1981; Harris, 1983). As each component in a model has been identified, studies have been undertaken to demonstrate that poor readers are either deficient or inefficient in that component area. The thrust of this research has been to specify the "cognitive disorders" (Jorm, 1983) that differentiated disabled readers from "normals"— to locate "the psychological underpinnings of reading disability" (Stanovich, 1986). As such, this research represents a continuation of earlier efforts to locate the source of the problem exclusively within the individual.

Over time, many single-factor accounts of disability have emerged. At present, the deficits presumed to underlie reading disability fall into at least six large classes: (1) visual-processing deficits, (2) phonological and semantic recoding deficits, (3) short-term memory deficits, (4) deficits in ability to use context, (5) language deficiencies, and (6) metacognitive deficiencies. Of these, only the sixth account of disability, metacognitive deficiencies, will be discussed in any detail here because, unlike the others, it is not described fully elsewhere in this volume.

Although space does not permit a fuller treatment of single-factor accounts of disability, it is instructive to consider the nature of research conducted in the service of these accounts. Most early investigations of the cognitive aspects of disability involved correlational studies. Correlational research involving single factors has been used to investigate every conceivable aspect of human cognition, some directly linked to reading and some only obliquely related to reading. More recently, researchers have focused on a variation of the correlational design known as *good-poor reader research*. This research paradigm has been used to demonstrate differences between good and poor readers and is clearly based on the assumption that the factors that differentiate these two groups of readers are the causes of poor readers' disability.

Taken as a whole, the research on single-factor correlates has suggested that many different abilities differentiate good and poor readers, but the results have often been equivocal and/or contradictory. Performance often depends on the nature of the task and the extent to which other possible factors have been controlled. For example, it appears that one possible reason for observed differences on memory tasks is that poor readers are less automatic in word recognition and, therefore, use more available memory space simply to accomplish the mechanical aspects of reading (Massaro & Miller, 1983).

Similar equivocal results have been reported for most single-factor accounts, and the adequacy of good-poor reader paradigms has been widely debated (Backman,

Mamen, & Fergusen, 1984); such results have led to disenchantment with disability research. The rash of criticism has been directed at both the methodological and conceptual frameworks used to investigate reading disability, including concerns about subject selection, rigor of reporting, instrumentation, research design, and generalizability (Applebee, 1981; Hallahan & Cruickshank, 1973; Torgesen, 1980). These concerns are not described in any detail; rather, this discussion focuses on the ways in which research from this paradigm has caused difficulties for the construction of a model of disability.

The first major problem has to do with the assumption of causality. As Willson (1986) has noted, this design generally starts by comparing "experts" to others who are not expert. Specific characteristics are assumed to be causally related to success. When differences are observed between the expert and the inexpert, these differences are used as proof that the causal relation exists. Finally, "these salient variables are promoted as efficacious for remedying the deficiencies of the novice" (p. 2). The tendency to assume a causal link from observed group differences has resulted in a number of erroneous conclusions about the nature of disability and the consequent proposal of a number of fallacious instructional suggestions (Stanovich, 1986).

The second major concern has to do with the degree to which good-poor reader research has masked potential variability within the reading-disabled population by averaging performance to make group comparisons (Carr, 1981; Stanovich, 1986). Thus, the *group* might appear to have a specific difficulty even though not all members do. Alternatively, the group may appear to have deficits in many areas, each experienced by only some of the members. Both educators and researchers have recognized that disabled readers probably represent a heterogeneous (versus homogeneous) population. However, current practices bury variation. In addition, such practices have masked possible developmental factors, including the possibility that some components are critical at some developmental points but not at others. The focus on single etiologies without attention to possible heterogeneity within the group has led several researchers to conclude that this line of research is like the six blind men and the elephant, each cause accounting for one part of a complex whole (Carr, 1981; Harris, 1983)

The plethora of linkages uncovered by correlational and good-poor reader studies and the relatively meager implications for instruction has encouraged the trend toward examining and identifying possible multiple syndromes of disability. Subtype research initiated within the medical and psychoeducational perspectives has been recast within an information-processing perspective.

Considerable variability among subtypes has been reported, and it is important to understand that *subtype research* has proceeded within a construct that relies heavily on previous single-factor investigations. For example, early clinical subtype studies tended to emphasize modality preference, adopting the prevailing single-factor explanations (Boder, 1973; Johnson & Myklebust, 1967). These early efforts produced distinguishably different profiles, as evidenced by patterns of behavior on verbal and performance IQ measures. However, other clinical data suggested that conclusions about identifiable and distinct "syndromes" should proceed cautiously. Denckla (1972), for example, reported that only 30 percent of a large clinical sample fell into identifiable subtypes and even these did not always demonstrate cognitive difficulties.

More recently, researchers have applied sophisticated statistical techniques to the identification of subtypes among reading-disabled populations. Using techniques like cluster analysis and Q-factor analysis, researchers have attempted to identify subgroups among learning-disabled subjects. However, like the earlier clinical subtyping efforts, these researchers have generally relied on traditional neuropsychological tests, resulting in clusters along verbal and/or perceptual dimensions (Satz & Morris, 1981).

The work of Doehring and associates is distinctive among studies on subtypes of reading disability, because it clearly does not presume a neurological deficit. Doehring and Hoshko (1977) used the Q technique of factor analysis to analyze the data obtained from 31 tests of "reading-related skills." This battery included four clusters of tasks: (1) visual matching tests (number, letter, syllable, and word); (2) tests that required matching of spoken and written stimuli (letters, syllables, and words); (3) tests of oral reading (letter, syllable, word, and sentence); and (4) visual scanning tests (number, letters, syllables, and words). The result of the Q-factor analysis supported the formation of three subtype groups characterized by the following: "poor oral reading" of syllables, words, and sentences; slow matching of spoken and written letters; and poor matching of spoken and written syllables and words. These results were validated by Doehring, Hoshko, and Bryans (1979), who compared the results of a Q-technique classification system with a cluster analysis. Two of the three groupings were upheld, using either statistical treatment of the data.

This work by Doehring and associates represents a shift in focus that makes the research more instructionally meaningful. For example, the battery of tests is somewhat related to reading. In addition, the subtypes are characterized by performance on a task (e.g., "poor oral reading") and not as cognitive deficits (e.g., "linguistic deficiency"). Thus, an instructional program devised for individuals in this subtype would necessarily include work on reading tasks requiring this skill.

Perhaps the greatest contribution of subtype research is the reconciliation of at least some of the previous single-factor accounts. The representation of different factors as subtypes within a disabled population helps to explain why some studies identified one component as causal, while others identified different causal factors. However, statistical approaches to subtyping yield varying numbers of subtypes that are often unrelated.

Clearly, the measures used to evaluate performance have a profound influence on the subtypes that emerge from the data. In a review and critique of 15 representative subtype studies, Kavale and Forness (1987) noted that the correlation between the names of tests and the names of subtypes is almost perfect ($r = .98$), leading them to conclude that ". . . subtypes are actually defined in terms of the functions being assessed" (p. 376). This is particularly important when one realizes that the vast majority of subtype research has employed traditional neuropsychological, but not reading, measures.

There is some evidence to suggest that when reading measures are a strong component of the statistical subtyping, there is much more heterogeneity within each subtype (Watson, Goldgar, & Rychon, 1983). Relying on performance tasks more closely related to reading certainly could inform understanding of reading disability. For example, Carr (1981, 1985) used profiles of readers' performances on a battery of component skill measures. Carr and his colleagues identified three distinct subgroups of readers: balanced readers, active comprehenders, and phonological recoders. The three types of reader showed distinctly different patterns of strength, and the correlations between their component strengths and other measures of reader-related competence are also distinct. From the data it was possible to infer the conditions under which they were likely to be successful and the conditions under which they were likely to fail. Although the authors acknowledge the limitations of their data, continued explorations of such within-group differences may suggest appropriately differentiated interventions for different subgroups of readers and the degree to which subgroup differences may be attributable to different types of initial instruction (cf. Olson, Kliegl, Davidson, & Foltz, 1985).

Subtype research efforts are likely to continue because they hold some promise of pointing toward differential instructional interventions. Indeed, McKinney and his colleagues propose a research agenda to validate subtype classifications by examining subtype by treatment interactions (McKinney & Speece, 1986). The utility of subtype research will depend in large measure on the development of theoretically sound measures of reading. As McKinney and Speece (1986) have noted:

> Although recent research has demonstrated the feasibility of subdividing [learning-disabled] LD samples into more homogeneous subtypes. . . . [T]he problem still remains to demonstrate the developmental and academic consequences associated with subtype membership. . . . [E]mpirical classification techniques such as Q-factor analysis and cluster analysis merely group individuals who show a similar pattern of response on a given set of variables; *they do not ensure that the clusters are psychologically and educationally meaningful or that they predict different developmental and academic outcomes* [italics added]. (p. 366)

Finally, all of the subtype studies report at least some children who do not fit into any of the classified subgroups. In their evaluation of the subtype research, Kavale and Forness (1987) estimated that an average of 30 percent of all subjects across studies did not fit into any deficit subtype. Among subjects who do not fit into any subtype, other factors must be considered. Instructional, motivational, environmental, and constitutional factors are conspicuously absent from all subtyping efforts.

A Metacognitive View

Over the past two decades, research within a cognitive view of ability-disability has led to a related, but somewhat different, vision of the etiology of reading disability. Whereas cognitive views posit a lack of ability in one or more component areas of cognitive processing, a *metacognitive view* posits a lack of strategy *use*, the so-called *production deficiency* (Brown, 1974).

> The central idea in the conceptualization of the learning disabled (LD) child as an "inactive learner" is that many of these children fail to learn because they do not efficiently utilize the intact abilities available to them. This idea contrasts with some traditional views that indicate that LD children suffer from specific enduring and relatively isolated ability deficits which interfere with their capacity to process information and learn. (Torgesen & Licht, 1983, p. 3)

Thus, while the cognitive research is focused on what might be called "elementary processes" (Newell & Simon, 1972) or "microcomponents" (Sternberg, 1977), the metacognitive research has focused on "control," or "executive," processes (Brown, 1975; Flavell, 1977; Ryan, 1981).

Having made this distinction, it should be noted that the two views are clearly not exclusive of one another. Failure to recruit and/or employ available strategies (production deficiencies) may be due to processing deficits or desire. The realization that effective performance relies on knowledge, control, and motivation has gradually led to a rapprochement in the psychological-educational community so that constructs of reading disability increasingly have moved from an either/or position to a recognition that effective performance requires *both* skill and will (Paris, Lipson, & Wixson, 1983). This, in turn, has led to more complex models of ability-disability.

The construct of metacognition is quite fluid at the moment and is discussed more fully elsewhere (e.g., Paris, Wasik, & Van der Westhuizen, 1988). Typically, however, metacognition is used to refer to the ability to reflect on one's thinking (awareness). It also typically includes some reference to the ability to manage one's learning actions (executive feature). Thus, metacognition involves both knowledge structures and control mechanisms. Skilled reading is viewed as the result of effective selection, application, and monitoring of strategies (Brown, 1975; Paris, Lipson, & Wixson, 1983). Therefore, a metacognitive account of reading disability hypothesizes a deficit in either knowledge and skill or in control mechanisms used to coordinate knowledge and skill.

Metacognitive research on ability-disability shares many of the features of cognitive research. For example, correlational studies have frequently been used to examine metacognitive awareness; and research has been designed to establish relationships between metacognitive factors and reading performance measures (Forrest-Pressley & Waller, 1984; Garner & Kraus, 1981–1982). In general, the results of this line of research suggest a positive relationship between levels of metacognitive awareness and reading comprehension. In addition, such studies have demonstrated that active engagement during reading is associated with better comprehension. For example, Beebe (1980) examined reader miscues and correction rates to demonstrate the relationship between monitoring errors and use of corrective strategies. There were significant positive correlations between spontaneous reader corrections and comprehension of text. Thus, researchers established the dual aspects of metacognition—awareness and control—as related to reading performance.

Metacognitive research has also relied heavily on the good-poor reader research paradigm described previously. In this case, research has been designed to establish relationships between reading ability (good and poor readers) and metacognitive awareness. For example, in one of the earliest studies of good and poor readers' metacognitive awareness, Paris and Myers (1981) interviewed fourth-grade students to compare the knowledge about reading reported by able and less-able readers. Paris and Myers also examined the comprehension and monitoring behaviors of these students, measuring ability both to recall and to detect errors in text. Their results indicated that good readers knew more about reading strategies than poor readers. Good readers also detected more errors and had better memory for text than did poor readers.

A variety of such contrasts has emerged, leading to the conclusion that poor readers' problems are rooted in "metacognitive deficits" (Baker, 1982). Results of research over the past decade suggest that poor readers fail to recruit resources and select appropriate strategies, even when they are available (Ryan, 1981; Torgesen, 1977). In addition, the ability to monitor and control cognitive activity differentiates skilled from less-skilled readers (August, Flavell, & Clift, 1984; Ryan, 1981). Similarly, poor readers do not appear to adjust their reading for different purposes nor do they adapt plans to changing conditions (Forrest-Pressley & Waller, 1984).

The problems associated with the good-poor reader research paradigm discussed previously are, of course, inherent in much of the work on metacognition and reading disability. However, differences in this construct also have resulted in some research advances. For example, much of the metacognitive research has examined reading behavior in the context of reading some connected text, with an increased interest in establishing the connection to performance on transfer tasks (see Brown & Campione, 1986). In addition, good-poor studies in the area of metacognition have generated relatively new research methods.

Because of the difficulty associated with measuring metacognitive aspects of reading (Jacobs & Paris, 1987), there has been wide use of techniques such as introspective and retrospective verbal reports, or *think-aloud measures*, to provide descriptions of the strategies and processes used by skilled readers and to compare good and poor readers (Garner, 1982; Olshavsky, 1976–1977). Thorough reviews of the problems surrounding verbal report data are available elsewhere (see Afflerbach & Johnston, 1984; Cavanaugh & Perlmutter, 1982; Nisbett & Wilson, 1977). However, for the purposes of comparing reading-disabled students with "normals," data from such studies should be viewed cautiously. In particular, since it appears that some, perhaps even a large portion, of the learning-disabled population has difficulty with linguistic tasks (see Vellutino, 1979), it is possible that the demands of this approach may mask or distort reading activity.

In an attempt to examine strategy use during reading, a number of other researchers have turned to *on-line measures*, using microcomputer technology (Lipson, Irwin, & Poth, 1986). For example, August, Flavell, and Clift (1984) examined the monitoring tactics of skilled and less-skilled fifth-grade readers as they read flawed stories on a microcomputer. Dependent measures included reading time, look-backs, and verbal reports of error detection. Even when on-line data suggested that less-able readers had detected some problem, they were less likely than able readers to report missing pages, place missing information correctly, or repair the selection. However, anomalous data from some able and less-able readers suggested that comprehension may proceed without conscious awareness.

Metacognitive research using the good-poor reader paradigm has led to the assumption of causality in much the same way it has in other perspectives. Correlational and comparative findings have been used to generate alternative conceptualizations of the sources of reading difficulty, and the journals are currently replete with reports of instructional attempts to remedy presumed deficits in the areas of monitoring and regulation during reading. Unfortunately, the "rush to instruction" (Brown & Campione, 1986) has often preceded the validation of the construct.

Fortunately, another class of studies has emerged that has proved helpful in verifying the psychological basis for a metacognitive account of disability. Increasingly, researchers are employing an intervention or training study approach (e.g., Palincsar & Brown, 1984). These training studies attempt systematically to teach (or train) subjects to employ specific strategies, thereby demonstrating the "causal" link between absence of this strategy and reading performance.

A great deal of *intervention research* is currently underway. Training studies may be undertaken for three possible purposes: (1) to validate the construct, to test whether limited awareness or control accounts for learning-disabled students' reading difficulties; (2) to remediate presumed deficits; and (3) to demonstrate the effectiveness of a particular instructional approach. Intervention research designed to demonstrate that metacognitive deficits account for some learning disabilities have often provided encouraging results, suggesting that learning-disabled students' inactive approach to reading is more "malleable than assumed" (Olsen, Wong, & Marx, 1983, p. 303). This has fueled interest in testing out various instructional interventions. However, the growing literature focused primarily on instruction is not reviewed here (see Derry & Murphy, 1986; Paris, Wasik, & Van der Westhuizen, 1988). Instead, a description of several prototypic intervention studies designed to validate the construct is provided.

Wong and Jones (1982) used a training study "to investigate whether or not insufficient metacomprehension, stemming from deficient comprehension monitoring, is one cause of learning-disabled students' reading comprehension problems" (p. 229). Using a reading-level match design, one-half of the subjects were learning-disabled students from grades eight and nine, and one-half were normally achieving students in sixth grade. This study is somewhat unique because students from both the learning-disabled and the normally achieving groups were included in both the treatment and the control conditions.

Subjects in the treatment groups were trained in a self-questioning technique focused on identifying important ideas in text. Learning-disabled students who received training predicted more important idea units and performed better on comprehension tasks than did untrained learning-disabled students. There were, however, no differences between trained and untrained normally achieving students. The authors concluded that limited metacognitive understanding is one cause underlying learning-disabled students' comprehension problems. They argued that the data discount the notion that learning-disabled students have an ability deficit and support Torgesen's view that learning-disabled students are "inactive learners."

In a subsequent study, Olsen, Wong, and Marx (1983) reported results that are consistent with this interpretation. A carefully crafted instructional intervention increased learning-disabled children's awareness and use of trained strategies. Moreover, the trained group maintained the learned skills over time. However, they did not generalize these skills to new settings, reverting instead to pretest levels. The authors concluded, "the skills, once learned, seem to be task-specific" (p. 301).

The problem of transfer and generalized learning of strategic behavior has become a major issue facing the field. The results of a burgeoning corpus of metacognitive training studies are mixed (Brown, Campione, & Day, 1981; Dansereau, 1978; Weinstein & Underwood, 1985). Although the results of training studies designed to develop task-specific behaviors (e.g., underlining) suggest that control and coordination skills can be taught, improvements in trained skills have not always resulted in improved reading performance; nor have the skills always been durable (Torgesen & Licht, 1983). In a comprehensive review of strategy training research, Derry and Murphy (1986) concluded that executive skills are acquired over extended periods of time and require lengthy interventions involving rich programs of training. They cannot be taught in brief doses of direct instruction.

As several writers have recently noted, students may have comparable skill and still perform differently. Production deficiencies, the failure to use available skills, may be due to processing deficits or desire (Paris, Lipson, & Wixson, 1983). That is, increased skill in any component area (micro-, macro-, or metacomponents) is not helpful unless students also develop a desire to use this skill and knowledge. Increasingly, researchers and model builders are suggesting that the information-processing construct must account for individual variability in motivation.

Adaptive cognitive behavior is an important area of interface between affect and cognition so that an LD child's self-confidence, expectations for success, and emotional commitment to learning may be as important determinants of adaptive cognitive behavior as actual metacognitive knowledge. Therefore, future training studies should focus not only on the metacognitive deficiencies of these children but also on the affect and attitudes that may determine their responses to learning tasks (Torgesen & Licht, 1983, p. 26).

A Motivational View

Motivational accounts of disability are somewhat unique among information-processing perspectives because they do not generally assume a single etiology of disability. Rather, they assume an interactive connection with cognitive, and increasingly with metacognitive, factors. Indeed, researchers in this area use terms such as "motivated cognitions" (Covington, 1983) and describe their work as a "social-cognitive approach" to learning (Dweck, 1986; Weiner, 1983). Educators and researchers have long recognized the potential influence of motivation on learning. Aspects of motivation that have been investigated in relation to achievement include beliefs, attitudes, attribution, and expectations.

In a continuous line of research, Diener and Dweck (1978, 1980) have demonstrated repeatedly that motivational patterns contribute to individual differences in performance. These authors argue that variability in performance can be accounted for by two distinct patterns of behavior: "adaptive" and "maladaptive" motivational patterns. These behavior patterns have been studied as children interact with failure and success experiences. Over time, repeated experiences with failure appear to generate increasingly negative attitudes, beliefs, and expectations (Dweck & Bempechat, 1983; Kurtz & Borkowski, 1984). These patterns may lead to a syndrome variously labeled "learned helplessness" and "passive failure" (Johnston & Winograd, 1985).

Much of the research on motivation has involved general cognitive problem-solving tasks. However, recent research provides insights into the relationship between motivational factors and performance on measures of reading. For example, Butkowsky and Willows (1980) demonstrated that poor readers had significantly lower initial expectations for success than did average and good readers. When these same readers were confronted with repeated exposure to failure on a task defined by the experimenters as a reading test, the good and average readers demonstrated greater persistence than did the poor readers. In addition, 68 percent of the poor readers attributed their failures to low ability, while only 12 to 13 percent of the good and average readers did so. The poor readers appeared to stop trying because they believed that they would fail no matter how hard they tried. These results are an example of the type of maladaptive pattern described by Dweck (1986).

As with metacognitive views, intervention research has been used to inform the motivational models of disability. For example, Dweck and her colleagues have clearly demonstrated that it is possible to change both children's expectations and their approach to problem-solving tasks, including persistence in the face of difficult problems (see Dweck & Bempechat, 1983). What is less clear, is how these changes in attribution, belief, or expectation interact with other cognitive components.

One promising line of research is described by Borkowski, Weyhing, and Turner (1986), using an approach that combines attribution retraining and metacognitive strategy instruction. The results of their research indicate that motivational factors account for the failure of some students to transfer and employ learned skills and strategies. These results suggest that motivation needs to be considered in terms of students' perceptions of the value of the learning task and also their ability to succeed (Lipson & Wixson, 1986). As Covington (1983) has pointed out, relationships between affect and cognition are probably reciprocal. Motivation *can* and *does* influence cognition. However, information-processing factors might influence and mediate affect as well.

Current evidence from Hiebert, Winograd, and Danner (1984) that children's attributions for success and failure in reading may vary across reading situations suggests that motivational factors may have a differential effect on students' performance in various reading situations. Indeed, research in the area of causal attributions, attitude, and persistence has generated conflicting findings and differential patterns, depending on such factors as sex (Licht et al., 1985), experimental manipulation (Covington, 1983), and developmental age (Oka & Paris, 1986). The relatively recent work in motivation has only begun to address exactly how affect influences students' performance in reading (see Oka & Paris, 1986).

Summary

The information-processing perspectives of today generally include three large components: (1) knowledge, (2) skill and strategy, and (3) belief or motivation. Research using a single-factor approach has identified a large number of within-reader factors that may contribute to reading disability, and there is reasonably good evidence that at least some reading/learning-disabled children have specific problems related to processing skills that are not under conscious control (see Vellutino & Denckla, Chapter 21 in this volume). In addition, however, research suggests that many less-skilled readers have a limited awareness of the factors that influence reading performance and of the strategies likely to improve their performance. They also approach tasks passively and fail to employ skills and strategies even when they are available. Finally, many reading/learning-disabled children have negative expectations for future performance, attribute their failure to inappropriate sources, and generally demonstrate limited motivation for reading tasks.

Although metacognitive and motivational studies have provided fresh approaches to researching issues in disability, and despite the possibility that these approaches may encourage even richer instructional paradigms, there are concerns about this type of research. Researchers may simply have located a new presumed source of deficit, one that may also be viewed as static and invariable. That is, although the types of suspected difficulties are qualitatively different, nevertheless it is assumed that these abilities are stable. This perpetuates traditional assumptions about the appropriate manner in which to cast reading difficulties, even though the evidence suggests that reading is interactive, variable, and dynamic (Anderson, Hiebert, Scott, & Wilkinson, 1985; Wixson & Peters, 1984).

The wealth of research from an information-processing perspective points to the fact that individual differences in reading ability are multiply determined and that many factors can, and probably do, interact to result in severe forms of disability. In the future, studies will need to address not only the relationships between metacognition, motivation, and cognition, but also whether changes in affect and strategy use have enduring benefits for reading achievement.

Children's motivations, attributions, and strategies develop and are learned in home, school, and community environments and children generate their sense of efficacy through experience. Recently, several authors have noted that good and poor readers simply do not have comparable school experiences. For example, Torgesen (1980) noted that the one thing all poor readers have in common is repeated experience with failure. In the next section, a construct is examined that views disability from within this larger social context.

Social Perspectives

There are a variety of social perspectives on reading and reading disability, including those referred to as sociolinguistic, sociocultural, sociohistorical, and sociocommunicative. For the most part, the distinctions among the various social perspectives are not important for the purposes of this review. However, the one key distinction that cannot be overlooked is the one between evaluative and literal perspectives on reading disability (cf. Mosenthal, 1986). *Evaluative perspectives* view the concept of reading disability as an artifact of the social values within a particular community, rather than as a literal fact. For this reason, the term "reading disability" is eschewed in favor of references to success and failure in literacy acquisition. Other social perspectives view the existence of reading disability as a literal fact and emphasize the role of social variables in etiology and remediation. What all of these perspectives have in common is the belief that literacy (reading and writing) and literacy acquisition are social phenomena.

Evaluative social perspectives suggest that the way literacy skills are defined, measured, and instructed or remediated can only be understood in terms of the values that exist within a particular social context. Support for this view comes from socio-cultural comparisons of literacy practices within different cultures (e.g., Schieffelin & Cochran-Smith, 1984; Wagner, 1986), and sociohistorical accounts of changes in the definition of literacy and literacy practices within a society over time. For example, Cook-Gumperz (1986) chronicled the changing views of literacy in Western society. Her analysis sets the stage for understanding many of today's literacy practices: "the transformation of literacy from a moral virtue to a cognitive skill is the key to the twentieth-century changes in literacy ideology" (p. 37). Literacy in today's culture is viewed as synonymous with schooled literacy—a system of decontextualized knowledge validated through test performances (Cook-Gumperz, 1986).

Evaluative social perspectives view reading as a process that is embedded in, and influenced by, instructional and communicative processes and events (Green & Weade, 1987). Research within evaluative social perspectives is grounded in principles and constructs from fields such as anthropology, linguistics, and sociology, and focuses on a variety of aspects of everyday life in classrooms and other educational settings. These include the ways in which social and academic life in educational settings is conducted and constructed through the social interactions of participants, what is learned from such participation, and how participation influences performance and assessment of student ability. The work in this area seeks to understand what members of a classroom need to know, understand, produce, predict, and evaluate in order to participate appropriately and gain access to learning. Researchers use analytic approaches such as conversational analysis, discourse analysis, ethnography of communication, and socio-linguistic methods to explore the nature of the classroom as a social system and to understand how teaching and learning are realized through face-to-face interactions among participants (Green & Bloome, 1983; Green & Weade, 1987).

Reading ability and disability are examined within the multiple layers of social and cultural contexts provided by classrooms, schools, homes, and communities. It is recognized that schooling is not the only context for learning to read; neither is it the first nor necessarily the most enduring influence on people's reading acquisition. Although literacy test scores are the products of schooling, literacy is not and cannot be solely the outcome of schooling (Cook-Gumperz, 1986). Of equal importance, however, is the recognition that schools define what counts as literacy and control literacy acquisition. As Gavelek and Palincsar (1988) note, "Society defines the curriculum and representatives of society inhibit or facilitate what learners can derive from the curriculum" (p. 280).

Students must acquire the "literate frameworks of schooling"; that is, "they must learn how to participate in reading, what effective reading means, and the definitions of reading held by the teacher and school" (Green & Bloome, 1983, p. 23). Research conducted as part of the School/Home Ethnography Project at the University of California at Berkeley indicates that to be regarded as literate in school, children must be able to shift from the face-to-face conversational discourse strategies appropriate in the home to the written strategies of discursive prose. The evidence suggests that some children come to school with an oral discourse style that is at variance with the teacher's literate style. These children, over time, often do not gain access to the kind of instruction and practice required to develop a more literate discourse style resulting in less-skilled performance in school-based literacy activities.

As part of the Berkeley project, Michaels (1981) found that the narrative styles demonstrated by first-grade children during "sharing time" were culturally patterned. When the child's discourse style matched the teacher's literate style and expectations, collaboration was successful, and sharing time served as "oral preparation for literacy." In contrast, when the child's narrative style was at variance with the teacher's expectations, collaboration was frequently unsuccessful and often led to negative assessments of ability and sanctions of student performance.

Related research has provided insights into how experiences in the home can produce a mismatch between the expectations of the student and the teacher. Research in this area has demonstrated that mismatches between the expectations of the student and the teacher can lead to misevaluation of student ability, inappropriate instruction, and/or limited access to certain types of school-related literacy activities (cf. Rist, 1970; Mehan, 1979). For example, Gilmore's (1987) three-year study of a predominantly low-income, black urban community demonstrated the ways in which selected students were allowed differential access to literacy based on teachers' assessments of their "attitude." All of the children observed displayed extensive literacy and language skills in peer and nonschool contexts; however, only some were admitted to the special academic programs and higher-track classes that maximized opportunities for literacy success. Many children were never seen as possessing literacy competence, because demonstrations of their competencies were contextualized and embedded in attitudinal displays that were considered inappropriate. Although the teachers believed that they were selecting students on the basis of their ability to handle certain skills, analysis of the data showed that they were in fact using a very different and unconscious set of social criteria based largely on communicative style to form their evaluations. Gilmore (1987) concluded, "the issue seemed not to be the *acquisition of literacy* . . . instead it appeared to be an exchange of appropriate attitudes for what can more accurately be described as an *admission to literacy*" (p. 98).

A related body of research, much of which was conducted from a more literal social perspective, supports the view that institutional practices such as *ability grouping* may perpetuate communicative mismatches, misevaluations of student ability, and limited access to the activities most highly related to literacy success. Rosenbaum (1980) noted that student groups created according to ability level are entities that have social properties and implications. The social properties of ability groups are derived, at least in part, from the fact that students are grouped with those defined to be similar and separated from those defined to be different. Group placement is based on socially valued criteria, so that group membership immediately identifies some individuals as better than others. Therefore, high- and low-ranked reading groups create unique instructional-social contexts that influence learning among individuals within those groups.

Reviews of research on ability grouping for reading instruction suggest that instructional and social experiences do differ for students in high- and low-ranked reading groups and that these differences influence student learning (e.g., Allington, 1983; Hiebert, 1983). For example, McDermott (1977) found that low-ranked groups spent approximately a third as much time in actual reading tasks as high-ranked groups. He also observed that the patterns of interaction in the high group were characterized by orderly turn taking and teacher questions were focused on text meaning, whereas the interactions in the low group were characterized by less orderly turn taking and questions usually concerned word identification rather than comprehension. It has also been observed that students in high-ability groups read silently much more than they read orally, while students in low-ability groups read orally much more frequently than silently (Allington, 1983). Teachers also interrupt students following oral reading errors proportionally more often in low-ability than high-ability groups (Allington, 1980).

These and other observations suggest differences in the ways students in different ability groups may be evaluated. Most important, perhaps, is the evidence that ability grouping provides students with messages about their potential for success in reading, and that children are aware of these messages and internalize them in ways that influence their learning (R. S. Weinstein, 1986). From her review of studies on ability grouping and self-concept, Rosenbaum (1980) concluded that average and low-ability students give lower self-evaluations if they are in ability groups than if they are not.

Such conclusions raise another important issue addressed by research conducted from an evaluative social perspective: the extent to which students of various social and cultural groups choose to perform in the context of school-related literacy activities. McDermott (1976) argued that reading takes its place in the classroom social organization as part of the teacher's "ecology of games." To read is to accept these games and all the statuses and identities that accompany them. Not to read is to accept peer group games and their accompanying statuses and identities; that is, given a particular social organization, reading failure may be a social achievement.

Social perspectives on reading and reading acquisition also provide a framework for research on instruction and remediation. This framework suggests that teaching and learning cannot be explained primarily in cognitive terms, because cognition is carried out by social persons whose thinking is interactively bound with, and inseparable from, sociocultural, sociohistorical, and sociocommunicative influences (Coles, 1984; Gavelek & Palincsar, 1988). Support for this view comes from research demonstrating the importance of cultural compatibility in the patterns of interaction between teachers and students in reading lessons. Using Vygotsky's (1978) notion that the child's development proceeds on the basis of experiences in the social world, Au (1980) observed that Hawaiian children were more successful in reading lessons that used the participation structures of the talk story, which is an important nonschool speech event for these students. This pattern of interaction was then contrasted with the conventional recitation pattern commonly used in reading lessons with children from the mainstream culture (Au & Mason, 1981). The results of this comparison indicated that the lessons of the teachers using these two participation structures were clearly different kinds of social events, and that Hawaiian students demonstrated much higher levels of achievement-related behavior in the lessons incorporating the culturally compatible talk story pattern.

An ambitious longitudinal study by Heath (1981, 1982) demonstrates both the impact of language patterns on school success and the ways in which socially acquired patterns of interaction affect both instruction and learning. Heath (1982) studied the patterns of language use related to books in three literate communities in the southeastern United States. The results of this study indicated that the patterns of language use and paths of language socialization differed strikingly for children in homes from these communities. In "Maintown," a middle-class, school-oriented community, the focus of literacy-related activities was on labeling, explaining, and learning appropriate interactional patterns of displaying knowledge. Children learned how to use language in literacy events and were socialized into the interactional sequences that are central features of classroom lessons.

Families in "Roadville," a white working-class community, also focused on labeling and explanations; however, they did not link these ways of taking meaning from books to other aspects of their environment. Consequently, children from these homes were well prepared for the literal tasks of early reading instruction, but not for reading assignments that called for reasoning and affective responses.

The third group of homes under investigation were located in "Trackton," a black working-class community. The children in these homes were not taught labels or asked for explanations; rather, they were asked to provide reasons and express personal responses to events in their lives. As a consequence, these children were unprepared for the types of questions often used in beginning reading instruction and unfamiliar with the interaction patterns used in reading lessons.

In a more detailed analysis, Heath (1981) reported on the uses of questions in three situations: the black working-class community (Trackton), the classrooms attended by children of this community, and the homes of teachers from these classrooms. The predominant characteristic of teachers' questions was to pull attributes of things out of context and name them. Trackton parents did not ask the children these kinds of questions, and Trackton children had different techniques for responding to questions. Teachers reported that it was difficult to get responses from Trackton students, Trackton parents reported that teachers did not listen or that "we don't talk to our children the way you do," and Trackton children reported that teachers asked "dumb" questions they already knew about.

Heath then shared with the teachers examples of how Trackton children inter-acted at home, and teachers incorporated questions similar to those the children were familiar with in their instruction. As a result, the children participated much more frequently and, in time, the teachers were able to involve them in more traditional question answering as well. As Gavelek and Palincsar (1988) note, this research illus-trates the point that the children from these homes were initially disabled by virtue of the fact that they had not engaged in the type of interaction that is characteristic of classroom instruction, but that their disabilities were remediated by the social interac-tion they subsequently experienced with their teachers.

The implications of a social perspective on remedial instruction have begun to receive more extensive attention. For example, Coles (1984) examined the social relationships in the learning of an illiterate adult during a clinical session. The evidence indicated that the student's learning was not simply a function of how he comprehended the content of the lesson. Rather, learning reflects the interrelationships among ele-ments such as personal interactions, previous interactions and their effects, educational materials, and influences from the broad social context in which the learning situation existed. The analysis further suggested that there were junctures where one direction led to continued successful learning, and another to learner frustration, problems, and even failure. Coles (1984) noted that although these junctures may be created by any number of elements, the learning difficulties at these times have often been interpreted as symptomatic of the learner's dysfunctional cognition, rather than as part of instruc-tional interrelationships and interactions. The essence of Coles's (1984) argument is that social relationships need to be regarded as the context in which disabled cognition is created and embedded.

Support for Coles's view comes from case studies by Johnston (1985) of three reading-disabled adults. He observed that a complex set of conditions involving concep-tual problems, strategy knowledge and usage, anxiety, attributions for success and failure, and goals and motivations were inextricably interwoven with cognitive activity. He too maintains that rather than the neurological and processing deficit explanations currently in vogue, explanations that stress combinations of anxiety, attributions, mal-adaptive strategies, inaccurate or nonexisting concepts about reading, and a variety of motivational factors need to be considered more seriously. He concludes that it is perfectly reasonable to suppose that these factors are likely to cause or serve as a catalyst for children's reading problems, given instructional practices such as ability grouping, and the present competitive social context equating literacy with intellect.

Summary

Current perspectives on reading disability represent a range of views from those that focus primarily on the nature of reader deficits to those that focus primarily on the role of social context. Research from information-processing perspectives examines various cognitive, metacognitive, and motivational components of the reader with little regard for the social contexts in which disability is manifest. Conversely, research from a social perspective examines the development and maintenance of disability within the social contexts in which it is defined with little regard for individuals' information-processing abilities. The final section of this review describes the movement within each of these current perspectives toward a more unified, interactive view of reading disability.

AN EMERGING PERSPECTIVE

The emergence of an interactive perspective on reading provides the basis for an interactive view of reading disability. Just as the medical and the psychoeducational perspectives came together in an information-processing perspective, the information-processing and social perspectives are now beginning to merge in an interactive view. An *interactive perspective* recognizes the need for a more complete theory of reading disability that encompasses factors both internal and external to the reader. As this review has indicated, this perspective is not entirely new. However, what is new is an empirical base that enables us to move away from the current emphasis on "the search for pathology" (Sarason & Doris, 1979), and toward the specification of the conditions under which a student can and will learn (Lipson & Wixson, 1986).

The term "interactive," as it applies to reading, is associated most closely with the work of Rumelhart (1977). Rumelhart characterized reading as an "interactive process" in which readers vary their focus along a continuum, from primarily text-based processing to primarily reader-based processing. According to this view, the processing of text is a flexible interaction of the different information sources available to the reader; and information contained in higher stages of processing can influence the analysis that occurs at lower stages of analysis, as well as the other way around. As readers process print they may rely on any one or more of the following information sources as their primary clues to meaning: general context, semantic context, syntactic environment, or surrounding letters.

Although Rumelhart's work has served as the basis for thinking about reading as an interactive process in recent years, this model still is lodged primarily within the reader and has a distinct "bias for explaining word identification" (Samuels & Kamil, 1984). Clearly, other factors also interact during the processing of print to influence reading. Current research indicates that the reading process varies as a function of the interaction among many factors, including the reader's prior knowledge (Anderson, Reynolds, Schallert, & Goetz, 1977), motivation and interest (Asher, 1980; Butkowsky & Willows, 1980), sociocultural background (McDermott, 1977), type of discourse (Kintsch & van Dijk, 1978; Meyer, 1975), task demands (McConkie, Rayner, & Wilson, 1973), and contextual factors (Frederiksen, 1975; Spiro, 1977). Full understanding of the reading process requires an understanding of the ways in which the various knowledge sources of the reader interact with one another and with the text and the context of the reading situation.

An interactive view suggests that reading ability *and* disability are not absolute properties of the reader, but rather are relative properties of the interaction among specific reader, text, and contextual factors (Wixson & Lipson, 1986). Support for this view comes from a review of the literature by Lipson and Wixson (1986) that examined students' performance on measures of word recognition and comprehension that are used traditionally to differentiate good from poor readers. This review indicated that the performance of *both able and disabled students* varies as a function of the conditions of the reading situation, suggesting the importance of the interaction between reader and nonreader factors in determining ability and disability.

The emergence of an interactive view of reading (dis)ability has resulted in the recognition of the need for changes in research. As Samuels suggests, researchers need "to abandon the attempt to find simple, all-embracing laws which can generalize. Instead, we need to specify the conditions under which particular processes occur" (1984, p. 391). An interactive perspective on reading (dis)ability suggests that research must focus on the variability within groups and subgroups and the interactive effects of different reading conditions on the learning and performance of individual readers. This means that research on reading (dis)ability must deal with the factors that are known to influence reading as valuable sources of information, as opposed to confounding factors that need to be controlled.

Although little research on reading disability has been conducted from an interactive perspective, this is not unexpected given that this view of reading has emerged only recently. As Coles (1987) has noted, "when we abandon an explanation that for decades has been the primary formulation for research, an alternative theory will almost certainly carry limited evidence, at least initially. This limitation is almost a given in the progress toward acceptance of theories of greater explanatory promise than those older but still inadequate ones that have received the most empirical attention" (p. 137–138).

One way in which evidence supporting an interactive perspective is growing is through research that expands on existing models. For example, Juel, Griffith, and Gough (1986) proposed an information-processing model of literacy acquisition that included a component external to the reader called *exposure to print*. This model was tested in a longitudinal study in an elementary school with a large minority, low-SES population of children from first through fourth grade. In analyzing the factors that seemed to keep poor readers from improving, Juel (1988) posited a vicious cycle between poor decoding skill and exposure to print. Children who did not develop good word recognition skill in first grade began to dislike reading and read considerably less than good readers both in and out of school. As a result, they lost the avenue to develop the knowledge and skills fostered by wide reading, which in turn contributed to a steadily widening gap in reading comprehension and writing skills. She concluded that these data illustrate the phenomenon of "Matthew Effects" described by Stanovich (1986). Taking its name from the Bible verse, "The rich get richer and the poor get poorer," Stanovich's analysis suggests that children enter school with differential ability to take advantage of what is offered. Their experiences then multiply and compound so that over time, some children appear to have multiple deficits.

Support for an interactive view of reading (dis)abiliity also comes from studies based on an interactive view of learning and instruction rather than reading. For example, Pascarella and Pflaum (1981) examined the interaction between locus of attribution and instructional methods for teaching the use of context cues in oral reading among learning disabled and "normal low" readers. Students initially high in internal control benefitted more under an instructional condition in which they were encouraged to determine the correctness of their responses. Conversely, students initially low in internal control benefitted more from a condition in which the teacher determined the correctness of their responses.

Another example of this type is provided by a study in which Johnston and Afflerbach (1983) used multiple baseline data to track the oral reading performance of a small group of disabled readers in relation to specific teacher practices. The resulting individual profiles revealed that changes in teacher responses to oral reading miscues, such as the timing of feedback (immediate, delayed) and the point of feedback (before, at, or following the next sentence break), resulted in dramatic changes in students' self-correction behaviors.

Evidence based on a interactive view of reading ability and disability is also emerging. One type of evidence comes from research emphasizing the multidimensional factors known to influence reading. For example, an exploratory study by Hric, Wixson, Kunji, and Bosky (1988/1989) examined the variability that exists within a group of ten less-able readers with comparable scores on a standardized reading test. This was done by assessing students' performance under reading conditions representing different combinations of familiarity, text type, length, and mode of reading. The results indicated that each of these variables made an important difference in the performance of at least one student, and that the performance of each student was affected in important ways by at least one of the variables. Based on the 75 percent criterion for "passing" that is commonly used in informal comprehension assessments, seven of the ten students' scores differed between acceptable and unacceptable levels as a function of the different reading conditions under which they performed.

In addition to multidimensional investigations, there is evidence from interactive research. For example, the guiding hypothesis of the Institute for the Study of Learning Disabilities Research at Columbia University Teachers College is that "academic failure experienced by learning-disabled children results from an interaction between the way they process information and the information-processing demands of the instructional methods in use in their classrooms" (Connor, 1983, p. 23).

A study conducted by Kimmel and MacGinitie (1984) at this LD institute identified a subgroup of disabled readers who consistently formed a hypothesis about the meaning of text at the outset of reading, then rigidly maintained that interpretation despite disconfirming information in subsequent text. The results of this research indicated that readers using this perseverative processing strategy had more difficulty comprehending text in which the main point was presented at the outset (deductive) as compared to text in which the initial sentences were used to lead up to the main point (inductive).

The increased acceptance of an interactive view of reading (dis)ability has resulted in the development of new assessments. For example, the 1986 National Assessment of Educational Progress (NAEP) young adult assessment (Kirsch & Jungeblut, 1986) was based on the recognition that "There is no single measure or specific point on a scale that separates the 'literate' from the 'illiterate' " and that "literacy is inextricably linked with home, school, work, and social environments" (Kirsch & Jungeblut, 1986). Other large-scale test efforts consistent with an interactive perspective include the development of new statewide reading tests in Michigan and Illinois. The assessments are of interest because they employ full-length intact texts that are representative of the texts students read in classrooms, and that provide interpretive information regarding readers' topic familiarity, metacognitive knowledge, and attitudes about reading (Valencia & Pearson, 1987; Wixson, Peters, Weber, & Roeber, 1987).

In addition, several interactive approaches to individual assessment are being developed, including a commercial informal reading inventory designed to evaluate students' prior knowledge of passage topics and to determine how students perform under different text conditions (Leslie & Caldwell, 1990), and dynamic assessment procedures that evaluate how students actually learn within a domain rather than the past knowledge that is typically assessed by traditional measures (e.g., Cioffi & Carney, 1983; Paratore & Indrisano, 1987; Lidz, 1987). As with previous perspectives, the development of appropriate assessment instruments is likely to result in additional research on an interactive view of reading (dis)ability.

As described here, an interactive perspective unites the reader and nonreader factors emphasized by various literal perspectives on reading disability. A more far-reaching interactive perspective would unite literal and evaluative perspectives on reading disability. Such a perspective has been proposed by Coles (1987) as an "interactivity theory of learning disabilities." Citing Bronfenbrenner, Coles (1987) argues that many interaction approaches in psychology and education display a marked asymmetry that focuses on the properties of the person and considers the environment to be only a passive context for the active subject who, when learning, "interacts" with the environment.

Coles maintains that the *cause* of a child's failure to learn must be explored by looking both at and beyond the immediate teacher-child interaction to other interactions that might not be readily apparent. He notes, for example, that it is important to consider the experiences that might have led a teacher to instruct as he or she does, and to know about the school's influence on classroom instruction and relationships. It is also necessary to identify, to the extent possible, the economic, social, political, and cultural forces that affect the school, the child, and the teacher. Finally, the child's biological functioning and how that has worked on other elements in the interactions must be assessed.

The basic assumption of interactivity theory is that every aspect of learning failure is related to broad social, economic, political, and cultural influences that are not always immediately apparent. Coles suggests that there are a number of scenarios in which children might become learning disabled either through school or nonschool experiences. For example, a teacher's negative response to a child might be affected by the child's personal qualities, such as physical appearance, that are independent of cognitive abilities; or a student's lack of application to an academic task central to the teacher-student interaction might be a consequence of disruptive family relationships. Conversely, the interplay of various factors may actually prevent various scenarios from producing a learning disability. For example, adverse family relationships and language difficulties may be overcome by a skilled, committed teacher; or confident, motivated children and supportive families may compensate for potentially destructive classroom interactions.

Summary

Interactive perspectives hold promise for integrating previous perspectives into a unified view of reading disability that is educationally meaningful. However, it is also important to recognize that although an interactive perspective can accommodate most instances of reading disability, it still lacks enough precision to make the predictions that are necessary for change in educational practices. Therefore, there is a pressing need for additional research that examines reading disability from the larger perspective of the interaction among a variety of reader and nonreader factors.

CONCLUSION

Research on reading disability has been shaped by the perspectives from which it has been conducted. This chapter reviews the research conducted within the major perspectives from which reading disability has been examined since the turn of the century. Specifically, this chapter reviews long-standing medical and psychoeducational perspectives, current information-processing and social perspectives, and an emerging interactive perspective.

Reviewed in this way, it is apparent that the various perspectives on disability have influenced research in a number of ways. First, the philosophical or theoretical perspective from which research is conducted influences what will be examined. Second, the perspective influences the focus of research, in terms of both the types of measures and the types of methods employed. Finally, the perspective influences the types of inferences drawn from research about both the etiology and the instruction of reading disability.

Although research within each perspective has contributed to the understanding of reading disability, there is still a need for a unified perspective on the causes and treatments for reading disability. In part because researchers and educators want to reduce the number of factors they consider as they explore reading disability (see Mosenthal, 1984, in press), research within each of the established perspectives has examined some, but not other, aspects of reading performance and achievement. The difficulty with such a reductionist (Poplin, 1988) approach is that it may distort the phenomena under examination.

The final concern of this chapter is how progress can be made in research on reading disability in the next decade. In his provocative paper, Mosenthal (1984) poses several critical questions regarding progress in research in reading that should also be applied to reading disability. Researchers and educators must ask themselves two questions as they characterize their own work: (1) What is the definition of reading (dis)ability? and (2) What are the possible definitions of reading (dis)ability? Furthermore, if researchers in areas such as special education, reading education, cognitive and developmental psychology, and linguistics are to avoid the spurious conclusions of the past, two additional questions must be addressed: (1) What should be the definition of reading (dis)ability? and (2) Who determines which definition of reading (dis)ability defines instructional programs? From the review in this chapter, it should be apparent that there are presently a number of theoretical and philosophical perspectives on reading disability competing for currency.

Mosenthal (in press) further suggests that reading researchers have operated in the past as a largely divided community and have attempted to define progress by considering the questions of what reading is and what reading ought to be as independent problems. The result has been a proliferation of independent and sometimes competing solutions. In independently pursuing these problems, reading researchers have tended to place the integrity of their specific research community above that of the reading-research community as a whole.

In conclusion, we agree with Mosenthal's (in press) assessment that progress will require reading researchers to see themselves as members of a common community with a common cause; that they will need to determine what common goals tie them to the reading research discipline. To do this, they will need to find a common level of discourse where the questions of what is reading, what are possible definitions of reading, what ought to be the definition of reading, and who should define reading can be entertained from a unified perspective. At the very least, for the field to progress, research on reading disability must include policy research; research directed toward defining the domain; research designed to develop innovative assessment tools; and much more longitudinal, multidimensional, and interactive research.

REFERENCES

Afflerbach, P., & Johnston, P. (1984). Research methodology on the use of verbal reports in reading research. *Journal of Reading Behavior, 16,* 306–321.

Allington, R. L. (1980). Teacher interruption behaviors during primary grade oral reading. *Journal of Educational Psychology, 72,* 371–377.

Allington, R. L. (1983). The reading instruction provided readers of differing reading abilities. *Elementary School Journal, 83,* 548–558.

Anderson, R. C., Hiebert, E. H., Scott, J. A., & Wilkinson, I. A. G. (1985). *Becoming a nation of readers: The report of the commission on reading.* Washington, DC: National Institute of Education.

Anderson, R. C., Reynolds, R. E., Schallert, D. L., & Goetz, E. T. (1977). Frameworks for comprehending discourse. *American Educational Research Journal, 14,* 367–381.

Applebee, A. N. (1981). Research in reading retardation: Two critical problems. *Journal of Child Psychology and Psychiatry, 12,* 91–113.

Asher, S. (1980). Topic interest and children's reading comprehension. In R. J. Spiro, B. C. Bruce, & W. F. Brewer (Eds.), *Theoretical issues in reading comprehension* (pp. 525–534). Hillsdale, NJ: Erlbaum.

Au, K. H. (1980). Participation structures in a reading lesson with Hawaiian children: Analysis of a culturally appropriate instructional event. *Anthropology and Education Quarterly, 11,* 91–115.

Au, K. H., & Mason, J. M. (1981). Social organizational factors in learning to read: The balance of rights hypothesis. *Reading Research Quarterly, 17,* 115–167.

August, D. L., Flavell, J. H., & Clift, R. (1984). Comparison of comprehension monitoring of skilled and less-skilled readers. *Reading Research Quarterly, 20,* 39–53.

Backman, J. E., Mamen, M., & Fergusen, H. B. (1984). Reading level design: Conceptual and methodological issues in reading research. *Psychological Bulletin, 96,* 560–568.

Baker, L. (1982). An evaluation of the role of metacognitive deficits in learning disabilities. *Topics in Learning and Learning Disabilities, 2,* 27–36.

Bakker, D. J. (1973). Hemispheric specialization and stages in the learning-to-read process. *Bulletin of the Orton Society, 23,* 15–27.

Bakker, D. J. (1979). Hemispheric differences and reading strategies: Two dyslexias? *Bulletin of the Orton Society, 29*, 84–100.

Bakker, D. J., Teunissen, J., & Bosch, J. (1976). Development of laterality-reading patterns. In R. M. Knights, & D. J. Bakker (Eds.), *The neuropsychology of learning disorders* (pp. 207–220). Baltimore: University Park Press.

Beebe, M. J. (1980). The effect of different types of substitution miscues on reading. *Reading Research Quarterly, 15*, 324–336.

Bennett, C. C. (1938). *An inquiry into the genesis of poor reading.* New York: Teachers College, Columbia University.

Benton, A. L. (1975). Developmental dyslexia: Neurological aspects. In W. J. Friedlander (Ed.), *Advances in neurology* (Vol. 7, pp. 1–47). New York: Raven Press.

Betts, E. A. (1934). A physiological approach to the analysis of reading disabilities. *Educational Research Bulletin, 13*, 135–140, 163–174.

Boder, E. (1973). Developmental dyslexia: A diagnostic approach based on three atypical reading-spelling patterns. *Developmental Medicine and Child Neurology, 61*, 471–483.

Bond, G. L. (1935). *The auditory and speech characteristics of poor readers* (Teachers College Contributions to Education, No. 657). New York: Teachers College, Columbia University.

Bond, G. L., & Tinker, M. A. (1967). *Reading difficulties* (2nd ed.). New York: Appleton-Century-Crofts.

Borkowski, J. G., Weyhing, R. S., & Turner, L. A. (1986). Attributional retraining and the teaching of strategies. *Exceptional Children, 53*, 130–137.

Brown, A. L. (1974). The role of strategic behavior in retardate memory. In N. Ellis (Ed.), *International review of research in mental retardation* (Vol. 7, pp. 55–113). New York: Academic Press.

Brown, A. L. (1975). The development of memory: Knowing, knowing about knowing, and knowing how to know. In H. Reese (Ed.), *Advances in child development and behavior* (Vol. 10, pp. 104–153). New York: Academic Press.

Brown, A. L., & Campione, J. (1986). Psychological theory and the study of learning disabilities. *American Psychologist, 14*, 1059–1068.

Brown, A. L., Campione, J., & Day, J. (1981). Learning to learn: On training students to learn from texts. *Educational Researcher, 10*, 14–22.

Buswell, G. T. (1922). *Fundamental reading habits: A study of their development* (Supplementary Educational Monographs, No. 21). Chicago: University of Chicago, Department of Education.

Butkowsky, S., & Willows, D. (1980). Cognitive-motivational characteristics of children varying in reading ability: Evidence for learned helplessness in poor readers. *Journal of Educational Psychology, 72*, 408–422.

Carr, T. H. (1981). Building theories of reading ability: On the relation between individual differences in cognitive skills and reading comprehension. *Cognition, 9*, 73–114.

Carr, T. H. (1985, February). *Component skills analysis and the cognitive contexts of reading acquisition.* Paper presented at the Bush Program in Child Development and Social Policy's Conference on Psychological and Educational Issues in Reading Instruction, Ann Arbor, MI.

Cavanaugh, J. C., & Perlmutter, M. (1982). Metamemory: A critical examination. *Child Development, 53*, 11–28.

Chall, J. (1983). Literacy: Trends and explanations. *Educational Research, 12*, 3–8.

Chall, J., & Mirsky, A. F. (Eds.). (1978). *Education and the brain.* Chicago: University of Chicago Press.

Cioffi, G., & Carney, J. J. (1983). Dynamic assessment of reading disabilities. *Reading Teacher, 36*, 764–768.

Coles, G. S. (1984). The polyphony of learning in the learning disabled. *Learning Disability Quarterly, 7*, 321–328.

Coles, G. S. (1987). *The learning mystique.* New York: Pantheon Books.

Connor, F. P. (1983). Improving school instruction for learning-disabled children: The Teachers College Institute. *Exceptional Education Quarterly, 4*, 23–44.

Cook-Gumperz, J. (1986). Literacy and schooling: An unchanging equation? In J. Cook-Gumperz (Ed.), *The social construction of literacy* (pp. 16–44). Cambridge, Eng.: Cambridge University Press.

Covington, M. V. (1983). Motivated cognitions. In S. G. Paris, G. M. Olson, & H. W. Stevenson (Eds.), *Learning and motivation in the classroom* (pp. 139–164). Hillsdale, NJ: Erlbaum.

Dansereau, D. F. (1978). The development of a learning strategy curriculum. In H. F. O'Neill, Jr. (Ed.), *Learning strategies* (pp. 1–29). New York: Academic Press.

Dearborn, W. F., & Anderson, I. H. (1938). Aniseikonia as related to disability in reading. *Journal of Experimental Psychology, 23*, 559–577.

Denckla, M. B. (1972). Clinical syndromes in learning disabilities: The case for "splitting" vs. "lumping." *Journal of Learning Disabilities, 5*, 401–406.

Derry, S. J., & Murphy, D. A. (1986). Designing systems that train learning ability: From theory to practice. *Review of Educational Research, 56*, 1–39.

Diener, C., & Dweck, C. (1978). Analysis of learned helplessness: Continuous changes in performance, strategy, and achievement cognitions following failure. *Journal of Personality and Social Psychology, 36*, 451–462.

Diener, C. I., & Dweck, C. S. (1980). An analysis of learned helplessness II: The processing of success. *Journal of Personality and Social Psychology, 39*, 940–952.

Doehring, D. G., & Hoshko, I. M. (1977). Classification of reading problems by the Q-technique of factor analysis. *Cortex, 13*, 281–294.

Doehring, D. G., Hoshko, I. M., & Bryans, B. G. (1979). Statistical classification of children with reading problems. *Journal of Clinical Neuropsychology, 1*, 5–16.

Downing, J., & Leong, C. K. (1982). *Psychology of reading*. New York: Macmillan.

Duffy, F. H., Denckla, M. B., Bertels, P. H., & Sandini, G., (1980). Dyslexia: Regional differences in brain electrical activity by topographic mapping. *Annals of Neurology, 7*, 412–420.

Duffy, F. H., Denckla, M. B., Bartels, P. H., Sandini, G., & Kiessling, L. S. (1980). Dyslexia: Automated diagnosis by computerized classification of brain electrical activity. *Annals of Neurology, 7*, 421–428.

Dweck, C. S. (1986). Motivational processes affecting learning. *American Psychologist, 41*, 1040–1048.

Dweck, C. S., & Bempechat, J. (1983). Children's theories of intelligence: Consequences for learning. In S. G. Paris, G. M. Olson, & H. W. Stevenson (Eds.), *Learning and motivation in the classroom* (pp. 239–258). Hillsdale, NJ: Erlbaum.

Flavell, J. H. (1977). *Cognitive development*. Englewood Cliffs, NJ: Prentice-Hall.

Forrest-Pressley, D. L., & Waller, T. G. (1984). *Metacognition, cognition, and reading*. New York: Springer-Verlag.

Frederiksen, C. H. (1975). Effects of context-induced processing operations on semantic information acquired from discourse. *Cognitive Psychology, 7*, 139–166.

Galaburda, A. M., & Eidelberg, D. (1982). Symmetry and asymmetry in the human posterior thalamus (II): Thalamic lesions in a case of developmental dyslexia. *Archives of Neurology, 39*, 333–336.

Galaburda, A. M., & Kemper, T. L. (1979). Cytoarchitectonic abnormalities in developmental dyslexia: A case study. *Annals of Neurology, 6*, 94–100.

Garner, R. (1982). Verbal report data on reading strategies. *Journal of Reading Behavior, 14*, 159–167.

Garner, R., & Kraus, C. (1981–1982). Good and poor comprehenders' differences in knowing and regulating reading behaviors. *Educational Research Quarterly, 6*, 5–12.

Gates, A. I. (1927). *The improvement of reading*. New York: Macmillan.

Gates, A. I., & Bond, G. L. (1936). Relation of handedness, eye-sighting, and acuity dominance to reading. *Journal of Educational Psychology, 27*, 450–456.

Gavelek, J. R., & Palincsar, A. S. (1988). Contextualism as an alternative worldview of learning disabilities: A response to Syanson's "Toward a metatheory of learning disabilities." *Journal of Learning Disabilities, 21*, 278–281.

Gilmore, P. (1987). Sulking, stepping, and tracking: The effects of attitude assessment on access to literacy. In D. Bloome (Ed.), *Literacy and schooling* (pp. 98–120). Norwood, NJ: Ablex.

Gough, P. C. (1972). One second of reading. In J. F. Kavanagh & I. G. Mattingly (Eds.), *Language by ear and eye* (pp. 331–358). Cambridge, MA: MIT Press.

Gray, W. S. (1915). *Oral reading paragraph test*. Bloomington, IN: Public School Publishing.

Green, J., & Bloome, D. (1983). Ethnography and reading: Issues, approaches, criteria, and findings. In J. A. Niles & L. A. Harris (Eds.), *Searches for meaning in reading/language processing and instruction* (Thirty-second Yearbook of the National Reading Conference) (pp. 6–30). Rochester, NY: National Reading Conference.

Green, J., & Weade, R. (1987). In search of meaning: A sociolinguistic perspective on lesson construction and reading. In D. Bloome (Ed.), *Literacy and schooling*. Norwood, NJ: Ablex.

Guthrie, J. T. (1973). Models of reading and reading disability. *Journal of Educational Psychology, 65*, 9–18.

Hallahan, D. P., & Cruickshank, W. M. (1973). *Psycho-educational foundations of learning disabilities*. Englewood Cliffs, NJ: Prentice-Hall.

Hammill, D. D., & Larsen, S. C. (1974). The effectiveness of psycholinguistic training. *Exceptional Children, 41*, 5–14.

Hammill, D. D., Leigh, J. E., McNutt, G., & Larsen, S. C. (1981). A new definition of learning disabilities. *Learning Disability Quarterly, 4*, 336–342.

Harris, A. J. (1983). How many kinds of reading disability are there? In G. M. Senf & J. K. Torgesen (Eds.), *Annual Review of Learning Disabilities, 1*, 50–54.

Harris, A. J., & Sipay, E. R. (1985). *How to increase reading ability* (8th ed.). White Plains, NY: Longman.

Harris, T. L., & Hodges, R. W. (Eds.). (1981). *A dictionary of reading and related terms*. Newark, DE: International Reading Association.

Heath, S. B. (1981). Questioning at home and at school: A comparative study. In G. Spindler (Ed.), *Doing ethnography: Educational anthropology in action* (pp. 102–131). New York: Holt, Rinehart, & Winston.

Heath, S. B. (1982). What no bedtime story means: Narrative skills at home and school. *Language in Society, 11*, 49–76.

Hiebert, E. F. (1983). An examination of ability grouping for reading instruction. *Reading Research Quarterly, 18*, 231–255.

Hiebert, E. H., Winograd, P. N., & Danner, F. W. (1984). Children's attributions for failure and success in different aspects of reading. *Journal of Educational Psychology, 76*, 1139–1148.

Hinshelwood, J. (1917). *Congenital word-blindness*. London: Lewis.

Holmes, J. A. (1953). *The substrata-factor theory of reading*. Berkeley, CA: Berkeley Book Co., Multilithed. (Out of print).

Hric, K. A., Wixson, K. K., Kunji, M., & Bosky, A. B. (1988/1989). Individual variability among less-able readers. *Reading, Writing, and Learning Disabilities, 4,* 49–67.

Hynd, G. W., & Hynd, C. R. (1984). Dyslexia: Neuroanatomical/neurolinguistic perspectives. *Reading Research Quarterly, 19,* 482–498.

Jacobs, J. E., & Paris, S. G. (1987). Children's metacognition about reading: Issues in definition, measurement, and instruction. *Educational Psychologist, 22,* 255–278.

Johnson, D., & Myklebust, H. R. (1967). *Learning disabilities: Educational principles and practices.* New York: Grune & Stratton.

Johnston, P. (1985). Understanding reading disability: A case study approach. *Harvard Educational Review, 55,* 153–177.

Johnston, P., & Afflerbach, P. (1983). Measuring teacher and student change in a remedial reading clinic. In J. A. Niles & L. A. Harris (Eds.), *Searches for meaning in reading/language processing and instruction* (Thirty-second Yearbook of the National Reading Conference) (pp. 304–312). Rochester, NY: National Reading Conference.

Johnston, P., & Winograd, P. N. (1985). Passive failure in reading. *Journal of Reading Behavior, 4,* 279–301.

Jorm, A. F. (1983). *The psychology of reading and spelling disorders.* London: Routledge & Kegan Paul.

Juel, C. (1988). Learning to read and write: A longitudinal study of fifty-four children from first through fourth grade. *Journal of Educational Psychology, 80,* 437–447.

Juel, C., Griffith, P. L., & Gough, P. B. (1986). Acquisition of literacy: A longitudinal study of children in first and second grade. *Journal of Educational Psychology, 78,* 243–255.

Judd, C. H. (1907). Photographic records of convergence and divergence. *Psychological Review Monograph Supplements, 8,* 370–423.

Just, M. A., & Carpenter, P. A. (1987). *The psychology of reading and language comprehension.* Boston: Allyn & Bacon.

Kavale, K. A., & Forness, S. R. (1987). The far side of heterogeneity: A critical analysis of empirical subtyping research in learning disabilities. *Journal of Learning Disabilities, 20,* 374–382.

Kimmel, S., & MacGinitie, W. H. (1984). Identifying children who use a perseverative text-processing strategy. *Reading Research Quarterly, 19,* 162–172.

Kinsbourne, M., & Hiscock, M. (1978). Cerebral lateralization and cognitive development. In Chall, J. S., & Mirsky, A. F. (Eds.), *Education and the brain.* Chicago: University of Chicago Press.

Kintsch, W., & van Dijk, T. (1978). Toward a model of text comprehension and production. *Psychological Review, 85,* 363–394.

Kirk, S. A., McCarthy, J. J., & Kirk, W. D. (1968). *Illinois Test of Psycholinguistic Abilities* (rev. ed.). Urbana: University of Illinois Press.

Kirsch, I. W., & Jungeblut, A. (1986). *Literacy: Profiles of America's young adults.* Princeton, NJ: Educational Testing Service.

Kurtz, B. E., & Borkowski, J. G. (1984). Children's metacognition: Exploring relations among knowledge, process, and motivational variables. *Journal of Experimental Child Psychology, 37,* 335–354.

LaBerge, D., & Samuels, S. J. (1974). Toward a theory of automatic information processing in reading. *Cognitive Psychology, 6,* 293–323.

Leong, C. K. (1982). Promising areas of research into learning disabilities with emphasis on reading disabilities. In J. P. Das, R. F. Mulcahy, & A. E. Wall (Eds.), *Theory and research in learning disabilities* (pp. 3–26). New York: Plenum.

Leslie, L., & Caldwell, J. (1990). *Qualitative reading inventory.* Glenview, IL: Scott-Foresman.

Lidz, C. (1987). *Dynamic assessment.* Hillsdale, NJ: Erlbaum.

Lipson, M. Y., Irwin, M., & Poth, E. (1986). The relationship between metacognitive self-reports and strategic reading behavior. In J. Niles & R. Lalik (Eds.), *Solving problems in literacy: Learners, teachers, and researchers* (Thirty-fifth Yearbook of the National Reading Conference) (pp. 214–221). Rochester, NY: National Reading Conference.

Lipson, M. Y., & Wixson, K. K. (1986). Reading disability research: An interactionist perspective. *Review of Educational Research, 56,* 111–136.

McConkie, G. W., Rayner, K., & Wilson, S. J. (1973). Experimental manipulation of reading strategies. *Journal of Educational Psychology, 65,* 1–8.

McDermott, R. P. (1976). Achieving school failure: An anthropological approach to illiteracy and social stratification. In H. Singer & R. B. Ruddell (Eds.), *Theoretical models and processes of reading* (pp. 389–428). Newark, DE: International Reading Association.

McDermott, R. P. (1977). The ethnography of speaking and reading. In R. W. Shuy (Ed.), *Linguistic theory: What can it say about reading?* (pp. 153–185). Newark, DE: International Reading Association.

McKinney, J. D., & Speece, D. L. (1986). Academic consequences and longitudinal stability of behavioral subtypes of learning-disabled children. *Journal of Educational Psychology, 78,* 365–372.

Massaro, D. W. (1984). Building and testing models of reading processes. In P. D. Pearson et al. (Eds.), *Handbook of reading research* (Vol. 1, pp. 111–146). White Plains, NY: Longman.

Massaro, D. W., & Miller, J. (1983). Working memory and individual differences in comprehension and memory of text. *Journal of Educational Psychology, 75,* 314–318.

Mehan, H. (1979). *Learning lessons: Social organization in the classroom.* Cambridge, MA: Harvard University Press.

Meyer, B. J. F. (1975). *The organization of prose and its effects on memory.* Amsterdam: North-Holland.

Michaels, S. (1981). "Sharing time: "Children's narrative styles and differential access to literacy. *Language in Society, 10,* 423–442.

Monroe, M. (1932). *Children who cannot read.* Chicago: University of Chicago Press.

Morgan, W. P. (1896). A case of congenital word blindness. *British Medical Journal, 2,* 1612–1614.

Mosenthal, P. B. (1984). The problem of a partial specification of translating reading research into practice. *Elementary School Journal, 85,* 1–28.

Mosenthal, P. B. (1986). Defining good and poor reading—the problem of artifactual lamp posts. *Reading Teacher, 40,* 858–861.

Mosenthal, P. B. (in press). Three approaches to defining progress in reading research. In R. J. Spiro (Ed.), *Reading research into the 90s.* Hillsdale, NJ: Erlbaum.

Myklebust, H. R. (1964). *The psychology of deafness: Sensory deprivation, learning, and adjustment.* New York: Grune & Stratton.

Myklebust, H. R. (1965). *Development and disorders of written language: Picture Story Language Test* (Vol. 1). New York: Grune & Stratton.

Newcomer, P., & Hammill, D. D. (1975). ITPA and academic achievement: A survey. *Reading Teacher, 28,* 731–741.

Nisbett, R. E., & Wilson, T. D. (1977). Telling more than we can know: Verbal reports on mental processes. *Psychological Review, 84,* 231–259.

Oka, E. R., & Paris, S. G. (1986). Patterns of motivation and reading skills in underachieving children. In S. J. Ceci (Ed.), *Handbook of cognitive, social, and neuropsychological aspects of learning disabilities* (Vol. 2, pp. 115–145). Hillsdale, NJ: Erlbaum.

Olsen, J. L., Wong, B. Y. L., & Marx, R. W. (1983). Linguistic and metacognitive aspects of normally achieving and learning-disabled children's communication process. *Learning Disabilities Quarterly, 6,* 289–304.

Olshavsky, J. E. (1976–1977). Reading as problem solving: An investigation of strategies. *Reading Research Quarterly, 12,* 654–674.

Olson, R., Kliegl, R., Davidson, B., & Foltz, G. (1985). Individual and developmental differences in reading disability. In G. MacKinnon & T. Waller (Eds.), *Reading research: Advances in theory and practice* (Vol. 4, pp. 1–64). London: Academic Press.

Orton, S. T. (1925). Word blindness in school children. *Archives of Neurology and Psychiatry, 14,* 582–615.

Osgood, C. E. (1957). A behavioristic analysis of perception and language as cognitive phenomena. In J. S. Bruner (Ed.), *Contemporary approaches to cognition* (pp. 75–118). Cambridge, MA: Harvard University Press.

Palincsar, A. S., & Brown, A. L. (1984). Reciprocal teaching of comprehension fostering and monitoring activities. *Cognition and Instruction, 1,* 117–175.

Paratore, J. R., & Indrisano, R. (1987). Intervention assessment of reading comprehension. *Reading Teacher, 40,* 778–783.

Paris, S. G., Lipson, M. Y., & Wixson, K. K. (1983). Becoming a strategic reader. *Contemporary Educational Psychology, 8,* 293–316.

Paris, S. G., & Meyers, M. (1981). Comprehension monitoring, memory, and study strategies of good and poor readers. *Journal of Reading Behavior, 13,* 5–22.

Paris, S. G., Wasik, B. A., & Van der Westhuizen, G. (1988). Meta-metacognition: A review of research on metacognition and reading. In J. E. Readence & R. S. Baldwin (Eds.), *Dialogues in literacy research* (Thirty-seventh Yearbook of the National Reading Conference) (pp. 143–166). Chicago: National Reading Conference.

Pascarella, E. T., & Pflaum, S. W. (1981). The interaction of children's attributions and level of control over error correction on reading instruction. *Journal of Educational Psychology, 73,* 533–540.

Pirozzolo, F. J., & Rayner, K. (1977). Hemispheric specialization in reading and word recognition. *Brain and Language, 4,* 248–261.

Poplin, M. S. (1988). The reductionist fallacy in learning disabilities: Replicating the past by reducing the present. *Journal of Learning Disabilities, 21,* 389–400.

Rist, R. C. (1970). Student social class and teacher expectations: The self-fulfilling prophecy in ghetto education. *Harvard Educational Review, 40,* 411–451.

Robinson, H. M. (1946). *Why pupils fail in reading.* Chicago: University of Chicago Press.

Roediger, H. L., III (1980). Memory metaphors in cognitive psychology. *Memory and Cognition, 8,* 231–246.

Rosenbaum, J. E., (1980). Social implications of educational grouping. In D. C. Berliner (Ed.), *Review of Research in Education* (Vol. 8). Washington, DC: American Educational Research Association.

Rumelhart, D. (1977). Toward an interactive model of reading. In S. Dornic (Ed.), *Attention and performance* (Vol. 6, pp. 573–603). Hillsdale, NJ: Erlbaum.

Ryan, E. B. (1981). Identifying and remediating failures in reading comprehension. In T. G. Waller & G. E. MacKinnon (Eds.), *Advances in reading research* (Vol. 1). New York: Academic Press.

Samuels, S. J. (1984). Resolving some theoretical and instructional conflicts in the 1980s. *Reading Research Quarterly, 19,* 390–392.

Samuels, S. J. (1987). Information-processing abilities and reading. *Journal of Learning Disabilities, 20,* 18–22.

Samuels, S. J., & Kamil, M. L. (1984). Models of the reading process. In P. D. Pearson et al. (Eds.),

Handbook of reading research (Vol. 1, pp. 185–224). White Plains, NY: Longman.

Sarason, S. B., & Doris, J. (1979). *Educational handicap, public policy, and social history.* New York: Fress Press.

Satz, P., & Morris, R. (1981). Learning disability subtypes: A review. In F. J. Pirozzolo & M. C. Wittrock (Eds.), *Neuropsychological and cognitive processes in reading* (pp. 109–141). New York: Academic Press.

Satz, P., Taylor, G., Friel, J., & Fletcher, J. (1978). Some developmental and predictive precursors of reading disabilities: A six-year follow-up. In A. L. Benton & D. Pearl (Eds.), *Dyslexia: An appraisal of current knowledge* (pp. 313–347). New York: Oxford University Press.

Satz, P., & van Nostrand, G. (1973). Developmental dyslexia: An evaluation of a theory. In P. Satz & J. Ross (Eds.), *The disabled learner: Early detection and intervention.* Rotterdam: Rotterdam University Press.

Schank, R. (1975). *Conceptual information processing.* Amsterdam: North-Holland.

Schieffelin, B. B., & Cochran-Smith, M. (1984). Learning to read culturally: Literacy before schooling. In H. Goelman, A. A. Oberg, & F. Smith (Eds.), *Awakening to literacy* (pp. 3–23). Exeter, NH: Heinemann.

Shuell, T. J. (1986). Cognitive conceptions of learning. *Review of Educational Research, 56,* 411–436.

Spiro, R. J. (1977). Remembering information from text: The "state of schema" approach. In R. C. Anderson, R. J. Spiro, & W. E. Montague (Eds.), *Schooling and the acquisition of knowledge* (pp. 137–165). Hillsdale, NJ: Erlbaum.

Stanovich, K. E. (1986). Matthew effects in reading: Some consequences of individual differences in the acquisition of literacy. *Reading Research Quarterly, 21,* 360–407.

Sternberg, R. J. (1977). *Intelligence, information processing, and analogical reasoning: The componential analysis of human abilities.* Hillsdale, NJ: Erlbaum.

Thorndike, E. L. (1914). The measurement of ability in reading. *Teachers College Record, 15,* 207–227.

Thorndike, R. L. (1963). *The concepts of over- and underachievement.* New York: Teachers College, Columbia University.

Tinker, M. A. (1933). Use and limitations of eye-movement measures of reading. *Psychological Review, 40,* 381–387.

Torgesen, J. K. (1977). The role of nonspecific factors in the task performance of learning-disabled children: A theoretical assessment. *Journal of Learning Disabilities, 10,* 27–34.

Torgesen, J. K. (1980). Conceptual and educational implications of the use of efficient task strategies by learning-disabled children. *Journal of Learning Disabilities, 13,* 364–371.

Torgesen, J. K., & Licht, B. (1983). The learning-disabled child as an inactive learner: Retrospect and prospects. In J. McKinney & L. Feagans (Eds.), *Topics in learning disabilities* (Vol. 1, pp. 3–31). Norwood, NJ: Ablex.

Uhl, W. L. (1916). The use of the results of reading tests as bases for planning remedial work. *Elementary School Journal, 17,* 266–275.

Valencia, S., & Pearson, P. D. (1987). Reading assessment: Time for a change. *Reading Teacher, 40,* 726–732.

Valtin, R. (1978–1979). Dyslexia: Deficit in reading or deficit in research? *Reading Research Quarterly, 14,* 201–221.

Vellutino, F. R. (1979). *Dyslexia: Theory and research.* Cambridge, MA: MIT Press.

Vygotsky, L. S. (1978). *Mind in society.* Cambridge, MA: Harvard University Press.

Wagner, D. A. (1986). When literacy isn't reading (and vice versa). In M. E. Wrolstad & D. F. Fisher (Eds.), *Toward a new understanding of literacy* (pp. 319–331). New York: Praeger.

Watson, B. U., Goldgar, D. E., & Ryschon, K. L. (1983). Subtypes of reading disability. *Journal of Clinical Neuropsychology, 5,* 377–399.

Weiner, B. (1983). Some thoughts about feelings. In S. G. Paris, G. M. Olson, & H. W. Stevenson (Eds.), *Learning and motivation in the classroom* (pp. 165–178). Hillsdale, NJ: Erlbaum.

Weinstein, C. E., & Underwood, V. L. (1985). The teaching of learning strategies. In J. Segal, S. Chipman, & R. Glaser (Eds.), *Relating instruction to basic research* (pp. 241–258). Hillsdale, NJ: Erlbaum.

Weinstein, R. S. (1986). Teaching reading: Children's awareness of teacher expectations. In T. E. Raphael (Ed.), *Contexts of school-based literacy* (pp. 233–252). New York: Random House.

Willson, V. L. (1986, December). *Methodological limitations of the application of expert systems methodology in reading.* Paper presented at the Annual Meeting of the National Reading Conference, Austin, TX.

Witty, P., & Kopel, D. (1936). Factors associated with the etiology of reading disability. *Journal of Educational Research, 29,* 449–459.

Wixson, K. K., & Peters, C. W. (1984). Reading redefined: A Michigan Reading Association position paper. *Michigan Reading Journal, 17,* 4–7.

Wixson, K. K., Peters, C. W., Weber, E. M., & Roeber, E. D. (1987). New directions in statewide reading assessment. *Reading Teacher, 40,* 749–754.

Wixson, K. K., & Lipson, M. Y. (1986). Reading (dis)abilities: An interactionist perspective. In T. E. Raphael (Ed.), *Contexts of school-based literacy* (pp. 131–148). New York: Random House.

Wong, B. Y. L., & Jones, W. (1982). Increasing metacomprehension in learning-disabled and normally achieving students through self-questioning training. *Learning Disabilities Quarterly, 5,* 228–240.

Zirbes, L. (1918). Diagnostic measurement as a basis for procedure. *Elementary School Journal, 18,* 505–512.

21

COGNITIVE AND NEUROPSYCHOLOGICAL FOUNDATIONS OF WORD IDENTIFICATION IN POOR AND NORMALLY DEVELOPING READERS

Frank R. Vellutino
and Martha B. Denckla

Printed word identification is a rather complex skill that involves the coordinated action of most of the child's cognitive abilities.[1] In order to identify a single word, the child must attach a name and conceptual meaning to visual characters representing that word. If the word is printed in a writing system based on an alphabet, he/she must also attach the sounds that make up the spoken form of the word to each of the characters that make up its printed counterpart. And because each printed word represents a word in a spoken language, which, by definition, has a unique function in sentences, he/she must invest each with the type of functional meaning implicitly associated with a word's form class.

In more technical parlance, the process of learning to identify printed words requires that the child store visual representations of uniquely arrayed sets of letter characters, and attach to particular sets of characters the semantic, phonological, and syntactic-grammatical properties of the words they represent. This attachment process is something that most children manage with comparatively little difficultly, despite its complexity. However, there are a number of children who, for one reason or another, have difficulty in establishing the necessary links between the visual and linguistic components of printed words and are therefore encumbered in their efforts at learning to read. A small group of children who are so encumbered (often called *dyslexics* or *disabled readers*) are particularly interesting because their difficulties in learning to read occur in the midst of apparently normal development in all other domains. Because the scientific analysis of their reading difficulties promises to teach us something about the cognitive and neuropsychological processes that underlie word identification, such children have attracted the attention of professionals in cognitive science and neuroscience, as well as that of students of the reading process. Each of these disciplines has approached the problem from a slightly different perspective, and the research they have conducted has yielded important insights that have both theoretical and practical value.

In the present chapter we discuss some of this research, focusing on hypothesized deficiencies in the systems and processes involved in word identification. We first discuss these systems and processes and thereafter evaluate theories of reading disability that have implicated one or another. We then discuss the neurological foundations of word identification and conclude our exposition with a brief discussion of the relative merits of the cognitive and neuropsychological approaches to the study of reading and reading disability.

SYSTEMS AND PROCESSES UNDERLYING
WORD IDENTIFICATION

As we indicated earlier, learning to identify printed words, in essence, involves attaching to visual characters the conceptual and linguistic properties already attached to units of natural language. This type of learning, by definition, involves linguistic and visual coding operations; but because beginning reading typically involves oral execution and is typically accompanied by oral and written spelling as related enterprises, the motor systems are also involved to some degree. In addition, a number of cognitive processes facilitate and support these coding operations and learning in general. It would therefore seem that deficiencies which impair the use of any of these mechanisms would lead to difficulties in learning to read; and, in fact, particular theories of reading disability have implicated one or another.

However, given the population of children of particular interest here—that is, impaired readers who are otherwise normal—the probable causes of reading disability would seem to more circumscribed. We document this point of view in the sections that follow.

Representational Systems in Word Identification

Language Systems

A printed word is gradually invested with several different types of linguistic properties that may be more or less salient during the course of the child's learning, depending on his/her stage of development. These properties are derived from corresponding linguistic *codes*, which are abstract entities that represent the different attributes of the units of language: *semantic codes*, *phonological codes*, and *syntactic-grammatical codes*.

Semantic coding.   Semantic codes are representations of the meanings assigned to units of language. They have reference either to the meanings of individual words (e.g., *playing*) or to the broader meanings conveyed by groups of words (*The children are playing*). In order to learn a natural language, the child must have the ability to acquire an adequate vocabulary of spoken words that he/she must learn to use appropriately in sentences. The more words a child acquires and the more he/she learns about those words, the more efficient he/she becomes in categorizing them and, thus, in retrieving them for appropriate and effective use—in communicating, in thinking, and so forth. He/she will also become increasingly efficient in discriminating between and among them. This process, of course, entails development, elaboration, and differentiation of what is often called the *semantic network*.

If the ability to acquire an adequate vocabulary is important for learning a natural language, it is equally important for learning to read. In order to learn to associate a spoken word with its counterpart in print, the child must have an adequate grasp of the meaning of that word, both in and out of sentence contexts. He/she must also be able to make clear-cut distinctions between the word's meaning and the meanings of other words—for example, words that are similar either in referential meaning (e.g., *cat* vs. *kitten*) or functional meaning (e.g., *add/plus*; *him/he*). Put another way, he/she must have a sufficiently elaborate and well-differentiated semantic network to readily access the meanings, and thereby the names, of words that he/she is attempting to learn to identify. An adequate level of semantic development is important at the beginning stage of reading, when the child relies so heavily on word meanings in learning to identify words initially encountered (Gough & Hillinger, 1980). It becomes increasingly important as the number of new words encountered in print expands, especially in learning to identify those that cannot be readily "decoded" using spelling-sound correspondence rules (e.g., *was*, *saw*, *their*, and so on). It follows that a child with a limited vocabulary may have difficulty learning to read. In fact, we suggest that learning to identify printed words as integrated wholes, making effective use of word meanings to aid the process, is one of several complementary subskills that the child must acquire in order to become an effective reader. Whole-word/meaning-based word identification is often called the *direct access* method of word identification.

Phonological coding.   Phonological codes are abstract representations of the sound attributes of spoken and written words in the form of individual units of speech—called *phonemes*—along with implicit "rules" for ordering those units (Chomsky & Halle, 1968). In their synthesized ("blended") form, the phonemes corresponding with a printed word represent the name of that word. In their segmented form, they correspond with the individual letters (*graphemes*) in that word or with certain combinations of those letters (e.g., *th*, *ing*). In order to acquire words in a language, children must be able to discriminate and represent the phonemes of the language. They must also be able to represent unique sequences of phonemes corresponding with the names of things. In other words, they must be able to code information phonologically.

Phonological coding ability is also important in learning to identify printed words and supports this enterprise in several different ways. One way is to aid the process of associating a name with a printed word as a whole unit. A second is to aid segmentation of spoken and printed words to facilitate detection and functional use of grapheme-phoneme and other spelling-sound invariants that can be used for word decoding (e.g., *cat*, *fat*, *train*, *pain*).

A third is to facilitate use of letter sounds to aid in discriminating and sequencing letters in words (e.g., *pot* vs. *top*). Still another is to facilitate development of morphophonemic production rules that help a child render correct pronunciations of derived words having common root morphemes, but varying with respect to form class (e.g., *bomb*, *bombadier*, *bombard*). A fourth is to aid the process of attaching the appropriate sounds to common subword units such as bound morphemes (*-ed*, *-ing*) and syllables (*ove* in *love* and *dove*).

In an orthography based on an alphabet, words are made up of combinations of letters that are often highly redundant. This property of the writing system has the potential for a good deal of visual confusion, unless the child acquires the means for capitalizing on spelling-sound redundancies such as those we have mentioned. This approach to word processing has alternately been called the *code-oriented* or *indirect access* method of word identification. In our estimation, the word-analytic subskills inherent in the use of code-oriented approaches to word processing are critically important for learning to identity printed words and complement the whole-word/meaning-based method of word identification.

Syntactic-grammatical coding.   Syntactic codes are abstract representations conforming with rules for ordering words in the language. Grammatical codes are representations of a word's form class (e.g., noun, verb, and so on), and together they define its function in sentences. Related to both of these codes are representations of bound morphemes that modify words for case, gender, tense, mood, and so forth. In order to comprehend and generate sentences, the child must learn to apply syntactic "rules" to segment sentences into their grammatical constituents and thereafter determine how those constituents are related to one another. The grammatical constituents contain the substantive components of a sentence, and the syntactic rules order them in ways that facilitate comprehension. For example, syntactic analysis uses word order rules and word meanings to determine whether active and passive sentences contain the same information.

Comprehension of the grammar and syntax of a natural language facilitates word identification in at least three different ways. First, by facilitating sentence comprehension, it aids the child in using sentence context to anticipate words that might appear in given sentence frames as well as to monitor accuracy in word identification. Second, it aids the process of assigning to printed words what might be called *function codes*. Function codes are representations that define, or "mark," a word's unique role in sentences. They are especially important in distinguishing among noncontent words such as *if, and, but, for, from, of*, and so forth. They, along with phonological codes, are also important in acquiring production rules that facilitate correct pronunciations of derived words such as *bomber* and *bombardier*, and inflections such as *-ed*, and *-ing*.

A child who has difficulty in representing the grammar and syntax of the language will, quite likely, have difficulty in sentence comprehension; and this, in turn, will impair his/her ability to use sentence contexts to aid word identification. He/she may also have difficulty discriminating functional differences in words, particularly those of a more abstract nature (i.e., noncontent words); and this, too, could impair word identification. Moreover, the child who does not adequately represent bound morphemes will tend to be imprecise in identifying words that are modified by these units, as exemplified in cases where words are not properly inflected (e.g., calling dogs /dog/).

Visual System

The role of the visual system in learning to read would seem to be straightforward: to store representations of printed words that one comes to recognize reliably. If the child is equipped with a good visual memory, then he/she should have little difficulty learning to read. Word identification in this case is simply a matter of remembering what a word looks like and then associating it with a word in one's vocabulary. This simple account, of course, misrepresents the enormity of the visual learning task set before the child when he/she begins to read. Not only must he/she come to discriminate among (literally) thousands of printed words, some differing in only a single letter feature (*snow/show*), or in the way their letters are ordered (*was/saw*), but he/she must also come to discriminate words written in different cases, fonts, and writing styles. How can the developing reader accomplish this feat relying on visual memory alone?

The answer is that he/she does not rely on visual memory alone, simply because he/she cannot do so—at least not in an alphabetic orthography where there is so much visual similarity. The load on visual memory is much too formidable, and a case could be made that the child who does attempt to rely exclusively on visual memory for words as wholes will encounter significant difficulties in learning to read. We suggest that the developing reader ultimately negotiates the complexities of the orthography by acquiring a number of synthesizing strategies that reduce the load on visual memory, and does so with the aid of the language systems, especially the phonological system. Provided that the child is exposed to instruction that facilitates discovery and functional use of the alphabetic principle, and assuming adequate ability in phonological coding, he/she soon learns to take advantage of spelling-sound redundancies as a vehicle for (1) storing rules for constraining the order in which letters may occur in the orthography; (2) storing rules for ordering the letters in words (e.g., graphophonemic rules); (3) storing representations of redundant combinations of letters with invariant spellings and pronunciations (e.g., *at* in *cat* and *fat*); (4) making increasingly fine-grained discriminations among visually similar words; (5) storing unitized representations of subword morphophonemic units that have invariant spellings and pronunciations (e.g., *-ing*, *-tion*); (6) storing unitized representations of redundant combinations of letters (e.g., *th*, *sh*, *ch*); and (7) identifying new words permutatively and generatively. Each of the foregoing strategies helps to reduce the load on visual memory in a slightly different way. Collectively they constitute a powerful set of mechanisms that not only aid the child in negotiating the writing system, but also assist in the necessary process of internalizing completely specified representations for identifying both words that are familiar and those that are unfamiliar.

Yet, there are many words in English orthography that contain elements which do not conform with typical pronunciations (e.g., *have* vs. *gave* and *save*; *bread* vs. *bead* and *beak*), and these pose special problems for the developing reader. Word elements that are especially problematic are the vowels, which are more complexly encoded and less predictable than the consonants (Fowler, Liberman & Shankweiler, 1977). The child cannot rely exclusively on phonetic decoding ability to identify words containing atypically pronounced vowels and must therefore generate a variety of mnemonics to learn to identify them with precision. Indeed, it is because of vowel complexity in particular that the child must come to diversify his/her processing strategies, if he/she is to fully specify and integrate the visual and linguistic components of printed words. For example, in learning to identify atypically pronounced words such as *have* and *bread*, the child must come to rely more heavily on the meanings and functional properties of these words than on their phonemic properties to effect precision in identification.

It should be apparent that, in our estimation, the visual system takes its lead from the language systems in word identification, this relationship being dictated by the nature of the reading process. It is the language systems that confer meaning and valence on the visual symbols representing printed words and determine how they will be analyzed and thereafter represented. It is also the language systems and the heuristics and algorithms generated by the language systems that facilitate synthesis of the vast amounts of visual information that must be stored in order for the child to acquire fluency in word identification. This suggests that reading may be an enterprise that can tolerate a wide range of individual differences in visual ability, provided that the child has the linguistic coding abilities that would facilitate his/her ability to capitalize on the spelling-sound redundancies inherent in the orthography, and to utilize code-oriented as well as meaning-based strategies for word identification.

Motor Systems

Insofar as the child typically learns to read using an oral reading method, he/she learns to relate visual symbols to representations of the speech-motor executions used in vocalizing the names associated with those symbols. It is therefore likely that such representations become part of the description of a printed word. If this assumption is made, then it might be reasonably inferred that a child who has significant difficulty in pronouncing words in the language, because of an articulation disorder, might have difficulty acquiring speech-based reading skills such as phonetic decoding ability; and this, in turn, could lead to difficulties in word identification.

Similarly, written spelling depends, in part, on a child's ability to execute the visual-motor programs necessary to form individual letters; and it would seem that visual-motor dysfunction could conceivably impair word identification, by impeding the child's ability to use written spelling as a vehicle for acquiring fully specified representations of printed words.

While we have no doubt that speech-motor and visual-motor representations do normally become part of the description of a printed word in memory, we are inclined to believe that success in word identification does not depend significantly on availability of high-quality representations of speech-motor and visual-motor executions. We do not deny the possibility (nor do we accept the certainty), that children with severe disorders in these areas progress more slowly than do normally developing children; but we assume that these abilities are secondary to the higher-level language skills that are central to reading. For example, we think it is more important for the child to grasp the concept that letters have sounds, as a prerequisite to success in alphabetic mapping, than to physically articulate these sounds. Similarly, it is more important for a child to attach a name and meaning to a printed word than to pronounce that name articulately in reading it. Moreover, a child can learn to spell a word without having to execute the motor programs necessary to write it, though it is certainly advantageous to be able to do so.

At the same time, a number of pedagogical devices can be used to compensate for even severe motor deficits that might interfere with reading instruction, as is clearly demonstrated by the fact that most children with cerebral palsy become quite literate, despite their motor difficulties and provided that other cognitive and linguistic systems are developing normally. It is also important that they be schooled in an educational program that allows them adequate opportunity to learn to read.

Finally, motor-deficit theories of reading disability have not been given strong confirmation in the literature (Vellutino, 1979). It would therefore seem that internalization of high-quality motor representations is not a significant determinant of success in word identification.

Cognitive Processes Involved in All Learning

In addition to the representational systems and processes that are specifically involved in reading, several cognitive processes are involved in all learning and not only in learning to read. These might be profitably discussed, both to enhance our understanding of the word identification process, and because dysfunction in each of these processes has been hypothesized to be a cause of reading disability.

Attention

It is a truism that our ability to learn any new relationship depends, initially, on our ability to attend selectively to the distinguishing attributes of the entities we are attempting to relate. It is also important that we come to distinguish between variant and invariant dimensions in these entities so as to become increasingly efficient in how we search for their distinguishing attributes. Gibson (1969) calls this type of processing *perceptual learning* to underscore one's tendency to become increasingly efficient in attending selectively. However, as she points out, such efficiency is not ensured by simply looking at or listening to the things one attempts to discriminate, but, instead, requires an extensive period of analysis, the course of which is determined by three related contingencies: (1) one's ability to attend as determined by one's affective or emotional state; (2) one's motivation or interest in attending; and (3) the extent to which one has acquired knowledge that would facilitate selective attention of the sort that leads to critical discriminations.

The first contingency relates to the intactness of those components of the central nervous system that are responsible for degree of emotional arousal. There is reason to believe that attention and concentration are contingent on degree of arousal, such that either underarousal or overarousal leads to poor attention and limited learning (Mirsky, 1978). Some children are, in fact, hampered by limited attention span and poor concentration; and children so impaired do, indeed, have difficulty learning to read (Dykman, Ackerman, & Holcomb; 1985; Harter, Anllo-Vento, Wood, & Schroeder, 1988).

The second contingency relates to the child's volition and deliberate intent. Without sufficient interest in acquiring knowledge in a given domain, it becomes difficult to attend in a way that optimizes the probability of success in learning. There are, no doubt, large numbers of children who have difficulty learning to read because of a lack of inherent motivation. This, of course, poses a special challenge not only for educators responsible for teaching them, but also for researchers attempting to distinguish the prospective sources of reading disability. Researchers studying the etiology of specific reading disabilities have traditionally controlled for attention deficits associated with motivational problems by excluding children from their research samples, if there is any indication, either in their school histories or through psychometric analysis, that they are impaired in reading because of such problems.

The third contingency is more subtle and refers to the role of prior knowledge in determining one's processing attitudes in new learning situations. To illustrate, the young child who is familiar with the printed word *lion*, on being first presented with the new word *loin*, is apt to misname this word because of his/her prior experience with its visually similar counterpart. When he/she adds *loin* to his/her vocabulary, he/she begins to attend to the way in which its medial letters and those in *lion* are ordered (perhaps in part, by virtue of the different phoneme values attached to these letters), and his/her means of processing these two words will change in such a way as to ensure selective attention to the order of their medial letters. During the initial stages of discrimination, this type of processing requires a good deal of cognitive effort, but over time it becomes automated. LaBerge and Samuels (1974) have documented that accurate discrimination of distinguishing attributes and selective and effortless attention to those attributes are related benchmarks of automatic processing of letters and words. Conversely, less-accurate discrimination of distinguishing attributes and nonselective and effortful attention in searching for those attributes are benchmarks of nonautomatic processing. It follows that the child who does not steadily and systematically acquire the types of knowledge that will allow him/her to more precisely analyze the orthography (e.g., word meanings, spelling-sound rules, and so on), will have difficulty selectively attending to critical differences in the letters and words he/she encounters. The child who does steadily acquire such knowledge becomes increasingly more efficient in attending selectively to such distinctions.

Associative Learning

The ability to associate one entity with another is a rather basic cognitive mechanism that is critically important for learning in general and word identification in particular. In a very real sense it defines one of the most rudimentary and ubiquitous of all of our cognitive abilities—specifically, the ability to symbolize. When we symbolize, we have one thing represent another and each may prompt a reaction common to both, as in attaching the same meaning to a word, regardless of whether it is spoken or printed. How one learns *associative relationships*, whether such learning is a matter of "insightful discovery" of distinguishing and mediating attributes or of gradual accretion of connective bonds through practice and reinforcement, is a controversial issue with a long history, and we need not address the issue here (Gibson, 1969). Contemporary theories of learning and memory suggest that each of these conceptualizations may have some validity. Associative learning does seem to involve something akin to a search for, and "discovery" of, implicit mediators (often called *retrieval cues*) that may link two associates in the semantic network (Tulving & Pearlstone, 1966). Moreover, such learning often does appear to be gradual. This fact is explained by the need to eliminate competition from associates with similar attributes, which entails explication and encoding of distinguishing attributes, and which may require several "passes" through the semantic network.

What is not controversial, however, is the fact that we come by this capability quite naturally, assuming that we are developing normally. Indeed, even subhuman species can symbolize and learn associative relationships, as anyone who owns a domesticated animal can readily testify.

Cross-Modal Transfer

When associative bonds are established between encoded information stored in different representational systems, and when accessing one type of information from memory becomes the occasion for accessing the other, we have an instance of what has been alternately called *cross-modal transfer* and *intersensory integration* (Bryant, 1974; Gibson, 1969). Learning to identify printed words is one type of cross-modal learning, insofar as it entails associating visual symbols with linguistic symbols.

The ability to associate symbols stored in different representational systems is also a rather basic mechanism for learning that is available very early in life (Bryant, 1974; Gibson, 1969). Reading typically involves the use of rather arbitrary sets of visual symbols, but it could as readily involve the use of other types of symbols, as in learning to read tactile symbols such as Braille. Moreover, the types of cross-modal equivalences established will vary with the writing system. For example, the types of equivalences established in a logographic writing system, such as Chinese, differ from those established in an alphabetic writing system, such as English; and the way in which those equivalences are established is different in each system. Whereas logographic systems rely primarily on word names and meanings to form connective bonds between the visual and linguistic symbols used in those systems, alphabetic systems rely more heavily on redundant letter sounds to do so.

Pattern Analysis and Rule Learning

One of the most important of all of our cognitive abilities is the ability to detect *patterned invariance*. Gibson (1969) suggests that humans are naturally inclined to "search for invariance" in new learning situations to aid them both in reducing the amount of information they would otherwise be required to store, and to facilitate detection of distinguishing attributes in things having overlapping features. She also suggests that humans are naturally endowed with mechanisms that allow them to store representations of invariant relationships in the form of *rules* and *algorithms* that can be used generatively. In regard to reading, she argues that the ability to detect and utilize patterned invariance makes word identification, as a developmental enterprise, something more than simple paired-associate learning. Thus, she suggests that the developing reader will eventually detect and utilize spelling-sound correspondences and other forms of orthographic redundancy, even if he/she is not explicitly attuned to such redundancy, because he/she is naturally "programmed" to search for invariance.

We are inclined to agree with this analysis. Indeed, we intuit that the ability to detect and represent invariance may well be the very foundation of all cognitive abilities and intelligent behavior in general.

Serial Memory

A question of some importance to students of cognition and practitioners alike is just how one remembers the order in which things occur. A related question is whether or not memory for the elements in a given array or system is a process that is psychologically and neurologically distinct from memory for the order in which those elements occur. Some suggest that *serial memory* is a generalized ability that determines the order in which all information is processed. For example, largely on the basis of the clinical study of neurologically impaired adults (e.g., Luria, 1973), some investigators have assumed that serial memory, in the general sense, is a neurologically distinct capability that depends upon the integrity of the left hemisphere (Das, Kirby, & Jarman, 1975). According to this point of view, the left hemisphere has the rather ubiquitous responsibility of representing and processing ordered information of all types. This entails representing such diverse types of information as the order in which elements of a stimulus array are presented on memory tasks, and the ordering rules for complex systems such as the language systems, mathematical systems, and so forth. By the same account, the right hemisphere is responsible for representing and processing simultaneously arrayed information—for example, spatial concepts. This division of labor has been called *successive* and *simultaneous processing* respectively, following Luria (1973).

An alternative view of serial memory is that different neurological structures support modality-specific sequencing abilities (Johnson & Myklebust, 1967). Thus, the ability to sequence visual information is seen as distinct from the ability to sequence auditory information and so forth.

While clinical descriptions of ordered recall have fostered the idea that serial memory may either be a general ability or a collection of modality-specific abilities, research conducted by cognitive psychologists would lead to a different conclusion. In fact, certain generalizations have emerged from this research which suggest that serial processing is a rather generic cognitive function that varies with the type of information serialized. The evidence suggests that the ways in which one represents the particular items (units) in an ordered set and the serial order in which those items occur are distinctly different. This facet of cognition is rather handily illustrated in the distinction between the semantic and syntactic components of a natural language, the former embodying the meanings of words in the language, in terms of their conceptual attributes, and the latter embodying abstract rules and algorithms that set constraints on the ways in which those words may be ordered. A more relevant illustration, in the present context, is the distinction between the letters that make up a printed word and the invariant order in which those letters appear. It is clear that the rules for serializing the letters in these words are not inherent in the encoded representations of the letters themselves, but, rather, in the writing system in the form of orthographic conventions that, in large measure, are determined by the various ways in which the alphabetic characters map onto their sound counterparts.

Experimental evidence that item and order information are represented separately is provided by results from several studies that have appeared in the literature. Thus, Bower and Minaire (1974) and Houston (1976) were able to create circumstances whereby subjects lost item and order information selectively. Similarly, Healy (1974) found that item and ordered recall yielded different-shaped curves, when either the items used as stimuli, or the order in which those items were presented, was held constant. Ordered recall yielded the typical bow-shaped curves associated with performance on serial memory tasks, while item recall yielded learning curves that were more nearly linear.

A second important generalization that has emerged from the study of item and order processing is that there is no invariant means by which one serializes information. Patterned information is typically serialized by implicit ordering devices in the form of rules or principles that are inherent in a particular representational system. For example, the syntactic rules that order the words in a language are quite different from the mathematical rules that order the quantities in a number system and so forth. Thus, learning to serialize a given type of information necessitates acquisition of the ordering rules inherent in the system representing that information. However, when one is confronted with information for which there are no inherent ordering rules, then serialization strategies must be devised; and those employed will vary both with the unique properties of the ordered set and with one's particular organizational and coding abilities. Such strategies will, therefore, be highly individualized.

The strategies one uses in serializing randomly ordered arrays has, in fact, been the object of extensive inquiry by memory researchers (see Bower & Hilgard, 1981, for a review), but space does not permit detailed discussion of this research. It will suffice to point out that the two strategies most often used to serialize random arrays are *chunking* and *recoding*, which are typically used in concert with one another. Chunking involves reducing the size of an array into units that more readily lend themselves to position coding. Recoding involves assigning these units superordinate codes that facilitate recovery of position as well as item information. This is essentially what we do when we learn the order of digits in new phone numbers or the letters and numerals imprinted on new license plates.

These latter points bring into focus a third and final generalization that has emerged from the study of serial memory in cognitively based research—specifically, that serial recall is almost always rule based. If the material to be ordered does not exceed the limit of short-term memory and provided that it is reasonably familiar (memory span for nonsense words is less than memory span for digits and meaningful words), then verbatim serial recall is readily accomplished without the aid of organizational and coding devices. But when the material to be ordered does exceed short-term memory limits, it is ordered by rules and algorithms that are implicit, induced, or invented anew.

Summary

The acquisition of skill in word identification depends on one's ability to acquire facility in both whole-word naming and letter-sound mapping as alternative and complementary vehicles for accessing a word's name and meaning. Success in acquiring each of these subskills depends, in turn, on adequate development in the semantic, syntactic-grammatical, and phonological domains of language. It also depends on intact functioning in the major cognitive abilities employed in most forms of representational learning—in particular, attention, associative learning, cross-modal transfer, pattern analysis, rule learning, and serial memory. Thus, limitations in one or another of these processes would theoretically impair one's ability to learn to read.

HYPOTHESIZED CAUSES OF READING DISABILITY

Logical Considerations and Weak Hypotheses

As we indicated earlier, there is a small but significant number of children who have extraordinary difficulty learning to read, despite apparently normal functioning in other areas. As studied in the laboratory, such children typically have average or above-average intelligence and are free from uncorrected sensory acuity problems and from serious physical, neurological, or emotional disorders. Moreover, they do not have frequent absences from school and typically come from middle- to upper-middle-class neighborhoods. We also pointed out that dysfunction in each of the systems and processes just discussed has been implicated as a possible cause of such difficulty. However, in the population of poor readers just described, certain of the hypothesized causes of reading disability can be ruled out on logical grounds alone. We refer here to theories of reading disability which suggest that the disorder might be caused by generalized deficiencies in attention, associative learning, cross-modal transfer, pattern analysis/rule learning, or serial memory.

For one thing, it is logically inconsistent to suggest that such children can be deficient only in reading and related skills such as spelling on the one hand, and generally deficient in one or more of these foundational processes on the other. Moreover, with the exception of the attention deficit explanation of reading disability, each of these theories is also contraindicated by the fact that the children to whom they are applied, by definition, have at least average intelligence. Indeed, it is difficult to imagine a child who scores in the average or above-average range on an intelligence test, who has generalized deficits in cognitive processes such as associative learning, cross-modal transfer, rule learning, or serial memory. It is therefore not surprising that these theories have received very little empirical support (Vellutino, 1979, 1987).

The possibility that poor readers may be impaired by generalized deficiencies in associative learning was independently suggested by Brewer (1967) and by Gascon and Goodglass (1970), on the basis of studies in which normal readers were found to perform better than poor readers on paired-associates learning tasks. However, all of the tasks used in these studies involved verbal learning. This is significant because in studies conducted subsequently (Rudel, Denckla, & Spalten, 1976; Vellutino, 1979), poor readers were found to be less proficient than normal readers on verbal learning tasks, but not on nonverbal learning tasks. Such findings rule out generalized deficits in association learning as a cause of reading disability and suggest, instead, that observed differences between poor and normal readers on paired-associates tasks were most likely due to verbal coding deficits in the poor readers.

Failure to control for verbal coding deficits has also equivocated the results of studies that purportedly document the cross-modal and serial deficit theories of reading disability. Thus, Birch and Belmont (1964) found that poor readers performed below normal readers on auditory-visual matching of rhythmic patterns and offered these results as evidence that poor readers are deficient in establishing cross-modal equivalence. However, Blank and Bridger (1966) found that poor readers performed below normal readers on intramodal as well as intermodal matching tasks and produced evidence that both sets of results were attributable to the fact that the poor readers were less facile than the normal readers in generating verbal mnemonics to aid recall (see Vellutino, 1979, for an extensive review of this work).

Similarly, Vellutino (1979) reviewed research evaluating serial deficit theories of reading disability and found that results from these studies were inconclusive, not only because they failed to control for verbal coding deficits in the poor readers, but also because they uniformly compounded recall of the items presented on serial memory tasks, with recall of the order in which those items occurred. Moreover, a later study that did employ such a control (Manis & Morrison, 1982) produced no evidence for a serial processing deficit in the poor readers evaluated. At the same time, other studies have provided strong evidence that serial memory deficits would be observed in poor readers only when the number of items to be recalled exceeds the upper limit in short-term memory and only when these items are verbally codable (Katz, Shankweiler, & Liberman, 1981; Vellutino & Scanlon, 1989).

As regards the pattern analysis/rule-learning deficit theory of reading disability, it will suffice to point out that this theory has received no compelling empirical support and is based primarily on studies conducted by Morrison and Manis (1982), in which it was found that poor readers were deficient in learning arithmetic rules as well as grapheme-phoneme correspondence rules. Vellutino and Scanlon (1982) criticized these studies on sampling and methodological grounds, pointing out that it is not uncommon to find children who have difficulties in acquiring arithmetic as well as reading subskills, especially if they have generalized learning problems that might be attributed to other causes such as attentional or motivational deficits. Moreover, in a separate study addressing the question (Vellutino, 1979), poor and normal readers were compared on visual-verbal and visual-visual rule-learning tasks; and it was found that the poor readers were less proficient than the normal readers only on the visual-verbal task. These results suggest that poor readers are not generally impaired in pattern analysis and rule learning, but may be found to be deficient in performing these operations only on tasks that depend heavily on verbal coding ability.

Finally, attention deficits (if, indeed, they do exist) should affect all school learning and not only reading. It is therefore incumbent upon researchers interested in specific reading disability to attempt to distinguish between poor readers whose reading difficulties are caused by attention deficits and poor readers whose reading difficulties occur in the absence of such deficits. Some recent research has, in fact, provided evidence that these two groups can be distinguished on the basis of both neurophysiological and psychological behaviors. Thus, using the *event-related potential (ERP) procedure*[2], Harter, Anllo-Vento, Wood, and Schroeder (1988) found that brain wave patterns, in terms of ERP amplitudes, were different in reading-disabled (RD) children and children with attention deficit disorder (ADD). Dykman, Ackerman, and Holcomb (1985) obtained similar results. These researchers also found that RD subjects performed better than ADD subjects on tasks that required vigilance and cognitive effort, while ADD subjects performed better than RD subjects on language and verbal memory measures. Insofar as they provide documentation for the RD-ADD distinction we are making (see also Duffy et al., 1980), such results add substance to our contention that specific reading disability is not logically characterized as the result of attention deficits.

Summary

If one defines reading disability as a specific learning disorder that occurs in an otherwise adequate learner, then it is logically inconsistent to suggest that the problem may be caused by generalized deficiencies in cognitive processes that underlie learning in general. We therefore conclude that deficiencies in attention, association learning, cross-modal transfer, pattern analysis/rule learning, and serial memory are not significant causes of specific reading disability.

Traditional and Current Conceptualizations

Visual Perceptual and Visual Memory Deficits

By far the most popular explanation of reading disability in young children—certainly the one with the longest history—is that the problem is caused by dysfunction in the visual system characterized by visual perception and visual memory deficits. The most common explanation is that reading disability is caused by optical reversibility ("seeing" letters and words in reverse) as manifested in orientation and sequencing errors, such as reading *b* for *d* or *was* for *saw*. This idea was initially suggested by Orton (1925), who hypothesized that such dysfunction is an outgrowth of a maturation lag characterized by the failure to establish hemispheric dominance for language.

A weaker version of the perceptual deficit explanation is that of Hermann (1959), who contended that orientation and sequencing errors are caused by a genetically determined tendency toward visual-spatial confusion, which impairs one's ability to maintain left-to-right scanning and correct orientation in processing written symbols of all types. Other investigators have suggested that at least some poor readers encounter difficulty in word identification because of limitations in their ability to visualize objects and symbols. Still others suggest that such difficulty extends from more basic dysfunction in perceiving visual stimuli as unified wholes, or gestalts.

Despite their currency in the popular media, these hypotheses have not fared very well in controlled laboratory research. Vellutino (1979) reviewed the evidence for the various visual deficit theories of reading disability and found that the studies evaluating such theories produced no strong evidence to support them. Moreover, in seminal research conducted by Vellutino and his colleagues (Vellutino, 1979, 1987), it was found that severely impaired readers (grades 2 through 8) could accurately perceive and visually reproduce printed words (e.g., *was, loin, calm*) presented for brief exposures (500 ms), even though they confused these same words with their visually similar counterparts (*saw, lion, clam*) on a reading task presented subsequently. They also reproduced geometric designs as well as normal readers (Figure 21.1). Furthermore, on the reading task, subjects were asked to "spell out" the letters in each word (again from visual memory) directly after naming that word as a whole; it was found that the poor readers could spell out the letters of a word in a correct order even after misnaming the word. It was concluded from these findings that the poor reader's tendency to make *b/d* and *was/saw* type errors in reading and spelling is quite likely the result of weak verbal encoding rather than deficiencies in visual perception and visual memory.

This conclusion was reinforced by a second series of studies in which poor readers were found to be comparable to normal readers in visual recall and recognition of letters and words printed in Hebrew (Figure 21.2), which for these subjects was an unfamiliar writing system (Vellutino, 1979, 1987). As would be expected, neither group performed as well as children learning to read and write Hebrew. Because the poor readers in these studies made no more orientation or sequencing errors than did the normal readers, the investigators concluded that directional scanning and orientation problems are, in all probability, consequences of reading disability rather than manifestations of visual-spatial confusion that causes reading disability. These and other findings (Vellutino, 1979, 1987) lead us to conclude that visual-processing deficits, by themselves, are not significant causes of specific reading disability.

Verbal Deficits

We indicated earlier that the ability to learn to read depends, in great measure, on one's ability to employ units of language to code and encode the visual counterparts of printed words. We also indicated that in our view of things, success in beginning reading is largely a matter of acquiring alternative vehicles for word identification and that this, in turn, depends on adequate development in the semantic, phonological, and syntactic/ grammatical domains of language. Thus, it was suggested that the child must learn to use word meanings, letter sounds, and sentence contexts as complementary devices for word identification. It follows that difficulties in acquiring knowledge of the meanings and/or functions of printed words, in accessing or analyzing their sound attributes, or in comprehending sentences containing those words could lead to difficulties in learning to identify them.

REAL WORDS

Three Letter	Four Letter	Five Letter
fly	loin	blunt
bed	form	drawn
was	calm	chair

SCRAMBLED LETTERS

Three Letter	Four Letter	Five Letter
dnv	jpyc	ztbrc
hbd	gzfs	yfpqg
mcw	qvlt	qldnr

NUMBERS

Three Digit	Four Digit	Five Digit
382	4328	96842
974	3724	31579
296	9156	86314

GEOMETRIC DESIGNS

Two Items   Three Items

FIGURE 21.1   Visual stimuli presented to poor and normal readers on both visual reproduction and naming tasks. Reprinted with permission of the publisher from Vellutino, F. R., Smith, H., Steger, J. A., & Kaman, M. (1975), ''Reading Disability: Age Differences and the Perceptual Deficit Hypothesis,'' *Child Development, 46,* p. 490.

Semantic deficits.   The possibility that inadequate knowledge of word meanings may be causally related to deficiencies in word identification seems intuitively sound, given the importance of meaning in any new learning enterprise. Suggestive evidence for this possibility comes from a number of studies reporting substantial correlations between measures of reading ability and measures of vocabulary development. Such correlations tend to be strong, regardless of whether reading ability is measured by tests of reading comprehension (Ravenette, 1961; Stanovich, Nathan, & Zolman, 1988) or by tests of facility in word identification (Stanovich et al., 1988). They are reinforced by studies demonstrating that poor readers tend to perform below normal readers on measures of vocabulary and verbal concept formation (Vellutino, 1979; Vellutino & Scanlon, 1987a). Equally supportive are results from longitudinal studies indicating that measures of vocabulary development, administered to kindergartners, tend to be

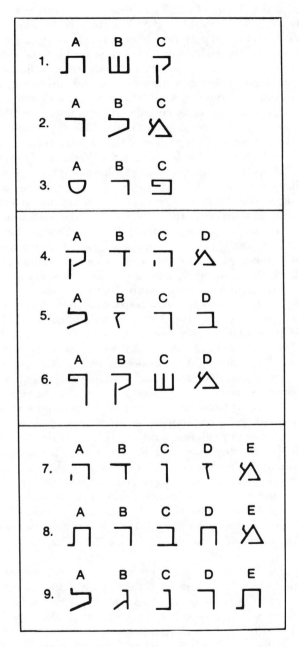

FIGURE 21.2 Hebrew words presented to poor and normal readers for visual reproduction. Reprinted with permission of the publisher from Vellutino, F. R., Pruzek, R., Steger, J. A., & Meshoulam, U. (1973), "Immediate Visual Recall in Poor and Normal Readers as a Function of Orthographic-Linguistic Familiarity," *Cortex, 9,* p. 373.

reasonably good predictors of facility in word identification in first and second grade (deHirsch, Jansky, & Langford, 1966; Vellutino & Scanlon, 1987b). Finally, poor readers have been found to perform below normally developing readers on a variety of semantic memory tasks, performance on which could certainly be affected by knowledge of word meanings, as we shall see momentarily (Vellutino & Scanlon, 1985).

Of course, such evidence is correlational and, therefore, provides only indirect support for a causal relationship between vocabulary deficits and reading disability. However, an experiment recently completed by Vellutino and Scanlon (1989) provides more direct support for this possibility. On the basis of previous studies that found that poor readers were generally less proficient than normal readers on both auditory-verbal memory tasks and visual-verbal learning tasks (Vellutino & Scanlon, 1985), Vellutino and Scanlon (1989) raised the question of whether reader group differences on such tasks could have been due, in part, to group differences in semantic development. Common to success on both auditory-verbal memory and visual-verbal learning tasks (such as word identification) is the ability to use the semantic network to store and retrieve name codes. Thus, it was reasoned that one major determinant of the reader group differences typically observed on memory and learning tasks is group differences in knowledge of the meanings of the words used as stimuli on these tasks.

To evaluate this possibility, poor and normal readers in second and sixth grade were compared on both an auditory-verbal memory task and a visual-verbal learning task that used the same words as verbal responses. However, on each task subjects were presented with two lists of words that were individualized with respect to degree of meaning. One list contained only words that were high in meaning for a given subject and another list contained only words that were low in meaning for that subject. To minimize variability that might be associated with visual complexity, Chinese ideographs were used as stimuli on the visual-verbal learning task rather than letter strings (simulating learning to read in a logographic system). It was reasoned that if deficiencies in semantic development had been an important determinant of previously observed differences between poor and normal readers on verbal memory and visual-verbal learning tasks, then poor readers should be in close approximation to normal readers on these tasks under the high-meaning list condition. Because previous research had shown that normal readers were better than poor readers in learning lists of nonsense words (Vellutino & Scanlon, 1987b), the poor readers were not expected to perform as well as the normal readers under the low-meaning condition. All subjects were expected to perform better under the high- than under the low-meaning condition, and performance on the auditory memory task was expected to be positively correlated with performance on the visual-verbal learning task. These expectations were confirmed (see Figure 21.3).

Such results make it clear that knowledge of word meanings is directly related to performance on tasks that make many of the same cognitive demands as word identification. They also provide strongly suggestive evidence that deficiencies in knowledge of word meanings may, in given cases, be a source of difficulty in word identification. Noteworthy, however, are the large differences between poor and normal readers on the low-meaning list. This finding indicates that deficiencies in semantic development are not the only source of reader group differences on verbal memory and visual-verbal learning tasks. Vellutino and Scanlon (1989) suggested that these differences were attributable to greater facility on the part of normal readers in phonological coding. We discuss this possibility momentarily, but we wish to make one other point about the semantic deficit explanation of reading disability before doing so.

We think it doubtful that vocabulary deficits would be a significant source of reading difficulty in most beginning readers who come from home and school environments that are rich in language stimulation. Vocabulary deficits as a source of reading

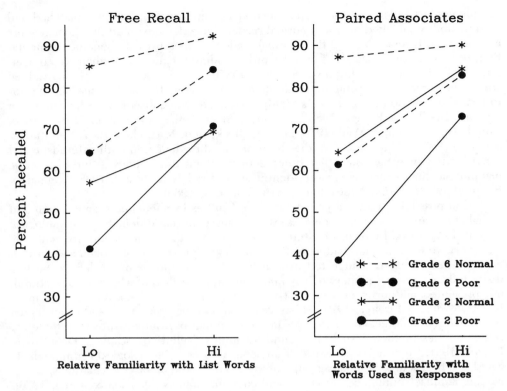

FIGURE 21.3 Performance of poor and normal readers in second and sixth grade on free recall and visual-verbal association learning tasks using the same sets of high- and low-meaning words. Reprinted with permission of the publisher from Vellutino, F. R., & Scanlon, D. M. (1989), "Auditory Information Processing in Poor and Normal Readers." In J. J. Dumont & N. Naken (Eds.), *Learning Disabilities: Vol. 2. Cognitive, Social and Remedial Aspects*. Amsterdam/Lisse, Netherlands: Swets & Zeitlinger.

difficulty in beginning readers should be more prevalent in children who are not exposed to language-rich environments. However, in either case, such deficits will inevitably accrue as a consequence of prolonged difficulties in reading and should compound the reading difficulties (Nagy & Anderson, 1984).

Phonological deficits.   Perhaps the most convergent evidence in research evaluating the etiology of reading disability comes from studies documenting that poor readers, as a group, tend to be inept on tasks that depend on proficiency in processing the phonological attributes of printed words. Moreover, the evidence for causal relationships between phonological deficits and deficiencies in word identification is more direct than the evidence for causal relationships involving the other domains of language. In fact, there is reason to believe that word identification problems, in the majority of cases, is caused by deficiencies in alphabetic mapping and phonetic decoding associated with deficiencies in phoneme segmentation (defined as the ability to explicate individual sounds in spoken and written words). Moreover, there is evidence that such deficiencies, in many cases, is caused by basic ineptitude in phonological coding.

That deficiency in phoneme segmentation and alphabetic mapping are directly and causally related to deficiencies in word identification comes from three types of complementary evidence. First, cross-sectional comparisons of both age-matched and reading-ability-matched poor and normal readers have demonstrated that poor readers are significantly less proficient than normal readers on measures of phoneme segmentation, as well as on measures of pseudoword decoding (Stanovich, Nathan, & Zolman, 1988; Vellutino, 1979; Vellutino & Scanlon, 1987b). Second, a number of longitudinal studies have recently documented that phonemic segmentation ability, measured prior to formal instruction in reading, is highly correlated with subsequent achievement in reading (Bradley & Bryant, 1983; Liberman, Shankweiler, Fischer, & Carter, 1974; Lundberg, Olofsson, & Wall, 1980; Perfetti, Beck, Bell, & Hughes, 1987; Vellutino & Scanlon, 1987b). Third, a few studies have provided evidence, in both naturalistic and experimental investigations, that training in phoneme segmentation and alphabetic mapping facilitates success in word identification (Bradley & Bryant, 1983; Treiman & Baron, 1980; Vellutino & Scanlon, 1987b; Williams, 1980).

The possibility that the poor reader's difficulties in phonemic segmentation and alphabetic mapping may, in some cases, be caused by basic deficits in phonological coding is supported by results of studies demonstrating that poor readers are generally less sensitive than normal readers to the phonological attributes of spoken and written words. This quality is manifested in a distinct tendency for poor readers to be less disrupted than normal readers by rhyming stimuli, regardless of whether these stimuli are presented auditorily or visually (Byrne & Shea, 1979; Shankweiler, Liberman, Mark, Fowler, & Fischer, 1979). It has also been observed that poor readers are much more inclined to detect commonalities in the meanings of printed words than to detect commonalities in their visual and sound attributes (Vellutino, Scanlon, DeSetto, & Pruzek, 1981; Vellutino, Scanlon, & Tantzman, in press). Phonological coding deficits could also be a source of reader group differences observed on tasks evaluating speed of naming familiar stimuli such as colors and common objects (Denckla & Rudel, 1976).

However, more direct evidence that poor readers are impaired by phonological coding deficits is provided by research demonstrating that poor readers have extraordinary difficulty storing and retrieving names when they cannot rely on meaning to aid this process. Recall that in the study discussed earlier, Vellutino and Scanlon (1989) found that poor readers more closely approximated normal readers on auditory memory and visual-verbal learning tasks when words were high in meaning than when they were low in meaning. Similarly, in studies conducted previously, poor readers were found to be much less able than normal readers on auditory memory and visual-verbal learning tasks, when the verbal stimuli employed were nonsense words (Vellutino, 1979; Vellutino & Scanlon, 1987b). And in one of these studies (Vellutino & Scanlon, 1987b), performance on a simulated word identification task that used alphabetic characters and nonsense words as paired associates was found to be highly correlated with performance on an auditory recall task that presented subjects with the same nonsense words presented on the associated learning task. These studies show that poor readers' deficiencies in word identification are directly related to difficulties they apparently encounter in using a word's phonological attributes to aid in storing and retrieving its name. Thus, they provide strong evidence that phonological deficits are a major cause of deficiencies in word identification, and may affect whole-word naming as well as alphabetic mapping.

Syntactic/grammatical deficits.   If the types of syntactic and grammatical knowledge we discussed earlier are important for word identification, and if at least some poor readers are characterized by gaps in such knowledge, then it might be expected that they would be found to be deficient on measures that directly evaluate syntactic and grammatical competence. There is, in fact, growing evidence that knowledge and use of syntactic and grammatical conventions is deficient in at least some poor readers even at an early point in skills development. Thus, young poor readers (grades 1 to 4) have been found to be less well developed than normal readers in expressive language abilities, as demonstrated in elicited language samples yielding measures evaluating complexity of sentences produced, adherence to syntactic and grammatical conventions, mean length of utterances, and number and types of words used (Fry, Johnson, & Meuhl, 1970). Poor readers have also been found to be less well developed than normal readers in comprehending sentences and in distinguishing between grammatically well-formed and ill-formed sentences, particularly those that are syntactically complex, such as passives, embedded clauses, and relative clauses (Byrne, 1981; Mann, Shankweiler, & Smith, 1984; Vellutino & Scanlon, 1987a). In addition, they have been found to encounter more difficulty than normal readers in learning to identify noncontent words such as *there* and *but* that have no referential meaning (Blank, 1985).

Finally, a number of studies have shown that poor readers take longer than normal readers in acquiring generative "rules" for correct use of inflectional morphemes (Brittain, 1970; Vellutino & Scanlon, 1987a). Facility in using inflectional morphemes has also been shown to be a good predictor of achievement in beginning reading (Vellutino & Scanlon, 1987b).

These results are consistent with our suggestion that reading difficulties in at least some poor readers are due, in part, to limited command of the grammar and syntax of the language. There is, however, need to quality this hypothesis. First, given the fact that children do not begin to encounter complex sentences in print until second or third grade, it is unlikely that deficiencies in sentence comprehension associated with immature syntactic and grammatical development would be a significant cause of reading difficulties at the rudimentary stages of reading. Such deficiencies would, of course, complicate initial learning difficulties at later stages, but are probably not a basic cause of these difficulties. On the other hand, severe deficiencies in syntactic and grammatical development are likely to be associated with more basic deficits in phonological and/or semantic development, which are more probable causes of reading difficulties at the initial stages of learning.

A second point we wish to make is that, except in cases where language deficits could be a consequence of basic constitutional limitations, pronounced deficiencies in syntactic and grammatical development are quite likely a consequence of an impoverished linguistic environment. This, in effect, means that deficiencies in representing and using the grammar and syntax of the language are probably not a significant cause of reading difficulties in most children who come from language-rich environments.

Deficiencies in word identification subskills.   We have been arguing that developing readers must acquire both whole-word/meaning-based and code-oriented strategies for word identification in order to become fluent in reading, and that deficiencies in the semantic, syntactic-grammatical, and phonological domains of language will differentially impair the acquisition of these subskills. But, although we have presented documentation that poor readers may be impaired in acquiring the linguistic knowledge necessary for acquiring given subskills, we have thus far presented no evidence for our suggestion that wholistic/meaning-based and code-oriented strategies are, by themselves, necessary but *not* sufficient conditions for the acquisition of skill in word identification. Such evidence comes from three sources.

The first source comes from naturalistic studies demonstrating that instructional philosophies biased toward either meaning-based or code-oriented approaches to word identification tend to limit the acquisition of facility in word identification. Thus, Chall (1967) found that children exposed to meaning-based programs acquired an initial corpus of "sight words" more rapidly than those exposed to code-oriented programs, but those exposed to code-oriented programs were better able than those exposed to meaning-based programs to identify new words. Similarly, Calfee and Piontkowski (1981) observed first graders exposed to programs that varied from extreme emphasis on meaning to extreme emphasis on decoding; and it was found that children exposed to meaning-oriented programs were better at reading passages than at reading words in isolation, especially new words. In contrast, children exposed to code-oriented programs manifested the opposite pattern. And, in classrooms where teachers were seen as supplementing programs with narrow emphases to effect greater balance, students made better progress. A study conducted later by Evans and Carr (1985) obtained similar results.

The second source of support for the word identification subskills notion comes from laboratory studies evaluating the idea that word-processing strategies can differentially affect performance in word identification. For example, Baron (1979) provided documentation that poor readers could be divided into subgroups with preferential tendencies toward, and differential facility in, either whole-word ("word-specific") or phonetic ("rule-based") approaches to word identification. Similar results were obtained in later studies conducted by Bryant and Impey (1986) and Freebody and Byrne (1988).

More direct evidence for the idea that word-processing strategies can differentially affect word identification comes from an experiment conducted by Vellutino and Scanlon (1987b). In this study, poor and normal readers (grades 2 and 6) were given training to facilitate either whole-word/meaning-based naming or alphabetic mapping in processing analogues of printed words (comprising novel characters), and it was found that each of these treatments had a positive effect on word identification relative to control subjects. However, of special interest is the fact that each treatment had different effects at different stages of learning. Subjects exposed to the whole-word naming condition performed better during initial learning trials than did subjects exposed to the alphabetic mapping condition, but subjects exposed to the alphabetic mapping condition performed better on transfer learning trials and made fewer generalization errors (e.g., *was/saw* type reversals) than did subjects exposed to the whole-word naming condition. Moreover, subjects exposed to both treatment conditions performed better overall and demonstrated more flexible processing strategies than did subjects exposed to only one or the other condition. These patterns were evident in poor as well as in normal readers.

A final source of support for the word identification subskills notion comes from retrospective analysis of subskills deficiencies in poor and normally developing readers. Table 21.1 presents profile analyses of psychometric test results of second- and sixth-grade poor and normal readers who were subjects in studies conducted by Vellutino and his associates from 1979 to 1988. The data presented are taken from tests evaluating vocabulary knowledge, as measured by the WISC-R Vocabulary subtest (Wechsler, 1974), and phonetic decoding ability as measured by a test of pseudoword decoding respectively. Table 21.1 also presents proportions for performance on the WISC-R Object Assembly subtest, which evaluates visual analysis and synthesis. Poor and normal readers were, in all instances, dichotomized on the basis of oral reading ability; and poor readers were, on average, at or below the tenth percentile on the oral reading test.

It is clear from these results that most poor readers are deficient in pseudoword decoding ability, although sizeable proportions are deficient in vocabulary or in both vocabulary and pseudoword decoding ability. Collapsing the vocabulary and visual categories, the percentage totals for pseudoword decoding ability are 83% and 70% for second- and sixth-grade poor readers respectively. Collapsing across pseudoword de-

TABLE 21.1   Percentages for Number of Second- and Sixth-Grade Poor and Normal Readers Receiving Either High or Low Scores (and Combinations Thereof) on Measures Evaluating Vocabulary, Pseudoword Decoding, and Visual-Processing Ability

| | LOW PSEUDOWORD DECODING | | | |
| | LOW VOCABULARY | | HIGH VOCABULARY | |
	LOW VISUAL ABILITY	HIGH VISUAL ABILITY	LOW VISUAL ABILITY	HIGH VISUAL ABILITY
Grade 2 Poor (N = 174)	4.02	9.20	13.79	55.75
Normal (N = 189)	.53	.53	.53	7.94
Grade 6 Poor (N = 252)	6.75	14.68	12.70	35.71
Normal (N = 232)	.00	.43	.86	7.33
	HIGH PSEUDOWORD DECODING			
	LOW VOCABULARY		HIGH VOCABULARY	
	LOW VISUAL ABILITY	HIGH VISUAL ABILITY	LOW VISUAL ABILITY	HIGH VISUAL ABILITY
Grade 2 Poor	1.15	1.72	1.15	13.22
Normal	2.11	5.29	6.35	76.72
Grade 6 Poor	1.98	5.95	10.71	11.51
Normal	.43	1.29	14.22	75.43

Note. A low score on decoding is equal to one standard deviation or more below the normal reader mean at a given grade level. Scores on Vocabulary and Visual-Spatial skills are based on the Vocabulary and Object Assembly subtests of the WISC-R with a scaled score of 8 or below constituting the low score on each. If a scaled score of 9 is used as the criterion, the percentages corresponding to the total number of subjects in each of these categories doubles, but the magnitude of the differences between poor and normal readers remains the same.

coding and visual–spatial ability, the percentage totals for children who are deficient in vocabulary are 16% for the second-grade poor readers and 29% for the sixth-grade poor readers. The percentage totals for those who are deficient in both vocabulary and pseudoword decoding (collapsing across visual ability) are 13% for second-grade poor readers and 21% for sixth-grade poor readers. Only 2% of the second-grade poor readers are deficient only in vocabulary, while 6% of the sixth-grade poor readers are deficient only in vocabulary. These patterns suggest that the largest majority of poor readers is deficient in the phonological domain of language, although a significant number may be found to be deficient in the semantic domain as well. They also suggest that semantic deficits would be greater and more prevalent in older than in younger poor readers, no doubt as a partial consequence of prolonged reading disability.

The proportion of poor readers who are deficient only on the visual-processing measure is very small at the second-grade level (1%) but increases significantly at the sixth-grade level (11%). However, the majority of poor readers are adequate in visual analysis and synthesis. And although the proportion of poor readers who are low on the task measuring this skill is greater than the proportion of normal readers who are low on this task (20%–2P; 10%–2N; 32%–6P, 16%–6N), there are sizeable proportions of normal readers who are also low on the task, suggesting that a high level of visual analysis and synthesis is not a requirement of either beginning or relatively skilled reading.

Finally, a small proportion of poor readers have adequate vocabulary, pseudoword decoding ability, and visual analysis and synthesis ability (13%–2P; 12%–6P). This group may be composed largely of children whose experiences incline them toward overanalytic processing that impairs their ability to identify words as meaningful wholes. That is, these children were significantly impaired in oral reading despite normal development in these latter areas, suggesting that their reading difficulties may originate in the strategies they employed in learning to read, rather than from any basic language or visual deficit.

In contrast to the poor readers, most normal readers have adequate ability in pseudoword decoding and vocabulary. It is also clear that a very small number of children at both grade levels are developing normally in reading despite poor ability in pseudoword decoding (10%–2N; 9%–6N). Yet, those normal readers who are poor in pseudoword decoding tend to have good visual ability as well as good vocabularies, suggesting that these abilities may compensate to some extent for deficiencies in pseudoword decoding. Some normal readers also have below par vocabularies (8%–2N; 2%–6N), but the number of such children is considerably less than it is in poor readers. Very few were deficient in both pseudoword decoding and vocabulary development (1%–2N; 0.5%–6N).

Coupling these findings with results from the naturalistic and experimental studies discussed, we have what appears to be strong evidence for our suggestion that reading disability may be caused by specific deficits in either wholistic/meaning-based or code-oriented approaches to word identification. That these deficits are associated with impairments in language is strongly suggested in the increasingly large number of studies documenting either specific or generalized language deficits in poor readers. The present data also suggest that visual-processing deficits are not a significant cause of reading disability, but could certainly compound reading difficulties caused by basic language deficits.

Finally, it is interesting to note that a clinical study conducted by Denckla (1977) yielded results that were similar to the retrospective study just discussed. In brief, it was found that of 52 cases of poor readers studied, 34 (65%) were characterized by either specific or general language deficits, six (12%) were deficient only in speech articulation, five (10%) were deficient in verbal memory (implying phonological and/or semantic memory deficits), and only two (.04%) were deficient on measures of visual-processing ability. Moreover, both of these latter children also had language deficits. The remaining five children had no apparent deficits and could not be classified. Thus, as regards the hypothesized causes of reading disability, extensive evaluation of both children in normal classroom settings and children referred for neurological evaluation yields compatible results; and both data sets provide documentation for the existence of language-based reading difficulties, while providing no strong support for visual-processing deficits as a source of such difficulties.

Summary

Verbal deficit explanations of reading have implicated the semantic, phonological, and syntactic-grammatical domains of language; and there is some reason to believe that deficiencies in one or another of these domains may directly or indirectly impair different aspects of the word identification process. However, the data rather strongly suggest that the largest proportion of poor readers are impaired in the phonological domain of language and that deficiencies in the semantic or syntactic-grammatical domains may not be the sole cause of word identification problems in most beginning readers. Evidence was also presented which suggests that proficiency in word identification is contingent upon adequate development of both whole-word/meaning-based and code-oriented approaches to word identification and that the failure to acquire functional use of one or the other of these approaches may be directly or indirectly related to language deficits and/or to word-processing strategies fostered through limited instructional programs.

BRAIN SYSTEMS UNDERLYING
WORD IDENTIFICATION

Representational Systems

Clinical Studies

Most of what we know about how specific brain systems are involved in word identification comes from the loss of function seen after brain injury, mainly in adults. Thus, until very recently, our model of brain/reading relationships was built of negative images or subtractions from putative normalcy. Even today, when technical advances have permitted us to examine the physiological aspects of what is happening in the living adult who is reading, we have very little evidence bearing upon the learning-to-read process in the developing brain. We are limited to making analogies and using observable dysfunction (e.g., naming deficits) as mediating variables, when we attempt to extrapolate from the adult brain (in the case of someone reading well or reading poorly) to the developing brain dynamically acquiring a repertoire of reading skills.

With these caveats in mind, let us nonetheless lay out whatever we do know about the brain and reading. First, from the by-now classic method of correlating clearly defined neural pathology with documented functional loss, we have a century of evidence that the left side of the brain's cerebral cortex is more important than the right in subserving the skills of reading; and that the posterior (temporoparietal) cortical association areas of the left hemisphere—the very regions of importance to understanding and formulating language (see Figure 21.4)—are critical for normal reading. In fact, many experts in the field of behavioral neurology would argue that virtually all acquired *alexia* (as the loss of reading is called) is either a subtle form of *aphasia* (loss of some aspect of language competence) or a disconnection of some other information-bearing system from the language comprehension or formulation regions. In cases of left posterior cortical lesion, the reading dysfunction may be the most important symptom. Reading is also abnormal in some cases of brain lesions, which are more anterior (frontal) in location—a point of interest when we come to modern physiologic data—but the reading loss in anterior cases is embedded in such dramatic speech or kinetic disruption that the separate status given alexia has not been conferred, largely because it is not the chief complaint.

Perhaps the most extensive research evaluating the neurological foundations of reading ability in adult clinical populations has been conducted by neuropsychologists studying acquired dyslexia associated with head trauma, cerebral vascular accident (stroke), or degenerative diseases. It will suffice to point out that this work has defined two major types of dysfunction in word identification: one characterized by primary inability to identify printed words using spelling-sound mapping rules, alternatively called *phonological dyslexia* and *deep dyslexia* (Coltheart, Patterson, & Marshall, 1980); and a second characterized by primary inability to identify printed words as integrated wholes, most often called *surface dyslexia* (Patterson, Marshall, & Coltheart, 1985).

Deep dyslexics retain some ability to identify words as wholes through direct access from print to meaning, but have extraordinary difficulty decoding pseudowords. Surface dyslexics retain some ability to identify words using letter-sound correspondence rules, but have extraordinary difficulty identifying words as wholes. These disorders are associated with a variety of types of lesions and lesion sites, but most often entail damage to temporal and parietal lobe structures in the left hemisphere. Extensive

594

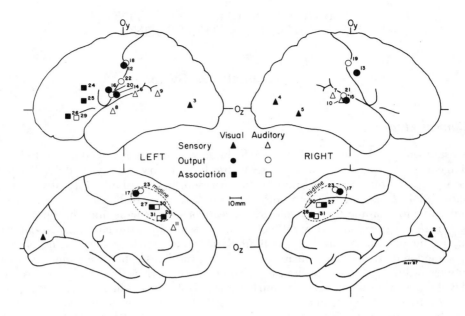

Sensory Tasks

Visual
1. Striate cortex (L)
2. Striate cortex (R)
3. Extrastriate cortex (L)
4. Extrastriate cortex (R)
5. Inferior lateral occipital cortex (R)

Auditory
6. Posterior superior temporal cortex (L)
7. Temporal cortex (R)
8. Anterior superior temporal cortex (L)
9. Temporoparietal cortex (L)
10. Lateral temporal cortex (R)
11. Inferior anterior cingulate cortex (L)

Output Tasks

Visual
12. Mouth region, rolandic cortex (L)
13. Rolandic cortex (R)
14. Buried sylvian cortex (L)
15. Lateral sylvian cortex (R)
16. Premotor cortex (L)
17. Supplementary motor area (SMA)

Auditory
18. Mouth region, rolandic cortex (L)
19. Rolandic cortex (R)
20. Buried sylvian cortex (L)
21. Lateral sylvian cortex (R)
22. Premotor cortex (L)
23. SMA

ASSOCIATION TASKS

Visual
24. Dorsolateral prefrontal cortex (L)
25. Lateral prefrontal cortex (L)
26. Inferior prefrontal cortex (L)
27. Anterior cingulate
28. Inferior anterior cingulate

Auditory
29. Inferior prefrontal cortex (L)
30. Anterior cingulate
31. Inferior anterior cingulate

FIGURE 21.4   Regions of the left and right hemispheres of the brain that were activated by sensory, output, and association tasks when stimuli were presented either visually or auditorily. Reprinted with permission of the publisher from Petersen, S. E., Fox, P. T., Posner, M. I., Mintun, M., & Raichle, M. E. (1988), "Position Emission Tomographic Studies of the Cortical Anatomy of Single-Word Processing," *Nature*, 331, pp. 585–588. Copyright © 1988 by Macmillan Journals Limited.

study of these patients, using both neurological and cognitive measures, has provided documentation for *dual-access theories* of word identification, which, in brief, suggest that, depending on task and stimulus variables, skilled readers may identify printed words either through direct (semantic) access or through phonologically mediated access to word names and meanings (Baron, 1979; Coltheart et al., 1980; LaBerge & Samuels, 1974; Patterson et al., 1985).

Finally, we should mention the anatomical studies conducted by Galaburda and his associates (e.g., Galaburda & Kemper, 1979) in postmortem analyses of the brains of deceased adolescents and young adults who had a long history of severe reading disability. The important findings from these studies are the observation of structural anomalies in language-related areas of the left hemisphere, and the unusual development of right hemisphere structures, rather than the more typical asymmetry between left and right hemisphere development. Although these studies are inconclusive as to the specific neurological structures that might be involved in learning to read, they provide the first anatomical evidence that developmental reading disability may be associated with anamolous brain structures.

To recapitulate, the inferences from cases of classical acquired alexia and dyslexia (from adult-onset damage in a person who knew how to read) have implicated, as essential to *maintenance* of skilled reading, primarily left-sided, language and speech-related areas of the cerebral cortex, the language (posterior) areas being more clearly and more "purely" implicated in reading. In contrast, the speech (anterior) areas are more incidentally implicated in reading. These inferences are reinforced by regional blood flow studies conducted more recently.

Regional Blood Flow Studies

Regional cerebral blood flow studies (RCBF) (Lassen, Ingvar, & Skinkoj, 1978), using xenon 133 (a decade ago injected, more recently inhaled)[3] have given us computer-generated, color-coded pictures of brain areas activated in normal adults, both when they are reading aloud and when they are reading silently. When subjects were reading aloud, RCBF studies showed that the left hemisphere was no more strongly activated than the right hemisphere. Reading aloud looked much like the state of speaking, involving bilateral activation of the auditory cortex; the face, tongue, and mouth areas of sensorimotor cortex; the speech association area in the lower rear frontal lobe (on the left it is called Broca's area); the upper premotor cortex; the visual association cortex; and the frontal eye fields (see Figure 21.4). Only the last two, the visual and eye-movement components of activation, differentiated the reading-aloud state from the speaking state. Six discrete cortical regions on each side, forming a z-shaped figure of activation on the surface of each hemisphere, were simultaneously active during reading aloud.

Reading silently, however, appears to be a state in which the face-tongue-mouth sensorimotor and auditory regions are *not* activated. Yet of the four regions activated during silent reading in the normal adult reader (*visual association, frontal eye field, supplementary motor/premotor,* and *Broca's speech association*), the anterior frontal regions account for three of the four zones demanding greatest blood flow during reading.

More recent RCBF studies, using inhaled rather than injected xenon 133, have produced two other findings that further document these different aspects of reading physiology (Flowers, Wood, & Naylor, 1989; Rumsey et al., 1987). Specifically, it was found that both sides of the brain were equally activated in normal readers during a reading task that involved semantic classification (e.g., one of a set of four words is "odd man out"). It was also found that the left temporoparietal region was activated far more than its right homologue during an orthographic discrimination task that involved deciding whether or not a word presented auditorily contained four letters. This task required processing of a word's structural and surface features, and specifically entailed phoneme segmentation and alphabetic mapping. Thus, of the multiple regions activated during silent reading, it is only when the reading task is oriented towards analysis of surface feature details that the left-side blood flow is decidedly the more prominent. In contrast, bilateral activation and bilateral increases in blood flow accompany semantically oriented reading.

Results such as these suggest that the different aspects of reading are supported by diverse, localized, and highly specialized neurological structures that must be orchestrated in the performance of the total enterprise. This possibility is even more clearly demonstrated by a study recently conducted by Peterson, Fox, Posner, Mintun, and Raichle (1988) using Positron Emission Tomography (PET) to measure RCBF. This study evaluated brain regions activated when high-frequency nouns were presented visually and auditorily. Subjects were adult volunteers. Tasks presented in each modality formed a three-level "subtractive hierarchy" such that each task at the next level in the hierarchy added a small number of operations to those of its subordinate. The subordinate task therefore served as the control for the task at the next level. This, in effect, meant that brain regions activated by tasks at a given level in the hierarchy were activated along with brain regions activated by tasks at lower levels. The procedure therefore allowed the investigators to ascertain the effects of tasks at one level by "subtracting" the effects of tasks at lower levels (see Table 21.2).

The first task involved passive processing of nonverbal stimuli presented either visually or auditorily. The second involved passive processing of word stimuli presented visually or auditorily. The third required that the subject repeat a word seen or heard, and the fourth required that he/she indicate a use for each word seen or heard. The important finding were as follows.

First, passive stimulation (input task) activated brain regions that were specific to a modality (see Figure 21.4). No regions were activated on both visual and auditory presentations. Of special interest is the fact that on both visual and auditory presentations, different brain regions were activated by nonverbal and verbal stimuli, respectively. Thus, in the visual modality, the striate area was activated by nonverbal stimuli, while the extrastriate area was activated by word stimuli. This conforms with clinical

TABLE 21.2   The "Subtraction" Method of Stimulus Presentation Used to Evaluate Brain Regions Activated by Sensory, Output, and Association Tasks.

SUBTRACTION	CONTROL STATE	STIMULATED STATE	TASK
Sensory task	Fixation point only	Passive words	Passive sensory processing Modality-specific word code
Output task	Passive words	Repeat words	Articulatory code Motor programming Motor output
Association task	Repeat words	Generate uses	Semantic association Selection for action

Note. The rationale of the three-level stepwise paradigm design is shown. At the second and third level, the control state is the stimulated state from the previous level. Some hypothesized cognitive operations are represented in the third column. Reprinted with permission of the publisher from Petersen, S. E., Fox, P. T., Posner, M. I., Mintun, M., & Raichle, M. E. (1988), "Positron Emission Tomographic Studies of the Cortical Anatomy of Word Processing," *Nature, 331*, p. 585. Copyright © 1988 by Macmillan Journals Limited.

studies insofar as lesions in the extrastriate area have been associated with word recognition problems in adults (Damasio, 1985). In the auditory modality, the temporoparietal and anterior superior temporal regions (among others) were activated by word stimuli, but not by nonword stimuli. This is of interest because lesions of the superior temporal gyrus (often called Wernicke's area) have been associated with phonological deficits (Shallice, McLeod, & Lewis, 1985), which suggests that this region may support phonological coding operations.

When words presented had to be pronounced (output task), visual and auditory stimuli activated identical regions of the brain, most of which appear to support articulatory and motor programming (Figure 21.4). Since the pronunciation tasks, by definition, also involved word naming, certain of these regions may support name-retrieval operations as well. A good candidate may be the temporoparietal region, which, as we said, may support phonological coding operations and facilitate the connection and integration of phonological and semantic features.

In addition to the brain regions activated by lower-level tasks, the association tasks activated two areas of cerebral cortex (among others) that were common to both visual and auditory presentations (Figure 21.4). One—the left inferior frontal area—quite likely supports semantic association. The second—the anterior cingulate gyrus—appears to be related to selective attention. The latter possibility is suggested by results of a companion study in which it was found that anterior-cingulate activation was much stronger for lists containing many targets than for those with few targets, indicating that this region is more strongly activated when sustained attention is required.

One of the most interesting aspects of this research is the possibility that skilled readers may apprehend the meaning of a printed word through direct visual access rather than through phonologically mediated access as hypothesized by some researchers (e.g., Gough, 1972). This possibility is consistent with the finding that visual presentations of items on the association tasks activated brain regions believed to support semantic processing (inferior frontal cortex), but not those regions that presumably support phonologic processing (temporoparietal area). Thus, for the first time, we have neurological data based on the study of normal (not brain-damaged) subjects that support a conceptualization of skilled word identification favored by the bulk of the evidence derived from cognitive studies addressing the question (see Vellutino, 1982, for a more thorough discussion of the latter evidence).

Electrophysiological Studies with Children

Because of the invasive nature of RCBF and PET procedures, studies of brain functioning in developing readers have utilized noninvasive procedures that evaluate electrophysiological changes rather than regional blood flow. These studies have utilized *Event-Related Potentials* (ERP), which are changes in brain wave patterns measured while the subject is engaged in a particular task (see Note 2).

The studies conducted with children using these techniques generally compared normally developing control children with children who were having difficulty in school learning. Consistent with the RCBF data, summarized above, is the finding of substantial activation, *bilaterally* and *anteriorly*, in young, normally developing readers (male, prepubertal), with *left*-sided accentuations in both language areas (temporoparietally) and speech areas (anteriorly) according to specific task demands (Duffy, Denckla, Bartels, & Sandini, 1980). This observation was based on measurements taken when children were engaged in language and visual-verbal association-learning tasks. The bilateral anterior activation—echoing the normative adult RCBF in the involvement of frontal eye fields and supplementary motor areas—was initially the most surprising insight into normally developing readers' brain activity. While not specific to reading, these anterior activations appear to be importantly related to reading skill acquisition. This is inferred from the fact that these patterns occurred on tasks that made many of the same cognitive demands as word identification.

Studies of Hemidecorticate Children

Another body of data giving us indirect yet powerfully suggestive models of the developing brain in reading acquisition comes from longitudinal studies of hemidecorticate children (Dennis, 1982). The children studied were suffering from Sturge-Weber Syndrome, a condition characterized by one very abnormal side of the brain giving rise to uncontrollable epileptic seizures. Early removal of the abnormal hemisphere (hemidecortication) cures epilepsy and allows remarkably normal development. From the point of view of understanding specific contributions of the left and right hemispheres to the acquisition of skill in reading, these cases are of great interest.

Although the children studied all had low-average general intelligence, they differed in their sensitivity to various aspects of written language. Those children who learned to read with only a right hemisphere (left hemidecorticate) were found to be deficient in all the fundamental components of structural analysis and phonetic decoding. Each left-hemidecorticate child experienced difficulty in sound analysis, manipulation of internal structures of words, decoding nonsense words, and judging the statistical structure of permissible sequences of spelling in their native (written) language. Working within the limits of the right hemisphere, they were weak in applying morphophonemic and phonotactic rules. Because she followed these children into adolescence, Dennis (1982) generated a detailed portrait of the limitations of an isolated right hemisphere in handling fundamental procedures and rules that relate speech sounds to graphemic representations. Compensation, then, even in a developing brain, seems to encounter a "ceiling effect" that implies specialized left-hemisphere mechanisms in manipulating what Dennis (1982) calls "lower-order" defcits, involving what we have called "surface-feature, within-word-detail" type processing.

The good news from the hemidecorticate studies is that the left-hemidecorticate child, who learns to read with the right hemisphere alone, achieves useful reading comprehension. Skills underlying connected prose comprehension appear to be acquired to a degree far greater than might have been predicted from the decoding skills asymmetry. When the material is more complex, however, a superior capacity for capitalizing on syntactic higher-order structures gives the edge to the isolated left hemisphere (right hemidecorticate) in terms of the speed and automaticity with which the text is processed and comprehended.

The picture derived from Dennis's (1982) data is that the right hemisphere alone can support and sustain a functional and reasonably adequate level of reading, in which meaning can be derived from written text. However, both at the lower-order level (phonological) and the higher-order level (syntactic), specific contributions are made by the left hemisphere that are not readily compensated by the isolated right hemisphere. Thus, the particular processing characteristics of each hemisphere are revealed in these highly unusual developing readers. Without a left hemisphere, there is inevitably poor reading of unfamiliar words, due to poor phonological skills, and a poor grasp of the larger syntactic relationships that facilitate comprehension of complex texts. Evidently, the left hemisphere not only analyzes sequential within-word phonological components but, at the higher-order level, synthesizes large chunks of text via syntactic appreciation. (Note that this higher-order capacity has never been studied with physiological monitoring, so its localization within the left hemisphere is unknown.)

Other Cognitive Processes

Serial Memory

These latter points again bring into focus our previous discussion of sequential ordering as a cognitive process. As we indicated earlier, one of the neuropsychological/cognitive deficits often reported to be associated with poor reading is dysfunction in sequencing. Since sequencing difficulties are often observed on both serial memory (e.g., serializing digits) and oral language tasks (calling *elephant ephelant*), as well as on reading and spelling tasks, some have speculated, in line with the successive/simultaneous dyad mentioned earlier, that sequencing problems may be attributed to dysfunction in either a ubiquitous ordering mechanism that serializes all information, or modality-specific mechanisms that serialize sensory-based information (Das et al., 1975; Johnson & Myklebust, 1967).

Although we have questioned these conceptualizations on both logical and empirical grounds, it may, nevertheless, be inquired whether there is any neural substrate known from human brain-behavior data that is relevant to oral and written language sequencing. Two dichotomies of brain may, in fact, be related to the successive/simultaneous dyad. One that is usually associated with the dyad is, of course, the "left/right" brain dichotomy; the other is a "front/back" dichotomy, which seems to be less well known. To attempt a simplification, the left hemisphere of the human brain does appear to subserve more sequential, bit-by-bit, part-oriented, temporally organized types of processing that support both comprehension and production of spoken and written language. In contrast, the right hemisphere's contribution to cognition is more characteristically "simultaneous," involving, it would appear, relational, contextual, and spatially organized processing and production. However, *within* each side, left *and* right, the posterior/basal functional systems are more processing related, and the anterior convexity systems are more production related. Logically, also, production is more often sequential and temporally organized, and for the types of production supporting schoolwork (which relies so heavily on language), far more left hemisphere dependent. Hence, for the relevant neural substrate operationalizing *most*, although certainly not all, types of behavior, the anterior quadrant of the left hemisphere seems to be especially important.

However, we should point out once again that there is neither one "master sequencer" nor several modality-specific sequencers in the brain, but, rather, somewhat different functional components of the anterior/frontal regions of both hemispheres, which are preferentially responsible for sequencing different types of information. The types of neural structures that allow one to sequence words in a sentence so as to understand that sentence appear to be different from the types of structures that allow one to sequence the phonemes in a word so as to recognize and understand that word. Moreover, both of these involve neural structures different from those that allow one to articulate that word. And although there is reason to believe that the mechanisms uniquely supporting each of these functions emanate from, or depend upon, the left hemisphere, the "rules" for ordering each type of information are qualitatively distinct. This facet of neural functioning is not accurately reflected in typical conceptualizations of the successive/simultaneous dyad.

Associative and Cross-Modal Transfer

Thus far we have discussed the neurological structures that appear to underlie the linguistic, visual, motor, and sequential aspects of word identification and have not specifically discussed neural structures that may support the other foundational processes involved in reading that we discussed earlier—in particular, associative learning, cross-modal transfer, pattern analysis, rule learning, and attention. When one attempts to delineate the brain regions or mechanisms that underlie these processes, the rudimentary nature of our knowledge of brain functioning immediately becomes evident. This is because these processes, for the most part, entail collaboration among the representational systems that are specifically involved in reading, all of which are highly specialized and localized. In contrast, the neural structures and processes that underlie and facilitate such collaboration are less apt to be localized.

For example, learning to identify the printed version of a meaningful word, by definition, involves both associative learning and cross-modal transfer and entails the establishment of connecting links between neurological structures supporting representations of the word's meaning, its name, and its component letters ordered invariantly. Fluent identification of the word implies that these links have been firmly established— which is to say that different types of coded information now represent the same concept. Although it is common to think of associative and cross-modal learning in terms of spatial metaphors, whereby neural "pathways" are laid down from one region of the brain to another, the fact is that we know very little about how such learning takes place. Moreover, it is possible that associative and cross-modal learning is not simply a matter of establishing neural pathways from one representational system to another. Each may also involve the operation of highly specialized recoding mechanisms that transcend particular systems and that are responsible for transforming information from one system into the "language" of the other, not unlike the type of computational mechanisms involved in transforming computer "software" routines into the machine "language" that allows it to function.

However, we are not completely devoid of insight, and there is some reason to believe that certain neural structures may be instrumental in facilitating collaboration between and among given systems. For example, in an extensive study of epileptic patients whose brains were surgically bifurcated, Sperry (1964) adduced evidence that the corpus callosum (midbrain) connecting the two hemispheres may not simply be connecting tissue having no functional utility, as was previously thought to be the case, but may actually be instrumental in transmitting information between the two hemispheres. These researchers found, for example, that a printed word stimulating only the right hemisphere (through visual half-field presentations) could be copied (drawn) by the split-brain patients, but could not be named. However, the same word could be both named and copied when only the left hemisphere was stimulated. Since vision is supported in both hemispheres, left-hemisphere stimulation gave the patients access to a name code; but the fact that they were denied such access when only the right hemisphere was stimulated strongly suggests that the corpus callosum may play a significant role in coordinating the flow of information between the hemispheres.

Additional support for this possibility was garnered by Geschwind and Fusillo (1966), who found that patients with lesions in the callosal regions of the brain were found to have difficulties on both reading and color-naming tasks. Studies such as these are important in revealing the neural mechanisms that may be involved in at least certain types of associative and cross-modal learning, but it should be clear that research of this type is seminal.

Pattern Analysis and Rule Learning

As regards pattern analysis and rule learning, results from both the physiological and clinical studies cited earlier strongly suggest that the lower-level operations involved in feature analysis and feature encoding take place in the sensory systems that support higher-level representational learning of the types unique to those systems. Results from these studies are also consistent with the possibility that what we have been calling *rule learning* may also involve coding operations that are endemic to those systems. However, the question of rule learning also brings into focus the more general question of whether or not we are equipped with some general faculty for detecting and representing patterned invariance and for conceptual learning in general. There is some suggestion that higher-order reasoning and conceptualization is disrupted by frontal lobe damage, but such data are inconclusive and could simply reflect our ignorance of how more specialized regions of the brain collaborate. Moreover, frontal lobe deficit does not measurably decrease psychometric intelligence but rather impairs general "control" processes, which, in turn, could affect higher-order functions such as concept formation (Wang, 1988).

Currently in usage is the term *executive dysfunction*, the neuropsychological equivalent of what some researchers call *metacognitive control processes*. Because they are impaired in generating "sifting" strategies, in making choices among alternatives, and in maintaining focal attention to incoming stimuli, persons who suffer from executive dysfunction secondary to frontal deficit fail when new information must be approached in an organized fashion and when old information must be analyzed or synthesized in new ways. Thus, insofar as metacognitive and other higher-order thinking skills are dependent upon the integrity of the frontal lobes and their connections, frontal lobe damage could have an indirect rather than a direct effect on rule learning, although the two possibilities are not mutually exclusive. As aptly stated in one treatment of the subject: "The human frontal cortex attends, integrates, formulates, executes, monitors, modifies, and judges all nervous system activities" (Stuss & Benson, 1987).

Attentional Processes

As regards the neural structures that might support attentional processes, we are only slightly more informed. Brain systems supporting attention have been subsumed under several sets of dichotomies: (1) *matrix*, or *state*, functions (tonic, diffuse, primary) versus (2) *vector*, or *channel*, functions (phasic, selective, secondary). State functions refer to overall information-processing capacity, detection efficiency (as in signal/noise ratio), focusing power, vigilance level, and resistance to interference; these functions appear to be associated with the reticular activating system of the brainstem and midbrain levels of the central nervous system. Channel functions refer to one's ability to separate figure from ground and, more generally, to efficiency in maintaining selective attention within visceral, extrapersonal, and semantic fields; these functions are apparently associated with more rostral (upper) portions of the central nervous system—the neocortex in particular.

Starting from the "bottom up," the pontomesencephalic brainstem (midbrain) contributes noradrenergic, upward-flowing pathways (from locus caeruleus and serotonergic to midline raphe nuclei). The noradrenergic system enhances signal-to-noise ratio, and the pharmacologic stimulants (Dexedrine, Ritalin) that increase central noradrenergic transmission certainly enhance attentiveness. Activation of the midbrain reticular core is necessary, but not sufficient, for wakefulness and alertness, sending major ascending cholinergic pathways to thalamic and neocortical targets; this provides excitation of widespread regions (thalamic, cortical) in a way that enhances overall information processing.

The thalamus, located just under the cortex, provides important relays, particularly in the reticular nucleus, which seem to act as a sort of valve for orienting one to focal stimuli, for receiving cortical input, and for inhibiting other thalamic nuclei, but (uniquely) giving no feedback directly to the cortex. Thus, the frontal cortex, by activating the reticular nucleus of the thalamus, can inhibit other thalamic regions that shut out stimuli other than the ones to which the frontal cortex is oriented; here we see the foundations of selectivity. These more complex aspects of attention are coordinated at the level of cortex that is polymodal (i.e., not confined to one sensory modality; not just auditory, visual, haptic/tactile, and so on) and privy to "motivational" connections from the limbic/paralimbic (more primitive, drive-related) cortex. Association neocortex of this polymodal type in the posterior parietal, ventral, temporal, and—preeminently—prefrontal areas thus simultaneously facilitates sensitivity to abstract and motivational features of incoming stimuli.

The single most crucial structure in the maintenance of attention (involved in both the state/matrix and the target/selective poles of the dichotomies) is the *frontal lobe*. Here attentional filterings occur at a quite advanced stage of information processing, not barring more peripheral sensory influx, but allowing fluidity and flexibility "on-line." Attention to all that is complex and anything that is novel necessitates the participation of the frontal lobe.

Furthermore, it is the right side that is more influential with respect to both the overall tone and the directed aspects of attention. Thus, in the hierarchy "bottom to top," the spotlight falls upon the right frontal lobe as the most crucial element. (The *striatum*, a portion of basal ganglia that is in the cerebral hemisphere if not the cortex, must be considered as intimately intertwined with the corresponding frontal cortex when one speaks of the frontal lobe as a three-dimensional volume of brain tissue.)

Let us recapitulate. In the attentional loops, arousal necessarily involves the brainstem/midbrain reticular activating system; motivation necessarily involves the limbic system; and selective-directed attention involves frontal lobe input (right more than left), which, in turn, has significant two-way connections to and from posterior parietal, thalamic, and striatal areas.

It is beyond the scope of this chapter to delve into the growing distinction between *attention* and *intention* (the motor activation and preparedness to act); suffice it to say here that the frontal-striatal and frontal-thalamic loops of the hierarchy may be discussed under *intention* in writings that the reader may encounter (see Damasio, 1985; Heilman & Valenstein, 1985; and Mesulam, 1985, for excellent discussions of this and other topics related to the neurological bases of attention).

Summary

What do we know about what goes on in the brain of a developing (or accomplished) reader? We know that both sides of the brain can and do participate in the processes and that anterior, motor-related, attention-related systems, as well as traditional "language" areas, are highly participatory. We know that certain left-hemisphere-based contributions are more prominent than right-hemisphere-based contributions and that excellence in reading—over and above adequacy in reading—may require these distinctive left-hemisphere-based contributions more fully. Still unknown are the developing brain/developing reading neurophysiologic relationships; large-scale longitudinal studies would be required to map out such a landscape.

CONSTITUTIONAL VERSUS EXPERIENTIAL CAUSES OF DEVELOPMENTAL READING DISABILITY

Terms such as *reading disability*, *specific reading disability*, and *dyslexia* (which we have used interchangeably) currently carry the implication that children who encounter difficulties in learning to read are impaired by constitutional limitations of neurological and/or genetic origin. Yet, the fact remains that there are currently no definitive criteria that allow one to distinguish between constitutionally and experientially based causes of developmental reading disability. Commonly used definitions of reading disability attempt to distinguish between these two etiologies through the use of exclusionary criteria designed to separate those children whose reading problems are due to such factors as low general intelligence, sensory deficits, emotional disorders, and/or socio-cultural deficits on the one hand, from those whose reading problems cannot be attributed to any of these factors on the other. Unfortunately, such definitions have not been very successful in making the constitutional-experiential distinction.

For one thing, neurological assessment does not always distinguish between poor readers who are identified on the basis of these criteria, and so-called "garden variety" poor readers who do not meet these criteria, since many of the children from this latter group have also been found to be impaired neurologically (Rutter, Tizard, & Whitmore, 1969). More important is the fact that virtually all of the research available has failed to evaluate or adequately control for the environmental and/or educational deficits that may cause a reading disorder. Clay (1987) makes this point quite compellingly. She reports results which indicate that 80 percent to 90 percent of a population of beginning readers, who were identified as significantly impaired in reading, were brought up to grade level after only 14 to 20 weeks of daily tutoring. She also suggests that those children who did not respond readily to remediation may have been the "hard core" organically impaired readers and advocates the conjoint use of longitudinal and intervention studies as the means of generating neurological and psychometric markers that may ultimately distinguish between constitutionally and experientially impaired readers.

Clay's points are well taken and are buttressed by the classroom observation studies, discussed earlier, which provide documentation that narrowly conceived pedagogical philosophies can impair the development of reading subskills (Calfee & Piontkowski, 1981; Chall, 1967; Evans & Carr, 1985). Yet, there is enough suggestive evidence to support the possibility that some poor readers are constitutionally impaired. The most compelling evidence comes from genetic studies which have documented that (1) reading disability occurs more often in near relatives than in the population at large; (2) it occurs more often in twins than in siblings; and (3) it has a much higher concordance rate in monozygotic twins than in dizygotic twins (DeFries, Fulker, & LaBuda, 1987). Also compelling is the fact that boy/girl ratios for disabled readers range anywhere from 4:1 to 10:1, suggesting that reading disability in some children may be a sex-linked disorder. Moreover, these studies have tentatively localized a gene for reading disability on chromosome 15, although this finding has not yet been replicated (Smith, Kimberling, Pennington, & Lubs, 1983).

Both electrophysiological studies (e.g., Duffy, Denckla, Bartels, & Sandini, 1980; Dykman et al., 1985; Harter et al., 1988) and clinical-neurological studies (Denckla, 1977; Dennis, 1982; Galaburda & Kemper, 1979) are also suggestive and are consistent with the possibility that reading difficulties in some children may be associated with dysfunction in language-related areas of the left hemisphere. Their findings are complemented by neuropsychological studies of adult patients with acquired dyslexia (Coltheart et al., 1980; Patterson et al., 1985), as well as by the regional blood flow studies of adult skilled readers (Petersen et al., 1988); both suggest that the language areas of the left hemisphere are the foundations of skilled word identification.

Given this degree of concordance in genetic and neurological studies of skilled and developing readers, it is significant that extensive study of reading impairment in developing readers, using psychometric measures exclusively, has clearly shown that facility in word identification is strongly correlated with intact language functioning and, conversely, that dysfunction in word identification is strongly correlated with deficiencies in language. Results from both areas of inquiry are also consistent with a description of the skilled reader as one who has alternative vehicles for word identification, and with a description of the deficient reader as one who has limited and imperfect vehicles for word identification because of deficiencies in reading subskills.

Thus, it is clear that cognitive and neuropsychological approaches to the study of both normal and impaired reading can be complementary and should become more so as the technology in each of these domains improves.

GENERAL SUMMARY

Word identification is a highly complex skill that recruits most of the major cognitive abilities involved in representational learning. The acquisition of skill in word identification implies adequate development in language as well as adequate ability to: (1) discriminate and recognize visual symbols; (2) associate and integrate visual and linguistic symbols; and (3) detect and represent patterned invariance. Of lesser importance are the speech-motor and visual-motor abilities involved in vocalizing and writing words one is learning to identify.

Skill in word identification also implies adequate development of language-based subskills that allow one alternative vehicles for accessing the lexicon. Whether words are encountered in connected text or in isolation, word identification, in essence, entails retrieval of word names and meanings. In a writing system based on an alphabet, words can be identified either through semantic-syntactic or phonologically mediated access to names and meanings. Research evidence suggests that while adult skilled readers most often use semantically and syntactically based vehicles for word identification, they are able to use phonologically based vehicles as well. Such evidence is consistent with the possibility that developing readers must have both vehicles for word identification in order to acquire any degree of fluency in reading.

Most children learn to read with relatively little difficulty, but there are a small number who have extraordinary difficulty in acquiring this skill, despite reasonably adequate environmental circumstances and adequate learning ability in all or most other areas. These children have been of special interest to researchers in the cognitive and neurosciences as well as to those in education, because serious study of the origins of their reading difficulties promises to enhance our understanding of the cognitive and neuropsychological foundations of all learning, while telling us something of the nature of the reading process and reading disability.

Research in this area of inquiry is consistent with our suggestion that reading disability, in otherwise normal children, is due, in most cases, to constitutionally and/or experientially derived deficiencies in language that lead to ineptitude in acquiring either meaning-based or code-oriented strategies for word identification, although the largest proportion appears to be deficient in the use of code-oriented strategies. Research supporting these inferences is complemented by experimental and naturalistic studies documenting the existence of pedagogical biases that differentially foster the development of word identification subskills. At the same time, the evidence suggests that visual and motor deficit theories of reading disability are weak at best. Theories citing deficiencies in foundational cognitive processes, such as associative learning, intersensory learning, and rule learning as sources of reading difficulty, can be questioned on logical as well as empirical grounds.

NOTES

1. Much of the research reported in this paper was funded by grants from the National Institute of Child Health and Human Development (R01HD09658) and the U.S. Office of Health, Education, and Welfare (G007604369). The authors express their appreciation to Melinda Taylor, Judy Moran, and Linda Riedlbauer, who typed and helped edit many drafts of this manuscript.

2. The ERP is technically defined as a transient series of voltage oscillations in the brain in response to a discrete stimulus. ERP's are defined in terms of their *polarity* (*p* or *n*), *latency* of onset in milliseconds, *amplitude* (magnitude of a change in polarity from some baseline), and the area of the brain from which measurements are taken in terms of placements of electrodes on the scalp. ERP's can also be classified on the basis of two other major properties: exogenous responses and endogenous responses. Exogenous responses are changes in voltage triggered by the onset of a stimulus. Such responses reflect the brain's sensitivity to physical attributes of stimuli such as intensity, sensory modality, and rate. In contrast, endogenous responses are determined by the processing demands of the task rather than the physical attributes of the stimuli. ERP's are interpreted in terms of all these properties, and the researcher's job is to document patterns of response that occur at different brain locations under particular stimulus conditions. The ultimate goal of such analysis is, of course, to relate cognitive processes to underlying brain functions in terms of the processing demands of theoretically rationalized tasks.

    Also noteworthy is a variant of the ERP method called *Brain Electrical Activity Mapping* (BEAM) developed by Duffy and his associates (Duffy, Denckla, Bartels, & Sandini, 1980). BEAM is essentially a computer program that averages a series of ERP's generated by a given stimulus and translates these measurements into a color-coded topographical map that depicts brain regions activated by the stimulus.

3. The RCBF method used over a decade ago by Larsen and associates (Larsen, Skinhoj, & Lassen, 1978; Lassen, Ingvar, & Skinhoj, 1978) was based upon the fact that blood flow in each tissue of the body varies as a function of the level of activity and metabolism going on in that tissue. Oxygen is supplied to each tissue via the bloodstream, and functional plus metabolic activity means a rise in oxygen demand that is in turn met by an increased flow to the active tissue of oxygenated blood. This fine-tuned responsiveness of blood flow continues even in isolated and denervated organs, so that it appears to be linked to local metabolic processes that release chemical "messages" in the tissue, calling for increased oxygenated blood flow as needed. Specifically true in brain tissue, this metabolic and blood flow linkage has been demonstrated on a localized basis; and it has been established that during a functional test involving focal processing, there is a correspondingly local change in nerve cell activity, hence in metabolic rate, that elicits an increased blood flow in the active region. The measurement of blood flow in discrete regions of the intact human brain, by means of radioactive isotopes, began with xenon 133 dissoved in sterile saline solution and then injected as a bolus into one of the main arteries serving the brain. The small volume of xenon 133 solution (2 to 3 milliliters containing between 3 and 5 millicuries of radioactivity) is tracked for one minute, from arrival to subsequent washout, with a gamma-ray camera consisting of 254 externally arrayed scintillation counters; each detector scans approximately one square centimeter of brain surface. A small digital computer processes the information from the 254 scintillation detectors and displays its output graphically on a color monitor, each blood flow level being assigned a different color. The injected radioactive xenon 133 technique detects radiation passing through the superficial layers of brain (cerebral cortex), but cannot detect significant activity (due to attenuation of radiation) from deeper brain structures.

    Later, by the early 1980s, the xenon 133 method was modified to one of inhalation of a gaseous mixture containing even less of a dose of radioactivity than that borne by xenon 133, and circumventing the injection into arteries that had limited the use of xenon 133 in saline solution. The principles, calculations, computer processing of data, and display of data via color-coded computer graphics remained unchanged; but the lessened risks of the inhalation method opened up the RCBF technique to wider use in research. Sensitivity of RCBF to cognitive manipulations has been well established and replicated (Rumsey et al., 1987).

REFERENCES

Baron, J. (1979). Orthographic and word specific mechanisms in children's reading of words. *Child Development*, 50, 60–72.

Birch, H. G., & Belmont, L. (1964). Auditory-visual integration in normal and retarded readers. *American Journal of Orthopsychiatry*, 34, 852–861.

Blank, M. (1985). A word is a word—or is it? In D. Gray and J. Kavanagh (Eds.), *Biobehavioral measures of dyslexia* (pp. 261–277). Parkton, MD: York Press.

Blank, M., & Bridger, W. H. (1966). Deficiencies in verbal labeling in retarded readers. *American Journal of Orthopsychiatry*, 36, 840–847.

Bower, G. H., & Hilgard, E. R. (1981). *Theories of learning.* Englewood Cliffs, NJ: Prentice-Hall.

Bower, G. H., & Minaire, H. (1974). On interfering with item versus order information in serial recall. *American Journal of Psychology, 87,* 557–564.

Bradley, L., & Bryant, P. E. (1983). Categorizing sounds and learning to read: A causal connection. *Nature, 303,* 419–421.

Brewer, W. F. (1967). *Paired-associate learning of dyslexic children.* Unpublished doctoral dissertation, University of Iowa, Iowa City, Iowa.

Brittain, M. D. (1970). Inflectional performance and early reading achievement. *Reading Research Quarterly, 6,* 34–48.

Bryant, P. E. (1974). *Perception and understanding in young children.* New York: Basic Books.

Bryant, P., & Impey, L. (1986). The similarities between normal readers and developmental and acquired dyslexics. *Cognition, 24,* 121–137.

Byrne, B. (1981). Deficient syntactic control in poor readers: Is a weak phonetic memory code responsible? *Applied Psycholinguistics, 2,* 201–212.

Byrne, B., & Shea, P. (1979). Semantic and phonetic memory codes in beginning readers. *Memory and Cognition, 7,* 333–338.

Calfee, R., & Piontkowski, D. (1981). The reading diary: Acquisition of decoding. *Reading Research Quarterly, 13,* 346–373.

Chomsky, N., & Halle, M. (1968). *The sound pattern of English.* New York: Harper & Row.

Chall, J. S. (1967). *Learning to read: The great debate.* New York: McGraw-Hill.

Clay, M. (1987). Learning to be learning disabled. *New Zealand Journal of Educational Studies, 22,* 155–173.

Coltheart, M., Patterson, K. E., & Marshall, J. C. (1980). *Deep dyslexia.* London: Routledge & Kegan Paul.

Damasio, A. R. (1985). The frontal lobes. In K. M. Heilman & E. Valenstein (Eds.), *Clinical neuropsychology* (2nd ed.) (pp. 339–376). New York: Oxford University Press.

Das, J. P., Kirby, J., & Jarman, R. F. (1975). Simultaneous and successive syntheses: An alternative model for cognitive abilities. *Psychological Bulletin, 82,* 99.

DeFries, J. C., Fulker, D. W., & LuBuda, M. C. (1987). Evidence for a genetic aetiology in reading disability of twins. *Nature, 329,* 537–539.

deHirsch, K., Jansky, J., & Langford, W. (1966). *Predicting reading failure.* New York: Harper & Row.

Denckla, M. B. (1977). Minimal brain dysfunction and dyslexia: Beyond diagnosis by exclusion. In M. E. Blank, I. Rapin, & M. Kinsbourne (Eds.), *Topics in child neurology* (pp. 243–260). New York: Spectrum Publications.

Denckla, M. B., & Rudel, R. (1976). Naming of pictured objects by dyslexic and other learning-disabled children. *Brain and Language, 39,* 1–15.

Dennis, M. (1982). The developmentally dyslexic brain and the written language skills of children with one hemisphere. In U. Kirk (Ed.), *The neuropsychology of language, reading, and spelling* (pp. 185–208). New York: Academic Press.

Duffy, F. H., Denckla, M. B., Bartels, R. H., & Sandini, G. (1980). Dyslexia: Regional differences in brain electrical activity by topographic mapping. *Annals of Neurology, 7,* 412–420.

Dykman, R. A., Ackerman, P. T., & Holcomb, P. J. (1985). Reading-disabled and ADD children: Similarities and differences. In D. B. Gray & J. F. Kavanagh (Eds.), *Biobehavioral measures of dyslexia* (pp. 47–62). Parkton, MD: York Press.

Evans, M. A., & Carr, T. H. (1985). Cognitive abilities, conditions of learning, and the early development of reading skill. *Reading Research Quarterly, 20,* 327–350.

Flowers, D. L., Wood, F. B., & Naylor, C. E. (1989). *Regional cerebral blood flow in adults diagnosed as reading disabled in childhood.* Unpublished manuscript.

Fowler, C. A., Liberman, I. Y., & Shankweiler, D. (1977). On interpreting the error patterns of the beginning reader. *Language and Speech, 20,* 162–173.

Freebody, P., & Byrne, B. (1988). Word-reading strategies in elementary schoolchildren: Relations to comprehension, reading time, and phonemic awareness. *Reading Research Quarterly, 23,* 441–453.

Fry, M. A., Johnson, C. S., & Muehl, S. (1970). Oral language production in relation to reading achievement among select second graders. In D. J. Bakker & P. Satz (Eds.), *Specific reading disability: Advances in theory and method* (pp. 123–146). Rotterdam: Rotterdam University Press.

Galaburda, A. M., & Kemper, T. L. (1979). Cytoarchitectonic abnormalities in developmental dyslexia: A case study. *Annals of Neurology, 6,* 94–100.

Gascon, G., & Goodglass, H. (1970). Reading retardation and the information content of stimuli in paired-associate learning. *Cortex, 6,* 417–429.

Geschwind, N., & Fusillo, M. (1966). Color-naming defects in association with alexia. *AMA Archives of Neurology, 15,* 137–146.

Gibson, E. J. (1969). *Principles of perceptual learning and development.* New York: Appleton-Century-Crofts.

Gough, P. B. (1972). One second of reading. In J. F. Kavanagh & I. G. Mattingly (Eds.), *Language by ear and by eye: The relationships between speech and reading* (pp. 331–358). Cambridge, MA: MIT Press.

Gough, P. B., & Hillinger, M. L. (1980). Learning to read: An unnatural act. *Bulletin of the Orton Society, 30,* 179–196.

Harter, M. R., Anllo-Vento, L., Wood, F. B., & Schroeder, M. M. (1988). Separate brain potential characteristics in children with reading disability and attention deficit disorder: Color and letter relevance effects. *Brain and Cognition, 7,* 115–140.

Healy, A. F. (1974). Separating item from order information in short-term memory. *Journal of Verbal Learning and Verbal Behavior, 13,* 644–655.

Heilman, K. M., & Valenstein, E. (1985). Neglect and related disorders. In K. M. Heilman & E. Valenstein (Eds.), *Clinical neuropsychology* (2nd ed., pp. 243–294). New York: Oxford University Press.

Hermann, K. (1959). *Reading disability.* Copenhagen: Munksgaard.

Houston, J. P. (1976). Item versus order information, proactive inhibition and serial recall. *American Journal of Psychology, 89,* 507–514.

Johnson, D., & Myklebust, H. (1967). *Learning disabilities: Educational principles and practices.* New York: Grune & Stratton.

Katz, R. B., Shankweiler, D., & Liberman, I. Y. (1981). Memory for item order and phonetic recoding in the beginner reader. *Journal of Experimental Child Psychology, 32,* 474–484.

LaBerge, D., & Samuels, S. J. (1974). Toward a theory of automatic information processing in reading. *Cognitive Psychology, 6,* 293–323.

Larsen, B., Skinhoj, E., & Lassen, N. A. (1978). Variations in regional cortical blood flow in right and left hemispheres. *Brain, 101,* 193–210.

Lassen, N. A., Ingvar, D. H., & Skinhoj, E. (1978). Brain function and blood flow. *Scientific American, 239,* 50–59.

Liberman, I. Y., Shankweiler, D., Fischer, F. W., & Carter, B. (1974). Explicit syllable and phoneme segmentation in the young child. *Journal of Experimental Child Psychology, 18,* 201–212.

Lundberg, I., Olofsson, A., & Wall, S. (1980). Reading and spelling skills in the first school years predicted from phonemic awareness skills in kindergarten. *Scandinavian Journal of Psychology, 21,* 159–173.

Luria, A. R. (1973). *Higher cortical functions in man.* New York: Basic Books.

Manis, F. R., & Morrison, F. J. (1982). Processing of identity and position information in normal and disabled readers. *Journal of Experimental Child Psychology, 33,* 74–86.

Mann, V. A., Shankweiler, D., & Smith, S. T. (1984). The association between comprehension of spoken sentences and early reading ability: The role of phonetic representation. *Journal of Child Language, 11,* 627–643.

Mesulam, M. M. (1985). Attention, confusional states, and neglect. In M. M. Mesulam (Ed.), *Principles of behavioral neurology* (pp. 125–168). Philadelphia: F. Davis.

Mirsky, A. (1978). Attention: A neuropsychological perspective. In J. S. Chall & A. F. Mirsky (Eds.), *Education and the Brain* (77th Yearbook of the National Society for the Study of Education [Part II]). Chicago: University of Chicago Press.

Morrison, F. J., & Manis, F. R. (1982). Cognitive processes and reading disability: A critique and proposal. In C. J. Brainerd & M. Pressley (Eds.), *Verbal processes in children* (pp. 59–93). New York: Springer-Verlag.

Nagy, W. E., & Anderson, R. C. (1984). How many words are there in printed school English? *Reading Research Quarterly, 19,* 304–330.

Orton, S. T. (1925). "Word-blindness" in school children. *Archives of Neurology and Psychiatry, 14,* 581–615.

Patterson, K. E., Marshall, J. C., & Coltheart, M. (1985). *Surface dyslexia—Neurological and cognitive studies of phonological reading.* London: Erlbaum.

Perfetti, C. A., Beck, I., Bell, L., & Hughes, C. (1987). Children's reading and the development of phonological awareness. *Merrill Palmer Quarterly, 33,* 39–75.

Petersen, S. E., Fox, P. T., Posner, M. I., Mintun, M., & Raichle, M. E. (1988). Position emission tomographic studies of the cortical anatomy of single-word processing. *Nature, 331,* 585–589.

Ravenette, A. T. (1961). Vocabulary level and reading attainment. *British Journal of Educational Psychology, 31,* 96.

Rudel, R. G., Denckla, M. B., & Spalten, E. (1976). Paired-associates learning of Morse code and Braille letter names by dyslexic and normal children. *Cortex, 12,* 61–70.

Rumsey, J. M., Berman, K. F., Denckla, M. B., Hamburger, S. D., Kruesi, M. J., & Weinberger, D. R. (1987). Regional cerebral blood flow in severe developmental dyslexia. *Archives of Neurology, 44,* 1144–1150.

Rutter, M., Tizard, J., & Whitmore, K. (1969). *Education, health and behavior.* Harlow, Eng.: Longman.

Shallice, F., McLeod, P., & Lewis, K. (1985). Isolating cognitive modules with the dual task paradigm: Are speech perception and production separate processes? *Quarterly Journal of Experimental Psychology, 37A,* 507–532.

Shankweiler, D., Liberman, I. Y., Mark, L. S., Fowler, C. A., & Fischer, F. W. (1979). The speech code and learning to read. *Journal of Experimental Psychology: Human Learning and Memory, 5,* 531–545.

Smith, S. D., Kimberling, W. J., Pennington, B. F., & Lubs, H. A. (1983). Specific reading disability: Identification of an inherited form through linkage analysis. *Science, 219,* 1345–1347.

Sperry, R. W. (1964). The great cerebral commissure. *Scientific American, 210,* 42–52.

Stanovich, K. E., Nathan, R. G., & Zolman, J. E. (1988). The developmental lag hypothesis in reading: Longitudinal and matched reading-level comparisons. *Child Development, 59,* 71–86.

Stuss, D. T., & Benson, D. F. (1987). The frontal lobes and control of cognition and memory. In E. Perecman (Ed.), *The frontal lobes revisited* (pp. 141–158). New York: IRBN Press.

Treiman, R., & Baron, J. (1983). Phonemic analysis training helps children benefit from spelling-sound rules. *Memory and Cognition, 11,* 382–389.

Tulving, E., & Pearlstone, Z. (1966). Availability versus accessibility of information in memory for words. *Journal of Verbal Learning and Verbal Behavior, 5,* 381–391.

Vellutino, F. R. (1979). *Dyslexia: Theory and research.* Cambridge, MA: MIT Press.

Vellutino, F. R. (1982). Theoretical issues in the study of word recognition: The unit of perception controversy reexamined. In S. Rosenberg (Ed.), *Handbook of applied psycholinguistics* (pp. 33–197). Hillsdale, NJ: Erlbaum.

Vellutino, F. R. (1987, March). Dyslexia. *Scientific American, 256*(3), 34–41.

Vellutino, F. R., & Scanlon, D. M. (1982). Verbal processing in poor and normal readers. In C. J. Brainerd & M. Pressley (Eds.), *Verbal processing in children* (pp. 189–264). New York: Springer-Verlag.

Vellutino, F. R., & Scanlon, D. M. (1985). Verbal memory in poor and normal readers: Developmental differences in the use of linguistic codes. In D. Gray & J. Kavanagh (Eds.), *Biobehavioral measures of dyslexia* (pp. 177–214). Parkton, MD: York Press.

Vellutino, F. R., & Scanlon, D. M. (1987a). Linguistic coding and reading ability. In S. Rosenberg (Ed.), *Advances in applied psycholinguistics* (Vol. 2, pp. 1–69). New York: Cambridge University Press.

Vellutino, F. R., & Scanlon, D. M. (1987b). Phonological coding, phonological awareness, and reading ability: Evidence from longitudinal and experimental study. *Merrill Palmer Quarterly, 33,* 321–363.

Vellutino, F. R., & Scanlon, D. M. (1989). Auditory information processing in poor and normal readers. In J. J. Dumont & H. Nakken (Eds.), *Learning disabilities (Vol. 2): Cognitive, social, and remedial aspects.* Amsterdam/Lisse, Neth.: Swets & Zeitlinger.

Vellutino, F. R., Scanlon, D. M., DeSetto, L., & Pruzek, R. M. (1981). Developmental trends in the salience of meaning versus structural attributes of written words. *Psychological Research, 43,* 131–153.

Vellutino, F. R., Scanlon, D. M., & Tanzman, M. S. (in press). Differential sensitivity to the meaning and structural attributes of printed words in poor and normal readers. *Learning and Individual Differences.*

Wang, P. L. (1988). Concept formation and frontal lobe function: The search for a clinical frontal lobe test. In E. Perecman (Ed.), *The frontal lobe revisited* (pp. 189–205). New York: IRBN Press.

Wechsler, D. (1974). *Wechsler Intelligence Scale for Children-Revised.* New York: Psychological Corporation.

Williams, J. P. (1980). Teaching decoding with an emphasis on phoneme analysis and phoneme blending. *Journal of Educational Psychology, 72*(1), 1–15.

22 THE DEVELOPMENT OF STRATEGIC READERS

Scott G. Paris, Barbara A. Wasik, and Julianne C. Turner

Expert readers use rapid decoding, large vocabularies, phonemic awareness, knowledge about text features, and a variety of strategies to aid comprehension and memory (Baker & Brown, 1984). Novice readers, in contrast, often focus on decoding single words, fail to adjust their reading for different texts or purposes, and seldom look ahead or back in text to monitor and improve comprehension. Such cognitive limitations are characteristic of young novices as well as older, unskilled readers. In addition, older yet poor readers may have motivational handicaps such as low expectations for success, anxiety about their reading, and unwillingness to persevere in the face of difficulty. Given the multidimensional differences between skilled and unskilled readers, why focus on *strategic reading* as a hallmark of expertise?

Strategic reading is a prime characteristic of expert readers because it is woven into the fabric of children's cognitive development and is necessary for success in school. There are six crucial reasons why strategic reading is fundamental to the development and education of children. First, strategies allow readers to elaborate, organize, and evaluate information derived from text. Second, the acquisition of reading strategies coincides and overlaps with the development during childhood of multiple cognitive strategies to enhance attention, memory, communication, and learning. Third, strategies are controllable by readers; they are personal cognitive tools that can be used selectively and flexibly. Fourth, strategic reading reflects metacognition and motivation because readers need to have both the knowledge and disposition to use strategies. Fifth, strategies that foster reading and thinking can be taught directly by teachers. And sixth, strategic reading can enhance learning throughout the curriculum.

Our special focus in this chapter is on the *development* of strategic reading. We describe changes in children's reading proficiency due to mental growth, motivation, instruction, and social guidance because all of these factors are related. A great deal of research in the past 20 years has shown that young and unskilled readers do not use strategies often or effectively without help (Brown, Bransford, Ferrara, & Campione, 1983). Garner (in press) has noted that these handicaps are particularly evident when (1) children fail to monitor comprehension; (2) they believe that the strategies will not make a difference in their reading; (3) they lack knowledge about text features; (4) they are disinterested in the text and unwilling to use strategies; and (5) they prefer familiar yet primitive strategies over less-familiar but more-effective tactics. Nonstrategic reading in these situations reflects a mixture of developmental naïveté, limited practice, lack of instruction, and motivational reluctance to use unfamiliar or effortful strategies. Be-

Our revisions were aided by the helpful comments of Peter Winograd and Peter Mosenthal. Research by the first author and development of many of the ideas in this paper were made possible by a Field Initiated Studies Program grant (No. G008610959) provided by the Office of Educational Research and Improvement (OERI), U.S. Department of Education. However, the findings and conclusions reported do not necessarily reflect the position or policy of the U.S. Department of Education.

609

cause no single factor can provide an adequate account of strategic reading, we try to provide a developmental and contextual perspective for understanding how children become strategic readers.

This chapter is organized in four major sections. In the first section, we describe common text-processing strategies that promote comprehension. The discussion emphasizes the strategic actions that readers might take before, during, and after reading. The second section includes a description of metacognitive differences among readers of different ages and abilities. We also describe how metacognitive instruction can promote strategic reading. In the third section, we discuss the relation between motivation and strategic reading with particular attention to the defensive strategies that some children adopt to circumvent thoughtful reading. We then show how children's perceptions of their own competence and control influence their emerging beliefs about reading and their dispositions to use effective strategies. The fourth section includes a discussion of the implications of strategic reading for innovations in curricula, instruction, and assessment. Although our sequential discussion of strategies, metacognition, and motivation corresponds to research trends during the past 15 years, these "layers" of reading variables should not be misconstrued as sequential factors in either developmental or instructional models of reading. Children's earliest encounters with literacy are influenced by their motivation, awareness, and strategies for reading and writing.

READING STRATEGIES

It would be helpful to begin with a concise definition of reading strategies, but unfortunately, there is no consensus among researchers. At least three problems persist. First, it is not clear how to differentiate *reading* strategies from other processes that might be called thinking, reasoning, perceptual, study, or motivational strategies. Weinstein and Mayer (1986) define cognitive strategies as a broad array of actions that help to control behavior, emotions, motivation, communication, attention, and comprehension. Although each kind of strategy might influence reading, not all researchers would classify them as reading strategies. A second problem concerns the scope of strategies—are they global or specific? Levin (1986) argues that strategies include multiple components that must be carefully analyzed, whereas Derry and Murphy (1986) distinguish strategies as general learning plans that are implemented through specific tactics. Strategies are difficult to demarcate when they are embedded in complex sequences of behavior or hierarchies of decisions. A third problem involves intentionality and consciousness. Consider these opposing viewpoints. "To be a strategy, the means must be employed deliberately, with some awareness, in order to produce or influence the goal" (Wellman, 1988, p. 5). "Also, it is now recognized that strategy functioning at its best occurs without deliberation. It is more reflexive than voluntary" (Pressley, Forrest-Pressley, & Elliot-Faust, 1988, p. 102).

Although the definition and parameters of reading strategies merit discussion, we cannot reconcile the different perspectives briefly. Thus, our discussion of reading strategies is broad and inclusive; we consider a wide range of tactics that readers use to engage and comprehend text. Our purpose is not to list these tactics by category or age, because they are neither uniformly defined nor acquired. Instead, we examine how children develop better understanding and control of these tactics in order to become motivated, self-regulated readers. To this end, we offer a distinction between reading skills and strategies that will clarify the developmental and instructional importance of strategic reading.

Skills refer to information-processing techniques that are automatic, whether at the level of recognizing grapheme-phoneme correspondence or summarizing a story.

Skills are applied to text unconsciously for many reasons including expertise, repeated practice, compliance with directions, luck, and naive use. In contrast, *strategies* are actions selected deliberately to achieve particular goals. An emerging skill can become a strategy when it is used intentionally. Likewise, a strategy can "go underground" (cf. Vygotsky, 1978) and become a skill. Indeed, strategies are more efficient and developmentally advanced when they become generated and applied automatically as skills. Thus, strategies are "skills under consideration" (see Paris, Lipson, & Wixson, 1983). Because they are conscious and deliberate, strategies are open to inspection; they can be evaluated for their utility, effort, and appropriateness privately or publicly. This characteristic of reading strategies is fundamental in our developmental analysis because mutual discussion of strategies underlies social guidance of early reading and classroom instruction, whereas private examination of strategies is the foundation of self-regulated reading.

Many reading strategies can be recruited for different purposes, but we will begin with prototypical text-processing strategies that promote comprehension. These can be organized taxonomically according to strategies applied before, during, or after reading, but the recursive nature of looking forward and backward through text while reading allows similar strategies to be applied at different times. Our taxonomy serves two purposes. First, it provides a framework to review a wide variety of cognitive strategies that aid comprehension. Second, it calls attention to the successive choices that readers make as they engage text. Strategic readers are not characterized by the volume of tactics that they use but rather by the selection of appropriate strategies that fit the particular text, purpose, and occasion.

Preparing to Read

There are many strategies that students can use before reading begins. For example, they can preview the material by skimming text, looking at pictures, or examining the title and subheadings. Previews of text help to increase students' comprehension of explicit and implicit information (Graves & Cooke, 1980). It may be a particularly useful strategy for unsuccessful readers who do not engage in strategies spontaneously. Graves, Cooke, and LaBerge (1983) helped fifth- and seventh-grade poor readers preview text material. They developed students' interest by asking questions, presenting statements, and encouraging a discussion about the topic before reading the story. Then a summary was presented along with the characters and part of the plot. These activities provided a link between familiar information and the topic of the story. Students who examined and discussed topics of stories before reading answered significantly more factual and inferential questions than students who simply read the text. In addition, previewing helped to generate a more positive attitude toward the text.

Previewing includes many components. One important aspect is the activation of prior knowledge. For example, Ogle (1986) advocates the use of a "K-W-L" approach to reading. Students learn to ask "What do I *know*?, What do I *want* to learn?, and, What did I *learn*?" This line of self-questioning helps students to think about relevant background information and to make predictions about text. Preparing to read also involves setting a purpose. This the first step in Directed Reading as Thinking Activity (DRTA) (Stauffer, 1969) and is critical for flexible, strategic reading. Students need to understand their learning goals and the criteria for success. They need to form hypotheses and generate good questions about the text before they begin to read.

A great deal of research has shown that prior knowledge influences comprehension. For example, Lipson (1983) has shown that children's familiarity with religious customs influences their comprehension and memory when they read a passage on a religious topic like communion. Pearson, Hansen, and Gordon (1979) observed that the effects of prior knowledge were greater on script-implicit than text-explicit questions. The schemata provided by prior knowledge apparently guide readers to make inferences and elaborations while reading. Activating prior knowledge can be stimulated by many instructional procedures, such as a group discussion of the key concepts in text (Langer, 1981). Langer (1984) found that activating prior knowledge significantly improves comprehension and does not simply motivate children's interest in reading.

There are two important problems with prereading strategies, however. First, they are difficult to execute spontaneously. Many students do not understand the value of previewing text, titles, and pictures, nor the importance of thinking about the topic before beginning to read. Even if the strategies are known, they are sometimes avoided as time consuming or unnecessary. Thus, a fundamental problem for teachers is to increase students' understanding of the value of the strategy so that it can be applied spontaneously without teacher support and prompting. A second problem with prereading strategies is that they depend on children's knowledge about text. Some strategies, like previewing, may be relatively independent of the content of text but other strategies may be driven by the nature of the material. For example, semantic mapping, which provides graphic descriptions of the relations among key ideas in text, varies with text genre and domain (Heimlich & Pittelman, 1986). Knowledge of story grammars for narrative text and knowledge of expository structures such as enumeration, compare/contrast, and hierarchical organization all contribute to the effectiveness of mapping and organizing text information before reading (Calfee & Chambliss, 1987). Thus, using effective strategies before reading involves knowledge about text genre and structure, knowledge about relevant strategies, and motivation.

Constructing Meaning While Reading

Many tactics for embellishing text information help readers elaborate the ideas suggested by text and make the information personally significant. Inferring characters' traits, connecting causal and temporal chains of events, and integrating information across sentences are all examples of constructive reasoning while reading. We discuss three paradigmatic examples of on-line reading strategies: identifying main ideas, making inferences, and looking forward and backward in text.

Identifying main ideas.   Identifying main ideas has been described as the "essence of reading comprehension" (Johnston & Afflerbach, 1985; Pearson & Johnston, 1978). Finding the main idea requires readers to (1) understand what has been read, (2) make judgments about the importance of information, and (3) consolidate information succinctly. But young readers have difficulty recognizing, recalling, or constructing the gist, central theme, or main idea from prose passages (e.g., Baumann, 1981, 1982; Johnston & Afflerbach, 1985; Smiley & Brown, 1979; Taylor & Williams, 1983; Winograd & Bridge, 1986). Even 12- and 13-year-old students do not easily discriminate relevant from irrelevant information in text nor generate topic sentences about paragraphs. In contrast, expert adult readers refine and revise their ideas continually while reading as they "crunch the data" to find the gist (Johnston & Afflerbach, 1985).

Several instructional studies, however, have demonstrated that students can be taught to improve main idea comprehension. Baumann (1984) used direct explanation to teach students five steps to construct main ideas: introduction, examples, direct instruction, teacher-directed application, and independent practice. Baumann (1984) found that sixth graders who were taught these steps were more skillful at comprehending explicit and implicit main ideas in passages than students who received traditional basal lessons.

Schunk and Rice (1987) explained the value of finding main ideas in text to remedial readers. There were three training conditions: General strategy value information (e.g., using these steps will help to answer questions in passages), specific strategy value information (e.g., using these steps will help to answer questions about the main ideas in the passage), and a combination of both general and specific value information. The effect that strategy use had on children's self-efficacy was also measured. The results showed that children who were given a combination of specific and general strategy value information were significantly better at identifying main ideas in passages. They also rated their self-efficacy higher than children in the other two groups. Understanding *why* the strategy was important helped children to identify main ideas and made them feel capable of completing the task. Similar success in teaching main ideas to learning-disabled students were also found by Williams, Taylor, Jarin, and Milligan (1983).

Various text-based factors influence readers' ability to construct main ideas from text. For example, readers are better at finding main ideas in passages when they are stated explicitly rather than implicitly (Baumann, 1984). Readers are more adept at identifying a main idea that appears at the beginning of a paragraph than when it is embedded in the text (Baumann, 1986; Taylor & Williams, 1983). Thus, both text properties and developmental reading skills contribute to the identification of main ideas.

Making inferences.   A second category of on-line strategies, making inferences, helps readers to construct meaning. Inferential comprehension is frequently automatic, but young children and beginning readers may benefit from strategies that promote inferences. For example, considerable research has shown that children have more difficulty answering inferential than literal comprehension questions (Hansen & Pearson, 1983; Raphael & Pearson, 1985). In addition, it appears that very little instructional time is spent teaching inferential comprehension skills in the classroom (Hare & Pulliam, 1979).

Research on inferential comprehension has focused on how young and beginning readers benefit from training that promotes inference making during reading. Hansen (1981) compared two approaches for teaching inferential comprehension. In one approach, children were trained to use an inferential-thinking strategy. In another approach, students practiced answering inferential questions. Students in both approaches improved their ability to make inferences significantly more than students in an untreated control. Hansen and Pearson (1983) trained good and poor fourth-grade readers (1) to be aware of the importance of making inferences, (2) to utilize prior knowledge, and (3) to ask inferential questions. Poor readers benefited from the training but the good readers did not.

Raphael and Pearson (1985) trained high-, average-, and low-reading sixth graders in the question-answer relationship (QAR) paradigm to investigate its effect on both literal and inferential comprehension. Although questions with answers explicitly stated in the text were more easily answered than questions with answers implied, the QAR training did increase students' inferential skills. A similar study was done by Raphael and McKinney (1983) with good and poor readers in the sixth and eighth grade. Although sixth graders' inferential comprehension improved, the eighth graders appeared to be unaffected by the training. Apparently, the eighth graders were unmotivated to use the strategy over the ten weeks of instruction and appeared to need only a 10-minute orientation in order to understand the strategy.

Dewitz, Carr, and Patberg (1987) taught fifth graders a variety of strategies to improve inferential comprehension. Three treatment groups received special instruction. One group was taught to use structured overviews to identify key information and hierarchical information in text. A second group learned to fill in appropriate words in a cloze passage and to use self-monitoring techniques to check their answers. A third group was trained with both the structured overviews and the cloze procedures. The three training groups were then compared to a treated control group who received vocabulary instruction and supplementary activities. Students trained in the cloze procedure made more inferences and transferred the strategies better than other students. Thus, children, particularly young or unskilled readers, can be taught to improve their inferential comprehension.

    Text inspection.   As readers encounter new words and ideas in text, they may need to inspect text already read or skip ahead to use context to discern difficult information. Text inspection comprises a third category of on-line strategies. Garner (1987) describes backtracking in text as a strategy that develops substantially between sixth and tenth grade. Looking back in text for information may be difficult for students because they may (1) not realize they have a comprehension problem and (2) be unfamiliar with text structure that can guide their backtracking. Garner and Reis (1981) found that skilled readers in eighth grade used backtracking but less-skilled readers read the text only once in a linear fashion. They apparently believed it was "illegal" or unnecessary to reread information. Direct instruction provided over five days to re-medial readers improved children's strategic backtracking in text (Garner, Hare, Alexander, Haynes, & Winograd, 1984).

    In summary, strategic reading includes many tactics that can be applied while reading. On-line reading strategies help readers go beyond text information by adding inferences and elaborations from their background knowledge and the text itself. Using context, making predictions, and backtracking all help to monitor the construction of meaning and to fill in gaps in students' understanding. These critical strategies are seldom used by beginning readers or unskilled readers, who may be unaware of how to use them or unconvinced of their importance.

Reviewing and Reflecting after Reading

Beginning readers and unsuccessful students may not think about text after the last word is read. Some readers eagerly move on to the next task without reflecting on their reading. "Did I meet my goal? What did I learn? Were my predictions accurate? Did everything make sense? Can I summarize the main points?" Good readers ask questions like these and invoke strategies to review the text and their comprehension. Of course, postreading strategies may involve the repeated application of tactics used before and during reading because strategic readers revise their understanding recursively. Therefore, checking one's plan, monitoring meaning, making inferences, and so forth can occur on subsequent passes through text. But some strategies can be applied only after the entire text has been processed. As an example, we consider the developmental changes in summarizing text information.

    Researchers have documented clear developmental trends in summarizing. In general, older and more expert readers summarize better than younger and less-skilled readers. Brown and Day (1983) evaluated fifth, seventh, and tenth graders' and college students' summarizing, using a modification of Kintsch and van Dijk's (1978) model. Fifth- and seventh-grade students deleted irrelevant information and reported ideas verbatim, whereas high school and college students collapsed and combined information across paragraphs and provided synopses in their own words. Younger students' summaries usually conformed to the sequence of the text; older students more frequently ordered text by topic or idea units. In addition to a difference in rule use, Brown and Day (1983) noted that older students planned their summaries more. Fifth and seventh graders would frequently "run out of space" before they had completed summaries. However, the few young students who were able to plan their summaries performed like college students.

Taylor (1986), in an investigation of fourth and fifth graders' summarization skills, found that more-capable summarizers planned before they wrote, used text structure as an aid in selecting and generalizing important ideas, recorded information in their own words, and monitored the text to evaluate their own accuracy. Students who had trouble selecting and generalizing important information were unfamiliar with cues in expository text structure and unable to use them as they wrote. Winograd (1984) found similar patterns with eighth graders. When asked to select the most important sentences in a text, poor readers chose sentences that were "interesting" and rich in detail. In contrast, fluent readers used text cues and background knowledge to identify important elements in text.

Despite the apparent lack of sophistication shown by many young students, Brown, Day, and Jones (1983) found that students could be trained to follow the rules that older and more-skilled summarizers use. For example, when constrained to a 20-word summary, fifth graders were as adept as older students in selecting the most important ideas for inclusion in summaries. Rinehart, Stahl, and Erickson (1986) instructed sixth graders to summarize social studies texts. Students who received strategy training took notes that contained more important ideas and improved their abilities to summarize main ideas that were stated explicitly. Hare and Borchardt (1984) also found that high school students were able to improve their use of explicit main ideas in summarizing. However, in neither study were students able to select and include ideas implicitly stated in text. These studies show that both text structure and explicitness of main ideas affect summarizing skills.

Day (1986) demonstrated the importance of metacognitive skills in summarizing. Average and below-average writers in junior college participated in one of four training conditions. Those who received both summarization and self-management instruction showed the most improvement in strategy use. Higher-level students profited more from instruction than lower-level writers, suggesting that more explicit training in complex rules may be necessary for some students. Self-monitoring was most effective when the rules were of moderate difficulty. Day suggests that until strategies become routine, students may be unable to use and monitor them simultaneously.

In summary, strategic readers use a variety of tactics before, during, and after reading to foster comprehension. Although longitudinal data on strategic reading are sorely needed, several developmental trends can be identified. First, children acquire a vast array of strategies between 7 and 13 years of age. Many tactics are taught explicitly, but others are discovered or generated through practice with increasingly complex text. Second, beginning readers require social guidance and assistance to use strategies, whereas children past the age of 10 exhibit progressive spontaneous, selective, and self-controlled use of strategies. Third, young readers tend to read in a linear fashion from beginning to end, but by adolescence they learn to look ahead and back in text, use context, and reread as recursive comprehension strategies. Fourth, strategies are initially applied most easily to small segments of well-organized text that contain explicit ideas and relations. Even adolescents have difficulty using strategies to make inferences, examine a long passage or book, or comprehend convoluted and disorganized text. The progressive acquisition and control of reading strategies is partly due to children's emerging metacognition about literacy, schooling, and themselves.

METACOGNITION AND STRATEGIC READING

The term *metacognition* was coined in the 1970s and it generated immediate interest and research on reading strategies. In fact, Baker and Brown (1984) entitled their chapter in the first volume of *Handbook of Reading Research* "Metacognitive Skills and Reading" in order to emphasize the knowledge and regulation that students exercise over reading strategies. In that chapter, they discuss much of the research conducted between 1975 and 1982 on strategies for enhancing comprehension and memory. Between 1980 and 1987, more than 200 articles were written on metacognition and reading (Paris, Wasik, & van der Westhuizen, 1988). But surprisingly, less than half of those have been empirical analyses of metacognition, and there is no apparent increase in the publication rate over the last several years. The majority of publications on metacognition and reading have been conceptual papers or advice to teachers on how to incorporate metacognition into classroom instruction.

There have been three distinct foci in research on metacognition and reading. One area involves what readers know about the task of reading. Students' conceptual awareness is often assessed with interview questions such as "What is reading?" "What makes someone a good reader?" and "What makes reading difficult?" A second area of interest has been how readers regulate their own thinking. These two dimensions of metacognition are referred to as *knowledge and control, awareness and regulation,* or *self-appraisal and self-management* (Brown, 1987; Paris & Winograd, in press). The third area of interest has been intervention studies in which different instructional approaches have promoted students' knowledge and control over their own reading. We consider each of these three areas in the following sections.

The Development of Reading Awareness

Children learn a great deal about reading and writing before they begin formal instruction in school. Most children are exposed to a wide variety of print in signs, advertisements, newspapers, and television. Parents and children also engage in joint book-reading activities that help children understand the relation between oral language and print (Snow & Ninio, 1986). These scaffolded interactions may provide crucial opportunities for learning initial concepts about print and reading that are relevant to emergent literacy (Clay, 1967; Teale & Sulzby, 1986). It has been argued that children who come to school with meager literacy experiences are often confused about the functions of letters, words, and print (Dyson, 1984). Ferreiro and Teberosky (1982) suggest that children who enter school without a strong connection between oral and written language experiences do not learn to read as quickly as children with richer literacy experiences. Thus, children's early awareness about the conventions of print and the nature of reading are critical for the effectiveness of early instruction and reading achievement.

Early research on emergent literacy by Clay (1967, 1973) revealed that 4- and 5-year-old children begin to understand that reading proceeds from left to right and top to bottom, that punctuation marks are different from words, and that the spaces between letters indicate word boundaries. Hiebert (1981) analyzed the development of preschool children's awareness of print. Whereas 3-year-olds scored less than 50 percent correct on letter naming and visual and auditory discrimination tasks, 5-year-olds were correct on 70 percent of the items. Hiebert notes that 3-year-olds know something about sound/symbol correspondences and letter naming, but their awareness improves sharply between the ages of 3 and 4.

Children's awareness of print conventions is related to measures of reading ability. For example, children's scores on the Concepts about Print Test (Clay, 1979), Written

Language Awareness Test (Evans, Taylor, & Blum, 1979), and Linguistic Awareness in Reading Readiness (LARR) Test (Downing, Ayers, & Schaefer, 1983) all correlate with measures of children's early reading ability. These conceptual or metacognitive measures may predict early reading as well as basic skills such as segmenting words into syllables, letter naming, and matching oral and written language (Ehri & Wilce, 1985). Lundberg, Frost, and Peterson (1988) taught preschoolers about the phonological structure of language and observed significant improvements in phonemic segmentation and metalinguisitic skills that persisted for several years. Phonemic awareness, measured by children's ability to segment, blend, delete, and substitute phonemes, correlates highly with word recognition scores at the end of first grade, $r = .83$ and second grade, $r = .71$ (Juel, Griffith, & Gough, 1986). Bradley and Bryant (1983) observed a longitudinal relation between preschoolers' ability to detect phonemic similarities and differences in words and their reading and spelling abilities measured four years later. The correlations ranged from .44 to .57 and led the authors to conclude "that the awareness of rhythm and alliteration which children acquire before they go to school, possibly as a result of their experiences at home, has a powerful influence on their eventual success in learning to read and to spell" (p. 421). Thus, many studies have shown that children's early concepts about print conventions and their phonemic awareness predict subsequent reading achievement.

Another dimension of children's early awareness about literacy involves their concepts about reading. Some beginning readers remain confused about the purposes and processes of reading. They are often not sure whether one reads the pictures or other marks on the page, and they cannot differentiate retelling a story from reading it (Clay, 1973; Reid, 1966). In contrast to the early awareness of print, children's understanding of the nature of reading may develop more slowly. For example, when one second-grade student was asked to explain reading, he described it as a "stand up, sit down" activity because the teacher made him stand up to read and he would sit down when he made a mistake (Johns, 1984).

Several interview studies have been employed to assess children's awareness about the nature of reading. Weintraub and Denny (1965) asked first graders "What is reading?" Only 20 percent of the children described reading as a cognitive activity that helps learning. Most were vague in their explanations or reported "I don't know." Reid (1966) and Downing (1970) also observed that young children frequently knew they could not read but had little idea of the skills they lacked. Hiebert (1981) observed that 3-year-olds understand some of the processes and purposes for reading, but that awareness improves substantially at age 4. This dawning awareness coincides with emerging skills that 2- to 4-year-old children exhibit in their treatment of books as discrete objects and in the ways they fit their own language to print in order to weave a story across the pages (Sulzby, 1985).

A comprehensive developmental study of children's awareness of reading was conducted by Lomax and McGee (1987). They administered 18 measures of print concepts and word reading to 81 children ranging from 3 to 7 years of age. The authors clustered their measures into five components believed to be related to early reading. The components included concepts about print, graphic awareness, phonemic awareness, grapheme-phoneme correspondence knowledge, and word reading. The purpose of administering this variety of reading tasks was to assess the relations between the different measures and to establish a developmental sequence of acquisition. Lomax and McGee (1987) observed that performance increased with age on each of the 18 tasks. On the five measures of children's concepts about print, the largest differences were observed between 3- and 4-year-olds, consistent with Hiebert (1981). Five and 6-year-olds were similar in their understanding but did not reach ceiling levels. Most of the other tasks revealed a similar pattern in which 3- and 4-year-olds were more different from each other than 5- and 6-year-olds were. Thus, this study confirms the dramatic acquisition of concepts about literacy and emerging skills by age 4 with progressive, but more modest improvement later.

Lomax and McGee (1987) proposed a model to describe the development of early reading and concluded that (1) the ability to discriminate letters and words visually depends upon the development of concepts about print; (2) phonemic awareness is primarily determined by the acquisition of graphic awareness; (3) grapheme-phoneme correspondence depends on the development of concepts about print and of phonemic awareness; and (4) word reading depends upon the knowledge of grapheme-phoneme correspondence. Thus, the data established a developmental sequence in which concepts about print and phonemic awareness assume a primary role in the subsequent development of reading.

These data confirm the importance of children's initial awareness about print conventions and the nature of reading. It should be noted that the developmental sequence of knowledge and skills does not necessarily mean that one causes the other. Lomax and McGee also suggest that it is not useful to think of *mastering* each component before moving on to the next. Rather, it makes more sense to interpret the relations among constructs as factors that facilitate growth in other aspects of reading. The developmental model proposed by Lomax and McGee (1987) is consistent with developmental trends noted by others. For example, Hiebert, Cioffi, and Antonak (1984) reanalyzed Hiebert's (1981) data and found that graphic awareness is a precursor of other print concepts. Other researchers have also found that graphic and phonemic awareness precedes other concepts about reading (Ehri, 1979; Juel, Griffith, & Gough, 1986; Mason, 1980). The finding that concepts about print directly influence grapheme-phoneme correspondence knowledge is consistent with the developmental sequence suggested by Ferreiro and Teberosky (1982), who note that children first differentiate print and pictures, then attend to salient graphic properties, and finally match graphemes and phonemes. Thus, letter-sound relationships are encouraged by children's awareness about print.

Reading awareness continues to develop beyond age 7, although there have been relatively few research studies with older students. For example, Johns and Ellis (1976) interviewed 1,655 students from grades one to eight and asked them the following questions: "What is reading?" "What do you do when you read?" and "If someone didn't know how to read, what would you tell him he would need to learn?" Johns and Ellis found that only 15 percent of the students defined reading as constructing meaning and most of those responses were from students in grades 7 and 8. In response to the second question, only 20 percent of the students indicated that they tried to create meaning as they read. Again, most of these appropriate responses came from students in junior high. In response to the third question, more than half of the students emphasized word recognition or decoding as the fundamental skills to be acquired for reading. In a reanalysis of the data, Johns (1984) confirmed that more than 80 percent of the students interviewed were confused about the nature of reading. The overwhelming majority of students at all grade levels regarded reading as classroom procedures that are nurtured by skills for recognizing and decoding words. Comprehension and thought getting were mentioned rarely by any except the oldest students.

Myers and Paris (1978) examined the knowledge that 8- and 12-year-olds have about person, task, and strategy variables related to reading. The 12-year-olds understood the structure of text and various goals of reading better than 8-year-olds. Older children also knew more about using strategies to construct meaning and to resolve comprehension failures. Eight-year-olds often regard reading as interpreting symbols and words and have incomplete ideas about the existence, value, or need to use strategies for constructing meaning (Paris & Jacobs, 1984).

Data from a wide variety of studies show that preschoolers have a rudimentary understanding of the task of reading (see Garner, 1987, and Jacobs & Paris, 1987, for critical evaluations of methods used to assess metacogniton about reading). Their emergent knowledge about literacy reflects incomplete concepts about the nature of reading, print conventions and processes, and purposes for reading. During elementary school, these concepts become more refined, but reading remains a mysterious activity for many students who receive daily instruction. It is clear that even 12-year-olds do not have well-articulated concepts about reading nor fully developed knowledge about effective strategies to enhance comprehension. Part of readers' metacognitive development includes more detailed knowledge about what strategies are available, how they function, when they should be applied, and why they help comprehension. This information is the declarative, procedural, and conditional knowledge acquired through reading experiences and instruction (Paris, Lipson, & Wixson, 1983). It is critical for monitoring and repairing comprehension. Children's knowledge about reading develops concurrently with their understanding and control of strategies, and these factors become more congruent with increasing age and skill (Cross & Paris, 1988). In the following section, we describe how metacognition facilitates self-regulated reading.

Monitoring, Managing, and Regulating Reading Comprehension

The importance of metacognition and strategic reading is evident in the tactics readers use to monitor comprehension. One of the problems of nonstrategic readers is that they often proceed on "automatic pilot," oblivious to comprehension difficulties (Duffy & Roehler, 1987). Baker and Brown (1984) said, "any attempt to comprehend must involve comprehension monitoring" (p. 344). Wagoner (1983) describes comprehension monitoring as "an executive function, essential for competent reading, which directs the readers' cognitive process as he/she strives to make sense of the incoming information" (p. 328). In this section we consider how this important function of reading develops.

Initial interest in comprehension monitoring was derived from studies of listening comprehension and communication. Markman (1977, 1979), for example, showed that young children failed to detect inconsistencies as they listened to stories and procedures. They realized their lack of understanding only when they tried to imitate the action or explain the story. Research on children's communication (e.g., Flavell, Speer, Green, & August, 1981) revealed that young children often do not ask questions following incomprehensible messages. Thus, many communication breakdowns are due to failures by listeners and speakers to monitor the meaningfulness of their exchanges (Schmidt & Paris, 1984; Shatz, 1983).

The illusion of understanding is evident in studies of reading comprehension also. For example, Paris and Myers (1981) compared the spontaneous comprehension monitoring of good and poor fourth-grade readers as they read aloud. Students read paragraphs that contained nonsense words and phrases and were prompted to underline anything in the text that did not make sense. Less than half of the errors were detected, and poor readers were able to detect as many inconsistencies as good readers only when the passages were simplified. Garner and Kraus (1982) and Grabe and Mann (1984) also found that poor readers had difficulties identifying inconsistencies in text.

In addition to sharp differences in the comprehension monitoring of good and poor readers, there are also developmental differences in monitoring. Garner and Taylor (1982) asked second, fourth, and sixth graders to edit passages that contained internal inconsistencies. Younger children did not find the errors in the passages spontaneously, and even older children had difficulty finding all the problem. Baker (1984) asked 9- and

11-year-olds to read passages that contained semantic inconsistencies. For example, students read a story about koalas that in one sentence described them as sleeping in trees and in a later sentence described them as sleeping on the ground. Nine-year-olds had difficulty detecting these kinds of contradictions, a finding similar to Markman and Gorin's (1981) study of listening comprehension.

Research on comprehension monitoring has clearly revealed both age and ability differences in the accuracy of children's comprehension monitoring. Several factors contribute to the effects. First, young children may not believe that there are mistakes in text. They hesitate to question the authority of print. Second, so much attention might be given to understanding the words that there are not enough cognitive resources left to construct, integrate, monitor, and evaluate the meaning. Third, many young readers do not understand the standards that can be used to evaluate comprehension. Fourth, some children may notice the problem but make inferences about missing or inaccurate text in order to construct a sensible interpretation rather than report a comprehension failure (August, Flavell, & Clift, 1984).

Because students often do not use good monitoring strategies, training helps considerably. Miller (1987) trained fifth graders to use a self-verbalization routine that provided purpose, guidance, evaluation, and feedback. Self-instructed statements occurred before, during, and after reading in order to enhance monitoring. Error detection was even better on delayed posttests, and the gains were largest for above-average students. Gambrell and Bales (1987) taught poor readers in fourth and fifth grade to use mental imagery to improve constructive processing while reading. After training in mental imagery, students detected significantly more explicit and implicit inconsistencies in text than the control group. Thus, good and poor readers differ in their spontaneous comprehension monitoring, but training students to use self-verbalization, mental imagery, and other monitoring tactics improves comprehension.

Several researchers have compared spontaneous and directed comprehension monitoring. For example, Markman and Gorin (1981) varied the instructions given to 8- and 10-year-old children who were listening to stories that contained inconsistencies. Half the children in each group were informed that the essay had some problems. The other half were also told that some of the statements would actually be false and examples were provided. When provided with explicit instructions about the nature of errors, young children increased their detection of inconsistencies in text. Paris and Myers (1981) found that detection of errors increased substantially when students were directed to underline any words or sentences in the story that they did not understand. Thus, monitoring by younger or less skilled readers improves when explicit instructions and examples are provided.

Baker (1984) noted that there were developmental differences in the types of standards that children used to evaluate comprehension. Young children focused on problems with individual words, whereas older children combined multiple standards to evaluate the passages. Baker (1984) found that comprehension monitoring of 9- and 11-year-olds could be improved when they were provided multiple standards for judging problems, internal consistency, and external consistency. Garner (1981) found that fifth-grade poor readers evaluated problems in text according to word meaning rather than larger units of text. The focus on word meaning is consistent with developmental trends in children's understanding of purposes of reading and text structure.

It is also possible that young children do not monitor meaning while reading because all of their attention is directed at decoding and analyzing meaning. Vosniadou, Pearson, and Rogers (1988) hypothesize that one of the difficulties in detecting errors in text is the construction of a general representation of the meaning of the passage. For example, Vosniadou et al. (1988) asked first, third, and fifth graders to detect familiar falsehoods and unfamiliar factual contradictions in narrative text. Children were able to detect familiar falsehoods more easily than unfamiliar contradictions. When familiarity was controlled in another experiment, no differences among age groups were observed in the degree of inconsistency detection. However, when children's recall was compared to their comprehension monitoring, it was found that detection of inconsistencies was poorest for those texts on which recall was also poorest. The authors argue that children may not differ in their ability to compare and evaluate text information once it is understood and represented, but they may differ in their ability to form coherent mental representations of text. Paris and Myers (1981) also observed that poor readers' low rate of error detection was correlated with more disorganized recall and fewer questions answered correctly about the passages. Thus, comprehension monitoring reflects strategies for constructing meaning, knowledge about criteria for evaluating text, and coherent recall and organization of text information.

In summary, it appears that young children and less-skilled readers have difficulty monitoring comprehension that is partly due to their lack of awareness about appropriate standards for evaluating their own comprehension. Younger and less-skilled readers emphasize understanding of words; they tend to evaluate lexical consistency and appropriateness when they examine problems in text. They also use single standards rather than multiple standards for monitoring comprehension. Older and more-skilled readers, in contrast, use multiple standards flexibly and focus on the meaning of text. They are also more likely to construct coherent representations of the text and benefit from examples and explanations of standards to use for evaluating text. Despite these developmental improvements, it should be noted that even 12-year-old good readers do not detect a large number of errors and inconsistencies inserted into meaningful text. We consider how instruction can promote more effective monitoring in the following section.

Interventions That Promote Reading Awareness and Comprehension Monitoring

Because students have many misconceptions about the nature of reading and incomplete awareness of strategies for monitoring and regulating comprehension, many researchers have tried to foster better metacognition and reading comprehension through direct instruction. Baker and Brown (1984) said

> An essential aim is to make the reader aware of the active nature of reading and the importance of employing problem-solving, trouble-shooting routines to enhance understanding. If the reader can be made aware of (a) basic strategies for reading and remembering, (b) simple rules of text construction, (c) differing demands of a variety of tests to which his background knowledge may be put, and (d) the importance of attempting to use any background knowledge that he may have, he cannot help but become a more effective reader. Such self-awareness is a prerequisite for self-regulation, the ability to monitor and check one's own cognitive activities while reading. (p. 376)

A variety of instructional approaches have been designed to enhance students' metacognition (see Paris, Wasik, & van der Westhuizen, 1988). Basically, the approaches can be grouped into interventions that teach and measure metacognition directly and instruction that promotes metacognition indirectly by teaching specific strategies. The following two sections describe examples of each type of intervention.

Direct Explanation

Some of the initial studies that taught children to use cognitive strategies relied on coercion rather than pedagogy. For example, children were directed to use unfamiliar or unlikely strategies to remember items, or they were persuaded to follow the behavior of a model who used such a strategy. Unfortunately, children who were compliant often did not change their understanding or evaluation of the strategy and thus avoided using it when it was not required. More recent training studies have added detailed explanations about the effectiveness and importance of strategies in order to persuade children that they should use the strategies independently. For example, memory strategies are maintained and generalized when children evaluate them as important and appropriate (Fabricius & Hagen, 1984; O'Sullivan & Pressley, 1984; Paris, Newman, & McVey, 1982). Schunk and Rice (1987) have shown that children are more likely to adopt strategies for finding the main idea when they understand the utility of the strategy and their own efficacy in using it.

As a consequence of these studies, several investigators have created classroom interventions to promote students' metacognition about reading. For example, Paris, Cross, and Lipson (1984) taught students in third and fifth grade declarative, procedural, and conditional knowledge about a variety of comprehension strategies. Group discussions of the strategies were prompted by the use of metaphors such as "Plan your reading trip" and "Be a reading detective." These dialogues helped make the strategies concrete and sensible to students who then practiced using them as they read. The intervention included considerable practice with feedback; combinations of reading, writing, listening, and speaking; and application of the strategies in content area reading. After four months, or approximately 30 hours, of metacognitive instruction on reading strategies, students displayed significant increases in their awareness about reading, comprehension monitoring, and strategic reading (Paris & Jacobs, 1984). Similar increases in metacognition and strategic reading were observed in a follow-up study with 50 third- and fifth-grade teachers (Paris & Oka, 1986).

A different approach was taken by Duffy, Roehler, and their colleagues. They trained teachers to provide more detailed explanations of reading strategies than were taught as part of students' regular basal reading instruction. In one study, fifth-grade teachers were taught to recast their prescribed basal skills as text-processing strategies and were told how to provide declarative, procedural, and conditional knowledge to their students (Duffy et al., 1986). After six months, the researchers found that teachers provided more detailed explanations about reading strategies to students and that students' metacognition about their reading lessons increased.

In a follow-up study, Duffy et al. (1987) taught third-grade teachers to provide more detailed explanations of reading strategies to their low readers. Again, the training helped teachers to describe strategies more precisely so that students could see the value and importance of using them. Following the intervention, third graders increased their understanding of strategies as well as their skills for word study and oral reading. The studies by Duffy, Paris, and colleagues improved children's metacognition and strategic reading but did not alter their standardized reading scores. Although this finding appears to minimize the effects of the instruction, it is possible that (1) longer or more concentrated intervention can alter standardized test performance, or (2) standardized tests may not assess strategic reading, which was the focus of the interventions.

Winograd and Hare (1988) described five critical elements of direct explanation. First, instruction must describe strategies so that they are sensible and meaningful to students. Second, students need to understand why the strategy should be learned and the potential benefits of using it. Third, teachers should explain how to use strategies step-by-step. Fourth, students need to understand the circumstances under which strategies should be employed and the contexts in which they are appropriate. Fifth, good instruction will teach students to evaluate their use of strategies so that they can monitor and improve their own strategic reading. In this fashion, instruction enhances awareness of strategic reading so that students can plan, evaluate, and regulate their own thinking.

Cooperative and Scaffolded Learning

Some interventions to increase strategic reading do not address students' awareness of strategies directly. Instead, they promote children's strategic reading with sets of procedures or organizational arrangements that may indirectly foster better appreciation of the usefulness of strategies. For example, reciprocal teaching is a method designed by Palincsar and Brown (1984) in which students take turns acting as leaders and followers in joint reading activities. In reciprocal teaching, unsuccessful seventh-grade readers were taught to use predicting, questioning, clarifying, and summarizing as comprehension strategies. As students took turns reading and using these strategies, they provided models for their peers and also provided encouragement, feedback, and correction. Thus, the social arrangements facilitated the use of four powerful reading strategies. The poor readers who received 20 days of intensive training with the strategies showed significant improvements in summarizing relevant information and detecting errors in text. They also transferred these strategies to lessons in science and social studies (Palincsar & Brown, 1984). However, there were no significant differences between treatment and control students in the improvement of standardized reading scores or rating the importance of information. Unfortunately, no data were collected on students' awareness about reading strategies, and so it is not clear whether reciprocal teaching enhanced metacognition or not.

Cooperative learning provides another opportunity for students to model, discuss, and evaluate the usefulness of comprehension strategies while reading. Stevens, Madden, Slavin, and Farnish (1987) designed a cooperative and integrated language arts program for third and fourth graders. The interventions included cognitive modeling, direct explanation, peer tutoring, and cooperative activities. Oral reading and peer conferences for planning, revising, and editing each other's compositions were common. Although no measures of metacognition were collected, students who received this eclectic treatment showed significant improvements on measures of reading comprehension, vocabulary, language, spelling, and writing. Cooperative learning provides opportunities for metacognitive exchanges among students as they discuss the content and processes of reading. There are also numerous opportunities to reduce anxiety, direct attention, and provide positive motivational support among peers. Thus, improved awareness about reading may be an outcome of effective instruction whether or not metacognition is the target or vehicle for instruction.

We believe that both direct and indirect attempts to increase students' metacognition promote the five essential components of effective instruction outlined by Langer and Applebee (1986): ownership, appropriateness, structure, collaboration, and transfer of control. First, students need to develop a sense of personal ownership about the information they read and write. Second, effective instruction is developmentally appropriate to individual skills and interests. Third, effective instruction calls attention to the structure of the task and provides a meaningful framework for learning. Fourth, effective instruction promotes collaboration among peers and teachers so that knowledge can be shared about effective learning strategies. Fifth, the ultimate goal of instruction is to transfer control to students so that they take the responsibility for their own self-regulated learning (Corno, 1986).

In summary, metacognition is an important component of the development of strategic reading. Nonreading preschoolers develop an orientation to print that can foster their motivation and emergent literacy. Rudimentary understanding is facilitated by social interactions with parents as well as direct instruction on letter-sound correspondences and the conventions of print. Numerous studies of emergent literacy reveal that students who adopt a perspective of constructing and monitoring meaning while reading develop literacy skills more quickly (Teale & Sulzby, 1986). Our review also indicates that metacognition improves substantially during elementary school years, but that many young adolescents still have incomplete and mistaken knowledge about reading strategies and the nature of reading. That may be why such a variety of instructional arrangements effectively promote children's metacognition and strategic reading in childhood and even adulthood. Apparently, children's poor concepts and regulatory skills may help explain why many children have difficulty maintaining and generalizing appropriate reading strategies to content area reading. As we shall see in the next section, though, knowledge and practice are not sufficient to assure independent strategic reading. A sense of confidence and competence helps to motivate students to learn and apply appropriate strategies while reading.

MOTIVATION FOR STRATEGIC READING

Research on strategic reading has focused almost exclusively on cognitive tactics for planning, monitoring, elaborating, and revising meaning constructed from reading. These text-processing strategies are, however, only some of the strategies that influence children's reading comprehension. There are also executive control strategies and tactics for managing time, attention, and anxiety. These tactics are motivational as well as cognitive because they mediate readers' investment of effort, perceptions of competence, and satisfaction with reading. In the next section, we discuss self-serving motivational strategies that students sometimes adopt to avoid reading or to minimize thinking about text. In the second section, we discuss how students' perceptions of competence and control influence their motivational and cognitive strategies.

Tactics That Avoid Strategic Reading

The predominant focus on cognitive strategies has led researchers to characterize novice and poor readers as nonstrategic by dint of knowledge deficiencies—for example, naïveté, misconceptions, or lack of practice. But many teachers know that students who are capable of reading well sometimes adopt strategies for avoiding failure rather than strategies for processing text thoroughly. There are a variety of defensive tactics available to ingenious students (see, for example, Covington, 1983; Covington & Beery, 1976; deCharms, 1976; Dweck, 1986) and we note them briefly here.

One group of self-serving strategies often observed in reading leads to cognitive disengagement. Some students simply withdraw participation; they give up or remain passive in their attempts to read (Johnston & Winograd, 1985). Other students may feign interest or try to appear involved when they are not. False effort avoids thinking as neatly as nonparticipation. Other students may devalue reading as an activity and compensate by investing greater effort in other endeavors such as mathematics or sports. All of the strategies minimize the effort devoted to reading and preclude learning. A second group of self-serving tactics shifts the blame for reading failure from the self to external factors. Students who read poorly may complain about the task difficulty, noise, feeling ill, interference by other students, teachers who pick on them, or just bad luck. The complaints and attributions to anything except the students' effort or ability are designed to protect positive self-perceptions of ability despite the evident failure to read well.

Third, some students guarantee reading failure by avoiding the task completely. They may neglect to take the book home, read the wrong pages, or just "forget" the assignment. Task avoidance and disengagement are often coupled with elaborate excuses that suggest circumstances beyond the students' control. Others may procrastinate or waste time so that there is insufficient time left for reading. Or some students, both good and poor readers, may invite inevitable failure by setting inappropriate goals or choosing very difficult texts. Although they may fail to read the texts, their tactics preserve their good intentions and positive perceptions of their own ability because external factors were the cause of the difficulty.

Finally, some students guarantee success but avoid thoughtful, strategic reading by choosing simple texts to read or by cheating. Low aspirations and easy reading bypass effort and bring cheap success without challenge. Success with low effort is a way of "beating the system." Some students even take perverse pride in success that results from cheating, copying, or peer assistance rather then personal skill. After all, low challenge minimizes effort, protects one from evaluations of low ability, and frequently pays off. Beating the system, whether successful or not, can be a badge of nonconformity that is worn with bravado.

All of these self-serving strategies are antithetical to the mastery-oriented, text-processing strategies that we want children to use before, during, and after reading. Why do students use them? They are seductive because they lead to short-term success. They minimize effort and protect readers from loss of self-esteem when failure occurs. Moreover, these tactics diminish students' anxiety, guilt, and shame. They provide temporary relief, but the cumulative effects are devastating. Students who remain passive, dodge thoughtful reading, and make excuses will, over time, fail to learn the skills and content necessary for further achievement in school. They are *failure-prone* (Covington, 1984) because their behavior exacerbates their ineffective reading and leads to greater failure. Too often, students end up devoting increasing amounts of time and energy to strategies that are designed to stave off short-term failure in reading. As a consequence, there is little time left to actually read or to learn effective text-processing strategies. Dissonance increases between students' actual reading abilities and their delusions of competence; and eventually there is a humiliating collapse of confidence and self-worth that cannot be easily overcome. This typically occurs between 12 and 16 years of age, when remedial education may be difficult and time consuming. That is precisely why an early emphasis on strategic reading may help students to avoid self-serving, defensive tactics that minimize effort devoted to reading. In the following section we discuss how students' confidence and self-control contribute to strategic reading.

Strategic Reading Depends on Perceptions of Competence and Control

Strategic readers regard themselves as competent in the classroom. Because they have multiple tactics available to monitor and improve comprehension, they know how to learn effectively rather then just "try harder." Students who perceive themselves as academically successful are usually intrinsically motivated and confident in their own abilities (Harter & Connell, 1984). They regard themselves as responsible for the outcomes of their learning and believe that they have the ability to achieve desired outcomes (Weiner, 1986). Personal agency (Bandura, 1987) and self-efficacy (Schunk, 1987) are also key components of a positive sense of self-esteem. In a similar vein, Covington (1987) describes the student's emerging sense of self-worth as partly dependent on self-perceptions of competence in classroom settings. These positive views of ability and responsibility contrast sharply with the defensive strategies of students who avoid challenges of thoughtful reading.

One important characteristic of students' confidence and competence is the control they exert over their environments. Students who feel little control over their learning may feel incompetent, helpless, or passive, which may lead to negative affect and defensive strategies such as nonparticipation, excuses, and cheating (Stipek & Weisz, 1981). Students' beliefs about control can have powerful effects on achievement (Bandura, 1986).

Children's notions of control develop during middle and late childhood. Connell (1985) asked children in third through ninth grade to select the causes of various academic outcomes. Choices included themselves as causes (internal control); others as causes (powerful others); and uncertainty about causes (unknown). Upper elementary and junior high students tended to see their own actions and capacities (internal control) as causes of events rather than those of others, and this pattern solidified with age. However, many children are unaware of who or what causes outcomes in school. Children high in the "unknown control" dimension "tend to see themselves as less (cognitively) competent . . . have less mastery motivation, and are less willing to make their own judgments about their classroom work" (Connell, 1985, p. 1033).

Measures of perceived control are significantly and positively correlated with standardized achievement scores (Connell, 1985) and with peers' perceptions of their classmates (Harter, 1985). Thus, by adolescence, perceptions of control become strong and positive predictors of academic success. It seems plausible that perceived control leads to greater effort in the use of particular learning strategies. Successful students persist in the face of failure and choose appropriate tactics for challenging tasks more often than students who do not understand what controls learning outcomes (Rohrkemper & Corno, 1988). The implication for reading is clear: instruction in strategic reading will help students learn how to manage their own reading behavior.

Just as the perception of control is positively correlated with academic success, the perceived lack of control is correlated with academic failure. When students perceive that they have few opportunities to influence academic outcomes by their own effort, they develop an orientation to school that has been labelled *learned helplessness* (Abramson, Seligman, & Teasdale, 1978) or *passive failure* (Johnston & Winograd, 1985). These labels describe children who, after repeated failure experiences, begin to believe that they are incapable of achieving their goals (Elliott & Dweck, 1988). "Passive" or "helpless" readers reason that effort is useless in the face of their certain failure and attempt to preserve a sense of worth by avoiding reading tasks, reacting with hostile or anxious responses, or trying half-heartedly at best (Covington, 1983). Poor readers who believe they have no control over their achievement outcomes establish a cycle of diminished task persistence, low expectations for future success, and low self-esteem (Butkowsky & Willows, 1980).

This pattern of failure has been observed consistently in reading, where children are often confused about what they can do to control reading outcomes. For example, if students confuse effort and ability, are unaware of effective comprehension strategies, and are unsure what to do when told to try harder, then they may choose disengagement, excuses, cheating, or faint-hearted effort when given a reading assignment. A study by Borkowski, Weyhing, and Carr (1988) illustrates the powerful role that beliefs about control exert on students. In this study, 75 reading-disabled children from 10 to 14 years of age participated in a series of conditions designed to train them in the use of summarizing strategies. The researchers found that learning-disabled students could learn summarizing strategies but attributional training that focused on self-control was critical. Only the attributional training plus informed training led to long-term maintenance of summarization strategies. Although it was not possible to change long-standing beliefs that students held about their own abilities in reading, short-term training did influence the effectiveness with which they learned to use summarizing strategies.

Kistner, Osborne, and LeVerrier (1988) analyzed learning-disabled children's achievement attributions and compared their academic progress over a two-year span to nondisabled children. The learning-disabled children often attributed failures to themselves, but those students who attributed failures to controllable causes made the greatest achievement gains and were rated by teachers as exhibiting the most appropriate classroom behavior. In other words, children who perceived themselves as being in control of academic events performed significantly better than students who perceived themselves as having no control. These researchers, in contrast to others, found that there was no self-perpetuating failure cycle for LD children and that with increasing age the learning-disabled and nondisabled children had more similar attributions. It appears that as children adapt to school settings, they learn to attribute outcomes to controllable causes. The researchers suggest that the causal relation between children's beliefs and their performance might be altered by specific instruction such as the short-term intervention conducted by Borkowski, Weyhing, and Carr (1988).

Borkowski, Carr, Rellinger, and Pressley (in press) demonstrated that motivational factors such as attributions to effort and perceived control clearly differentiated achievers and underachievers in reading. After training was provided about the utility of strategies and the importance of effort in using them, students generalized the reading strategies and changed their attributions for success and failure in reading. Achievers were more willing to use strategies and believed in their utility because they attributed success to effort that they could control. Thus, successful intervention programs must not only provide knowledge about reading strategies, but also the motivation to use them by convincing students that they control the instrumental effectiveness of these strategies.

In summary, students who believe they can exercise control over academic tasks and outcomes show greater effort in school and greater success as measured by grades, teacher ratings, and peer perceptions about their competence. Four features of control appear critical. First, students must believe that they are the active agents of their own learning. They must assume responsibility for their performance and believe that they have the self-efficacy to accomplish the tasks (Schunk, 1986; Weiner, 1986). Second, students must believe that they can choose their own goals and set their own standards for learning. Elliott and Dweck (1988) describe *mastery-oriented children* as those intrinsically motivated students who select goals of task mastery, whereas children who are labelled *learned helpless* select extrinsic goals or comply with the goals supplied by other people. Third, students must believe in the instrumental value of specific strategies for accomplishing selected goals (Skinner, Chapman, & Baltes, 1988). And fourth, students must realize the contingencies between their own actions and the desired outcomes. As children grow older they develop a greater understanding of what causes outcomes and how they can control their own achievement (Connell, 1985). Thus, a successful student is aware of the strategies to use, attributes success to the strategies and appropriate effort, and feels a sense of control for engineering the desired outcomes. In essence, students become self-regulated learners who establish positive self-esteem by exercising control over their own learning.

SOCIAL GUIDANCE PROMOTES STRATEGIC READING AND MOTIVATION

Strategic reading develops over many years, initially nurtured by parents and others at home and later by teachers and classmates at school. Social assistance in learning to read enhances children's metacognition and motivation for reading. It serves as a bridge or scaffold from other-regulated to self-regulated learning (Vygotsky, 1978). Parents, peers, and teachers are all instrumental in this process.

Parental Influences in Reading

Parents play an important role in promoting the development of strategic readers. In most cases, children's early literacy experiences are promoted by interactions with parents in joint book reading. Pelegrini, Brody, and Siegel (1985) found that children who showed a greater ability to read and discuss stories engaged their parents more often in reading activities, thus promoting a richer early literacy experience. In fact, one of the clearest predictors of early reading ability is the amount of time spent reading with parents (Mason & Allen, 1986). Mason and McCormick (1981) found in a parent survey that low-SES parents spent less time fostering reading and writing activities than did professional families. Based on these findings, McCormick and Mason (1987) conducted an intervention program to improve prereading skills of kindergarteners. Children in the experimental group were given simple books to take home, and their parents were advised how to help their children learn to read. These children showed significant improvement in prereading skills. Similar findings have been observed in studies by Ninio and Bruner (1978), Snow (1983), and others.

Parental expectations also play a significant role in children's preliteracy skills. Hiebert and Adams (1987) asked 44 mothers and fathers to predict their 3- and 4-year-old children's performance on letter naming, auditory discrimination, writing, and general interest in reading. Comparisons of parental predictions and the children's actual performance on these measures revealed that parents significantly overestimated both the children's skills and their interest in reading. Undoubtedly, some of the early encouragement that parents from middle- and high-SES backgrounds provide their children reflects their high expectations for literacy development and their positive value for reading and writing activities. If optimism is contagious, then both parents and students can be optimistic about the role of motivation and cognition in early literacy development.

Peer Interactions

Peers can also have a great deal of influence on both children's achievement and motivation in school. Research on cooperation in classrooms has shown that student help seeking and help giving are adaptive and important learning skills (Ames, 1983; Nelson-LeGall, 1985). Nelson-Le Gall describes mastery-oriented help seeking as an achievement behavior. When students work in an atmosphere in which they are encouraged to take responsibility for their own learning, they are more likely to persist in difficult tasks and undertake more challenging tasks (Nelson-LeGall, 1985). Help seeking also fosters students' self-efficacy and their perceptions of themselves as goal achievers. Students are more likely to feel in control of their academic work when they are allowed to select and pursue personally relevant goals and make their own decisions about how to achieve them. Webb (1980) reports that high school students who took the roles of active solicitors of help *and* explainers for others showed the greatest achievement gains in problem solving. When students act as teachers and help providers, they are learning effective ways to master academic tasks.

The skill that children show in seeking and using help increases with age. For example, 4- and 5-year-olds use help more effectively than 3-year-olds (Wood, Bruner, & Ross, 1976), and sixth graders reported that they would use more help than second graders (Myers & Paris, 1978). Young children have more difficulty recognizing the need for help, and when they do, tend to solicit answers rather than explanations. In addition, they place a higher priority on nurturance and kindness than competence, thus sometimes passing over the best helpers. In reading, young students and poor readers may not monitor their comprehension and seek help appropriately; instead, they focus on looking busy and following procedures. Better metacognitive appraisal of personal ability, task complexity, and choice of appropriate helper may allow older students to assess the need for help better than 6- to 8-year-olds.

Teachers' Beliefs

Some teachers regard reading as rules for decoding and interpreting text, whereas others stress creative, aesthetic, and strategic aspects of reading (Winograd & Johnston, 1987). Different views of reading and teachers' expectations for students' learning are apparent in the classroom. Teachers who believe that all children can learn will promote literacy development while those who believe that lack of ability is a stable state will produce a debilitating environment (Eccles & Wigfield, 1985).

Teachers also communicate learning goals to students by their instruction. Rigid adherence to basal readers and heavy emphasis on test scores convey a sense of reading as task completion (Doyle, 1983). Products are more important than process in this orientation. Ability-based reading groups assign status according to comparative reading achievement, which can diminish cooperation and help seeking. But flexible grouping and variable methods of instruction promote student collaboration. Some teachers emphasize metacognition and reading strategies in an integrated language arts curriculum, but many do not (Durkin, 1978–1979). When teachers convey a conceptualization of reading ability as a repertoire of knowledge that can be developed continuously and when teachers value individual differences and minimize social comparison, they communicate positive expectations about reading development to their students (Marshall & Weinstein, 1984).

Classroom Climate

Multidimensional classrooms avoid normative evaluations and stratification of students by abilities (Rosenholtz & Simpson, 1984). They provide meaningful literacy tasks, employ a variety of instructional methods, apply multiple performance standards, and afford all students opportunities for success (Winograd & Smith, 1987). The structure and variety of academic tasks contribute to students' motivation and achievement. When tasks are repetitive or unidimensional, allowing only certain types of students to become involved and successful, students lose interest and cease to believe in their own abilities. When academic evaluation is salient in classrooms, kindergarten children rate their competence and future attainment lower than children who are in classrooms where evaluation is not salient (Stipek & Daniels, 1988). Blumenfeld and Meece (1988) have shown that meaningful task structures have an influence on cognitive engagement and students' use of strategies. Fourth, fifth, and sixth graders in science classes reported that their interest and involvement were stimulated most by the procedures or forms of the tasks and the products they were asked to produce rather than the lesson content or social grouping used.

Variety of method, like multiple tasks, offers different students the opportunity to participate and learn. Morine-Dershimer (1983), analyzed third and fourth graders' responses in reading lessons and found that instructional methods helped determine classroom status. Students attained status depending on whether they were able to supply the type of response that conformed to the instructional format. Because teachers' methods and expectations varied, different types of students were able to attain status with the teacher and with their peers in each classroom studied. This study suggests that a variety of methods will provide more students with opportunities for participation and achievement.

Different reading tasks and varied instructional methods afford students multiple opportunities for success. Rosenholtz and Simpson (1984) demonstrated that multidimensional classrooms promote students' academic self-concepts and positive perceptions about school better than unidimensional classrooms, in which there is only one way to achieve competence and pride. Single-standard classrooms work to the disadvantage of most students, because those who excel do so at the expense of the rest of the class. Multidimensional classrooms, in contrast, encourage a variety of different performance standards so that different students can excel on different kinds of tasks. Fewer students feel incompetent and there is less stratification of students when multiple tasks are available, non-normative evaluations are used, and grades are narrowly dispersed (MacIver, 1988). These dimensions of classrooms are very important for reading instruction because ability grouping and public evaluation are common.

Ability Grouping

Ability grouping in reading, ubiquitous in American classrooms for nearly 50 years, is a common practice in the unidimensional classroom (Venezky, 1986). Although there is a limited amount of research to support ability grouping (Slavin, 1987), it is often used as the basis for later school tracking and as a surrogate measure for overall school achievement. In addition to these long-term consequences, ability grouping also has short-range effects on students. Assignment to a group frequently seems to dictate instructional methods and standards, limiting the ways students can establish competence and achieve.

Standards are different depending on group membership. Allington (1980) observed teachers working with good and poor readers during oral reading and found that teachers interrupted poor readers more often when they made pronunciation errors. They frequently directed their instruction at surface-level skills rather than teaching the comprehension strategies reserved for better readers. This differential instructional treatment has been observed by Eder (1982) and Englert and Semmel (1981). Eder (1982) observed that twice as much time is spent attending to managerial tasks in low reading groups, thus reducing the time for instruction. Haskins, Walden, and Ramsey (1983) reported that teachers used more drill work with low-ability reading groups. Thus, a great deal of research indicates that children in low reading groups are perceived as inferior readers and students by peers, receive lower levels of instruction, and receive less instructional time from teachers.

However, even students in middle and high reading groups suffer from judgments that imply unidimensional criteria for success. Rosenholtz and Wilson (1980) surveyed 15 fifth- and sixth-grade classrooms. Students who were in classrooms that had little differentiation of task structure, poorly organized materials, little student autonomy, and little teacher evaluation had few opportunities to demonstrate their competence in reading. Because reading was so narrowly defined in the classroom, only a few students could demonstrate their talents adequately.

Marshall and Weinstein's (1984) interactive model of classroom structure describes the multidimensional classroom well. In this classroom, teachers believe that all students can learn. They value individual differences so that there are multiple ways to display competence. Teachers support these beliefs by creating noncompetitive learning environments, flexible grouping, opportunities to achieve in a variety of areas, mastery-oriented learning, and assessments based on individual progress rather than social comparison. A classroom of this type facilitates student motivation and self-perceptions of competence by allowing students to manifest their skills and strengths in different ways.

It is clear that student motivation for reading is influenced by a variety of factors. Students' perceptions of their own competence and the perceptions of the control they exercise in classrooms will influence the effort that they expend recruiting and using different reading strategies. In addition, the attitudes and expectations that are conveyed by parents, teachers, and peers shape students' views of themselves as learners, which further mediate the investment of personal resources and energy. In particular, students who view themselves as competent, in control, and comfortable in their social relationships will be more likely to give and seek help in a classroom, thus promoting collaborative learning and academic achievement. Teachers can promote students' motivation to read by providing multidimensional classrooms that have a wide variety of opportunities to exhibit academic strengths and by minimizing social comparisons and competition for limited rewards. Academic goals that promote mastery learning, task involvement, and cooperation facilitate both motivation and reading skill (Covington, 1983; Elliott & Dweck, 1988; Nicholls, 1984; Paris & Winograd, in press).

IMPLICATIONS OF STRATEGIC READING FOR EDUCATIONAL REFORM

During the 1980s, public education has endured critical scrutiny, public indictments, and multiple pleas for reform. Part of the problem is the disparity between traditional practices and new methods that enhance strategic reading and independent learning. Dramatic and genuine changes in the field of reading education have begun, however. The new agenda in reading education is based on recent research for reforming educational practices (Anderson et al., 1986). The research reviewed in this chapter reflects substantial evidence for helping children to become competent and confident learners. The long-term educational objectives of enhancing critical literacy skills of well-informed citizens can be met in part by an emphasis on strategic reading. In particular, there are three areas of educational reform that follow directly from research on strategic reading: a balanced curriculum for literacy, thought-provoking instruction, and assessment of a large range of reading abilities.

Changing the Curriculum

More than 90 percent of America's schoolchildren use basal readers as the primary source of reading material. This overwhelming reliance on published and programmatic instructional materials has emerged during the last 40 years of American education (Paris, Wixson, & Palincsar, 1986; Venezky, 1987). Although many children become successful readers with these programs, criticisms of basal reading series are becoming more frequent and strident (Goodman, Shannon, Freeman, & Murphy, 1988). For example, commercial materials often teach literacy as decontextualized and disconnected skills that miscommunicate the nature of reading (Jensen & Roser, 1987). The selections are often insipid and boring rather than rich examples from children's literature. Too often, commercial materials minimize the decision making of teachers by relegating them to roles of technicians or managers in a delivery system (Duffy, Roehler, & Putnam, 1987). Shannon (1987) argues that commercial materials "deskill" teachers and inhibit meaningful interactions with text by both teachers and students. Commercial materials need to be modified to enhance individual strategies and control in children's reading.

A second area of curriculum reform involves the integration of strategic reading with the rest of the curriculum. The California State Department of Education issued the *California English-Language Arts Framework* (1987) for kindergarten through twelfth grade, which provides evidence of active reform as well as the need to involve policy makers. Some of the effective features emphasized in the new curriculum include a literature-based program; the integration of listening, speaking, reading, and writing; the teaching of language skills in meaningful contexts; instructional programs that guide all students through a range of thinking processes; a developmental language arts program from kindergarten through grade twelve; a systematic oral language and writing program that is integrated with reading; and an early phonics emphasis that is simple and can be taught in meaningful contexts.

As others have noted (e.g., Winograd & Greenlee, 1986), reading cannot be taught as a set of decontextualized and isolated skills. Strategic reading is a companion to strategic writing, strategic listening, and strategic speaking because the strategies, metacognition, and motivation are interwoven in the same developmental and educational experiences. They have been disassembled and fractionated in many curricula that focus on components of reading; yet, research shows that they must be reassembled in order to be sensible and useful for students.

A third emphasis of curriculum reform concerns thinking skills. The cornerstone of strategic reading is a thoughtful reader who is aware of the parameters of reading, chooses plans selectively, monitors comprehension while reading, and reflects on both content and process following reading. These aspects of strategic reading have been emphasized as critical dimensions of thinking (Marzano et al., 1988). But, we do not advocate separate courses to teach thinking. Instead, principles of strategic reading and thinking can and should be interwoven in all subjects.

As research has illuminated the developmental aspects of strategic reading, it has become clear that existing curricula are disjointed and incompatible with strategic, metacognitive, and motivated aspects of reading. Basal materials need to be redesigned and the curriculum for reading needs to be integrated with writing and language arts. The cognitive strategies emphasized in a balanced language arts curriculum transfer readily to content area reading and become learning strategies that can be used independently by students.

A New Agenda for Reading Instruction

Instructional research during the 1980s has revealed a variety of methods that enhance teaching effectiveness. One important characteristic is the nature of explanations provided by teachers. Research by Duffy and his colleagues has demonstrated convincingly that teachers can be taught to provide better explanations of the cognitive and motivational strategies that students must learn to use. A second feature of effective instruction is an emphasis on strategies for constructing meaning. Good teachers model and demonstrate strategies used by experts. They also provide explanations and practice using these strategies. For example, reciprocal teaching demonstrates four effective text-processing strategies and provides extended practice for students to use these strategies jointly as they read and discuss text information (Palincsar & Brown, 1984). Ineffective instruction has focused on isolated skills and repeated practice on worksheets, whereas effective instruction orients students to the task of constructing meaning from text and provides a variety of tactics to use before, during, and after reading.

A third characteristic of effective instruction in reading is the use of Socratic methods. Students and teachers engage in discussions about effective strategies so that they can exchange declarative, procedural, and conditional knowledge about them.

Erroneous conceptions of strategies can be assessed and addressed directly. Interactive dialogues also permit teachers to address self-defeating, negative expectations and attitudes about strategic reading. Students also have the opportunity to learn from each other when cooperation and reciprocity are encouraged. The Socratic method of teaching emphasizes both cognitive and motivational aspects of strategic reading and has been compared to "cognitive coaching" and "apprenticeship" (Paris, 1986). Metaphors of Socratic dialogues and cognitive coaching stand in sharp contrast to other metaphors of Calvinistic teaching (Venezky, 1986), management of academic work (Doyle, 1983), or diagnostic/prescriptive teaching based on skill deficiencies.

Instructional Validity in the Assessment of Reading

Testing is a mainstay of U.S. education, and students endure a wide variety of criterion-referenced and norm-referenced tests every year. But educational tests of reading have not changed to conform with our notion of strategic reading. Instead, they are surprisingly uniform. The common format of most reading tests requires the students to read brief paragraphs and answer multiple-choice questions about them. Although decoding, vocabulary, syntax, and other features of language are often tested, comprehension scores are usually derived from reading several short paragraphs. Most of these paragraphs are disembodied prose—they do not have titles, pictures, or structures like the selections used in basal reading instruction or text encountered in content areas. That is precisely why new tests generated by the State Departments of Education in Michigan, Illinois, and Wisconsin have mandated that reading will be assessed with authentic and meaningful passages. The multiple-choice questions used to measure comprehension are derived from analyses of structurally important information and not on the basis of psychometric patterns of errors (Wixson & Peters, 1987).

A second aspect of new reading assessment tests is measuring students' background knowledge of the test passages. These measures will help teachers interpret students' comprehension scores on both expository and narrative passages more accurately. Research has shown that prior knowledge is a central factor in reading comprehension. Studies have also shown that comprehension is superior when readers use strategies to activate appropriate background knowledge. Yet, most standardized tests of reading comprehension do not include measures of prior knowledge or any assessment of children's familiarity with the topics that they read. If the concepts and vocabulary of the reading selections are unfamiliar or uninteresting to students, their comprehension scores may suffer.

Despite the long-standing interest in reading strategies and the importance of them for independent learning, standardized reading tests do not measure strategic reading. This is not simply a case of disparity between a test and classroom instruction, it may be the insurmountable obstacle in educational reform. The common axiom that "Testing drives the curriculum" means that new forms of assessment in reading must make teachers and students accountable for strategic reading. This position has been stated well in the *California English-Language Arts Framework* (1987):

> With the revised curriculum in place, assessment of its effectiveness must depend on tests that reflect the purposes of the curriculum. Teachers and others responsible for assessment will create tests based on significant works whose meanings have import for all students: tests will integrate all of the language arts by including significant reading and writing and reflecting the student's oral skills as well; and tests will focus on students' meaning not on formalistic features such as plot and character. Good assessment practices will include informal daily activities in which students commend each other for their strengths, teachers

create environments in which students can succeed, and parents support their children's progress as part of evaluation. (p. 33)

Many researchers advocate the use of a portfolio of reading assessments that includes criterion-referenced tests that are linked to curriculum objectives, as well as creative assessments of students' use of strategies, students' awareness of reading and writing processes, and students' motivation and literacy experiences. A rich variety of formal and informal assessments can be more useful to teachers, parents, and students. An assessment program that is aligned with a revised curriculum and new instructional objectives will provide a better evaluation of learning and will increase students' and teachers' attention to critical dimensions of strategic reading.

SUMMARY

Twenty years ago, the development of skilled reading was viewed as a linear accumulation of skills. When children were developmentally ready, they learned sound-symbol correspondence, followed by sight words and decoding, followed by interpretation of sentences and text. This reductionistic and additive model of learning has been challenged by researchers and educators from diverse backgrounds (Winograd & Smith, 1987). An overemphasis on elementary skills led to repeated practice with decontextualized language and isolated component skills. Neither teachers nor students enjoy reading and writing in approaches that emphasize skills at the expense of meaningful involvement with text.

Research during the past 20 years has contributed directly to a different view of the development of reading. Current models emphasize the importance of authentic language activities that are integrated within a language arts and communication model. From their early encounters with literacy, children try to make sense of print as they read and write. Research on cognitive strategies has illuminated the rich variety of tactics that readers can use to enhance comprehension. We began our review with some examples of strategies that children use before, during, and after reading. Even nonreaders can be exposed to these strategies as they bridge speaking and listening with reading and writing, but it is obvious that strategies such as examining text, constructing main ideas, and summarizing important points continue to develop over many years.

The development of strategic reading is fostered by cognitive development, practice, and instruction. Research on metacognition, for example, has illuminated how children acquire declarative, procedural, and conditional knowledge about strategies. The awareness of tactics for appraising and managing one's reading, however, does not guarantee that students will use these strategies spontaneously and effectively. There is growing recognition that the development of strategic reading depends on personal motivation to select and apply persistently strategies that are appropriate to the task. Such motivation requires knowledge about the instrumental value of strategies, different purposes for reading, confidence in one's self-efficacy, and beliefs about the ability to control reading to achieve a desired goal. In our review, we discussed many of the classroom experiences that contribute to the development of positive self-concepts and strategic reading as well as self-defeating patterns of failure, avoidance, and guilt.

Reading research and reading instruction are changing dramatically. Previous models of reading skills are being replaced by models that emphasize cognitive, metacognitive, motivational, and affective dimensions of reading. The failure of a significant proportion of U.S. schoolchildren to learn to read with enjoyment and success has helped alter our views of reading and instructional practices. However, the impetus for change has also been provided by research programs that show successful interventions that promote strategic reading in the classroom. A variety of methods, including modeling, direct explanation, cognitive coaching, peer tutoring, and cooperative learning, have been used to stimulate children's knowledge about reading and their motivation to regulate their own learning. The success of these initial projects is encouraging and attests to the viability of reading instruction that combines cognitive and motivational approaches.

One of the hallmarks of education and literacy is the ability to read thoughtfully and flexibly. The development of strategic reading is a lifelong endeavor that is supported by parents, peers, and teachers who instill enthusiasm, knowledge, and confidence in students. As students learn to regulate their own reading and to use strategies for different purposes, they become independent learners who read with confidence and enjoyment. Thus, strategic reading contributes directly to lifelong education and personal satisfaction.

REFERENCES

Abramson, L. Y., Seligman, M. P., & Teasdale, J. D. (1978). Learned helplessness in humans: Critique and reformulation. *Journal of Abnormal Psychology, 87,* 49–74.

Allington, R. L. (1980). Teacher interruption behaviors during primary-grade oral reading. *Journal of Educational Psychology, 72,* 371–377.

Ames, R. (1983). Help-seeking and achievement orientation: Perspectives from attribution theory. In B. DePaulo, A. Nadler, & J. Fisher (Eds.), *New directions in helping: Vol. 2. Help-seeking* (pp. 165–186). New York: Academic Press.

Anderson, R. C., Hiebert, E. H., Scott, J. A., & Wilkinson, I. A. G. (1986). *Becoming a nation of readers: The report of the Commission on Reading.* Washington, DC: U. S. Department of Education, NIE.

August, D. L., Flavell, J. H., & Clift, R. (1984). Comparison of comprehension monitoring of skilled and less-skilled readers. *Reading Research Quarterly, 20,* 39–53.

Baker, L. (1984). Spontaneous versus instructed use of multiple standards for evaluating comprehension: Effects of age, reading proficiency, and type of standard. *Journal of Experimental Child Psychology, 38,* 289–311.

Baker, L., & Brown, A. L. (1984). Metacognitive skills and reading. In P. D. Pearson, M. Kamil, R. Barr, & P. Mosenthal (Eds.), *Handbook of reading research* (Vol. 1, pp. 353–394). White Plains, NY: Longman.

Bandura, A. (1986). From thought to action: Mechanisms of personal agency. *New Zealand Journal of Psychology, 15,* 1–17.

Bandura, A. (1987). Self-regulation of motivation and action through goal systems. In V. Hamilton, G. H. Bowen, & N. H. Frijda (Eds.), *Cognition, motivation, and affect: A cognitive science view.* Dordrecht, Neth.: Martinus Nijhoff.

Baumann, J. F. (1981). Effect of ideational prominence on children's reading comprehension of expository prose. *Journal of Reading Behavior, 13,* 49–56.

Baumann, J. F. (1982). Research on children's main idea comprehension: A problem of ecological validity. *Reading Psychology, 3,* 167–177.

Baumann, J. F. (1984). The effectiveness of a direct instruction paradigm for teaching main idea comprehension. *Reading Research Quarterly, 20,* 93–117.

Baumann, J. F. (1986). Effect of rewritten content textbook passages on middle grade students' comprehension of main ideas: Making the inconsiderate considerate. *Journal of Reading Behavior, 18,* 1–21.

Blumenfeld, P., & Meece, J. (1988). Task factors, teacher behavior, and students' involvement and use of learning strategies in science. *Elementary School Journal, 88,* 235–250.

Borkowski, J. G., Carr, M., Rellinger, E., & Pressley, M. (In press). Self-regulated cognition: Interdependence of metacognition, attributions, and self-esteem. In B. F. Jones & L. Idol (Eds.), *Dimensions of thinking and cognitive instruction* (Vol. 1). Hillsdale, NJ: Erlbaum.

Borkowski, J. G., Weyhing, R. S., & Carr, M. (1988). Effects of attributional retraining on strategy-based reading comprehension in learning-disabled students. *Journal of Educational Psychology, 80,* 46–53.

Bradley, L., & Bryant, P. (1983). Categorizing sounds and learning to read: A causal connection. *Nature, 301,* 491–521.

Brown, A. L. (1987). Metacognition, executive control, self-regulated and other more mysterious mechanisms. In F. Weinert & R. Kluwe (Eds.), *Metacognition, motivation, and understanding* (pp. 65–116). Hillsdale, NJ: Erlbaum.

Brown, A. L., Bransford, J. D., Ferrara, R. A., & Campione, J. C. (1983). Learning, remembering, and understanding. In J. H. Flavell & E. M. Markman (Eds.), *Carmichael's manual of child psychology* (Vol. 1). New York: Wiley.

Brown, A. L., & Day, J. D. (1983). Macrorules for summarizing texts: The development of expertise. *Journal of Verbal Learning and Verbal Behavior, 22,* 1–14.

Brown, A. L., Day, J., & Jones, R. (1983). The development of plans for summarizing texts. *Child Development, 54,* 968–979.

Butkowsky, I. S., & Willows, D. M. (1980). Cognitive-motivational characteristics of children varying in reading ability: Evidence of learned helplessness in poor readers. *Journal of Educational Psychology, 72,* 408–422.

Calfee, R. C., & Chambliss, M. J. (1987). The structural design features of large texts. *Educational Psychologist, 22,* 357–375.

California English-Language Arts Framework (1987). Sacramento: California State Department of Education.

Clay, M. M. (1967). The reading behavior of five-year-old children: A research report. *New Zealand Journal of Educational Studies, 2,* 11–31.

Clay, M. M. (1973). *Reading: The patterning of complex behavior.* Auckland, New Zealand: Heinemann.

Clay, M. M. (1979). *The early detection of reading difficulties.* Auckland, New Zealand: Heinemann.

Connell, J. P. (1985). A new multidimensional model of children's perceptions of control. *Child Development, 56,* 1018–1041.

Corno, L. (1986). The metacognitive control components of self-regulated learning. *Contemporary Educational Psychology, 11,* 333–346.

Covington, M. V. (1983). Motivated cognition. In S. Paris, G. Olson, & H. Stevenson (Eds.), *Learning and motivation in the classroom* (pp. 139–164). Hillsdale, NJ: Erlbaum.

Covington, M. V. (1984). The motive for self-worth. In C. Ames & R. Ames (Eds.), *Research on motivation in education* (Vol. 1, pp. 77–113). New York: Academic Press.

Covington, M. V. (1987). Achievement motivation, self-attributions on exceptionality. In J. D. Day & J. G. Borkowski (Eds.), *Intelligence and exceptionality: New directions for theory, assessment, and instructional practices* (pp. 173–213). Norwood, NJ: Ablex.

Covington, M. V., & Beery, R. (1976). *Self-worth and school learning.* New York: Holt, Rinehart & Winston.

Cross, D. R., & Paris, S. G. (1988). Developmental and instructional analyses of children's metacognition and reading comprehension. *Journal of Educational Psychology, 80,* 131–142.

Day, J. D. (1986). Teaching summarization skills: Influence of student ability level and strategy difficulty. *Cognition and Instruction, 3,* 193–210.

deCharms, R. (1976). *Enhancing motivation: Change in the classroom.* New York: Irvington.

Derry, S. J., & Murphy, D. A. (1986). Designing systems that train learning ability: From theory to practice. *Review of Educational Research, 56,* 1–39.

Dewitz, P., Carr, E. M., & Patberg, J. P. (1987). Effects of inference training on comprehension and comprehension maintaining. *Reading Research Quarterly, 22,* 99–121.

Downing, J. (1970). Children's concepts of language in learning to read. *Educational Research, 12,* 106–112.

Downing, J., Ayers, D., & Schaefer, B. (1983). *Linguistic awareness in reading readiness (LARR) test.* Windsor, Eng.: NFER-Nelson.

Doyle, W. (1983). Academic work. *Review of Educational Research, 53,* 159–200.

Duffy, G., & Roehler, L. (1987). Improving classroom reading instruction through the use of responsive elaboration. *Reading Teacher, 40,* 514–521.

Duffy, G. D., Roehler, L. R., Meloth, M. S., Vavrus, L. G., Book, C., Putnam, J., & Wesselman, R. (1986). The relationship between explicit verbal explanations during reading skill instruction and student awareness and achievement: A study of reading teacher effects. *Reading Research Quarterly, 21,* 237–252.

Duffy, G., Roehler, L., & Putnam, J. (1987). Putting the teacher in control: Basal reading textbooks and instructional decision making. *Elementary School Journal, 87,* 357–366.

Duffy, G., Roehler, L., Sivan, E., Rackliffe, G., Book, C., Meloth, M., Vavrus, L., Wesselman, R., Putnam, J., & Bassiri, D. (1987). Effects of explaining the reasoning associated with using strategies. *Reading Research Quarterly, 22,* 347–368.

Durkin, D. (1978–1979). What classroom observations reveal about reading comprehension instruction. *Reading Research Quarterly, 14,* 481–533.

Dweck, C. S. (1986). Motivational processes affecting learning. *American Psychologist, 41,* 1040–1048.

Dyson, A. H. (1984). Emerging alphabetic literacy in school contexts: Toward defining the gap between school curriculum and child mind. *Written Communication, 1,* 5–55.

Eccles, J., & Wigfield, A. (1985). Teacher expectations and student motivation. In J. B. Dusak (Ed.), *Teacher expectations* (pp. 185–217). Hillsdale, NJ: Erlbaum.

Eder, D. (1982). The management and turn-allocation activities in student performance. *Discourse Processes, 5,* 151–162.

Ehri, L. C., & Wilce, L. S. (1985). Movement into reading: Is the first of printed word learning visual or phonetic? *Reading Research Quarterly, 20,* 163–179.

Ehri, L. C. (1979). Linguistic insight: Threshold of reading acquisition. In T. G. Waller & G. E. MacKinnon (Eds.), *Reading research: Advances in theory and practice,* Vol. 1 (pp. 63–114). New York: Academic Press.

Elliott, E. S., & Dweck, C. S. (1988). Goals: An approach to motivation and achievement. *Journal of Personality and Social Psychology, 54*, 5–12.

Englert, C. S., & Semmel, M. I. (1981). The relationship of oral reading substitution miscues to comprehension. *Reading Teacher, 35*, 273–280.

Evans, M., Taylor, N., & Blum, I. (1979). Children's written language awareness and its relation to reading acquisition. *Journal of Reading Behavior, 11*, 331–341.

Fabricius, W. V., & Hagen, J. W. (1984). Use of causal attributions about recall performance to assess metamemory and predict strategic memory behavior in young children. *Developmental Psychology, 20*, 975–987.

Ferreiro, E., & Teberosky, A. (1982). *Literacy before schooling.* Exeter, NH: Heinemann.

Flavell, J. H., Speer, J. R., Green, F. L., & August, D. L. (1981). The development of comprehension monitoring and knowledge about communication. *Monographs of the Society for Research in Child Development, 192*, 1–65.

Gambrell, L. B., & Bales, R. J. (1987). Mental imagery and the comprehension-monitoring performance of fourth- and fifth-grade poor readers. *Reading Research Quarterly, 21*, 454–564.

Garner, R. (1981). Monitoring of passage inconsistency among poor comprehenders: A preliminary test of the "piecemealing process" explanation. *Journal of Educational Research, 74*, 159–162.

Garner, R. (1987). *Metacognition and reading comprehension.* Norwood, NJ: Ablex.

Garner, R. (in press). Children's use of strategies in reading. In D. Bjorklund (Ed.), *Children's strategies: Contemporary views of cognitive development.* Hillsdale, NJ: Erlbaum.

Garner, R., Hare, V. C., Alexander, P., Haynes, J., & Winograd, P. (1984). Inducing use of a text lookback strategy among unsuccessful readers. *American Educational Research Journal, 21*, 789–798.

Garner, R., & Kraus, C. (1982). Good and poor comprehenders' differences in knowing and regulating reading behaviors. *Educational Research Quarterly, 6*, 5–12.

Garner, R., & Reis, R. (1981). Monitoring and resolving comprehension obstacles: An investigation of spontaneous text lookbacks among upper-grade good and poor readers' comprehension. *Reading Research Quarterly, 16*, 569–582.

Garner, R., & Taylor, N. (1982). Monitoring of understanding: An investigation of attentional assistance needs at different grade and reading proficiency levels. *Reading Psychology, 3*, 1–6.

Goodman, K. S., Shannon, P., Freeman, Y. S., & Murphy, S. (1988). *Report card on basal readers.* Katonah, NY: Richard Owen.

Grabe, M., & Mann, S. (1984). A technique for the assessment and training of comprehension monitoring skills. *Journal of Reading Behavior, 16*, 131–144.

Graves, M. F., & Cooke, C. L. (1980). Effects of previewing difficult short stories for high school students. *Research on Reading in Secondary Schools, 6*, 28–54.

Graves, M. F., Cooke, C. L., & La Berge, H. J. (1983). Effects of previewing difficult and short stories on low-ability junior high school students' comprehension, recall, and attitude. *Reading Research Quarterly, 18*, 262–276.

Hansen, J. (1981). The effects of inference training and practice on young children's reading comprehension. *Reading Research Quarterly, 16*, 391–417.

Hansen, J., & Pearson, P. D. (1983). An instructional study: Improving the inferential comprehension of good and poor fourth-grade readers. *Journal of Educational Psychology, 75*, 821–829.

Hare, V., & Borchardt, K. (1984). Direct instruction of summarization skills. *Reading Research Quarterly, 20*, 62–78.

Hare, V., & Pulliam, C. A. (1979). Teaching questioning: A verification and an extension. *Journal of Reading Behavior, 12*, 69–72.

Harter, S. (1985). Competence as a dimension of self-evaluation: Toward a comprehensive model of self-worth. In R. L. Leahy (Ed.), *The development of the self* (pp. 55–121). New York: Academic Press.

Harter, S., & Connell, J. P. (1984). A model of the relationships among children's academic achievement and their self-perceptions of competence, control, and motivational orientation. In J. Nicholls (Ed.), *The development of achievement motivation* (pp. 219–250). Greenwich, CT: JAI.

Haskins, R., Walden, T., & Ramsey, C. T. (1983). Teacher and student behavior in high- and low-ability groups. *Journal of Educational Psychology, 6*, 865–876.

Heimlich, J. E., & Pittelman, S. O. (1986). *Semantic mapping: Classroom applications.* Newark, DE: International Reading Association.

Hiebert, E. H. (1981). Developmental patterns and interrelationships of preschool children's print awareness. *Reading Research Quarterly, 16*, 236–260.

Hiebert, E. H., & Adams, C. S. (1987). Fathers' and mothers' perceptions of their preschool children's emergent literacy. *Journal of Experimental Child Psychology, 44*, 25–37.

Hiebert, E. H., Cioffi, G., & Antonak, R. A. (1984). A developmental sequence in preschool children's acquisition of reading readiness, skill, and print awareness concepts. *Journal of Applied Developmental Psychology, 5*, 115–126.

Jacobs, J. E., & Paris, S. G. (1987). Children's metacognition about reading: Issues in definition, measurement, and instruction. *Educational Psychologist, 22*, 313–332.

Jensen, J. M., & Roser, N. (1987). Basal readers and language arts programs. *Elementary School Journal, 87*, 375–383.

Johns, J. (1984). Students' perceptions of reading: Insights from research and pedagogical implications. In J. Downing & R. Valtin (Eds.), *Language awareness and learning to read* (pp. 57–77.) New York: Springer-Verlag.

Johns, J., & Ellis, D. W. (1976). Reading: Children tell it like it is. *Reading World, 16*, 115–128.

Johnston, P., & Afflerbach, P. (1985). The process of constructing main ideas from text. *Cognition and Instruction, 2*, 207–232.

Johnston, P., & Winograd, P. (1985). Passive failure in reading. *Journal of Reading Behavior, 17*, 279–301.

Juel, C., Griffith, P., & Gough, P. (1986). The acquisition of literacy: A longitudinal study of children in first and second grades. *Journal of Educational Psychology, 78*, 243–255.

Kintsch, W., & van Dijk, T. A. (1978). Toward a model of text comprehension and production. *Psychological Review, 85*, 363–394.

Kistner, J. S., Osborne, M., & Le Verrier, L. (1988). Causal attributions of learning-disabled children: Developmental patterns and relation to academic progress. *Journal of Educational Psychology, 80*, 82–89.

Langer, J. (1981). From theory to practice: A prereading plan. *Journal of Reading, 25*, 152–156a.

Langer, J. (1984). Examining background knowledge and text comprehension. *Reading Research Quarterly, 19*, 468–481.

Langer, J. A., & Applebee, A. N. (1986). Reading and writing instruction: Toward a theory of teaching and learning. In E. Rothkopf (Ed.), *Review of research in education* (Vol. 13, pp. 171–194). Washington, DC: American Educational Research Association.

Levin, J. R. (1986). Four cognitive principles of learning-strategy instruction. *Educational Psychologist, 21*, 3–17.

Lipson, M. (1983). The influence of religious affiliation on children's memory for text information. *Reading Research Quarterly, 8*, 448–457.

Lomax, R. G., & McGee, L. M. (1987). Young children's concepts about print and reading: Toward a model of word reading acquisition. *Reading Research Quarterly, 22*, 237–256.

Lundberg, I., Frost, J., & Peterson, O. (1988). Effects of an extensive program for stimulating phonological awareness in preschool children. *Reading Research Quarterly, 23*, 263–284.

McCormick, C., & Mason, J. M. (1987). Intervention procedures for increasing preschool children's interest in and knowledge about reading. In W. H. Teale & E. Sulzby (Eds.), *Emergent literacy: Writing and reading* (pp. 90–115). Norwood, NJ: Ablex.

MacIver, D. (1988). Classroom environments and the stratification of pupils' ability perceptions. *Journal of Educational Psychology, 80*, 495–505.

Markman, E. M. (1977). Realizing that you don't understand: A preliminary investigation. *Child Development, 48*, 986–992.

Markman, E. M. (1979). Realizing you don't understand: Elementary school children's awareness of inconsistencies. *Child Development, 50*, 643–655.

Markman, E. M., & Gorin, L. (1981). Children's ability to adjust their standards for evaluation comprehension. *Journal of Educational Psychology, 73*, 320–325.

Marshall, H., & Weinstein, R. (1984). Classroom factors affecting students' self-evaluations: An interactional model. *Review of Educational Research, 54*, 301–325.

Marzano, R., Brandt, R., Hughes, C., Jones, B., Presseisen, B., Rankin, S., & Suhor, C. (1988). *Dimensions of thinking.* Alexandria, VA: Association for Supervision and Curriculum Development.

Mason, J. (1980). When do children begin to read: An exploration of four-year-old children's letter and word reading competencies. *Reading Research Quarterly, 15*, 203–227.

Mason, J., & Allen, J. (1986). A review of emergent literacy with implications for research and practice in reading. In E. Rothkopf (Ed.), *Review of research in education in America* (Vol. 13, pp. 3–47). Washington, DC: American Educational Research Association.

Mason, J., & McCormick, C. (1981). *An investigation of prereading instruction from a developmental perspective: Foundations for literacy* (Tech. Rep. No. 224). Urbana: University of Illinois, Center for the Study of Reading (ERIC Document Reproduction Service No. ED 212 988).

Miller, G. E. (1987). The influence of self-instruction on the comprehension monitoring performance of average and above average readers. *Journal of Reading Behavior, 19*, 303–316.

Morine-Dershimer, G. (1983). Instructional strategy and the "creation" of classroom status. *American Educational Research Journal, 20*, 645–661.

Myers, M., & Paris, S. G. (1978). Children's metacognitive knowledge about reading. *Journal of Educational Psychology, 70*, 680–690.

Nelson-LeGall, S. (1985). Help-seeking behavior in learning. In E. Gordon (Ed.), *Review of research in education* (Vol. 12, pp. 55–90). Washington, DC: American Educational Research Association.

Nicholls, J. (1984). Achievement motivation: Conceptions of ability, subjective experience, task choice, and performance. *Psychological Review, 91*, 328–346.

Ninio, A., & Bruner, J. (1978). The achievement and antecedents of labeling. *Journal of Child Language, 5*, 5–15.

Ogle, D. M. (1986). K-W-L: A teaching model that develops active reading of expository text. *Reading Teacher, 39*, 564–570.

O'Sullivan, J. T., & Pressley, M. (1984). Completeness of instruction and strategy transfer. *Journal of Experimental Child Psychology, 38,* 275–288.

Palincsar, A. S., & Brown, A. (1984). Reciprocal teaching of comprehension-fostering and comprehension-monitoring activities. *Cognition and Instruction, 1,* 117–175.

Paris, S. G. (1986). Teaching children to guide their reading and learning. In T. Raphael (Ed.), *Contexts of school-based literacy* (pp. 115–130). New York: Random House.

Paris, S. G., Cross, D. R., & Lipson, M. Y. (1984). Informed strategies for learning: A program to improve children's reading awareness and comprehension. *Journal of Educational Psychology, 76,* 1239–1252.

Paris, S. G., & Jacobs, J. E. (1984). The benefits of informed instruction for children's reading awareness and comprehension skills. *Child Development, 55,* 2083–2093.

Paris, S. G., Lipson, M. Y., & Wixson, K. K. (1983). Becoming a strategic reader. *Contemporary Educational Psychology, 8,* 293–316.

Paris, S. G., & Myers, M. (1981). Comprehension monitoring, memory, and study strategies of good and poor readers. *Journal of Reading Behavior, 13,* 5–22.

Paris, S. G., Newman, R. S., & McVey, K. A. (1982). Learning the functional significance of mnemonic actions: A microgenetic study of strategy acquisition. *Journal of Experimental Child Psychology, 34,* 490–509.

Paris, S. G., & Oka, E. R. (1986). Children's reading strategies, metacognition, and motivation. *Developmental Review, 6,* 25–56.

Paris, S. G., Wasik, B., & van der Westhuizen, G. (1988). Meta-metacognition: A review of research on metacognition and reading. In J. Readance & S. Baldwin (Eds.), *Dialogues on literacy research* (pp. 143–166). Chicago: National Reading Conference.

Paris, S. G., & Winograd, P. (in press). How metacognition can promote academic learning and instruction. In B. F. Jones & L. Idol (Eds.), *Dimensions of thinking and cognitive instruction* (Vol. 1). Hillsdale, NJ: Erlbaum.

Paris, S. G., Wixson, K. K., & Palincsar, A. S. (1986). Instructional approaches to reading comprehension. In E. Rothkopf (Ed.), *Review of research in education* (Vol. 14, pp. 91–128). Washington, DC: American Educational Research Association.

Pearson, P. D., Hansen, J., & Gordon, C. (1979). The effect of background knowledge on young children's comprehension of explicit and implicit information. *Journal of Reading Behavior, 11,* 201–209.

Pearson, P. D., & Johnston, D. D. (1978). *Teaching reading comprehension.* New York: Holt, Rinehart & Winston.

Pelegrini, A. D., Brody, G. H., & Sigel, I. E. (1985). Parents' book-reading habits with their children. *Journal of Educational Psychology, 77,* 323–340.

Pressley, M., Forrest-Pressley, D., & Elliott-Faust, D. (1988). What is strategy instructional enrichment and how to study it: Illustrations from research on children's prose memory and comprehension. In F. Weiner & M. Perlmutter (Eds.), *Memory development: Universal changes and individual differences* (pp. 101–130). Hillsdale, NJ: Erlbaum.

Raphael, T. E., & McKinney, J. (1983). An examination of fifth- and eighth-grade children's question answering behavior: An instructional study in metacognition. *Journal of Reading Behavior, 14,* 67–86.

Raphael, T. E., & Pearson, P. D. (1985). Increasing students' awareness of sources of information for answering questions. *American Educational Research Journal, 22,* 217–235.

Reid, J. F. (1966). Learning to think about reading. *Educational Researcher, 9,* 56–62.

Rinehart, S. D., Stahl, S. A., & Erickson, L. G. (1986). Some effects of summarization training on reading and studying. *Reading Research Quarterly, 21,* 422–438.

Rohrkemper, M., & Corno, L. (1988). Success and failure on classroom tasks: Adaptive learning and classroom teaching. *Elementary School Journal, 88,* 297–312.

Rosenholtz, S. R., & Simpson, C. (1984). The formation of ability conceptions: Developmental trend or social construction? *Review of Educational Research, 54,* 31–63.

Rosenholtz, S. R., & Wilson, B. (1980). The effect of classroom structure on shared perceptions of ability. *American Educational Research Journal, 17,* 75–82.

Schmidt, C. R., & Paris, S. G. (1984). The development of verbal communicative skills in children. In H. Reese (Ed.), *Advances in child development and behavior* (Vol. 18, pp. 1–47). Orlando, FL: Academic Press.

Schunk, D. H. (1986). Verbalization and children's self-regulated learning. *Contemporary Educational Psychology, 11,* 347–369.

Schunk, D. H. (1987). Peer models and children's behavioral change. *Review of Educational Research, 57,* 149–174.

Schunk, D. H., & Rice, J. H. (1987). Enhancing comprehension skill and self-efficacy with strategy value information. *Journal of Reading Behavior, 3,* 285–302.

Shannon, P. (1987). Commercial reading materials, a technological ideology, and the deskilling of teachers. *Elementary School Journal, 87,* 307–329.

Shatz, M. (1983). Communication. In J. J. Flavell & E. M. Markman (Vol. Eds.) and P. H. Mussen (Gen. Ed.), *Handbook of child psychology: Cognitive development* (Vol. 3, pp. 841–889). New York: Wiley.

Skinner, E. A., Chapman, M., & Baltes, P. B. (1988). Control, means-ends, and agency beliefs: A new conceptualization and its measurement during childhood. *Journal of Personality and Social Psychology*, *54*, 117–133.

Slavin, R. E. (1987). Ability grouping and student achievement in elementary schools: A best-evidence synthesis. *Review of Educational Research*, *3*, 293–336.

Smiley, S. S., & Brown, A. L. (1979). Conceptual preference for thematic and taxonomic relations: A nonmonotonic age trend from preschool to old age. *Journal of Experimental Child Psychology*, *28*, 249–257.

Snow, C. E. (1983). Language and literacy: Relationships during the preschool years. *Harvard Educational Review*, *53*, 165–189.

Snow, C. E., & Ninio, A. (1986). The contracts of literacy: What children learn from learning to read books. In W. H. Teale & E. Sulzby (Eds.), *Emergent literacy: Writing and reading* (pp. 116–138). Norwood, NJ: Ablex.

Stauffer, R. G. (1969). *Directing reading maturity as a cognitive process*. New York: Harper & Row.

Stevens, R. J., Madden, N. A., Slavin, R. E., & Farnish, A. M. (1987). Cooperative integrated reading and composition: Two field experiments. *Reading Research Quarterly*, *22*, 433–454.

Stipek, D., & Daniels, D. (1988). Declining perceptions of competence: A consequence of changes in the child or in the educational environment? *Journal of Educational Psychology*, *80*, 352–356.

Stipek, D., & Weisz, J. (1981). Perceived personal control and academic achievement. *Review of Educational Research*, *51*, 101–137.

Sulzby, E. (1985). Children's emergent reading of favorite storybooks: A developmental study. *Reading Research Quarterly*, *20*, 458–481.

Taylor, K. (1986). Summary writing by young children. *Reading Research Quarterly*, *21*, 193–208.

Taylor, M. B., & Williams, J. P. (1983). Comprehension of learning-disabled readers: Task and text variations. *Journal of Educational Psychology*, *75*, 743–751.

Teale, W. H., & Sulzby, E. (1986). *Emergent literacy: Writing and reading*. Norwood, NJ: Ablex.

Venezky, R. L. (1986). Steps toward a modern history of American reading instruction. In E. Rothkopf (Ed.), *Review of research in education* (Vol. 13, pp. 129–167). Washington, DC: American Educational Research Association.

Venezky, R. L. (1987). A history of the American reading textbook. *Elementary School Journal*, *87*, 247–265.

Vosniadou, S., Pearson, P. D., & Rogers, T. (1988). What causes children's failures to detect inconsistencies in text? Representation versus comparison difficulties. *Journal of Educational Psychology*, *80*, 27–39.

Vygotsky, L. S. (1978). *Mind in society*. Cambridge, MA: Harvard University Press.

Wagoner, S. A. (1983). Comprehension monitoring: What it is and what we know about it. *Reading Research Quarterly*, *28*, 328–346.

Webb, N. (1980). Group process and learning in an interacting group. *Quarterly Newsletter of the Laboratory of Comparative Human Cognition*, *2*, 10–15.

Weiner, B. (1986). *An attributional theory of motivation and emotion*. New York: Springer-Verlag.

Weinstein, C., & Mayer, R. (1986). The teaching of learning strategies. In M. Wittrock (Ed.), *Handbook of research on teaching* (pp. 315–327). New York: Macmillan.

Weintraub, S., & Denny, T. P. (1965). What do beginning first graders say about reading? *Childhood Education*, *41*, 326–327.

Wellman, H. M. (1988). The early development of memory strategies. In F. Weiner & M. Perlmutter (Eds.), *Memory development: Universal changes and individual differences* (pp. 3–29). Hillsdale, NJ: Erlbaum.

Williams, J. P., Taylor, M. B., Jarin, D. C., & Milligan, E. S. (1983). *Determining the main idea of expository paragraphs: An instructional program for learning disabled and its evaluation* (Tech. Rep. No. 25). New York: Research Institute for the Study of Learning Disabilities, Teachers College, Columbia University.

Winograd, P. (1984). Strategic difficulties in summarizing texts. *Reading Research Quarterly*, *19*, 404–425.

Winograd, P., & Bridge, C. (1986). The comprehension of important information in written prose. In J. F. Baumann (Ed.), *Teaching main idea comprehension* (pp. 18–48). Newark, DE: International Reading Association.

Winograd, P., & Greenlee, M. (1986). Students need a balanced reading program. *Educational Leadership*, *43*, 16–21.

Winograd, P., & Hare, V. C. (1988). Direct instruction of reading comprehension strategies: The nature of teacher explanation. In C. Weinstein, E. Goetz, & P. Alexander (Eds.), *Learning and study strategies: Issues in assessment, instruction and evaluation* (pp. 121–139). San Diego, CA: Academic Press.

Winograd, P., & Johnston, P. (1987). Some considerations for advancing the teaching of reading comprehension. *Educational Psychologist*, *22*, 213–230.

Winograd, P., & Smith, L. (1987). Improving the climate for reading comprehension instruction. *Reading Teacher*, *41*, 304–310.

Wixson, K. K., & Peters, C. W. (1987). Comprehension assessment: Implementing an interactive view of reading. *Educational Psychologist*, *22*, 333–356.

Wood, P., Bruner, J., & Ross, G. (1976). The role of tutoring in problem solving. *Journal of Child Psychology and Psychiatry*, *17*, 89–100.

23 DIAGRAMS IN THE COMPREHENSION OF SCIENTIFIC TEXTS

Mary Hegarty, Patricia A. Carpenter, and Marcel Adam Just

Diagrams accompanied by text have been a common means of recording and conveying scientific and technical information since the 15th century. Illustrated technical books originated in engineers' notebooks and manuals of technical processes. These books relied heavily on graphics, and when they included text, it served to explain the pictures. The invention of the printing press in the 15th century made these illustrated books available to a large audience. Some historians have suggested that their availability may have been a major cause of the large technological advances between the 16th and 18th centuries (Ferguson, 1977).

In recent years, there has been an analogous advance in the capabilities of graphic technologies, as well as their availability. Graphics innovations, such as animation software, computer-aided drawing, and plotting programs, have made the techniques of graphic communication available to an ever-growing community of users. These innovations have made clear the need for a theory of communication that would specify which media are suited to conveying different types of information, where and when graphics should be included, and the extent to which information in graphics and text should overlap (Bertin, 1983). But such prescriptions must be grounded in a theory of the processes in understanding texts and diagrams.

This chapter describes the beginnings of such a theory, focusing on how readers understand technical texts and diagrams, particularly diagrams that have a close correspondence to their concrete referents. Of course, the processes in text comprehension have been the focus of considerable research in the last 15 years (Just & Carpenter, 1987; Pearson, Barr, Kamil, & Mosenthal, 1984; van Dijk & Kintsch, 1983). In this chapter, we build on what is known about text processing to describe how the process changes when diagrams accompany the text. Our discussion focuses on how text comprehension is influenced by the diagram, how the diagram itself is processed, and how information from the two sources is integrated. But a psychological analysis that considered only the properties of the text and diagram would miss a significant component of the story. As we will show, the processes in understanding a text accompanied by diagrams also depend on the reader's profile of cognitive aptitudes, so that the theory must take into account the differences among individuals.

The chapter has two main sections. The first describes the properties of diagrams and how they are related to their accompanying text, suggesting ways in which these properties influence processing. The second considers the unique characteristics of text comprehension when the text is accompanied by diagrams, focusing on how readers coordinate the activities of reading the text and inspecting the diagram and how this coordination process is affected by individual differences.

THE NATURE OF DIAGRAMS
AND THEIR RELATIONS TO TEXTS

A Taxonomy of Diagrams

Although the main focus of this chapter is on the interaction of texts and diagrams, we must first sketch the general terrain of graphic material, particularly the types of graphic material found in scientific and technical material. Such a framework is useful for understanding how the existing research on diagrams fits together. Moreover, a taxonomy of the graphic material suggests several features that may be relevant to how such material is processed when it accompanies text. For our current purposes, scientific and technical graphics can be classified into three broad categories: iconic diagrams, schematic diagrams, and charts and graphs. These categories are distinguished by the type of information that is depicted and the way in which it is depicted.

In a pictorial drawing, or *iconic diagram*, the referent is typically concrete and the spatial relations of the referent object are isomorphic to the spatial relations in the graphic depiction. This category includes photographs and line drawings of objects; some examples from biology, psychology, and physics are shown in Figure 23.1. The spatial relations among parts of the object, such as position, orientation, shape, and size, generally correspond to the spatial relations depicted in the diagram. An example par excellence of an iconic diagram is a drawing of a mechanical device or system (see Figure 23.3). The system is concrete and its structural features can be mapped fairly directly onto the iconic drawing. This category of graphic will be of primary concern in this chapter. We decided to focus on this type of diagram because such diagrams appear less dependent on convention for interpretation than do other types, such as schematic diagrams or various graphs. Of course, even iconic drawings may depend on some important conventions for their interpretation. For example, engineering and architectural drawings can be drawn from different points of view, such as the side, top, or front of the object, as shown in Figure 23.2. Also, the diagram may be made using either converging or parallel line projections. The convention must be understood to correctly interpret the drawing in order to represent the spatial relations in the referent. However, the more typical iconic diagrams accompanying technical texts are less conventionalized, and the spatial relations among components are more easily interpreted.

Interestingly, as the physical sciences developed beyond mechanics so that the functional information was no longer closely tied to spatial structure, so too did the graphic conventions evolve to reflect nonstructural relations, such as electrical conductance. The evolution of such conventions can be seen in the domain of electronics. Early circuit drawings, in the 1880s and 1890s, emphasized the visual appearance of the components, such as a lamp or resistor. But in 20 years, by 1900, symbols were developed for such electronic components. Moreover, the organization of the components in the diagram changed from representing physical position to the functional features of electrical connectivity (Gregory, 1970, pp. 156–159). Thus, conventions developed to indicate both the components and their organization. Diagrams that depict very abstract concepts and rely on such conventions to depict both the components and their organization constitute a second category of graphics that we will refer to as *schematic diagrams*.

In addition to electrical circuit diagrams, the category of schematic diagrams includes examples such as organizational charts, Venn diagrams, flow charts, and linguistic tree diagrams. In contrast to iconic diagrams, the entities depicted in schematic diagrams are typically not physical ones; consequently, the physical attributes of the components in the depiction do not necessarily have any special significance. Moreover,

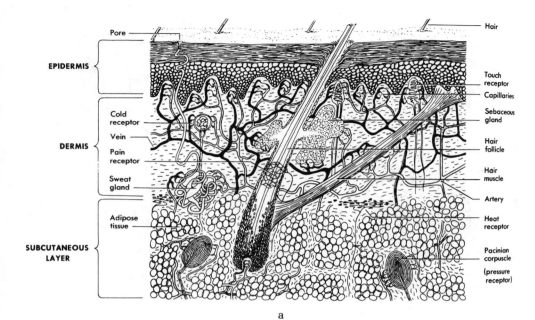

a

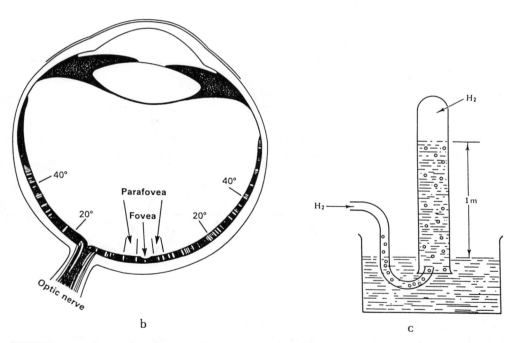

b   c

FIGURE 23.1   Examples of iconic diagrams in biology, psychology, and physics textbooks: (a) A cross-section of the skin (from *Biology* by J. Kimball. Menlo Park, CA: Addison-Wesley, 1965. Reprinted by permission of Addison-Wesley Publishing Company, Inc.); (b) A cross-section of the eye (from *The psychology of reading and language comprehension* by M. Just and P. Carpenter. Newton, MA: Allyn & Bacon, 1987. Reprinted by permission); (c) An illustration of dynamics in fluids (from *Fundamentals of university physics* by W. McCornick. Toronto, Ontario: MacMillan, 1969. Reprinted by permission).

644

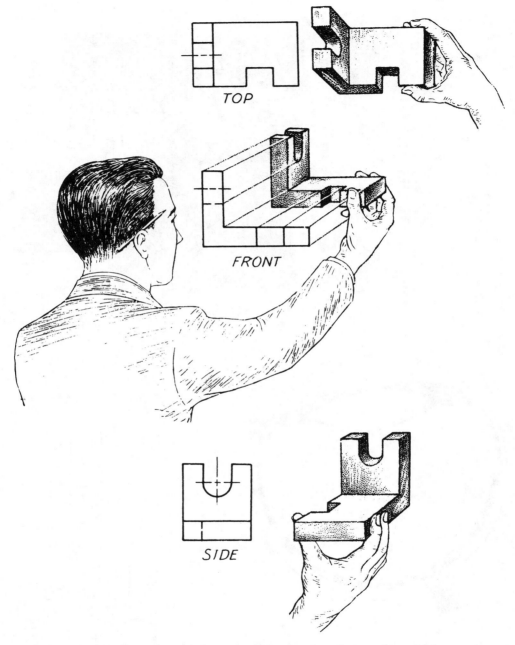

FIGURE 23.2 An illustration of the various perspectives that can be used to generate specific types of iconic diagrams: a top view, front view, and side view of an object. To correctly interpret one of these views and relate it to the representation of the three-dimensional object, the reader must understand the conventions that were used to generate that perspective. Source: From Warren J. Lugader, *Basic graphics: For design, analysis, communications, and the computer*, © 1968, p. 88. Reprinted by permission of Prentice-Hall, Inc., Englewood Cliffs, NJ.

the interpretation of the functional relation signaled in the diagram is obviously dependent on convention for interpretation. A student has to learn how to read a linguistic tree diagram and to interpret the links as indicating grammatical relations, not physical position.

A third category, *charts and graphs*, is commonly encountered in the social and physical sciences. In a chart or graph, the referent to be depicted is some set of related facts or records that are typically quantitative. These attributes are mapped onto some quantifiable attribute of the graph, such as position on a coordinate space, coloring, and shading. This category includes line graphs, polar charts, and pie graphs. A frequent type of graph in nonscientific publications, particularly newspapers, is the one-dimensional plot, such as a bar chart, time-series plot, or data map (Tufte, 1983). Of course, much more complex graphs are frequently used in scientific publications.

Interest in statistical graphics has accelerated over the last 20 years, reflecting both the graphic revolution mentioned in the introduction to this chapter and also, in part, the increasingly quantitative nature of the social sciences. Like schematic diagrams, the interpretation of most complex types of graphs depends heavily on learning their conventions. Indeed, there are a number of seminal analyses of graphics conventions, both by graphic designers (Bertin, 1983; Tufte, 1983), and by researchers interested in psychological processes, such as perceptual illusions in graphs (see the bibliographies in MacDonald-Ross & Smith, 1977; Levie, 1987). However, the interpretation of graphs will not be the focus of this chapter.

A survey of three introductory college textbooks that were representative of the textbooks in their discipline, one in biology (Kimball, 1965), one in physics (Genzer & Youngner, 1969), and one in psychology (Hilgard, Atkinson, & Atkinson, 1979), suggested that iconic diagrams constitute a sizable proportion of their graphic illustrations: .73 in the biology textbook, .49 in the physics textbook, and .69 in the psychology textbook, respectively. However, the purposes of iconic diagrams differed in predictable ways among the three disciplines. Structural relations are crucial to understanding the function of most biological systems. Consequently, the iconic diagrams in the biology textbook were typically central to the text's exposition. For example, to understand nerve conductance in the central nervous system, it is necessary to understand the structural relations among neurons.

By contrast, many of the iconic diagrams in the psychology and physics textbooks were less central to the exposition of the underlying processes in those areas. In the psychology textbook, many of the iconic diagrams were photographs (30%) or cartoons (12%). Their purpose was often to provide a context for the explanation of some psychological process, typically by illustrating some everday situations in which the psychological process occurred. For instance, the discussion of frustration was accompanied by a photograph of a long line of traffic on a freeway. Similarly, the physics book included iconic diagrams depicting everyday situations in which physics principles applied—for example, a drawing of a person pulling a heavy weight up a ramp illustrated the trade-off of force and distance to accomplish the same amount of work. The physics diagrams that were most central to the exposition in the text were usually illustrating more abstract concepts; hence, they were more clearly considered as schematic drawings or graphs. In both the physics and psychology textbooks, the iconic diagrams that were most central to the text were those that depicted experimental setups (or stimuli in the case of psychology).

These three categories of graphic types are not mutually exclusive. A statistical map that shows, for example, the median age of people in the United States as a function of geographic location, has properties both of a graph and an iconic diagram.

Hence, the processes in interpreting such a graph undoubtedly overlap with the processes of interest in this chapter. Also, the boundary between iconic diagrams and schematic diagrams can be difficult to sharply define in domains, such as physics, where both abstract relations (such as force) and concrete relations (distance) are important. Indeed, the three categories should be conceptualized as based more on family resemblances than on a logically necessary or sufficient criterion. Nevertheless, this brief survey suggests the diversity among graphic conventions, and these contrasts help situate the iconic diagrams in the larger field of graphic processing.

In the current chapter, we will be concerned primarily with iconic diagrams that contribute to the explanation of the text beyond providing some general orientation or example of the text's description, although the diagrams may accomplish these goals as well. In any case, this brief survey supports the idea that iconic diagrams are both a prominent and an important category of illustration in technical domains. However, their exact function in an exposition may depend on the subject matter; they are more likely to play a central role in domains such as mechanics, biology, and architecture, where the spatial structure is integrally related to the function.

Features of Iconic Diagrams

The category of iconic diagrams permits further subdivisions that are undoubtedly important in comprehending such diagrams when they accompany text. In particular, iconic diagrams can vary in their realism, from photographic quality to caricatures, even though such diagrams generally depict the appearance of objects. If the purpose of the drawing is not simply decoration, then the type of distortion may reflect the particular goal of the text. Simplification or distortion may be used to emphasize certain information. For example, the diagram of the pulley in Figure 23.3a is stylized to emphasize the configuration of components of the pulley system, rather than their detailed appearance. Such diagrams might be most useful to people who already are familiar with pulley systems. However, the diagram might not be immediately recognized by someone who is unfamiliar with pulleys or the conventions for this type of diagram. Such a person might need to examine a more realistic diagram, such as the one in Figure 23.3b, to recognize a pulley system before studying its configuration. More generally, the visual properties of the drawing may orient the reader to particular salient aspects of the objects that may also be discussed in the text.

Iconic diagrams can also depict objects that are not visible, either because they are too small (or too large) to be observed unaided or because they are not typically visually accessible, such as the structure of a cross section of the skin. The problem of visual accessibility is also addressed by a type of iconic diagram called the *exploded view*, which originated with Leonardo da Vinci (Ferguson, 1977), an example of which is shown in Figure 23.4. The exploded view depicts the individual components of a machine in their relative spatial locations, even if some of the components would not be visible in an assembled machine. To understand an exploded view of a machine, readers have to mentally translate their representations of the components in the diagram to construct a representation of the assembled machine.

An iconic diagram may incorporate some conventions for depicting abstract entities, such as the superimposition of arrows to represent direction of movement or force. The use of arrows to represent direction is very familiar, but other conventions may be less familiar and may require verbal labels or an explanation in the text. In addition, such drawings can vary in the amount of information they convey, from being a comprehensive compendium to a simple sketch.

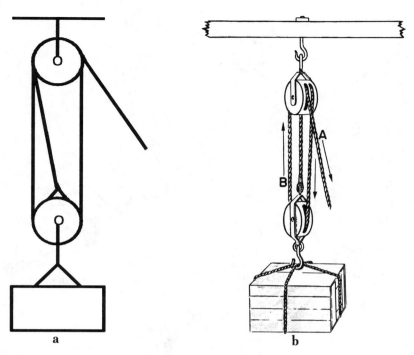

FIGURE 23.3 Different types of iconic diagrams in mechanical texts to illustrate the difference between (a) a more stylized diagram of a pulley system, and (b) a more realistic diagram (from the Bureau of Naval Personnel, 1971).

One important dichotomy among iconic diagrams is whether they are meant only to depict static features of the objects or dynamic properties that can be "read off" of the diagram, as least by the sophisticated viewer. Alternatively, a dynamic process may be depicted by a series of static diagrams, as shown in Figure 23.5. Finally, animation graphics make it possible to animate the display, a topic we will return to in a later section of the paper.

The different features of an iconic diagram may be related to different purposes of the diagram or different purposes of the text and diagram as a unit. Of particular concern in this chapter are those cases in which readers are using the text and drawing to learn new information about some scientific or technical topic. Moreover, our primary focus is on cases in which the drawing has a functional role, beyond its role in providing decoration, some general orientation, or example of the issues being described. This research focus stands in contrast to the literature on the role of pictures in early reading books, where the informational role of illustrations is more global, rather than providing specific structural or functional information. We will now consider more precisely the role of the drawing in technical and scientific texts.

Relation between Text and Diagrams

Because we are interested in how diagrams are processed when they are accompanied by text, it is also important to consider the relation between a text and diagram. Again, depending on the content and purpose of a text, this relation can differ. We will consider three main possibilities:

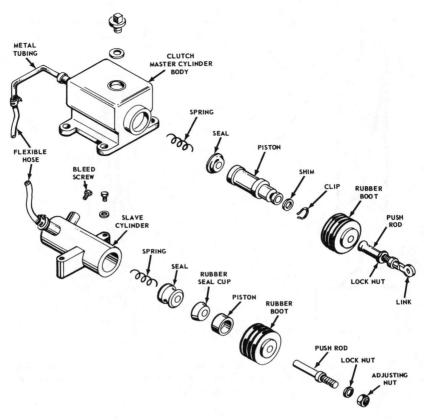

FIGURE 23.4   An example of an iconic diagram that illustrates components that are typically hidden from view. This is an exploded view of a hydraulic clutch (from the Bureau of Naval Personnel, 1971).

- Text and diagrams can complement each other by providing different information about the same object.
- Text and diagrams can be redundant by providing similar information in different formats.
- The text can provide information that is specific to the processing of the diagram itself.

Text and Diagrams That Are Complementary

Text and diagrams may provide different types of information about the same referent. For example, a description of a mechanical device might include both a diagram showing the configuration of parts of the device, and a text describing its overall function, its application, or its development. Differences in the type of information expressed in texts and diagrams can be related to differences in their structure and their processing.

The visual properties of iconic diagrams make them particularly useful if the purpose of the text is to help the reader perform some task that is dependent on the visual properties of the referent. This would include tasks such as navigating a route, or assembling, operating, or repairing some mechanical device. The fact that the iconic diagram provides a visual representation may help the reader construct a more accurate internal representation of those aspects that rely on visual appearance or structure. The diagram may help a reader understand spatial features of an object or system that the text could provide only through an awkward or lengthy description. If these attributes were only described, the reader would have to use the description to form a visual representation, a process that can be subject to severe limitations in the accuracy of initial formation (Carpenter & Just, 1986; Kosslyn, 1980).

Although diagrams are an excellent means for conveying approximate or relative spatial attributes of shape, size, or position, exact spatial dimensions typically cannot be accurately encoded from a visual display alone (see Baird, 1970). These must be provided on the diagram, in an accompanying table, or in the text itself (MacDonald-Ross, 1977).

Text and Diagrams That Are Redundant

Text and diagrams can also be used to convey the same information in different formats. This is useful in situations in which different aspects of the information are more easily encoded from text and diagrams. For example, general numerical trends are easily encoded from a graph, whereas exact numbers are more easily encoded from a table (MacDonald-Ross, 1977); if it were important that readers process both the relational and absolute data, the results could be presented in both tabular and graphic formats.

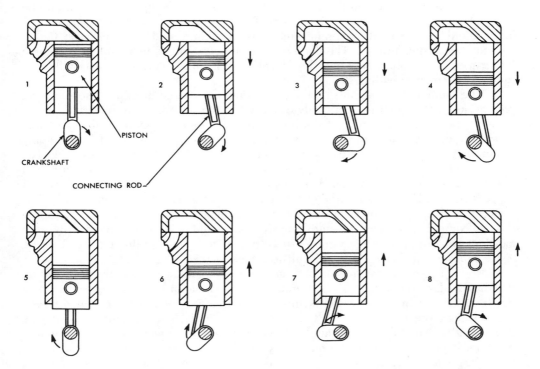

FIGURE 23.5   A series of static diagrams can be configured to convey dynamic information about a process. This particular series shows several views of a piston, connecting rod, and crank on a crankshaft as the crankshaft turns one revolution (from the Bureau of Naval Personnel, 1971).

Also, the presentation of information in more than one medium can help readers who have difficulty encoding information from either texts or diagrams alone. For example, redundant information in a text and diagram can draw readers' attention to information in a diagram that they may not notice otherwise.

Because the two media are suited to different types of information, texts and diagrams can differentially affect performance. Although a diagram is particularly useful for spatial and configural information, a text may be a better source of specific details. The speed and accuracy of abstracting the two kinds of information can be affected by the medium in which the information is presented. This type of trade-off was found in a task that required students to assemble a device from information contained either in a text or in a diagram (Bieger & Glock, 1982). The students were more accurate when the text contained the spatial information about the location and orientation of components, presumably because the text afforded more accuracy in the detailed information. However, they assembled the device more quickly when spatial information was presented in a diagram, presumably because general configural information could be encoded more quickly from the diagram.

As the assembly task illustrates, many types of information can be represented in more than one way. If two representations contain the same information, they may be considered informationally equivalent. However, abstracting the information from the two media requires different types of computations and so the processes are not necessarily computationally equivalent (Larkin & Simon, 1987). For example, one can represent the location of a house by depicting its spatial relation to landmarks, or as a sequence of verbal directions for how to go there. The former representation would be easily communicated in a map, and it is useful for a variety of starting locations. The latter would be more easily communicated in a text, and it would be more closely tied to a particular starting location. The degree of match between the medium in which some information is communicated and the reader's use for that information may influence the ease of comprehending it.

The sequential constraints on the processing of texts and diagrams also affect the type of information that is most easily conveyed in the two forms. In particular, there are few inherent constraints on the order in which the information in the diagram must be extracted. This stands in marked contrast to text processing, which at least initially has inherent sequential constraints that require generally left-to-right processing. Because of the lack of constraint, iconic diagrams may permit more efficient search and visual comparisons than text. Diagrams may reduce the knowledgeable viewer's search by presenting information in predictable spatial locations (Larkin & Simon, 1987). For example, a diagram of a particular geometric configuration can permit the viewer to directly compare particular structural features that would be described in very different locations in a text. Thus, the diagram may be potentially useful for finding or comparing visual information that is more difficult to access in the text.

The left-to-right structure of texts makes them suitable for presenting information that has analogous sequential constraints, such as a causal sequence of events or a strictly linear argument. However, sequential information can also be presented graphically, using a linear arrangement and arrows (or an equivalent convention) to indicate directionality. Moreover, some kinds of information with sequential aspects may also have nonsequential features (hierarchical or cyclic) that are easily depicted diagrammatically. In fact, diagrams have been found to be useful instructional tools for teaching the concept of biological cycles (Winn, 1987).

Even though diagrams have fewer inherent sequential constraints on their processing, that does not mean that diagrams are "immediately apprehended." A statement by William Playfair, one of the founders of statistical graphics, exemplifies this common misconception of how graphics are comprehended:

> Information that is imperfectly acquired is generally as imperfectly retained; and a man who has carefully investigated a printed table finds, when done, that he has only a very faint and partial idea of what he has read; and that like a figure imprinted on sand, it is soon totally erased and defaced. . . . On inspecting one of these charts attentively, a sufficiently distinct impression will be made, to remain unimpaired for a considerable time, and the idea which does remain will be simple and complete, at once including the duration and the amount. (Playfair, 1801).

Our data argue against any blanket application of the view that diagrams, even iconic diagrams, are "immediately apprehended." If the information in diagrams were immediately apprehended, then readers would have to inspect a diagram only once in order to extract the relevant information. However, this prediction is contradicted by experiments in which we have recorded the eye fixations of readers who are inspecting iconic diagrams in conjunction with reading a text. In several such studies, the readers typically inspect the diagram in some detail. In some cases, they fixate different parts of the diagram, suggesting that they are encoding new information from the diagram; and in some cases, they repeatedly fixate the same part. Thus, the eye fixations of readers suggest that the processing of diagrams is not immediate. The fixations reflect complex cognitive processes, in addition to the more automatic processes that are part of perceptual processing. A similar characterization arises from research on how viewers inspect pictures of complex scenes, such as a picture of a college campus or a city intersection. Often viewers can abstract the general topic of a picture after a short exposure (less than 300 milliseconds) (Biederman, Rabinowitz, Glass, & Stacy, 1974); but further fixations on different parts of the picture are needed to acquire more detailed information, and these fixations improve their recognition memory for the picture (Loftus, 1981).

Texts That Guide the Processing of Diagrams

The text can provide information about the diagram itself. Often the text identifies the objects in the diagram by labeling them, and the text may provide other information about the conventions embodied in a diagram. The text also can direct the processing of diagrams by referring to them in the appropriate places. This is an important function because in some contexts, students do not examine illustrations because they believe that they can get all the information they need from the text alone (Winn, 1987). For example, in a study of students learning about the nitrogen cycle from text and diagrams, students who viewed diagrams alone outperformed students who read text accompanied by diagrams (or text alone), because students who were given the text with the diagrams did not attend to the diagrams (Holliday, 1976).

The amount of attention paid to a diagram is also influenced by its proximity to the part of the text that refers to it. It has been found that readers pay more attention to diagrams if the diagrams are presented immediately after the sentence in which they are first referenced, than if the diagrams are distributed throughout the text (Whalley & Fleming, 1975). The convention of publishing a diagram on the backside of the accompanying text is particularly detrimental to overall comprehension. If readers do process the diagram, it involves effortful place keeping as they turn the page back and forth to integrate the information in the text and diagram; alternatively, comprehension also suffers if readers simply skip the diagram entirely.

Our survey of various types of graphics distinguished among three general types: iconic diagrams, schematic diagrams, and graphs. Iconic diagrams are distinguished from the other categories because there is a close isomorphism between the spatial properties of the concrete referent and the spatial properties of the diagram. This makes them particularly suited for conveying structural information. Diagrams also differ in their relation to their accompanying text—in particular, whether their relation is complementary or redundant and the degree to which the text directs attention to the diagram. We will now consider in more detail how texts and diagrams are processed when they occur together in a technical exposition, and the influence of individual differences on their processing.

COMPREHENSION OF SCIENTIFIC TEXTS ACCOMPANIED BY DIAGRAMS

Understanding a situation or object from a technical description involves constructing a representation of that object or situation, which we will call the *referential representation*. When this description includes both a text and a diagram, the reader must read the text, interpret the diagram, and combine the information extracted from the two media into a single representation of the referent. In this section, we will briefly review how representations are constructed from text, in order to suggest ways in which this process differs when the text is accompanied by diagrams and how the process is affected by individual differences.

Incremental Construction of the Representation

When people read a text, they construct the referential representation incrementally (Just & Carpenter, 1980, 1987; Kintsch & van Dijk, 1978). The text commonly unfolds by presenting new information that is grounded in what has already been established. Successive clauses and sentences refer to certain objects or events that are central to the content, presenting some elaboration or relational information about them. Readers construct a representation of each section of text and integrate this with their representation of what they have read up to that point.

When the text is accompanied by a diagram, the comprehension process is more involved because the information that readers have to integrate is presented in two different media. Furthermore, as we pointed out earlier, the computations required to abstract information from a text and diagram are different, so that readers have to coordinate two qualitatively different encoding processes. Because each medium is suited to displaying different types of information, this coordination process might involve evaluating the type of information presented at each stage of a text to determine whether it would be useful to examine the diagram. Thus, the coordination process involves alternation between reading the text and inspecting the diagram. The decision about when to alternate is influenced by the text, the diagram, and the current state of the reader's representation.

Effects of Individual Differences on the Reading Process

The reading process is constrained by characteristics of readers, including differences in basic information-processing capacities and their knowledge of the domain. One basic processing capacity that influences how an individual integrates information from successive clauses of text is the amount of information an individual can store in working memory while processing a text (Daneman & Carpenter, 1980, 1983; Carpenter & Just, 1989). If the information is in working memory, it is easier to integrate successive clauses of the text that refer to that information. The information may be in working memory because it was recently processed or because it is the central theme of the text (Kintsch & van Dijk, 1978). A reader with a large working memory capacity who can maintain more recent and central information in working memory will find it easier to process the text than a reader with less capacity. If the relevant information is no longer in working memory, the reader must reactivate parts of the existing representation from long-term memory, reread an earlier part of the text, or suffer some decrement in comprehension.

When a text is accompanied by a diagram, the relevant information could be reactivated by inspecting the diagram rather than rereading the text. A diagram might be particularly helpful if the various pieces of information to be related were presented in adjacent locations or easily identified locations. For example, in mechanical systems, components that directly affect each other's motions are always spatially contiguous; hence, a diagram might be especially useful for integrating information about the motions of individual components to construct a global model of how the components interact dynamically.

Diagrams can be used to compensate for working memory limitations only if the reader can process the diagram itself. The processes of encoding and reactivating information from the diagram may be subject to further information-processing limitations specific to the processing of spatial information, such as capacity limitations on how much detail can be retained in a spatial representation (Carpenter & Just, 1986; Kosslyn, 1980). In addition, some types of information may be more difficult to represent than other types. For example, metric information and complex irregular forms are more difficult to encode and process (Baylor, 1971; Just & Carpenter, 1985; Yuille & Steiger, 1982). Finally, it is difficult to use a static diagram to form a dynamic representation of the object in action, to "mentally animate" the diagram. Some spatial transformations, like mental rotation, are very difficult to execute accurately for people with low spatial skills, as assessed by standard psychometric tests (Just & Carpenter, 1985; Shepard & Metzler, 1971).

Reading researchers are already familiar with the effects of domain knowledge on text comprehension. Background knowledge, or explanation in the text itself, is also required to interpret diagrams. The role of such knowledge is obvious for graphs, charts, and schematic diagrams, because these often use highly specialized symbols and conventions. But iconic diagrams may also require background knowledge or concurrent information in the text. Prior knowledge or the text itself can direct the reader's attention to the relevant information in a diagram; the text may provide labels and describe interrelations among the components. Several studies that we will describe in the next section suggest that background knowledge is necessary to successfully use a diagram if this information is not given by the text.

In conclusion, the processing of technical texts that include diagrams differs from processing a text alone because it requires readers to integrate information in two different formats by coordinating two different modes of information processing. Second, readers of technical texts are constrained by the limitations of spatial information processing, in addition to the normal memory demands involved in integrating different sections of a text. Finally, readers of technical texts require different kinds of background knowledge, especially knowledge of the conventions for displaying information in diagrams. We will now report some empirical data showing how these factors affect processing of texts accompanied by diagrams.

Empirical Studies of Processing Text and Diagrams

In the remainder of the chapter, we will summarize a number of studies of how readers comprehend texts accompanied by diagrams. We will focus on research that studied the comprehension process itself by monitoring readers' eye fixations while they read texts accompanied by diagrams. We will also draw on research that studied this comprehension process less directly, by observing how the outcomes of the comprehension process were affected by task differences and individual differences. We will use the results of this research to propose a preliminary model of how readers construct representations from texts and iconic diagrams by coordinating their processing of the two media.

Methodology

The processes in constructing a representation from a technical text can be studied by monitoring readers' eye fixations as they process a text (Just & Carpenter, 1980, 1987). This methodology is particularly suitable for studying the integration of information from text and diagrams because it reveals when in the course of reading the text the reader inspects the diagram, as well as the parts of the diagram that are inspected. The content of the text and the inspected parts of the diagram may indicate whether information is being reactivated or whether the reader is seeking new information.

The eye-fixation studies that we summarize here are concerned with how people process text and diagrams to understand the working of a simple machine, such as a pulley system (Hegarty, 1988; Hegarty & Just, 1989). In a typical experimental trial, a subject reads a description, such as the one in Figure 23.6 (Hegarty, 1988). The text and diagram are presented simultaneously on a CRT screen so that subjects are free to switch between reading the text and processing the diagram as often as they wish. The text is expository and descriptive, describing the components of the machine, their configuration, how the components move when the machine is in operation, and how these motions achieve the function of the machine. The diagram is iconic but also somewhat schematic because it emphasizes the configural and functional relations between components and gives little detail of their surface appearance. There is some redundancy between the information in the text and diagram, because both provide information about the configuration of components of the system. Each medium also provides information that is not present in the other. For example, the diagram may indicate the exact spatial locations and sizes of the components, while the text may describe the motions of the components.

The influence of limitations of the cognitive architecture and knowledge can be studied by observing how subjects with different cognitive abilities process the text and diagram. In this chapter, we will report processing differences among students who differ in *spatial ability* and *mechanical ability*, as assessed by common psychometric tests. Accounts of spatial ability (Just & Carpenter, 1985; McGee, 1979; Smith, 1964) suggest that this ability relates to the process of accurately constructing and maintaining a representation of a mechanical system from diagrams. Mechanical ability includes the ability to differentiate relevant from irrelevant attributes of a machine, and the knowledge of how to combine information about different attributes of a machine (Hegarty, Just, & Morrison, 1988). Mechanical ability reflects experience interacting with machines, as well as formal instruction in mechanics. Mechanical and spatial ability are highly correlated (Smith, 1964; Bennett, 1969), so that differences in processing text

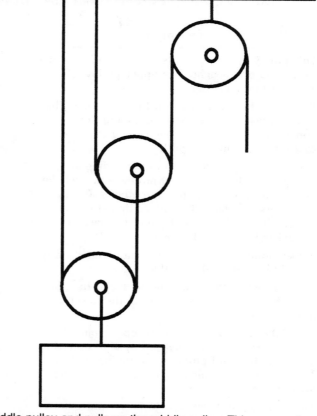

This pulley system consists of three pulleys, two ropes and one weight. The upper pulley is attached to the ceiling. The other pulleys are free to move up and down. The upper rope is attached to the ceiling at one end, goes under the middle pulley and over the upper pulley, and is free at the other end. The lower rope is attached to the ceiling at one end. It goes under the lower pulley and is attached to the middle pulley at the other end. The crate is suspended from the lower pulley. When the free end of the upper rope is pulled, the rope moves over the upper pulley and under the middle pulley and pulls up the middle pulley. This causes the lower rope to move under the lower pulley and to pull up the crate.

FIGURE 23.6   An example of texts and accompanying diagram used to analyze how readers process the diagrams when reading technical material. The text and diagram describe a relatively complex pulley system, consisting of three pulleys and two ropes (from Hegarty, 1988).

and diagrams between readers with different mechanical ability might also reflect differences in basic spatial information-processing capacities.

A Sample Protocol

To provide a context for the analysis, it is useful to consider some of the features of a typical sequence of gazes on the text and diagram. Table 23.1 presents one for a college student who had low spatial and mechanical skills, who was reading the description in Figure 23.6. The sequence is presented from top to bottom, with the left side of the table showing the sections of text that the subject read, and the right side listing the parts of the diagram that he inspected.

The protocol is typical of how readers process the text and accompanying diagram (Hegarty, 1988). First, the subject switched between reading the text and processing the diagram numerous times—a total of seven times while reading a 17-clause text. We

TABLE 23.1   Sequence of Fixations on a Text and Diagram by a Subject
Reading the Text in Figure 23.6

TEXT READ	PART OF DIAGRAM INSPECTED
This pulley system consists of three pulleys, two ropes, and one weight. The upper pulley is attached to the ceiling.	(upper pulley)
The upper pulley is attached to the ceiling. The other pulleys are free to move up and down. The upper rope is attached to the ceiling at one end, goes under the middle pulley.	(right lower rope) (middle pulley)
The upper rope is attached to the ceiling at one end, goes under the middle pulley, and over the upper pulley and is free at the other end. The lower rope is attached to the ceiling at one end. It goes under the lower pulley and is attached to the middle pulley at the lower end.	
It goes under the lower pulley and is attached to the middle pulley at the other end.	(lower pulley)
and is attached to the middle pulley at the other end. The crate is suspended from the lower pulley.	(right lower rope) (middle pulley)
When the free end of the pull rope is pulled, the rope moves over the upper pulley and under the middle pulley and pulls up the middle pulley. This causes the lower rope to move under the lower pulley.	(crate)
This causes the lower rope to move under the lower pulley and to pull up the crate.	(lower pulley)
	(lower pulley) (middle pulley) (upper pulley) (pull rope) (upper pulley) (right upper rope) (upper pulley) (right upper rope) (left upper rope) (left lower rope) (left upper rope) (middle pulley) (right lower rope) (middle pulley) (right lower rope) (middle pulley) (left upper rope)

find that readers typically inspect the diagram about once every three or four clauses. This result suggests that when people read technical text accompanied by diagrams, they attempt to integrate the information in the text and diagram frequently as they progress through the text.

Another typical feature of the subject's performance was the central role that the text played in controlling the reader's attention. The subject's inspections occurred at the ends of sentences and clauses. About 80 percent of all diagram inspections occurred at sentence and clause boundaries. This finding indicates that readers attempt to interpret a sentence or clause before checking the representation of that clause against the diagram. Another typical pattern, evident in Table 23.1, was that in the diagram, the subject examined components that had been referred to in the preceding clause. Across all of the subjects, about 80 percent of the inspections on the diagrams were on components mentioned in the last three clauses that the subject read before looking at the diagram.

The inspections on the diagram were of two types. The subject's first six inspections, which occurred while he was reading the text, were relatively short, and each inspection focused on one or two components of the pulley system. By contrast, the final inspection of the diagram was much longer and included 17 distinct gazes on the various pulleys and ropes of the system. These two types of diagram inspection will be called *local* and *global* inspections. The difference suggests that two processes are involved in forming a representation from a text and a diagram. The first may reflect the formation of a detailed representation of parts of the system, and it may entail integrating the information from the text and the diagram. The second type may reflect combining the more local, detailed representations to derive a global representation of the whole pulley system. When subjects are reading texts of this type, about 70 percent of subject's inspections are local and 30 percent are global. In this protocol, the global inspection occurred at the end, which was the most common place. However, sometimes readers inspected the diagram globally in the middle or even early in the text, indicating that subjects alternate between these different processes to form the referential representation.

In sum, this protocol suggests that the process of constructing a representation from text and diagrams is directed by the text, particularly for a reader who has less knowledge of the domain. Information is added to the representation in the order in which it is read in the text, and the diagram is inspected only as required by this representation process. The construction of the referential representation consists of forming detailed representations of parts of the mechanical system, and combining these to form a representation of the whole system.

Coordinating Reading and Diagram Inspection Processes

Readers frequently switch between reading text and inspecting the diagram. Essentially, these switches imply that at each step of reading the text, the reader must decide whether to continue reading or to inspect the diagram. There are several possibilities why readers might interrupt their reading to inspect a diagram:

- Because they have difficulty abstracting some information from the text alone
- Because they want to check the accuracy of a spatial representation of the system that they have constructed from the text
- Because they want to reactivate some information that they read earlier but which is no longer in working memory
- Because they want to encode new information that they have not yet read in the text

Our research suggests that each of these reasons plays a role in deciding to inspect the diagram, although the importance of any one factor depends on the content of the text and the abilities of the reader.

Use of a diagram to encode spatial information. A reader might choose to inspect the diagram to encode spatial information that is difficult to encode from the text, particularly because diagrams are suited to communicating certain spatial information, such as configuration, shape, and size. Diagrams can contribute to the comprehension process by providing readers with the spatial information more directly than the text alone.

Because diagrams are used to construct spatial representations in this way, readers inspect diagrams more often when they read texts that require them to encode more spatial information. This is true when the referent of the text is more spatially complex because it contains more components and there are more connections between these components. For example, Figure 23.7 shows that both low- and high-ability subjects inspected a diagram more often while reading descriptions of more-complex pulley systems, than while reading descriptions of less-complex pulley systems. Thus, the more spatially complex the referent, the more a reader uses a diagram that displays this configural information.

Figure 23.7 also shows that low-spatial-ability readers consistently inspected the diagram more often than high-ability subjects. People with low spatial ability may use a diagram more often than high-ability people when reading descriptions of objects that are spatially complex because they have more difficulty forming an accurate spatial representation. This is consistent with accounts of spatial ability (e.g., McGee, 1979).

The eye-fixation studies suggest that when students read a text that is accompanied by a diagram, they first attempt to construct the representation from the text and inspect the diagram to verify this representation, or they may inspect the diagram if they have difficulty constructing the representation from the text alone. Subjects inspect the diagram on average after reading every three or four clauses, suggesting that they construct preliminary spatial representations from the text and check these periodically against the diagram. At the same time, subjects may inspect a diagram immediately after reading a clause if they have difficulty forming a preliminary representation of the clause.

These conclusions were suggested by an analysis in which we assessed whether the parts of a diagram that a reader fixated were referred to in the most recently read section of text. If readers inspect the diagram because they have difficulty representing a particular clause, they should look at the parts of the diagram that were referred to in that clause. If they hold a temporary representation of two or three clauses in a temporary memory buffer before checking this representation against the diagram, they might inspect the referents in any of those clauses. About 42 percent of subjects' diagram inspections are referred to in the most recently read clause, while a further 37 percent were referred to in the preceding two clauses, suggesting that readers sometimes retain the representations of two or three clauses in working memory before checking these representations against the diagram. This may be a particularly efficient strategy because consecutive clauses of a text typically present information that is related. By keeping the representation of a number of related clauses in working memory before checking them against the diagram, subjects can use the diagram to integrate these representations.

Assuming that readers first attempt to construct the referential representation from the text alone, a diagram may not affect comprehension if the text and diagram are redundant and the relevant spatial information can be easily derived from the text. This interpretation may explain the findings of a study of junior high school students reading about the water cycle (Koran & Koran, 1980). A flow diagram included in the text helped seventh-grade students but not eighth-grade students. Even among seventh-grade students, the diagram primarily helped students who received low scores on a test of general intelligence and reasoning ability. The diagrams may not have been helpful to

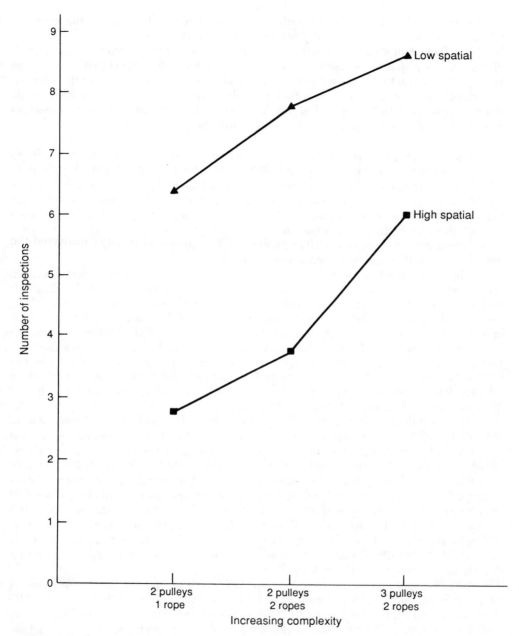

FIGURE 23.7   The graph shows the number of inspections of the diagram as a function of the complexity of the pulley system that is being described and depicted. Both high- and low-spatial-ability subjects make more inspections as the complexity increases. In addition, low-ability subjects make more fixations than the higher-ability subjects on all three types of displays (from Hegarty, 1988).

more mature and more intelligent students because they may have been able to derive the information presented in the diagram from the text alone.

In conclusion, subjects sometimes switch between reading a text and inspecting a diagram to form spatial representations. The eye-fixation data suggest that readers first attempt to construct representations from the text alone. They may inspect the diagram to verify these representations or if they have difficulty forming these representations. Because readers with low spatial ability have more difficulty forming representations from text alone, they inspect the diagrams more often.

Use of a diagram to reorganize information.   A diagram can also be used to reactivate information that readers have already represented, allowing them to reorganize or integrate parts of the existing representation. One of the main processes a reader has to carry out when reading a text is to relate the information presented at different parts of the text. Because working memory capacity is limited, this integration process may involve reactivating information that has been represented previously, but which is no longer in working memory. A diagram can aid this integration by reducing the search for information that has been represented previously.

This reorganization process is particularly important for scientific texts because these texts are often used to solve problems or to think creatively about the material, rather than to memorize the information in a verbatim or rote manner. For example, a text describing how electrical circuits work might be useful in understanding the cause of a broken circuit or in designing a new circuit. These kinds of activities require the reader to reorganize and make inferences from the information presented in the text. Diagrams can enhance readers' understanding by helping them to focus on the relevant information in a text, to reorganize this information, and to integrate it with their existing knowledge. Consequently, diagrams facilitate conceptual understanding of texts but not verbatim recall (Mayer, in press).

Mayer and his colleagues studied the effects of diagrams on comprehension of texts that explained the functioning of different types of systems, including mechanical systems, such as brakes (Mayer, in press); physics principles, such as Ohm's law (Mayer, 1983); and biological systems, such as the nitrogen cycle (Mayer, Dyke, & Cook, 1984). In each of the descriptions, the diagrams provided a model of the system being described: it illustrated the system's major parts, states, and actions and how a change in state of one part of the system affected another part. In all cases, the inclusion of a diagram improved the readers' recall of the concepts explained in the text and their ability to transfer to problem-solving situations, and the diagram had negative effects on their ability to recall the text word for word. Thus, diagrams are useful in promoting deeper understanding of the concepts.

This integration process can be observed in the sequence of eye fixations of subjects inspecting a diagram, such as the sequence shown earlier in Table 23.1. We pointed out that there were two types of inspections: short, local inspections and longer, global inspections. The function of the longer, global inspections, such as the final inspection of the diagram in Table 23.1 might be to aid in integrating the representations of parts of the pulley system constructed at earlier stages of the reading process.

Although a diagram can be helpful in organizing information, there are limitations to how much a diagram can help. If the text is highly disorganized, only readers with high mechanical ability successfully compensated for the disorganization of the text by inspecting a diagram more often (Hegarty, 1988). In an experiment on the effect of text organization, the *organized* text could be divided into sections of consecutive clauses describing the same pulley system component. In the *disorganized* text, clauses describing the configuration of the pulley system were presented in a scrambled order, so that clauses describing the same component were not presented consecutively. It was predicted that subjects who read the disorganized text would inspect the diagram more often to integrate the information presented at different parts of the text. However, only high-ability subjects inspected the diagram more often when the text was disorganized. In contrast, low-ability subjects actually inspected the diagram less often if they read the disorganized text. Because low-ability subjects were unable to make this compensation, their comprehension of the text was poorer, as assessed by questions after the text was read. These results suggest that only subjects with more expertise in a domain may be able to use a diagram to integrate information presented at different parts of a disorganized text.

In sum, readers can use diagrams in technical texts to help them integrate information presented at different parts of the text and to reorganize this information. Consequently, they may form a better conceptual understanding of the text, allowing them to apply the information in the text in novel, problem-solving situations. However, the ability to use the diagram in this way may depend on the expertise of the reader.

Use of a diagram to encode new information.   A diagram can provide new information to augment the representation formed from the text. So far, our discussion has concentrated on the processing of text and diagrams that are largely redundant; and under these circumstances, processing of the diagram is primarily text directed. However, diagrams and text can communicate different information about the same referent. In these cases, processing of the diagram cannot be directed by the text.

Subjects with low domain-specific ability or expertise may not be able to encode new information from a diagram without direction from an accompanying text. This was suggested by a study that compared the eye fixations of subjects who read one of two texts which differed in redundancy with their accompanying diagrams (Hegarty & Just, 1989). One text described the components, configuration, and movements of a mechanical system; this text was accompanied by a diagram that also showed the components and configuration of the system. The other text just described the components and movement of the system; the diagram was the only source of information about the configuration of components. As Figure 23.8 shows, subjects who scored high on a test of mechanical ability spent more time inspecting the diagram when its accompanying text included less redundant information, indicating that these subjects were able to encode information from a diagram without direction from an accompanying text. In contrast, low-ability subjects spent more time inspecting the diagram if it was accompanied by the text that was highly redundant with the diagram, indicating that they needed the text to direct their processing of the diagram.

Subjects with low mechanical ability may not be able to encode information from a diagram alone because they are not able to select the relevant information from a diagram. Various analyses of expertise indicate that low-ability subjects are less likely to know what information is relevant. For example, college students who score high on tests of mechanical knowledge typically know which parts of a mechanical system are relevant to its mechanical functioning. By contrast, low-scoring students often incorrectly believe that an irrelevant property, such as the height of a pulley system, is relevant to its mechanical advantage (Hegarty, Just, & Morrison, 1988). Consequently, low-ability subjects may not attend to the important information in a diagram and they may not know a component's relation to the system's function.

Because low-ability subjects have difficulty identifying relevant information in a diagram, they do not always benefit from detailed and realistic diagrams, even those that closely resemble their referents. Some studies have demonstrated positive effects of realistic diagrams on learning, especially for low-verbal subjects (e.g., Holliday,

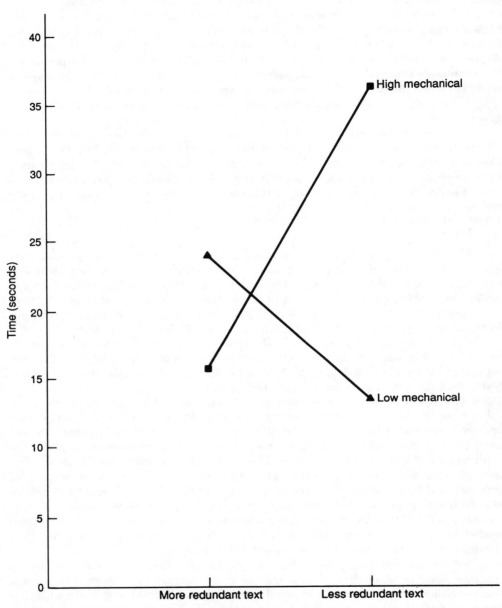

FIGURE 23.8   The graph shows the time subjects of high or low mechanical ability spent inspecting a diagram, depending on whether the text was more or less redundant with the diagram. Low-mechanical-ability subjects are directed by the text, so that if the text refers to the diagram less, they look at the diagram less. High-mechanical-ability subjects can compensate for deficiencies in the text, so if the text provides less information, they can rely more on the diagram (from Hegarty & Just, 1989).

Brunner, & Donais, 1977). In contrast, other studies found negative effects of realism on learning for low-ability subjects (Parkhurst & Dwyer, 1983). In Parkhurst and Dwyer's study, undergraduates were given diagrams of the heart, ranging from realistic pictures to line drawings, as part of a programmed instruction study. The realism of the pictures helped high-IQ students but hindered low-IQ students. A similar conclusion was reached in a study in which field dependence was the individual difference measure differentiating the two groups of students (Canelos, Taylor, & Gates, 1980). These results may again reflect low-ability subjects' inability to differentiate relevant from irrelevant information.

Another reason why low-ability subjects might have more difficulty extracting information from a detailed diagram is that they might encode diagrams in terms of smaller chunks of information (Chase & Simon, 1973; de Groot, 1965, 1966). An individual who is mechanically knowledgeable might encode a mechanical diagram in larger chunks of information. For example, a pulley system might be coded in units that include multiple components, while low-scoring subjects encode pulley systems in terms of their elementary components (Hegarty, Just, & Morrison, 1988). The expertise literature therefore leads to the prediction that high-ability subjects will encode more information and more relevant information, and so might benefit from realistic diagrams more than low-ability subjects.

In sum, readers can augment the representations that they construct from technical texts by encoding additional information from diagrams. Some knowledge of the subject domain may be necessary for a reader to differentiate the relevant from the irrelevant information in a diagram and thus to be able to abstract information from a diagram without direction from an accompanying text.

The Role of Animated Displays in Comprehension

In the previous sections, we have focused on the role that static diagrams play in the comprehension of technical information. Movement and the interrelation among moving components was not a primary aspect of the systems that have been the focus of this research. However, movement can be a central feature of various mechanical or biological systems—for example, it is central to the function of the circulatory system; and in physics, the analysis of movement is a large domain that has its own name, *kinematics*. The comprehension of concepts involving movement can be seen as involving *mental animation*—that is, the internal representation of motion. Such topics provide an opportunity to analyze a different kind of display—namely, an animated display and its role in text comprehension. Another reason to examine this area is that recent technological advances in computer animation have made it much easier to generate and display animation, so that it is now possible to examine the processes in standard laboratory settings.

We have recently begun a series of studies on the interplay between the text and diagram, contrasting certain types of animated displays to the processing that occurs with static displays (Carpenter, Just, & Fallside, 1988; Fallside, 1988). An intuitive feel for the comprehension processes of interest can be gained by inspecting the device in Figure 23.9, called a ratchet device, and reading the description of the device.

In addition to representing structural information, a crucial part of understanding this device is representing the motions of the various components. For example, when examining the ratchet, some people report imaging what happens to the upper bar in the ratchet device when the handle is pulled. Such actions occur at the *joints*, where one component meshes with another; the comprehension process often involves mentally animating that joint. However, it is insufficient to understand individual compo-

This machine makes a gear wheel turn when the handle is pumped. The machine consists of a handle linked by a system of levers and bars to the gear wheel. When the handle is pulled, the upper bar turns the gear while the tooth in the lower bar slides over the gear teeth. When the handle is pushed, the lower bar turns the gear while the tooth on the upper bar slides over the gear teeth.

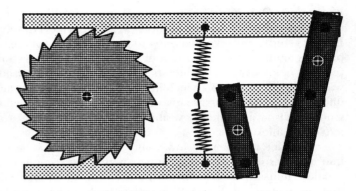

FIGURE 23.9   An example of the text and accompanying diagram used to analyze how readers process kinematic descriptions. In this case, the diagram is static; in some conditions, the readers were able to animate all or part of the display presented on a computer-controlled screen (from Carpenter, Just, & Fallside, 1988).

nents or joints. Rather, the reader must construct an integrated representation of the device. This might be done by tracing through a sequence of components starting at the input force and going through to the output; this sequence will be referred to as a *line of action*. For example, the ratchet device has two lines of action. One line of action is determined by the handle's connection to the upper bar and from there, to the gear. The second line is a "lower route" that goes through the small levers and lower bar to the gear. The diagram and description are prototypical of the materials used to study the role of animation. The passages were patterned after the descriptions found in magazines such as *Popular Mechanics* or typical self-help manuals designed for the interested layman. In some cases, the diagram is static (as it is in Figure 23.9). In other cases, the subject can press a button and the whole device (or some subset of its parts) is animated on the screen.

The major focus of the research was the role played by the text and the diagram in the understanding process. In an eye-fixation study, we contrasted the role of static and animated diagrams in understanding mechanical devices. After reading a description such as the one in Figure 23.9, the subjects were given questions that probed for information that was either in the text or had to be inferred from the diagram, using the text. The devices are somewhat more complex than simple machines and so some knowledge might be needed to know how to trace the lines of action in a diagram. Indeed, we found that subjects who were more mechanically knowledgeable spent more time on the diagram (about 40 seconds) than the less-knowledgeable subjects, who averaged about 35 seconds. Both high- and low-ability subjects inspected an animated display longer than a static diagram. Correspondingly, the high-ability subjects spent less time on the text (about 35 seconds) than the low-ability subjects (about 45 seconds). Thus, here is a case in which the expertise of the more mechanically able subjects permitted them to encode more information directly from the display.

There were also differences in their comprehension scores. The subjects who scored high on a test of mechanical ability were able to use the static diagram to answer about 60 percent of the questions concerning the motions and interactions among the mechanical components. By contrast, low-ability subjects who were given a static diagram performed very poorly, answering only 18 percent of those questions. However, when the low-ability group read a description accompanied by an animated display, their performance was greatly improved; they could answer 40 percent of the questions about the device's motion. Thus, the animated display helped the low-ability subjects to correctly encode motions that they were unable to infer based on the information in the static diagram. Finally, the high- and low-ability readers differed much less on questions that probed for information that was in the text. In sum, animated displays help ameliorate the spatial and mechanical processes that appear to be a bottleneck for lower-ability subjects who are trying to understand descriptions about interacting mechanical devices.

Another set of studies addressed how the text might guide the interpretation of a mechanical diagram. Our initial hypothesis was that the text could improve comprehension by pointing out a line of action and instructing the reader to mentally trace the mechanical interactions of the joints along the line of action. Thus, the major instructional manipulation was whether instructions directed the reader to trace through the lines of action (the Directed condition) or whether it was a more standard text (the Normal condition). In one experiment, we asked subjects to talk aloud as they were processing the text and diagram. To our surprise, the instruction to trace through a line of action, by itself, did not lessen the difference between the two groups. The high-ability subjects continued to perform much better than low-ability subjects on a comprehension test.

An analysis of what the readers said while reading the text and looking at the diagram revealed that low-mechanical subjects had difficulty imagining the action at a joint in the device. Consequently, in a further experiment, we used a display that could be used to show an animation of the movement of two components and their shared joint. We hypothesized it would be less effortful and more accurate to perceptually encode the motion of mechanical components, rather than internally generate the animation. The ability to perceive a joint in its animated condition at the appropriate point in a test did compensate for much (but not all) of the differences in mechanical knowledge. However, the low-mechanical-ability subjects required guidance from the text. If they were simply free to peruse a display that was entirely animated, they did not show the same improvement in comprehension. Thus, the difficulty is not simply spatial ability but using the spatial information in the service of constructing an integrated representation of the mechanical device. This is the beginning of an analysis of the role of animated displays in text comprehension. Nevertheless, it suggests that animation and other types of specialized displays may ameliorate some of the difficulties experienced by individuals who lack specific domain knowledge. These displays could have important instructional applications in technical and scientific domains.

A Model of Coordinating Text and Diagram Processing

The empirical studies reported here point to the multiplicity of processes involved in processing text accompanied by diagrams. At least for individuals who have relatively little domain knowledge, it appears that the comprehension process is driven by the text itself. The text may be necessary to direct the reader's attention to the particular part of the diagram, and it may provide crucial information concerning the interpretation of the diagram. Finally, the state of the subject's working memory—that is, the information that is activated from the text—plays a large role in determining both when the diagram is fixated and what is fixated. But clearly the nature of the display itself has an important role in the comprehension process. In several cases, the presence of the diagram, in conjunction with the text, has large effects on understanding. Moreover, the character-ization of the diagram-inspection process as being text directed arises partially from our focus on lower-ability subjects or younger students. Experts in a domain may already know the conventions for interpreting a diagram; and hence, they are more free to choose the medium that best suits their particular reading goals.

Individual differences clearly modulate the comprehension process at several points. For example, spatial ability could affect the difficulty of forming a representation from a verbal statement in the text. The reader's verbal skill could influence his or her tendency to rely on diagrams for information, particularly if the diagram uses only more-familiar conventions. In addition, a subject's expertise can affect when his or her temporary memory buffer is full, because more-expert subjects encode information in larger chunks. Individual differences can also affect the extent to which diagram inspections can fulfill their goal. The ability to integrate the representations of clauses presented in different parts of the text is limited by expertise and the subject's reading ability. Finally, the ability to encode new information from a diagram is also related to the reader's expertise.

The fact that such a large variety of types of diagrams are used in scientific and technical texts suggests that diagrams are a particularly suitable means of conveying scientific and technical information. Some scientists (Ferguson, 1977; Shepard, 1978; Smith, 1964) have gone beyond this to claim that visual and spatial representations are essential to scientific thought. The literature reviewed in this chapter suggests that diagrams can be effective in instruction because they provide the reader with spatial representations that are often difficult to derive from text, because they enable the reader to reorganize information in new ways, and because they can provide additional information to the text. However, the optimal medium for communicating scientific information also depends on the skills of the reader. A diagram may be most useful if the reader has the knowledge necessary to extract the relevant information from the diagram and if the topic is sufficiently complex that the reader cannot visualize spatial representations of the information without a diagram.

The emphasis in this chapter and in the literature has been on the processing of texts accompanied by iconic diagrams. Compared to graphs and schematic diagrams, we might expect iconic diagrams to be relatively easy to interpret because they depict the appearance of the objects that they signify. Yet we have found that even iconic diagrams are dependent on knowledge of the subject matter or on the text itself for their interpretation. Background knowledge or an accompanying text may be even more important in guiding comprehension of schematic diagrams and graphs.

In the first section of this chapter we reviewed the variety of ways in which diagrams use space to convey information. Compared to this variety, the empirical studies have focused on only a small section of the space of possible diagrams that can accompany technical text. We have presented the beginnings of a theory of how technical texts are understood. There are numerous remaining issues, such as how comprehension processes differ for different types of diagrams, the precise causes of individual differences in comprehending text and diagrams, and the specification of the optimal medium of communication for different types of information.

REFERENCES

Baird, J. C. (1970). *Psychophysical analysis of visual space*. Oxford, Eng.: Pergamon Press.

Baylor, G. (1971). *A treatise on the mind's eye: An empirical investigation of visual mental imagery*. Doctoral dissertation. Carnegie Mellon University, Pittsburgh.

Bennett, G. K. (1969). *Bennett mechanical comprehension test*. New York: Psychological Corporation.

Bertin, J. (1983). *Semiology of graphics*. Madison: University of Wisconsin Press.

Biederman, I., Rabinowitz, J. C., Glass, A. L., & Stacy, E. W. (1974). On the information extracted from a glance at a scene. *Journal of Experimental Psychology, 103*, 597–600.

Bieger, G. R., & Glock, M. D. (1982). *Comprehension of spatial and contextual information in pictures and text* (Tech. Rep. No. 6). Department of Education, Cornell University.

Bureau of Naval Personnel. (1971). *Basic machines and how they work*. New York: Dover.

Canelos, J. J., Taylor, W. D., & Gates, G. B. (1980). The effects of three levels of visual complexity on the information processing of field dependents and field independents when acquiring information for performance of three types of instructional objectives. *Journal of Instructional Psychology, 7*, 65–70.

Carpenter, P. A., & Just, M. A. (1986). Spatial ability: An information-processing approach to psychometrics. In R. Sternberg (Ed.), *Advances in the psychology of human intelligence* (Vol. 3, pp. 221–253). Hillsdale, NJ: Erlbaum.

Carpenter, P. A., & Just, M. A. (1989). The role of working memory in language comprehension. In D. Klahr & K. Kotovsky (Eds.), *Complex information processing: The impact of Herbert A. Simon* (pp. 31–68). Hillsdale, NJ: Erlbaum.

Carpenter, P. A., Just, M. A., & Fallside, D. C. (1988). *The role of animation in understanding descriptions of kinematics*. Pittsburgh: Carnegie Mellon University.

Chase, W. G., & Simon, H. A. (1973). Perception in chess. *Cognitive Psychology, 4*, 55–81.

Daneman, M., & Carpenter, P. A. (1980). Individual differences in working memory and reading. *Journal of Verbal Learning and Verbal Behavior, 19*, 450–466.

Daneman, M., & Carpenter, P. A. (1983). Individual differences in integrating information between and within sentences. *Journal of Experimental Psychology: Learning, Memory and Cognition, 9*, 561–584.

de Groot, A. (1965). *Thought and choice in chess*. The Hague: Mouton.

de Groot, A. (1966). Perception and memory versus thought: Some old ideas and recent findings. In B. Kleinmuntz (Ed.). *Problem solving* (pp. 19–50). New York: Wiley.

Fallside, D. C. (1988). *Understanding machines in motion*. Unpublished doctoral dissertation. Carnegie, Mellon University, Pittsburgh.

Ferguson, E. S. (1977). The mind's eye: Nonverbal thought in technology. *Science, 197* (4306), 827–836.

Genzer, I., & Youngner, P. (1969). *Physics*. Morristown, NJ: Silver Burdett Co.

Gregory, R. L. (1970). *The intelligent eye*. New York: McGraw-Hill.

Hegarty, M. (1988). *Comprehension of diagrams accompanied by text*. Unpublished doctoral dissertation, Carnegie Mellon University, Pittsburgh.

Hegarty, M., & Just, M. A. (1989). Understanding machines from text and diagrams. In H. Mandl & J. Levin (Eds.) *Knowledge acquisition from text and picture* (pp. 171–194). Amsterdam: North-Holland.

Hegarty, M., Just, M. A. & Morrison, I. R. (1988). Mental models of mechanical systems: Individual differences in qualitative and quantitative reasoning. *Cognitive Psychology, 20*, 191–236.

Hilgard, E. R., Atkinson, R. L., & Atkinson, R. C. (1979). *Introduction to psychology* (7th ed.) New York: Harcourt Brace Jovanovich.

Holliday, W. G. (1976). Teaching verbal chains using flow diagrams and texts. *Audio-Visual Communication Review, 24*, 63–78.

Holliday, W. G., Brunner, L. L., & Donais, E. L. (1977). Differential cognitive and affective responses to flow diagrams in science. *Journal of Research in Science Teaching, 14*, 129–138.

Just, M. A., & Carpenter, P. A. (1980). A theory of reading: From eye fixations to comprehension. *Psychological Review, 87*, 329–354.

Just, M. A., & Carpenter, P. A. (1985). Cognitive coordinate systems: Accounts of mental rotation and individual differences in spatial ability. *Psychological Review, 92*, 137–172.

Just, M. A., & Carpenter, P. A. (1987). *The psychology of reading and language comprehension*. Newton, MA: Allyn & Bacon.

Kimball, J. W. (1965). *Biology*. Palo Alto, CA: Addison-Wesley.

Kintsch, W., & van Dijk, T. A. (1978). Toward a model of text comprehension and production. *Psychological Review, 85*, 363–394.

Koran, M. L., & Koran, J. (1980). Interaction of learner characteristics with pictorial adjuncts in learning from science text. *Journal of Research in Science Teaching, 17*, 477–483.

Kosslyn, S. M. (1980). *Image and mind*. Cambridge, MA: Harvard University Press.

Larkin, J. H., & Simon, H. A. (1987). Why a diagram is (sometimes) worth ten thousand words. *Cognitive Science, 11*, 65–99.

Levie, W. H. (1987). Research on pictures: A guide to the literature. In D. M. Willows & H. A. Houghton (Eds.). *The psychology of illustration* (pp. 1–50). New York: Springer-Verlag.

Loftus, G. R. (1981). Tachistoscopic simulations of eye fixations on pictures. *Journal of Experimental Psychology, 7*, 369–376.

Macdonald-Ross, M. (1977). Graphics in texts. *Review of Research in Education, 5*, 49–85.

Macdonald-Ross, M., & Smith, E. (1977). *Graphics in text: A bibliography*. Milton Keynes, Eng.: Open University, Institute of Educational Technology.

McCornick, W. W. (1969). *Fundamentals of university physics*. Toronto, Ontario: Macmillan.

McGee, M. G. (1979). Human spatial abilities: Psychometric studies and environmental, genetic, hormonal, and neurological influences. *Psychological Bulletin, 86*, 889–918.

Mayer, R. E. (1983). Can you repeat that? Qualitative effects of repetition and advance organizers on learning from science prose. *Journal of Educational Psychology, 75,* 40–49.

Mayer, R. E. (in press). Systematic thinking fostered by illustrations in scientific text. *Journal of Educational Psychology.*

Mayer, R. E., Dyke, J., & Cook, L. K. (1984). Techniques that help readers build mental models from science text: Definitions, training, and signaling. *Journal of Educational Psychology, 76,* 1089–1105.

Parkhurst, P. E., & Dwyer, F. M. (1983). An experimental assessment of students' IQ and their ability to benefit from visualized instruction. *Journal of Instructional Psychology, 10,* 9–20.

Pearson, P. D., Barr, R., Kamil, M. L., & Mosenthal, P. (Eds.). (1984). *Handbook of reading research* (Vol. 1). White Plains, NY: Longman.

Playfair, W. (1801). *The statistical breviary.* London: Corry.

Shepard, R. N. (1978). Externalization of mental images and the act of creation. In B. S. Randhava & W. E. Coffman (Eds.), *Visual learning, thinking, and communication.* New York: Academic Press.

Shepard, R. N., & Metzler, J. (1971). Mental rotation of three-dimensional objects. *Science, 171,* 701–703.

Smith, I. M. (1964). *Spatial ability: Its educational and social significance.* London: University of London Press.

Tufte, E. R. (1983). *The visual display of quantitative information.* Cheshire, CT: Graphics Press.

van Dijk, T. A., & Kintsch, W. (1983). *Strategies of discourse comprehension.* New York: Academic Press.

Whalley, P. C., & Fleming, R. W. (1975). An experiment with a simple recorder of reading behaviour. *Programmed Learning and Educational Technology, 12,* 120–123.

Winn, W. D. (1987). Charts, graphs, and diagrams in educational materials. In D. M. Willows & H. A. Houghton (Eds.), *The psychology of illustration* (pp. 152–198). New York: Springer-Verlag.

Yuille, J. C., & Steiger, J. H. (1982). Nonholistic processing in mental rotation: Some suggestive evidence. *Perception & Psychophysics, 31,* 201–209.

24 BASIC LITERACY SKILLS IN THE WORKPLACE

Larry Mikulecky and Rad Drew

A large and growing amount of literacy activity in developed nations occurs in the workplace. By the late 1970s, survey research of adult reading habits had established that most American adults spent more time reading and writing in the workplace than they did anywhere else (Murphy, 1975; Mikulecky, Shanklin, & Caverly, 1979). Since a majority of adult reading is performed upon workplace-related material, the nature, difficulty, and prevalence of these functional reading tasks is particularly important to understanding the reading demands encountered by adults and their abilities to meet such demands.

WHAT IS BASIC TO FUNCTIONAL LITERACY IN THE WORKPLACE?

Most attempts to define literacy or establish a criterion for what is basic functional literacy tend to become muddled. Part of the explanation for this muddled situation is that literacy is not easily defined. In a recent paper for the U.S. Office of Educational Research and Improvement, Valentine (1986) addressed issues central to definitions of literacy. He pointed out that much of the confusion derives from the fact that there is little agreement on what skills comprise literacy. For example, one unresolved question is which clusters of skills comprising reading and writing are essential.

One can sidestep the issue of what skills comprise reading and writing and simply look at materials that people are able or unable to read and write. This, however, creates another problem of definition: Literacy means being able to read and write which materials? Bormuth (1975) suggested that the list of materials will always differ from person to person and situation to situation, and therefore offered the definition of literacy as "the ability to respond competently to real-world reading tasks" (p. 65). Guthrie (1983) expanded on this idea by noting that the "reader's literacy depends on the context of the situation, not on a specific achievement level" (p. 669).

Some writers have focused on specialized forms of literacy. Sticht (1975) differentiated externally imposed literacy tasks from internally imposed tasks and defined functional literacy as

> the possession of those literacy skills needed to perform some reading task *imposed by an external agent* between the reader and a goal the reader wishes to obtain. (pp. 4–5).

Such definitions create new problems. Kirsch and Guthrie (1977–1978) pointed out that reading the same material (i.e., a newsmagazine) is functional for some people and leisure reading for others. Valentine (1986) suggested functional literacy is the area of overlap between print literacy and functional tasks. Presumably job literacy would be the overlap between print literacy and the myriad of functional tasks apparent in jobs ranging from forklift driver to surgeon. Valentine left it to others to define exactly what comprises print literacy.

Rush, Moe, and Storlie (1986) referred to *occupational literacy*, which they defined as "the ability to competently read required, work-related materials." They further note that

> . . . by definition, functional literacy varies according to individual demands of divergent roles, settings and materials. Occupational literacy competencies comprise a subset of functional literacy. Required competencies vary from occupation to occupation and from job to job within occupations. (p. 1)

A good deal of research on the difficulty levels of workplace reading material has suggested that the difficulty level of running prose (i.e., memos, manuals, correspondence, and so on) averages high school difficulty levels (Mikulecky, 1982; Sticht & Mikulecky, 1984; Rush, Moe, & Storlie, 1986). Since a good deal of workplace reading material is not running prose, however, using such grade-level indicators is somewhat problematic.

The problem of establishing a sensible grade-level indicator becomes even more problematic when the role of reader background is considered. Some workers can competently read work-related material that averages one to two grade levels above the difficulty levels of the general newspaperlike material that they successfully comprehend (Diehl & Mikulecky, 1980; Mikulecky 1982). The authors attributed this seeming higher ability with work reading to familiarity with the topic and format of job-related material. Sticht et al. (1986) presented military data that indicate a range of four grade levels of tested reading ability between the reading abilities required for job-related reading by highly experienced workers and workers with no experience on the reading topic. This suggests that background knowledge can account for up to four grade levels of reading ability with a given topic and print format. Grade-level definitions of literacy levels are particularly ineffective as readers' background knowledge increases.

Mosenthal and Kirsch (1987) pointed out another difficulty in using a simple grade level as an indicator of material difficulty. Their analysis of errors made by adults in the National Assessment of Educational Progress (NAEP) Adult Functional Literacy study reveals a pattern in errors. Reading difficulty can, to a degree, predict whether mistakes will be made. Mosenthal and Kirsch found information-processing demands to be an even better predictor of mistakes made on the NAEP study, however. The number of columns needing to be scanned, the pieces of information needing to be stored in memory, and the processing steps needed to locate and use information were better predictors of functional literacy task difficulty than were more traditional indicators of reading difficulty such as complexity of materials.

LITERACY DEMANDS IN THE WORKPLACE
AND WORKPLACE TRAINING

Two decades of civilian and military research have documented and examined the range of literacy demands in the workplace. Though there are a small and shrinking number of jobs requiring little or no literacy, the amount and complexity of literacy demands appears to be increasing in most sectors of the workplace.

Workplace Literacy Demands

Research has revealed that reading, writing, and computation in the workplace is ubiquitous and at a relatively high level. Diehl and Mikulecky (1980) examined 100 workers for a representative cross-section of occupations ranging from executive vice president to forklift driver. Only two percent of the occupations examined required no reading or writing. Time spent reading print, charts, graphs, and computer terminals averaged nearly two hours daily. Difficulty levels of 70 percent of the running prose reading materials on the job ranged from ninth- to twelfth-grade levels. This finding also concurs with the work of Rush, Moe, and Storlie (1986). In addition, Sticht (1982) reported similar reading times and difficulty levels for military jobs and reading materials. Mikulecky (1982), in a comparison study of school and workplace literacy demands, found high school juniors spent less time reading, including time spent doing homework, than all categories of workers except blue-collar workers. In addition, the difficulty levels of work materials were generally as difficult or more difficult than high school materials.

In addition to their inability to deal with fairly difficult on-the-job reading materials and training materials, many high school students are unprepared for how literacy skills are used in the workplace. Most workplace reading, writing, and computation is done to accomplish tasks and make assessments. Rather than reading from a single text, workers must gather information from several sources to solve problems, provide services, and perform tasks. Research by Mikulecky and Winchester (1983) and Mikulecky and Ehlinger (1986) provided evidence of a strong relationship between higher-level metacognitive and problem-solving reading abilities and job performance across differing occupations. The ability to set purposes, self-question, summarize information, monitor comprehension, and make useful notes distinguishes superior job performers from merely adequate job performers.

An examination of workplace literacy surveys and analyses (Diehl & Mikulecky, 1980; Heath, 1980; Jacobs, 1982; Kirsch & Guthrie, 1984; Mikulecky, 1982; Mikulecky & Winchester, 1983; Mikulecky & Ehlinger, 1986; Miller, 1982; Rush, Moe, & Storlie, 1986; Sticht, 1975, 1982) produces several generalizations about the nature of literacy in the workplace.

> Most jobs call for literacy and computation (Diehl & Mikulecky, 1980; Mikulecky, 1982; Rush, Moe, & Storlie, 1986).
>
> Workers use a variety of materials while high school students usually do not (Mikulecky, 1982).
>
> Literacy and computation on the job are necessary for performing tasks (Mikulecky, 1982; Mikulecky & Ehlinger, 1986; Rush, Moe, & Storlie, 1986; Sticht, 1982).
>
> Workplace literacy and computation are often social phenomena involving asking questions and gathering some information from other workers (Heath, 1980; Jacobs, 1982; Mikulecky, 1982; Mikulecky & Ehlinger, 1986; Mikulecky & Winchester, 1983).
>
> Workplace literacy calls for regular use of higher-level application and metacognitive reading skills (i.e., setting purposes, self-questioning, summarizing, and monitoring), while school reading is predominantly fact gathering (Guthrie, 1988; Mikulecky & Ehlinger, 1986; Mikulecky & Winchester, 1983).
>
> The majority of workplace literacy is reading-to-do, as opposed to textbook reading-to-learn (Miller, 1982; Mikulecky, 1982; Sticht, 1982).

The results of the above research reflect the increased level of literacy demands in both training and the workplace. This is true both of existing jobs and of new jobs created as the work world changes and expands.

Literacy Demands of Job Training

Though workplace literacy demands are high, the literacy demands of vocational training are even higher. Mikulecky (1982), Rush, Moe, and Storlie (1986), and Sticht (1975) found that reading was a daily requirement of students in training courses and in the workplace. Mikulecky (1982) found that students in job-training programs actually spent more time reading texts and manuals than did high school juniors (135 minutes daily versus 97 minutes daily).

Rush, Moe, and Storlie (1986) studied training program courses for 10 occupations. They found that student reading time ranged from 42 minutes to six hours per day, depending on the occupation. They also found that students in training programs used primarily reading-to-learn strategies, and that textbooks, reference books, and sets of complex instructions were part of the daily required reading. Students often encountered information in book-length and graphic formats as well as shorter materials (e.g., quizzes, instruction sets, chalkboard notes) in combinations of text and graphic formats in the classroom and laboratory.

In addition, Rush, Moe, and Storlie observed that the reading requirements were varied and ranged from informal notes in the classroom to highly technical prose in textbooks. Specialized vocabulary—both true technical words and common words with special occupational meanings—was present in reading materials and was encountered in each of these types of reading. Rush, Moe, and Storlie also studied job-training materials to see how easily understood or readable they were. Readability formulas indicated that training materials ranged in difficulty from eighth-grade to college-graduate level. The authors pointed out that the high reading levels of materials are an additional demand on the learner, but that they are sometimes partially offset by the students' interest, motivation and familiarity with a given subject matter.

Given the amount of reading required in both training and work settings, and the highly demanding printed material that students are required to read, it is clear that an individual's success in the classroom and the workplace is dependent, in part, on an ability to read and apply information obtained from complex textual and graphic materials. More than the ability to simply read for facts is required both of workers and of students in training programs. Literacy skills in vocational training and work settings include reading to solve problems and make judgments.

LITERACY SKILLS DEMANDS HAVE BEEN INCREASING WITH SOME EXCEPTIONS

Each major war during this century has brought with it increased literacy demands for military performance. During World War II, the U.S. Army found it necessary to set a minimum criterion of a fourth-grade reading level for acceptance into the Army. A special 1947 census defined literacy as five years of schooling and found 13.5 percent of the population illiterate. By the 1960s, the U.S. Office of Education had raised the level of acceptable literacy to eight years of schooling. Even this level was considered too low in the 1970s, when the Adult Performance Level study was released (Cook, 1977).

During the early 1980s, a survey of citizens in Milwaukee reported the type of materials residents considered essential to normal functioning (Negin & Krugler, 1980).

These materials provide a reasonable idea of what current functional literacy means to a cross-section of adults. Though these materials were not specific to the workplace, the difficulty level of materials outside the workplace tends to reflect the difficulty levels of those in the workplace. Frequently mentioned materials in the Milwaukee study ranged from relatively simple items such as street and traffic signs and medicine bottle directions to more complex items such as bank statements, health and safety pamphlets, loan applications, and product-warning and antidote directions. Difficulty levels of the more complex safety instructions and economic statements were at the twelfth-grade level and higher (Negin & Krugler, 1980).

Current estimates of occupational demands for literacy indicate that over 90 percent of occupations call for some reading and writing (Diehl & Mikulecky, 1980; Mikulecky, 1982). This is up from not more than 10 percent in the first decennial census undertaken in 1790 (Tyler, 1978).

The difficulty levels of occupational reading are quite high. Nearly every civilian and military study cited above indicates levels at the high school level or above. Even blue-collar workers average more than one and one-half hours of daily job reading. Though having a wealth of background knowledge on a topic can effectively lower reading difficulty levels, the heaviest job-related reading is performed by new workers learning new jobs (Kern, 1985). New workers are the least likely to have a wealth of background experience. This expectation of demanding reading for new workers is a dramatic change from earlier times, when one out of 10 workers performed the literacy tasks for others.

Fields, Hull, and Sechler (1987) used a case study approach to study seven industry-based literacy training programs. Two training manager observations from these case studies graphically capture the impact of these literacy changes for low- and middle-level workers. In describing changes for low-level workers, a training manager observed

> Materials handlers are the guys that pick up boxes and move them from here to over there. Twenty-five years ago . . . you hired people with muscles. . . . All you needed to do was lift . . . and be honest. Easy to hire. Now those guys—same guys, same job grade, same badges, muscles are a little weaker—sit in chairs and run computers that monitor automated warehouses. And they keep real-time inventories; they do real-time quality control. . . . And they've got a much more important role in the management of the operation intellectually than they ever did. . . . And that's what's happening all across jobs. Grunt jobs are turning into head jobs. (p. 35)

The increased literacy demands have an impact well beyond the "grunt" jobs described by the first trainer. A second trainer notes that the same phenomenon occurs with middle-level jobs.

> This is a whole group of people who in the past thirty years have made it into the working middle class with only marginal cognitive skills. Their inferencing is weak, their generalization is weak. Those are reading skills the new jobs call [for]. You have to be able to read data, synthesize it, and predict trends. . . . The general education course in the 1950s . . . did not give [them] an adequate base for the kind of work that is done in the workplace today. (p. 36)

There are a few exceptions to the general trend of higher literacy requirements in the workplace. For example, some low-paying jobs can be simplified through fragmentation and automation. In West Germany, cost-effectiveness has resulted by breaking down complex tasks to simple tasks done repeatedly by an individual worker. This method is not as cost effective as having a worker who is literate and can adjust flexibly to new tasks when the operation for which he or she has been trained is temporarily halted. However, fragmentation can be cost effective if the worker is paid an extremely low wage, as are the immigrant "guest workers" in West German industries.

In the United States, where no legal guest-worker option exists, fragmented jobs tend to be shipped out of the country, leaving Americans with low literacy abilities without employment. Some fast-food chains in the United States have eliminated the need for much literacy among employees by using pictures on cash-register keys and computerized pricing. A trained manager must be knowledgeable and available in the event of equipment difficulties, but the system works as long as less-capable workers can accept extremely low pay for their severely limited performances. Similar approaches are being used in the automating of oil pipeline monitoring gauges and holographic package readers in grocery stores. The grocery store example is useful for examining this low-skill job trend. Fewer mistakes and hold-ups mean faster lines and, therefore, the need for fewer low-paid check-out personnel and packaging personnel to run and check prices. Computerized inventories also lower the need for massive warehousing and many of the warehouse jobs associated with such operations. Several middle-skill-level jobs have been created for building, marketing, and servicing the holographic price readers (Harste & Mikulecky, 1984).

Problems Related to High Literacy Skill Demands

In the early 1980s, there were several indications from industry that the educational levels of new and existing workers were inadequate. According to a Center for Public Resources survey (Henry & Raymond, 1982),

> over 65 percent of responding companies note that basic skill deficiencies limit the job advancement of their high school graduate employees, and 73 percent responded that deficiencies inhibit the advancement of nongraduates. (p. 23)

Percentages of basic skills difficulties reported by employers in the survey were the following:

Secretaries having difficulty reading at the level required by the job	30 percent
Managers and supervisors unable to write paragraphs free of mechanical errors	50 percent
Skilled and semiskilled employees, including bookkeepers, unable to use decimals and fractions in math problems	50 percent

The *Wall Street Journal* (Hymowitz, 1981) cited industry reports that indicate increased economic problems resulting from workers who are unable to meet the literacy skills demands of their jobs. William Barnes, Vice President of Finance of JLG Industries, reported that "poorly educated workers are our number-one problem, the main factor slowing our growth" (p. 1). JLG Industries reported having spent over $1 million to correct worker literacy mistakes. Similarly, Mutual of New York reported "an estimated 70 percent of the insurance firm's correspondence must be corrected or retyped at least once." Concerns regarding the safety of workers who cannot read warnings and follow written directions have been issues in a growing number of court cases and have led to several firings at Westinghouse Electric Corporation's defense gear plant in Sunnyvale, California (Hymowitz, 1981).

In many industries, workers with low literacy skills are being replaced. For example, following the lead of the Japanese, U.S. employers in automobile industries have substantially replaced unskilled workers with robots. In 1981, General Motors reported one skilled worker for every 5.6 assembly-line workers (Hymowitz, 1981). By late in the decade, General Motors was approaching its goal of a one-to-one ratio of skilled and nonskilled workers (i.e., an 80 percent reduction in nonskilled positions).

THE CHANGING NATURE OF WORK

One indication of the changes in literacy skills required to participate in society is the changing nature of work in the United States and other industrialized countries. As new jobs are created and old jobs disappear, new levels and types of literacy skills for employment are also created. In addition, the occupational mix within industries also changes. For example, in *Workforce 2000*, Johnston and Packer (1987) reported that the insurance industry requires far more accountants and lawyers and many fewer cashiers. Industry employs more scientists and engineers and fewer tool and die makers. Professional, managerial, sales, and service jobs have far outstripped opportunities in other fields, while jobs as machine tenders, assemblers, miners, and farmers have actually declined.

Low-literacy-skill jobs are decreasing in availability. In addition, many other nonskilled production jobs are being moved off-continent, where nonskilled workers perform tasks for considerably lower salaries than do Americans. Johnston and Packer (1987) have analyzed the language, reasoning, and mathematics skills ratings of jobs in decline and jobs on the increase. They reported that

> . . . only four percent of the new jobs can be filled by individuals with the lowest levels of skills, compared to 9 percent of jobs requiring such low skills today. At the other end of the scale, 41 percent of the new jobs will require skills ranked in one of the top three categories compared with only 24 percent that require such proficiency at present. (p. 99)

These projections indicate that it will be increasingly difficult for workers to find adequate employment in jobs that require a low level of literacy skills. In addition, a significant percentage of existing middle-level workers will need to increase their skills as their jobs change or increase in difficulty.

U.S. Department of Labor data do not suggest that all new jobs will involve high technology, such as lasers or robots, and call for years of specialized training. Rumberger (1984a, 1984b) reported that the greatest number of new jobs are unrelated to high technology. Between 1978 and 1990, the United States will have needed 672,000 new janitors and sextons but only 199,000 new computer systems analysts. These janitorial positions, however, usually require the ability to read manuals, manage the directions on chemical solvents, handle new equipment, and do a good deal more than simply sweep floors.

Though years of training will not be required for all new jobs, it is likely that higher minimum levels of literacy skills will be required. The growing service industries require a good deal more paperwork and regular managing of information to solve problems than did higher-paying "muscle work" production industries.

This is some disagreement about which skills will be needed in the future. For example, Rumberger (1984b) has suggested that there is no evidence to support the "myth" that high technology will be the primary source of new jobs in our economy in the future. Instead, he contends that most new jobs will not be in high-technology fields in the future economy, and technology will not require a vast upgrading of workers' skills, because the primary impact of technology will be to reduce the skill requirements of jobs.

Others (Mikulecky, 1987; Rush, Moe, & Storlie, 1986; Sticht & Mikulecky, 1984) have maintained that though it is true that high-tech jobs will make up only a small percentage of future jobs, jobs that have traditionally required minimal basic skills are becoming more complex, demanding higher-level reading, writing, and computational skills. Some jobs will show a decrease in skill requirements, but most jobs will move from low-skill to middle-skill levels.

RELATIONSHIP OF LITERACY SKILLS TO JOB PERFORMANCE

An underlying assumption behind concern about literacy-skill levels in the workplace is that job performance is related to workers' literacy-skill levels. The research (Mikulecky & Ehlinger, 1986; Sticht, 1975) suggests that there is a relationship but that it is by no means overwhelming or direct.

Most research about the relationship of literacy to job performance is sketchy and based upon information obtained from military studies. Kulp (1974), in a controlled study, found that performance of an assembly task decreased significantly when worker reading skills were more than two grade levels below the difficulty level of instructions.

Sticht (1975), in *Reading for Working*, reported correlations of reading ability to job sample performance that range from $r = .26$ to $r = .37$. These correlations are significant but explain only from 8 percent to 13 percent of the job performance variance. A good deal more than basic reading ability as measured by a reading test is needed to explain job performance ability. Sticht's (1982) review of basic skills training in the military noted that

> the most highly skilled, non-high school graduates in one study had a job success rate equal to those having the lowest basic skill levels among high school graduates. Thus basic skills competence per se does not appear to be the overriding determinant of success in the military. (p. vii)

As one would expect, the degree of correlation between literacy and cognitive measures and job performance varies somewhat from occupation area to occupation area. The U.S. Department of Defense (1984), in comparing job performance to performance on the *Armed Services Vocational Aptitude Battery*, notes the following correlation ranges:

.36 to .52 for jobs in communications,

.39 to .77 for jobs in data processing, and

.53 to .73 for clerical and supply specialties.

Hunter and Hunter (1984) meta-analyzed the results of hundreds of studies designed to predict job performance and found reading ability to be a significant predictor of job performance. Though Hunter and Hunter did not directly address literacy skills tests, they did include tests of reading ability in the general category of "cognitive measures." Hunter and Hunter claimed that cognitive measures tend to correlate at the $r = .5$ to $r = .6$ level (25 percent to 36 percent shared variance) with job performance.

Literacy and cognitive performance do not totally explain job performance. Even the highest correlations only explain about 50 percent of the variance for job performance. Research does suggest, however, that literacy ability is a better predictor of job performance than many other variables. Hunter and Hunter (1984) found that in every job family without exception, cognitive measures were predictors of job performance superior to measures of either perceptual or motor abilities. Indeed, cognitive measures were more effective predictors of job performance than biographical inventories, biographical interviews, expert recommendation, or amount of previous education.

Some research has attempted to identify how reading abilities interact with job performance. In studies of the relationship between performance and literacy abilities among nurses (Mikulecky & Winchester, 1983) and among electronic technicians (Mikulecky & Ehlinger, 1986), the researchers noted a low-level relationship between simple, literal-level reading ability and job performance. A much higher relationship was noted, however, between job performance and the ability to apply and use reading, writing, and computation skills critically.

Guthrie (1988) analyzed the cognitive strategies involved in the workplace reading task of locating information in documents. His conclusion, based on the results of two task performance studies, was that locating information in documents appears to warrant a unique cognitive process model that is more similar to analytical reasoning than to language processing or visual search. This identification of higher-level use of literacy skills may explain the high relationship between cognitive measures of ability and job performance presented by Hunter and Hunter (1984).

Stedman and Kaestle (1987), in examining the research of Sticht (1975), Mikulecky (1981), and Heath (1980), noted that "severe reading deficiencies would interfere with the ability to acquire and hold many jobs, but above a certain threshold, reading level as measured by standardized tests has little to do with job performance" (p. 39). This conclusion is supported, in part, by Heath's (1980) observation that many workers at lower levels have personnel officers fill out job application forms and are given instructions orally.

The survey by the Center for Public Resources (Henry & Raymond, 1982) takes a different perspective on the role of basic skills and job performance. Survey respondents were not as concerned about overall correlations between general basic skills levels and performance as they were about costly one-time mistakes resulting from low basic skills. Examples cited include workers accidently killed because of an inability to read warning signs, costly mistakes made because of an inability to comprehend correspondence, and time lost due to the need to give regular lectures on the use of equipment as opposed to step-by-step written instructions (p. 18). Low ability levels in applied computation and measurement, according to respondents, regularly accounted for losses in production, quality, and general corporate performance (p. 20).

To summarize, literacy skills do appear to be related to job performance in at least two ways. Reading ability, as indicated by higher-level problem-solving and metacognitive skills, rather than factual-level reading ability, appears to be a significant predictor of overall job performance. In addition, extremely low-level basic skills appear to be related to costly and dangerous mistakes in the workplace. The best workers can communicate and use print to solve problems. The least effective workers do not use print in such ways and may be prone to costly, dangerous errors in situations calling for the use of basic skills.

HOW GENERIC AND TRANSFERABLE
ARE LITERACY SKILLS?

It has been clear for quite some time that increased literacy-skills training is a require-ment of good job training. What has not been as clear is how to most cost-effectively provide such training. During the 1970s and early 1980s, experts had limited knowledge of how to most effectively design programs to incorporate literacy skills into job training. The usual procedure was to send students to remedial programs to get better at reading, computation, and whatever else they needed. The assumption was that once the "basics" had been learned, they could easily transfer to the workplace or vocational training. A major challenge for this approach was determining exactly what was basic. Determining key competencies and devising curricula were thus central tasks. A second line of thought noted that people tended to learn better when the basics were integrated with actual job training, and that "school work" did not seem to transfer very well to actual workplace applications. Researchers even questioned the assumption that there were "generic" transferable skills. Instead, some researchers concluded that people learned what they are taught and not a lot more.

Researchers from each school of thought share the goal of improving the literacy-skills competence of vocational students. Research has begun to accumulate that par-tially supports the assumptions of each position. For example, analysis of the documents and observations of workers from several occupations reveals many seemingly shared skills that cross occupational lines (Greenan, 1982; Greenan & Smith, 1981). On the other hand, there appear to be considerable limitations on the degree to which reading learned in one setting can easily be transferred to other settings (e.g., reading a story or a workbook is of little help in reading a manual or following a troubleshooting guide).

Problems of Transfer

Even though it is possible to note similarities across occupational and school settings, researchers have found transfer on the part of learners to be severely limited. They observe that one problem with generalizable skills approach is that skills differ so much from task to task. A skill used one way for one task, may be used differently to complete a similar task in a different job context. For example, Duffy (1985) noted

> To the extent that the newspaper and the job manual have different subject matter (the concepts discussed), different information access or referencing systems, and different writing styles and information display strategies, there will indeed be little transfer. If we consider how the function of graphics differs between a technical manual and a newspaper, we find that strategies one might teach for using graphics to understand (or find information in) a newspaper might even hinder (produce negative transfer) effective use of technical manuals. . . . The point is that reading is not a unitary concept. Transfer from one reading task to another depends on the similarity of the components—the processing require-ments—of the tasks. If instruction in reading the technical manual does not transfer to reading the newspaper, literacy instruction based on the newspaper would probably not transfer to the technical manuals (and reading the technical manuals is, indeed, the goal of the instruction). (pp. 449–450)

Mikulecky and Ehlinger (1986) have also pointed out problems related to skills transfer from classroom to workplace. The differences between job literacy and school literacy may explain, in part, the disturbing phenomena of limited transfer from gains in the general school literacy abilities to comparable gains in the workplace.

Much schooling is based, both consciously and unconsciously, on the assumption that basic learnings and skills easily transfer from one situation to another. In school, student reading is largely limited to a relatively small amount of textbook reading (Mikulecky, 1982; Smith & Feathers, 1983). Only three percent of student writing is as long as a paragraph in length, and the majority of writing is in response to text or worksheet questions (Applebee, 1981). It is generally assumed that students who perform such school literacy activities adequately will transfer their abilities and be prepared for literacy demands outside of school.

Research results on the transferability of training challenge these assumptions, however. For example, military research (Sticht, 1982) indicates that recruits given traditional literacy-skills training make gains while in class but tend to revert and lose their skills within eight weeks. Specific job-related literacy- and computational-skills programs are exceptions to this pattern. For example, Sticht reported that

> personnel retained 80% of their end-of-course gain in job literacy training, and only 40% of their end-of-course gain in general reading. (p. 40)

Most recently Kirsch and Jungeblutt (1986) reported limited correlations between individuals' abilities to read prose, documents, and forms, and read material calling for use of computation. Test scores for these different reading tasks tend to correlate at the $r = .5$ level. This suggests about 25 percent shared variance among tasks. It may indeed be that there is some transfer or generalizability among skills but that it is limited to only about 25 percent. The rest of performance ability may be explained by background knowledge, experience, general intelligence, and a host of other factors, as noted above.

Until more evidence accumulates on the degree of transfer and which skills are generic and to what extent, caution is in order. It is useful to know similarities across occupations, but it is not warranted to assume that observed similarities imply transfer of training. Indeed, the most effective job literacy-training programs (Business Council for Effective Literacy [BCEL], 1987; Mikulecky & Strange, 1986; Sticht & Mikulecky, 1984) appear to integrate literacy-skills training with actual job training, thereby avoiding the risk of mistakenly assuming transfer or mistakenly counting on generic skills.

EFFECTIVE TRAINING PROGRAMS

Fields, Hull, and Sechler (1987) used a case study methodology to examine seven industry-based adult literacy programs. They report that programs established since 1980 are viewed primarily as instruments for achieving the company's advanced technology goals. Involvement is usually voluntary, but persons in need of training were less likely to be considered for promotion and more likely than other workers to be laid off. In nearly every literacy program examined, enrollment increased after the initial cycle, when employees saw the benefits.

A key characteristic of effective workplace literacy programs is a job-oriented approach that employs tasks, materials, and training directly linked to the functional context in the workplace. This increases the likelihood of transfer and continued practice of skills and strategies mastered in training (Sticht & Mikulecky, 1984).

A number of successful basic skills programs in the military employ a job-oriented approach to training personnel. One of the first to apply a functional literacy approach using reading materials found in the workplace was the U.S. Army Functional Literacy Training (FLIT) program, which found occupation-specific approaches using actual job materials to be successful (Sticht, 1975, 1982).

The FLIT program developed materials based on the results of interviews with military personnel, who were asked to identify the reading tasks performed on the job in the last 48 hours. Teaching materials were developed using the tables of contents, indexes, tables and graphs, forms, procedural information, and so on, that were needed to perform on the job. Evaluation data (Sticht, 1982) for more than 700 students showed that

> Students made three times the improvement in job-related reading as in general reading, indicating that they were learning what was being taught.
>
> Students in the FLIT program performed three times better than comparable students in other Army and Air Force programs, indicating that general literacy training does not make as much impact on job-related reading as does job-related reading training.
>
> Retention studies indicated that eight weeks after FLIT training, personnel retained 80 percent of their end-of-course gain in job-related reading but only 40 percent of their end-of-course gain in general reading.
>
> Many students in the FLIT program made little gain and failed to master or even attempt some instructional modules and activities, suggesting the need for a longer period of development for some Army personnel.

Another highly successful military program is the U.S. Navy's Job-Oriented Basic Skills (JOBS) program, the military's first attempt to apply FLIT's functional literacy development principles to basic skills in preparation for highly technical areas. The JOBS objective is to provide instruction "that would enable lower-aptitude personnel to increase their mastery of selected basic skills and knowledge enough to permit them to enter and complete" apprentice-level training (Duffy 1985).

The Army's FLIT curriculum has been described by Duffy as an "exemplary program" (Duffy, 1985) and has been a model for developing other programs in the Navy, Air Force, Marines, and National Guard. An occupation-specific approach has been applied to more highly technical areas, such as the Navy's JOBS program described above. Other programs include the Army's recruit-level lower-literate program, BSEP I and II, as well as its comprehensive basic skills curriculum, JSEP I and II. The Air Force's Job-Oriented Basic Skills Assessment and Enhancement System and the Army's STARS program both have been developed with an occupation-specific approach that requires students to read job-related materials and solve problems in simulated workplaces. STARS employs videodisc technology and makes the learner a member of a space team with a number of tasks to perform. Students are required to read written instructions from notes and warnings on the wall, follow directions, and monitor supplies. Student responses provide assessments of skill levels and branch to the appropriate levels on the video disc.

Other basic skills programs that apply the functional literacy approach to teaching and integrating basic skills have been developed in the public and private sectors (Mikulecky & Strange, 1986; Sticht & Mikulecky, 1984). For example, a joint public-private venture trained CETA-eligible word-processor operators in a program that integrated basic skills training with job training and used performance levels of employed word-processor operators as criteria for program completion. Training applicants were carefully recruited and screened, with special emphasis placed on selecting individuals who were not only CETA eligible but who were also likely to succeed. Classes of 30 to 35 trainees were accepted into the program. These individuals were paid to attend training 40 hours per week. Each day included language training, typing and word-processing training, work habits training, and individual study time. Three full-time teachers (a reading specialist, a word-processing specialist, and a business specialist) worked with students throughout the day and planned assignments that integrated language and machine skills. Much of the classroom work simulated actual job demands: Students composed business communication that other students edited and later produced in final form on word-processing equipment. A good deal of the work involved using actual business communication that was handwritten in rough draft with editing notations.

The most clear-cut differences between this program and traditional basic skills programs related to the application and integration of training. Trainees actually used up-to-date word-processing equipment and were aware of the industry standards they had to meet. Their training in language, work habits, and machine use was integrated so that they received focused practice to meet those standards. Unlike much current schooling, the cooperative program assumed no guaranteed transfer of basic skills training; instead, the program used job simulation as a major training device.

The time needed for trainees to reach job-level competence varied. The earliest trainees were able to find employment in 14 weeks of training. The average time needed for the screened applicants to reach the preset standards was 20 weeks, and a few trainees took nearly 28 weeks. In spite of economic difficulties that adversely affected hiring in the area, slightly more than 70 percent of trainees found word-processing employment within six months after completing the program.

Another successful program integrating basic skills and job training (Mikulecky & Strange, 1986) involved the retraining of workers for the new basic skills and technical demands of a job that was changing. An urban municipality had recently opened a new waste-water treatment plant as a result of new clean-water guidelines. The plant incorporated several technical innovations, and workers who needed little technical training to work in the old treatment plant now faced an entirely different situation. Before workers could be transferred to the new plant, they needed to be retrained in how the new process and equipment functioned, what safety precautions to use when working with a variety of dangerous gases, and how to maintain the microorganisms essential to the waste-water treatment.

An engineering consulting firm set up a cooperative relationship with a university consultant and hired a university-trained reading specialist to develop a basic skills component for the retraining program. The major academic goal was to help trainees gain mastery of technical vocabulary, concepts, and materials. The reading specialist set up special study guides to break down assignments into manageable tasks, and in some cases rewrote or redesigned training materials to lower difficulty levels. By working cooperatively with the reading specialist, teachers made modifications to traditional reading assignments and introduced key vocabulary prior to making those assignments.

The basic skills component of the retraining program can be judged a success by several standards. Nearly half the students who took special basic skills training passed their technical class posttests. It was the consensus of both technical instructors and of the reading specialist that fewer than five percent of these students would have passed without the special attention they received. Of the students who attended sessions, 70 percent were able to summarize materials in their own words by the end of training. Retention of students receiving special basic skills training was actually higher than that of students who only attended technical classes. Gains in general reading ability were less encouraging. Only about 10 percent of the students taking special training made noticeable gains in their ability to read general material or new material for which they had received no direction or purpose provided by the teacher. According to the reading specialist, students making the most significant gains in job and general reading ability invested five or more hours per week in outside reading of material at an appropriate difficulty level.

Characteristics of Effective Programs

Several conclusions are suggested by the civilian case studies and military programs. It does appear possible to make fairly rapid gains in the ability to comprehend technical material if training is focused on that material. General literacy improvement, however, was not a noticeable, direct by-product of any programs but did occur with sufficient time on-task (five hours per week) in the waste-water treatment program with appropriate general material. Best results seemed to occur when basic skills training was integrated with technical training. Training that employed job simulations and literacy applications increased trainee time on task. In the civilian programs, actively involved students received up to three times more practice per paid day than did traditionally trained students. The integrated program, therefore, is also more attractive from a cost-effectiveness perspective.

Probably the most significant conclusion to be drawn from programs in the private sector is that successful technical and basic skills training programs are beginning to emerge in the vacuum left unfilled by traditional schooling. Where schools are unwilling or unable to match basic skills training and materials to specific occupational needs, private consulting firms are successfully filling the gap. They are successful to the degree that they do not assume transfer from general basic skills training to specific job training. Matching training to the application required on the job appears to be key.

MODIFYING LITERACY DEMANDS
VIA JOB PERFORMANCE AIDS

Most of the research reported thus far has focused upon the relationships between workers' literacy abilities, workplace literacy demands, and effective workplace literacy training programs. Training is not the only way to narrow the gap between worker literacy abilities and workplace demands. In addition, one can restructure information so that it is more accessible and comprehensible to workers. This restructured information, designed to help workers perform tasks, is often called a *job performance aid* (JPA).

Job performance aids are typically based on a task analysis of the steps of jobs. While they vary in format (i.e., checklists, flowcharts, step-by-step instructions, computerized guidance, and so on), they all are designed to improve job performance and lower the time needed for training. Initial research addressing the effectiveness of JPAs was predominantly performed in the military.

The effectiveness of JPAs has been documented by a number of studies. Elliott and Joyce (1971), for example, found that high school students with 12 hours of training in how to use a JPA for diagnosing electrical problems were able to spot errors at a level comparable to fully trained technicians with an average of seven years of experience. Kammann (1975) found that an algorithmic (or flowchart) format increased comprehension and reduced errors and reading time. Swezey (1977) reports that high-aptitude workers using JPAs significantly outperformed high-aptitude workers using traditional print materials. Medium-aptitude workers using JPAs outperformed high-aptitude workers without JPAs on some measures, while performance by the two groups was the same on other measures.

Mockovak (1981) and Smillie (1985) report on several studies which suggest that workers prefer training built around the use of JPAs and that JPAs encourage increased use of training manuals after training is completed. Johnson, Thomas, and Martin (1977) report that 78.7 percent of military technicians trained in the use of JPAs liked the JPAs better than the manuals they replaced. Though over half of technicians reported they would be irritated if required to use JPAs for every job, 58 percent preferred JPAs for nonroutine jobs.

Existing research on JPAs indicates that workplace literacy problems can be addressed, in part, by modifying and developing new materials. Further examination of the effectiveness and limitations of JPAs and restructured information in the workplace is clearly in order.

Needed Research

Though a good deal of research related to workplace literacy is available, a great deal remains to be done. Five areas calling for particular attention are

1. developing workplace literacy process models,
2. determining the generalizability and limits of transfer for literacy strategies in the workplace,
3. examining the cost-effectiveness of workplace literacy training efforts,
4. technology's role in workplace literacy training, and
5. economic and political issues related to race and social class.

Developing Workplace Literacy Process Models

To date, little research has attempted to determine the nature of the literacy *process* in the workplace. Early military research by Sticht (1975) established the fact that the purposes of job literacy were predominantly *reading-to-do* and *reading-to-learn* while performing tasks. Diehl and Mikulecky (1980) and Mikulecky (1982) were able to confirm these reading purposes for civilian jobs and expand them to include *reading-to-assess*. In addition, Kirsch and Guthrie (1984) have added to the understanding of reading processes and text-search strategies of technical workers. Guthrie's (1988) work on search strategies for locating information in documents suggests that problem-solving models may be more effective in explaining workplace literacy than traditional language models.

Only suggestions and exploratory discussions of workplace literacy models have appeared in print. Sticht has proposed and modified a developmental information-processing model for literacy as it is used in the workplace. The most recent version of this proposed model is available in Sticht (1987). Mikulecky, Ehlinger, and Meenen (1987) have adapted the Flowers' and Hayes' (1984) composing model to explain the literacy process in the workplace. This model is essentially a problem-solving model.

Though these models are interesting for discussion purposes, serious research needs to test and examine the degree to which these and subsequent models reflect and explain the mental processes used by workers using literacy in the workplace. Research does indicate that literacy use in the workplace differs considerably from literacy use in schools. Tested models of how one reads most effectively in the workplace are needed to guide instruction and help prepare educators to deal with the massive training and retraining of adults in the decades to come.

Transfer and Generalizability of Training

This topic was discussed at some length earlier. More research needs to be done to determine the degree to which training transfers. For example, to what degree do literacy training and performance in one occupational area transfer to other occupational areas? To what extent does the cognitive ability factor identified by Hunter and Hunter (1984) limit the degree of transfer? To what degree are metacognitive and problem-solving strategies identified by researchers (Guthrie, 1988; Mikulecky & Ehlinger, 1986; Mikulecky & Winchester, 1983) transferable from one job setting to others? There is currently very little research and many untested assumptions relating to transfer and generalizability of training.

Cost-Effectiveness of Job Literacy Training

No coherent body of research exists on the cost-effectiveness of basic skills and work-place literacy training. Some initial work has attempted to estimate the cost of low-level literacy to society in general and to business in particular.

Newspaper accounts and some survey information suggest that worker literacy mistakes cost a great deal in dollars and injuries (Henry & Raymond, 1982; Hymowitz, 1981). Kozol (1985) has attempted to draw broad inferences on the national cost to the United States of functionally illiterate adults, and the Canadian Business Task Force on Literacy (1988) has attempted more systematic estimates of costs to Canadian business and society. A survey of Canadian expert opinion and projections from known costs place estimated illiteracy costs to Canadian business at $4 billion annually. Using the traditional 10:1 ratio for U.S.-Canadian conversions, this would suggest a figure approaching $40 billion annually for the United States. Societal costs, including fractions of costs for incarceration and social insurance programs, are estimated at $10 billion annually in Canada ($100 billion by extension to the United States).

No systematic attempt has been made, however, to determine the cost of work-place literacy deficiencies in terms of

> accidents and mistakes,
> lost worker time while avoiding print and seeking oral information, and
> lost manager time in terms of repeating oral explanations.

Such baseline information is needed to determine the cost-effectiveness of training.

A related issue considered by business training departments is who is worth training. Traditionally, educators have taken the position that everyone should learn as much as possible; and the role of the educator is to teach and facilitate that learning. Workplace training is often concerned with the cost-benefit ratio of training. Military research (Sticht, 1982) indicates that a grade-level gain in reading ability takes approximately 100 hours of engaged literacy training time. Focusing on job-specific training can cut the time, but ability gains may be limited somewhat to job-specific reading materials (Sticht, 1987). More research needs to be done to determine the amount and types of literacy training required for needed worker improvement and upon the cost-effectiveness of a mixture of training, redesigning materials, and redesigning jobs.

The Role of Technology in Job Literacy Training

Duffy (1985) has described the computer and videodisc technology used for basic skills simulations in military programs. There are promising possibilities inherent in using computer and video technology to devise expert systems to model and diagnose difficulties with a variety of job literacy tasks. Turner (1988) and Young and Irwin (1988) have documented the high value adults place upon such computer learning benefits as privacy, feedback, flexibility, and control. The ability to teach when the learner rather than the teacher is available is extremely attractive to employers. Though a good deal of promising research is currently in process at this writing, we have much to learn about the effectiveness and limits of technological literacy training in the workplace.

Economic and Political Issues Related to Race and Social Class

Most of the research reported above has dealt with issues of language, cognition, and performance. Almost no research discussed here has addressed workplace literacy in terms of economic and political issues related to race and social class. As a society, we increasingly face the challenge of what to do with individuals who are not equipped to participate productively. The increasing complexity of job literacy tasks has joined with the inequities in our education and social systems to create several dilemmas. Given the increasing literacy demands in the workplace and differential ethnic performance on national literacy tests, it appears that the gap is widening between opportunities available to the average white youth and the average black and Hispanic youth. Access to employment and income are key to most other societal functions. The methods we are currently using to teach youth and to train adults are inadequate to the tasks of preparing many minority-group members to actively and productively participate in society. From both ethical and pragmatic perspectives, it is crucial for educational and policy research to address the issue of how best to halt, or at least slow, our split into two unequal societies.

Multistranded Approaches

There appear to be at least three major workplace literacy problem areas, each calling for a slightly different solution. These problem areas relate to

1. extreme low-level literates (i.e., those unable to function independently with even simple print),
2. new and experienced workers who can read at a moderate level (i.e., as high as the sports page), consider themselves to be literate, but derive little benefit from expensive training because of insufficient reading, computing, and study abilities, and
3. workers at nearly all ability levels who make some job-related literacy mistakes that influence safety, productivity, and promotability.

The first problem area involves the smallest number of workers (below 5 percent) and is yet foremost in the public mind. Surveys of corporate literacy training indicate that approximately 10 percent of businesses fund basic education training and that this percentage may be increasing (Lusterman, 1977; Mikulecky & Cousin, 1982). This training ranges from in-plant basic education programs (BCEL, 1987) to funding for employees to attend community basic-skills education and General Educational Development (G.E.D.) classes.

The second problem area (i.e., low basic skills that limit training effectiveness) is less recognized but affects a larger percentage of workers. The vast majority of workers in many industries hold high school diplomas and do not perceive themselves as having literacy difficulties. Management expectations of increased training and performance, however, often reveal that worker self-perceptions are inaccurate. For example, a recent survey of a manufacturing concern (Condit, Drew, & Mikulecky, 1988) revealed that over a half million dollars was spent on yearly training for 700 employees. For hourly employees, most of whom had graduated from high school, training involved taking specialized courses from a local technical college. Nearly 20 percent of hourly employees were unable to meet the technical college's minimal reading and mathematics entrance requirements (approximately an eighth-grade level of achievement). Most of these workers considered themselves to have no literacy problems, but their tested reading and math abilities were below minimum levels needed for successful ongoing training. Further, both technical college and in-plant instructors commented upon the marginal benefits of training and mastery of skills for workers who *did pass* minimum entry standards, but just barely. One in as many as four or five hourly workers may be ill prepared to benefit from required technical training.

The third area of literacy problems (i.e., literacy mistakes related to safety, productivity, or promotability) can happen at any literacy level. Literacy task analysis or literacy audits of key job tasks may be required to determine the extent to which literacy-based mistakes are endangering lives or costing money (Drew & Mikulecky, 1988; Mikulecky, 1985; U.S. Departments of Education and Labor, 1988). Henry and Raymond (1982) identify literacy-related safety mistakes to be the major literacy problem reported by employers. Literacy-related productivity problems involve mistakes (i.e., the need to redo correspondence or other paperwork) and the inability to implement new productivity innovations. For example, low literacy levels can limit the productivity of quality circle meetings in which hourly employees address productivity and quality control problems. These meetings are used in many industries and are designed to increase the responsibility of workers in spotting problems and developing solutions. To encourage open discussion, it is often desirable for management to be absent from such meetings. At these meetings, notes are taken and key ideas submitted in written form. At a major manufacturing concern, nearly 25 percent of quality circle groups had no employee capable of taking and writing notes that could communicate to a person not attending the meeting (Condit et al., 1988). Similar problems occur with suggestion boxes or federal "whistle-blower" programs that request workers to submit written ideas about safety infractions or improved productivity.

Most work sites experience all three of the above problem areas. It is unlikely that a single approach will solve all problems. What is called for is a *multistranded approach*. Such an approach offers varying solutions to varying problems.

The most prevalent strand is designed for low-level literates. Such workers need long-term support for improving their basic skills. It may take several hundred hours of instruction before a worker who can barely read a product label is able to troubleshoot by using a manual for computerized equipment. Economic support for basic education is one way that employers can help provide such long-term support. Some employers also offer in-plant basic skills programs with time contributed by both employer and worker. Such programs have the advantage of making workplace materials more easily accessible to instructors and communicating to workers the value management places upon a capable work force.

The second workplace literacy program strand is directed toward middle-level literates who are ill equipped for technical training. The needs of these workers can often be addressed by integrating basic skills training with technical training. Technical schools and in-plant instructors can organize class periods to briefly teach such study skills as how to use textbooks or how to take notes related to the technical material covered. Such instruction can be managed in 10- to 15-minute sessions in which the instructor demonstrates how to take notes or gather key information from a text. Technical instructors can also be taught to make use of the host of tested ideas available to content area reading specialists (i.e., developing study guides, preteaching key concepts, individualized assignments, alternate readings, etc.). The implication here is clearly that trainers working with the bottom 25 percent of the work force may need to receive some retraining in their own right.

The final workplace literacy training strand is directly related to local safety and productivity issues. It implies a careful analysis of the key workplace tasks involving basic skills and is likely to lead to custom-designed materials and training. Such analyses may identify areas where workers need training, documents that need to be redesigned, or job descriptions that need to be rewritten. Several suggestions for how to develop such a strand have appeared in print (Cornell, 1988; Drew & Mikulecky, 1988; Mikulecky, 1985; U.S. Departments of Education and Labor, 1988). All involve some form of on-site analysis and diagnosis of the tasks, strategies, and materials needed to perform competently.

CONCLUSIONS

There is a gap between the literacy abilities needed to be productive in the workplace and the ability levels of a significant percentage of workers. This gap is largely the result of a general increase in the demands of most jobs that has occurred at the same time that many very low-skilled jobs have been disappearing or shifted to nations where labor is less expensive.

A disproportionate percentage of black and Hispanic workers from low economic backgrounds are among those with the most inadequate skills. Demographic projections indicate that this population segment is growing more rapidly than any other segment. Our ability to thrive economically and our ability to maintain many of our democratic ideals may be determined by our ability to enable this segment of our population to contribute productively in the workplace.

Accomplishing this goal will require us to gather more information about the effectiveness of workplace literacy training methods. It will also require us to recognize that there are several literacy problems which call for differing solutions and that the workplace of the 1990s is likely to require as many of our educational resources as does the schoolhouse.

REFERENCES

Applebee, A. (1981). *Writing in the secondary school* (NCTE Research Report No. 21). Urbana, IL: National Council of Teachers of English.

Bormuth, J. R. (1975). Reading literacy: Its definition and assessment. In J. B. Carroll & J. S. Chall (Eds.), *Toward a literate society* (pp. 61–100). New York: McGraw-Hill.

Business Council for Effective Literacy. (1987). *Job-related basic skills: A guide for planners of employee programs.* New York: Author.

Canadian Business Task Force on Literacy. (1988). *Measuring the costs of illiteracy in Canada.* Toronto, Ontario: Author.

Condit, L., Drew, R., & Mikulecky, L. (1988). *Indiana workplace literacy partnership.* An unfunded proposal to the U.S. Department of Education, Washington, DC.

Cook, W. (1977). *Adult literacy education in the United States.* Newark, DE: International Reading Association.

Cornell, T. (1988). Characteristics of effective occupational literacy programs. *Journal of Reading, 31,* 654–657.

Diehl, W., & Mikulecky, L. (1980). The nature of reading at work. *Journal of Reading, 24,* 221–227.

Drew, R. A., & Mikulecky, L. J. (1988). *How to gather and develop job-specific literacy materials for basic skills instruction.* Bloomington, IN: Office of Education and Training Resources, School of Education, Indiana University.

Duffy, T. M. (1985). Literacy instruction in the military. In *Armed Forces and Society, 11,* 437–467.

Elliott, T. K., & Joyce, R. P. (1971). An experimental evaluation of a method for simplifying electronic maintenance. *Human Factors, 13,* 217–227.

Fields, E. L., Hull, W. L., & Sechler, J. A. (1987). *Adult literacy: Industry-based training programs.* Columbus, OH: National Center for Research in Vocational Education.

Flower, L., & Hayes, J. (1984). Images, plans, and prose: The representation of meaning in writing. *Written Communication, 1,* 129–160.

Greenan, J. P. (1982). The development of generalizable skills instruments for identifying the functional learning abilities of students in vocational education programs. *Journal of Industrial Teacher Education, 20,* 19–36.

Greenan, J. P., & Smith, B. B. (1981). *Assessing the generalizable skills of post-secondary vocational students: A validation study.* Minneapolis: University of Minnesota, Minnesota Research and Development Center.

Guthrie, J. T. (1983). Equilibrium of literacy. *Journal of Reading, 26,* 668–670.

Guthrie, J. T. (1988). Locating information in documents: Examination of a cognitive model. *Reading Research Quarterly, 23,* 178–199.

Harste, J., & Mikulecky, L. (1984). The context of literacy in our society. In Purves, A., & Niles, O. (Eds.), *Becoming readers in a complex society.* Chicago: University of Chicago Press.

Heath, S. B. (1980). The functions and uses of literacy. *Journal of Communication, 30,* 123–133.

Henry, J. F., & Raymond, S. (1982). *Basic skills in the U.S. work force.* New York: Center for Public Resources.

Hunter, J., & Hunter, R. S. (1984). Validity and utility of alternative predictors of job performance. *Psychological Bulletin, 96,* 72–98.

Hymowitz, L. (1981). Employers take over where school failed to teach the basics. *Wall Street Journal* (Jan. 22, 1981), p. 1.

Jacobs, E. (1982). *Literacy of the job: Ethnographic component of the industrial project.* Washington, DC: Center for Applied Linguistics.

Johnson, R. C., Thomas, D. L., & Martin, D. J. (1977). *User acceptance and usability of the C-144 job guide technical order system* (AFHRL-TR-77-31). Dayton, OH: Wright-Patterson Air Force Base, Air Force Human Resources Laboratory.

Johnston, W. B., & Packer, A. E. (1987). *Workforce 2000.* Indianapolis, IN: Hudson Institute.

Kammann, R. (1975). The comprehensibility of printed instructions and the flowchart alternative. *Human Factors, 17,* 183–191.

Kern, R. P. (1985). Modeling users and their use of technical manuals. In T. M. Duffy & R. Waller (Eds.) *Designing usable texts* (pp. 341–375). New York: Academic Press.

Kirsch, I., & Guthrie, J. T. (1978). The concept of measurement of functional literacy. *Reading Research Quarterly, 13,* 485–507.

Kirsch, I., & Guthrie, J. (1984). Prose comprehension and text search as a function of reading volume. *Reading Research Quarterly, 19,* 331–342.

Kirsch, I., & Jungeblutt, A. (1986). *Literacy: Profiles of America's young adults.* Princeton, NJ: National Assessment of Educational Progress at Educational Testing Service.

Kozol, J. (1985). *Illiterate America.* Garden City, NY: Anchor Press.

Kulp, M. (1974). *The effects of position practice and readability level on performance.* Unpublished master's thesis. San Diego State University, San Diego, California.

Lusterman, S. (1977). *Education in industry.* New York: Conference Board.

Mikulecky, L. (1981). The mismatch between school training and job literacy demands. *Vocational Guidance Quarterly, 30,* 174–180.

Mikulecky, L. (1982). Job literacy: The relationship between school preparation and workplace actuality. *Reading Research Quarterly, 17,* 400–419.

Mikulecky, L. (1985). *Literacy task analysis: Defining and measuring occupational literacy demands.* A paper presented at the annual meeting of the American Educational Research Association, Chicago, IL, March 31, 1985 (ERIC Document Reproduction Service No. ED262206).

Mikulecky, L. (1987). The status of literacy in our society. In J. Readance & S. Baldwin (Eds.), *Research in literacy: Merging perspectives* (Thirty-sixth yearbook of the National Reading Conference) (pp. 211–235). New York: National Reading Conference.

Mikulecky, L., Shanklin, N., & Caverly, D. (1979). Adult reading habits, attitudes, and motivations: A cross-sectional study. *Teaching and Learning Series Monograph.* Bloomington, IN: Indiana University, School of Education.

Mikulecky, L., & Cousin, P. (1982). Literacy training in business: A survey of Fortune 500 training programs. *Performance and Instruction, 21,* 29–30.

Mikulecky, L., & Winchester, D. (1983). Job literacy and job performance among nurses at varying employment levels. *Adult Education Quarterly, 34,* 1–15.

Mikulecky, L., & Ehlinger, J. (1986). The influence of metacognitive aspects of literacy on job performance of electronics technicians. *Journal of Reading Behavior, 18,* 41–62.

Mikulecky, L., & Strange, R. (1986). Effective literacy training programs for adults in business and municipal employment. In J. Orasanu (Ed.), *A decade of reading research: Implications for practice.* Hillsdale, NJ: Erlbaum.

Mikulecky, L., Ehlinger, J., & Meenan, A. (1987). Training for job literacy demands: What research applies to practice. *Monograph of the Institute for the Study of Adult Literacy.* University Park, PA: Pennsylvania State University.

Miller, P. (1982). Reading demands in a high-technology industry. *Journal of Reading, 26,* 109–115.

Mockavok, W. P. (1981). Integrating training and manual design using job aids. *Educational Technology, 23,* 21–23.

Mosenthal, P., & Kirsch, I. (1987). *The constructs of adult literacy.* Paper presented at the annual meeting of the National Reading Conference, St. Petersburg, FL.

Murphy, R. T. (1975). Assessment of adult reading competence. In A. Nielson & J. Hjelm (Eds.), *Reading and career education* (pp. 50–61). Newark, DE: International Reading Association.

Negin, G., & Krugler, D. (1980). Essential literacy skills for functioning in an urban community. *Journal of Reading, 24,* 109–115.

Rumberger, R. W. (1984a). The growing imbalance between education and work. *Phi Delta Kappan, 65,* 342–346. (ERIC Document Reproduction Service No. EJ 291 592).

Rumberger, R. W. (1984b). *Demystifying high technology* (Occasional paper No. 97). Columbus: Ohio State University, National Center for Research in Vocational Education.

Rush, T., Moe, A., & Storlie, R. (1986). *Occupational literacy.* Newark, DE: International Reading Association.

Smillie, R. J. (1985). Design strategies for job performance aids. In T. Duffy & R. Waller (Eds.), *Designing usable texts* (pp. 213–243). New York: Academic Press.

Smith, F., & Feathers, K. (1983). Teacher and student perceptions of content area reading. *Journal of Reading, 26,* 348–354.

Stedman, L., & Kaestle, C. (1987). Literacy and reading performance in the United States, from 1880 to the present. *Reading Research Quarterly, 22,* 32–46.

Sticht, T. G. (1975). *Reading for working: A functional literacy anthology.* Alexandria, VA: Human Resources Research Association.

Sticht, T. G. (1980). *Literacy and human resources development at work.* Alexandria, VA: Human Resources Research Organization.

Sticht, T. G. (1982). *Basic skills in defense.* Alexandria, VA: Human Resources Research Organization.

Sticht, T. G. (1987). *Functional context education.* San Diego, CA: Applied Behavioral and Cognitive Sciences.

Sticht, T. G., Amijo, L., Weitzman, R., Koffman, N., Robertson, K., Chang, F., & Moracoo, J. (1986). *Teachers, books, computers, and peers: Integrated communications technologies for adult literacy development.* Monterey, CA: U.S. Naval Postgraduate School.

Sticht, T. G., & Mikulecky, L. J. (1984). *Job-related basic skills: Cases and conclusions* (Information Series No. 285). Columbus: Ohio State University, National Center for Research in Vocational Education.

Swezey, R. W. (1977). Performance aids as adjuncts to instruction. *Educational Technology, 17,* 27–32.

Turner, T. (1988). Using the computer for adult literacy instruction. *Journal of Reading, 31,* 643–647.

Tyler, R. W. (1978). *Education for functional literacy: Old problems, new problems.* Paper presented at the Conference on Functional Illiteracy, Indiana University, Bloomington, IN.

U.S. Department of Defense. (1984). *Counselor's manual for the armed services vocational aptitude battery, form 14.* Washington, DC: Author.

U.S. Departments of Education and Labor. (1988). *The bottom line: Basic skills in the workplace.* Washington, DC: Office of Public Information, Employment and Training Administration, U.S. Department of Labor.

Valentine, T. (1986). *Issues central to the definition of adult functional literacy* (Contract No. OERI-P-86-3014). Paper presented to the U.S. Department of Education.

Young, D., & Irwin, M. (1988). Integrating computers into adult literacy programs. *Journal of Reading, 31,* 648–653.

25 WORD MEANINGS

Richard C. Anderson
and William E. Nagy

> Words have often been called slippery customers, and many scholars have been distressed
> by their tendency to shift their meanings and slide out from under any simple definition. A
> goal of some clear thinkers has been to use words in more precise ways. But though this is
> an excellent and necessary step for technical jargon, it is a self-defeating program when
> applied to ordinary words. It is not only that words are shifters; the objects to which they
> must be applied shift with even greater rapidity. (Labov, 1973, p. 341)

This chapter addresses the nature of the knowledge people possess about word
meanings, and how this knowledge is acquired and used in reading comprehension.
Drawing on philosophy, linguistics, and psychology as well as education, the chapter
attempts to describe gaps in knowledge and controversies as well as marshaling the
reasoning and evidence for what can be accepted as truths. Although we have incorporated some original thinking of our own and have been contentious about some issues,
our fundamental purpose has been to present a state-of-the-art synthesis.

SOME BASIC DISTINCTIONS

As Labov said, words, and in particular, their meanings, are "slippery customers."
Words about word meanings are no exception; if anything, they have proved more
slippery than most. In a field as old as the study of word meanings, it should come as no
surprise that the words used to talk about meanings themselves have many meanings.
Thus, no discussion of word meaning can proceed fruitfully without a definition of
terms. We will use *meaning* as an everyday, pretheoretical term, and *sense, reference,
connotation*, and *denotation* as technical vocabulary. We would not care to say that all of
these terms are needed to adequately characterize word meanings. They are needed,
though, to talk about the distinctions maintained by philosophers, linguists, and others
who theorize about semantics.

We will define the *reference* of a word as the thing or things "picked out" by the
word on a particular occasion of use as, for instance, the word *dog* in the sentence *The
black dog looks mean*, in a situation in which there are several dogs, one of which is
black. Of course, the words in two or more utterances have the same reference if they
pick out the same thing.

This occasion-specific use of the term reference is now fairly common (cf. Lyons,
1977), but it must be distinguished from an older and even more common use to mean

The authors gratefully acknowledge the criticisms and suggestions offered by Patricia Herman, Margaret
McKeown, Peter Mosenthal, Stephen Norris, Judith Scott, Diane Stephens, and Gordon Wells. The
preparation of this paper was supported by the Office of Educational Research and Improvement (OEG 0087–
C1001).

all of the things a word might stand for; in this usage *dog* would be said to refer to all dogs. To maintain a distinction between specific and general reference, we will use the traditional term *denotation* to indicate the entire class of entities associated with a word. (An alternative term for the entire class that we could have chosen is *extension*.) Of course, the reference and the denotation of a word can be identical, as in *I'm not afraid of dogs*.

The construct *denotation* applies most felicitously to concrete nouns; for example, the denotation of apple is the set of all apples. The construct is extended by analogy to other types of words; for example, the denotation of *red* can be defined as the set of all red objects; the denotation of *migrate* as the set of all instances of migrating. The denotation of a word is the set of all potential referents for a word, imaginary as well as real. Thus, we take the position that the denotations of *unicorn* and *griffin* are different, even though both sets happen to be empty in the known universe.

Notice that a person's internal representation of the denotation of a word could not be just a list of members in the set, because the denotations of most words are indenumerable. How, for instance, could apples from next year's crop be listed? Instead, what people must have in their heads is some basis for determining membership in the set. We will use the traditional term *connotation* (we could have used *intension*) for the distinctions, or rule, for deciding whether an object, action, or property belongs to the set that constitutes the denotation of a word. (This use of connotation should not be confused with the everyday meaning of affective coloration.)

We will define the *sense* of a word as the distinctions the word conveys in a particular circumstance of use. A more common usage is to equate sense with connotation as we have just defined it; that is, as the distinctions which it is supposed are conveyed on any and all circumstances in which the word is used in a serious, literal-minded fashion.

The four terms we have introduced are related according to the paradigm below:

Language Function	One Occasion	All Occasions
Pointing	Reference	Denotation
Attributing	Sense	Connotation

Sense and reference are context bound, whereas denotation and connotation are context free. Ordinarily, but not always, the reference of a word is included within its denotation. The sense and the connotation of a word are related but, if we are right, they are seldom identical.

Although all four of these concepts may not be necessary for a satisfactory characterization of word meaning, either the sense/reference distinction or, alternatively, the connotation/denotation distinction is required. The distinction is necessary to account for the fact that two expressions can refer to the same individual or object, and yet clearly be different in meaning. In a classic paper, Frege (1892; translation, 1966) made the case for the distinction using the sentence *The morning star is the evening star*. Of course, the referent of the two expressions is the same; both refer to the planet Venus. Yet the meaning—more precisely, the sense—is different; one is about a heavenly body visible in the morning, the other about a heavenly body visible in the evening. Hence, the sentence is potentially informative instead of being tautological and, hence, uninformative. For another example, compare *triangle* and *closed three-sided figure*. The two expressions denote the same geometric figures. But *triangle* brings to mind angularity, whereas *closed three-sided figure* highlights, promotes, or calls attention to the feature of sidedness. Contrasts such as these demonstrate that the distinction between sense and reference is a real one, and contribute to the case that both concepts are necessary to adequately represent word meanings.

MEANINGS OF DIFFERENT TYPES OF WORDS

Any reasonable theory of word meaning has to take into account the fact that there are fundamentally different types of words. An obvious distinction is that between function words and content words. Whatever sort of meanings one wants to attribute to the words *if* and *the* will be different in nature from the meanings of words like *ostrich* or *panic*. Likewise, words like *Hello* and *Gesundheit*, to the extent that they could be said to have meaning, have meaning of a quite different sort.

We adopted as a basic definition of the connotation of a word, the distinctions, or rule, for deciding whether an object, action, or property is a member of the class of objects, actions, or properties that constitutes the denotation of the word. However, this definition requires some refinement in order to deal with problems posed by different types of words.

Proper names are a case where some refinement is needed. On the one hand, proper names are used generatively; seen from different distances, from different angles, or on different occasions, even the same individual does not look exactly the same. In that sense, one has some sort of strategy or rule for recognizing an individual.

On the other hand, whatever means people may have for recognizing an individual, these do not constitute the meaning, or sense, of that individual's name. Traditionally, therefore, proper names have been said to have reference but not sense. They refer to specific individuals, but the reference is by convention, not by rule.

One way to clarify what constitutes the connotation of a word has been on the basis of necessity. That is, the connotation of a word is taken as the set of necessary and sufficient conditions for inclusion in the denotation. This provides a basis for the claim that proper names do not have sense. For example, your friends may recognize you on the basis of the size of your nose, the color of your hair, and the presence or absence of a mustache; but changing any or all of these would not change your name. More generally, no particular fact about you is necessarily true; therefore, no such fact can be considered part of the meaning—that is, the connotation—of your name.

On the same basis, it can be argued that there are other categories of words that do not have connotation, as we have defined it. In particular, Kripke (1972) and others have argued that this is true of natural kind terms. For example, the word *dog* denotes, by convention, a particular species of animal. There are various ways we can distinguish dogs from other species of animals, but none of these are the meaning, or connotation, of the word *dog*. Changes in the breeding of cats and woodchucks might result in a world in which the only reliable test for doghood was careful chemical testing of chromosomes; but the meaning of the word *dog* would not therefore come to be defined in terms of such a test. The word *dog* simply denotes, by convention, a particular kind of being; the nature of that kind of being, and the tests used to distinguish that kind from others, are part of our knowledge of the world, but not part of the meaning of the word.

Green (1984) argues that what has been claimed about natural kind terms applies as well to many other types of words, so that most words should not be considered to have connotation, as we have defined it. However, Green does not extend this claim to all words in the language; she agrees that there are some words that refer not simply by convention, but by describing.

It is clear that phrases can refer by describing rather than by convention. For example, someone can refer to a given individual either by name (Grover Cleveland) or by a description (the only person to serve two nonconsecutive terms as president of the United States). According to Green, some kinds of words, those which Putnam (1975) calls one-criterion words, also refer by describing—for example, *bachelor* or *orphan*. In the case of *dog* or *gold*, it is reasonable to say that there is a certain kind of entity, conventionally denoted by a particular name, and that knowledge of particular facts about these kinds (e.g., that gold has a particular atomic weight, or that dogs are mammals) is knowledge of the world, not knowledge of the language. In the case of *orphan*, however, it cannot reasonably be said that there is a particular kind of individual, and that among the facts we happen to know about members of this kind is that they do not have living parents.

In summary, the point is that one cannot expect a simple, unified theory of word meaning to work for all types of words. As Putnam says, "To look for any one uniform link between word or thought and object is to look for the occult" (1975, p. 290).

THE STANDARD MODEL
OF WORD MEANING

The standard model of word meaning, briefly stated, equates word meaning with connotation, and defines connotation in terms of the necessary and sufficient conditions for inclusion in the denotation. A primary purpose of this chapter is to explore the properties of this model, then present a variety of arguments exposing its weaknesses and shortcomings.

It might seem that we are not only setting up a straw man but beating a dead horse: It would be difficult to find anyone at present who would espouse the entire standard model as we will define it. However, we consider this mode of presentation worthwhile, for three reasons:

First, dissatisfaction with the standard model is perhaps the most accurate representation of the current consensus. That is, scholars concerned with word meanings concur in their rejection of aspects of the standard model, but not on any model to replace it.

Second, the horse is not dead, or, to switch figures, the straw man is still very seductive. To some extent, the standard model we define comes close to reflecting a commonsense view of word meaning that forms the implicit basis for much of the thinking that is done about word meanings, especially in applied areas such as reading and vocabulary instruction.

Third, although it might be hard to find anyone who would hold to all the attributes of the standard model, for most of the individual attributes we will be able to find contemporary proponents.

We want to make it clear that we are looking for a psychologically real and pedagogically relevant model of word meanings; thus, the standards we set for a theory of word meaning are not necessarily those adopted by all of its proponents. Nevertheless, contemporary proponents of various aspects of the standard model include psycholinguists as well as philosophers; and, as we have said, whatever its origins, the standard model of word meaning continues to influence educational practice.

The core of the standard position is that word meanings can be characterized in terms of *criterial features*—that is, necessary and sufficient conditions for inclusion in the denotation of a word. This means, for example, that the ability to fly could not be part of the meaning of the word *bird*, because it is neither necessary nor sufficient; not all birds fly, and not everything that flies is a bird. The notion of criteriality follows from assumptions of abstractness and parsimony. These two interrelated properties are fundamental to the standard model of word meaning; we discuss them in turn in the following sections.

Abstractness

Learning word meanings entails more than acquiring names for a large number of individual persons, objects, actions, and qualities. Even the concrete object names that constitute a large proportion of children's first words are not names for individuals, but for classes of objects. The overgeneralizations sometimes observed in children's language—for instance, a child using the word *dog* for a *cow*—are interesting in the way that they may reflect differences between child and adult representations of word meanings. But they are also interesting in that they highlight a more basic property of word meanings. To know what a word means is somehow to know a generative rule, a rule that allows a person to map a given sequence of sounds or letters onto a potentially infinite but still restricted class of possible referents. Overgeneralization errors of the sort children make are not like mistakenly calling your friend Mike by the name John. Rather, they reflect the child's attempt to induce a rule.

Some level of *abstractness*, then, is necessary to account for the ability people have to apply words to novel instances—for example, to recognize an Irish setter as a dog, even though they may never have seen a dog of that variety before. What is in question is the degree and nature of the abstraction in the internal representation of word meanings. There are three ways in which information about a word meaning could be stored in the mental lexicon:

1. Knowledge of a word's meaning is stored exclusively in the form of a rule or generalization defining the set of entities or events to which this word can be applied. No information about individual examples is stored permanently in the mental lexicon.
2. Knowledge of a word's meaning is stored exclusively in terms of a set of examples of the use of that word, along with the situations in which these examples are embedded. No rule is stored, but ordinarily one can be quickly derived from the examples when needed to interpret a new use of the word.
3. Knowledge of a word's meaning is stored both in terms of examples and in terms of a rule, perhaps an incomplete one, that helps determine the set of possible uses of the word.

These three alternatives lead to somewhat different predictions about how people will process word meanings, and what sort of relationships among word meanings can be expected in the language. Of course, the first alternative is embodied in the standard model.

Parsimony

The level of abstraction postulated for word meanings depends in part on the extent to which *parsimony* of representation plays a role in one's theory of word meaning. The standard theory comes down on the side of maximal parsimony; it is inherent in the equation of word meaning with a set of necessary and sufficient conditions.

The commitment to parsimony is a pretheoretical assumption that reflects a belief about what counts as an elegant theory. Parsimony has always been a criterion applied to scientific theories. Explicit formulation of this criterion goes back at least to William of Occam (1300–1349). It is an axiom of scientific inquiry that the broader the sweep of explanations the better, and that redundant, piecemeal explanations should be avoided. In other words, according to the criterion of parsimony, principles should be stated in the most general form allowed by the data.

However, there is no convincing a priori reason to assume that, in representing word meanings, the human mind avoids redundancy and strives for parsimony of representation. The question that we shall raise is whether the data on words and their meanings allows as much parsimony as the standard model supposes.

CONTEXTUAL VARIATION IN WORD MEANING

The criterion of parsimony becomes problematical as soon as one tries to account for different meanings (or shades of meaning) that words display on different occasions. A number of psycholinguistic studies appear to show that the meaning of terms can vary according to context. For example, consider the meaning of the term *nurse* in the following two sentences:

> *Nurses have to be licensed.*
> *Nurses can be beautiful.*

The first sentence emphasizes the fact that a nurse is a health professional, whereas the second emphasizes the femaleness of nurses. Anderson and Ortony (1975) obtained evidence of the psychological reality of this difference in emphasis. They found that *doctor* was a better cue for recall of the first sentence, while *actress* was a better cue for the recall of the second.

Considering results such as the foregoing, Anderson et al. (1976) propose that

> a word does not have *a* meaning, but has, rather, a *family* of potential meanings. When comprehended in context, the meanings of the words in an utterance are further articulated in a process of inferential interpolation based on schemata which embody one's knowledge of the world. The effect with respect to nouns is usually to limit the scope of reference to a subset of the cases which would otherwise be denoted. If the context is rich and if the message is processed deeply, a noun may be identified with a single real or imagined thing. This process will be called *instantiation*. . . . [A] close analysis will show that a word can have a somewhat different sense in each use. (p. 667)

Johnson-Laird and his colleagues (Tabossi & Johnson-Laird, 1980) have also found evidence for the psychological reality of context-based variation in meaning. However, Johnson-Laird (1981, 1983, 1987; see also Perfetti & McCutchen, 1986) has objected to the claim of Anderson and his colleagues that both the sense and reference of terms depend upon context. Johnson-Laird argues that except in the case of "genuinely polysemous words"—for instance, *bank*, which can mean a financial institution, the side of a river, or to tilt and turn an airplane—the sense of words remains fixed on every occasion of use, and only the reference changes.

Johnson-Laird's position is motivated by a desire to maintain parsimony in the representation of word meanings. He asserts this explicitly when he says

> In fact, there has been too much emphasis on polysemy and in consequence a mistaken view about the mechanism of instantiation. . . . [T]he crucial psychological criterion is whether or not it is necessary to postulate more than one semantic representation for a word in order to account for the interpretations of the sentences in which it occurs. Instead

of asking how many different meanings can be squeezed out of the word, psycholinguists need to ask what is the minimum number of different senses that are necessary to cope with all of its different uses. (p. 196)

Continuing, Johnson-Laird writes

If *eat* were truly polysemous then the sentence *He eats the food* should be highly ambiguous. It should have many wholly distinct senses. Yet it remains unequivocal. What is true, however, is that the sentence in common with others can be truthfully asserted of an infinite number of different situations: *he* can refer to any male individual, *food* can designate an indefinite number of different types of foods served in an indefinite number of different conditions, and the manner by which the food is eaten can vary in an indefinite number of different ways from chewing it like cud to straining through the teeth. This indeterminacy of reference is not sufficient to establish ambiguity because, if it were, all open-class words would be infinitely ambiguous and their meanings could not be contained by a finite brain. Hence, the sentence above, which truly applies to a variety of situations, is referentially indeterminate, but not ambiguous. Its syntax is unambiguous and its words are unambiguous; they each have in ordinary usage a single sense, but these senses suffice, as do the senses of all words, to embrace many different situations. The sentence requires only a single representation of its meaning. (pp. 196–197).

Thus, Johnson-Laird's explanation for shifts in meanings of words is that the reference, but not the sense, of a word may vary from context to context. With respect to the sentences about nurses shown above, presumably Johnson-Laird would say that the set of nurses referred to in the first sentence is not identical to the set of nurses referred to in the second sentence. For instance, he might point out with regard to the second sentence that some nurses are male. Notice, though, that if one were to say about a male nurse, *That nurse certainly is beautiful*, it would not be for the purpose of drawing attention to his status as a health professional!

But rather than quibble over debatable cases, let us consider contexts in which the reference of certain terms is undeniably the same:

All the nurses at Massachusetts General Hospital are licensed.
All the nurses at Massachusetts General Hospital are beautiful.

These uses of *nurse* differ in sense even though the reference is identical.

One way to save the concept of fixed word connotation, and at the same time explain the rich interpretation usually made of words in context, is to distinguish sharply between linguistic knowledge and world knowledge. In this realization, connotation is pure linguistic meaning, or *core meaning*; it is the decontextualized and presumably invariant concept associated with a word. And sense (as we are using the term) is what might be called the *contextual meaning;* it is connotation, onto which are embroidered inferences based on the circumstances of use and relevant world knowledge.

Thus, it may be possible to postulate a single connotation or core meaning for *nurse* and to account for the type of variation in the above examples in terms of some general principles for incorporating inferences based on world knowledge, that would also apply to analogous cases involving words like *secretary, receptionist, doctor, carpenter,* and so on. In some cases, then, a distinction between connotation, or core meaning, on the one hand, and sense, or contextual meaning, on the other, may make it possible to maintain a single parsimonious representation of word connotation, even in the face of what appears to be genuine contextual variation in meaning.

There are two rejoinders to this apparently successful attempt to preserve the parsimony of representations of word meaning. The first is to point out the steep price of parsimony. The notion of core linguistic meaning is now at least one more step removed from the data about meaning gathered in experiments like those of Anderson et al. (1976). As we will attempt to show in detail later, ultimately the notion of literal core meaning can be maintained only by divorcing it from phenomenological and experiential senses of "meaning."

The second response is that while distinguishing core meaning and contextual meaning may seem to work in the examples just discussed, it will not work in a large number of other cases. Consider the problems that arise when one attempts to arrive at any fixed representation of the meaning of the verb *give*. The first connotation of this word listed in *Webster's New Third International Dictionary* (1964) is "to confer ownership of something without receiving a return." This definition works just fine with *John gave Mary a present*, but already there is a problem with *John gave Mary $10 and she gave him $2.57 change*. The putative fixed connotation fails to cope with the fact that "receiving a return" in goods or service, as well as a return of change, is expected in this context. The problem is even more acute in *John gave Mary a kiss*. *Gave* seems to be used here in a perfectly ordinary way, but does one really want to mean that John "conferred ownership" of a kiss?

Examine most entries in a large dictionary such as *Webster's Third New International* and you will see how unwieldy the concept of a fixed, context-free word connotation is. *Webster's* recognizes that *give* is, in Johnson-Laird's phrase, "genuinely polysemous" by according it two main entries. The secondary entry lists two related senses: (1) "tendency to yield to force" and (2) "state of being springy." The primary entry begins with "to confer ownership . . ." and continues with no less than 56 other related senses in 14 major groupings, as well as a number of idioms.

The issue of parsimony must be looked at in terms of degrees and types of relatedness among words. Everyone would agree that there are instances of homophony—for example, the three different meanings of *bank*—that must be described by postulating distinct connotations. Similarly, we would agree with Johnson-Laird that there are some instances of contextual variation in meaning that might be characterized in terms of a fixed core meaning, and principles of inference and instantiation that result in a more elaborated, context-specific sense. However, there remain cases of related meanings, such as the subentries listed under one of the main entries of *give*.

The principle of parsimony of representation, applied strictly, makes the following claim: Any two senses that are genuinely related (i.e., not instances of homophony) can be accounted for by a single, more general, core meaning, and general principles of inference and instantiation that account for contextual variation in word meanings. We argue that this claim can be falsified in many specific cases. Not only that, but we argue that a broad look at the English lexicon shows that it is characterized more by redundancy than by parsimony, and that parsimony is at most a secondary consideration in determining the nature of semantic representations. Therefore, even when a parsimonious representation of word meaning in terms of a single core meaning is *possible*, such a representation generally is not the most psychologically realistic.

THE FAMILY RESEMBLANCE MODEL
OF WORD SENSE

It is instructive to consider some of the senses listed under the primary entry for *give* in *Webster's*: (3d) "to administer as a medicine"—e.g., *give her a shot of penicillin*; (4c) "to perform the action necessary or appropriate for a public performance or production"—

e.g., *give a concert*; (6a) "to yield or furnish as a product, consequence, or effect"—e.g., *the candle gave its final flicker*; (8a) "to deliver or deal by some bodily action"—e.g., *give him a shove*; (9b) "to deliver verbally"—e.g., *give a warm greeting*; (10c) "to make known, or impart knowledge or information about"—e.g., *give a valid argument*; (12f) "to allow to have or take"—e.g., *give him permission.*

All of these senses of *give* are related, to be sure. What is not true, though, is that the senses are related because they embody a single fixed connotation, or core meaning. If the sense of the different uses of the term were identical, it would be possible to substitute the same synonym in each expression and preserve the meaning. However, you can say *set forth a valid argument*, but you cannot, in any normal situation, say *set forth a warm greeting*; you can say *grant him permission*, but you cannot say *grant him a shove.*

Instead, the relationship among the senses of *give* in various contexts is better characterized as one of "family resemblance," to borrow Wittgenstein's (1953) insightful metaphor. In a human family there is a greater or lesser degree of resemblance among the members. The nature of the resemblance shifts from member to member, without there necessarily being any one clear respect in which all are alike. The same is true of the meanings of most words in actual use. The features that are important shift from use to use. A feature that is essential in one use may be unimportant or even absent in another.

We recognize that there are some cases in which a core meaning, plus general principles of inference and instantiation, *can* account for contextual variation in word meaning. As Johnson-Laird says, "All open-class words . . . are closer to being pronouns than is commonly recognized; they provide a relatively simple semantic framework that can be enriched by inferences based on knowledge. These inferences concern the situation designated by the sentence, and different linguistic contexts highlight different aspects of lexical meaning" (1987, p. 187).

However, we deny that it is possible to set up a "relatively simple semantic framework" to account for much of the variation in meaning represented by related senses found in dictionaries. A problem with stretching a single word sense to cover every related use is that the sense necessarily becomes increasingly abstract—that is to say, bland and vague. No meaning of *give* that is general enough to cover all the clearly related senses would account for the fact that you can give, but not grant, someone a shove. In general, the effect of stretching word senses to make them maximally inclusive is to cede any linguistic basis for explaining nuance. All richness and particularity of understanding is left to be explained in terms of knowledge of the world.

The proposal that word senses are fashioned to be maximally inclusive and parsimonious also leads to a psychologically implausible picture of vocabulary acquisition, in that learning new senses of a word would have to diminish the amount of information in one's lexical representations. Say, for example, a person knew the word *deliver* only in the sense of delivering mail. If that person then learns the senses of *deliver* for delivering babies and delivering speeches, his or her knowledge of the word *deliver* becomes general to the point of being vacuous.

Furthermore, although a general core meaning might, with the help of general principles of inference and instantiation, account for the range of meanings that a word can take on, this approach will generally not account for *which* specific meanings a given word actually does and does not take on. Consider the dictionary entries for the words *gusset* and *gore* (entry no. 2) from *Webster's Third New International* (unabridged):

gusset:

1a: a piece of chain mail or plate at the openings of the joints in a suit of armor

1b: a usually triangular or diamond-shaped insert [as of cloth or leather] placed in a seam [as of a sleeve, pocketbook, glove] to give ease or expansibility; also, a similar piece made by adding stitches at the heel of hose

1c: any V-shaped or triangular insert [as in a sail or skirt]: as: (1) an elastic insert in a shoe upper [as for providing a snug fit] (2) gusset tongue: bellows tongue

1d: a pleat or fold esp. in bookbinding

2: something resembling a gusset, as:

2a: a gore of land

2b: (1) gusset plate: a connecting or reinforcing plate that joins the truss members in a truss joint or fits at a joint of a frame structure or set of braces, (2) gusset stay: a bracket or angular piece of iron for strengthening angles of a structure [as an airplane or a bridge]

3: a pretended abatement in heraldry consisting of either side of a pall without the top opening

gore:

1a: a small usually triangular piece of land

1b: a relatively small unassigned or disputed tract of land lying between larger political divisions [as townships]

1c: a minor unorganized and usually sparsely settled or uninhabited part of a county [as in Maine and Vermont]

2a: (1) a tapering or triangular piece of cloth (2) one of several flared lengthwise sections of a garment [as a skirt]

2b: gusset 1c

3a: one of the triangular pieces of the covering of a dome, umbrella, balloon, or similar object

3b: one of the series of related sections of a map that is applied to the surface of a sphere in the making of a terrestrial globe

4: a heraldic bearing imagined as two curved lines drawn respectively from the sinister or dexter chief and from the lowest point of the shield to meeting in the fess point

These two words illustrate the inadequacy of the construct of core meaning. There are obvious similarities among the meanings of *gusset* and *gore*, but no set of features in common to the meanings of each that would distinguish them from each other, or from a more general meaning such as "triangle." These two words show clearly that the family-resemblance pattern of related meanings is not restricted to high-frequency words like *give*.

Even if a core meaning *could* be constructed for each of these words, this core meaning could not predict *which* particular meanings each of these words has taken on. There may be some historical reasons why *gusset* took on some meanings and *gore* took on others; but as far as a description of present-day English is concerned, it is an arbitrary fact that these words have the specific meanings they do. Likewise, it is a historical accident, so to speak, that the webs in the feet of ducks and other water birds have not come to be called *gores* or *gussets*, or that *gore* did not take on the meaning of *shim*; these possible extensions seem no less reasonable than the ones that actually occurred.

Both high-frequency verbs like *give* and low-frequency nouns like *gore* and *gusset* have related meanings with a family-resemblance structure that cannot be adequately characterized by means of a single core meaning. One can attempt to accommodate these cases in the standard model of word meaning by deviating from the strict position of parsimony and allowing separate entries for related but distinct meanings; the difficulty is that there are no principled boundaries between uses involving the same sense, related but distinguishable senses, and wholly distinct senses. Anyway, wherever the lines are drawn, forcing different uses of words into categories will obliterate fine distinctions in sense to which people are sensitive.

Our claim is that *give, gore* and *gusset* are typical, rather than exceptional. What constitutes a normal situation for English vocabulary is an anomaly in the standard model of word meaning. The assumption of parsimony does not characterize the way word meanings are actually organized in human memory.

ACCOUNTING FOR CONTEXTUAL VARIATION
WITHIN THE STANDARD MODEL

There are several avenues by which one might try to maintain some version of a core meaning approach to the multiple senses one finds for a verb like *give*, as in the sentences

> *John gave Frank five dollars.*
> *John gave Mary a kiss.*
> *The doctor gave the child an injection.*
> *The orchestra gave a stunning performance.*

The initial problem, of course, is to postulate a general meaning for *give* that would account for these four sentences. At first glance, this seems next to impossible, since the intersection of the four senses of *give* here seems close to empty. However, it is not logically necessary for core meanings to simply be the intersection of the features of all their contextual realizations. One can conceive of rules of contextual modification of meaning that change features, as well as rules that add them. Such a rule would, in effect, provide an algorithm for answering the question, "Given the core meaning of *give* [which could be fairly specific], what meaning is the word *give* likely to have in this context?" Essentially, such rules would be principles of metaphor.

Such rules are not inconceivable. Take for example the meaning of *high* in *high mountains, high prices, high morale*, and *high opinion*. The intersection of the meanings of *high* in these various contexts is presumably something very general, something like "positive polarity," which would not be sufficient to distinguish *high* from other positive polarity words like *large, great, tall*, or *good*, especially since others of these presumably would also need very vague core meanings, if core meanings were defined simply in terms of the features common to all uses. However, one could also account for the meanings of *high* in the phrases mentioned by giving it a fairly concrete literal definition (e.g., "positive polarity with respect to the vertical dimension") and then stipulate a principle of semantic extension that says something like this: "When terms having positive or negative polarity do not literally fit their contexts, preserve their polarity and adjust the scale on which the polarity is expressed to fit the context."

In the case of *give a kiss*, it is a little harder to state the principle explicitly, but the point is the same. Given some core meaning of *give*, which could be fairly specific, someone who knew anything about kissing, but had never heard the phrase *give (someone) a kiss*, could easily figure out what *give* means in this context using principles of metaphorical extension.

The notion of core meaning plus metaphorical extension fits awkwardly with the standard model, however. Logically speaking, within the standard model it would be expected that a meaning derived by metaphorical extension would be based on criterial features, since these features *are* the core meaning of the word in this model. However, as a matter of fact, metaphorical extensions are typically based on noncriterial features. Birds are not free by definition; nor is craftiness a criterion for being a fox.

And of course, even where the idea of a core meaning plus metaphorical extension is highly plausible, this does not guarantee that a person does not also store contextual variants. For example, the use of the phrase *the White House* to refer to the executive branch of the U.S. government is part of a predictable pattern of metonymy (cf. the Kremlin, the Vatican, No. 10 Downing Street). But that does not mean that the extended meaning of *the White House* is not lexicalized—that is, permanently stored in the person's lexicon.

The problem is not that the relationship between the meanings of words is so opaque; in fact, we have just considered the possibility that it is predictable, given the contexts. The specific evidence against the core meaning approach in the case of *give*, for instance, has to do with distribution; the fact that you can *give* someone a shove, but not *grant* someone a shove; you can *give* a performance, but not *donate* one, at least not in the same sense.

One way to solve the problem is to include in the lexical entry, along with the core meaning, a specification of the contexts in which the word is used. For example, *give* {permission, kisses, performances, medical treatment, . . . }; *grant* {permission, favors, . . .}. This move to salvage a parsimonious "core meaning" model seems to work satisfactorily in a number of cases. And, some will believe that it is inherently more satisfying to account for the differences in usage of *give*, *grant*, and *donate* as conventionalized restrictions on their distribution, rather than in terms of subtle differences in meaning.

But representing the distribution of these meanings in the lexicon, however it is done, necessarily compromises the principles of abstractness and parsimony; exemplars of the uses of words are being incorporated into lexical entries. In terms of the overall parsimony of the model, there is a trade-off between specifying distribution and postulating subtle distinctions in sense. If you are allowed to specify the contexts in which the word occurs, you can often get by with a vaguer, more generic account of its meaning. Conversely, more precise formulation of related meanings of a word will, at least in some cases, account for the word's distribution in the language. Which way is most parsimonious is not clear a priori. Nor is it apparent that the two alternatives— having separate senses of *give* for *give a kiss* and *give a recital*, or having one sense, but listing the specific contexts in which this one sense may occur—are any more than notational variants.

However, some facts about language usage appear to require including information about contexts in the mental lexicon. For example, the fact that in German you can have *high punishment (hohe Strafe)*, while in English punishment would be called *severe*, does not seem to be a fact about the meanings of the words *high* and *punishment* in English and German, but simply arbitrary facts about stock phrases in the two languages that must be recorded in the lexicon, if people are to use the words appropriately. Similarly, sometimes contextual information must be included in lexical entries for syntactic reasons. For example, it must be represented in the lexicon that *donate*, unlike the related verb *give*, cannot take an indirect object without a preposition; one does not normally say *He donated the museum a large sum of money.*

Not even the compromised model, in which the contexts in which a word is used are specified along with a core meaning, saves the standard theory from the embarrassment of multiple related senses. Often two or more senses must be postulated because a word can have different meanings in identical contexts. For example, the sentence *The doctor delivered the baby* is potentially ambiguous, since this sentence could be used to refer to a situation in which the doctor brought the baby to a house in his station wagon.

In summary, we argue that it is typical of natural language that there are arbitrary, conventional restrictions on how words are combined in sentences; our knowledge of words must therefore include exemplars of their usage, in some form or another. The fact that words have multiple, contextually contingent meanings is an anomaly for the standard model. Moves to account for contextual variation in meaning within the standard model are at best partially successful.

On the other hand, family-resemblance relationships among meanings are the natural consequence of a model of meaning in which the meaning of a word is represented not in terms of a maximally abstract generalization that covers all members of the set, but in terms of specific uses of the word. That is, for example, the application of a word like *game* to a new activity (say, knocking bottles off a fence by throwing rocks at them) may be based not on a consideration of whether that activity meets some general criteria for games, but on the basis of its similarity, say, to bowling.

SEMANTIC DECOMPOSITION

In the standard model of word meaning, the connotation of a word consists of the set of necessary and sufficient conditions required for the serious, literal use of the word. Thus, the standard model of meaning presupposes some type of semantic decomposition, the analysis of meanings into conditions, or semantic features. We intend *semantic feature* to be an unproblematical and theoretically neutral term, although of course the expression has taken on a patina of meaning because of the way it has been used by various theorists.

A well-known example of feature analysis is the decomposition of *bachelor* into HUMAN, ADULT, MALE, NEVER MARRIED (Katz & Fodor, 1963). The features are capitalized (or marked in some other way such as <human> <adult>) to indicate these are conceptual distinctions instead of just other words in English.

Any attempt to analyze word senses into component distinctions, however modest and informal, could be called *semantic feature analysis*. Some type of semantic decomposition is almost unavoidable in the description of word meanings. That is, it would be difficult to deny that the meanings of some words overlap. One could hardly deny that some concepts are complex and therefore reducible to simpler concepts. Nor could one deny that there are groups of words that share common elements of meaning. For example, one would scarcely want to argue that people have multiple, totally independent theories of gender, one for the word *mother*, one for the word *uncle*, one for the word *niece*, one for the word *grandfather*, and so on.

However, the assertion that some words share semantic content does not amount to a theory of semantic features. Any theory of semantic features necessarily involves stronger claims. A feature theory strong enough to be interesting will have at least several of the following properties:

Criterial: Word meanings can be characterized in terms of a set of necessary and sufficient components.

Atomic: Semantic features are not further reducible within the linguistic system.

Sense based: Features can be defined in terms of sensorimotor constructs.

Binary: Features have two mutually exclusive and opposite values.

Unstructured: Word meanings can be described in terms of unstructured or unordered sets of features—e.g., a bachelor is someone who is human, and adult, and male, and unmarried.

Exhaustive: All word meanings in a language can be analyzed exhaustively into semantic components.

Parsimonious: The set of semantic features necessary to describe the vocabulary of a language is small, at the very least smaller than the number of the words in the language.

Universal: All word meanings in every language can be mapped onto a single universal alphabet of semantic features.

Sufficient to account for sentence semantics: Notions of sentence semantics such as synonymy, analyticity, ambiguity, meaningfulness, and anomaly can be adequately characterized in terms of semantic features.

Causally involved in comprehension: Word meanings are understood by decomposing them into their semantic features.

Convergent: The elements of meaning that are primitive in a description of adult linguistic knowledge will also be developmentally primitive and computationally primitive—i.e., the units of on-line comprehension.

Although it is often extremely convenient to talk in terms of components or features when discussing word meanings, one does not have a theory of semantic features at all unless one can maintain at least some of these properties. And strong objections have been raised to any theory of semantic features defined with enough precision to have any teeth; each of the above properties can be shown to be problematic.

Can Semantic Features Capture Necessary and Sufficient Conditions?

In the strongest versions of standard semantic theory, the goal is to specify the semantic features that are individually necessary and jointly sufficient for the sober, good-faith use of a term. As we have already discussed, this goal has turned out to be impossible in principle for natural-kind terms (Putnam, 1975) and perhaps inappropriate for other sorts of words as well (Green, 1984).

Some words may be considered to have truly necessary features. It does seem, for example, that a person's being unmarried is a necessary condition for literally calling this person a *bachelor*. However, this fact does not force one to the conclusion that even the meanings of these words can be described in terms of necessary and sufficient conditions. Continuing the example, the meaning of *bachelor* is influenced by a complex social milieu that is changing before our very eyes. The boundaries of its meaning are fuzzy and constantly shifting. Does a man become a bachelor if he remains unmarried past his twenty-first birthday? Or not until his thirtieth? Does a young man have to move out of his parents' home to be called a bachelor? Can a divorced man properly be called a bachelor? Is a man in "a long-term relationship" with a woman a bachelor? Is a man in a gay "marriage" a bachelor? Is a middle-aged woman who has never been married a bachelor? Has the meaning of the term shifted so that one now has to say *confirmed bachelor* to get across what was once communicated by *bachelor* alone?

Are Semantic Features
Atomic and Sense Based?

A feature is *atomic*, or *primitive*, if it is not further reducible. A feature is *sense based* if its presence or absence can be directly determined using the eyes, ears, nose, or fingertips. Looking again at the representation of the meaning of *bachelor* as a string of features, MALE is perhaps sense based, but it seems to be a bundle of separable characteristics rather than one irreducible feature. Obviously, NEVER MARRIED fails on both counts. It would be impossible to tell from looking at a man whether he had ever been married. Marriage is a complex social form that should be reducible to more primitive elements. NEVER is a peculiar, or at least special, modifier; yet the simpler NOT does not quite work, because a man who is divorced or a widower is not (usually) called a bachelor. *Bachelor* is not an exceptional case. Few of the semantic features that appear in published analyses appear to be both atomic and sense based.

Are Semantic Features Binary?

Semantic features are usually treated as *binary*. It is customary to indicate that a word has a feature with a plus sign and that it does not have a feature with a minus sign. Words coded plus on a feature usually denote the presence of some attribute; those coded minus denote the absence or relative absence of the attribute. When pairs of words with contrasting values on a feature are examined, the ones coded plus usually are linguistically *unmarked*, whereas the ones coded minus may be *marked*. A word is marked if it contains a prefix, typically one indicating negation such as *un-* or *in-*; for example, *friendly* and *unfriendly*, *animate* and *inanimate*, and *relevant* and *irrelevant*. When a word coded plus and a word coded minus on a feature are used in a compound expression, the preferred order is the plus word before the minus word; thus, we say *good or bad* instead of *bad or good* and *husband and wife* instead of *wife and husband*.

The tradition of representing meanings as strings of binary, or two-valued, features coded plus or minus lays traps for the unwary. VERTICAL seems to be atomic, sense based, and universal. What + VERTICAL means is intuitively clear. Putting it in words, it means, roughly, perpendicular to the plane of the earth's surface. However, there is an indefinite range of possibilities for − VERTICAL. It decidedly does not mean horizontal. Nor does − BLACK mean white, since many shades of gray are possible.

In general, a determinate meaning for a word coded minus on a feature is warranted only when the feature divides the world into two mutually exclusive and exhaustive categories. Thus, strictly speaking, − TRUE cannot be equated with false because statements may be partly true, answers not entirely wrong, and so on. Yet, stipulating that TRUE and FALSE are to be taken as mutually exclusive and exhaustive is a simplifying assumption that powerfully aids reasoning. Similarly, it can be argued that equating − MALE with female is a serviceable approximation to reality, despite the existence of bisexuals, transvestites, and hermaphrodites.

Some scholars have modified semantic feature theory by treating some semantic features essentially as continuous variables (e.g., Labov, 1973; Lakoff, 1972). Although allowing features to apply to varying degrees may appear to be a relatively minor extension of the notion of "semantic feature," this extension in fact impacts on the notion of criteriality of features, which is at the very core of the standard model of word meaning.

Can Word Meanings Be Described as Unordered Sets of Features?

The simple versions of feature theory assume that word meanings are unordered sets of features. However, it is easy to show that some sort of internal structure is needed to represent many word meanings. An example is *husband*. To say that this word is coded +ADULT and +MALE is merely to express boundary conditions; the distinctive semantic content is that a husband is the spouse of some woman and, reciprocally, that this woman is his spouse. Just writing down SPOUSE does not reveal who is related to whom, and what characteristics they must have to enter into the relationship.

Various methods have been proposed for representing the internal structure of word senses. One is in *meaning postulates* (Carnap, 1947; Gordon & Lakoff, 1971), which attempt to formalize meanings in logical notation. Another way is in terms of *case structures*. This approach was used by Fillmore (1968) in an informative analysis of verbs of judging, such as *accuse, blame, criticize,* and *praise*. Each of the capitalized words in the following represents a case or role. Verbs of judging involve a Situation, which is an action, deed, or state of affairs that may impact favorably or unfavorably upon the Affected. The Situation may have been caused by a Defendant. A Judge renders a moral judgment about the Situation or the Defendant's responsibility. To illustrate, Fillmore gave the role structure of *accuse* as "A Judge tells an Addressee that a Defendant is responsible for a bad Situation."

According to Fillmore, a *role* is a variable to be assigned a value—or a slot to be instantiated—based on information from utterances being interpreted. For example, in the sentence *Sara accused Rick of leaving the gift*, the Judge is Sara and the Defendant is Rick. The Addressee is not clear; perhaps this role is also filled by Rick. Though leaving a gift is not ordinarily bad, it must fill the bad Situation role; otherwise, the sentence will not make sense. This leads to the further inferences: Sara is accusing in a playful manner, the gift is something outrageous, or Rick left the gift someplace where it should not have been left (e.g., at home instead of bringing it to a birthday party). Fillmore is making the same point frequently made by schema theorists: People strive for coherence; they fill slots with the information given when possible, by inference when necessary.

The point here is that there are groups of words—such as *buy* and *sell*; or *accuse, blame,* and *criticize*—whose meanings differ not in which features they contain, but in the structure into which these features are organized.

Can Semantic Features Be Both Exhaustive and Parsimonious?

Can a set of features be constructed that both exhaustively describes the vocabulary of a language, and that is substantially smaller than that vocabulary? Analysis of the words in a language into semantic features is a reasonable enterprise only if the number of semantic features turns out to be smaller than the number of words they describe (Fodor et al., 1980). Knowing whether this is the case depends on an exhaustive and detailed semantic analysis of at least one language, something that is unlikely to be available in the foreseeable future.

There is reason to doubt that semantic feature analysis will result in a vocabulary of features considerably smaller than the vocabulary of words. Having a relatively small number of features depends on the features required to make distinctions in any one semantic domain applying in several other domains.

For example, an absolute minimum of eight semantic features would be necessary to describe the meanings of *swagger, strut, stride, saunter, pace, amble,* and *stroll*—one feature, at least, for what they share, and at least one feature each that distinguishes them from the others. This semantic feature analysis will result in a set of features smaller than the vocabulary it describes only if these features are used elsewhere. For example, if there were an adverb for each of these verbs that exactly captures how the verb differs from the base verb *walk* (that is, if the word *arrogantly* expresses exactly that which distinguishes *swagger* from *walk*, *vigorously* that which distinguishes *stride* from *walk*, and so on), then there would be fourteen words (not counting *walk*), and only eight features.

Whether analysis of meanings into semantic features would actually result in such economy depends on two things. First, there is the question of whether or not one is satisfied with definitions such as "walk arrogantly" for *swagger*. Similarly, one can argue that *bachelor* means more than "unmarried adult male." One can add features such as "eligible" in the attempt to capture the subtleties of word sense that simple clusters of features do not capture, but this diminishes the chances that the number of semantic features postulated will be smaller than the number of words.

Second, there is the question whether the fine-grained distinctions necessary in any given domain will be applicable in any other domain. For example, the semantic difference between *roller skate* and *skateboard*, whatever it is, is not likely to play a role in very many other semantic domains. One could even go through the labor of trying to specify the semantic feature, perhaps INDIVIDUATED FOR SYMMETRICAL BODY PARTS, and trying to find other pairs of words that seem to be distinguished in terms of the feature—for instance, *mittens* versus *muffs*, *culottes* versus *skirts*, and, maybe, *skis* versus *toboggans*. Still, this leaves unvitiated the force of the argument that there will be an unmanageably large number of extremely specialized features if one tries to account for all of the fine distinctions in the vocabulary of a language.

One way to try to get around this problem is to recognize two types of semantic features. An example of such a division is Katz and Fodor's (1963) distinction between *semantic markers*—features that occur in many word meanings—and *distinguishers*—the semantic content unique to the word, that cannot be further analyzed into features that recur in other meanings.

It should be noted first of all that such a move involves abandoning several of the properties often postulated for a theory of semantic features. Taken together, semantic markers and distinguishers are no longer necessarily fewer in number than the words in the vocabulary of the language they describe. But semantic markers alone do not exhaustively describe the meanings of words. On the other hand, there may be a little more hope for having semantic markers (but not distinguishers) meet some of the other conditions postulated for semantic features, for instance, being atomic and universal.

Katz and Fodor had set as the basic goal of their theory accounting for the sentence-level semantic phenomena of ambiguity, analyticity, meaningfulness, anomaly, and synonymy. They had attempted to constrain their semantic theory by claiming that these phenomena could be described in terms of semantic markers, with no reference to the information in distinguishers. Bolinger (1965) argued cogently that this claim could not be maintained, effectively putting an end to the use of this distinction.

Are Semantic Features Universal?

Some semantic features, such as CAUSE, recur in the descriptions of numerous languages, reflecting, presumably, either innate properties of human cognition, or universal properties of human experience. While it is reasonable to suppose that *some* features are universal, any strong claim of universality of features would be incompatible with the criterion of exhaustiveness.

A strong test of universality would be to show that there is no semantic distinction between two words in any one language that cannot be expressed in terms of features independently motivated for many other languages. To carry out such a test for even a single semantic distinction in a well-researched domain, such as, for instance, kinship terms, would be a daunting task.

Are Semantic Features Sufficient to Account for Sentence Semantics?

In addition to providing a gloss on the meanings of individual words and furnishing the differentia for sets of related words, features are invoked to explain a variety of other aspects of meaning and language understanding. According to Katz and his associates (Katz & Fodor, 1963; Katz & Postal, 1964; Katz, 1972), whose seminal writings can be credited with the surge of interest in semantic feature analysis beginning in the mid-1960s, features play a pivotal role in resolving such matters as whether sentences are ambiguous, anomalous, or tautological.

The treatment of anomaly is illustrated by the sentence *The dream was tall*. It does not make sense because dreams are not the sorts of things that can be tall. According to the theory, the problem is that *dream* does not have the feature + PHYSICAL OBJECT, which is required for the use of *tall*. It is the violation of this so-called "selection restriction" that is said to make the sentence anomalous.

The comprehensiveness of the feature theory proposed by Katz and his associates makes it very appealing and, at one and the same time, opens it to telling criticism. It can be argued that the theory sweeps under its skirts issues that cannot be, or should not be, decided solely on the basis of knowledge of the language. Feature theory glosses the sentence *She is the father of her children* as anomalous because *father* is marked + MALE, whereas *she* and *her* are marked − MALE. The sentence expresses a riddle to be sure, but the difficulty is not in understanding the assertion. Instead, the obstacle to comprehension is conceiving a situation in which the sentence could be a good-faith utterance. A mundane possibility is a single woman who has to roughhouse with her sons, teach them to play ball, and so on. Matched to this scenario *father* is being used metaphorically. With just a little more imagination it is possible to envision a setting for the sentence in which *father* has a literal meaning: Suppose a transvestite with a family has a sex-change operation (see Lyons, 1977, p. 305).

Are Semantic Features Causally Involved in Comprehension?

The weakest claim that could be made for some sort of semantic feature theory as a model of meaning is that of what Chomsky (1965) would call *observational adequacy*. That is, the semantic features are hypothetical constructs that attempt to describe the content, although not necessarily the form, of people's knowledge of word meanings.

For example, at this level, saying that words such as *brother, uncle,* and *bachelor* have the feature + MALE is simply an assertion that anyone who knows what these words mean applies them (seriously and literally, at least) only to male individuals.

A stronger claim about semantic features can be made—namely, that they describe not only the content of people's word knowledge but also the form it takes. From this perspective, features are psychologically real. A person who knows what a word means has this meaning represented in his or her mind as a set of semantic primitives.

This stronger claim, that the componential representation of word meaning is somehow isomorphic to the cognitive representation and processes involved in knowing and understanding words, gives rise to specific predictions about language processing—for instance, that speed and difficulty of processing should be predictable from the number and nature of semantic features involved in a word's meaning. Despite numerous experiments, unequivocal support for any strong version of this claim has not been found (Fodor et al., 1980; Kintsch, 1974).

Are Semantic Features Convergent?

Can there be a convergent theory of semantic features? That is, can one postulate a single set of features that are developmentally primitive (features that are acquired early, and out of which later meanings are constructed), computationally primitive (the elements involved in on-line comprehension), and definitionally primitive (the set of features out of which all meanings in adult language can be constructed)?

Carey (1982) points out that the classical view of semantic features assumes this kind of convergence (p. 351). As we have just argued, there is no evidence that semantic features are computationally primitive at all. Carey argues further that the features which would best describe distinctions among adult word meanings are not likely to be developmentally primitive (p. 367). Some of the distinctions among word meanings known by adults can be described only in terms of theories of the world that the young child does not yet possess. Hence, it does not seem possible for the same set of features to underlie children's acquisition of word meanings and adults' use of them.

SEMANTIC FEATURES
AS LEXICAL ORGANIZERS

Our discussion of what is known about semantic features has left us with something of a paradox. On the one hand, some notion of semantic decomposition is almost unavoidable in any discussion of word meanings. As we said, it is hard to believe (by way of example) that a speaker of English would have separate, independent theories of gender for each term in the language that involved specification of a person being male or female. In other words, such terms must share common semantic elements. On the other hand, as we argued, any of the specific claims for a theory of semantic features that would be strong enough to have some teeth to it is problematic.

One step towards resolving this paradox is to attribute a more limited role to semantic features in the internal representation of word meanings. Semantic features can be treated as generalizations about the overlap in meaning among words. In this treatment, knowledge of the meaning of individual words is not necessarily embodied in features. An implication is that children initially could learn to use words such as *father, mother, sister,* and *brother* correctly without fully recognizing the semantic relationships among them. Only later would they come to understand the features that structure kinship terms.

Several researchers in the area of child language acquisition have suggested essentially this position. For example, Nelson (1988), after reviewing a range of language development research, says, "All of these findings suggest a system that is at first characterized by independent lexemes, that are related to experientially based concepts but are not related directly to other lexemes, subsequently becoming reorganized in terms of relations between lexical items, a process that in turn leads to new insights into both the linguistic and the conceptual systems" (p. 226). Nelson describes language acquisition in terms of three phases. "The third period is one of revision, reorganization, and consolidation of lexical items within domains of related words" (p. 225).

Similarly, Gleitman and Wanner (1982), summarizing research on the acquisition of word meanings, say that "each early word is an unopened package; only much later does productive lexical analysis begin to appear" (p. 12). Gleitman and Wanner's point applies most obviously to the internal morphological structure of words. That is, children may learn the word *Thanksgiving*, and use it with some degree of appropriateness, before they appreciate that it has anything to do with giving thanks. However, the point applies equally well to the internal semantic structure of words. Bowerman (1982) gives specific cases of children learning to appropriately use semantically complex words like *drop* and *break*, which involve the notion of causation. But only later do they show, through overextensions in their use of other words, that they have recognized that the feature CAUSE has recurrent organizational significance in the English lexicon.

One way in which this perspective on semantic features differs from a stronger theory is that it abandons the claim of exhaustiveness. That is, it does not assume that words can be exhaustively analyzed into semantic features. Rather, the point is that *some* parts of word meanings may be factored out, so to speak. Bowerman (1982) theorizes that distinctions which have recurrent organizational significance may function differently from those that do not. "Meaning distinctions that are relevant only to one or a small handful of language forms may typically be left implicit, even if the child might in some sense recognize them. . . . In contrast, meaning distinctions that run systematically through a variety of forms . . . may be pulled out for special attention under certain circumstances" (p. 129).

The point is that there are good reasons to distinguish conceptual distinctions a child is able to make from the subset of those distinctions that come to play a role in the organization of the child's word knowledge. Carey (1978) explains this in the following way: "The child already knows the words *big* and *little* before he learns any of the specialized spatial adjectives. Since the core comparative structure [including polarity] is part of his early representations of *big* and *little*, these features are already available as lexical organizers when the child encounters a word like *wide* or *low*. By 'available as a lexical organizer,' I mean already part of the lexical entry of some word. Although the features underlying the dimensionality of spatial extent are part of the child's conceptual system, their linguistic relevance might not yet be recognized. That is, the child might not yet realize that the spatial concepts mark contrasts between words. . . . It is not unreasonable to assume that features available as lexical organizers are mapped onto new words more easily than those that are not yet so available" (pp. 281–282).

A key assumption is that recognition of the semantic relationships among words, and hence of those parts of word meanings that are shared, is not a prerequisite for appropriate use of words and some level of understanding of them. As Gleitman and Wanner (1982) put it, "Internal analysis of the word unit is a late and variable step in cognitive-linguistic development." (p. 13). Explicit representation of semantic relationships may be an asymptote that adults approach, rather than a characteristic of linguistic representation at all ages. Thus, Carey (1978) hypothesizes: "It is possible that even some adults do not discover all the regularities in the domain, never fully representing, for example, how *fat*, *wide*, and *thick* differ, although they know very well some paradigm cases of things that can be each" (p. 288).

In the perspective being outlined here, then, semantic features are in some sense optional. People can, and often do, use and understand words correctly without recognizing the relationships that hold among them. If this is so, one can then justifiably ask, What function do semantic features have? An answer is that a knowledge of features facilitates word learning. In Carey's (1978, 1982) research, for instance, learning a new color word was easier if the construct of a color word was already part of child's semantic system. Similarly, learning the word *niece* should be easier if one already knows that gender plays a systematic role in differentiating kinship terms.

If analysis of meanings into semantic features is optional but aids in word learning, one might expect the tendency to recognize semantic features to be associated with greater facility in word learning. Van Daalen Kapteijns and Elshout-Mohr (1981, 1987) argue that the tendency to analyze word meanings into components is associated with higher verbal ability. They make this claim on the basis of their analysis of protocols from a task in which subjects had to infer the meaning of a novel word from a series of context sentences. The task paralleled the one used by Werner and Kaplan (1952), except that in this experiment, the novel words represented novel, complex concepts. In trying to integrate information from succeeding sentences, the higher-ability subjects treated their initial hypothesis about the word's meaning as a decomposable structure, adjusting the meaning to fit other contexts by keeping some parts constant and varying others. The lower-ability subjects, on the other hand, tended to treat word meanings as unanalyzable wholes; if the meaning they chose for the first sentence did not fit the second, they would start from scratch rather than try to alter parts of their first hypothesis.

In this section, we have outlined an alternative perspective on semantic features. Semantic features are theorized to represent not essential conditions for comprehension and successful use of words, but attributes useful for organizing knowledge of word meanings. The evidence cited in this section is consistent with the position that we outlined earlier about the role of abstractness and parsimony in lexical representations: We do not deny that people see similarities among word meanings and represent generalizations about these similarities in some way. What we deny is that word meanings are represented exclusively, or even primarily, at the maximal level of abstractness.

SENTENCE MEANING

Associated with the standard model of word meaning is the view that sentences have a literal, compositional meaning independent of world knowledge, context, or speaker's intentions. That is to say, the standard position is that the meaning of a sentence is determined by core word meanings, syntactic rules, and nothing else. We will attack this view in two ways: First, we will argue that for a large number of English sentences, the literal sentence meaning is not a compositional function of the meanings of the component words. Second, we will argue that the concept of literal meaning itself is not tenable.

Sentence Compositionality

One of the fundamental insights of generative grammar was the creativity of normal language use. As has been pointed out repeatedly by Chomsky (1965) and others, knowing English (or any other language) does not consist in knowing a list of specific sentences. Rather, the rules of syntax can be applied creatively, so that many of the sentences one speaks or hears, although fully understandable, are occurring for the first time in the history of the language. This is no doubt true, for example, of the vast majority of the sentences in this chapter; to the extent that the reader understands them, it is not because these exact sentences have been read or heard before.

We do not deny that understanding and producing English involves creative use of the syntactic rules of the language. However, the fact that language use is *truly* creative does not mean that it is *fully* creative. Although the grammar of a language must specify how words are put together to form sentences, it does not follow that when speakers or writers form sentences, they start from the smallest units, building phrases from individual words, and sentences from phrases. On the contrary, the frequency of idioms, collocations, clichés, and stock phrases in normal language use shows that normal speech is often more like baking a cake from a mix than like baking a cake from scratch.

Normal language use is full of prefabricated units. Such units, since they function as units, tend to take on meanings above and beyond what is predictable from the meanings of their component parts. This is most obvious at the level of words. The fact that an iceman brings the ice, but a snowman is made out of snow, for example, cannot be determined on the basis of the meanings of *ice, snow,* and *man* alone. It would be safe to say that a large proportion of the complex words in the language, and the majority of the most frequent ones, have meanings that convey something beyond what is predictable on the basis of the meanings of the parts alone. However, there is also rampant semantic irregularity above the level of the word. The idiosyncrasy of the meaning of a phrase is sometimes minor; the fact that one says *ham and eggs* instead of *eggs and ham* may encode only the fact that ham and eggs is a traditional combination of foods, unlike, for example, eggs and broccoli. But there is a continuum of semantic irregularity, ranging from phrases like *ham and eggs* to fully opaque expressions like *kick the bucket,* or *by and large.*

In between are a variety of fixed phrases like *flew the coop, change one's mind, toe the line, make ends meet, pay one's own way, make oneself at home,* or *to think better of* something. In some sense, the in-between cases are the most problematic for a compositional model of sentence meaning. On the one hand, the meaning of the phrase is more than, or different from, the sum of its parts; on the other hand, it cannot be treated simply as a long word, because there is a recognizable internal structure, and some of the items within these phrases do have their usual meanings. Furthermore, the number and frequency of this type of phrase in normal language use is far greater than most people are aware. *Take your chances* and *make yourself at home* may sound like examples of perfectly regular, literal phrases, until you realize that *take your risks* and *make yourself at house,* although presumably similar in meaning, do not sound like normal English.

For a substantial proportion of the phrases used in English, then, it is simply not possible to treat their meanings as a compositional function of the meanings of their parts. Rather, the meaning of the phrase, or at least some aspects of its meaning, must be considered to be associated with the phrase as a whole. This raises the possibility that even for some of the phrases that have fully predictable meanings, the meaning of the phrase as a whole is also stored in memory, rather than being computed from scratch every time the phrase is used. Of course, for truly novel phrases, meanings will have to be computed. But there is little reason to cling to an a priori notion of parsimony that would necessitate, for a phrase with a perfectly regular meaning, that the listener compute its meaning afresh on the fifth, tenth, or hundredth time he or she heard it.

Indirect speech acts also pose a problem for the concept of literal sentence meaning. The sentence *Can you pass the salt?* literally asks whether someone is able to pass the salt, but what it actually means is please pass the salt. A somewhat similar problem is posed by idioms. The sentence *He kicked the bucket* literally declares that someone struck a blow with his foot against a type of container, but what it ordinarily means is that someone died.

The way proponents of compositional theory propose to deal with indirect speech acts and idioms is to distinguish between *sentence meaning* and *utterance meaning.* Utterance meaning is so called because the sentence is supposed to have been uttered by some speaker in some situation for some reason. Thus, *Do you have change for a dollar?* is a question at the level of sentence meaning but usually is a request at the level of utterance meaning. Sentence meaning is supposed to be the unadorned linguistic interpretation, while utterance meaning includes elaborations based on linguistic context, situational context, and background knowledge. The distinction between literal sentence meaning and utterance meaning parallels the distinction between *core word meaning* (connotation) and *contextual word meaning* (sense) we discussed in an earlier section.

In compositional theories of language processing, it is supposed that people first compute sentence meaning and then ascertain utterance meaning. It follows that it should take longer to understand sentences containing expressions like *kick the bucket* when the expressions are used idiomatically than when they are used literally. The reasoning is that it will take time to activate and then reject the literal meaning which, in expressions such as this, is misaligned with utterance meaning. Gibbs (1986) was unable to confirm this prediction. Nor did he find that it took people longer to process sentences such as *Can you pass the salt?* in contexts that invited an indirect speech act interpretation as compared with contexts that invited a literal interpretation (Gibbs, 1983).

One way to save compositional theory from the predictions that went unfulfilled in the Gibbs experiments is to assume that people treat familiar idioms and conventional indirect requests as long words. Accordingly, to die is one sense, undoubtedly the primary one, of the whole phrase *kick the bucket*. There is evidence that all of the distinct senses of a word are activated when it is encountered, and then the ones that do not fit the context quickly fade (Swinney, 1979). Thus, if such expressions are treated as long words, it may be possible to explain Gibbs's findings within the standard framework.

We are, of course, willing to accept the consequence that a large number of prefabricated sentences and sentence fragments will be stored in memory. However, the attempt to salvage a compositional theory of sentence processing by redefining idioms and indirect speech acts as complex words is somewhat self-defeating. That is, any apparently nonliteral utterance meaning that is not associated with an increase in processing time becomes a literal sentence meaning, by definition, and a noncompositional one, at that. This amounts to simply defining away any counterexamples to the claim of compositional theory that nonliteral meanings should require additional processing time.

Literal Sentence Meaning

Our fundamental quarrel is with the construct *literal sentence meaning*. Specifically, we reject the claim that there is a sentence meaning, constructed prior to and apart from the application of background knowledge to determine utterance meaning, which constitutes a literal understanding of the sentence.

First of all, we question whether there can be a strict ordering of types of processing, with background knowledge being called into play only after all strictly linguistic processing has been completed. Certainly there are *some* bottom-up processes in reading comprehension that operate prior to and independent of the reader's knowledge or expectations. For example, as we have mentioned, it appears that all distinct senses of a word are immediately activated, before contextual selection of sense takes place. But we know of no persuasive evidence that a linguistically based selection of senses—for example, distinguishing between the senses of *rose* on the basis of its syntactic function—always occurs before a knowledge-based selection of senses. (For the contrasting view that lexical access is "impenetrable" to the influence of world knowledge, see Perfetti & McCutchen, 1986.)

Secondly, we claim that the ordinary experience of understanding a sentence corresponds to the concept of utterance meaning, and necessarily involves the utilization of world knowledge. There is no experience of sentence meaning that does not involve the application of background knowledge in some way. This can be illustrated with examples of several types.

Consider the following set of sentences, all containing what in any parsimonious version of the standard model would constitute the same sense of the verb *cut*

Bill cut the grass.
The barber cut Tom's hair.
Sally cut the cake.

A normal reading of these sentences produces envisionments, or scenarios, that go beyond what might be said to be literally contained in the words. Everyone's envisionments will include the instruments by which the cutting is done. The word *cut* is used in the same sense in these sentences, meaning roughly to physically separate into parts using a more-or-less sharp object.

Yet as Searle (1979) has observed, "crazy misunderstandings" will be likely if that is all there is to the meaning of *cut* in these sentences: Sally's cutting the cake with a lawn mower would be no less acceptable than her using a knife. In other words, a person asked to determine the literal meaning of the sentence *Sally cut the cake* would not have in mind an abstract representation of the situation that was equally applicable to cutting the cake with a lawn mower and with a knife.

It is true that, with some conscious effort, a person can imagine a representation of the "meaning" of the sentence *Sally cut the cake* that is so abstract as to apply equally well to either of these situations. It seems peculiar, though, to cling to the position that the result of such mental gymnastics has more right to be called the meaning of the sentence than what comes spontaneously to the mind of the normal reader taking the sentence at face value.

It might appear that the problem posed for the concept of literal meaning by the preceding example could be dealt with simply by postulating multiple senses of the word *cut*. If there are three senses of *cut*—something like "to mow, as with a lawn mower," "to trim, as with scissors," and "to separate into serving portions"—then one might be able to equate literal meaning with the normal understanding of these sentences. However, such a move would ultimately require an appeal to background knowledge in the disambiguation of *cut*, as we explained at length in the section on contextual variation.

Another type of example involves sentences that are not fully comprehensible unless one is able to bring to bear extralinguistic knowledge. In this example, unlike the preceding one, distinctions in the sense of individual words do not play a crucial role. Try to determine the literal meaning of the following sentences:

The haystack was important because the cloth ripped.
The notes were sour because the seams split.
The party stalled because the wire straightened.

These sentences are well known to psycholinguists from the work of Bransford and Franks (1976), but if you have not seen them before you probably experienced difficulty in coming up with anything you would want to call the sentence meaning. To be sure, these are especially contrived sentences. But they are not defective like *Colorless green ideas sleep furiously*. The syntax is straightforward. The words are used in ordinary ways. And, each of the sentences does have a legitimate and readily understandable interpretation.

Now, consider some clues that provide additional information for interpreting the sentences. The clues are *parachute, bagpipe,* and *corkscrew* for the three sentences, respectively. If any of the clues enabled the "click of comprehension" for you, the source of difficulty with the sentences ought to be clear: The obstacle to comprehension is envisioning possible situations onto which the sentences could map. The question is whether, if you failed to come up with the defective parachute envisionment, for instance, you would want to say that you were in possession of the meaning of the haystack sentence? We believe the answer is No, but not everyone agrees.

Let us sharpen the issue. The question is whether sentences have a *zero-context*, literal meaning—that is, a meaning that does not depend in any way on analysis of the linguistic context, in any way on analysis of the situation, or in any way on world knowledge. The zero- or null-context meaning of a sentence is supposed to depend solely on its wording and syntax (and maybe other linguistic machinery, as long as no contextual analysis or world knowledge creeps in).

Our experience is that educators do not appreciate the force of weird counterexamples against what are presented as universal claims, because they so often have to deal with claims that no one in their right mind would mistake as being universal in scope. The sentences above about haystacks and so on might be discounted because they are a little weird. We turn, therefore, to the exquisitely simple sentence below:

The cat is on the mat.

This sentence has been debated at length by Searle (1979), who upholds the constructivist position, and Katz (1981), who defends what we are calling the standard position. Katz claims to know the zero-context meaning of *The cat is on the mat.* He says, "The sentence . . . has a literal compositional meaning. Unlike *Itches drink theorems*, its selection restrictions are in order. Its meaning is, roughly, that some [contextually specified] cat is vertically positioned over some [contextually specified] mat and that the aforementioned cat is also positioned so that its bottom is in contact with the top of the mat" (p. 220).

Katz completely gives away his argument in this passage. Bear in mind that he is not merely suggesting the usual meaning of the sentence, or pointing to one among several possible meanings. He is declaring the literal meaning based on the sentence's wording alone, with what he alleges is absolutely no reliance on context or world knowledge. Thus, to display a legitimate interpretation different from Katz's is to prove him wrong. And this is easily done. Katz says the sentence means that the cat is vertically positioned over the mat, but consider the possibility that the mat is being used as a wall hanging and that the cat has jumped up and grabbed the mat with its claws. Katz says that the sentence means that the cat is also positioned so that it is in contact with the top of the mat; but imagine the possibility of a cat balancing on the edge of a rolled, stiff, upright mat standing in a corner. As for the cat, its bottom does not need to be in contact with the mat in order to satisfy the sentence; it could be standing or it could be lying on its side.

It is plain to see that what Katz holds up as the zero-context, literal meaning of this sentence depends heavily on assumptions about the customary positions of mats and the usual postures of cats. We assert as a general rule that the literal meaning of a sentence is parasitical on assumptions about normal states of the world. It follows that there is no such thing as a zero-context meaning for a sentence.

The idea of literal meaning as the first derivative in language understanding has had an almost irresistible appeal for information-processing psychologists committed to the concept of automaticity. Basically they argue that a fast, fluent process could not involve much reasoning or complicated choices among alternatives. For a good exposition of this position, which goes over some of the same ground as this chapter, see Perfetti and McCutchen (1986).

For a different reason, the idea of literal meaning also has appeal to linguists. Consider the sentence *Flying planes can be dangerous*. It has two distinct meanings, at least in some sense of meaning, depending on whether one sees *planes* as the underlying subject or underlying object of *flying*. The concept of utterance meaning does not provide the right level of analysis for dealing insightfully with ambiguities of this type, however. But if linguists were to adopt a construct of literal sentence meaning for talking about such examples, they would have to (we argue) avoid identifying that construct with any actual representation of sentences by real listeners or readers.

We believe that both the assumption of fixed core meanings, which are automatically accessed, and the assumption of invariant parsing rules, which are automatically applied, are faulty, for the reasons set forth in the preceding sections. This is not to say that word senses do not get accessed or that sentences do not get parsed, and that these steps happen fairly early and fairly routinely during sentence interpretation. The mistake is to identify these transient linguistic throughputs with meaning.

WHY IS THE STANDARD MODEL SO ATTRACTIVE?

If the standard model of word meaning is wrong on so many counts, and if there is such a substantial consensus among scholars that it is inadequate, why is it so attractive?

One reason is that the standard model serves as an ideal for scientific terminology, or in fact, terminology in any domain in which communication is intended to be as explicit and precise as possible. In some sense, then, the standard model reflects what many scientists and philosophers wished the language were, and tried to make it. Watson and Olson (1987) argue that a standard model of meaning, in which words are defined in terms of criterial features, follows naturally from the need for communication in a modern, literate society to be successful without personal contact, when there is no guarantee of shared assumptions.

The standard model reflects the time when scholars, at least, still thought of language primarily as written language. It might have been acknowledged that word meanings in oral language were vague and variable, but this was looked upon as exactly what good writers would want to avoid. There is, of course, a long tradition of a *prescriptive approach* towards language, treating the language not in terms of what it is, but in terms of a conception of what it should be. It is really only relatively recently that linguists have explicitly focused on oral, rather than written, language as primary. A prescriptive approach to language is still firmly entrenched in popular thinking, as can be seen from the nature of the debates about dictionaries, such as the one surrounding the publication of *Webster's Third*.

The Relationship between Linguistic and Conceptual Categories

To some extent, the attractiveness of the standard model, and its failure, can be understood in terms of two different ways of thinking about the relationship between language and the world, or more precisely, between linguistic and conceptual categories.

One we could call the *grid model*. In this model, the relationship between word meanings and the world can be thought of as analogous to the imposition of national and state boundaries on a map of, say, North America. In this analogy, state boundaries represent word meanings, national boundaries represent superordinate categories, and the whole map represents the conceptual domain—say, the universe of all animals, or of all colors, or of all emotions.

Criteriality is a logical consequence of the grid model. It follows from the fact that the conceptual domain is exhaustively categorized. The label given to an entity identifies what category the entity is in, but not its position within that category.

An alternative way of thinking might be called the *scattered-points model*. Word meanings are associated with points in a conceptual space in this model. To use another geographical metaphor, imagine a world in which almost all of the population lives in widely dispersed cities. Although the cities are clearly named, the lack of substantial population outside the cities has made it quite unnecessary, in most cases, to draw boundaries between them. There is a lot of territory that does not belong to any particular city. When an area near an established city is settled, the region is sometimes simply counted as part of the city, even though it may not be physically contiguous.

There is no reason to identify criterial features in the second model. There are a hundred ways one can differentiate Boston from New York; but there is no need to determine which of them uniquely identifies the essence of either city.

There are some cases of naming in which the grid model is better. For example, a biologist trying to come up with terms—say, at the mid-levels of a biological taxonomy—is essentially trying to impose a grid on a conceptual domain. The terms must be chosen so that they allow one to exhaustively categorize known animals. However, the taxonomy must not be so bound to idiosyncratic properties of individual species that the discovery of a new related species would necessitate major reorganization.

More generally, it could be said that the grid model is the standard for scientific terminology, especially at the level of superordinate terms. The scattered-points model, on the other hand, deals more comfortably with basic-level terms used in ordinary language: There is maximal similarity among members of a basic-level category and maximal dissimilarity between members of this category and other categories (Rosch & Mervis, 1975).

The nature of the relationship between linguistic and cognitive categories has long been a matter of debate. Whorf (1956) is associated with a strong claim about this relationship, in which linguistic categories are seen as primary. According to what has come to be called the *Sapir-Whorf hypothesis*, it is claimed that languages can differ radically in the way that they categorize and structure the world, and that linguistic categories determine cognitive categories. Thus, the structure of one's language determines how one perceives and thinks about the world. In slightly different terms, the linguistic system is both an embodiment of the worldview of a culture, and a necessary and sufficient means of inculcating it in new members.

Part of the attractiveness of the Sapir-Whorf hypothesis was that it constituted an instantiation of the insight that existing knowledge structures have a profound effect on cognition and perception, one that predated the most recent incarnation of the schema theory. The distinctive element of the Sapir-Whorf hypothesis, however—the primacy of *linguistic* structure—has never met with wide acceptance.

But despite the fact that the Sapir-Whorf hypothesis has never achieved the status of a consensus opinion, there is reason to believe that some of the assumptions underlying this hypothesis have influenced thinking about word meanings, and in fact, constitute part of the foundation for the standard model of word meaning; in particular, the assumption that experience of the world is inherently unstructured or continuous, and that language plays a primary role in structuring and categorizing it. This idea motivated James's famous description of the infant's experience of the world as a "blooming, buzzing confusion." Thus, until Berlin and Kay's (1969) work, the rainbow was often taken as a metaphor of the relationship between language and the world. The physical reality is an undifferentiated continuum; it is language that imposes boundaries.

The grid metaphor, then, can be seen as flowing out of a way of looking at the relationship between language and the world. It is most appropriate in those instances in which word meanings do serve to exhaustively categorize some semantic domain—which is sometimes the case, especially for superordinate categories.

The grid metaphor, however, depends crucially on the assumption that experience is essentially undifferentiated, and that it is language which imposes structure. Recently, increasing evidence has been brought forward that in numerous domains, conceptual structure is independent of or prior to linguistic categories (see Au, 1988, for a review of such evidence). For example, in the domain of color, although physically a rainbow is a continuum of wavelengths, the human perceptual apparatus in fact defines certain focal colors as being perceptually salient. Linguistic systems differ in interesting ways in how they categorize colors, but within constraints reflecting the structure imposed by the human perceptual system (Berlin & Kay, 1969). Perceptually, the rainbow is not a continuum; and there is no reason to believe that people from different language groups see different rainbows.

Nelson (1988), Clark (1983), and others have suggested that the extremely rapid rate of early word growth is due to the fact that once children have figured out what naming is about, they already have a very rich conceptual structure, and lots of concepts to learn the names for. It may be relevant in this regard that Nagy, Anderson, and Herman (1987) found that, in learning new words incidentally while reading, schoolchildren learned words for which they already had concepts, but did not learn words that represented new concepts.

We are not arguing that the grid model *never* fits the relationship between linguistic and conceptual categories. There are domains, as we have indicated, such as biological taxonomies, where exhaustive categorization is an important function of language. However, we would argue that meanings are not *typically* structured into exhaustive and mutually exclusive categories arranged into taxonomic hierarchies.

Let's take, for an example, the average person's knowledge of names for tools. Do the tool names known by most people exhaustively categorize the universe of tools or any subparts of that universe? Hardly. We can imagine, and we think we have seen, numerous tools that do not fit into any of our existing tool categories. Even for people with rich tool vocabularies, it seems likely that a new tool could be invented which would not be a special subcategory of existing tools.

For most people, if our experience is representative, the vocabulary of tool names contains a preponderance of basic-level categories (e.g., saw, hammer, drill), with a few subcategories (hacksaw, coping saw), and few if any true superordinates. These terms in no way exhaustively categorize the universe of possible tools.

Does this example simply reflect a fact about tools: the fact that linguistic categories cannot anticipate all possible technological breakthroughs? Let us take a different example, then: the set of verbs that describe human motion unaided by mechanical devices: verbs like *walk, run, skip, hop, dance, crawl,* and so on. Do such verbs divide possible human motion into a taxonomic hierarchy of mutually exclusive and exhaustive categories?

Not without violence to the normal meanings of the words. Again, there appears to be a lack of true superordinates—for example, is there a label for the category that includes *walk* and *run*? The common category names do not exhaustively categorize the space of possible human movement. For example, a cartwheel does not seem to fit into any more general category, nor does to walk on one's hands.

The world is structured because there is a lot of empty space in it. There are few if any tools halfway between a saw and a screwdriver. A farm does not include a continuum of animals ranging from sheep to cows. People talk and they sing, but in normal life in our culture they usually do one or the other; daily experience does not include a lot of things intermediate between the two.

To conclude, the scattered-points metaphor provides a better picture than the grid metaphor of the relationships between words and thoughts and objects. Names for things in natural languages have redundant, noncriterial features because there is empty space between categories.

DEFINITIONS AND WORD MEANING

Almost all conventional vocabulary instruction involves definitions in some way. Students look up definitions, memorize them, select the appropriate one from several alternatives, or arrive at them through discussion. Indeed, it is hard to imagine explicit instruction about word meanings that does not either begin or end with some sort of statement or description of the meaning of the word being learned.

Vocabulary instruction generally involves definitions that reflect many of the characteristics of the standard model of word meaning. The very term *definition* implies criteriality, abstractness, and parsimony of statement. Very often, the definitions used in vocabulary instruction and in glossaries are even shorter, more abstract, and less likely to include examples and information about contextual constraints than those found in regular dictionaries. Especially in such cases, the theoretical weaknesses of the standard model translate into pedagogical shortcomings.

Definitions and Meanings

A fundamental fact to be accounted for by any theory of word meaning is that people are, for the most part, not able to articulate their knowledge of word meanings quickly or easily (Johnson-Laird, 1987). This fact implies that a distinction has to be made between knowledge of word meanings and knowledge of definitions.

The fact that word knowledge normally does not take the form of definitions is a matter of logical necessity in the last analysis. Definitions map words onto other words, and at some point this circularity must be broken (Fodor et al., 1980). Familiar words that have been learned from experience in context are especially difficult to define. When familiar, everyday words are cast in definitions, it must be in terms of much less familiar words (Johnson-Laird, 1987).

But even for those words that are more amenable to definition, the distinction between knowing the meaning of the word and knowing its definition must be maintained. For most words one knows, producing a definition requires a substantial amount of reflection, whereas understanding what the word means during reading takes about a quarter of a second (McConkie, Reddix, & Zola, 1985).

Knowing a definition is neither a necessary nor sufficient condition for knowing the meaning of a word. Children successfully understand and use many words before they have the linguistic or cognitive sophistication to either produce or understand any sort of formal definition (Watson, 1985). Even for adults, the task of producing a definition for a known word is not trivial.

Nor can the gap between knowing meanings and knowing definitions be attributed simply to problems in expressing one's self. When selecting the right alternative on a multiple-choice vocabulary test or looking up a familiar word in the dictionary, one often has the sense that some insight was gained. Thus, one can know a word well enough and still feel that one has learned something by seeing an explicit definition. This would not happen if the definition already constituted understanding of the word.

Not only is knowledge of a definition not a necessary condition for knowing the meaning of a word, it is not a sufficient one either. Miller and Gildea's (1987) examples of the sort of sentences children produce on the basis of definitions make the point forcefully. For instance, given the definition of *correlate* as "to be related one to the other," one child wrote, "Me and my parents correlate, because without them I wouldn't be here."

That definitions are not sufficient for knowing the meanings of words is also forcefully illustrated by the widespread failure of definition-based instruction in word meanings to improve comprehension of text containing the instructed words (Graves, 1986; McKeown, Beck, Omanson, & Pople, 1985; Mezynski, 1983; Stahl & Fairbanks, 1986).

Attributes of the Standard Model Reflected in Definitions

The chief pedagogical difficulties with definitions arise from the properties of parsimony and abstractness. These properties are a consequence both of the standard model of meaning and of the nature of dictionaries. Dictionaries are designed as reference works, not as a teaching aids, and the practical consideration of length limits their informativeness.

The need to be brief pushes writers and editors of definitions to use very sophisticated and abstract language. Definitions are commonly shortened by using abstract nouns, which allows stating a predicate without specifying the arguments. For example, in a basal glossary, *habits* is defined as "usual behavior" rather than "what a person or animal usually does." Although the more abstract wording saves space, it diminishes the pedagogical usefulness of definitions. The linguistic devices used in definitions are not likely to be familiar to many younger and less-able learners, the very ones most likely to need help with word meanings.

Dictionaries tend to be biased toward use by readers, rather than by writers; the alphabetical arrangement assumes that the word is given, and that the meaning is in question. In this situation, there is less necessity for detailed information on how a word is to be used; the reader already has the context available.

Another problem is that a brief definition often simply does not contain sufficient information about a word. As we have argued earlier, any attempt to reduce the variety of contextual meanings of a word by stipulating a core meaning results in substantial loss of semantic content and precision. Unless illustrative sentences are included, definitions do not provide sufficient information about how a word is actually used. And comprehension is no respecter of the line between linguistic knowledge and general knowledge, wherever one draws that line. Understanding a text always depends on knowledge that goes beyond any narrow conception of word meanings.

Definitions and Instruction

Definitions—even short ones—can make a contribution to the process of word learning. Definitions can convey information that may not be available from the natural contexts in which a word appears. Thus, learning the definition for a word may serve as a foundation for making more effective use of subsequent encounters with that word in context, or help in organizing and synthesizing information gained from prior encounters.

However, real word knowledge is less abstract than the information provided in a definition, and includes representations of the contexts in which a word appears. This type of word knowledge can be inferred from a definition, but usually only if a sufficient number of illustrative contexts are also available to the learner. Studies such as those of McKeown et al. (1985) show that intensive vocabulary instruction, but not definitional instruction alone, improves text comprehension. These studies demonstrate that vocabulary instruction only produces gains in real uses of language when the students have engaged in activities that foster the translation of definitions into a working knowledge of meanings.

The process of arriving at definitions of words through, for instance, class discussion, though it can be time consuming, is probably productive in the long run. One benefit is the insight students gain into the process of making explicit knowledge that has formerly been tacit. But, to reiterate, the ability to recognize or even state definitions is a symptom of word knowledge, not its essence.

In summary, although explanations of the meanings of words are certainly a part of vocabulary instruction, the conventions that constrain traditional definitions make them of limited pedagogical value. The information in definitions must be supplemented by experience with the words to be learned in natural contexts. Teaching word meanings via definitions alone is analogous to trying to teach someone to cook by having them heat TV dinners.

Beyond Definitions: Treating Word Meanings as Complex, Ill-Structured Knowledge

Much of this chapter has been devoted, in effect, to the point that to truly know the meaning of a word is to possess complex and ill-structured knowledge. According to Spiro and his colleagues (Spiro, Vispoel, Schmitz, Samarapungavan, & Boerger, 1987; Spiro, Feltovich, & Coulson, in press), one aspect of ill-structuredness is the contextual interaction of concepts. For example, the flow of blood in the circulatory system depends not just on the properties of the heart, veins, arteries, and capillaries, it depends on how these components fit together as a system. Likewise, the meaning of a sentence is not a simple compositional function of the core meanings of individual words.

A second aspect of ill-structuredness is irregularity. In an ill-structured domain, knowledge of the domain cannot be reduced to a single generalization or organizational scheme. The family-resemblance structure of related word meanings is exactly this kind of case.

Spiro, Coulson, Feltovich, and Anderson (1988) argue that advanced knowledge acquisition in a complex and ill-structured domain requires viewing the domain from multiple perspectives, a case-based rather than an abstraction-based approach, and a commitment to avoiding oversimplification. Spiro and his colleagues have been concerned with, for example, the learning of biomedical concepts by medical students. However, we want to argue that their formulation is equally well applicable to the learning and teaching of word meanings.

In the vocabulary instruction, multiple examples have proved desirable. The research literature shows that more effective learning is associated with multiple exposures to a word (Stahl & Fairbanks, 1986). Furthermore, in improving comprehension, multiple exposures involving varied contexts, rather than just multiple exposures to definitions, seem necessary (McKeown, Beck, Omanson, & Pople, 1985).

Likewise, in vocabulary instruction there is much to be said for a case-based rather than abstraction-based approach. As we have already suggested, the widespread existence of family-resemblance clusters of word meanings indicates that people extend word meanings to new cases on the basis of specific known cases, rather than on the basis of some more abstract and general representation. Pedagogically, this principle suggests that instead of definitions being seen as central, and illustrative examples of words in context as supplementary, the opposite ought to be the rule.

In vocabulary learning, as in medicine and the other fields Spiro and his associates have examined, oversimplification is an ever-present danger; and it is a danger that often arises because of overreliance on abstract generalizations. To borrow another example from Miller and Gildea (1987), given the definition of *meticulous* as "very careful or too particular about small details," a student apparently took the meaning to be "very careful" and wrote the sentence "I was meticulous about falling off the cliff."

The whole point of vocabulary learning is flexible application—"reasoning with, and applying, the material learned," in Spiro's phrase. Word meanings are learned to serve as tools for comprehension and new learning, not simply as facts to be remembered. The truth is that students are seldom called on to apply knowledge, say, of the Civil War, other than in answering test questions. Really knowing a word, on the other hand, always means being able to apply it flexibly but accurately in a range of new contexts and situations. Thus, it can be argued that there is no knowledge addressed in school in which application is more crucial than knowledge of word meanings. The challenge for educators is to provide instruction of the sort that will lead to flexible application of word knowledge.

CONCLUSION

What we have mainly done in this chapter is take a close look at the standard theory of word meanings. We have concluded that every element of the theory is open to serious challenge. No one has yet been able to specify a set of semantic features that are atomic, sense based, and universal in application; that provide an exhaustive and satisfying analysis of word meanings; or that give a firm foundation for sentence semantics; nor is there good reason to hope that these goals are even achievable. In its very attempt to provide a parsimonious, general account of semantics, standard theory falls woefully short of a linguistically adequate and psychologically realistic characterization of meaning.

There is general dissatisfaction with standard theory among semantic theorists. Yet this chapter is, we submit, more than an exercise in beating dead horses. Versions of the standard theory do have current-day proponents among scholars concerned with language, notably among information-processing psychologists trying to account for the speed and fluency with which people process language. More important, considering the primary audience of this chapter, something resembling standard theory seems to characterize the conventional wisdom about word meanings in the field of reading education.

Standard semantic theory seems to provide the tacit foundation for several common practices in vocabulary instruction. To the extent that the foundation is weak, the practices may be of dubious value. We hope that exposing the assumptions of prevailing semantic theory to close scrutiny will make some contribution to raising the level of consciousness of the field, informing debate, refocusing research, and informing practice.

One instructional practice that is widespread is to preteach unfamiliar vocabulary before commencing a reading selection. The assumptions seem to be that (1) words have fixed, context-free meanings and (2) that the meaning of a text is a compositional function of the meanings of its constituent words. As we have argued at length, both assumptions are shaky. We believe that apprehending the gist of a story is as likely or even more likely to assist in learning the meanings of unfamiliar words than vice versa.

A second widespread practice is reliance on the definitions in dictionaries and glossaries as sources for the meanings of unfamiliar words. But if we are correct, and word meanings are context sensitive, a dictionary is a questionable aid for an inexpert language learner. In fact, independent empirical evidence shows that dictionaries often fail to provide children with much help (Miller & Gildea, 1987).

Finally, there is the practice of attempting to promote vocabulary growth by providing direct instruction, drill, and practice on lists of isolated, unrelated words. In another line of research, we have established that the size of the vocabulary-learning task is simply too large to make much headway teaching words one at a time, 10 at a time, or even 100 at a time (Nagy & Anderson, 1984; Nagy, Anderson, & Herman, 1987; Nagy & Herman, 1987; Nagy, Herman, & Anderson, 1985). The theoretical analysis presented in this chapter provides independent, converging reasons for being suspicious about the value of instruction involving lists of isolated words: Word meanings are difficult to capture in the abstract; nuance of meaning, especially, depends upon setting and context.

The most obvious implication of our analysis is as follows: For enhancement of children's vocabulary growth and development, there can be no substitute for voluminous experience with rich, natural language.

REFERENCES

Anderson, R. C., & Ortony, A. (1975). On putting apples into bottles: A problem of polysemy. *Cognitive Psychology, 7,* 167–180.

Anderson, R. C., Pichert, J. W., Goetz, E. T., Schallert, D. L., Stevens, K. W., & Trollip, S. R. (1976). Instantiation of general terms. *Journal of Verbal Learning and Verbal Behavior, 15,* 667–679.

Au, T. K. (1988). Language and cognition. In R. L. Schiefelbusch and L. L. Lloyd (Eds.), *Language perspectives: Acquisition, retardation and intervention* (2nd ed., pp. 125–146). Austin, TX: Pro-ed.

Berlin, B., & Kay, P. (1969). *Basic color terms: Their universality and evolution.* Berkeley and Los Angeles: University of California Press.

Bolinger, D. (1965). The atomization of meaning. *Language, 41,* 555–573.

Bowerman, M. (1982). Starting to talk worse: Clues to language acquisition for children's late speech errors. In S. Strauss (Ed.), *U-shaped behavioral growth.* New York: Academic Press.

Bransford, J., & Franks, J. J. (1976). Toward a framework for understanding learning. In G. Bower (Ed.), *The psychology of learning and motivation* (Vol. 10, pp. 93–127). New York: Academic Press.

Carey, S. (1978). The child as word learner. In M. Halle, J. Bresnan, & G. Miller (Eds.), *Linguistic theory and psychological reality* (pp. 264–293). Cambridge, MA: MIT Press.

Carey, S. (1982). Semantic development: The state of the art. In E. Wanner & L. Gleitman (Eds.), *Language acquisition: The state of the art* (pp. 347–389). Cambridge, Eng.: Cambridge University Press.

Carnap, R. (1947). *Meaning and necessity.* Chicago: University of Chicago Press.

Chomsky, N. (1965). *Aspects of the theory of syntax.* Cambridge, MA: MIT Press.

Clark, E. (1983). Meanings and concepts. In J. H. Flavell & E. M. Markman (Eds.), P. H. Mussen (Series Ed.), *Handbook of child psychology: Vol. 3, Cognitive Development* (pp. 787–840). New York: Wiley.

Elshout-Mohr, M., & van Daalen-Kapteijns, M. (1987). Cognitive processes in learning word meanings. In M. McKeown & M. Curtis (Eds.), *The nature of vocabulary acquisition* (pp. 53–71). Hillsdale, NJ: Erlbaum.

Fillmore, C. J. (1968). The case for case. In E. Bach & R. T. Harms (Eds.), *Universals in linguistic theory* (pp. 1–88). New York: Holt, Rinehart & Winston.

Fodor, J. A., Garrett, M. F., Walker, E. C. T., & Parkes, C. H. (1980). Against definitions. *Cognition, 8,* 263–367.

Frege, G. (1892; translation, 1966). On sense and reference. In P. Geach and M. Black (Eds.), *Translations from the philosophical writings of Gottlob Frege* (pp. 56–78). Oxford: Blackwell.

Gibbs, R. W. (1983). Do people always process the literal meanings of indirect requests? *Journal of Experimental Psychology: Learning, Memory, and Cognition, 9,* 524–533.

Gibbs, R.. W. (1986). Skating on thin ice: Literal meaning and understanding idioms in conversation. *Discourse Processing, 9,* 17–30.

Gleitman, L., & Wanner, E. (1982). Language acquisition: The state of the state of the art. In E. Wanner & L. Gleitman (Eds.), *Language acquisition: The state of the art* (pp. 3–48). Cambridge, Eng.: Cambridge University Press.

Gordon, D., & Lakoff, G. (1971). Conversational postulates. In *Papers from the 7th Regional Meeting, Chicago Linguistics Society* (pp. 63–84). Chicago: Chicago Linguistics Society.

Graves, M. (1986). Vocabulary learning and instruction. In E. Z. Rothkopf and L. C. Ehri (Eds.), *Review of research in education* (Vol. 13, pp. 49–89). Washington, DC: American Educational Research Association.

Green, G. (1984). *Some remarks on how words mean* (Tech. Rep. No. 307). Urbana: University of Illinois, Center for the Study of Reading.

Johnson-Laird, P. N. (1981). Mental models of meaning. In A. K. Joshi, B. L. Webber, & I. A. Sag (Eds.), *Elements of discourse understanding* (pp. 106–126). Cambridge, Eng.: Cambridge University Press.

Johnson-Laird, P. N. (1983). *Mental models: Towards a cognitive science of language, inference, and consciousness.* Cambridge, Eng.: Cambridge University Press; Cambridge, MA: Harvard University Press.

Johnson-Laird, P. N. (1987). The mental representation of the meanings of words. *Cognition, 25,* 189–211.

Katz, J. J. (1972). *Semantic theory.* New York: Harper & Row.

Katz, J. J. (1981). Literal meaning and logical theory. *Journal of Philosophy, 78,* 203–234.

Katz, J. J., & Postal, P. M. (1964). *An integrated theory of linguistic descriptions.* Cambridge, MA: MIT Press.

Katz, N., & Fodor, J. (1963). The structure of a semantic theory. *Language, 39,* 170–210.

Kintsch, W. (1974). *The representation of meaning in memory.* Hillsdale, NJ: Erlbaum.

Kripke, S. (1972). Naming and necessity. In G. Harman & D. Davidson (Eds.), *The semantics of natural language* (pp. 254–355). Boston: Reidel.

Labov, W. (1973). The boundaries of words and their meanings. In C. J. Bailey & R. Shuy (Eds.), *New ways of analyzing variation in English* (pp. 340–373). Washington, DC: Georgetown University Press.

Lakoff, G. (1972). Hedges: A study in meaning criteria and the logic of fuzzy concepts. In *Papers from the Eighth Regional Meeting, Chicago Linguistics Society* (pp. 183–228). Chicago: Chicago Linguistics Society.

Lyons, J. (1977). *Semantics* (Vols. 1 and 2). Cambridge, Eng.: Cambridge University Press.

McConkie, G. W., Reddix, M. D., & Zola, D. (1985, November). Chronometric analysis of language processing during eye fixations in reading. Unpublished paper presented at the annual meeting of the Psychonomic Society.

McKeown, M., Beck, I., Omanson, R., & Pople, M. (1985). Some effects of the nature and frequency of vocabulary instruction on the knowledge and use of words. *Reading Research Quarterly, 20,* 522–535.

Mezynski, K. (1983). Issues concerning the acquisition of knowledge: Effects of vocabulary training on reading comprehension. *Review of Educational Research, 53*(2), 253–279.

Miller, G. A., & Gildea, P. (1987). How children learn words. *Scientific American, 257*(3), 94–99.

Nagy, W., & Anderson, R. (1984). How many words are there in printed school English? *Reading Research Quarterly, 19,* 304–330.

Nagy, W., Anderson, R., & Herman, P. (1987). Learning word meanings from context during normal reading. *American Educational Research Journal, 24*(2), 237–270.

Nagy, W., & Herman, P. (1987). Breadth and depth of vocabulary knowledge: Implications for acquisition and instruction. In M. McKeown & M. Curtis (Eds.), *The nature of vocabulary acquisition* (pp. 19–35). Hillsdale, NJ: Erlbaum.

Nagy, W., Herman, P., & Anderson, R. (1985). Learning words from context. *Reading Research Quarterly, 20,* 233–253.

Nelson, K. (1988). Constraints on word learning? *Cognitive Development, 3,* 221–246.

Perfetti, C. A., & McCutchen, D. (1986). Schooled language competence: Linguistic abilities in reading and writing. In S. Rosenberg (Ed.), *Advances in applied psycholinguistics* (pp. 105–141). Cambridge, Eng.: Cambridge University Press.

Putnam, H. (1975). The meaning of meaning. In H. Putnam (Ed.), *Mind, language, and reality* (pp. 215–271). New York: Cambridge University Press.

Rosch, E., & Mervis, C. B. (1975). Family resemblances: Studies in the internal structure of categories. *Cognitive Psychology, 7,* 573–605.

Searle, J. (1979). Literal meaning. In J. Searle (Ed.), *Expression and meaning.* Cambridge, Eng.: Cambridge University Press.

Spiro, R., Coulson, R. L. Feltovich, P. J., & Anderson, D. K. (1988). *Cognitive flexibility theory: Advanced knowledge acquisition in ill-structured domains* (Tech. Rep. No. 441). Urbana, IL: Center for the Study of Reading, University of Illinois.

Spiro, R., Feltovich, P. J., & Coulson, R. L. (in press). Multiple analogies for complex concepts: Antidotes for analogy-induced misconception in advanced knowledge acquisition. In S. Vosniadou & A. Ortony (Eds.), *Similarity and analogical reasoning.* Cambridge, Eng.: Cambridge University Press.

Spiro, R., Vispoel, W. L., Schmitz, J. Samarapungavan, A., & Boerger, A. (1987). Knowledge acquisition for application: Cognitive flexibility and transfer in complex content domains. In B. C. Britton & S. Glynn (Eds.), *Executive control processes.* Hillsdale, NJ: Erlbaum.

Stahl, S., & Fairbanks, M. (1986). The effects of vocabulary instruction: A model-based meta-analysis. *Review of Educational Research, 56,* 72–110.

Swinney, D. A. (1979). Lexical access during sentence comprehension: (Re)consideration of context effects. *Journal of Verbal Learning and Verbal Behavior, 18,* 427–440.

Tabossi, P., & Johnson-Laird, P. N. (1980). Linguistic context and the priming of semantic information. *Quarterly Journal of Experimental Psychology, 32,* 595–603.

van Daalen-Kapteijns, M., & Elshout-Mohr, M. (1981). The acquisition of word meanings as a cognitive learning process. *Journal of Verbal Learning and Verbal Behavior, 20,* 386–399.

Watson, R. (1985). Towards a theory of definitions. *Journal of Child Language, 12,* 181–197.

Watson, R., & Olson, D. (1987). From meaning to definition: A literate bias on the structure of word meaning. In R. Horowitz & S. J. Samuels (Eds.), *Comprehending oral and written language* (pp. 329–353). New York: Academic Press.

Webster's Third New International Dictionary of the English Language. (1964). Unabridged. Springfield, MA: G. & C. Merriam Co.

Werner, H., & Kaplan, E. (1952). *The acquisition of word meanings: A developmental study.* Monograph of the Society for Research in Child Development (Vol. 15, Serial 51[1]).

Whorf, B. (1956). J. B. Carroll (Ed.), *Language, thought, and reality: Selected writings of Benjamin Lee Whorf.* Cambridge, MA: MIT Press.

Wittgenstein, L. (1953). *Philosophical investigations.* New York: Macmillan.

PART FOUR

Literacy and Schooling

Section Editor: P. David Pearson

26 EMERGENT LITERACY

Elizabeth Sulzby and William Teale

$\mathbf{M}$uch research during the past decade and a half has been based on new ways of conceptualizing the reading and writing development of young children. Along with this new perspective on reading and writing development came a new term, *emergent literacy*, which appears for the first time as a chapter title in this second volume of the *Handbook*. In the first volume of the *Handbook*, Mason's (1986) chapter was called "Early Reading from a Developmental Perspective," which already showed a shift from the idea of reading readiness toward emergent literacy. The term emergent literacy evolved during the early 1980s. It was derived in part from Marie Clay's (1966, 1967) influential research and from increasing references to emergent literacy in books and articles. During this period, other research appeared that did not use the term but still contributed to the reconceptualization of what young children are learning about reading, writing, and print prior to schooling. Terms were proliferating—such as *metalinguistic awareness, print awareness, early literacy, concepts about print, literacy before schooling*—and there was a felt need to unify the research under a common term.

Emergent literacy was nominated and has gained currency as a term both in the research community and among practitioners, as well as in the popular press (Marzollo & Sulzby, 1989–1990; Vobejda, 1987; Wells, 1988). The term is now found as a descriptor in the ERIC and CIJE data bases, as a chapter title in *Becoming a Nation of Readers* (Anderson, Hiebert, Scott, & Wilkinson, 1985), and in volumes aimed at researchers (Teale & Sulzby, 1986) and teachers (Strickland & Morrow, 1989). Emergent reading and emergent literacy began to appear as section headings in the *34th Yearbook of the National Reading Conference* in 1985 and have continued since then; they were the topics of the invited research review of the *36th Yearbook* (Teale, 1987). The lead review chapter in the *13th Review of Research in Education* (Mason & Allen, 1986) was also on emergent literacy. Articles with emergent literacy in the title or text now appear regularly in major educational, psychological, linguistic, and anthropological journals. School districts are building curricula and assessment based on emergent literacy principles and practices. Educational publishers are now using the concept widely in reading, language arts, and early childhood materials. Such developments have prompted a need for a close look at the research that has contributed to this perspective on early childhood literacy learning.

In the introductory chapter of *Emergent Literacy: Writing and Reading* (Teale & Sulzby, 1986), we detailed a history of educational and research perspectives on young children's literacy development. A historical perspective is not repeated in this chapter; instead, we critically review recent studies for what they tell us about the nature and course of young children's literacy learning and some implications from this body of research. We are not attempting to duplicate the efforts of Mason and Allen's (1986) and Teale's (1987) quite extensive reviews, but instead to take those reviews further by casting new light on studies previously reported, adding newer research, and framing all of the research in light of what we currently know and its significance to the research and practice communities.

EMERGENT LITERACY: DEFINITIONS AND BACKGROUND

We have stated that emergent literacy is a new way of conceptualizing early reading and writing development. As a technical definition, Sulzby (1989) describes emergent literacy as "the reading and writing behaviors that precede and develop into conventional literacy." For the present purposes, we have focused specifically on just what is new about the newer ways of conceptualizing early reading and writing development found in current research and theory. To do so, let us examine what guides emergent literacy research—what issues and questions are addressed, what methodologies are employed, what theoretical orientations guide the research.

Issues and Questions

Emergent literacy is concerned with the earliest phases of literacy development, the period between birth and the time when children read and write conventionally. The term emergent literacy signals a belief that, in a literate society, young children—even 1- and 2-year-olds—are in the process of becoming literate. This literacy is seen in not-yet-conventional behaviors; underlying the behaviors are understandings or hypotheses about literacy. Literacy learning is seen as taking place in home and community settings, in out-of-home care settings, and in school settings such as Head Start, prekindergarten, and kindergarten. In short, an emergent literacy perspective ascribes legitimacy to the earliest literacy concepts and behaviors of children and to the varieties of social contexts in which children are becoming literate. As such, it has moved the focus of research to younger and younger children; it is now fairly common to see studies of the reading and writing of 2-, 3-, and 4-year-olds.

Emergent literacy has expanded the purview of the research from reading to *literacy* because theories and findings have shown that reading, writing, and oral language develop concurrently and interrelatedly in literate environments. The locus of research has expanded beyond the laboratory and classroom into the home and community because it has been shown that so much of early literacy development arises out of these more informal settings. Perhaps most significantly, researchers have reoriented their points of view on early literacy learning. Instead of regarding young children's literacy concepts, behaviors, and attitudes merely as gradual approximations of those present in literate adults, researchers are interpreting results from the children's perspectives. Early reading and writing concepts, behaviors, and attitudes are seen as children's constructions that take place within the influences of a social environment that immerses them, to varying degrees, in a range of literacy activities.

In this sense, emergent literacy research has benefited from the research in oral language development dating from the early 1970s and has taken the orientation toward the child as an active constructor of concepts further into the new domain of written language. It has clearly benefited from the work in children's development by pioneers such as Dewey (1938) and Piaget (1959). The obvious outcome of this research is a description of, and growing theoretical framework for, children's emerging literacy; another key outcome has been a reexamination of the previously accepted operational definitions of when a child is "really reading" or "really writing"—a reexamination of *conventional literacy* (see Sulzby, 1989, for further discussion of this distinction). In this review, we draw attention back to the continuity of development and research between emergent and conventional literacy.

The concept of development has always been a central concern of reading research and theory; but as a result of these newer ways of framing research on young children's emergent literacy, the nature of literacy development and thus the ways of researching it are being reconceptualized. Clearly, an emergent literacy perspective ascribes to the child the role of constructor of his or her own literacy. Unlike previous work, the central issues now being addressed are the nature of the child's contributions (i.e., individual construction), the role of the social environment in the process (i.e., social construction), and the interface between the two.

Methodological Considerations

The methods for researching these issues are multiple and often combined with a single research project, many of which are longitudinal and multifaceted. As with educational research in general, naturalistic, particularly ethnographic, techniques have been popular ways of striving for ecological validity. Young children often refuse to engage in reading and writing in artificially contrived situations. Thus, an understanding of the context of the research and its relationship to the child is essential in order to interpret the child's behaviors and infer the concepts and intentions behind those behaviors. For these reasons, emergent literacy research has tended to make much use of descriptive methodologies using naturalistic observation, particularly in studies focused on home and community settings. Also, interview techniques, including Piagetian clinical interviews, have been applied in inventive ways to reveal young children's concepts about reading and writing. The research has also led to the employment of innovative— although often simple—tasks, such as asking a nonconventional reader to "read your own way." Such methods contribute to the goal of understanding the process of literacy development from the children's perspectives. When experimental methods are used, they tend to be tempered by concerns for ecological validity and guided by findings from more naturalistic methodologies. Readers new to the field of emergent literacy will find the experimental methods used similar to many used in studies of child language acquisition focused at oral language development. In almost all studies, perhaps because the field is so new, researchers have come to include many examples as a way of *showing* descriptive data in addition to, or occasionally instead of, traditional avenues, such as tables of means, standard deviations, and figures showing distributions, interactions, or regression lines. Finally, because researchers have been forced to devise new means of measuring and showing the child's knowledge and development, research reports often focus upon the development of new means of analysis rather than being able to depend upon a body of widely accepted measurement tools.

Theoretical Perspectives

Just as multiple research perspectives are used in designing the research studies, a number of theoretical perspectives guide the research, most of which address development. First is the perspective seen most recently in early child language acquisition research, that the child is somehow innately predisposed to becoming literate and all the adult has to do is to provide an environment rich in literacy artifacts and activities. In its extreme, this position takes an almost Rousseauian stance that the child's efforts are to be honored and should be not tampered with. The second perspective is derived from the work of Piaget and focuses upon the child's active construction of literacy through interactions with the environment. This perspective emphasizes how children's concepts are constructed, how they change, and how they differ from adult concepts. The third perspective extends Vygotsky's ideas on literacy and on learning in general. This perspective stresses the social interaction between a literate adult and the young child, claiming that children acquire literacy through conversations and supported, purposeful engagements in literacy events. Closely tied to this position is the idea of *scaffolding*, in which a more knowledgeable adult supports the child's performance across successive engagements, gradually transferring more and more autonomy to the child. Also relevant, but less immediately so, are models of reading/writing processing organized around the descriptors top-down, bottom-up, and interactive (see Rumelhart, 1977). These theories tend to ignore development, except in a simplistic fashion, but do draw attention to details of proficient processing of conventional text. Many researchers currently draw upon aspects from a number of these perspectives. We return to a discussion of the needs of merging, or at least acknowledging the challenging, of many perspectives at the end of this review.

Overall, we can see much that is new in research based upon the emergent literacy perspective. However, the issue of when and how children become able to read and write is as old as educational research itself. Emergent literacy builds upon previous work and thought but clearly is taking certain new directions, applying new methodologies, and addressing the issue of development from multiple perspectives. In short, emergent literacy brings to research a fresh way of looking at young children's literacy development. This fresh way of looking at literacy development is now a vigorous, if not yet entirely rigorous, area of research, which we review in the sections that follow.

We have broken our review into four areas. The first three—emergent storybook reading, emergent writing, and emergent literacy and the home—have become somewhat traditional areas of research synthesis. In the fourth section, we urge that the research on metalinguistic awareness—in particular, phonemic awareness—be reexamined from an emergent literacy perspective in order to broaden both research arenas. Thus we devote somewhat more space to this topic than this subset of development would ordinarily receive. Finally, we conclude the chapter with a look to the future in research, theory, and application.

STORYBOOK READING AS AN EMERGENT PHENOMENON

Historically, storybook reading as an aspect of young children's literacy experience has received more research attention than any other. Correlational studies of storybook reading were predominant from the 1950s through the 1970s. They utilized retrospective interview data and showed significant, positive relations between early childhood experience in being read to at home and such factors as vocabulary development (Burroughs, 1972; Fodor, 1966; Templin, 1957), level of language development in children viewed as prereaders (Burroughs, 1972; Chomsky, 1972; Foder, 1966; Irwin, 1960; MacKinnon, 1959), children's eagerness to read (Mason & Blanton, 1971), becoming literate before formal schooling (Clark, 1976), and success in beginning reading in school (Durkin, 1974–1975).

In more recent years researchers have continued to study storybook reading intently. However, the research has evolved in at least four significant ways. First, as is true in all areas of emergent literacy research, the methodology has become heavily descriptive to analyze what actually goes on during the activity. Researchers have moved toward using methods that analyze the language and social interaction of storybook reading to help provide clues about causal (and not merely correlational) relationships.

A second noticeable change in storybook-reading research is an expansion of the storybook-reading situations being studied. Much of the early storybook-reading research focused upon the more intimate one-to-one (or one-to-few) readings typical of the parent-child readings of the home. Now many studies focus on group storybook readings like those that usually occur in classrooms (one adult reading to groups of 15 to 30 or so children). In this way similarities and differences between home and school literacy situations and learning can be examined.

A third important shift is that storybook-reading research has been a focus upon children's independent "readings" of books during the early years, in addition to the focus on adult-child interactions. In other words, young children's storybook-reading experiences are now viewed as consisting both of being read to and trying out reading by themselves. Researchers focus upon children's independent reading attempts in order to infer what concepts the child is internalizing and using in reading situations.

Finally, we see most recently that descriptive methodologies and experimental designs are beginning to be used in a complementary fashion. Researchers apply insights from descriptive studies to plan intervention studies and to examine the effects of those interventions upon storybook-reading practices and, ultimately, upon children's literacy development. Results from the naturalistic observational research are also used to design more ecologically valid tasks and elicitation techniques that serve to amass sufficient data to confirm or disconfirm hypotheses.

Because of these four developments, we stand a better chance of understanding what is actually happening in children's development that led to the previously reported correlations between storybook reading and subsequent achievement. Additionally, we can begin to understand how storybook reading contributes to children's concurrent writing, intellectual, emotional, and oral language development. A reasonably comprehensive review of storybook-reading research was provided by Teale (1987). Therefore, the purpose of this section of the chapter is to focus on recent insights about storybook reading. The discussion is organized around five major conclusions that emerge from the literature:

Storybook reading is a socially created, interactive activity.

Storybook reading with very young children is typically routinized in dialogue cycles.

Patterns of storybook reading change over time with children's increasing age, knowledge, and experience.

Young children's independent, not-yet-conventional readings of books grow out of interactive readings and serve to advance children's literacy development.

Variations in storybook-reading patterns of interaction affect children's development differentially.

Storybook Reading as a Socially Created Activity

A central finding from descriptive studies of parent-child storybook reading (e.g., Bloome, 1985; DeLoache, 1984; DeLoache & DeMendoza, 1987; Heath, 1982; Miller, Nemoiaunu, & DeJong, 1986; Ninio, 1980; Ninio & Bruner, 1978; Snow, 1983; Snow & Goldfield, 1982, 1983; Snow & Ninio, 1986; Sulzby & Teale, 1987; Taylor, 1986; Teale & Sulzby, 1987; Yaden, Smolkin, & Conlin, 1989) and of classroom storybook-reading studies (e.g., Cochran-Smith, 1984; Green & Harker, 1982; Green, Harker, & Golden,

1986; Martinez & Teale, 1987; Mason, Peterman, Powell, & Kerr, 1989; Peterman, 1987; Peterman, Dunning, Eckerty, & Mason, 1987; Teale & Martinez, 1986, 1989; Teale, Martinez, & Glass, 1989) is that the act of reading books aloud to a child is characteristically a socially created activity. In the situations and cultures studied, children almost never encounter solely an oral rendering of the text of the book in a storybook-reading situation. Instead, the words of the author are surrounded by the language of the adult reader and the child(ren) and the social interaction among them. During this interaction the participants cooperatively seek to negotiate meaning through verbal and nonverbal means. Viewing storybook reading as social interaction has revealed that reading books aloud to children is fundamentally an act of construction. The language and social interaction that surround the text are critical to the nature of this construction; in fact, they appear to be good candidates for what makes storybook reading so powerful an influence in young children's literacy development.

Storybook Reading as a Routinized Activity

Ninio and Bruner (1978) examined the readings of picture books by a mother and her very young child (age 8 months–1½ yr). They found that the interaction consisted of dialogue cycles and a standard action format. Snow (1983; Snow & Goldfield, 1983) also emphasized the routinized nature of storybook reading in her analysis of one parent-child pair's readings of a picture dictionary and alphabet books. Sulzby and Teale (1987) and Heath (1982) reported that picture-word-book or alphabet-book-reading episodes with young children are most often played out similarly to the routine patterns described by Ninio and Bruner (1978).

The finding that certain storybook-reading practices are characterized by routines helps explain how storybook reading contributes to literacy learning. It also links the storybook-reading literature with oral language acquisition literature (e.g., Snow, 1977). Routines create highly predictable contexts. As these contexts recur, children can utilize a strategy of saying what they have heard others say in that same context. The usefulness of routines such as dyadic games, caretaking routines, and interactive play and request sequences as contexts for oral language acquisition has been documented by a number of researchers (e.g., Bruner, 1975; Bruner & Sherwood, 1976; Snow, Dubber, & Blauw, 1982).

The routines of storybook reading also provide predictable, but not rigid, formats that help children learn how to participate in the activity. These recurring situations serve to scaffold (Wood, Bruner, & Ross, 1976) the activity for the child, thus helping the child complete a task that is beyond his or her individual capability. This scaffolding involves the adult's " 'controlling' those elements of the task that are initially beyond the learner's capability, thus permitting him to concentrate upon and complete only those elements that are within his range of competence" (Wood, Bruner, & Ross, 1976, p. 90). It is theorized that through these routinized interactions the child develops expectations of the kinds of language that will be found both in specific books and books in general. Later, these expectations are used as the child begins independent reenactments; and, eventually, they operate to help guide and confirm the child's attempts at decoding.

Patterns of Change in Storybook-Reading Interactions

A number of studies indicate that storybook interactional patterns change over time. Additionally, the interactional patterns seem to be different with different genres and across some social groups. In general, scaffolding appears to be a useful concept to help describe the changes. However, the dynamic and interactive nature of scaffolding is a critical feature. A static view of scaffolding sees the parents as adults helping children to perform conventionally. With storybook reading as with much of oral language, however, it is as if parents develop a moving target of performance for children that takes into account their development.

A closer look at a few studies helps clarify the appropriateness of the scaffolding concept for describing changes in storybook reading. Sulzby and Teale (1987) documented shifts in the interactional patterns of parent-child readings in their study of eight Hispanic and Anglo families. They found that parents scaffolded the storybook readings and gradually provided a shift in responsibility for accomplishing the reading that was responsive to the child's development. The earliest readings, with children aged 1½ through 3 were highly interactive; gradually, interactive patterns shifted to address larger chunks of text and, finally, parents began to read almost all of a given storybook without interruption. (Eventually, as we discuss later, all of the children in the study gave independent reenactments of whole texts.)

Heath (1982) had also found that, at around the time their children were 3, her samples of middle-class and lower-income white parents began to discourage the highly interactive, dialogic readings that had been characteristic when the children were younger and instead insisted that the children sit and listen as an audience. Few interruptions, either by adult or child, occurred during the reading of the text. After the text was completed, however, parents often asked questions about the book or engaged children in prolonged discussions.

In a study of repeated readings across social situations, Martinez and Roser (1985) studied effects on young children's responses to literature. Looking both at parent-child home storybook reading and teacher storybook reading in a day-care setting with 4-year-olds, they found that (a) children talked more when the story was familiar, (b) the forms of talk shifted when the story was familiar, and (c) the responses to the story indicated an increased depth of processing in repeated readings.

The next study also looked at change over time and used children's familiarity with being read to as a grouping variable. The authors found differences according to familiarity with being read to. In a set of studies of Dutch 3-year-old day-care children from low socioeconomic status (LSES) families, Bus and Van IJzendoorn (1989) used storybooks, all with well-formed story structures. They found that mothers of children who had been read to frequently had to take part in far fewer disciplinary or controlling behaviors than did mothers of children who were read to infrequently. In a related intervention study with small samples ($N = 9$ each) of children who had been read to infrequently, they found that, after mothers read to their children frequently (reading many of the same books repeatedly), children became more active and mothers less active during the readings. Although active, the children were focused on the storybook task and did not need their mothers to call them to attention. Overall, the children who were read to had fewer problematic interactions than did the control group, which played games with their mothers.

DeLoache and DeMendoza (1987) examined the structure and content of picturebook interactions of 30 mothers and their 12-, 15-, or 18-month-old infants. Although structural features of the interactions remained relatively constant across the age levels (mothers controlled the interactions and determined what pictures would be discussed), the content of the interactions varied as a function of age. The mothers structured the interaction so that the child performed at his or her highest level. Older infants initiated significantly more turns related to the discussion of a particular object, children's input to the interaction became increasingly verbal, and the information supplied by the mother became increasingly complex.

Snow (1983; Snow & Goldfield, 1982) examined a mother-child pair's repeated readings of *Richard Scarry's Storybook Dictionary* over a period of approximately 11 months. She reported a move from discussion concentrating on items, item elaborations, events, and event elaborations in the early and middle phases of the study to a much greater focus on motive/cause issues at the end. Similarly, Teale and Sulzby (1987) described changes across time in the language and social interaction that took place over a 14-month period in a mother-child dyad's readings of a counting book. Four interactive readings of the book were tape recorded. Changes in the level of discussion from the beginning to the end of the period showed a shift from counting and naming of items in the early readings to adding elaborations on the items by discussing their colors or the sounds they made in later readings. Finally, the child "read" the book to her doll.

Sulzby and Teale (1987) found similar shifts in the interactional patterns of parent-child readings in all eight Hispanic and Anglo families they studied. But they found that an additional factor—type of text—confounded understanding of the true nature of the shifts. Picture/label books and alphabet books lent themselves to the dialogic interaction pattern described by Ninio and Bruner (1978), even when some children as old as 4 or 5 were being read to. However, when stories were read, the parents' scaffolding resulted in speech episodes more like those described in Sulzby's (1985a, 1988) work with independent reenactments. The parent would often focus the very young child on identifying specific objects or characters in the pictures of the book rather than on the overall story, especially if the parent believed the story was too complex. As children became toddlers, the parent would sometimes tell the overall gist of each page or two-page spread (rather than read the words); or read only selected parts of the story, sometimes switching between storytelling and reading. Thus, readings of narratives to young children may be a kind of hybrid of the format of reading label, or ABC, books, dialogic exchanges, and fuller story reading. Readings of narratives to older children become much less dialogic and more monologic.

In an earlier study of interactions between mothers and 1½-, 3½- and 5½-year-olds, Bus and Van IJzendoorn (1988) also showed that different types of texts affect the nature of the storybook-reading experience. They found much more "reading instruction" focusing on letters and sounds occurring with an ABC book containing multiple topics than readings of *Where's Spot? (Waar Is Dribbel?)* which emphasized a question-answer pattern in the text, with lift-up flaps hiding a little dog that has hidden.

Pellegrini, Perlmutter, Galda, and Brody (1990) varied familiar and unfamiliar narrative and expository texts during interactive reading between LSES black Head Start children and their mothers. They found different patterns of interaction across narrative and expository genres, with exposition gaining more initiation on the part of the children and leading mothers to be more supportive of children's efforts. Thus, in order to draw conclusions about changes in storybook or other kinds of reading interactions over time, text type must be taken into consideration.

Most of these studies interpreted their results using Vygotsky's (1978) theoretical framework of cognition as internalized social interaction. The changes observed in the adults' and children's roles in the readings across time can be seen as examples of scaffolding. A facilitative framework within which the child can operate (i.e., a routine) was provided in the readings; but subsequent readings proved to be not mere repetitions, but repetitions with variation. Thus, the child had a generalized framework but also freedom within that framework. The child gradually took over more and more of the interaction, but the adult also raised the ante and changed the interaction as she or he saw the child's capabilities growing. The endpoint of the process is internalization of the interaction, an ability to conduct the task independently; this leads to the next major conclusion emanating from the storybook literature: children's independent functioning with storybooks.

Independent Functioning with Storybooks

Independent reenactments, often called *emergent storybook readings*, are occasions when children read familiar books (books that have previously been read repeatedly to them—i.e., "bedtime stories") in ways that are not yet conventional reading. Children reenact books (or "read" books) spontaneously and show behaviors that indicate their growing awareness of features of written language. These behaviors appear to play an integral part in the process of learning to read; and as the studies in the previous section indicate, they grow out of interactive storybook readings.

Sulzby (1985a, 1988) found that when children aged 2 to 6 years were asked to read favorite storybooks in a longitudinal study, they produced speech that could be categorized as acts of reading. The speech was clearly differentiated prosodically, syntactically, and topically from the child's conversation surrounding the reading event. She described these reading attempts by a classification scheme consisting of 11 categories of emergent storybook readings.

This scheme appeared to have developmental properties (Sulzby, 1988) and demonstrated children's growing understandings of oral and written language distinctions. No 2-year-old attended to print as the source to be read from, but many 5- and most 6-year-olds treated the print as the source of the story, and some read conventionally. Furthermore, as data from these independent reenactments were analyzed longitudinally, individual children were seen to move from (a) strategies of labeling and commenting on items in discrete pictures, to (b) weaving an oral recount over the pictures in order, to (c) creating a story with the prosody and wording of written language, to (d) using print in preconventional ways to read the story, and finally to (e) reading the story conventionally. Some of the children became conventional readers during this study, moving across the higher levels of the classification scheme into reading independently from print.

Purcell-Gates (1988, 1989), using the framework of Chafe's (1982) work in oral and written language relationships, investigated the speech of kindergartners who had been read to frequently during their preschool years. She found that such children seem to have abstracted identifiable lexical and syntactic knowledge about written narrative and that they then used this knowledge to create language for wordless picturebooks.

Sulzby's and Pappas's research (Pappas, 1986, 1987; Pappas & Brown, 1987) provide insights into how children learn the registers of written language during the preschool years. As Pappas (1987) concluded, "the approximation observed in reading-like behavior cannot be explained simply in terms of rote memory. The ontogenesis of the register of written language, instead, appears to be just as much a constructive process as we have seen in other areas of children's cognitive/linguistic development" (pp. 174–175). Similarly, Sulzby (1985a) described her subcategory of "reading verbatim-like story" as showing that "the child is not delivering a rote memorization; rather, the child is using strategic, effortful, conceptually driven behaviors . . ." (p. 470). These behaviors include overgeneralization of written-language-like patterns and self-corrections, prior to the time the child is attending to print in the reading attempt.

Pappas's most recent work extends the examination of emergent reading to the domain of expository text (Pappas, 1988) and continues to examine the written language registers. Analyses indicated that kindergartners showed an increasing sensitivity to the registers of information books across three readings of the same book, and thus it was concluded that learning to use the information book genre is also a meaning-driven, constructive process.

Sulzby and Teale (1987) conducted a two-part longitudinal study relating parent-child storybook interaction and children's independent functioning. In one part of the study focusing on parent-child interaction of low- and middle-income Hispanic and

Anglo toddlers and preschoolers, they found that all eight of the children in the study began spontaneous emergent readings. In the second part of their study, involving a large sample of low-income preschoolers and kindergartners, incipiently bilingual children read emergently from the same storybook in both English and Spanish forms, with approximately the same level of emergent storybook reading in both languages, showing a generalization of emergent literacy understandings across languages.

Overall, the research indicates that children's independent reenactments of books seem to play an important role in the ontogeny of literacy. Independent reenactments offer opportunities for the child to practice what has been experienced in interactive storybook-reading events. In addition, they allow children to develop new understandings through such explorations of books. Studies of reenactments provide insights into reading in general and into increased ability to read the particular book being dealt with. For some children, reenactments become the primary avenue into conventional reading from print, thus raising questions for advocates of simplified texts for young children.

Variability in Storybook Reading

Variability in parent-child storybook reading is well documented in the literature. Heath and her colleagues (Heath 1982, 1983; Heath & Branscombe, 1985), Ninio (1980), Teale (1984), and Sulzby and Teale (1987) have described differences among parents reading the same book to their children. The Ninio (1980) and Heath (1982) research suggests, furthermore, that some ways of reading have more positive effects on children's vocabulary development and school achievement than do others. Examining vocabulary acquisition in the context of joint picture-book reading for high socio-economic-status (SES) versus low-SES mother-infant dyads, Ninio (1980) found relationships between dyadic interaction styles and language development. Low-SES mothers were less skilled in eliciting words from their children. The eliciting style of reading (mother asks *what* questions; new information is provided in form of feedback utterances) used predominately by higher-SES mothers was positively associated with the development of productive vocabulary.

Heath (1982) found that both mainstream and white working-class parents in her study read books to their children. Mainstream parents interacted with their children during readings in ways that helped the children learn the basic concepts of reading; and the parents linked information from books, and even the book reading experiences themselves, to other contexts in the children's lives. However, the working-class parents tended not to extend the information or skills of book reading beyond its original context. Part of Heath's conclusions were that these patterns of literacy socialization appeared to be linked to the children's future school achievement in reading. Children from both communities tended to do well in the early years of reading instruction in their school, where there was a focus on recitation and low-level skills. But once they reached the upper elementary school and the curriculum proceeded beyond an emphasis upon decoding, sight word recognition, and factual recall to higher-level comprehension, the working-class children fell significantly behind mainstream families in reading achievement.

Heath's work suggests that it is not merely the presence or absence of storybook reading that affects the child's literacy development; parents in both social groups read to their children. The ways in which mainstream parents mediated the book for their children—the language and social interaction surrounding the text—had a strong impact on the children's ultimate attainment of literacy.

In addition to home studies, research on group storybook reading in early childhood classrooms also has revealed variability in the way in which adults read to children.

Teale and Martinez (1986, 1980; Teale, Martinez, & Glass, 1989; Martinez & Teale, 1987) have analyzed three kindergarten teachers' readings of the same four books. Developing an analytic system that took into account the language and social interaction of the teacher and children vis-à-vis the content of the story, they found that there were describable differences in the ways in which the teachers read to their students. Furthermore, the teachers demonstrated their characteristic reading styles consistently across stories and occasions, leading to the conclusion that teachers have characteristic storybook reading styles (see also Mason, Peterman, Powell, & Kerr, 1989; Morrow, 1988).

Dickinson and Keebler (1989) also found that although the familiarity and complexity of the books being read affected how three day-care teachers read to 3- and 4-year-olds, each teacher nonetheless assumed a characteristic storybook-reading style. Moreover, analysis of the children's talk during the readings indicated that they tailored their contributions to each teacher's style, suggesting that the teacher's style affected how the children responded to books. In another study, Green, Harker, and Golden (1986) applied three different analytical perspectives to two teachers' readings of the same book to primary-grade students and showed that the organization, participation structures, and foci of the two readings differed markedly.

Thus, it appears that a key factor in the effect of storybook reading across home and school is how the adult mediates the reading in response to the child's reactions and initiations. The important link between social interaction and cognition seems to be manifested as the relation between the adult's mediation of the book and the child's learning or internalization. The adult mediator seems to have a definite effect on what the child takes from the reading situation. And, as the work of Pellegrini, Brody, and Sigel (1985) points out, parents respond to their children's statuses and needs.

The finding of variability in storybook-reading style and the indication that style of reading differentially affects young children's literacy learning has prompted a number of intervention studies of storybook reading. These studies have primarily been directed at home intervention programs, but seem to have implications for classroom intervention studies and teacher education studies as well.

Edwards (in press) and Heath (Heath with Thomas, 1984) demonstrated that parents can be taught to read to their children in the interactive fashion described as *facilitative*. In a study of infants, Whitehurst et al. (1988) trained parents of 21- to 35-month-old children from middle socioeconomic status (MSES) families to increase their rates of asking open-ended questions, commenting on functions and attributes, and expanding children's contributions and to decrease questions that could answered simply by pointing. This technique showed a significant increase in immediate posttest expressive language and longer-term growth on some measures of language ability.

EMERGENT WRITING

Compared with a decade or so ago, we now know much more about important features of emergent writing. In contrast with emergent storybook reading, however, the findings are meager. The major findings are that, just as with storybook reading, (1) children write in preconventional, or emergent, forms (such as scribbling, drawing, nonphonetic letterings and phonetic spelling) long before they write conventionally, and (2) they develop into conventional writers. A growing number of researchers (e.g., Allen et al., 1989; Bissex, 1980; Chomsky, 1972; Clay, 1975; Dyson, 1982a, 1982b, 1984, 1987; Ferreiro, 1978, 1986; Ferreiro & Teberosky, 1982; Gundlach, 1982; Gundlach, McLane, Stott, & McNamee, 1985; Harste, Woodward, & Burke, 1984; King & Rentel, 1981; Martlew, 1988; Nurss, 1988; Read, 1970, 1975; Stewart & Mason,

1989; Sulzby, 1985b; Sulzby, Barnhart, & Hieshima, 1989; Sulzby & Teale, 1985; Teale & Martinez, 1989; Tolchinsky-Landsmann & Levin, 1985, 1987; Wolf & Gardner, 1981) have begun investigating children's early writing development. This body of research has, however, varied greatly in the questions asked and methodologies and theories used. In this review, we focus first upon how the term *writing* has been interpreted, both historically and currently. Second, we examine the forms of writing that young children use. Finally, we take a look at how children develop as composers in social environments, including schools.

Definitions of Writing

Writing has many definitions. It can refer to handwriting as well as to composition; similarly, it can refer to the encoding of a composition by another (dictation). Studies of early writing as readiness focused upon letter formation and other mechanical aspects of writing; there are few current relevant studies except for Simner's (1981, 1982) works on letter formation. He showed that children have consistent tendencies toward letter formation that they revert to for free writing, even following careful direct instruction.

The advent of theory and research in the *Language Experience Approach* (LEA) (Allen & Allen, 1966; Stauffer, 1970) was an important precursor to current research in emergent writing. LEA theorists pointed out the importance of children coming to understand that the print on paper had been composed by some real person like themselves; and that children themselves could produce such writing speech. In this approach, dictation became a prevalent way in which children "wrote" prior to the time they could write conventionally; in dictation, a teacher or other adult served as a "scribe" for the young child. More recent work in oral and written language relationships (Dyson, 1982a, 1983; King & Rentel, 1981; Levin, Scheffler, & Snow, 1982; Olson, 1977; Purcell-Gates, 1988, 1989; Rubin, 1978; Scollon, 1988; Simons & Murphy, 1983; Sulzby, 1985a, 1986a, 1987; see also Tannen, 1984; Florio-Ruane, 1988) has provided evidence contrary to the oft-quoted claim that written language is "just speech written down." Currently researchers have emphasized that part of children's emerging literacy is the understanding of the ways in which written language is different from, but related to, oral language.

Dictation from child to adult continues to be an important research tool (King & Rentel, 1981; Sulzby, 1987), when contrasted with children doing their own emergent writing. Other strands of emergent writing research focus upon dictation from the adult to child. Ferreiro and Teberosky (1982) and Barnhart (1986) have contrasted the child's writing of dictated words with dictated sentences in order to infer underlying conceptions of writing. Reading Recovery research (see Pinnell et al., 1986), with low-achieving first graders, has used the method of adult-to-child dictation to investigate and teach writing and reading strategies.

Other definitions of writing (see Dyson, 1985, 1988; Sulzby, 1985b, 1989; Rowe, 1986, 1987, 1988; Vekulich & Edwards, 1987, 1988) focus upon children as composers and upon composition of connected discourse as the primary research product. It is this definition of writing that we emphasize in this review, although we include research using children's writing from adult dictation and judgments about what counts as writing.

Forms of Writing

Most researchers of emergent writing have studied children's composition, or creation, of their own stories, letters, and other pieces. Read's (1970, 1975) influential study of invented spelling used multiple methods, including experiments of speech perception, but his initial design was based upon hypotheses coming from retrospective reports and naturalistically gathered writing samples from parents of preschoolers. These parents reported that their children had begun to write stories and other compositions with readable, but not-yet-conventional spellings prior to schooling. Similarly, Clay (1975) displayed voluntary compositions by young children. Sulzby (1983) and Harste, Woodward, & Burke (1984) have elicited story compositions by young children by encouraging and accepting any form of writing produced by the child. Dyson (1982b, 1984) has focused upon task assignments by teachers and upon how children compose differently within those task constraints and negotiate those tasks for their own purposes and interpretations.

While a number of researchers have described the external forms that children use, they are in agreement that it is insufficient simply to look at the forms of writing that children use; we must look at the underlying conceptualizations behind the forms of writing. Among the researchers who have studied this issue extensively are Clay (1975), Ferreiro (1985, 1986), and Sulzby (1983, 1985b). While Dyson (1984, 1986, 1988) has also contributed to our understandings of children's writing forms, we reserve discussion of her work until the section on social interaction, particularly since she typically takes the teachers' assignments as the starting point in her analyses.

Clay was the first to focus upon the patterns that could be inferred as underlying many different forms of writing. In *What Did I Write?* (Clay, 1975), she displayed examples of children's use of writing forms, including scribble, drawing, strings of letters, copying, and readable invented spelling. This book was not designed as a formal research report, yet it provided the impetus for much subsequent research. Clay made a number of inferences about children's understandings about writing just from examining the forms the children used. She often also used children's statements about their writing in order to infer the principles they were displaying, but she did not systematically present the rereading nor the compositional language that surrounded the pieces of writing.

Ferreiro, a Piagetian scholar, has studied Argentinian and Mexican children's concepts about reading and writing. She (1978, 1985, 1986; Ferreiro & Gómez Palacio, 1982; Ferreiro & Teberosky, 1982) has investigated children's interpretations of how different pieces of writing can be read and has asked children to produce writing. Additionally, researchers from many countries (e.g., Brazil, France, Israel, Italy, Spain, United States, and Venezuela) have used her techniques. In Ferreiro's tasks, researchers ask children to write given words or sentences (dictation from adult to child) and to read these items back. The adults then interview the children about the relationship between the forms of their writing, their rereadings, and the symbolic relationships involved, using clinical interviews.

Ferreiro's work does not furnish an inventory of writing forms as such. Her category systems are constantly emerging (personal communication, October 1988), but they revolve around an assumption that children are moving in somewhat linear, hierarchical fashion toward conventional literacy, represented best in Spanish by the *alphabetic principle*. The alphabetic principle for Ferreiro is phonetic since her language is Spanish; thus the alphabetic principle she refers to would not fit English directly. The following descriptions of children's underlying conceptualizations were drawn from her work with Teberosky in 1979, published in English in 1982; the data were drawn from low- and middle-income children from Buenos Aires, when children were asked to write words or sentences dictated by an adult:

Level 1: The child treats the writing as having some "figurative correspondence" to whatever the child is writing about, even though the actual markings may not display those features to anyone except the child.

Level 2: The child notes that if different things are to be written, the markings must be different. From a basic stock of elements (now usually letters or letterlike in form), the child reorders the elements in order to create new "words," following dual principles that a piece of writing must have a minimum number of elements and that these elements must be reordered to express different meanings.

Level 3: The child attempts to have each written symbol stand for a different "sound" at the syllable level, whether or not the symbol-sound relationships are conventional.

Level 4: The child begins to extend the syllabic hypothesis below the syllable level and runs into conflict with "known" words that s/he knows as "stable units" (in particular, the child's name).

Level 5: The child discovers the alphabetic principle that each separate character has a correspondence to some part of the sound of the intended message.

Ferreiro's work is intriguing, and other researchers (Barnhart, 1986; Barnhart & Sulzby, 1986; Sulzby, 1986b) report seeing vestiges of these behaviors in a variety of tasks with U.S. English-speaking children, even though the children's primary concepts appear to be much more advanced. Ferreiro's work can be characterized by an analysis primarily focused at the word level, although she has conducted some research into children's concepts for different text genres.

Sulzby (1983, 1985a, 1989; Sulzby, Barnhart, & Hieshima, 1989) has conducted a number of studies focusing upon the forms of writing used by young children when teachers and researchers accepted all forms that the children used. In a reanalysis of data from 1981, Sulzby (1985b) noted that a group of 24 kindergarten children used the following not-yet-conventional forms when asked to write stories in one-to-one interviews: drawing, scribbling, letterlike forms, well-learned elements (later called *patterned letterstrings*), and invented spelling. She was not convinced that this survey captured all of the forms used by young children nor the effects of the writing contexts. Data from another study (Sulzby, 1983) showed that many children used different forms of writing when asked to write stories, if the setting were varied from in-classroom writing to out-of-classroom individual interviews. Additionally, a number of children seemed to use a less-mature form of writing such as scribble in order to accomplish a more-mature compositional task; their subsequent rereading would also be high level.

Children seem to use different writing forms for different tasks at the same point in development (Allen et al., 1989; Barnhart, 1986; Barnhart & Sulzby, 1989; Sulzby, 1983). Yet there is growing evidence of within-task stability (Dyson, 1984; Ferreiro & Teberosky, 1982; Sulzby, 1983; Sulzby, Barnhart, & Hieshima, 1989). Kindergarten children tend to use invented spelling and/or what appear to be conventional spellings to write short, familiar words, and to branch out to less-mature-appearing forms when asked to write sentences, and to even less-mature-appearing forms when asked to write stories or other pieces of connected discourse (Sulzby, 1983; Barnhart, 1986). Barnhart (1986) also found that even though children from the United States may produce invented or conventional spellings in word- or sentence-writing tasks, some still give explanations of the relationship between graphics, speech, and meaning that fit Ferreiro's lower-level categories.

Because the developmental patterns in writing appear quite complex, some researchers (Allen et al., 1989; Sulzby, 1989; Sulzby, Barnhart, & Hieshima, 1989) have moved to longitudinal designs with multiclassroom samples. In Sulzby's (1989) study of five classrooms, children were invited to write "your own way" after a discussion and modelling of ways in which kindergartners often write. Scribble, drawing, nonphonetic letter strings, invented spelling, and conventional orthography were the major forms used throughout the study, although rebus, abbreviation, and idiosyncratic forms showed up on rare occasions, usually in first grade. Children moved only gradually toward the use of *conventionally readable writing* (defined as writing in full, invented spelling and/or conventional orthography); they did not immediately read conventionally themselves from this conventionally readable writing. Throughout the study they continued to move back and forth across forms of writing as well, even to the point of conventional writing. What did appear to change was the language that surrounded the writing—the compositional language and, in particular, the ways in which children reread their stories. By the end of first grade, however, all the children were writing conventionally.

Similar patterns of development have been reported by Allen et al. (1989) in their large-sample longitudinal study of writing in whole-language classrooms. Both studies documented findings from other sources—that kindergartners and first graders can and will write when asked to, that they will reread from their writing, and that teachers and researchers can interpret these emergent writing/reading behaviors. Vukelich and Edwards (1987, 1988) found similar patterns in weekly writing samples from children in a university-run kindergarten.

In the fall of kindergarten in the Sulzby study, children primarily used scribble, drawing, and letter strings. This is similar to findings in the Allen et al. study. The primary rereading form was the "written monologue," in which both wording and intonation are written languagelike. By the middle of kindergarten, children were using all five of the major forms of writing. Scribble, drawing, and letter strings continued to be used in first grade, although decreasing in frequency, through midyear. By spring of first grade, all the children were writing readable text (invented and conventional spellings).

Scribbling (as well as drawing) continued to be used more frequently and for longer than expected, lasting through the kindergarten year and into first grade for some children. Children used patterns in scribble that had previously been found only in invented spelling. For example, they used hyphens, darkened blocks, column display, and large dots within the scribble as if to indicate spacing. Children also used composing language with scribble. Many children used a stable rereading of the same scribble with the same speech over time. Some tracked the scribble and making finger, voice, and scribble end simultaneously.

Invented spelling appeared relatively late, in late kindergarten for some children but not until mid to late first grade for others. When children first began to use invented spelling, they often did not use phonetic decoding in order to reread this writing (Kamberelis & Sulzby, 1988), even though they had been observed to encode the same text phonetically. When asked to reread, many children did not track the print. Some began tracking the print for a few words and then stopped. Others, when asked to locate a given word (*bike* written as BK), would locate it in the entire written text, in larger parts of the text (not necessarily including BK), and/or would not locate it in the same place over repeated requests (cf. Barnhart, 1986; Ferreiro & Teberosky, 1982).

Vukelich and Edwards (1987) reported similar findings in a study in which children's readable text was manipulated across three versions: the child's original writing with illustrations, the child's original writing without illustrations; and the child's writing transformed into conventional orthography. While the Sulzby system described in Sulzby, Barnhart, and Hieshima (1989) was used to code writing and rereading behaviors, drawing that accompanied text in letters was treated consistently as illustration, rather than as an alternative form of writing. Children wrote once a week for four weeks, with delayed rereadings of their altered and original texts. In an analysis of individual differences, Vukelich and Edwards found that the most advanced children could read equally well across these forms. One was aided by the conventional spelling, while others were aided more by their own writing with illustrations.

Social Interaction and Aesthetic Composition

In the studies just reviewed, we have focused upon form, even though children's language about the forms and their language in interaction with the forms was used to interpret the forms. Now we turn to research that focuses directly upon the child and the child's composition from social and aesthetic points of view. Dyson's (1984, 1987, 1988) work has approached this topic through the use of ethnographic techniques in school settings in the rural South and in a multicultural school in California. Dyson views a child's writing as one world among many that the child is constructing. She takes issue with a research focus that defines development as the movement toward highly decontextualized text (Olson, 1977). Instead, Dyson claims that the child is constantly dealing with and negotiating contexts. This position echoes findings from Harste, Woodward, and Burke (1984) and predates the work of Rowe (1986) with 3- and 4-year-olds.

Dyson's research technique typically consists of longitudinal observation in classrooms, using ethnographic procedures. She takes observational notes, collects work samples, and makes audiotapes of the child's speech during composition. From these data, she constructs case studies. She also examines the classroom context and how children negotiate tasks that teachers set for them.

Dyson's work raises a number of key issues about school contexts. First, the tasks set by the teacher are clearly not the tasks as perceived by the child (see also Harste, Woodward, & Burke, 1984). Second, teachers may cut off options through assignments such as "draw a picture and then write," "write with rebus," or, as seen in other studies (e.g., Buhle, 1986), telling children that they must write with letters, not scribble. Third, children's lives are whole, not just governed by tasks. During the creation of a text, they tend to interact with peers, to take breaks to deal with other issues that they think are important (such as planning a trick to play on another child on the playground later), to come and go from active composing, and to import issues from their everyday life into a seemingly different text setting. Dyson (1988) calls this a *multiple worlds perspective*. Studies of home literacy (Sulzby, Teale, & Kamberelis, 1989) convince us that taking such a perspective is very important in our understanding of children's emergent literacy.

Rowe (1986, 1987, 1988) studied writing as a participant observer, using methods similar to those of Dyson. The children she studied, however, were aged 3 and 4. Rowe became known to the children as an assistant teacher. The method that she used to interact with the children involved writing messages with them. The transcripts and field notes indicate that the children saw Rowe writing and making comments about her writing; similarly, they shared their writing with her and with peers, asking questions and making comments about the writing. From a number of analyses of this social situation, Rowe was able to demonstrate that these children entered into compositional tasks in a classroom setting, practicing and sharing rich knowledges about writing and reading. In one analysis (Rowe, 1987), she demonstrated the children's awareness of and memory for multiple texts and text events, or *intertextuality*.

In a review of the literature contrasting home and school emergent writing, Sulzby, Teale, and Kamberelis (1989) discussed five themes about children's writing drawn from observations in literacy-rich homes and how these themes may differ in the school setting, depending upon how literacy-rich the school environment is. In literacy-rich homes, children show (1) transcience in participating in writing. They also (2) negotiate power with their parents and siblings and develop a sense of self that endures frustration as well as pleasure in writing. Children continue to (3) write with many forms, moving across forms at a given time and only gradually beginning to write conventionally. In literacy-rich homes, children often have time and space to become engrossed in (4) multimedia projects that take lots of time and in (5) aesthetic creation. The authors argue that, even in a literacy-rich school environment, the social situation in a classroom in which 25 to 30 children use and model all varieties of forms of writing and language surrounding writing is quite different from most home situations (see Cochran-Smith, 1984; Hiebert, 1988). We need actual comparative longitudinal research across home and school settings for the same children in order to understand more fully differences due to home-school social situations.

From these studies of emergent writing, we conclude that children engage in writing at multiple levels; they use numerous forms of writing to perform increasingly complex compositional tasks; they progress toward conventional writing; and they become writers in social situations in which aesthetic creation may play a key function. Much remains to be learned about emergent writing. The fact that all writing also involves reading creates a tension that researchers need to address more clearly—we can view writing as a tool for becoming conventional and competent readers, or we can view writing as the process and product of the child as composer. We need research in both areas, and studies that focus upon the child as reader/writer—or literate person.

EMERGENT LITERACY AND THE HOME

Attempts to understand the influence of the home and family on early reading and writing are by no means new. For decades researchers in sociology and psychology have studied the relationships between reading achievement and family environment measures such as SES, including parental education levels, language of the home, availability of reading materials in the home, and reading habits of the family (see Wigfield & Asher, 1984, for a review.) Studies generally show positive, moderate correlations between such variables and reading achievement. In more recent years correlational studies of family environment have swung away from the use of proxy variables like SES to a focus on actual home activities (see Clark, 1983; or Marjoribanks, 1979). Thus, the trend has been to look more at what families *do* with children that promotes literacy development than at who the families *are*. For example, Wells's (1985) examined preschool literacy-related activities of children from the age of 15 months to 3½ years in the Bristol Language Development Research Programme. He found that listening to stories read aloud had the highest correlation with knowledge of literacy at age 5 and reading comprehension achievement at age 7.

Within the older research, a specific line developed around the issue of the home background of early readers, children who learn to read before having formal reading instruction in school (Durkin, 1966; Clark, 1976). These studies can be traced back almost 40 years. Teale (1978, 1980) reviewed the body of research on early readers that had been conducted to the mid-1970s and concluded that four home factors were repeatedly associated with early conventional reading: (1) a range of printed materials were available, (2) reading was "done" by adults and older children in the home, (3) writing instruments and materials were readily accessible to the children, and (4) other persons in the home responded to the children's reading and writing activities.

Since that time additional early-reader studies have been conducted, most notably one by Tobin and Pikulski (Pikluski & Tobin, 1988; Tobin, 1981; Tobin & Pikulski, 1988), which followed subjects from a group of 30 early readers and 30 matched nonearly readers for a period of six years (kindergarten through the end of sixth grade). Their findings on home background factors mirror those of earlier studies. Using a multiple-discriminant cross-validation analysis, they found that parental assistance was the most important factor associated with early reading achievement.

Thus, the correlational analyses that identified home background factors associated with reading achievement and the early-reader studies both suggest a significant role for the home in promoting literacy growth. However, because of their methodologies, these studies leave certain questions about the relation between home background and reading unanswered. A significant recent development in studies of the home and emergent literacy has been the influence of anthropological research methods. Historical evidence (e.g., Goody, 1977; Schmandt-Besserat, 1978) and anthropological and psychological research (e.g., Reder & Green, 1983; Scollon & Scollon, 1981; Scribner & Cole, 1981) suggest that it is useful to view literacy in terms of its contribution to the ongoing attempts of people to understand and deal with their world. Much of the recent research on home background and early literacy has also taken such a perspective. These studies involve families being willing for researchers to visit their homes over a period of time.

One general conclusion from these studies is that literacy is deeply embedded in the culture of the family and community, functioning primarily as an aspect of human activity rather than a set of isolated skills. Heath's ethnography of communication in two working-class communities (one white, one black) and one mainstream community (black and white mixed) in the Piedmont Carolinas, for example, showed reading and writing to be intimately connected both with the histories and day-to-day lives of the members of each community (Heath, 1983).

In other longitudinal ethnographic research, Taylor (1983) studied the family literacy of six white middle-class suburban families around New York City. She also found that the families used reading and writing to solve practical problems and to maintain social relations. Taylor and Dorsey-Gaines (1988) studied six urban black families living in poverty. They concluded that literacy was part of the social world in which these children lived, just as it was for the middle-class families of Taylor's initial study. All of the types and uses of literacy identified by Heath were in evidence in the families Taylor and Dorsey-Gaines studied.

Research that Teale and colleagues at the Laboratory of Comparative Human Cognition conducted in the San Diego area focused on the literacy occurring in the lives of 24 low-income Anglo, black, and Mexican-American children (Teale, 1986). Findings on the functions and uses of literacy in the families reflected the results of Heath and Taylor. Literacy in the households mediated nine domains of activity, including Daily Living Activities, Entertainment, School-Related Activities, Work, Religion, Interpersonal Communication, Participating in Information Networks, Storybook Time, and Literacy for the Sake of Teaching/Learning Literacy. The vast majority of the time literacy mediated an activity for which the goal went beyond reading or writing itself (e.g., to pay bills, be entertained, transmit information). Only in the domain of Literacy for the Sake of Teaching/Learning Literacy was literacy itself the focus of the activity, and this context constituted but 19.8 percent of the events observed and accounted for only 11.6 percent of the time that families were engaged in literacy-related events.

Such findings are important to emergent literacy research for a number of reasons. First, they show that studying literacy development is basically an investigation of the acquisition of culture. The task for researchers is not merely to study in isolation the cognitive operations of children, but rather to understand cognition in terms of the social systems for utilizing literacy. In other words, motives, goals, and conditions are intrinsic parts of the processes of reading and writing (and of becoming readers and writers); and they cannot be abstracted away without losing characteristics essential to the attempts to analyze literacy and literacy development.

The theory of *activity*, developed by Soviet psychologists (especially by Leont'ev, 1981), provides a framework for this conceptualization. Leont'ev viewed activity as "the molar unit of life" for the individual. Activity orients the individual in the world. Neither the external, objective world, on the one hand, nor the person, on the other hand, is solely responsible for the person's developing knowledge of the world (Wertsch, 1981). Rather, the individual develops knowledge by the processes through which he or she enters into practical contact with the objective world. By conceptualizing literacy development as learning how to participate in a socially organized set of practices involving the use of written materials, we are better able to understand what is involved in young children's literacy learning.

Although research in home literacy has revealed much of the social nature of literacy, including which literacy events (e.g., storybook reading) are routinized structures in some cultures, much remains to be learned. Additionally, studies of home literacy have tended to ignore previous and ongoing work on children's development in other areas. One group of researchers (Bus & Van IJzendoorn, 1988, 1989) have begun to examine the storybook-reading interaction between securely attached children and their parents and those who are not securely attached and the differential emergent literacy development of such children.

Thus, research shows that the home plays a key role in emergent literacy. For literacy education, perhaps the most striking implication is the extreme importance of getting literacy embedded in children's social lives. It is this fundamental orientation that provides the foundation for subsequent academic growth in literacy. In fact, Teale (1988) has argued that essentially the first step in children's literacy is learning that literacy serves to mediate a variety of cultural activities in their everyday lives. However, insufficient research has been done with children in homes and cultures in which children are not heavily involved in literacy. We also do not have research about cultures in which literacy is not heavily embedded; perhaps the day for such studies is almost past.

METALINGUISTIC AWARENESS

In the previous section on home literacy, we stressed that literacy is embedded in ongoing family life and that children develop toward conventional literacy within home literacy interactions. In the process of becoming conventionally literate, whether it be purely from home influences or also includes schooling, children learn to reflect upon language as an object, in addition to using language to comprehend and produce ideas. The transition into conventional literacy entails a growing objectification of language: treating language as the object of thought and manipulation. Reflection upon language is known as *metalinguistic awareness*, and it encompasses a wide range of abilities from language play (e.g., pig Latin) and the appreciation of linguistic jokes to the separation of words into their constituent phonemes. It is useful to think of the ability to reflect on language as occurring on four levels: (1) phonemic (phonological) awareness, (2) word awareness, (3) form awareness, and (4) pragmatic awareness (Tunmer & Bowey, 1984). Phonemic awareness and word awareness refer to awareness of the subunits of language, while form awareness and pragmatic awareness refer to the ability to reflect on the meanings and acceptability of larger units of language (phrases, sentences, texts).

All levels of metalinguistic awareness are important in becoming literate; however, we have chosen in this review to focus mainly on the issue of *phonemic awareness*, the conscious ability to segment spoken words into their constituent phonemes and manipulate phonemes. Research in the broad area of metalinguistic awareness (e.g., Goodman, 1984; Mickish, 1974; Papandropoulos & Sinclair, 1974; Pontecorvo, Orsolini, Zucchermaglio, & Rossi, 1987; also see Yaden & Templeton, 1986) has been part of emergent literacy research; but when a field of inquiry is new (as emergent literacy is) there is a tendency to stress that which is new and different, to generate new vocabulary and definitions, and to ignore the contributions of other related fields. Phonemic awareness, with its ties to the school practice of teaching phonics and other decoding skills, has been neglected thus far in work in emergent literacy, in part because of the tendency to view this area of research as traditional and bottom-up in theory. Yet emergent literacy research illustrates that children are acquiring literacy at all levels, from the phonetic and phonemic to the genre and pragmatic areas, not from bottom up. Researchers in emergent literacy and in phonemic awareness are now beginning to look for ways in which these areas of emphasis can inform each other. In the section that follows, our language shifts in part to use language that has long been in place in more traditional views of "beginning reading" (see Juel, Chapter 27, this volume).

Development of Phonemic Awareness

Our reason for focusing on phonemic awareness is threefold. First, phonemic awareness in the sense just described is directly related to the issue of understanding the pronunciation clues of written language, one of the key features of becoming conventionally literate. In order to develop fluency in utilizing the alphabetic and/or morphophonemic principles of written language, children must develop conscious, analytic knowledge of how phonetic and graphic elements map onto phonemes (Adams, 1988). Second, two decades of research have shown that skill in phonemic analysis is related to efficient decoding for children of a variety of ages (Bond & Dykstra, 1967; Bradley & Bryant, 1983; Ehri, 1979; Juel, Griffith, & Gough, 1986; Lundberg, Olofsson, & Wall, 1980; Olofsson & Lundberg, 1983; Tunmer, Herriman, & Nesdale, 1988), and decoding, as we have stated in less traditional terminology, is one of the essential elements of conventional reading. Also some studies show a relationship between phonemic awareness and spelling (Perin, 1983; Rohl & Tunmer, 1988) that is clearly evident in the research in invented spelling. Finally, as Tunmer, Herriman, and Nesdale (1988) argue, phonemic awareness implies word awareness because the ability to reflect on phonemes presupposes the ability to reflect on words. Therefore, we feel that in dealing with phonemic awareness we are, implicitly, addressing the issue of word awareness.

Some have argued that the ability to deal with the codes of alphabetic languages does not simply and automatically emerge out of environmental print awareness (Dickinson & Snow, 1987; Mason, 1980; Masonheimer, Drum, & Ehri, 1984). They claim that young children must be helped to notice that words encode sounds as well as meaning.

Researchers in phonemic awareness tend to use the language of *prerequisites*, meaning prerequisites to conventional literacy. As we have implied throughout this review, there is a sense in which the term prerequisite is a moot point, since children are gradually building all of the knowledges that have previously been treated as prerequisites to "real literacy." However, the issue of what contributes to conventional literacy is an important one. There are at least three possible conceptualizations of the link between phonemic awareness and early conventional reading and spelling. The first is that phonemic awareness is a causal precursor of learning to read and write conventionally. That is to say, the ability to segment words into their constituent phonemes may be a necessary prerequisite for conventional reading and spelling. The second possibility is that phonemic awareness is a consequence of reading and spelling ability and that knowledge of reading and the orthographic system enables children to deal with individual phonemes. The third possibility is an interactive model: phonemic awareness is neither simply precursor nor consequence, but rather some basic level of phonemic awareness is required for acquiring certain emergent reading and spelling abilities (while others precede phonemic awareness), which, in turn, stimulate more advanced phonemic awareness skill. (There is also what might be considered a fourth conceptualization about the relation: the idea espoused by Stanovich (1986) that certain facets of literacy shift in their contribution at different points in development. Such a notion partially subsumes the interactive position just discussed.)

Data from a longitudinal study by Juel, Griffith, and Gough (1986) led them to conclude that children do not make substantial improvement in spelling-sound knowledges unless they have some phonemic awareness. Studies by Bradley and Bryant (1983) and Torneus (1984) also support the theory that phonemic awareness is a necessary first step in becoming an independent reader. But work by Ehri and her colleagues (Ehri, 1984, 1986; Ehri & Wilce, 1985) led her to conclude that phonemic awareness is a consequence of literacy because children's reports of the number of phonemes in words are affected by their orthographic knowledge. The results of Morais, Cary, Alegria, and Bertelson (1979) are also often used to support the *consequence* point of view. They found that although phoneme addition and deletion tasks were easy for literate adults, illiterate adults could not add or delete phonemes from words.

The more interactive notion of the relation between phonemic awareness and orthographic knowledge may prove to be the most useful model for understanding the relationship. Juel (1986) herself suggests that "It may be that, while a certain amount of phonemic awareness is prerequisite to learning to read and spell, phonemic awareness can increase through exposure to printed words" (p. 242). Recent studies by Morais and his colleagues, whose work has been used to support phonemic awareness as a consequence of literacy (e.g., Morais, Bertelson, Cary, & Alegria, 1986; Kolinsky, Cary, & Morais, 1987), leaves room for an interpretation involving reciprocal causation also.

A study by Yopp (1988) that focused on establishing the reliability and validity of phonemic awareness tests can be used to shed light on some reasons for the conflicting precursor/consequence findings. In her work, factor analyses utilizing results from 10 tests of phonemic awareness revealed two related factors underlying phonemic awareness as it is measured in young children. One was simple phonemic awareness—the ability to segment, blend, and isolate one sound. The other, compound phonemic awareness, involved phoneme deletion and word-to-word matching (isolating a sound in a given position in a second word and comparing it with a sound already isolated in a first word). Thus, though phonemic awareness was found to be a valid concept, it is not simply a monolithic ability that children either have or do not have.

The notion of two "levels" of phonemic awareness helps explain how the reciprocal causation model could apply. Simple phonemic awareness clearly seems to be a necessary prerequisite for (i.e., a causal factor in) what Sulzby (1985a, 1989) calls *aspectual reading*, with a letter-sound emphasis in which children temporarily focus on sounding out words, often blending to nonsense syllables. Aspectual reading (which has two other forms, one with a word identification focus and the second with a comprehension focus) is a precursor to early conventional reading. Simple phonemic awareness is obviously necessary for writing with invented spelling. Aspectual and conventional reading and writing with invented spelling build increased orthographic knowledge which, in turn, effects more advanced (compound) phonemic awareness. The reciprocal causation interpretation also fits with Perfetti, Beck, Bell, and Hughes's (1987) longitudinal study of first graders' development of phonemic awareness and reading. They found that phoneme blending (simple phonemic awareness for Yopp) was a cause of early reading proficiency while ability to delete phonemes (compound phonemic awareness) was better described as a result of early reading.

Instruction in Phonemic Awareness

Because the research has established a correlation between phonemic awareness and literacy learning and because the relationship appears to be, at least in certain respects, causal in nature, the issue of teaching children phonemic awareness inevitably is raised in discussions of early childhood literacy education. Studies by Lundberg and colleagues (Olofsson & Lundberg, 1983; Lundberg, Frost, & Petersen, 1988) indicate that young children can be trained to develop phonemic awareness outside the context of reading instruction.

Bradley and Bryant (1983) utilized individual tutoring sessions focusing on comparing beginning, middle, and ending sounds of words to develop phonemic awareness in 4- and 5-year-olds. They found that the children were able to increase significantly in phonemic awareness and that the children scored higher in reading comprehension than peers who did not receive phonemic training. However, the differences in reading scores were not large enough or consistent enough to be statistically significant. Another experimental group in this study received phonemic awareness training *and* were taught how sounds relate to letters of the alphabet. Reading scores for this group were significantly higher than those of peers not receiving phonemic awareness training.

Thus, research indicates that young children can be trained in phonemic awareness prior to formal instruction in conventional reading, provided they have a certain amount of letter knowledge when the instruction begins (Ehri & Wilce, 1985). Unresolved, however, are issues of major significance in the area of early literacy instruction. One relates to the children themselves. Who can benefit from instruction for phonemic awareness? The studies just reviewed seem to suggest that children as young as 4 years of age can. But the training in the Bradley and Bryant work was spread over two years, and the authors do not indicate how many 4-year-olds were in the training groups or the extent of children's learning at various ages. Thus, the issue of the age at which such training can be effective is not clear, nor is the amount and kind of prior knowledge that children need for any given intervention.

Thus, perhaps even more important is the issue of children's prior experience with literacy, which, it can be assumed, plays a determining role in the effectiveness of phonemic awareness training. Teale (1989) contends that the first development in the literacy-learning process is one in which children develop a basic understanding of the functions and uses of literacy and form initial attitudes about the enjoyment and utility of written language in their lives (described above as the mediation of cultural activities). He says that such knowledge and attitudes grow primarily from children's literacy experiences in their home and community—for example, storybook reading, language play, and seeing parents and other literate persons use written language in everyday cultural practices. Without such fundamental understandings, he contends, learning about aspects of literacy like the code will not progress readily. Thus, all the good phonemic awareness instruction in the world may be useless unless children have the experiential background to profit from it.

In another sense prior knowledge is an important factor in the degree to which phonemic awareness training will take in children. As Sulzby (1989) has argued, children develop letter-name and letter-sound knowledges gradually over the years (simultaneously with word knowledge and comprehension schemata) from infancy through beginning school, through both home and school experiences. These knowledges gradually become visible and explicit in activities such as storybook reading or emergent writing, although they can also be seen in isolated tasks and play directly with letters and sounds. Training in phonemic awareness, for children with such experience, provides an organization of knowledge, rather than an initial teaching of this knowledge. Prior experience is thus essential for phonemic awareness training to advance children. Therefore, the question becomes one of how much formal instruction is needed, if any, in addition to tacit exploration. We believe that most children profit from some instruction, perhaps at different points in development, to help the child reorganize knowledge and to provide needed metalinguistic terms.

A second issue of extreme importance pedagogically is the nature of the activities designed to help children become phonemically aware. In an experimental study of short duration under controlled conditions, less-than-engaging activities may be tolerated by the children. But if we are to design a curriculum that will work in the classroom, the activities for the children must be interesting and motivating. They must also "fit" with the overall curriculum in the kindergarten or prekindergarten.

Another finding seems clear from the research. Phonemic awareness by itself is not the sole factor that helps children become fluent in, and confident with, the code of alphabetic languages. Bradley and Bryant's (1983) research suggests that both phonemic awareness in the oral/aural sense and opportunities to explore the relations between sound and letter are needed to have a marked effect on reading ability. Thus, the curriculum must provide children with a variety of emergent reading and writing experiences in order to help them make sense of and use their developing phonemic awareness.

On top of all these issues we come to the question of "Should we?" Are phonemic-awareness training activities important enough that children should be engaged in them *rather* than something else? From a curriculum perspective and policy view, do the nature and size of the effects of phonemic-awareness training activities justify changes in the preschool curriculum?

The body of research growing around the topic of phonemic awareness is an extremely significant one for the area of emergent literacy. The challenge for the 1990s is to address issues like those raised here and thereby clarify the nature and extent of the effects of phonemic awareness. We need researchers knowledgeable about children's total emergent literacy development who will collaborate with researchers specializing in phonemic awareness and conduct rigorous classroom-based research on phonemic-awareness training and its relation to the overall early childhood curriculum.

A Look to the Future

We have mentioned a number of needs for research in the previous discussion. One strength of emergent literacy research currently is the openness of researchers to use many different methodologies. One always needs methodology for some purpose, of course. We think that two overarching purposes or outcomes are useful to organize our thinking about this topic. In emergent literacy research, we need to build a sense of the child and a sense of the field. It seems as if descriptions of the individual child, children, or children, in general, get lost in the methodologies being used in much of the research. In others, we seem to have so much detail about individual children that growth of understanding of the field of research is obscured. The body of research is beginning to have sufficient volume and quantity to allow us to begin to piece together a sense of the child and a sense of the field. In this review, we indicate that useful information is being gained in both areas, but we have suggestions for next steps.

We have a number of detailed case studies of children (Bissex, 1980; Dyson, 1984, 1988; Hoffman, 1981; Sulzby, 1983). We have a few longitudinal studies (Allen et al., 1989; Sulzby, 1983) and some studies that are both longitudinal and cross-sectional

(Ferreiro & Teberosky, 1982; Sulzby & Teale, 1987). Such research builds the base for our beginning to construct a detailed, theoretically oriented description of the child, including children as individuals, both at a given point in time and across time, as children become conventionally literate.

In our depictions for the child, we often read case studies that are either school based or home based but do not cross both boundaries. Taylor's (1983) study is an example of an ethnographic study that attempted to cross these boundaries but without actual observations in the school setting. Additionally, there are certain areas of child development and family interaction that researchers currently are treating (and may have to treat) as inaccessible. We need to go beyond the depictions of early readers as wonderfully well-rounded, inquisitive children, to depictions of children who have survived in spite of dreadful odds and negative circumstances (Taylor & Dorsey-Gaines, 1988). We need more information about the home circumstances of families such as the low-income families in Sulzby and Teale (1987) who dropped out of a longitudinal study of family literacy. We may not be able to gain needed information due to family and individual needs for privacy, but we can begin to build a picture through indirect means, at least at first, such as life histories and historical documents. For example, we need to understand the literacy development (as well as many other parts of development) of children born of drug-addicted or HIV-infected parents.

We definitely need more research, but more than that we need to begin to consolidate what we do know. We have noted, in some published studies, a dearth of citations across research groups and viewpoints. While we are sympathetic with editors' needs to cut space, we think this is a detriment in a field that needs to consolidate and relate across studies; journal editors and reviewers can be more diligent in urging authors to present more inclusive and relevant research review, both in introductions and discussions. We urge researchers to begin to design studies that specifically address issues raised by other researchers and to use the discussion section more extensively to relate findings across studies. Studies by McGee (McGee, Lomax, & Head, 1988) and Pappas (Eller, Pappas, & Brown, 1988; Pappas & Brown, 1988) are exemplary in this regard.

We think it is particularly important for writers of ethnography and case studies to relate their research to findings from other researchers and paradigms. The reverse is certainly true as well, but the space needed to write up naturalistic observations sometimes imposes space constraints that are harmful to our understanding of the child. Finally, all researchers of emergent literacy should search across the studies of writing for its relation to reading and vice versa.

Most of us are aware of the need for longitudinal research to address longitudinal questions, yet many of the most promising research methods tend to be very labor intensive. Longitudinal research also tends to yield multiple results, but sometimes the data are richer than our abilities to write about them, so there is a lag time between research and published research. We urge researchers to consider more economical designs, such as combining longitudinal and cross-sectional research aimed at more discrete issues. More sensitive uses of experimental designs can contribute much, given our base in naturalistic observation. We do not want to be misconstrued as suggesting the fragmentation of a field that has made contributions by being more wholistic, but we think we are at a point where specific issues must be addressed. The day for exploratory studies seems to be ending rapidly, from our review.

While we are addressing the needs of emergent literacy to become a better-defined and more-articulated field of research, we must not neglect the need to put the research into application. We were heartened in our review to find how many studies are beginning to be based in child-care and school settings and to include collaboration with teachers and parents. We applaud this trend and urge that researchers address application more specifically in future research, including increasing the age range of longitudinal research well past the time when children become conventionally literate, tracking the progress of similar children who were allowed to enter conventional literacy with a firm foundation in emergent literacy with children who had different kinds of instruction at different points in emergent literacy development. So, we conclude this review by raising again the need for research that investigates the fit between instruction and development.

REFERENCES

Adams, M. (1989, February). *Phonics and beginning reading instruction.* Final Report. Champaign, IL: Reading Research and Education Center.

Allen, J. B., Clark, W., Cook, M., Crane, P., Fallon, I., Hoffman, L., Jennings, K. S., & Sours, M. A. (1989). Reading and writing development in whole-language kindergartens. In J. Mason (Ed.), *Reading and writing connections* (pp. 121–146). Needham Heights., MA: Allyn & Bacon.

Allen, R. V., & Allen, C. (1966). *Language experiences in reading: Teachers' resource book.* Chicago: Encyclopaedia Britannica Press.

Anderson, R. C., Heibert, E. H., Scott, J. A., & Wilkinson, I. A. G. (1985). *Becoming a nation of readers: The report of the Commission on Reading.* Washington, DC: National Institute of Education.

Barnhart, J. E. (1986). *Written language concepts and cognitive development in kindergarten children.* Unpublished doctoral dissertation, Northwestern University, Evanston, IL.

Barnhart, J. E., & Sulzby, E. (1986, April). *How Johnny can write: Kindergarten children's uses of emergent writing systems.* Paper presented at the annual meeting of the American Educational Research Association, San Francisco, CA.

Barnhart, J. E., & Sulzby, E. (1989). Written language concepts in kindergarten children: Patterns and developmental influences. Submitted for publication.

Bissex, G. (1980). *GNYS at work: A child learns to write and read.* Cambridge, MA: Harvard University Press.

Bloome, D. (1985). Bedtime story reading as a social process. *National Reading Conference Yearbook, 34,* 287–294.

Bond, G. L., & Dykstra, R. (1967). The cooperative research program in first-grade reading instruction. *Reading Research Quarterly, 2,* 5–142.

Bradley, L., & Bryant, P. E. (1983). Categorizing sounds and learning to read—a causal connection. *Nature, 301,* 419–421.

Bruner, J. S. (1975). Language as an instrument of thought. In A. Davies (Ed.), *Problems of language and learning* (pp. 61–88). London: Heinemann.

Bruner, J. S., & Sherwood, V. (1976). Peekaboo and the learning of rule structures. In J. S. Bruner, A. Jolly, & K. Sylva (Eds.), *Play: Its role in development and evolution* (pp. 277–285). Harmondsworth, Eng.: Penguin.

Buhle, R. (1986). *A study of implementation of emergent literacy by kindergarten teachers.* Unpublished master's thesis, Northwestern University, Evanston, IL.

Burroughs, M. (1972). *The stimulation of verbal behavior in culturally disadvantaged three-year-olds.* Unpublished doctoral dissertation, Michigan State University, East Lansing, MI.

Bus, A. G., & van IJzendoorn, M.H. (1988). Mother-child interactions, attachment, and emergent literacy: A cross-sectional study. *Child Development, 59,* 1262–1272.

Bus, A. G., & van IJzendoorn, M. H. (1989, April). *Storybook reading, attachment, and emergent literacy; Some experimental studies with children from lower socioeconomic status families.* Paper presented at the biennial meeting of the Society for Research in Child Development, Kansas City, MO.

Chafe, W. A. (1982). Integration and involvement in speaking, writing, and oral literature. In D. Tannen (Ed.), *Spoken and written language: Exploring orality and literacy* (pp. 35–54). Norwood, NJ: Ablex.

Chomsky, N. (1972). Stages in language development and reading exposure. *Harvard Educational Review, 42,* 1–33.

Clark, M. M. (1976). *Young fluent readers: What can they teach us?* London: Heinemann.

Clark, R. M. (1983). *Family life and school achievement: Why poor black children succeed or fail.* Chicago: University of Chicago Press.

Clay, M. M. (1966). *Emergent reading behavior.* Unpublished doctoral dissertation, University of Auckland, Auckland, NZ.

Clay, M. M. (1967). The reading behavior of five-year-old children: A research report. *New Zealand Journal of Educational Studies, 2,* 11–31.

Clay, M. M. (1975). *What did I write?* Auckland, NZ: Heinemann.

Cochran-Smith, M. (1984). *The making of a reader.* Norwood, NJ: Ablex.

DeLoache, J.S. (1984). What's this? Maternal questions in joint picturebook reading with toddlers. *Quarterly Newsletter of the Laboratory of Comparative Human Cognition, 6,* 87–95.

DeLoache, J. S., & DeMendoza, O. A. P. (1987). Joint picturebook interactions of mothers and 1-year-old children. *British Journal of Developmental Psychology, 5,* 111–123.

Dewey, J. (1938). *Experience and education.* New York: Macmillan.

Dickinson, D., & Keebler R. (1989). Variation in preschool teachers' styles of reading books. *Discourse Processes, 12,* 353–375.

Dickinson, D., & Snow, C. (1987). Interrelationships among prereading and oral language skills in kindergartners from two social classes. *Early Childhood Research Quarterly, 2,* 1–25.

Durkin, D. (1966). *Children who read early.* New York: Teachers College Press.

Durkin, D. (1974–1975). A six-year study of children who learned to read in school at the age of four. *Reading Research Quarterly, 10,* 9–61.

Dyson, A. H. (1982a). Reading, writing, and language: Young children solve the written language puzzle. *Language Arts, 59,* 829–839.

Dyson, A. H. (1982b). The emergence of visible language: Interrelationships between drawing and early writing. *Visible Language, 16,* 360–381.

Dyson, A. H. (1983). The role of oral language in early writing. *Research in the Teaching of English, 17,* 1–30.

Dyson, A. H. (1984). Learning to write/learning to do school: Emergent writer's interpretations of school literacy tasks. *Research in the Teaching of English, 18,* 233–264.

Dyson, A. H. (1985). Individual differences in emergent writing. In M. Farr (Ed.), *Advances in writing research, Vol. 1: Children's early writing development* (pp. 59–126). Norwood, NJ: Ablex.

Dyson, A. H. (1987). Individual differences in beginning composing: An orchestral vision of learning to compose. *Written Communication, 4*(4), 411–442.

Dyson, A. H. (1988). Negotiating among multiple worlds: The space/time dimensions of young children's composing. *Research in the Teaching of English, 22*(4), 355–390.

Edwards, P. A. (in press). Supporting lower-SES mothers' attempts to provide scaffolding for bookreading. In J. B. Allen & J. Mason (Eds.), *Reading the risks for young learners: Literacy practices and policies.* Portsmouth, NH: Heinemann.

Ehri, L. C. (1979). Linguistic insight: Threshold of reading acquisition. In T. G. Waller & G. E. MacKinnon (Eds.), *Reading research: Advances in theory and practice* (Vol. 1, pp. 63–116). New York: Academic Press.

Ehri, L. C. (1984). How orthography alters spoken language competencies in children learning to read and write. In J. Downing & R. Valtin (Eds.), *Language awareness and learning to read* (pp. 119–147). New York: Springer.

Ehri, L. C. (1986). Source of difficulty in learning to spell and read. In M. L. Wolraich & D. Routh (Eds.), *Advances in development and behavioral pediatrics* (Vol. 7, pp. 121–195). Greenwich, CT: JAI Press.

Ehri, L. C., & Wilce, L. S. (1985). Movement into reading: Is the first stage of printed-word learning visual or phonetic? *Reading Research Quarterly, 20,* 163–179.

Eller, R. G., Pappas, C. C., & Brown, E. (1988). The lexical development of kindergartners: Learning from written content. *Journal of Reading Behavior, 20,* 5–20.

Ferreiro, E. (1978). What is written in a written sentence? A developmental answer. *Journal of Education 160,* 25–39.

Ferreiro, E. (1985). Literacy development: A psychogenetic perspective. In D. Olson, N. Torrance, & A. Hildyard (Eds.), *Literacy, language, and learning* (pp. 217–228). Cambridge, Eng.: Cambridge University Press.

Ferreiro, E. (1986). The interplay between information and assimilation in beginning literacy. In W. H. Teale & E. Sulzby (Eds.), *Emergent literacy: Writing and reading* (pp. 15–49). Norwood, NJ: Ablex.

Ferreiro, E., & Gómez Palacio, M. (1982). *Análisis de las perturbaciones en el proceso aprendizaje de la lectoescritura* [Analysis of variations in the process of literacy development]. (5 vols.) Mexico City: Office of the Director General of Special Education.

Ferreiro, E., & Teberosky, A. (1982). *Literacy before schooling.* Exeter, NH: Heinemann.

Florio-Ruane, S. (1988). How ethnographers of communication study writing in school. *National Reading Conference Yearbook, 37,* 269–283.

Fodor, M. (1966). *The effect of systematic reading of stories on the language development of culturally deprived children.* Unpublished doctoral dissertation. Cornell University, Ithaca, NY.

Goodman, Y. (1984). The development of initial literacy. In H. Goelman, A. Oberg, & F. Smith (Eds.), *Awakening to literacy.* Exeter, NH: Heinemann.

Goody, I. (1977). *The domestication of the savage mind.* Cambridge, Eng.: Cambridge University Press.

Green, J. L., & Harker, J. O. (1982). Reading to children: A communicative process. In J. A. Langer & M. T. Smith-Burke (Eds.), *Reader meets author/Bridging the gap: A psycholinguistic and sociolinguistic perspective* (pp. 196–221). Newark, DE: International Reading Association.

Green, J., Harker, J., & Golden, J. (1986). Lesson construction: Differing views. In G. W. Noblit & W. T. Pink (Eds.), *Schooling in social context: Qualitative studies* (pp. 46–77). Norwood, NJ: Ablex.

Gundlach, R. (1982). Children as writers: The beginnings of learning to write. In M. Nystrand (Ed.), *What writers know: The language, process, and structure of written discourse* (pp. 129–148). New York: Academic Press.

Gundlach, R., McLane, J. B., Stott, F. M., & McNamee, G. D. (1985). The social foundations of children's early writing development. In M. Farr (Ed.), *Advances in writing research, Vol. 1: Children's writing development* (pp. 1–58). Norwood, NJ: Ablex.

Harste, J. E., Woodward, V. A., & Burke, C. L. (1984). *Language stories and literacy lessons.* Portsmouth, NH: Heinemann.

Heath, S. B. (1982). What no bedtime story means: Narrative skills at home and school. *Language in Society, 11,* 49–76.

Heath, S. B. (1983). *Way with words: Language, life, and work in communities and classrooms.* Cambridge, MA: Harvard University Press.

Heath, S. B., & Branscombe, A. (1985). "Intelligent writing" in an audience community: Teachers, students, and researcher. In S. W. Freedman (Ed.), *The acquisition of literacy: Revision and response.* Norwood, NJ: Ablex.

Heath, S. B., with Thomas, C. (1984). The achievement of preschool literacy for mother and child. In H. Goelman, A. Oberg, & F. Smith (Eds.), *Awakening to literacy* (pp. 51–72). Exeter, NH: Heinemann.

Hiebert, E. H. (1988). The role of literacy experiences in early childhood programs. *Elementary School Journal, 89,* 161–171.

Hoffman, S. J. (1981). *Preschool reading related behaviors: A parent diary.* Unpublished doctoral dissertation, University of Pennsylvania, Philadelphia.

Irwin, D. (1960). Infant speech: Effect of systematic reading of stories. *Journal of Speech and Hearing Research, 3,* 187–190.

Juel, C., Griffith, P. L., & Gough, P. B. (1986). Acquisition of literacy: A longitudinal study of children in first and second grade. *Journal of Educational Psychology, 78,* 243–255.

Kamberelis, G., & Sulzby, E. (1988). Transitional knowledge in emergent literacy. *National Reading Conference Yearbook, 37,* 95–106.

King, M., & Rentel, V. (1981). *How children learn to write: A longitudinal study* (Final report to the National Institute of Education, RF Project 761861/712383 and 765512/711748). Columbus, OH: Ohio State University Research Foundation.

Kolinsky, R., Cary, L., & Morais, J. (1987). Awareness of words as phonological entities: The role of literacy. *Applied Psycholinguistics, 8,* 223–232.

Leont'ev, A. N. (1981). The problem of activity in psychology. In J. Wertsch (Ed.), *The concept of activity in Soviet psychology* (pp. 37–71). Armonk, NY: M. E. Sharpe.

Levin, H., Scheffler, C. A., & Snow, C. E. (1982). The prosodic and paralinguistic features of reading and telling stories. *Language and Speech, 25,* 43–54.

Lomax, R. G., & McGee, L. M. (1987). Young children's concepts about print and reading: Toward a model of word-reading acquisition. *Reading Research Quarterly, 22,* 237–256.

Lundberg, I., Frost, J., & Petersen, O. P. (1988). Effects of an extensive program for stimulating phonological awareness in preschool children. *Reading Research Quarterly, 23,* 264–284.

Lundberg, I., Olofsson, A., & Wall, S. (1980). Reading and spelling skills in the first school years predicted from phonemic awareness skills in kindergarten. *Scandinavian Journal of Psychology, 21,* 159–173.

McGee, L., Lomax, R., & Head, M. (1988). Young children's written language knowledge: What environmental and functional print reading reveals. *Journal of Reading Behavior, 20,* 99–118.

MacKinnon, P. (1959). *How do children learn to read?* Montreal, Quebec, Canada: Copp Publishing.

Marjoribanks, K. (1979). Family environments. In H. J. Walberg (Ed.), *Educational environments and effects* (pp. 15–37). Berkeley, CA: McCutchan Publishing Corp.

Martinez, M., & Roser, N. (1985). Read it again: The value of repeated readings during storytime. *Reading Teacher, 38,* 782–786.

Martinez, M., & Teale, W. H. (1987). The ins and outs of a kindergarten writing program. *Reading Teacher, 40,* 444–451.

Martlew, M. (1988). Children's oral and written language. In A. D. Pellegrini (Ed.), *Psychological bases for early education* (pp. 77–122). Chichester, Eng.: Wiley.

Marzollo, J., & Sulzby, E. (1988–1990). See Jane read! See Jane write! In J. S. McKee & K. M. Paciorek (Eds.), *Annual editions: Early childhood education 89–90.* Guilford, CT: Dushkin Publishing. (Reprinted from *Parents,* 1988, 63[7], 80–84.)

Mason, G., & Blanton, W. (1971). Story content for beginning reading instruction. *Elementary English, 48,* 793–796.

Mason J. M. (1980). When do children begin to read: An exploration of four-year-old children's letter- and word-reading competencies. *Reading Research Quarterly, 15,* 203–227.

Mason, J. M. (1986). Prereading: A developmental perspective. In P. D Pearson et al., (Eds.), *Handbook of reading research* (Vol. 1, pp. 505–543). New York: Longman.

Mason, J. M., & Allen, J. B. (1986). A review of emergent literacy with implications for research and practice in reading. *Review of Research in Education, 13,* 3–47.

Mason, J. M., Peterman, C. L., Powell, B. M., & Kerr, B. M. (1989). Reading and writing attempts by kindergartners after book reading by teachers. In J. M. Mason (Ed.), *Reading and writing connections* (pp. 105–120). Needham Heights, MA: Allyn & Bacon.

Masonheimer, P. E., Drum, P. A., & Ehri, L. C. (1984). Does environmental print identification lead children into word reading? *Journal of Reading Behavior, 16,* 257–271.

Mickish, V. (1974). Children's perception of written word boundaries. *Journal of Reading Behavior*, 6, 19–22.

Miller, P., Nemoianu, A., & DeJong, J. (1986). Early reading at home: Its practice and meaning in a working-class community. In B. Schieffelin & P. Gilmore (Eds.), *The acquisition of literacy: Ethnographic perspectives* (pp. 3–15). Norwood, NJ: Ablex.

Morais, J., Bertelson, P., Cary, L., & Alegria, J. (1986). Literacy training and speech segmentation. *Cognition*, 24, 45–64.

Morais, J., Cary, L., Alegria, J., & Bertelson, P. (1979). Does awareness of speech as a sequence of phonemes arise spontaneously? *Cognition*, 7, 323–331.

Morrow, L. M. (1988). Young children's responses to one-to-one story readings in school settings. *Reading Research Quarterly*, 23, 89–107.

Ninio, A. (1980). Picture-book reading in mother-infant dyads belonging to two subgroups in Israel. *Child Development*, 51, 587–590.

Ninio, A., & Bruner, J. (1978). The achievement and antecedents of labelling. *Journal of Child Language*, 5, 1–15.

Nurss, J. R. (1988). Development of written communication in Norwegian kindergarten children. *Scandinavian Journal of Educational Research*, 32, 33–48.

Olofsson, A., & Lundberg, I. (1983). Can phonemic awareness be trained in kindergarten. *Scandinavian Journal of Psychology*, 24, 35–44.

Olson, D. R. (1977). From utterance to text: The bias of language in speech and writing. *Harvard Educational Review*, 47(3), 257–281.

Papandropoulos, I., & Sinclair, H. (1974). What is a word? Experimental study of children's ideas on grammar. *Human Development*, 17, 241–258.

Pappas, C. C. (1986). *Learning to read by reading: Exploring text indices for understanding the process* (Final report to the Research Committee for the Research Foundation of the National Council of Teachers of English [No. R85:21]). Lexington: University of Kentucky.

Pappas, C. C. (1987). Exploring the textual properties of "protoreading." In R. Steele & T. Threadgold (Eds.), *Language topics: Essays in honour of Michael Halliday* (Vol. 1, pp. 137–162). Amsterdam, Neth.: John Benjamins.

Pappas, C. C. (1988, December). *Exploring the ontogenesis of the registers of written language: Young children tackling the "book language" of information books.* Paper presented at the 38th annual meeting of the National Reading Conference, Tucson, AZ.

Pappas, C. C., & Brown, E. (1987). Learning to read by reading: Learning how to extend the functional potential of language. *Research in the Teaching of English*, 21, 160–184.

Pappas, C. C., & Brown, E. (1988). The development of children's sense of the written story language register: An analysis of the texture of "pretend reading." *Linguistics and Education*, 1, 45–79.

Pellegrini, A. D., Brody, G. H., & Sigel, I. E. (1985). Parents' book-reading habits with their children. *Journal of Educational Psychology*, 77(3), 332–340.

Pellegrini, A. D., Perlmutter, J. C., Galda, L., & Brody, G. H. (1990). Joint book reading between black Head Start children and their mothers. *Child Development*.

Perfetti, C. A., Beck, I., Bell, L., & Hughes, C. (1987). Phonemic knowledge and learning to read are reciprocal: A longitudinal study of first-grade children. *Merrill-Palmer Quarterly*, 33, 283–319.

Perin, D. (1983). Phonemic segmentation and spelling. *British Journal of Psychology*, 74, 129–144.

Peterman, C. L. (1987). *The effects of storyreading procedures collaboratively designed by teacher and researcher on kindergartners' literacy learning.* Unpublished doctoral dissertation, University of Illinois, Champaign-Urbana.

Peterman, C. L., Dunning, D., Eckerty, C., & Mason, J. M. (1987, April). *The effects of storyreading procedures collaboratively designed by teacher and researcher on kindergartners' literacy learning.* Paper presented at the annual meeting of the American Educational Research Association, Washington, DC.

Piaget, J. (1959). *The language and thought of the child* (3rd ed.). London: Routledge & Kegan Paul.

Pikulski, J. J., & Tobin, A. W. (1988). *Factors associated with long-term reading achievement of early readers.* Paper presented at the annual meeting of the National Reading Conference, Tucson, AZ.

Pinnell, G. S., et al. (1986, July). *The Ohio Reading Recovery Project: Columbus Project, Year Two.* Columbus: The Ohio State University.

Pontecorvo, C., Orsolini, M., Zucchermaglio, C., & Rossi, F. (1987, December). *Metalinguistic skills in children: What develops?* Paper presented at the National Reading Conference, St. Petersburg, FL.

Purcell-Gates, V. (1988). Lexical and syntactic knowledge of written narrative held by well-read-to kindergartners and second graders. *Research in the Teaching of English*, 22(2), 128–160.

Purcell-Gates, V. (1989). The ability of well-read-to kindergartners to decontextualize/recontextualize experience into a written-narrative register. Manuscript submitted for publication.

Read, C. (1970). *Children's perceptions of the sound of English.* Unpublished doctoral dissertation, Harvard University, Cambridge, MA.

Read, C. (1975). *Children's categorizations of speech sounds in English* (NCTE Res. Rep. No. 17). Urbana, IL: National Council of Teachers of English.

Reder, S., & Green, K. R. (1983). Contrasting patterns of literacy in an Alaska fishing village. *International Journal of the Sociology of Language*, 42, 9–39.

Rohl, M., & Tunmer, W. E. (1988). Phonemic segmentation skill and spelling acquisition. *Applied Psycholingusitics, 9*, 335–350.

Rowe, D. W. (1986). *Preschoolers as authors: Literacy learning in the social world of the classroom.* Unpublished doctoral dissertation, Indiana University, Bloomington, IN.

Rowe, D. W. (1987). Literacy learning as an intertextual process. *National Reading Conference Yearbook, 36,* 101–112.

Rowe, D. W. (1988, April). *The impact of author/audience interaction on preschoolers' literacy learning.* Paper presented at the annual meeting of the American Educational Research Association, New Orleans, LA.

Rubin, A. D. (1978). *A theoretical taxonomy of the differences between oral and written language* (Tech. Rep. No. 35). Urbana-Champaign: University of Illinois, Center for the Study of Reading.

Rumelhart, D. E. (1977). Toward an interactive model of reading. In S. Dornic (Ed.), *Attention and performance VI* (pp. 573–603). London: Academic Press.

Schmandt-Besserat, D. (1978). The earliest precursor of writing. *Scientific American, 238,* 50–59.

Scollon, R. (1988). Storytelling, reading, and the micropolitics of literacy. *National Reading Conference Yearbook, 37,* 15–33.

Scollon, R., & Scollon, S. B. K. (1981). *Narrative, literacy, and face in interethnic communication.* Norwood, NJ: Ablex.

Scribner, S., & Cole, M. (1981). *The psychology of literacy: A case study among the Vai.* Cambridge, MA: Harvard University Press.

Simner, M. L. (1981). The grammar of action and children's printing. *Developmental Psychology, 17,* 866–871.

Simner, M. L. (1982). Printing errors in kindergarten and the prediction of academic performance. *Journal of Learning Disabilities, 15*(3), 155–159.

Simons, H. D., & Murphy, S. (1983). Oral and written language differences in becoming literate. *Claremont Reading Conference Yearbook,* 193–204.

Snow, C. E. (1977). Mothers' speech research: From input to interaction. In C. E. Snow & C. A. Ferguson (Eds.), *Talking to children: Language input and acquisition* (pp. 31–49). Cambridge, Eng.: Cambridge University Press.

Snow, C. E. (1983). Literacy and language: Relationships during the preschool years. *Harvard Educational Review, 53*(2), 165–189.

Snow, C. E., Dubber, C., & Blauw, A. D. (1982). Routines in other-child interaction. In L. Feagans & D. C. Farran (Eds.), *The language of children reared in poverty* (pp. 53–72). New York: Academic Press.

Snow, C. E., & Goldfield, B. A. (1982). Building stories: The emergence of information structures from conversation. In D. Tannen (Ed.), *Analyzing discourse: Text and talk* (pp. 127–141). Washington, DC: Georgetown University Press.

Snow, C. E., & Goldfield, B. A. (1983). Turn the page, please: Situation-specific language acquisition. *Journal of Child Language, 10,* 535–549.

Snow, C. E., & Ninio, A. (1986). The contracts of literacy: What children learn from learning to read books. In W. H. Teale & E. Sulzby (Eds.), *Emergent literacy: Writing and reading* (pp. 116–138). Norwood, NJ: Ablex.

Stanovich, K. (1986). Matthew effects in reading: Some consequences of individual differences in the acquisition of literacy. *Reading Research Quarterly, 21,* 360–407.

Stauffer, R. G. (1970). *The language-experience approach to the teaching of reading.* New York: Harper & Row.

Stewart, J., & Mason, J. (1989). Preschool children's reading and writing awareness. In J. Mason (Ed.), *Reading and writing connections* (pp. 219–236). Needham Heights, MA: Allyn & Bacon.

Strickland, D. S., & Morrow, L. M. (Eds.). (1989). *Emerging literacy: Young children learn to read and write.* Newark, DE: International Reading Association.

Sulzby, E. (1983, September). *Beginning readers' developing knowledges about written language* (Final report to the National Institute of Education [NIE-G-80-0176]). Evanston, IL: Northwestern University.

Sulzby, E. (1985a). Children's emergent reading of favorite storybooks: A developmental study. *Reading Research Quarterly, 20,* 458–481.

Sulzby, E. (1985b). Kindergartners as writers and readers. In M. Farr (Ed.), *Advances in writing research, Vol. 1: Children's early writing development* (pp. 127–199). Norwood, NJ: Ablex.

Sulzby, E. (1986a). Writing and reading: Signs of oral and written language organization in the young child. In W. H. Teale & E. Sulzby (Eds.), *Emergent literacy: Writing and reading* (pp. 50–87). Norwood, NJ: Ablex.

Sulzby, E. (1986b). Young children's concepts for oral and written texts. In K. Durkin (Ed.), *Language development during the school years* (pp. 95–116). London: Croom Helm.

Sulzby, E. (1987). Children's development of prosodic distinctions in telling and dictating modes. In A. Matsuhashi (Ed.), *Writing in real time: Modeling production processes* (pp. 133–160). Norwood, NJ: Ablex.

Sulzby, E. (1988). A study of children's early reading development. In A. D. Pellegrini (Ed.), *Psychological bases for early education* (pp. 39–75). Chichester, Eng: Wiley.

Sulzby, E. (1989). Assessment of writing and of children's language while writing. In L. Morrow & J. Smith

(Eds.), *The role of assessment and measurement in early literacy instruction* (pp. 83–109). Englewood Cliffs, NJ: Prentice-Hall.

Sulzby, E., Barnhart, J., & Hieshima, J. (1989). *Forms of writing and rereading from writing: A preliminary report*. In J. Mason (Ed.), *Reading and writing connections* (pp. 31–63). Needham Heights, MA: Allyn & Bacon. (Also Tech. Rep. No. 20, Center for the Study of Writing, University of California, Berkeley, CA.)

Sulzby, E., & Teale, W. H. (1985). Writing development in early childhood. *Educational Horizons, 64*, 8–12.

Sulzby, E., & Teale, W. H. (1987, November). *Young children's storybook reading: Longitudinal study of parent-child interaction and children's independent functioning* (Final report to the Spencer Foundation). Ann Arbor: University of Michigan.

Sulzby, E., Teale, W. H., & Kamberelis, G. (1989). Emergent writing in the classroom: Home and school connections. In D. S. Strickland & L. M. Morrow (Eds.), *Emerging literacy: Young children learn to read and write* (pp. 63–79). Newark, DE: International Reading Association.

Tannen, D. (1984). *Conversational style: Analyzing talk among friends*. Norwood, NJ: Ablex.

Taylor, D. (1983). *Family literacy*. Exeter, NH: Heinemann.

Taylor, D. (1986). Creating family story: "Matthew! We're going to have a ride!" In W. H. Teale & E. Sulzby (Eds.), *Emergent literacy: Writing and reading* (pp. 139–155). Norwood, NJ: Ablex.

Taylor, D., & Dorsey-Gaines, C. (1988). *Growing up literate: Learning from inner-city families*. Portsmouth, NH: Heinemann.

Teale, W. H. (1978). Positive environments for learning to read: What studies of early readers tell us. *Language Arts, 55*, 922–932.

Teale, W. H. (1980). *Early reading: An annotated bibliography*. Newark, DE: International Reading Association.

Teale, W. H. (1984). Reading to young children: Its significance in the process of literacy development. In H. Goelman, A. Oberg, & F. Smith (Eds.), *Awakening to literacy* (pp. 110–121). Exeter, NH: Heinemann.

Teale, W. H. (1986). Home background and young children's literacy development. In W. H. Teale & E. Sulzby (Eds.), *Emergent literacy: Writing and reading* (pp. 173–206). Norwood, NJ: Ablex.

Teale, W. H. (1987). Emergent literacy: Reading and writing development in early childhood. *National Reading Conference Yearbook, 36*, 45–74.

Teale, W. H. (1988). Developmentally appropriate assessment of reading and writing in the early childhood classroom. *Elementary School Journal, 89*, 173–183.

Teale, W. H. (1989). The promise and challenge of informal assessment in early literacy. In L. M. Morrow & J. K. Smith (Eds.), *Assessment for instruction in early literacy* (pp. 45–61). Englewood Cliffs, NJ: Prentice-Hall.

Teale, W. H., & Martinez, M. (1986). Teachers' storybook reading styles: Evidence and implications. *Reading Education in Texas, 2*, 7–16.

Teale, W. H., & Martinez, M. (1989). Connecting writing: Fostering emergent literacy in kindergarten children. In J. Mason (Ed.), *Reading and writing connections* (pp. 177–197). Needham Heights., MA: Allyn & Bacon.

Teale, W. H., Martinez, M. G., & Glass, W. L. (1989). Describing classroom storybook reading. In D. Bloome (Ed.), *Classrooms and literacy* (pp. 158–188). Norwood, NJ: Ablex.

Teale, W. H., & Sulzby, E. (Eds.). (1986). *Emergent literacy: Writing and reading*. Norwood, NJ: Ablex.

Teale, W. H., & Sulzby, E. (1987). Literacy acquisition in early childhood: The roles of access and mediation in storybook reading. In D. A. Wagner (Ed.), *The future of literacy in a changing world*. (pp. 111–130). New York: Pergamon Press.

Templin, M. (1957). *Certain language skills in children*. Minneapolis: University of Minnesota Press.

Tobin, A. W. (1981). *A multiple discriminant cross-validation of the factors associated with the development of precocious reading achievement*. Unpublished doctoral dissertation, University of Delaware, Newark, DE.

Tobin, A. W., & Pikulski, J. J. (1988). A longitudinal study of the reading achievement of early and nonearly readers through sixth grade. *National Reading Conference Yearbook, 37*, 49–58.

Tolchinsky-Landsmann, L., & Levin, I. (1985). Writing in preschoolers: An age-related analysis. *Applied Psycholinguistics, 6*, 319–339.

Tolchinsky-Landsmann, L., & Levin, I. (1987). Writing in four- to six-year-olds: Representation of semantic and phonetic similarities and differences. *Journal of Child Language, 14*, 127–144.

Torneus, M. (1984). Phonological awareness and reading: A chicken and egg problem? *Journal of Educational Psychology, 76*, 1346–1358.

Tunmer, W. E., & Bowey, J. A. (1984). Metalinguistic awareness and reading acquisition. In W. E. Tunmer, C. Pratt, & M. L. Herriman (Eds.), *Metalinguistic awareness in children: Theory, research, and implications* (pp. 144–168). Berlin: Springer-Verlag.

Tunmer, W. E., Herriman, M. L., & Nesdale, A. R. (1988). Metalinguistic abilities and beginning reading. *Reading Research Quarterly, 23*, 134–158.

Tunmer, W. E., & Nesdale, A. R. (1985). Phonemic segmentation skill and beginning reading. *Journal of Educational Psychology, 77*, 417–427.

Vobejda, B. (1987, August 10). "Emergent literacy" in scribbles of young. *Washington Post*, p. A3.

Vukelich, C., & Edwards, N. (1987, December). *Young children's writing and reading; or, If I have to have words, can I have a picture too?* Paper presented at the National Reading Conference, St. Petersburg, FL.

Vukelich, C., & Edwards, N. (1988). The role of context and as-written orthography in kindergartners' word recognition. *National Reading Conference Yearbook, 37,* 85–93.

Vygotsky, L. S. (1978). *Mind in society: The development of higher psychological processes.* Cambridge, MA: Harvard University Press.

Wells, C. G. (1985). Preschool literacy-related activities and success in school. In D. Olson, N. Torrance, & A. Hildyard (Eds.), *Literacy, language, and learning: The nature and consequence of literacy* (pp. 229–255). Cambridge, Eng.: Cambridge University Press.

Wells, M. (1988). The roots of literacy. *Psychology Today, 22,* 20–22.

Wertsch, J. (Ed.). (1981). *The concept of activity in Soviet psychology.* Armonk, NY: M. E. Sharpe.

Whitehurst, G. J., Falco, F. L., Lonigan, C. J., Fischel, J. E., DeBaryshe, B. D., Valdez-Menchaca, M. C., & Caulfield, M. (1988). Accelerating language development through picturebook reading. *Developmental Psychology, 24,* 552–559.

Wigfield, A., & Asher, S. R. (1984). Social and motivational influences on reading. In P. D. Pearson, Barr, R., Kamil, M. L., & Mosenthal, P. (Eds.), *Handbook of reading research* (Vol. 1, pp. 423–452). White Plains, NY: Longman.

Wood, D., Bruner, J. S., & Ross, G. (1976). The role of tutoring in problem solving. *Journal of Child Psychology and Psychiatry, 17,* 89–100.

Wolf, D., & Gardner, H. (1981). On the structure of early symbolization. In R. L. Schiefelsbusch (Ed.), *Early language: Acquisition and intervention* (pp. 287–327). Baltimore, MD: University Park Press.

Yaden, D. B., Smolkin, L. B., & Coulon, A. (1989). Preschoolers' questions about pictures, print conventions, and story text during reading aloud at home. *Reading Research Quarterly, 24,* 188–214.

Yaden, D. B., & Templeton, S. (Eds.). (1986). *Metalinguistic awareness and beginning literacy.* Portsmouth, NH: Heineman.

Yopp, H. K. (1988). The validity and reliability of phonemic awareness tests. *Reading Research Quarterly, 23,* 159–177.

27 BEGINNING READING

Connie Juel

One day a good fortune befell him, for he hit upon Lane's translation of *The Thousand Nights and a Night*. He was captured first by the illustrations, and then he began to read, to start with, the stories that dealt with magic, and then the others; and those he liked he read again and again. He could think of nothing else. He forgot the life about him. He had to be called two or three times before he would come to his dinner. Insensibly he formed the most delightful habit in the world, the habit of reading. . . . (Maugham, 1915/1963, p. 37)

W e know surprisingly little about the transition from what has been termed *emergent literacy* to beginning reading. We know too little about the cognitive, social, and instructional forces that enable a child to grow from labeling the letters of the alphabet and "reading" environmental print to reading a page from a book that the child has never seen before. Our ignorance is partly the result of governmental and organizational funding policies, and the consequent research focus in the past decade (at a minimum) on "higher-order" reading processes. Such an emphasis reflects legitimate concern over the poor performance of many *older* students on national assessments of higher-order reading and writing skills (e.g., National Assessment of Educational Progress [NAEP]). This focus also reflected a feeling that we were doing an adequate job teaching "lower-order" decoding skills and that the earlier debate over whether to include phonics in early instruction had been resolved in favor of phonics (Anderson, Hiebert, Scott, & Wilkinson, 1985).

Ignorance of a critical initial step in an ongoing process is likely to obscure full understanding of the total process, and we are highly likely to draw erroneous conclusions if we start with inaccurate assumptions. Reading skill may not be developed as quickly or as well in the primary grades as is believed (Gough & Hillinger, 1980). We are just beginning to detect the dire consequences that a poor initial start with reading has on later reading development (cf. Stanovich, 1986). Certainly, the debate over initial reading methods continues.

THE STATE OF MODELS OF THE READING ACQUISITION PROCESS

In 1983 Gough, Juel, & Roper-Schneider found it curious that Singer and Ruddell's (1976) collection of models of reading did not contain one of reading acquisition. The 1985 edition still lacks any thorough model of the reading acquisition process.

This is not to say we know nothing about reading acquisition; although we know much, our knowledge is selective. We clearly lack a comprehensive model of reading acquisition, one that would incorporate the various psychological, social, and instructional components that contribute to the process of learning to read.

Compared to the paucity of reading acquisition models, there are numerous models of the reading process of the *skilled* reader. These models usually emphasize psychological processes. It is not clear how such models of fluent reading relate—if at all—to the beginning of the process of reading. Three fairly common assumptions of the highly skilled reading process are presented below.

First, several models of *skilled* word recognition indicate that words frequently are not processed phonologically prior to identifying the meaning of the word (Kleiman, 1975; Massaro, 1975; Rumelhart, 1985). That is, words are identified without mediated processing of spelling-sound characteristics. Phonological equivalents of orthographic strings (if needed to aid in short-term memory retention and comprehension) may be produced as by-products of lexical access. It is tenuous to assume that beginning readers have built up sufficient orthographic information (through frequent exposures to words) to allow much of this type of nonmediated, nonphonological, word processing (Juel, 1983).

Second, La Berge and Samuels (1974) describe the *fluent* reader as one whose decoding processes are "automatic," requiring no conscious attention. When a reader is fluent, he or she is more able to deploy his or her attention *selectively*, which obviously can facilitate ongoing comprehension and integration of material with prior knowledge. This is not true for the beginning reader. Samuels (1979) has suggested that repeated readings of text allow the beginner to approximate, or possibly mimic, the automatic decoding of the fluent reader and thus appear to be concentrating attention on comprehension. It is not clear how closely the beginner approximates the experienced reader in these experiences. Furthermore, it is not clear *which* decoding subprocesses become "automatic." Is it the decoding of the whole word or some orthographic constituent of words such as phonograms, common letter combinations like *st*, or spelling-sound generalizations? Can we state with certainty that such automatic decoding is the same for both experienced and beginning readers?

Third, the fluent reader is one who actively searches for, and constructs meaning from, text. Prior knowledge of language and subject matter is actively used by the fluent reader to predict, confirm, and create meaning (K. S. Goodman, 1976; Tierney & Pearson, 1984). The question of whether meaning exists in the text or in the reader seems to be both hopelessly philosophical (who knows how to derive conclusively the *absolute* meaning of anything?) and educationally irrelevant (if we knew where "absolute meaning" resides, would it change pedagogy?). On the other hand, the degree to which both the fluent and the nonfluent reader search for meaning using similar cognitive processes and similar sources of knowledge *is* important. The understanding of how readers make sense of text would clearly be useful pedagogically and *can* be determined through empirical study. It may be that the relatively inexperienced reader relies *more* on prior knowledge than does the experienced reader to actively "construct" meaning from text; whereas the skilled reader is more prone to "reconstruct" text meaning after reflection on the text and its fit with the reader's prior knowledge.

Models of Reading Acquisition

In their 1975 book, *The Psychology of Reading*, Gibson and Levin state:

> Despite all the current emphasis on literacy, the wealth of programs commercially available, the "learning specialists" who have set up in shopping centers, and the arguments over phonics or whole-word [today one might add whole-language] methods, it is the beginning phase of learning to read that we seem to know least about. All the talk is of what

the teacher does or should do and not of what happens or should happen in the child. (p. 264)

Indeed, since this 1975 quote appeared, much of the progress we have made in understanding the reading acquisition process has occurred precisely because we *did* start to focus on what happens *inside the child's mind*. That is, we began to focus more on which processes, traits, or skills *the child* actually learns as he or she becomes literate. This focus is useful; when we know what and how the child learns we can better facilitate the passage to literacy.

The focus (on teacher and methods) seems less useful in understanding the acquisition process per se. Let me illustrate. Suppose we believe that phonics is superior to other methods. We may therefore infer that the process of learning to read involves the learning of the type of letter-sound correspondences taught in phonics programs. It may be, however, that the actual spelling-sound relations used by readers bear little or no resemblance to what is taught in phonics (Gough & Hillinger, 1980). Rather, phonics may be useful to some children because it suggests to them a strategy of looking for sound patterns in words, and they then discover the real "rules" for themselves. On the other hand, phonics may be successful because of factors quite unrelated to its content, such as its emphasis on direct instruction (Resnick, 1979).

This is not to imply research on methods is unimportant. It is tremendously important. Teachers need reliable information on what forms of reading instruction work best in particular situations. The synthesis and interpretation of studies on methods, as in the classic *Learning to Read: The Great Debate* by J. S. Chall (1967), need to be continued. Rather it is to suggest that the lens through which we view reading instruction should be opened more widely to include not just the method in isolation, but factors that accompany the method. Time spent reading, the kinds of texts that are read, the social setting for instruction, and patterns of interaction are examples of such factors. Recent reviews of reading instruction seem to take this broader picture (see Barr, 1984; Venezky, 1986).

To better understand literacy acquisition, the focus needs to be centered on the child and what the child is actually learning, rather than on what the teacher (or parent) appears to be teaching. It is this focus on the child (and how the child interacts with and makes sense of his or her own written communication) that seems to underlie the promising research in emergent literacy (see Ferreiro & Teberoksy, 1982; Y. M. Goodman, 1980, 1986; Mason, 1984; Mason & Allen, 1986; Sulzby & Teale, this volume, Chapter 26; Teale & Sulzby, 1986).

By focusing on the child during the preschool years, or the period in which, as Y. M. Goodman (1980) says, "the roots of literacy" develop, one sees that the development of literacy starts well before formal schooling. Insights about the world of print arise over time, often through interaction with storybooks in the home and printed materials in the environment. Exactly what insights are gained, how they arise, and whether insights about print tend to develop in a sequential order have been, and are being, researched (e.g., Hiebert, 1981; Lomax & McGee, 1987; Mason, 1980; Sulzby, 1985).

A fundamental insight that most children appear to learn in the emergent literacy period is that *print* has a communicative function (Ferreiro & Teberosky, 1982; Y. M. Goodman, 1980, 1986; Lomax & McGee, 1987). Such understanding does not come quickly, however (see Hiebert, 1981; Mason & Allen, 1986). The importance of the individualized, underlying meaning of the "objects" attached to print (which includes the environmental context in which the print is embedded) tends to obscure the specific, impersonal role of the print itself. The child calls "signs of Burger Chef, Burger King, and MacDonald's all MacDonald's" (K. S. Goodman & Y. M. Goodman, 1979) or labels the printed word "Crest" on a tube of toothpaste as "toothpaste" or "brush your teeth" (Harste, 1980). While one can philosophize that "brush your teeth" is the "true" meaning of the printed word "Crest" for a particular individual, at some point in life the individual must also be able to identify the generalized, impersonal word "Crest."

This chapter will discuss models of reading acquisition that are concerned with *how* the child moves from contextually bound "readings" of print to noncontextually bound readings (i.e, models concerned with how the child reads "Crest" when it is not embedded on a tube of toothpaste, or how the child can read "Crest" as "Crest" *in addition to* any personalized, connotative meaning the word may evoke). This chapter also builds on much of what the child has learned about print, such as its communicative functions, in the emergent literacy period described by Sulzby and Teale in the prior chapter.

Two basic paradigms have been used for modeling reading acquisition. In one paradigm the reading process is viewed as the same process whether the reader is experienced or inexperienced. For both the beginner and the experienced reader, it is emphasized, reading is the search for meaning. This search is best accomplished by using knowledge about language and the world (or syntactic and semantic knowledge), rather than specific graphic information about a printed word. *Quantitative* growth in language and world knowledge are seen as the primary factors that distinguish the reading of the skilled from the beginning reader. (See Ehri, 1978; K. S. Goodman, 1976; K. S. Goodman & Y. M. Goodman, 1979; Smith, 1971, 1973).

The second paradigm is based on the belief that there are *qualitative* differences in reading processes between beginning and experienced readers. Qualitative differences emerge over time as the reader gains new and more efficient ways to identify printed words. The differences in how words are identified are thought to be more related to knowledge about orthography than to improved syntactic or semantic knowledge. This view has generated "stage" models of reading. Each stage reflects an additional (and usually more efficient) way to identify printed words. In "stage" models differences are seen in the actual processes readers use, and not just in their control of these processes. (See Chall, 1979, 1983; Ehri & Wilce, 1985, 1987; Gough & Hillinger, 1980; Mason, 1980.)

It should be emphasized that the goal of reading in both paradigms is the construction of meaning. The paradigms differ in their views of how this comprehension is normally or most easily accomplished. The first paradigm suggests that the reader is most successful if *minimal* orthographic information is used. It suggests that the beginner, as well as the experienced reader, uses as little graphic information as possible to construct meaning. In contrast, in the second paradigm it is the increasingly rapid and efficient use of *maximal* orthographic information that is seen as leading to better comprehension. The child progresses through stages in which graphic information is more speedily and efficiently used to identify printed words.

The next section will more extensively detail nonstage models. It will be followed by a section on stage models. Then some questions raised by both these types of models will be addressed.

Nonstage Models of Reading Acquisition

K. S. Goodman and Y. M. Goodman (1979) state: "There is only one reading process. Readers may differ in the control of this process but not in the process they use" (p. 148). In this view, the primary advantage of skilled readers is their increased knowledge of the world and language. The better reader uses syntactic and semantic information to form hypotheses about the content of text, with minimal reliance on orthographic information. K. S. Goodman (1976) captures this view when he asserts that "Skill in reading involves not greater precision, but more accurate first guesses based on better sampling techniques, greater control over language structure, broadened experiences and increased conceptual development" (p. 504). Children frequently show these "guesses" both when they miscue (e.g., substitute *big* for *large*) as they read orally and when they are more able to read words embedded in text than when they occur in isolation (K. S. Goodman, 1965).

Reading development is thought to parallel language development, being a natural process that evolves because of the need to communicate. Y. M. Goodman (1980) suggests that "Language development is natural whether written or oral. It develops in a social setting because of the human need to communicate and interact with the significant others in the culture" (p. 3).

Increased reading skill comes from increased language skill. Reading skill will therefore be facilitated by exposure to text that is rich in natural language (i.e, not a controlled vocabulary). In this model, reading skill will not be helped by focusing on parts of words. K. S. Goodman and Y. M. Goodman (1979) explain why: "Since we view language as a personal-social invention, we see both oral and written language as learned in the same way. In neither case is the user required by the nature of the task to have a high level of conscious awareness of the units and system" (p. 139).

Ehri (1978) developed a model of acquisition that drew on many of the ideas that were part of K. S. Goodman's portrayal of skilled reading as a "psycholinguistic guessing game in which the reader processes and coordinates simultaneously three types of information—graphic, syntactic, and semantic" (Ehri, 1978, p. 1). Ehri, however, distinguishes her approach from Goodman's. She states that it "differs from Goodman's in that it focuses upon the child's linguistic system rather than upon information-processing strategies he learns to use in his reading, and it identifies word recognition as the major hurdle faced by the beginner" (Ehri, 1978, p. 2).

In her 1978 model Ehri suggests that the beginner relies strongly on syntactic and semantic cues in initial reading. She attributes this reliance partly to the unreliable nature of letter-sound relations and partly to the relatively rich semantic and syntactic knowledge the child brings to the reading task (as compared to decoding skill knowledge). When the child is exposed to words *in context*, the child will eventually add graphic and phonological information to the semantic and syntactic information about a word. The child will then have available a range of information stored about a word from which multiple and various cues can be used for identification (i.e., syntactic, semantic, graphic, and phonological). Ehri (1978) describes the acquisition process:

It appears that initially the identities imposed upon a new word are primarily syntactic and semantic rather than phonological, that these cues are amalgamated with only some graphic symbols in the word, and that only gradually the full printed form becomes associated with the abstract form stored in the lexicon. (p. 17)

Smith (1971) proposes perhaps the most radical of the nonstage models in minimizing the role that graphic information plays in reading:

The more difficulty a reader has with reading, the more he relies on the visual information; this statement applies to both the fluent reader and the beginner. In each case, the cause of the difficulty is inability to make full use of syntactic and semantic redundancy, of nonvisual sources of information. (p. 221)

Smith (1971) sees the reader as "predicting" the way through the text. Smith and Holmes (1971) provocatively question how often readers even identify words.

Smith (1973) suggests, "Readers do not use (and do not need to use) the alphabetic principle of decoding to sound in order to learn or identify words" (p. 105). Smith (1971, 1973, 1978) proposes that when readers do identify specific unpredictable words, they do so much in the way Gibson (1965) suggested they learn to identify letters.

Gibson (1965) suggested that letters are identified on the basis of their distinctive features: "Regarding each letter, one asks, for example, 'Is there a curved segment?' and gets a yes or no answer" (p. 1068). Letters are identified by asking the minimal number of questions that will distinguish one letter from another. Just as Gibson (1965) proposed feature lists for letters, Smith (1971) proposed them for words. Recognizing *horse* will involve asking the minimal number of questions about its distinctive features that distinguish it from other printed words. Individual letters within words are not identified. Rather, the printed gestalt functions like a Chinese ideogram. Smith (1973) suggests that ". . . in fact we can read as efficiently as most of us do only because we treat our written language as if it were ideographic . . ." (p. 118).

Stage Models of Reading Acquisition

In stage models it is the understanding of the *alphabetic* nature of written (alphabetic) languages that is seen as the major hurdle for the beginning reader. While spelling-sound correspondences are not thought to be easily learned, they are thought to considerably reduce what must be learned to read an alphabetic, as compared to a nonalphabetic, writing system.

Though stage models share the notion that understanding the alphabetic system is at the heart of learning to read, they differ in what is learned and how what is learned is used in the reading process. This section will concentrate on the stage models of Gibson (1965, 1972), Chall (1979, 1983), Mason (1980), Gough and Hillinger (1980), and Ehri (1985, 1987).

Gibson (1965) describes the learning-to-read process as consisting of three different stages:

> Once a child begins his progression from spoken language to written language, there are, I think, three phases of learning to be considered. They present three different kinds of learning tasks, and they are roughly sequential, though there must be considerable overlapping. These three phases are: learning to differentiate graphic symbols; learning to decode letters to sounds ("map" the letters into sounds); and using progressively higher-order units of structure. (p. 1067)

Gibson's approach to learning letters by learning their distinctive features has been described in the section on nonstage models. (Indeed, her view of feature analysis in letter identification has been the starting point for many psychological models of word recognition.) Gibson continues: "When the graphemes are reasonably discriminable from one another, the decoding process becomes possible" (p. 1069).

Gibson views learning to decode as a search for patterns and the induction of rules:

> It is my belief that the smallest component units in written English are spelling patterns. . . . By a spelling pattern, I mean a cluster of graphemes in a given environment which has an invariant pronunciation according to the rules of English. These rules are the regularities which appear when, for instance, any vowel or consonant or cluster is shown to correspond

with a given pronunciation in an initial, medial, or final position in the spelling of a word. (p. 1071)

Gibson believes that the child at first reads in fairly short units but "that the size and complexity of the spelling patterns which can be perceived as units increase with development of reading skill" (1965, p. 1072). She stresses that the mapping rules are not "simply one letter for one phoneme" (1972, p. 12). Rather, ". . . the correspondence rules are morphophonemic and abstract" (p. 13).

Chall (1979, 1983) proposed a developmental stage model of reading. She believes her model to be more macroscopic than microscopic in scope, since it provides broad outlines of the major transitions from prereading through college-level reading, rather than precise descriptions of the processes at work in each stage. Similar to Piaget's notion of stages, each stage in her model is seen as differing in a *qualitative* fashion from other stages. Of most interest to the current review are the major distinguishing characteristics between Stage 0 (Prereading Stage—Preschool to Kindergarten), Stage 1 (initial Reading or Decoding Stage—Grade 1–2), and Stage 2 (Confirmation, Fluency, Ungluing from Print—Grades 2–3).

In Stage 0 children develop the prerequisite visual, visual-motor, and auditory skills required to learn to read. For example, in this stage children are seen as learning "that spoken words may be segmented, that the parts may be added to designated spoken words, that some parts of words sound the same (rhyme and alliteration), and that word parts and sounds can be blended (synthesized) to form whole words" (Chall, 1979, p. 38). The critical passage to Stage 1 reading occurs *when children associate letters with sounds.* "The qualitative change that occurs at the end of this stage is the insight gained about the nature of the spelling system of the particular alphabetic language used" (1979, p. 39).

In Stage 2 of Chall's model, reading fluency is gained. "Although some additional, more complex phonic elements and generalizations are learned during Stage 2 and even later, it appears that what most children learn in Stage 2 is to use their decoding knowledge, the redundancies of the language, and the redundancies of the stories read. They gain courage and skill in using context and thus gain fluency and speed" (1979, p. 41).

Mason (1980) was interested in how 4-year-old preschool children approach reading. She followed two classrooms of preschool children over a nine-month period. Mason suggested a natural hierarchy of three "stages" through which the children seemed to progress. (The word *stages* is herein used to better equate Mason's work with others, but she uses the term *levels*.) In the first stage, children are "context-dependent readers." They read only signs or labels embedded in environmental context (e.g., stop signs). In the second stage, children can recognize a few words out of context. In this "visual recognition" stage, children "seem to be learning to analyze words into their letters" (p. 217). In the third stage, children were reading many words by way of "letter-sound analysis." Mason found few preschool children in the third stage and believes that formal reading instruction is usually necessary for this stage to arrive.

Gough and Hillinger (1980) proposed two qualitatively different stages through which the child passes in learning to read. A parallel is seen between the first stage, called the *paired-associate stage*, and other initial learning tasks involving *selective learning*, "a kind of problem solving in which the learner seeks some attribute of the stimulus which will distinguish it from its competitors" (Greeno, James, DaPolito, & Polson, 1978) (p. 181). In the paired-associate stage, the child will associate a known spoken word with a selected, arbitrary attribute of its printed form. Such selective attributes may be the first letter in a word (e.g., *cat* is remembered by the initial *c*) or distinctive letters (e.g., *moon* is recalled by the two circles) or distinctive visual cues (e.g., the distinctive font in which the word *Budweiser* is printed or the length of the word *elephant*).

The child can easily learn some words by selective association. Gough and Hillinger (1980) suggested the number may be around 40, but individual variations no doubt exist. In the course of their study, Juel, Griffith, and Gough (1986) found one first-grade child who appeared to recall approximately 400 basal words in a paired-associate fashion. Whatever the number that can be so recalled, it is likely that at some point the paired-associate system will break down as selective cues used to differentiate one word from the next become progressively more difficult to find (i.e., *c* for *cat* will no longer work when *cap* is introduced). With every new word, reading becomes increasingly difficult until a new, less arbitrary, system for word recognition is found.

In the second stage, called *cryptanalysis* or *cipher reading*, the child discovers that there is some systematic (albeit not perfect) relationship between printed letters and sounds. Whether skilled readers use such correspondences in fluent reading is not settled. Gough and Hillinger believe the child has no choice but to use these correspondences because (1) "It defies imagination that the child could learn 50,000 items as arbitrary associations" (p. 186); (2) "The argument that English spelling is frequently irregular overlooks the fact that the irregularities are not arbitrary: we do not pronounce *one* /hæm/ or *of* eləfant/" (p. 186); (3) Context is not as helpful to the child as some would like us to believe as "the words which are predictable will tend to be those words which the child already recognizes, and the novel words which he now must recognize are exactly the ones which context will *not* enable him to predict" (p. 186).

Since the 1978 model described in the nonstage section, Ehri seems to have modified her stance on phonological processing and apparently advocates that phonological processing occurs almost at the very onset of word reading. Ehri and Wilce (1985, 1987) now view reading acquisition as occurring in three stages. In the first stage (which is labeled *prereading* and is populated by children who cannot read preprimer words), environmental and visual cues are used for print recognition. In the second stage, when children (labeled "novice readers") can read a few preprimer words, partial knowledge about spelling-sound associations is used to identify words. In this second stage, children frequently use the sounds captured in the letter names to identify and spell words (e.g., spelling *light* as *lt*). Finally, in the third stage, the "veteran" early reader not only can phonologically recode, but more importantly can store sight words in memory by establishing phonological access routes which connect the letters in spellings to phonemes used in the pronunciation of words (see Ehri, this volume, Chapter 15).

Ehri and Wilce (1985, 1987) provide evidence that prior to entry to the third stage, children use partial phonetic cues (often stemming from the sound provided in letter names) to recall words. They propose this *phonetic-cue stage* as intermediate between the paired-associate and the cipher stage of Gough and Hillinger (1980). In this intermediate stage, children use partial phonetic cues as mnemonics for recall (e.g., reading the word *jail* by associating the names of the letters *j* and *l* with sounds heard in *jail*). The documented existence of such cueing is intriguing and suggests another explanation for the well-known positive correlation between knowing the names of the letters of the alphabet and learning to read in first grade.

There is some disagreement on how soon a decoding stage develops, or how lasting it is in the models discussed so far; yet they all assign great importance to the child learning to decode words. The stage nature of all the models suggests that over time the child learns to read in qualitatively different ways.

Although the stage models presented in this section may have used different labels for stages, may lump some stages together, or may represent some variations in processes in a particular stage, they paint a remarkably similar picture of beginning reading. After the child discovers that print itself carries meaning, the process of identifying or remembering specific printed words appears to involve at least two qualitatively different stages.

In the first stage, the *selective-cue stage* child identifies words by attending to *random* features of either the environment in which the print occurs (i.e., place on a page) and/or to some features of the print itself (e.g., distinctive letters). In this stage the child attends to minimum graphic information and maximum contextual information (Ehri, 1987; Ehri & Wilce, 1985; Gough & Hillinger, 1980; Mason, 1980).

In the second stage, the *spelling-sound stage* child identifies unknown words by attending to maximum graphic information. Early in this stage, the child may "glue to print" (cf. Chall, 1979, 1983). During this phase the child's attention may be overtly directed to spelling-sound relationships.

While "sounding out" words affords the child some independence in early reading, it is thought that the concentrated attention on the letters during that process eventually allows the child to circumvent such explicit use of spelling-sound correspondences. *Either* the visual/orthographic representation of the word has now been amalgamated to its sound and meaning (Ehri, 1978, 1984; Ehri & Wilce, 1985), *or* the application of spelling-sound information becomes rapid and automatic (Gough & Hillinger, 1980). The speed at which good readers can name pseudowords (e.g., *nuv*, *cleef*) suggests just how automatic the process of phonological recoding can become. Gough and Hillinger (1980) see such automatic processing of phonetic elements as creating the true "cipher" reader, and as such do not separate automatic processing out into a new stage.

When viewed as a qualitative change in how a word is recognized, and not simply a quantitative change in speed of applying spelling-sound information, a third or "automatic" stage of word recognition is seen. From this view most words are seen as recognized "wholistically" through automatic processing of their "visual" orthographic features (Ehri 1987). Two questions involving "automaticity" seem to require further research (Juel, 1983). First, the question of what units become automatic is central: whether the whole word is the unit which becomes automatically recognized or some subset of the word. Second, the question of how whatever unit is processed is critical. If, like Gough and Hillinger (1980), the processing is viewed as the automatic application of spelling-sound knowledge, then another qualitatively different stage from the spelling-sound stage need not be delineated. If the processing is seen as now involving more purely "visual" orthographic information about the whole word, then another stage is seen (Ehri, 1987).

Whatever the processing reason behind the increased speed with which words can be identified, the freedom from deliberate attention to word identification allows the child to attend more to meaning, to use contextual information to facilitate the construction of meaning, and to reflect more broadly upon the content that is read. This redirection of attention has been viewed as distinct enough from the employment of attention in earlier processing stages to qualify as a new "automatic" stage (Chall, 1979, 1983). When many words can be recognized automatically, the child is more likely to engage in wide reading. With wide reading the child accumulates even more spelling-sound knowledge. This information can be applied to new words until they too become automatically recognized. Venezky (1976) indicates that spelling-sound knowledge continues to grow at least through eighth grade.

Fluent readers very seldom are required to divert their attention from the meaning of what they are reading to conscious reflection on word identification. When they do so it is usually to identify a rare or a foreign word. At such moments the experienced reader may mimic the beginner. The adult may be conscious of adopting a selective-cue strategy (e.g., when reading a Russian novel and recalling a strange and long name for a character by recalling the letter it starts with) or consciously using spelling-sound knowledge (e.g., to assign a phonological equivalent to the character's name).

In terms of the stage models, reaching the automatic stage is seen as ending the beginning reading period. Though it marks the end of the early literacy period, it certainly is not seen as the end of literacy learning.

Questions Raised by the Models

There are at least four major issues raised by the stage description of reading acquisition. The first issue concerns the very existence of *qualitative* changes with each stage. The second issue is whether the stages are "natural" or simply artifacts of school instruction. The third issue is the criticality often assigned to the spelling-sound stage. The fourth issue is the emphasis stage models place on the early development of word recognition skill. Each of these issues will be examined.

Is There Evidence for Qualitative Stages?

Stage models are based upon the idea that there are qualitative differences in how children approach print at different times (or stages) in their development. In each stage a different strategy or process may be dominant in identifying words not immediately recognized (e.g., the use of systematic spelling-sound relationships in stage two). Qualitative, rather than quantitative, changes are viewed as leading to progress in reading. It is hypothesized that advances in reading ability occur as new processes or strategies for word identification can be employed.

In the first stage (the selective-cue stage) the child learns to recognize a word by selecting some cue that distinguishes it from other words the child has seen before. Different types of cues may be used with different words. On occasion, environmental features may be used, such as recognizing the golden arches in MacDonald's or the red color of the stop sign. Children in this stage may not recognize the printed word (e.g., STOP) when it is removed from its environment (Masonheimer, Drum, & Ehri, 1984). Sometimes obvious or memorable visual features of the printed word may be used—features like the double *oo* in *moon* or the dot in the middle of *pig* (Gates & Boeker, 1923). Frequently, the first and last letters appear to be used as recall cues in this early reading stage (Samuels & Jeffrey, 1966). Sometimes a letter might be selected as a cue because it is associated with a word's sound, as in the *b* in *bee* (Ehri & Wilce, 1985, 1987).

Gough (in preparation) performed two simple, yet intriguing, experiments with preschool children that demonstrate the selective-cue stage. He taught a group of nonreaders to identify four words that were printed on flashcards. Half the children learned a set of similar words (*bag, bat, rag,* and *rat*), the other half a set of dissimilar words (*box, leg, sun,* and *rat*). For each child, there appeared a noticeable thumbprint on one of the cards. The standard method of paired-associate learning with anticipation and correction was used until the child read all four words right twice in a row.

While the dissimilar set was learned faster than the similar set, the "thumbprinted" word was learned most rapidly in each set. Apparently the children quickly associated the word with the thumbprint. In doing so they seemed to ignore all other cues. When the children were shown a card bearing the same word without the thumbprint, few of them could identify the word. On the other hand, most of the children "read" a card that appeared with *only* the thumbprint as the old word.

In a second experiment, Gough (in preparation) asked a different group of preschoolers to learn to read four words (*duck*, *fish*, *pony*, and *lamb*), in the same manner as in the first experiment (except with no highly visible cue like the thumbprint on the card). After reaching criterion, the children were asked to recognize each word when part of it was hidden (either the first part of the word or the last part). Gough reasoned that if a child was learning to recognize these words by selecting one distinguishing cue (such as the "tail" on *pony*), the child would ignore the other cues (and thus recognize only the half of the word from which the cue came). He found that when a child recognized the one half of the word, that child was not likely to recognize the other half. These results, along with the ones from the thumbprint study, suggest that the child begins to learn to recognize words through selective association of *one* cue that distinguishes each word from the others in the set.

Gough, Juel, and Roper-Schneider (1983) found that in reading a story, first-grade children in the selective-cue stage (defined as children without spelling-sound knowledge as demonstrated by their inability to read pseudowords like *buf* or *cleef*) (1) made reading errors in inverse proportion to the number of times they had previously seen a word in their basal, and (2) these errors were usually substitutions of other words they had seen in their basal readers. In contrast, the reading errors of first-grade children in the spelling-sound stage (i.e., children who could read many pseudowords) were (1) relatively impervious to the number of times the word had previously appeared in their basal, and (2) more likely to be nonwords or nonbasal words. Spelling-sound stage children made many fewer errors overall.

Selective-cue stage children appear to read by reaching into mental storage for words they know are likely candidates for a printed word and retrieving one that contains some of the letters of the unrecognizable word. When reading words in isolation, this strategy is very evident. Juel, Griffith, and Gough, (1985) found that in response to the word *rain* the reading errors of first-grade children with little spelling-sound knowledge were *ring, in, runs, with, ride, art, are, on, reds, running, why,* and three *ran*'s. Also revealing are the spelling errors of these same children. Lacking spelling-sound knowledge, the children must spell by either (1) recalling all the letters in a word; (2) recalling some of the letters in a word, the approximate length of the word, and then writing random letters (or other symbols) to fill in for the unrecalled letters; (3) substituting another real word for the target. In response to *rain* used in a sentence, the spelling errors of selective-cue stage children were *weir, rach, yes, uan, ramt, fen, rur, Rambl, wetn, wnishire, Rup,* five *ran*'s, and one drawing of raindrops. There is clearly a wide range of errors among these children. The child who spelled *rain* as *ran* may be either recalling most of the letters or using the sounds of letter names to spell the word. The child who uses the sound equivalents of letter names to spell is further along toward the spelling-sound stage than the child who draws raindrops or writes *yes*.

When the child makes use of spelling-sounds correspondences and moves from the selective-cue to spelling-sound stage, different types of responses are made. Whereas the child had been associating spoken words with only selected parts of printed words, now the child will attempt to map a string of phonemes onto the string of letters. Juel, Griffith, and Gough (1985) found that first-grade children with good spelling-sound knowledge made many fewer reading and spelling errors than children without such knowledge. The form of their errors appeared to show *qualitative* differences in processing print. When *these* children made word recognition errors on words in isolation, they frequently substituted a nonsense word reflecting unsuccessful attempts to "sound out" the target (e.g., *rannin* for *rain*). When they made *spelling* errors for words used in sentences, the errors were often homophonous nonword versions of the target word (e.g., *raine* and *rane* for *rain*).

Biemiller (1970) examined the oral reading errors of 42 children in two first-grade classrooms through the school year. Biemiller identified three main phases of development. In the first phase, children's oral reading errors were predominantly contextually constrained; that is, their errors made sense syntactically and semantically. Children who were not making good progress in reading stayed in this phase for much of the year.

After two and a half months the predominant form of errors of children who were making good progress were *nonresponses* (i.e., silence when faced with an unknown word). Biemiller suggested this nonresponse phase may mark (1) the child's realization that each printed word is associated with one specific oral word; (2) the child's increased attention to graphic information; and (3) the child's realization that the graphic information provided by a specific printed word could not be identified.

Finally, the good readers entered a third phase, where most of their errors were constrained both graphically and contextually. Biemiller concluded that with increased speed and mastery of the graphic skills, the child's attention could be more fully allocated to the content and structure of what was being read (p. 94).

As children advance into the third, "automatic" stage, they typically do not reflect on word recognition strategies. At this point children can automatically recognize a large number of high-frequency words, either as well-rehearsed orthographic patterns or through automatic phonological processing. Several experiments have shown that by second or third grade, children can recognize many words while their attention is focused on another task—a sign that word recognition is automatic (Doehring, 1976; Golinkoff & Rosinski, 1976; Guttentag & Haith, 1978, 1979, 1980; Rosinski, 1977; Rosinski, Golinkoff, & Kukish, 1975; West & Stanovich, 1979). As was mentioned when discussing models of skilled reading in the first part of this paper, we do not know which variables become automatic in word recognition (e.g., whether phonetic elements, spelling patterns, or "whole" words as graphic units). When graphic information can be processed without deliberate effort, the reader is freed to attend to, and reflect on, the meaning of the content itself. From the primary to the upper elementary grades, more and more words appear to be recognized automatically (Doctor & Coltheart, 1980; Backman, Bruck, Hebert, & Seidenberg, 1984; Juel, 1983).

Are Stages "Natural" or Artifacts of School Instruction?

Those who do not view reading in terms of stages tend to see the nonsense word errors of young children (e.g., *rannin* for *rain*), the laborious "sounding out" of words, and mid-year first-grade children's use of more graphic and less contextual information to identify words (cf. Biemiller, 1970), as unnatural products, or side effects, of formal school instruction. Typical reading instruction in school, with its emphasis on word parts, on short, dull texts, and its frequent separation from communicative writing and book sharing, is seen as interrupting the "natural" development of literacy that ostensibly starts at home, frequently creating an unnatural "stage" of reading in which children lose sight of reading as a process of constructing meaning (Bondy, 1985; Tovey, 1976). In this view, children are hypothesized to lose the insight that print is meaningful and communicative, and to enter an unnatural phase induced by school instruction, where they equate reading with "sounding out" words.

Ferreiro and Teberosky (1979/1982), in a longitudinal study of first-grade children, interpret nonsense word errors of mid-year first-grade children in just such a manner:

. . . the phenomena of divorcing deciphering from meaning and of rejecting meaning at the expense of deciphering are school products. They are the consequence of reading instruction which forces children to forget meaning until they have mastered the mechanics of deciphering. On their own, children are not inclined toward such dissociation. (p. 98)

As already discussed, Biemiller (1970) also found such dissociation. But Biemiller concluded

Data presented in this study indicate that the child's first task in learning to read is mastery of the use of graphic information, and possibly, of the notion that one specific spoken word corresponds to one written word. The child's early use of contextual information does not appear to greatly facilitate progress in acquiring reading skill. The longer he stays in the early, context-emphasizing phase without showing an increase in the use of graphic information the poorer reader he is at the end of the year. (p. 95)

Chall (1979) agrees with Biemiller's interpretation. Her Stage 0 preschoolers know little about print but engage in "pseudoreading" (i.e., retelling a familiar story with the aid of storybook pictures). These children are not "glued" to print. But to enter Chall's Stage 1 (or my Stage 2, the spelling-sound stage):

To advance, to build up the skill for making choices, beginners have to let go of their pseudomaturity. They have to engage, at least temporarily, in what appears to be less mature reading behavior—becoming glued to the print—in order to reach the real maturity later. They have to know enough about the print in order to leave the print. (pp. 40–41)

This observation, that children in mid-first grade are frequently "glued" to the print, has been viewed either as an undesirable product of formal reading instruction or as a necessary step on the way to becoming a mature reader. The question thus arises whether without formal instruction children will skip this glued stage. What evidence there is seems to suggest they would not. In some accounts of children who learn to read before they enter school, there are descriptions of children—apparently without *formal* letter-sound instruction—paying particular attention to letters and word parts and sometimes slowly "sounding-out" words.

Söderbergh (1977) used the Doman method to teach her daughter (between the ages of 2.4 and 3.6) to read Swedish. The Doman method involves no formal instruction in letter-sound relationships. Initial teaching involves showing the child flashcards with the words *mother, father*, and other vocabulary with which the child is familiar (e.g., the child's toys). After learning some words, short books are presented and the child arranges the word cards to form the sentences in the book. Names of the letters of the alphabet are taught, but not their sounds.

Söderbergh reports that the words were first learned visually, by discriminating on the basis of length, some letters (particularly initial letters), and position of letters. Söderbergh describes one of the child's first verbal comparisons between words:

In the third month of reading the girl learnt the word 'precis' [exactly]. She then observed: "precis liknar pappa" (precis is like pappa)—pointing at the 'p' in 'precis'—"men i 'pappa' e de dtre stycken" (but in 'pappa' there are three of them). (p. 24)

By the fourth or fifth month this visual learning led the girl to approach new words in one of three ways: (1) she would either not read them at all—if they were too different from other words learned; 2) she would substitute an old word that resembled the new word (e.g., *mugg* for *mun*); or (3) she would find that the new word contained earlier words or word parts (e.g., *bäcken* read as a combination of the previously learned *bäck* and *en*) (p. 37).

This last type of reading forms the beginnings of what Söderbergh terms *analytical reading*. Analytical reading initially involved free and bound morphemes. After about one year, a radical change occurred. At this time, "she begins to use a quite new analytical technique when trying to read new words that cannot be read by means of adjunctions etc. of previously learnt words or morphemes: she 'sounds' the words letter by letter" (p. 40). Suddenly (during the month of October) the child stops making many substitutions (of old words for new) and makes many more analytical readings. The analytical readings are now based more on grapheme-phoneme correspondences than morphemes—resulting in increased numbers of nonsense pronunciations and sounding out of words. Söderberg continues:

> The development towards analytical reading on the graphematic level is clearly illustrated by the fact that during the three last days of October the reader overlooks in many cases a more simple way of reading a word—through analysis into morphemes—and makes a more complicated graphematic reading. (p. 97)

Söderberg's daughter also shows the gluing phase of Stage 2, in her case by sounding out, letter by letter, words which were previously identified through analysis into morphemes. Söderbergh cites the child responding to "bakåt" with /ba:-k:t/ instead of the simpler (and earlier) analysis into morphemes, such as "bak–åt" (p. 97).

The qualitative change in reading processes produces quantitative changes in reading ability. Each month the child was presented about 130 to 140 new words. In October her increased reading ability allowed her mother to present 180 new words. Söderberg describes the progression from April to October:

> In April 43% of the readings are correct. During the following months the percentage of correct readings fluctuates between 39% and 48%, and no significant increase is made until October, the month when the code is broken and when 70% of the readings are correct. (p. 39)

Thus in a very detailed study of a preschool child learning to read, we see evidence for at least two qualitatively different stages. These stages mirror the selective-cue (Stage 1) and spelling-sound stage (Stage 2) previously described.

Söderberg's daughter also shows the gluing phase of Stage 2, in which her extra attention to letter-sound information seems to be a regression from analysis into morphemes. This phenomenon of apparent regression seems analagous to the over-learning or overgeneralizing of grammatical rules phase in language development—for example, in those cases in which *goed, buyed* and *breaked* are substituted for *went, bought,* and *broke* (cf. Clark & Clark, 1977, p. 343). This phenomenon implies that during reading acquisition the child is actively formulating rules, but in this case, about the spelling-sound system. (This is similar to processes during the acquisition of grammatical morphemes.)

Bissex (1980) followed the writing and reading development of her son, Paul, from age 5 to 11. His mother did not teach him to read directly or formally. Paul's early reading emerged from his own writings (e.g., invented spellings)—which will be discussed in a later section—and from having his parents read to him. Despite this "natural" introduction to reading, Bissex compares Paul's reading development in his fifth year to the stages found by Biemiller (1970) in first-grade children:

> Paul's reading development so far seems broadly to have followed the same progression of strategies Biemiller (1970) observed in beginning readers: Initially, a dependence on context cues; then an increasing use of graphic information and decreased use of context; and finally, after the graphic strategies are practiced, adding to them contextual strategies. (p. 130)

Bissex describes how hard her son worked at reading:

> Picture and rhyme cues probably helped him at 5:8 to read most of the answers in his "Electric Company" *Nitty Gritty Rhyming Riddles Book* when he first got it. (I must have read the riddles to him.) But the next day he sat down with it for a long time—perhaps forty-five minutes—trying to figure out every word. Unless he was sure of a word right off, he would sound it out to himself and then say it aloud. (p. 127)

Sulzby (1985) studied the emergent reading attempts of 24 kindergarten children who were given no formal reading or writing instruction. She documented their attempts through the year to "read" a favorite storybook to an adult. She described several "stages" of development, ranging from picture-governed attempts (with increasing sophistication in ability to produce a story) to print-governed attempts. She found four subcategories in the print-governed stage. These subcategories "appear to be ordered thus: (a) Refusing to read based on print awareness; (b) Reading aspectually; (c) Reading with strategies imbalanced; and (d) Reading independently" (p. 471).

There are clear overlaps in strategies found in Sulzby's (1985) kindergarten sample, Söderbergh's daughter, and Biemiller's (1970) first-grade sample. The most obvious overlap in these studies is the nonresponse stage. All three researchers found children who became aware that they should read the print rather than the pictures; when they could not, they simply refused to read.

Sulzby identified "aspectual" reading as the stage when a child "often starts to focus upon one or two aspects about print to the exclusion of other aspects (p. 471). In this regard, aspectual reading sounds very like paired-associate (or selective-cue) reading (Gough & Hillinger, 1980). Sulzby (1985) further delineates this phase:

> Here, as with the high-level refusal, the child's "reading" may seem to regress. The child who was reciting entire texts with reading intonation may stop attending to meaning and just recite words s/he can recognize on the page. One of our children recited: "Grandma, the, and, the a, and," for page after page while at this print-governed, "aspectual" level of emergent reading. Other children focus attention on sounding-out words; others upon memory for text; others upon combinations of these. (p. 472)

A "strategy imbalance" was seen when a child began to rely excessively on one strategy (e.g., the child became overly dependent on sounding out words, producing uncorrected nonsense words). This imbalance period may be similar to the glued-to-print phase of what was termed the spelling-sound stage earlier in this chapter.

In the last observed stage, the "independent" reader was more flexible and less text bound, but also more able to read the author's actual words. This child was able to integrate strategies, as could the child in Biemiller's (1970) final stage. Sulzby (1985) found only three children who had entered this stage at the end of kindergarten.

Finally, Chall (1983) reminds us of

> . . . Sartre's (1964) memory of how he taught himself to read. He recalls persisting and struggling with a favorite book. Determined to read it to himself, he was "grunting" and sounding the syllables for hours until—with what seemed to be a flash of insight—he could read! He let out a loud roar and shouted the news for all to hear. (p. 16)

There is some evidence that a "gluing-to-print" phase and/or a laborious "sounding-it-out" phase occurs independently of formal instruction. This phase does not appear to be an overly long one in either the home or school environment, however. Biemiller (1970) found that by the end of the first grade, children were fairly consistent in combining the products of spelling-sound knowledge with contextual checks for appropriateness. Gough, Juel, and Roper-Schneider (1983) found that first-grade spelling-sound stage readers were not insensitive to semantic appropriateness, making as many self-corrections based on context as selective-cue readers. Lesgold and Curtis (1981) found that the oral reading errors of children in "code-emphasis" programs were almost always contextually appropriate—even by the middle of first grade.

How Critical Is It to Learn Spelling-Sound Correspondences?

Most of the researchers who have portrayed reading acquisition in stage models see the spelling-sound stage as *the* critical hurdle for the child. These researchers agree that in order to progress from rudimentary reading skill to reading large numbers of words, the child must learn to decipher.

There is indeed considerable evidence that the primary difference between good and poor readers lies in the good reader's rapid ability to use spelling-sound knowledge to identify words (Barron, 1981; Curtis, 1980; Gough, Juel, & Roper-Schneider, 1983; Juel, 1988; Liberman & Shankweiler, 1985; Perfetti, 1985; Rozin & Gleitman, 1977; Stanovich, 1980). Juel, Griffith, and Gough (1986) found that spelling-sound knowledge at the end of first grade (as evidenced by the ability to read pseudowords such as *buf, dit,* and *cleef*) was correlated .82 with ability to read real words (from the Wide Range Achievement Test [WRAT]). WRAT word recognition was correlated .74 with Iowa reading comprehension. The substantial correlation between reading ability and spelling-sound knowledge (as measured by the ability to read pseudowords) has been found, even when the effects of IQ (Stanovich, Cunningham, & Feeman, 1984) and amount of reading (i.e., where the child is in a basal series; Souther, 1986) are partialled out.

There is little evidence that the difference between good and poor readers lies in good readers' better use of context for word recognition. First, good readers are able to recognize words on the basis of purely graphic information faster than they can generate predictions as to what the word is based on contextual information (McConkie & Rayner, 1976; Rayner, 1975; Samuels, Begy, & Chen, 1975–1976; Wildman & Kling, 1978–1979). Second, numerous studies have shown that it is the *poor* reader who must use context for word recognition (see Stanovich, 1980, 1986, for extensive listings of such studies). Third, eye-movement studies indicate skilled readers look not only at almost every individual word in text, but also process their component letters (McConkie, Kerr, Reddix, & Zola, 1978; McConkie & Zola, 1981). There is no indication from these three sources of data that skilled readers use context to reduce processing of graphic information.

There is an upper limit to improvement in use of context. *At best* adult readers can accurately predict one out of four words in context (Gough, Alford, & Holley-Wilcox, 1981). Those words that can be predicted on the basis of context are frequently function words (which are of such high frequency that context is rarely needed to recognize them) (Alford, 1980). Content words are predictable in running text only about 10 percent of the time (Gough, 1983). So it is the content words—those words that carry the meaning in text—that can be least accurately *predicted* and that require the most *decoding* skill.

The principle advantage of an alphabetic language is that there is some degree of correspondence between graphemes and phonemes. Whether these correspondences are learned as "rules" or are formulated by an analogical mechanism is not known (Gough & Juel, 1989). Whatever their nature (and however imperfect they are), the evidence presented above suggests that they form more reliable and important cues for word identification than does context. (Perfetti (1985) summarizes this view:

The main failing of this approach [Goodman's 1970/1976 "psycholinguistic guessing game"] is that it does not recognize that one of the "cueing systems" is more central than the others. A child who learns the code has knowledge that can enable him to read no matter how the semantic, syntactic, and pragmatic cues might conspire against him. No matter how helpful they are to reading, these cues are not really a substitute for the ability to identify a word. (p. 239)

How Important Is Early Word Recognition Skill?

Learning the abstract rules that underlie alphabetic writing systems is deemed neither easy (Gibson & Levin, 1975, p. 265) nor "natural" (Gough & Hillinger, 1980, p. 180). A strong focus on word recognition, therefore, might stifle or impair a child's interest in learning to read. Given this possibility, why is an early focus on word recognition skill considered so important?

It is considered important because early attainment of decoding skill very accurately predicts later reading comprehension. Lesgold and Resnick (1982) found that a child's speed of word recognition in first grade was an excellent predictor of that child's *reading comprehension* in second grade. In a longitudinal study of 54 children from first through fourth grade, Juel (1988) found that there was a .88 probability that a child at the bottom quartile on the Iowa Reading Comprehension subtest at the end of first grade, would still be a poor reader at the end of fourth grade. Of 24 children who remained poor readers through four grades, only two had average decoding skills. Likewise, the probability of remaining an average or good reader in fourth grade, given average or good reading ability in first grade, was .87. In each grade good readers had considerably more decoding skill than poor readers. Similarly in a longitudinal study of children learning to read in Sweden (where formal schooling does not start until a child is 7 years old), Lundberg (1984) found that of 46 children with low phonological awareness of words and low reading achievement in first grade, 40 were still poor readers in sixth grade.

Clay (1979) discusses the results of a study of children learning to read in New Zealand, where reading instruction begins at age 5:

> There is an unbounded optimism among teachers that children who are late in starting will indeed catch up. Given time, something will happen! In particular, there is a belief that the intelligent child who fails to learn to read will catch up to his intelligent classmates once he has made a start. Do we have any evidence of accelerated progress in late starters? There may be isolated examples which support this hope, but correlations from a follow-up study of 100 children two and three years after school entry lead me to state rather dogmatically that where a child stood in relation to his age-mates at the end of his first year at school was roughly where one would expect to find him at 7:0 or 8:0. (p. 13).

While certainly not definitive, the findings of Clay (1979), Lundberg (1984), and Juel (1988), suggest that despite age of school entry (whether age five, six, or seven), language (English or Swedish), and perhaps method (as there was a difference in emphasis on phonics, etc., in the research schools), a child who does poorly in reading in the first year is likely to continue to do poorly. It is unlikely that as poor and good readers age they will change positions. The NAEP (1985) assessment found that good 9-year-old readers from previous assessments were likely to remain good readers through secondary school (p. 33).

Poor decoding skill can limit what the child reads. Juel (1988) found that in first grade good decoders were exposed to about twice as many words in basal running text as poor decoders (18,681 words vs. 9,975 words). Clay (1967) estimated that a child who was in the high reading group read about 20,000 words, while the low-middle reading group child read 10,000 words, and the low-group child read only 5,000 words. Allington (1984) and Biemiller (1977–1978) have found similar differences among ability groups in exposure to print.

Juel (1988) found that the in-school differences in print exposure continue in subsequent grades. By fourth grade the good readers had read approximately 178,000 words in running text in their basal readers, while the poor readers had read less than lhalf of that—about 80,000 words. These in-school differences in exposure to print were further compounded by out-of-school differences in reading. In first and second grade neither the good nor the poor readers read much out of school. By fourth grade the average good reader reported reading at home almost four nights per week; the average poor reader reported reading at home about once a week. Interviews with the fourth-grade children revealed that the poor readers read little because they now disliked reading (or possibly the failure experiences associated with it in school).

Nagy and Anderson (1984) suggest that "beginning in about third grade, the major determinant of vocabulary growth is amount of free reading" (p. 327). Stanovich (1986) describes how the poor reader becomes involved in a downward spiral:

> The effect of reading volume on vocabulary growth, combined with the large skill difference in reading volume, could mean a "rich get richer," or cumulative advantage, phenomenon is almost inextricably embedded within the developmental course of reading progress. The very children who are reading well and who have good vocabularies will read more, learn more word meanings, and hence read even better. Children with inadequate vocabular-ies—who read slowly and without enjoyment—read less, and as a result have slower development of vocabulary knowledge, which inhibits further growth in reading ability (p. 381).

Efficient, automatic word recognition appears to lead to better comprehension, rather than vice versa (Calfee & Piontkowsky, 1981; Lesgold, Resnick, & Hammond, 1985; Shankweiler & Liberman, 1972). Early word recognition skill may be especially important to the development of later reading comprehension for children who enter school with relatively weak oral language skills (e.g., poor oral vocabularies).

The Juel (1988) study occurred in a low socioeconomic status (SES) neighborhood school with a racially mixed population of children. Entering first-grade children scored poorly on the Metropolitan Readiness Test School Language and Listening Comprehension subtest. Things did not improve much through first grade. After first grade, however, a substantial improvement in listening comprehension occurred in children who became good decoders. Good decoders finished first grade with a grade equivalent of 1.5 on the Iowa listening comprehension subtest, but they finished fourth grade with a grade equivalent of 5.2 on this subtest. Poor decoders scored a 1.4 grade equivalent on this subtest at the end of first grade, and only 2.6 at the end of fourth grade. The "Matthew effect" described above by Stanovich (1986) may be operating (although the correlational data of this particular study prevent making a causal link between the growth in reading ability and growth in listening comprehension).

This section has focused on (a) the centrality of learning to decipher when beginning to learn to read—partly because context is not as useful as we once believed it to be in word identification; and (b) on the qualitatively different stages through which the beginner appears to pass in learning to read. Given the above, we need to address (a) how a child moves from one stage to another, and (b) how to balance learning of the "cipher" and reading for enjoyment and meaning. This balance is especially critical as learning to decipher does not appear to be an easy task. Gough (1981) sums up:

I conclude that Goodman is dead wrong about what separates the skilled adult from the beginning reader, and hence about what must be accomplished in reading acquisition. The most conspicuous difference between good and poor readers is found in the swift and accurate recognition of individual words, in decoding, and the mastery of this skill is at the heart of reading acquisition (cf. Gough & Hillinger, 1980). But it should not be inferred from this that I completely disagree with Goodman's views on reading instruction. I believe that Goodman's insistence on reading for meaning is exactly right. Our problem is to find a way to teach the child to decode while doing just that. (p. 95)

WHAT FACTORS MOVE A CHILD FROM PREREADING TO READING?

A common question of preschoolers who "teach themselves to read" is "What's this word?" (Clark, 1976; Durkin, 1966). Such a question reveals certain information about the child. First, we know the child knows what a word is. Second, we know the child has some knowledge about the form of written communication—that it consists of words printed between spaces. Third, we know the child knows something about the function of printed words—that they carry the meaning of a text.

Downing (1979) views the learning-to-read process as consisting in "the rediscovery of (a) the functions and (b) the coding rules of the writing system; their rediscovery depends on the learner's linguistic awareness of the same features of communication and language as were accessible to the creators of the writing system . . . " (p. 37). Explaining the first of these two rediscoveries (a), Downing states, "the two original chief functions of writing or print remain the same today as ever: (1) to communicate a message to another; (2) to communicate with oneself for purposes of remembering words or ideas" (p. 45). Explaining the second rediscovery (b), Downing states:

> . . . the primary technical relationship between writing and speech is the code of graphemes (letters or letter groups) for phonemes (basic sound units) within larger units called "words." Therefore, seven concepts are obviously needed to understand this first technical feature of written English: (1) the concept that the continuous flow of *speech can be segmented* into parts; (2) the concept of the *spoken word*; (3) the concept of the *phoneme*; (4) the concept of *code*—that an abstract symbol can represent something else; (5) the concept of the *written word*; (6) the concept of the *grapheme*; (7) the concept of the *letter*. (p. 71)

The child who asks "What's this word?" is on the road to discovering the coding rules of the writing system. The child knows the prerequisite concepts of a "spoken word" and a "written word." What the child does not yet know is how to translate a particular word from its written to its oral equivalent.

Enough answers to "What's this word?" provide the pairings of spoken and printed words (or "data"), which form one of the four conditions that Gough and Hillinger (1980) believe are necessary to enable the child to enter the cipher stage of reading. A second condition that Gough & Hillinger view as necessary for learning the cipher is that the child has cryptanalytic intent; the child must understand that print is encoded speech (similar to Downing's concept 4 above). Third, the child must have alphabetic understanding; the child must understand that words are composed of letters (similar to Downing's concepts 5, 6, and 7). Fourth, the child must have phonemic awareness; the child must be aware that words are composed of phonemes (similar to Downing's concepts 1, 2, and 3).

It is presumed that, with phonemic awareness, alphabetic understanding, and cryptanalytic intent, *and* enough pairings of spoken and written words, the child should be able to induce the cipher. Thus, when the answers to "What's this word?" include *see, feet, tree*, and *tweet*, the child will, over time, induce the sound of *ee*.

Of the above four conditions the most "unnatural," or the hardest one to attain, seems to be that of phonemic awareness. *Phonemic awareness* is the realization that oral words are sequences of meaningless sounds (i.e., phonemes) which occur in many different words the child hears and says every day. This understanding is not necessary for understanding or producing speech. In speech production there is no clear distinction between phonemes, as one phoneme overlaps another. (In the word *cat*, pronunciation of the /a/ begins before /k/ ends.)

Phonemic awareness is not merely a solitary insight or ability. Being able to judge which is a longer word in spoken duration, rhyming words, syllable sense, knowing that *cat* is composed of three distinctive—albeit overlapping and abstract—sounds, is a partial list. Some phonemic abilities (such as phoneme blending) appear to be prerequisites to learning to read, while other abilities (such as identifying the number of phonemes in a word) are later augmented by print exposure (Perfetti, Beck, Bell, & Hughes, 1987). There is considerable evidence from both experimental and longitudinal studies conducted in several countries that some form of phonemic awareness is necessary for successfully learning to read alphabetic languages (Blachman & James, 1985; Bradley & Bryant, 1983; Elkonin, 1963, 1973; Fox & Routh, 1975; Juel, Griffith, & Gough, 1986; Lundberg, Olofosson, & Wall, 1980; Share, Jorm, Maclean, & Matthews, 1984; Tornéus, 1984; Treiman & Baron, 1981; Tunmer & Nesdale, 1985; Williams, 1984).

Phonemic awareness is important because it is linked to the ability to decode, which is linked to reading comprehension. Tunmer and Nesdale (1985) showed that in first grade phonemic awareness affects reading comprehension indirectly, through phonological recoding (as measured by pseudoword naming). Lundberg (1984) found that linguistic awareness of words and phonemes in first grade correlated .70 with reading achievement in sixth grade.

Juel, Griffith, and Gough (1986) found that most of the children who did not learn to decode well in first grade had entered that grade with little phonemic awareness. Although their phonemic awareness steadily grew in first grade, they left first grade with less phonemic awareness than that which the children who became average or good decoders possessed upon *entering* first grade. This appeared to contribute to a very slow start in learning spelling-sound correspondences and, consequently, a difficult time learning to recognize words. Juel, Griffith, and Gough found that phonemic awareness contributed .49 to predicting WRAT word recognition at the end of first grade—after accounting for the effects of IQ and listening comprehension (i.e., oral language comprehension). They found that phonemic awareness contributed .24 to predicting Iowa reading comprehension at the end of first grade, after accounting for the effects of the same factors.

The shift from a spelling-sound stage to a stage where most words are recognized "automatically," without overt attention directed to spelling-sound elements, would appear to come about only after the reader has read a lot (Samuels, 1988). Some readers may never arrive at this stage. Downing (1979) suggested that

> . . . the periodic conflict between teachers and the public over the incidence of "illiteracy" probably arises because many pupils manage at school on minimal standards. Overlearning has not taken place. Therefore, on leaving school and practicing even less, their skill deteriorates until they become exliterate. The same phenomenon was found in UNESCO's

earlier adult "Literacy Campaigns" in developing countries when the brief instruction period was not followed up by adequate practice. (p. 35)

WHAT SHOULD BEGINNING READING INSTRUCTION LOOK LIKE?

The research presented in this chapter provides considerable evidence that children move through stages in their reading development. Some of the insights or skills that move a child through the stages have been discussed. No doubt there are various routes a child might take to gain the information necessary to advance as a reader. These routes will be shaped by *both* home and school experiences.

Entering the Selective-Cue Stage

The first critical insight that the child must gain is understanding the communicative function of print. Such understanding frequently seems to arrive in the preschool years through exposure to environmental print and being read to at home (see Sulzby and Teale, Chapter 26 in this volume). In-school practices that may foster such understanding include (1) the common labeling of objects in classrooms with printed signs (e.g., "door"); (2) "language experience" activities, where students "dictate" words, sentences, or stories to the teacher to write; (3) the use of "Big Books," where children can clearly see the print as their teachers read it (cf. Holdaway, 1979); and (4) the use of patterned, predictable text in chart stories and so forth, which can facilitate the "feel" for and enjoyment of reading, as well as induce some sight word recognitions (Bridge, 1986). The above activities are probably sufficient to induce the child to enter a selective-cue stage of print recognition.

Entering the Spelling-Sound Stage

A Prerequisite: Phonemic Awareness

As previously indicated, there is compelling evidence that some degree of phonemic awareness is necessary for advancing to the next stage of learning spelling-sound correspondences. Phonemic awareness can be fostered in preschool and kindergarten.

Lundberg, Frost, and Peterson (1988) showed that preschool children can be successfully trained to discover and manipulate the phonological elements in words. Their eight-month training program involved a variety of games, nursery rhymes, and rhymed stories. (A typical game designed to foster syllable synthesis included a "troll" who had a peculiar way of speaking, who tried to tell children what they would get as presents. The troll produced the words representing the presents, syllable by syllable. Each child had to figure out what the troll actually meant to offer.) Danish children who went through the training program showed dramatic gains in certain phonemic-awareness skills, such as phoneme segmentation skill, compared to children who did not go through the program. The preschool training had a facilitating effect on reading and spelling acquisition through second grade.

The use of patterned, rhymed text (such as found in nursery rhymes and many Dr. Seuss books) in oral story reading as well as in chart stories or Big Books, probably would foster phonemic awareness. In a 15-month longitudinal study of British children from the age of 3 years, 4 months, Maclean, Bryant, and Bradley (1987) found (1) a strong relationship between children's early knowledge of nursery rhymes and their later development of phonemic awareness; and (2) that phonemic awareness predicted early reading ability. Both relationships were found after controlling for the effects of IQ and SES.

Clay (1979) found that many 6-year-old children who were not making adequate progress in learning to read could not hear the sound sequences in words. She proceeded to adapt a phonemic awareness training program developed by the Russian psychologist Elkonin to train these children (Elkonin, 1973). She found that the children could learn and apply the strategy of analyzing the sound sequences of words. Such phonemic analysis is now part of her Reading Recovery program, where it is ultimately connected to sounding out and writing words. Clay (1987) describes her thinking on phonemic awareness, and one of the initial recovery procedures.

> For many decades and in many different programmes teachers have tried to teach children a sound to go with a letter they can see. The children who succeeded in those programmes were able to do just that, and those who failed were probably unable to hear the sound sequences in words anyway.
>
> For children who cannot hear the order of sounds in words the teacher can act as analyser of the words. She articulates the word slowly, but naturally, and gradually develops the same skill in her pupils. It is an essential feature of the theory behind this tutoring to hear sounds in words in sequence. The child's first lessons take place *in the absence of letters or printed words*. The child must *hear* the word spoken, or speak it himself and try to break it into sounds by slowly articulating it. He is asked to show what he can hear with *counters* not *letters*. (pp. 64–65)

As an example, the teacher would have cards on which squares were drawn for each phoneme (not letter) in words with up to four sounds. As the teacher slowly articulates the word, the child puts counters into the squares when a new sound is heard. The child then articulates the word and fills in the counters.

Building Spelling-Sound Knowledge through Writing

Once children have some degree of phonemic awareness and know some letter names, they frequently display what has been termed *invented spelling* (Read, 1971, 1975, 1986). Invented spellings often use the sounds captured in letter names to represent phonemes (e.g., *MI* for *my*). Spelling-sound knowledge can emerge from these attempts to write. Sometimes this will happen spontaneously; sometimes a bit of extra attention at school can foster it. Both situations will be discussed.

Bissex (1980) gives a wonderful example of how a child learned spelling-sound correspondences through writing at home. Two examples of 5-year-old Paul's questions while attempting to write words illustrate this route:

PAUL: What makes the *ch* (in *tech*)
MOTHER: *c-h*
PAUL: What makes *oo*?
MOTHER: *o-o*
PAUL: in *to*
MOTHER: Only one *o* (p. 12)

PAUL: What makes the *uh* sound?
MOTHER: In what word?
PAUL: *Mumps*
MOTHER: *u* (p. 13)

It is clear Paul has phonemic awareness, cryptanalytic intent, alphabetic understanding, and "data." He also has a very special one-to-one partner in learning. Bissex describes how Paul's "basic beginning reading strategy involved using letter-sound relationships (through writing he had a lot of practice with 'phonics') plus context rather than sight word recognition" (p. 171).

Paul apparently was able to induce the spelling-sound system from his questions concerning how words were written and his mother's answers to them. What is less clear is whether children who had to rely solely on a teacher in a school setting, given the school time available for such questioning, could make as rapid growth. Certainly this is an area that needs to be explored.

Clay (1987) describes one systematic technique that teachers might use for children who need it. It follows the development of phonemic awareness in her Reading Recovery program. When a child can do the task with the counters (described in the previous section), and after the child knows letters, the child can get help writing words for stories with an extension of the counter method. The child can say the word slowly and move counters into (or simply point to) the squares as before. Then the child can (with the teacher's help as needed) write the appropriate letters in the squares.

Clay (1979) describes how this approach may replace more formal instruction in letter-sound correspondences:

> A strategy of analysing spoken words into sounds, and then going *from sounds to letters* may be a critical precursor of the ability to utilize the heuristic tricks of phonics. And many children may not need phonic instruction once they acquire and use a sound sequence analysis strategy. (p. 65)

Building Spelling-Sound Knowledge through Explicit Reading Instruction

Formal and explicit instruction in spelling-sound correspondences has been quite controversial in reading instruction. This may be the case in part because such correspondences have traditionally been taught through reading instruction rather than through the child's own writing (as in the examples in the previous section). As discussed earlier in this chapter, the issue has also stemmed from different views of how reading skill is acquired. Nonstage models, with their emphasis on improved oral language skills as the primary vehicle for improving early reading, necessarily must deemphasize the importance of decoding skills. Proponents of such models want early reading materials that are rich in vocabulary and meaning. Those who have emphasized the importance of early learning of spelling-sound correspondences, on the other hand, tend to favor reading materials with vocabulary that lays bare the alphabetic principle. Resnick (1979) describes the ensuing conflict:

> It lies in part in a fundamental competition between code and language demands in early reading. Learning the code requires a controlled vocabulary—but language processing requires a rich language with which to work. This conflict cannot be wished away. (p. 330)

One point raised by several researchers (e.g., Mason, 1980) is that formal instruction may facilitate the understanding and use of spelling-sound associations that are needed to decipher. For some children such instruction may even be essential. Ehri and Wilce (1985), referring to a study by Masonheimer, Drum, and Ehri (1984), describe why ". . . movement into effective printed word learning requires a qualitatively different way of processing printed words, one that prereaders do not naturally hit upon as they encounter print in their environment. The problem is that they habitually process context and configurational cues, and this precludes their attending to phonetic cues which must be done to begin reading words reliably" (pp. 174–175).

It is clear some children (like Paul) can induce the code solely from random, rich exposure to print (Bissex, 1980; Durkin, 1966; Ehri, 1978; Y. M. Goodman, 1980). It is also apparent that explicit phonics instruction—particularly when it is paired with stories to read that contain a bulk of words that can be decoded based on what has been taught—can speed acquisition of these generalizations and influence word recognition (Barr, 1972, 1974, 1974–1975; Beck 1981; Chall, 1967; DeLawter, 1970; Elder, 1971; Evans & Carr, 1983; Guthrie et al., 1976; MacKinnon, 1959; Resnick, 1979; Williams, 1979).

It is unfortunate that many basal series treat phonics lessons as if they had no relation to story reading (Beck, 1981). Children may receive a phonics lesson on the short *o* sound (e.g., as in *top*) and then read text with few short *o* words to practice upon—or even worse, encounter words that violate what they were just taught (e.g., *come*). Children in such a situation frequently abandon their attempts to "sound out" words (Juel & Roper-Schneider, 1985).

How can we create controlled texts without making them so limited in vocabulary that they appear as dull and tongue-twisting as most phonics-based texts? There are at least two approaches that might help.

First, multiple letters that often correspond to the same sound can be introduced together (e.g., the long *e* pattern as in *me, sea, see, neat, green,* and *Pete*). Simultaneous teaching of different sounds of the same letters (e.g., *how, bow*) will also foster a more varied initial vocabulary for stories. There is some evidence that concurrent teaching of two sounds for a single letter promotes better learning than the successive teaching of the two sounds (Levin & Watson, 1963; Williams, 1968). Such teaching may even foster a "set for diversity" that helps children understand English orthography (Levin & Watson, 1963). Certainly we need more research on the effectiveness of simultaneous versus concurrent teaching of letter-sound patterns.

Second, not all the words in a story need to be decodable exclusively on the basis of what has been taught in phonics. Beck (1981) found that several phonics texts used in the first third of first grade had between 69 percent and 100 percent of such decodable words, while basal readers have had no more than 13 percent. Research is needed to see if these percentages are the same in current series, and how lowering the percentage of decodable words in phonics texts affects learning. High-frequency words used since kindergarten (e.g., *green, girl*) would seem natural additions to the phonics texts. Patterned text and nursery rhymes (e.g., *How now, brown cow*) could also be used. The well-known or well-rehearsed text can be "read," with attention going to the words that exemplify the spelling-sound patterns of the day.

Perhaps phonics is successful with some children because it fosters both phonemic awareness and *cryptanalytic intent* (cf. Gough & Hillinger, 1980). In other words, phonics may (perhaps inadvertently) foster an attitude in the child of being a detective, a detective who is trying to break the "code." This attitude may help the child become an active problem solver with regard to graphic information. Certainly the child will need such a spirit when faced with words that cannot be entirely decoded using the phonic rules the child has been taught. The child will also need to realize that the teacher can only give clues to the code and that there is an inexact match between the actual sounds of letters and the sounds that are taught in phonics.

The child may get the idea of what to look for in matching letters to sounds through relatively few examples of spelling-sound correspondences. Juel and Roper-Schneider (1985) found that first-grade children who read from a phonics basal were quicker (and more likely) to induce *un*taught spelling-sound correspondences than were children who read from a basal series with higher-frequency, but less regularly spelled, words. This type of induction will be necessary in any case, for it appears that the rules covered by phonics instruction cannot account for the mastery of several hundred "rules" by the skilled reader (Honeycutt, n.d.; Venezky, 1967). Some explicit instruction in spelling-sound relationships may point the child in the right direction, however.

Results of the Juel and Roper-Schneider study suggest that fairly minimal explicit phonics instruction (i.e., instruction during the first few months of first grade in initial and final consonants and short vowels) was sufficient for the induction of untaught spelling-sound relationships (i.e., long vowels and vowel pairs). There is some evidence that a little explicit phonics instruction goes a long way—at least when the text children are exposed to contains a number of "regular" decodable words that can facilitate implicit learning. Further research is certainly needed on how much, and what types, of spelling-sound instruction and texts will facilitate this inductive learning. The less time spent teaching phonic rules per se (rules that at best are only crude approximations) and more time spent actually reading, would seem optimal for maintaining interest in reading.

Entering the Automatic Stage

Keeping reading interesting is critical if we want children to read enough to become "automatic" at word recognition. *Automaticity* in almost any skill (e.g., skipping rope) results from overlearning. Repeated practice frees up one's attention so that it does not have to be focused on the mechanics involved in the specific activity (e.g., on the coordination of jumps and rope swings).

One problem we face is that we do not know exactly what it is about word recognition that becomes automatic. This too is an area in which more research is needed. It seems likely that certain high-frequency words are recognized automatically. It also seems likely that our response to common spelling-sound patterns becomes automatic (as suggested by the speed with which we can read pseudowords like *bleef*, *tup*, and *fevcate*). The trend in basal series appears to be toward more diverse vocabularies, with less repetition of the same words (Beck, 1981). It would be interesting to determine the effect this trend has on developing automatic word recognition skill. It is possible that fewer encounters with the same words (and more exposure to unknown words) will produce (a) less automatic recognition of basal vocabulary; and (b) more frustrated beginning readers who then read less. On the other hand, seeing more diverse vocabulary may be helpful if (a) what becomes "automatized" are spelling-sound relations; and/or (b) it creates more interesting stories, more motivation for reading, and therefore more reading.

CONCLUSIONS

We have yet to develop a comprehensive model of the reading acquisition process. We do have promising leads toward understanding of the process. It appears the child passes through stages in reading development which reflect qualitatively different ways of identifying printed words. In the first stage, the selective-cue child relies upon random, environmental (e.g., location on a page), and visual cues (e.g., distinctive letters) to identify words. In the second stage the child gains use of the spelling-sound information that underlies the particular alphabetic language being learned. In the third stage, many words that were "sounded out" in the second stage, elicit either automatic phonological recodings or become recognizable purely on the basis of "visual" ortho-graphic features. Certain cognitive insights and instructional procedures were discussed that might facilitate the child's passage through these stages.

More research is needed to better understand and define how reading skill develops. The three stages discussed in this chapter are only generally outlined and defined. We need research that better defines and interrelates the insights and abilities required in these stages of reading. We need to know how the psychological, social, and instructional components influence, interact with, and affect a child's desire and pro-gress in learning to read. We must attack those problems that are associated with how children learn to read as early as possible since the research indicates there is a strong relationship between a child's later reading skill and comprehension and his or her earliest progress in reading.

REFERENCES

Alford, J. A. Jr. (1980). *Lexical and contextual effects on reading time*. Unpublished doctoral dissertation, University of Texas at Austin.

Allington, R. L. (1984). Content coverage and contextual reading in reading groups. *Journal of Reading Behavior, 16*, 85–96.

Anderson, R. C., Hiebert, E. H., Scott, J. A, & Wilkinson, I. A. G. (1985). *Becoming a nation of readers: The report of the Commission on Reading*. Washington, DC: National Institute of Education.

Backman, J., Bruck, M., Hebert, M., & Seidenberg, M. S. (1984). Acquisition and use of spelling-sound correspondences in reading. *Journal of Experimental Child Psychology, 38*, 114–133.

Barr, R. (1972). The influence of instructional conditions on word recognition errors. *Reading Research Quarterly, 7*, 509–529.

Barr, R. (1974). Influence of instruction on early reading. *Interchange, 5 (4)*, 13–21.

Barr, R. (1974–1975). The effect of instruction on pupil reading strategies. *Reading Research Quarterly, 4*, 555–582.

Barr, R. (1984). Beginning reading instruction: From debate to reformation. In P. D. Pearson, R. Barr, M. L. Kamil, & P. Mosenthal (Eds.), *Handbook of reading research* (Vol. 1, pp. 545–581). New York: Longman.

Barron, R. W. (1981). Development of visual word recognition: A review. In T. G. Waller & G. E. MacKinnon (Eds.), *Reading research: Advances in theory and practice* (Vol. 3, pp. 119–158). New York: Academic Press.

Beck, I. L. (1981). Reading problems and instructional practices. In G. E. MacKinnon & T. G. Waller (Eds.), *Reading research: Advances in theory and practice* (Vol. 2, pp. 53–95). New York: Academic Press.

Biemiller, A. (1970). The development of the use of graphic and contextual information as children learn to read. *Reading Research Quarterly, 6*, 75–96.

Biemiller, A. (1977–1978). Relationships between oral reading rates for letters, words, and simple text in the development of reading achievement. *Reading Research Quarterly, 13*, 223–253.

Bissex, G. L. (1980). *Gnys at Wrk*. Cambridge, MA: Harvard University Press.

Blachman, B. A., & James, S. L. (1985). Metalinguistic abilities and reading achievement in first-grade children. In J. Niles & R. Lalik (Eds.), *Issues in literacy: A research perspective* (pp. 280–286). Rochester, NY: National Reading Conference.

Bondy, E. (1985, April). *Children's definitions of reading: Products of an interactive process*. Paper presented at the meeting of the American Educational Research Association, Chicago, IL.

Bradley, L., & Bryant, P. E. (1983). Categorizing sounds and learning to read—a causal connection. *Nature, 301*, 419–421.

Bridge, C. A. (1986). Predictable books for beginning readers and writers. In M. R. Sampson (Ed.), *The pursuit of literacy*. Dubuque, IA: Kendall/Hunt Publishing Company.

Calfee, R. C., & Piontkowski, D. C. (1981). The reading diary: Acquisition of decoding. *Reading Research Quarterly, 16*, 346–373.

Chall, J. S. (1967). *Learning to read: The great debate*. New York: McGraw-Hill.

Chall, J. S. (1979). The great debate. Ten years later, with a modest proposal for reading stages. In L. B. Resnick & P. A. Weaver (Eds.), *Theory and practice of early reading* (Vol. 1, pp. 29–55). Hillsdale, NJ: Erlbaum.

Chall, J. S. (1983). *Stages of reading development.* New York: McGraw-Hill.

Clark, H. H., & Clark, E. V. (1977). *Psychology and language.* New York: Harcourt Brace Jovanovich.

Clark, M. (1976). *Young fluent readers.* London: Heinemann Educational Books.

Clay, M. M. (1967). The reading behaviour of five-year-old children: A research report. *New Zealand Journal of Educational Studies, 2 (1)*, 11–31.

Clay, M. M. (1979). *Reading: The patterning of complex behaviour.* Auckland, N.Z.: Heinemann Educational Books.

Clay, M. M. (1987). *The early detection of reading difficulties* (3rd ed.). Hong Kong: Heinemann Publishers.

Curtis, M. E. (1980). Development of components of reading skill. *Journal of Educational Psychology, 72,* 656–669.

DeLawter, J. (1970). *Oral reading errors of second-grade children exposed to two different reading approaches.* Unpublished doctoral dissertation, Teachers College, Columbia University.

Doctor, E., & Coltheart, M. (1980). Children's use of phonological encoding when reading for meaning. *Memory and Cognition, 8,* 195–209.

Doehring, D. G. (1976). Acquisition of rapid responses. *Monographs of the Society for Research in Child Development, 41* (2, Serial No. 165).

Downing, J. (1979). *Reading and reasoning.* New York: Springer-Verlag.

Durkin, D. (1966). *Children who read early.* New York: Teachers College Press.

Ehri, L. C. (1978). Beginning reading from a psycholinguistic perspective: Amalgamation of word identities. In F. B. Murray (Ed.), *The development of the reading process* (pp. 1–33). International Reading Association Monograph No. 3. Newark, DE: International Reading Association.

Ehri, L. C. (1984). How orthography alters spoken-language competencies in children learning to read and spell. In J. Downing & R. Valtin (Eds.), *Language awareness and learning to read* (pp. 119–147). New York: Springer-Verlag.

Ehri, L. C. (1987). Learning to read and spell words. *Journal of Reading Behavior, 19,* 5–31.

Ehri, L. C. & Wilce, L. S. (1985). Movement into reading: Is the first stage of printed word learning visual or phonetic? *Reading Research Quarterly, 20,* 163–179.

Ehri, L. C., & Wilce, L. S. (1987). Cipher versus cue reading: An experiment in decoding acquisition. *Journal of Educational Psychology, 79,* 3–13.

Elder, R. D. (1971). Oral reading achievement of Scottish and American children. *Elementary School Journal, 71,* 216–230.

Elkonin, D. B. (1963). The psychology of mastering the elements of reading. In B. Simon & J. Simon (Eds.), *Educational psychology in the U.S.S.R.* (pp. 165–179). London: Routledge & Kegan Paul.

Elkonin, D. B. (1973). U.S.S.R. in J. Downing (Ed.), *Comparative reading* (pp. 551–579). New York: Macmillan.

Evans, M. A., & Carr, T. H. (1983). *Curricular emphasis and reading development: Focus on language or focus on script?* Symposium conducted at the biennial meeting of the Society for Research on Child Development, Detroit.

Ferreiro, E., & Teberosky, A. (1982). *Literacy before schooling* (K. Goodman Castro, Trans). Exeter, NH: Heinemann Educational Books. (Original work published in 1979).

Fox, B., & Routh, D. K. (1975). Analyzing spoken language into words, syllables, and phonemes: A developmental study. *Journal of Psycholinguistic Research, 4,* 331–342.

Gates, A.I., & Boeker, E. (1923). A study of initial stages in reading by preschool children. *Teachers College Record, 24,* 469–488.

Gibson, E. J. (1965). Learning to read. *Science, 148,* 1066–1072.

Gibson, E. J. (1972). Reading for some purpose. In J. F. Kavanagh & I. G. Mattingly (Eds.), *Language by ear and by eye* (pp. 3–19). Cambridge, MA: MIT Press.

Gibson, E. J., & Levin, H. (1975). *The psychology of reading.* Cambridge, MA: MIT Press.

Golinkoff, R. M., & Rosinski, R. R. (1976). Decoding, semantic processing, and reading comprehension skill. *Child Development, 47,* 252–258.

Goodman, K. S. (1965). A linguistic study of cues and miscues in reading. *Elementary English, 42,* 639–643.

Goodman, K. S. (1970/1976). Reading: A psycholinguistic guessing game. In H. Singer & R. Ruddell (Eds.), *Theoretical models and processes of reading* (pp. 497–508). Newark, DE: International Reading Association.

Goodman, K. S. & Goodman, Y. M. (1979). Learning to read is natural. In L. B. Resnick & P. A. Weaver (Eds.), *Theory and practice of early reading* (Vol. 1, pp. 137–154). Hillsdale, NJ: Erlbaum.

Goodman, Y. M. (1980). The roots of literacy. In M. P. Douglass (Ed.), *Claremont Reading Conference Forty-Fourth Yearbook* (pp. 1–32). Claremont, CA: Claremont Reading Conference.

Goodman, Y. M. (1986). Children coming to know literacy. In W. H. Teale & E. Sulzby (Eds.), *Emergent literacy: Writing and reading* (pp. 1–14). Norwood, NJ: Ablex.

Gough, P. B. (1981). A comment on Kenneth Goodman. In M. L. Kamil (Ed.), *Directions in reading: Research and instruction* (pp. 92–95). Washington, DC: National Reading Conference.

Gough, P. B. (1983). Context, form, and interaction. In K. Rayner (Ed.), *Eye movements in reading: Perceptual and language processes.* New York: Academic Press.

Gough, P. B., Alford, J. A., Jr., & Holley-Wilcox, P. (1981). Words and contexts. In O. J. L. Tzeng & H. Singer (Eds.), *Perception of Print* (pp. 85–102). Hillsdale, NJ: Erlbaum.

Gough, P. B., & Hillinger, M. L. (1980). Learning to read: An unnatural act. *Bulletin of the Orton Society, 30*, 179–196.

Gough, P. B., & Juel, C. (1989). Les premières étapes de la reconnaissance des mots. In L. Rieben & C. Perfetti (Eds.), *L'apprenti lecteur*, (pp. 85–102). Neuchâtel and Paris: Delachaux et Niestlé.

Gough, P. B., Juel, C., & Roper-Schneider, D. (1983). A two-stage model of initial reading acquisition. In J. A. Niles & L. A. Harris (Eds.), *Searches for meaning in reading/language processing and instruction* (pp. 207–211). Rochester, NY: National Reading Conference.

Greeno, J. G., James, C. T., DaPolito, F., & Polson, P. G. (1978). *Associative learning: A cognitive analysis.* Englewood Cliffs, NJ: Prentice Hall.

Guthrie, J. T., Samuels, S. J., Martuza, V., Seifert, M., Tyler, S. J., & Edwall, G. A. (1976). *A study of the locus and nature of reading problems in the elementary school.* Washington, DC: National Institute of Education.

Guttentag, R. E., & Haith, M. M. (1978). Automatic processing as a function of age and reading disability. *Child Development, 49*, 707–716.

Guttentag, R. E., & Haith, M. M. (1979). A developmental study of automatic word processing in a picture classification task. *Child Development, 50*, 894–896.

Guttentag, R. E., & Haith, M. M. (1980). A longitudinal study of word processing by first-grade children. *Journal of Educational Psychology, 72*, 701–705.

Harste, J. (1980, April). Written language learning as a social event. Paper presented at the meeting of the American Educational Research Association, Boston, MA.

Hiebert, E. H. (1981). Developmental patterns and interrelationships of preschool children's print awareness. *Reading Research Quarterly, 16*, 236–260.

Holdaway, D. (1979). *The foundations of literacy.* New York: Ashton Scholastic.

Honeycutt, S. (n.d.) *Phonological rules for a text-to-speech system.* Natural Language Processing Group, MIT. Undated manuscript.

Juel, C. (1983). The development of mediated word identification. *Reading Research Quarterly, 18*, 306–327.

Juel, C. (1988). Learning to read and write: A longitudinal study of fifty-four children from first through fourth grades. *Journal of Educational Psychology, 80*, 437–447.

Juel, C., Griffith, P. L., & Gough, P. B. (1985). Reading and spelling strategies of first-grade children. In J. A. Niles & R. Lalik (Eds.), *Issues in literacy: A research perspective* (pp. 306–309). Rochester, NY: National Reading Conference.

Juel, C., Griffith, P. L., & Gough, P. B. (1986). Acquisition of literacy: A longitudinal study of children in first and second grade. *Journal of Educational Psychology, 78*, 243–255.

Juel, C., & Roper-Schneider, D. (1985). The influence of basal readers on first-grade reading. *Reading Research Quarterly, 20*, 134–152.

Kleiman, G. M. (1975). Speech recoding and reading. *Journal of Verbal Learning and Verbal Behavior, 14*, 323–339.

LaBerge, D., & Samuels, S. J. (1974). Toward a theory of automatic information processing in reading. *Cognitive Psychology, 6*, 293–323.

Lesgold, A. M., & Curtis, M. E. (1981). Learning to read words efficiently. In A. M. Lesgold & C. A. Perfetti (Eds.), *Interactive processes in reading* (pp. 329–360). Hillsdale, NJ: Erlbaum.

Lesgold, A. M., & Resnick, L. B. (1982). How reading disabilities develop: Perspectives from a longitudinal study. In J. P. Das, R. Mulcahy, & A. E. Wall (Eds.), *Theory and research in learning disability.* New York: Plenum.

Lesgold, A. M., Resnick, L. B., & Hammond, K. (1985). Learning to read: A longitudinal study of word skill development in two curricula. In G. E. Mackinnon & T. G. Waller (Eds.), *Reading research: Advances in theory and practice* (Vol. 4, pp. 107–138). New York: Academic Press.

Levin, H., & Watson, J. (1963). The learning of variable grapheme-to-phoneme correspondence. In *A basic research program on reading* (Final report, Project No. 639). New York: Cornell University and U.S. Office of Education.

Liberman, I. Y., & Shankweiler, D. (1985). Phonology and the problems of learning to read and write. *Remedial and Special Education, 6 (6)*, 8–17.

Lomax, R. G., & McGee, L. M. (1987). Young children's concepts about print and reading: Toward a model of word reading acquisition. *Reading Research Quarterly, 22*, 237–256.

Lundberg, I. (1984). Learning to read. *School Research Newsletter* (August). National Board of Education (Sweden).

Lundberg, I., Frost, J., & Petersen, O. (1988). Effects of an extensive program for stimulating phonological awareness in preschool children. *Reading Research Quarterly, 23*, 263–284.

Lundberg, I., Oloffson, A., & Wall, S. (1980). Reading and spelling skills in the first school years predicted from phonemic awareness skills in kindergarten. *Scandinavian Journal of Psychology, 21*, 628–636.

Maclean, M., Bryant, P., & Bradley, L. (1987). Rhymes, nursery rhymes, and reading in early childhood. *Merrill-Palmer Quarterly, 33*, 255–281.

MacKinnon, A. B. (1959). *How do children learn to read?* Toronto: Copp Clark.

Mason, J. M. (1980). When do children begin to read: An exploration of four-year-old children's letter- and word-reading competencies. *Reading Research Quarterly, 15*, 203–227.

Mason, J. M. (1984). Early reading from a developmental perspective. In P. D. Pearson, R. Barr, M. L. Kamil & P. Mosenthal (Eds.), *Handbook of reading research*, Vol. I, pp. 505–543 (White Plains, NY: Longman).

Mason, J. M., & Allen, J. A. (1986). A review of emergent literacy with implications for research. In E. Z. Rothkopf (Ed.), *Review of Research in Education, 13*, 3–47.

Masonheimer, P. E., Drum, P. A., Ehri, L. C. (1984). Does environmental print identification lead children into word reading? *Journal of Reading Behavior, 26*, 257–271.

Massaro, D. W. (1975). *Understanding language: An information-processing analysis of speech perception, reading, and psycholinguistics*. New York: Academic Press.

Maugham, W. S. (1963). *Of human bondage*. Middlesex, Eng.: Penguin. (Original work published in 1915.)

McConkie, G. W., Kerr, P. W., Reddix, M. D., & Zola, D. (1987). *Eye-movement control during reading: The location of initial eye fixations on words* (Tech. Rep. No. 406). Champaign, IL: Center for the Study of Reading, University of Illinois.

McConkie, G. W., & Rayner, K. (1976). Identifying the span of effective stimulus in reading: Literature review and theories of reading. In H. Singer & R. B. Ruddell (Eds.), *Theoretical models and processes of reading* (2nd ed., pp. 137–162). Newark, DE: International Reading Association.

McConkie, G. W., & Zola, D. (1981). Language constraints and the functional stimulus in reading. In A. M. Lesgold & C. A. Perfetti (Eds.), *Interactive processes in reading* (pp. 155–175). Hillsdale, NJ: Erlbaum.

Nagy, W. E., & Anderson, R. C. (1984). How many words are there in printed school English? *Reading Research Quarterly, 19*, 304–330.

National Assessment of Educational Progress. (1985). The reading report card, progress toward excellence in our schools: Trends in reading over four national assessments, 1971–1984 (Report No. 15-R-01). Princeton, NJ: Educational Testing Service.

Perfetti, C. A. (1985). *Reading Ability.* New York: Oxford University Press.

Perfetti, C. A. Beck, I., Bell, L. C., & Hughes, C. (1987). Phonemic knowledge and learning to read are reciprocal: A longitudinal study of first-grade children. *Merrill-Palmer Quarterly, 33*, 283–319.

Rayner, K. (1975). The perceptual span and peripheral cues in reading. *Cognitive Psychology, 7*, 65–81.

Read, C. (1971). Pre-school children's knowledge of English phonology. *Harvard Educational Review, 41*, 1–34.

Read, C. (1975). *Children's categorization of speech sounds in English.* Urbana, IL: National Council of Teachers of English.

Read, C. (1986). *Children's creative spelling.* London: Routledge & Kegan Paul.

Resnick, L. B. (1979). Theories and prescriptions for early reading instruction. In L. B. Resnick & P. A. Weaver (Eds.), *Theory and practice of early reading* (Vol. 2, pp. 321–338). Hiillsdale, NJ: Erlbaum.

Rosinski, R. R. (1977). Picture-word inference is semantically based. *Child Development, 48*, 643–647.

Rosinski, R. R., Golinkoff, R. M., & Kukish, R. S. (1975). Automatic semantic processing in a picture-word interference task. *Child Development, 46*, 247–263.

Rozin, P., & Gleitman, L. (1977). The structure and acquisition of reading: II. The reading process and the acquisition of the alphabetic principle. In A. Reber & D. Scarborough (Eds.), *Toward a psychology of reading* (pp. 55–141). Hillsdale, NJ: Erlbaum.

Rumelhart, D. E. (1985). Toward an interactive model of reading. In H. Singer & R. B. Ruddell (Eds.), *Theoretical models and processes of reading* (3rd ed., pp. 722–750). Newark, DE: International Reading Association.

Samuels, S. J. (1979). The method of repeated readings. *Reading Teacher, 32 (4),* 403–408.

Samuels, S. J. (1988). Decoding and automaticity: Helping poor readers become automatic at word recognition. *Reading Teacher, 41*, 756–760.

Samuels, S. J., Begy, G., & Chen, C. C. (1975–1976). Comparison of word recognition speed and strategies of less skilled and more highly skilled readers. *Reading Research Quarterly, 11*, 72–86.

Samuels, S. J., & Jeffrey, W. E. (1966). Discriminability of words and letter cues used in learning to read. *Journal of Educational Psychology, 57*, 337–340.

Shankweiler, D., & Liberman, I. Y. (1972). Misreading: A search for causes. In J. F. Kavanagh & I. G. Mattingly (Eds.), *Language by ear and by eye* (pp. 293–317). Cambridge, MA: MIT Press.

Share, D. L., Jorm, A. F., Maclean, R. & Matthews, R. (1984). Sources of individual differences in reading achievement. *Journal of Educational Psychology, 76*, 1309–1324.

Singer, H., & R. B. Ruddell (1985). *Theoretical models and processes of reading* (3rd ed.). Newark, DE: International Reading Association.

Smith, F. (1971). *Understanding reading.* New York: Holt, Rinehart & Winston.

Smith, F. (Ed.). (1973). *Psycholinguistics and reading.* New York: Holt, Rinehart & Winston.

Smith, F. (1978). *Understanding reading* (2nd ed.). New York: Holt, Rinehart & Winston.

Smith, F., & Holmes, D. L. (1971). The independence of letter, word, and meaning identification in reading. *Reading Research Quarterly, 6*, 394–415.

Söderberg, R. (1977). *Reading in early childhood: A linguistic study of a preschool child's gradual acquisition of reading ability.* Washington, DC: Georgetown University Press.

Souther, A. F. (1986). *A two-stage model of early reading development.* Unpublished doctoral dissertation, University of Texas at Austin.

Stanovich, K. E. (1980). Toward an interactive-compensatory model of individual differences in the development of reading fluency. *Reading Research Quarterly, 16*, 32–71.

Stanovich, K. E. (1986). Matthew effects in reading: Some consequences of individual differences in the acquisition of literacy. *Reading Research Quarterly, 21*, 360–406.

Stanovich, K. E., Cunningham, A. E., & Freeman, D. J. (1984). Intelligence, cognitive skills, and early reading progress. *Reading Research Quarterly, 19*, 278–303.

Sulzby, E. (1985). Children's emergent reading of favorite storybooks: A developmental study. *Reading Research Quarterly, 20*, 458–481.

Teale, W. H., & Sulzby, E. (Eds.). (1986). *Emergent literacy.* Norwood, NJ: Ablex.

Tierney, R. J., & Pearson, P. D. (1984). Toward a composing model of reading. In J. M. Jensen (Ed.), *Composing and comprehending* (pp. 33–45). Urbana, IL: National Council of Teachers of English.

Tornéus, M. (1984). Phonological awareness and reading: A chicken and egg problem? *Journal of Educational Psychology, 76*, 1346–1358.

Tovey, D. R. (1976). Chilren's perceptions of reading. *Reading Teacher, 29*, 536–540.

Treiman, R., & Baron, J. (1981). Segmental analysis ability: Development and relation to reading ability. In T. G. Waller & G. E. MacKinnon (Eds.), *Reading research: Advances in theory and practice* (Vol. 3, pp. 159–198). New York: Academic Press.

Tunmer, W. E., & Nesdale, A. R. (1985). Phonemic segmentation skill and beginning reading. *Journal of Educational Psychology, 77*, 417–427.

Venezky, R. L. (1967). English orthography: Its graphical structure and its relation to sound. *Reading Research Quarterly, 2*, 75–106.

Venezky, R. L. (1976). *Theoretical and experimental base for teaching reading.* The Hague: Mouton.

Venezky, R. L. (1986). Steps toward a modern history of American reading instruction. In E. Z. Rothkopf (Ed.), *Review of Research in Education, 13*, 129–167.

West, R. F., & Stanovich, K. E. (1979). The development of automatic word recognition skills. *Journal of Reading Behavior, 11*, 211–219.

Wildman, D. M., & Kling, M. (1978–1979). Semantic, syntactic, and spatial anticipation in reading. *Reading Research Quarterly, 14*, 128–164.

Williams, J. P. (1968). Successive vs. concurrent training of multiple grapheme-phoneme correspondences. *Journal of Educational Psychology, 59*, 309–314.

Williams, J. P. (1979). Reading instruction today. *American Psychologist, 34*, 917–922.

Williams, J.P. (1984). Phonemic analysis and how it relates to reading. *Journal of Learning Disabilities, 17*, 240–245.

28 CONDITIONS OF VOCABULARY ACQUISITION

Isabel Beck and Margaret McKeown

V ocabulary is among the oldest areas of interest in educational research. Yet the first volume of the *Handbook of Reading Research* (Pearson, Barr, Kamil, & Mosenthal, 1984) did not include a separate vocabulary chapter. The omission, in part, reflects the fact that in the 20-year period preceding the planning for the first volume, little vocabulary research had been conducted. However, the last decade has shown an active resurgence of vocabulary research. Indeed, this chapter is the second major review of vocabulary research to appear in the last four years. The first was a notable review by Graves in 1986, which, because of its breadth, was particularly useful in defining the "space" of vocabulary research—that is, what topics can be considered within the boundaries of the field.

David Pearson alludes to the resurgence of vocabulary research in his introduction to the first volume, where he suggests that the omission of a separate vocabulary chapter, in large part, occurred because vocabulary was among the topics that had "only very recently come to stand alone as extant lines of research" (p. xxiii). Pearson's comments imply a promise for a separate vocabulary chapter in the second volume of the *Handbook*. So let us start the promised chapter by considering what early vocabulary research was like, what might account for the 20-year hiatus, and why the 1980s have been an active period of vocabulary research.

A HISTORICAL CONTEXT

Clifford (1978) points to the publication in 1921 of Thorndike's *The Teacher's Word Book* as an early landmark in vocabulary research. The book, which ranked words by frequency of occurrence in general reading materials, was both a product of, and an impetus for, gaining some understanding of words used in common discourse, of how many words people know, and of what both of those mean for learning and instruction. In the period that produced *The Teacher's Word Book*, the foci of vocabulary research were vocabulary size at various ages and educational levels, the relationship between vocabulary ability and general mental ability, which words were most useful to know, and the development of a corpus of words for use in creating more readable texts. From about the turn of the century until the early 1950s, these questions dominated vocabulary research.

These early vocabulary topics had a huge impact on instructional practice, chiefly through the implementation of readability formulas and the choice of words to be taught to beginning readers. Some of that was good, but some of it may not have been so good. The positive side was that consideration was being given to directing materials to the level of the learner. Unfortunately, the movement institutionalized the virtually exclusive use of vocabulary frequency and sentence length to control readability. Although these two features are predictive of easier reading materials, their use does not bring about greater ease in grasping the concepts represented or in establishing relations among concepts (Beck & McKeown, 1986; Davison & Kantor, 1982; Duffy & Kabance, 1981; Rubin, 1985).

Clifford (1978) suggests that this early period of vocabulary research was driven by a fascination with "the relationship between one's stock of words and one's stock of ideas" (p. 108). Yet, it seems that the complexity of that fundamental relationship was not pursued. Much of the research did not address the mental processes involved in that relationship beyond a simple match between a word and an idea. Perhaps one reason for the hiatus in vocabulary research was that benefits from further studies of this type would have been limited until some understanding of the complexities of the mental processes involved in relating words to ideas was gained. In a similar vein, Calfee and Drum (1978) and Clifford (1978) pegged the hiatus in vocabulary research to the lack of a coherent theory underlying the topic. One caveat to that conclusion, however, is that a coherent theory of vocabulary research cannot exist of itself but must draw from theories that concern the full range of language comprehension and production.

It is our assertion that a major reason for renewed interest in vocabulary research is rooted in the shift to an information-processing orientation in psychology, which provided rich theory from which to draw in conceiving the relationship between words and ideas. Scientific inquiry turned away from the view that memory was built sequentially from associations between elements to the notion that making meaning requires more than accumulation of "the facts" about specific elements. The large role of inference and organization of information came to be recognized, and the processes in which learners engaged became the focus of research attention. These revolutionary ideas of the late 1950s and 1960s (e.g., Bruner, 1957; Miller, 1965) grew to be the dominant perspective of the 1970s and 1980s. Current research in vocabulary acknowledges vocabulary acquisition as a complex process that involves establishing relationships between concepts, organization of concepts, and expansion and refinement of knowledge about individual words. It should be acknowledged before leaving the discussion of why vocabulary research lapsed that there were some studies, particularly during the 1940s and 1950s, that did embody the depth and complexity of vocabulary development issues. For example, Calfee and Drum (1978) cite work on qualitative variations in vocabulary (Cronback, 1943; Feifel & Lorge, 1950; Gerstein, 1949; Russell & Saadeh, 1962; Templin, 1957). But a line of iterative research in this direction did not take hold. Perhaps a lack of richness of the early work had already taken its toll and other interests had come to the forefront—for example the focus on syntax in linguistics and psycholinguistics (e.g., Chomsky, 1957; Miller, 1962; Slobin, 1966).

AN ORIENTATION

When the complexity of vocabulary acquisition is considered, any question on vocabulary, be it how readily words are learned, how many words are known by individuals, or what kind of instruction works best, must be answered by "it's conditional; it depends on the situation." For this volume, we were charged with examining instructional aspects of vocabulary. However, given the conditional nature of vocabulary acquisition, discussion of vocabulary instruction in isolation is not productive. For instructional issues to be meaningful, one needs to first consider the goals of vocabulary acquisition, how and how readily words are typically learned, and whether instruction can augment that process. Toward a decision about the role of instruction, one must also understand something about the array of student abilities and vulnerabilities. The goal of this chapter, then, is to examine vocabulary learning and instruction through a discussion of notions from current research on vocabulary acquisition and the conditions under which those notions apply.

This chapter is divided into two sections: Issues Underlying Vocabulary Learning and Sources of Vocabulary Learning. The first section includes three topics, beginning with what it means to know a word. Here the point is that word knowledge is not an all-or-nothing proposition. The second topic involves issues of vocabulary size and growth. The main points here are that there are problems associated with various estimates of people's vocabulary stock, and different investigators champion different estimates. A point of particular emphasis is that there are huge individual differences in both size and growth. The third topic is concerned with how word knowledge is measured. This issue is closely intertwined with the first two in that we cannot know the size of people's vocabulary without understanding how knowing a word has been measured. The second major section, on sources of vocabulary learning, considers first, context, and then direct instruction. The context section explores the puzzle of why, although context seems the most likely source for vocabulary learning, evidence of its effects on learning has been so scant. The direct instruction section investigates how instruction can play a productive role in vocabulary learning.

ISSUES UNDERLYING VOCABULARY LEARNING

Answers to questions about vocabulary learning must acknowledge some fundamental underlying issues. Perhaps the most pervasive issue is what constitutes *word knowledge*. Any hypotheses posed or conclusions drawn about vocabulary learning and instruction carry with them assumptions about what it means to know a word. The size and rate of growth of an individual's vocabulary is another fundamental issue because it embodies implications about how vocabulary is learned and whether intervention in the acquisition process can be productive. And interpretations of the implications of vocabulary size and growth vary according to what aspects of vocabulary knowledge are measured. In this section we attempt to lay the groundwork for interpreting notions about vocabulary learning and instruction by considering what it means to know a word, estimates of the size and growth of an individual's vocabulary, and how word knowledge is assessed.

What It Means to Know a Word

The question of what it means to know a word draws two kinds of responses: One pertains to how information about word meanings is represented in memory. The other response involves the extent or dimensions of knowledge that people may have about individual words. The latter response is our focus here because it has more direct consequences for learning and instruction, and because the former is addressed by Anderson and Nagy in this volume (see Chapter 25).

Simply put, knowing a word is not an all-or-nothing proposition; it is not the case that one either knows or does not know a word. Rather, knowledge of a word should be viewed in terms of the extent or degree of knowledge that people can possess. Such differential knowledge was described by Dale (1965) in terms of four stages: Stage 1—never saw it before; Stage 2—heard it, but doesn't know what it means; Stage 3—recognizes it in context as having something to do with. . . ; Stage 4—knows it well.

Another description of the extent of an individual's knowledge about a word involves the notion that word knowledge falls along a continuum from no knowledge; to a general sense, such as knowing *mendacious* has a negative connotation; to narrow, context-bound knowledge; to having knowledge but not being able to access it quickly; to rich, decontextualized knowledge of a word's meaning, its relationship to other words, and its extension to metaphorical uses (Beck, McKeown, & Omanson, 1987; Beck, Perfetti, & McKeown, 1982).

Closely related to descriptions of the extent of knowledge are descriptions of the dimensions of knowledge and ability involved in knowing a word. Probably the earliest such description is Cronbach's (1942). The dimensions he discussed were *generalization*, the ability to define a word; *application*, the ability to select or recognize situations appropriate to a word; *breadth*, knowledge of multiple meanings; *precision*, the ability to apply a term correctly to all situations and to recognize inappropriate use; and *availability*, the actual use of a word in thinking and discourse. Calfee and Drum (1986) offer a description that covers much the same territory as Cronbach, but theirs includes some additional dimensions such as facile access and appreciation of metaphor, analogy, and wordplay.

A conceptualization of the kind of information one must have about a word in order to produce and understand it appropriately is provided by Miller (1978). Unique to Miller's scheme is explicit mention of the relationship of a word to other concepts and pragmatic constraints, such as topics to which the word can apply and the kinds of discourse in which the word is typically found.

Kameenui, Dixon, and Carmine's (1987) discussion of dimensions of knowledge adds an interesting facet, which they labeled *derived knowledge*. That is, an individual may derive enough information about a word to understand it in the context being read or heard, but not remember the information, and thus does not "learn" the word.

As the work discussed above evidences, what it means to know a word is a complicated, multifaceted arena. As such, statements that imply vocabulary knowledge, such as notions of how words are learned, number of words known, and effects of instruction, can only be interpreted in light of what evidence is being accepted as "knowing a word."

The Size and Growth of Vocabulary

Vocabulary Size

The size of an individual's vocabulary is probably the oldest focus of vocabulary research, dating back to the end of the nineteenth century. While interest in the topic remains keen, the amount of research done in measuring vocabularies has declined significantly in recent decades. Clifford (1978) reports that by 1907, 118 studies of vocabulary size had been cited; and by 1957, nearly 100 more were added. Yet since 1960, there seem to have been only six studies related to vocabulary size (Dupuy, 1974; Graves, Brunetti, & Slater, 1982; Graves & Slater, 1987; Loban, 1963; Lorge & Chall, 1963; Nagy & Anderson, 1984). Of those six, only four report new data, and three of those are based on a very limited corpus.

The most striking characteristic of the pre-1960s work was the huge discrepancy in estimates of vocabulary size. For example, estimates of total vocabulary size for first graders ranged from about 2,500 (Dolch, 1936; M. E. Smith, 1926) to about 25,000 (Shibles, 1959; M. K. Smith, 1941), and for college students from 19,000 (Doran, 1907; Kirkpatrick, 1891) to 200,000 (Hartman, 1946). The reasons for these wide variations are generally traced to three sources. One is the definition of what constitutes a word. For example, should proper names be included? To what extent are inflected and derived forms the same or different words? That is, should individuals who know *walk* be credited with knowing *walking*? What about the relationship between *judge* and *adjudicate*?

Another source of discrepancy is the issue discussed earlier as underlying all queries about vocabulary learning, what does it mean to know a word. In order to measure which words people know, researchers have most often asked learners either to recognize a word's definition from among several choices, or to define the word. Yet how word knowledge is measured and what constitutes knowing a word strongly influence estimates of vocabulary size.

A third source of discrepancy in vocabulary size is that different studies have used different corpuses to represent English vocabulary, including a variety of dictionaries and frequency lists. And, because an entire dictionary or frequency list cannot be tested, a sample must be selected. Creation of a sample raises two issues: The first is the influence on the eventual estimates of vocabulary size exerted by the size of the dictionary or the number of frequency levels used. For example, if a sample of 50 words was tested from a dictionary of 50,000 words, for every test item passed the learner would be given credit for knowing 1,000 words. If the same sample were taken from a dictionary of 100,000 words, then each correct item would credit the learner with 2,000 words known. A related implication of corpus size is that, for the smaller dictionary, learners could be credited with a vocabulary of not more than 50,000 words. The second issue concerned with sampling from dictionaries is that, because dictionaries are not random samples of the language, creating an unbiased sample is problematic. Dictionaries contain greater proportions of frequent words and devote more space to these words, both of which can bias estimates.

Two of the sources of discrepancy in vocabulary size estimates have been addressed by contemporary thinking. The question of what is to be counted as a distinct word was investigated by Nagy and Anderson (1984), because they viewed discrepancies in this area to be the greatest culprit in the widely different estimates of vocabulary size. In developing criteria for what constitutes a word, Nagy and Anderson took the perspective that *how* words are counted depends on *why* they are counted. Their *why* was to understand the size and nature of the task students faced when learning the vocabulary of school texts. The authors structured their investigation by asking about the relative ease or difficulty students would have in learning new forms of a familiar word. For example, if a student knows *tyrant*, how likely is it that s/he can immediately understand *tyrants*, *tyrannical*, *tryannosaurus*? It seems clear that understanding *tyrannosaurus* will be less likely than understanding *tyrants*. Thus, an important part of Nagy and Anderson's work involved assessing degrees of semantic relatedness.

The result of Nagy and Anderson's effort is a system of classifying word types and word relatedness that can be applied to discover how many different words exist in any corpus. They used the term *word family* to describe a set of morphologically related words within which knowledge of one of the words makes figuring out the meanings of other family members relatively easy, if even a low level of contextual information is provided. Words that are morphologically related to a family but whose relationship is not helpful in figuring out the meaning of new words are labeled *semantically opaque* and comprise distinct word families. For example, *hookworm* comprises a distinct family from *hook*. Nagy and Anderson then applied their notions to Carroll, Davies, and Richman's (1971) *Word Frequency Book*, which is based on a sample of printed school materials for grades three through nine. This resulted in an estimation of about 88,000 word families in printed school English.

Nagy and Anderson (1984) concluded that some of the more conservative estimates of vocabulary size "substantially underestimate the number of words children know" (p. 1) because the definition of *word* has led to an underestimation of the word stock of English. They use as an example of this problem Dupuy (1974), who adopted a rather restricted concept of *basic word*, as evidenced by his count of just 12,300 basic words in English.

Although Nagy and Anderson's work indicated that some early estimates of vocabulary size should be raised, work on another source of discrepancy in estimates indicated that some estimates should be lowered. Lorge and Chall (1963) took issue with the use of dictionaries as the dominant source from which to develop samples of English vocabulary. Lorge and Chall examined a study by Seashore and Eckerson (1940), which used an unabridged dictionary to develop its sample, and found that the sample used in the study was biased in favor of high-frequency words. It seems that the unabridged dictionary contained many words with more than one entry, and thus a greater probability of being selected; and these multiple-entry words are the more common words. The Seashore and Eckerson test was found to contain both a disproportionate share of higher-frequency words and twice as many words with multiple entries, compared to a sample that Lorge and Chall selected to eliminate the multiple-entry factor. Lorge and Chall concluded that Seashore and Eckerson's results, and estimates of vocabulary size based on similar sampling procedures or on the widely used test that Seashore and Eckerson developed, should be drastically reduced. Such a reduction would bring estimates of vocabulary size more in line with earlier work, such as M. E. Smith's (1926) reckoning that first graders knew approximately 2,500 words.

Where do widely varying estimates of vocabulary size, followed by both upward corrections due to a rethinking of what should be counted as a word and downward corrections promoted by the identification of problems in sampling procedures, lead us in estimating vocabulary size? About as precise an estimate as can be given is to place vocabulary size for 5- to 6-year-olds at between 2,500 and 5,000 words. Writers who have reviewed the topic since the 1960s fall within that range, although different writers vary widely in their interpretation of whether current estimates of vocabulary size are larger or smaller than those done earlier.

The only studies of vocabulary size done since 1960 include Loban's (1963) longitudinal study, two small-scale studies by Graves and his colleagues (Graves, Brunetti, & Slater, 1982; Graves & Slater, 1987), and Dupuy's (1974) work, mentioned earlier. Of these, all but Dupuy's fall within the 2,500–5,000 range for 5- to 6-year-olds. So we now understand problems of older work on vocabulary size, but have no recent, large-scale studies that correct these problems. The figures offered in recent writings, except for those few studies noted, are hypothetical, based on the effect certain corrections in earlier procedures might make.

Although absolute statements about vocabulary size of various populations cannot be made, some rather strong statements can be made about individual differences within populations. Studies that have compared high- and low-ability learners have found huge individual differences (Graves, Brunetti, & Slater, 1982; Graves & Slater, 1987; Seashore & Eckerson, 1940; M. K. Smith, 1941). For example, M. K. Smith reported that high school seniors near the top of the distribution knew about four times as many words as their classmates at the bottom of the distribution; and even more remarkably, higher-performing third graders had vocabularies about equal to lowest-performing twelfth graders. More recently, Graves and Slater (Graves, Brunetti, & Slater, 1982; Graves & Slater, 1987) found that the vocabulary of upper SES first graders was about twice the size of their lower SES peers. Thus, estimates of a given student's vocabulary size cannot be stated with much precision, but it can be said with some confidence that the student knows many more or many fewer words than his or her age peers.

Vocabulary Growth

An issue closely related to vocabulary size is the rate of growth of an individual's vocabulary. References are commonly made to the notion that, particularly during the school years, growth is very rapid (Just & Carpenter, 1987; Miller, 1977, 1985; Nagy & Herman, 1987). Specific estimates of vocabulary growth, not surprisingly, vary widely. Miller (1985) uses data from a study by Templin (1957) to arrive at the rather astounding conclusion that students may be learning 20 words a day. Just and Carpenter, using M. K. Smith's study, and Nagy and Herman, using recalibrations of older work, including M. K. Smith's, put the figure at between 2,700 and 3,000 words per year, or about seven new words per day. Another figure, cited by Clifford (1978), is about 1,000 words a year, or about three per day. This estimate comes from Joos (1964), but Joos cites no data for it. Let us work with the middle figure of seven words per day, as it seems to be reasonably well supported.

The notion of rapid vocabulary growth, and seven words per day is indeed rapid growth, needs to be tempered by at least two considerations. The first is the issue of individual differences mentioned earlier. Even if *some* students are learning as many as seven new words a day, many others may be learning only one or two.

A second consideration when looking at vocabulary growth is, What does it mean that a child may "know" seven new words at the end of a day? Such a possibility seems at odds with the kind of effort it appears to take in order to learn a word in a way that makes it a useful part of one's vocabulary. This seems to be true for learning words whether it be through direct instruction or from context (Jenkins, Stein, & Wysocki, 1984; McKeown, Beck, Omanson, & Pople, 1985; Nagy, Herman, & Anderson, 1985). A way to understand this apparent contradiction between rapid growth and effortful learning might be to consider Carey's (1978) concept of word learning as consisting of fast and extended mapping. *Fast mapping* is an initial mapping of the meaning of a new word that includes some syntactic and semantic properties and occurs rather easily. After fast mapping, however, "protracted further experiences" (p. 274) are needed in order to complete the learning, or *extended mapping*. Carey characterizes the slowness of attaining full mapping as surprising. In her research she found this to be true even for the learning of simple color terms when the information for full mapping was repeatedly presented. Carey hypothesizes that at any point throughout the school years, a child may be working on 1,600 mappings. It may take quite some time before new words affect a child's ability to comprehend and use language. Perhaps, then, it is more realistic to say that school-aged children may become aware of seven new words per day, but from there they have a long way to go in completing the task of learning the words.

Assessment of Vocabulary Knowledge

Consideration of vocabulary growth in terms of its effects on a student's verbal functioning evokes once again the issue of what it means to know a word. In order to examine how this issue interacts with estimations of vocabulary size and growth, let us take it out of a theoretical realm to the more practical question of how word knowledge can be assessed, or what kind of measures allow judgment that a word is known.

Limitations of Multiple-Choice Test Measurement

The most widely used measure of word knowledge, for both vocabulary research and school testing, is the *multiple-choice format*, in which one selects a brief definition or synonym for a target word from among several choices. The assessment of an individual's word knowledge resulting from a multiple-choice test may be greatly influenced by the nature of the *distractors*. As Anderson and Freebody (1981) and Cronbach (1943) have pointed out, distractors may present confusions that interfere with what a student knows about a word. On the other hand, if there is great semantic distance between distractors and the target word, a correct response can be obtained from knowing merely the general domain of the word.

The changeable nature of multiple-choice tests can be used to advantage as in Nagy, Herman, and Anderson's (1985) manipulation of distractors to create test items that tapped varying levels of word knowledge. However, in most applications multiple-choice tests require only a low level of knowledge, and they can make vocabulary knowledge appear "flat," as if all words are either known to the same level or unknown. That is, correct responses do not differentiate between words that are known well and words that are known vaguely; and incorrect responses do not distinguish between completely unfamiliar words and words about which one has a glimmer of knowledge, but not enough to distinguish a correct meaning choice.

Kameenui, Dixon, and Carnine (1987) evaluated multiple-choice tests in the most pessimistic light by concluding from issues such as those outlined that "such multiple-choice vocabulary tasks are useless at best and dangerous at worst" (p. 138). Further, they suggest that because so many conclusions about vocabulary learning are drawn from such tasks, one might well question what is really known about vocabulary.

Another, more positive view of multiple-choice tests is taken by Curtis (1987), who argues that, despite their drawbacks, they do provide some useful information. They give reliable indications of the relative range of an individual's vocabulary and correlate rather strongly with measures of reading comprehension and intelligence. As a school assessment measure they give useful information on where a student stands in vocabulary development in relation to his or her peers.

Alternatives to Multiple-Choice Test Measurement

In sorting out issues related to assessment of vocabulary knowledge, it is useful to return to the notion that word knowledge falls along a continuum, and to consider where along the continuum word knowledge is assessed by different measures. Curtis (1987) has demonstrated that different pictures of word knowledge emerge from different criteria by testing fifth graders on a set of words using several different measures. She found that on a checklist, where students were to respond *yes* if they knew a word, students did so an average of 80 percent of the time. When asked to explain the meaning of the words, 70 percent could pass a very easy criterion such as describing *invent* as "to invent a machine." When the criterion involved giving an example or partial explanation, 50 percent of the responses were correct. Only 20 percent were correct for a conservative criterion that required synonyms or complete explanations. Interestingly, Curtis's administration of a multiple-choice test yielded an average score of 50 percent, comparable to the measure that revealed partial knowledge.

It makes sense to suggest that where along the continuum a measurement is taken should be dictated by what one wants to know about a learner's knowledge of words. Even if classic multiple-choice tests are acknowledged as useful, it is still the case that they do not measure the full continuum of word knowledge. Clearly, information needed by researchers and educators often goes well beyond what can be learned from multiple-choice tests.

There have been several attempts to create assessment techniques that tap various aspects of vocabulary knowledge. As early as 1942, Cronbach pointed out the need to determine the degree to which a student's understanding of a word was complete rather than merely whether the word was known or unknown. Cronbach (1943) then devised a test based on what he viewed as components of true understanding of a word, which included recognizing examples of its use and how it contrasts with semantically related words. In Cronbach's test, students were asked to distinguish between examples of a word and nonexamples that might be confused with the word. For instance, an item to test an understanding of the concept *element* asked students to choose examples of elements from among the following: brass, iron, water, sulfur, fire, and oxygen. Cronbach envisioned the test, which he labeled "multiple true-false," as a useful measure of precision of knowledge for technical or content-specific vocabulary. But he also noted its limitations, including difficulty in testing verbs, abstract nouns, and words referring to large entities.

The assessment of precision of word knowledge was also examined by Curtis and Glaser (1983). Their approach involved first presenting items that required only a minimal degree of familiarity with a word, followed by items that required discrimination among related concepts. For example, an item that tested minimal familiarity might require selection of a synonym for *desist* from among the following: *stop, review, consider, debate*. A more discriminating item for *desist* might then present the following choices: *pause, halt, prevent, discontinue*.

The notion of assessing both vague and precise recognition of word meanings was used by Marshelek (1981) to investigate aspects of vocabulary knowledge in high school seniors. Students' knowledge was assessed through vague-recognition items, in which all distractors were semantically unrelated to the correct choice; accurate-recognition items, in which all distractors were semantically related; and a test of ability to provide definitions for words. This variety of measures allowed examination of the distribution of words in various states of knowledge. Marshelek found that many words could be recognized or defined vaguely but not accurately, or recognized but not defined. More specifically, it was found that often students could give a correct example of a word's use but inferred incorrect defining features, and that low-ability students had more words in partial knowledge states than did high-ability students.

A similar finding that completeness or precision of word knowledge differentiates high- and low-ability individuals resulted from a study by Curtis (1981). In that study, undergraduates took a traditional multiple-choice test and then were interviewed about the tested words. Curtis's interview included measures of *semantic range* (i.e., whether students could produce *any* correct associations to a word); and *semantic depth* (i.e., whether they could produce a synonym or correct explanation). Curtis found that low-ability students not only knew fewer of the tested words and had less practice knowledge of the words they knew, they also were able to produce correct explanations for only about half the words they had gotten correct on the multiple-choice test.

Precision or completeness of word meaning is described as a qualitative aspect of vocabulary knowledge. Another qualitative aspect of vocabulary is the character of associations a learner has to known words, and this too has received research attention. Work in this direction was based on the finding (Feifel & Lorge, 1950) that definitions produced by 6- and 7-year-olds tended to include more information on literal features, such as function and concrete description, while those of 10- to 14-year-olds contained more abstract features. These differences in definition quality led Russell and Saadeh (1962) to investigate developmental differences in understanding words in terms of three levels: concrete, functional, and abstract. The researchers designed a test that offered a concrete, a functional, and an abstract meaning alternative for each word, as well as an incorrect distractor. For example, the meanings offered for the word *count* were, at the concrete level, "to find how many pennies are in your pocket"; at the functional level, "to find the number of things in a group"; and at the abstract level, "to say numbers in order—upward or downward." The results for third-, sixth-, and ninth-grade students showed the dominance of concrete and functional choices for third graders, and the decline of concrete choices along with increases in functional and abstract choices for sixth and ninth graders. Thus, Russell and Saadeh's work provides another demonstration of how knowledge about words is not the simple present/absent conceptualization that traditional multiple-choice tests most often measure.

Earlier we implied that perhaps the most immediate need for assessing a full range of word knowledge was for studies measuring vocabulary size and growth. A study by Graves (1980) compared the number of words children knew on different dimensions of knowledge. Three tasks were used to assess three different aspects of the reading vocabulary of primary-grade children. The tasks included a multiple-meanings task in which children were asked to produce more than one definition for a word, a meanings-in-context task that required children to explain what a word meant within a sentence, and a precision-of-meanings task that required children to give meanings of two semantically similar words. The three different subtask scores presented a richer picture of the extent of children's knowledge of words than do traditional, single-measurement approaches. The results illustrate the multifaceted picture of vocabulary size that can emerge if different dimensions are considered.

The work discussed in this section on varying approaches to assessing vocabulary knowledge suggests that neither the problem nor attempts to solve it are new. The issue has been widely discussed, and many intriguing solutions have been offered. Yet, the use of alternative assessment measures has mostly been limited to small-scale tests of their effectiveness and experimental learning studies (e.g., Jenkins, Stein, & Wysocki, 1984; McKeown, Beck, Omanson, & Pople, 1985; Nagy, Anderson, & Herman, 1985). We concur with Graves's call (1986) for large-scale studies that characterize the configurations of words in various states of knowledge within individuals and across individuals of different ages and abilities. Only with such information can we better understand how words are learned, the processes involved in learning and using words, and the extent of benefits from contextual exposures and from instruction.

SOURCES OF VOCABULARY LEARNING

Questions about how people learn the words they know have long been of interest to those who think about vocabulary. The psychologist's focus on "how" is primarily on the cognitive processes involved in acquiring a word and on how that word is represented in memory. The practitioner's focus on "how" is more concerned with ways to arrange conditions that enhance the learning of words. Of course, the two interests overlap, and one place of convergence is consideration of the sources of word learning. These sources can be distinguished as incidental and intentional learning situations. In an incidental learning situation, the major purpose for the interaction with the particular environment is not to learn words. Sources of incidental learning include oral environments such as conversations, movies and television, and written environments, from signs and letters to magazines and books.

Intentional sources for learning vocabulary are ones in which the explicit purpose of an interaction is to learn the meaning of a word. These include a learner's decision to consult a source, such as a dictionary or more knowledgeable person, and direct instruction on the meanings of specific words. In this section we consider the sources that have been the focus of attention for research on vocabulary development during the school years, that is, written contexts and direct instruction in classrooms.

Context

Educational research has considered issues about acquiring vocabulary from context almost exclusively in terms of written contexts. This probably is because vocabulary research has existed as a strand of reading research while studies of oral language development tend to have been the domain of developmental psychologists interested in how young children begin to acquire language. The result is a gap in research on the later influence of oral language on vocabulary development. Although it is intuitively obvious that oral language continues to be a source for the acquisition of vocabulary beyond the preschool years, there are few, if any, investigations of it.

The assumption that reading is a major source for the acquisition of vocabulary has long been prominent, with Huey (1908) and Thorndike (1917) two of its early proponents. However, research spanning several decades has failed to uncover strong evidence that word meanings are routinely acquired from context. It seems that the role of *context* in vocabulary acquisition is prominent by default, as it is well accepted that its closest contender for explaining vocabulary growth, direct instruction, is not adequate to account for the vocabulary children learn.

One of the earliest studies of the role of context in the acquisition of vocabulary was by Elivian (1938). Elivian found that fifth- and sixth-grade students who read stories containing unknown words that were defined within the context could identify meanings of an average of only 22 percent of the words. Reading level made a substantial difference, however, with children of high reading ability able to identify meanings of 52 percent of the words.

Similar outcomes resulted from later work by Rankin and Overholser (1969) and Quealy (1969). In those studies, students correctly identified word meanings an average of 50 percent and 42 percent of the time, respectively. Again, substantial differences were found among ability levels for both studies. The studies also showed that success in identifying meaning differed as to the type of information offered by the context that served as clues to word meaning.

Types of context clues were a focus of the work of Artley (1943), McCullough (1943, 1945, 1958), and Ames (1966–1967), all of whom developed classification schemes for kinds of context clues. The classification schemes were intended to serve as a basis for developing instruction in using context clues to derive word meaning. Although Ames's scheme was the most comprehensive, there was a fair degree of overlap among the three, including such categories as synonym, mood or tone, and familiar expressions.

The current decade has seen a resurgence in research on the acquisition of vocabulary from context. Current work has continued examination of earlier issues, such as kinds of context clues and the contribution of an individual's reading ability to deriving meaning from context. The newer work has also been concerned with the processes in which readers engage when deriving word meanings from context and has examined the natural versus artificial nature of the experimental task and text and the effects on a variety of outcome measures.

The issue of natural versus artificial experimental conditions has been raised in terms of the distinctions between what has been called *deliberate* versus *incidental word learning* (Jenkins, Stein, & Wysocki, 1984; Nagy, Herman, & Anderson, 1985). Deliberate learning refers to a reader's ability to derive meaning from context when directed to do so. Incidental learning refers to whether readers learn words during normal reading.

Deliberate Learning from Context

Studies by Carnine, Kameenui, and Coyle (1984); Beck, McKeown, and McCaslin (1983); and Schatz and Baldwin (1986) examined deliberate learning from context through the use of tasks that explicitly asked readers to derive the meaning of an underlined word appearing in a text passage. Carnine et al. used experimental passages designed to present clues to specific words and control for distance between the clue and the target word. They found that fourth- and sixth-grade subjects were better able to identify meanings of words presented in context than of words presented in isolation. However, even the best performance, that of sixth graders, showed a success rate of only 40 percent, with type and distance of clue making a difference. Synonym clues provided better results than clues requiring an inference, and clues closer to the target word were more helpful than those far away. Clues that both required inferences and were distant from the target word yielded correct outcomes only 17 percent of the time.

Beck et al. (1983) used natural text to test their hypothesis of a continuum of effectiveness of natural contexts for deriving word meaning. They identified four points along the continuum: misdirective contexts, which seem to direct a reader toward an incorrect meaning; nondirective contexts, which offer no direction for word meaning; general directive contexts, which offer correct but general clues; and directive contexts, which seem to lead to a correct, specific meaning for a word. The researchers presented adults with stories from fourth- and sixth-grade basal readers in which target words were blacked out and asked them to supply the word or a synonym. The results varied greatly by context type. Correct responses were given for 3 percent of the misdirective contexts, 27 percent of the nondirective contexts, 49 percent of the general directive contexts, and 86 percent of the directive contexts. Hence, Beck et al. concluded that not all contexts are created equal.

Passages used by Schatz and Baldwin (1986) were also from natural texts. In three separate experiments, using a variety of text types, including passages from literature, newspaper articles, and history and science texts, the researchers found that context offered no assistance in deriving word meaning for eleventh and twelfth graders. Schatz and Baldwin acknowledged that previous research has shown that students can use context clues when available but contended that difficult words in naturally occurring prose may not generally lend themselves to inferring meaning from context.

Incidental Learning from Context

The question of whether readers learn words incidentally from context through normal reading was examined in studies by Jenkins, Stein, and Wysocki (1984) and by Nagy and Herman and their colleagues (Herman, Anderson, Pearson, & Nagy, 1987; Nagy, Anderson, & Herman, 1987; Nagy, Herman, & Anderson, 1985). The tasks used in these studies reflected a more natural reading situation in that readers were not told that the purpose was related to word learning, and the target words were not identified.

Although the reading situation was more natural in the Jenkins et al. study, the contexts were specifically created to strongly imply the word's meaning and often provided a synonym. Fifth-grade students received preexposure to the meaning of half the target words in order to capture the role of partial prior knowledge in learning from context. The researchers also varied the number of encounters with the words, providing conditions of two, six, and ten encounters. The results did indicate learning from context effects. However, the effects occurred only for words encountered six or ten times unless there had been preexposure to meaning. The effects also varied as to outcome measure and reader ability. Significant effects were found on measures that required readers to select and supply definitions, but not on a measure requiring selection of a completion for a sentence containing a target word. Ability differences again appeared, with higher-ability readers learning more word meanings than lower-ability students.

Nagy and Herman initiated a program of research with the assumption that evidence of learning from context was not captured by most studies because such learning proceeds in small increments that the measures used in many studies have failed to capture (Herman, Anderson, Pearson, & Nagy, 1987; Nagy et al., 1987; Nagy et al., 1985). To examine this assumption, Nagy et al. (1985) employed a variety of measures designed to capture partial knowledge. The researchers had seventh and eighth graders read passages containing target words and then respond to three levels of multiple-choice tests, the easiest of which required only that the reader have some very general knowledge of a word, in that knowledge of its part of speech or its general category was sufficient to get the item correct. An interview task was also used in which readers were asked to give definitional information. The study yielded small but robust effects for learning from context. Based on their results, Nagy et al. calculated that the probability of learning a word from a single contextual encounter was between .05 and .11, depending on the learning criterion used.

Nagy et al. (1985) point to the issue of measurement sensitivity in discussing their finding of effects for single contextual exposures in contrast to Jenkins et al.'s conclusion that at least more than two exposures were needed. Only the most difficult level of Nagy et al.'s range of multiple-choice items was comparable to the difficulty level of the multiple-choice test used by Jenkins et al. And, although both groups of researchers asked students to produce definitions, the scoring criteria were much more lenient for Nagy et al.'s interview responses.

In later studies, Nagy and Herman considered other text and reader characteristics that could affect learning from context. Herman et al. (1987) found that learning from context was facilitated by conceptually explicit text and higher reading ability. Nagy et al. (1987) found that the conceptual difficulty of a word or of the text diminished learning the word. But they failed to find an effect for reading ability, which is a departure from findings about the relationship between ability and learning from context reached by many previous studies.

The studies discussed so far seem to indicate that some learning from context does occur, but that the effect is not very powerful. However, a most interesting facet of the literature in this area is that the power of contextual effects is interpreted in markedly different ways by different researchers. Nagy et al. (1985) characterize the effect as "substantial" and hypothesize that the overall influence of context on vocabulary learning is large because the volume of reading students typically do allows for a great accumulation of encounters with unknown words and, ultimately, learning of substantial numbers of words. On the other hand, Schatz and Baldwin (1986) suggest that Nagy et al.'s findings occur because of an extremely powerful design and characterize the effects as "statistically significant—but minute" (p. 448). Jenkins, Stein, and Wysocki (1984) conclude that learning from context does not come easily or in large quantities, and cast doubt upon context as accounting for the kind of large gains in vocabulary that are frequently claimed to occur during the school years.

Process of Word-Meaning Acquisition

The studies just described asked students to read passages containing new words and then tested whether the words were learned. Another perspective for understanding the effects of context on learning vocabulary is to examine the processes in which readers engage when asked to derive the meaning of a word. Three such studies will be discussed: two from this decade (van Daalen-Kapteijns & Elshout-Mohr, 1981; McKeown, 1985) and one classic study by Werner and Kaplan from 1952. In one sense, the findings of these studies are similar to those just discussed. That is, learning from context was found to occur, but the extent of that learning was not impressive, particularly for less-skilled learners. Beyond these similar findings, these studies describe the components of the word-meaning acquisition process and where the process is most vulnerable.

Werner and Kaplan (1952) examined the development of how children use context to assign meanings to words. They tested 9- to 13-year-olds on sets of six sentences containing an unknown (actually an artificial) word. Their findings showed that performance improved with age, and immature processes were characterized by inability to integrate information in order to derive a single meaning for all six sentences, and lack of differentiation between word and the larger context. For example, in the sentence "Jimmy *libdered* stamps from all countries," *libder* might be defined by a younger student as "collect stamps."

Van Daalen-Kapteijns and Elshout-Mohr (1981) conceptualized the word-meaning acquisition process as beginning with the formulation of a rough notion, or model, of a word's meaning accompanied by empty slots reserved for more specific information. They asked college students to derive the meaning of a word from a series of sentences in which the word was used. The researchers found that learners did initially form a rough notion of word meaning and that the integration of specific information into this model differed between higher and lower verbal learners. The lower verbal learners had difficulty readjusting their model of word meaning when new information from subsequent sentences required it.

In McKeown's (1985) study of the word-meaning acquisition process, fifth graders were asked to derive the meaning of artificial words from a series of sentences that provided progressively stronger clues to the meaning of the word. McKeown found that lower verbal learners, especially, had difficulty understanding the relationship between a word and context, particularly that a context sets limits on what a word may mean, and in integrating information across multiple contexts.

Research on the process of acquiring word meaning from a context suggests that learning a word is not simply a matter of lifting the meaning from a context. Rather, it is a complex process of developing a meaning in which a series of steps must contribute to achieve a successful outcome.

Attempts to Teach Ability to Use Context

An issue that many researchers have considered is whether students' ability to use printed contexts as a source for vocabulary learning can be upgraded. Recommendations abound that context skills should be taught. Yet, studies in which students were instructed in using context to derive word meaning have yielded limited results. The earliest attempt to teach skills for deriving word meaning from context was a month-long experiment with fifth graders that produced no results for instruction (Hafner, 1965). However, recent work has been somewhat more successful. Carnine, Kameenui, and Coyle (1984) found that teaching a "rule" about examining context for clues to an unknown word and providing practice applying the rule yielded improved ability to use context.

Patberg, Graves, and Stibbe (1984) replicated Carnine et al.'s study but used more active teaching and explanation in the instruction. The technique yielded reliable differences on one of two dependent measures. Yet a follow-up study (Patberg & Stibbe, 1985) found no effects for the instructional procedure. Limiting factors in the Carnine et al. and Patberg et al. outcomes are that the instruction presented only two types of context clues, synonym and contrast, and the tasks that measured learning provided artificially rich contexts.

In a very recent study, Jenkins, Matlock, and Slocum (1988) taught fifth graders a system for using context. The system involved class discussion in which teachers presented contexts containing unfamiliar words and asked students to offer possible meanings for the word and to examine the fit of those meanings to the context. Significant effects of the instruction were found; but as the authors note, scores on the outcome measures were low, and the differences in favor of instruction were small.

A theoretically driven program of research on learning word meaning from context has been undertaken by Sternberg. Sternberg and Powell (1983) developed a theory of learning from context that involves three components: the process applied to the task; types of context clues available in texts; and variables that mediate success in using context, such as the number of occurrences of a word within a text. Sternberg subsequently designed instruction aimed at each of these components of the theory. Research on the instruction is still ongoing, but summary results of two experiments are available (Sternberg, 1987). The first, which trained high school students on one component of the theory, types of context clues, yielded what the researcher describes as disappointingly weak effects. The second experiment, with adults, examined instruction that targeted each of the three components of Steinberg's theory: clue types, the process of deriving word meaning, and mediating variables. Significant gains were found for all three types of instruction, with clue types showing the weakest effects.

There are two caveats regarding Sternberg's research thus far. One is that descriptions of the experiments that are currently available do not provide details on the test passages, making it impossible to evaluate the level of contextual support provided. The second is that it is unclear whether such procedures are appropriate for learners younger than high school age.

Some Conclusions

From the research that has been done, what can be concluded about the role of printed context in accounting for vocabulary growth during the school years? The ubiquitous finding that learning word meanings from context does not seem to occur with particular ease suggests three possible explanations to account for vocabulary growth: One is that learners encounter such a huge number of contextual word-learning opportunities that impressive growth is possible even when the effect of each opportunity is minute. A second explanation is that oral contexts continue to play the major role in vocabulary learning throughout the school years. A third explanation is that vocabulary size and growth have been substantially overestimated. Because available data do not allow selecting with confidence among those three explanations, there seems to be a clear need for research that will clarify the issues. Research is needed that will give some insight into the contribution of oral context to vocabulary growth. Also needed are large-scale studies of vocabulary size that correct for the problems of earlier research in that area.

Investigations of instruction in using context to derive word meaning have shown that such skill is not easily affected. At best, researchers have found admittedly small gains. Jenkins et al. (1988) and Carnine et al. (1984) both mention that more powerful instructional procedures are likely needed if stronger effects are to occur. These observations seem to match the notion from studies of the meaning-acquisition process: that the process is a complex one with many possible vulnerabilities. The potential importance of context as a vocabulary-learning source and the apparent difficulty in fully utilizing that source warrant a continued search for more effective instruction.

Direct Instruction

Direct vocabulary instruction describes situations in which word-meaning information is intentionally made available to the student. This includes teacher-led instruction and independent work with printed material. Among the stronger forms of direct instruction are those in which the teacher engages students in a discussion about a word's meaning; a weaker form is when students are directed to look words up in the dictionary.

We initiate our discussion of vocabulary instruction by considering where in school curricula it occurs. Vocabulary is not a subject matter in itself, and one might find teachers bringing attention to the meaning of a word in any subject, including math. But "general" vocabulary development traditionally falls within the domain of reading and language arts instruction. In the reading program, vocabulary instruction appears to be most often associated with a textual selection that the students will read and can occur prior to reading the selection, as well as during and after reading (Beck, McKeown, McCaslin, & Burkes, 1979). It appears, however, that most vocabulary instruction occurs prior to reading (Blachowicz, 1987).

Search for a Best Method

Because prereading vocabulary instruction usually introduces words important for the upcoming selection, teachers are concerned with effective methods for teaching new words. Researchers have also been concerned with this issue, and the literature contains investigations of, and recommendations for, methods bearing a variety of labels. The two most prominent methods are the dictionary, or definition, method, and the context method, but references are also found to concept methods. More recently, the key word method, semantic mapping, and semantic features analysis have appeared in the literature.

The quest for a best method, however, has not been successful. Although specific investigations that compared methods have reported findings that favor one over another, the results have not necessarily held up. For example, in Gipe's 1978–1979 comparative study, the context method was found to be superior to several others, yet in a later study the effect was not found (Gipe, 1981). Similarly, semantic mapping was found to be superior to semantic features analysis (Johnson, Toms-Bronowski, & Pittelman, 1982); but both were found to be inferior to the key word method (Levin et al., 1984). The inability to find a best method was well illustrated by Petty, Herold, and Stoll (1986), who concluded from their analysis of 80 studies that the search for "the most satisfactory methods" was a "wide-open area of research."

One key to why a best method has not been identified is that the same label can be used to describe a very different set of activities. Indeed, it has been found that methods with a particular label have included features that would be considered the eminent domain of another method. For instance, the context method used by Gipe (1978–1979) included explicit definitions of the words. But the context methods used in studies by Quealy (1969) and Rankin and Overholser (1969) included no definitional information. Relatedly, students in Gipe's context method were required to produce a novel example for each target word. Yet the context method used by Margosein, Pascarella, and Pflaum (1982) did not include the production activity.

Certainly, studies that remedy the problems discussed above can be developed; however, we assert that this would not be productive unless the goals for the instruction are specified. That is, in order to determine what kind of vocabulary instruction is optimal, the criterion behavior at which the instruction is aimed needs to be specified. If, for example, the criterion behavior is what we refer to as *word learning*, that is, the ability to associate a word with a definition or synonym as in a typical multiple-choice test, then there are some reliable findings.

From some recent work, most notably, Graves's review of the field (1986) and analyses by Stahl and Fairbanks (1986) and Mezynski (1983), the following four statements about the effects of vocabulary instruction on word learning can be made with a high degree of confidence: First, all instructional methods produce better word learning than no instruction. Second, no one method has been shown to be consistently superior. Third, there is advantage from methods that use a variety of techniques. Fourth, there is advantage from repeated exposures to the words to be learned. The simple version of these findings is that people tend to learn what they are taught, and more attention to what is being taught is useful.

The paramount issue, however, is that increasing students' word knowledge to the level of their being able to match word and definition is not an end in itself. Such a limited goal may produce *inert knowledge*, that is, knowledge that has a low probability of being activated in appropriate situations. (For discussion of inert knowledge and its effects, see Bereiter & Scardamalia, 1985; Bransford, Sherwood, Vye, & Rieser, 1986; Brown, 1985; Brown, & Campione, 1981). Instead it seems reasonable to suggest that the goal of vocabulary instruction is to enhance students' ability to engage in complex language situations. The complex language situation that has received the most attention from both practitioners and researchers is reading comprehension.

Relating Vocabulary Knowledge to Comprehension

Interest in the relationship between vocabulary and reading comprehension has a long history, and the relationship is intuitively obvious. Moreover, psychometric support for the relationship between vocabulary knowledge and comprehension has been strong. In factor analytic studies of reading comprehension, vocabulary knowledge has consistently emerged as a major component (Davis, 1944, 1968; Singer, 1965; Spearrit, 1972; Thurstone, 1946), correlating very highly with comprehension ability. The robust nature of this correlation has raised the question of whether there is a causal link between vocabulary knowledge and reading comprehension. One way of studying whether a causal link exists has been to test comprehension of texts that contain very low-frequency vocabulary, that is, words that are likely to be unknown to the readers. Studies by Marks, Doctorow, and Wittrock (1974) and by Anderson and Freebody (1983) showed that the presence of difficult vocabulary does diminish text comprehension. However, the proportion of low-frequency to high-frequency words apparently needs to be quite high before the effect is demonstrated. In the Marks et al. study, 15 percent of the text was low-frequency words; and in Anderson and Freebody's study one in three content words was replaced with low-frequency substitutes before effects were realized.

Given the strong correlational relationship between vocabulary and comprehension and hints of a causal connection, a most intriguing question for researchers has been whether increasing vocabulary knowledge through instruction would improve reading comprehension. But, prior to this decade, evidence of comprehension improvement from vocabulary instruction had been elusive with most studies finding no effects (Jackson & Dizney, 1963; Jenkins, Pany, & Schreck, 1978; Tuinman & Brady, 1974). For the most part, the kind of instruction studied focused on establishing associations between words and definitions. One marked exception, which did yield comprehension effects, was Draper and Moeller's (1971) rather comprehensive approach to vocabulary via radio broadcasts and an assortment of follow-up activities.

The Role of Active Processing in Comprehension

As researchers sought to understand why instruction had generally not brought comprehension improvement, a theme began to emerge which suggested that, in order to affect comprehension, instruction may need to go beyond simply establishing accuracy of associations between words and definitions (e.g., Beck, Perfetti, & McKeown, 1982; Kameenui, Carnine, & Freschi, 1982; Margosein, Pascarella, & Pflaum, 1982). This theme reflected an information-processing orientation, in which reading is viewed as a complex process consisting of a variety of concurrent, interacting subprocesses. The implication of the processing complexity is that the lexical and semantic aspects of comprehension may require more than the ability to associate words and definitions.

The most explicit attention to the implication of an information-processing orientation for vocabulary instruction was reflected in Beck et al.'s (1982) work. These researchers considered the semantic processes involved in reading comprehension to require fluency of access to word meanings and richness of semantic network connections, in addition to accuracy of word-meaning knowledge; they then designed instruction to affect these three features. The instruction included frequent encounters with each word, instructional strategies that entailed elaboration and discussion of word meaning, and opportunities to use the taught words outside of the classroom. The instruction was found to affect all three components in that students learned the word meanings, had faster access to the words, and had better comprehension of text that used the taught words.

Since the Beck et al. (1982) study, there have been two reviews that examined the question of whether vocabulary instruction can influence comprehension by analyzing features of instruction in studies that both succeeded and failed to affect comprehension. Mezynski (1983) reviewed eight studies and concluded that three features seemed to differentiate those that succeeded in improving comprehension. These were amount of practice, breadth of information about the words, and activities that encouraged active processing of information. Stahl and Fairbanks (1986) conducted a meta-analysis of about 30 studies and reached similar conclusions. Specifically, they found that successful instruction provided more than one or two exposures to each word, presented both definitional and contextual information, and engaged students in deeper processing.

The theoretical underpinnings of the importance of deep processing during vocabulary instruction derive from the notion that instruction that requires the learner to actively generate information improves retention because it helps to build semantic network connections between new and prior information (Anderson & Reder, 1979; Craik & Tulving, 1975). It follows that comprehension is affected by deep processing because the number and variety of connections that are formed facilitate access to components of word meaning that are relevant for the variety of contexts in which a word might be encountered (Beck et al., 1982).

A study by McKeown, Beck, Omanson, and Pople (1985) directly compared instruction that was designed to engage active processing with instruction that focused on practice of definitions. High and low frequencies of encounters with the words were also investigated for both types of instruction. The investigators found that for accuracy of knowledge as measured by a multiple-choice test, high frequency of instruction led to better results, but whether instruction emphasized active processing or practice of definitions did not make a difference here. On measures of comprehension, type of instruction did make a difference. Instruction that encouraged active processing of words held a modest advantage in recall of stories containing taught words. And it showed a substantial advantage on a measure of *context interpretation*, which is defined as the ability to incorporate a word's meaning into the surrounding context to develop an appropriate representation of the context as a whole. The results of the study support the conclusions from Mezynski's (1983) and Stahl and Fairbanks's (1986) work, that is, encouraging active or deeper processing distinguishes instruction that affects comprehension.

Integrating Active Processing into Instruction

Let us now consider how active processing has been manifested in specific instructional techniques. Although the labels and specific activities differ, these differences are less significant than the shared features that all involve active processing.

Semantic features analysis and semantic mapping are two instructional techniques that engage active processing by having students examine how words are related (Johnson & Pearson, 1978, 1984). In *semantic features analysis* (SFA), both words and concepts or features associated with the words are presented on a grid. The teacher introduces the words and concepts, and then students fill in the grid by deciding whether the concepts or features are positively or negatively related to each word. Anders, Bos, and Filip (1984) found that SFA yielded improvements in reading comprehension. *Semantic mapping* instruction aims to tie new words into networks of related known words by making explicit the shared and unique features of members of a group. For example, Margosein et al's (1982) use of the technique presented the word *solitude* by discussing how it compared to *alone, lonely,* and *quiet.* Margosein et al. found that semantic mapping instruction resulted in improved comprehension.

Instruction developed for the Beck and McKeown studies (Beck et al., 1982; McKeown et al., 1983; McKeown et al., 1985) used an assortment of activities to engage student processing. Words were presented in semantically related groups to encourage students to compare and contrast. For example, students were asked if they would *berate* someone who had *inspired* them, or if a *tyrant* could be a *miser.* Students were asked to consider uses of the words, such as applying them to contexts or creating contexts for them. For example, one activity required students to discover that *baffle* described a situation in which a boy could not figure out a riddle. Another activity asked students to consider what a *hermit* might have a nightmare about.

Kameenui, Carnine, and Freschi (1982) hypothesized that in order for knowledge of a word to affect comprehension, learners may need explicit help to integrate the word's meaning within a context. A component of the instruction in Kameenui et al.'s study was designed to teach *passage integration.* After initial learning of word meanings, students read passages containing the new words. When students encountered a new word, an experimenter stopped them and asked them to define the word and to answer a question that required knowing the meaning. Kameenui et al. found that instruction using the passage integration technique held some advantage on measures of comprehension effects.

A common thread running through these examples of instruction that encourages active processing is that activities do not merely call for entering new information in memory. Rather, students are required to use information by comparing it to, and combining it with, known information toward constructing representations of word meaning.

Some Conclusions

Although recent research has demonstrated the importance of considering the semantic processes involved in reading comprehension for designing instruction, our understanding of the relationship between vocabulary and comprehension is far from complete.

The effects of vocabulary instruction on comprehension have tended to be rather small; and most measures of comprehension have relied upon contrived passages, which poorly represent texts students meet in natural reading situations. Thus, the results of instructional studies indicate that vocabulary learning does affect comprehension, but the parameters of that effect have not yet been identified.

Several studies have provided some hints about the aspects of comprehension that are affected by vocabulary instruction. One such hint was Kameenui et al.'s (1982) finding that instruction involving passage integration, the component that encouraged active processing, tended to have a greater effect on questions that required inferences to be drawn. However, the differences were significant in only one of two experiments.

A study by Wixson (1986) also has relevance to this issue. In teaching 5 out of 22 unfamiliar words from a 1,500-word story to students, Wixson found that although overall comprehension, as tested by story recall, was not affected, understanding of specific ideas related to the instructed words was shown. This suggests that the effect of vocabulary knowledge on comprehension may be localized, and that broad measures of comprehension may not be sensitive to the effects.

Another hint was offered by McKeown et al. (1983). In addition to finding reliable differences in amount of recall of stories containing taught words, the researchers examined quality of recall. They constructed prototypical recalls from the text propositions that were best recalled by experimental and control groups. The prototypical recalls of the experimental group were found to constitute coherent summaries of the stories while those of the control group omitted key elements from each story's setting, conflict, and resolution.

Another insight about the contribution of vocabulary to comprehension was provided by McKeown et al. (1985). They found that instruction that encouraged active processing had less effect on a measure of recall than on a measure that required students to reason with the words in order to create an interpretation of a context.

From the hints that these studies provide, we can speculate that the effect of vocabulary instruction on comprehension may seem small when measured in quantitative ways, but its significance may be revealed when the quality of understanding is considered. Thus, the issue to be pursued is, Under what conditions will better comprehension be demonstrated? or even more importantly, In what way can an individual's ability to comprehend be improved by vocabulary instruction?

DISCUSSION

The theme that has been echoed throughout this chapter is that vocabulary acquisition is a complex verbal process. Within this theme any question on vocabulary, be it how readily words are learned, how many words are known by individuals, or what kind of instruction works best, must be answered by "it's conditional; it depends on the situation."

In the case of what it means to know a word, interpretation of notions about how many words are known, how words are learned, and how effective instruction is, all depend on what is intended by knowledge of a word. The notion of "it depends" applies in two ways to the size of an individual's vocabulary. First, estimates of vocabulary size depend on the sample that is tested and on what is considered a word, as well as on what knowing a word is taken to mean. Second, whichever of the hugely discrepant estimates of vocabulary size one accepts significantly influences beliefs about how easily words are learned and the role that instruction can play. The assessment of vocabulary knowledge depends on what one wants to know about that knowledge. Different assessment measures tap different levels and aspects of knowledge, and thus studies have shown large differences in student knowledge of the same set of words. An understanding of the role of context in learning vocabulary depends on conditions such as whether the context is oral or written, the type of learner, and the amount of support provided by the context. It also depends on what is meant by learning. And finally, the question of whether direct instruction works depends on whether "works" means enabling students' ability to associate words with definitions or affecting more complex verbal functions.

Given the conditional state of what is known about vocabulary learning, it is not surprising that a variety of conclusions on how to best promote vocabulary learning can be reached. And, indeed, a variety of positions has been taken by different researchers. We examine four positions that have received some prominence. It is important to note that none of these positions is espoused to the complete exclusion of others, but the degree of emphasis among various researchers is quite different.

The first position is based on the belief that students learn vocabulary from context during reading and has led to a laissez-faire view of instruction (e.g., Nagy & Herman, 1987). As a substitute for instruction, the promotion of wide reading is espoused. A second position shares the belief in context as the primacy source of vocabulary learning, but registers concern with the effectiveness of learning from context. Thus, instruction in deriving word meaning from context is recommended (e.g., Jenkins, Stein, & Wysocki, 1984; Sternberg, 1987). A third position takes the view that context hinders deriving word meaning as often as it helps, and therefore emphasizes encouraging students to use the dictionary (e.g., Schatz & Baldwin, 1986). Finally, a position holds that no matter what context contributes, direct instruction can play an important role in vocabulary development (e.g., Beck et al., 1987; Graves, 1986, 1987; Stahl & Fairbanks, 1986).

All four positions have merit, and all of the strategies they promote should be part of the educational environment. But, in concert with this chapter's theme, the effectiveness of each strategy is dependent on certain conditions. Let us consider the strategies in terms of some of those conditions.

The goal of wide reading for all students is an excellent one, not only for vocabulary development but for general language development and learning about the world. Yet, there are several problems on the way to achievement of this goal, and they lie in the realm of "the rich get richer." Highly skilled students are likely to embrace the idea of increasing their reading, while less-skilled students are apt to be reluctant to do so. Even if less-skilled students are motivated to read, they will probably not be able to reach the same breadth of experience as their high-skilled counterparts nor will their comprehension be as rich. A corollary to this is that their skills in deriving word meaning from context will not be as effective. The point of these comments is certainly not to discourage the practice of wide reading but to question whether it can be relied upon to enhance vocabulary development for all students.

The issue of whether students use context effectively brings us to the position that they need to be taught to do so. And research seems to indicate that people's ability to derive word meaning from context can be improved. We offer two conditions, however: First, the research in this area to date demonstrates rather small gains, which indicates a need to seek more effective instructional procedures. Second, it is not only the ability to use contextual information that stands in the way of deriving word meaning; often, natural texts do not reveal sufficient clues. Thus we urge that instruction in context skills include helping students to understand that context may reveal a little or a lot about a word's meaning and to recognize when information should be considered tentative or incomplete.

Because natural contexts often do not contain information sufficient for deriving word meaning, encouragement to use a dictionary is an obvious recommendation. Yet, learners are often reluctant to interrupt their reading for a trip to the dictionary; so motivation is a big obstacle. An additional obstacle is that once we get students to the dictionary, what they find may not be particularly helpful. Dictionary definitions are often difficult formats from which to learn (Miller, 1985). As Nagy and Herman (1987) have noted, "definitions almost seem to be written in a secret code, accessible only to those with the inside knowledge" (p. 29). Yet, people with voracious appetites for words do consult dictionaries and do expand vocabulary knowledge through their use. Thus, we see two areas in which work is needed. One is to arrange conditions that enable students to see the benefits of searching out the meanings of unknown words. The other area is to consider whether dictionary definitions can be transformed into more effective vehicles for vocabulary learning.

Lastly we consider what direct instruction can contribute to vocabulary development. The major arguments against a significant role for direct instruction are that (a) there are too many words to teach, given what it takes for effective instruction; and (b) people learn vocabulary readily on their own. The second is arguable, in that no definitive figures on vocabulary growth have been reached, and individual differences are wide. The first point is true, *if* the intent is to teach all words. Yet we assert that an important condition in considering the significance of direct instruction is that not all words need attention. For example, common words in everyday vocabulary such as *school, road*, and *grandfather* are learned as part of initial language acquisition and do not require instruction about their meanings.

Words that are the most appropriate targets of instruction for general vocabulary development are those of high frequency in a mature vocabulary and of broad utility across domains of knowledge. Because of the role such words play in a language user's verbal repertoire, direct instruction of these words might have significant impact on verbal functioning. Thus, the problem that effective instruction takes time can be alleviated by targeting instruction toward the most useful words.

The goal for vocabulary development is to insure that students are able to apply their knowledge of words to appropriate situations and are able to increase and enrich their knowledge through independent encounters with words. The body of research discussed here seems to indicate that the best way to reach this goal is to help students add to their repertoires both specific words and skills that promote independent learning of words, and also to provide opportunities from which words can be learned.

REFERENCES

Ames, W. S. (1966–1967). The development of a classification scheme of contextual aids. *Reading Research Quarterly, 2*, 57–62.

Anders, P., Bos, C., & Filip, D. (1984). The effect of semantic feature analysis on the reading comprehension of learning-disabled students. In J. A. Niles & L. A. Harris (Eds.), *Changing perspectives on research in reading/language processing and instruction*. Rochester, NY: National Reading Conference.

Anderson, R. C., & Freebody, P. (1981). Vocabulary knowledge. In J. T. Guthrie (Ed.), *Comprehension and teaching: Research reviews* (pp. 77–117). Newark, DE: International Reading Association.

Anderson, R. C., & Freebody, P. (1983). Reading comprehension and the assessment and acquisition of word knowledge. In B. Hutton (Ed.), *Advances in reading/language research: A research annual*. Greenwich, CT: JAI Press.

Anderson, J. R., & Reder, L. M. (1979). An elaborative processing explanation of depth of processing. In L. S. Cermak & F. I. M. Craik (Eds.), *Levels of processing in human memory* (pp. 385–404). Hillsdale, NJ: Erlbaum.

Artley, A. S. (1943). Teaching word-meaning through context. *Elementary English Review, 20*, 68–74.

Beck, I. L., & McKeown, M. G. (1986). Instructional research in reading: A retrospective. In J. Orasanu (Ed.), *Reading comprehension: From research to practice* (pp. 113–134). Hillsdale, NJ: Erlbaum.

Beck, I. L., McKeown, M. G., & McCaslin, E. S. (1983). Vocabulary development: All contexts are not created equal. *Elementary School Journal, 83,* 177–181.

Beck, I. L., McKeown, M. G., McCaslin, E. S., & Burkes, A. M. (1979). *Instructional dimension that may affect reading comprehension: Examples from two commercial reading programs.* Pittsburgh: University of Pittsburgh, Learning Research & Development Center.

Beck, I. L., McKeown, M. G., & Omanson, R. C. (1987). The effects and uses of diverse vocabulary instructional techniques. In M. G. McKeown & M. E. Curtis (Eds.), *The nature of vocabulary acquisition.* Hillsdale, NJ: Erlbaum.

Beck, I. L., Perfetti, C. A., & McKeown, M. G. (1982). The effects of long-term vocabulary instruction on lexical access and reading comprehension. *Journal of Educational Psychology, 74,* 506–521.

Bereiter, C., & Scardamalia, M. (1985). Cognitive coping strategies and the problem of "inert" knowledge. In S. Chipman, J. W. Segal, & R. Glaser (Eds.), *Thinking and learning skills: Current research and open questions* (Vol. 2, pp. 65–80). Hillsdale, NJ: Erlbaum.

Blachowicz, C. Z. (1987). Vocabulary instruction: What goes on in the classroom? *Reading Teacher, 2,* 132–137.

Bransford, J., Sherwood, R., Vye, N., & Rieser, J. (1986). Teaching thinking and problem solving: Research foundations. *American Psychology, 10,* 1078–1089.

Brown, A. L. (1985). Mental orthopedics, the training of cognitive skills: An interview with Alfred Binet. In S. Chipman, J. Segal, & R. Glaser (Eds.), *Thinking and learning skills* (Vol. 2, pp. 77–165). Hillsdale, NJ: Erlbaum.

Brown, A. L., & Campione, J. C. (1981). Inducing flexible thinking: A problem of access. In M. Friedman, J. P. Das, & N. O'Connor (Eds.), *Intelligence and learning* (pp. 515–529). New York: Plenum.

Bruner, J. S. (1957). Going beyond the information given. In H. Gruber et al. (Eds.), *Contemporary approaches to cognition.* (pp. 41–70). Cambridge, MA: Harvard University Press.

Calfee, R. C., & Drum, P. A. (1978). Learning to read: Theory, research, and practice. *Curriculum Inquiry, 8,* 183–249.

Calfee, R. C., & Drum, P. A. (1986). Research on teaching reading. In M. C. Wittrock (Ed.), *Handbook of research on teaching* (3rd ed., pp. 804–849). New York: Macmillan.

Carey, S. (1978). The child as word learner. In M. Halle, J. Bresman, & G. Miller, (Eds)., *Linguistic Theory and Psychological Reality* (pp. 265–293). Cambridge, MA: MIT Press.

Carnine, D., Kameenui, E. J., & Coyle, G. (1984). Utilization of contextual information in determining the meaning of unfamiliar words in context. *Reading Research Quarterly, 19,* 188–202.

Carroll, J. B., Davies, P., & Richman, B. (1971). *Word frequency book.* New York: American Heritage.

Chomsky, N. (1957). *Syntactic structures.* The Hague: Mouton.

Clifford, G. J. (1978). Words for schools: The application in education of the vocabulary researches of Edward L. Thorndike. In P. Suppes (Ed.), *Impact of research on education: Some case studies* (pp. 107–198). Washington, DC: National Academy of Education.

Craik, F. I. M., & Tulving, E. (1975). Depth of processing and the retention of words in episodic memory. *Journal of Experimental Psychology: General, 104,* 268–294.

Cronbach, L. J. (1942). An analysis of techniques for systematic vocabulary testing. *Journal of Educational Research, 36,* 206–217.

Cronbach, L. J. (1943). Measuring knowledge of precise word meaning. *Journal of Educational Research, 36,* 528–534.

Curtis, M. E. (1981). Word knowledge and verbal aptitude. Unpublished manuscript.

Curtis, M. E. (1987). Vocabulary testing and instruction. In M. G. McKeown & M. E. Curtis (Eds.), *The nature of vocabulary acquisition* (pp. 37–51). Hillsdale, NJ: Erlbaum.

Curtis, M. E., & Glaser, R. (1983). Reading theory and the assessment of reading achievement. *Journal of Educational Measurement, 20,* 133–147.

Dale, E. (1965). Vocabulary measurement: Techniques and major findings. *Elementary English, 42,* 895–901, 948.

Davis, F. B. (1944). Fundamental factors in reading comprehension. *Psychometrika, 9,* 185–197.

Davis, F. B. (1968). Research in comprehension in reading. *Reading Research Quarterly, 3,* 499–545.

Davison, A., & Kantor, R. (1982). On the failure of readability formulas to define readable texts: A case study from adaptations. *Reading Research Quarterly, 17,* 187–210.

Dolch, E. W. (1936). How much word knowledge do children bring to grade 1? *Elementary English Review, 13,* 177–183.

Doran, E. W. (1907). A study of vocabularies. *Pedagogical Seminar, 14,* 177–183.

Draper, A. G., & Moeller, G. H. (1971). We think with words (therefore to improve thinking, teach vocabulary). *Phi Delta Kappan, 52,* 482–484. (ERIC Document Reproduction Service No. ED 036 207)

Duffy, T. M., & Kabance, P. (1981). *Testing a readable writing approach to text revision.* San Diego: Navy Personnel Research and Development Center.

Dupuy, H. P. (1974). *The rationale, development, and standardization of a basic word vocabulary test* (DHEW Publication No. HRA 74-1334). Washington, DC: U.S. Government Printing Office.

Elivian, J. (1938). Word perception and word meaning in student reading in the intermediate grades. *Education, 59,* 51–56.

Feifel, H., & Lorge, I. (1950). Qualitative differences in the vocabulary responses of children. *Journal of Educational Psychology, 41,* 1–18.

Gerstein, R. A. (1949). A suggested method for analyzing and extending the use of Bellevue-Wechsler vocabulary responses. *Journal of Consulting Psychology; 13*, 366–370.

Gipe, J. P. (1978–1979). Investigating techniques for teaching word meaning. *Reading Research Quarterly, 14*, 624–644.

Gipe, J. P. (1981, April) *Investigation of techniques for teaching new words*. Paper presented at the meeting of the American Educational Research Association, Los Angeles.

Graves, M. F. (1980, April). *A quantitative and qualitative study of students' reading vocabularies*. Paper presented at the meeting of the American Educational Research Association, Boston.

Graves, M. F. (1986). Vocabulary learning and instruction. In E. Z. Rothkopf (Ed.), *Review of Research in Education, 13*, 91–128.

Graves, M. F., Brunetti, G. J., & Slater, W. H. (1982). The reading vocabularies of primary-grade children of varying geographic and social backgrounds. In J. A. Harris & L. A. Harris (Eds.), *New inquiries in reading research and instruction* (pp. 99–104). Rochester, NY: National Reading Conference.

Graves, M. F., & Slater, W. H. (April 1987). *The development of reading vocabularies in rural disadvantaged students, inner-city disadvantaged students, and middle-class suburban students*. Paper presented at the meeting of the American Educational Research Association, Washington, DC.

Hafner, L. E. (1965). A one-month experiment in teaching context aids in fifth grade. *Journal of Educational Research, 58*, 471–474.

Hartman, G. W. (1946). Further evidence on the unexpected large size of recognition vocabularies among college students. *Journal of Educational Psychology, 37*, 436–439.

Herman, P. A., Anderson, R. C., Pearson, P. D., & Nagy, W. E. (1987). Incidental acquisition of word meaning from expositions with varied text features. *Reading Research Quarterly, 22*(3), 263–284.

Huey, E. B. (1908). *The psychology and pedagogy of reading*. New York: Macmillan.

Jackson, J. R., & Dizney, H. (1963). Intensive vocabulary training. *Journal of Developmental Reading, 6*, 221–229.

Jenkins, J. R., Matlock, B., & Slocum, T. A. (1988, April). *Effects of specific vocabulary instruction in deriving word meaning from context*. Paper presented at meeting of the American Educational Research Association, New Orleans.

Jenkins, J. R., Pany, D., & Schreck, J. (1978). *Vocabulary and Reading Comprehension: Instructional Effects* (Tech. Rep. No. 100). Urbana: University of Illinois, Center for the Study of Reading. (ERIC Document Reproduction Service No. ED. 160 999).

Jenkins, J. R., Stein, M., & Wysocki, K. (1984). Learning vocabulary through reading. *American Educational Research Journal, 21*, 767–787.

Johnson, D. D., & Pearson, P. D. (1978). *Teaching reading vocabulary*. New York: Holt, Rinehart & Winston.

Johnson, D. D., & Pearson, P. D. (1984) *Teaching reading vocabulary* (2nd ed.). New York: Holt, Rinehart & Winston.

Johnson, D. D., Toms-Bronowski, S., & Pittelman, S. D. (1982). *An investigation of the effectiveness of semantic mapping and semantic feature analysis with intermediate grade level children* (Program Report No. 83-3). Madison, WI: Wisconsin Center for Education Research.

Joos, M. (1964). Language and the school child. *Harvard Educational Review, 34*, 203–210.

Just, M. A., & Carpenter, P. A. (1987). *The psychology of reading and language comprehension*. Newton, MA: Allyn & Bacon.

Kameenui, E. J., Carnine, D. W., & Freschi, R. (1982). Effects of text construction and instructional procedures for teaching word meanings on comprehension and recall. *Reading Research Quarterly, 17*, 367–388.

Kameenui, E. J., Dixon, R. C., & Carnine, D. W. (1987). Issues in the design of vocabulary instruction. In M. G. McKeown & M. E. Curtis (Eds.), *The Nature of Vocabulary Acquisition* (pp. 129–145). Hillsdale, NJ: Erlbaum.

Kirkpatrick, E. A. (1891). The number of words in an ordinary vocabulary. *Science, 18*, 107–108.

Levin, J. R., Johnson, D. D., Pittelman, S. D., Levin, K. M., Shriber, L. D., Toms-Bronowski, S., & Hayes, B. L. (1984). A comparison of semantic- and mnemonic-based vocabulary-learning strategies. *Reading Psychology, 5*, 1–16.

Loban, G. (1963). *The language of elementary school children*. Champaign, IL: National Council of Teachers of English.

Lorge, I., & Chall, J. (1963). Estimating the size of vocabularies of children and adults: An analysis of methodological issues. *Journal of Experimental Education, 32*, 147–157.

Margosein, C. M., Pascarella, E. T., & Pflaum, S. W. (1982, March). *The effects of instruction using semantic mapping on vocabulary and comprehension*. Paper presented at the meeting of the American Educational Research Association, New York.

Marks, C. B., Doctorow, M. J., & Wittrock, M. C. (1974). Word frequency and reading comprehension. *Journal of Educational Research, 67*, 259–262.

Marshalek, B. (1981). *Trait and process aspects of vocabulary knowledge and verbal ability* (Tech. Rep. No. 15). Stanford, CA: Stanford University, School of Education.

McCullough, C. (1943). Learning to use context clues. *Elementary English Review, 20,* 140–143.

McCullough, C. M. (1945). The recognition of context clues in reading. *Elementary English Review, 22,* 1–5, 40.

McCullough, C. M. (1958). Context aids in reading. *Reading Teacher, 11,* 224–229.

McKeown, M. G. (1985). The acquisition of word meaning from context by children of high and low ability. *Reading Research Quarterly, 20,* 482–496.

McKeown, M. G., Beck, I. L., Omanson, R. C., & Perfetti, C. A. (1983). The effects of long-term vocabulary instruction on reading comprehension: A replication. *Journal of Reading Behavior, 15,* 3–18.

McKeown, M. G., Beck, I. L., Omanson, R. C., & Pople, M. T. (1985). Some effects of the nature and frequency of vocabulary instruction on the knowledge and use of words. *Reading Research Quarterly, 20,* 522–535.

Mezynski, K. (1983). Issues concerning the acquisition of knowledge: Effects of vocabulary training on reading comprehension. *Review of Educational Research, 53,* 253–279.

Miller, G. A. (1962). Some psychological studies of grammar. *American Psychologist, 17,* 748–762.

Miller, G. A. (1965). Some preliminaries to psycholinguistics. *American Psychologist, 20,* 15–20.

Miller, G. A. (1977). *Spontaneous apprentices: Children and language.* New York: Seabury Press.

Miller, G. A. (1978). Semantic relations among words. In M. Halle, J. Bresnan, & G. A. Miller (Eds.), *Linguistic theory and psychological reality* (pp. 61–118). Cambridge, MA: MIT Press.

Miller, G. A. (1985). Dictionaries of the mind. *Proceedings of the 23rd Annual Meeting of the Association for Computational Linguists* (pp. 305–314). Chicago: Author.

Nagy, W. E., & Anderson, R. C. (1984). How many words are there in printed school English? *Reading Research Quarterly, 19,* 304–330.

Nagy, W. E., Anderson, R. C., & Herman, P. A. (1985). *The influence of some word and text properties on learning from context.* Unpublished manuscript, University of Illinois at Urbana-Champaign, Center for the Study of Reading.

Nagy, W. E., Anderson, R. C., & Herman, P. A. (1987). Learning word meanings from context during normal reading. *American Educational Research Journal, 24,* 237–270.

Nagy, W. E., & Herman, P. A. (1987). Depth and breadth of vocabulary knowledge: Implications for acquisition and instruction. In M. G. McKeown & M. E. Curtis (Eds.), *The nature of vocabulary acquisition* (pp. 19–35). Hillsdale, NJ: Erlbaum.

Nagy, W., Herman, P., & Anderson, R. (1985). Learning words from context. *Reading Research Quarterly, 20,* 233–253.

Patberg, J. A., Graves, M. F., & Stibbe, M. A. (1984). Effects of active teaching and practice in facilitating students' use of context clues. In J. A. Niles & L. A. Harris (Eds.), *Changing perspectives on reading/language processing and instruction.* Rochester, NY: National Reading Conference.

Patberg, J. A., & Stibbe, M. A. (1985, December). *The effects of contextual analysis instruction on vocabulary learning.* Paper presented at the meeting of the National Reading Conference, San Diego, CA.

Pearson, P. D., Barr, R., Kamil, M. L., & Mosenthal, P. (Eds.). (1984). *Handbook of reading research* (Vol. 1). White Plains, NY: Longman.

Petty, W. T., Herold, C. P., & Stoll, E. (1968). *The state of knowledge about the teaching of vocabulary.* Champaign, IL: National Council of Teachers of English.

Quealy, R. J. (1969). Senior high school students' use of context aids in reading. *Reading Research Quarterly, 4,* 512–532.

Rankin, E. F., & Overholser, B. M. (1969). Reaction of intermediate-grade children to contextual clues. *Journal of Reading Behavior, 1,* 50–73.

Rubin, A. (1985). How useful are readability formulas? *Reading education: Foundations for a literate America* (pp. 61–84). Washington, DC: D.C. Heath.

Russell, D. H., & Saadeh, I.Q. (1962). Qualitative levels in children's vocabularies. *Journal of Educational Psychology, 53,* 170–174.

Seashore, R. H., & Eckerson, L. D. (1940). The measurement of individual differences in general English vocabularies. *Journal of Educational Psychology, 31,* 14–38.

Schatz, E.K., & Baldwin, R. S. (1986). Context clues are unreliable predictors of word meanings. *Reading Research Quarterly, 21,* 439–453.

Shibles, B. H. (1959). How many words does the first-grade child know? *Elementary English, 31,* 42–47.

Singer, H. (1965). A developmental model of speed of reading in grade 3 through 6. *Reading Research Quarterly, 1,* 29–49.

Slobin, D. I. (1966). Grammatical transformations and sentence comprehension in childhood and adulthood. *Journal of Verbal Learning and Verbal Behavior, 5,* 219–227.

Smith, M. E. (1926). An investigation of the development of the sentence and the extent of vocabulary in young children. *University of Iowa Studies in Child Welfare, 5,* 219–227.

Smith, M. K. (1941). Measurement of the size of general English vocabulary through the elementary grades and high school. *Genetic Psychological Monographs, 24,* 311–345.

Spearrit, D. (1972). Identification of subskills of reading comprehension by maximum likelihood factor analysis. *Reading Research Quarterly, 8,* 92–111.

Stahl, S. A., & Fairbanks, M. M. (1986). The effects of vocabulary instruction: A model-based meta-analysis. *Review of Educational Research, 56,* 72–110.

Sternberg, R. J. (1987). Most vocabulary is learned from context. In M. G. McKeown & M. E. Curtis (Eds.), *The nature of vocabulary acquisition* (pp. 89–105). Hillsdale, NJ: Erlbaum.

Sternberg, R. J., & Powell, J. S. (1983). Comprehending verbal comprehension. *American Psychologist, 38,* 878–893.

Templin, M. C. (1957). *Certain language skills in children.* Minneapolis: University of Minnesota Press.

Thorndike, E.L. (1917). Reading and reasoning. A study of mistakes in paragraph reading. *Journal of Educational Psychology, 8,* 323–332.

Thorndike, E. L. (1921). *The teacher's word book.* New York: Teachers College.

Thurstone, L. L. (1946). A note on a re-analysis of Davis' reading tests. *Psychometrika, 11,* 185–188.

Tuinman, J. J., & Brady, M. (1973, December). *How does vocabulary account for variance on reading comprehension tests?* Paper presented at the National Reading Conference, Houston.

van Daalen-Kapteijns, M. M., & Elshout-Mohr, M. (1981). The acquisition of word meaning as a cognitive learning process. *Journal of Verbal Learning and Verbal Behavior, 20,* 386–389.

Werner, H., & Kaplan, E. (1952). The acquisition of word meanings: A developmental study. *Monographs of the Society for Research in Child Development, 15* (Serial No. 51, No. 1).

Wixson, K. K. (1986). Vocabulary instruction and children's comprehension of basal stories. *Reading Research Quarterly, 21*(3), 317–329.

29 COMPREHENSION INSTRUCTION

P. David Pearson and Linda Fielding

In the fast-paced world of educational research, traditions rise and fall with incredible speed. Just a decade ago, there were no existing reviews of research about reading comprehension instruction. But today we can honestly introduce our review as yet another in a rich "tradition" of reviews of research about instruction intentionally designed to improve reading comprehension.

Where that tradition begins depends upon how one chooses to define reading comprehension and how one chooses to define instruction. Most would probably fix its start with the publication, in 1978, of Pearson and Johnson's book, *Teaching Reading Comprehension*. *Teaching Reading Comprehension* is allegedly a book about how to teach children to understand what they read; but a careful reading reveals that the only chapter that even comes close to what we have, in the last decade, come to regard as comprehension instruction is Chapter 9, "Interaction Strategies for Teaching Comprehension."

Others would fix the starting point of this tradition with the publication, in 1981, of the Santa and Hayes monograph for the International Reading Association, *Children's Prose Comprehension: Research and Practice*. Included are two chapters of particular relevance to our topic: a chapter by Levin and Pressley with the relevant title "Improving Children's Prose Comprehension: Selected Strategies That Seem to Succeed" and a chapter by Barrett and Johnson describing the kinds of comprehension skills presented within the leading basal series. This paper is important because it represents one of the earliest attempts in what is now a legitimate line of research in its own right: research about instructional materials (see Chall and Squire, Chapter 7 in this volume).

Still others would point to Durkin's 1978–1979 article in *Reading Research Quarterly* about the complete lack of reading comprehension instruction in middle-grade classrooms. Durkin's work revealed that there was nothing "instructive" about our instruction. Instead, instruction consisted primarily of giving students opportunities to demonstrate, by answering questions, completing workbook pages, or taking tests, whether they could perform the various comprehension tasks that form the basis of school reading curricula. Durkin found precious little in the way of teachers offering students any sort of advice about *how* to actually carry out any of the skills included in the curricula. Although others have questioned the severity of her criteria for determining what counts as instruction (Hodges, 1980; Heap, 1982), Durkin's paper, more than any other single book or article, motivated other researchers to design and carry out research about instruction that was instructive by her, or anyone else's, definition.

And some would take the view that it really all began with the revolution in the way scholars think about language and cognition (Anderson, 1977; Anderson & Pearson, 1984; Pearson, 1986). This is the revolution that took its toll on behavioral views of language and cognition (Chomsky, 1959) and spawned the fields of psycholinguistics, cognitive psychology, and cognitive science (see Gardner, 1985). And, in an important sense, this view is absolutely correct. Without changes in the basic paradigm through which cognition was viewed, it is doubtful that educational researchers would ever have had any reason to ask the questions about comprehension instruction that were asked in the late 1970s.

But whatever the starting point, it is clear that within the last decade we have experienced an explosion in research about comprehension instruction. Furthermore, that research has been reviewed on several occasions in just the last few years. Two questions naturally arise out of this situation. First, how does our review fit into that tradition? Second, what perspective does our review add that is not already captured by one of our ancestors? We begin with our answer to the first question; we will end this chapter with our answer to the second.

THE TRADITION

In trying to characterize the tradition of which our review is the latest entrant, we really begin our review of the instructional research per se. After all, we cannot discuss the reviews without discussing their content and structure. Also, there are now so many reviews that they almost constitute a viable category of scholarship in their own right.

While several earlier reviews might be called reviews of reading comprehension (e.g., Davis, 1944, 1968; Simons, 1971; Collins, Brown & Larkin, 1980), the 1981 Levin and Pressley chapter, as we indicated earlier, probably qualifies as the first complete review of the then-existing work on comprehension strategy instruction. They decomposed strategies according to when in the course of a reading lesson the strategy is to be invoked (before or after reading) and by whom (the teacher or the reader). Those strategies that are invoked before reading were labelled stage-setting strategies; those that are invoked during or after reading were labelled storage/retrieval strategies. The second dimension of their category scheme was also dichotomous: either the primary thrust of the intervention was prose dependent (it was something the text author, materials designer, or teacher did) or processor dependent (it was something the reader did or was asked to do). Examined with the hindsight of nearly a decade, their review is interesting in several respects. First, it is clear that Levin and Pressley approached their task from the then-dominant verbal-learning perspective within the field of educational psychology; this perspective is revealed both in their category structure and in the range of studies they chose to review. Second, many of the studies that they considered instructive would not meet Durkin's criterion that comprehension instruction include offering students advice about how to understand texts; in fact, most of the instructional studies completed through 1980 involved little more than students *responding* to stimuli or activities under the control of either the author or the teacher. Third, since it is less than a decade old, the review underscores just how *recent* the explosion in genuinely instructional research has been.

Chronologically, the next important reviews came out in 1983 and 1984. In their 1984 landmark chapter, which appeared in the first volume of this *Handbook*, Tierney and Cunningham assembled what is likely to remain the most exhaustive review of reading comprehension instruction ever attempted. The review is notable on a number of counts, but most important is the major distinction they made between research that examines ways to increase comprehension and learning from prose and that which examines ways to increase students' *ability* to comprehend and learn from prose. Within the section about increasing comprehension and learning, Tierney and Cunningham employed a before, during, and after reading breakdown reminiscent of the Levin and Pressley work in 1981. What is so different about the Tierney and Cunningham piece, however, is the range of research studies reportable in 1984 (in contrast to 1981);

furthermore, in the section on improving students' ability to comprehend on their own, nearly every one of the more than 20 entries were published too late to have been included in the Levin and Pressley review. The Tierney and Cunningham review is also noteworthy for raising some cautionary flags about this whole endeavor of instruction. Specifically, they were very concerned about the mechanistic character of much of the research, particularly the strategy instruction research, wondering whether the emphasis on the systematic and sequential had been achieved at the expense of the aesthetic aspects of reading.

In a 1983 issue of *Contemporary Educational Psychology*, two important reviews of reading comprehension instruction work appeared. In "The Instruction of Reading Comprehension," Pearson and Gallagher took a very different approach to reviewing research about reading comprehension instruction; they decomposed the relevant research into categories based upon methodological distinctions. *Existential descriptions*, they argued, are attempts to describe what is "out there" in schools and curricula, like Durkin's 1978–1979 study of what teachers do in the name of comprehension instruction or Johnson and Barrett's (1981) analysis of comprehension skills taught in basal readers. *Existential proofs*, in contrast, attempt to prove the existence of relationships among variables—for example, that good readers are more aware of the problems they encounter when reading than are poor readers (e.g., Paris & Myers, 1981) *or* that the background knowledge students bring to reading influences their comprehension (e.g., Anderson, Reynolds, Schallert, & Goetz, 1977; Pearson, Hansen, & Gordon, 1979). *Pedagogical experiments* are more like what Tierney and Cunningham classified as attempts to increase students' *ability* to comprehend and learn from prose; they represent the heart of reading comprehension instructional research (e.g., Hansen, 1981; Hansen & Pearson, 1983; Gordon & Pearson, 1983; Dewitz, Carr, & Patberg, 1987). Their last category, *program evaluations*, includes attempts to evaluate the influence of a variable when it becomes a part of a larger curriculum rather than the focus of a controlled experiment. Examples would include evaluations of the comprehension instruction in the Kamehameha Early Education Project (Tharp, 1982) and the Informed Strategy Learning (really metacognitive strategy training) project of Paris and his colleagues (Paris, Cross, & Lipson, 1984; Paris & Jacobs, 1984).

Pearson and Gallagher come out foresquare in favor of what they label a model of explicit instruction, in which teachers demonstrate to students how to carry out particular strategies, then engage them in guided practice, followed by independent practice. Finally, students apply the strategies on their own while *reading* regular texts. Pearson and Gallagher tried to summarize their preferred approach by adapting a visual model from Campione (1981) to create what has become a widely used conceptualization of instruction known as the *gradual release of responsibility* (see Figure 29.1).

The Paris, Lipson, and Wixson (1983) piece, "Becoming a Strategic Reader," is noteworthy for our present purposes on two counts. First, what they labelled as metacognitive instructional research is very similar to what others label as comprehension instruction research. Second, they introduced an important set of distinctions for instruction and instructional research: the triad of declarative, procedural, and conditional knowledge. It has proven to be very useful in helping researchers and instructional designers conceptualize their instructional strategies. Declarative knowledge is knowledge of *what*—for example, knowledge of what a summary is. Procedural knowledge is knowledge of *how*—for instance, a delineation of the specific steps one might go through to create a summary (see, e.g., Brown & Day, 1983). But it was the addition of conditional knowledge, knowledge of *why* and *when* (e.g., why and when it is useful to compose summaries), that truly set the Paris, Lipson, and Wixson review apart from predecessors.

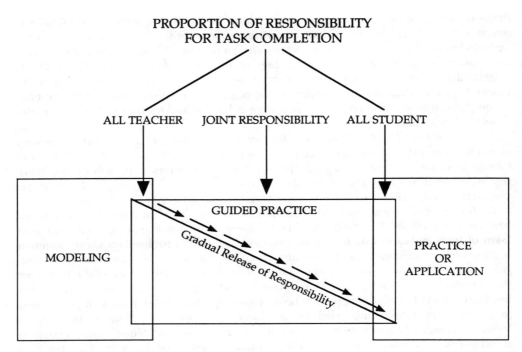

FIGURE 29.1   A model of explicit instruction (from Pearson & Gallagher, 1983).

About this same time, two "popular" reviews of comprehension instruction re-search appeared. In 1985 Pearson published "Changing the Face of Reading Compre-hension Instruction" in *The Reading Teacher*, a journal popular with many reading educators. In 1986, Gersten and Carnine published "Direct Instruction in Reading Comprehension" in *Educational Leadership*, a journal read by many administrators and curriculum specialists. The focus of both reviews was on how to use these exciting new research findings as a basis for curriculum change within schools. But they are notewor-thy because their publication implies that the research base in this domain had reached a new and significant plateau, a plateau at which generalizations about practice were acceptable to the community of school practitioners. Perhaps most noteworthy in this regard is the Commission on Reading's publication, in 1985, of *Becoming a Nation of Readers* (Anderson, Hiebert, Scott, & Wilkinson, 1985), a synthesis of the instructional implications from reading research; it may be the most widely read document about reading in recent history. Although the scope of the book extends to all aspects of read-ing instruction, the content emphasizes the central role of comprehension instruction.

Very recently, Pressley and his colleagues have produced several reviews of the strategy instruction literature, including reading comprehension strategies (Pressley, Johnson, Symons, McGoldrick, & Kurita, in press; Pressley, Goodchild, Fleet, Zajchowski, & Evans, 1989; Pressley, Symons, Snyder, & Cariglia-Bull, 1989; Lysynchuk, Presley, d'Ailly, Smith & Cake, 1989). They are convinced that we know enough to recommend to teachers that comprehension strategies can and should be taught using a direct explanation approach (Duffy et al., 1987) quite reminiscent of Pearson and Gallagher's (1983) explicit instructional model. In the Lysynchuk et al. piece, they evaluated the 40 major pieces of strategy instructional research for methodological adequacy according to criteria of both internal and external validity (Campbell &

Stanley, 1966). While these studies met most of the criteria fairly well, they were, as a group, woefully inadequate on certain criteria, such as random assignment, appropriate units of analysis, and provision for assessing transfer to new situations.

Pearson and Dole (1987), after reaching much the same conclusions as Pearson and Gallagher (1983) and Pressley and his colleagues about what models of instruction appear to be effective, pointed out possible shortcomings of the model they advocate. First, they noted that there is very little research evaluating the effectiveness of the explicit instruction model as a teacher education tool. Second, they raise some unresolved questions about the body of research upon which they and others have based their advocacy of the explicit instruction model. Most relevant to our present purposes, they wondered whether a simple strategy of focusing student attention on the structure of the information in the text at hand might not obviate the need for explicit content-free strategy instruction.

Our review fits this evolving tradition in several ways. First, we, like our predecessors, are careful to distinguish between attempts to improve students' comprehension of texts and attempts to improve students' ability to comprehend texts independently. Second, we will be illustrative rather than exhaustive in our attempt to characterize this domain of research; given our characterization of the last few years as frenetic in its pace, we could not possibly present an exhaustive review anyway. Third, we have focused primarily upon studies designed to determine methods of comprehension instruction that are associated with improvement on *some measure of comprehension*—a story retelling or text summary, a measure of text interpretation or response to literature, answers to comprehension questions, and so on. We have systematically and intentionally avoided descriptive "state-of-the-art" studies of what comprehension instruction looks like in classrooms and sociolinguistic studies of teacher-student interactions during comprehension instruction because they are not our primary focus here. We refer readers to several other chapters in this volume for such discussions: Chapter 33, Alvermann and Moore's discussion of secondary reading instruction; Chapter 26, Sulzby and Teale's discussion of emergent literacy; Chapter 30, Roehler and Duffy's analysis of classroom reading instruction; and Chapter 7, Chall and Squire's essay on instructional materials (including basal reader teachers' manuals).

We will differ from our predecessors in one important way: we have selected very different categories in which to "decompose" the domain. We have adopted a hybrid classification scheme. Our first goal is to characterize comprehension research in terms of the type of text to which it is addressed. Within those broad categories, we then have tried to characterize the particular text feature, set of text features, or strategy on which the instruction is focused.

One other procedural matter: We have made a concerted effort to review work not previously included in major "archival" reviews; hence our focus is clearly upon work completed in the last decade, especially in the last five years. For the most part, we have been successful, but occasionally a few "classics" have crept into our discussion. For work completed prior to 1983, the reader is urged to consult one of the reviews addressed in the "tradition" we have discussed.

IMPROVING TEXT COMPREHENSION

We leave the issue of whether the organizational features of different genres of text are, at some basic, primitive level of analysis, truly different from one another to other reviewers in this volume (see, for example, Chapter 10 by Weaver & Kintsch, and

Chapter 8 by Graesser, Golding, & Long in this volume). However, we will divide our review of research into separate categories for narrative and expository text. This division is more pragmatic than conceptual; those who have conducted the research have tended to regard their pet instructional strategies as peculiarly suited to either one or the other, but not both, genres.

Narratives, for us, are largely stories—pieces written to excite, enthrall, and entertain us as readers. In fact, our search for instructional research targeted on narrative text turned out to deal exclusively with stories. But, had we found research on biography, for example, we would have included it in the narrative section. Expository texts, for us, are written largely to inform—textbooks, essays, most magazine writing. (We acknowledge the complexity underlying this apparently simple dichotomy; it is seldom the case that discourse force—entertainment, information, persuasion, aesthetic—applies exclusively to a particular type of text structure. Novelists persuade and inform just as essayists sometimes entertain [see Brewer, 1980].)

For each text type, narrative and expository, we will examine the entire range of instructional research completed in the past several years, both studies in which the focus has been on improving students' comprehension of the texts in which the instruction is embedded (where the concern is for what we will call *local effects*); and studies in which the focus has been on improving comprehension of texts students will encounter on their own after the instruction has been completed (where the concern is for *transfer effects*). After reviewing the research specific to narrative and expository texts, we will turn our efforts to comprehension instruction studies that have attempted to help students acquire generic comprehension strategies that are, presumably, applicable to all texts (e.g., reciprocal teaching, inference training, and comprehension monitoring, or just reading).

Narrative Texts

Attempts to improve narrative text comprehension and to build strategies for reading narrative texts generally fall into two categories. Studies are designed to

a.   Build or activate background knowledge of story structure or the themes and topics important in a given narrative.
b.   Alter the kinds of questions children are asked or discussions that they have during and after reading.

These categories form the sequence for organizing our review of studies designed to improve narrative comprehension.

Interventions Designed to Build or Activate Background Knowledge

Perhaps no other phenomenon has influenced instructional research in the last decade as pervasively as our increased understanding of the powerful role of background knowledge in reading comprehension (e.g., Anderson, 1977; Anderson & Pearson, 1984). In fact, the general goal of a number of narrative instruction investigations was either to activate or build pertinent background knowledge or, in some cases, to teach children how to activate and use it themselves. For stories, the requisite background knowledge takes at least two forms: knowledge of the structure underlying typical stories; and knowledge about the topics, themes, and experiences that are important in understanding a given story.

Story structure knowledge.   Instructional studies designed to activate or build readers' knowledge of the structure of stories typically are grounded in story grammar research. *Story grammars* (e.g., Mandler, 1978; Mandler & Johnson, 1977; Stein & Glenn, 1979) are abstract linguistic representations of the ideas, events, and personal motivations that comprise the flow of narratives. The assumption behind the psychological research stemming from story grammars is that the abstract hierarchical structures that can be used to characterize stories linguistically represent structures that readers can use to encode and store information in long-term memory. The validity of story grammars as psychological models of comprehension and memory rests on findings that adults' and children's story retellings match the sequential structure set forth in story grammars and that the frequency with which given information is recalled is correlated with its hierarchical position in the story grammar (Mandler & Johnson, 1977; Rumelhart, 1975; Stein, 1978; Stein & Glenn, 1979; Thorndyke, 1977).

In the instructional interventions designed to build children's story schemata, children generally get instruction in a simplified version of story grammar categories (e.g., *setting, problem, goal, action, outcome*), and practice in identifying category-relevant information in stories (see Idol, 1987). Although Dreher and Singer argued in 1980 that story grammar instruction was unnecessary for the fifth-grade students in their study, a number of researchers since then have explored the conditions under which either instruction about story structures or story questions based on story structure are helpful to readers.

In a number of studies, comprehension improvement after instruction in story structures has been noted both beyond the specific stories used during instruction and in "natural" storybooks (or at least in unaltered basal reader stories) instead of specially constructed or altered stories (Gordon & Pearson, 1983; Greenewald & Rossing, 1986; Idol, 1987; Morrow, 1984b; Nolte & Singer, 1985). For Gordon and Pearson's (1983) fifth-grade students and Morrow's (1984b) kindergarten students, improvement was instruction specific: Groups whose instructional focus was on story structure performed better on measures sensitive to story structure knowledge, while groups whose instructional focus was on more traditional questions (Morrow, 1984b) or scriptal inference questions (Gordon & Pearson, 1983) performed better on those measures. In both cases, these specific effects of instruction extended to new, independently read stories. Comprehension improvement was more general in studies by Greenewald and Rossing (1986), Nolte and Singer (1985), and Singer and Donlan (1982). In each of these studies, story structure instruction was combined successfully with some other training oriented toward independence of use. Greenewald and Rossing's (1986) intermediate students also received training in monitoring their own understanding of story categories while reading. Nolte and Singer's (1985) intermediate students and Singer and Donlan's (1982) high school students learned to use general story structure knowledge to generate their own specific questions about stories. In all but Singer and Donlan's (1982) study, improvement extended to new, independently read stories. Singer and Donlan did not test for such transfer and, in fact, argued that transfer of sorts was evident, anyway, because their students were tested throughout the study on all story elements, although instruction focused on only one element per day.

Idol's (1987) study is notable in that learning-disabled and low-achieving readers participated in the same instructional groups with heterogeneously grouped intermediate students, showing and maintaining comprehension improvement as a result of story structure instruction, even though instructional and testing materials were a year or more above their measured instructional reading levels. Idol argued that these results were achieved by employing two key instructional features: the model → lead → -test teaching paradigm (similar to the direct instruction principles espoused by Gersten & Carnine, 1986), and "criterion" levels of performance to determine when instruction should cease.

Carnine and Kinder (1985), however, found no special effects of story structure instruction for intermediate-grade poor readers reading short basal reader stories. Students who were trained through modeling, fading, and corrective feedback to ask themselves four structure-based questions about a story's content performed no better on free recall and multiple-choice transfer measures than a "generative" group, who learned simply to "make a picture" of story events in their minds at selected intervals. Each group did improve in comprehension from the beginning to the end of the study and maintained improvement after the instruction ended. Carnine and Kinder interpreted these findings as support for both story structure and generative training. It should be noted, though, that there was no control group to use for comparison; thus both groups' improvement could be attributable to the fact that they retold the instructional stories and got corrective feedback on their retellings daily.

Story structure instructional studies focused on intermediate-grade poor readers (Buss, Ratliff, & Irion, 1985; Fitzgerald & Spiegel, 1983; Short & Ryan, 1984) have shown comprehension improvement maintained beyond the texts used for instruction. For Short and Ryan (1984), who combined story structure instruction and effort attribution training, trained poor readers were indistinguishable from untrained good readers on a posttest. It is disappointing, though, that all three of these studies of poor readers used specially constructed or shortened, adapted stories for most instructional and all testing materials. Whether improved comprehension would extend to unedited basal reader stories or, especially, to tradebook stories remains to be seen.

Knowledge of topics and themes.   Besides general knowledge about story structure, story comprehension can be influenced by one's knowledge about and experience with the specific topics and themes of a given story. "Building background knowledge" relevant to a story is a common feature of the instructional suggestions in basal reader teacher's manuals; however, critics like Beck, Omanson, and McKeown (1982) have demonstrated that it is not background knowledge in general but knowledge about important story ideas in particular that influences comprehension.

In story reading, one's own experiences can be used to generate expectations about upcoming story events. That, in fact, was the notion behind two studies by Hansen, in which second-grade average readers (Hansen, 1981) and fourth-grade good and poor readers (Hansen & Pearson, 1983) participated in prereading discussions designed to teach them to generate expectations about what the story characters might do based on their own experiences in similar situations. Along with a steady diet of inferential story questions, which required integration of background knowledge with text ideas, this technique led to improved comprehension for both young and poor readers on a variety of measures, including understanding new, uninstructed stories. Fourth-grade good readers' performance was not improved strongly; but the explanation for that could be that because of their instructional history or their ability to make generalizations, explicit instruction in making story inferences was not necessary. What is interesting in Hansen and Pearson's study is that trained poor readers' performance was indistinguishable from the performance of good readers who got more traditional basal instruction.

While Hansen's techniques for background knowledge activation had positive effects beyond the stories children actually read during instruction, other methods of attending to background knowledge have been evaluated only for their effects on the instructed stories. In two recent studies (Prince & Mancus, 1987; Thames & Readence, 1988), improvements over a traditionally instructed control group have resulted from the simple ploy of reorganizing the typical basal reader lesson so that what the teacher's edition calls *enrichment activities* were carried out before reading instead of after. The investigators argued that the enrichment activities function to help children build and integrate background knowledge and, thus, are more effective when done before reading.

Another, more elaborate incarnation of background knowledge building is a *story preview*, in which background knowledge of specific story events is built before reading via orally presented previews that stimulate student discussion, link story events to readers' experiences, and give a synopsis of events up to the climax. Graves, Cooke, and LaBerge (1983), already having noted the positive effects of such previews for middle-grade and high school students of a range of ability levels, found positive effects on a variety of comprehension and attitude measures when very poor junior high school readers heard previews. In an extension of the existing research, Neuman (1988) recently found, however, that story previews were helpful to fourth-grade readers only when orally presented by the teacher and accompanied by group discussion and prediction. Written, silently read previews were no more effective than traditional basal reader background-building lessons.

In two other studies, the emphasis was on using writing as a means of recalling one's own background knowledge and using it to anticipate story information. McGinley and Denner (1987), dissatisfied with the amount of specific story information given away in typical previews (they often are anywhere from 15 percent to 50 percent as long as the stories they accompany), tried instead developing a short list of key words or phrases representing a story's significant events and themes that students could connect together before reading by writing their own story. For students in a range of elementary and junior high grades, they found positive effects for the writing activity, especially for poor readers. It is not the accuracy of the match between students' stories and target stories that is related to students' improved story understanding, they argue, but instead cognitive engagement that comes from the act of using one's own background knowledge and experiences in writing one's own story and later comparing it to the author's story. Marino, Gould, and Haas (1985) also found that writing a story about a situation similar to the one in the upcoming story led to significantly better story recall, even though their students did not even know (when they were writing their own stories) that they later would be reading and recalling stories about similar events. In both of these studies, weak control groups compromise the educational significance of the results—control groups either did nothing or wrote about topics unrelated to the target stories before reading and recalling the target stories.

One other method of improving story comprehension does not fit neatly into our categories but can be explained with reference to the importance of background knowledge. Although traditionally viewed as a *measure* of comprehension, *story retelling* recently has been used by some investigators as a way to improve story comprehension (see Morrow et al., 1986, for a review). The rationale is that retelling helps children learn about typical story structure and gives them a tool for planning and organizing their own comprehension when they listen to or read stories. Morrow (1984a, 1985, 1986), for example, found that frequent practice in retelling, bolstered by adult feedback focused on story structure, improved kindergarten children's story comprehension, their understanding of story structure, and even their oral language complexity and ability to produce their own stories. Similar results have been found for intermediate-grade readers, even without as much adult feedback (e.g., Gambrell, Pfeiffer, & Wilson, 1985; Koskinen, Gambrell, Kapinus, & Heathington, 1988).

Changing Story Discussions

A decade ago, Durkin (1978–1979, 1981) asserted that story discussion questions in typical basal readers did more to assess than to enhance children's comprehension. Since then, a number of investigators have tried to design more facilitative teacher-posed story questions. In most of these studies, the notion is that teachers' questions shape the model of meaning children construct for what they read; questioned information is seen as more important and is remembered better. The goal, then, is to ensure that questions highlight the desired parts of the story, and the desired parts usually involve making inferences important to the coherence of the story.

Golden (1988) argues that in group story-reading situations, as important as the *literary* text itself is, the crucial text is the *instructional* text that is created by teacher and student as they discuss, amplify, and interweave ideas with the original text. In separate analyses of two first-grade teachers' oral reading and discussion of the same story, both Golden (1988) and Harker (1988) concluded that the teacher is a powerful influence in shaping students' text reconstructions. The teachers in the study talked nearly the same amount, elicited similar amounts of talk from their students, and were both sensitive to the story's episodic structure in planning breaks for discussion. One teacher, however, had twice as much story-related discussion as the other. That teacher structured her discussion to move from general book features (title, author, and so on) to discussion of story content and theme, while the other teacher focused on the animals in the story and students' experiences. While both teachers asked questions that went beyond literally stated story information, there were differences in these questions as well. The teacher who focused on the story asked more complex story-related questions and provided assistance in the form of prompts, when necessary, to help students form answers. The teacher who focused on the animals asked more expansion questions, questions that emphasized self-expression and application of story ideas to one's own experiences. While the two groups of students recalled nearly equal amounts about the first part of the story (the part about the animals), the students whose teacher focused on the story itself recalled almost three times more of the theme-related events in the second part of the story.

Focus on inferential questions.   Recently, *inference questions* have achieved a special status in story discussions. Two reasons are commonly cited for studying the incidence of inference questions: (1) inference questions represent a kind of thinking about stories that is less familiar to school children because they have few opportunities to respond to them, and (2) because they involve more thorough processing of the text and integration of text ideas with background knowledge, they may enhance story understanding. In her first study, Hansen (1981) found that for many of her comprehension measures, simply asking more inference questions was nearly as effective as teaching students how to make inferences by connecting their background experiences to their reading. Sundbye (1987) found that asking inference questions about relationships between characters, their goals, and their actions enhanced third-grade children's story comprehension as much as modifying the stories so that these relationships were stated explicitly in the text. It is important to note, though, that in both of her experimental conditions, instructional overkill was possible. For example, in the inference question condition, somewhere around 50 inference questions were asked per story!

Prediction questions, a special case of inference questions in which readers are encouraged to predict upcoming story events using prior text, personal experiences, and story structure knowledge, have proven to be effective components of story-reading lessons (e.g., Hansen, 1981; Hansen & Pearson, 1983). Anderson, Wilkinson, Mason, and Shirey (1987) found that they enhanced story memory and interest over word-level questions. In a more stringent test of the effects of prediction questions, Fielding, Anderson, & Pearson (1990) found that they were more effective than typical basal reader questions as long as predictions were compared with text ideas upon further reading. In a study designed to teach third-grade students a variety of metacomprehension activities, Schmitt (1988) found that prediction was the most frequently reported behavior of experimental children, who outperformed control children on an independently read story after the instructional sessions had ended.

Focus on important ideas.   Taking a different approach, Beck and her associates (Beck, Omanson, & McKeown, 1982; Omanson, Beck, Voss, & McKeown, 1984) demonstrated that the centrality of *story ideas* provides an effective basis for deciding which ideas to target with questions. Almost from their inception, one of the criticisms of story grammars was that while readers do seem to use some representational scheme to guide the encoding of story information, this representational system may be described more accurately as a text-based, not a schema-based, chain of causal networks of events and their relations. Various researchers have demonstrated that although story grammars have some validity, recall data is better explained by the centrality of a story proposition to the story's central event sequence or by its inclusion in a causal chain of events rather than by its membership in a certain story grammar category. Beck et al. (1982) made a number of revisions in basal reader story lessons based on flaws they had noted in the lessons suggested in teacher's manuals. One of these involved changing the inserted postreading questions such that they focused on information that was part of the story's central event sequence according to Omanson's (1982) narrative analysis. Third-grade students instructed individually with the revised lessons performed better on free recall of the instructed stories than students instructed with the original basal lessons. Follow-up analyses indicated that the revised questions were one of two revisions that exerted the most influence on comprehension (Omanson et al., 1984).

The work of Beck and her associates represents the traditional notion that before broader story ideas and themes can be explored, readers must have an understanding of important explicit story information and simple relationships among explicitly stated story ideas. Au and Kawakami (1984) have noted, however, that in successful lessons with high-risk Hawaiian children, teachers regularly use high-level questions effectively by regarding them as general probes or problems to be followed up with a subsequent set of simpler questions that lead back to an answer to the more difficult question. Shake (1988) observed remedial reading tutors using a similar technique, and she argued that this "slicing" (Pearson & Johnson, 1978) of difficult questions served an instructional function through which poor readers could learn to integrate information in order to answer such questions.

Focus on constructing an interpretation.   Much of the research about story comprehension discussed so far either glosses over or ignores the very real possibility of multiple interpretations of the same text—a possibility that becomes increasingly likely when students read full-length, unedited pieces of fiction instead of edited stories or those written for special experimental purposes. There is some belief that teachers' questions, even when one single answer is not designated as the "correct" one, could serve to reveal and sanction the teacher's theory of what the story is about and thus could constrain children's thinking as much as expand it (e.g., Dillon, 1982, 1983; Weber, 1986). Studies by Golden (1986) and Rogers (1988) point to the importance of avoiding the constraints of teacher questions. Golden (1986), in fact, described short story discussions among eighth-grade students and their teacher as "social construction" of the text. While each reader came to the discussion with his or her own interpretation based upon a private reading, the discussion led to the construction of a group text. Students confirmed, modified, or abandoned their original interpretations about plot, character, narrator, and reader in the text through hearing others' viewpoints, referring to other texts and others' experiences, and using the original text as a reference point for clarifying confusions.

Rogers (1988) explored how the nature and content of high school students' short story discussions influenced their theory of interpretation. Products of a New Criticism-based mode of discussion in which the teacher served as interpretive authority, the high-ability students in her study originally interpreted undiscussed stories analytically, with a focus on textual information—structure and characters. After repeated opportunities to engage in discussions that emphasized using multiple sources of data for text interpretation (other texts, author information, personal experiences and reactions, and other students' and critics' interpretations), the students came to use these other sources more in forming their own independent interpretations and to value more highly the interpretations of critics who made use of multiple data sources.

Summary

Overall, two themes run through the majority of research in improving children's narrative comprehension. One is the powerful role of background knowledge, which is at the heart of interventions designed to sensitize children to story structure, to activate or build their knowledge and experiences related to story themes and topics, and to increase their opportunities to think inferentially. The other recurrent theme has to do with deciding which story ideas to focus on instructionally. The majority of research suggests that the ideas that are identified as important in a story grammar or central story content analysis, especially if they are implied but not stated, should receive instructional focus. As our review shows, we think it is important to consider the likelihood of several kinds of transfer in evaluating this research about narrative comprehension. One kind is transfer of improved comprehension to independently read stories; another is transfer from improved comprehension of highly structured stories adapted especially for the research to improved comprehension of school materials and "real" children's literature. Such demonstrations of transfer are crucial because, as has been pointed out many times, real stories frequently do not conform to the sequence suggested by a story grammar or do not state explicitly certain important information, such as character motives (e.g., Bruce, 1984; Bruce & Newman, 1978). As the use of real short stories and full-length novels becomes more widespread in reading instruction, we also think it will be important for investigators to ask whether the same instructional interventions that have worked so far will continue to hold up (e.g., Walmsley & Walp, 1990). Finally, we want to point out that investigators have become remarkably sophisticated at designing comprehension measures that are sensitive to their interventions. While this is as it should be, it is always important to remember that if the criteria for "success" were to be expanded or changed, our picture of effective story comprehension instruction might change, too. What if, for example, increased individual text interpretation among students, or increased voluntary choice of fiction reading, were considered as important as ability to recall a story or answer someone else's questions about it?

Expository Texts

Our review of instructional research designed to improve the comprehension of expository text is divided into two major sections: Attempts to teach students how to use the *structure* of the text to improve comprehension of, and memory for, the ideas presented in the text, and attempts to teach students how to *summarize* text.

Text Structure Instruction

In one sense, research about expository text structure instruction is as old as research about study skills because all of the work on the effects of underlining, outlining, note-taking, or summary instruction is an attempt to sensitize students to the usefulness of focusing on, representing, or rerepresenting the author's arguments as an aid to comprehending, learning, and remembering information (see Anderson & Armbruster, 1984, for a summary of the classic studying research). In another sense, the research is very young, covering just over a decade and following close on the heels of the extensive work on the recent cognitive and linguistic schemes for analyzing text structure (see Meyer & Rice, 1984; Weaver & Kintsch, Chapter 10 in this volume).

Summaries of the traditional studying research (Anderson & Armbruster, 1984; Goetz, 1984) suggest that studying techniques that foster attention to text structure facilitate comprehension, learning, and remembering in direct proportion to the similarity between the training task and the outcome measure (usually a transfer task of some sort). In other words, if the outcome measure is some sort of diffuse comprehension task (e.g., answering detailed multiple-choice questions or short-answer tasks), then attempts to focus on text organization have little advantage (sometimes a disadvantage) over simple rereading or skimming. By contrast, if the outcome measure requires readers, for example, to summarize a new text, to build a schematic representation of a text, or to rate the importance of ideas related to the text, then these attempts have a distinct (but task-specific) advantage over vague strategies such as rereading (see Anderson & Armbruster, 1984, for a complete development of this argument).

As indicated earlier, most of the work on text structure instruction has been conducted since the advent of text analysis schemes, such as those developed by Meyer (1975) and Kintsch and van Dijk (1978). Undoubtedly the search for direct instructional strategies for teaching text structure as an aid to comprehension was fueled by two consistently encouraging findings. First, students who are knowledgeable about and/or follow the author's structure in their attempts to recall a text remember more than those who do not (Bartlett, 1978; McGee, 1982; Meyer, 1979; Meyer, Brandt, & Bluth, 1980; Richgels, McGee, Lomax, & Sheard, 1987). Second, more good than poor readers follow the author's structure in their attempts to recall a text (Taylor, 1980). Attempts to teach text structure have included hierarchical summaries (Taylor, 1982; Taylor & Beach, 1984) and visual representations, such as conceptual maps, visual organizers, and networks (Armbruster & Anderson, 1980; Armbruster, Anderson, & Ostertag, 1987; Holley & Dansereau, 1984a; Gallagher & Pearson, 1989; Geva, 1983; Long, Hein, & Coggiola, 1978), as well as very general and diffuse attempts to sensitize students to text structure (e.g., Davis, Lange, & Samuels, 1988; Bartlett, 1978; Slater, Graves, & Piche, 1985).

Hierarchical summaries. Taylor and her colleagues (Taylor, 1982; Taylor & Beach, 1984; Taylor & Berkowitz, 1980) have examined the usefulness of engaging middle-grade students in the process of building hierarchical summaries of textbook material. In the hierarchical summary training, teachers use a model → guided practice → independent practice procedure to show students how to turn the headings, sub-headings, and paragraph topics of textbook prose into verbal summaries. In the modeling phase, teachers show students how they apply the strategy to a text segment, thinking out loud the entire time in order to share their on-line problem-solving strategies. In the guided practice phase, teachers and students work together, sharing think-aloud opportunities as well as completed summaries with one another. Finally, in independent practice students work on their own to complete their summaries.

In all of the work completed to date (Taylor, 1982; Taylor & Beach, 1984; Taylor & Berkowitz, 1980), Taylor has found that hierarchical summarization training helps students to recall text information better than do other studying strategies, such as answering questions or additional study. Additionally, the technique transfers to unin-structed texts on the same, but not on different, topics (Taylor & Beach, 1984).

Visual representations. It is difficult to fix an exact starting date for the begin-nings of the instructional tradition of trying to improve students' comprehension of text by getting them either to study or create visual representations of key ideas in text. On the one hand, visual displays have been a part of textbooks for as long as we have had the technology available to use nontext information in books. On the other hand, the research evaluating the usefulness of *re*representing textual information in a visual format is fairly recent (see Moore & Readance, 1980 or 1984, for reviews of research on graphic organizers; see Holley & Dansereau, 1984c, for a complete volume devoted to this matter). Perhaps it is no surprise that the instructional work on visual organizers began in earnest fairly soon after several attempts to represent basic knowledge struc-tures (e.g., Collins & Quillian, 1969; Lindsay & Norman, 1977) and text structures (e.g., Kintsch & van Dijk, 1978; Meyer, 1975; Thorndyke, 1977) diagrammatically. Not surprising either is the fact that these sorts of conceptualizations of human knowledge or text structure are often used in setting up computer simulations of cognitive processes (e.g., Fijda, 1972; Minsky, 1975; Schank, 1972; Schank & Abelson, 1977).

Within the recent iteration of this sort of research, the earliest tradition we have been able to document is *networking* by Dansereau and his colleagues (see Holley & Dansereau, 1984b, for a complete summary) and Long and Aldersley (1984). Beginning in the middle 1970s, the group at Texas Christian University (Holley, Dansereau, and a host of students) began to teach groups of college students enrolled in a variety of courses (psychology, educational psychology, learning strategies, nursing and statistics, to name a few) to use networking as a way of representing visually the important ideas in the texts assigned in their courses. The key to networking is teaching students to represent text using a set of six links (relationships) between ideas; these links fall into three basic structures. There are two hierarchical linking structures (*Part*—A is a *part* of B; and *Type*—A is an *example of* B), one chain structure (usually a *causal* or an *enabling* relationship—A *leads to* B), and three cluster structures (*Analogy*—A *is like* B; *Characteristic*—A has B as a feature; and *Evidence*—A provides *evidence* or *support for* B).

Using a combination of clear cases (completed examples of well-done network representations), real-time modeling by the teacher of the steps required to complete a network, and interactive peer modeling (pairs of students work together, serving in either the networker or the critic role), teachers attempt to bring students to the point at which they can complete networks on their own.

In comparison to control groups in which students engage in whatever study, reading, and strategies they wish, the results have been quite positive for the networking training on a variety of outcome measures: recall, essay tests, short-answer main idea and detail questions, concept cloze tests, and multiple-choice measures. Perhaps the most interesting application of networking has been Long and Aldersley's work (1984) with hearing-impaired students. Of particular interest, of course, with deaf students is the expectation that they will respond better to visually than verbally organized information. Consistent with the focus on relationships, the most robust effects favoring networking have been found for main idea rather than detail-focused tasks. Also, with some exceptions, the task has proved to be more successful for lower-than higher-ability readers, indicating, perhaps, that good readers voluntarily adopt some of the strategies that occur to poor readers only with painstaking instructional care. While Long and Aldersley have been able to demonstrate substantial pretest to posttest comprehension improvement as a function of using networking, they have not illustrated its effects in comparison to competing strategies.

The advantage of networking for low-achieving and exceptional college students is consistent with Geva's (1983) research evaluating a related strategy that she calls flowcharting. *Flowcharting*, like networking, focuses upon relationships between specific, but important, ideas in the text. Links between ideas include topic, elaboration, cause-effect, process, example, and so on. On both local measures (recall of ideas in the texts that were flowcharted) and broad transfer measures (the Nelson-Denny standardized reading test), Geva found aptitude-treatment interactions favoring the use of the flowcharting treatment only for the lowest-ability students. Geva, like others, has raised the possibility that high-ability students are capable of developing their own strategies, whereas low-ability students require more instructional assistance. One other noteworthy aspect of Geva's work is that she was able to establish a link between improved outcome performance and more precise use of the flowcharting technique, indicating that strategy use was implicated in the improvement.

Vaughan's *Con Struct* (Concept Structuring) procedure is thematically related to networking and flowcharting, but it differs in two important ways (Vaughan, 1984): (1) it makes no assumptions about any minimal levels of prior knowledge needed by students, and (2) it makes no attempt to teach specific relationships among ideas. Instead, the reader engages in stages of reading and rereading in an attempt to build some sort of graphic overview of the text, each time adding more detail to the visual summary. In the three studies completed to date, students (including medical students as well as eighth- and tenth-grade students) who have been trained to use the Con Struct procedure have outperformed conventionally instructed (read, answer questions, and discuss) control students on transfer tasks in which students read new, topically related texts and responded to test questions designed to tap their comprehension of ideas that exist at different conceptual levels (superordinate, subordinate, and specific) in the texts. In all of the studies, Con Struct students performed better than control students on overall comprehension on both immediate and delayed posttests. The locus of the Con Struct effect appears to be on the top two conceptual levels, with no differences between groups on learning specific information.

Armbruster and her colleagues at Illinois (Armbruster & Anderson, 1980; Armbruster & Anderson, 1985; Armbruster, Anderson, & Ostertag, 1987; Armbruster, Anderson, & Meyer, in press) have completed several studies evaluating the efficacy of their mapping and conceptual frames approach to dealing with text organization. While their earlier work on *mapping* (Armbruster & Anderson, 1980) focused upon microstructural relations and was quite reminiscent of networking, their recent work on *conceptual frames* has focused upon repetitive macrostructures, such as problem-solution, description, and conflict frames. The logic of their effort is that content area textbooks tend to present information within these recurring top-level organization patterns. So, for example, in history texts there are many conflict frames representing situations in which two groups have competing goals and engage in competing actions that result in a common outcome (usually with one winner and one loser or else some sort of compromise). By instructing students in ways of recognizing opportunities to use frames and methods of constructing them, they reason that students will learn and remember information better. Armbruster and Anderson have identified several recurring frames—among them description, action, problem-solution, explanation, system, and the like—but the major research efforts have been limited to only the problem-solution frame.

In their initial study (Armbruster, Anderson, & Ostertag, 1987), they used a model → guided practice → feedback → independent practice instructional framework to present the frame instruction to fifth-grade students over an 11-day period. The framing group was compared to a control group in which students discussed and answered questions on the same material in which the framing instruction had been embedded. Differences favoring the framing group were found on two of three transfer measures; the framing students wrote superior essays and summaries, but they performed no better than the control group on short-answer questions. In a recent follow-up to the initial study, Armbruster, Anderson, and Meyer (in press) have extended the framing instruction over a longer stretch of time and content (several chapters in the social studies text) with students and teachers in grades four and five. Compared to students whose teachers simply followed the teachers' manual, students in the framing group achieved higher scores on criterion tests of information gained during the reading/studying activities. The locus of the training group difference, however, was in the fifth-grade classrooms; fourth-grade students in the framing group were indistinguishable from those in the teachers' manual group. Armbruster and her colleagues attributed the grade by treatment interaction to the structural differences in the content of the two social studies texts; in the fourth-grade text the various chapters were fairly straightforward descriptions of regions, while the content of the fifth-grade text was American history, a topic much more complex and subtle and, hence, more likely to be enhanced by some sort of visual rerepresentation of ideas.

In the final category of visual representation studies, we find a potpourri of efforts, none of which seem to fit neatly into any of our other categories. For example, Bean, Singer, Sorter, and Frazee (1986), working with high-ability tenth-grade history students, found that instruction on the use of *graphic organizers* (their graphic organizers appear to be something in between Armbruster's frames and Geva's flowcharting), when it followed a unit on summarization training, produced results consistently superior to solo versions of either graphic organizer instruction or outlining on both multiple-choice tests of the content in which the instruction was embedded and written recalls of difficult transfer passages. Draheim (1984), working with college freshmen, found that a combination of a *directed reading-thinking* lesson and *conceptual mapping* (similar to Vaughn's ConStruct) helped students write better essays when the criterion was the number of main ideas from the article included in their essays; there was no effect for the number of subordinate ideas, permitting the inference that the instruction had an impact only on students' comprehension of top-level text structures. Darch, Carnine, and Kameenui (1986) contrasted graphic organizer instruction with directed reading-thinking instruction and study strategy training in two different social settings (cooperative learning versus individualized learning). They found an instructional strategy by social setting interaction, indicating a special advantage for graphic organizer instruction in the cooperative learning setting.

Additionally, several studies have examined the effects of using visual organization devices such as semantic mapping, cognitive webbing, and semantic feature analysis (see Johnson & Pearson, 1984) as pre- and/or postreading conceptual organizers. Closely related to vocabulary instruction research (see Beck and McKeown, Chapter 28 in this volume), these studies (e.g., Anders, Bos, & Filip, 1984; Carr & Masur-Stewart, 1988; Johnson, Toms-Bronowski, & Pittelman, 1982; Levin et al., 1984) have consistently shown an advantage for such conceptual/vocabulary organizational schemes on measures of text-specific comprehension—for example, answers to text-based questions, recall of text ideas, or the inclusion of key concepts in free recall.

Of special interest because of their more extensive treatment periods, application to naturally occurring texts, and concern for both local and transfer effects are studies by Berkowitz (1986) and Gallagher and Pearson (1989). Berkowitz trained classroom teachers to teach sixth-grade students to apply one of four study procedures (constructing a semantic map of key concepts, studying a semantic map prepared by someone else, answering text-based questions, and just rereading) to passages taken from a social studies textbook. After 12 weeks (one 45-minute session per week) of instruction, all students read three new texts, recalled them, and wrote short answers to questions. On two of the three short-answer tests and on two of the three main-idea recall measures, map construction emerged as the most effective strategy, although the question-answering group often proved superior to the map study and rereading groups. Only when the analysis was limited to those students who, in the course of instruction, exhibited *mastery* of the study strategy to which they were assigned did the map construction group exhibit a clear advantage over the question-answering group. These results, coupled with occasional advantages of the question-answering group over the map study group, led Berkowitz to adopt an *active comprehension* (Doctorow, Wittrock, & Marks, 1978) explanation of the data. Active comprehension, she argued, leads to greater depth of processing (Craik & Lockhart, 1972) and, hence, better encoding and retrieval performance.

In a series of studies, Gallagher and Pearson (1989) compared lessons organized around text-based questions to lessons organized around incomplete visual displays as alternative means for guiding discussions of science material (a booklet on insect societies) for fourth-grade students. The question group engaged in what was dubbed *discrete instruction*—finding and discussing the answer to a question after each discrete section of text was read. The visual display group engaged in what was labelled *integrative instruction* because the visual displays (much akin to Armbruster's frames) served as a framework for discussing the interrelationships among ideas presented in both smaller units (paragraphs and sections) and larger units (from one chapter to another) of the material. A control group simply read the material and answered a range of questions—text based, inferential, and applications of ideas presented in the text. After three weeks of instruction, students responded to a range of local measures (knowledge acquisition), near and far transfer measures (free recalls of independently read passages that were closely related, moderately related, and unrelated to the insect society topic), and process measures (text search strategies, sensitivity to text organization, and the like). The integrative group outperformed the other two groups consistently and dramatically. As the type of measure deviated from the instructional passages, the effect sizes decreased consistently; however, the effects were statistically reliable even for the unrelated passages, with effect sizes ranging from .75 to 3.15 standard deviation units.

Other attempts to teach text structure. No matter how rich the category structure one uses to describe a domain, a few important pieces of work seem not to fit the structure. A handful of text structure instruction studies do not fit our scheme, mainly because neither summarization nor visual portrayal of information appeared central to the instruction provided. In all of them, there is a decided attempt to teach students something about the nature of abstract text structures and how they can be used to organize text information while reading or studying. In the earliest, Bartlett (1978) taught ninth-grade students how to identify and use four top-level structures (e.g., cause-effect, problem-solution, and the like) to organize their reading and studying of text; he found that the instruction benefitted their ability to identify novel instances of text organized in each of the structures as well as the amount of text-related information they were able to recall. Slater, Graves, and Piche (1985), in a more experimentally robust modification of the Bartlett study (also with ninth-grade students), found that if the general structural organizer information was supported with an outline-like study guide (lists with blanks to fill in), both comprehension and recall were facilitated; however, the structural organizer instruction by itself was no more effective (in some cases, less effective) than simply taking notes while reading. Barnett (1984), working with college students, found that providing students with top-level information about structure before reading elicited superior delayed recall and better recognition of both verbatim and paraphrased text-based idea units when compared to similar instruction provided after reading or to a read-only control group. In two studies, one with English-speaking college students reading a scientific article in English (Samuels et al., 1987) and one with English-speaking students reading a scientific article in French (Davis, Lange, & Samuels, 1988), Samuels and his colleagues found strong local effects for text structure instruction. In both studies instruction was factorially crossed with text order (normal versus scrambled); interestingly, with English texts, the instruction was equally facilitative for both normal and scrambled texts while with French texts, the instruction was facilitative only for the normal texts. This difference between the two studies suggests that there may be a threshold level of linguistic functioning below which instruction fails to make any appreciable difference.

An approach by Carnine and Kinder (1985) actually might have as much to do with instruction about general knowledge structures as instruction about text structures in particular. Having noted that many science passages center on a rule that explains why a phenomenon occurs as it does, they developed a procedure for reading science texts that focused on understanding and applying the cause-effect principle that was explained in the text (e.g., that water and air move from a place of high pressure to a place of low pressure). In the same study (reviewed earlier, see p. 822) in which they taught low-performing middle-grade students a comprehension strategy based on narrative structure, they taught the students this strategy for understanding science texts. As in the narrative portion of the study, Carnine and Kinder compared this structure-based instruction to generative instruction, in which teachers simply encouraged children to make a picture of text events in their minds at selected junctures. For the most part, results were the same for the expository as for the narrative strategies—both the structure and the generative groups improved in comprehension from the beginning to the end of the study, but neither strategy emerged as more effective overall. However, students who learned the expository text-reading strategy did outperform the generative instruction group on the maintenance test after the completion of the study.

Summary.   In general, we have found incredibly positive support for just about any approach to text structure instruction for expository text. It appears that any sort of systematic attention to clues that reveal how authors attempt to relate ideas to one another or any sort of systematic attempt to impose structure upon a text, especially in some sort of visual rerepresentation of the relationships among key ideas, facilitates comprehension as well as both short-term and long-term memory for the text.

Summarizing

The early history of research about summarizing stands in stark contrast to more recent work. Prior to 1980, it is difficult, if not impossible, to locate studies finding a comparative advantage for summarization over simple rereading on measures of either comprehension or recall (e.g., Arnold, 1942; Germane, 1921a, 1921b; Howe & Singer, 1975; Stordahl & Christensen, 1956). Anderson and Armbruster (1984) explained this anomalous finding by pointing out that most of the outcome measures in these early studies consisted of low-level multiple-choice tests of textual information, hardly the type of information that is likely to be encoded during summary writing.

The more recent work in summarization training is consistently positive, variously demonstrating improved comprehension for texts in which the summarization training is embedded (McNeil & Donant, 1982), transfer to summarizing new texts (Bean & Steenwyk, 1984; Day, 1980; McNeil & Donant, 1982), increased summarizing efficiency (Hare & Borchardt, 1984), increased recall (Doctorow et al., 1978; Linden & Wittrock, 1981; Rinehart, Stahl, & Erickson, 1986), and even improved standardized test scores (Bean & Steenwyk, 1984).

Direct summary instruction. There are several dimensions distinguishing the earlier (and ineffective) work from the more recent (and effective) work. Day's (1980) study is a good starting point. Day and her colleagues (Brown & Day, 1983; Brown, Day, & Jones, 1983) had observed that summarizing does not come easily at any age, especially at younger ages. However, they did find a natural progression of rule application across age levels. They identified five basic rules (Brown & Day, 1983) corresponding roughly to van Dijk and Kintsch's (1978) macrorules—basic operations for comprehending and remembering prose. The first rule is to delete trivial or irrelevant information, which even fourth- or fifth-grade students do fairly well. The second is to delete redundant information, a more challenging venture. The third is to provide a *superordinate term* for members of a category (e.g., substitute animals for dogs, cats, and cows). The last two relate to main ideas. Rule four is to *find and use any main ideas* you can; rule five is to *create your own* when the author has not provided one. Examined developmentally, Brown and Day's (1983) results indicate that even fifth-grade students used the deletion rules, but were not at all adept at the others. By grade seven, the substitution and selection rules are under student control, but even college students use the invention rule in only about half of the appropriate situations.

Working with low-achieving community college students, Day (1980) embedded instruction for these five rules in a self-monitoring instructional milieu designed to promote students' independent monitoring of their own rule use. Over several sessions, summary-writing ability improved dramatically; Day did not test for effects on recall or comprehension. Day's work is important for three reasons: First, the rules that she adapted have been used, in modified form, in a number of other studies. Second, her instructional strategies included specific attention to self-regulatory activities; metacognitive concerns were uppermost in her work. Third, the instruction worked well; students who were offered systematic instruction along with metacognitive monitoring routines learned how to summarize texts remarkably well.

Day's work was quickly followed by a host of attempts to teach students how to summarize texts. McNeil and Donant (1982) used a set of summarization rules similarly adapted from van Dijk and Kintsch's work with grade-five students. The training group received instruction on how to apply the rules to simple (grade-three) passages. One control group got the rules on a card but no guidance from the teacher; the other control group simply read the passages. Effects were found favoring the training group on both a summary-writing activity for a new passage and a comprehension test for that passage. Using an intuitive ("do whatever seems right") discovery approach, Cunningham (1982) trained fourth-grade students to apply his "getting the GIST" procedure. In GIST students receive continuing feedback about the appropriateness of the very short (15-word) summaries they compose for short passages. In comparison to a placebo control that practiced word-level tasks, GIST students wrote markedly superior summaries after nine short training sessions. Working with sixth graders, Bean and Steenwyk (1984) compared the rule-governed approach of McNeil and Donant with the intuitive procedure of Cunningham and a group advised to focus on main ideas. After twelve 30-minute sessions spread out over five weeks, either approach proved markedly superior to the control group on a task requiring them to summarize a short paragraph and on a standardized test of reading comprehension.

Working with high-aptitude, low-income urban students, Hare and Borchardt (1984) taught them to apply Day's (1980) rules and self-monitoring procedures. Using a pre-post design, they found no appreciable differences in the quality of students' summaries; however, they did find a dramatic increase in summary-generating efficiency.

Rinehart, Stahl, and Erickson (1986) taught sixth-grade students to apply three of Day's rules (the selection rule and the two deletion rules) and one general "relate main ideas to supporting details" rule derived from Taylor's work (1982; Taylor & Beach, 1984). They found strong effects favoring the summarizing group over a "business-as-usual" basal control group on recall of major, but not minor, information from the transfer paragraphs for which students were asked to prepare summaries. The unique contribution of the Rinehart et al. work was that they tried to pinpoint the locus of the summary facilitation effect by including processing measures (preparation time and quality of notes prepared during reading) in their design. Since the quality-of-notes measure was more strongly related to recall of major information, they concluded that the summarization effect stems from the fact that trained students focus attention on important information.

Indirect summarization instruction.   One could mount a convincing argument that all of the instruction reviewed thus far in the expository text section is, at heart, instruction in summarization. After all, what is an abstract account of the structure of a text, whether it exists in verbal or visual form, but a summary of that text? This argument is especially applicable to the work of Taylor and her colleagues on hierarchical summaries instruction reviewed earlier (Taylor, 1982; Taylor & Beach, 1984; Taylor & Berkowitz, 1980); in fact, the whole set of studies could have been included just as well within the summary section of this review as in the text structure section. That this line of work could be so easily moved emphasizes our basic point: representations of text structure can be viewed as just another form of summarization.

There have been a few related studies focused on main idea instruction rather than summary instruction; in effect, these studies involve teaching Day's selection and invention rules. Baumann (1984) compared sixth-grade students who were directly taught a strategy for how to find and/or create main ideas with a basal control group, which focused upon practicing main-idea worksheets, and a placebo control, which completed vocabulary activities. While there were no group differences on transfer measures of free recall, there were significant differences favoring the strategy group over the other groups on both *near-transfer* (finding-the-main-idea) tasks and *far-transfer* (outlining) *tasks*; additionally the basal approach was superior to the placebo control on the near-transfer tasks. Schunk and Rice (1987) added an interesting twist to their main-idea strategy instruction, embedding it within a systematic examination of the importance of teachers' social/metacognitive interactions with students. They wanted to know whether remedial readers' strategy acquisition and application would be influenced by teachers' comments about the usefulness of the specific strategy being learned (specific value), the usefulness of strategies like this one (general value), or feedback about the general effectiveness of the strategy. What they found, consistent with Brown's conclusions about the importance of self-regulation and monitoring (Baker & Brown, 1984; Brown & Day, 1983), was that the more information and the more specific the information students received about the value of the strategy, the better they were able to perform on posttests measuring strategy application.

One final indirect application of summary instruction occurs within Palincsar and Brown's (1984; Palincsar, Brown, & Martin, 1987) reciprocal teaching approach to improving text comprehension (cf. p. 841). In *reciprocal teaching*, students work in a cooperative learning milieu to learn how to apply four strategies consistently to text segments they read. The four strategies are summarizing, asking important questions, clarifying unclear segments, and predicting what will be discussed next. In a set of studies completed with students ranging in age from 5 to 15 and in ability from low to high (see Palincsar, Brown, & Martin, 1987), this combined strategy has exhibited consistently robust and positive effects, both on local and broad transfer measures. Since at least two of the strategies, summarizing and generating questions about important ideas, focus directly on summarizing-like behaviors, the research provides yet more indirect support for summarizing as a broad-based comprehension training strategy.

Summary.   It is clear from our review of recent work that helping students learn how to summarize the texts they read has a positive effect on their comprehension and recall of text; yet, just a decade ago, very few summary studies showed any positive effects at all (Anderson & Armbruster, 1984). What accounts for the sudden shift in their proven effectiveness? Two things, we think. First, Anderson and Armbruster were undoubtedly right in their assessment of the mismatch between what students in those pre-1980 studies were being trained to do and what they were accountable for on outcome measures. In nearly all of the post-1980 studies, the ability to summarize new texts is the primary outcome measure; hence educationally and statistically significant effects are more likely to show up than they were in the earlier studies. But there is more. The second difference stems from the nature of the training itself. The newer studies are better designed. The instruction is better designed, it endures for longer instructional periods, and it includes conscious attempts on the part of the teacher to let students in on the "metacognitive" underpinnings of the instruction: the *what, how, why,* and *when.*

GENERIC STRATEGIES AND PRACTICES

The studies reviewed up to this point have been focused on a particular kind of text (expository versus narrative) to which they are most applicable or on a particular goal they are intended to accomplish (e.g., summarizing, understanding narrative structure, and so on). We turn now to strategies that we term as more *generic* in one or both of two senses: (1) they are applicable to a wide range of text types and sometimes even disciplines (e.g., math and reading); or (2) they are an amalgamation of several techniques or activities. We find that most of the studies included in this section can be characterized by one of the following descriptors, which we will use as organizers:

a.   Attempts to get students actively involved in their own learning
b.   Attempts to engage students and teachers in cooperative ventures
c.   Attempts to increase students' opportunities to read connected text

Active Involvement

One of the lasting contributions of cognitive psychology in general and schema theory in particular to our current view of the reading process is the idea that reading is not a passive activity; it demands that readers engage in an *active search for meaning* (e.g., Doctorow et al., 1978; Anderson & Pearson, 1984). That may explain why getting students independently and actively engaged in the act of comprehending is a major goal of several generic strategies and practices, including self-questioning, generative learning, and self-monitoring.

Self-Questioning

Questioning oneself while reading seems to be a characteristic activity of good readers (Collins, Brown, & Larkin, 1980). Smith (1975, p. 34), in fact, has called comprehension ". . . the condition of having one's cognitive questions answered," and Singer (1980) characterized what he called "active comprehension" as a movement away from readers answering questions and toward readers asking questions about texts. Self-questioning studies have existed parallel to adjunct questioning studies for many years (see Tierney & Cunningham, 1984, for a review of both lines of work), but advances in our thinking about the nature of comprehension instruction merit another look at this broad area of research.

In a comprehensive review of the self-questioning instructional research up to that time, Wong (1985) criticized much of the existing work for the lack of a theoretical perspective on what kinds of questions are useful ones to ask oneself and why they could conceivably be useful. She was much more sanguine about two more recent, and more theoretically satisfying, lines of self-questioning research focused, respectively, on the metacognitive construct of self-monitoring (e.g., Palincsar & Brown, 1984; Wong & Jones, 1982) and the schema-theoretic construct of linking text information to background knowledge (e.g., Singer & Donlan, 1982). She concluded that it is not self-questioning per se, but the cognitive processes that are induced by one's own questions (e.g., making inferences, monitoring understanding, attending to narrative structure) that matter. She believes that two nonmethodological factors may account for the success or lack of success that readers have with using self-questioning as a way to enhance text comprehension: readers' background knowledge about the topic and their ability to self-monitor. Beyond that, Wong believes, methodological issues may account for the degree of success various self-questioning interventions have achieved, including whether students reach a criterion level of performance in generating their own questions, whether they are given explicit instruction in how to generate questions (see Pearson & Gallagher, 1983), whether they are given enough time to read a passage and generate questions about it, and whether the criterion measures are sensitive to the likely benefits of self-questioning. Two recent studies are especially interesting when considered in light of Wong's points.

Yopp (1988) concluded that the active nature of self-questioning was an important component in its success by comparing groups differentiated by *who* asked the questions during lessons—self or teacher. Instruction for all three groups of fifth-grade students in Yopp's study focused on background knowledge of story structure. In experimental groups, students generated their own questions, while teachers asked questions of the control group. One experimental group also learned a metacognitive strategy for answering their own questions based on classifying each question in a manner similar to Raphael's (Raphael & McKinney, 1983; Raphael & Pearson, 1985; Raphael & Wonnacut, 1985), according to the source of information needed for answering it. By the third week of instruction and on a delayed test after the study's completion, experimental groups performed better than the control group on multiple-choice tests. What is especially interesting in this study is the window it provides into why self-questioning was effective. For each tested story, Yopp collected during-reading think-aloud protocols from a subset of students in each group and also interviewed them about how they got their answers to comprehension questions. Interviewed students from both experimental groups reported thinking about possible questions while reading the test stories—a kind of thinking that undoubtedly was helpful, given that Yopp's criterion measure was an objective test. Control group students reported thinking about a summary of the events in the story and elaborations on story events—kinds of thinking to which a multiple-choice test may not be sensitive. Interviews also showed that the experimental students who learned a procedure for answering their own questions were better than the other experimental group and the control group in explaining how they got their answers to the criterion measure; this ability did not, however, translate into better question-answering performance in comparison to the other experimental group (again the objective test may have had an influence).

A study by King, Biggs, and Lipsky (1984) directly addresses the issue of the criterion measure's sensitivity to the intervention. When college study-skills students who learned to ask themselves questions were compared to those taught to generate a summary and those simply told to take notes, success depended on the criterion measure. On objective and free recall measures, the experimental groups performed equally well; but on an essay measure, the summary group outperformed the self-questioning group. What is interesting is that the summary group learned summarization rules that differed from Brown and Day's (1983) rules in one important way: they also learned to search for details that supported main ideas; this may have been an especially useful way of organizing one's thinking for essay writing and also may have helped them learn the details typically tested with objective items.

Generative Learning

Wittrock and his associates (e.g., Doctorow et al., 1978; Linden & Wittrock, 1981; Wittrock, 1974; Wittrock, Marks, & Doctorow, 1975) use the term *generative learning* to describe how comprehension occurs when readers build relationships among various parts of a text and between the text and their background knowledge and experiences. They have demonstrated in several studies that these relationships can assume a number of realizations, including images, summaries, inferences, elaborations, analogies, and metaphors; the basic thesis is that instruction which promotes the generation of virtually any association can improve comprehension. Linden and Wittrock (1981), for example, found that fifth-grade children instructed to generate such relationships did in fact generate more relationships and had better text comprehension than children who received no instructions to generate associations or who were in classrooms where teachers were permitted to teach any procedures they wished. The instruction in generation was not elaborate, consisting, it seems, of little more than directing children to generate relationships of a certain kind (images, summary sentences, or metaphors and analogies) on each of the three days of instruction, and collecting evidence that such generations were actually performed. Linden and Wittrock did not ascertain whether their instruction resulted in increased generations and better comprehension for texts other than those used during instruction.

Self-Monitoring

Monitoring one's own comprehension involves using procedures to check on whether comprehension is occurring and employing fix-up strategies when it is not. Self-monitoring is a hallmark of skilled reading (e.g., Collins & Smith, 1982), and many of the comprehension-fostering strategies already discussed in this chapter also can function as self-monitoring strategies (e.g., summarizing, self-questioning, predicting) when they are used properly (see Palincsar & Brown, 1984; Paris, Cross, & Lipson, 1984).

A body of work by Miller and her associates (1985, 1987; Miller, Giovenco, & Rentiers, 1987) also suggests that both average and below-average middle-grade readers can improve in their ability to monitor their own comprehension through self-instruction training. In general, *self-instruction training* consists of learning to internalize statements about the routines to follow to detect inconsistencies while reading. These statements are about such activities as defining what the task is, designing an approach for its completion, evaluating the approach taken, and deciding whether the task has been completed. Two important features of self-instruction training emerge from Miller's research. First, the *informed* nature of the training (see Brown, Campione, & Day, 1981; Paris, Cross, & Lipson, 1984) is crucial to its success; in other words, students should be informed about how the strategy is supposed to improve their comprehension ability. Second, instruction to encourage the children to self-verbalize is even more crucial. Generally, children taught to self-verbalize performed better even than those children who learned the identical routines for self-monitoring and received the same kind of feedback on their performance, but were not taught how to self-verbalize. The one-to-one nature of the instruction and the somewhat artificial nature of the passages weaken the generalizability of Miller's results; nevertheless, it is noteworthy that the treatment effects generally persisted even on delayed tests and for detection of text inconsistencies different in nature from those in the training passages. Furthermore, in the Miller et al. (1987) study, trained, below-average readers performed as well as higher-ability readers on transfer measures.

Raphael and her colleagues (1984; Raphael & McKinney, 1983; Raphael & Pearson, 1985; Raphael & Wonnacut, 1985) taught students a procedure for answering questions that was motivated by children's generally poorer performance in answering inferential than literal questions. But the strategy also can be seen as a way for children to monitor their own comprehension. In essence, students learned to adapt their comprehension strategies according to the task demands of teacher-posed (and later, their own) questions about a text. In trying to answer questions, middle-grade students learned to figure out whether the question and answer came from the same sentence in the text or different parts of the text, or whether the question related to the text but had to be answered using information in one's background knowledge. Although there were differences across age levels in the amount and type of training needed, taken as a whole Raphael et al.'s studies show that students who learned about question-answer relationships were better able to monitor their comprehension and understand independently read texts. Furthermore, it was found that the strategy could be used successfully with the real materials children already were reading in their classrooms.

Other Attempts to Increase Involvement

We close this section with a review of two instructional studies that illustrate especially well the importance of active involvement. Following up on an earlier study (Carr, Dewitz, & Patberg, 1983), DeWitz et al. (1987) compared the effectiveness of two methods of inference training that differed in terms of the level of "activity" in the role played by the reader. In the more-active condition, fifth-grade students got instruction and practice in making inferences via cloze exercises that required integrating prior knowledge with text; in the less-active condition, students learned what the relationships between text and prior knowledge were via structured overviews. The inference-training group had better comprehension of instructional and transfer material than either the structured-overview group or an untrained group who got only a self-monitoring checklist; moreover, their self-reports about the strategies they used to answer text questions revealed more strategic methods of comprehension monitoring (e.g., evaluating the sense of their answers, selective rereading). By contrast, the other groups reported rereading the entire text as their primary strategy for answering test questions. In the Dewitz et al. work, instruction plus active involvement seemed to provide the optimal combination of ingredients for fostering learning.

In Schmitt's (1988) study, third-grade students were trained to gradually assume responsibility for carrying out their own directed reading activity—they learned to activate their own prior knowledge, set their own reading purposes, ask and answer their own prequestions, verify or reject their predictions, and monitor their own success in meeting purposes and summarizing. The experimenter/instructor gradually played a less and less prominent role in the experimental group's reading lessons. In the control group, the teacher exercised typical teacher-directed basal reader control of activities as suggested in the teacher's manual. The experimental group outperformed the control group on all posttests which, notably, were from independently read basal reader selections not used during instruction. Moreover, children in the experimental group reported more extensive use of monitoring strategies. Schmitt credited the experimental group's success to the contextualized nature of their instruction, the focus on metacomprehension, and the gradual release of responsibility to the students themselves.

Working Together to Comprehend Texts

A growing concern in comprehension instructional research is how to take into account those social aspects of instruction that influence cognitive outcomes. The two social aspects of comprehension instruction whose cognitive consequences have been investigated most frequently are peer interaction and student-teacher dialogue.

Peer Interaction

Students working together to complete academic tasks is the focus of both cooperative learning and peer tutoring. Both have been investigated in a variety of academic disciplines and with a focus on social and personal development as well as cognitive outcomes.

The general finding of the vast literature about *cooperative learning*, including, of course, studies in a variety of disciplines besides reading instruction, is that both high-achieving and low-achieving students benefit from the opportunity to learn together in mixed-ability groups or pairs. Several recent reviews of this literature point to specific features of cooperative learning that enhance both cognitive and social outcomes. In many cases, successful cooperative learning interventions are "appended to" teacher-directed activities as follow-ups. In general, successful groups work toward group goals while monitoring the success of each individual's learning as a criterion of group success; also associated with positive growth are peer interactions that emphasize offering explanations rather than right answers (e.g., Johnson & Johnson, 1975, 1985; Slavin, 1987a, 1987b; Webb, 1985). In his review, Bossert (1988–1989) points out that mediating variables, such as the kind of cognitive processing and reasoning strategies that different cooperative methods engender, have not been studied sufficiently in the bulk of cooperative learning research.

Two recent studies illustrate the application of cooperative learning techniques in prose comprehension research. According to Dansereau (1987), whose research involves college students studying textbook material, the specific nature of student interactions affects outcomes. In what he has called *cooperative teaching*, pairs of students take turns at playing a primarily teacher or a primarily learner role for alternating sections of text that only the "teacher" has read before the cooperative interaction. By contrast, in cooperative learning, students take turns performing various cooperative activities on texts that both have read. He concluded that while cooperative teaching results in better learning of jointly studied texts, cooperative learning transfers better to independent reading and studying. He has also suggested that among the various cooperative activities performed, error detection and correction result in more learning from target texts, while elaborations result in greater transfer to independent learning.

In a recent study aimed specifically at language arts instruction, Stevens, Madden, Slavin, and Farnish (1987) investigated the consequences of arranging third- and fourth-grade students into heterogeneous cooperative groups for practice and follow-up activities after their teacher conducted instruction in homogeneous reading groups. After 12 weeks, cooperatively grouped classrooms outperformed control classrooms (where students received traditional basal reader instruction in homogeneous groups, including lots of independent practice) on several standardized measures of reading and language skills. It should be noted that although these results are consistent with those from more controlled investigations of cooperative learning, the experimental classroom practices differed from control classroom practices in several important respects besides the presence or absence of cooperative learning. For instance, experimental students got more integrated (as opposed to isolated) reading/writing instruction, were assigned more reading of connected text, and completed more "active" practice activities such as predicting, summarizing, and other metacomprehension activities. Any of these differences between control and experimental groups may have been responsible for the differences on the outcome measures.

The opportunity it provides for peer tutoring is believed to be an important component in the success of cooperative learning, but peer tutoring also has been studied separately from cooperative learning. In various studies, different tutor/tutee relationships have been examined. Average or high-achieving tutors have been paired with younger or less-able tutees. Students with learning difficulties have tutored other students with learning difficulties. Or, more recently, older learning-disabled students have tutored younger average-achieving students in need of some extra help. Generally tutors as well as tutees learn more lesson content than students not involved in peer tutoring, and tutors especially show growth in self-esteem (see Cohen, Kulik, & Kulik, 1982; or Jenkins & Jenkins, 1987, for reviews).

The bulk of the peer-tutoring research in reading instruction involves word-level or low-level comprehension activities. For example, in Top and Osguthorpe's (1987) recent study of reverse-role tutoring, middle-grade, low-achieving handicapped students learned how to tutor low-achieving, first-grade readers. The instruction given to the tutors focused on tutoring methods rather than reading skills, and most of the instruction they offered to the first graders focused on word-attack skills instead of comprehension. Even so, tutors outperformed nontutor peers in follow-up measures of comprehension as well as decoding. Furthermore, tutored students outperformed untutored students in measures of word attack without declines in comprehension, even though their tutoring activity focused on decoding. Because time in reading was held constant for all groups, there is reason to believe that being involved in the tutoring relationship in either role, rather than increased time by itself, was responsible for increases in learning.

In a noninstructional study, Garner, Wagoner, and Smith (1983) used peer tutoring as an alternative to verbal reports to externalize the question-answering strategies of good and poor readers reading expository texts. Although Garner et al. did not measure the effects of peer tutoring on comprehension, they did learn that tutors and tutees talked to each other about their comprehension strategies in this setting. For Garner et al., this was important because of the window it provided to permit them to examine the comprehension strategies good and poor readers use; but we think it also suggests one of the important benefits peer tutoring provides in comprehension instruction: the opportunity for poor comprehenders to become aware of the strategies of good comprehenders.

Judy, Alexander, Kulikowich, and Willson (1988) trained average to gifted sixth-grade students to reason by analogy using either a direct instruction or an inquiry approach and then assigned a subset of these trained students to tutor peers matched in reading ability. Students trained by teachers using either method outperformed a control group on analogical reasoning measures and on a reading comprehension transfer measure. Contrary to the bulk of peer-tutoring findings, there was only a nonsignificant trend for tutors to outperform nontutors; but, consistent with other research, tutees performed as well or better than their teacher-instructed peers on a variety of analogical reasoning tasks in spite of the fact that some of the inquiry-trained tutors gave their tutees inaccurate information. Again, the very involvement in a peer-tutoring situation seemed to override specific lesson focus or accuracy.

A recent extension of Palincsar and Brown's (1984) research about reciprocal teaching provides important information about the processes through which cooperative learning and peer tutoring achieve their effectiveness. *Reciprocal teaching*, in which students learn under an adult's guidance to take turns leading peers through four comprehension-fostering and comprehension-monitoring activities (summarizing, asking questions, clarifying, and predicting), has proved to be a highly effective form of instruction that involves a good deal of peer interaction in and of itself. Palincsar, Brown, and Martin (1987) more recently took the peer interaction component of reciprocal teaching one step further by training teachers to train peer tutors to carry out these four activities with their tutees. To measure the effects of peer tutoring structured around the four reciprocal-teaching activities, Palincsar, Brown, and Martin collected not only product measures of comprehension but also process measures of group dynamics. Classroom teachers who had used the reciprocal-teaching procedure successfully in the past taught the four activities to classes of seventh-grade poor comprehenders using teacher-directed instruction and worksheet practice but not reciprocal-teaching techniques. Then they taught selected peer tutors within these classes how to conduct the reciprocal-teaching sessions. After this instruction, the peer tutors conducted reciprocal-teaching dialogues with their group of tutees. Consistent with the original approach, they also gave daily performance feedback on independently read test passages to their tutees. Tutors quite quickly reached ceiling on daily comprehension measures, and tutees made and maintained substantial comprehension gains similar to those achieved by poor comprehenders in Palincsar and Brown's (1984) work, even though in the previous studies reciprocal-teaching dialogues were led by an experimenter or trained teacher. Importantly, these gains were not realized by tutees after their classroom teacher's instruction or after worksheet practice in the four reciprocal-teaching activities; only engagement in the reciprocal-teaching dialogues with their peer tutors prompted such gains. Process measures indicated that peer tutors were effective in modeling, giving practice, giving specific feedback, and adjusting the level of support that they provided their tutees.

Student-Teacher Dialogue

The knowledge that explicit instruction in how to comprehend is more effective than massed practice and assessment was a significant discovery in the last decade, and it spawned much of the comprehension instructional research we have reviewed in this chapter. However, recent thinking suggests that it is not explicit instruction per se, but the nature and content of the interactions that occur between teacher and students during instruction that count. Two features of teacher-student interactions are especially interesting: the degree of student control in discussions, and the teachers' instructional scaffolding (Applebee & Langer, 1983; Palincsar, 1986; Wood, Bruner, & Ross, 1976)—in other words what teachers say and do to enable children to complete complex mental tasks they could not complete without assistance.

A few recent investigations of classroom participation structures suggest that how children learn to think about what they read may be as much a function of how they interact with the teacher and with one another and how much responsibility they take for initiating questions and topics of discussion as it is a function of the cognitive demands of teacher-directed interventions and teacher-posed questions (Au & Mason, 1981; Bloome & Green, 1984; Cazden, 1986; Green, Harker, & Golden, 1987; O'Flahavan, 1989; Weber, 1986). In most of the studies reviewed in this chapter, discussion, when it occurs, usually takes the shape familiar in most U.S. classrooms— the teacher initiates an interaction by asking a question, a student responds, and the teacher evaluates the response (Cazden, 1986); in fact, the practice is so prevalent that it has achieved acronymous status—the *IRE* (for *initation-response-evaluation*). However, discussion that is initiated and controlled more by student than teacher, and that allows for a variety of text interpretations, is being investigated (e.g., Atwell, 1987; Hansen, 1987; O'Flahavan, 1989).

Much of this work describes observations about the change process, made by the teachers themselves (e.g., Atwell, 1987) or by participant observers (e.g., Hansen, 1987). O'Flahavan (1989) has examined the effects of alternative participation structures on children's cognitive, social, and affective behavior in a very direct fashion. O'Flahavan compared traditional discussions, based on the IRE format, with discussions in which the teacher discards his or her traditional role in favor of a more "supportive" role—empowering students to take responsibility for initiating topics, monitoring the relevance of comments, taking turns, and deciding when to shift discussions to another matter. In the experimental discussion groups, he encouraged teachers to model the discussion norms and participation structures found in everyday conversations; hence the name *Conversational Discussion Groups* (CDGs) for the nontraditional groups. While he found no differences on recall and interpretation measures, he did find several differences favoring the CDGs on measures of attention, group process knowledge, locus of control, and perceptions of the role and value of discussions. The CDG students attended to more central information in transfer stories. Additionally, the CDG students were far superior to the traditional students in offering advice about how other students could solve problems that arose in videotaped segments of discussions, and they perceived themselves as much more in charge of and able to control the flow of discussions. Finally both the students and the teachers in the CDGs experienced substantial shifts in their views about discussions; they perceived discussions as more valuable and more central to literacy learning. Additionally, in the CDG groups there was a greater match between teachers' and students' perceptions about the function of discussions.

According to Brown, Collins, and Duguid (1989) and Collins, Brown, and Newman (in press), much of the cognitive activity in complex mental tasks is made artificial when we try to make it excessively explicit. They argue that real learning of complex mental tasks takes place gradually, over time, in the performance of authentic activities, not through procedural instruction. They use the term *cognitive apprenticeship* to highlight two important features of such learning: that activity on the part of the student is central to learning; and that situated modelling, coaching, and fading on the part of the teacher are what enable and shape student cognitive activity. *Authentic* and *situated* are the operative terms here, the notion being that students learn how to perform complex mental tasks when there is a real need to do so and when they are allowed to participate in the whole act of task completion even before they can carry out the entire process independently.

While there are some similarities between the master teacher in this cognitive apprenticeship model (the provider of models and feedback) and a teacher who serves as the deliverer of planned instruction in a direct or explicit instruction model, there are significant differences. The most important is that in situated learning, the teacher's role is redefined every time the teacher, one or more students, and a text come together. Collins, Brown, and Newman (in press) describe several successful teaching methods in math, writing, and reading as embodying the principles of cognitive apprenticeships. Since one of the methods is reciprocal teaching, Collins et al. provide a fresh perspective from which to view Palincsar and Brown's (1984) approach. Collins, Brown, and Newman think that the activities of reciprocal teaching help students form a new constructive model of reading by engaging them in the authentic task of reading comprehension; and the responsibility for making meaning is shared among adult teacher, student "teacher," and students, with the adult teacher providing just enough tailored feedback to decompose each task to the degree necessary to permit a given student to succeed at it.

A set of investigations suggests that a quite similar role is played by successful teachers in the Kamehameha Early Education Project in Hawaii (Au & Kawakami, 1984; Au & Mason, 1981; Tharp, 1982; Tharp & Gallimore, 1989a, 1989b). Earlier investigations had established the importance of soliciting students' dialogue about their own experiences as they are related to the text and allowing students to respond in culturally compatible styles instead of waiting to be called on by the teacher (Au & Mason, 1981; Tharp, 1982). More recently, an increased focus on the nature and content of student-teacher dialogues highlights the importance of what Tharp and Gallimore (1989a, 1989b) call *responsive teaching*, or *instructional conversations*. They contrast instructional conversations with the recitation format so prevalent in classroom text discussions; in recitations teachers rarely respond to student input or use it to help students develop more complete ideas, relying instead on prepared teacher questions for which single student responses are accepted. Instructional conversations, on the other hand, mirror the natural learning of the home in that activities are goal directed, enough help is provided so that even young and poor readers can participate in complex mental activities (like reading whole texts) before they can do them on their own, and instruction is embedded in task completion, not separate from it. Reminiscent of O'Flahavan's (1989) conversational discussion groups, in instructional conversations, the teacher's role is to use student input into discussions and student interpretations of texts to help all students move to higher levels of comprehension than they could attain independently. In text comprehension lessons, for example, a teacher would prepare not by reading the lesson in the teacher's edition but by reading the student text carefully, with an eye toward anticipating the entire range of possible student interpretations and responses, exploring all instructional possibilities, and developing discussion prompts (questions and challenges) that will maximize student input during discussion. Tharp and Gallimore use lesson transcripts to demonstrate that responsive teaching is both an explicit and implicit goal of many teachers in the successful Kamehameha Early Education Project *and* that teachers learn responsive teaching techniques from the responsive instruction of their supervisors.

Increasing Opportunities to Read Connected Text

The more we learn about the job of instruction in reading comprehension the more daunting it appears. In that light, we have saved for the end of our review a brief discussion of several practices that require little more of the teacher than setting up the opportunities for students simply to read connected text. Volume of reading has been associated with various measures of reading achievement and growth in reading (Anderson, Wilson, & Fielding, 1988; Greaney, 1980; Greaney & Hegarty, 1984; Kirsch & Guthrie, 1984; Krashen, 1988; Lehr, 1988); in fact, Heyns (1978) found that how far a child lived from the public library was the strongest predictor of retention of learning over the summer months. It is surprising, then, that several methods designed to increase the amount of contextual reading children do have met with only mixed success.

Elley and Mangubhai (1983) and Ingham (1982) both carried out what they called *book floods*, in which classrooms were equipped with paperback book libraries. For Elley and Mangubhai's middle-grade, non-native English speakers, this exposure to English storybooks through sustained silent reading and shared book experiences (Holdaway, 1979) produced large gains in measures of English reading and listening. For Ingham (1982), results of a book flood in British elementary schools were positive but less dramatic, supporting Elley and Mangubhai's theory that book floods may be most effective in settings where very few books exist prior to the intervention.

Morrow and Weinstein (1986) found that they could increase second-grade children's selection of book reading as a voluntary, in-school, free-time activity with two simple strategies: (a) restocking and sprucing up the library corner, and (b) spending about 20 minutes per day on various book enjoyment activities, such as reading to children, talking about books, and group silent reading. This voluntary use of the library during free-choice time did not, however, transfer to increased out-of-school reading, and no measures were collected of how increased reading related to comprehension improvement.

When opportunity to read has been provided via sustained silent reading (McCracken, 1971), results have been mixed. School *sustained silent reading* (SSR) programs have been associated with better attitudes toward reading and more library use (Cline & Kretke, 1980), and faster movement through basal materials, with no loss in spelling and English achievement (C. Collins, 1980), even though these classes were cut short to provide time for reading. Manning and Manning (1984) have provided the only evidence that SSR is related to achievement—however, in that situation, SSR was accompanied by peer and teacher interaction about books. Because individualized and other literature-based reading programs are becoming increasingly popular, we expect that the conditions under which in-school independent silent book reading is related to reading growth will become an even more important research question in the coming years. As such research expands, we must remember that providing books and time to read them does not guarantee that students will be actively engaged in reading (e.g., Rosenshine & Stevens, 1984); and it is engagement in silent reading that is, undoubtedly, the operative factor in these opportunity to read studies.

Repeated Reading

Another way to increase reading volume is by engaging students in repeated reading of the same text. A regular and valued feature of the storybook experiences of young children (see Chapter 26 by Sulzby & Teale in this volume) and a natural form of recreational reading for many avid readers, *repeated reading* of the same text also is believed to improve some aspects of reading ability for older readers. Although repeated reading originally was viewed as a way to improve word identification, reading speed, and fluency (see Dahl & Samuels, 1979), its connections to improved comprehension also have been established through several direct and indirect measures (see Dowhower, 1987, for a review). A compelling explanation, offered by Schreiber (1980, 1987), is that the lack of prosodic information in printed text—pitch, stress, and juncture cues that help listeners get meaning from spoken language—can be compensated for by repeated reading, through which readers learn to read in the kinds of meaningful phrases people use in speech.

Using the proportion of semantically inappropriate miscues as an indirect measure of comprehension (the lower the proportion, the higher the comprehension is assumed to be), both Koskinen and Blum (1984), with third-grade poor readers, and Herman (1985), with middle-grade poor readers, found improvement as a result of repeated readings. For Herman, the improvement was maintained on new passages as well as within reread ones. Taylor, Wade, and Yekovich (1985) found that fifth-grade poor readers were nearly indistinguishable from good readers in passage recall after repeated readings. In Dowhower's (1987) study, accurate but slow primary-grade readers improved both within and between passages in comprehension as a result of either read-along or independent practice, especially when they read several stories a few times each instead of one story many times.

O'Shea, Sindelar, and O'Shea (1985) found some goal-specific effects for third-grade average readers instructed to reread either for improved fluency or improved comprehension: Although both groups improved in fluency and comprehension after repeated readings, each group made greater gains in their goal area. Rashotte and Torgesen (1985) compared two methods of repeated reading, one designed to provide maximum overlap of words and the other, minimum overlap of words, with a third method that merely provided the opportunity to read new texts each time. None was more effective than others in improving third-grade learning-disabled children's comprehension.

Taking a different approach, Amlund, Kardash, and Kulhavy (1986) evaluated repeated reading as a study strategy for college students; their logic for selecting it as an experimental approach was interesting in that they had typically found it being used as a kind of "poor sister" control strategy against which more elaborate cognitive strategies could be compared. They found that although the number of readings affected the amount of recall, initial encoding errors were remarkably resistant to change. With more than two rereadings, students tended to remember more passage details but not to correct original misunderstandings.

Summary

We have attempted to confine our review of the research about each generic strategy or practice to that which has to do with improving reading comprehension. In so doing, we have found that although some practices have considerable research support in general, there is plenty of room for additional research about their use in improving reading comprehension in particular. Generative learning, cooperative learning, and peer tutoring are several good examples. In this regard, Palincsar et al.'s (1987) reciprocal teaching research provides an appropriate model to follow. In examining the role of peer interaction in reciprocal teaching, they focused on four reading activities that their past research (Palincsar & Brown, 1984) had indicated were associated with improved comprehension, and went on to demonstrate that peer dialogues centered around these activities were as effective as teacher-student dialogues and more effective than teacher-led instruction and practice without reciprocal dialogues. We applaud this technique of applying the strategy of interest to the learning of comprehension skills that already have a strong foundation in theory and practice.

Because many of the strategies reviewed in this section are so broad based, we have found it difficult in some cases to pinpoint a particular feature that accounts for the success (or lack thereof) of the strategy. Attempts like those of Dansereau (1987) to determine which kinds of cooperative interactions are associated with which kinds of comprehension, and of Miller (1985, 1987; Miller et al., 1987), to determine which components of self-instruction training are the most important, are noteworthy exceptions. In evaluating the research about each strategy, it also is important to consider whether there were provisions for ascertaining whether and how the strategy as a whole or its various components actually were used by readers. Use of observation, special tests, think-aloud protocols, self-reports, or interviews helped some researchers to determine the degree to which the strategies and activities of interest actually were used by their subjects (e.g., Dewitz et al., 1987; Linden & Wittrock, 1981; O'Flahavan, 1989; Palincsar & Brown, 1984; Palincsar et al., 1987; Raphael & McKinney, 1983; Raphael & Pearson, 1985; Raphael & Wonnacott, 1985; Schmitt, 1988; Tharp & Gallimore, 1989a, 1989b; Yopp, 1988). In contrast, much of the opportunity-to-read research that we reviewed would benefit greatly by the addition of such components to determine whether contextual reading or repeated reading actually was engaged in during the time allocated for it. In short, a major responsibility of instructional researchers is to index "fidelity" to the intended instructional strategy.

SUMMARY AND CONCLUSIONS

Summarizing trends and drawing conclusions about a corpus of research as large and diverse as the one we have reviewed thus far is a formidable task. First, in the right circumstances or situations, nearly every possible approach to instruction can be shown to work to benefit students' comprehension. Finding the right words to say, "Everything works," without incurring the judgment that we are simply taking the easy and diplomatic way out, is not simple. Second, summarizing inevitably leads to simplification, and simplification to oversimplification.

Nonetheless, we will attempt to summarize by discussing two dominant features of the reading comprehension instructional research of the last decade. One is the apparent convergence on a corpus of reading activities and accompanying cognitive behaviors whose performance is associated with measured improvement in comprehension. The second is an increased focus on certain instructional principles that define the role of the teacher, the student, and the task in reading comprehension instruction. Thus, we shall attempt to sum up what we have learned in two ways. First, we highlight the particular strategies that consistently rise to the surface as associated with overall comprehension improvement. Second, we attempt to recontextualize the research we have examined according to the instructional principles (be they intentional or unintentional) that are represented in successful strategies. Finally, we will speculate about next steps in reading comprehension instructional research that might advance our inquiry to a more sophisticated level.

Consistently Successful Strategies

Although we examined narrative and expository approaches separately, we found several common themes. The first two broadly applicable generalizations concern background knowledge. First, students of a variety of ages and abilities benefit when teachers take the time to help them either recall or build knowledge of text structure by paying systematic attention to it. Be it a set of questions that leads through the "story line" of a narrative, a focus on the categories of information typically present in stories, a summary of the macrostructural relations in a textbook chapter, or a visual rerepresentation of almost any selection, students' comprehension is enhanced when teachers help them pay attention to the structural relationships among the important or central ideas in the text. Further, in some studies, such instruction actually aids comprehension of transfer texts presented after the instructional phase has ended.

Second, students' comprehension, particularly inferential comprehension, is improved when relationships are drawn between students' background knowledge and experiences and the content included in reading selections. This may involve invoking appropriate knowledge structures before reading, making and verifying predictions before and during reading, or answering inferential questions during or after reading. Further there is evidence that when students develop an expectation that they should try to understand what is new in terms of what they already know, their comprehension of new and unguided selections is improved.

A third warranted generalization is that students understand what they read and learn how to understand what they read in the process of learning how to monitor their comprehension. This finding should be predictable from our first two conclusions about knowledge structures—after all, when students monitor comprehension, asking whether or not what they have read makes sense to them, their ultimate criterion for "making sense" is nothing more or less than what they already know about the topic or text genre under consideration.

A fourth general finding centers on summarization. When students are taught to recast what they have read by ferreting out the important from the unimportant information, their comprehension and recall of the text is enhanced. Further, there is some evidence (see the reciprocal teaching and the hierarchical summaries sections) that summarization training transfers to new texts.

We have discussed these findings as related to one another because we think that, taken together, they reveal a more general conclusion about comprehension instruction. Singer (1980) called it active comprehension, Wittrock and his associates (e.g., Doctorow et al., 1978) have labelled it generative learning, Pearson and Johnson (1978) called it relating the new to the known. But whatever the label, the principle seems clear: Students understand and remember ideas better when they have to transform those ideas from one form to another. Apparently it is in this transformation process that *author's* ideas become *reader's* ideas, rendering them more memorable. Examined from the teacher's perspective, what this means is that teachers have many options to choose from when they try to engage students more actively in their own comprehension; summarizing, monitoring, engaging relevant knowledge, creating visual rerepresentations, and requiring students to ask their own questions all seem to "generate learning."

Principles of Comprehension Instruction

While we believe that research has helped us reach some consensus about the reading activities and cognitions associated with improved comprehension, we still find instruction to be operationalized in a variety of forms. What instruction actually looks like varies along several dimensions, each of which we see as a continuum. Three, in particular, are most relevant to our corpus of studies: task control, task authenticity, and teacher's role. By *task control*, we mean who decides what kinds of learning tasks students will engage in, how the tasks will get carried out, and how they will be evaluated. *Authenticity* refers to how much like real-life reading the texts and tasks are. The *teacher's role* varies according to how much teacher participation there is at various points and what the nature of that participation is. We argue that what a student learns about comprehension as a result of instruction depends as much upon where instruction falls on these continua as it does upon the precise nature of the comprehension activities that comprise the instruction.

Although we find examples of comprehension instruction that have produced comprehension gains at nearly every combination of points on the continua, we do notice several trends that characterize recent comprehension instructional research with respect to these dimensions, particularly for teacher's role and task control.

Traditionally, the most typical role for the teacher has been task director: directing recitations, written practice, and study activities about texts. Our review of research suggests several shifts *away* from this time-honored tradition. The first trend is subtle; it could be characterized as an attempt to embed implicit instruction within the typical recitation or practice format. In some recent studies involving teacher-posed questions and assignments, the teacher's questions or directions for written activity are designed not only to review text ideas but also to impart an implied message about how readers construct meaning from what they read. We reviewed studies in which the teacher's questions or their assignments to students: (a) consistently focused on text structure or central text content; (b) encouraged students to connect background knowledge to text ideas to make inferences, predictions, and elaborations; or (c) prompted students to ask their own questions about the text (e.g., Beck et al., 1982; Fielding et al., 1990; Graves et al., 1983; one condition in Hansen, 1981; Koskinen et al., 1988; McGinley & Denner, 1987; Marino et al., 1985; Morrow, 1984a, 1984b, 1985, 1986; Neuman, 1988; Prince & Mancus, 1987; Sundbye, 1987; Thames & Readence, 1988). The hope in studies such as these is that repeatedly exposing children to activities that give them implied messages about how skilled readers construct meaning will help them develop their own model for how to construct meaning. We found that interventions like these were usually at least moderately successful in improving children's comprehension of the text at hand and occasionally even in improving their performance in reading a text independently; however, such transfer was almost never tested for. Most of these studies went no further than to demonstrate that when teacher's questions, comments, and directions to students are backed by a theory of text comprehension, students usually perform better than when there is no particular theory behind the text-related activities that teachers direct students to engage in. What is almost never clear in implicit instruction studies like these is how the teacher is supposed to relinquish his or her role, which tends to be quite directive; and how students are supposed to carry out the same tasks independently.

Probably the largest share of research attention in recent years has gone to the role of the teacher as a deliverer of explicit instruction in how to perform comprehension skills and strategies; this is a trend that has persisted and escalated since Tierney and Cunningham's (1984) review of comprehension instruction in the first volume of this handbook. In the most recent explicit instruction studies, teacher modeling and explaining of thought processes (what Paris, 1986, calls making thinking public) has replaced an earlier focus on stating rules or procedures; in other words, didactic "telling" has been replaced by an increased emphasis on learning strategies fully—ensuring that students understand *when* and *why* the comprehension strategies are helpful and providing feedback at key points in the learning process (see Chapter 30 by Roehler & Duffy on instruction and Chapter 22 by Paris, Wasick, & Turner on metacognitive strategy development, both in this volume).

In our corpus, most of the research that was designed to teach students about text structures, inferences, summarizing, self-monitoring, and self-questioning put the teacher in this explicit instruction role. The logic of the instructional model is as follows: (a) in the early stages of explicit instruction the teacher plays a central role by modeling and sharing cognitive secrets; (b) the teacher gradually turns over more responsibility to students (see Figure 29.1); and (c) the ultimate goal is for the teacher to fade out of the picture so that students can apply the strategy independently. This has proved to be a highly effective role for teachers in teaching students to perform a variety of strategies when reading texts independently, at least when the dependent measure closely resembles the trained task, and sometimes on more general measures of comprehension.

In the vast majority of explicit instruction studies, one of two patterns of instructional delivery was present: (a) either a heterogenous group of students received the instruction and its relative effects for students of various initial abilities were evaluated; or (b) a group of students for whom the instruction was especially tailored were guided through a series of lessons by the teacher. What has almost universally remained unspecified about the teacher's role in these studies is exactly how the teacher is supposed to know where to start, or how and when to turn over more responsibility to students.

The third trend we have noticed centers on the scaffolding construct. In a small number of studies we reviewed, the teacher's role was to provide instructional scaffolding that enables children to carry out comprehension activities that they would not be able to do on their own (Applebee & Langer, 1983; Palincsar, 1986; Paris, Wixson, & Palincsar, 1986; Wood, Bruner, & Ross, 1976). In scaffolded instruction, the teacher determines the difference between what students can accomplish independently and what they can accomplish with more expert guidance, and then designs instruction that provides just enough scaffolding for them to be able to participate in tasks that are currently beyond their reach. Providing appropriate scaffolding requires teachers to engage in an ongoing, dynamic interaction with students. Each response provided by a student or students gives teachers information about what they do and do not understand; these responses become cues to the teacher concerning the level and kind of feedback the teacher should give and the step or steps that should be taken next. When scaffolded instruction operates according to plan, two things happen: first, the tasks and texts of the moment gradually come more and more under the learner's control; and second, more difficult tasks and texts become appropriate bases for further teacher-student interaction.

Tharp and Gallimore (1989a, 1989b) have demonstrated that teachers provide such scaffolding when they carry out responsive teaching, or instructional conversations; and it also is at the heart of cognitive apprenticeships (Brown, et al., 1989; Collins et al., in press). Palincsar (1986; Palincsar et al., 1987) also demonstrated that scaffolding, as revealed in student-teacher dialogues, is fundamental in reciprocal teaching and that successful peer tutors used scaffolding in carrying out reciprocal teaching activities.

The differences between the teacher's role in this setting and in what we have called explicit instruction are subtle but important. Most notably, in scaffolded instruction, the teacher's instruction grows at least as much out of an analysis of the learner's ongoing understanding as it does out of an analysis of the text or task at hand. Furthermore, in contrast to much of the explicit instruction research, the issue of possible multiple interpretations of texts is addressed. Children's text interpretations are not automatically considered wrong if they are different from the teacher's interpretation; rather, they are considered to be potentially valid, definitely informative, and the starting point for instruction firmly grounded in student performance.

The fourth trend, just beginning to surface, is toward the teacher as a facilitator of learning and as a coequal with students in a literary community. In this view, readers hold the ultimate authority (and bear the ultimate responsibility) for meaning. Teachers can demonstrate their own uses of literacy tools but they cannot tell anyone what to do or when to do it. They can share their interpretation of a story, but they must respect alternative interpretations provided by students. The changes in interaction patterns and text interpretations that occur when teachers relinquish their role as discussion director or interpretive authority and replace it with the role of facilitator have been demonstrated in studies of text discussions (e.g., Golden, 1986; O'Flahavan, 1989; Rogers, 1988); such changed roles for the teacher also are paramount in what has been termed the Whole Language movement (e.g., Goodman, 1986; Smith, 1981; Short & Burke, in press) and in other efforts to put individual student choice, talk, and inter- pretation at the heart of comprehension instruction (e.g., Atwell, 1987; Hansen, 1987). Ironically, this growing view of the role of the teacher is in many ways the antithesis of the teacher-as-deliverer-of-explicit-instruction view, and the desired outcomes and preferred modes of research in the two are so different that they tend to be supported by separate communities whose research is difficult to compare. In our view, scaffolded instruction, especially as operationalized in responsive teaching and cognitive appren- ticeships, may be the bridge that spans the chasm that currently exists between explicit instruction and these more student-centered views of teachers' roles.

Most of the research in our corpus that does not address one of the issues or patterns discussed thus far is focused upon students' practice opportunities. The opportunity-to-read studies (e.g., book floods, sustained silent reading, and repeated reading) fit this category, as do the cooperative learning and peer-tutoring studies. We have been unable to uncover any special set of trends in this research, but we highlight it here because we believe that precisely the ingredient lacking in these opportunity-to- read and social learning studies is a careful description of the role of the teacher.

The conflicting results of much of the opportunity-to-read research actually have been very informative because they have pointed to the importance of the context in which opportunities for practice in independent reading are provided. At present, it seems that the optimal context for independent contextual reading practice may be one in which practice is preceded by instruction for those who need it, is carried out on appropriate materials, is monitored to insure that students actually are engaged in the activity during the time allotted for it, and is accompanied by opportunities to talk about or otherwise respond to what was read in a literary community (e.g., Five, 1986). Likewise, cooperative learning and peer tutoring seem to be most successful as practice- oriented adjuncts to other kinds of instruction instead of as total instructional packages. Although largely successful, they are usually short-term in duration and there is some question about whether the novelty of working with peers instead of the cognitive and social activity they engender accounts for most of the success.

A final trend we notice in our corpus is the move toward the use of more and more authentic texts and tasks in research. While much of the earliest research about comprehension and comprehension instruction was based on artificial texts that were intentionally created to demonstrate a point, we were pleased to find that much of the recent comprehension research uses authentic texts throughout instruction, and even those that use special texts during instruction usually evaluate transfer to *authentic texts*—the kind adults and children actually read in or out of school. Of course, there is some debate about what counts as an authentic text; many would argue against includ- ing school textbooks and basal readers in this category. By far the majority of studies have defined authentic texts as textbook and basal reader materials (which now are most often adaptations or excerpts from children's books) instead of children's books per se. Because we see a trend toward more and more use of children's literature, including full-length works, in school reading instruction, we expect to see a corresponding trend toward the use of children's literature in comprehension instruction research.

Next Steps

While we have learned much about the nature of comprehension and comprehension instruction in the past two decades, there is even more to learn. We close by raising but a few of the possible issues that, if carefully addressed, will advance this line of inquiry substantially.

Carver (1987) has questioned whether direct or explicit comprehension instruction is necessary at all. While he grounds his conclusions in empirical data (questioning, in fact, the significance of some of the findings we have reported in this chapter), he could just as easily have based his argument on conceptual grounds.

It could be, for example, that simple practice is a viable alternative to direct instruction. In fact, both the conventional basal approach that Durkin found so loathesome and the opportunity-to-read studies (book floods, sustained silent reading, and repeated reading) rely on a practice principle. The logic seems to be that if you engage students in the criterion activity (i.e., what you want them, ultimately, to be able to do) for a sufficient period of time, eventually they will infer the structure of the system and learn how to control it on their own. Whether such an approach will prove to be more effective than explicit explanations and instruction remains to be seen. The danger, always, in explicit training studies is that the explanations and the self-reflections will become more complicated than the task itself, leading to the possibility that students will become trapped in introspective nightmares (see Pearson & Dole, 1987). The danger in leaving students to "their own devices" is that in the process we will do little except exacerbate the already wide gaps between successful and unsuccessful comprehenders, unintentionally eliciting another Matthew effect—the rich get richer and the poor get poorer (see Stanovich, 1986). What we need are more studies—both natural descriptions and controlled experiments—examining what it is students learn when there is no direct attempt to teach them to do anything in particular except to make sure that things make sense.

Second, it is possible that by focusing upon the content in the text, teachers could eliminate the need for explicit instruction. From an instructional research point of view, a critical issue is whether content- or context-free structures or strategies ever have to be taught at all. Carver, for example, raises the possibility that if teachers did nothing more than to help students understand the text at hand as well as they possibly could, all of the so-called comprehension strategies and generic structures would "take care of themselves." Put differently, he is asking whether the best way to develop context-free knowledge is to teach as though all knowledge was inherently context-bound (see also Pearson & Dole, 1987).

A related, and equally unsettled, issue in comprehension research is whether there is any substantive difference between text structure and knowledge structure. Clearly, the proponents of each have made convincing arguments concerning the importance of their endeavors (see, for example, Chapter 10 by Weaver and Kintsch, on expositions; and Chapter 8 by Graesser, Golding, and Long on narratives, in this volume); however, the relationship between the two kinds of knowledge remains clouded, at best. For example, when a teacher holds a prereading discussion about the upcoming chapter in a social studies book, is she focusing on knowledge structure or text structure? Are the two ever really independent of one another? Or, does one always entail the other? This issue is as interesting from a theoretical as it is from an instructional point of view.

A final set of issues comes not from potential problems with the explicit explanation perspectives, but from interesting but unanswered questions arising from some of the generic comprehension strategy work reviewed earlier. Of particular interest to us are the issues that arise from the acceptance and application of a social learning model. Such a model explicitly underlies all of the work reviewed about reciprocal teaching, cooperative learning, cognitive apprenticeships, and discussion groups. And several other lines of research, including work completed in the direct and explicit instructional traditions, could be examined from a social learning perspective. We find it regrettable that so few researchers have examined *concurrently* the social factors and social and aesthetic outcomes of instruction on the one hand and its cognitive outcomes on the other hand. We still have much to examine regarding what is learned (and what is learned differently) when students and teachers work together rather than alone on cognitive tasks. It is also possible that a social learning environment might create a situation in which students can learn naturally what can only be taught artificially in a more conventional environment. And the question of what types of students benefit most from a social learning environment is not completely settled.

These represent but a few of the fascinating and important tasks to be completed within the comprehension instruction research tradition. The progress we have made in the last decade and a half, as significant as it is, pales in comparison to the prospect of what we have yet to learn.

REFERENCES

Amlund, J. T., Kardash, C. A. M., & Kulhavy, R. W. (1986). Repetitive reading and recall of expository text. *Reading Research Quarterly, 21,* 49–58.

Anders, P. L., Bos, C. S., & Filip, D. (1984). The effect of semantic feature analysis on the reading comprehension of learning-disabled students. *Changing perspectives on research in reading/language processing and instruction* (Thirty-third yearbook of the National Reading Conference) (pp. 162–172). Rochester, NY: National Reading Conference.

Anderson, R. C. (1977). The notion of schemata and the educational enterprise. In R. C. Anderson, R. J. Spiro, & W. E. Montague (Eds.), *Schooling and the acquisition of knowledge* (pp. 415–431). Hillsdale, NJ: Erlbaum.

Anderson, R. C., Hiebert, E. H., Scott, J. A., & Wilkinson, I. (1985). *Becoming a nation of readers.* Washington, DC: National Institute of Education.

Anderson, R. C., & Pearson, P. D. (1984). A schema-theoretic view of basic processes in reading comprehension. In P. D. Pearson, R. Barr, M. L. Kamil, & P. Mosenthal (Eds.), *Handbook of reading research* (Vol. 1, pp. 255–291). White Plains, NY: Longman.

Anderson, R. C., Reynolds, R. E., Schallert, D. L., & Goetz, E. T. (1977). Frameworks for comprehending discourse. *American Educational Research Journal, 14,* 367–382.

Anderson, R. C., Wilkinson, I. A. G., Mason, J. M., & Shirey, L. (December 1987). Prediction versus word-level questions. In R. C. Anderson (chair), *Experimental investigations of prediction in small-group reading lessons.* Symposium conducted at the 37th meeting of the National Reading Conference, St. Petersburg Beach, FL.

Anderson, R. C., Wilson, P. T., & Fielding, L. G. (1988). Growth in reading and how children spend their time outside of school. *Reading Research Quarterly, 23,* 285–303.

Anderson, T. H., & Armbruster, B. B. (1984). Studying. In P. D. Pearson, R. Barr, M. L. Kamil, & P. Mosenthal (Eds.), *Handbook of reading research* (Vol. 1, pp. 657–679). White Plains, NY: Longman.

Applebee, A. N., & Langer, J. A. (1983). Instructional scaffolding: Reading and writing as natural language activities. *Language Arts, 60,* 168–175.

Armbruster, B. B., & Anderson, T. H. (1980). *The effect of mapping on the free recall of expository text* (Tech. Rep. No. 160). Urbana: University of Illinois, Center for the Study of Reading.

Armbruster, B. B., & Anderson, T. H. (1985). Frames: Structures for informative text. In D. H. Jonassen (Ed.), *The technology of text* (Vol. 2, pp. 90–104). Englewood Cliffs, NJ: Educational Technology Publications.

Armbruster, B. B., Anderson, T. H., & Meyer, J. L. (in press). *The framing project: A collaboration to improve content area reading using instructional graphics* (Tech. Rep.). Urbana: University of Illinois, Center for the Study of Reading.

Armbruster, B. B., Anderson, T. H., & Ostertag, J. (1987). Does text structure/summarization instruction facilitate learning from expository text? *Reading Research Quarterly, 22,* 331–346.

Arnold, H. F. (1942). The comparative effectiveness of certain study techniques in the field of history. *Journal of Educational Psychology, 33,* 449–457.

Atwell, N. (1987). *In the middle.* Montclair, NJ: Boynton/Cook.

Au, K. H., & Kawakami, A. J. (1984). Vygotskian perspectives on discussion processes in small-group reading lessons. In P. L. Peterson, L. C. Wilkinson, & M. Hallinan (Eds.), *The social context of instruction* (pp. 209–225). Orlando, FL: Academic Press.

Au, K. H., & Mason, J. M. (1981). Social organizational factors in learning to read: The balance of rights hypothesis. *Reading Research Quarterly, 17,* 115–152.

Baker, L., & Brown, A. L. (1984). Metacognitive skills and reading. In P. D. Pearson, R. Barr, M. L. Kamil, & P. Mosenthal (Eds.), *Handbook of reading research* (Vol. 1, pp. 353–394). White Plains, NY: Longman.

Bartlett, B. J. (1978). *Top-level structure as an organizational strategy for recall of classroom text.* Unpublished doctoral dissertation, Arizona State University, Tempe.

Barnett, J. E. (1984). Facilitating retention through instruction about text structure. *Journal of Reading Behavior, 16,* 1–13.

Baumann, J. F. (1984). Effectiveness of a direct instruction paradigm for teaching main idea comprehension. *Reading Research Quarterly, 20,* 93–108.

Bean, T. W., Singer, H., Sorter, J., & Frazee, C. (1986). The effect of metacognitive instruction in outlining and graphic organizer construction on students' comprehension in a tenth-grade world history class. *Journal of Reading Behavior, 15*(2), 153–169.

Bean, T. W., & Steenwyk, F. L. (1984). The effect of three forms of summarization instruction on sixth graders' summary writing and comprehension. *Journal of Reading Behavior, 15,* 297–306.

Beck, I. L., Omanson, R. C., & McKeown, M. G. (1982). An instructional redesign of reading lessons: Effects on comprehension. *Reading Research Quarterly, 17,* 462–481.

Berkowitz, S. J. (1986). Effects of instruction text organization on sixth-grade students' memory for expository reading. *Reading Research Quarterly, 21,* 161–178.

Bloome, D., & Green, J. (1984). Directions in the sociolinguistic study of reading. In P. D. Pearson, R. Barr, M. L. Kamil, & P. Mosenthal (Eds.), *Handbook of reading research* (Vol. 1, pp. 395–421). White Plains, NY: Longman.

Bossert, S. T. (1988–1989). Cooperative activities in the classroom. In E. Z. Rothkopf (Ed.), *Review of research in education* (Vol. 15, pp. 225–250). Washington, DC: American Educational Research Association.

Brewer, W. F. (1980). Literary theory, rhetoric, and stylistics: Implications for psychology. In R. Spiro, B. Bruce, & W. F. Brewer (Eds.), *Theoretical issues in reading comprehension* (pp. 221–239). Hillsdale, NJ: Erlbaum.

Brown, A. L., Campione, J. C., & Day, J. (1981). Learning to learn: On training students to learn from texts. *Educational Research, 10,* 14–21.

Brown, A. L., & Day, J. D. (1983). Macrorules for summarizing texts: The development of expertise. *Journal of Verbal Learning and Verbal Behavior, 22*(1), 1–14.

Brown, A. L., Day, J. D., & Jones, R. (1983). The development of plans for summarizing texts. *Child Development, 54,* 968–979.

Brown, J. S., Collins, A., & Duguid, P. (1989). Situated cognition and the culture of learning. *Educational Research, 18*(1), 32–42.

Bruce, B. (1984). A new point of view on children's stories. In R. C. Anderson, J. Osborn, & R. J. Tierney (Eds.), *Learning to read in American schools: Basal readers and content texts* (pp. 153–174). Hillsdale, NJ: Erlbaum.

Bruce, B., & Newman, D. (1978). Interacting plans. *Cognitive Science, 2,* 195–233.

Buss, R. R., Ratliff, J. L., & Irion, J. C. (1985). Effects of instruction on the use of story structure in comprehension of narrative discourse. In J. A. Niles & R. B. Lalik (Eds.), *Issues in literacy: A research perspective,* (Thirty-fourth Yearbook of the National Reading Conference) (pp. 55–58). Rochester, NY: National Reading Conference.

Campbell, D. T., & Stanley, J. C. (1966). *Experimental and quasi-experimental designs for research.* Chicago: Rand McNally.

Campione, J. C. (April 1981). *Learning, academic achievement, and instruction.* Paper delivered at the Second Annual Conference on Reading Research of the Study of Reading, New Orleans.

Carnine, D., & Kinder, D. (1985). Teaching low-performing students to apply generative and schema strategies to narrative and expository material. *Remedial and Special Education, 6*(1), 20–30.

Carr, E. M., Dewitz, P., & Patberg, J. P. (1983). Effect of inference training on children's comprehension of expository text. *Journal of Reading Behavior, 15*(3), 1–17.

Carr, E. M., & Mazur-Stewart, M. (1988). The effects of the vocabulary overview guide on vocabulary comprehension and retention. *Journal of Reading Behavior, 20,* 43–62.

Carver, R. P. (1987). Should reading comprehension skills be taught? In J. E. Readence & R. S. Baldwin (Eds.), *Research in literacy: Merging perspectives* (Thirty-sixth Yearbook of the National Reading Conference) (pp. 115–126). Rochester, NY: National Reading Conference.

Cazden, C. (1986). Classroom discourse. In M. C. Wittrock (Ed.), *Handbook of research on teaching* (3rd ed.) (pp. 432–462). New York: Macmillan.

Chomsky, N. (1959). Review of Skinner's verbal behavior. *Language, 35*(1), 26–58.

Cline, R. K., & Kretke, G. L. (1980). An evaluation of long-term sustained silent reading in the junior high school. *Journal of Reading, 23,* 503–506.

Cohen, P. A., Kulik, J. A., & Kulik, C. C. (1982). Educational outcomes of tutoring: A meta-analysis of findings. *American Educational Research Journal, 19,* 237–248.

Collins, A., Brown, J. S., & Larkin, K. M. (1980). Inference in text understanding. In R. Spiro, B. Bruce, & W. F. Brewer (Eds.), *Theoretical issues in reading comprehension* (pp. 385–407). Hillsdale, NJ: Erlbaum.

Collins, A., Brown, J. S., & Newman, S. E. (in press). Cognitive apprenticeship: Teaching the craft of reading, writing, and mathematics. In L. B. Resnick (Ed.), *Knowing, learning, and instruction: Essays in honor of Robert Glaser.* Hillsdale, NJ: Erlbaum.

Collins, A., & Smith, E. E. (1982). Teaching the process of reading comprehension. In D. K. Detterman & R. J. Sternberg (Eds.), *How and how much can intelligence be increased?* (pp. 173–185). Norwood, NJ: Ablex.

Collins, A. M., & Quillian, M. R. (1969). Retrieval time from semantic memory. *Journal of Verbal Learning and Verbal Behavior, 8,* 240–247.

Collins, C. (1980). Sustained silent reading periods: Effect on teachers' behaviors and students' achievement. *Elementary School Journal, 81,* 108–114.

Craik, F. I. M., & Lockhart, R. S. (1972). Levels of processing: A framework for memory research. *Journal of Verbal Learning and Verbal Behavior, 11,* 671–684.

Cunningham, J. W. (1982). Generating interactions between schemata and text. In J. A. Niles & L. A. Harris (Eds.), *New inquiries in reading research and instruction* (pp. 42–47). Rochester, NY: National Reading Conference.

Dahl, P. R., & Samuels, S. J. (1979). An experimental program for teaching high-speed word recognition and comprehension skills. In J. E. Button, T. C. Lovitt, & T. D. Rowland (Eds.), *Communications research in learning disabilities and mental retardation.* Baltimore, MD: University Park Press.

Dansereau, D. F. (1987). Transfer from cooperative to individual studying. *Journal of Reading, 30,* 614–619.

Darch, C. B., Carnine, D. W., & Kameenui, E. J. (1986). The role of graphic organizers and social structure in content area instruction. *Journal of Reading Behavior, 18,* 275–295.

Davis, F. B. (1944). Fundamental factors of comprehension in reading. *Psychometrica, 9,* 195–197.

Davis, F. B. (1968). Research in comprehension in reading. *Reading Research Quarterly, 3,* 499–545.

Davis, J. N., Lange, D. L., & Samuels, S. J. (1988). Effects of text structure instruction on foreign language readers' recall of a scientific journal article. *Journal of Reading Behavior, 20,* 203–214.

Day, J. D. (1980). *Training summarization skills: A comparison of teaching methods.* Unpublished doctoral dissertation, University of Illinois, Urbana-Champaign.

Dewitz, P., Carr, E., & Patberg, J. (1987). Effects of inference training on comprehension and comprehension monitoring. *Reading Research Quarterly, 22,* 99–119.

Dillon, J. T. (1982). The effect of questions in education and other enterprises. *Journal of Curriculum Studies, 14,* 127–152.

Dillon, J. T. (1983). *Teaching and the art of questioning* (Fastback Series No. 194). Bloomington, IN: Phi Delta Kappa.

Doctorow, M. J., Wittrock, M. C., & Marks, C. B. (1978). Generative processes in reading comprehension. *Journal of Educational Psychology, 70,* 109–118.

Dowhower, S. L. (1987). Effects of repeated reading on second-grade transitional readers' fluency and comprehension. *Reading Research Quarterly, 22,* 389–406.

Draheim, M. E. (1984). Facilitating comprehension and written recall of exposition through DRTA instruction and conceptual mapping. In J. A. Niles & L. A. Harris (Eds.), *Changing perspectives on research in reading/language processing and instruction* (Thirty-Third Yearbook of the National Reading Conference, pp. 167–172). Rochester, NY: National Reading Conference.

Dreher, M. J., & Singer, H. (1980). Story grammar instruction unnecessary for intermediate grade students. *Reading Teacher, 34,* 261–268.

Duffy, G. G., Roehler, L. R., Sivan, E., Rackliffe, G., Book, C., Meloth, M. S., Vavrus, L. G., Wesselman, R., Putnam, J., & Bassiri, D. (1987). Effects of explaining the reasoning associated with using reading strategies. *Reading Research Quarterly, 23*(3), 347–368.

Durkin, D. (1978–1979). What classroom observations reveal about reading comprehension instruction. *Reading Research Quarterly, 15,* 481–533.

Durkin, D. (1981). Reading comprehension instruction in five basal reading series. *Reading Research Quarterly, 16,* 515–544.

Elley, W., & Mangubhai, F. (1983). The impact of reading on second language learning. *Reading Research Quarterly, 19,* 53–67.

Fielding, L. G., Anderson, R. C., & Pearson, P. D. (January 1990). *How discussion questions influence children's story understanding* (Tech. Rep. No. 490). Urbana: University of Illinois, Center for the Study of Reading.

Fijda, N. H. (1972). Simulation of human long-term memory. *Psychological Bulletin, 77,* 1–31.

Fitzgerald, J., & Spiegel, D. L. (1983). Enhancing children's reading comprehension through instruction in narrative structure. *Journal of Reading Behavior, 15*(2), 1–17.

Five, C. L. (1986). Fifth graders respond to a changed reading program. *Harvard Educational Review, 56,* 395–405.

Gallagher, M., & Pearson, P. D. (August 1989). *Discussion, comprehension, and knowledge acquisition in content area classrooms* (Tech. Rep. No. 480). Urbana: University of Illinois, Center for the Study of Reading.

Gambrell, L. B., Pfeiffer, W., & Wilson, R. (1985). The effects of retelling upon reading comprehension and recall of text information. *Journal of Educational Research, 78*, 216–220.

Gardner, H. (1985). *The mind's new science: A history of the cognitive revolution.* New York: Basic Books.

Garner, R., Wagoner, S., & Smith, T. (1983). Externalizing question-answering strategies of good and poor comprehenders. *Readers Research Quarterly, 18*, 439–447.

Germane, C. E. (1921a). Outlining and summarizing compared with reading as methods of studying. In G. M. Whipple (Ed.), *20th Yearbook of the National Society for the Study of Education, Part II.* Bloomington, IL: Public School Publishing Co.

Germane, C. E. (1921b). The value of the written paragraph summary. *Journal of Educational Research, 3*, 116–123.

Gersten, R., & Carnine, D. (1986). Direct instruction in reading comprehension. *Educational Leadership, 43*(7), 70–78.

Geva, E. (1983). Facilitating reading comprehension through flowcharting. *Reading Research Quarterly, 15*, 384–405.

Goetz, E. T. (1984). The role of spatial strategies in processing and remembering text: A cognitive information-processing analysis. In C. D. Holley & D. F. Dansereau (Eds.), *Spatial learning strategies: Techniques, applications, and related issues* (pp. 47–77). New York: Academic Press.

Golden, J. M. (1986). Story interpretation as a group process. *English Quarterly, 19*, 254–266.

Golden, J. M. (1988). The construction of a literary text in a story-reading lesson. In J. Green & J. Harker (Eds.), *Multiple perspective analyses of classroom discourse* (pp. 71–106). Norwood, NJ: Ablex.

Goodman, K. (1986). *What's whole in whole language?* Portsmouth, NH: Heinemann.

Gordon, C. J., & Pearson, P. D. (1983). *The effects of instruction in metacomprehension and inferencing on children's comprehension abilities* (Tech. Rep. No. 277). Urbana: University of Illinois, Center for the Study of Reading.

Graves, M. F., Cooke, C. L., & LaBerge, M. J. (1983). Effects of previewing difficult short stories on low ability junior high school students' comprehension, recall, and attitudes. *Reading Research Quarterly, 28*, 262–276.

Greaney, V. (1980). Factors related to amount and type of leisure time reading. *Reading Research Quarterly, 15*, 337–357.

Greaney, V., & Hegarty, M. (1984). *Correlates of leisure-time reading.* Unpublished manuscript, Educational Research Centre, St. Patrick's College, Dublin.

Green, J. L., Harker, J. O., & Golden, J. M. (1987). Lesson construction: Differing views. In G. W. Noblit & W. T. Pink (Eds.), *Schooling in social context: Qualitative studies* (pp. 46–77). Norwood, NJ: Ablex.

Greenewald, M. J., & Rossing, R. L. (1986). Short-term and long-term effects of story grammar and self-monitoring training on children's story comprehension. In J. A. Niles & R. V. Lalik (Eds.), *Solving problems in literacy: Learners, teachers, and researchers* (Thirty-Fifth Yearbook of the National Reading Conference) (pp. 210–213). Rochester, NY: National Reading Conference.

Hansen, J. (1981). The effects of inference training and practice on young children's reading comprehension. *Reading Research Quarterly, 16*, 391–417.

Hansen, J. (1987). *When writers read.* Portsmouth, NH: Heinemann.

Hansen, J., & Pearson, P. D. (1983). An instructional study: Improving the inferential comprehension of good and poor fourth-grade readers. *Journal of Educational Psychology, 75*, 821–829.

Hare, V. C., & Borchardt, K. M. (1984). Direct instruction of summarization skills. *Reading Research Quarterly, 20*, 62–78.

Harker, J. O. (1988). Contrasting the content of two story-reading lessons: A propositional analysis. In J. Green & J. Harker (Eds.), *Multiple perspective analyses of classroom discourse* (pp. 49–70). Norwood, NJ: Ablex.

Heap, J. L. (1982). Understanding classroom events: A critique of Durkin, with an alternative. *Journal of Reading Behavior, 14*(4), 391–411.

Herman, P. (1985). The effect of repeated readings on reading rate, speech pauses, and word recognition accuracy. *Reading Research Quarterly, 20*, 553–565.

Heyns, B. (1978). *Summer learning and the effects of schooling.* NY: Academic Press.

Hodges, C. A. (1980). Commentary: Toward a broader definition of comprehension instruction. *Reading Research Quarterly, 15*(2), 299–306.

Holdaway, D. (1979). *The foundations of literacy.* Portsmouth, NH: Heinemann.

Holley, C. D., & Dansereau, D. F. (1984a). The development of spatial learning strategies. In C. D. Holley & D. F. Dansereau (Eds.), *Spatial learning strategies: Techniques, applications, and related issues* (pp. 3–19). New York: Academic Press.

Holley, C. D., & Dansereau, D. F. (1984b). Networking: The technique and the empirical evidence. In C. H. Holley & D. F. Dansereau (Eds.), *Spatial learning strategies: Techniques, applications, and related issues* (pp. 81–108). New York: Academic Press.

Holley, C. D., & Dansereau, D. F. (Eds.) (1984c). *Spatial learning strategies: Techniques, applications, and related issues.* New York: Academic Press.

Howe, M. J. A., & Singer, L. (1975). Presentation variables and students' activities in meaningful learning. *British Journal of Educational Psychology, 45*, 52–61.

Idol, L. (1987). Group story mapping: A comprehension for both skilled and unskilled readers. *Journal of Learning Disabilities, 20*, 196–205.

Ingham, J. (1982). *Books and reading development: The Bradford book flood experiment* (2nd ed.). Exeter, NH: Heinemann.

Jenkins, J. R., & Jenkins, L. M. (1987). Making peer tutoring work. *Educational Leadership, 44*(6), 64–68.

Johnson, D. D., & Barrett, T. C. (1981). Prose comprehension: A descriptive analysis of instructional practices. In C. M. Santa & B. L. Hayes (Eds.), *Children's prose comprehension* (pp. 72–102). Newark, DE: International Reading Association.

Johnson, D., & Johnson, R. (1975). *Learning together and alone.* Englewood Cliffs, NJ: Prentice Hall.

Johnson, D., & Johnson, R. (1985). The internal dynamics of cooperative learning groups. In R. Slavin, S. Sharon, S. Kagan, R. Hertz-Lazarowitz, C. Webb, & R. Schmuck (Eds.), *Learning to cooperate, cooperating to learn* (pp. 103–124). New York: Plenum Press.

Johnson, D. D., & Pearson, P. D. (1984). *Teaching reading vocabulary* (2nd ed.). New York: Holt, Rinehart & Winston.

Johnson, D. D., Toms-Bronowski, S., & Pittelman, S. D. (1982). *An investigation of the effectiveness of semantic mapping and semantic feature analysis with intermediate grade level children* (Program Rep. No. 83–3). Madison, WI: Wisconsin Center for Education Research.

Judy, J. E., Alexander, P. A. Kulikowich, J. M., & Wilson, V. L. (1988). Effects of two instructional approaches and peer tutoring on gifted and nongifted sixth-grade students' analogy performance. *Reading Research Quarterly, 23,* 236–256.

King, J. R., Biggs, S., & Lipsky, S. (1984). Students' self-questioning and summarizing as reading study strategies. *Journal of Reading Behavior, 16,* 205–218.

Kintsch, W., & van Dijk, T. A. (1978). Toward a model of text comprehension and production. *Psychological Review, 85,* 363–394.

Kirsch, I. S., & Guthrie, J. T. (1984). Prose comprehension and text search as a function of reading volume. *Reading Research Quarterly, 19,* 331–342.

Koskinen, P., & Blum, I. (1984). Repeated oral reading and the acquisition of fluency. In J. A. Niles & L. Harris (Eds.), *Changing perspectives on research in reading/language processing and instruction* (Thirty-Third Yearbook of the National Reading Conference) (pp. 183–187). Rochester, NY: National Reading Conference.

Koskinen, P. S., Gambrell, L. B., Kapinus, B. A., & Heathington, B. S. (1988). Retelling: A strategy for enhancing students' reading comprehension. *Reading Teacher, 41,* 892–896.

Krashen, S. D. (1988). Do we learn to read by reading? The relationship between free reading and reading ability. In D. Tannen (Ed.), *Linguistics in context: Connecting observation and understanding* (Lectures from the 1985 LSA/TESOL and NEH Institutes) (pp. 269–298). Norwood, NJ: Ablex.

Lehr, S. (1988). The child's developing sense of theme as a response to literature. *Reading Research Quarterly, 23,* 337–357.

Levin, J. R., Johnson, D. D., Pittelman, S. D., Levin, K. M. Shriberg, L. K., Toms-Bronowski, S., & Hayes, B. L. (1984). A comparison of semantic- and mnemonic-based vocabulary-learning strategies. *Reading Psychology, 5,* 1–16.

Levin, J. R., & Pressley, M. (1981). Improving children's prose comprehension: Selected strategies that seem to succeed. In C. M. Santa & B. L. Hayes (Eds.), *Children's prose comprehension* (pp. 44–71). Newark, DE: International Reading Association.

Linden, M., & Wittrock, M. C. (1981). The teaching of reading comprehension according to the model of generative learning. *Reading Research Quarterly, 17,* 44–57.

Lindsay, P. H., & Norman, D. A. (1977). *Human information processing: An introduction to psychology* (2nd ed.). New York: Academic Press.

Long, G., & Aldersley, S. (1984). Networking: Application with hearing-impaired students. In *Spatial learning strategies: Techniques, applications, and related issues* (pp. 109–125). New York: Academic Press.

Long, G., Hein, R., & Coggiola, D. (1979). *Networking: A technique for understanding and remembering instructional material* (Tech. Rep.). Rochester, NY: Department of Educational Research and Development, National Technical Institute for the Deaf, Rochester Institute of Technology.

Lysynchuk, L. M., Presley, M., d'Ailly, H., Smith, M., & Cake, H. (1989). *A methodological analysis of reading comprehension strategy instruction research.* London, Ont.: University of Western Ontario, Department of Psychology.

McCracken, R. A. (1971). Initiating sustained silent reading. *Journal of Reading, 14,* 521–524, 582–583.

McGee, L. M. (1982). Awareness of text structure: Effects on children's recall of expository text. *Reading Research Quarterly, 17,* 581–590.

McGinley, W. J., & Denner, P. R. (1987). Story impressions: A prereading/writing activity. *Journal of Reading, 31,* 248–253.

McNeil, J., & Donant, L. (1982). Summarization strategy for improving reading comprehension. In J. A. Niles & L. A. Harris (Eds.), *New inquiries in reading research and instruction* (pp. 215–219). Rochester, NY: National Reading Conference.

Mandler, J. M. (1978). A code in the node: The use of a story schema in retrieval. *Discourse Processes, 1,* 14–35.

Mandler, R. M., & Johnson, N. S. (1977). Remembrance of things parsed: Story structure and recall. *Cognitive Psychology, 9,* 111–151.

Manning, G. L., & Manning, M. (1984). What models of recreational reading make a difference? *Reading World, 23,* 375–380.

Marino, J. L., Gould, S. M., & Haas, L. W. (1985). The effects of writing as a prereading activity on delayed recall of narrative text. *Elementary School Journal, 86,* 199–205.

Meyer, B. J. F. (1975). *The organization of prose and its effect on memory.* Amsterdam: North-Holland Publishing Co.

Meyer, B. J. F. (1979). Organizational patterns in prose and their use in reading. In M. L. Kamil & A. J. Moe (Eds.), *Reading research: Studies and applications* (pp. 108–117). Clemson, SC: National Reading Conference.

Meyer, B. J. F., Brandt, D. M., & Bluth, G. J. (1980). Use of top-level structure in text: Key for reading comprehension of ninth-grade students. *Reading Research Quarterly, 16,* 72–103.

Meyer, B. J. F., & Rice, G. E. (1984). The structure of text. In P. D. Pearson, R. Barr, M. L. Kamil, & P. Mosenthal (Eds.), *Handbook of reading research* (Vol. 1, pp. 319–351). White Plains, NY: Longman.

Miller, G. E. (1985). The effects of general and specific self-instruction training on children's comprehension monitoring performances during reading *Reading Research Quarterly, 20,* 616–628.

Miller, G. E. (1987). The influence of self-instruction on the comprehension monitoring performance of average and above-average readers. *Journal of Reading Behavior, 19,* 303–317.

Miller, G. E., Giovenco, A., & Rentiers, K. A. (1987). Fostering comprehension monitoring in below-average readers through self-instruction training. *Journal of Reading Behavior, 19,* 379–394.

Minsky, M. (1975). A framework for representing knowledge. In P. H. Winston (Ed.), *The psychology of computer vision.* New York: McGraw-Hill.

Moore, D. W., & Readence, J. E. (1980). A meta-analysis of the effect of graphic organizers on learning from text. In M. L. Kamil & A. L. Moe (Eds.), *Perspectives on reading research and instruction* (Twenty-Ninth Yearbook of the National Reading Conference). Washington, DC: National Reading Conference.

Moore, D. W., & Readence, J. E. (1984). A quantitative and qualitative review of graphic organizer research. *Journal of Educational Research, 78,* 11–17.

Morrow, L. M. (1984a). Effects of story retelling on young children's comprehension and sense of story structure. In J. A. Niles & L. A. Harris (Eds.), *Changing perspectives on research in reading/language processing and instruction* (Thirty-Third Yearbook of the National Reading Conference) (pp. 95–100). Rochester, NY: National Reading Conference.

Morrow, L. M. (1984b). Reading stories to young children: Effects of story structure and traditional questioning strategies on comprehension. *Journal of Reading Behavior, 16,* 273–288.

Morrow, L. M. (1985). Retelling stories: A strategy for improving young children's comprehension, concept of story structure, and oral language complexity. *Elementary School Journal, 85,* 647–661.

Morrow, L. M. (1986). Effects of story retelling on children's dictation of original stories. *Journal of Reading Behavior, 18,* 135–152.

Morrow, L. M., Gambrell, L., Kapinus, B., Koskinen, P., Marshall, N., & Mitchell, J. N. (1986). Retelling: A strategy for reading instruction and assessment. In J. A. Niles & R. Lalik (Eds.), *Solving problems in literacy: Learners, teachers, and researchers* (Thirty-Fifth Yearbook of the National Reading Conference) (pp. 73–80). Rochester, NY: National Reading Conference.

Morrow, L. M., & Weinstein, C. S. (1986). Encouraging voluntary reading. The impact of a literature program on children's use of library corners. *Reading Research Quarterly, 21,* 330–346.

Neuman, S. (1988). Enhancing children's comprehension through previewing. In J. Readence & R. S. Baldwin (Eds.), *Dialogues in literacy research* (Thirty-Seventh Yearbook of the National Reading Conference) (pp. 219–224). Chicago, IL: National Reading Conference.

Nolte, R., & Singer, H. (1985). Active comprehension: Teaching a process of reading comprehension and its effects on achievement. *Reading Teacher, 39,* 24–31.

O'Flahavan, J. O. (1989). *Second graders' social, intellectual, and affective development in varied group discussions about narrative texts: An explanation of participation structures.* Unpublished doctoral dissertation, University of Illinois, Urbana-Champaign.

Omanson, R. C. (1982). Analysis of narratives: Identifying central, supportive, and distracting content. *Discourse Processes, 5,* 195–224.

Omanson, R. C., Beck, I. L., Voss, J. F., & McKeown, M. G. (1984). The effects of reading lessons on comprehension: A processing description *Cognition and Instruction, 1,* 45–67.

O'Shea, L. J., Sindelar, P. T., & O'Shea, D. J. (1985). The effects of repeated readings and attentional cues on reading fluency and comprehension. *Journal of Reading Behavior, 17,* 129–142.

Palincsar, A. S. (1986). The role of dialogue in providing scaffolded instruction. *Educational Psychologist, 21,* 73–98.

Palincsar, A. S., & Brown, A. L. (1984). Reciprocal teaching of comprehension-fostering and comprehension-monitoring activities. *Cognition and Instruction, 1,* 117–175.

Palincsar, A. S., Brown, A. L., & Martin, S. M. (1987). Peer interaction in reading comprehension instruction. *Educational Psychologist, 22,* 231–253.

Paris, S. G. (1986). Teaching children to guide their reading and learning. In T. E. Raphael (Ed.), *The contexts of school-based literacy* (pp. 115–130). New York: Random House.

Paris, S. G., Cross, D. R., & Lipson, M. Y. (1984). Informed strategies for learning: A program to improve children's awareness and comprehension. *Journal of Educational Psychology, 76,* 1239–1252.

Paris, S. G., & Jacobs, J. E. (1984). Benefits of informed instruction for children's reading awareness and comprehension skills. *Child Development, 55*, 2083–2093.

Paris, S. G., Lipson, M., & Wixson, K. (1983). Becoming a strategic reader. *Contemporary Educational Psychology, 8*, 293–316.

Paris, S. G., & Myers, M., II. (1981). Comprehension monitoring, memory, and study strategies of good and poor readers. *Journal of Reading Behavior, 13*(1), 5–22.

Pearson, P. D. (1985). Changing the face of reading comprehension instruction. *Reading Teacher, 38*, 724–738.

Pearson, P. D. (1986). Twenty years of research in reading comprehension. In T. E. Raphael (Ed.), *The contexts of school-based literacy* (pp. 43–62). New York: Random House.

Pearson, P. D., & Dole, J. A. (1987). Explicit comprehension instruction: A review of research and a new conceptualization of instruction. *Elementary School Journal, 88*(2), 151–165.

Pearson, P. D., & Gallagher, M. C. (1983). The instruction of reading comprehension. *Contemporary Educational Psychology, 8*, 317–344.

Pearson, P. D., Hansen, J., & Gordon, C. (1979). The effect of background knowledge on young children's comprehension of explicit and implicit information. *Journal of Reading Behavior, 9*, 201–210.

Pearson, P. D., & Johnson, D. (1978). *Teaching reading comprehension.* New York: Holt, Rinehart, & Winston.

Pressley, M., Goodchild, F., Fleet, J., Zajchowski, R., & Evans, E. D. (1989). The challenges of classroom strategy instruction. *Elementary School Journal, 89*(3), 301–342.

Pressley, M., Johnson, C. J., Symons, S., McGoldrick, J. A., & Kurita, J. A. (in press). Strategies that improve children's memory and comprehension of what is read. *Elementary School Journal.*

Pressley, M., Symons, S., Snyder, B. L., & Cariglia-Bull, T. (1989). Strategy instruction research comes of age. *Journal of the Council for Learning Disabilities: Learning Disability Quarterly, 12*(1), 16–31.

Prince, A. T., & Mancus, D. S. (1987). Enriching comprehension: A schema-altered basal reading lesson. *Reading Research and Instruction, 27*(1), 45–54.

Raphael, T. E. (1984). Teaching learners about sources of information for answering comprehension questions. *Journal of Reading, 27*, 303–311.

Raphael, T. E., & McKinney, J. (1983). An examination of fifth- and eighth-grade children's question-answering behavior: An instructional study in metacognition. *Journal of Reading Behavior, 15*(1), 67–86.

Raphael, T. E., & Pearson, P. D. (1985). Increasing students' awareness of sources of information for answering questions. *American Educational Research Journal, 22*, 217–236.

Raphael, T. E., & Wonnacott, C. A. (1985). Heightening fourth-grade students' sensitivity to sources of information for answering comprehension questions. *Reading Research Journal, 20*, 282–296.

Rashotte, C., & Torgesen, T. (1985). Repeated reading and reading fluency in learning-disabled children. *Reading Research Quarterly, 20*, 180–188.

Richgels, D. J., McGee, L. M., Lomax, R. G., & Sheard, C. (1987). Awareness of four text structures: Effects on recall of expository text. *Reading Research Quarterly, 22*(2), 177–196.

Rinehart, S. D., Stahl, S. A., & Erickson, L. G. (1986). Some effects of summarization training on reading and studying. *Reading Research Quarterly, 21*, 422–438.

Rogers, T. (1988). *Students as literary critics: A case study of the interpretive theories, processes, and experiences of ninth-grade students.* Unpublished doctoral dissertation, University of Illinois, Urbana-Champaign.

Rosenshine, B., & Stevens, R. (1984). Classroom instruction in reading. In P. D. Pearson, R. Barr, M. L. Kamil, & P. Mosenthal (Eds.), *Handbook of reading research* (Vol. 1, pp. 745–798). White Plains, NY: Longman.

Rumelhart, D. (1975). Notes on a schema for stories. In D. G. Bobrow & A. M. Collins (Eds.), *Representation and understanding: Studies in cognitive science* (pp. 211–236). New York: Academic Press.

Samuels, S. J., Tennyson, R., Sax, L., Mulcahy, P., Schermer, N., & Hajovy, H. (1987). *Adults' use of text structure in the recall of a scientific journal article.* Unpublished manuscript.

Santa, C. M., & Hayes, B. L. (Eds.), (1981). *Children's prose comprehension.* Newark, DE: International Reading Association.

Schank, R. C. (1972). Conceptual dependency: A theory of natural language understanding. *Cognitive Psychology, 3*, 552–631.

Schank, R. C., & Abelson, R. P. (1977). *Scripts, plans, goals, and understanding,* Hillsdale, NJ: Erlbaum.

Schmitt, M. C. (1988). The effects of an elaborated directed reading activity on the metacomprehension skills of third graders. In J. E. Readance & R. S. Baldwin (Eds.), *Dialogues in literacy research* (Thirty-Seventh Yearbook of the National Reading Conference) (pp. 167–181). Chicago, IL: National Reading Conference.

Schreiber, P. A. (1980). On the acquisition of reading fluency. *Journal of Reading Behavior, 12*, 177–186.

Schreiber, P. A. (1987). Prosody and structure in children's syntactic processing. In R. Horowitz & S. J. Samuels (Eds.), *Comprehending oral and written language* (pp. 243–270). New York: Academic Press.

Schunk, D. H., & Rice, J. M. (1987). Enhancing comprehension skill and self-efficacy with strategy value information. *Journal of Reading Behavior, 19*, 285–302.

Shake, M. C. (1988). Questioning during remedial reading instruction. *Questioning Exchange, 2,* 219–225.

Short, E. J., & Ryan, E. B. (1984). Metacognitive differences between skilled and less-skilled readers: Remediating deficits through story grammar and attribution training. *Journal of Educational Psychology*, 76, 225–235.

Short, K. E., & Burke, C. L. (in press). New potentials for teacher education: Teaching and learning as inquiry. *Elementary School Journal*.

Simons, H. D. (1971). Reading comprehension: The need for a new perspective. *Reading Research Quarterly*, 6, 338–363.

Singer, H. (1980). Active comprehension: From answering to asking questions. In C. M. McCullough (Ed.), *Inchworm, inchworm: Persistent problems in reading education* (pp. 222–232). Newark, DE: International Reading Association.

Singer, H., & Donlan, D. (1982). Active comprehension: Problem-solving schema with question generation for comprehension of complex short stories. *Reading Research Quarterly*, 17, 166–186.

Slater, W. H., Graves, M. H., & Piche, G. H. (1985). Effects of structural organizers on ninth-grade students' comprehension and recall of four patterns of expository test. *Reading Research Quarterly*, 20, 189–202.

Slavin, R. E. (1987a). Cooperative learning and the cooperative school. *Educational Leadership*, 45(3), 7–13.

Slavin, R. E. (1987b). Cooperative learning: Where behavioral and humanistic approaches to classroom motivation meet. *Elementary School Journal*, 88, 29–37.

Smith, F. (1975). *Comprehension and learning*. New York: Holt, Rinehart, & Winston.

Smith, F. (1981). Demonstrations, engagement, and sensitivity: A revised approach to language learning. *Language Arts*, 58(1), 103–122.

Stanovich, K. E. (1986). Matthew effects in reading: Some consequences of individual differences in the acquisition of literacy. *Reading Research Quarterly*, 21, 360–407.

Stein, N. L. (1978). *How children understand stories: A developmental analysis* (Tech. Rep. No. 69). Urbana: University of Illinois, Center for the Study of Reading.

Stein, N. L., & Glenn, C. (1979). An analysis of story comprehension in elementary school children. In R. O. Freedle (Ed.), *New directions in discourse processing: Vol. II. Advances in discourse processes* (pp. 53–120). Norwood, NJ: Ablex.

Stevens, R. J., Madden, N. A., Slavin, R. E., & Farnish, A. M. (1987). Cooperative integrated reading and composition; Two field experiments. *Reading Research Quarterly*, 22, 433–454.

Stordahl, K. E., & Christensen, C. M. (1956). The effect of study techniques on comprehension and retention. *Journal of Educational Research*, 49, 561–570.

Sundbye, N. (1987). Text explicitness and inferential questioning: Effects on story understanding and recall. *Recall Research Quarterly*, 22, 82–98.

Taylor, B. M. (1980). Children's memory for expository text after reading. *Reading Research Quarterly*, 15, 399–411.

Taylor, B. M. (1982). Text structure and children's comprehension and memory for expository material. *Journal of Educational Psychology*, 74, 323–340.

Taylor, B. M., & Beach, R. W. (1984). The effects of text structure instruction on middle-grade students' comprehension and production of expository texts. *Reading Research Quarterly*, 19, 134–146.

Taylor, B. M., & Berkowitz, S. (1980). Facilitating children's comprehension of content area material. In M. Kamil & A. Moe (Eds.), *Perspectives on reading research and instruction* (pp. 64–68). Washington, DC: National Reading Conference.

Taylor, N. E., Wade, M. R., & Yekovich, F. R. (1985). The effects of text manipulation and multiple reading strategies on the reading performance of good and poor readers. *Reading Research Quarterly*, 20, 566–574.

Thames, D. G., & Readence, J. E. (1988). Effects of differential vocabulary instruction and lesson frameworks on the reading comprehension of primary children. *Reading Research and Instruction*, 27(2), 1–12.

Tharp, R. G. (1982). The effective instruction of comprehension: Results and description of the Kamehameha Early Education Program. *Reading Research Quarterly*, 17, 503–527.

Tharp, R. G., & Gallimore, R. (1989a). *Rousing minds to life: Teaching, learning, and schooling in social context*. New York: Cambridge University Press.

Tharp, R.G., & Gallimore, R. (1989b). Rousing schools to life. *American Educator*, 13(2), 20–25, 46–52.

Thorndyke, P. W. (1977). Cognitive structures in comprehension and memory of narrative discourse. *Cognitive Psychology*, 9, 77–110.

Tierney, R. J., & Cunningham, J. W. (1984). Research on teaching comprehension. In P. D. Pearson, R. Barr, M. L. Kamil, & P. Mosenthal (Eds.), *Handbook of reading research* (Vol. 1, pp. 609–655). White Plains, NY: Longman.

Top, B. L., & Osguthorpe, R. T. (1987). Reverse-role tutoring: The effects of handicapped students tutoring regular class students. *Elementary School Journal*, 87, 413–423.

van Dijk, T. A., & Kintsch, W. (1978). Cognitive psychology and discourse: Recalling and summarizing stories. In W. U. Dressler (Ed.), *Current trends in textlinguistics* (pp. 61–80). New York: de Gruyter.

Vaughan, J. L. (1984). Concept structuring: The technique and empirical evidence. *Spatial learning strategies: Techniques, applications, and related issues* (pp. 127–147). New York: Academic Press.

Walmsley, S. A., & Walp, T. (1990). Integrating literature and composing into the language arts curriculum: Theory and practice. *Elementary School Journal*, 90, 251–279.

Webb, N. R. (1985). Student interaction and learning in small groups: A research summary. In R. E. Slavin, S. Sharan, S. Kagan, R. Hertz-Lararowitz, C. Webb, & R. Schmuck (Eds.), *Learning to cooperate, cooperating to learn* (pp. 147–172). New York: Plenum.

Weber, R. M. (1986). *The constraints of the questioning routine in reading instruction.* Paper presented at the annual meeting of the American Educational Research Association, San Francisco, CA.

Wittrock, M. C. (1974). Learning as a generative process. *Educational Psychologist, 11,* 87–95.

Wittrock, M. C., Marks, C. B., & Doctorow, M. J. (1975). Reading as a generative process. *Journal of Educational Psychology, 67,* 484–489.

Wong, B. Y. L. (1985). Self-questioning instructional research: A review. *Review of Educational Research, 55,* 227–268.

Wong, B. Y. L., & Jones, W. (1982). Increasing metacomprehension in learning-disabled and normally-achieving students through self-questioning training. *Learning Disabilities Quarterly, 5,* 228–240.

Wood, D. J., Bruner, J. S., & Ross, G. (1976). The role of tutoring in problem solving. *Journal of Child Psychology and Psychiatry, 17,* 89–100.

Yopp, R. E. (1988). Questioning and active comprehension. *Questioning Exchange, 2,* 231–238.

30

TEACHERS'
INSTRUCTIONAL ACTIONS
Laura R. Roehler and Gerald G. Duffy

In this chapter, we try to answer the question, What actions do teachers take to communicate the curriculum of literacy to students in school? The chapter is organized into two major sections: (1) effective instructional actions and (2) the role these actions play in current instructional models.

BACKGROUND

A Historical Context

Instruction has historically centered on drill-and-practice, which fit nicely with the then-prevailing theory that learning was a matter of shaping overt student behavior by providing reinforcement within a stimulus-response cycle. Teachers exterminated incorrect responses through punishment and established correct responses through reinforcement and repetition.

In reading, drill-and-practice often took the form of skills management systems (Otto, Wolf, & Eldridge, 1984), in which reading was conceptualized as a list of skills. Teachers tested students on each skill in turn, providing corrective feedback as needed and retesting until the students "mastered" the individual skill. Then they moved to the next skill in the list and repeated the process. Commercial programs such as DISTAR (Direct Instruction Systems for Teaching Arithmetic and Reading) emphasized such drill-and-practice through use of scripted lessons, small-group instruction, use of physical teacher signals to cue students to correct responses, choral student responses, and extrinsic reinforcement. Teacher-effectiveness research (see Brophy, 1979; Dunkin & Biddle, 1974; Hoffman, Chapter 32 in this volume; Rosenshine, 1979) tended to support drill-and-practice types of instruction because they were associated with high standardized test scores. Consequently, instruction centered on recitation (Duffy, 1983; Duffy & Roehler, 1982; Mehan, 1979), in which students practice or answer questions after limited amounts of explanation, development, or assistance (Brophy & Good, 1986; Duffy & McIntyre, 1982; Durkin, 1978–1979; Herrmann, 1986; Stallings, Needles, & Stayrook, 1979). Bereiter and Scardamalia (1987) refer to such instruction as the *exercise model* (p. 12).

Current theories of learning, however, call for instruction that goes beyond the exercise model. Specifically, research on cognitive psychology and associated work in information processing emphasizes organization, coherence, and connectedness in which " . . . knowledge is structure . . . not a 'basket of facts.' " (R. C. Anderson, 1984, p. 5). Two distinctions are particularly important. First, in order for learners to move information from short- to long-term memory, they must transform information into meaningful concepts that can be referenced and stored in organized ways. Hence, the focus is organization of knowledge, not memory for knowledge. Second, processes can be either self-regulated or automatic (Frederiksen, 1984). *Automatic* means that an individual does not consciously control thought; in contrast, *self-regulation* means that one assumes conscious control of cognitive processing, often referred to as *metacognition* (Baker & Brown, 1984; Flavell, 1976). The result is a focus on understanding (Brophy, in press) rather than low-level memory outcomes.

This shift in emphasis has recently influenced instruction. Instruction based on drill-and-practice is no longer adequate because it does not promote understanding and self-regulation of learning. Resnick (1981) characterized what was needed as follows:

> . . . today's assumptions about the nature of learning and thinking are interactionist. We assume that learning occurs as a result of mental constructions of the learner. These constructions respond to information and stimuli in the environment, but they do not copy or mirror them. This means that instruction must be designed not to put knowledge into learners' heads, but to put learners in positions that allow them to construct well-structured knowledge. (p. 660)

Others make similar calls for new kinds of instruction (Fennema, Carpenter, & Peterson, 1986). For instance, Jones (1986) argues for *cognitive instruction*, in which the teacher or the instructional materials help students process information in meaningful ways; Tharp and Gallimore (1988) call for *assisted performance*, in which teachers guide students through stages; and Bereiter and Scardamalia (1987) call for an *intentional learning model*, in which students gradually take over all the goal-setting, context-creating, motivational, strategic, analytical, and inferential actions that are initially carried out by the teacher. Others call for *propleptic teaching*, in which students are actively involved with teachers, who socially mediate students' emerging understandings (Collins, Brown, & Newman, 1986; Palincsar, 1986; Rogoff & Gardner, 1984). Langer and Applebee (1986) describe it as follows:

> In propleptic teaching, the student carries out simpler aspects of the task while observing and learning more complex forms from the adult, who serves as a model. (p. 181)

Examples include apprenticeship approaches, where students are encouraged to acquire skills by working with a master (Collins & Brown, in press), and collaborative instruction, in which students learn by participating in the solution of problems (Greeno, 1986). Still another example is the *cognitive mediational paradigm* (Winne, 1985), or the *mediating process paradigm* (W. Doyle, 1980), in which instruction is seen not as a direct influence on student achievement outcomes but as an experience that causes students to think in particular ways which, in turn, mediate what they learn. As summarized by Shulman (1986):

> The learner does not respond to the instruction per se. The learner responds to the instruction as transformed, as actively apprehended. Thus, to understand why learners respond (or fail to respond) as they do, ask not what they were taught, but what sense they rendered of what they were taught. The consequences of teaching can only be understood as a function of what that teaching stimulates the learner to do with the material. (p. 17)

Studies by Weinstein (1983), Winne and Marx (1982), and Blumenfeld and colleagues (Blumenfeld, Pintrich, & Meece, 1983; Blumenfeld, Pintrich, Meece, & Wessels, 1982) demonstrate that students cognitively mediate instructional events and interpret teachers' intended instructional messages in various ways. To be successful, therefore, a teacher must influence students' cognitive activities during instruction. As Pearson, Dole, Duffy, and Roehler (in press) point out, students construct meaning in response to instruction much as readers construct meaning embedded in text. In cognitive mediational paradigm terms, readers mediate text and, as a result, may construct meaning differently from what the author intended. Similarly, students mediate instructional experiences, constructing curricular meaning that may or may not be precisely what the teacher intended. *Instruction, then, should direct a learner's internal cognitive events so as to increase the probability that intended meanings will be constructed.*

In general, therefore, movement is away from drill-and-practice, in which teachers emphasize repetition, and toward a cognitive model, in which teachers provide information and mediate student mental processing. Lampert (1986) describes it as follows:

> They [students] need to be treated like sense-makers rather than rememberers and forgetters. They need to see connections between what they are supposed to be learning in school and things they care about understanding outside of school, and these connections need to be related to the substance of what they are supposed to be learning. (p. 340)

Such instruction is distinct from drill-and-practice in two ways. First, the instructional objective is students' active cognitive processing designed to result in understanding, organized information, networks of connections, and self-regulated learning. Second, instruction demands more from teachers than simply eliciting student responses in a drill-and-practice mode. As Shulman (1987) says, instruction involves:

> . . . transforming [one's] own comprehension of the subject matter, [one's] own skills of performance or desired attitude values, into pedagogical representations and actions. There are ways of talking, showing, enacting, or otherwise representing ideas so that the unknowing can come to know, those without understanding can comprehend and discern, the unskilled can become adept. (p. 7)

The purpose of this chapter is to identify those "pedagogical representations and actions."

Criteria for Selecting
Teachers' Instructional Actions

Despite recent emphasis on cognitively oriented instructional approaches, murky definitional parameters make it difficult to locate research about teachers' specific instructional actions in the literature. To avoid such murkiness here, we list five criteria that guided our search for teachers' instructional actions.

First, because of our desire to emphasize cognitively oriented instruction associated with understanding and because earlier instructional models have been reviewed extensively in the past (e.g., Brophy & Good, 1986; Rosenshine & Stevens, 1984), we do not review them here. This is not to say that drill-and-practice is no longer relevant to literacy instruction. To the contrary, it continues to be important for certain automatized outcomes. However, our focus is cognitive outcomes. Second, because instruction is an intentional effort to create specified curricular outcomes in students, we did not review studies in which children learned or developed independently of instruction. Instead, we focused on intentional efforts to create curricular outcomes. Third, while classroom management is crucial to effective instruction (Doyle, 1986), we make a distinction here between management and instruction. *Management* is what teachers do to insure students' attention; *instruction* is what teachers do to create desired curricular outcomes once students are attending. This chapter focuses on the latter. Fourth, while instruction often includes materials, we focus here on teachers. Instructional materials are not examined. Fifth, while it is possible for parents and peers to conduct instruction, we examine only teachers. Finally, we emphasize "actions" rather than "behaviors" or "procedures" in order to highlight the intentional and cognitive aspects of instruction as opposed to the technical and routinized aspects of instruction. In sum, then, this chapter takes a particular focus. It examines teachers' instructional actions as they occur in the context of intentional efforts in classrooms to develop specified curricular outcomes consistent with cognitive orientations to literacy learning.

TEACHERS' INSTRUCTIONAL ACTIONS

Teachers' instructional actions are reviewed in four subsections: planning actions, motivating actions, information-giving actions, and teacher mediation actions.

Teacher Actions Associated with Planning

Teacher planning has been studied since the 1970s with emphasis on teachers' *preactive thinking* (Clark & Peterson, 1986). While this research yields little specific information about teacher actions, it does suggest (1) that teachers engaged in a rich variety of planning, much of which is directed toward simplification and routinization of schooling rather than toward substantive instructional issues (Yinger, 1977); (2) that planning of daily lessons is seldom emphasized by teachers (Clark & Yinger, 1979); (3) that planning plays a heavy role early in the year and that early plans are seldom changed or modified as the year progresses (Anderson & Evertson, 1978; Clark & Elmore, 1979); and (4) that standard linear models for rational planning taught in most preservice teacher education institutions are unlike what teachers actually do when they plan (Clark & Peterson, 1986).

Other lines of research suggest three foci for teacher planning: transforming knowledge, selecting academic work to assign, and selecting appropriate activity structures.

Transforming knowledge. Planning transforms published curriculum into teacher actions. Shulman (1986) describes this as the "missing paradigm" because there is so little research on how teachers transform knowledge about what is to be learned into instructional content. Wilson, Shulman, and Richert (1987) hypothesize that this transformation involves critical interpretation in which teachers (1) review instructional materials in light of their own understanding; (2) create alternative representations of the subject matter as reflected in a repertoire of metaphors, analogies, illustrations, activities, and examples teachers use when teaching; (3) create adaptations to fit content to general characteristics of their students; and (4) tailor materials to individual student characteristics.

More specifically, teachers transform content into *critical features*, such as when Beck, Omanson, and McKeown (1982) break stories to be read into "silent reading units" representing critical features of story structure. The importance of determining critical features has often been substantiated (Engelmann & Carnine, 1982; Leinhardt & Smith, 1985; Paris, Cross, & Lipson, 1984; Wood, Bruner, & Ross, 1976). Teachers also transform content by *simplifying* it. That is, on the basis of critical features, teachers simplify the task to expedite students' efforts to learn it (Englemann & Carnine, 1982; Leinhardt & Smith, 1985; Wood, Bruner, & Ross, 1976). Finally, teachers transform content by *selecting examples* that highlight critical features (Baumann, 1984; Englemann & Carnine, 1982; Leinhardt & Smith, 1985). In sum, when teachers plan they identify critical features, simplify the task, and create effective examples, all of which transform the published curriculum into instructional content.

Academic work.   Planning also includes deciding what *academic work* students will do (Bossert, 1979; Doyle, 1983; Marx, 1983; Winne, 1985). In reading, for instance, students may be asked to answer comprehension questions after reading a story, or to complete a worksheet about letter-sound associations, or to describe personal feelings after listening to the teacher read *Charlotte's Web*. What they learn depends in large part on what the academic work (or task) leads them to think. That is, the answers teachers require students to produce (and the cognition students must engage in to produce those answers) determines what is learned. For instance, Doyle (1984) examined the tasks and events leading to the creation of academic products in six junior high school classrooms and concluded that the academic work directed students to employ memory and other low-level cognitive processing. In writing, this phenomenon is observed in the strategies students activate (Flower, 1987), and in mathematics in how features of academic work produce either procedure-oriented or understanding-oriented results (Putnam, 1987). A good illustration from reading is a descriptive study of first-grade seatwork (Anderson, Brubaker, Alleman, & Duffy, 1985). Researchers observed students as they pursued daily seatwork, noting their behaviors, and audio-taping their responses to informal interviews. Results indicated that potentially at-risk students demonstrated virtually no understanding that seatwork was supposed to help them be better readers. Instead, they thought the primary goal was "to get done." In effect, the academic work in these classrooms encouraged low-aptitude students to think about how to finish, not about how to make sense out of text. Hence, selecting academic work is an important part of teacher planning because it directs students to certain learnings (i.e., students acquire the operations necessary to accomplish the task).

Activity structures.   A third teacher planning action involves *structuring lesson activity*. Leinhardt and Greeno (1986) note that teachers divide lessons into subunits, each of which is characterized by a particular activity. In a standard basal text lesson, for example, activity structures often include subunits such as introducing vocabulary words, silent reading, postreading discussion of story content, presentation of an associated skill lesson, assignment of a workbook page, independent completion of the workbook page, and group checking of the accuracy of workbook answers. Such structures dictate certain procedures and social patterns (Blumenfeld, Mergendoller, & Swartout, 1987). For instance, if a lesson's activity structure calls for individual completion of workbook pages, individual student effort is encouraged; if a lesson's activity structure calls for cooperative learning, collaborative student effort is encouraged. In short, students cognitively mediate not only academic work but also the social and procedural demands associated with how an activity is structured.

Activity structures also establish an instructional rhythm. For instance, Leinhardt and Greeno (1986) studied eight expert mathematics teachers and four novice undergraduate student teachers. The experts' lessons were based in routine activity structures that expedited lesson flow because both teachers and students operated from a familiar format. As Leinhardt and Greeno (1986) point out:

When we consider the massive amount of information that teachers and students must deal with in the course of a single . . . class, it becomes clear that some techniques must be used to structure the information and limit its complexity. (p. 94)

Summary.   Research on teachers' planning actions is largely descriptive. It suggests that teacher planning includes (1) transforming content knowledge into instruction by identifying critical features, simplifying tasks, and creating appropriate examples; (2) assigning academic tasks that encourage students to engage in cognitive activity appropriate for the outcome; and (3) employing activity structures that reduce instructional complexity and encourage students to engage in behaviors appropriate for the outcome.

Teacher Actions Associated with Motivation

From the teacher's standpoint, *motivation* requires initiating, sustaining, and directing students' enthusiasm and perseverance in the pursuit of curricular goals. Teacher actions designed to achieve motivation include setting expectations, developing metacognitive awareness, and employing cooperative learning.

Expectancy.   Current views of motivation rely heavily on *expectancy*. That is, motivation results from an expectancy to attain a goal and its associated value (Wigfield & Asher, 1984) and from teachers' actions in setting these expectancies. For instance, in a study involving 200 fourth-, fifth-, and sixth-grade students, Weinstein (1985) reported that all students perceived teachers to be giving low achievers more directions, rules, work, and negative feedback while high achievers were given more freedom of choice and opportunity, findings that a more recent study (Marshall & Weinstein, 1986) substantiated, particularly for older students. Similarly, in a review of teacher expectations, Brophy (1986) found that teachers' expectations have a powerful influence on achievement. While Dreeban and Barr (1987) argue that at least some of these expectations are rooted in class composition, research nevertheless suggests that what teachers say and do sets expectancies for students, and that these are powerful motivators.

Metacognitive aspects of motivation.   The recent surge of research knowledge about metacognition suggests interesting connections between motivation and cognition. Pressley, Snyder, and Cariglia-Bull (1987) report that metacognition encourages students to be consciously aware of (1) what they have learned, (2) situations where it would be useful, and (3) processes involved in using it; by becoming aware in this way, students are empowered, or develop ownership (Langer & Applebee, 1986), and, ultimately, are motivated. Further support comes from correlational studies such as one by Sivan and Roehler (1986) which indicates that teacher statements about the usefulness of what is to be learned raise student consciousness and thereby promote motivation.

A particularly intriguing aspect of the connection between motivation and metacognition is presented by Rohrkemper and Corno (1988). They describe a proactive approach to motivation in which students are helped to develop "adaptive behavior" through a metacognitive form of "inner speech" that helps students modify self and/or task when confronted with stress. Teacher actions in developing such adaptive behavior are presumed to be instrumental in creating motivation.

Cooperative learning as motivation.   *Cooperative learning* involves conducting instruction in heterogeneous groups structured to promote collaboration in learning academic content (Cohen, 1980; Slavin, 1980). Cooperative learning is a highly motivating approach to instruction presumably because of the grouping format itself, the high levels of success that result, the fact that students both give and receive help by alternatively assuming the role of teacher and student, and the emphasis on social solidarity and joint responsibility. The work of Slavin and associates (Slavin, 1984; Slavin, 1987; Slavin & Karweit, 1984) is of particular interest because of its focus on literacy and its results that indicate that students in cooperative learning classrooms are more motivated and less anxious than students in traditional classrooms.

Summary of motivational actions. Teachers' actions can motivate students. However, motivation results not from a single action but rather from *patterns* of actions over time. For instance, Brophy's (1986; Brophy & Kher, 1985) critical reviews of motivation research suggest patterns of actions that include support of students' efforts, assignment of appropriately difficult tasks, and specification of how learning is useful. Of particular importance, however, is Brophy's (1986) convincing argument that the major teacher action in motivation is explicit and salient modeling of learning as a rewarding, self-actualizing activity resulting in personal satisfaction and an enriched life.

Teacher Actions Associated with Giving Information

Information giving is often associated with lecturing. However, we found no reference to lecturing in the literature on literacy instruction. Instead, information giving is discussed in tandem with student participation (Duffy & Roehler, in press-a), in which information communicated through students' instructional experience is the raw material used to construct schemata about reading and how it works. Teacher information-giving actions focus on explanations and modeling, which help students interpret instructional experiences in ways that encourage construction of intended curricular goals (Marx, 1983). Winne and Marx (1982) summarize the argument by pointing out:

> . . . if teachers do not communicate clearly the relationships between what they are teaching, how they are teaching, and how students should be thinking, students' learning may not be optimal. (p. 514)

Explanations. *Explanations* are explicit teacher statements about what is being learned (declarative or propositional knowledge), why and when it will be used (conditional or situational knowledge), and how it is used (procedural knowledge) (Duffy, Roehler, Meloth, & Vavrus, 1986; Paris, Lipson, & Wixson, 1983). Explanation has been associated with positive results in numerous studies (Adams, Carnine, & Gersten, 1982; Armbruster, Anderson, & Ostertag, 1987; Baumann, 1984; Day, 1986; Durin & Graves, 1987; Leinhardt & Smith, 1985; O'Sullivan & Pressley, 1984; Palincsar, 1986; Paris & Oka, 1986; Readance, Baldwin & Head, 1986; Rinehart, Stahl, & Erickson, 1986; Scardamalia & Paris, 1985, Smith & Goodman, 1984; Tharp, 1982). However, three recent experimental studies are particularly illustrative.

The first examined the effects of directly explaining to low-group students how to use repair strategies to remove blockages to meaning while reading (Duffy et al., 1987). Randomly selected treatment teachers were taught to directly explain reasoning involved in using such strategies while treated-control teachers implemented basal text prescriptions. Results substantiate that treatment teachers provided more explicit explanations than control teachers, and that students of treatment teachers (1) demonstrated more awareness of lesson content and (2) achieved better on a variety of traditional and nontraditional measures of reading achievement.

Similarly, Bereiter and Bird (1985) taught reading strategies to 40 seventh and eighth graders from both rural and urban settings and demonstrated that direct explanation, combined with modeling and guided participation, is more effective than modeling alone or guided participation alone.

Third, Stevens, Madden, Slavin, and Farnish (1987) also demonstrate the effectiveness of explanations. Specifically, when explanations are embedded within cooperative learning, treatment group students perform better on reading and writing measures than their control group counterparts.

However, two words of caution are offered about explanations. First, direct explanation may not be equally effective with all learning. Carnine, Kameenui, and Coyle (1984) found that when the content to be learned is easy, explanations and practice together were not as effective as practice alone. Second, statements about conditional or situational knowledge may play a particularly important role in student learning. Brown, Bransford, Ferrara, and Campione (1983); Duffy and Roehler (in press-b); O'Sullivan and Pressley (1984); and Paris, Lipson, and Wixson (1983) all cite evidence suggesting that statements explicitly directing students to *why* the learning is useful and *when* to apply it are of particular importance. Indeed, several experiments have shown that the addition of conditional knowledge increases the likelihood that a strategy will be used following instruction (Brokowski, Levers, & Gruenenfelder, 1976; Cavanaugh & Borkowski, 1979); and post hoc discriminatory analysis of experimental data about teacher explanations suggests that teachers' conditional knowledge statements may contribute more to treatment students' success than either declarative or procedural statements (Meloth & Roehler, 1987).

Modeling.   *Modeling* is what teachers do to show students how to do a curricular task. As described by Collins, Brown, and Newman (1986), modeling is "an expert carrying out a task so that students can observe and build a conceptual model of the processes that are required to accomplish the task" (p. 22). It has long been recommended as an effective way to provide students with instructional information. As Bandura (1986) says:

. . . most human behavior is learned through modeling. By observing others, one forms rules of behavior, and on future occasions this coded information serves as a guide for action. Because people can learn approximately what to do through modeling before they perform any behavior, they are spared the costs and pain of faulty effort. (p. 47).

Modeling varies depending upon how much information is explicitly provided. For instance, in *Uninterrupted Sustained Silent Reading* (USSR), information is implicit in the experience, but is not explicitly stated. The teacher models by reading books of his or her choice while students do likewise, but students do not receive explicit information about how reading works. For instance, students must infer what cognitive processes are involved and how to engage in these processes. This characteristic may explain why the effects of USSR are difficult to document (Berglund & Johns, 1983; Evans & Towner, 1975; Guiser, 1986; Levine, 1984).

Talk-alouds are a second kind of modeling which, unlike techniques such as USSR, involves teacher statements. Relatively nonexplicit talk-alouds are found in the studies of Gordon and Pearson (1983), Hansen and Pearson (1983), and Raphael and Wonnacott (1985). In the Hansen and Pearson inferencing study, for instance, teachers modeled by saying aloud questions such as, "What do I know about this? What can I predict here? and How can I combine it with what is in the text?" but they did not model the thinking one does to answer these questions. A relatively more explicit form of talk-aloud modeling involves *front-loading* explicit procedures into the beginning of a lesson. Much of the recent laboratory research demonstrating effectiveness of cognitive strategy instruction employs this kind of modeling, usually with the teacher demonstrating how to follow a fixed set of steps (e.g., Miller, 1987). As described by Baumann and Schmitt (1986), this kind of modeling begins with a teacher specifying certain steps for students to follow:

> Here are three steps we will use to figure out unstated paragraph main ideas. [Teacher displays these on a chart or a transparency.]
>   1. First, decide what the *topic* of the paragraph is. The topic is like a short title and is usually one or two words that tell what the whole paragraph is about.
>   2. Next, decide what is said about the topic. . . . (p. 642)

Note that the teacher makes oral statements about the steps to follow but that students must infer the thinking a reader does in performing those steps. Even when modeling individual steps, cognitive processing is not specified:

> Step 1 says to decide what the topic of the paragraph is. I will read through the paragraph and try to think of one or two words that tell what the whole paragraph is about. [Teacher reads the paragraph aloud in a thoughtful manner.] I think the topic is *solar system*, because it is mentioned in just about every sentence. (Baumann & Schmitt, 1986, p. 643)

Note that the teacher emphasizes the presence of "solar system" in the text and the implicit "rule" that frequency of appearance in the text is associated with topic, but does not describe any reasoning. The emphasis is on procedural steps and tangible text cues. Other instructional studies also employ talk-aloud modeling (Rinehart, Stahl, & Erickson, 1986; Stevens, Madden, Slavin & Farnish, 1987).

Think-alouds, a third type of modeling, go beyond talking aloud about procedural steps and tangible text cues by including descriptions of reasoning readers engage in when performing the task. Meichenbaum (1985), who studied how to help impulsive children use strategies to control their behavior, developed this technique by having teachers model a series of self-statements and then rehearsing students in the use of such statements. Meichenbaum and Goodman (1971) provide the following example:

> Okay, what is it I have to do? I have to copy the picture with the different lines. I have to go slowly and carefully. Okay, draw the line down, down, good; and then to the right, that's it; now down some more and to the left. Good, I'm doing fine so far. Remember, go slowly. Now back up again. No, I was supposed to go down. That's okay. Just erase the line carefully. . . . Good. Even if I make an error I can go on slowly and carefully. I have to go down now. Finished. I did it! (p. 117)

Two examples illustrate how think-alouds have been applied to school learning. The first is from Duffy, Roehler, and Herrmann (1988), who, based on a post hoc descriptive analysis of data collected in an experiment favoring treatment group students who received such modeling (Duffy et al., 1987), argue for *mental modeling*, in which teachers reduce the inferencing students must do when learning cognitive tasks by thinking aloud about the reasoning they themselves engage in when doing the task. They cite the following example of a think-aloud:

> I want to show you what I look at when I come across a word I don't know the meaning of. I'll talk out loud to show you how I figure it out. Then I will help you do this. [reading] "The cocoa steamed fragrantly." Hmm, I've heard that word "fragrantly" before, but I don't

really know what it means here. I know one of the words right before it though—
"steamed." I watched a pot of boiling water once and there was steam coming from it. That
water was hot so this must have something to do with the cocoa being hot. OK, the pan of
hot cocoa is steaming on the stove. That means steam coming up and out, but that still
doesn't explain what fragrantly means. Let me think again about the hot cocoa on the stove
and try to use what I already know about cocoa as a clue. Hot cocoa bubbles, steams and
. . . smells! Hot cocoa smells good. [reading] "The cocoa steamed fragrantly." That means it
smelled good! [addressing the students] Thinking about what I already knew about hot
cocoa helped me figure out what that word meant. (p. 765)

Similarly, Scardamalia (1984) illustrates think-aloud modeling when teaching students
how to begin writing an essay on the topic of "modern rock stars:"

I don't know a thing about modern rock stars. I can't think of the name of even one rock
star. How about David Bowie or Mick Jagger? . . . But many readers won't agree that they
are modern rock stars. I think they are both as old as I am. Let's see, my own feelings about
this are . . . that I doubt if today's rock stars are more talented than ever. Anyway, how
would I know? I can't argue this . . . I need a new idea . . . An important point I haven't
considered yet is . . . ah . . . well . . . what do we mean by talent? Am I talking about
musical talent or ability to entertain—to do acrobatics? Hey, I may have a way into this
topic. I could develop this idea by . . . (p. 17)

In sum, modeling is an effective teacher action. While cognitive processes associated with literacy ought not to be modeled in isolation from content (Pearson, 1985;
Tierney & Cunningham, 1984), research indicates that modeling is effective when the
cognitive processes are simultaneously applied in connected text (Duffy et al., 1987;
Roehler, Duffy, & Meloth, 1986; Roehler, Duffy, & Johnson, 1988).

Summary on giving information.   Information giving is an important teacher
action because the more explicit the teacher is in helping students interpret information
inherent in experience, the better students achieve (Anderson, Stevens, Prawat, &
Nickerson, 1988; Baumann, 1984; Day, 1986; Duffy et al., 1987; Pearson, 1985; Stevens
et al., 1987). In providing information, teachers reduce the inferences students must
make and thereby help them construct desired curricular understandings.

Teacher Actions Associated
with Mediation of Student Learning

Students cannot be passive receivers of information. They must be involved in constructing understandings. Students interpret information presented during instruction
much as they interpret information authors present in text. However, teachers, unlike
authors, respond to students' interpretations, modifying instructional information in
subsequent interactions to increase the likelihood that students will construct intended
understandings. What teachers do to mediate students' construction of schemata about
curricular outcomes is crucial (Collins, Brown, & Newman, 1986; Palincsar & Brown, in
press; Raphael, Englert, & Anderson, 1987; Roehler & Duffy, 1986; Roehler, Duffy, &
Warren, 1988). Two teacher actions associated with mediation are: (1) asking questions;
and (2) gradually releasing responsibility to students.

Asking questions to mediate student understanding.   While *question asking* has
long been valued as a teacher instructional action (Raphael & Gavelek, 1984), most
research focuses on the fact that teachers ask low-level questions, particularly with low-

group students (Gambrell, 1983; Guzak, 1967; Pearson, 1983). As a result, teachers have been urged to ask higher-level questions (Rodgers, 1972), although research on the effect of asking questions generally and on asking higher-level questions particularly is ambivalent at best. For instance, a metanalysis by Winne (1979) found that questions had no effect on student achievement, while one by Redfield and Rousseau (1981) found that questions had a positive effect on student achievement. Similarly, Dillon (1982), after coding the cognitive level of all utterances in 27 high school discussion classes and computing the percent of agreement between level of student responses and level of teacher questions and statements, concluded that there was little correspondence between levels of teacher questions and student responses. Recent research suggests that standard question-and-answer patterns may be most effective in creating *memory* for information and less effective in facilitating students' construction of schemata and networks among schemata. For instance, process-product research indicates that teachers who ask many academically focused low-level questions produce students who score high on tests of basic skills (i.e., they remember more) (Brophy & Good, 1986; Rosenshine, 1983); and Wixson (1983) found that students recall information best if they directly answer questions about it.

However, mediating student understanding demands more of teachers than questions that demand memory. For instance, two studies indicate that teachers should precede questioning with a presentation of information. In one study, Vavrus (1987) conducted a post hoc microethnographic study of the elicitation patterns of effective and less-effective elementary reading teachers and concluded that questions are most effective in mediating student understanding when preceded by explicit presentation of information; and, in another study, Dillon (1982) noted that students produce higher-order cognition when teachers make statements than they do when teachers ask questions, a phenomenon he attributed to the fact that questions serve to limit inquiry by requesting specified information while statements invite inquiry because respondents can accept them, modify them, or reject them. Further, to mediate student understanding, teachers must ask different kinds of questions, questions that assist students in constructing understandings. For instance, when teaching students to activate prior knowledge, the teacher may wish to avoid asking an assessment question such as "Are you activating knowledge?" or a memory question such as "What knowledge should be activated?" and instead ask questions that help students construct understandings about how to activate prior knowledge such as "What do you already know about this story and what does your knowledge make you think will happen here?" Tharp (1982) refers to these as *regulatory questions*. The Kamehameha Early Elementary Program (KEEP) in Hawaii embeds regulatory questions in comprehension lessons to help students establish relationships between their experience, the text, and the relationships between the two (Au, 1979). To illustrate, note how a teacher's questions direct students' thinking during a fourth-grade lesson using a story about a grandmother who helps her grandchild understand the natural cycle of birth, life, and death (Au & Kawakami, 1986):

TEACHER: But she also compared it when she said—
JOEY: The cactus.
TEACHER: Okay, tell me about the cactus, Joey.
JOEY: Oh, I know about the cactus.
TEACHER: What did you find about cactus?
JOEY: (*Reading from the text*) "The cactus did not bloom forever. Petals dried and fell to earth."
TEACHER: Okay, what is she trying to tell Annie by using that analogy of the cactus?

Ross: That people die of old age. That people just don't die when they say so.
Teacher: Well, yeah, okay, that's—that's true. But what did they mean when they said, "The cactus did not bloom forever?"
Ross: That people, they got to die.
Kent: That means that when it starts blooming a life will start, but when it falls the life will end. (pp. 70–71)

The distinction between assessment of memory questions on the one hand and questions that help students mediate understanding on the other is highlighted by Lampert (1986) when describing her studies of her own mathematics instruction:

> In my discussions with students, I almost always followed an unexplained answer with a question to probe how the student "figured it out." This strategy has two purposes. One is to give me some sense of the procedures students are using to arrive at their answers and how they are warranted; the other is to develop a habit of discourse in the classroom in which work in mathematics is referred back to the knower to answer questions of reasonability. This habit needs to be developed because, in the traditional culture of classroom interaction, students have learned to rely on the authority of a book or a teacher to "know" if their answers are right or wrong rather than asking themselves whether either the answer or the procedure they used to arrive at it makes sense. (p. 317)

Gradual release of responsibility.   Pearson (1985) coined the phrase *gradual release of responsibility* to describe how teachers can mediate students' understandings by gradually weaning them away from teacher assistance until they can perform a task independently. Reflective of the Vygotskian principle of moving students gradually from the point where they are directed by an adult or someone acting like an adult to the point where they can take control of their own learning (Gavelek, 1986; Vygotsky, 1978; Wertsch, McNamee, McLare, & Budwig, 1980), directives and questions are gradually reduced until students can independently regulate their own learning. These principles have been used with excellent student achievement results in several studies (Duffy et al., 1987; Palincsar & Brown, 1984; Paris & Oka, 1986; Scardamalia & Bereiter, 1985). Two teacher actions associated with gradually releasing responsibility are (1) scaffolding and (2) coaching.

Scaffolding is support teachers provide to help students carry out a task (Collins, Brown, & Newman, 1986; Langer, 1984). It was first described by Bruner (1978) as a technique that

> . . . reduces the degrees of freedom with which the child has to cope, concentrates his efforts into a manageable domain, and provides models of the expected dialogue from which he can extract selectively what he needs for filling his role in discourse. (p. 254).

Whether taking the form of verbal directives and supports (Roehler, Duffy, & Warren, 1988; Palincsar & Brown, 1984) or of combined physical and verbal support (Scardamalia, Berieter, & Steinbach, 1984; Raphael, Englert, & Anderson, 1987), scaffolding normally occurs in dialogues of structured interactional sequences in the midst of instruction. For instance, Palincsar (1986) cites the following reciprocal teaching dialogue as an example of scaffolding. Note that beginning in line 7 the teacher accepts the student's contribution but also mediates students' construction of understanding by directing them to think of a question that can be answered using the text and by then modeling such a question, beginning in line 12:

1 T: I need someone to ask a question about the new information I just shared with
       you.
2 S2: How does the sea horses . . . carry their babies in their pouch?
3 T: Okay. Does someone remember the answer?
4 S5: Um, that's the only way they can carry them. They don't have any hands or
       anything.
5 T: Now, was he doing a little bit of predicting or figuring out how that sea horse is
       able to do that? Did the story really tell why they carry them in their pouches?
6 S5: Or they might drowned. They might not be able to swim and they might
       drowned.
7 T: You are right in all of your answers and thinking. Your question was a good
       question in that it got us thinking about why they did have pouches and why they
       carry their babies there, but you were going a little bit further than the written
       word. You were pretty smart to figure that out. Can anyone think of a question that
       they did give us the answer to in the story?
8 S4: Um, what kind of animals are they?
9 S6: Um . . . sea horses.
10 T: What else did they see besides the sea horses?
11 S6: Um . . . crawfish.
12 T: See, what you might have wanted to ask, and C——— might have wanted to
       ask, "Why were they called unusual fish or animals?" Why do they call a sea horse
       unusual? (p. 88)

Studies of writing instruction also provide excellent examples of such scaffolding (Applebee, 1986; Langer & Applebee, 1986; Raphael, Englert, & Anderson, 1987).

   Coaching requires teachers to observe students while they carry out a task and to
offer feedback, modeling, reminders, explanations, and clues designed to help them
successfully complete the task. For instance, Duffy and Roehler (1987) demonstrate
how effective teachers coach by providing elaborative explanations in response to
students' restructuring:

T: What do you think is going to happen next here? I mean, you're reading the story.
     What happens next? Candy?
S: [*Gives a response*]
T: Oh, okay. What do you think, Matt?
S: [*Gives a response*]
T: Interesting. Why do you think what you think? How can you make these predic-
     tions like this? How can you predict what's going to happen next in the story?
S: I thought about the story and Roberto and his problem.
T: Yes, but how did you use that to predict? Did you use your own experience?
S: Yeah. I thought about what I thought would probably happen.
T: That's right. Because you've been thinking about the story and you've been
     thinking about Roberto and his problem. And that's part of what reading is. It's
     making predictions about what's going to happen next. (p. 519)

   Summary of teacher mediation.   Mediation of student understanding requires
more of teachers than the standard classroom elicitation pattern of asking students for a
response, giving feedback, and then asking for another response. Instead, teachers must
(1) create questions that help students build understandings and (2) gradually diminish
assistance through scaffolding and coaching. Because many of these actions are generated spontaneously in response to instructional interactions, they may be the most
demanding of instructional actions.

Summary of Teachers' Instructional Actions

Instructional research suggests four major categories of teacher actions: planning, motivating, providing information, and mediating student learning. Each of these categories, in turn, is made up of subactions that, together, represent what effective teachers do to create intended student outcomes. Combinations of these actions have been tested as instructional strategies or models.

THE USE OF TEACHER ACTIONS IN INSTRUCTIONAL MODELS

We describe here six well-researched instructional models. Planning, motivating, information giving, and mediating student understandings are part of each model; but varying emphases are placed on one or another of these actions, particularly in terms of information giving and teacher mediation.

Instructional Models Placing Relatively Heavy Emphasis on Information Giving

Three instructional models place relatively heavy emphasis on information giving: the Direct Explanation Model, the Informed Strategies for Learning Model, and the Cooperative Integrated Reading and Composition Model.

The Direct Explanation Model.   The *Direct Explanation Model* was designed to investigate the effects of directly explaining the mental acts associated with strategic reading to low-group readers (Duffy et al., 1987). The central tenets of this model are that teacher explanations affect student awareness and achievement, and that teachers can adjust basal textbook prescriptions in order to create explanations that are effective with low-group students. Within the context of a basal text story, the teacher explicitly states what strategy is being taught, when in the story it will be used, and a think-aloud model of the reasoning involved when using the strategy. The teacher then mediates student acquisition of the strategy, providing students with gradually reduced instructional scaffolding and coaching so that students will gain control, and success will be high. Teachers then move students directly to the reading of the basal selection where students apply the strategy while reading to comprehend.

Information giving is emphasized in this model. Teacher talk must be explicit, consistent, and tailored to students' needs, even during teacher mediation when teachers continue to provide supplementary information for students to use in creating intended curricular outcomes. In addition, however, planning actions are also important; teachers make their own plans instead of being provided with scripts because scripts connote a single way to explain and the Direct Instruction Model assumes that all explanations must be adapted to individual student backgrounds. Similarly, motivation is emphasized, particularly by creating supportive environments that demonstrate the utility of reading and by emphasizing the usefulness of strategies.

Naturalistic classroom experimental research indicates that the Direct Explanation Model is effective in creating significant student growth (Duffy et al., 1987). Success was attributed to (1) providing explicit information about the reasoning readers use when strategies are employed and (2) assisting and supporting students' mediation of learning.

The Informed Strategies for Learning Model (ISL). The *Informed Strategies for Learning Model* emphasizes the relationship between children's awareness about reading strategies and their reading skills (Paris, Cross, & Lipson, 1984; Paris & Jacobs, 1984). Using a supplementary curriculum, teachers provide explanations to the entire class and mediate through discussions. The central tenet of ISL is that students will use strategies appropriately and spontaneously in subsequent reading if they perceive them to be sensible and useful courses of action. As its name implies, there is heavy emphasis on informing, particularly through use of metaphors (e.g., "being a reading detective"). The instructional cycle consists of three lessons: the first two introduce a metaphor, describe a strategy, explain how to use it while reading, and provide group practice, feedback, and individual practice with texts and worksheets; the third is a bridging lesson to other curricular areas such as social studies or science. Motivation is emphasized in ISL through appealing metaphors, colorful bulletin boards depicting strategy information, and usefulness statements; planning is less emphasized since researchers expect teachers to follow prescribed modules. The heaviest emphasis is on information giving through explanation and modeling of each module.

Regarding the impact of ISL on students, a recent study involving 46 teachers in 18 schools indicated that small, but significant, improvements were obtained for awareness measures and informal reading achievement measures, but not for standardized measures of reading achievement (Paris & Oka, 1986). The success of the ISL model is attributed to informing students of strategies and how they work, although the role of motivation and teacher mediation is also acknowledged.

The Cooperative Integrated Reading and Composition Model (CIRC). The CIRC model (Stevens, Madden, Slavin, & Farnish, 1987) focuses on cooperative learning as a vehicle for utilizing state-of-the-art instructional practices derived from basic research. The central tenets of CIRC are that students are motivated by the opportunity to work together and that they benefit from direct assistance from teachers prior to beginning cooperative efforts. Each instructional cycle begins with direct teacher explanation and modeling, continues with peers doing much of the coaching in pairs and in cooperative groups, and closes with quizzes.

Motivation is a central feature of this model (Slavin, 1987) and is accomplished by giving students responsibility for practicing and using what they learn in cooperative groups. However, there is also a strong emphasis on information giving through explanations and modeling at the beginning of each cycle of instruction and as needed during various forms of practice. Teacher mediation receives relatively less emphasis, primarily because most of the mediation is presumed to occur in cooperative groups. Similarly, teacher planning is not emphasized; instead, teachers are provided with a detailed manual to follow.

Research results support the effectiveness of the CIRC model (Stevens et al., 1987). Achievement as measured by standardized tests and informal reading inventories show significant growth for decoding and comprehension for CIRC students, and growth in writing and language is consistently positive. Success is attributed to the use of teacher-supervised explanation and practice within a framework of cooperative learning.

Instructional Models Placing Relatively Heavy Emphasis on Teacher Mediation

Three instructional models emphasize teacher mediation more than information giving: the Reciprocal Teaching Model, the Kamehameha Early Education Program, and the Procedural Facilitation Model.

The Reciprocal Teaching Model.   Reciprocal teaching is designed to improve text comprehension through instruction in four strategies that facilitate monitoring of comprehension: predicting, questioning, summarizing, and clarifying (Palincsar & Brown, 1984). In reciprocal teaching, teachers and students take turns directing strategic processes in a dialogue format that moves from other- to self-regulation. The central tenet of this model is that the dialogue between teachers and students facilitates learning. While instruction begins with initial teacher explanations and modeling of the four strategies, such information giving receives relatively little emphasis. Instead, dialogues are emphasized, with the teacher providing large amounts of scaffolded assistance initially and gradually diminishing it as students begin to control the four strategies.

The emphasis is on teacher mediation through scaffolding, coaching, and reduction of teacher assistance during an interactive dialogue. Planning is based on material provided by researchers about lesson structure, initial explanation, general format, and guidelines for conducting reciprocal dialogues; but these materials are not highly prescriptive and leave considerable room for teacher modification. Motivation is assumed to result from experiencing the role of teacher.

Reciprocal teaching has been effective with slow learners of junior high school age and with first graders (Brown & Palincsar, 1985; Palincsar & Brown, 1984; Palincsar, 1986). Several studies have yielded impressive gains for comprehension, including a transfer measure administered three months after the conclusion of a study. Success is attributed to the reciprocal teaching dialogue that promotes student mediation of strategy use in real reading by allowing him or her to be both critic and producer in the dialogue.

The Kamehameha Early Education Program (KEEP).   The Kamehameha Early Education Program focuses on comprehension instruction that is culturally compatible with native Hawaiian students. It is based on three premises: First, two-thirds of the instructional time is spent in comprehension activities, which center around a "talk-story" format matching the discussion patterns of the Hawaiian culture (Au, 1985). Second, teachers follow a three-step format in which they activate students' experiences, read the text, and relate student experiences to the content of the text. Third, the teacher asks regulatory questions in a gradual progression from other- to self-regulation (Au & Kawakami, 1984).

Mediation is heavily emphasized through regulatory questioning and talk-story formats, while information giving receives less emphasis. Teachers do not follow scripts but, instead, receive extensive staff development. Motivation is assumed to result from a supportive, encouraging environment and through use of the culturally compatible style of instructional interactions.

One experimental study, conducted in four first-grade classrooms in the public schools of Hawaii, resulted in findings favoring students in the KEEP program (Tharp, 1982). These results tend to corroborate field-based ethnography that has produced encouraging descriptive findings (Au & Kawakami, 1984). Success is attributed primarily to heavy comprehension emphasis and to teacher mediation factors such as regulatory questions asked within the context of a culturally compatible system of social interaction.

The Procedural Facilitation Model

The *Procedural Facilitation Model* focuses on developing students' self-regulatory planning and revision processes during writing, particularly in terms of helping students switch attention back and forth from executive control of composing to an executive mechanism for editing (Scardamalia & Bereiter, 1985; Scardamalia, Bereiter, & Steinbach, 1984). While teachers do a form of think-aloud modeling, the emphasis is on mediation in which students use prompts placed on cue cards to develop self-regulation, a form of scaffolded assistance that is gradually removed. After the teacher models, various individual students try out the use of cue cards, while the teacher and other students assess and discuss how to resolve any problems. Scardamalia and Bereiter (1985) say the teacher's role is more like a conductor's relationship to a soloist than a puppeteer's relationship to a puppet.

The emphasis is on teacher mediation of learning by providing spontaneous coaching and scaffolding as students use cue cards during lessons. Information giving is emphasized less, and planning receives relatively little emphasis because the approach has not yet been implemented with regular classroom teachers. Motivation is assumed to result from the cue cards, which encourage risk taking and promote success.

Experimental studies indicate that students instructed using the Procedural Facilitation Model compose texts that are significantly superior in thought content. Success is attributed primarily to teacher mediation of students' understanding that writing is nonlinear, involves planning and revision, and can be controlled through use of planning and revision mechanisms.

Summary of Instructional Models

Analysis of these six instructional models suggests that disagreement continues regarding the relative roles of information giving and mediation. Some instructional models, assuming that it is difficult to bring to the surface some students' intuitive understandings and the information implicit in instructional experiences, place relatively more emphasis on information giving; other models, assuming that it is relatively easy to bring to the surface all students' intuitive understandings and the information implicit in instructional experiences, place relatively more emphasis on teacher mediation. Overall, however, all models call for planning, motivation, information giving, and mediation of student understanding.

CONCLUSIONS AND IMPLICATIONS

Research supports direct and explicit teacher action associated with planning, motivating, information giving, and mediating student understandings. Conversely, there is no research support for inexplicit teacher actions or for instruction in which teachers assume passive or covert roles.

However, this should not be interpreted to mean that a technology of instruction now exists, and that teachers can be directed to engage mindlessly in specified teacher actions, confident that effective instruction will result. To the contrary, emerging studies on the nature of teaching (Buchmann, 1986; Floden & Clark, 1988; Lampert, 1986) suggest that instruction is a complex, fluid endeavor, and that teachers engage in creative orchestration rather than rigid direction following. That is, teachers' planning, motivating, information giving, and mediating actions are blended into integrated patterns that are modified in an infinite number of ways in order to meet an infinite number of challenges. For instance, plans become obsolete as soon as a lesson begins; motivation is not a set procedure but a pattern adjusted to conditions; information giving is not a matter of reading a script but of hooking information to students' individual backgrounds; and teacher mediation is a series of spontaneous teacher decisions in response to students' emerging understandings. The key to instructional effectiveness, therefore, is not development of a technology packaged in prescriptions, scripts, or commercial programs. The key is helping teachers flexibly adapt their instructional actions to fit particular situations.

From this perspective, the important future research questions about teachers' instructional actions are not Which actions work? or What directions, prescriptions, or scripts should we give to teachers? Rather, the questions of the future are What patterns and combinations of teacher actions are most effective in various situations? and How can teachers be helped to orchestrate instructional actions so that meaningful linkages are made according to situational demands?

Research to answer such questions must account for three particularly important conditions: First, naturalistic experimental research must be emphasized. As it now stands, virtually all instructional research is conducted under pseudoclassroom conditions that short-circuit the naturally occurring events of real classroom life, thereby making it very difficult to determine if findings can be generalized to real teachers in real classrooms. We need more research on teachers' instructional actions in true experiments in which subjects are randomly assigned (Pressley, Snyder, & Cariglia-Bull, 1987) and in which real teachers are observed teaching under natural conditions over long durations of time (Barr, 1986). Second, the language of instructional research must become more precise. For instance, Slavin and his colleagues (Stevens et al., 1987) and Tharp (1982) both describe their instruction as "direct instruction," even though they are clearly doing different things; while Miller (1987) labels her intervention "self-instruction," even though the teacher is heavily involved and students are not instructing themselves at all. All such terminology problems impede understanding about teacher actions and cry out for semantic precision. Finally, all instructional actions should be documented by reference to lesson excerpts. In the absence of descriptive lesson excerpts, it is difficult to determine exactly what action a teacher is taking, and instructional actions are open to multiple interpretations.

The research conducted to date has been effective in identifying teacher instructional actions. Hopefully, however, the third volume of this handbook will contain a chapter on instruction which, by virtue of more rigorous language and research, provides more sophisticated answers to the question, What actions do teachers take to communicate the curriculum of literacy to students in school? These answers, we are sure, will document not only the interactive nature of instructional actions and the way patterns of actions are modified to respond to various situations but also that the key to effective instructional actions is not a technician who follows prescribed directions reflecting a technology of teaching, but rather, a teacher who metacognitively controls the process of creating and modifying patterns of instructional actions.

REFERENCES

Adams, A., Carnine, D., & Gersten, R. (1982). Instructional strategies for studying content area texts in the intermediate grades. *Reading Research Quarterly, 18*, 27–55.

Anderson, L., Brubaker, N., Alleman-Brooks, J., & Duffy, G. (1985). A qualitative study of seatwork in first grade classrooms. *Elementary School Journal, 86*(2), 123–140.

Anderson, L., & Evertson, C. (1978). *Classroom organization at the beginning of school: Two case studies.* Paper presented to the American Association of Colleges for Teacher Education, Chicago.

Anderson, L., Stevens, D., Prawat, R., & Nickerson, J. (1988). Classroom task environments and students' task-related beliefs. *Elementary School Journal, 88*(3), 281–296.

Anderson, R. C. (1984). Some reflections on the acquisition of knowledge. *Educational Researcher, 13*(8), 5–10.

Applebee, A. N. (1986). Problems in process approaches: Toward a reconceptualization of process instruction. In A. R. Petrosky and D. Bartholomae (Eds.), *Eighty-Fifth Yearbook of the National Society for the Study of Education: The teaching of writing* (pp. 95–113). Chicago: University of Chicago Press.

Armbruster, B. B., Anderson, T. H., & Ostertag, J. (1987). Does text structure/summarization instruction facilitate learning from expository text? *Reading Research Quarterly, 22*, 331–346.

Au, K. H. (1979). Using the experience-text-relationship method with minority children. *Reading Teacher, 32*(6), 677–679.

Au, K. H. (1985, April). *Instruction: The implications of research in the Kamehameha approach to developing reading comprehension ability*. Paper presented at the annual meeting of the American Educational Research Association, Chicago.

Au, K. H., & Kawakami, A. J. (1984). Vygotskian perspectives on discussion processes in small-group reading lessons. In P. L. Peterson, L. C. Wilkinson, & M. Hallinan (Eds.), *The social context of instruction: Group organization and group processes*. New York: Academic Press.

Au, K. H., & Kawakami, A. J. (1986). Influence of the social organization of instruction on children's text comprehension ability: A Vygotskian perspective. In T. Raphael (Ed.), *The contexts of school-based literacy* (pp. 63–77). New York: Random House.

Baker, L., & Brown, A. L. (1984). Metacognitive skills and reading. In P. D. Pearson, R. Barr, M. L. Kamil, & P. Mosenthal (Eds.), *Handbook of reading research* (Vol. 1, pp. 353–394). White Plains, NY: Longman.

Bandura, A. (1986). *Psychological modeling: Conflicting theories*. Chicago: Aldine-Atherton.

Baumann, J. F. (1984). The effectiveness of a direct instruction paradigm for teaching main idea comprehension. *Reading Research Quarterly, 20*(1), 93–115.

Baumann, J. F., & Schmidt, M. C. (1986). The what, why, how, and when of comprehension instruction. *Reading Teacher, 39*(7), 640–647.

Beck, I. L., Omanson, R. C., & McKeown, M. G. (1982). An instructional redesign of reading lessons: Effects on comprehension. *Reading Research Quarterly, 17*(4), 462–481.

Bereiter, C., & Bird, M. (1985). Use of thinking aloud in identification and teaching of reading comprehension strategies. *Cognition and Instruction, 2*, 131–156.

Bereiter, C., & Scardamalia, M. (1987). An attainable version of high literacy: Approaches to teaching higher-order skills in reading and writing. *Curriculum Inquiry, 17*(1), 9–30.

Berglund, R., & Johns, J. (1983). A primer on uninterrupted sustained silent reading. *Reading Teacher, 36*(6), 534–539.

Blumenfeld, P., Mergendoller, J., & Swarthout, D. (1987). Task as a heuristic for understanding student learning and motivation. *Journal of Curriculum Studies, 19*(2), 135–148.

Blumenfeld, P., Pintrich, P., & Meece, J. (1983, April). *The relation of student characteristics and children's perceptions of teacher and peers in varying classroom environments*. Paper presented at the annual meeting of the American Educational Research Association, Montreal.

Blumenfeld, P., Pintrich, P., Meece, J., & Wessels, K. (1982). The formation and role of perceptions of ability in elementary school classrooms. *Elementary School Journal, 82*, 401–420.

Borkowski, J. G., Levers, S. R., & Gruenenfelder, T. M. (1976). Transfer of mediational strategies in children: The role of activity and awareness during strategy acquisition. *Child Development, 47*, 779–786.

Bossert, S. (1979). *Tasks and social relationships: A study of instructional organization and its consequences*. New York: Cambridge University Press.

Brophy, J. (1979). Teacher behavior and its effects. *Journal of Educational Psychology, 71*, 733–750.

Brophy, J. (1986). *Socializing student motivation to learn* (Research Series No. 169). East Lansing, MI: Michigan State University, Institute for Research on Teaching.

Brophy, J. (Ed.). (in press). *Advances in research on teaching, Vol. I: Teaching for understanding and self-regulated learning*. Greenwich, CT: JAI Press.

Brophy, J., & Good, T. (1986). Teacher behavior and student achievement. In M. Wittrock (Ed.), *The handbook of research on teaching* (3rd ed.). Riverside, NJ: Macmillan.

Brophy, J., & Kher, N. (1985). Teacher socialization as a mechanism for developing student motivation to learn. In R. Feldman (Ed.), *Social psychology applied to education*. Cambridge, Eng.: Cambridge University Press.

Brown, A. L., Bransford, J. D., Ferrara, R. A., & Campione, J. C. (1983). Learning, remembering and understanding. In J. H. Flavell and E. M. Markman (Eds.), *Handbook of child psychology, Vol. 3: Cognitive development* (pp. 77–166). New York: Wiley.

Brown, A. L., & Palincsar, A. M. (1985). *Reciprocal teaching of comprehension strategies: A natural history of one program for enhancing learning* (Tech. Rep. No. 334). Champaign, IL: Center for the Study of Reading.

Bruner, J. S. (1978). The role of dialogue in language acquisition. In A. Sinclair, R. J. Jarvelle, & W. J. M. Leveet (Eds.), *The child's conception of language*. New York: Springer.

Buchmann, M. (1986). Role over person: Morality and authenticity in teaching. *Teacher College Record, 87*(4), 531–541.

Carnine, D., Kameenui, E. J., & Coyle, G. (1984). Utilization of contextual information in determining the meaning of unfamiliar words. *Reading Research Quarterly, 19*, 188–204.

Cavanaugh, J. C., & Borkowski, J. G. (1979). The metamemory-memory "connection": Effects of strategy training and maintenance. *Journal of General Psychology, 101*, 161–174.

Clark, C., & Elmore, J. (1979). *Teacher planning in the first weeks of school* (Research Series No. 56). East Lansing, MI: Michigan State University, Institute for Research on Teaching.

Clark, C., & Peterson, P. (1986). Teachers' thought processes. In M. Wittrock (Ed.), *Handbook of research on teaching* (3rd ed., pp. 255–296). New York: Macmillan.

Clark, C., & Yinger, R. (1979). *Three studies of teacher planning* (Research Series No. 55). East Lansing, MI: Michigan State University, Institute for Research on Teaching.

Cohen, E. G. (1980, September). A multi-ability approach to the integrated classroom. Paper presented at the annual meeting of the American Psychological Association, Montreal.

Collins, A., & Brown, J. (in press). The new apprenticeship: Teaching students the craft of reading, writing, and mathematics. In L. B. Resnick (Ed.), *Knowing and learning: Issues for a cognitive science of instruction*. Hillsdale, NJ: Erlbaum.

Collins, A., Brown, J. S., & Newman, S. E. (1986). Cognitive apprenticeship: Teaching the craft of reading, writing, and mathematics (Report No. 6459). Cambridge, MA: BBN Laboratories.

Day, J. D. (1986). Teaching summarization skills: Influences of student ability level and strategy difficulty. *Cognition and Instruction*, 3, 193–210.

Dillon, J. (1982). Cognitive correspondence between question/statement and response. *American Educational Research Journal*, 19(4), 540–551.

Doyle, W. (1980). *Student mediation responses in teaching effectiveness* (Final Report). Denton, TX: North Texas State University.

Doyle, W. (1983). Academic work. *Review of Educational Research*, 53(2), 159–199.

Doyle, W. (1984, April). *Patterns of academic work in junior high school science, English, and mathematics classes*. Paper presented at the annual meeting of the American Educational Research Association, New Orleans.

Doyle, W. (1986). Classroom organization and management. In M. Wittrock (Ed.), *Handbook of research on teaching* (3rd ed., pp. 392–431). New York: Macmillan.

Dreeban, R., & Barr, R. (1987). *Class composition and the design of instruction*. Paper presented at the annual meeting of the American Educational Research Association, Washington, DC.

Duffy, G. (1983). From turn-taking to sense-making: Broadening the concept of teacher effectiveness. *Journal of Educational Research*, 76(3), 134–139.

Duffy, G., & McIntyre, L. (1982). A naturalistic study of instructional assistance in primary grade reading. *Elementary School Journal*, 83(1), 15–23.

Duffy, G., & Roehler, L. (1982). The illusion of instruction. *Reading Research Quarterly*, 17, 438–445.

Duffy, G., & Roehler, L. (1987). Improving classroom reading instruction through the use of responsive elaboration. *Reading Teacher*, 40(6), 514–521.

Duffy, G., & Roehler, L. (in press-a). The tension between information giving and mediation: New perspectives on instructional explanation and teacher change. In J. Brophy (Ed.), *Advances in research on teaching*. Greenwich, CT: JAI Press.

Duffy, G., & Roehler, L. (in press-b). Why strategy instruction is so difficult and what we need to do about it. In M. Pressley, C. McCormick, & G. Miller (Eds.), *Cognitive strategy research*. New York: Springer-Verlag.

Duffy, G., Roehler, L., & Herrmann, B. (1988). Modeling mental processes helps poor readers become strategic readers. *Reading Teacher*, 41(8), 762–767.

Duffy, G., Roehler, L., Meloth, M., & Vavrus, L. (1986). Conceptualizing instructional explanation. *Teaching and Teacher Education*, 2(3), 197–214.

Duffy, G., Roehler, L., Sivan, E., Rackliffe, G., Book, C., Meloth, M., Vavrus, L., Wesselman, R., Putnam, J., & Bassiri, D. (1987). Effects of explaining the reasoning associated with using reading strategies. *Reading Research Quarterly*, 22(3), 347–368.

Durin, A. H., & Graves, M. F. (1987). Intensive vocabulary instruction as a prewriting technique. *Reading Research Quarterly*, 22, 311–330.

Durkin, D. (1978–1979). What classroom observation reveals about reading comprehension instruction. *Reading Research Quarterly*, 14, 481–533.

Engelmann, S., & Carnine, D. (1982). *Theory of instruction: Principles and applications*. New York: Irvington Publishers.

Evans, H., & Towner, J. (1975). Sustained silent reading: Does it increase skills? *Reading Teacher*, 29, 155–156.

Fennema, E., Carpenter, T. P., & Peterson, P. L. (1986). Teachers' decision making and cognitively guided instruction: A new paradigm for curriculum development. Paper presented at the Seventh Annual Psychology of Mathematics Education Conference, London, England.

Flavell, J. H. (1976). Metacognitive aspects of problem solving. In L. B. Resnick (Ed.), *The nature of intelligence*. Hillsdale, NJ: Erlbaum.

Floden, R., & Clark, C. (1988). Preparing teachers for uncertainty. *Teacher College Record*, 89(4), 505–524.

Flower, L. (1987, June). *The role of task representation in reading-to-write* (Tech. Rep. No. 6). Berkeley, CA: University of California–Berkeley, Center for the Study of Writing.

Frederiksen, N. (1984). Implications of cognitive theory for instruction in problem solving. *Review of Educational Research*, 54(3), 363–407.

Gambrell, L. (1983). The occurrence of think-time during reading comprehension instruction. *Journal of Educational Research*, 77(2), 77–80.

Gavelek, J. R. (1986). The social contexts of literacy and schooling: A developmental perspective. In T. E. Raphael (Ed.), *The contexts of school-based literacy* (pp. 1–26). New York: Random House.

Gordon, C., & Pearson, P. D. (1983). The effects of instruction in metacomprehension and inferencing on children's comprehension abilities (Tech. Rep. No. 277). Urbana, IL: University of Illinois, Center for the Study of Reading.

Greeno, J. (1986). Collaborative teaching and making sense of symbols: Comment on Lampert's "Knowing, Doing, and Teaching Multiplication." *Cognition and Instruction, 3*(4), 343–347.

Guiser, D. (1986). *An examination of the relationship between recreational reading and reading achievement for eighty-six fifth- and sixth-grade students.* Unpublished doctoral dissertation, Michigan State University.

Guzak, F. (1967). Teacher questioning and reading. *Reading Teacher, 21,* 227–234.

Hansen, J., & Pearson, P. D. (1983). An instructional study: Improving the inferential comprehension of fourth-grade good and poor readers. *Journal of Educational Psychology, 75,* 821–829.

Herrmann, B. A. (1986). Reading instruction: Dealing with classroom realities. *Community College Review, 13*(1), 28–34.

Hoffman, J. (1991). Teacher and school effects in learning to read. In R. Barr, M. Kamil, P. Mosenthal, & P. D. Pearson (Eds.), *Handbook of reading research* (Vol. 2, pp. 950–991). New York: Longman.

Jones, B. F. (1986). Quality and equality through cognitive instruction. *Educational Leadership, 43*(7), 4–11.

Langer, J. (1984). Literacy instruction in American schools: Problems and perspectives. *American Journal of Education, 92,* 107–132.

Langer, J. A., & Applebee, A. N. (1986). Reading and writing instruction: Toward a theory of teaching and learning. In E. Rothkopf (Ed.), *Review of Research in Education: 13* (pp. 171–194). Washington, DC: American Educational Research Association.

Leinhardt, G., & Greeno, J. (1986). The cognitive skill of teaching. *Journal of Educational Psychology, 78*(2), 75–95.

Leinhardt, G., & Smith. D. A. (1985). Expertise in mathematics instruction: Subject matter knowledge. *Journal of Educational Psychology, 77,* 247–271.

Levine, S. (1984). USSR: A necessary component in teaching reading. *Journal of Reading, 28,* 394–400.

Marshall, H., & Weinstein, R. (1986). Classroom context of student-perceived differential teacher treatment. *Journal of Educational Psychology, 78*(6), 441–453.

Marx, R. (1983). Student perception in classrooms. *Educational Psychologist, 18*(3), 145–164.

Mehan, H. (1979). *Learning lessons: Social organization in the classroom.* Cambridge, MA: Harvard University Press.

Meichenbaum, D. (1985). Teaching thinking: A cognitive behavioral perspective. In S. Chipman, J. Segal, & R. Glaser (Eds.), *Thinking and learning skills: Current research and open questions* (Vol. 2, pp. 407–426). Hillsdale, NJ: Erlbaum.

Meichenbaum, D., & Goodman, J. (1971). Training impulsive children to talk to themselves: A means of developing self-control. *Journal of Abnormal Psychology, 77,* 115–126.

Meloth, M., & Roehler, L. (1987). *Dimensions of teacher explanation.* Paper presented at the annual conference of the American Educational Research Association, Washington, DC.

Miller, G. (1987). The influence of self-instruction on the comprehension-monitoring performance of average and above-average readers. *Journal of Reading Behavior, 19*(3), 303–318.

O'Sullivan, J., & Pressley, M. (1984). Completeness of instruction and strategy transfer. *Journal of Experimental Child Psychology, 38,* 275–288.

Otto, W., Wolf, A., & Eldridge, R. (1984). Managing instruction. In P. D. Pearson, R. Barr, M. L. Kamil, & P. Mosenthal (Eds.), *Handbook of reading research* (Vol. 1, pp. 799–878). White Plains, NY: Longman.

Palincsar, A. M. (1986). The role of dialogue in providing scaffolded instruction. *Educational Psychologist, 2,* 73–98.

Palincsar, A. M., & Brown, A. L. (1984). Reciprocal teaching of comprehension-fostering and monitoring activities. *Cognition and Instruction, 1*(2), 117–175.

Palincsar, A. M., & Brown, A. L. (in press). Classroom dialogues to promote self-regulated comprehension. In J. Brophy (Ed.), *Advances in research on teaching, Volume I: Teaching for understanding and self-regulated learning.* Greenwich, CT: JAI Press.

Paris, S. G., Cross, D. R., & Lipson, M. Y. (1984). Informal strategies for learning: A program to improve children's reading awareness and comprehension. *Journal of Educational Psychology, 76,* 1239–1252.

Paris, S. G., & Jacobs, J. E. (1984). The benefits of informed instruction for children's reading awareness and comprehension skills. *Child Development, 55,* 2083–2093.

Paris, S., Lipson, M., & Wixson, K. (1983). Becoming a strategic reader. *Contemporary Educational Psychology, 8,* 293–316.

Paris, S. G., & Oka, E. R. (1986). Self-regulated learning among exceptional children. *Exceptional Children, 53,* 103–108.

Pearson, P. D. (1983). A critique of F. J. Guzak's study: "Teacher gives timing and reading." In L. Gentile, M. Kamil, & J. Blanchard (Eds.), *Reading Research Revisited* (pp. 271–281). Columbus, OH: Merrill.

Pearson, P. D. (1985). Changing the face of reading comprehension instruction. *Reading Teacher, 38*(8), 724–738.

Pearson, P. D., Dole, J., Duffy, G., & Roehler, L. (in press). Developing expertise in reading comprehension: What should be taught and how should it be taught? In J. Farstrup & S. J. Samuels (Eds.), *What research has to say to the teacher of reading* (2nd ed.) Newark, NJ: International Reading Association.

Pressley, M., Snyder B., & Cariglia-Bull, T. (1987). How can good strategy use be taught to children? Evaluation of six alternative approaches. In S. Cormier & J. Hagman (Eds.), *Transfer of learning: Contemporary research and application* (pp. 81–120). Orlando, FL: Academic Press.

Putnam, R. (1987). Structuring and adjusting content for students. *American Educational Research Journal*, 24(1), 13–48.

Raphael, T. E., Englert, C. S., & Anderson, L. M. (1987). *What is effective instructional talk? A comparison of two writing lessons.* Paper presented at the annual meeting of National Reading Conference, St. Petersburg Beach, FL.

Raphael, T. E., & Gavelek, J. R. (1984). Question-related activities and their relationship to reading comprehension: Some instructional implications. In G. Duffy, L. Roehler, & J. Mason (Eds.), *Comprehension instruction: Perspectives and suggestions* (pp. 234–250). New York: Longman.

Raphael, T. E., & Wonnacott. (1985). Metacognitive training in question-answering strategies: Implementation in a fourth-grade developmental reading program. *Reading Research Quarterly, 20,* 282–296.

Readance, J. E., Baldwin, S. R., & Head, M. H. (1986). Direct instruction in processing metaphors. *Journal of Reading Behavior, 28,* 325–339.

Redfield, D., & Rousseau, E. (1981). A meta-analysis of experimental research on teacher questioning behavior. *Review of Educational Research, 51,* 237–245.

Resnick, L. (1981). Instructional psychology. In M. R. Rosenzweig & L. W. Porter (Eds.), *Annual review of psychology* (Vol. 32, pp. 659–704). Palo Alto, CA: Annual Reviews.

Rinehart, S. D., Stahl, S. A., & Erickson, L. G. (1986). Some effects of summarization training on reading and studying. *Reading Research Quarterly, 21,* 422–438.

Rodgers, V. (1972). Modifying questioning strategies of teachers. *Journal of Teacher Education, 23,* 58–62.

Roehler, L. R., & Duffy, G. G. (1986). Why are some teachers better explainers than others? *Journal of Education for Teaching, 12*(3), 273–284.

Roehler, L. R., Duffy, G. G., & Johnson, J. (1988, April). *The instructional challenge in reading: How to put the student in control of getting meaning from text.* Paper presented at the annual meeting of the American Educational Research Association, New Orleans.

Roehler, L. R., Duffy, G. G., & Meloth, M. (1986). What to be direct about in direct instruction in reading. In T. Raphael & R. Reynolds (Eds.), *Contexts of school-based literacy* (pp. 79–96). New York: Random House.

Roehler, L. R., Duffy, G. G., & Warren, S. (1987). Adaptive explanatory actions associated with effective teaching of reading strategies. In J. Readance and S. Baldwin (Eds.), *Dialogues in literacy research* (Thirty-Seventh Yearbook of National Reading Conference) (pp. 339–346). Chicago: National Reading Conference.

Rogoff, B., & Gardner, W. (1984). Adult guidances of cognitive development. In B. Rogoff & J. Love (Eds.), *Everyday cognition* (pp. 95–116). Cambridge, MA: Harvard University Press.

Rohrkemper, M., & Corno, L. (1988). Success and failure on classroom tasks: Adaptive learning and classroom teaching. *Elementary School Journal, 88*(3), 297–312.

Rosenshine, B. (1979). Content, time, and direct instruction. In P. Peterson & H. Walberg (Eds.), *Research on teaching: Concepts, findings, and implications* (pp. 28–56). Berkeley, CA: McCutchan.

Rosenshine, B. (1983). Teaching functions in instructional programs. *Elementary School Journal, 83,* 335–351.

Rosenshine, B., & Stevens, R. (1984). Classroom instruction in reading. In P. D. Pearson, R. Barr, M. L. Kamil, & P. Mosenthal (Eds.), *Handbook of reading research* (Vol. 1, pp. 745–798). White Plains, NY: Longman.

Scardamalia, M. (1984, April). *Knowledge telling and knowledge transforming in written composition.* Paper presented at the American Educational Research Association, New Orleans.

Scardamalia, M., & Bereiter, C. (1985). Fostering the development of self-regulation in children's knowledge processing. In S. Chipman, W. Segal, & R. Glaser (Eds.), *Thinking and learning skills: Research and open questions* (Vol. 2, pp. 563–578). Hillsdale, NJ: Erlbaum.

Scardamalia, M., Bereiter, C., & Steinbach, R. (1984). Teachability of reflective processes in written composition. *Cognitive Science, 8,* 173–190.

Scardamalia, M., & Paris, P. (1985). The function of explicit discourse knowledge in the development of text representations and composing strategies. *Cognition and Instruction, 2,* 1–39.

Shulman, L. (1986). Paradigms and research programs in the study of teaching: A contemporary perspective. In M. Wittrock (Ed.), *Handbook of research on teaching* (3rd ed., pp. 3–36). New York: Macmillan.

Shulman, L. (1987). Knowledge and teaching: Foundations of the new reform. *Harvard Educational Review, 57,* 1–22.

Sivan, E., & Roehler, L. R. (1986). Factors which inhibit or enhance change. In J. Niles & R. Lalik (Eds.), *35th Yearbook of the National Reading Conference.* Rochester, NY: National Reading Conference.

Slavin, R. E. (1980). Cooperative learning. *Review of Educational Research, 50,* 315–342.

Slavin, R. E. (1984). Students motivating students to excel: Cooperative incentives, cooperative tasks, and student achievement. *Elementary School Journal, 85,* 53–63.

Slavin, R. E. (1987). Cooperative learning: Where behavioral and humanistic approaches to classroom motivation meet. *Elementary School Journal, 88,* 29–37.

Slavin, R. E., & Karweit, N. (1984). Mastery learning and student teams: A factorial experiment in urban general mathematics classes. *American Research Educational Journal, 21*(4), 725–736.

Smith, E. E., & Goodman, L. (1984). Understanding written instruction: The role of an explanatory schema. *Cognition and Instruction, 1,* 359–396.

Stallings, J., Needles, M., & Stayrook, N. (1978). *The teaching of basic reading skills in secondary schools, Phase II* (Final Report). Menlo Park, CA: SRI International.

Stevens, R. J., Madden, N. A., Slavin, R. E., & Farnish, A. M. (1987). Cooperative integrated reading and composition: Two field experiments. *Reading Research Quarterly, 22,* 433–454.

Tharp, R. (1982). The effective instruction of comprehension: Results and description of the Kamehameha Early Education Program. *Reading Research Quarterly, 17*(4), 462–481.

Tharp, R., & Gallimore, R. (1988). *Rousing minds to life: Teaching, learning, and schooling in social context.* Cambridge, Eng.: Cambridge University Press.

Tierney, R., & Cunningham, J. (1984). Research on teaching reading comprehension. In P. D. Pearson, R. Barr, M. L. Kamil, & P. Mosenthal (Eds.), *Handbook of reading research* (Vol. 1, pp. 609–656). White Plains, NY: Longman.

Vavrus, L. (1987). *The functional role of teacher elicitations in instructional sequence interactions during low group reading skill lessons of more effective and less effective fifth grade teachers.* Unpublished dissertation, Michigan State University.

Vygotsky, L. S. (1978). *Mind in society: The development of higher psychological processes* (M. Cole, V. John-Steiner, S. Scribner, & E. Souberman, Eds. & Trans.). Cambridge, MA: Harvard University Press.

Weinstein, R. (1983). Student perceptions of schooling. *Elementary School Journal, 83,* 287–312.

Weinstein, R. (1985). Student mediation of classroom expectancy effects. In J. Dusek (Ed.), *Teacher Expectancies* (pp. 329–352). Hillsdale, NJ: Erlbaum.

Wertsch, J. V., McNamee, G. W., McLare, J. B., & Budwig, N. A. (1980). The adult-child dyad as a problem-solving system. *Child Development, 51,* 1215–1221.

Wigfield, A., & Asher, S. R. (1984). Social and motivational influences on reading. In P. D. Pearson, R. Barr, M. L. Kamil, & P. Mosenthal (Eds.), *Handbook of reading research* (Vol. 1, pp. 423–452). White Plains, NY: Longman.

Wilson, S. M., Shulman, L. S., & Richert, A. E. (1987). "150 different ways" of knowing: Representations of knowledge in teaching. In J. Calderhead (Ed.), *Exploring teachers' thinking* (pp. 104–124). London: Cassell.

Winne, P. (1979). Experiments relating teachers' use of higher cognitive questions to student achievement. *Review of Educational Research, 49,* 13–50.

Winne, P. (1985). Steps toward promoting cognitive achievements. *Elementary School Journal, 85*(5), 673–693.

Winne, P., & Marx, R. (1982). Students' and teachers' views of thinking processes for classroom learning. *Elementary School Journal, 82,* 493–518.

Wixson, K. (1983). Questions about a text: What you ask about is what children learn. *Reading Teacher, 37*(3), 287–294.

Wood, D., Bruner, J. S., & Ross, G. (1976). The role of tutoring and problem solving. *Journal of Child Psychology and Psychiatry, 17,* 89–100.

Yinger, R. (1977). *A study of teacher planning: Description and theory development using ethnographic and information processing methods.* Unpublished doctoral dissertation, Michigan State University.

31 GROUPING STUDENTS FOR READING INSTRUCTION

Rebecca Barr and Robert Dreeben

G rouping students on the basis of ability for reading instruction is pervasive in American schools. Despite the prevalence of this practice, or possibly because of it, many have taken it for granted. Recently, however, several forces have converged to make us reconsider how we organize students for reading. Important among these is the ideological position that identifies ability grouping as a practice that violates the principle of equal educational opportunity. The recent court decision, *Moses v. Washington Parish School Board* (1971), objected to ability grouping in theory on the grounds that educational research does not justify its use. Particularly within the field of reading, the movement toward a more unified language arts curriculum and against fragmentation and compartmentalization, has had a bearing on our thinking about ability grouping. Whatever the reason, we are now in a period in which we are reevaluating this long-standing practice.

In order to understand the practice of ability grouping, we must consider its origins. An examination of grouping in the United States and in other nations reveals it to be a response to the problem of how aggregations of students should be organized so that knowledge can be imparted.

In the first two sections of this chapter, we describe the constellation of conditions that led to ability grouping in the United States, and then we show how similar issues have been treated in other industrialized nations.

The educational research community began to study the nature and consequences of ability grouping soon after the practice became entrenched during the first quarter of the twentieth century. With the advantage of hindsight, it becomes clear that most researchers have treated ability grouping simply as a dispute over the efficacy of alternative pedagogical techniques (homogeneous and heterogeneous grouping) or as a scheme that either violates or supports the principle of equal educational opportunity. The technical and ideological narrowness of these controversies obscures the broad range of educational questions that lie behind ability grouping. In the third section of the chapter, we consider this body of research. During the past two decades researchers have addressed a broad set of issues both in elementary and high schools. Not only does this research show the connections between school and class characteristics, grouping and instruction, but it also suggests how the progression through an ability-grouped system for reading instruction in elementary schools may lay the basis for tracking in the content areas in high schools. Thus, ability grouping can be viewed as a sorting process begun during the first years of schooling that continues through high school and beyond. We consider the research pertaining to elementary schools in the fourth section of the chapter and that for high schools in the fifth.

We will argue, in the concluding section, that research in the future must focus on the conditions of schools and classes that lead to grouping, the characteristics of the groups formed, the knowledge imparted through instruction, and the consequence of grouping and instruction for learning. In sum, the purpose of this chapter is to provide a broad perspective for viewing the practice of ability grouping.

HISTORICAL OBSERVATIONS

According to Aries (1962),

> Medieval schools lacked gradation in the curriculum according to difficulty of the subject-matter, the simultaneity with which the subjects were taught, the mixing of the ages, and the liberty of the pupils. (p. 145)

Anachronistically, we can refer to this form of schooling as a type of "grouping" where complexity and type of knowledge had no visible connection to age or maturation, and where the time for instruction was indeterminate. "The medieval school was confined to the tonsured, to the clerics and the religious. From the end of the Middle Ages, it extended its teaching to ever-wider sections of the population" (p. 141).

Under different historical circumstances, contrasting forms of school organization appeared. In late-18th-century England, the French Revolution kindled a demand for schooling among the poor that outstripped the resources of church schools and Sunday schools. As conservative fears about the social and political dangers of educating the poor abated, reformers like Joseph Lancaster devised a financially viable scheme by which older students were employed to maintain discipline and provide instruction to hundreds of younger students. According to Kaestle (1973),

> The monitorial scheme provided constant activity, immediate reinforcement, and individual pupil progress. Unlike the later graded system, pupils were classified separately in reading, writing, spelling, and arithmetic, and were promoted to a new group whenever they had demonstrated their competence. (p. 7)

The factory-like and proto-bureaucratic character of these schools, by contrast to their medieval predecessors, showed concern with the standardization of subject matter, the capacities of students, and the rate of their progress.

It should not surprise us that curricular developments accompanied the development of the monitorial scheme. The first readers, characterized by increasing levels of difficulty, were written by Samuel Wood early in the 19th century, probably for the Lancasterian schools (Venezky, 1988). Curriculum and evaluation considerations were less visible in earlier forms of schooling, but they have come to be problematic and the subject of educational debate and experimentation from that time forward.

Schools in the first four decades of the 19th-century United States were prevalent in the North, and in rural as well as in urban areas. In rural areas, schooling was tied to the agricultural cycle, and the age for starting school was not standardized (Fuller, 1982). According to Kaestle (1983),

> Most teachers attempted to group children into "classes" based on the level of their primers, but this was often frustrated by the diversity of texts owned by parents. By jealously defended tradition, children studied from the texts their families sent with them to school (p. 17; see also Fuller, 1982).

The impulse to regularize education goes back at least to the 1830s. According to Tyack (1974), Horace Mann was greatly impressed by the "supervision, graded classes, [and] well-articulated curriculum" (p. 35) he found in Prussian schools; but his efforts to have such provisions instituted in the urban schools of Boston met fierce opposition from local interests. The first graded school was, however, established in Boston in 1847. Series of readers "in which a book was definitely prepared for each different school grade" (Smith, 1965, p. 83) became common during the period between 1840 and 1860. The regularizing of texts, curricula, and timing, and later the consolidating of school districts were also responses to conflicts arising among highly localized and divergent practices in rural schools (Fuller, 1982).

Mann and others were proponents of the common school movement. Kaestle (1983) states that during this period in the United States, opposition to popular schooling was far less intense than in England, a reflection of prevailing

> republican, Protestant, and capitalist values. . . . The reform version of this ideology called for state-regulated common schools to integrate and assimilate a diverse population into the nation's political, economic, and cultural institutions. (p. x)

While the development of a system of common schooling did not occur without opposition, its later institutionalization meant that schools, especially as they later became concentrated in urban areas, would have to accommodate intellectually, economically, and culturally diverse populations of students and provide them with instruction. (For descriptions of equality of U.S. social conditions relative to Europe, and of the widespread acceptance of egalitarian social principles, see Cremin [1951].) What has come down to us as the problem of grouping in the 20th century originates in these institutional questions rooted in the larger society.

The tendency to standardize education extended beyond Mann's time. William T. Harris, an advocate of standardization, provided major impetus to the bureaucratization of the schools. According to Tyack (1974),

> Urban schoolmen . . . wanted to divide the cities into attendance districts; calibrate upgraded primary and grammar schools into distinct classes in which children were segregated according to their academic progress; train and certify teachers for specific tasks within these graded schools; design a sequential curriculum . . . ; devise examinations which would test the achievement of pupils and serve as a basis of promotion. . . . (pp. 43–44)

It is not surprising that ability grouping into classes was first documented in 1862 in the St. Louis schools, where Harris was superintendent (Otto, 1932). Through the testing of achievement, schoolmen became aware of wide individual differences among students within grade levels. Harris also favored instituting a standardized humanities curriculum consisting of "grammar, literature and art, mathematics, geography and history . . . the means by which the culture of the race would be transmitted to the vast majority of Americans" (Kliebard, 1986, p. 17).

One can view the controversies over standardization, and its ultimate emergence as an organizing principle governing attendance, deportment, curricular content, and student progress, as responses to different philosophical positions about what the nature of schooling should be, to the rise of an industrializing economy, to the growing application of scientific considerations to educational matters, to the growth of urbanization, and to the growing diversity of the population over a prolonged period of foreign immigration. Standardization had important implications for the operation of schools.

The common school movement prevailed and attendance became widespread even without mandatory enforcement (Richardson, 1980). With the advance of education to promote an intelligent citizenry, school officials at the end of the 19th century turned their attention to matters of educational quality. As part of the Progressive Era, the realities of the educational enterprise were expressed ideologically by spokesmen with contrasting views about the nature of curriculum, instruction, and schooling. Some defended the importance of standard bodies of knowledge, some the principles of psychological development, some the principles of economic efficiency, and others the appropriate ways to organize classes and carry out instruction (Cremin, 1988; Kliebard, 1986).

In his famous book, *Laggards in Our Schools*, Ayres (1909) identified "the elimination of pupils from school and the cognate matter of retardation [repeating grades]" (p. 8) as important educational problems. His evidence showed that retardation was attributable—over and above population change, mortality, and the legal school-leaving age—to ethnic differences among students and to poor attendance. He also believed that courses in the curriculum were

> not fitted for the average child. They are so devised that they may be followed by the unusually bright pupil substantially as mapped out. The really exceptional child may even advance faster than the scheduled rate but the average child cannot keep up with the works as planned and the slow child has an even smaller chance of doing so. (p. 218)

While Ayres thought about this situation as a problem in educational inefficiency to be dealt with by better management techniques (especially proper record keeping), in actuality the retardation question posed a larger set of issues concerning the definition of satisfactory progress, whether progress appropriate to one group of students was so for another, and how the curriculum should be adapted to the capacities of students. Issues of this kind do not usually arise when schools are ungraded, the school year varied in length, the curriculum idiosyncratic to the school or even to school children who bring their own books from home (Fuller 1982), and students homogeneous in social background because of their residential proximity in very small communities.

It is interesting to note that some of the changes in reading programs during this period involved the creation of easier stories through increased word control and repetition and the addition of preprimers (Smith, 1965). To provide appropriate instruction to individuals within classes, moreover, teachers began to teach smaller groups of children with similar abilities. Although it is difficult to date the emergence of this practice, one of the earliest references, found in the *Story Hour Readers Manual* (American Book Company, 1913), suggests separate groups for those who "progress rapidly" and for those who are "slow and need more assistance."

As reading groups within classes became more common, basal reading programs during the 1920s and 1930s became more comprehensive and included workbooks for skill practice and teacher's guides (Smith, 1965). Indeed, the comprehensiveness of the basal programs used with ability groups for reading instruction, and instruction of total classes in spelling, writing, and other language arts may have fostered the separation of reading instruction from the other language arts.

Reading programs for groups of different ability did not appear until several decades later in the 1950s and 1960s in the form of supplementary readers (Macmillan), easy and more difficult versions of the same program (American Book Company), and two parallel series (Scott Foresman) (Smith, 1965). Earlier, teachers were encouraged to use the same materials with *all* their groups so that the program would be consistent and teachers would be more able to shift students from group to group (Smith, 1965, p. 241).

In sum, what becomes clear in hindsight is that the educational system posed a set of problems for which no solution removed all difficulties. Ability grouping, along with a variety of 20th-century school reforms—the educational plans with their eponymous cities (Joplin, Detroit, Winnetka, Denver, Gary, Dalton); the platoon school; individualized instruction; graded and nongraded schooling; schemes for regulating the number of years required to complete elementary school according to student performance; schemes for enriching and extending the curriculum without changing the time for program completion; automatic promotion, skipping, and retention; mastery learning; the formation of special classes; team teaching; the specialization of teachers and departmentalization of schools; continuous progress; reading groups—are all attempts to impart knowledge in grouped settings so that all students benefit. Each attempts in different ways to accomplish this goal by altering the time set aside for completing a program, the criterion for deciding when the curriculum has been mastered sufficiently to justify moving onward, the difficulty and richness of curricular content, the frequency of promotion, and the composition of groups, classes, and grades (Otto, 1932; Purdom, 1929).

These issues were by no means peculiarly American; educational systems in all societies dealt with them; and different societies have arrived at varying solutions, depending upon their social, religious, ethnic, and historical circumstances, their commitment to universal education, and their traditions.

CROSS-NATIONAL COMPARISONS

Schools in various countries have served a variety of functions: education for the masses of young children, formation of governing and social elites, entrance into the labor force, and inculcation of moral values. Even though there has been a secular trend across countries toward universalizing education at successively higher levels, this trend has not everywhere followed the same course. National differences in historical experience have led in various ways and in different degrees to the extension of common school principles governing elementary education to higher levels, the fusion of separate principles distinguishing elementary from higher levels, and the weakening of elite principles of school organization (Clark, 1985). As the result of these processes, different kinds of schools have developed from country to country, along with different boundary lines between one level and another as well as contrasting notions about curricular content and eligibility for admission. (See Chapter 2 by Foster and Purves in this volume for a description of schooling in developing nations.)

In the U.S. system, for example, with its tradition of common schooling organized in local districts, public elementary schools serve all students residing in a catchment area. At the secondary level, although comprehensive high schools are the norm (a continuation of the common school principle), one also finds distinctions among public secondary schools according to type of curriculum (e.g., vocational and academic) and to selectivity. While most U.S. schools are public, there is a private sector at both the elementary and secondary levels; and private schools tend to be distinguished by the wealth, religion, ability, and ethnicity of their clienteles as well as by religious affiliation, social eclat, restrictiveness of disciplinary environment, and philosophical orientation.

British education outwardly resembles the U.S. situation in certain respects, approaching it, however, through different historical circumstances. Three differences are particularly significant. The first is the existence, until recently, of an examination given to students at age 11 to determine their future education. The second, "streaming" in the elementary schools, represents a device comparable to some forms of ability grouping and tracking in U.S. schools (Barker-Lunn, 1970; Central Advisory Council for Education, [CACE], 1967; Daniels, 1961a, 1961b; Douglas, 1964; Galton, Simon, & Croll, 1980; Jackson, 1980). The third is the prominence of private schools attended by the socially elite.

At issue in Great Britain, as in virtually all other school systems, is the fact that schools must serve the multiple functions of providing for the welfare of individual students; imparting at least some core of a standardized curriculum; determining what elements of the educational process should fall within the provinces of elementary and secondary schools, academic and vocational forms of further education and training, or assigned to noneducational institutions engaged in economic production that require trained labor; and screening and allocating students according to the quality of academic performance in anticipation of their later participation in a stratified labor force.

In the British case, the common schooling principle extended only until 11, a terminal age for many students, according to provisions of the Education Act of 1870. As secondary enrollments edged upward in the early part of the 20th century, so did the school leaving age. Unlike U.S. secondary schools, the British were distinguished by clientele into grammar, technical, and secondary modern schools with access to such schools governed by performance on a national examination at age 11 (Halsey, Heath, & Ridge, 1980, pp. 24–31; Kerckhoff, Campbell, & Trott, 1982).

From the 1930s onward, following guidelines set down in a series of legislative acts and reports, the class-bound character of the British educational system declined in prominence, though it was surely not eliminated (see Keddie, 1971). The 1944 Education Act moved the system in the direction of making secondary education (for students aged 11 to 15) available to all, but divided it into selective grammar and unselective secondary modern schools. Over the next decade, the wisdom of selecting students at age 11 was seriously questioned; and in time the 11 + examination was abolished, and comprehensive secondary schools increased in number (Halsey, Heath, & Ridge, 1980, p. 27; Maden, 1985, pp. 77–81).

Similar distinctions among types of secondary schools were, and remain, common in continental Europe. A major difference between U.S. and British and other European secondary schools, then, consists in the fact that the former characteristically provide for diversity in school populations through curricular-track divisions within schools, while the latter more frequently cope with them by differentiating among types of schools (Clark, 1985, p. 293).

Tawney stated in 1931 that "The hereditary curse upon English education is its organization upon lines of social class" (p. 142). In both the United States and Great Britain, an elite, independent sector of schools has long existed providing education for a monied and socially prominent minority with disproportionate access to positions of governmental importance (Cookson & Persell, 1985; Weinberg, 1967; Wilkinson, 1964). Over time, however, students of less-than-privileged background in both countries have gained access to such schools.

In Japan, common schooling runs through the ninth grade. According to Rohlen (1983), a cluster of societal conditions in Japan (relative income equality compared to the industrial West, ethnic homogeneity, a low divorce rate, late marriage age, a small proportion of mothers working outside the home, and high rates of kindergarten attendance) support substantial equality of educational opportunity, in undifferentiated schools and classrooms, in a highly uniform, centralized, and competitive system (see also Brinton, 1988).

According to Cummings (1980), heterogeneous classroom grouping is common in Japanese elementary schools.

Under no circumstances do the teachers consciously form groups stratified by ability as is the practice in growing numbers of American schools. Although the teachers recognize differences in ability among their students, they feel it is their responsibility as public school teachers in a democratic society to try to bring all the students up to a common level. (p. 127)

Japanese schools, nevertheless, confront problems associated with variations in student ability, but by different means: maintenance of instructional similarity within classes, an institutionalized system of out-of-school tutoring, substantial parental involvement in home instruction, and differentiation of secondary schools.

The Japanese system is unique among industrialized nations in its nondifferentiation of students at the elementary level. "All of this," according to Rohlen (1983), however,

is reversed at the high school level, where entire schools are differentiated by the presumed ability of their students, where tracking is the essential ingredient *in the overall structure of schools*, and where instead of offering equal education, high school offerings are responsive to and limited by specific abilities of their students. From lumping, the system shifts to splitting. (p. 121, our italics)

Competitive examinations represent the key to entering an advantageous high school that increases the likelihood of attending a prestigious university.

In general, where secondary schools are distinguished by type and ability (like those respectively in Great Britain and the Continent, and in Japan), one does not usually find a differentiated curriculum within the schools. By contrast, when secondary schools are of the comprehensive type (as in the United States and to a lesser extent in Great Britain) designed to serve highly diverse student populations, tracking and curricular differentiation within schools are prevalent. In the United States tracking is almost universal, though controversial, in the public sector, and rare in the private and parochial sectors. (See Cohen [1985] for a thorough historical and contemporary treatment of curriculum differentiation and the disputes surrounding it.)

From the vantage point of current educational practice, it is easy to see how grouping has been understood as a mechanism internal to schools for dealing with diverse school populations. The schools themselves, however, must also be seen as groups related to larger units in the structure of national educational systems. Clark (1985) argues that a key consideration in defining the character of secondary schools is whether they are more closely integrated to the system of higher education (as on the Continent) than to the primary schools (as in the United States). In the former case, one finds clear lines drawn between elite schools, staffed by academically prominent faculty, that provide direct access to university (often through a specialized subject, like mathematics) and schools for everyone else; selection into elite schooling, moreover, occurs at the boundary of primary and secondary schools. In the latter case, unspecialized comprehensive schools provide a mélange of courses under rather loose internal tracking systems with a marginally professionalized teaching force; selection into elite universities occurs at the boundary between secondary school and university.

The definition of what schools are represents an important aspect of what educational grouping means. The formation of different *kinds of schools*, with differing points of entry and exit and different curricular offerings, serving different student populations, and occupying different places in the overall sequence of schooling represents one form of grouping. The internal division of schools into smaller units is another. The now virtually universal practices of dividing schools by level and age-related grades are cases in point. Beyond the alignment of curricular content with age, other forms of within-school grouping not only exist but represent at the same time topics of educational controversy and matters of settled practice. Among the most prominent of these is grouping by ability.

RESEARCH ON ABILITY GROUPING AND TRACKING

Although ability grouping has taken many different forms, we focus on two major variants: *between*-class and *within*-class grouping. The most common, as described in the U.S. literature of the 1920s and 1930s, refers to the assignment of students to classes or tracks on the basis of ability to increase homogeneity within classes. Within-class grouping occurs in elementary school classes, mainly for reading instruction, less frequently for math instruction, and rarely for other subjects. This practice also emerged early in the 20th century.

Within- and between-class ability grouping differ in flexibility and peer interaction. For *within*-class grouping, group membership can theoretically be modified over time since all groups are taught by single teachers, and different groups can be formed for different content areas. Further, in those subject areas in which the class is instructed as a unit, children have the opportunity to interact with classmates who vary in ability. Ability grouping *between* classes (e.g., ability-grouped classes, cross-class grouping or departmentalization, cross-grade grouping, tracking) requires the agreement of several teachers to make changes. Further, in ability-grouped classes, the same grouping is used for all subjects, and students interact only with other students of similar ability; this is typically not true for cross-class or cross-grade grouping for particular subjects or tracking.

Most traditional studies of ability grouping have addressed questions of prevalence and effectiveness. Unfortunately, what is meant by "ability grouping" in this research is often not clearly delineated. For example, classes formed so as to be heterogeneous may be characterized by ability groups within classes; yet, this condition is described as nonability grouped. Thus, the results are difficult to interpret.

Prevalence

It is generally accepted that elementary reading instruction in U.S. schools is a content area that is almost universally subject to ability grouping within and/or between classes. What systematic evidence supports this impression? Generally, where descriptions of ability grouping exist, they are based on nonrandom and often nonrepresentative samples. As important, it is not often clear whether "ability group" means grouping within or between classes (see, for example, NEA, 1961; Wilson & Schmits, 1978).

Probably the most reliable and frequently cited source on the prevalence of ability grouping is Austin and Morrison (1963). Through interviews and observations, they found that most teachers (in 35 of 51 schools studied) instructed classes heterogeneous in ability, with children placed in groups on the basis of reading ability within classes. Similarly, Goodlad (1984) claims that three highly stable ability groups established during the first months of first grade are typical in primary-grade reading, but that total class instruction is dominant in the intermediate grades. One study frequently cited to support the prevalence of ability grouping (Pikulski & Kirsch, 1979) is not based on regular classrooms, but on compensatory reading groups.

The observational research literature from the past two decades also suggests that grouping occurs frequently within classes for reading instruction (Barr & Dreeben, 1983; Anderson, Evertson, & Brophy, 1979; Mason & Osborn, 1982; Stallings, 1975) but somewhat less frequently in the intermediate grades, particularly when classes are grouped by ability for reading instruction (Barr & Sadow, 1989; Hallinan & Sørensen, 1983; Sirotnik, 1983). Slavin (1987), in his metanalysis of the ability-grouping literature, found no examples of completely heterogeneously grouped reading instruction. Because of the unsystematic nature of the evidence on ability grouping for reading instruction between and within classes, we are left with the belief that it is pervasive; but we have little basis for determining its prevalence and for plotting trends over time.

Effectiveness

The research on effectiveness has typically examined achievement outcomes and sometimes attitudinal results for students grouped into classes on the basis of ability in comparison to those heterogeneously grouped into classes. This work is limited in several ways. Most important, the instruction that intervenes between the division of classes into groups and outcomes is not systematically described, even though it is of major significance in understanding the relationship. Further, ability grouping within classes is typically not considered even though its presence may confound the comparison.

Researchers since the early decades of the century have inquired about the consequence of ability grouping for the learning and feelings of students. The literature contains two major waves of reviews: one in the early 1930s (Billet, 1932; Kelliher, 1931; Miller & Otto, 1930; Rock, 1929; Whipple, 1936; Wyndham, 1934) and another in the 1960s (Eash, 1961; Ekstrom, 1961; Goldberg, Passow, & Justman, 1966; Goodlad, 1960; Morgenstern, 1966; Yates, 1966). The reviewers of both periods criticized the adequacy of the studies they discussed, emphasizing the inconsistency in results and the conclusion that ability grouping per se is not effective unless the content and techniques of instruction are appropriately differentiated. The early reviewers were, however, unique in their conclusion that ability grouping benefited "slow" pupils. As Otto (1941) states, "The evidence indicates greatest relative effectiveness for dull children, next greatest for average children, and least (frequently harmful) for bright children" (p. 440). These generalizations may have arisen, in part, from the difficulty of the curricula of the time. As discussed earlier, Ayres (1909) believed that courses in the curriculum were "not fitted for the average child."

Some studies during this early period went beyond examining the effectiveness of ability grouping to inquire about the nature of the groups formed and their instruction. Researchers, particularly from Teachers College, challenged whether ability grouping significantly narrowed the range of class ability (Burr, 1931; Hartill, 1936; West, 1933). They found that student ability in one area of knowledge was not highly correlated with that in another; and hence classes formed on the basis of results in one subject area were not appropriate for instruction in another. This evidence led to questioning the usefulness of grouping students into classes by ability. Other evidence showed that measures of ability were not reliable and therefore questionable for forming stable class groups. These same studies documented student diversity within classes and the overlap in distributions in low- and high-ability classes. The diversity of classes underscores the difficulty in matching instruction to some average within a group because of its inappropriateness for those deviating from the mean.

Research on ability grouping appears to have declined from 1935 to 1955 as indicated by the number of published reports. Some, like J. W. McDermott (1976),

Persell (1977), and Winn and Wilson (1983) claim that the *practice* of ability grouping also diminished during this period due to the criticisms of the 1930s. Others (Noland, 1985) argue that this decline was largely illusory; ability grouping may have been as common, but not of interest to researchers.

The late 1950s through the 1980s are marked by a resurgence of interest in instructional grouping. Technological preoccupation with its effectiveness in earlier decades gave way to concerns for equality of educational opportunity. Questions arose in part from the possibility that court-ordered desegregation might be undermined by ability grouping and tracking, leading to de facto resegregation within schools. Following the *Brown v. Board of Education of Topeka* (1954) decision, the *Hobson v. Hansen* (1967) decision challenged the use of IQ tests as a valid basis for identifying the academic ability of disadvantaged students, and raised questions about social and ethnic stratification. The *Moses v. Washington Parish School Board* (1971) decision went even further by objecting to ability grouping in theory on the grounds that educational research does not justify its use.

While reviewers of the 1960s acknowledged inconsistency in results and no difference "on the average" between grouping alternatives similar to earlier reviewers, some discerned a tendency for high achievers in homogeneous groups to learn more than comparable students in heterogeneous groups, but for low achievers to do less well in homogeneous than in heterogeneous groups (Borg, 1965; Dahllöf, 1971; Esposito, 1973; Findley & Bryan, 1971; Heathers, 1969). For the first time, the equivocal results were used to assert that there is little positive justification for segregating students according to achievement or ability (Eash, 1961; Esposito, 1973; Findley & Bryan, 1970; Yates, 1966).

The number of traditional studies comparing the achievement and/or attitudinal outcomes of ability-grouped students with those not grouped has declined in recent years (Noland, 1985). Yet, new methods of summarizing the evidence have been brought to bear. Ability-grouping studies undertaken from 1967 to 1983 were the focus of a meta-analysis by Noland (1985). A set of 50 studies comparing homogeneously with heterogeneously grouped students in grades kindergarten through twelve was identified and described in terms of such characteristics as grade level, gender, racial and ethnic composition, ability level, content area, and time allocated to instruction. The results for all content areas combined yielded results that differed from those for reading. Generally, ability-grouped students scored lower on affective, but not on achievement, measures. For reading, no affective measures were included for students in grades kindergarten through three; however, low-achieving ability-grouped students benefited over their nongrouped counterparts, whereas high-achieving ability-grouped students did less well. In grades four to six, low- and average-ability groups did less well than their nongrouped peers, but high groups did better. Unlike most other areas of instruction, which showed a decline on affective measures associated with ability grouping, students who were ability grouped for reading instruction scored higher on affective measures. These results show that content area influences the effectiveness of ability grouping. The results, however, should be treated with caution since some studies contributed many outcomes (as many as 63), and others only one.

In a second review, Slavin (1987) undertook a "best-evidence synthesis" combining features of meta-analysis with those of narrative review. Slavin included all studies of ability grouping in grades one through six that established the initial comparability of comparison groups, used standardized achievement tests, occurred for at least a semester, and involved at least three experimental and three control teachers. The analysis is particularly useful because the findings are organized in terms of the forms of grouping frequently employed in elementary schools, results are reported for each study separately, and distinctions are made concerning the subject areas of focus (reading vs. mathematics) and the grade level of students. He did not consider the consequence of ability grouping for affective measures.

Several trends emerge from Slavin's review. Based on mixed results from 13 well-designed studies, he concludes that the superiority of ability-grouped class assignment in terms of enhanced learning was *not* demonstrated. There was no support for the assertion that high achievers benefit from being streamed into homogeneous ability classes or that low achievers suffer from it. Results based on three studies were similarly equivocal for departmentalized forms of instruction in comparison with heterogeneously grouped classes. He did find, however, that students grouped across grades for reading instruction learned more than comparable students in self-contained classes in nine of eleven studies. Further, low-achieving students as well as those of higher achievement levels learned more when instructed in cross-grade groups than did similar students instructed in reading groups in self-contained classrooms. The effectiveness of cross-grade grouping may come about through two conditions: The groups resulting from cross-grade patterns are likely to be more homogeneous than those for other patterns. This is because students from grade to grade overlap considerably in achievement; consequently, when the same number of groups is established, cross-grade grouping results in narrower ranges of proficiency than single-grade groupings. This greater homogeneity, in turn, should make it easier for teachers to design appropriate instruction. Beyond this, achievement is influenced by the difficulty of the curricular tasks assigned. Typically, a greater range of curricular materials is available in cross-grade grouping involving two or more grades than in forms of grouping involving a single grade. Thus, greater opportunity exists for high achievers to be given sufficiently demanding work and lower achievers to be met at their precise reading level.

Slavin found no study in which the achievement of ability groups within classes for reading instruction was compared to that for students receiving ungrouped instruction in heterogeneous, self-contained classes. This is probably because of the widespread practice of grouping students for reading instruction on the basis of achievement. While the advantage of ability-grouped instruction within classes that was found for math instruction may also hold for reading, we lack evidence on this point.

A third meta-analysis focused on the results from studies of junior and senior high school tracking. Kulik and Kulik (1982) identified 52 studies conducted with appropriate control groups and no major methodological flaws. Conclusions were based on composite achievement measures from all studies, and on self-concept and attitudinal measures from some studies. The achievement benefits of tracking were small but favored ability grouping, particularly in 14 studies of talented and gifted students who received a demanding curriculum in honors classes. Results were mixed for self-concept, but ability-grouped students showed more positive attitudes than ungrouped students towards the subjects they studied. The results were not, however, reported for ability groups considered separately; thus, average effects may have masked differences within groups (Marsh, 1984; see also Slavin, 1984).

The results from the meta-analyses are not more informative than the narrative reviews from earlier periods. Similar to earlier reviews, these analyses yield, for the most part, equivocal and inconsistent results. Why researchers should expect more is interesting. A social arrangement, in and of itself, does not lead directly to achievement or attitudinal outcomes; rather, it is the activities and knowledge that students experience as part of instruction that bear directly on what they learn and how they feel about their learning. We should have learned from this long history of research that we need to document systematically the instruction students receive and the nature of their curricular exposure. While group characteristics may set outside limits on what can occur during instruction, we have not begun to examine the extent to which group characteristics constrain instruction (for further discussion of this issue, see Dreeben & Barr, 1988a; Gamoran, 1987a).

The research on ability grouping has, however, become more varied in recent years. In the following two sections, we consider newer strands of research on grouping in elementary schools and on tracking in secondary schools.

GROUPING IN ELEMENTARY SCHOOLS

Research of the most recent period examines grouping in more broadly conceived ways and focuses on the instruction that ability groups receive. Concern with equality spawned several lines of inquiry, some going beyond narrow ideological concerns and leading to conceptualizations of ability grouping as part of the social systems of classrooms. Some of the more interesting research of the 1970s and 1980s stems from concern with the mechanisms through which social background influences education and life chances. Cohen and associates (1984, 1986; Rosenholtz & Cohen, 1983) consider how traditional versus more individualized forms of teaching influence classroom authority, collaboration among teachers, friendship among students, and the attribution of status. They argue that traditional forms of instruction (restricted curricular tasks, ability grouping, and comparative grading) serve as the occasion for attributing low status to low achievers, thereby depressing their interaction and learning. Similarly, Bossert (1979) shows how the task structure of classes influences the leadership of teachers and the friendship choices of students.

Along somewhat different lines, Barr and Dreeben (1983) argue that most past research fails to examine the instructional events that mediate the influence of grouping (heterogeneous versus homogeneous) on achievement and that these events must be understood. Ability grouping, and other forms of it, are the means teachers use to match instruction to the characteristics of a diverse group of students. Grouping patterns (number, relative size, diversity, and overlap among groups) reflect class composition and curricular materials. The rate of curricular presentation is responsive to group ability; and it, in turn, influences the learning of students. (For similar formulations, see Dahllöf, 1971; Dreeben & Gamoran, 1986; Gamoran, 1986; Hallinan & Sørensen, 1983; Rowan & Miracle, 1983; Sørenson & Hallinan, 1986).

Most research conducted in elementary schools during the past two decades, however, has examined limited aspects of these events. Some studies reminiscent of the descriptive studies from the 1930s focus on the criteria used in organizing groups, at least in part to determine whether minority students are overrepresented in low-ability classes and groups. Some consider the stability of grouping arrangements once formed. Others pursue the question of equality by determining whether certain groups are discriminated against through the quality of their instruction. In the following sections, we consider this research on the organization, stability, and instructional interaction of ability groups within elementary school classrooms.

Organization of Reading Groups

Forming groups at the beginning of the school year appears to represent an interactive decision in which a tentative grouping pattern is fitted to the characteristics of students. Not only are students placed in groups, but the grouping pattern itself may undergo change in response to the characteristics of students. Sørensen and Hallinan (1984) found, for example, that high-ability groups tended to be larger in classrooms that were racially mixed, thereby giving black students more of a chance to be assigned to the high group. This observation suggests that the creation of a larger high group may represent the teacher's response to the racial composition of the class. The form of grouping may also be influenced by the nature of curricular materials and the tasks teachers have planned. Barr (1975), for example, described how the availability of workbook materials determined whether heterogeneous total class or smaller ability groups were used for this aspect of reading instruction.

Several investigators using simulated information on students have examined the evidence that teachers use in forming ability groups (Borko, Shavelson, & Stern, 1981). Russo (1978) and Borko (1982) found that teachers consider such information as reading achievement, sex, participation during instruction, and problematic behavior.

Earlier investigators such as Rist (1970) have argued that teachers group students according to their conception of "ideal" students—that is, those who are clean and non-aggressive. Haller and Davis (1980, 1981) explored the extent to which extraneous characteristics such as social class influenced group placement. They asked teachers to consider how students in their classes should be grouped for reading in the following year. Teachers' comments during the grouping process indicated that decisions were more strongly influenced by achievement-related than by social class considerations.

Extension of this work focused on grouping decisions in racially mixed classes (Haller, 1985; Haller & Waterman, 1985) and failed to reveal evidence of racial bias, although more black students were placed in lower groups on the basis of their lower reading achievement. For both black and white students, teachers relied most heavily on reading ability, followed by general ability. Some mentioned work habits and behavior/personality, but few commented on home background. Haller and Waterman (1985) found that when students of similar ability fell close to the margin between reading groups, considerations such as work habits and behavior/personality had an increased bearing. Home background was crucial in very few cases. Similarly, Sørensen and Hallinan (1984) found no direct effect of race on the assignment of students to ability groups with achievement controlled. The latter study is particularly important because it examined what teachers do, not what they say they do. These results suggest that most teachers assign students to groups on the basis of achievement and work habits and are not influenced by home background.

Stability

The assertion is repeatedly made that ability groups, once established, are highly stable (Austin & Morrison, 1963; Goodlad, 1984). While this conclusion seems more likely to be true for ability-grouped classes and other forms of grouping between classes, it may also hold for ability groups *within* classes. Recent observational evidence, however, suggests more movement than might be expected. Barr and Dreeben (1983) found an average of about a 30 percent change between December and May in first-grade classes, with group change occurring in two ways: shifting individuals from one group to another and changing the group structure by eliminating or adding a group. Hallinan and Sørensen (1983) report that the average was a 5 percent change for each of five time periods in grades four to seven, suggesting about a 25 percent change for the year. These findings are similar to the earlier results based on observation by Groff (1962) and Hawkins (1966): change in group membership during the beginning months of the school year varied from 20 percent to 35 percent in grades one to four, but less than 10 percent in grades five to six. Since these estimates were based on less than a semester, the amount of change for the school year must be higher. This observational evidence conflicts with the frequent assertion of little change in group membership.

Teachers can be characterized by different patterns of group change, some with a tendency to move more students up than down, some more down than up, and some with balanced changes among groups. The pattern characterizing more-effective teachers appears to involve that of moving students up so that near the end of the school year, high-ability groups are relatively larger than earlier, while low groups are smaller (Barr & Dreeben, 1983; Rupley, Blair, & Wise, 1982).

In contrast to the study of the stability of groups during the school year, there has been relatively little documentation of the stability of ability-group membership from year to year. Some evidence comes from desegregation court cases. As part of the *Hobson v. Hansen* case, evidence on grouping in the Washington, D.C., schools revealed that placements were permanent for 90 percent of students (*Hobson v. Hansen*, 1967, p. 16,760, as cited in Rosenbaum, 1984). It is not clear, however, how this figure was derived and whether it applies to elementary as well as secondary students. Gamoran (in press), in examining change from first to second grade, found that schools differed in the extent to which first-grade basal placement versus standardized test results predicted second-grade group placement. Barr and Sadow (in press) reported that the ability groups they studied in fourth-grade classes were highly overlapping in reading comprehension and speculated that the groupings initially established in kindergarten or first grade on the basis of skill in learning print were perpetuated into fourth grade, where other criteria (comprehension) should have distinguished them.

Based on evidence of the stability of grouping in elementary schools, reading groups within classes appear to be alterable rather than entrenched arrangements. Overall, however, the evidence is thin.

Group Placement and Instructional Interaction

Once students are placed in ability groups for reading, does this placement influence the quality of their instruction? Does the instruction of ability groups differ—and if so, how? A body of naturalistic research compares the social participation and academic task characteristics of high and low reading groups (Allington, 1983; Barr, 1989; Calfee & Piontkowski, 1987; Hiebert, 1983; Good & Marshall, 1984). While groups are composed to facilitate differential instruction, the question is whether different instruction constitutes effective instruction. Rist (1970), in one of the earliest ethnographic studies of ability groups, observed that the groups within the class he observed during their kindergarten, first-, and second-grade years were treated differently. Children in the low-status groups communicated less with the teacher, were less involved in class activities, and received infrequent instruction in comparison with high-status children.

Other research has documented the differential treatment of low and high reading groups. R. McDermott (1976), in his study of instruction in a first-grade class, found that low-group children spent less time on reading instruction than high-group ones partly because their turn-taking procedures diverted attention from the instructional task and because of frequent interruptions by other class members. McDermott suggests that the agendas for the two groups may differ, with the low group avoiding the frustration and embarrassment associated with getting through the reading lesson. Others have reported that the instruction of low-group members tends to be characterized by a greater number of intrusions (Eder, 1981, 1982), less time (Hunter, 1978), and less time-on-task (Gambrell, 1984; Gambrell, Wilson, & Gnatt, 1981; Good & Beckerman, 1978; Haskins, Walden, & Ramey, 1983; Martin & Evertson, 1980). Some, however, have not found differential time allocations (Weinstein, 1976; Collins, 1985).

Beyond characterizations of instructional time, other researchers have found that the work by low and high groups differs. Low-group members typically read less material and complete simpler assignments (Allington, 1984; Barr, 1974, 1975; Barr & Dreeben, 1983; Clay, 1967; Hart, 1982); focus on smaller units of print and have decoding rather than meaning emphasized (Allington, 1980; Alpert, 1974; DeStefano, Pepinsky, & Sanders, 1982; Duffy & Anderson, 1981; Hart, 1982); are given more drill, skillwork, and oral reading (Collins, 1986; DeStephano, Pepinsky, & Sanders, 1982; Haskins, Walden, & Ramey, 1983); are asked more questions that require recall of information rather than reasoning (Seltzer, 1976); receive different prompts from teachers (Allington, 1980; Hoffman & Baker, 1981); and are provided more structure through advanced organizers for lessons and motivational exercises (Duffy & Anderson, 1981; Hart, 1982; Russo, 1978) than are students in higher-achieving groups.

Although it has long been the wisdom in the field of reading that children learn best in small homogeneous groups, little systematic evidence exists to support or refute this practice. The research of the past two decades describes the instruction that low- and high-group members receive, but there are several major problems in drawing conclusions based on this evidence. First, few of the case studies describe the learning of students in a systematic fashion; and without outcome measures it is impossible to judge the consequence of instruction for learning. Second, few involve more than one or several cases studied intensively; there are no appropriate instructional contrasts on which to base conclusions. It is not appropriate to generalize solely from a comparison of the instruction that low- and high-group members receive. That the instruction of high and low groups should differ is not unexpected; indeed, one reason for forming groups that are more homogeneous in reading than the class as a whole is so that instruction can be more appropriate. The research, nevertheless, raises two major issues, one having to do with the nature of instruction and the second with the composition of groups.

With respect to the first, and in view of current normative models of "good" reading instruction (Anderson, Hiebert, Scott, & Wilkinson, 1985), it is not clear that reading fewer stories and more isolated letters and words and responding to informational questions constitutes "more appropriate" instruction. Because few studies provide evidence on low-group members who receive alternative forms of instruction, we have no firm basis for concluding that the instruction currently provided for low-group members is less effective than alternatives. However, a few studies provide comparative evidence. Research by Barr and Dreeben (1983) suggests that when low groups receive extra instructional time to accomplish more contextual reading, they demonstrate higher achievement. (See Dreeben and Barr [1988b] for additional evidence on the importance of time for the instruction of low-group students.) Indeed, the contribution of progress within the basal program (content coverage) to reading achievement is of the same magnitude as group ability (see also Gamoran, 1986). Similarly, direct instructional procedures have been shown to enhance the progress of low-achieving students (Anderson, Evertson, & Brophy, 1979; Fisher et al., 1978; Stallings, 1975). More research is needed, particularly that in which low-achieving groups are treated more like high groups. The assumption that ability grouping leads to more appropriate tasks and instruction for lower-achieving children needs to be tested directly.

The recent body of descriptive research provides extensive evidence of the relation between group composition and interactional characteristics. There are social consequences of placing children who have difficulty learning a task in the same group, not least of which is the tendency for more intrusions to erode the time spent on reading. An obvious alternative is to group children heterogeneously for reading instruction; yet, there is the strong belief, particularly among teachers, that ability grouping is necessary. Two conditions may influence the need to group by ability: whether the task allows a range in prerequisite abilities or not, and the range of proficiency represented within a group. With respect to the first, progress in the beginning stages of learning to read may demand a closer match between ability and task than later reading when comprehension tasks allow greater diversity in background knowledge (Barr & Anderson, 1988). With respect to the second, it is well established that diversity in reading increases as students progress through school.

In any case, for whatever reason, there is little research documenting the reading instruction and learning of students in diverse groups. An exception is that of Eldridge and Butterfield (1984, 1986), who compared second graders instructed in heterogeneous groups with those using a traditional basal instructed in ability groups. The same reading selections were used for all students in the experimental classes; consequently, the method of instruction needed to be modified to involve peer-supported oral reading for the poorer readers. The results showed no achievement or attitudinal differences for the two groups; the equivalent results suggest that heterogeneous grouping will not interfere with the progress of young readers (i.e., second graders). Unfortunately, results were not analyzed for students of different ability to compare low-ability students in the two grouping situations. MacKinnon (1959) also describes the beginning stages of learning to read in heterogeneous groups.

Studies involving cooperative peer groups as part of reading instruction also show that learning to read is not impaired by using heterogeneous forms of grouping, and that it is often enhanced (Rosenholtz & Cohen, 1983). Darch, Carnine, and Kameenui (1986) found that sixth-grade students learned more from peer-group practice using a graphic organizer following total class instruction than from individual practice. Further, none of the experimental studies reviewed by Slavin (1983) found that learning was depressed by peer-group work. Three involving reading tasks (DeVries, Mescon, & Shackman, 1975; Hamblin, Hathaway, & Wodarski, 1971; Slavin & Karweit, 1981), as well as a more recent field study (Stevens, Madden, Slavin, & Farnish, 1987) all showed higher achievement for students working in peer groups than individually. The results from the experimental studies need to be further tested for classroom reading instruction over the course of the school year.

In sum, there is a clear need for more research on elementary-grade reading that examines group composition, size, and stability in relation to instruction, achievement, and attitudinal outcomes. Past research has examined either group characteristics in relation to outcomes or group characteristics in relation to instruction; neither provides a comprehensive basis for understanding the consequence of ability grouping. Until all three components are examined in the same study, we have little basis for evaluating the conditions under which ability grouping may be advantageous or destructive.

The counterpart to ability grouping in elementary schools is tracking in high schools. Because there are no longitudinal studies that trace the group membership of students from elementary schools into high schools, there is no basis for knowing with certainty the extent to which reading-group membership forecasts membership in basic, regular, and honors track classes. It seems plausible, however, that early reading proficiency may relate directly to content area reading proficiency in high school. In the next section, we consider the research on tracking in high schools in order to obtain a more complete picture of the grouping enterprise.

SECONDARY SCHOOL TRACKING

In high schools, reading is not an ordinary subject as it is in elementary schools. For that reason, levels of reading ability or of achievement do not serve by themselves as criteria for classifying students and placing them in course programs. Ability to read, however, as part of a cluster of considerations that includes previous courses taken and level of performance in them no doubt influences the content and difficulty of the high school program that each high school student undertakes.

Despite the patent differences between elementary-school grouping in reading and secondary school tracking, based on a number of considerations, both phenomena resemble each other in function. They should be seen as forms of educational organization designed to cope with problems that originate in the matching of curricular knowledge to the aggregate capacities of groups of students. As indicated earlier, secondary school tracking is largely a U.S. phenomenon; school systems in other countries more frequently deal with the matching problem by the use of different kinds of schools that tend to be internally undifferentiated. British comprehensive schools, however, represent a partial exception to that generalization to the extent that they resemble American high schools.

Perspectives on Tracking

In the commonly accepted view, *tracking* is a division of the school into distinct curricular programs. Hollingshead (1949), in his widely read book *Elmtown's Youth*, referred to college preparatory, general, and commercial *courses* to indicate that each course represents a category of school organization and that each student is enrolled in only one. The courses are not only distinct, they are stratified by virtue of the fact that each emphasizes knowledge valued to a greater or lesser degree, and each caters to different socioeconomic sectors of the community. Parsons (1959) takes a similar perspective in distinguishing the college preparatory from all other curricula in his discussion of the relation between schooling and both adult attainment and adolescent peer-group relations.

The idea that tracks are categories of school organization has been overwhelmingly influential in the design of research on tracking, particularly those employing large-scale survey research methods. This view, however, has come under critical scrutiny in the work of Rosenbaum (1976, 1980), who found disagreements between students' reports of their track location and the school's official designation of it. In trying to explain such subjective departures from the presumed actuality of official track placement, Rosenbaum implicates guidance counselors, who are alleged to provide inadequate information about the connection between school and occupational destinations more often to noncollege- than to college-track students. While this no doubt can happen, the disagreements can have other origins. Among them is the fact that many high schools are not tracked in the commonly believed way, relying more on individual student programs, whose constituent courses vary in how demanding they are, than on rigid, stratified track distinctions.

Garet and DeLany (1980), discussing the nature of tracking, indicate that the structure of tracking schemes varies from school to school. While in some cases the school might be categorically stratified, in others the basis of tracking is premised on student programs. The school offers a variety of courses in each subject, differing in content and difficulty; and students elect them according to their interests and past record of preparation and performance. This scheme allows students to prepare themselves for college and other post-high school destinations, but it represents a different organizational solution to the problem of matching students to curricular knowledge (along with the variety of Continental and Asian formats that vary the school agenda and distinguish types of schools).

Tracking has arisen in the U.S. educational system out of old and continuing disputes about who should learn what, and about what knowledge the schools should provide (see Cohen, [1985] on The Committee of Ten and The Cardinal Principles). Note that these disputes contain a component that pertains to the organization of schools around categories of knowledge. In the latter regard, it is important to recognize that one part of the school's task is to impart knowledge to students; another part, though vastly neglected, is to establish what represents legitimate knowledge and its embodiment in the curriculum. (For discussions of this question, see Keddie, 1971; Meyer, 1977).

According to D. K. Cohen (1985), in the two decades before 1900, a debate arose between the defenders of a classical secondary education (emphasizing Latin and Greek) and Charles W. Eliot, whose views were later embodied in the 1893 report of the Committee of Ten, which advocated a broadening of the curriculum to include modern subjects (e.g., science and modern languages); and the introduction of student choice (among academic electives), but that would preclude practical and vocational subjects). While Eliot defended a curriculum acceptable to the colleges, his views were challenged by G. Stanley Hall, who advocated further broadening of the curriculum to make it appropriate to the majority of students attending high school, according to their "nature and needs." Cohen (1985) states that

> Between them, Eliot and Hall had politely laid out the greatest issue that divided American educators at the time: could all students be expected to pursue an intellectually demanding program of academic study, or should most be given an easier and more practical curriculum? (pp. 243–244)

The introduction of tracking early in the 1900s represented a strategy for addressing this basically unresolvable controversy.

The existence of a tracking system, or other methods for differentiating curricular exposure among different students, means that on the supply side, the schools institutionalize different kinds of knowledge for various segments of student populations; and on the demand side, student exposure to knowledge will vary in such a way that the post-high school destinations of students will, on average, differ accordingly. This discussion lays the issue out in a general and formalistic way. In particular school districts and schools, actual decisions are made about precisely what knowledge will be made available in each track, how selective the tracks will be, how much curricular overlap there will be in course offerings across tracks, and to what extent students of similar capacities will be found in different tracks (see Sørensen, 1970).

Studies of Tracking

Empirical studies of tracking have been included in ethnographic investigations of small U.S. cities, the best-known of which were reported in Warner, Havighurst, and Loeb's (1944) well-known essay, *Who Shall Be Educated?* and Hollingshead's (1949) *Elmtown's Youth.* A major theoretical statement about tracking appeared in an essay of Parsons (1959). These works noted especially how assignment to high school tracks was related to the socioeconomic background of students and how tracking influenced students' later occupational placement in the labor force. This line of work failed to generate continuing interest in tracking, but its emphasis on socioeconomic status coalesced with a growing trend in sociology to examine social mobility and particularly the contribution of schooling to the process by which the social status of parents influenced the future educational, social, and economic life chances of their children.

As part of this second line of development, attention returned to tracking, influenced by the increasing concern about equality of educational opportunity during the late 1960s and throughout the 1970s. One of the main questions addressed was whether the socioeconomic status of students influenced their placement in curricular tracks (Alexander, Cook, & McDill, 1978; Garet & DeLany, 1988; Hauser, Sewell, & Alwin,

1976; Heyns, 1974; Jencks & Brown, 1975; Rehberg & Rosenthal, 1978; Rosenbaum, 1976). The weight of evidence from these studies on track placement supports the view that the direct effects of student ability are more important than those of socioeconomic status.

The track-placement question, though important, has been limited in scope and aroused less interest over the course of time than two other questions: What is the effect of tracking on the future life chances of students? and By what mechanisms does tracking work its effects? The first question is an outgrowth of a long tradition of sociological research on social mobility that traces the life course of individuals from the background influences of the family (with particular reference to race, sex, ability, and socioeconomic status) through the experiences of schooling (including the influences of teachers and peers, track locations, and levels of aspiration and achievement) and toward adult occupational status and earnings. The evidence generally indicates that track location influences aspiration for education beyond high school as well as the actual attainment of it (Alexander & Cook, 1982; Alexander, Cook, & McDill, 1978; Alexander & Eckland, 1975; Alexander & McDill, 1976; Hauser, Sewell, & Alwin, 1976; Heyns, 1974; Rehberg & Rosenthal, 1978; Vanfossen, Jones, & Spade, 1987). Track location also influences achievement (basic cognitive skills and subject matter knowledge), though the evidence is mixed; however, as it accumulates and research designs become more sophisticated, there is increasing reason to believe that patterns of course taking related to track location contribute to academic achievement (Alexander, Cook, & McDill, 1978; Gamoran, 1987b; Garet & DeLany, 1988; Jencks & Brown, 1975; Lee & Bryk, 1988).

In recent years, attention to tracking has expanded beyond the limited perspective of its impact on the life chances of individual students. There has been increasing recognition that the stratification of secondary schools, by tracking or other devices, is an organizational and an institutional phenomenon (Bidwell & Kasarda, 1980; Bidwell & Friedkin, 1988). Individualistic approaches to the impact of schooling on students have characteristically treated school tracks and curricula as attributes of individuals through their membership (say, in the college preparatory or vocational program), along with a combination of other characteristics (socioeconomic status, ability, aspiration, encouragement, level of achievement, and so on). It has become clear that membership in the college preparatory track, for example, does not necessarily mean the same thing in different schools, or indeed, even in the same school. Across tracks and curricula from school to school and within them in the same school, the educational experiences of students (even those with similar abilities and past levels of achievement) can vary markedly, depending on the level and quality of the curricular materials used, the capabilities of teachers, and the aggregate characteristics of students from class to class. This is to say that the internal variation in the availability and use of educational resources within and between schools can be as important to the production of educational outcomes as the characteristics of students viewed individually.

At issue here are the educational opportunities that schools provide, as conceptually distinct from those that individual students experience. (The two, of course, are hardly unrelated empirically.) As a case in point, one can find identically labeled tracks or curricula in schools that differ according to the inclusiveness of their membership or according to whether track membership is elected by students or assigned by the school (Sørensen, 1970). Distributions of students can vary in the same track across different schools. Beyond that, as Garet and DeLany (1988) demonstrate, markedly different proportions of comparable students enroll in courses of similar difficulty in different schools. Garet and DeLany show that a student at the seventy-fifth percentile in mathematics achievement had a 4 percent chance of taking geometry at School A, a 58 percent chance at School B, a 46 percent chance at School C, and a 32 percent chance at School D. (p. 71)

In other words, schools, through their tracking schemes, provide different levels of educational opportunity for comparably able students. Taking the organizational side of schooling into account, in other words, helps explain the rather weak and inconsistent relationships between track placement and achievement when both are construed at the individual level.

A variation on the theme of school differences grows out of the recent comparisons between public and private (mainly Catholic) schools. Lee and Bryk (1988), for example, draw attention to the organizational differences between public and parochial schools and how they shape educational opportunity. Primary among them is the tendency of parochial schools to provide less highly differentiated curricula so that patterns of course taking are less strongly related to family background than in public schools. In effect, the organization of parochial schools works to reduce student choice and to provide more homogeneous curricular opportunity biased in the direction of academic rather than vocational and remedial study.

Much work on tracking has dwelt upon questions inspired by the issue of social equality, both in the schooling experience and in the way schooling contributes to future life changes. Some of it, however, has been concerned with matters of school organization and its inner workings (Gamoran & Berends, 1987). Cicourel and Kitsuse (1963), in treating the guidance function in high schools, observe that counselors not only influence the process by which the future educational careers of the more- and less-able students are determined, they define in the first place what "more able" and "less able" mean. In short, defining the terms by which students are distinguished and sorting them on the basis of the definition become important organizational events that shape the educational experiences of students, including what knowledge they will encounter. (See also Rosenbaum, 1976.)

Recent work on the importance of tracking and the differentiation of curricula has built upon the efforts of Alexander and his colleagues (Alexander, Cook, & McDill, 1978; Alexander & Cook, 1982), who looked at patterns of course taking. Although the impact of track-related course taking has been related to achievement and subject-matter learning among individual students (Gamoran, 1987b; Lee & Bryk, 1988; Vanfossen, Jones, & Spade, 1987), attention has broadened to include how schools make different kinds of knowledge available through the curriculum and instruction, and to whom. At issue is how schools shape opportunity to learn as distinct from what students actually learn. Oakes (1985), in the tradition of earlier work by Cusick (1973) and Rosenbaum (1976), compares higher- and lower-track students and finds that the former are usually exposed to a more interesting and challenging educational diet composed of more demanding curricular materials, more interesting classroom activities, and teachers who appear to use class time more productively. In short, upper-track students have greater opportunities for exposure to more highly valued academic knowledge (Meyer, 1977).

One of the difficulties that arises in research that compares higher and lower tracks is the tacit assumption that such categories have the same meaning from school to school. It is quite possible that the general-track curriculum available in one school is as intellectually demanding as the college preparatory curriculum of another. To the extent this is true, an observer must consider the characteristics of schools carefully—the selectivity and homogeneity of tracks, the internal variation of curricular offerings within tracks and programs, and the level of curricular offerings of each track. Garet and

DeLany (1988) pay particular attention to such issues by considering how much course enrollment can be explained by student characteristics, and with that component taken into account, how much can be explained by characteristics of the schools.

CONCLUSIONS

A historical view of grouping, at least in the industrial nations, reveals that when school populations are socially and intellectually diverse in their composition, the educational system makes provision for variations among students by providing different kinds of educational experiences. Educational systems provide distinct kinds of schools that either accommodate a variety of students or that specialize in certain kinds according, for example, to social background, religion, ethnicity, and academic performance. Which alternative a nation selects depends on its own culture and history. Educational systems also differ in how they define the stages of schooling, in the eligibility of students to progress from one stage to the next, in the selectivity of students, and in the curriculum content and difficulty characteristic of each stage. Although it is customary to think of grouping as if it pertained primarily to ability differences found among students in the same school or classroom, grouping is actually a phenomenon of far larger scope that extends to educational provisions based upon major lines of social demarcation in societies at large.

Over the past half century, little of this larger conception has entered into the treatment of grouping, which has been concerned predominantly with the division of school grades into classes distinguished by ability and the division of classes into ability groups primarily, though not exclusively, for instruction in reading. The research literature has been largely practical in orientation (What is the best way to organize instruction?) and ideological in tone (Does grouping foster or undermine democracy or social equality?). In both respects, the conventional question asked has led to the comparison of cognitive and attitudinal outcomes among students instructed under grouped and ungrouped conditions. For the most part, work done in the area has paid little attention to the properties of ability groups, the principles underlying their formation, the nature of the instruction they have received, and the connection between grouping and other aspects of the educational enterprise, particularly those pertaining to the administration of schools and the curriculum. The results of this narrow set of preoccupations—until quite recently, when a broader set of issues has emerged—has been a rather dull, inconsistent, inconclusive, and noncumulative body of knowledge. It has largely distracted us from more important general questions of how knowledge is imparted through instruction to various populations of students.

Although it is common knowledge that ability groups are used in most U.S. elementary schools for reading instruction, there is a dearth of systematic documentation on many important questions: What is the prevalence of alternative forms of grouping? How stable are grouping patterns once they are established? What is the connection between the groups students belong to one year with those they join in subsequent years? What is the relation between elementary-school grouping and secondary-school tracking? To what extent does ability grouping narrow or broaden the variation in reading proficiency among group members at the primary and intermediate levels? What is the nature of curricular tasks and instruction provided to students in similar and in different groups and tracks across schools? How do these instructional differences influence attitudes and learning? These questions should be viewed as items on an agenda of grouping issues in which only beginning efforts have been made.

REFERENCES

Alexander, K. L., & Cook, M. A. (1982). Curricula and coursework: A surprise ending to a familiar story. *American Sociological Review, 47,* 626–640.

Alexander, K. L., Cook, M. A., & McDill, E. L. (1978). Curriculum tracking and educational stratification: Some further evidence. *American Sociological Review, 43,* 47–66.

Alexander, K. L., & Eckland, B. K. (1975). Contextual effects in the high school attainment process. *American Sociological Review, 40,* 402–416.

Alexander, K. L., & McDill, E. L. (1976). Selection and allocation within schools. *American Sociological Review, 41,* 963–980.

Allington, R. L. (1980). Teacher interruption behaviors during primary-grade oral reading. *Journal of Educational Psychology, 72,* 371–377.

Allington, R. L. (1983). The reading instruction provided readers of differing reading ability. *Elementary School Journal, 83,* 548–559.

Allington, R. L. (1984). Content coverage and contextual reading in reading groups. *Journal of Reading Behavior, 16,* 85–96.

Alpert, J. L. (1974). Teacher behavior across ability groups: A consideration of the mediation of Pygmalion effects. *Journal of Educational Psychology, 66,* 348–353.

American Book Company (1913). *Story hours readers manual.* New York: American Book Co.

Anderson, L., Evertson, C., & Brophy, J. (1979). An experimental study of effective teaching in first-grade reading groups. *Elementary School Journal, 79,* 193–223.

Anderson, R. C., Hiebert, E. H., Scott, J. A., & Wilkinson, I. A. G. (1985). *Becoming a nation of readers.* Washington, DC: National Institute of Education.

Aries, P. (1962). *Centuries of childhood.* New York: Knopf.

Ayres, L. P. (1909). *Laggards in our schools.* New York: Russell Sage.

Austin, M., & Morrison, C. (1963). *The first R: The Harvard report on reading in the elementary school.* New York: Macmillan.

Barker-Lunn, J. C. (1970). *Streaming in the primary school.* London: National Foundation for Educational Research in England and Wales.

Barr, R. (1974). Instructional pace differences and their effect on reading acquisition. *Reading Research Quarterly, 9,* 526–554.

Barr, R. (1975). How children are taught to read: Grouping and pacing. *School Review, 75,* 479–498.

Barr, R. (1989). Social organization of reading instruction. In C. Emilhovich (Ed.), *Locating learning across the curriculum: Ethnographic perspectives on classroom research.* Norwood, NJ: Ablex.

Barr, R., & Anderson, C. S. (1988). *Grouping students for instruction in elementary schools.* Unpublished report. Elmhurst, IL: North Central Regional Educational Laboratory.

Barr, R., & Dreeben, R. (1983). *How schools work.* Chicago: University of Chicago Press.

Barr, R., & Sadow, M. (1989). Influence of basal programs on fourth-grade reading instruction. *Reading Research Quarterly, 24,* 44–71.

Bidwell, C. E., & Friedkin, N. E. (1988). The sociology of education. In N. J. Smelser (Ed.), *The handbook of sociology.* Beverly Hills, CA: Sage Publications.

Bidwell, C. E., & Kasarda, J. D. (1980). Conceptualizing and measuring the effects of school and schooling. *American Sociological Review, 40,* 55–70.

Billett, R. O. (1932). *The administration and supervision of homogeneous grouping.* Columbus, OH: Ohio State University Press.

Borg, E. R. (1965). Ability grouping in the public schools. *Journal of Experimental Education, 34*(2), 1–97.

Borko, H. (1982). Teachers' decision policies about grouping students for reading instruction. In J. A. Niles & L. A. Harris, (Eds.), *New inquiries in reading research and instruction* (Thirty-First Yearbook of the National Reading Conference) (pp. 220–226). Rochester, NY: National Reading Conference.

Borko, H., Shavelson, R. J., & Stern, P. (1981). Teachers' decisions in the planning of reading instruction. *Reading Research Quarterly, 16,* 449–466.

Bossert, S. T. (1979). *Tasks and social relationships in classrooms.* New York: Cambridge.

Brinton, M. C. (1988). The social-institutional bases of gender stratification: Japan as an illustrative case. *American Journal of Sociology, 94,* 300–334.

Brown v. Board of Education of Topeka (1954). 347 U.S. 483, 493.

Burr, M. Y. (1931). *A study of homogeneous grouping.* New York: Teachers College Press.

Calfee, R. C., & Piontkowski, D. C. (1987). Grouping for teaching. In M. J. Dunkin (Ed.), *The international encyclopedia of teaching and teacher education.* Oxford, Eng.: Pergamon Press.

Central Advisory Council for Education (1967). *Children and their primary schools, Vol. 1* (The Plowden Report). London: Her Majesty's Stationery Office.

Cicourel, A. V., & Kitsuse, J. I. (1963). *The educational decision-makers.* Indianapolis, IN: Bobbs-Merrill.

Clark, B. R. (1985). Conclusions. In B. R. Clark (Ed.), *The school and the university.* Berkeley: University of California Press.

Clay, M. (1967). The reading behaviour of five-year-old children: A research report. *New Zealand Journal of Educational Studies, 2,* 11–31.

Cohen, D. K. (1985). Origins. In A. G. Powell, E. Farrar, & D. K. Cohen (Eds.), *The shopping mall high school*. Boston: Houghton Mifflin.

Cohen, E. G. (1984). Talking and working together: Status, interaction, and learning. In P. Peterson, L. C. Wilkinson, & M. Hallinan (Eds.), *The social context of instruction*. Orlando, FL: Academic Press.

Cohen, E. G. (1986). On the sociology of the classroom. In J. Hannaway & M. E. Lockhead (Eds.), *The contribution of the social sciences to educational policy and practice: 1965–1985*. Berkeley, CA: Mc-Cutchan.

Collins, J. (1986). Differential treatment in reading instruction. In J. Cook-Gumperz (Ed.), *The social construction of literacy*. Cambridge, Eng.: Cambridge University Press.

Cookson, P., & Persell, C. H. (1985). *Preparing for power*. New York: Basic Books.

Cremin, L. A. (1951). *The American common school*. New York: Teachers College.

Cremin, L. A. (1988). *American education: The metropolitan experience, 1876–1980*. New York: Harper & Row.

Cummings, W. K. (1980). *Education and equality in Japan*. Princeton, NJ: Princeton University Press.

Cusick, P. A. (1973). *Inside high school*. New York: Holt, Rinehart & Winston.

Dahllöf, U. S. (1971). *Ability grouping, content validity, and curriculum process analysis*. New York: Teachers College Press.

Daniels, J. C. (1961a). The effects of streaming in the primary school: 1. What teachers believe. *British Journal of Educational Psychology, 31*, 69–78.

Daniels, J. C. (1961b). The effects of streaming in the primary school: 2. Comparison of streamed and unstreamed schools. *British Journal of Educational Psychology, 31*, 119–127.

Darch, C., Carnine, D., & Kameenui, E. (1986). The role of graphic organizers and social structure in content area instruction. *Journal of Reading Behavior, 28*, 275–295.

DeStefano, J., Pepinsky, J., & Sanders, T. (1982). Discourse rules for literacy learning in a first-grade classroom. In L. C. Wilkinson (Ed.), *Communicating in the classroom*. New York: Academic Press.

DeVries, D. L., Mescon, I. T., & Shackman, S. L. (1975). *Teams-Games-Tournament (TGT) effects on reading skills in the elementary grades*. Center for Social Organization of Schools, Johns Hopkins University (Report No. 200).

Douglas, J. W. B. (1964). *The home and the school*. London: MacGibbon and Kee.

Dreeben, R., & Barr, R. (1988a). Classroom composition and the design of instruction. *Sociology of Education, 61*, 129–142.

Dreeben, R., & Barr, R. (1988b). The formation and instruction of ability groups. *American Journal of Education, 97*, 34–61.

Dreeben, R., & Gamoran, A. (1986). Race, instruction, and learning. *American Sociological Review, 5*, 660–669.

Duffy, G., & Anderson. L. (1981). *Final report: Conceptions of reading project*. Unpublished report, Institute for Research on Teaching, Michigan State University.

Eash, M. J. (1961). Grouping: What have we learned? *Educational Leadership, 18*, 429–434.

Eder, D. (1981). Ability grouping as a self-fulfilling prophecy: A micro-analysis of teacher-student interaction. *Sociology of Education, 54*, 151–161.

Eder, D. (1982). Differences in communicative styles across ability groups. In L. C. Wilkinson (Ed.), *Communicating in the classroom*. New York: Academic Press.

Eldredge, J. L., & Butterfield, D. (1984). *Sacred cows make good hamburger: A report on a reading research project titled "Testing the Sacred Cows in Reading."* (ERIC Document Reproduction Service No. ED 255 861).

Eldredge, J. L., & Butterfield, D. (1986). Alternatives to traditional reading instruction. *Reading Teacher, 40*, 32–37.

Ekstrom, R. B. (1961). Experimental studies of homogeneous grouping: A critical review. *School Review, 69*, 216–229.

Esposito, D. (1973). Homogeneous and heterogeneous ability grouping: Principal findings and implications for evaluating and designing more effective educational environments. *Review of Educational Research, 43*, 163–179.

Findley, W., & Bryan, M. C. (1970). *Ability grouping: 1970—II. The impact of ability grouping on school achievement, affective development, ethnic separation, and socioeconomic separation*. Athens, GA: Center for Educational Improvement, University of Georgia.

Fisher, C. W., Filby, N. N., Marliave, R. S., Cahen, L. S., Dishaw, M. M., Moore, J. E., & Berliner, D. C. (1978). *Teaching behaviors, academic learning time, and student achievement: Beginning teacher evaluation study* (Final Rep. Phase III-B). San Francisco: Far West Laboratory for Education Research and Development.

Fuller, W. E. (1982). *The old country school*. Chicago: University of Chicago Press.

Galton, M., Simon, B., & Croll, P. (1980). *Inside the primary classroom*. London: Routledge & Kegan Paul.

Gambrell, L. (1984). How much time do children spend reading during teacher-directed reading instruction? In J. Niles & L. Harris (Eds.), *Changing perspectives on research in reading/language processing and instruction* (Thirty-Third Yearbook of the National Reading Conference). Rochester, NY: National Reading Conference.

Gambrell, L., Wilson, R., & Ganatt, W. (1981). Classroom observations of task-attending behaviors of good and poor readers. *Journal of Educational Research, 74*, 400–404.

Gamoran, A. (1986). Instructional and institutional effects of ability groups. *Sociology of Education, 59*, 185–198.

Gamoran, A. (1987a). Organization, instruction, and the effects of ability grouping: Comment on Slavin's "best-evidence synthesis." *Review of Educational Research, 57*, 341–345.

Gamoran, A. (1987b). The stratification of high school learning opportunities. *Sociology of Education, 60*, 135–155.

Gamoran, A. (1989). Rank, performance, and mobility in elementary school grouping. *Sociological Quarterly, 30*, 109–123.

Gamoran, A., & Berends, M. (1987). The effects of stratification in the secondary schools: Synthesis of survey and ethnographic research. *Review of Educational Research, 57*, 415–435.

Garet, M., & DeLany, B. (1988). Students, courses, and stratification. *Sociology of Education, 61*, 61–77.

Goldberg, M., Passow, A. H., & Justman, J. (1966). *The effects of ability grouping.* New York: Macmillan.

Good, T. L., & Beckerman, T. M. (1978). Time on task: A naturalistic study in sixth-grade classrooms. *Elementary School Journal, 78*, 192–201.

Good, T. L., & Marshall, S. (1984). Do students learn more in heterogeneous or homogeneous groups? In P. L. Peterson, L. C. Wilkinson, & M. Hallinan, (Eds.), *The social context of instruction.* New York: Academic Press.

Goodlad, J. I. (1960). Classroom organization. In C. W. Harris (Ed.), *Encyclopedia of educational research.* New York: Macmillan.

Goodlad, J. I. (1984). *A place called school.* New York: McGraw-Hill.

Groff, P. J. (1962). A survey of basal reading grouping practices. *Reading Teacher, 15*, 136–140.

Haller, E. J. (1985). Pupil race and elementary school ability grouping: Are teachers biased against black children? *American Educational Research Journal, 22*, 465–483.

Haller, E. J., & Davis, S. A. (1980). Does socioeconomic status bias the assignment of elementary school students to reading groups? *American Educational Research Journal, 17*(4), 409–418.

Haller, E. J., & Davis, S. A. (1981). Teachers' perspectives, parental social status, and grouping for reading instruction. *Sociology of Education, 54*, 162–174.

Haller, E. J., & Waterman, M. (1985). The criteria of reading group assignments. *Reading Teacher, 38*, 772–782.

Hallinan, M., & Sørenson, A. B. (1983). The formation and stability of instructional groups. *American Sociological Review, 48*, 838–851.

Halsey, A. F., Heath, A. F., & Ridge, J. M. (1980). *Origins and destinations.* London: Oxford University Press.

Hamblin, R. L., Hathaway, C., & Wodarski, J. S. (1971). Group contingencies, peer tutoring, and accelerating academic achievement. In E. Ramp and W. Hopkins (Eds.), *A new direction for education: Behavior analysis.* Lawrence, KS: University of Kansas, Department of Human Development.

Hart, S. (1982). Analyzing the social organization for reading in one elementary school. In G. Spindler (Ed.), *Doing the ethnography of schooling: Educational anthropology in action.* New York: Holt, Rinehart & Winston.

Hartill, R. M. (1936). *Homogeneous grouping.* New York: Teachers College Press.

Haskins, R., Walden, T., & Ramey, C. T. (1983). Teacher and student behavior in high- and low-ability groups. *Journal of Educational Psychology, 75*, 865–876.

Hauser, R. M., Sewell, W. H., & Alwin, D. F. (1976). High school effects on achievement. In W. H. Sewell, R. M. Hauser, & D. L. Featherman (Eds.), *Schooling and achievement in American society.* New York: Academic Press.

Hawkins, M. L. (1966). Mobility of students in reading groups. *Reading Teacher, 20*, 136–140.

Heathers, G. (1969). Grouping. In R. L. Ebel (Ed.), *Encyclopedia of educational research.* New York: Macmillan.

Heyns, B. (1974). Social selection and stratification within schools. *American Journal of Sociology, 79*, 1434–1451.

Hiebert, E. H. (1983). An examination of ability grouping for reading instruction. *Reading Research Quarterly, 18*, 231–255.

Hobsen v. Hansen (1967). 269 F. Supp. 401 (DC).

Hoffman, J. V., & Baker, C. (1981). Characterizing teacher feedback to student miscues during oral reading instruction. *Reading Teacher, 34*, 907–913.

Hollingshead, A. B. (1949). *Elmtown's youth.* New York: Wiley.

Hunter, D. (1978). *Student on-task behavior during reading group meeting.* Unpublished dissertation, University of Missouri, Columbia, MO.

Jackson, B. (1980). *Streaming.* London: Routledge & Kegan Paul.

Jencks, C. S., & Brown, M. D. (1975). Effects of high schools on their students. *Harvard Educational Review, 45*, 273–324.

Kaestle, C. F. (Ed.). (1973). *Joseph Lancaster and the monitorial school movement.* New York: Teachers College Press.

Kaestle, C. F. (1983). *Pillars of the republic.* New York: Hill & Wang.

Keddie, N. (1971). Classroom knowledge. In M. F. D. Young (Ed.), *Knowledge and control.* London: Collier-Macmillan.

Kelliher, A. V. (1931). *A critical study of homogeneous grouping.* New York: Teachers College.

Kerckhoff, A. C., Campbell, R. C., & Trott, J. M. (1982). Dimensions of educational and occupational attainment in Great Britain. *American Sociological Review, 42,* 347–364.

Kliebard, H. M. (1986). *The struggle for the American curriculum 1893–1959.* Boston: Routledge & Kegan Paul.

Kulik, C. C., & Kulik, J. A. (1982). The relationship between self and achievement/performance measures. *American Educational Research Journal, 19,* 415–428.

Lee, V. E., & Bryk, A. S. (1988). Curriculum tracking as mediating the social distribution of high school achievement. *Sociology of Education, 61,* 78–94.

McDermott, J. W., Jr. (1976). The controversy over ability grouping in American education. Unpublished doctoral dissertation, Temple University.

McDermott, R. (1976). Kids make sense: An ethnographic account of the interactional management of success and failure in one first-grade classroom. Unpublished doctoral dissertation, Stanford University.

MacKinnon, A. (1959). *How do children learn to read?* Toronto: Copp Clarke.

Maden, M. (1985). England and Wales. In B. R. Clark (Ed.), *The school and the university.* Berkeley: University of California Press.

Marsh, H. W. (1984). Self-concept, social comparison, and ability grouping: A reply to Kulik and Kulik. *American Educational Research Journal, 21,* 799–806.

Martin, J., & Evertson, C. M. (1980). Teachers' interactions with reading groups of differing ability levels (Tech. Rep. No. R-4093). Austin: University of Texas, Research and Development Center for Teacher Education.

Mason, J. M., & Osborn, J. (1982). *When do children begin "reading to learn?": A survey of classroom reading instruction practices in grades two through five* (Tech. Rep. No. 261). Urbana: University of Illinois, Center for the Study of Reading.

Meyer, J. W. (1977). The effects of education as an institution. *American Journal of Sociology, 83,* 55–77.

Miller, W. S., & Otto, J. (1930). Analysis of experimental studies in homogeneous grouping. *Journal of Educational Research, 21,* 95–102.

Morgenstern, A. (1966). Historical survey of grouping practices in the elementary school. In A. Morgenstern (Ed.), *Grouping in the elementary school.* New York: Pitman.

Moses v. Washington Parish School Board (1971). 330 F. Supp. 1340 (E.D. La.).

National Education Association, Research Decision (1961). *Administrative practices in urban school districts, 1958–1959* (Research report 1961-R10). Washington, DC: National Educational Association.

Noland, T. K. (1985). The effects of ability grouping: A meta-analysis of research findings. Unpublished doctoral dissertation, University of Colorado at Boulder.

Oakes, J. (1985). *Keeping track.* New Haven: Yale University Press.

Otto, H. J. (1932). *Current practices in the organization of elementary schools.* Evanston, IL: Northwestern University, School of Education.

Otto, H. J. (1941). Elementary children II. Organization and administration. In W. S. Monroe (Ed.), *Encyclopedia of educational research.* New York: Macmillan.

Parsons, T. (1959). The school class as a social system. *Harvard Educational Review, 29,* 297–318.

Persell, C. (1977). *Education and inequality: The roots and results of stratification in America's schools.* New York: Free Press.

Pikulski, J. J., & Kirsch, I. S. (1979). Organization for instruction. In R. C. Calfee & P. A. Drum (Eds.), *Compensatory reading survey.* Newark, DE: International Reading Association.

Purdom, T. L. (1929). *The value of homogeneous grouping.* Baltimore: Warwick & York.

Rehberg, R. A., & Rosenthal, E. R. (1978). *Class and merit in the American high school.* New York: Longman.

Richardson, J. G. (1980). Variations in the date of enactment of compulsory school attendance laws. *Sociology of Education, 53,* 153–163.

Rist, R. (1970). Student social class and teacher expectations: The self-fulfilling prophecy in ghetto education. *Harvard Educational Review, 40,* 411–451.

Rock, R. T. (1929). A critical study of current practices in ability grouping. *Educational Research Bulletin of the Catholic University of America, 4,* 5–132.

Rohlen, T. P. (1983). *Japan's high schools.* Berkeley: University of California Press.

Rosenbaum, J. (1976). *Making inequality: The hidden curriculum of high school tracking.* New York: Wiley.

Rosenbaum, J. E. (1980). Track misperceptions and frustrated college plans: An analysis of the effects of tracks and track perceptions in the National Longitudinal Survey. *Sociology of Education, 53,* 74–83.

Rosenbaum, J. E. (1984). The social organization of instructional grouping. In P. L. Peterson, L. C. Wilkinson, & M. Hallinan, (Eds.) *The social context of instruction.* New York: Academic Press.

Rosenholtz, S. J., & Cohen, E. G. (1983). Back to basics and the desegregated school. *Elementary School Journal, 83,* 515–527.

Rowan, B., & Miracle Jr., A. W. (1983). Systems of ability grouping and the stratification of achievement in elementary schools. *Sociology of Education, 56,* 133–144.

Rupley, W., Blair, T., & Wise, B. (1982). Specification of promising teacher-effectiveness variables for reading instruction. In J. Niles and L. Harris (Eds.), *New inquiries in reading research and instruction* (Thirty-First Yearbook of the National Reading Conference). Rochester, NY: National Reading Conference.

Russo, N. (1978). *The effects of student characteristics, educational beliefs, and instructional task on teachers' preinstructional decisions in reading and math*. Unpublished doctoral dissertation, University of California, Los Angeles.

Seltzer, D. A. (1976). A descriptive study of third-grade reading groups. *Dissertation Abstracts, 36*, 5811 (University Microfilms No. 76–6345).

Sirotnik, K. A. (1983). What you see is what you get: Consistency, persistency, and mediocracy in classrooms. *Harvard Education Review, 53*, 16–31.

Slavin, R. E. (1983). *Cooperative learning*. New York: Longman.

Slavin, R. E. (1984). Meta-analysis in education: How has it been used? *Educational Researcher, 13*(8), 6–15, 24–27.

Slavin, R. E. (1987). Ability grouping: A best-evidence synthesis. *Review of Educational Research, 57*, 293–336.

Slavin, R. E., & Karweit, N. (1981). Cognitive and affective outcomes of intensive student team learning experience. *Journal of Experimental Education, 50*, 29–35.

Smith, N. B. (1965). *American reading instruction*. Newark, DE: International Reading Association.

Sørensen, A. B. (1970). Organizational differentiation of students and educational opportunity. *Sociology of Education, 43*, 355–376.

Sørensen, A. B., & Hallinan, M. (1984). Effects of race on assignment to ability groups. In P. L. Peterson, L. C. Wilkinson, & M. Hallinan, (Eds.), *The social context of instruction*. New York: Academic Press.

Sørenson, A. B., & Hallinan, M. (1986). Effects of ability grouping on growth in academic achievement. *American Educational Research Journal, 23*, 519–542.

Stallings, J. (1975). Implementation and child effects of teaching practices in follow-through classes. *Monographs of the Society for Research in Child Development, 40*.

Stevens, R. J., Madden, N. A., Slavin, R. E., & Farnish, A. M. (1987). Cooperative integrated reading and composition: Two field experiments. *Reading Research Quarterly, 12*, 433–454.

Tawney, R. H. (1931). *Inequality*. London: Unwin.

Tyack, D. (1974). *The one best system*. Cambridge, MA: Harvard University Press.

Vanfossen, E. E., Jones, J. D., & Spade, J. Z. (1987). Curriculum tracking and status maintenance. *Sociology of Education, 60*, 104–122.

Venezky, R. L. (1988). The American reading script and its nineteenth-century origins. The first Marilyn Sadow memorial lecture, Department of Education, University of Chicago.

Werner, W. L., Havighurst, R. L., & Loeb, M. (1944). *Who shall be educated?* New York: Harper & Row.

Weinberg, I. (1967). *The English public schools*. New York: Atherton Press.

Weinstein, R. S. (1976). Reading group membership in first grade: Teacher behaviors and pupil experience over time. *Journal of Educational Psychology, 68*, 103–116.

West, P. (1933). *A study of ability grouping in the elementary school*. New York: Teachers College, Columbia University.

Whipple, G. M. (1936). *The grouping of pupils* (Thirty-Fifth Yearbook, Part 1, National Society for the Study of Education). Chicago: University of Chicago Press.

Wilkinson, R. (1964). *Gentlemanly power*. Oxford, Eng.: Oxford University Press.

Wilson, B., & Schmits, D. (1978). What's new in ability grouping? *Phi Delta Kappan, 59*, 535–536.

Winn, W., & Wilson, A. P. (1983). The affect and effect of ability grouping. *Contemporary Education, 54*(2), 119–125.

Wyndham, H. S. (1934). *Ability grouping*. Melbourne: Melbourne University Press.

Yates, A. (1966). *Grouping in education*. New York: Wiley.

32 TEACHER AND SCHOOL EFFECTS IN LEARNING TO READ

James V. Hoffman

R eading educators work with students in schools to affect growth in literacy. They believe that what they do and how well they do it can make a positive contribution to student learning. My purpose in writing this chapter is to explore the scientific basis for this belief. At a very superficial level, the task I face in presenting the science of teaching and school effects on learning to read is one of surveying the existing research that explores these issues. The complexity of the task is much greater than this, however. No simple listing or summary of studies, factors, and findings would come close to capturing the peculiarities or power of this research literature; nor would such a linear strategy serve to raise some of the most important questions for future research to address. In the final analysis it is perhaps more in the evolution of ways in which researchers and research communities have studied teaching and schooling effects than in the simple accumulation of findings that one discovers the important lessons to be learned (Shulman, 1986).

This review considers research that has been conducted in elementary classrooms and schools and focused on the nature of teaching and learning in developmental reading programs. In some cases, studies included in this review are discussed in other chapters of this handbook as well. While every attempt has been made to reduce redundancy and duplication, it would be an error to not include them here again, for each plays a critical role in the unfolding of the research movement. The organization of this chapter reflects the kinds of questions that guided the initial search of the literature. One set of guiding questions related to the historical roots for research into teaching and school effects in reading. How have the basic questions asked and methods employed in research changed over time? Is each new generation of reading researchers simply rediscovering what others have known before, but packaged under a different set of labels? The first section of this review focuses on the significant roots of research into teaching and school effects in learning to read. Another set of guiding questions is related to the nature of, and findings from, current research studies into teaching and school effects. What are the issues being explored and what have we learned about teaching and school effects in learning to read? What paradigms and methodologies dominate this field of inquiry? The second section of this review relates to the findings from recent research. A final area of guiding questions is related to the identification of critical areas of need for future research. What have we learned from research about how to conduct research? What important questions remain to be answered or even addressed in this field? The final section focuses on an analysis of the shortcomings of current research and possible directions for the future.

THE ROOTS OF RESEARCH INTO TEACHING
AND SCHOOL EFFECTS IN LEARNING TO READ

Studies related to the roots of research into teaching and school effects in learning to read will be described in four sections. The first section includes implementation and evaluation studies conducted in the 1920s, 1930s, and 1940s. The second section includes a series of survey studies conducted in the 1950s and 1960s. The third section includes studies that adopted a methods-comparison framework conducted in the 1960s. And the fourth section includes a series of studies conducted in the 1960s that will be described as research anomalies.

Implementation and Evaluation Studies

Numerous studies were conducted during the 1920s, 1930s, and 1940s on the initiative of individual school districts as part of a general reading improvement plan. In some cases, these studies were undertaken as a cooperative effort between leading figures in reading in the academic arena and the instructional leaders in major school districts. Often these studies were designed to investigate the problems of implementing into classrooms what research had demonstrated to be true in clinical settings (e.g., Buswell, 1922). In other cases, researchers who were actively involved in basic research attempted to "test-out" their theories in the real world of classrooms (e.g., Gates, 1937). Two programs of research conducted in this period will be described in some detail, as they appear to be representative of this kind of early research into the teaching of reading and its effects.

In 1925, the members of the Educational Research Committee of the Commonwealth Fund supported a study by William S. Gray into the improvement of reading instruction in schools. The purposes of the study were:

1. To determine ways and means of reorganizing and improving the teaching of reading in harmony with the results of scientific studies.
2. To study the character of the administrative, supervisory, and teaching difficulties encountered in a supervisory campaign planned to improve instruction in reading.
3. To determine the effect, if any, on the achievement of pupils that accompanies and follows vigorous efforts to improve teaching. (Gray, 1933, p. 2)

The study took over five years to complete and involved a large number of school districts and schools in the northern Illinois area. The first part of the study involved a survey of all of the participating districts and schools to determine the status of reading in the schools, the nature of the reading activities provided, the amount and character of the free reading of the pupils, and the achievement of the pupils at the end of the school year. The second part of the study involved each school making changes in their reading program that would accommodate the needs of the students they served. In each school, the pupils were tested at the beginning of the school year. These test scores were analyzed for what they revealed about pupil needs. The research literature was then consulted and discussed among teachers to identify desirable changes in the instructional program. Administrative, supervisory, and teaching problems encountered in making these changes were observed and analyzed. At the end of the school year, all of the pupils were tested once again to determine gains. For this second part of the study, there were five experimental schools participating in the change effort. Four other schools served as the controls.

The data collected through the initial survey were quite exhaustive and included not only demographic information but also information specific to classroom instruction. For example, the amount of reading done by pupils was monitored. This included reports from teachers collected three times a year on the number of pages read in class under the teacher's direct supervision and on the number of books read by students independently during story time. At the upper grade levels, students completed brief reports over their independent reading that called for information on where they got the book, how difficult the vocabulary was, and judgments about its quality.

Extensive descriptions of the various experiences in the schools are provided by Gray. These document the activities of supervisors and administrators in supporting change in their schools from the time of the analysis of the achievement scores in the fall, through the reading of the professional literature, to the implementation of program changes. The test scores from the fall and the spring are reported and interpreted as supporting the claim that the changes were beneficial to students learning to read. "The evidence is conclusive that notable progress can be made in improving teaching through the study and application of the results of scientific investigations relating to reading" (1933, p. 208). Gray identifies several *factors* that he believes contribute to successful change efforts. Among the points noted: the improvement of teaching needs to be viewed as a cooperative effort between the supervisory staff and teaching faculty; roles and responsibilities should be clearly defined; the best place to start is where you are and work to make improvements; continuous help and guidance is necessary; and recognition should be afforded to those who make outstanding progress. He believes that certain *processes* are supportive of successful change. Among these are a survey of existing practices, goals, and student performance levels; the cooperative study of the data collected to determine areas of need and identify priorities; the intensive study of the problem that is to be addressed first; a critical reading of the professional literature for insights and ideas on what to do; the drawing of a clear definition of what is to be done; the use of demonstrations, observations, and discussions to support the change process; and continuous study of the progress achieved.

Gray also identifies several *conditions* that appear critical to successful change efforts. Among these are capable leadership within the schools; a competent and professionally minded staff; familiarity with current trends and the results of scientific study; the need for continued research; and the importance of time. The latter point refers to the fact that school improvement is a complex process. Success is achieved in small steps that may unfold over quite a long period of development.

The second program of research that is also representative of the studies conducted during this early period consists of a series of investigations into oral reading instruction. Until the turn of the century, practically all of the reading instruction in schools was conducted with oral reading being the dominant mode for practice. A debate over the relative merits of oral versus silent reading modes began in early 1900s, when the findings from several research and evaluation studies suggested that silent reading produced better comprehension and that practice in silent reading led to improved performance on standardized reading achievement tests (Smith, 1965). The debate reached its peak in the 1930s. Perhaps the most extreme advocate of silent reading over oral reading was McDade in his nonoral reading method, based on two cardinal rules: (1) the positive rule was that there must always be an association of the printed word and its meaning (e.g., every time the child would read "door," a door must be dealt with in some fashion; and (2) the negative rule was that there must never be an association of the printed word with the vocal word (McDade, 1944).

McDade conducted a number of different experiments with this method. The first experiment (1935) was in a single first-grade classroom, where the approach was tried for a year. The results were regarded as so good by McDade that two other classes were identified and tested for comparison purposes. The nonoral class was found to be far superior in achievement as compared to traditional classes. During the ten-year period from 1935 to 1945, the Chicago Public Schools carried on an experiment in nonoral reading. The following gives a breakdown of its use: 1935 (1 class), 1936 (11 classes), 1939 (470 classes), 1945 (137 of 346 elementary schools). All together more than 70,000 pupils were taught in this way. The method also received heavy criticism. Rohrer (1943) wrote a devastating critique of the methodology used in McDade's first study and asserted that its conclusions were meaningless. Rohrer argued that the nonoral method violated the psychological principle of the motor theory of consciousness. Basically, this theory holds that it is impossible to have thinking, and hence learning, unless there is bodily movement. Rohrer argued that in the beginning stages of learning to read there should be a maximum of oral activity. Pronouncing is important for the beginner, not only because of the link with speech, but because the fullest range of motor expression is a tremendous asset in all childhood learning.

Buswell (1945) reported on an attempt to evaluate the effectiveness of McDade's nonoral approach in the Chicago Public Schools. Although the approach was used only through grade three, Buswell focused the evaluation on students who were in grade six, arguing that if differences in performance could be found at this point then the effects of the method were indeed substantial. He identified students who had come through one approach (nonoral) and the other (traditional) and then set up a matched-set comparison for the two groups on achievement and lip movement during silent reading. No statistically significant differences were found on any of these measures. Interest in the nonoral method dissipated rapidly after this point.

Research in this early period like Gray's seemed to reflect a prevailing view that classrooms and schools are (or at least should be) consumers of good ideas and insights that have grown out of clinical research studies. On occasion, as with McDade and Buswell, classrooms and schools served as contexts to test out theories and to resolve scholarly debates. Classrooms and schools, however, were not seen as research contexts in which to actually develop theories about teaching and schooling effects. Problems in implementation were seen as the major bottleneck in bringing positive changes in instruction.

Survey Studies

In the late 1950s and early 1960s, the climate for research changed as a "crisis of confidence" arose over the status quo of reading instruction (Smith, 1965). Motivated by widespread concerns over the quality of teaching in schools, Austin and Morrison (1961) initiated a study into the collegiate preparation of prospective teachers of reading. This study of teacher preparation revealed that for the most part the teachers graduating from undergraduate programs were not fully prepared to assume responsibility for classroom reading instruction. The authors offered numerous recommendations for reform in teacher preparation. At the same time, they raised questions about how well the public schools were assuming responsibility for directing the development of these inadequately prepared teachers through staff development and in-service programs.

To explore this question further, the authors initiated a second national survey study focused this time on instructional practices in the teaching of reading at the elementary school. This study (Austin & Morrison, 1963) included an examination of the administrative structure for reading programs as well as consideration of the staff development and supervisory support available to classroom teachers. This report provides a remarkably detailed sketch of reading instruction in the late 1950s and early 1960s.

Two sources of data were relied on in this study. The first source was based on questionnaire surveys sent to all school systems located in cities and counties through-out the United States where the population exceeded 10,000. The questionnaires focused on numerous factors associated with instructional practices, program features, and administrative structures. Among these were approaches and materials used in beginning reading instruction, grouping and management practices, attention to indi-vidual differences and services to those in special need, evaluation of pupil progress, support for professional development, and the role of administrators.

The second data source was direct contact with a representative sample of the 1,023 school districts responding to the survey. A total of 51 districts that represented a balance of geographic and demographic types (e.g., rural vs. urban vs. suburban) were visited. Administrators and teachers were interviewed and observed. Observations were conducted in approximately 1,800 classrooms in 225 schools. Teachers were interviewed in group settings (2,000+), while district administrators (271) and princi-pals (225) were interviewed individually. While there was a great range in practices across the schools sampled, the striking feature is one of similarity. Basal reader systems formed the core of the developmental reading program in the vast majority of schools surveyed. Sixty-four percent reported reliance on a single series, while another 31.4 percent reported that multiple series were in use. Workbooks were in wide use (50% of the schools), and where they were not in use the teachers were asking for them. Word recognition was taught following the guidelines provided by basals, although many teachers used supplementary phonics materials to augment instruction in decoding. Ability grouping for reading instruction (both intraclass and interclass) was commonly practiced, the rationale given being that in this way the individual needs of pupils could be better addressed. Oral reading dominated over silent reading in the early primary grades, while silent reading surpassed oral reading in the middle and upper grades. The most commonly cited frustration for teachers was in dealing with and meeting the needs of pupils who were experiencing difficulty. A minimum of support services was found in the schools to help teachers in their work with children.

The survey of administrators focused on the perceived roles and responsibilities of various individuals in guiding and supporting the reading program. The focus was on eleven major functions: (1) development of reading goals; (2) implementation of the reading program; (3) appraisal of the success or failure of the reading program; (4) recruitment of personnel involved in the reading program (other than the classroom teachers); (5) selection of reading materials for classroom use; (6) supervision of class-room teaching; (7) diagnostic testing in reading; (8) providing remedial instruction; (9) supervision of the reading program in all elementary schools; (10) supervision of the reading program in an individual school; and (11) interpretation of the reading program to parents.

Among the roles examined were the elementary supervisor, the assistant superin-tendent, the curriculum director, the reading consultant, the remedial reading teacher, the classroom teacher, and the school principal. Of course, not all school districts included in the survey had individuals serving in each of these roles, but nevertheless the findings revealed certain trends. Respondents were asked to designate who had primary responsibility in their district for each of the functions identified above. The authors comment that in looking at the general array of assignment of functions within school districts, there appears to be considerable confusion about who is doing what. Some general trends were inferred, however, by looking across all of the data for all schools.

Various degrees of satisfaction were found to be evident with respect to adminis-trative decision making. Those who were responsible for the creation of policy appeared to be far more satisfied with the status quo than those who were expected to implement it. Teachers as a group expressed many concerns over the quality of the reading programs in which they were working. They were troubled by children not reading up to expectations, by the inadequate supply of materials, by the content of readers that were dull, by the workbooks that did not contain enough phonics, and so on.

The research staff independently rated the 51 programs they visited on overall quality. They judged 17 as good, 26 as fair, and 8 as poor. To their dismay, administrators in these 51 programs rated their quality as 13 excellent, 34 good, 4 fair. These data on perceived quality, combined with the information on roles and responsibilities, suggested that radical improvements may not be forthcoming. Nonetheless, the authors offer specific suggestions for improvement around the areas of a challenging developmental program for all children, better provisions for individual differences, more stimulating programs for the gifted reader, improved teacher preparation, and more effective leadership at the administrative level.

Following closely on the heels of the publication of the Austin and Morrison studies, Jeanne Chall reported the findings of her investigation into beginning reading instruction (Chall, 1967). She examined the existing research literature for evidence related to the question of the best way to approach beginning reading instruction. She also examined the existing evidence related to the best time to begin formal instruction and the kinds of failure experienced by children working in the various methods. Additional data sources (beyond the critical review of the research literature) included interviews with leading proponents of the various approaches; observations in schools using these approaches; and a systematic analysis of the readers, workbooks, and teachers' guidebooks from the two most widely used reading series in the United States during the late 1950s and early 1960s. This was a monumental effort, the scope of which is sometimes lost by critics focusing on the controversial conclusion she draws from her critical analysis of existing research comparing different approaches to beginning reading.

Chall begins her treatment with a description of the "consensus" that had developed from the 1930s through the early 1950s in the United States around the task of teaching beginning reading. She describes the challenges to that consensus which became rampant and widespread in the mid 1950s and coalesced into a "crisis" over the best way to teach beginning reading. Chall analyzed 22 beginning reading programs that had been widely discussed and/or researched in the literature. Based on this analysis, she derived nine common labels by which the programs were classified: conventional basal; phonics programs: partial phonics-first programs; complete; linguistics approach; initial teaching alphabet; responsive environment; individualized reading; language experience; and programmed learning. Of the 22 programs analyzed, she described all as directed toward the "ultimate goal" of meaning. At the "beginning stages" though she described 14 as being "code emphasis" and the remaining 8 as being "meaning emphasis" from the start. She reviewed the existing experimental literature that contrasted the effects of these various methods and summarized her results in terms of a dichotomy (which she stressed is one of "emphasis") between findings with approaches that emphasize code from the beginning and those that emphasize meaning. She concluded from this review that "A code emphasis tends to produce better overall reading achievement by the beginning of fourth grade than a meaning emphasis" (p. 137). Code emphasis, she explains, does not equate to systematic phonics, since approaches like the linguistic emphasize the child's own discovery of letter-sound relationships.

Chall's conclusions regarding beginning instruction were challenged by many (e.g., Rutherford, 1968). Some critics pointed to the questionable validity of most of the research studies that formed the basis for this review. Others argued that the classification of systems into the code- and meaning-emphasis categories was arbitrary and simplistic. Still others attacked the position taken on the grounds that the measures used to judge reading "achievement" were too biased toward code-emphasis approaches. No one denied the significance of the report, however, in terms of its almost immediate impact on the field of reading education from the level of the classroom to the level of research itself. The report focused the attention of the professional community on the issue of the "best way to teach beginning reading" and contributed to a polarization on the importance of decoding versus meaning in beginning reading instruction. Chall is quite clear in the book that, while she believes the existing evidence points toward the benefits of an emphasis on code in instruction at early stages, her goal is to encourage the development of a scientific basis for reading instruction through expanded research efforts.

Methods-Comparison Studies

During the late 1950s and early 1960s there were abundant proposals on how to resolve the perceived crisis in the quality of reading instruction. Most of these proposals took the form of advocacy for new methods (or old methods relabeled) for teaching reading that were touted as more effective. Research was seen as the way to test out the validity of the methods. In this period, therefore, one finds rampant testing of one approach to reading versus another in controlled studies designed to demonstrate superiority. Downing (1963), Mazurkiewicz (1964), and others examined the effectiveness of i.t.a. (the initial teaching alphabet) over traditional instruction. Sparks and Fay (1957), McDowell (1953), Bear (1964), and others examined the effectiveness of systematic or synthetic phonics over traditional approaches. Most of the studies conducted in this "methods-comparison" paradigm seemed to show support for the experimental method over the control condition. While numerous concerns were raised over methodology, there was no widespread questioning of the value of a research paradigm directed toward the discovery of *the best* way to teach.

This line of methods-comparison research reached its zenith in the form of a large-scale investigation into beginning reading. The Cooperative Research Program in First-Grade Reading Instruction (commonly referred to as the "First-Grade Studies") was a research effort funded by the U.S. Office of Education and coordinated by Guy Bond and Robert Dykstra at the Minnesota Coordinating Center. Each of the 27 individual projects that comprised the cooperative research program formed a complete study in its own right. Most of the projects investigated instructional methodology. The data were analyzed within each project and then sent to the University of Minnesota for aggregation and analysis across research sites. The program was designed to explore three basic questions:

1. To what extent are various pupil, teacher, class, school, and community characteristics related to pupil achievement in first-grade reading and spelling?
2. Which of the many approaches to initial reading instruction produces superior reading and spelling achievement at the end of the first grade?
3. Is there any program uniquely effective or ineffective for pupils with high or low readiness for reading? (Bond & Dykstra, 1967, p. 9)

Each of the instructional comparison studies contrasted a traditional basal program with one or more of the following: (1) basal-plus-phonics, (2) i.t.a., (3) linguistic, (4) phonic-linguistic, and (5) language experience. Certain design features and measures were common across all of the studies.

Data collected on pupils included sex, age, amount of preschool experience, and absences during the experimental treatment. Pretesting of children included, but was not limited to, measures of intelligence (Pintner-Cunningham Primary Test), auditory discrimination (Murphy-Durrell Phonemes Test), letter naming (Murphy-Durrell Letter Names Test), and listening comprehension (Metropolitan Listening Test). Posttesting focused on measuring silent reading ability, word identification, vocabulary, spelling, and word study skills (Stanford Achievement Battery). A sample of students from each research site was tested further with the Gates Word Pronunciation Test, the Fry Phonetically Regular Words Test, and the Gillmore Oral Reading Test.

Data collected on teachers included age, degrees, certification, years teaching experience, and years of experience teaching at first grade, marital status, number of children, attitude toward teaching, absences during the treatment period, and a global rating of effectiveness by supervisors.

Data collected about the community included the median education of adults in the community, median income, population, and type of community. Data collected on the schools included the number of children enrolled in first grade, length of the school day, length of the school year, number of classes in each school, number of classes in the district, availability of library services, and per-pupil costs for education.

The length of the experimental program across all sites was designed to be 140 instructional days. Project directors were "encouraged to take whatever steps would be necessary to control for the Hawthorne Effect" (Bond & Dykstra, 1967, p. 33), although there were no requirements for random assignment of teachers to treatments. It was ". . . assumed that, within each project, treatments were assigned at random to a set of classes. It was assumed that identical treatments were used in each project" (p. 47).

These data were used to analyze relationships among pupil characteristics and end-of-year achievement. Of particular interest for this review are the findings related to the effects of the various methods studied. Data from only 15 of the studies were used in the methods-comparison analysis. Separate analyses were conducted for studies that compared the traditional basal with one or another of the targeted experimental programs (e.g., i.t.a.). The data analysis and subsequent interpretation of findings was made difficult in many cases due to the project-by-treatment interactions found. Where these interactions were found, it was nearly impossible to make sense of the effects across all of the studies. While many attempts were made to eliminate these interactions through the use of various covariates in the analysis, these efforts were not always successful. As an alternative, the data from each of the projects were analyzed independently on the various postmeasures and then interpretations were based on the consistency of findings across studies.

The authors conclude that in general the treatment approaches as a group tended to produce pupils with better word recognition skills than did the basal programs. Differences with respect to paragraph meaning, spelling, and reading accuracy were less consistent. Variability in the data did not seem to suggest that the experimental or control methods had an effect on students' growth as a function of entering ability. The only exception to this were findings related to the language experience method. The variability increased within this group, with the students entering at higher levels of ability doing better than those in the traditional basal approach, while the students with lower entering ability benefitted more from the traditional basal. Overall, though, no strong conclusions could be drawn. Bond (1966) states, "We have found no one approach so distinctly better in all situations and respects than the others that it should be considered the one best method nor to be used exclusively" (p. 8) (cited in Chall, 1967, p. 136). He continues:

> There are, however, many indications that no matter what the underlying method is, word-study skills need to be emphasized and taught systematically. This is best shown by the superiority of the approaches which augmented the basal reader, with a phonetic (phonic)

emphasis as compared with basal readers as usually taught. (p. 9) (cited in Chall, 1967, p. 136)

   The authors interpret the large number of project-by-treatment interactions to suggest that "reading achievement is influenced by factors peculiar to school systems." They also conclude that the wide variation within treatments suggests the importance of elements over and above the methods employed. Interesting with respect to these elements is the analysis of the teacher and school-community data collected. The categorical data on teachers (e.g., type of certificate held) was found to be unrelated to achievement. The teacher efficiency rating was "not utilized because of lack of objectivity which raised questions about reliability and validity, and because it was related to only a slight degree to pupil success in reading" (Bond & Dykstra, 1967, p. 31). The authors report that there was little in the school or community data that would indicate that these factors had a relationship to achievement.

   The findings, interpretations, and significance of the First-Grade Studies have been debated over the years. There is some small measure of support in these data for Chall's assertions regarding the superiority of code-emphasis approaches on achievement based on the findings from the basal-plus-phonics and the phonic-linguistic groups. On the other hand, even these results are subject to challenge on the grounds that the "real" differences are small in magnitude, the measures were biased toward code-emphasis programs, there was no consistent definition for the treatment in many of the experimental groups (e.g., language experience), there was no monitoring of implementation, there was no effective control for the Hawthorne Effect in most studies, and there were many cases in which the assignment of treatment to teacher and students to treatment was not random.

   Perhaps one of the most important outcomes of the First-Grade Studies was that this experience forced the research community to look at the ways in which research questions were being framed. The failure of the First-Grade Studies to provide a satisfactory answer to the "big question" marked the end of one era and ushered in a new one. It should be noted that even entering into the planning of the first studies many scholars had cautioned about the emptiness of the methods-comparison framework (Gray, 1960. Russell & Fea, 1963).

Research Anomalies

Three studies that were both outside the dominant paradigm for their time and remarkable in the way in which they foreshadowed the trends to come in research are deserving of attention. These studies will be presented in this fourth and final section of the early reading research root. Interestingly, two of these efforts were initiated as part of the First-Grade Studies, though neither was involved directly in the methods-comparison question.

   Most of the methods-comparison studies conducted in the field of reading operated under the assumption that teachers, once told or trained in what to do, would do just that. Seldom were teachers actually observed in the implementation of the method, nor was much consideration given to what the individual teacher already knew or believed about the method. It was also assumed in these studies that, aside from the experimental manipulation, all teachers were doing pretty much the same thing in their classrooms. Chall and Feldman (1966) designed a study to explore these issues and assumptions more carefully. The study was conducted in first-grade classrooms serving children from socially disadvantaged neighborhoods. It was one of the First-Grade

Studies, but it was not a part of the larger study in which various methods were contrasted with the "common" basal reader approach. The authors describe the study as being conducted in a "natural," as contrasted to an experimental, situation. A questionnaire, designed to elicit beliefs and practices concerning the teaching of reading in the first grade, was administered to the teachers participating in the study. Based on this survey, each teacher was rated on a continuum ranging from "meaning" to "sound-symbol" types. The twelve teachers originally chosen to participate divided equally between the meaning and the sound-symbol types. For the study, the teachers continued following the same reading program they had been working with in the past. The teachers were observed in their classrooms on a regular basis. A "Classroom Observation Inventory," developed to rate teacher characteristics and practices, was used for these observations. Interviews were also conducted with the teachers.

The children in these classes were tested in October of 1964 with the same tests administered in the other First-Grade Studies. Posttesting was conducted after 140 instructional days. In all, the data included 45 measures of pupil skills and 83 measures of teacher characteristics. The teacher data were derived, for the most part, from the Classroom Observation Inventory, and the remainder from the interviews.

Several teacher characteristics were found to be significantly related to pupils' reading achievement at the end of the first grade, even when the entering differences were statistically adjusted through an analysis of covariance. Teacher characteristics included teacher competence, approach to learning, a sound-symbol emphasis in reading, and using an appropriate level of lessons. These significant achievement relationships held true only for those tests that combined decoding and meaning tasks, but not for the "meaning only" test (i.e., the Stanford Achievement Vocabulary Test).

There were at least two quite unexpected findings. The amount of teacher "attention given to individual differences" was negatively related to achievement scores. "The less attention paid to individual differences, the higher the pupil achievement." A second surprise came with the finding that there was no significant relationship between the ranking of the teacher's professed method (sound-symbol vs. meaning) and the method emphasized in instruction.

Chall and Feldman conclude that ". . . what teachers do does make a difference in pupil achievement, even when initial skills and their own teaching experience is accounted for" (p. 574). They argue that the great variation in implementation of professed method observed in this study makes it necessary for researchers in the future to take direct measure of teacher characteristics and implementation characteristics.

The second study of note as a research anomaly during this same period was the CRAFT project (Harris & Serwer, 1966). This project was part of the Cooperative First-Grade Study Program and in many ways resembled the others in terms of design. The study was designed to assess the relative effectiveness of two major approaches to teaching beginning reading to disadvantaged pupils: a skills-centered approach and a language-experience approach. There were actually four treatment methods, with two variations on each of the basic approaches. In one treatment, the skills approach was prescribed with a rigid following of a basal design for instruction. In the second treatment, the skills approach also used the basal readers but substituted the phono-visual method for teaching word attack for the basal recommendations. In the third treatment, the language-experience approach was followed using the oral language of the children to create the instructional materials. In the fourth treatment group, the language-experience method was also used, but it was supplemented with audiovisual skills procedures. The study was directed toward several effectiveness questions but in addition examined whether the success a teacher has with a method depends on how faithfully it is used.

There were 12 elementary schools involved in the study, all serving pupils from severely disadvantaged neighborhoods. The investigators were able to achieve random assignment of methods to schools (two to each), random assignment of teachers to method within a school, and random assignment of students to method. Forty-eight teachers were recruited into the project with the understanding that they would be willing to implement any of the four methods they were assigned. Training sessions were begun in the summer and continued for 21 sessions during the year. The 1,378 children completed the same battery of pretests used in all of the other First-Grade Studies.

Each teacher was required to maintain a log of instructional time. In addition, teachers were observed during "representative lessons." The Observation Scale and Rating-Reading (OScAR-R) was used as an "objective" way of recording teacher behavior. The instrument was developed by Donald M. Medley specifically for use in this study. The "static" side of the recording form was used to represent the variety of materials and activities that the teacher was observed using. The "dynamic" side was used to record teacher-pupil verbal interaction behaviors. Each teacher was observed eight times.

In general, the results showed a slight but statistically significant advantage for the pupils working in the basal approach. The analysis went on to focus on the issue of instructional time spent in reading activities and its relationship to approach and growth. The primary source for the time data was the logs the teacher maintained. The total amount of time spent in reading was about the same for the two approaches. However, a distinction was made at this point between reading time and supportive time. Thus, time spent drawing a picture for a chart was regarded as supportive time in the language-experience approach, whereas time spent reading the chart was reading time. Based on this distinction, large differences were found between the approaches, with the basal approach yielding higher levels of "reading time." There was also great variation between the teachers in the amount of time they were able to devote to reading time regardless of approach. Analyses of the amount of time spent in reading time and its relation to achievement yielded strong positive findings. Those teachers who were able to achieve the greatest amount of time in reading produced students with the highest gains. "When teachers of reading spend substantial amounts of time on activities that involve little or no practice in reading, the results in reading achievement tended to be unfavorable" (p. 56).

The third and final study to be described as a research anomaly was a study into the kinds of questions that teachers ask about reading assignments (Guszak, 1967). Guszak's primary interest was in discovering whether the patterns in questioning used by teachers promote the development of good thinking skills. The focus for the study was the reading group. Four teachers each from second-, fourth-, and sixth-grade levels and their students were studied. At the second- and fourth-grade levels there were three reading groups (high, average, and low) in each class. At the sixth-grade level only one class had three groups. All of the groups were observed over a three-day period. Sessions were tape recorded and later transcribed for analysis purposes. Questions were categorized according to the following types: recognition, recall, translation, conjecture, explanation, and evaluation. The total number of questions observed was 1,857 (878 in grade two, 725 in grade four, and 254 in grade six). Teachers spent most of their time engaging students in questions at the literal level (71.3%) that included both recognition and recall types. In analyzing the response patterns of pupils to teacher questions, Guszak examined "congruence," or whether the response was correct or not. He found that the students' responses were "congruent" over 90 percent of the time on the first student try. Guszak laments the failure of teachers to use questioning in a manner that might promote good thinking.

Summary

The roots of research in teaching and school effects on learning to read reveal many shifts in focus and method. Four research paradigms stand out as one looks across the studies conducted in this period. Research began slowly over the decades of the 1920s, 1930s, and 1940s. The first paradigm consisted of occasional implementation and evaluation studies in schools designed to test out various applications of basic research. The crisis of confidence in the quality of instruction in the 1950s was a transitional period. The bridging paradigm to the next generation of research took the form of a series of large-scale descriptive studies of reading education. Research was being used to respond to public and professional concerns over the quality of instruction. These survey studies attempted to represent practice in a way that could be examined and evaluated by whatever standards one chose to apply. However, there was little in the way of data collected through these studies that would permit learning outcomes to be used as one standard. This limitation gave rise to a third paradigm in the 1960s. Reading research came to be viewed as the ultimate tool in determining the best way to teach reading through methods comparison studies. The "big" question of "What best?" was asked. The data yielded inconclusive results at best and contradictory findings at worst. The fourth paradigm, more of an anomaly than a trend, consisted of the small set of studies in which researchers began to directly investigate the nature of instruction in classrooms. These studies suggested that there was a good deal to be learned from research that ventured into classrooms to study teaching effects.

RESEARCH INTO EFFECTIVE TEACHING

A large number of factors came together in the mid-1960s and early 1970s that contributed to the emergence of the field of research in teaching. The period is marked by a shift in research from a focus on teachers and teacher characteristics to a focus on teaching and teaching processes. The research prior to the 1960s was pursued primarily by supervisors and administrators interested in identifying the characteristics of effective teachers. These data were seen as important in making decisions about the hiring, firing, and promotion of faculty. For the most part, studies in this genre attempted to identify through correlational procedures the relationship between teacher characteristics and the ratings of effectiveness made by principals and supervisors. The results of these studies yielded information that was of questionable value at either a theoretical or a practical level (Barr et al., 1955). Seldom did these studies involve the direct observation of teachers in classrooms for any significant period. Further, the criteria for judging effectiveness were subjective and therefore suspect.

As the field moved toward a focus on classroom processes, a new paradigm for research was developed. Most of the research in this area was conducted by individuals outside the mainstream traditions of reading education who were concerned about effective teaching in general and not teaching/learning relationships specific to reading. The fact that reading achievement was often used as a dependent variable for studying the effects of teaching makes this body of research relevant to a review of teaching effects on learning to read.

Pioneering Efforts

Several researchers were at the vanguard of this movement and through their initial studies set the tone for research that was to follow. Ned Flanders, with his work in the study of classroom interaction patterns, was one of the most influential figures. Flanders was interested in discovering how verbal interaction patterns influenced pupil development. This line of research has its own peculiar history dating back to the work of Anderson (1939) in his studies of dominating and integrative teacher behaviors. Flanders's interest was primarily in the development of pupil attitudes toward schools, although he investigated academic learning as well. Using the observation instrument he developed, the FIAC (Flanders Interaction Analysis Categories), teachers were observed in classrooms to determine their direct or indirect style of interaction. Flanders found consistent relationships between what he labeled an indirect style of teaching and the development of positive learning attitudes. The relationship between indirectness and academic learning was less clear (Flanders, 1965, 1970). Critics of this research pointed out the limitations of the instrument used in the observation. For example, in one study using the Flanders system, Furst and Amidon (1965) reported that "the reading teacher responded most often to a student communication by posing a question" (p. 285). This pattern could in fact represent an inappropriate slice of language interaction. The student communication may itself have been a response to another teacher question. And the "response" by the teacher may in fact have been a new question to a different student on a different topic.

Despite such limitations, Flanders's research and that of his colleagues marked the first time that the observation of teachers had received such prominent and systematic attention. The instrument itself was widely disseminated and modified for use in numerous other studies of classroom practices.

Rosenthal and Jacobson's (1968) study of the relationship between teacher expectations and pupil achievement raised hopes and set a direction for many researchers to follow. In their "Pygmalion in the Classroom" study, these researchers monitored the academic performance of at-risk children over the course of a year. Participating teachers were told that a low-achieving child in their classroom had been identified through a newly developed test as a potential "late bloomer." The pupil was tested at the beginning of the year and again at the end to assess growth. The name of the pupil was given to the teacher early in the year. Another child in the same classroom, of comparable academic ability, was also tested at the beginning and ending of the year to assess growth. The teacher was not aware that this second pupil had been tested. In fact, there was no "late-bloomer" test. The pupil identified as a potential late bloomer had been randomly selected from the matched pair for that classroom.

Other than the identification of the targeted pupil and the explanation of the results of the late-bloomer test, no contact was made with the teacher during the year. The comparisons made on pupil academic growth at the end of the year revealed that the child who had been identified as a late bloomer outperformed his or her classroom counterpart. These results were interpreted to mean that teacher expectations shape if not determine pupil success in learning.

This study did seem to demonstrate quite clearly and powerfully to skeptics that teaching can make a difference. The study has been roundly criticized on ethical and methodological grounds. But, like the work of Flanders noted earlier, its real contribution was in the formulation of a research agenda. The findings from the Rosenthal and Jacobson study were tantalizing to those interested in exploring how expectations were being mediated in the classroom. What was it that teachers were doing or not doing that would account for the learning differences observed?

Research Syntheses

As a single document, the *Second Handbook of Research on Training* (Travers, 1973), marks for many the beginning of the field. The various authors in this handbook struggle to pull together what little research there was on teaching into a coherent framework. It is a tribute to these authors that they were able to do so. They established in the process the baseline and direction for subsequent research. Of particular note in this handbook is a chapter by Rosenshine and Furst (1973) in which they report on a comprehensive review of all of the research conducted up to that time focusing on the relationships among teacher behaviors and student learning. They identify nine areas in which research had revealed a consistent relationship between teacher behavior and student achievement:

1.   clarity
2.   variability
3.   enthusiasm
4.   task oriented and/or businesslike
5.   criticism (a negative correlation to achievement)
6.   teacher indirectness
7.   student opportunity to learn criterion material
8.   use of structuring comments
9.   multiple levels of questions or cognitive discourse

In calling for continued research, the authors advocate programs of study that follow a descriptive, correlational, experimental loop. In other words, descriptive studies of classroom practices lead to the identification of significant correlates of teaching behaviors to learning outcomes. Where significant relationships are discovered, these are then tested through direct manipulation of variables in classroom experiments. It is clear that this chapter set a course for much of the research in the decade to follow. Whether its popularity was because the "behaviorist" leanings of educational psychology lined up well with this view of research in teaching, or because this strategy seemed to offer some hope for answering the question of what is effective, is difficult to determine.

In 1974, Dunkin and Biddle wrote a book entitled *The Study of Teaching*. In this book the authors develop a framework for representing research in teaching as well as report their findings of a review of existing literature using this framework. The framework was quickly adopted by writers and researchers in the field. According to these authors, there are four major categories of variables that are of interest in research in teaching: (1) presage variables, (2) context variables, (3) process variables, and (4) product variables.

Presage variables refer to those personal characteristics, experiences, or qualities that the teacher brings to the classroom (e.g., sex, educational background, personality, etc.). *Context variables* refer to the surrounding conditions that are "givens" to the teacher entering the classroom (e.g., class size, pupil background, community characteristics, the prescribed curriculum, the daily and yearly schedule, etc.). *Process variables* refer to what teachers and students do in the classroom (e.g., asking questions, giving answers, explaining assignments, correcting inappropriate behavior, etc.). *Product variables* refer to what is learned as a function of participating in classroom events. These products can be short term (e.g., specific skills) or long term (e.g., reading achievement). They can be academic or attitudinal. The model is depicted in Figure 32.1.

Dunkin and Biddle also refer to six classes of knowledge that can be informed through research in teaching. The first class is research into the conceptualization of the processes of teaching. Here a researcher might be investigating classification schemes for such teacher behaviors as questioning or offering feedback to pupil errors. The second class is research into the rates of occurrence of these processes (e.g., questions

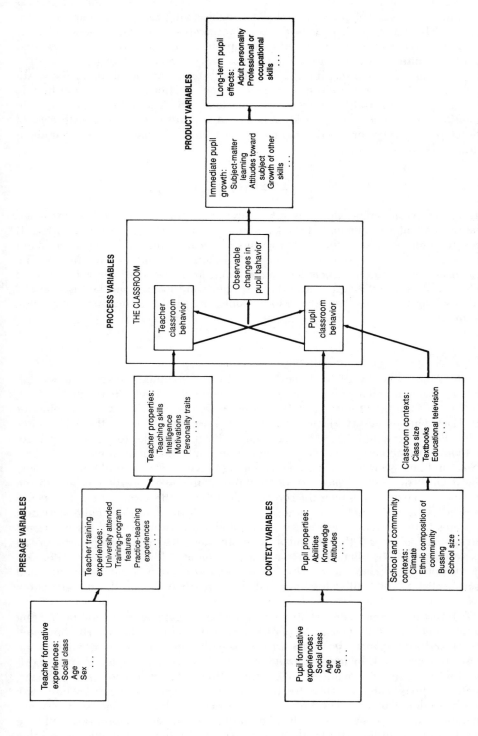

FIGURE 32.1 A model from the study of classroom teaching. SOURCE: from *The Study of Teaching* by Michael Dunkin and Bruce Biddle. Copyright © 1974 by Holt, Rinehart and Winston, Inc. Reprinted by permission of the publisher.

per minute or questions per story). The third class is research into context-process relationships (e.g., types of questions to low vs. high reading groups; questions in high-SES vs. low-SES classrooms). The fourth class is research into presage-process relationships (e.g., the types of questions asked by comprehension-oriented vs. code-oriented teachers). The fifth class is research into process-process relationships (e.g., question characteristics and the differential responses of pupils to extended wait time). The sixth and final class refers to research into process-product relationships (e.g., questioning characteristics and growth in reading comprehension level). The utility of the model in framing research questions was quickly recognized within the field. The sixth class of knowledge (i.e., process-product) came to represent the dominant research paradigm for the decade to follow.

Programs of Research

During the 1970s and on into the early 1980s, several programs of research were carried out that were significant in terms of the large number of findings that were reported. It is easiest to describe these in terms of programs of research since they were carried out by several individuals and typically encompassed more than one or two studies. The discussion of this research is included at this point as a root of research in teaching and school effects on reading because these studies were focused on the discovery of generic teaching strategies that related to outcome, or "product," measures of reading achievement.

Soar and Soar

In the late 1960s and early 1970s, Robert and Ruth Soar conducted several studies that focused on teacher behaviors and student achievement (Soar & Soar, 1979). They adapted and refined the observational techniques developed by Flanders to account for several classroom process variables that they felt were hidden by the FIAC. For example, they distinguished between emotional climate variables (e.g., teacher affective responses to students) and the managerial (or control) strategies used.

Soar and Soar worked within the developing process-product tradition. Typically in their studies, they would measure pupil abilities and then observe teachers in the classroom four to eight times over the course of the year. In the spring, the pupils would be assessed once again and then an analysis was performed to determine statistical relationships between teaching processes and pupil growth. In terms of the emotional climate of the classroom, they found a generally negative relationship between an oppressive or negative climate and pupil achievement. However, the relationship between a positive climate and pupil achievement was not significant. This suggested that a poor climate can inhibit learning, but that a positive climate did not guarantee success.

With respect to management strategies, the Soars discovered several interesting interactions between strategy use and pupil learning. They found that a fairly controlled and structured management style was associated with pupil success in learning in the lower primary grades and with fifth-grade pupils who were disadvantaged and experiencing difficulty with the material. They found this relationship to be curvilinear, however. The benefits for a highly structured and tightly controlled learning task were positive for students up to a point, but there is a level at which this relationship becomes dysfunctional. At this point the benefits of more time spent on recitation and drill-type tasks disappear. In studies with third- through sixth-grade pupils, the Soars found that there was a strong positive relationship between high cognitive level activities and pupil learning. Here there were benefits associated with less teacher control over tasks.

The Texas Teacher Effectiveness Studies

The initial stage in this program of research was to identify teachers who were "stable" in terms of their effects on pupil achievement. Brophy (1973) studied the achievement data on pupils from 165 second- and third-grade teachers for a three-year period. Gain scores (averaged across pupils in a class) were calculated for each teacher for the three years. Low to moderate positive correlations with gain scores were found. These correlations were interpreted to mean that there was, at least among this group of teachers, evidence for a stable effect on pupils related to the teacher. A similar analysis was performed across several subtests included in the achievement battery. The correlations among subtest scores were found to be much higher within a given year than from one year to the next. This difference was interpreted to mean that the individual teachers were exerting a substantial impact on pupil growth.

Of the original 165 teachers, approximately one-half were found to be quite stable in their effects over the years on pupil growth. Thirty-one of these teachers were identified and each observed for 10 hours in the first year of this stage of the research. Twenty-eight teachers were observed for 30 hours in the second year. Nineteen of the 28 had been observed the first year as well. A combination of low-inference and high-inference observation systems was used to measure classroom processes. Thousands of correlations were computed between scores on process measures and student gain.

General patterns in teacher effectiveness were interpreted by these researchers. The classrooms of effective teachers were businesslike in their orientation. There was a strong sense of task and direction for both teachers and students. The climate was not found to be stern or oppressive. The teachers who were most effective expressed a "can do" attitude about teaching and pupil learning. They had high expectations for all of their students, and when failure was experienced they redoubled their efforts. The authors note that this level of persistence was particularly in evidence with those teachers working in low-SES environments.

The management skills of the more effective teachers were found to be strong, with high levels of pupil engagement. The teachers were proactive in anticipating and preventing disruptions. When disruptions did occur they were dealt with quickly and in accordance with preestablished consequences. The use of harsh criticism toward behavior was rare among the more effective teachers, and overall negatively correlated with gain. The more effective teachers tended to rely more on moderate amounts of specific praise to encourage and to motivate. If criticism was used effectively, it was in the high-SES context and focused on poor academic performance, not behavior.

A significant positive effect was found for teacher questioning on pupil achievement. More precisely, the effect was for literal-level questions. The frequency of higher-level questions was so low that the effect of these kinds of questions could not be determined reliably. A curvilinear relationship was found between teacher questions followed by a correct response and the SES characteristics of the class. For the high-SES classes, the optimum level was around 70 percent of the questions answered correctly, while for the low-SES classes the optimum level was found to be around 80 percent. In general, the probing of incorrect responses (termed "sustaining response") was found to be a more effective strategy than simply calling on someone else or the teacher giving the answer (a "terminal response").

An analysis of effective strategies for the low-SES classroom revealed several interesting patterns. Teacher warmth and affect seemed to be important in establishing a positive working environment, whereas, in the high-SES classrooms, teacher warmth and affect were found to be unrelated to effectiveness. In the more effective low-SES classrooms, the teachers tended to rely a great deal on teaching to overlearning.

Anderson, Evertson, and Brophy (1979) reported the results of an experimental investigation of first-grade reading group instruction in which the findings from their own process-product research were compiled into a set of 22 principles for organizing, managing, and instructing small groups. These principles included recommendations ranging from maintaining involvement during the lesson, to trying to improve unsatisfactory answers through probes, to calling on pupils by ordered turns rather than at random during recitations. The principles, along with brief explanations, were organized into a manual. First-grade teachers from nine schools were assigned randomly (by school) to one of three groups: treatment-observed ($N = 10$), treatment-nonobserved ($N = 7$), and control ($N = 10$). The treatment-observed groups were trained in the principles and observed periodically during the year. The treatment-nonobserved groups were also trained but were not observed. The control group teachers were not trained but were periodically observed. Achievement data on groups indicated that the pupils in the treatment-observed and treatment-nonobserved conditions outperformed the pupils in the control condition. There were no significant differences between the observed and unobserved conditions. The researchers found that within the group of teachers trained in the principles, the implementation was uneven. The teachers were most successful in implementing feedback, and moderate use of praise. They were less successful with principles related to suggestions about beginning lessons with an overview, repeating new words, giving clear explanations, or breaking up the group based on instructional need. Process-product analyses revealed that higher levels of achievement were associated with such factors as more time spent in reading groups and in active instruction, shorter transitions, introduction of lessons with an overview, the presentation of new words with phonic clues, and the follow-up by the teacher to incorrect responses with attempts to improve upon them.

This program of research, spanning almost a decade, is regarded by many followers of the process-product paradigm as noteworthy, if not exemplary in its progression from observational, to correlational, to experimental studies.

The Follow-Through Studies

The Follow-Through Program was initiated by the federal government in response to the findings from studies of the effects of Head Start Programs on children's learning. These studies seemed to indicate that there were substantial effects for children who participated in Head Start Programs, but that these effects disappeared by the end of kindergarten or first grade in the regular school curriculum. The Follow-Through Program provided for continuous support for these children through the third grade.

The research design associated with the Follow-Through Program permitted comparisons of several different approaches and methods (represented in seven different instructional models) for working with these students. Twenty-two Follow-Through Programs were implemented in sites across the country. The particular models implemented in these sites ranged from direct instruction (DISTAR) models, to Individually Prescribed Instruction (IPI) models, to more affective and open classroom orientation models. The analysis of the effects of these various approaches and related classroom processes involved teachers and students in 108 first-grade and 58 third-grade classrooms (Stallings & Kaskowitz, 1974). The classrooms were observed for three consecutive days. Achievement data on students for both mathematics and reading were collected and analyzed.

The teachers were highly successful in implementing the various models in their classrooms. This success in implementation, coupled with the fact that the models were so diverse in terms of their orientation and characteristics, yielded results with greater variation than is the case in most studies of "typical" classrooms. Overall, the strongest gains in both reading and mathematics were associated with the two programs that had the strongest academic focus.

There were a large number of significant findings associated with the analysis of classroom processes and student achievement gain. For example, in reading 118 of the 340 correlations run at the first-grade level were found to be statistically significant. Among the process variables positively correlated to gain were time spent in academic activities, frequency of small-group instruction in basic skills, and frequency of supervised seatwork activities. Among the process variables negatively associated with gain were time spent in nonacademic activities and time spent in informal interactions among students

Due to the nature of the Follow-Through Program, most of the students involved in this study were from a low-SES background. Nonetheless, several significant interactions were found with respect to SES level within the sample. In general it was found that the lowest SES students benefited most from intense, small-group instruction.

The findings suggested that instruction involving traditional recitation formats—direct questions (literal-level particularly) with direct feedback by the teacher—are associated with high levels of progress in learning basic skills for children from disadvantaged backgrounds. Applications of these principles in experimental studies and longitudinal follow-up studies offer support for the findings from the Follow-Through correlational research base (Becker, 1977; Meyer, 1974).

The Beginning Teacher Evaluation Study (BTES)

Beginning in 1974 and running through 1978, the Far West Laboratory directed the Beginning Teacher Evaluation Study. This study was partially funded by the California State Department of Education and the National Institute of Education. The purpose of the study, as it was originally envisioned, was to gather data on the characteristics of teachers who are effective so that better teacher education programs could be designed. There were several different phases to this study incorporating different data sets and different methodologies. For the purposes of this review, the focus will be on the field study associated with Phase III (Fisher et al., 1980).

Twenty-five second-grade and 21 fifth-grade classrooms were the focus for this study. These classrooms were selected because they each contained at least six "target" children from an earlier phase of the project whose achievement levels in reading and mathematics fell between the 30th and 60th percentiles. Student achievement was assessed three times over the course of the academic year. The classes were observed for one entire day once a week for 20 weeks. The focus for the observation was on the "target" pupils. Their activity (e.g., content focus, engagement, and success rate) was coded every four minutes. If the teacher happened to be interacting with one or more of these students, then his or her behavior was coded according to three functions: presenting, monitoring, and feedback. In addition to these data the teachers were also interviewed and required to keep daily logs.

Several important constructs emerged from the analyses of these data. Time allocated to academics across these classes was found to be 58 percent of the school day. Time for nonacademic activities (music, art, storytime, etc.) was 24 percent, and time for procedural activities was 18 percent of the school day. Enormous variation, however, was found between classes. The more-effective teachers were found to have high levels of allocated time to academics *with low standard deviations*. Engagement (or "on-task" behavior) was also found to be significantly related to pupil learning. Across all classes, students were engaged an average of 70 percent to 75 percent of the total time allocated to academics. Here again there was tremendous variation among teachers in terms of their ability to generate high levels of engagement. High success rates on tasks were also found to be associated with high learning gains. As with the Brophy and

Evertson and Soars studies, there appeared to be several interactions between success rate and learning rates (e.g., for low-ability students the optimum success rate was higher than for the high-ability students).

The variables of allocated time to academics, engaged time, and success rate were combined statistically by the researchers to create a composite variable labeled Academic Learning Time (ALT). This ALT variable was found to be a stronger predictor of achievement gains than any of the other three considered in isolation. The findings with respect to the characteristics of instruction did not correlate significantly with the achievement gains, but did correlate significantly with the ALT composite variable (e.g., frequent use of structured lessons). The findings were interpreted to support the Carroll (1963) model for learning that emphasized the role of time and engagement as a key variable of instruction to affect learning.

Summary

There are at least two major themes that relate to effective teaching to be found in these studies. The first is the important role teachers play in organizing and managing the instructional environment in a way that serves to maximize student engagement in academics. The second is the important role teachers play in presenting academic content in a way that promotes learning. Rosenshine and Stevens (1984) have summarized and integrated findings that relate to the academic function of teaching. This involves:

1. A short demonstration in which the new material or skill is presented to the group.
2. Guided practice, in which the practice is guided by the teacher through factual or process questions and/or teacher demonstration. During this practice, the teacher provides feedback, evaluates understanding, and provides additional demonstration if necessary.
3. Independent practice, where the students practice without teacher guidance and continue until their responses are rapid and firm. If necessary, the specific stages are recycled, although if the instruction consists of small steps and explicit direction, there should be little need to do so. (pp. 758–759)

Each aspect of the model is supported through the process-product research literature. The model is consistent with what is commonly referred to as the "direct instruction" model for effective teaching.

RESEARCH INTO EFFECTIVE SCHOOLS

In the mid 1960s, President Johnson became convinced that one key to successfully addressing the problem of poverty in America was through improved efforts to educate the children of disadvantaged families. He believed that by focusing massive amounts of federal dollars on improving the quality of schooling, the basis for gains on social equality could be laid and the disparity between racial and ethnic groups could be reduced. For this reason, a large number of the War on Poverty and Great Society Programs were focused on education. In preparation for the implementation of these programs, a national study of education and its effects was commissioned by Congress in 1964. This study, entitled *The Equality of Educational Opportunity*, or the Coleman Report, was directed toward the following basic questions:

1. What is the extent to which racial and ethnic groups are segregated one from the other?
2. Do schools offer equal educational opportunity in terms of input characteristics?
3. How much do students learn as measured by standardized reading tests?
4. What is the relationship between achievement and school characteristics?

It was believed by both those who commissioned the study as well as those who conducted it, that the answers to these questions were pretty well known. Their effort was simply one of gathering the data to document what was believed and set the stage for the programs to follow. When the final results were in, however, the answers were in many cases counter to their intuitions (Coleman et al., 1966). The basic findings were as follows:

1. Most black and white Americans attend different schools.
2. There are major discrepancies in academic achievement between ethnic groups. These differences become greater as these groups progress through school.
3. There are no major discrepancies in resource allocations to black and white schools.
4. Where discrepancies in resource allocations did exist, there was little effect on either black or white students' performance on standardized tests.

The Coleman Report represented in part an attempt to document, at a very gross quantitative level, the effects of teaching and school characteristics on academic achievement. The fact that no relationships among school factors and achievement were found suggested that the school level may not be a very fertile area for study or reform. For many researchers this became a challenge to begin to study schools in an effort to document and characterize the effects of school characteristics on learning.

Perhaps the most intriguing paradigm for research in school effects, in terms of its impact on practice, has been the study of "outlier" schools. The term *outlier* is one borrowed from statisticians. For them, outliers are those cases or data points in a study that do not conform to the general pattern of findings. The outlier studies of program effectiveness rely first on the identification of individual schools that are successful in terms of high pupil achievement levels, where the school context would typically lead one to predict failure (e.g., low-SES community, minority children). These "exceptional" schools are then studied on an intensive basis in an effort to describe those features and processes that appear to contribute to success. This approach is in stark contrast to the "input-output" type studies of which the Coleman Report is a prime example. The input-output studies tend to focus on the measurement of variables that are easily quantified (i.e., counted) and then correlated to measures of pupil achievement.

Weber's (1971) study of effective schools was the first to be reported using an outlier paradigm. Weber set out with the express purpose of showing that it is possible for inner-city schools to teach basic reading successfully. Weber focused his search for effective schools on inner-city settings. He set two criteria for effectiveness in terms of pupil success: first, a national grade norm median achievement level on a standardized reading achievement test; and second, a low number of "gross reading failures." Weber sought out nominations for effective schools on a national scale from reading experts and school district officials. A total of 95 schools were nominated. Weber personally visited 17 of these schools. Six of the schools did not meet the reading success criterion. Seven of the schools did not meet the inner-city criterion. Four schools met both. Two of these schools were in New York City, one in Kansas City, and one in Los Angeles. Weber visited each school site. He observed and interviewed both teachers and administrators.

Using these data, Weber identified the following set of factors as common to the successful schools:

1. Strong curriculum leadership (in three cases it was the principal, and in the other case the superintendent)
2. High expectations for students
3. Good atmosphere (sense of purpose, quiet, orderliness)
4. Strong emphasis on reading (focus on basics, additional reading personnel)
5. Use of phonics
6. Individualization (attention and responsiveness within the curriculum to needs of students)
7. Careful evaluation of pupil progress

Weber also commented on several factors that he described as "nonessential" features of a successful program: small class size, ability grouping, the quality of individual teaching, ethnic background of the teacher and the principal, the presence of preschool programs, and building characteristics (i.e., the physical plant).

The reading specialists in these schools were primarily involved in staff development and curriculum coordination. Very little time if any was spent on "pull-out" instruction for disabled readers. Weber also noted that in every case the program leaders were responsible for beginning a new reading program in the school where they worked. The interviews also revealed that the process of becoming a successful school took a number of years (from 3 to 9 years in this sample of schools).

Wilder (1977) reported the findings from a study of effective schools that was conducted as part of a national study of compensatory reading programs funded by the U.S. Office of Education. Seven hundred and forty-one elementary schools were randomly selected from the original sample. A combination of questionnaires, interviews, and testing was used to identify five of the most effective schools. Additional on-site visits were made to these schools in order to conduct additional observations and interviews. The effective schools were found to be quite diverse in the types of reading programs used, ranging from ECRI (intensive, direct instruction in basic skills) to traditional basal to LEIR (a language-experience approach). The following factors were common to all of these schools:

1. reading being identified as an important instructional goal
2. leadership in the reading program (either the principal or the reading specialist)
3. attention to basic skills
4. breadth of materials available
5. communication of ideas across teachers in a school often catalyzed by the program leader (the reading specialist or the principal)

Wilder noted that there did not appear to be a concentration of high-quality teachers in these highly effective schools.

Venezky and Winfield (1979) studied program factors related to success in teaching reading with disadvantaged students. Two urban schools with high minority student representations were studied. The two schools had experienced contrasting patterns in achievement since 1971. One school had surpassed national norms in reading achievement by 1975, with 60 percent of the students reading above grade level. The other school had remained substantially below national norms in terms of student reading achievement. Data on these schools were collected using extensive interviews, classroom observations, analyses of school records and memos, and the examination of reading specialists' logs.

Two major factors were identified as distinguishing these two schools: curriculum leadership and instructional efficiency. With respect to curriculum leadership, the influence of the principal on the instructional program was found to be much stronger in the more effective school. The principal of this school had targeted the reading program as a high-priority area of concern. He set a high-risk goal (i.e., 60% of the students achieving above the national norms in reading) and announced this to his faculty. They describe the principal as being "task-oriented" in terms of raising pupil achievement in reading. He was responsible for promoting one of his own best teachers to a full-time reading specialist and turned over responsibility for program development and coordination to her. This was in contrast to the principal of the less-effective school, who was much more concerned with human relations. He worked to involve parents, to create a positive school image, and to organize special programs for the children. He also relied on the district coordinator for leadership in the reading program.

The term "instructional efficiency" was used to describe the utilization of resources to achieve maximal student outcomes. Resources included time, materials, personnel, and money. Two specific aspects of efficiency were identified: accountability and consistency. Accountability refers to the degree to which each student received the instruction he or she needs. In the more-effective school, accountability was achieved in a number of ways: homogeneous grouping to restrict the range of abilities facing the teacher, monitoring of student progress, and the availability and coordination of support personnel toward student needs. Consistency was achieved through stability (with the same program in use for many years) and compatibility (across grades with continuing progress).

The studies that have been discussed are representative of the significant inquiries into effective schools. Other noteworthy examples include Armor, Osegura, Cox, King, McDonnell, Pascal, Pauly, and Zellmon (1975); Austin, 1978; Wellisch, MacQueen, Carriere, and Duck (1978); Brookover and Lazotte (1979); Brookover, Beady, Flood, Schweitzer, and Wisenbaker (1979); and New York State Office of Education (1974). The findings from these studies are quite consistent with those already identified in that they have been successful in documenting that effective schools (i.e., those that succeed in the teaching of basic skills where pupil and community characteristics would predict failure) do exist.

The literature also suggests a number of programmatic features common to these effective schools. These features have been summarized often and are referred to in terms of the eight concepts that underlie effective schools (e.g., Shavelson & Berliner, 1988). These features are (1) a clear school mission; (2) effective instructional leadership and practices; (3) high expectations; (4) safe, orderly, and positive school environment; (5) ongoing curriculum improvement; (6) maximum use of instructional time; (7) frequent monitoring of student progress; and (8) a positive home-school relationship.

Hoffman and Rutherford (1984) have summarized this same literature, specific to reading, in terms of three major areas (see Table 32.1). With respect to program characteristics, all of the programs described through the effective schools research were unique in some aspect. The instructional themes that emerge are suited to almost any "method" or "approach" to reading instruction. Issues related to importance of strong instructional leadership appear critical in the effective schools literature. The leader is typically the principal with considerable expertise in reading or the principal working closely with a reading specialist. The role expectations for the reading specialist in such circumstances relate primarily to program issues and only secondarily to direct instruction in clinical settings. Finally, in terms of psychological conditions, effective schools appear to have a personality all their own.

TABLE 32.1   Effective Reading Program (from Hoffman & Rutherford, 1984)

1. **Program Characteristics**
   A. *Explicitness:* The programs are well articulated and even formalized in terms of specific objectives and role expectations.

   B. *Continuity:* The programs provide for continuous student progress through the curriculum. Typical grade-level structures and other organizational variables present no significant barriers to continuous progress.

   C. *Flexibility:* The programs are adaptable to individual differences such that students can be matched easily to appropriate materials and instruction.

   D. *Stability:* The programs are established and in place a relatively long time before the effects on achievement become apparent. It is this longevity that makes the world predictable for both students and instructional personnel and makes possible the establishment of routines. These routines permit attention to be focused on the quality of instruction.

2. **Leadership Behaviors**
   A. *Sets goals and standards:* The leader establishes reading improvement as a program priority and often sets explicit goals for the school in terms of pupil achievement.

   B. *Possesses knowledge:* The leader knows a great deal about reading instruction and has often made a conscious commitment toward a particular approach or method of teaching reading. In a large number of the effective schools, the program leader brought with him or her, or was in some way directly responsible for, the implementation of a new reading program.

   C. *Participates in and facilitates instructional decisions:* The program leader is actively—though not autocratically—involved in all decisions made within the program. He or she encourages individual initiative and cross-fertilization of ideas.

   D. *Monitors students:* The program leader establishes and actively maintains a system of testing that permits continuous monitoring of student progress in the program.

   E. *Evaluates teachers:* The program leader is constantly involved in observing classroom instruction and offering feedback to teachers. Some of the studies suggest that this strong evaluation role leads directly to the attrition of unproductive faculty.

3. **Psychological Conditions**
   A. *Attribution:* The source or cause of failure in learning to read is viewed not so much in terms of pupil background as in terms of shortcomings in the school program.

   B. *Expectation:* The instructional staff and the leadership of the school believe that the students they face will be successful in learning to read if they do their job.

   C. *Order:* Effective schools are consistently described as calm and businesslike without being oppressive in terms of their atmosphere or what some term "climate."

   D. *Commitment:* The instructional staff and the leadership are committed to the successful implementation of the reading program in their school.

   E. *Community:* There is a sense of cooperation and working together among the staff. This relationship seems to extend into the local community in terms of parental involvement.

Summary

The findings from this "school effects" research have been, for the most part, enthusiastically endorsed by policy makers and administrators. Odden and Dougherty (1982) reported that most states had underway a school improvement program of one form or another that reflected features of the effective schools literature. Edmunds (1983) described some of the staff development efforts already underway in major school districts and states across the country.

Within the research community, the response has been more cautious if not critical (e.g., Purkey & Smith, 1983; Ralph & Fennessey, 1983; Hoffman & Rutherford, 1984). Concerns over methodology, generalizability, validity, and so on, have led many to argue for restraint in implementing programs that draw on the findings from these studies. Perhaps the most common criticisms of this literature are (1) the failure of researchers to describe the ways in which school and program characteristics are influencing classroom instruction; and (2) the paucity of data relative to the process by which schools become effective.

RECENT RESEARCH INTO TEACHING AND SCHOOL EFFECTS IN LEARNING TO READ

The research in teaching and school effects conducted during the 1970s and early 1980s outside the field of reading set the stage for research into the teaching of reading that was qualitatively different from earlier work. This research wil be presented around the various topics and issues that have been explored.

Managing Reading Instruction

With the perspective only time can give, it seems fair to assign the beginning of this period with Barr's (1974) research into the effects of instructional grouping and pace on reading achievement (see Farr & Weintraub, 1974, p. 23). The study was conducted in the first-grade classrooms of three schools. The schools had been selected because they represented very different patterns of grouping and pacing for reading. These differences offered optimal conditions under which to observe the effects of such factors on reading acquisition. Two of the schools were located very close to one another and served the children of families from a suburban-middle to upper-middle-class neighborhood. The three teachers in one school (A) taught their classes as a whole, with no ability grouping. The two teachers in the other school (B) each had three reading groups homogeneously grouped by ability. The third school (C) was urban and served children of families from a lower- to lower-middle-class neighborhood. Most of the children in this school were black. The four first-grade teachers in this school grouped children by ability (three groups) for reading instruction.

The children from each class were tested on several reading measures, including a basal word list (a test developed by Barr from the basal series the children were working in), the WRAT (a standardized word recognition test), and the Gates-McGinitie (a standardized test used to assess reading comprehension). Two tests of reading aptitude were administered, the Word Learning Tasks and the Metropolitan Readiness Test. Pace was defined operationally in terms of the number of new basal words introduced to a student within a given time period. The pacing data were collected twice from the teachers during the course of the year (once in December and once in May) with specific reference to the level and page in the basal reader that the child had made it up to at that point in time. Informal testing with the basal word list and the WRAT was conducted in December and May, with the Gates-McGinitie being administered in

May. The aptitude measures were administered either prior to the start of the school year (in two schools at the end of kindergarten) or at the beginning of first grade (in the remaining school).

The data were analyzed for relationships between grouping and pacing patterns and the students' performance on the three reading measures. These analyses were conducted for each of the reading measures, with the three ability levels considered for differential effects. For the most part, the data were analyzed separately for the three schools. The variation in pacing within the homogeneous (i.e., the whole-class instruction) school (A) was found to be small in comparison to the variation within the school with ability grouping (B). There was considerable variation in pacing between the four classes in the third school (C).

In terms of relationships to the reading outcome measures, Barr found that word learning was higher for both the average- and high-ability students in differentially paced classrooms than for comparable students in a homogeneous (whole-class) or a slow-paced context. In general, a faster rather than a slower pace was found to be facilitating. In addition to the finding that pacing has a substantial affect on word learning at the end of the first grade, her analysis revealed that this word learning accounted for a significant portion of the variance in word recognition measured at the end of the first grade. Follow-up testing a year later on a sample of the original group of students revealed that word learning at the end of the first grade also accounted for a significant portion of the variance in vocabulary and comprehension measured at the end of second grade. Barr found that all of the low-ability groups were paced slowly. She concluded that the differential pacing designed to accommodate the needs of these children does not appear to hold any promise or pay off in terms of successful reading development.

The Teaching of Good and Poor Reading Groups

Barr's findings relative to differences in instruction associated with reading groups overlap with several programs of research exploring the differences in teaching associated with good and poor reading groups. One notable characteristic of these programs is the diversity of research paradigms that have been utilized to study teaching.

McDermott (1976, 1977) studied two reading groups (one high achieving, one low achieving) over the course of one year. He combined both macro and micro ethnographic approaches to the study of teacher-pupil interaction patterns. At the macro level, he visited the classroom several times each week as a participant observer of instruction. He interacted freely with the students and the teacher in an effort to uncover intentions and understandings of instruction. At the micro level, McDermott filmed the high and low reading groups during instruction. These films were subjected to a frame-by-frame analysis of verbal participation as well as nonverbal behaviors of teachers and students. Based on these extensive analyses, he was able to document differences in the instructional environment for each group. In the high group, the students were found to be engaged three times as much as the students in the low group. In the high group, ordered turns for oral reading with a set amount of reading for each student was the rule, In the low group, there was a bidding for turns with no fixed order. It was observed that certain students in the low group (the poorest reader in particular) might not get a chance to read at all in a group session. Interruptions in the low-reading-group session were found to be twenty times more common than in the high group.

McDermott argues that the social organization of the low group makes it a difficult context in which to learn to read. He does not believe that the differential treatment was consciously imposed by the teacher. Rather, the differences reflect the negotiations between the teacher and the struggling students to avoid embarrassment and complete the work for the day with some semblance of order.

McDermott's research (and most of the sociolinguistic classroom research of this period) challenges the notion that teaching effects can be studied in a unidirectional pattern. Teaching effects are interactive and reflect negotiated behaviors and working relationships.

Allington (1978) conducted a study into the content of teacher verbal behaviors during reading instruction and the impact these actions had upon the development of reading ability. The specific focus for the study was on teacher interruption behaviors during oral reading sessions. Twenty primary-grade teachers participated in this study. Two reading group sessions were audiorecorded for each teacher: one with a group identified by the teacher as his or her best and one with a group identified by the teacher as his or her worst. Copies of the reading materials used in these sessions were collected and analyzed for number of pages read, number of words read in the text, and the errors made by each child while reading. All responses that did not agree with the text were counted as errors. Teacher interruption behaviors were coded in terms of two dimensions: point of interruption (at the error, after the error but before the next phrase or sentence break, and at the next phrase or sentence break); and direction of interruption (graphic, phonemic, semantic/syntactic, teacher pronounce, and other). Significant differences were found in the proportion of interruptions with the poor readers interrupted at a higher rate (68% of the errors for the lows, 24% of the errors for the highs). Poor readers were also more likely to be interrupted at the point of the error. Poor readers were found to have read more pages but fewer words than the good readers. Allington suggests that the differential treatment afforded to poor readers might be a contributing cause to their disability.

Hoffman and Clements (1984) found that the less-skilled second-grade readers in their study of oral reading interactions were given less time in reading groups, had less engaged time in actual reading, and experienced less task success (i.e., a higher error rate) than the more-skilled readers. They described the more-skilled readers in their study as making mainly substitution-type miscues that affected meaning only slightly and did not resemble the grapho-phonic characteristics of the text word being read. The more-skilled readers were likely to continue reading in the text after a miscue of this type without bothering to self-correct and without interruption from the teacher. With more difficult words, the more-skilled readers were likely to mispronounce—showing strong use of grapho-phonic analysis—and then immediately self-correct or make repeated attempts at the word, again without interruption from the teacher until the word was successfully identified. Less-skilled readers also made primarily substitution miscues; however, these miscues did resemble the grapho-phonic features of the text word and also substantially affected text meaning. In such instances, the teacher was likely to interrupt immediately to give the correct word. With more difficult words, the less-skilled readers hesitated and all but waited for assistance, which the teacher quickly obliged by giving the text word. Hoffman and Clements suggest that these interactive patterns are best interpreted in terms of the ways in which teachers and students are each influencing the behavior of the other. They propose that teachers and student groups have tacitly negotiated an efficient system to make it through the task of oral reading of basal materials such that there is a minimum of disruption to activity flow within the lesson and a maximum amount of content coverage.

In a subsequent field-based study of 22 second-grade teachers interacting with their high and low reading groups over an entire semester, Hoffman et al. (1984) found similar patterns of behavior. They discovered strong ties between pupil oral-reading behaviors and teacher verbal-feedback behaviors. These interactive patterns were interpreted as logically reinforcing of one another and supportive of the development of stable behavioral routines. The long-term effects (in terms of reading strategies and achievement) were shown to be debilitating to the low-skilled reader.

Studies of this type suggest something of the mechanisms for the ways in which management and instruction seem to set in motion vectors for achievement in reading that are powerful. Stanovich (1986) has recently described this phenomenon in terms of the "Matthew effect," or "the rich get richer and the poor get poorer." What manifest themselves as small ability differences in first grade (perhaps a function of individual developmental differences) become the basis for decisions (e.g., grouping for instruction) that set in motion certain patterns of instruction (e.g., a differentiated curriculum, reduced time for reading, disabling feedback to reading performance, etc.) that result in different rates of learning. The differences that were small at the beginning of the first grade become substantial by the end of the first grade, and perhaps unremedial by the end of primary grades.

Sources of Influence on Teaching Behavior

Several programs of research have been designed to identify the sources of influence on teacher behaviors as they engage in instructional decision making. The two areas that have received the most attention are (1) teacher beliefs and (2) curricular materials.

It has been assumed that teachers, as they engage in their professional role, are influenced by their knowledge, beliefs, and commitments regarding students, the curriculum, and classrooms. At least two instruments have been developed with the goal of assessing teachers' beliefs. The first of these is the DeFord (1978, 1985) Theoretical Orientation to Reading Profile (TORP), which contains items reflecting accepted practices and beliefs about reading. The TORP was designed within the framework proposed by Harste and Burke (1977). Research with this instrument indicates that it is a one-factor test measuring instruction in reading characterized by a continuum from isolation to integration of language. Research findings also indicate a fairly high agreement between teacher profiles generated by this instrument and holistic ratings made by independent observers of selected teachers during actual instruction. The second instrument was developed as part of the Conceptions of Reading Project at the Institute for Research in Teaching. The purpose of this instrument is to characterize teacher beliefs about reading in terms of standard instructional models (i.e., basal text, linear skills, natural language, interest-based, and integrated curriculum models). Research with the Proposition about Reading Instructional Inventory (PRI) has led the authors to conclude that it is an efficient and reliable tool for assessing teacher beliefs about reading (Duffy & Metheny, 1979).

Buike, Burke, and Duffy (1980) reported a large-scale study of teacher beliefs and their relationship to teaching practices using the PRI. This study attempted to relate the reading conceptions of 23 elementary school teachers to instructional practices. They found only superficial support for the hypothesis that teachers operate from implicit theories of reading during actual instruction. Teachers' decisions seemed more influenced by such factors as characteristics of the curriculum (i.e., the adopted basal series), features of the context (e.g., student ability, class size), and the pressure on teachers to manage classroom events (e.g., by attending to "activity flow," content coverage, etc.)

Several researchers have examined the influence of curriculum on teaching. Durkin (1984) conducted an investigation into the influence of suggestions in the basal teachers' guides on teaching. She observed teachers from three grade levels: first ($N = 5$), third ($N = 6$), and fifth ($N = 5$). The observations took place over two days for each teacher. She catalogued each activity observed in terms of (a) followed recommendation, (b) followed recommendation in altered form, or (c) not in manual. A follow-up interview was conducted with all teachers to explore motivations and confirm accuracy of data collection. She discusses several patterns in the use of basal recommendations by teachers. Teachers tended to ignore suggestions for prereading activities (e.g., vocabulary teaching, building conceptual background), and demonstrated a great deal of reliance on the guide for postreading activities (e.g., questioning, written practice assignments). There was a generous use of written practice in the form of worksheets and workbook pages. Across the different grade levels, she found more similarities than differences. Omission of activities suggested in the manuals was explained by teachers in terms of time constraints and lack of importance.

In a study focused on the influence of the basal manual on teacher instruction in reading groups, Shake and Allington (1985) examined the patterns of questioning. They studied six elementary teachers for three reading lessons each. They found that 79 percent of the questions asked were not included in the manual. The remaining 21 percent were found explicitly stated in the manual. It is not clear what portion this 21 percent is of the total number presented in the manual. These data suggest, though, that teachers do go beyond the manual in their question-asking strategies.

Barr and Sadow (1989) studied the use of two different basal reading programs by seven fourth-grade teachers in two school districts. They examined the organization of the basal materials, the use of the materials in relation to their design, the use of time, and the teachers' adherence to recommendations in the basal guidebooks. They found that the two basal series, while similar in content, differed greatly in terms of design complexity. Further, they found that the design characteristics had an influence on the extent to which materials were assigned and read. Both series had an emphasis on skills activities, and this was reflected in the instructional emphasis. Finally, there was considerable variance in the degree to which teachers seemed to rely on the basal for direction. Their data suggest that the degree of reliance on suggestions from the manual tends to vary from one teacher to another, but may be consistent for the individual teacher. For example, some teachers tended to rely heavily on the manual as the source of most of their questioning, while other teachers did not appear to be guided at all in their questioning by the manual. Barr and Sadow draw implications for their research into areas of staff development, program design features, and future research.

The research in this area has advanced our understanding of the sources of influence on teacher behaviors in instructional decision making. Teacher beliefs exert some influence, in particular when the orientation is strong and biased toward an extreme position. Often, though, the effects for beliefs are overwhelmed by features of the instructional context such as adopted materials. Studies suggest the important role that instructional materials exert over teacher instructional activities. The short-term effects are documented, in the case of the Barr and Sadow study, in terms of coverage of material and engaged time in various types of activities.

Comprehension Instruction

Durkin was responsible for a series of studies into the nature of reading comprehension instruction in the elementary grades. Durkin (1979) devised a definition of reading comprehension from her review of the existing literature, the findings from a pilot study, and her own theories and conceptions regarding the nature of reading. In her terms,

> Comprehension: instruction-teacher does/says something to help children understand or work out the meaning of more than a single, isolated word. (p. 488).

In addition to this definition for comprehension instruction, several other conceptual categories were devised. These included: comprehension: application; comprehension: assessment; comprehension: an assignment; comprehension: helps with assignment; comprehension: review of instruction; comprehension: preparation for reading;

and comprehension: prediction. Several categories for what Durkin terms "other kinds of instruction" were also developed. These included phonics (instruction, review, and application); structural analysis (instruction, review, and application); word meanings (instruction, review, and application); assignment (gives help with and checks); and study skills (instruction, review, application, and assignment).

The specific purpose for the study was to find out how much time was allotted to comprehension instruction in elementary schools. Observations were made of teachers during both reading periods and social studies periods. The project comprised three "substudies." The first substudy was focused on comprehension instruction in fourth-grade classrooms. The rationale offered for this focus was that the fourth grade is commonly regarded as a pivotal time in the transition of reading instruction from a focus on "learning to read" to a focus on "reading to learn." The second substudy examined comprehension instruction in grades three through six across a number of school sites to determine if there is a great deal of variation across different settings. The third substudy focused on individual children in an effort to describe comprehension instruction from the student's vantage point. The data for all three studies were drawn from observations in each classroom over a three-successive-day period.

In substudy one, 24 fourth-grade classrooms were observed for a total of 4,469 minutes in reading and 2,775 minutes in social studies. Durkin reports that less than one percent of the reading time was spent in "comprehension: instruction." No comprehension instruction was observed for the social studies period. For the reading period, the teachers spent their greatest amount of time in "comprehension: assessment" (17.65%); next was "noninstruction" (10.72%); followed by "transition" (10.75%); and then "listens to oral reading" (9.67%).

In substudy two, 12 classrooms in grades three through six were observed (four each in three schools). The total observation time for the reading period in these schools was: first school = 694 minutes; second school = 670 minutes; and third school = 810 minutes. "Comprehension: instruction" was observed only in the second school (4 minutes). No "comprehension instruction" was observed during this time in the other two schools. Overall, Durkin notes that the patterns observed for comprehension instruction were more similar than different for these schools and seemed to replicate what was found in the fourth-grade study.

Substudy three involved the direct observation of three students arbitrarily selected from average readers in three classrooms. Two of the students were girls (one from third grade and one from sixth). The other student was a fifth-grade boy. No administrators or teachers were aware that these children had been identified for observation. The classrooms were visited for observations approximately every three weeks on three successive days from September to May. The total time spent in observations of each of the children during the reading period was 1,548 minutes for the third grader, 1,957 minutes for the fifth grader, and 1,439 minutes for the sixth grader. For the third-grade student, the greatest amount of observed time was spent writing (32.75%), followed by listening (27.77%), noninstruction (9.24%), reading silently (8.91%), and transitions (4.07%). For the fifth-grade student, the greatest amount of observed time was spent writing (43.33%), followed by noninstruction (21.00%), reading silently (12.01%), listening (11.85%), and transitions (4.75%). For the sixth-grade student, the greatest amount of time was spent writing (39.05%), followed by listening (24.25%), noninstruction (11.40%), following another student reading orally (8.83%), and transitions (4.24%). Less than 1 percent of the total time for all students was spent listening to comprehension instruction. The analysis of the time these same three children spent during the social studies period was similar in terms of student engagement.

Durkin summarizes the findings from her research in terms of four points. First, there was practically no comprehension instruction observed. Second, other kinds of reading instruction were observed infrequently. She asserts that one cannot argue that comprehension instruction was not going on because teachers were busy doing something else. Third, rather than being comprehension instructors, teachers were more often found to be interrogators, assignment givers, and mentioners. Fourth, none of the teachers seemed to see social studies as a time to improve children's comprehension abilities. Durkin comments with surprise that teachers seemed to resort to the teacher's manuals only occasionally for direction. Rather, it was the materials that the students were expected to complete that seemed to be driving instruction.

As a follow-up to this observational study, Durkin (1981) conducted a detailed analysis of the directions for comprehension instruction included in five popular basal reading series. The rationale for this was that there is a widely held notion that basal manuals are driving instruction. Finding so little comprehension instruction going on in schools may be explained by the fact that teachers are not given enough direction or guidance in how to achieve this aspect of the curriculum.

The same taxonomy used for the classroom observations of reading comprehension instruction was adapted for use in the basal analysis. Each page of the manuals for the five series (kindergarten through sixth grade) was read and coded. Procedures related to comprehension were identified for each series. The procedures were categorized in terms of their type (i.e., instruction, review, application, practice, preparation, and assessment). While a great deal of variation is apparent in the statistics used to describe the frequency of occurrence in the five series, Durkin asserts that the similarities are more apparent than the differences. Similarities were apparent between the procedures targeted in the manual and the activities captured in the observational study. One common characteristic was the emphasis on practice exercises. Another common feature is the heavy reliance on assessment.

Criticism of Durkin's work has focused primarily on the restricted operational definition for comprehension instruction that may discount teacher actions that facilitate children's understanding of text (Hodges, 1980). It is clear, though, that Durkin's research generated an enormous amount of discussion in professional circles regarding why there is so little comprehension instruction in classrooms. The study does not have a great deal to say directly about teaching and learning if one assumes a process-product view of judging value. As Shulman (1986) points out, however, Durkin's observational study is a good example of how knowledge of teaching can be informed by taking a normative model for "good instruction" and examining its occurrence in the real world of classrooms. For this reason, it seems, Durkin's findings have been so widely accepted and so influencial. She represented the prevailing view of good comprehension instruction in her observational instrument and she carefully documented its absence in classroom instruction.

Story Discussions

Au (1980) and Au and Mason (1981) report on a series of investigations into teacher-pupil participation patterns during reading group lessons. This research was conducted with disadvantaged children enrolled in the Kamehameha Early Education Program (KEEP) in Hawaii. Au was interested in exploring the hypothesis that the difficulties minority children experience in schools can be attributed to the fact that the dominant social organization patterns for participation in schools are different from those the children have experienced in their own home culture.

Au's initial study was focused on an analysis of the participation structures used by one KEEP teacher during a reading group lesson. *Participation structures* refer to the different rules that govern speaking, listening, and turn taking at different points in an event. In contrast to the model for discussions represented in basal manuals, lessons taught in the KEEP reading program are designed to be similar to "talk story," a major speech event in Hawaiian culture. The talk story is characterized by mutual participation in conarration. The teacher, as the adult, assumes a receptive role. The purpose of the study was to examine the participation structures when a teacher was using this talk-story framework.

There were four children working with the teacher in the 20-minute lesson that was analyzed. Nine different participation structures were identified. The majority of the participation structures, and in particular those relied on most often, resembled the talk story in the sense that there was a great deal of joint verbal performance. Au notes that the typical context for talk story and the context of a typical lesson are quite different. Therefore, the teacher is constantly forced to say just enough in a controlling position to maintain order without becoming so intrusive as to discourage the free interchange of ideas. Lessons of this type, Au asserts, seem to encourage learning to read by allowing the children to engage in text discussion in participation structures compatible with those experienced outside the classroom.

In the second study, Au and Mason examined participation structures in reading group lessons under more experimentally controlled conditions. Videotapes of two teachers working with the same group of six disadvantaged second-grade Hawaiian students were analyzed. One teacher had little experience (Low Contact) in the past in working with native Hawaiian children, while the other teacher had considerable experience (High Contact) in working with this population. The teachers were similar in terms of years of formal education and overall teaching experience. The teacher with experience in working with Hawaiian children had a documented history of successful teaching in terms of the achievement gains made by her students over a three-year period. No information is provided on the expertise of the other teacher.

Each teacher conducted two reading lessons with the same group of students. There were four videotaped lessons in all. The teachers were directed to have the students read and discuss the story emphasizing comprehension. The analysis of the videotapes revealed a total of nine participation structures used by these two teachers. There was little overlap between the teachers in terms of the dominant structures relied on. For the most part, the High-Contact teacher tended to rely on joint participation structures that were consistent with the talk story framework. The Low-Contact teacher tended to rely mainly on more teacher-controlled and single participation structures.

Several proximal measures of performance were made in an effort to document the effects associated with the different participation structures used by these teachers. Engagement rate was lower in the Low-Contact teacher's lessons (43%) than in the High-Contact teacher's lessons (80%). Reading-related responses were 5.80 per minute in the Low-Contact teacher's lessons, and 10.08 per minute in the High-Contact teacher's lesson. Correct responses occurred at a rate of 5 per minute in the Low-Contact teacher's lessons and 9.13 per minute in the High. The rate of idea units discussed was 1.51 per minute for the Low-Contact teacher's lessons and 5.28 per minute in the High. This research suggests that different participation structures were used by these teachers and that the most positive effects were associated with the talk story framework.

Teacher Explanations

Duffy and Roehler and their colleagues at Michigan State University have been responsible for a series of studies into the explicitness of teacher explanations during reading instruction and its relationship to student development in reading. They were guided in this by the basic understanding that good readers and poor readers differ in their awareness of how to use comprehension strategies. Their goal was to determine whether explicitness in instruction was beneficial to the improvement of poor readers.

In one major field-based study, the subjects were 22 fifth-grade teachers and the students in their low reading groups (Duffy et al., 1986). All of the teachers were observed to document baseline practices with respect to management skills. Based on the findings from these observations, the teachers were stratified into three groups: high managers ($N = 8$), average managers ($N = 9$), and low managers ($N = 5$). Using these groups, teachers were then randomly assigned to treatment and control conditions. Student assignment to reading groups was made by the teachers based on Stanford Achievement Test scores from the previous years. All of the students in the low groups included in the study scored at least one year below their assigned grade level.

Each teacher was rated on "explicitness" of explanations. Two aspects of explanations were assessed, using the rating scale developed by these researchers. One aspect focused on what information was conveyed about the skills and processes being taught, and how this information was conveyed (what was said about the skill being taught, when it would be used, the features to attend to, the sequence to follow, and the examples used). The other aspect focused on the pedagogy, or the teacher's use of modeling, highlighting, feedback, review, practice, and application.

Student awareness data were obtained through interviews with five low-group students immediately following each of the four observed lessons subsequent to the baseline observation. Three questions were posed: What were you learning in the lesson I just saw? When would you use what was taught in the lesson? and, How do you do what you were taught to do? Overall achievement was measured using the Gates-McGinite on a pre/post basis. Treatment teachers received 10 hours of training on how to incorporate explicit explanations into their ongoing reading-skills instruction. The basic sequence of skills prescribed in the adopted basal series was followed. Five additional sessions (of two hours each) were conducted at approximately one-month intervals from November through March.

Results of the study indicated that the experimental teachers were successful in becoming more explicit in their explanations, surpassing the levels achieved by the control teachers. Students in the classes of the treatment teachers achieved higher awareness scores that those in the control. No significant difference was found, however, on the achievement measure.

In a subsequent study (Duffy et al., 1987), teacher explanations and their effects were again investigated in an experimental study. The subjects were 20 third-grade teachers and the students in their low reading groups. The methodology and focus were similar to those used in the first study, only additional measures of student achievement were utilized: two nontraditional measures, which reflected directly the skills and strategies taught; one standardized measure; and one maintenance measure administered five months after the end of the study. The results indicated that the treatment teachers did become more explicit than the controls and that the students in the treatment groups scored higher on awareness measures of skill and strategy use. Results on the achievement measures indicated statistically significant effects in favor of the experimental students on all measures.

Relating School Effects to Teaching Effects

The work of Barr and Dreeben (1983) is one of the few studies of teaching and school effects in reading that has investigated the kinds of mechanisms that bridge school and classroom processes. They propose a formulation for "how schools work," focused on the division of labor among levels of school organization. Decisions made at district and school levels appear to determine the resources available and other conditions that in turn influence the work of teachers. They argue that the larger organization plays a key role through control over the conditions under which teachers must operate. At the school level the role of the principal is crucial. "The principal's significant influence lies in the allocation and shaping of the schools' most basic resources: children's characteristics, learning materials, and time."

The principal deals the cards and the teacher must play the game with the hand that is dealt. One strategy teachers employ to "play the game" that seems to be of great influence on learning is that of forming and teaching reading groups. In their research, Barr and Dreeben observed "strikingly" large effects on learning that originate in the suborganization of classrooms in reading groups. Once the teacher forms reading groups, instruction is responsive to the mean aptitude of the group. This is reflected particularly and powerfully in the pace at which materials (e.g., basal books) are covered. Coverage in turn relates to numerous outcome measure (e.g., end-of-year achievement, basal words mastered).

Summary

These are the major research programs that have examined various aspects of teaching and schooling and their effects in learning to read. While not large in number, the findings have raised important issues regarding teacher effects in the organizing and pacing of instruction, in the differential treatment of good and poor reading groups, in comprehension instruction, in teacher explanations, and in the influence of curricular materials on instructional actions. Many of the studies reveal enormous discrepancies between the instruction offered in most classrooms and the kind of instruction that basic research suggests would most benefit learners. These studies also reveal that the fabric of instruction is tightly woven. While a particular study may focus on one source of influence (e.g., management concerns, curricular materials) or outcome of instruction (e.g., content coverage, strategy learning), the reality is that these influences and outcomes are always interacting as a part of any instructional experience. To study them is difficult. To isolate them is virtually impossible and likely undesirable.

SHORTCOMINGS OF CURRENT RESEARCH EFFORTS AND FUTURE DIRECTIONS

Considering the brief amount of time in which reading scholars have been actively investigating teaching and school effects, the results have been quite impressive. While the actual number of studies has been fairly small, the descriptive data base and the interpretations of them have been both informative and provocative. In the future, one would certainly hope to see even greater activity and productivity. There are several shortcomings that stand out when one looks back over this literature that, if addressed, may lead to even greater productivity.

The first shortcoming has to do with the fact that research into teaching and school effects in reading has been, by and large, atheoretical. The role of research is to affirm and inform scientific knowledge. Theories are our *representations* of scientific knowledge. They provide the *explanations* for what we observe, not merely descriptions of what we observe. The field has successfully moved beyond a "methods comparison" mentality for research, but the observational and even experimental studies of the past two decades often stop at description and then move directly on to discuss implications or applications related to practice. If a theoretical framework is drawn up, then it is often tied to models of learning or comprehension, not models for instruction, teaching, or schooling. The field of reading has prospered since the 1960s because scholars have made the effort to draw and test theories of the reading process. Many of these theories have been long abandoned, most have been modified, but most have contributed to programs of research that have had enormous payoff for the field. Research into teaching and school effects needs to become much more theoretical if it is to advance.

Initially, the move to a more theoretical orientation for research might take the form of some simple modeling of relationships among teaching and learning variables: not the kind of process-product studies correlating hundreds of teacher behaviors to some remote student achievement measures, but studies that examine more directly the relationships among classroom processes and the development of student strategies. Through subsequent studies designed to gather data that inform these models, the initial efforts can be refined into theoretical propositions.

The second shortcoming of research in the area of teaching reading is its preoccupation with what the teacher is doing or saying in classrooms. Whether it is counting the number of questions teachers ask or examining the praise statements offered by teachers, the focus is on the teacher's actions. The same holds true for the focus on what administrators do and say in schools. In part, this focus draws on the behavioristic, positivistic, quantitative traditions that have dominated educational research. In part, this focus draws on the process-product, input-output paradigms so popular in research in teaching and school effects during the 70s. The simple counts of behaviors and their correlation to achievement outcomes have yielded an enormous amount of data but not much insight into teaching, schooling, and learning. The lens of science has been focused on such a small area that the meaningfulness of the behaviors observed is lost without reference to the surrounding context. There is a growing consensus that this kind of research has taken us about as far as it can in understanding instruction and schools (Shulman, 1986).

The third shortcoming of research is the reliance one finds on quantitative experimental research traditions as the standard for good research. Deviations from this standard are viewed as flaws in the research program. The fact is that traditional quantitative research paradigms often do not apply well to important questions in research in teaching and program effects. The operationalization of outcome measures, the random selection of school sites and teachers from a broad population, the random assignment of teachers to treatments and of students to teachers, the systematic control over the application of a treatment condition and control conditions, and so on, create so many experimental demand characteristics as to make meaningful field-based research so incredibly expensive and nearly impossible that few participate. This is to say nothing of the fact that in creating such experimental conditions, the real processes of teaching and learning become hopelessly distorted. The field must become more eclectic and flexible in its research methods if broader participation and greater insights are to be achieved. Until the field is willing to embrace alternative research paradigms, both quantitative and qualitative, we are likely to continue to see precious few studies conducted and reported.

This is not to suggest that we should become in any way less rigorous. Slavin (1984) has suggested a quantitative paradigm described as "component building" that offers promise for studying complex innovations in teaching over time. Erickson (1986) proposes a framework and standards for qualitative research that are both challenging and insightful. Case study research (an area pioneered by researchers in the area of reading disabilities in the 1940s and 1950s) is to be valued. Single-subject experimental studies and time series designs are alternatives that are seldom used but potentially powerful in their capacity to inform field-based research. There is no perfect method for research into teaching and school effects. The method must be adapted to the nature of what is being studied. The situation we face today in research has much in common with the situation in teaching, where assessment techniques are driving instruction. The tail is wagging the dog. Questions derived from theoretical propositions should drive research so that the methods used are adapted to the situation.

Future Directions

Research into teaching and school effects must become more focused on important theoretical issues, more considerate of contextual factors implicit in field settings, and more adaptable in the use of research methods. These features must become the hallmark for the next generation of research if significant progress is to be made. There are any number of possible directions that research into teaching and school effects might take in the future. We may see an enormous increase in the number of large-scale evaluation studies as the pressure from the public for accountability increases. We may see a return to methods-comparison studies (under some new guise) as the debates in the professional literature over the best way to teach beginning reading continue. We may finally see the realization of the "teacher-as-researcher" movement that has remained on the fringes of educational research for so many years. While all of these and many others are possible, and some more promising than others, I will focus attention in this last section on just one direction for research that offers some promise for the future and lends itself to the criteria of being theoretical, contextual, and adaptable.

The TASK Framework for Research in Training and School Effects

The work of Doyle (1983) and others suggests that adopting a different perspective for looking in classrooms can lead to a quite different and potentially more complete view of teaching and learning relationships than has been achieved in the past. Rather than a focus on the teacher and what the teacher is doing, as in the process-product research perspective, the focus is on the learner and the "academic work" the learner is engaging in.

In the abstract, the academic-work view suggests a somewhat static model for teaching and learning. The teacher selects or develops work from the curriculum, structures work into tasks in ways appropriate to the context, and presents these to the students to complete. Active teaching occurs as the students are introduced to and guided through tasks. Learning arises in the student's association with and engagement in tasks. The teacher evaluates the students' learning based on the processes of engagement and the "products" they have generated.

In the reality of schools, in the dailiness of classroom life, the teaching-learning process is dynamic, not static. The dynamic process begins as the teacher engages in planning for instruction. For effective teachers this process is not as simplistic as consulting the teacher's guide, nor as idealistic as formulating an instructional objective and proceeding in some sort of linear planning model. The planning of teachers is interactive and unfolds in stages (Yinger, 1977). The dynamics of instruction continue in the negotiations that transpire between the teacher and the students as tasks are constructed and completed. The students negotiate from the point of reducing uncertainty in the learning environment. They seek a point of equilibrium between what they see themselves as capable of and willing to do and what the task demands are. The teacher negotiates from the point of creating uncertainty in the environment (in the form of task demands) in an effort to induce growth in ability.

How are the tasks negotiated? This would appear to be fertile ground for research. The students have at least one powerful negotiating point to use in their effort to reduce uncertainty: *cooperation*. In an ideal world, the teacher is after active engagement on the part of all students. But she or he will likely settle for cooperation in the task by some students as long as most are engaged. What the teacher cannot tolerate are high levels of uncooperative or disruptive behavior that threaten the work system of the classroom. Without the general tone of cooperation in the classroom the teacher has no basis from which to negotiate. The teacher can call on several strategies in the negotiation process. The teacher can reduce the risk associated with the task in any number of ways (e.g., reducing the number of items to be completed in a time period, allowing students of mixed ability to work together toward a common grade). The teacher can manipulate consequences (e.g., by announcing that performance on the task will not be graded at all, by assuring students that performance will not count toward a final grade, or by promising "extra credit" for effort and performance on the task). The teacher can reduce the ambiguity of the task (e.g., providing the students with a model of what is to be turned in, giving more explicit specifications for the product). Finally, the teacher can manipulate effort by adjusting the resources available to the students to perform the task (e.g., providing students with a collection of reference material, being available to respond to questions or concerns during task work).

If the teacher negotiates away too much, then the opportunity for significant learning may be lost. If the teacher fails to negotiate at all, then the teacher puts at risk the order of the classroom. The default option, and one that unfortunately is common in elementary schools today, is for the teacher to initially plan for and present tasks that are so low in risk, ambiguity, consequence, and effort demands that there is no real need for students to engage in negotiation. This is one explanation for why elementary classrooms are filled with academic work (typically ditto sheets) that is at a simple memory or recall level.

What kinds of tasks are presented to students during reading instruction? How are these tasks selected, structured, and negotiated with students? What processes of interaction and learning are associated with these tasks? These are the kinds of questions that our current research base does not shed much light on at all; and yet, from a task perspective, this information is central to understanding instruction.

The task framework is potentially useful in examining the relationship among classroom and school-level processes. As just one example, consider the system used by the principal to evaluate teachers. In states where observation systems have been derived from the process-product literature (e.g., Florida and Texas), the teacher who does best is the one who has a well-managed classroom and who engages students frequently in small- or large-group direct instruction. In order to perform well on such an appraisal instrument, it is the interest of the teacher to reduce the ambiguity, risk, consequence, and effort characteristics of tasks in order to achieve high levels of cooperation. Does such an evaluation system encourage the use of low-level memory tasks during instruction?

Adoption of the task framework for research in teaching and school effects is a direction that would help address the shortcomings of current research described earlier. In terms of a theoretical framework, the task and academic frameworks suggest important relationships among the key variables in instruction that are associated with learning. It is a basis upon which models of teaching, schooling, and learning can be posited. It can serve as the basis for extending and refining the seminal work of Carroll (1963) in his model of schooling and learning that focuses on the importance of pupils' behaviors and activities as central to their learning.

The task perspective encourages a contextualized view of instruction. Studies of tasks must take into consideration not just the teacher's behaviors, but also the nature of the curriculum, the characteristics of the work system in the classroom, the learning outcomes, and so on.

Finally, the task framework is one that is amenable to many different paradigms for research. From a qualitative framework, researchers might be interested in examining the conceptions of tasks from the perspective of the participants. What is the students' conception of the task? How might students with different entering experiences construct a different meaning for the same task represented by a teacher? What is the teacher's conception of the task? From a quantitative framework, researchers might be interested in examining the effects of participation and the structuring of tasks on learning. Perhaps most important, the task perspective can be used easily and effectively in small-scale carefully conducted studies.

Summary

Looking over the past two decades of research reports published in the *Reading Research Quarterly*, one finds only a handful that relate to the study of teaching and school effects. In contrast, out of the ten or so editorial commentaries that have appeared in this journal during the same two decades, over three-quarters focus on the need for more research in teaching and school effects. This investigation began with the goal of examining the scientific base for teaching and school effects. We must conclude that at this point in time the glass of "knowledge" is half full. Looking at where we are today as compared to three decades ago in our understanding of the relationships among teaching, schools, and learning, progress has been remarkable. Looking at where we are today in relation to the questions that still stand before us, one is less inclined to do much back patting. I choose to believe that we are on the edge of a breakthrough in research in teaching and school effects. The breakthrough will come as more researchers, without enormous resources, but with a scientific model, move into schools to observe and systematically study reading instruction and learning to read in classrooms.

REFERENCES

Allington, R. L. (1978). *Are good and poor readers taught differently? Is that why poor readers are poor readers?* Paper presented at the annual meeting of the American Educational Research Association, Toronto.

Anderson, H. H. (1939). The measurement of domination and of socially integrative behavior in teachers' contacts with children. *Child Development, 10,* 73–89.

Anderson, L., Evertson, C., & Brophy, J. (1979). An experimental study of effective teaching in first-grade reading groups. *Elementary School Journal, 79,* 193–223.

Armor, D., Osegura, P., Cox, M., King, N., McDonnell, L., Pascal A., Pauly, E., & Zellmon, G. (1975). *Analysis of the school preferred reading program in selected Los Angeles minority schools.* Los Angeles: Rand Corporation. (ERIC Document Reproduction Service No. ED 130 243).

Au, K. H. (1980). Participation structures in a reading lesson with Hawaiian children. Analysis of a culturally appropriate instructional event. *Anthropology and Education Quarterly, 11,* 91–115.

Au, K. H., & Mason, J. M. (1981). Social organization factors in learning to read: The balance of rights hypotheses. *Reading Research Quarterly, 17,* 115–152.

Austin, G. R. (1978). *Process evaluation. A comprehensive study of outliers.* Baltimore: Maryland State Department of Education.

Austin, M. C., & Morrison, C. (1961). *The torchlighters: Tommorrow's teachers of reading.* Cambridge, MA: Harvard University Press.

Austin, M. C. & Morrison, C. (1963). *The first "R": The Harvard report on reading in elementary schools.* New York: Macmillan.

Barr, A. S., Becholt, B., Coxe, W., Gage, N. L., Orleans, J., Remmers, H., & Ryans, D. Report of the Committee on the Criteria of Teacher Effectiveness. *Review of Educational Research, 22,* 238–263.

Barr, R. (1974). Instructional pace differences and their effect on reading acquisition. *Reading Research Quarterly, 9*(8), 526–554.

Barr, R., & Dreeben, R. (1983). *How schools work.* Chicago: University of Chicago Press.

Barr, R., & Sadow, M. W. (1989). Influence of basal programs on fourth-grade reading instruction. *Reading Research Quarterly, 24,* 44–71.

Bear, D. E. (1964). Two methods of teaching phonics: A longitudinal study. *Elementary School Journal, 64,* 273–279.

Becker, W. C. (1977). Teaching reading and language to the disadvantaged: What we have learned from field research. *Harvard Educational Review, 47,* 518–543.

Bond, G. L., & Dykstra, R. (1967). The cooperative research program in first-grade reading instruction. *Reading Research Quarterly, 2,* 10–141.

Brookover, W., Beady, C., Flood, P., Schweitzer, J., & Wisenbaker, J. (1979). *School social systems and student achievement.* New York: Praeger.

Brookover, W., & Lazotte, L. (1979). *Changes in school characteristics coincident with changes in student achievement* (Occasional paper No. 17) East Lansing, MI: Institute for Research in Teaching. (ERIC Document Reproduction Service No. ED 181 005)

Brophy, J. (1973). Stability of teacher effectiveness. *American Educational Research Journal, 10,* 245–252.

Buike, R., Burke, E., & Duffy, G. (1980, May). *Teacher conceptions of reading as they influence instructional decisions and pupil outcomes.* Paper presented at the annual conference of the International Reading Association, St. Louis.

Buswell, G. T. (1922). *Fundamental reading habits: A study of development.* Supplementary Educational Monographs. Chicago: University of Chicago Press.

Buswell, G. T. (1945). Non-oral reading: A study of its use in Chicago Public Schools. Supplementary Educational Monograph #60, Chicago, IL.: University of Chicago Press.

Carroll, J. (1963). A model of school learning. *Teachers College Record, 64.* 723–733.

Chall, J. S. (1967). *Learning to read: The great debate.* New York: McGraw-Hill.

Chall, J. S., & Feldman, S. (1966). First-grade reading: An analysis of the interactions of professed methods, teacher implementation, and child background. *Reading Teacher, 19,* 569–575.

Coleman, J., Campbell, E., Hobson, C., McPartland, J., Mood, A., Weinfield, F., & York, R. (1966). *Equality of educational opportunity.* Washington, DC: U.S. Government Printing Office.

DeFord, D. (1978). *A validation study of an instrument to determine teachers' theoretical orientation to reading instruction.* Unpublished doctoral dissertation, Indiana University.

DeFord, D. (1985). Validating the construct of theoretical orientation in reading instruction. *Reading Research Quarterly, 20*(3) 351–367.

Downing, J. A. (1963). *Experiments with Pitman's initial teaching alphabet in British schools.* London: Initial Teaching Publishing Company.

Doyle, W. (1983). Academic work. *Review of Educational Research, 53,* 159–199.

Duffy, G., & Metheny, W. (1979). The development of an instrument to measure teacher beliefs about reading. In M. Kamil & A. Moe (Eds.), *Twenty-Eighth Yearbook of the National Reading Conference.* Clemson, SC: National Reading Conference.

Duffy, G. G., Roehler, L. R., Meloth, M. S., Vavrus, L. G., Book, C., Putnam J., & Wesselman, R. (1986). The relationship between explicit verbal explanations during reading skill instruction and student awareness and achievement: A study of reading teacher effects. *Reading Research Quarterly, 21,* 237–252.

Duffy, G. G., Roehler, L. R., Sivan, E., Rackliffe, G., Book, C., Meloth, M. S., Vavrus, L. G., Wesselman, R., Putnam, J., & Bassiri, D. (1987). Effects of explaining the reasoning associated with using reading strategies. *Reading Research Quarterly, 20,* 347–368.

Dunkin, M., & Biddle, B. (1974). *The study of teaching.* New York: Holt, Rinehart & Winston.

Durkin, D. (1979). What classroom observations reveal about reading comprehension instruction. *Reading Research Quarterly, 14*(4), 481–533.

Durkin, D. (1981). Reading comprehension instruction in five basal reader series. *Reading Research Quarterly, 16,* 515–544.

Durkin, D. (1984) Is there a match between what elementary school teachers do and what basal manuals recommend? *Reading Teacher, 37,* 734–749.

Edmunds, R. R. (1983). *Progress of school improvement: An overview.* Paper presented at the Implications of Research on Teaching for Practice Conference, Airle House, Virginia.

Erickson, F. (1986). Qualitative methods in research on teaching. In M. Wittrock (Ed.). *Handbook of research in teaching* (3rd ed., pp. 119–161). New York: Macmillan.

Farr, R., & Weintraub, S. (1974) In this issue. *Reading Research Quarterly, 9.*

Fisher, C., Berliner, D., Filby, N., Marliave, R., Cahen, L., & Dishaw, M. (1980). Teaching behaviors, academic learning time, and student achievement: An overview. In C. Denham and A. Lieberman (Eds.), *Time to learn.* Washington, DC: National Institute of Education.

Flanders, N. (1965). *Teacher influence, pupil attitudes, and achievement* (Cooperative Research Monograph No. 12). Washington, DC: U.S. Office of Education.

Flanders, N. (1970). *Analyzing teacher behavior.* Reading, MA: Addison-Wesley.

Furst, N., & Amidon, E. (1965). Teacher-pupil interaction patterns in the teaching of reading in the elementary school. *The Reading Teacher, 18*(4), 283–287.

Gates, A. I. (1937). The necessary mental age for beginning reading. *Elementary School Journal, 37,* 497–508.

Gray, W. S. (1933). *Improving instruction in reading: An experimental study.* Chicago: University of Chicago Press.

Gray, W. S. (1960). The teaching of reading. In *Encyclopedia of Educational Research.* New York: Macmillan.

Guszak, F. J. (1967). Teacher questioning and reading. *Reading Teacher, 21,* 227–234.

Harris, A. J., & Serwer, B. L. (1966). The CRAFT Project: Instructional time in reading research. *Reading Research Quarterly, 2,* 27–56.

Harste, J., & Burke, C. (1977) A new hypothesis for reading teacher research: Both the teaching and learning of reading are theoretically based. In P. D. Pearson (Ed.), *Twenty-Sixth Yearbook of the National Reading Conference* (pp. 32–40). Clemson, SC: National Reading Conference.

Hodges, C. A. (1980). Toward a broader definition of comprehension instruction. *Reading Research Quarterly, 15,* 299–306.

Hoffman, J. V., & Clements, R. (1984). Reading miscues and teacher verbal feedback. *Elementary School Journal, 84,* 423–440.

Hoffman, J. V., O'Neal, S. F., Kastler, L. A., Clements, R. O., Segel, K. W., & Nash, M. F. (1984). Guided oral reading and miscue focused verbal feedback in second-grade classrooms. *Reading Research Quarterly, 19*, 367–384.

Hoffman, J. V., & Rutherford, W. L. (1984). Effective reading programs: A critical review of outlier studies. *Reading Research Quarterly, 20*, 79–92.

Mazurkiewicz, A. J. (1964). Teaching reading in America using the initial teaching alphabet. *Elementary English, 41*, 766–772.

McDade, J. (1944). Examination of a recent criticism of non-oral beginning reading. *Elementary School Journal, 44*, 343–351.

McDermott, R. (1976). *Kids make sense: An ethnographic account of the interactional management of success and failure in one first-grade classroom.* Unpublished doctoral dissertation, Stanford University.

McDermott, R. (1977). Social relations as contexts for learning in school. *Harvard Educational Review, 47*, 198–213.

McDowell, J. B. (1953). Report on the phonetic method of teaching children to read. *Catholic Education Review, 51*, 506–519.

Meyer, L. (1984). Long-term academic effects of the Direct Instruction Project Follow Through. *Elementary School Journal, 84*, 380–394.

New York State Office of Education Performance Review (1974). *School factors influencing reading achievement: A performance review.* Albany, NY. (ERIC Document Reproduction Service No. ED 089 211)

Odden, A., & Dougherty, U. (1982). *State programs of school improvement: A 50-state survey.* Denver, CO: Education Commission of the States.

Purkey, S., & Smith, M. (1983) Effective schools: A review. *Elementary School Journal, 83*(4), 427–452.

Ralph, J. H., & Fennessey, J. (1983). Science or reform: Some questions about the effective schools models. *Phi Delta Kappan, 64*(10), 689–694.

Rohrer, J. H. (1943). An analysis and evaluation of the (non-oral) method of reading instruction. *Elementary School, 43*, 415–421.

Rosenshine, B., & Furst, N. (1973). The use of direct observation to study teaching. In R. M. W. Travers (Ed.), *Second handbook of research on teaching* (pp. 122–183). Chicago: Rand McNally.

Rosenshine, B., & Stevens, R. (1984). Classroom instruction in reading. In P. D. Pearson, R. Barr, M. L. Kamil, & P. Mosenthal (Eds.), *Handbook of reading research* (Vol. 1) (pp. 745–798). White Plains, NY: Longman.

Rosenthal, R., & Jacobson, L. (1968). *Pygmalion in the classroom.* New York: Holt, Rinehart & Winston.

Russell, D. H. & Fea, H. (1963). Research on teaching reading. In N. L. Gage (Ed.) *Handbook of Research in Teaching* (pp. 865–928.) Chicago: Rand McNally.

Rutherford, W. (1968). Learning to read: A critique. *Elementary School Journal, 69*, 72–83.

Shake, M., & Allington, R. (1985) Where do teachers' questions come from? *Reading Teacher, 38*, 432–438.

Shavelson, R. J., & Berliner, D. C. (1988). Evasion of the education research infrastructure: A reply to Finn. *Educational Researcher, 17*, 9–11.

Shulman, L. S. (1986). Paradigms and research programs in the study of teaching: A contemporary perspective. In M. Wittrock (Ed.), *Handbook of research in teaching* (3rd ed., pp. 3–36). New York: Macmillan.

Slavin, R. E. (1984). Component building: A strategy for research-based instructional improvement. *Elementary School Journal, 84*, 255–269.

Smith, N. B. (1965). *American Reading Instruction.* Newark, DE: International Reading Association.

Soar, R. S., & Soar, R. M. (1979). Emotional climate and management. In P. Peterson and H. Walbert (Eds.), *Research on teaching: Concepts, findings, and implications.* Berkeley, CA: McCutchan.

Sparks, P. E., & Fay, L. C. (1957). An evaluation of two methods of teaching reading. *Elementary School Journal, 57*, 386–390.

Stallings, J., & Kaskowitz, D. (1974). *Follow through classroom observation evaluation 1972–1973* (SRI Project URU-7370). Stanford, CA: Stanford Research Institute.

Stanovich, K. E. (1986). Matthew effects in reading: Some consequences of individual differences in the acquisition of literacy. *Reading Research Quarterly, 21*, 360–407.

Travers, R. M. W. (Ed.). (1973). *Second handbook of research on teaching.* Chicago: Rand McNally.

Venezky, R. L., & Winfield, L. (1979). *Schools that succeed beyond expectations in teaching reading* (Technical Report No. 1). Newark, DE: Department of Educational Studies, University of Delaware.

Weber, G. (1971). *Inner city children can be taught to read: Four successful schools* (CGE Occasional Papers No. 18). Council for Basic Education, Washington, DC. (ERIC Document Reproduction Service No. ED 057 125)

Wellisch, J., MacQueen, A., Carriere, R., & Duck, G. (1978). School management and organization in successful schools. *School of Education, 51*, 211–226.

Wilder, G. (1977). Five exemplary reading programs. In J. T. Guthrie (Ed.), *Cognition, curriculum, and comprehension* (pp. 57–68). Newark, DE: International Reading Association.

Yinger, R. J. (1977). *A study of teacher planning: Description and theory development using ethnographic and information-processing methods.* Unpublished doctoral dissertation, Michigan State University, East Lansing, MI.

33 SECONDARY SCHOOL READING

Donna E. Alvermann
and David W. Moore

Efforts toward reforming secondary schools frequently center on issues such as graduation requirements and conduct codes. A key issue often ignored is the quality of daily instruction. Critics of reform movements such as Passow (1986) have challenged researchers and educators to focus on the daily interactions between teachers and students as they encounter subject matter. To meet this challenge requires an understanding of the research on secondary school teacher-student interactions specific to reading.

In this chapter we review the research on reading practices in grades 7 through 12. The review is by no means exhaustive. Secondary reading has been an academic specialty since the early 1940s (Moore, Readence, & Rickelman, 1983), and a great quantity of research has accumulated (e.g., see Alvermann, Moore, & Conley, 1987; Berger & Robinson, 1982; Dupuis, 1984; Singer, 1983; Witte & Otto, 1981).

We have divided this chapter into five sections. The first section consists of a brief rationale for the special treatment of secondary school reading. The second section reviews the experimental research on teaching strategies and learning strategies designed to affect secondary students' learning from text. The third section describes actual reading practices that have predominated in secondary schools. Observational, ethnographic, and survey methodologies are most common here. Next, the fourth section presents reasons for the predominance of certain secondary reading practices. Conceptual and historical studies inform much of the discussion in this part of the chapter. The last section concludes with implications for future research.

RATIONALE

Volume 1 of the *Handbook of Reading Research* (Pearson, Barr, Kamil, & Mosenthal, 1984) did not include a chapter on secondary school reading; a separate chapter is appropriate in Volume 2 for at least two reasons: Secondary schooling differs from elementary schooling, and reading achievement at the secondary level is a highly visible educational and political issue.

Secondary Schooling

Subject-matter specialization is a central difference between elementary and secondary schooling (Confrey, 1982; Squire, in press; Knott, 1986). Unlike the child-centered environment and self-contained structure of elementary schools, secondary schools are characteristically departmentalized according to subject matter specialties. Along with departmentalization, subject-matter specialization is manifested in secondary teachers' goals, educational preparation, and teaching practices. Secondary teachers' goals are bound to the contents and skills related to their disciplines, whereas elementary teachers focus on basic literacy and numeracy skills (Firestone & Herriott, 1982; Goodlad, 1984). Feistritzer (1986) reported that secondary teachers believed their college educations prepared them in subject matter knowledge better than in areas such as instructional methods and classroom management; for elementary teachers, the reverse was true. Comparisons of secondary and elementary teachers' self-reports about teaching practices also reveal differences. Secondary teachers report an acceptance and implementation of traditional, lecture-oriented teaching more frequently than do elementary teachers (von Eschenbach & Ley, 1984; Ryans, 1960). Clear differences also exist between elementary and secondary schools relative to the size of enrollments, variability of student backgrounds, and developmental levels of the students.

In sum, secondary teachers generally work as specialists in their particular disciplines who have relatively little training in how to impart their knowledge to students. Elementary teachers tend to work as specialists in methodology who have the common purpose of teaching basic skills.

Secondary Reading Achievement

During the 1980s substantial national attention was devoted to the reading achievement of secondary school students. The publication of *A Nation at Risk* (National Commission on Excellence in Education, 1983) stimulated much of this attention when it cited declining literacy rates among secondary school students as one of the indicators of a failing educational system. Following this report, numerous ones from the political arena (Education Commission of the States, 1983; Green, 1987) and from academia (Ekstrom, Goertz, & Rock, 1986; Gross & Gross, 1985) attempted to document the literacy decline and recommend ways to combat it.

Despite widespread belief in a marked decline in reading achievement at the secondary level, one noteworthy study (Stedman & Kaestle, 1987) concluded that the decline was only slight, although literacy problems still existed. For instance, Stedman and Kaestle reported that the performance of certain groups of people and the acquisition of specific reading strategies were deficient. Other studies have shown that basic reading skills of at-risk students have improved but still are depressed, and higher-level interpretive and evaluative reading performance for most students is unsatisfactory (National Assessment of Educational Progress, 1985; Applebee, Langer, & Mullis, 1988). In addition, many secondary students lack efficient and flexible learning strategies. High school students have indicated that memorizing and rereading are their most common study strategies (Schallert & Tierney, 1980), and even college-bound juniors tend to employ one general learning strategy regardless of the topic or their familiarity with the material (Higginson, 1987).

Secondary reading achievement also is problematic because the criteria of literacy increase as occupational and social demands for literacy increase (Clifford, 1984; Kaestle, 1985; Resnick & Resnick, 1977). Maintaining the same absolute level of reading ability in schools actually means falling behind when the workplace and society present increasingly complex tasks (Compaine, 1987; Harker, 1985; Venezky, Kaestle, & Sum, 1987; Willinsky, 1987). Current conceptions of literacy emphasize *activities* in which people engage rather than *skills* to be learned (Langer, 1988).

To recapitulate, a chapter on secondary school reading in the second volume of the *Handbook of Reading Research* is justifiable. Secondary and elementary schooling differ. Furthermore, the extent of a decline in literacy in secondary schools is debatable, but it is clear that reading achievement at the secondary level needs to keep pace with the demands for increased levels of literacy.

EXPERIMENTAL RESEARCH ON SECONDARY READING PRACTICES

In this section we review the experimental research on strategies aimed at improving secondary school students' learning from text. We begin by detailing the search procedure used in the review process. Following that, we describe the relative effectiveness and ineffectiveness of the recommended teaching and learning strategies. We conclude by discussing several limitations in the experimental research.

Search Procedure

Initially, we examined six secondary reading methods textbooks (Estes & Vaughan, 1978; Herber, 1978; Readence, Bean, & Baldwin, 1985; Singer & Donlan, 1985; Vacca & Vacca, 1986; Vaughan & Estes, 1986) and compiled a list of learning-from-text strategies that the authors of these texts recommended using with secondary school students. We added to this list any new strategies found in Chapters 20 and 21 of the first volume of the *Handbook of Reading Research* (Pearson, et al., 1984); chapters 3 through 8 in *Landscapes: A State-of-the-Art Assessment of Reading Comprehension Research, 1974–1984* (Crismore, 1985); and Chapter 28 of the *Handbook of Research on Teaching* (Wittrock, 1986).

Next, we searched the following data bases for studies involving one or more of the strategies on our list: *Citation Index to Journals in Education, Resources in Education,* and *Dissertation Abstracts International.* Each data base was searched by hand and by computer from its beginning date. We also hand-searched the two yearbook series published by the National Reading Conference and the American Reading Forum, as well as the two monograph series on secondary reading published by Syracuse University and the University of Arizona. In addition, we looked for relevant titles in the reference lists of reviews of literature in a variety of journals published prior to the beginning dates of the data bases named above. After securing copies of the studies, we read each study involving students in grades 7 through 12. In instances where we were unable to obtain a dissertation or a copy of a paper cited in *Resources in Education,* we read the abstracts.

Like the pedagogical experiments reviewed by Pearson and Gallagher (1983), many of the studies that we reviewed consisted of short-term interventions conducted in situations that were not representative of actual classrooms. We referred to these studies as *decontextualized experiments* to distinguish them from the more contextualized ones. This distinction between contextualized and decontextualized research became the basis for the last four questions listed below. Answers to all five questions were recorded on index cards as we read each study. Later, this information was transferred to Tables 33.1 and 33.2

1. Was the strategy effective, ineffective, or mixed?
2. Was the experimental treatment involving the strategy added onto, rather than incorporated into, the normal classroom routine?
3. Did the experimenter, rather than the classroom teacher, introduce the treatment?
4. Was the text used in the experiment borrowed from another source or constructed specifically for the experiment rather than selected from among the texts routinely used in class?
5. Was the strategy's effectiveness tested without first providing students with instruction in the use of it?

The greater the number of affirmative responses we gave to questions two through five, the more decontextualized a study became from our point of view.

By the end of the review process, two lines of research into recommended secondary reading practices had emerged. These included *teaching strategies*, which typically were content focused and teacher initiated, and *learning strategies*, which were student directed and intended for building independence in reading and studying (Weinstein & Mayer, 1986; Weinstein & Underwood, 1985). In selecting the studies to include in the following discussion of effective and ineffective teaching and learning strategies, we set two criteria. One criterion was that there had to be an instructional intervention; thus, studies that looked at developmental changes in students' spontaneous use of strategies (e.g., Brown & Smiley, 1978) did not qualify for inclusion. A second criterion was that the experimental design had to include a control or a comparison group. Preference was also given to studies that were published, although exceptions were made in the case of dissertations on strategies for which little other research existed.

Teaching Strategies

Statistically significant differences that favored a teaching strategy group over a control or comparison group were found in 62 percent of the studies in Table 33.1. No facilitative effects were found in 27 percent of the studies, and mixed results were reported in 12 percent of the studies (e.g., the strategy was effective for one ability level of reader or for one type of dependent measure but not for others).

A considerable body of research exists on guides and adjunct questions used with students at the secondary level. Although students of varying ability levels tended to benefit from the use of reading and writing guides (Bean & Pardi, 1979; Berget, 1973; Martin, Konopak, & Martin, 1986; Vacca, 1975, 1978), above-average readers benefited the most (Armstrong, Patberg, & Dewitz, 1988; Baker, 1977) with few exceptions (e.g., Bean, Singer, & Cowen, 1985). Similarly, facilitative effects were found for adjunct questions used with students of varying reading ability (Andre, Mueller, Womack, Smid, & Tuttle, 1980; Graves & Clark, 1981; Memory, 1983; Rothkopf & Bisbicos, 1967; Washburne, 1929), but especially with good readers (Watts & Anderson, 1971; Wood, 1986). It is important to note, however, that adjunct questions may generate strong question-specific effects at the expense of more general beneficial effects (see Gustafson & Toole, 1970, for a discussion of this possibility).

A review of the research on graphic organizers (Moore & Readence, 1984) suggests that more-able students (Baker, 1977) and students who construct their own organizers after reading a selection (Barron & Stone, 1974) benefit more than less-able students and students who are exposed to a teacher-made organizer before reading a selection (Barron, 1972; Barron & Cooper, 1973; Berget, 1977; Earle, 1969). Exceptions to these findings included studies in which either teacher-made graphic organizers were effective (Estes, Mills, & Barron, Experiment No. 2, 1969) or all students, regardless of reading ability, benefited from graphic organizers (Alvermann, 1981).

The conditions under which advance organizers are effective or ineffective are less clear. Question-specific facilitation appears more common than general facilitation (Proger, Taylor, Mann, Coulson, & Bayuk, 1970), although this finding varies for level of reading ability (Allen, 1970) and a variety of other contextual factors (see Barron, 1972; Estes, 1972; Pearson & Gallagher, 1983). Overall, advance-organizer research is an ill-structured domain. Definitions of advance organizers range from rather abstractly written previews (Jones, 1977) to relatively concrete oral previews (Graves, Cooke, & LaBerge, 1983; Smith & Hesse, 1969). Where advance organizers were found to be effective (Alvarez, 1983; Andrews, 1972–1973; Graves, Cooke, & LaBerge, 1983;

TABLE 33.1 Teaching Strategies

RESEARCH	TREATMENT CONDITION		INTERVENOR		TEXT		INSTRUCTION	
	Treatment Incorporated into Classroom Routine	Treatment Added; Contrived Condition	Teacher Introduced Treatment	Experimenter Introduced Treatment	Text Routinely Used in Class	Borrowed/Constructed Text for Experiment	Instruction in Strategy Use	No Instruction in Strategy Use
Guided Reading & Writing								
+ Armstrong et al. (1988)	●		●		●		●	
± Baker (1977)	●		●		●		●	
+ Bean & Pardi (1979)		●		●		●		●
± Bean et al. (1985)	●		●		●		●	
+ Berget (1973)		●		●		●		●
- Carney (1977)	●		●			●	●	
- Estes (1973)		●		●	●		●	
+ Martin et al. (1986)	●		●			●	●	
- Simon (1934)	●		●		●		●	
+ Vacca (1975)	●		●		●		●	
+ Vacca (1978)		●	●			●	●	
DRA & DR-TA								
- Manzo (1969)		●	●			●	●	
+ Wilkerson (1986)		●	●			●		●
Questioning (Placement)								
+ Graves & Clark (1981)		●		●		●		●
- Gustafson & Toole (1970)		●		●		●		●
+ Rothkopf & Bisbicos (1967)		●		●		●		●
- Santiesteban & Koran (1977)		●		●		●		●
+ Washburne (1929)		●		●		●		●
+ Watts & Anderson (1971)		●		●		●		●
+ Wood (1986)		●		●		●	●	

+ indicates strategy was effective   − indicates strategy was ineffective   ± indicates mixed results

Continued

TABLE 33.1 Continued

RESEARCH	TREATMENT CONDITION		INTERVENOR		TEXT		INSTRUCTION	
	Treatment Incorporated into Classroom Routine	Treatment Added; Contrived Condition	Teacher Introduced Treatment	Experimenter Introduced Treatment	Text Routinely Used in Class	Borrowed/Constructed Text for Experiment	Instruction in Strategy Use	No Instruction in Strategy Use
Questioning (Types, Levels)								
+ Andre et al. (1980)		●		●		●		●
+ Memory (1983)	●	●	●			●	●	
Reciprocal Teaching & Request								
+ Manzo (1969)		●	●	●		●	●	●
+ Palincsar & Brown (1984a)		●	●	●		●	●	
+ Palincsar & Brown (1984b)	●	●	●			●	●	
Advance Organizers								
± Allen (1970)		●		●		●		●
+ Alvarez (1983)		●		●		●		●
+ Andrews (1972 - 1973)		●		●		●		●
- Barron (1972)		●		●		●		●
- Barron & Cooper (1973)		●		●		●		●
- Estes (1972)		●		●		●		●
- Estes et al. (1969)		●		●		●		●
+ Graves et al. (1983)	●		●			●		●
+ Graves & Prenn (1984)	●		●			●		●
+ Jones (1977)		●	●			●		●
+ Karahalios et al. (1979)		●		●	●		●	
± Proger et al. (1970)		●		●		●		●
- Santiesteban & Koran (1977)		●		●		●		●
± Smith & Hesse (1969)		●		●		●		●

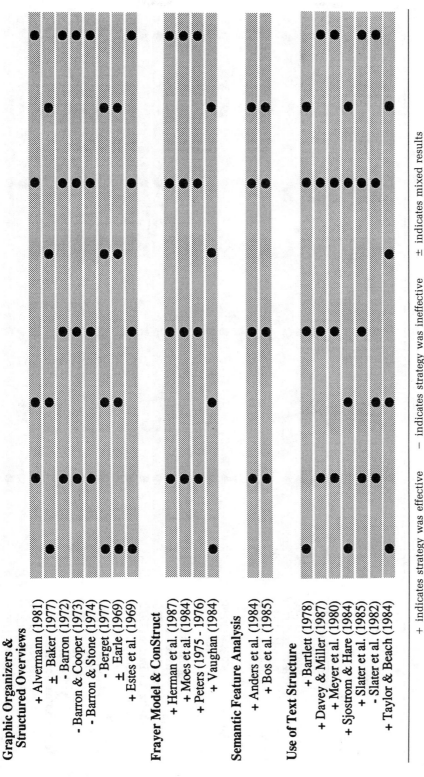

Graphic Organizers &
Structured Overviews

+ Alvermann (1981)
± Baker (1977)
- Barron (1972)
- Barron & Cooper (1973)
- Barron & Stone (1974)
- Berget (1977)
± Earle (1969)
+ Estes et al. (1969)

Frayer Model & ConStruct

+ Herman et al. (1987)
+ Moes et al. (1984)
+ Peters (1975 - 1976)
+ Vaughan (1984)

Semantic Feature Analysis

+ Anders et al. (1984)
+ Bos et al. (1985)

Use of Text Structure

+ Bartlett (1978)
+ Davey & Miller (1987)
+ Meyer et al. (1980)
+ Sjostrom & Hare (1984)
+ Slater et al. (1985)
- Slater et al. (1982)
+ Taylor & Beach (1984)

+ indicates strategy was effective   − indicates strategy was ineffective   ± indicates mixed results

957

TABLE 33.2 Learning Strategies

RESEARCH	TREATMENT CONDITION — Treatment Incorporated into Classroom Routine	TREATMENT CONDITION — Treatment Added; Contrived Condition	INTERVENOR — Teacher Introduced Treatment	INTERVENOR — Experimenter Introduced Treatment	TEXT — Text Routinely Used in Class	TEXT — Borrowed/Constructed Text for Experiment	INSTRUCTION — Instruction in Strategy Use	INSTRUCTION — No Instruction in Strategy Use
Underlining								
+ Dynes (1932)		●		●		●		●
− Mathews (1938)		●	●			●		●
Summarizing								
− Germane (1921a)		●		●		●	●	
+ Germane (1921b)		●		●		●		●
± Hare & Borchardt (1984)		●		●		●	●	
− Head & Buss (1987)		●		●	●			●
+ Rudolf (1949)	●		●		●		●	
+ Salisbury (1934)	●		●			●	●	
Notetaking								
+ Bretzing & Kulhavy (1979)		●		●		●		●
+ Dynes (1932)		●		●		●		●
+ Kulhavy et al. (1975)		●		●		●		●
− Mathews (1938)		●	●			●		●
+ Rudolf (1949)	●		●		●			●
+ Shimmerlik & Nolan (1976)		●		●		●	●	
− Schultz & DiVesta (1972)		●		●		●		●
+ Slater et al. (1985)		●		●		●		●
Mapping								
+ Armbruster & Anderson (1980)		●		●		●	●	
+ Barron & Stone (1974)		●		●		●	●	
− Bean et al. (1986)	●			●	●		●	
Metacognitive Training								
+ Bean et al. (1986)	●			●	●		●	
± Raphael & McKinney (1983)	●		●			●	●	
± Reis & Spekman (1983)		●		●		●	●	

Outlining

+ Barton (1930a)
+ Barton (1930b)
+ Barton (1930c)
- Bean et al. (1986)
+ Drum (1985)
+ Hansell (1978)
+ Jacobson (1932)
+ Rudolf (1949)
+ Salisbury (1934)

Analogy & Metaphor

+ Readence et al. (1983)
+ Hayes & Henk (1986)
± Hayes & Tierney (1982)

Self-Questioning

± Andre & Anderson (1978-79)
+ Frase & Schwartz (1975)
+ Jacobson (1932)
- Johnson & Bliesmer (1983)
+ MacDonald (1986)
+ Singer & Donlan (1982)
± Smith (1973)
+ Wong & Jones (1982)

Imagery

- Anderson & Kulhavy (1972)
- Cramer (1982)
- Gunston-Parks (1985)
+ Peters & Levin (1986)
- Rasco et al. (1975)
+ Weinstein (1982)
- Warner (1977)

+ indicates strategy was effective   − indicates strategy was ineffective   ± indicates mixed results

959

Graves & Prenn, 1984; Jones, 1977; Karahalios, Tonjes, & Towner, 1979), researchers almost always credited them with having provided a type of prereading assistance that enabled students to map new information onto existing knowledge structures.

Teaching students to use text structure in identifying (Sjostrom & Hare, 1984) and comprehending main ideas (Davey & Miller, 1987) is generally acknowledged as being an effective strategy, although students' familiarity with the topic of the text appears to mediate the effectiveness of the instruction (Taylor & Beach, 1984). However, it seems to make little difference whether readers simply follow the text structure used by the author (Bartlett, 1978; Meyer, Brandt, & Bluth, 1980) or employ adjunct aids to highlight that structure (Slater, Graves, & Piche, 1985); either way, their comprehension and recall of textual information improves.

Although few studies at the secondary school level involve the Directed Reading Activity (DRA), the Directed Reading-Thinking Activity (DR-TA), Reciprocal Teaching, ReQuest, the Frayer Model, ConStruct, and Semantic Feature Analysis (see Tables 33.1 and 33.2 for references), those that do exist indicate generally positive effects. One distinguishing feature of almost all of these teaching strategies is their emphasis on manipulating conceptual relationships. Other distinguishing features, though less inclusive, include the attention paid to predicting (DR-TA, Reciprocal Teaching) and to vocabulary building (Frayer Model, Semantic Feature Analysis).

In summary, the research on teaching strategies suggests moderate support for these strategies when they are used with secondary school students in situations similar to those described in the experimental conditions. Although the strategies have been tested and shown to be effective with students across a wide range of abilities, typically the more-able readers benefit the most. Regardless of ability level, the teaching strategies have their greatest effect when students are actively involved in manipulating conceptual relationships and integrating new information with old knowledge.

Learning Strategies

The research support for learning strategies is nearly identical to the support for teaching strategies. Statistically significant differences that favor a learning-strategy group over a control or comparison group were found in 61 percent of the studies in Table 33.2. No facilitative effects were found in 26 percent of the studies, and mixed results were reported in 12 percent of them.

Unlike teaching strategies, which depend on "the teacher presenting certain material at a certain time in a certain way" (Weinstein & Mayer, 1986, p. 316), learning strategies are designed to be student initiated and student directed. Learning strategies as categorized by Weinstein and Mayer (1986) include *rehearsing* (underlining, taking notes verbatim), *elaborating* (taking notes by paraphrasing text, forming a mental image, creating an analogy, summarizing), *organizing* (outlining, mapping), and *comprehension monitoring* (metacognitive training, self-questioning). They do not include study systems such as Robinson's (1941) SQ3R (Survey, Question, Read, Recite, Review), which combines one or more of the strategies from within and across the categories in Weinstein and Mayer's taxonomy of learning strategies. However, SQ3R was recommended in the methods textbooks on secondary reading that we examined. Readers may wish to consult Lawrence (1978) and Stahl (1983) for reviews of the literature on SQ3R, as well as Crewe and Hultgren (1969), Donald (1967), Spenser (1978), and Turner (1968) for individual studies involving SQ3R.

Recent reviews of the research on underlining (e.g., Anderson & Armbruster, 1984; Swafford, 1988) as well as earlier studies (e.g., Mathews, 1938) show it to be no more effective than having students read for understanding and recall. However, broad generalizations regarding the relative ineffectiveness of underlining as a learning strategy at the secondary school level are hardly justified, given that few studies exist, perhaps because students typically are discouraged from marking their textbooks.

Summarizing, outlining, and mapping require students to identify important information and to relate subordinate ideas to superordinate ones. Of the three, summarizing appears to be the most difficult strategy for students to master (Anderson & Armbruster, 1984). The chief reasons for the difficulty seem to stem from students' insensitivity to what is important in text (Germane, 1921a; Hare & Borchardt, 1984) and to their lack of interest in a topic or their poor writing ability (Head & Buss, 1987). Studies that have found summarizing to be an effective learning strategy have been ones in which either instruction was provided (Hare & Borchardt, 1984) over a substantial period of time (Rudolf, 1949) or instruction was scaffolded so that students received increasingly less support as they became more proficient in using the strategy (Germane, 1921b; Salisbury, 1934). Similar results have been reported for outlining studies (Anderson & Armbruster, 1984). Fairly extensive instruction in the process of outlining accounted for the effectiveness of this strategy in nearly all of the studies reviewed (Barton, 1930a, 1930b, 1930c; Jacobson, 1932; Rudolf, 1949; Salisbury, 1934). A more recent study in which outlining was found ineffective (Bean, Singer, Sorter, & Frazee, 1986) concluded that "it takes time, indeed, as much time as a year for students to internalize a new study strategy" (p. 161). Like outlining and summarizing, mapping (which here includes graphic organizing if taught as a student-directed learning strategy) is typically more effective when instruction is long term (Anderson & Armbruster, 1984; Armbruster & Anderson, 1980) rather than short term (Bean et al., 1986), but see Barron and Stone (1974) for an exception.

Note taking (by paraphrasing text) is generally an effective learning strategy for secondary school students (Swafford, 1988). Researchers have attributed its effectiveness to the cognitive effort and level of processing required (Bretzing & Kulhavy, 1979; Dynes, 1932; Kulhavy, Dyer, & Silver, 1975; Shimmerlik & Nolan, 1976) and to students' active involvement in using the strategy to master content (Rudolf, 1949; Slater, Graves, & Piche, 1985). Studies in which note taking was found to be an ineffective learning strategy (e.g., Mathews, 1938; Schultz & DiVesta, 1972) tended to have criterion tasks that did not reflect the kind of processing used in taking notes (see also Anderson & Armbruster, 1984).

The research on comprehension monitoring and self-questioning, both fairly common components of metacognitive training studies, suggests that individual differences in reading ability may influence the degree to which a strategy is considered effective or ineffective. Although comprehension monitoring typically has proven difficult for low-ability readers (Garner & Kraus, 1981–1982), seventh-grade poor comprehenders in the Reis and Spekman (1983) study improved in their ability to detect reader-based (but not text-based) inconsistencies after only two sessions of direct instruction in comprehension monitoring. Raphael and McKinney's (1983) work also suggests that older students, in this instance eighth graders, may benefit as much from a relatively short period of metacognitive training as from an extended one.

Generally, instruction in self-questioning improves students' processing of text (Haller, Child, & Walberg, 1988; Wong, 1985). However, those with low verbal ability and/or poor reading skills tend to profit more from this instruction than do those with high verbal ability and/or better reading skills (Andre & Anderson, 1978–1979; Wong & Jones, 1982). Although MacDonald's (1986) work provides additional evidence that improving below-average and average readers' self-questioning ability leads to improved recall, it appears to do so only for readers who possess certain prerequisite abilities, such as the ability to perform well on free-recall measures. MacDonald noted some instances in which self-questioning instruction actually depressed below-average students' performance. Regardless of students' ability level, successful self-questioning instruction typically involves either direct instruction in the strategy (Singer & Donlan, 1982; Wong & Jones, 1982) or explicitly written instructions with examples of good questions (Andre & Anderson, 1978–1979; Jacobson, 1932; Smith, 1973).

We were able to locate very few studies that did more than mention how students were to perform learning strategies involving analogies, metaphors, and imagery. Typically, the instruction consisted of a written set of directions (Hayes & Henk, 1986), practice in interpreting metaphorical statements as part of the treatment condition (Readence, Baldwin, & Rickelman, 1983), or specially prepared texts that included embedded analogies (Hayes & Tierney, 1982). Of the three imagery studies that included instruction in the strategy prior to testing its effectiveness, two reported positive findings. Weinstein (1982) found that scaffolded instruction in how to form images increased students' free recall, while Peters and Levin (1986) found that instruction in a two-step mnemonic strategy improved students' memory for text. However, simply telling readers to form images (Anderson & Kulhavy, 1972; Gunston-Parks, 1985; Rasco, Tennyson, & Boutwell, 1975) and using high image-evoking selections (Cramer, 1982) or imagery listening guides (Warner, 1977) did not significantly increase students' comprehension and recall.

In summary, with few exceptions, the research on learning strategies suggests that there is moderate support for these strategies when they are used by secondary school students in situations similar to those described in the experimental conditions under which they were tested. Learning-strategies instruction is generally most effective when it is direct and long term, although there is some evidence that shorter periods of instruction may be just as effective. Finally, due to the complexities of most learning strategies, scaffolding the instruction so that students acquire gradual control of a strategy has proved beneficial.

Limitations of the Experimental Research

The foremost conclusion to be drawn from this review of the experimental research on teaching and learning strategies related to secondary school reading is that most strategies are moderately effective *under the conditions tested*. After analyzing those conditions, we believe that certain limitations of the research warrant attention. For example, the majority of the experimental studies on secondary reading practices are decontextualized. As shown in Tables 33.1 and 33.2, 65 percent of the studies tested the effectiveness of a strategy under conditions that were part of neither the regular curriculum nor the classroom routine. The experimenter, rather than the regular classroom teacher, introduced the intervention in 62 percent of the studies. In 76 percent of the studies on teaching and learning strategies, the text used in the experiment was either borrowed from another source or written specifically for the experiment—that is, the text was not the one routinely used in class. Finally, in 50 percent of the studies, students received neither instruction nor practice in how to use the strategy under investigation prior to the start of the experiment. Perhaps, particularly in the case of the studies on learning strategies, the experimenters assumed that students had had previous experience in using the strategies.

Specific limitations related to the decontextualized nature of the research on secondary school reading practices are discussed next. These limitations raise a variety of concerns and suggest future directions in the research on secondary school reading.

Limited ecological validity.   Of primary concern is the degree to which we might expect to find the effective experimental treatments applied in real classrooms. This is a concern because the results of studies that pay students to participate (e.g., Frase & Schwartz, 1975; Rothkopf & Bisbicos, 1967), that require them to read a passage and then recall it orally (e.g., Drum, 1985), or that prevent them from looking back at previously read text (e.g., Andre et al., 1980) signal treatment conditions that most secondary school teachers would find foreign to their classrooms. Although most of the decontextualized studies reviewed here contained less-obvious threats to ecological validity than those just cited, they still presented problems. One way to avoid these problems is to adopt a stance similar to that of Armstrong, Patberg, and Dewitz (1988), who pointed out in their study of reading guides, "If we want teachers to use reading guides, we must demonstrate their effectiveness in actual classroom instruction, so we made every attempt to maintain the integrity of the existing classroom environment" (p. 526).

Limited teacher input.   Another concern is the relatively low input from classroom teachers during the design and implementation of the majority of the experimental treatments included in this review. In an effort to control for the teacher variable and its potentially biasing effect, researchers have typically excluded the classroom teacher from much of the research on learning from text. Yet, as Wade (1983) pointed out in her critique of the research on improving reading in social studies, successful treatments generally are those in which teachers have high input and are actively involved. We found a similar effect for high teacher input when we analyzed *who* introduced the treatment, the experimenter or the classroom teacher, in studies that had only positive or negative effects (see Tables 33.1 and 33.2). When it was the teacher, 61 percent of the studies reported finding a strategy effective, compared to only 48 percent when it was the experimenter.

Limited texts.   A further concern rests with the nature of the texts students were given to read in the studies we reviewed. As noted earlier, over three-fourths of those texts were either borrowed from another source or written specifically for the experiment. Many were on topics for which students had no readily available background knowledge. Although controlling for exposure to previously read material is important in experimental research, it may also interfere with students' ability to focus on the strategy under investigation. The importance of adequate domain knowledge for prompting strategy use (Pressley, Borkowski, & Schneider, 1987) is an issue that Wong (1985) addressed in her review of the self-questioning research. Wong found that without appropriate background knowledge, students typically experienced difficulty in generating questions on their own. Winograd's (1984) work on summarizing also pointed out the difficulties students may encounter when they lack sufficient background knowledge to identify what is important in texts. Perhaps of even greater concern than passage unfamiliarity was the brevity of many of the experimental passages. Because shorter texts are not representative of the texts routinely assigned in secondary schools, it cannot be assumed that strategies capable of facilitating students' learning from brief experimental passages will be equally effective with longer texts.

Limited instruction in strategy use.   A final concern lies with testing the effectiveness of a strategy without first instructing students in its use. It seems unreasonable to expect students to apply a strategy if they have had little or no previous experience in using it. The problem becomes magnified in studies involving multiple strategies (e.g., Estes et al., 1969; Mathews, 1938), although in some of these studies prolonged preinstruction with a strategy led to depressed scores on attitude measures (Estes, 1973) and metacognitive cuing tasks (Raphael & McKinney, 1983).

Summary

The experimental research on secondary reading practices suggests moderate support for most of the teaching and learning strategies reviewed here when they are used under conditions similar to those employed by the research. The limitations associated with this research reflect the tensions inherent in designing studies aimed at balancing researchers' concerns for both internal and ecological validity. Although the decontextualized nature of the majority of the experimental studies in secondary reading argues against making strong recommendations for classroom practice, this is not a condemnation of the research. Early (1982) would view such recommendations as inappropriate under any condition. According to Early, we should not expect research to dictate practice; rather, we should view research as contributing to the belief systems that teachers develop as they observe their own students in their own classrooms.

ACTUAL SECONDARY READING PRACTICES

Understanding the predominant daily reading practices of secondary teachers seems to be essential for those who wish to affect those practices. Just as maps of an area enable travelers to move about efficiently and confidently, descriptions of classroom teaching can benefit educators. Knowing the terrain enhances decision making before and during a journey. Understanding existing instructional conditions enables one to suggest practices that are compatible and stand a chance of being successful (Barr, 1986).

It is important to realize that the descriptions presented here are general. One reason for this generality is that in 1985 approximately 14,000,000 U.S. students in grades 9 through 12 were served by about 814,000 teachers (Center for Education Statistics, 1987). Detailing the reading practices that secondary teachers employ for every class each day of the school year is difficult at best. A second reason for the generality of these descriptions is that research into secondary reading practices is embryonic. Most of the studies reviewed in this section were published after 1976, and most were small-scale efforts. Fine-grained theory-infused descriptions of secondary school reading practices await further research.

Descriptions of everyday secondary school instruction reveal traditional activities that include some reading. As Holton (1982) stated, "The dominant instructional activity in the secondary school is a combination of lecture, textbook assignment, and classroom recitation" (p. 1693). Goodlad (1984) depicted typical school activities as follows:

> The data from our observations in more than 1,000 classrooms support the popular image of a teacher standing in front of a class imparting knowledge to a group of students. Explaining and lecturing constituted the most frequent teaching activities, according to teachers, students, and our observations. And the frequency of these activities increased steadily from the primary to the senior high school years. Teachers also spent a substantial amount of time observing students at work or monitoring their seat-work, especially at the junior high school level. (p. 105)

Our review of the research on actual secondary reading practices, which consisted of observational, ethnographic, and survey methodologies, produced two first-order and three second-order generalizations. The two first-order generalizations seem to characterize all of secondary reading; they are universal statements. The three second-order generalizations describe reading practices that are found regularly in secondary schools but that are quite malleable. Visitors to secondary classrooms could reasonably expect to observe the reading practices described in the second-order generalizations, although exceptions in type and amount certainly would occur.

Secondary Reading Universals

The two first-order generalizations about secondary school reading practices, which seem to be universal, are as follows:

1. Reading is connected with other forms of classroom communication.
2. Reading practices vary.

Reading and other forms of classroom communication.   Researchers have consistently found that reading is tightly connected with other forms of classroom communication. Secondary teachers and students combine reading with other language arts and with performance in order to accomplish numerous outcomes as they move through course content. As Doyle (1984) reported, "Content was typically presented by going over a worksheet or a section of a textbook using a combination of lecture, questions (often related to information learned previously), and oral exercises or examples" (p. 272). Greenewald and Wolfe (1981) found that reading was involved in instruction about 60 percent of all class time and that reading was incorporated into well-integrated systems of classroom communication.

The close connection between reading and other communication forms is suggested by the finding that continuous reading in classrooms is rare. Dolan, Harrison, and Gardner (1979) noted that approximately half of all classroom reading occurred in bursts of less than 15 seconds in any one minute. This preponderance of short-burst reading was mixed with listening, speaking, and writing activities. Mitman, Mergendoller, and St. Clair (1987) also found that students frequently spent their reading time locating bits of information rather than engaging in self-motivated and self-regulated reading for extended periods of time.

Examination of the partnership between classroom reading and other activities led Greenewald and Wolfe (1981) to conclude that reading most frequently played a supportive rather than a dominant role. It is important to realize that Greenewald and Wolfe studied all instances of reading, not just instances of textbook involvement. They found frequent occurrences of reading being used supportively in an instrumental fashion. Instrumental uses consist of practices such as following outlines to help structure oral or media presentations; completing worksheets, tests, or other testlike exercises without reference to additional print materials; and referring to a text to check the accuracy of a response. The frequency of such instrumental uses of reading has been noted by others (Alvermann, Dillon, O'Brien, Smith, 1985; Dolan et al., 1979; Mitman et al., 1987; B. Tye, 1985).

The supportive use of reading in classroom communication systems is defined further by the occasional role of print as an auxiliary source of subject matter. Reading is auxiliary when it provides only one route among many to learning required subject matter. Instead of relying on print, students frequently rely on teachers' presentations of subject matter through lectures, discussions, and films (Davey, 1988; Dolan et al., 1979; Hinchman, 1987; Ratekin, Simpson, Alvermann, & Dishner, 1985; Rieck, 1977; Smith & Feathers, 1983a, 1983b). To illustrate, the eight teachers observed by Ratekin et al. (1985) "used textbooks as a written verification—a safety net of sorts—for information presented via lecture and lecture-discussion" (p. 435). Many teachers orally highlight the textual information they consider appropriate for students to know. Heap

(1982) referred to this practice as certifying a "corpus of knowledge" (p. 406). The body of facts and ideas students are expected to learn might be contained in print, but many teachers indicate the relevance of that information through lecture and classroom interaction. Students frequently have access to textual information through listening as well as reading.

Finally, a noteworthy finding from the descriptive studies reviewed here is that practically no oral reading was observed. In the few instances that oral reading was mentioned, it was tightly connected with other communication forms. For example, Dillon (1989) reported a student's reaction to her teacher, Mr. Appleby, who connected oral reading with silent reading:

> I read with him [silently], but if I don't hear him I can't figure out the characters. When he reads I know what the characters look like. When Appleby read Lenny [Lenny's part from Steinbeck's *Of Mice and Men*] he sounded like a retarded person. He put meaning into it. He adds more fun to the characters—he uses his body and everything. He helps me learn by the way he tells the stories. When he read it [*The Old Man and the Sea*] I got interested in it. I wanted to understand it more. He read the book and got me into it. (p. 252)

In sum, reading in secondary schools is a common activity that is connected with other activities. The nature of the connection frequently places reading in a supportive role, as an instrument to accomplish tasks and as an auxiliary source of information. Because reading is connected with other communication forms, students who wish to succeed need to learn how to manipulate print to fit classroom communication systems. Research is needed into how students learn to incorporate reading into ongoing classroom communication systems. In addition, how teachers balance textual and nontextual information and how they indicate that balance to students await further research.

Reading practice variation.   Precisely defining the connection between reading and other communication forms is difficult because reading practices vary. Although large-scale surveys and observations of teachers (Goodlad, 1984; Wiley, 1977) convey the impression of uniform reading practices in secondary schools, comparisons of smaller studies indicate differences. For instance, reports about textbooks as sources of information differ substantially. One study reported that "Most classes rely on the textbook as the primary source of information" (Applebee, Langer, & Mullis, 1987, p. 3); and another claimed "The source of knowledge authority was not so much the teacher—it was the textbook. Teachers were prepared to intercede, to explain, but the direct confrontation with knowledge for most students was with printed information statements" (Stake & Easley, 1978, p. 13:59). In contrast, a third report indicated that "The teacher, not the text, was the primary source of information" (Ratekin et al., 1985, p. 435), and a fourth claimed

> In-depth critical reading was not required of students. Reading as an active process necessary to the search for information, ideas, and viewpoints was not emphasized. Reading even for literal level information did not play a significant role in these classes. Reading was not an essential or even central activity in the classes studied. (Smith & Feathers, 1983b, p. 266)

The disparity between these conclusions is striking. Textbooks or teachers are the primary source of information, depending on which study is read. One explanation of these divergent conclusions is that researchers might view primary sources of information differently. To illustrate, the text or the teacher might be considered primary when teachers recount information from a text or when teachers use a text to certify students' answers. Another explanation for the reported differences about the role of textbooks is that reading practices vary across at least four variables: teachers, content areas, curricular materials, and academic tracks.

Hinchman (1987) and Mitman et al. (1987) stressed the variation in textbook usage across teachers. In both studies teachers tended to use textbooks in a consistent manner from day to day, but they varied substantially in their reliance on textbooks. As Hinchman stated, "Uses appeared to range from the use of the text as a primary information source upon which tests were based to use of the text as a supplementary information and activity source" (p. 254). Mitman et al. (1987) concluded that teachers' substantive knowledge and self-confidence affected their reading practices. This conclusion is supported by Conley (1986a, 1986b), who found that teachers with expertise in Herber's (1978) reading guides adapted them to meet perceived changes in course content and course direction, whereas novices to Herber's model adapted guides more in reaction to classroom management concerns.

Reading practice variation across content areas was noted as early as 1930 by McCallister (1930a, 1930b). More recently, Eldridge and Muller (1986) supported this finding. They found that social studies teachers focused on lecturing, asking literal-level questions, and developing vocabulary meaning. English teachers taught isolated skills in language arts classes and focused on details about the plot and characters in literature classes. Science teachers asked higher-order questions and provided instruction in how to process information. Barnes, Britton, and Rosen (1971) found that history and English teachers asked a preponderance of questions that demanded facts rather than reasoning. Alvermann (1986) observed this phenomenon in a study involving social studies, English, science, and health teachers. The social studies and English teachers engaged students in recitations over facts from assigned readings, whereas the science and health teachers led discussions over these readings. It seems that reading practices vary across some content areas, with social studies and English teachers tending to stress the acquisition of literal information.

Evidence is also available that variations in reading practices occur with variations in curricular materials. Barr (1987) noted that when students read relatively easy short stories, the teacher asked questions that elicited interpretive responses. When the difficulty level of the selections increased, the teacher asked questions that focused on literal text-based information. Barr reasoned that the increased difficulty of the materials was responsible for the teacher's increased use of text-based questions.

Finally, reading practices seem to vary in relation to the academic track students enter. In reanalyzing Goodlad's (1984) data, Oakes (1985) found differences between high and low tracks with regard to the type of knowledge gained, the opportunities available for learning, classroom climate, and students' attitudes. Hargreaves (1967) concluded that upper-track students had more positive attitudes toward school than lower-track students partly as a function of the competence, teaching strategies, and attitudes of teachers assigned to the different tracks. And in a review of the ethnographic and survey research into the effects of stratification in secondary schools Gamoran and Berends (1987) found patterns of instructional differences that favored high-track students.

In short, teachers differ in reading practices such as relying on textbooks as a source of information and asking questions at certain levels of processing. Differences also exist relative to classroom climate, which affects reading expectations and behavior.

Variation in reading practices can be found across teachers of different expertise, content areas, curricular materials, and academic tracks. Researchers who seek to understand how reading fits the communication systems of secondary teachers should expect to encounter different systems.

Secondary Reading Regularities

The first-order generalizations presented above seem to characterize all secondary reading practices. The following second-order generalizations depict regular, but not universal, reading practices in secondary schools:

1. Textbooks predominate.
2. Teachers emphasize factual textual information.
3. Teachers govern students' encounters with print.

These three generalizations represent convergences of the research on actual secondary reading practices. An explanation of each follows.

Textbook predominance.   Class sets of a single required text predominate in secondary classrooms. This finding appeared in studies that ranged from national surveys (Applebee et al., 1987; Weiss, 1978) to a large-scale observational and self-report study (B. Tye, 1985) to small-scale observational studies (Ratekin et al., 1985; Smith & Feathers, 1983a, 1983b). For instance, Weiss found that 59 percent of grades seven through nine mathematics teachers reported using a single text throughout the school year and 72 percent of grades ten through twelve mathematics teachers reported doing the same. Slightly less than one-half of the seven through twelve science and social studies teachers reported using class sets of two or more textbooks during the year. Materials such as library books, brochures, and magazines rarely supplemented instruction. Although textbooks are highly visible instructional tools in secondary classrooms, the role they play is integrated and varied, but not well understood, as noted earlier.

Emphases on factual textual information.   When textbooks or other reading materials are used as a source of information, students typically employ them as storehouses of factual answers for oral or written questions. Recitation, a common form of oral questioning in which teachers already know the answers to the questions they ask (Dillon, 1984), occurs more frequently than discussion, a give-and-take dialogue in which teachers do not necessarily know the answers. For instance, Wiley (1977) reported that "the most common scene was not of 'liberated' discourse but of the teacher asking questions about the reading assignment, often requiring verbatim responses, stressing the value of good information from reliable sources, particularly the textbook" (p. 19:7).

Written responses to text also consist mostly of literal answers. Worksheets and end-of-chapter questions tend to require students to locate factual information, and tests encourage memorization of information presented earlier (Smith & Feathers, 1983a, 1983b). When study guides are used, they resemble traditional worksheets rather than Herber's (1978) model of guides (Ratekin et al., 1985). Indeed, it appeared to one group of researchers that a major role of reading was "to provide a set of basic facts" (Dolan et al., 1979, p. 124).

This emphasis on factual information tends to reward students who list facts and reproduce textual language. Bloome (1987) referred to listing facts as cataloging; and

McNeil (1986), who observed this phenomenon in teachers' lectures, called it fragmentation. When students or teachers list facts, they enumerate brief pieces of information in an attempt to describe a concept that might be better described if the pieces were explained in relation to the whole.

Teachers elicit factual textual information when they require students to phrase their answers in "book language" (Bloome, 1987, p. 128). Stake and Easley (1978) noted this same phenomenon, reporting that during recitations students' answers were given "in the stylish rhetoric of the textbook" (p. 13:60).

Governance of students' encounters with print.   Classroom interactions are characterized by centralized communications, with teachers owning the interaction (Edwards & Furlong, 1976; Marshall, 1989). The dominant pattern during whole-class presentations in secondary classrooms consists of the following moves: the teacher solicits a student to answer a question; the teacher listens to the student's response; and the teacher evaluates or modifies the student's response (Bellack, Kliebard, Hyman, & Smith, 1966; Sinclair & Coulthard, 1975). Student-initiated comments or questions are rare. This pattern of communication persists during postreading checks as well as during any other time set aside for whole-class presentations.

Along with being the most active participants during classroom interactions, teachers select the content to be presented and the materials and activities to be used (B. Tye, 1985; K. Tye, 1985). To paraphrase Flanders (1970), teachers tell students what to read, when to read, and what to do after reading. And after reading, students rarely work in small groups to collaborate in refining their responses. About half of the students in grades 7 and 11 reported never exchanging ideas in a group discussion after reading (Applebee et al., 1988). Indeed, reports of general classroom activities indicated that small-group work in secondary schools accounted for only 11 percent to 22 percent of the total activities (B. Tye, 1985; Weiss, 1978).

Despite the large amount of governance teachers exert over students' reading, little is done relative to preparation for reading or to instruction in reading skills. Observational data (Ratekin et al., 1985) and teacher survey data (Davey, 1988) have indicated that secondary teachers seldom preview concepts or provide students with learning objectives prior to reading (but see Applebee et al., 1988).

The amount of planned reading instruction that secondary teachers provide seems negligible. For instance, Eldridge and Muller (1986) reported that "Contrary to . . . the recent emphasis on the inclusion of teaching reading skills and strategies in content area classes, limited instruction in reading skills and strategies occurs" (pp. 16–17). This conclusion was supported by Gee and Forester (1988), who surveyed *Journal of Reading* subscribers. Of the 373 secondary teachers who responded, only about 18 percent reported having a program of reading instruction in the content areas, and the level of implementation of these programs was not documented.

In conclusion, the three second-order generalizations presented above indicate secondary reading practices that occur regularly. Exceptions certainly exist, but the practices described here seem to apply to a majority of secondary classrooms. Textbooks are the most common reading material, teachers generally emphasize factual information, and teachers typically govern students' encounters with print. These practices are highly controlled and routine, being consistent with many descriptions of overall secondary school instruction (Boyer, 1983; Cusick, 1973, 1983; Grant & Sleeter, 1986; Powell, Farrar, & Cohen, 1985; Silberman, 1970; Sizer, 1984). They are traditional, being consistent with a teaching style that has endured since at least the turn of the century (Cuban, 1984; Hoetker & Ahlbrand, 1969). Reasons for their prevalence are explored in the next section.

REASONS FOR SECONDARY READING REGULARITIES

Two points are important to keep in mind when examining reasons for secondary reading regularities. One point is that secondary school reading is part of the larger domain of secondary schooling. An understanding of the forces that affect secondary schooling in general is needed in order to understand reasons for particular reading practices (Barnes, 1976; Luke, DeCastell, & Luke, 1983; O'Brien, 1988; Stewart & O'Brien, 1989; White, 1974). A second point is that the conditions of teaching affect the practice of teaching (Lortie, 1975; Sarason, 1982; Waller, 1932). Over time teachers tend to adopt an ideology and an instructional repertoire that fit their work settings (Blase, 1985; Dreeben, 1973; Grant, 1988; Hoy, 1969; McArthur, 1978; Ryan, 1970). For instance, Blase (1985) reported that high school teaching was shaped in part by "constant and unrelenting encounters with routine problems over a long period of time" (p. 242).

Although the general tenor of individual secondary schools differs (Lightfoot, 1983; Perrone, 1985), the daily setting in which teachers work has many similarities (Center for Education Statistics, 1987; Cusick, 1973; Cypher & Willower, 1984). Students in grades seven through twelve demonstrate diverse abilities, attitudes, and paces at which they work. Teachers generally encounter students in classes of at least 20. The classes are devoted to specialties. Teachers typically meet about five classes per day during periods that last about one hour. On the average, teachers work 50 hours per week when extracurricular activities and coaching are included. The physical setting consists mainly of four-wall confines with cumbersome pupil desks. Classroom practices that fit this setting can be expected to dominate.

Classroom teaching also fits powerful forces from outside the classroom. Teachers and students interact amid a web of expectations produced by sources such as the media, community leaders, teacher educators, subject-matter specialists, accreditation organizations, postsecondary educational institutions, school administrators, parents, and personal backgrounds. Thus, teaching practices are influenced by conditions encountered inside and outside the classroom. Four demands that secondary teachers inherit from this situation involve order, accountability, socialization, and resources.

Order

Order means that students are behaving in such a way that discernible classroom events are being accomplished (Doyle, 1986). Order is a substantial concern of beginning teachers (Bullough, 1989; Veenman, 1984) as well as experienced teachers (Willower, Eidell, & Hoy, 1967). Physical safety, emotional well-being, and academic achievement are enhanced in orderly classrooms. Classroom order is accomplished by setting and enacting rules and procedures for general conduct as well as for classroom activities.

Negotiating treaties is one technique for maintaining order (Powell et al., 1985; Woods, 1983). Subject-matter treaties are understandings students and teachers reach implicitly about how far to lower subject-matter expectations in return for orderly behavior. Subject-matter treaties are emphasized by Cusick (1973, 1983) and are apparent in discussions of defensive teaching (McNeil, 1986) and classroom bargains (Sedlak, Wheeler, Pullin, & Cusick, 1986).

Doyle and Carter (1984) illustrated the conditions underlying a subject-matter treaty relative to the reading-writing tasks assigned by a junior high school teacher. The teacher had difficulty managing her class when her students wrote short-story reports and comparisons of short stories; however, the students were orderly and achieved high success rates when they completed grammar worksheets and word-study exercises. According to Doyle and Carter (1984), the teacher had "to choose between preserving conditions for students' self-direction and preserving order in the classroom. In most instances she reduced ambiguity to establish or sustain work involvement" (p. 146).

Secondary reading regularities, which emphasize brief factual information and are controlled by the teacher, prevail possibly due to subject-matter treaties that are stimulated by demands for order. Open questions, with their highly unpredictable answers, pose management problems for teachers (Hargreaves, 1984). Routinized, superficial reading practices allow teachers and students to move through the school day in an orderly manner.

Accountability

Expectations for student learning are held by the public, parents, school administrators, teaching colleagues, teachers, and students. Determining accountability for this learning is accomplished through formal measures such as test score and course grade reports (Resnick & Resnick, 1985; Wise, 1979). Informal means of holding teachers and students accountable for learning also prevail. For instance, colleagues might informally complain about and even scorn teachers who do not prepare students for the next year (Stake & Easley, 1978), and students in class are known to comment sarcastically about other students' poor performances (Delamont & Galton, 1987).

Regular reading practices in secondary schools satisfy demands of accountability in several ways. Most accountability systems require teachers to cover course contents expeditiously, and teachers who govern students' encounters with print seem to be more efficient at content coverage than teachers who give students free rein (Grant & Sleeter, 1986). Emphases on literal information also are compatible with demands for accountability because the acquisition of facts seems to be more easily accomplished and is more readily apparent than other cognitive operations. Teachers and students want to demonstrate progress; consequently, when teachers encounter students with learning difficulties, they tend to adapt their instruction by "organizing, structuring, objectifying, routinizing, and simplifying" (Blase, 1985, p. 243). These actions frequently are done out of "genuine sympathy for adolescents encountering problems and pressures" (Sedlak et al., 1985, p. 109). Another way accountability encourages regular reading practices is by stressing the need for a clear sequence. Teachers who rely on textbooks easily clarify where students have been, where they are, and where they are going (Edwards & Furlong, 1976; Grant & Sleeter, 1986; Smith & Geoffrey, 1968).

Secondary reading practices that occur regularly are associated with cognitive and affective outcomes of some consequence. Recitation-like interactions that follow assigned readings promote factual learning by allowing students to practice recalling the contents of a text and to receive feedback about their performance (Gall, 1984). Clear questions and structure increase student performance on achievement tests (Brophy & Good, 1986) and cue students to text contents that are likely to be included on a variety of assessments (Gall, 1984; Hinchman, 1987). Finally, teachers and students who engage in traditional question-answer routines demonstrate solidarity, or mutuality, as they jointly construct a body of information (Farrar, 1986).

In brief, traditional practices fit common systems of accountability. Relying on textbooks and following up reading assignments with highly controlled question-answer routines satisfy demands for accountability by contributing to content coverage, demonstrable progress, specific learning outcomes, and feelings of solidarity.

Socialization

Secondary schools are expected to do more than develop students' cognitive abilities; schools also are expected to socialize the young (Hamilton, 1984; Parsons, 1959). The impact of socialization on instruction was stated directly by Stake and Easley (1978): "Putting it in a nutshell, most teachers seemed to treat subject matter knowledge as evidence of, and subject materials as a means to, the *socialization* of the individuals in school" (p. 16:24). The reading regularities found in secondary schools are compatible with demands for socialization as well as order and accountability.

At a general level, socialization is "the process of learning the habits, norms, and ways of thinking essential for fitting into society" (Bowers, 1984, p. 33). This process leads to learning the academic heritage as well as the acceptable behaviors of a society (Minuchin & Shapiro, 1983). The academic heritage consists of a time-honored body of knowledge. For instance, in science, teachers present Ohm's law, the five steps of the scientific method, and the stages of mitosis. Other disciplines contain subject matter of similar stature. Instruction that allows students to independently explore self-selected topics is at risk of not conveying sanctioned information.

The acceptable behaviors of a society are taught through the hidden curriculum (Cornbleth, 1984; Jackson, 1968; Martin, 1976; Vallance, 1977). This curriculum seeks to develop students who are, among other things, industrious, reliable, neat, respectful, and restrained. These attributes allow individuals to fit into the existing social order.

The hidden curriculum of schools has been characterized variously as negative, positive, and neutral. A large body of literature presents a negative view of the hidden curriculum (Apple, 1987; Bourdieu & Passeron, 1977; Bowles & Gintis, 1976; Everhart, 1983; Giroux, 1983; Katz, 1968, 1975; McLaren, 1986; Violas, 1978). This view holds that schools reproduce class structures and impose capitalist values on the working class. Schools are not seen as instruments for the liberation of individuals from ignorance; instead, they are seen as institutions designed to bring students into line with customary social expectations. On the other hand, authorities such as Durkheim (1961) view the hidden curriculum as a positive force. Allowing individuals to function efficiently in society is seen as a mutually beneficial enterprise. Finally, others have argued that hidden curriculums are neutral, having little to do with socializing children to their roles in the larger society (Doyle, 1986; Selakovich, 1984). These authorities contend that teachers consider socialization to be necessary primarily for establishing and maintaining order in the present day.

The reasons for teachers' socialization practices remain to be determined; however, there is little doubt that teachers exert much effort conveying a sanctioned body of knowledge and making students' behaviors socially acceptable. Reading practices that are highly controlled and routine fit at least part of the demand for this socialization.

Resources

Along with demands for order, accountability, and socialization, resources seem to affect secondary school reading practices. Broadly speaking, resources consist of external and internal assets.

Two external resources are time and materials. A perceived absence of time to prepare and deliver instruction limits teachers' capabilities to develop ideas and cover content in depth (Blase, 1985; Guzzetti, 1989; Hinchman, 1987). Teachers frequently indicate that time does not affect their instruction (Weiss, 1978; Grant & Sleeter, 1986), but these teachers probably have adapted their practices to fit the time constraints. Little time is available for planning and preparing to teach, so pulling together multiple materials related to the same topic and planning projects related to the materials are difficult. Consequently, teachers tend to rely on a traditional textbook approach (Smith & Geoffrey, 1968).

Teachers' days are regulated by the changing of class periods, which has been termed the "tyranny of the bells" (Cypher & Willower, 1984, p. 23). Allowing students to explore topics in depth slows down content coverage within these periods. Evidence of this slowdown was presented by Dillon (1983), who noted that both teachers and students took increasingly longer times to express utterances that were at successively higher levels of cognition. For instance, defining a term was done more quickly than justifying a response.

Materials also play a role in determining secondary reading practices (Grant & Sleeter, 1986; Weiss, 1978). A problem with textbook materials is that their contents are dictated by concerns other than appeal and comprehensibility to students (Broudy, 1975; Coser, Kadushin, & Powell, 1982; Fitzgerald, 1979). Adults who serve on adoption committees, not students, are the market for textbook publishers. Comprehensiveness and value orientation play a large role in textbook selection, and this can make textbooks difficult for students to comprehend. However, the inconsiderateness of textbooks is not the entire problem. Frequently, students' general confusion about schooling spills over to their assigned readings. For example, Nicholson (1984) observed numerous instances in which students' everyday knowledge conflicted with the information in a text. Teachers have difficulty promoting nonliteral thinking when they use texts that pose problems for students.

An alternative view about the impact of time and materials is that these resources do not directly affect instruction. Teachers with different levels of external resources might teach the same way due to limited internal resources of pedagogical and subject-matter knowledge (B. Tye, 1985). Teachers require an extensive knowledge base to be successful (Shulman, 1987), but teacher education and staff development efforts frequently are insufficient for empowering teachers to use creative, flexible practices. From the moment they first entered elementary school as students, teachers have observed how instruction occurs. This apprenticeship of informal observation through the years dictates many of the traditional practices individuals implement when they assume the teacher's role (Lortie, 1975). In addition, limited subject-matter knowledge leads teachers to rely on texts and highly controlled presentations to insure accurate information. Hence, traditional teaching practices might prevail because they are what teachers know best.

A Final Word

When considering the reasons presented here for the secondary reading regularities, it is important to keep in mind two points that are in addition to the ones stated at the beginning of this section. First, one practice can satisfy many demands. Doyle (1986) named this phenomenon multidimensionality, and Lortie (1975) referred to it as indivisibility. For example, clear-cut text-based routines satisfy instructional as well as management concerns. Providing class time for students to copy answers found in a textbook simultaneously controls students' behavior and the type and amount of information to be covered. Secondary reading regularities seem to predominate partly because they satisfy multiple demands for control.

Second, research and theory explaining the prevalence of traditional reading practices are rudimentary: the ideas presented in this section were synthesized from disparate studies; the demands of order, accountability, socialization, and resources are more complex than presented here; other demands certainly exist; and the process by which instruction is driven remains to be determined. Notwithstanding these limitations, this section has documented some of the forces that are likely to be in a complete account of what shapes secondary reading.

CONCLUSIONS

As this chapter demonstrates, researchers are beginning to form a picture of secondary school reading, but much work remains. Progress has continued in explaining the effects of teaching strategies and learning strategies on learning from text under experimentally controlled conditions, but many areas of investigation await further research. From the experimental research on secondary reading practices, we know more about *what* needs to be done in order to learn from text than *how* teachers and students approach that learning.

A fruitful area of investigation will be to examine how teachers take strategies that are known to be effective in experimentally controlled settings and incorporate them into actual classroom settings. This area of research deserves considerable attention because, according to Doyle (1983), "Tasks which cognitive psychology suggests will have the greatest long-term consequences for improving the quality of academic work are precisely those which are the most difficult to install in classrooms" (p. 186). This chapter supports Doyle's conclusion. There is clear evidence that students in experimentally controlled settings benefit from strategies that promote active engagement with subject material. However, descriptions of actual practices in secondary school reading suggest that students rarely participate in such strategies. Convincing reasons for this situation are needed.

However convincing the reasons for actual reading practices in secondary schools might be, they still will not directly address the limitations of the experimental research on teaching and learning strategies discussed earlier. Advocates of naturalistic experimentation (e.g., Barr, 1986) have pointed out the need for a research methodology that actively involves teachers and documents what instruction is like in classrooms *prior* to and *following* teachers' decisions to incorporate new practices. Attempts to move toward this kind of methodology include studies in which researchers and teachers (Alvermann & Hayes, 1989; Conley, 1988; Dillon, O'Brien, & Ruhl, 1988; Lapp, Flood, & Alvarez, 1988) have documented the changes in context-specific secondary school reading practices.

Finally, if researchers are to form a more complete picture of secondary reading, they will need to tap a variety of sources. This chapter highlights information from several of those sources. The challenge is to bring together such information and form coherent ongoing research agendas. To be sure, practitioners and teacher educators need not wait for definitive answers before incorporating tested strategies into classroom practices. Their task is to adapt the strategies so they retain their outcomes yet fit an environment that rewards control.

REFERENCES

Allen, D. I. (1970). Some effects of advance organizers and level of question on the learning and retention of written social studies material. *Journal of Educational Psychology, 61,* 333–339.

Alvarez, M. C. (1983). Using a thematic pre-organizer and guided instruction as aids to concept learning. *Reading Horizons, 24,* 51–58.

Alvermann, D. E. (1981). The compensatory effect of graphic organizers on descriptive text. *Journal of Educational Research, 75,* 44–48.

Alvermann, D. E. (1986). Discussion versus recitation in the secondary classroom. In J. A. Niles & R. V. Lalik (Eds.), *Solving problems in literacy: Learners, teachers, and researchers* (35th Yearbook of the National Reading Conference) (pp. 113–119). Rochester, NY: National Reading Conference.

Alvermann, D. E., Dillon, D. R., O'Brien, D. G., & Smith, L. C. (1985). The role of the textbook in discussion. *Journal of Reading, 29,* 50–57.

Alvermann, D. E., & Hayes, D. A. (1989). Classroom discussion of content area reading assignments: An intervention study. *Reading Research Quarterly, 24,* 305–335.

Alvermann, D. E., Moore, D. W., & Conley, M. W. (Eds.). (1987). *Research within reach: Secondary school reading.* Newark, DE: International Reading Association.

Anders, P. L., Bos, C. S., & Filip, D. (1984). The effect of semantic feature analysis on the reading comprehension of learning-disabled students. In J. A. Niles & L. A. Harris (Eds.), *Changing perspectives on research in reading/language processing and instruction* (33rd Yearbook of the National Reading Conference) (pp. 162–166). Rochester, NY: National Reading Conference.

Anderson, R. C., & Kulhavy, R. W. (1972). Imagery and prose learning. *Journal of Educational Psychology, 63,* 242–243.

Anderson, T. H., & Armbruster, B. B. (1984). In P. D. Pearson, R. Barr, M. L. Kamil, & P. Mosenthal, (Eds.), *Handbook of reading research* (Vol. 1, pp. 657–679). White Plains, NY: Longman.

Andre, M. E. D. A., & Anderson, T. H. (1978–1979). The development and evaluation of a self-questioning technique. *Reading Research Quarterly, 14,* 605–623.

Andre, T., Mueller, C., Womack, S., Smid, K., & Tuttle, M. (1980). Adjunct application questions facilitate later application, or do they? *Journal of Educational Psychology, 72,* 533–543.

Andrews, L. (1972–1973). Reading comprehension and three modes of prereading assistance. *Journal of Reading Behavior, 5,* 237–241.

Apple, M. W. (1987). *Teachers and texts.* London: Routledge & Kegan Paul.

Applebee, A. N., Langer, J. A., & Mullis, I. V. S. (1987). *Literature and U.S. history: The instructional experience and factual knowledge of high school juniors.* Princeton, NJ: Educational Testing Service.

Applebee, A. N., Langer, J. A., & Mullis, I. V. S. (1988). *Who reads best? Factors related to reading achievement in grades 3, 7, and 11.* Princeton, NJ: Educational Testing Service.

Armbruster, B. B., & Anderson, T. H. (1980). *The effect of mapping on the free recall of expository text* (Tech. Rep. No. 160). Champaign, IL: University of Illinois, Center for the Study of Reading.

Armstrong, D. P., Patberg, J., & Dewitz, P. (1988). Reading guides—helping students understand. *Journal of Reading, 31,* 524–531.

Baker, R. L. (1977). The effects of informational organizers on learning and retention, content knowledge, and term relationships in ninth-grade social studies. In H. L. Herber & R. T. Vacca (Eds.), *Research in reading in the content areas: The third report* (pp. 134–150). Syracuse, NY: Syracuse University, Reading and Language Arts Center.

Barnes, D. (1976). *From communication to curriculum.* Harmondsworth, Eng.: Penguin.

Barnes, D., Britton, J., & Rosen, H. (1971). *Language, the learner, and the school* (rev. ed.). Middlesex, Eng.: Penguin.

Barr, R. (1986). Commentary: Studying classroom reading instruction. *Reading Research Quarterly, 21,* 231–236.

Barr, R. (1987). Classroom interaction and curricular content. In D. Bloome (Ed.), *Literacy and schooling* (pp. 150–168). Norwood, NJ: Ablex.

Barron, R. F. (1972). The effects of advance organizers and grade level upon the reception, learning, and retention of general science content. In F. P. Greene (Ed.), *Investigations relating to mature reading* (21st Yearbook of the National Reading Conference) (pp. 8–15). Milwaukee, WI: National Reading Conference.

Barron, R. F., & Cooper, R. (1973). Effects of advance organizers and grade level upon information acquisition from an instructional-level general science passage. P. L. Nacke (Ed.), *Diversity in mature reading: Theory and research* (22nd Yearbook of the National Reading Conference) (pp. 78–82). Boone, NC: National Reading Conference.

Barron, R. F., & Stone, V. F. (1974). The effect of student-generated graphic post organizers upon learning vocabulary relationships. In P. L. Nacke (Ed.), *Interaction: Research and practice in college adult reading* (23rd Yearbook of the National Reading Conference) (pp. 172–175). Clemson, SC: National Reading Conference.

Bartlett, B. J. (1978). *Top-level structure as an organizational strategy for recall of classroom text.* Unpublished doctoral dissertation, Arizona State University, Tempe, AZ.

Barton, W. A., Jr. (1930a). The experiment at the Horace Mann High School for Girls. In W. A. Barton, Jr. (Ed.), *Outlining as a study procedure* (Contributions to Education No. 411) (pp. 67–73). New York: Teachers College, Columbia University.

Barton, W. A., Jr. (1930b). The experiment at the Bayonne Junior High School. In W. A. Barton, Jr. (Ed.), *Outlining as a study procedure* (Contributions to Education No. 411) (pp. 74–83). New York: Teachers College, Columbia University.

Barton, W. A., Jr. (1930c). The experiment at the George Washington High School. In W. A. Barton Jr. (Ed.), *Outlining as a study procedure* (Contributions to Education No. 411) (pp. 84–90). New York: Teachers College, Columbia University.

Bean, T. W., & Pardi, R. (1979). A field test of a guided reading strategy. *Journal of Reading, 23,* 144–147.

Bean, T. W., Singer, H., & Cowen, S. (1985). Acquisition of a topic schema in high school biology through an analogical study guide. In J. A. Niles & R. V. Lalik (Eds.), *Issues in literacy: A research perspective* (34th Yearbook of the National Reading Conference) (pp. 38–41). Rochester, NY: National Reading Conference.

Bean, T. W., Singer, H., Sorter, J., & Frazee, C. (1986). The effect of metacognitive instruction in outlining and graphic organizer construction on students' comprehension in a tenth-grade world history class. *Journal of Reading Behavior, 18,* 153–169.

Bellack, A. A., Kliebard, H. M., Hyman, R. T., & Smith, F. L., Jr. (1966). *The language of the classroom.* New York: Teachers College Press, Columbia University.

Berger, A., & Robinson, H. A. (Eds.) (1982). *Secondary school reading: What research reveals for classroom practice.* Urbana, IL: ERIC Clearinghouse on Reading and Communication Skills and the National Conference on Research in English.

Berget, E. (1973). Two methods of guiding the learning of a short story. In H. L. Herber & R. F. Barron (Eds.), *Research in reading in the content areas: Second-year report* (pp. 53–57). Syracuse, NY: Syracuse University, Reading and Language Arts Center.

Berget, E. (1977). The use of organizational pattern guides, structured overviews and visual [*sic*] summaries in guiding social studies reading. In H. L. Herber & R. T. Vacca (Eds.), *Research in reading in the content areas: The third report* (pp. 151–162). Syracuse, NY: Syracuse University, Reading and Language Arts Center.

Blase, J. J. (1985). The socialization of teachers: An ethnographic study of factors contributing to the rationalization of the teacher's instructional perspective. *Urban Education, 20,* 235–256.

Bloome, D. (1987). Reading as a social process in an eighth-grade classroom. In D. Bloome (Ed.), *Literacy and schooling* (pp. 123–149). Norwood, NJ: Ablex.

Bos, C. S., Anders, P. L., Filip, D., & Jaffe, L. E. (1985). Semantic feature analysis and long-term learning. In J. A. Niles & R. V. Lalik (Eds.), *Issues in literacy: A research perspective* (34th Yearbook of the National Reading Conference) (pp. 42–47). Rochester, NY: National Reading Conference.

Bourdieu, P., & Passeron, J. C. (1977). *Reproduction in education, society, and culture.* Beverly Hills, CA: Sage.

Bowers, C. A. (1984). *The promise of theory.* New York: Teachers College Press, Columbia University.

Bowles, S., & Gintis, H. (1976). *Schooling in capitalist America: Educational reform and the contradictions of economic life.* New York: Basic Books.

Boyer, E. L. (1983). *High school: A report on secondary education in America.* New York: Harper & Row.

Bretzing, B. H., & Kulhavy, R. W. (1979). Notetaking and depth of processing. *Contemporary Educational Psychology, 4,* 145–153.

Brophy, J., & Good, T. (1986). Teacher behavior and student achievement. In M. C. Wittrock (Ed.), *Handbook of research on teaching* (3rd ed.) (pp. 328–375). New York: Macmillan.

Broudy, E. (1975). The trouble with textbooks. *Teachers College Record, 77,* 13–34.

Brown, A. L., & Smiley, S. S. (1978). The development of strategies for studying texts. *Child Development, 49,* 1076–1088.

Bullough, R. V., Jr. (1989). *First-year teacher: A case study.* New York: Teachers College Press, Columbia University.

Carney, J. J. (1977). The effects of separate vs. content-integrated reading training on content mastery and reading ability in the social studies. In H. L. Herber & R. T. Vacca (Eds.), *Research in reading in the content areas: The third report* (pp. 163–177). Syracuse, NY: Syracuse University, Reading and Language Arts Center.

Center for Education Statistics. (1987). *The condition of education.* Washington, DC: U.S. Government Printing Office.

Clifford, G. J. (1984). Buch und lesen: Historical perspectives on literacy and schooling. *Review of Educational Research, 54,* 472–501.

Compaine, B. M. (1987). The new literacy. In J. Y. Cole (Ed.), *Books in our future: Perspectives and proposals* (pp. 126–138). Washington, DC: U.S. Government Printing Office.

Confrey, J. (1982). Content and pedagogy in secondary schools. *Journal of Teacher Education, 33,* 13–16.

Conley, M. W. (1986a). The influence of training on three teachers' comprehension questions during content area lessons. *Elementary School Journal, 87,* 17–27.

Conley, M. W. (1986b). Teachers' conceptions, decisions, and changes during initial classroom lessons containing content reading strategies. In J. Niles & R. Lalik (Eds.), *Solving problems in literacy: Learners, teachers, and researchers* (35th Yearbook of the National Reading Conference) (pp. 120–126). Rochester, NY: National Reading Conference.

Conley, M. W. (1988, December). *Knowledge about pedagogical content: How practicing teachers come to understand content reading instruction.* Paper presented at the annual meeting of the National Reading Conference, Tucson, AZ.

Cornbleth, C. (1984). Beyond hidden curriculum? *Journal of Curriculum Studies, 16,* 29–36.

Coser, L. A., Kadushin, C., & Powell, W. W. (1982). *Books: The culture and commerce of publishing.* New York: Basic Books.

Cramer, E. H. (1982). Reading comprehension and attitude of high and low imagers: A comparison. In J. A. Niles & L. A. Harris (Eds.), *Inquiries in reading: Research and instruction* (31st Yearbook of the National Reading Conference) (pp. 37–41). Rochester, NY: National Reading Conference.

Crewe, J., & Hultgren, D. (1969). What does research really say about study skills? In G. B. Schick & M. M. May (Eds.), *The psychology of reading behavior* (18th Yearbook of the National Reading Conference) (pp. 75–78). Milwaukee, WI: National Reading Conference.

Crismore, A. (Ed.). (1985). *Landscapes: A state-of-the-art assessment of reading comprehension research, 1974–1984.* Bloomington, IN: Indiana University.

Cuban, L. (1984). *How teachers taught.* New York: Longman.

Cusick, P. (1973). *Inside high school.* New York: Holt, Rinehart & Winston.

Cusick, P. (1983). *The egalitarian ideal and the American high school: Studies of three schools.* New York: Longman.

Cypher, T. W., & Willower, D. J. (1984). The work behavior of secondary school teachers. *Journal of Research and Development in Education, 18,* 17–24.

Davey, B. (1988). How do classroom teachers use their textbooks? *Journal of Reading, 31,* 340–345.

Davey, B., & Miller, D. (1987, April). *Topicalization and the processing of expository prose of children: Mediating effects of cognitive styles and content familiarity.* Paper presented at the annual meeting of the American Educational Research Association, Washington, DC.

Delamont, S., & Galton, M. (1987). *Inside the secondary classroom.* London: Routledge & Kegan Paul.

Dillon, D. R. (1989). Showing them that I want them to learn and that I care about who they are: A microethnography of the social organization of a secondary low-track English-reading classroom. *American Educational Research Journal, 26,* 227–259.

Dillon, D. R., O'Brien, D. G., & Ruhl, J. D. (1988, December). *The construction of the social organization in one secondary content classroom: An ethnographic study of a biology teacher and his academic-track students.* Paper presented at the annual meeting of the National Reading Conference, Tucson, AZ.

Dillon, J. T. (1983). Cognitive complexity and duration of classroom speech. *Instructional Science, 12,* 59–66.

Dillon, J. T. (1984). Research on questioning and discussion. *Educational Leadership, 42,* 50–56.

Dolan, T., Harrison, C., & Gardner, K. (1979). The incidence and context of reading in the classroom. In E. Lunzer & K. Gardner (Eds.), *The effective use of reading* (pp. 108–138). London: Heinemann.

Donald, M. (1967). The SQ3R method in grade seven. *Journal of Reading, 11,* 33–35, 43.

Doyle, W. (1983). Academic work. *Review of Educational Research, 53,* 159–199.

Doyle, W. (1984). How order is achieved in classrooms: An interim report. *Journal of Curriculum Studies, 16,* 259–277.

Doyle, W. (1986). Classroom organization and management. In M. C. Wittrock (Ed.), *Handbook of research on teaching* (3rd ed.) (pp. 392–431). New York: Macmillan.

Doyle, W., & Carter, K. (1984). Academic tasks in classrooms. *Curriculum Inquiry, 14,* 129–150.

Dreeben, R. (1973). The school as a workplace. In R. M. W. Travers (Ed.), *Second handbook of research on teaching* (pp. 450–473). Chicago: Rand McNally.

Drum, P. A. (1985). Retention of text information by grade, ability, and study. *Discourse Processes, 8,* 21–52.

Dupuis, M. (Ed.). (1984). *Reading in the content areas: Research for teachers.* Newark, DE: International Reading Association.

Durkheim, E. (1961). *Moral education.* New York: Free Press.

Dynes, J. J. (1932). Comparison of two methods of studying history. *Journal of Experimental Education, 1,* 42–45.

Earle, R. A. (1969). Use of the structured overview in mathematics classes. In H. L. Herber & P. L. Sanders (Eds.), *Research in reading in the content areas: First-year report* (pp. 49–58). Syracuse, NY: Syracuse University, Reading and Language Arts Center.

Early, M. J. (1982). Epilogue: New students, new teachers, new demands. In A. Berger & H. A. Robinson (Eds.), *Secondary school reading: What research reveals for classroom practice* (pp. 193–202). Urbana, IL: ERIC Clearinghouse on Reading and Communication Skills and the National Conference on Research in English.

Education Commission of the States. (1983). *A summary of major reports on education.* Denver, CO: Author.

Edwards, A. D., & Furlong, V. J. (1976). *The language of teaching.* London: Heinemann.

Ekstrom, R. B., Goertz, M. E., & Rock, D. R. (1986). Student achievement. In J. Hannaway & M. E. Lockheed (Eds.), *The contributions of the social sciences to educational policy and practice: 1965–1985* (pp. 71–97). Berkeley, CA: McCutchan.

Eldridge, R., & Muller, D. (1986, June). *Content area teachers and reading skills instruction.* Paper presented at the annual University of Wisconsin Reading Symposium, Milwaukee.

Estes, T. H. (1972). The effect of advance organizers upon meaningful reception learning, and retention of social studies content. In F. P. Greene (Ed.), *Investigations relating to mature reading* (21st Yearbook of the National Reading Conference) (pp. 16–22). Milwaukee, WI: National Reading Conference.

Estes, T. H. (1973). Guiding reading in social studies. In H. L. Herber & R. F. Barron (Eds.), *Research in reading in the content areas: Second-year report* (pp. 58–63). Syracuse, NY: Syracuse University, Reading and Language Arts Center.

Estes, T. H., Mills, D. C., & Barron, R. F. (1969). Three methods of introducing students to a reading-learning task in two content subjects. In H. L. Herber & P. L. Sanders (Eds.), *Research in reading in the content areas: First-year report* (pp. 40–47). Syracuse, NY: Syracuse University, Reading and Language Arts Center.

Estes, T. H. & Vaughan, J. L. (1978). *Reading and learning in the content classroom.* Boston, MA: Allyn & Bacon.

Everhart, R. B. (1983). *Reading, writing and resistance.* London: Routledge & Kegan Paul.

Farrar, M. T. (1986). Teacher questions: The complexity of the cognitively simple. *Instructional Science, 15,* 89–107.

Feistritzer, C. E. (1986). *Profile of teachers in the U.S.* Washington, DC: National Center for Education Information.

Firestone, W. A., & Herriott, R. E. (1982). Prescriptions for effective elementary schools don't fit secondary schools. *Educational Leadership 40,* 51–53.

Fitzgerald, F. (1979). *America revised.* Boston: Little, Brown.

Flanders, N. (1970). *Analyzing teacher behavior.* Reading, MA: Addison-Wesley.

Frase, L. T., & Schwartz, B. J. (1975). Effect of question production and answering on prose recall. *Journal of Educational Psychology, 67,* 628–635.

Gall, M. (1984). Synthesis of research on teachers' questioning. *Educational Leadership, 42,* 40–47.

Gamoran, A., & Berends, M. (1987). The effects of stratification in secondary schools: Synthesis of survey and ethnographic research. *Review of Educational Research, 57,* 415–436.

Garner, R., & Kraus, C. (1981–1982). Good and poor comprehender differences in knowing and regulating reader behaviors. *Educational Research Quarterly, 6,* 5–12.

Gee, T. C., & Forester, N. (1988). Moving reading instruction beyond the reading classroom. *Journal of Reading, 31,* 505–511.

Germane, C. E. (1921a). The value of the written paragraph summary. *Journal of Educational Research, 3,* 116–123.

Germane, C. E. (1921b). The value of the controlled summary as a method of studying. *School and Society, 13,* 730–732.

Giroux, H. (1983). Theories of reproduction and resistance in the new sociology of education: A critical analysis. *Harvard Educational Review, 53,* 257–293.

Goodlad, J. I. (1984). *A place called school.* New York: McGraw-Hill.

Grant, C. A., & Sleeter, C. E. (1986). *After the school bell rings.* Philadelphia, PA: Falmer Press.

Grant, G. (1988). *The world we created at Hamilton High.* Cambridge, MA: Harvard University Press.

Graves, M. F., & Clark, D. L. (1981). The effect of adjunct questions on high school low achievers' reading comprehension. *Reading Improvement, 18,* 8–13.

Graves, M. F., Cooke, C. L., & LaBerge, M. J. (1983). Effects of previewing difficult short stories on low-ability junior high school students' comprehension, recall, and attitudes. *Reading Research Quarterly, 18,* 262–276.

Graves, M. F., & Prenn, M. C. (1984). Effects of previewing expository passages on junior high school students' comprehension and attitudes. In J. A. Niles & L. A. Harris (Eds.), *Changing perspectives on research in reading/language processing and instruction* (33rd Yearbook of the National Reading Conference) (pp. 173–177). Rochester, NY: National Reading Conference.

Green, J. (1987). *The next wave: A synopsis of recent education reform reports.* Denver, CO: Education Commission of the States.

Greenewald, M. J., & Wolfe, A. E. (1981, December). *Reading instruction and material in content area classes: A summary of three observational studies.* Paper presented at the meeting of the Secondary Reading Symposium, National Reading Conference, Dallas, TX.

Gross, B., & Gross, R. (Eds.). (1985). *The great school debate: Which way for American education?* New York: Simon & Schuster.

Gunston-Parks, C. A. (1985). *Effects of imagery ability and text-bound guided imagery on comprehension by low readers.* (From *Dissertation Abstracts International,* 1985, 47, University Microfilms No. 85-28, 762)

Gustafson, H. W., & Toole, D. L. (1970). Effects of adjunct questions, pretesting, and degree of student supervision on learning from an instructional text. *Journal of Experimental Education, 39,* 53–58.

Guzzetti, B. J. (1989). From preservice to inservice: A naturalistic inquiry of beginning teachers' practices in content reading. *Teacher Education Quarterly, 16,* 65–71.

Haller, E. P., Child, D. A., & Walberg, H. J. (1988). Can comprehension be taught? A quantitative synthesis of "metacognitive" studies. *Educational Researcher, 17* (9), 5–8.

Hamilton, S. F. (1984). The secondary school in the ecology of adolescent development. In E. W. Gordon (Ed.), *Review of research in education* (Vol. 11) (pp. 227–258). Washington, DC: American Educational Research Association.

Hansell, T. S. (1978). Stepping up to outlining. *Journal of Reading, 22,* 248–252.

Hare, V. C., & Borchardt, K. M. (1984). Direct instruction of summarization skills. *Reading Research Quarterly, 20,* 62–78.

Hargreaves, D. H. (1967). *Social relations in a secondary school.* London: Routledge & Kegan Paul.

Hargreaves, D. H. (1984). Teachers' questions: Open, closed, and half-open. *Educational Research, 26* (1), 46–52.

Harker, W. J. (1985). The new imperative in literary criticism. *Visible Language, 19,* 356–372.

Hayes, D. A., & Henk, W. A. (1986). Understanding and remembering complex prose augmented by analogic and pictorial illustration. *Journal of Reading Behavior, 18,* 63–77.

Hayes, D. A. & Tierney, R. (1982). Developing readers' knowledge through analogy. *Reading Research Quarterly, 17,* 256–280.

Head, M. H., & Buss, R. R. (1987). Factors affecting summary writing and their impact on reading comprehension assessment. In J. E. Readence & R. S. Baldwin (Eds.), *Research in literacy: Merging perspectives* (36th Yearbook of the National Reading Conference) (pp. 25–33). Rochester, NY: National Reading Conference.

Heap, J. L. (1982). Understanding classroom events: A critique of Durkin, with an alternative. *Journal of Reading Behavior, 14,* 391–412.

Herber, H. L. (1978). *Teaching reading in content areas* (2nd ed.). Englewood Cliffs, NJ: Prentice-Hall.

Herman, P. A., Anderson, R. C., Pearson, P. D., & Nagy, W. E. (1987). Incidental acquisition of word meaning from expositions with varied text features. *Reading Research Quarterly, 22,* 263–284.

Higginson, B. C. (1987). An investigation into the self-selected study strategies used by college-bound secondary students: Implications for the college reading specialist. *Journal of College Reading and Learning, 20,* 24–30.

Hinchman, K. (1987). The textbook and three content-area teachers. *Reading Research and Instruction, 26,* 247–263.

Hoetker, J., & Ahlbrand, W. P., Jr. (1969). The persistence of the recitation. *American Educational Research Journal, 6,* 145–167

Holton, S. M. (1982). Secondary education. In H. E. Mitzel (Ed.), *Encyclopedia of educational research* (5th ed.) (Vol. 4) (pp. 1683–1696). New York: Free Press.

Hoy, W. K. (1969). Pupil control ideology and organizational socialization: A further examination of the influence of experience on the beginning teacher. *School Review, 77,* 257–265.

Jackson, P. (1968). *Life in classrooms.* New York: Holt, Rinehart & Winston.

Jacobson, P. B. (1932). The effect of work-type reading instruction given in the ninth grade. *School Review, 40,* 273–281.

Johnson, G. S., & Bliesmer, E. P. (1983). Effects of narrative schema training and practice in generating questions on reading comprehension of seventh-grade students. In G. H. McNinch (Ed.), *Reading research to reading practice* (3rd Yearbook of the American Reading Forum) (pp. 91–94). Athens, GA: American Reading Forum.

Jones, E. E. (1977). The effects of advance organizers prepared for specific ability levels. *School Science and Mathematics, 77,* 385–390.

Kaestle, C. F. (1985). The history of literacy and the history of readers. In E. W. Gordon (Ed.), *Review of research in education* (Vol. 12) (pp. 11–54). Washington, DC: American Educational Research Association.

Karahalios, S. M., Tonjes, M. J., & Towner, J. C. (1979). Using advance organizers to improve comprehension of a content text. *Journal of Reading, 22,* 706–708.

Katz, M. (1968). *The irony of urban school reform.* Cambridge, MA: Harvard University Press.

Katz, M. (1975). *Class, bureaucracy, and schools* (expanded ed.). New York: Praeger.

Knott, G. (1986). Secondary school contexts of reading and writing instruction. *Theory into Practice, 25,* 77–83.

Kulhavy, R. W., Dyer, J. W., & Silver, L. (1975). The effects of notetaking and test expectancy on the learning of text material. *Journal of Educational Research, 68,* 363–365.

Langer, J. A. (1988). The state of research on literacy [Review of *Literacy and schooling, Literacy, society and schooling,* and *Literacy, language, and learning: The nature and consequences of reading and writing*]. *Educational Researcher, 17* (3), 42–46.

Lapp, D., Flood, J., & Alvarez, D. (1988, November). *Preservice teachers, secondary classroom teachers, and teacher educators: A model which promotes effective instruction and learning.* Paper presented at the annual meeting of the National Reading Conference, Tucson, AZ.

Lawrence, A. E. (1978). Study skills and study habits: A review of the research and literature at the secondary level. In J. L Vaughan & P. J. Gaus (Eds.), *Research on reading in the secondary schools* (Vol. 2) (pp. 3–22). University of Arizona, Tucson, AZ.

Lightfoot, S. L. (1983). *The good high school.* New York: Basic Books.

Lortie, D. C. (1975). *Schoolteacher: A sociological study.* Chicago: University of Chicago Press.

Luke, C., DeCastell, S., & Luke, A. (1983). Beyond criticism: The authority of the school text. *Curriculum Inquiry, 13,* 111–128.

MacDonald, J. D. (1986). Self-generated questions and reading recall: Does training help? *Contemporary Educational Psychology, 11,* 290–304.

Manzo, A. V. (1969). Improving reading comprehension through reciprocal questioning. (From *Dissertation Abstracts International,* 1970, *30,* University Microfilms No. 70-10,364)

Marshall, J. D. (1989). *Patterns of discourse in classroom discussions of literature* (Tech. Rep. No. 2.9) Albany: State University of New York at Albany, Center for the Learning & Teaching of Literature.

Martin, J. R. (1976). What should we do with a hidden curriculum when we find one? *Curriculum Inquiry, 6,* 135–151.

Martin, M. A., Konopak, B. C., & Martin, S. H. (1986). Use of the guided writing procedure to facilitate reading comprehension of high school text materials. In J. A. Niles & R. V. Lalik (Eds.), *Solving problems in literacy: Learners, teachers, and researchers* (35th Yearbook of the National Reading Conference) (pp. 66–72), Rochester, NY: National Reading Conference.

Mathews, C. O. (1938). Comparison of methods of study for immediate and delayed recall. *Journal of Educational Psychology, 29*, 101–106.

McArthur, J. (1978). What does teaching do to teachers? *Educational Administration Quarterly, 14*, 89–103.

McCallister, J. M. (1930a). Reading difficulties in studying content subjects. *Elementary School Journal, 31*, 191–201.

McCallister, J. M. (1930b). Guiding pupils' reading activities in the study of content subjects. *Elementary School Journal, 31*, 271–284.

McLaren, P. (1986). *Schooling as a ritual performance.* London: Routledge & Kegan Paul.

McNeil, L. M. (1986). *Contradictions of control.* London: Routledge & Kegan Paul.

Memory, D. M. (1983). Constructing main idea questions: A test of a depth-of-processing perspective. In J. A. Niles & L. A. Harris (Eds.), *Searches for meaning in reading/language processing and instruction* (32nd Yearbook of the National Reading Conference) (pp. 66–70). Rochester, NY: National Reading Conference.

Meyer, B. J. F., Brandt, D. M., & Bluth, G. J. (1980). Use of top-level structure in text: Key for reading comprehension of ninth-grade students. *Reading Research Quarterly, 16*, 72–103.

Minuchin, P. P., & Shapiro, E. K. (1983). The school as a context for social development. In P. H. Mussen (Ed.), *Handbook of child psychology* (4th ed.) (pp. 197–274). New York: Wiley.

Mitman, A. L., Mergendoller, J. R., & St. Clair, G. (1987, April). *The role of textbooks in middle grade science teaching.* Paper presented at the annual meeting of the American Educational Research Association, Washington, DC.

Moes, M. A., Foertsch, D. J., Stewart, J., Dunning, D., Rogers, T., Seda-Santana, I., Benjamin, L., & Pearson, D. (1984). Effects of text structure on children's comprehension of expository material. In J. A. Niles & L. A. Harris (Eds.), *Changing perspectives on research in reading/language processing and instruction* (33rd Yearbook of the National Reading Conference) (pp. 28–41). Rochester, NY: National Reading Conference.

Moore, D. W., & Readence, J. E. (1984). A quantitative and qualitative review of graphic organizer research. *Journal of Educational Research, 78*, 11–17.

Moore, D. W., Readence, J. E., & Rickelman, R. J. (1983). An historical exploration of content area reading instruction. *Reading Research Quarterly, 18*, 419–438.

National Assessment of Educational Progress. (1985). *The reading report card.* Princeton, NJ: Educational Testing Service.

National Commission on Excellence in Education. (1983). *A nation at risk: The imperative for educational reform.* Washington, DC: U.S. Government Printing Office.

Nicholson, T. (1984). Experts and novices: A study of reading in the high school classroom. *Reading Research Quarterly, 19*, 436–451.

Oakes, J. (1985). *Keeping track: How schools structure inequality.* New Haven: Yale University Press.

O'Brien, D. G. (1988). Secondary preservice teachers' resistance to content reading instruction: A proposal for a broader rationale. In J. E. Readence & R. S. Baldwin (Eds.), *Dialogues in literacy research* (37th Yearbook of the National Reading Conference) (pp. 237–243). Chicago: National Reading Conference.

Palincsar, A. S., & Brown, A. L. (1984a). Reciprocal teaching of comprehension-fostering and comprehension-monitoring activities. *Cognition and Instruction 1*, 117–175 (Study 1).

Palincsar, A. S., & Brown, A. L. (1984b). Reciprocal teaching of comprehension-fostering and comprehension-monitoring activities. *Cognition and Instruction, 1*, 117–175 (Study 2).

Parsons, T. (1959). The school class as a social system: Some of its functions in American society. *Harvard Educational Review, 29*, 297–318.

Passow, A. H. (1986). Beyond the commission reports: Toward meaningful school improvement. In A. Lieberman (Ed.), *Rethinking school improvement: Research, craft, and concept* (pp. 206–218). New York: Teachers College Press, Columbia University.

Pearson, P. D., Barr, R., Kamil, M. L., & Mosenthal, P. (Eds.). (1984). *Handbook of reading research* (Vol. 1). White Plains, NY: Longman.

Pearson, P. D., & Gallagher, M. C. (1983). The instruction of reading comprehension. *Contemporary Educational Psychology, 8*, 317–344.

Perrone, V. (1985). *Portraits of high schools.* Lawrenceville, NJ: Princeton University Press.

Peters, C. (1975–1976). The effect of systematic restructuring of material upon the comprehension process. *Reading Research Quarterly, 11*, 87–111.

Peters, E. E., & Levin, J. R. (1986). Effects of a mnemonic imagery strategy on good and poor readers' prose recall. *Reading Research Quarterly, 21*, 179–192.

Powell, A. G., Farrar, E., & Cohen, D. K. (1985). *The shopping mall high school: Winners and losers in the educational marketplace.* Boston: Houghton Mifflin.

Pressley, M., Borkowski, J. G., & Schneider, W. (1987). Cognitive strategies: Good strategy users coordinate metacognition and knowledge. In R. Vasta (Ed.), *Annals of child development* (Vol. 4) (pp. 89–129). Greenwich, CT: JAI Press.

Proger, B. B., Taylor, R. G., Jr., Mann, L., Coulson, J. M., & Bayuk, R. J., Jr. (1970). Conceptual pre-structuring for detailed verbal passages. *Journal of Educational Research, 64*, 28–34.

Raphael, T. E., & McKinney, J. (1983). An examination of fifth- and eighth-grade children's question-answering behavior: An instructional study in metacognition. *Journal of Reading Behavior, 15*(3), 67–86.

Rasco, R. W., Tennyson, R. D., & Boutwell, R. C. (1975). Imagery instructions and drawings in learning prose. *Journal of Educational Psychology, 67*, 188–192.

Ratekin, N., Simpson, M. L., Alvermann, D. E., & Dishner, E. K. (1985). Why content teachers resist reading instruction. *Journal of Reading, 28*, 432–437.

Readence, J. E., Baldwin, R. S., & Rickleman, R. J. (1983). The role of word knowledge in metaphorical interpretation. In J. A. Niles & L. A. Harris (Eds.), *Searches for meaning in reading/language processing and instruction* (32nd Yearbook of the National Reading Conference) (pp. 178–181). Rochester, NY: National Reading Conference.

Readence, J. E., Bean, T. W., & Baldwin, R. S. (1985). *Content area reading: An integrated approach* (2nd ed.). Dubuque, IA: Kendall/Hunt.

Reis, R., & Spekman, N. J. (1983). The detection of reader-based versus text-based inconsistencies and the effects of direct training of comprehension monitoring among upper-grade poor comprehenders. *Journal of Reading Behavior, 15*(2), 49–60.

Resnick, D. P., & Resnick, L. R. (1977). The nature of literacy: An historical exploration. *Harvard Educational Review, 47*, 370–385.

Resnick, D. P., & Resnick, L. R. (1985). Standards, curriculum, and performance: A historical and comparative perspective. *Educational Researcher, 14*(4), 5–21.

Rieck, B. J. (1977). How content teachers telegraph messages against reading. *Journal of Reading, 20*, 646–648.

Robinson, F. P. (1941). *Diagnostic and remedial techniques for effective study.* New York: Harper & Bros.

Rothkopf, E. L., & Bisbicos, E. E. (1967). Selective facilitative effects of interspersed questions on learning from written materials. *Journal of Educational Psychology, 58*, 56–61.

Rudolf, K. B. (1949). *The effect of reading instruction on achievement in eighth-grade social studies* (Contributions to Education, No. 945). New York: Teachers College, Columbia University.

Ryan, K. (1970). The first year of teaching. In K. Ryan (Ed.), *Don't smile until Christmas* (pp. 164–190). Chicago: University of Chicago Press.

Ryans, D. G. (1960). *Characteristics of teachers.* Washington, DC: American Council on Education.

Salisbury, R. (1934). A study of the transfer effects of training in logical organizations. *Journal of Educational Research, 28*, 241–254.

Santiesteban, A. J., & Koran, J. J. (1977). Instrumental adjuncts and learning science from written materials. *Journal of Research in Science Teaching, 14*, 51–55.

Sarason, S. B. (1982). *The culture of the school and the problem of change* (2nd ed.). Boston: Allyn & Bacon.

Schallert, D. L., & Tierney, R. J. (1980). *Learning from expository text: The interaction of text structure with reader characteristics* (Report No. 79-0167). Washington, DC: National Institute of Education. (ERIC Document Reproduction Service No. ED 221 833)

Schultz, C. B., & DiVesta, F. J. (1972). Effects of passage organization and note taking on the selection of clustering strategies and on recall of textual materials. *Journal of Educational Psychology, 63*, 244–252.

Sedlak, M., Wheeler, C., Pullin, D., & Cusick, P. (1986). *Selling students short: Classroom bargain and reform of the American high school.* New York: Teachers College Press, Columbia University.

Selakovich, D. (1984). *Schooling in America.* New York: Longman.

Shimmerlik, S. M., & Nolan, J. D. (1976). Reorganization and recall of prose. *Journal of Educational Psychology, 68*, 779–786.

Shulman, L. (1987). Knowledge and teaching: Foundations of the new reform. *Harvard Educational Review, 57*, 1–22.

Silberman, C. E. (1970). *Crisis in the classroom.* New York: Random House.

Simon, D. L. (1934). Developing desirable reading habits in studying citizenship. *School Review, 42*, 447–458.

Sinclair, J. McH., & Coulthard, R. M. (1975). *Towards an analysis of discourse.* London: Oxford University Press.

Singer, H. (1983). A century of landmarks in reading and learning from text at the high school level: Research, theories, and instructional strategies. *Journal of Reading, 26*, 332–342.

Singer, H., & Donlan, D. (1982). Active comprehension: Problem-solving schema with question generation for comprehension of complex short stories. *Reading Research Quarterly, 17*, 166–186.

Singer, H., & Donlan, D. (1985). *Reading and learning from text.* Hillsdale, NJ: Erlbaum.

Sizer, T. R. (1984). *Horace's compromise: The dilemma of the American high school.* Boston: Houghton Mifflin.

Sjostrom, C. L., & Hare, V. C. (1984). Teaching high school students to identify main ideas in expository text. *Journal of Educational Research, 78*, 114–118.

Slater, W. H., Palmer, R. J., & Graves, M. F. (1982). Effects of directions describing passage structure, signaling, and elaboration on reader's recall. In P. L. Anders (Ed.), *Research on reading in secondary schools* (Monograph No. 9) (pp. 1–25). Tucson: University of Arizona.

Slater, W. H., Graves, M. F., & Piche, G. L. (1985). Effects of structural organizers on ninth-grade students' comprehension and recall of four patterns of expository text. *Reading Research Quarterly, 20,* 189–202.

Smith, A. E. (1973). The effectiveness of training students to generate their own questions prior to reading. In P. L. Nacke (Ed.), *Diversity in mature reading: Theory and research* (22nd Yearbook of the National Reading Conference) (pp. 71–77). Boone, NC: National Reading Conference.

Smith, F. R., & Feathers, K. M. (1983a). Teacher and student perceptions of content area reading. *Journal of Reading, 26,* 348–354.

Smith, F. R., & Feathers, K. M. (1983b). The role of reading in content classrooms: Assumption vs. reality. *Journal of Reading, 27,* 262–267.

Smith, L., & Geoffrey, W. (1968). *The complexities of an urban classroom.* New York: Holt, Rinehart & Winston.

Smith, R. J., & Hesse, K. D. (1969). The effects of prereading assistance on the comprehension and attitudes of good and poor readers. *Research in the Teaching of English, 3,* 166–177.

Spenser, F. (1978). SQ3R: Several queries regarding relevant research. In J. L. Vaughan & P. J. Gaus (Eds.), *Research on reading in the secondary schools* (Vol. 2) (pp. 23–38). Tucson: University of Arizona.

Squire, J. R. (in press). The history of the profession. In J. Flood, J. Jensen, D. Lapp, & J. Squire (Eds.), *Handbook of research on teaching the English language arts.* New York: Macmillan.

Stahl, N. A. (1983). A historical analysis of textbook-study systems. *Dissertation Abstracts International, 45,* 480A. (University Microfilms No. 84-11,839)

Stake, R. E., & Easley, J. (1978). *Case studies in science education* (Vol. 2: Design, overview and general findings). Washington, DC: U.S. Government Printing Office.

Stedman, L. C., & Kaestle, C. F. (1987). Literacy and reading performance in the United States, from 1880 to the present. *Reading Research Quarterly, 22,* 8–46.

Stewart, R. A., & O'Brien, D. G. (1989). Resistance to content area reading: A focus on preservice teachers. *Journal of Reading, 32,* 396–401.

Swafford, J. (1988, December). *The use of study strategy instruction with secondary school students: Is there a research base?* Paper presented at the annual meeting of the National Reading Conference, Tucson, AZ.

Taylor, B. M., & Beach, R. W. (1984). The effects of text structure instruction on middle-grade students' comprehension and production of expository text. *Reading Research Quarterly, 19,* 134–146.

Turner, W. J. (1968). A study of the effectiveness of teaching methods of study to selected high school freshmen. *Dissertation Abstracts, 28,* 978A. (University Microfilms No. 67-10,777)

Tye, B. B. (1985). *Multiple realities: A study of 13 American high schools.* Lanham, MD: University Press of America.

Tye, K. A. (1985). *The junior high: A school in search of a mission.* Lanham, MD: University Press of America.

Vacca, R. T. (1975). The development of a functional reading strategy: Implications for content area instruction. *Journal of Educational Research, 69,* 108–112.

Vacca, R. (1978). The effect of expanded directions and adjunct aids on students' comprehension of world history text. In P. D. Pearson & J. Hansen (Eds.), *Reading: Disciplined inquiry in process and practice* (27th Yearbook of the National Reading Conference) (pp. 222–225). Clemson, SC: National Reading Conference.

Vacca, R. T., & Vacca, J. L. (1986). *Content area reading* (2nd ed.). Boston: Little, Brown.

Vallance, E. (1977). Hiding the hidden curriculum: An interpretation of the language of justification in nineteenth-century educational reform. In A. A. Bellack & H. M. Kliebard (Eds.), *Curriculum and evaluation* (pp. 590–607). Berkeley, CA: McCutchan.

Vaughan, J. L. (1984). Concept structuring: The technique and empirical evidence. In S. D. Holley & D. F. Dansereau (Eds.), *Spatial learning strategies* (pp. 127–147). New York: Academic Press.

Vaughan, J. L., & Estes, T. H. (1986). *Reading and reasoning beyond the primary grades.* Boston: Allyn & Bacon.

Veenman, S. (1984). Perceived problems of beginning teachers. *Review of Educational Research, 54,* 143–178.

Venezky, R., Kaestle, C., & Sum, A. (1987). *The subtle danger: Reflecting on the literacy abilities of America's young adults.* Princeton, NJ: Educational Testing Service.

Violas, P. C. (1978). *The training of the urban working class: A history of twentieth-century American education.* Chicago: Rand McNally.

von Eschenbach, J. F., & Ley, T. C. (1984). Differences between elementary and secondary teachers' perceptions of instructional practices. *High School Journal, 68,* 31–36.

Wade, S. E. (1983). A synthesis of the research for improving reading in the social studies. *Review of Educational Research, 53,* 461–497.

Waller, W. (1932). *The sociology of teaching.* New York: Wiley.

Warner, M. M. (1977). Teaching learning-disabled junior high students to use visual imagery as a strategy for facilitating recall of reading passages. *Dissertation Abstracts International, 38,* 7277A.

Washburne, J. (1929). The use of questions in social science material. *Journal of Educational Psychology, 20,* 321–359.

Watts, G. H., & Anderson, R. C. (1971). Effects of three types of inserted questions on learning from prose. *Journal of Educational Psychology, 62,* 387–394.

Weinstein, C. E. (1982). Training students to use elaboration learning strategies. *Contemporary Educational Psychology, 7,* 301–311.

Weinstein, C. E., & Mayer, R. E. (1986). The teaching of learning strategies. In M. C. Wittrock (Ed.), *Handbook of research on teaching* (3rd ed.) (pp. 315–327). New York: Macmillan.

Weinstein, C. E., & Underwood, V. L. (1985). Learning strategies: The *how* of learning. In J. W. Segal, S. F. Chipman, & R. Glaser (Eds.), *Thinking and learning skills, Volume I: Relating instruction to research* (pp. 241–258). Hillsdale, NJ: Erlbaum.

Weiss, I. R. (1978). *Report of the 1977 national survey of science, mathematics, and social studies education.* Washington, DC: U.S. Government Printing Office.

White, M. A. (1974). Is recitation reinforcing? *Teachers College Record, 76,* 135–142.

Wiley, K. B. (1977). *The status of pre-college science, mathematics, and social science educational practices in U.S. schools: An overview and summary of three studies.* Washington, DC: U.S. Government Printing Office.

Wilkerson, B. C. (1986). Inferences: A window to comprehension. In J. A. Niles & R. V. Lalik (Eds.), *Solving problems in literacy: Learners, teachers, and researchers* (35th Yearbook of the National Reading Conference) (pp. 192–198). Rochester, NY: National Reading Conference.

Willinsky, J. M. (1987). The seldom-spoken roots of the curriculum: Romanticism and the new literacy. *Curriculum Inquiry, 17,* 267–292.

Willower, D. J., Eidell, T. L., & Hoy, W. K. (1967). *The school and pupil control ideology* (Pennsylvania State Studies Monograph, No. 24). University Park: Pennsylvania State University Press.

Winograd, P. N. (1984). Strategic difficulties in summarizing texts. *Reading Research Quarterly, 19,* 404–425.

Wise, A. (1979). *Legislated learning: The bureaucratization of the American classroom.* Berkeley: University of California Press.

Witte, P. L., & Otto, W. (1981). Reading instruction at the postelementary level: Review and comments. *Journal of Educational Research, 74,* 148–158.

Wittrock, M. C. (Ed.). (1986). *Handbook of research on teaching* (3rd ed.). New York: Macmillan.

Wong, B. Y. L. (1985). Self-questioning instructional research: A review. *Review of Educational Research, 55,* 227–268.

Wong, B. Y. L., & Jones, W. (1982). Increasing metacomprehension in learning-disabled and normally achieving students through self-questioning training. *Learning Disability Quarterly, 5,* 228–240.

Wood, K. D. (1986). The effect of interspersing questions in text: Evidence for "slicing the task." *Reading Research and Instruction, 25,* 295–307.

Woods, P. (1983). *Sociology and the school.* London: Routledge & Kegan Paul.

34 REMEDIATION

Peter Johnston and Richard Allington

Language is always metaphorical and words carry more baggage than appears at first glance. The words we use to discuss the acquisition of reading are not excepted from this general principle. For instance, the word *remedial* is used by different individuals in different ways and to mean different things; and the several meanings, as well as the historical development of these, deserve some exploration. Each of the meanings involves an entire metaphor and attendant consequences. Exploring these metaphors is illuminating.

HOW REMEDIATION MEANS

The Language of Remedial Reading

The word *remedial* comes to us from the Latin roots *re*, meaning "again," and *mederi*, meaning "to heal." Literally, it means "to heal again." The word could have come to us from other roots. For example, it could have come from the Latin *mediare*, meaning "to divide in the middle." This would lead to an entirely different set of metaphors. Webster's Unabridged (2nd ed.) tells us that *mediation* (from *mediare*) means "intercession or friendly intervention, usually by consent or invitation." A further meaning of remedial, also stemming from *mediatus-mediare*, is the adverbial form "dependent on, acting by, or connected through some intervening agency; related indirectly: opposed to immediate." Using a similar analysis, Cole and Griffin (1986) have suggested that "*remediation* means a shift in the way that mediating devices regulate coordination with the environment" (p. 113) and assert that "Most of our children [here referring to participants in remedial reading instruction] do not have the slightest notion of what the system of mediation we call reading is about. The system of remediation most commonly used does not re-mediate the overall understanding of what reading is or is for . . ." (p. 127).

On the other hand, *Webster's New Collegiate Dictionary* brings home the narrower meaning of *remedial* as "intended as a remedy" or "concerned with the correction of faulty study habits and the raising of a pupil's general competence [reading courses]" and *remediation* is offered as "the act or process of remedying [of reading problems]." Here the meanings of *remedy*, too, are instructive.

1: a medicine, application, or treatment that relieves or cures a disease
2: something that corrects or counteracts an evil
3: the legal means to recover a right or to prevent or obtain redress for a wrong.

These meanings of *remedial* and related words differ in the location of the problem, valence, and the implicit nature of the problem to be remedied, and how one would act upon the problem. Of primary concern here is the term remedial and with its connotations of sickness. This association with sickness may have evolved from the early interest of the medical profession in children who did not acquire reading proficiency as a result of school attendance. Morgan's (1896) and Hinshelwood's (1917) reports on "word blindness" seemed to focus educational attention on locating the cause of an individual's failure to acquire reading proficiency (Pelosi, 1977; Critchley, 1964). Only 20 years later, following the development of the first standardized assessment instruments for measuring reading proficiency, Uhl (1916) introduced the term *remedial reading* (Smith, 1965) in an article entitled "The Use of Results of Reading Tests as Bases for Planning Remedial Work." Within a decade the term was popularized, aided by its use by W. S. Gray (1922) in "Remedial Cases in Reading: Their Diagnosis and Treatment," one of a series of monographs published by the University of Chicago Press. There is, however, a not-so-subtle shift in usage here—from *remedial* as a characteristic of instruction to a characteristic of the reader. While Webster's continues to define remedial as descriptive of instruction or other interventions, current educational use includes reference to "remedial readers." In addition, remedial is used, alas, to describe not simply a state but a trait.

Other words frequently associated with the term remedial are *diagnosis* and *clinic*. Once again, there are several meanings associated with these words. Returning to the roots, we find that diagnosis derives from the Greek words *dia*, meaning between or across; and *gnosis*, meaning to know. A useful interpretation with respect to children is thus simply to know between, or to know the ways children are the same or different from each other and how their way of knowing and being literate is similar to and different from that of mature proficient readers. However, how and what one knows about the similarities and dissimilarities is bounded by the lens one uses to examine the child. Sarason (1971), for instance, notes that the existing culture and its inherent structure and beliefs define the permissible options for examining goals or outcomes and that it is hard for those who operate in a culture to "recognize, create, or believe in alternative structures" (p. 12). In reference to the diagnosis of learning difficulties, Cummins (1986) points out but one limitation in current practice:

> If the psychologist's task is to discover the causes of a . . . student's academic difficulties and the only tools at his or her disposal are psychological tests, then it is hardly surprising that the child's difficulties will be attributed to psychological dysfunctions. (p. 39)

The metaphors that have dominated our attempts to diagnose difficulties in acquiring reading proficiency were borrowed from medicine and shaped by sociology and psychology. Critchley (1964) notes, "What had hitherto been a medical province or responsibility now became invaded by the sociologists and educational psychologists . . ." (p. 9). Both, however, advanced *deficit hypotheses*, in which the deficits were found in the child, though as a result of environment, experience, or heredity.

Pelosi (1977) suggests that there have been three different understandings in educational use of the term diagnosis. The earliest, as evidenced in the work of C. T. Gray (1922), was a "remedial" conception, with diagnosis presented as a "procedure which enables the teacher to determine the difficulties of those pupils who are below standards for their grade level" (p. 7). W. S. Gray (1922), Monroe (1936), and Robinson (1946), on the other hand, advanced a "causative" conceptualization of diagnosis in which one attempted to identify those factors that inhibited reading acquisition. While classroom, school, home, and community were not wholly ignored (they could have been identified as the source of the problem), the focus was on the identification of deficits in the child. A third perspective traced by Pelosi is the *research orientation*.

Here the focus was on development and refinement of diagnostic procedures and instruments to produce precision in diagnosis. This conceptualization was dominated by educational psychologists and resulted in a vast array of instrumentation one might use to diagnose the "sickness" inherent in children who failed to learn to read on society's schedule.

Like diagnosis, *clinic*, another word often associated with the term remedial, has a medical derivation from the Latin root (*clinicus*—a bedridden person). One treated at a clinic is deemed ill, or deficient, and in need of a remedy. The adjectival form, *clinical*, has come through positivistic medical science to mean "impersonal, sterile, and distant" (as in "his style is so clinical"). Smith (1965) notes that the first "clinic for remedial instruction" was established in 1921 at the University of California at Los Angeles by Grace Fernald. This effort evolved into the Clinic School, which was to become part of the University's Department of Psychology. Over the next decade several other reading clinics were established at universities and in large school systems. Many of these ventures were multidisciplinary, with a particular bent toward combining psychological, medical, and optometric procedures into the diagnostic and remedial processes.

We provide this review and analysis because we believe it useful to consider the kinds of words we use and their implications. Of major concern is the legacy of connotations of sickness that permeate the meanings we assign to the word remedial and associated words. *Diagnosis*, which originally was instructionally oriented, now means assessing an individual's performance on a very narrow range of psychometric instruments in an attempt to locate deficits and deficiencies. *Clinics* once, according to Gray (1922), were established "to provide classroom teachers with expert help," but now operate in relative isolation from the classroom, classroom instruction, and classroom curriculum (Johnston, Allington, & Afflerbach, 1985).

We argue that this language creates roles and one simply fills in the details of how to behave with such a person. In this case, the association with sickness suggests that those afflicted are relatively helpless and will require our help. While remedial once described instructional procedures, it is now used to describe children. We must examine what makes instruction remedial and what makes children remedial. We either need to acquire a new vocabulary or we need to more carefully use the vocabulary we have in place. In any case, we would suggest that the use of the terms *children-with-different-schedules-for-reading-acquisition*, or *children-we-have-failed-to-teach-to-read*, would result in different understandings of the issue than the use of the term remedial readers.

The Emergence of Remedial and Special Education

As most commonly understood in current usage, remedial readers are but a subset of the children who have failed to acquire proficient reading abilities in accordance with the schedule set by the assessment system. Essentially, what has evolved, especially over the past 20 years, is a system of categorical eligibility that sorts children we have failed to teach to read into one of two broad categories: remedial or special education. These categories have been broadly related to the supposed etiology of the teaching difficulty. Table 34.1 depicts the delineation of the categories and corresponding federal regulatory basis, indicates the key words used to describe the learners, and identifies the supposed etiologies and prognoses for learners. These two sets of categorical programs, remedial and special education, have emerged to address the problem of children we fail to teach to read in regular education. Historically, however, the fields derive from similar roots and have had similar concerns (Critchley, 1964; McGill-Franzen, 1987; Ysseldyke & Algozzine, 1982a).

TABLE 34.1 Delineation of Categorical Terms, Programs, Presumed Etiology, and Outcomes

REGULAR EDUCATION		
Remedial Education	Category	Special Education
Chapter 1 of ECIA of 1980	Program	EHA of 1975 (PL94–142)
Disadvantaged	Label	Disabled/Handicapped
Environmental/experiential	Etiology	Physiological/emotional/intellectual
Enriched education solves	Outcomes	Permanent deficit limits learning

Separation of remedial and special education is not a recent development, nor have the differences only recently emerged. Over a half-century ago, Arthur Gates (1937), writing for the National Society for the Study of Education (NSSE) Committee on Reading, noted that

Some decades ago, when attention was first directed to these children, such terms as "word-blindness" and "congenital alexis" were commonly used. These terms are now rarely employed, since they imply that the cases of extreme difficulty in reading are the result of specific organic defects and that the prognosis is far from hopeful. (p. 394)

Instead, the committee recommended the use of the term "extreme reading difficulty" for the "three to four children of each hundred that enter the first grade encountering difficulties so severe as to make expert diagnosis and remedial treatment advisable, if not absolutely necessary" (p. 392). On the other hand, in that same era, Gillingham and Stillman (1936) argued that it was not 3 to 4 percent of the population that experienced "severe difficulties," but 15 percent. She went on to explain her understanding of the etiology of acquisition difficulties in reading:

The essential difference between our point of view and that of the authorities to whom we have referred is that we find all of the cases in our school and those sent from outside, to be selective language disability cases, not merely non-readers. (Gillingham & Stillman, 1936, p. 170)

Gillingham and Stillman (1936) argue for considering the disability a permanent characteristic of the learner, suggesting that while specialized instruction can alleviate some of the difficulty, the disability is permanent and, therefore, basically irremediable. While many have written much on both remedial and special education, children's difficulties in the acquisition of reading are central to each educational strand. Even the early classic texts (e.g., Dolch, 1931) separated children experiencing reading acquisition difficulties into two categories, as in Table 34.1, and other texts focused solely on the problems of "handicapped" children (Dolch, 1948; Kirk, 1940). However, two subsequent developments have perpetuated that segregation.

First, the separation of children has become institutionalized, with the demarcations drawn by federal regulations and professional segregation (McLaughlin, 1982). Second, there has been an explosive growth in the proportion of children served in special education since the Education of All Handicapped Children Act (EHA) of 1975 (Algozzine, Ysseldyke, & Christenson, 1983; Foster, 1984). The growth in special education has occurred while the number of students served in federally funded remedial programs (Chapter 1 of the Educational Consolidation Act [ECIA] of 1980) has shrunk. This growth in special education has been a result of the "learning-disabled" classification expanding tremendously in the past 20 years (McGill-Franzen, 1987), an expansion such that today "learning-disabled" students represent nearly one-half of all special education classifications. McGill-Franzen (1987) provides a compelling analysis that suggests that children previously served in Chapter 1 remedial programs are now served in special education programs for the learning disabled.

There has been a more recent trend to provide special education students with services in the "least restrictive environment," or greater integration of these students into regular education classrooms (Wang, Reynolds, & Walberg, 1987). This integration has mixed regular, remedial, and special education students together in the schools; and, perhaps as a result of this mixing, similarities among students—particularly remedial and special education—have become the subject of research and discussion. Currently, the professional literature is rife with debate about the reliability, utility, and economics of separate systems for educating students with similar academic difficulties (Gartner & Lipsky, 1987; Reynolds, Wang, & Walberg, 1987; Stainback & Stainback, 1984; Will, 1986).

The debate focuses on three issues. First, etiology is problematic. Serious questions about the validity and reliability of the assessment instruments and procedures have been raised (Algozzine & Ysseldyke, 1983; Arter & Jenkins, 1979; Coles, 1987; Johnston, 1987a; Mehan, Hartweck, & Meihls, 1986; Messick, 1984). Second, separation of learners into groups with different educational profiles also seems problematic. On this issue there is substantial empirical evidence that children served in the various categorical programs differ on few, if any, commonly measured educational variables (Jenkins, 1987; Leinhardt, Bickel, & Pallay, 1982; Messick, 1984; Shepard, Smith, & Vojir, 1983; Ysseldyke, Algozzine, & Epps, 1983; Ysseldyke, Algozzine, Shinn, & McGue, 1982). Third, instructional needs differentiation by category has received little support from the research. Evidence has accrued that (1) reading-achievement gains by students in regular, remedial, or special education programs are related to instruction environments and activities that are similarly described (Crawford, Kimball, & Patrick, 1984; Larrivee, 1985; Leinhardt & Pallay, 1982; Morsink, Soar, Soar, & Thomas, 1986); and (2) reading-instructional activities in remedial and special education programs are similar, though seeming to differ from regular education instructional practice in several ways (Allington & McGill-Franzen, 1989b). Thus, the "different programs for different needs" rationale for the separation of students into remedial and special education categories is undermined by current practice (McGill-Franzen & Allington, 1990).

Remediation and remedial reading, as currently used, typically exclude special education interventions. The recent evidence noted above, however, suggests this traditional view is unnecessarily limiting. Hence, in this chapter we take a broader view of remediation efforts and remedial reading. In our view, remediation encompasses efforts to instruct any child whose reading development has, by some arbitrary standard, been deemed less than satisfactory, regardless of the supposed etiology or the source of funding for the instruction provided.

THE NATURE OF CURRENT REMEDIAL PROGRAMS

In opening this section, we would note, like Carter (1984), that, although there are individually coherent programs, there is no such thing as a typical remediation program, at least in the sense of a single organizational plan or prototypical approach to instruction. Rather, what exists, primarily, are funding patterns to support remediation and, in some cases, legislation or policy mandates to provide the same. While evaluations of remediation efforts have been routinely conducted by district, state, and federal agencies, the focus more often has been on evaluating compliance with regulations and policies than on the question of resolving reading difficulties. Light and Smith (1971),

Cooley (1981), Gartner and Lipsky (1987), and Slavin (1987b) are but a few who have argued that the traditional program evaluations were misdirected since they rarely focused on effective programs or attempts to discover why some programs seem to obtain more positive outcomes. What we do have is a series of studies that report proxies for effective educational environments, proxies that appear in regulatory language such as class size, contact time, teacher certification, and the like; but what we lack are careful descriptions of the educational interventions offered as remediation (though the recent Rowan & Guthrie [1989] and Lee et al. [1986] reports for the national evaluation of Chapter 1, and Clay and Cazden's [in press] and Pinnell's [1989] descriptions of Reading Recovery, begin to provide such descriptions).

Characteristics of organizational plans.   The primary organizational pattern for providing remediation is the small group withdrawn from the regular classroom setting. Remediation is rarely one-to-one tutorial instruction and rarely provided in groups larger than eight, at least in the elementary schools (Birman et al., 1987; Calfee & Drum, 1979; Stonehill & Anderson, 1982). Most remediation is offered at a site separate from the regular classroom but usually in the same building (Birman et al., 1987; Vanecko, Ames, & Archambault, 1980). In the case of students served in full-time special education classes, the figures shift a bit, with 10 to 12 students common, but again a separate classroom in a regular school building is the most common location. More recently, there have been suggestions that lower teacher-pupil ratios may be important considerations. For example, Carter (1984) found that in Chapter 1 programs, lower teacher-pupil ratios were more frequently associated with successful outcomes. Similarly, in the Reading Recovery project (Clay, 1985; Pinnell, 1989), one-on-one instruction has been shown to have considerable advantages, as would be predicted from the work of Bloom (1984). In addition, there has recently begun a shift away from the withdrawal approach toward in-class remedial interventions. This shift is associated with a changing role of the specialist teacher toward a more collaborative, consultative model.

A second characteristic of remediation is that typically it is provided by a teacher who has earned more graduate credits and who is more likely to hold a specialized teaching license (Allington, 1980; Ysseldyke & Algozzine, 1982a). These specialized licenses seem most frequently to be either a "reading teacher/specialist" or "special education/learning-disability" license, earned primarily through graduate professional training. On the other hand, most of the teacher aides found in schools today are funded with remedial or special education monies, and they work almost exclusively with participants in these programs. The apparent paradox of using paraprofessionals with limited instructional expertise to assist those children experiencing the greatest difficulties has not drawn much comment in the discussions of improving school programs for these learners.

Indeed, another characteristic of current remediation is that it is commonly, and often totally, funded with state or federal money. The emergence of these fiscal incentives is traced by McGill-Franzen (1987), who also notes some of the important influences the current incentives-disincentives bear on the design of remediation. A similar theme can be found in Allington and McGill-Franzen (1989a); Gartner and Lipsky (1987); Leinhardt, Bickel, and Pally (1982); Singer and Butler (1987); and Wang and Reynolds (1985), among others. While these fiscal incentives are generally overlooked in analyses of remediation, there is little evidence that remediation was well funded before the legislative initiatives produced the fiscal support. This support in turn brought with it regulations and audits that markedly influenced the nature of remedial programs and the population they serve. Later, we will attempt to describe briefly some of the influences of the current regulations.

A further characteristic of remedial programs is that they tend not to get under way until the student has been in school for a couple of years. There are several probable contributors to this situation. First, there is still a belief in the notion of "reading readiness," an idea which holds that some children are not maturationally ready to begin to learn to read in kindergarten or first grade. In a readiness view, the solution to difficulties in learning to read is to wait until the child is ready before beginning instruction; thus no remediation is required, though retention is often recommended to allow the "gift of time" (Smith & Shepard, 1988). This view seems to be the basis, for example, for the recent action by Georgia that put in place a test to prevent unready children from entering kindergarten. Unfortunately, the evidence consistently indicates that practices stemming from this view, such as retention or transition-room placement, rarely serve the children well (Shepard & Smith, 1986). A second possible contributor to the late beginning of remedial instruction is the difficulty in measuring, with any accuracy, children's early reading development using standardized tests. A third might be the operational definition of reading difficulty, which is often considered to be something like a full grade equivalent (or two) behind grade level. A fourth contributor might be the federal regulations for the Chapter 1 remedial program, which until recently applied to grades two through twelve.

Recently, however, a trend towards earlier intervention has become evident. This is probably related to reports of the success of early intervention programs such as the Hi/Scope project (Schweinhart, Weikart, & Larner, 1986), and the Reading Recovery project (Clay, 1985; Pinnell, 1989), and to an increasing acceptance of the emergent literacy view of early reading (Teale & Sulzby, 1987). In addition, there has been, in the last several years, a substantial increase in the funding available for the early identification and education of handicapped children in the preschool. Unfortunately, this trend may have reached problematic proportions, as in the Texas mandate for preschool testing to detect "dyslexics."

The segregation of remedial and special programs from the regular education program is yet another characteristic of current intervention efforts. Ironically, this unfortunate development was predicted a half-century ago:

> The success of a specialist in diagnostic and remedial work depends in no small measure upon his ability to work with, through, and for the teacher, and not independently of her. The danger is that the classroom teacher may feel that diagnosis and remedial instruction of extreme cases are matters too intricate for her to understand. In effect, therefore, she may wash her hands of the problem if a specialist is available; or if one is not she may say that the case is hopeless unless an expert is provided.
>
> On the other hand, the specialist is sometimes tempted to consider that extreme cases present highly specialized problems too complicated for the teacher to understand. In some cases his technical skill exceeds his ability to learn from the teacher. The result of such a situation is unfortunate in every way. Obviously both diagnosis and remediation are most effective when the specialist and the teacher cooperate. The teacher can give the specialist illuminating accounts of the pupil's difficulties and the methods that have been employed with him. . . . Remedial instruction should not disregard earlier classroom instruction, neither should it disregard subsequent classroom instruction. (Gates, 1937, pp. 413–414)

Unfortunately, the fragmentation of the instructional experiences of participants, as Gates foresaw, is now typical. Remediation efforts typically proceed separately from the regular education instruction, regardless of the categorical program (Allington, Stuetzel, Shake, & Lamarche, 1986; Allington & Johnston, 1989; Kimbrough & Hill, 1981; McGill-Franzen & Allington, 1990; Moore, Hyde, Blair, & Weitzman, 1981). Classroom teachers too often express little personal responsibility for the learning of children served by categorical programs (Winfield, 1986), most often shifting accountability to the specialist teacher and expressing either (1) a lack of expertise, or (2) a belief that such children cannot be expected to acquire reading proficiency. In addition, classroom teachers and specialist teachers share little knowledge of each other's instructional activities (Johnston, Allington, & Afflerbach, 1985). Participants in remediation efforts work in several different curricula, often with curricula that present philosophical and pedagogical conflicts as well as fragmentation. Good (1983) summarizes the result, "It seems unfortunate that students who have least adaptive capacity may be asked to make the greatest adjustment as they move from classroom to classroom" (p. 49).

This fragmentation of instruction has been attributed to the influence of federal regulations concerning the various intervention efforts (Kimbrough & Hill, 1981), to professional segregation and conventional wisdom (Moore et al., 1981), and to an interaction between the two (Allington & Johnston, 1989). The latter argument suggests that professional knowledge of an era drives regulatory language; and, once in place, regulatory language maintains the conventions established. Some have argued that in the era of the emergence of these federal intervention efforts (1960–1970), educators had little knowledge of how one might design effective remediation (Cooley, 1981). Thus, the university clinic model was accepted, with its specialist teacher, separate rooms, unique curriculum, and specialized instructional techniques. Since that time, professional knowledge has advanced and serious challenges to the most common organizational patterns for remediation have appeared (Jenkins, Pious, & Peterson, 1988; Slavin, 1987a; Top & Osguthorpe, 1987). However, "institutional learning" (Timar & Kirp, 1987) has not kept pace with the advancing professional knowledge.

Nonetheless, we now provide reading remediation to millions of children under an array of categorical programs, such as Chapter 1, special education, migrant education, bilingual education, and other noncategorical efforts. The most recent information on these interventions suggests that much of what seems to best describe effective educational practice does not describe remediation (Allington & Johnston, 1989; Cooley & Leinhardt, 1980; Gartner & Lipsky, 1987; Morsink et al., 1986; Will, 1986).

THE NATURE OF REMEDIAL READING

As we began to write this chapter, we had concerns about how to describe remedial reading instruction as quite distinct from regular instruction. Arthur Gates described the problem well in his book, *The Improvement of Reading* (1927):

> Remedial instruction, often conceived as an emergency measure, is frequently a form of teaching radically different in type and intent from ordinary measures. For this reason, in part, such follow-up methods are frequently of distinctive character. They are often novel "supplementary" devices partaking of the nature of "stunts." Indeed, some of the worst devices and most inadequate teaching methods are to be found in remedial reading instruction for pupils who, precisely because they have had difficulties with a subject, are most in need of the best possible teaching. The fact is that remedial teaching should follow the same general principles of learning that are, or should be, observed in any other type of instruction—with certain occasional departures to meet particular types of need. These variations represent not contradictions of the main principles but special applications of them which require unusual skill and understanding. Such comprehension is to be reached by a clear grasp of the main principles themselves. (Gates, 1927, p. 19)

If Gates was correct in his description, and recent evidence suggests that he was (Allington & Johnston, 1989; Larrivee, 1985), what is special about remedial reading instruction? Remedial instruction is still done separately from regular instruction and at least since the 1930s, it has been done increasingly by a different, more specialized teacher. There have been changes in what is done in the name of remediation, but the evidence available suggests several common characteristics of current remediation efforts.

Quantity of instruction. Remedial instruction funded under Chapter 1 is required to "supplement not supplant" regular instruction. Although this requirement is not placed on remediation funded under EHA, the intention of a greater overall amount of instructional time is evident (Will, 1986). However, few of the remedial or special education instructional interventions enhance the time allocated to learn to read in any reliable manner. Those who have studied instructional time allocations report that participation in Chapter 1 programs does not insure larger quantities of reading instruction (Carter, 1984; Birman et al., 1987; Stanly & Greenwood, 1983; Rowan & Guthrie, 1989; Vanecko et al., 1980). Those who have studied special education services for the mainstreamed student offer similar findings (Haynes & Jenkins, 1986; Ysseldyke, Thurlow, Mecklenburg, & Graden, 1984). Indeed, the available evidence suggests that, as often as not, children who are failing to learn to read on schedule receive *less* instruction than their on-schedule peers. For instance, Birman et al. (1987) note that children enrolled in schools with high levels of Chapter 1-eligible students received about 25 percent less classroom reading instruction than children in schools with few Chapter 1-eligible students. Even when Chapter 1 instructional time was included in the calculations, these children received less reading instruction. Vanecko et al. (1980) and Stanley and Greenwood (1983) reported similar results for children enrolled in schools with Chapter 1 programs and those enrolled in schools without a Chapter 1 effort. Zigmond, Vallecorsa, and Leinhardt (1980) noted that special education services for the learning disabled often reduced the reading instructional time; and Allington and McGill-Franzen (1989b) report that mainstreamed special education students routinely receive smaller amounts of classroom reading instruction than Chapter 1 participants, even when the special education services are included. Transition room programs, an increasingly popular alternative to categorical programs (Leinhart, 1980), likewise, do not routinely expand instructional time allocated to reading. In addition, participation in transition rooms, like retention in grade, has no demonstrated history of effectiveness in resolving achievement deficits, even though participation typically results in an additional year of school attendance (Holmes & Matthews, 1984).

Thus, one predictable characteristic of remediation seems to be that these efforts are more likely to reduce the quantity of reading instruction than increase it. Given the importance that "opportunity to learn," even when as crudely defined as the time allocated to instruction, plays in many conceptualizations of the effective teaching of reading (Allington & Johnston, 1989; Denham & Liberman, 1980; Harris & Serwer, 1966; Kiesling, 1978; Leinhardt, Zigmond, & Cooley, 1981; Wiley & Harnischfeger, 1974), it is surprising that the design of remedial instruction rarely results in increased reading instructional time.

This result comes about in a number of ways. For example, pullout programs require travel and set-up time, and participants usually leave during some portion of the classroom reading instruction period. Furthermore, the readers assigned to such programs tend to be placed in materials that are too difficult (Jorgenson, 1977); they read more slowly and are then more likely not to be involved in reading (Gambrell, Wilson, & Gannt, 1981) and are less inclined to pick up a book unless required to do so (Anderson, Wilson, & Fielding, 1988). In addition, the use of worksheets in the name of individualization reduces both time and motivation for real reading (Allington & McGill-Franzen, 1989b). Finally, teaching the skills this way takes longer with the less-competent readers, and thus they never get beyond the instructional materials to read literature (Walmsley & Walp, 1990).

Instructional emphasis. When groups of more- and less-able readers are held up for comparison, the differences that people have described are quite diverse. They are often found to differ in phonemic awareness, phonic analysis, concepts about print, comprehension, metacognition, attributions for success and failure, speed of reading, amount of time spent reading, enjoyment of reading, and so forth (Stanovich, 1986). When people set up instructional programs, their planned instructional emphases reflect their different priorities among these differences. A half-century ago, at the emergence of the notion of remediation (Whipple, 1925), the essential objectives of remedial instruction were laid out in the following order: First, "a rich and varied experience through reading"; second, "strong motives for, and permanent interests in, reading"; and third, "desirable attitudes and economical and effective habits and skills" (pp. 9–11). The order of importance appears to have changed substantially over time. Currently we find a major characteristic of remediation is that participation rarely involves the reading of stories, magazines, or books; in fact, children served by remedial programs typically spend less time reading any text and read less text during instruction than do nonparticipating peers (Allington & McGill-Franzen, 1989b; Haynes & Jenkins, 1986; Thurlow, Ysseldyke, Graden, & Algozzine, 1984; Ysseldyke & Algozzine, 1982b). Instead, remediation primarily involves the individual completion of worksheet tasks that rarely require reading more than a sentence or paragraph (Allington et al., 1986; Quirk, Trismen, Weinberg, & Nalin, 1976). The focus of remediation, and the classroom reading instruction for these readers, tends to be on attention to accuracy of print detail and not on the composition or construction of meaning (Allington, 1983; Hiebert, 1983; Stanovich, 1986). Perhaps it is because so little text reading is accomplished, and little of this reading is done silently, that led the most comprehensive study of remediation to note the virtual absence of instructional activities that offer opportunities "to engage in higher order academic skills" (Birman et al., 1987, p. 114). More instructional time is allocated to either specific skill seatwork or nonacademic activities (travel, management, and so on) than to comprehension-focused text reading (Allington, et al., 1986; Haynes & Jenkins, 1986; Quirk, Trismen, Weinberg, & Nalin, 1976; Zigmond, Vallecorsa, & Leinhardt, 1980). Another characteristic, then, of remediation is the emphasis on activities other than reading books, and on goals other than comprehension of texts.

Nature of instruction. Beyond the instructional emphases, one could also consider the nature of the teacher's instructional behavior during remedial sessions. Reports of teacher behavior during remediation suggest that there is often little teacher involvement beyond monitoring on-task behavior and providing feedback on the accuracy of responses. While different investigators have operationalized teaching, or instruction, differently, the lack of instructional explanation, modelling, or strategic prompts (Duffy et al., 1987) is obvious in the reports by Allington et al. (1986); Allington and McGill-Franzen (1989b); Haynes and Jenkins (1986); Quirk, Trismen, Nalin, and Weinberg (1975); and Rowan & Guthrie (1989). In remedial interventions incorporating teacher aides, the situation is even more dismal (McGill-Franzen & Allington, 1990; Rowan & Guthrie, 1989), and we are hard-pressed to explain the quite common use of relatively untrained teacher aides to provide instructional support to children experiencing difficulty in acquiring reading proficiency.

In addressing the nature of instructional interactions observed in remedial programs, McGill-Franzen and Allington (1990) have pointed out that *individualization*, as currently practiced, means that each child in a small group of children in a remedial setting will work, primarily alone, on a different skill sheet. The teacher moves about monitoring this activity and checking responses but rarely offers instructional explanation or strategic prompts. Each child receives but a few moments of teacher attention and that attention is most commonly feedback concerning the accuracy of responses. Cazden (1988b) describes the nature of such interactions as frequently "abrupt" and "perfunctory" help and "ritualized praise." She notes that such interactions might maintain high time on task but will not "stimulate a child's thinking or language development" (p. 20).

These descriptions do not portray instruction that emphasizes the student's interest and involvement in reading. Recall that these were at the top of the list in 1925. By involvement we do not mean simply "on-task behavior." Rather, we intend what Csikszentmihalyi (1977) calls *flow experiences*: the experience of "losing oneself in the activity." The experience is literally a losing of the "self" as action and awareness become one. This state is most likely to occur during *aesthetic* (Rosenblatt, 1978) *reading*—that is, reading that is done for the experience of reading itself rather than for what is remembered after having read. Aesthetic reading is least likely to occur in remedial reading because of the focus on skills; the lack of independence and choice on the part of the readers; the use of reading material prepared specifically for the conveying of skills; the lack of diversity of allowable response; and, where comprehension is considered, the oppressive concern for accurate recall.

Individualization and instruction. Remediation has come to mean primarily skills-based differential teaching within a reductionist framework. In our attempts to understand and remedy the reading acquisition difficulties, we have focused our attention on individual deficits and differences, but attended to a narrow range of traits. Accommodating individual learner differences is at the root of remediation. It is the supposed nature of the individual differences that results in the various labels applied to children and that are intended to imply differences in instructional technique. Some see these differences as relating to knowledge and skills. Others argue that the knowledge and skill deficits are caused by more fundamental learner differences. The most familiar of these arguments have come from the advocates of neurological interpretations of differences in children's learning. This view of differences has been institutionalized in the exclusionary definition of learning disability in PL94–142 (EHA). Individual differences in learning modality preferences, learning styles, and sensory (particularly visual) deficits have been the most prominent grounds for differential instruction. For example, there are still common beliefs (Allington, 1982) that different learners learn better through different sensory modalities (e.g., Fernald & Keller, 1921); that many learners learn best through multimodal presentation (Fernald, 1943); and that some learners are plagued by certain modalities that are too powerful and require blocking (Blau & Blau, 1968). These ideas have also been argued against for some time (e.g., Gates, 1927); and although the utility of the notion of modality preferences has persisted in the folk wisdom of special education, experimental research has not provided support for the concept (Arter & Jenkins, 1977). Reviews of research by Miller (1981), Tarver and Dawson (1978), and Ysseldyke (1973) and a recent metanalysis by Kavale and Forness (1987) make it clear that neither assessment nor instruction based on these notions seems to work. Other researchers (e.g., Carbo, 1987) have argued for individual learning-style differences between readers. However, individualized remedial instruction differentiated on the basis of learning style has received no more support than that based on modality preferences, though it continues to receive considerable popular press.

Another individual difference that has been the object of considerable attention, but that lacks research support is the notion of an *Attention Deficit Disorder* (ADD)

(Coles, 1987; Meents, 1989). Following the general discrediting of the Hyperactivity Syndrome, ADD has been proposed as a cause for some children failing to learn to read. Treatment involves administration of drugs and behavioral management rather than a careful consideration of the school context. For example, if the books that children read are uninvolving or if children consistently encounter failure, they would be predictably distractible.

One way to conceptualize individual differences is in terms of *aptitude-treatment interactions* (ATI). Some researchers (e.g., Cronbach & Snow, 1977) have argued that if we have good measures of individual differences, then instruction can be matched to those differences. While the theory sounds appealing, in practice there are many problems. In the first place, "good measures" are hard to come by. The most common measures are invalid, unreliable, and instructionally uninformative (Arter & Jenkins, 1979; Coles, 1987; Messick, 1984). Second, there are many different opinions about what should count as a meaningful psychological difference. For example, on top of the arguments for modality and style differences already noted, Rosenshine and Stevens (1984) have argued that achievement differences are a meaningful individual difference and that low-achieving students need instruction that is more direct and more structured, and that emphasizes greater accuracy and lower-level skills, than the instruction needed for higher-achieving students. Unfortunately, to complicate the issue, Anderson, Mason, and Shirey (1984) found that the effectiveness of such instruction in reading groups was heavily dependent on instructional time allocations, whereas in meaning-based instruction (the kind more frequently offered to higher-achieving students) the quantity of time was less important than the quality of the instructional engagement. Such confoundings lead us to suspect that improved instrumentation is unlikely to lead to improved instructional adaptation to individual differences.

Instructional interactions.   The testing involved in an ATI approach may even create more problems than it solves. Aside from the loss of instructional time to the testing, the depersonalization and categorization typically involved in testing may even decrease the quality of the instructional interaction for the individual student. Indeed, Cazden (1988b) suggests that

> It may be helpful to differentiate between individualization as a way of organizing a learning environment and personalization as quality of the interactions in that environment, however it is organized. (p. 30)

This distinction seems critical since, in the name of individualization, many remedial situations encourage depersonalization (e.g., computer-based drill and practice, specific skillsheets completed in the isolation of a study carrel, programmed texts, and other individual work). We believe that a more productive direction than testing students to detect aptitudes, achievement or otherwise, lies in focusing on the teacher as the evaluation expert (Johnston, 1987b). In order for teachers to be most instructionally effective, they need to be sensitive observers of children's literate activity. This expertise cannot be replaced by tests, and it includes the set of beliefs about students that teachers bring to both their observations and their instructional interactions.

Indeed, it is teacher beliefs about differences in learners, especially teacher perceptions of individual aptitude for, or style of, learning that make for the different instruction emphases and interactions that do exist (DeFord, 1985). Since the early and much-debated claims about the "Pygmalion effect" in classes (Rosenthal & Jacobson, 1968), there have been extensive demonstrations of the ways in which teachers' expectations influence the instructional interactions experienced by children (Cooper, 1979).

Naturally, the negative expectations are most likely to be associated with those who are in, or will be in, remedial reading situations. It seems that teachers' beliefs and expectations, particularly about individual differences between learners, have direct and indirect, positive and negative, influences on children's learning. For example, a teacher who believes a student has low ability will not wait as long for a response from that student as he or she will from a student perceived to be more able. The effect is to preempt the student's problem solving or self-correction and to simultaneously convey to the student the teacher's perception of his or her lack of ability. Winfield (1986) documents variations in the belief systems of urban teachers with respect to instructional responsibility and students' teachability. Considerable evidence is also accumulating on the influence of teachers' nonverbal behaviors on the perceptions and performance of students (e.g., Byers & Byers, 1972; Woolfolk & Brooks, 1985).

Recent evidence suggests that there are cultural differences in interaction patterns that can make it difficult for some children to learn in classrooms with conflicting social dynamics (e.g., Au, 1981; Cazden & Leggett, 1981; Philips, 1983). Au and her colleagues' (Au & Jordan, 1981) work, in particular, has shown the instructional advantage of adopting a classroom context and interactional style that is compatible with the home cultural pattern. However, Au's work is more useful for preventing failure in culturally homogeneous classrooms than in culturally diverse groups such as those normally occuring in the United States. In addition, Cazden (1988b) notes that upper- and lower-class children in her studies were found to give approximately similar amounts and kinds of information about objects presented to them, but the lower-class children needed to be prompted nearly twice as much in order to give it. She attributes this necessary prompting to differences in cultural interaction patterns, noting that many children in remedial programs come from low-income homes where referential language (talk about inanimate objects) is in short supply. Eliciting full representation of the information from these children required more requests from the teacher.

Some of these cultural differences result in the differential treatment of students. Cazden (1988b) presents evidence of consequent cross-cultural differential treatment of children in minority cultures, which makes it likely that they will become in need of remedial reading; and minority children are indeed overrepresented in remedial programs (Kennedy, Jung, & Orland, 1986). Cazden provides examples from both New Zealand and the United States in which minority children are not encouraged to speak at any length. Indeed, they are discouraged, which results in their being perceived as uncomprehending and at the same time perceiving the teacher as uncomprehending and themselves as having little of consequence to say. Cazden and Leggett (1981) propose some solutions. For example, they propose continuous ethnographic monitoring of classroom interactions, and the hiring of culturally relevant faculty who may be able to help understanding. They also encourage participation in the classroom by parents and grandparents from the local community, a point echoed by Comer (1988). Given the disproportionate representation of minorities in remedial reading programs, this is clearly something that needs our attention. It seems that the most effective approach to these issues is likely to be a more open, broader approach to early literacy development. If individual children are able to choose to participate through particular favored modalities and interaction patterns, yet at the same time be exposed to literate activity through alternative modalities and interaction patterns in a supportive, non-threatening context, they are less likely to encounter difficulties in learning.

Conflicts would seem most likely to arise in a highly teacher-directed, lockstep situation that prevents student choice and does not allow the teacher the time or the situation in which to observe the ways children go about their learning. Obviously this implies the possibility of having not only time but teachers who are sensitive observers and are able to acknowledge such differences. Bussis and her colleagues (1985) comment that, in appropriate conditions

> [Children] will keep on signaling what information they need in one way or another and will generally overlook those instances when unhelpful information is provided or needed information withheld. In other words, children don't appear to be put off or terribly harmed by a teacher's miscalculations in offering information. . . . But such benign consequences may not be the case if instruction deliberately or inadvertently focuses on children's styles. Instructional materials, direction, and intervention that in effect try to change or otherwise predetermine how children orchestrate knowledge will most likely be self-defeating. In the long run, such efforts may sever children's access to the very judgments that best enable them to make sense of text. (p. 197)

Al least one early advocate of a modalities approach argued similarly. Grace Fernald (1943) argued that to the extent that we close children's options for learning, we increase the risk that some children will fail to learn. Indeed, she argued for instruction that, as far as we can tell, is a forerunner of the "process" approach to writing instruction (Graves, 1983), the major difference being the failure to recognize invented spelling as a positive aspect of learning.

Cazden (1988a) suggests that group activities, particularly those that are less teacher dominated, are more likely to involve some minority children who are used to such social activities or to particular relationships to adults or other authority figures. It is also likely to make it easier for such children to express themselves in extended conversation, particularly since mainstream adults tend to have difficulty engaging in extended dialogue with minority children. Cazden notes that this is similar to what has been found with Hawaiian children in the Kamehameha project (Au & Jordan, 1981). It also happens to be similar to Philips's (1983) observations on the Warm Springs Indian Reservation in central Oregon. In other words, Cazden is arguing for a consideration of the different interactional styles of different cultural groups in the organization of instruction, pointing out that at least for some minority groups, highly teacher-directed instruction is counterproductive. This is not to deny the need for clear instruction on the various conventions and functions of written language, a point which Delpit (1988) argues is critical, particularly in the instruction of low-income minority children. Cazden (1988a) also advocates consideration of less teacher-dominated group learning. Again, this is not an argument for all group learning but certainly for diversity that includes group learning. However, note that no evidence suggests that the formation of such groups should be based on individual differences in reading achievement, which is what most commonly occurs in schools (Slavin, 1987a) and on which remedial reading participation is based.

Indeed, there is now considerable research suggesting that cooperative learning situations are more appropriate than competitive situations for mainstream children as well as minorities and for high-achieving as well as low-achieving children (e.g., Johnson & Johnson, 1975; Slavin, 1984). In other words mainstream and many minority children appear to benefit from a combination of group and individualized structures but no arguments are made in the research for the competitive contexts that are the norm. Indeed, the arguments against them are substantial (e.g., Ames, 1983; Nicholls, 1987; Johnston & Winograd, 1985; Winograd & Paris, 1988), many noting that such contexts are the primary cause of the need for remedial reading in the first place. Similarly the construction of cultural (and other) mismatches produces serious problems in learning as students resist the instructional imposition in various ways (e.g., Willis, 1977). Clearly these instructional issues relate at least as much to regular instruction as they do to remedial instruction since students spend at least as much time in the former as the latter.

CONSEQUENCES OF REMEDIAL INSTRUCTION

A clear and unfortunate characteristic of current remediation is the limited success the various efforts have had in resolving the difficulties of learners who have failed to learn to read on the school's schedule. While reports of spectacularly successful programs can be found in the professional literature, there exist relatively few large-scale longitudinal studies of the effects of remediation. Those that are available suggest that while participation in remediation has a small positive effect, most children who get off schedule in reading acquisition remain off schedule for their school careers (Carter, 1984; Cooley, 1981). Very simply, remediation has a small effect on enhancing standardized test performance generally, though presumably it has a large effect in a few cases. Slavin (1987b) reports that the few well-designed evaluations of Chapter 1 remedial programs suggest a three percentile annual gain, on average, for participants; while Glass (1986) suggests even more difficulties and less reliable effects on achievement for special education programs. Forbes (1984), on the other hand, offers some suggestive evidence supporting remediation efforts, generally by noting that NAEP achievement scores rose during the decade from 1970 to 1980 for historically lower-performing students—those attending poor rural or urban schools. He argues that these children are frequently served by remediation programs but provides no evidence that participation in remediation is linked to the achievement gains reported.

Other standards might be used for evaluating the effects of remediation, such as decline in school leaving, attendance improvement, return to regular education with no further need of remedial support, and so on. However, there is little data on such standards. Gartner and Lipsky (1987), Singer and Butler (1987), and Coles (1987) all note that children who begin participation in special education rarely return to regular education with no further participation in remediation. In a similar vein, McGill-Franzen (1987) notes that special education participation suggests a permanence of the problem and thus few even attempt to release children. In the case of Chapter 1 participants, the picture is not much brighter. Here some children attain test scores that make them ineligible for remediation in the following year, but many return in subsequent years and few participants ever attain reading proficiency (Carter, 1984; Cooley, 1981; Wang, 1980).

In general, remedial efforts have not been characterized by thoughtful reflection on their consequences. Doubtless this is related in part to assumptions about the nature of the problem to be solved. For example, Gillingham, while strongly advocating an intensive decoding emphasis in remedial instruction, was unmoved by its apparent failure. She comments that

> I feel that four years is the minimum [of this remedial instruction] but that really the child who has a specific language disability should be taught by special techniques of this kind throughout his entire school life. . . . (Gillingham, 1956, p. 189)
>
> Almost invariably, however, the pupil who as a little child has had trouble in acquiring mastery of the reading technique will all his life be a very slow reader, e.g., he will find courses in history which require a large amount of supplementary reading extremely laborious. Sometimes it will even be necessary to have some of the mass of subject matter read aloud to him. (Gillingham & Stillman, 1936, p. 170)

Seemingly it did not occur to Gillingham that the laborious decoding emphasis in the instruction may actually have produced the continuing slow reading, or that the displeasure created in reading by the instruction may have severely reduced the amount and frequency of actual reading that the child might do, and hence the automation of recognition. Indeed, she insisted that apart from words that the child's "drill" had thus far not covered, which were to be "pronounced quietly by [the teacher] before he has looked at them at all":

> words are to be sounded out and blended from phonetic units, increase in speed coming from greater and greater facility in blending, not from wider and wider recognition. Sentences thus slowly and painfully worked out, must be reread so as to give the thought, "to sound like real talking." (Gillingham, 1932, p. 124)

Neither did it occur to Gillingham that beliefs about the terminal nature of the problem might be subtly communicated to the student. Nor did she consider the possibility that the continued dependence of these children on such instruction might be a function of the instruction itself.

Perhaps we face a similar situation with current remedial techniques. Barr (1974–1975) argues that whereas more-able readers show little trace of instructional method past the second grade, less-able readers appear to learn narrowly what they are taught; indeed, they tend to show quite marked effects of their instructional focus. Barr was concerned at the time with the effects of a phonic emphasis versus a meaning emphasis in classroom instruction. However, descriptions of students who find themselves in remedial reading suggest that there may be additional consequences of remedial focus. For example, it has often been noted in the literature that the least successful learners exhibit a whole list of characteristics that distinguish them from their more successful peers. They tend to be unreflective and tend not to self-monitor or self-correct (Brown, 1980; Torgeson, 1982); less positive about reading and writing; less inclined to initiate reading or writing independently (Anderson, Wilson, & Fielding, 1988; Juel, 1988); less likely to actively construct meaning and patterns in their reading and writing activities (Johnston & Winograd, 1985; Vellutino, 1987); less persistent in the face of failure (Andrews & Debus, 1978; Chapin & Dyck, 1976); and less strategic (Diener & Dweck, 1978; Torgeson, 1977, 1982). In addition, they have frequently reported affective characteristics such as low self-esteem and resignation (Abramson, Garber, & Seligman, 1980); nervousness, defeatism, and chronic worry (Challman, 1939); an unmotivating belief that the way they do things has little to do with what happens to them (Abramson et al., 1980); and a tendency to make negative affective statements about themselves while performing tasks (Diener & Dweck, 1978). Yet the instruction they receive, and even that which is often recommended for them, appears likely to produce these very characteristics while also communicating that they lack ability. Our instruction reflects and reinforces everything that bothers us about these students. Indeed, there is reason to believe that we contributed to producing these characteristics in the first place. As Margaret Donaldson (1978) points out:

> Once the teaching of reading is begun, the manner in which it is taught may be of far-reaching significance. . . . [T]he process of becoming literate can have marked—but commonly unsuspected—effects on the growth of the mind. It can do this by encouraging highly important forms of intellectual self-awareness and self-control. (p. 97)

The instruction can presumably have the reverse effect too. The instructional interactions in which less-able readers engage while they are reading and regarding what they have read are documented as being different in ways that are likely to cause the problems attributed to these students (Allington, 1983; Eder & Felmlee, 1984; Hiebert, 1983). For example, if a teacher corrects a child's oral reading errors without allowing the child time to self-correct, as is commonly the case with less-able readers, the child will continue not to self-correct even after the instructional situation that produced the failure to self-correct (McNaughton, 1981). A related pattern has been found in the interactions between language-impaired children and their parents (Sammarco, 1984). In addition to such interactional patterns, less-able readers read substantially less than their more-able peers. There is every reason to believe that these students learn not to be metacognitively aware. It may simply be the case that metacognitive awareness follows competence. As learners read more and become more automatic in their reading, and as they read material with which they are more comfortable and talk about it, they may ordinarily develop metacognitive awareness. However, the less-able students rarely have the luxury of either reading more or talking about their reading. Furthermore, their interactions may well have set them up to conceive of reading in entirely different terms than their more able peers.

Children involved in remedial programs are also seen as less flexible and less likely to generalize instruction. On the other hand, remedial instruction, as we have already noted, is characterized by isolated skill work that may very well produce, or at least enforce, the characteristics attributed to them. As Arthur Gates noted in 1927:

> The difficulty with supplementary training of this [flash card] type is that the abilities so developed to be fruitful must transfer to other situations. Careful studies of the transfer of training in such cases show often a disappointing carryover. In one study, it was found that many of the important skills developed by flash card drill did not reappear appreciably in regular reading. In other studies, similar limitations have been found for certain types of phonetic drill. (p. 27)

The very narrowness and isolation of the instruction is likely to reinforce everything we may have already produced through common instructional practices in low reading groups (Stanovich, 1986).

It may be that, rather than narrowing remedial instruction, it needs instead to be broadened. For example, phonemic analysis is probably most meaningfully cast in the context of writing, in which the learners' task is to represent words by the sounds in them (Chomsky, 1970; Clay, 1979). There is also less likelihood they will fail since, if invented spelling is accepted, the interpretable representations of a given word allow greater flexibility than in reading where teachers are more likely to look for accurate conventional reading. For example, *coat* can be written as *kot*, *kote*, or even *ct* (among other possibilities) and still in context be successfully read by a teacher. Through writing there is also a greater likelihood learners will explore the representation system with consequently more flexible understanding of it. Unfortunately, in the process of focusing instruction, writing has not readily made it into remedial reading programs.

Perhaps the less-able readers learn exactly what they are taught in interaction; and the remedial interaction is, with the best of intentions, organized to maintain students' remedial status. A good analogy for remedial reading is the tourist who, having encountered people in a foreign culture who do not understand him, speaks more slowly and loudly—the consequence being rejection of not just the individual, but all that he is seen to stand for. Perhaps teachers, interpreting low performance as indicating low intellectual ability or willful inattention, are inclined to go more slowly, more oppressively, and in the process have a similar effect on the student. As instruction becomes more imperative, it becomes less flexible and less playful; and it will have different consequences for the student's development of higher cognitive processes.

The prospect that schooling actually causes the need for remedial reading was raised quite clearly by Gates in 1927. He describes research by Lois Meek, in which she studied several children of average or above intellect in their first (individual) reading lessons presented as a game. He noted that each was very interested in the word-learning game at the outset, but that as some children had difficulties "due to ineffective types of reactions to the words"

> their interest began to wane. Soon certain pupils showed every evidence of distaste for the task. One hid behind the piano when the investigator appeared; another refused to try when the task was set; another told her in no uncertain terms what she thought of "that old game." In such cases distaste and half-hearted effort were added disadvantageous modes of learning, each magnifying the other. Had such conditions been permitted to continue, the result would doubtless have been, in time, a serious "disability" in, and hatred of, reading. Doubtless many "disabilities" in reading arise in just this way; perhaps some of them originate in the very first lesson. (p. 23)

> Until our methods of initial teaching of reading become far more effective than they now are, difficulties may be expected and, consequently, remedial treatment will be needed. (p. 24)

Our review has brought us to the conclusions that in the first place, as Gates has pointed out, the need for remedial reading is generally a consequence of our early instructional efforts. In the second place, remedial reading is generally not very effective at making children more literate. The unavoidable conclusion, then, is that the most sensible way to improve remedial reading is to eliminate the need for it in the first place. Thus, our concluding section takes up the issue of eliminating remedial reading, which we believe to be the direction demanded by the research.

ELIMINATING REMEDIAL READING

Organizational issues. If we are to eliminate remedial reading, in whole or in part, several routes are open to us. If an increasing part of the problem to be dealt with is the psychological damage to the student classified as remedial, then the earlier we intervene, perhaps, the better. Gates's use of the words "remedial treatment" suggests the healing metaphor, and his arguments suggest that he meant just that in terms of psychological damage which may have been done by previously inappropriate instruction. Fernald (1943), too, was concerned with this issue, commenting that "the application of remedial techniques before the child has failed is one of the most important phases of clinical psychology" (p. 2). Early intervention appears to be a sensible recommendation. If problems can be detected and acted upon early enough, confusions and misconceptions may not be compounded by extensive failure, and the gap between the more and less able may be eliminated rather than continuing to widen. Earlier intervention has been favored by recent research (Carter, 1984; Clay, 1985; Guthrie, Seifert, & Kline, 1978). Clay (1985) documents one such program, *Reading Recovery*, which appears to be very effective. The program involves intensive early intervention by a highly trained specialist teacher after one year of schooling, for those children who appear to be most at risk in terms of their conceptual and strategic development in reading. Clay points out that if remedial instruction is to be effective in rapidly returning children to the regular classroom, the children who have been learning the slowest must learn *faster* than the other children so that they catch up to them and become able to benefit equally from normal classroom instruction. Note that this runs directly counter to the common beliefs about these students' learning abilities. Note also that it has been demonstrated to be possible (Clay, 1985; Pinnell, 1989).

The intensity of the program and speed of "recovery" begin to address an ongoing problem with remedial programs. Required by law to "supplement, not supplant," regular instruction, remedial reading programs have been required to classify some aspect of the regular classroom program as not relevant to reading instruction. Something must be supplanted in a fixed-length school day, be it independent reading, science lessons, or whatever. The problem is that the more content instruction is missed, the less background knowledge students have, and the more their reading of that material is impaired. If independent reading is missed, the less practice the student gets and the less automatic the strategies already learned become. The idea behind Clay's early intervention program is to return the student to the regular classroom as an average performing student as quickly as possible. The program requires substantial investment of resources at a time when these resources are not yet obviously necessary since obvious failure has not yet occurred. On the other hand, it promises considerable long-term savings in both human and financial terms if it is successful in returning participants to regular classroom instruction. However, as McDermott and Aron (1978) point out:

> to return [students] to the classrooms in which they experienced their original school failure may prove to be a cruel hoax, unless we understand and transform the dynamics of failure in our regular classrooms. (p. 61)

If failure is produced in part by the comparative nature of the classroom, then taking some students from the bottom and moving them to the middle simply places other students at the bottom as the new normative failures. In other words, early intervention is not enough. We are essentially faced with the need to improve regular classroom instruction no matter what. Prevention requires changing the classroom context so that children who are slower to acquire reading and writing are not handicapped in class, allowing them time and a supportive context in which they can continue to become literate without developing the debilitating characteristics typical of children in remedial programs: children who have been failed.

Major questions arise as to whether this is reasonable to pursue. Can we expect a regular classroom teacher, who must teach all subjects effectively to all 22 to 35 of his or her students, to teach reading to all children? Perhaps we could reduce the number of students in each class. Some positive effects on improving children's reading performance have been demonstrated, for example, in the use of Chapter 1 funds to reduce overall teacher-pupil ratios (Doss & Holley, 1982). These ratio reductions might be even more effective if they were more radical and if they were accompanied by the elimination of other barriers. For example, a simple proposal (Allington & McGill-Franzen, 1989a) might be to reduce the number of administrators and specialist teachers and place them in classrooms of their own. According to the U.S. Department of Education, the number of these two groups of educators has expanded enormously in the past 20 years (currently they outnumber classroom teachers nearly two to one). Making half of them into classroom teachers would reduce the teacher-pupil ratio to one teacher for every 12 to 17 children—a much more manageable situation. Those with special skills could work collaboratively with other classroom teachers to help plan for students not being served well by instruction, perhaps involving reciprocal support structures such as those demonstrated by Pugach and Johnson (1987) to be effective in substantially reducing the special education referral rate. Such a move would simultaneously eliminate the problem of instructional coordination between remedial and regular programs. It would also tend to make classrooms more personal and to increase teachers' ownership of instructional responsibility for students with special needs. On the other hand, simply reducing class size will not necessarily enhance mediocre instruction. Something must also be done to guarantee higher-quality instruction and eliminate the conditions that produce failure.

Reducing failure. The basis for children's participation in remedial reading programs is their status with respect to what is considered normal, particularly with respect to their performance on a standardized test. Many states mandate remedial instruction below a particular score on a given test. Thus, society has set up schedules for the development of particular abilities, and reading now has a very narrow and inflexible schedule. Tests differ in the aspects of reading they assess at different grade levels and hence produce somewhat different schedules. In the United States the overall schedule is quite different from the schedules in the Soviet Union, Great Britain, Sweden, and New Zealand, and their schedules are different from each other. Schedules and criteria differ from state to state and school to school within the United States so that a child considered a candidate for remedial intervention in one location would not be a candidate in another. Schedules also differ from time to time. For example, a recent renorming of the Degrees of Reading Power test (College Board) meant that children who by the norms of the previous year were comfortably on schedule (54 percentile), by the new norms were substantially behind (23 percentile) and eligible for remedial instruction (Office of Research, Evaluation, and Assessment, 1989).

Decisions as to what it means to be subnormal, or in need of remediation, are always arbitrary, though clearly moderated by the nature of the classroom and the degree of tolerance for diversity. Other criteria could always be used. For example, we could decide to be concerned if a student is not actively monitoring and self-correcting his or her reading, regardless of word recognition level; or we could become concerned if a student makes no progress over a period of two or three months, or perhaps if a student has read only five books in a given month or week or day. Alternatively, we could place writing in higher regard and allocate remedial resources when a student has difficulty with composing. Of course, the choice of what counts as progress will be a decision to be argued over because it will depend on how we keep track of the students' development—what we decide to count. These decisions relate to our instructional priorities and will certainly be understood by the students and teachers and will influence their definitions of themselves as being successful or unsuccessful, and their definition of literacy.

It is clear that the public expects a normal range of performance in intellect, speech development, athletic ability, and the like, but expects "on grade-level" performance in reading. In reading, it is only acceptable to perform at or above the median level for one's age group. By using tests that are specifically designed to produce a normal curve of ability estimates, we then reject half of the curve and assign a good proportion of that rejected group to remedial instruction because they are not learning to read according to society's schedule. This procedure guarantees a considerable amount of failure. It is rather like taking the measure of one foot that was originally normative—or at least based on the regal foot size—and arguing that all feet should be at least that size or be labelled deficient.

Consequently, the first step in reducing reading failure and the need for remedial reading is to remember that "success" and "failure" are constructs. As Nicholls (1987) has pointed out, "success is always a human construction and different criteria of success involve different immediate and ultimate goals as well as different beliefs about the causes of success" (p. 3). The child whose notions of success and failure depend on his relative standing with respect to the rest of his class will behave differently than the child whose definitions depend on whether or not he can become successfully involved in reading a book. Indeed, when students in remedial reading classes (or resource rooms and the like) "fail" at activities such as reading, they may well be successfully achieving their own goals, as Willis (1977), Labov (1982), and others have amply demonstrated. Such students, for example, choose failure in reading in order to remain part of a peer group that negatively values academic achievement. In addition, students who are not part of the culture of power often reject that culture and the instruction that it mandates, thus insuring the perpetuation of their remedial classification. Thus, the goals that are selected are critical, and goals of avoidance can be set just as easily as goals of approach.

How we define "ability" has implications for our choice of goals and beliefs about success and failure. Nicholls (1984) distinguishes between a differentiated view of ability and a nondifferentiated view. The differentiated view is one in which ability is more self-referenced in terms of one's own learning and subjective feelings of competence and satisfaction gained from the activity. The definitions of ability children choose are different in different situations. Take, for example, the difference between ego-involving and task-involving situations. *Task-involving situations* are those in which the individual becomes caught up in the activity, and in doing so defines him- or herself as successful, the activity becoming the means and the end. *Ego-involving situations* are those commonly public situations in which the nature of the situation causes one's ego to be exposed. In ego-involving situations, the differentiated, or capacity, view holds sway, whereas in task-involving situations, the less-differentiated view is operative. Students choose reading activities that will maximize the goal of demonstrating high ability and avoiding demonstrating low ability. Thus, when children are given the opportunity to choose their own books to read, they choose easier or more difficult books, depending on the public (ego-involving) or private (task-involving) nature of the reading they will be using them for (Danner, Hiebert, & Winograd, 1983). When children are placed in a linear sequence of books according to their ability, the possibility of simple, linear public comparisons is increased, along with the ego-involving nature of the task. By contrast, when children choose their own books to read, the possibilities for simple linear comparisons with each other and competitive contexts are reduced and the possibility of aesthetic reading (task-involved) is increased, along with the grounds for the less-differentiated, and more likely positive, view of ability. In other words, in task-involving situations, students' views of their own ability are likely to be based on their feelings of involvement with books rather than on comparisons with others. The consequences of this perceived competence are important. R. Ames (1983) has noted that when students perceive themselves to have low ability, they are unlikely to ask for assistance in an ego-involving situation because they see it as clear evidence of their own lack of capacity. On the other hand, in task-involving situations, they view help seeking as a demonstration of learning and are thus more likely to ask for assistance. If low-ability students see others, including the teacher, as sources of assistance, the amount of instruction that they receive is likely to increase.

In ego-involving situations, students with a low expectation of demonstrating high ability tend to direct their attention to the goal of avoiding demonstrating low ability. In the case of reading, then, they work to avoid engagement in reading activity. Other problematic goals are also possible. If children adopt the goal of survival in the classroom (vs. survival as adults in later life, or simply enjoyment of language), then a different behavior pattern is likely to emerge. The pattern may completely defeat the teacher's intentions. For example, students can withdraw from the situation, or they can change the situation by changing their definition of ability or by rejecting whatever it is that they see as producing the value structure responsible for their position. Alternatively, they can attribute the responsibility for their success or failure to factors that do not have implications for their ability such as an incompetent or malicious teacher. Research clearly points to the importance of task-involving situations rather than ego-involving situations (Ames & Ames, 1984; Nicholls, 1984; Johnston & Winograd, 1985; Winograd & Paris, 1988). This is particularly important for the less-able students. Unlike their more-able peers, their performance on tasks of average difficulty is severely impaired in ego-involving situations.

Instructional issues.   Although we have pointed out the problem of talking about "remedial readers," we have also been using the term "remedial instruction." Perhaps a better way to think of it is that it is indeed the instruction which needs to be remediated. We are not without direction for instruction that will eliminate remedial reading. We know that noncompetitive, task-involving contexts are likely to reduce feelings of failure and increase involvement and cooperation. We also know that accommodating individual differences is easier when children have some choice, when the program is not narrow, and when a reasonable portion of the time is spent in group participation without teacher domination. We know about the damaging effects of competitive contexts (Ames & Ames, 1984). We also know that sheer quantity of reading and writing has a big impact on development (Anderson, Wilson & Fielding, 1988), and that a major characteristic of children who are failing in these activities is that they do not engage in them often (Allington, 1983). If we could set contexts in which students continue to engage in reading and writing, and continue to explore reading and writing processes rather than avoiding them, what would happen? We know that, in general, these children in remedial programs do less reading and writing and get less instruction and less personal instruction. What would happen if we arranged for task-involving contexts so that children would solve problems for themselves and seek help from the teacher or peers as necessary, without encountering feelings of failure? This would represent a shift in the re-"mediation" metaphor to the meaning "intercession or friendly intervention, usually by consent or invitation."

The major dilemma, then, is, Can regular beginning literacy instruction (let us say the first four years) be organized to produce such a context in a highly competitive society? If we believe that it cannot, then we appear to require early intensive remedial instruction in order to restore children to healthy learner status and to prevent the development of further psychological damage. But how early is early enough? How much opportunity should children be given to become literate without invasive interventions? If children simply come from a background of limited literate experience, or initially have other things on their agenda, does it help to take evasive action at the outset? If we develop effective early intervention programs, does this simply remove the incentive to organize less failure-prone beginning programs?

Whichever way we go, we are faced with the fact that whatever needs to be accomplished, be it highly effective early remedial programs or classroom programs that prevent the need for remedial instruction, teacher expertise is at the heart of the matter. It would not be hard to get agreement on this, but to get agreement on what constitutes appropriate expertise will most certainly depend on who is asked. Beliefs about literacy, learning, and ability are as different and as consequential as other forms of political thought. We must, then, either examine ways to alter the instruction in spite of the beliefs, or find ways to alter those beliefs in directions that will facilitate changes in instruction. Since attitudes are part of the organization of behavior, and since teaching is not simply a collection of instructional techniques, we believe that changing the beliefs themselves is very important. If instruction must be organized against beliefs and expectations, it must consciously be so organized all of the time—a very difficult feat. Burns and Lash (1988) found that attempting to get teachers to teach, or even plan instruction against their instructional belief system, is next to impossible. If the belief can be altered, then the reorganization of instruction can be simplified dramatically.

There are ways to help teachers accomplish constructive changes in their teaching practice. For example, the Reading Recovery Program, which, as far as we can tell, is the most effective remedial intervention currently available, was devised by getting together a group of good teachers who watched each other work with students having difficulty and argued about the strategies they used (Clay, 1985). Over a period of time each picked up strategies from each other, and collectively they were able to put together an organized instructional framework upon which they agreed, and which had stood the test of their critical evaluation. Efforts such as these will require examining the conditions that allow for such development to take place. Teacher beliefs and teachers' efforts at self-improvement are at least partly determined by the structure of schooling and the accountability system. It takes great confidence or minimal threat for teachers to be able to take risks with their instruction and to open themselves up to peer evaluation.

In analyzing the consequences of our instruction and what counts as effective, we have tended to consider only achievement test data. However, we must consider the possibility that we may be influencing more than we are currently concerned about measuring. For example, Donaldson (1978) points out:

> The hope, then, is that reading can be taught in such a way as greatly to enhance the child's reflective awareness, not only of language as a symbolic system but of the processes of his own mind. . . . For instance, if the child is taught to operate with the decimal system without coming to understand that it is one system among other possible ones then, to quote Vygotsky, "he has not mastered the system but is, on the contrary, bound by it." (p. 99)

But of course some have argued that that is exactly the goal of remedial reading instruction—to have those children, usually those of the poor and of minority groups, bound by limited literacy and thus help to preserve a classed society (e.g., McDermott, 1974; McDermott & Aron, 1978; Postman, 1970). Indeed, this relationship between schooling and the structure and imperatives of the society at large must seriously be considered in our attempts to reorganize instruction (e.g., Bowles & Gintis, 1976; Giroux, 1981; Fraatz, 1987). If, as these writers suggest, remedial instruction is simply a lavishly concealed way of maintaining a classed society, and if that really is the principal mandate of schooling, then we should be aware that remedial instruction will be difficult to eliminate, and that if it is eliminated other means of maintaining the status quo will quickly take its place. If teachers are in an organizational context that makes it very difficult for them to service the needs of less-able students or to make changes in their instruction, then we cannot reasonably blame teachers for the problems.

REFERENCES

Abramson, L. Y., Garber, J., & Seligman, M. E. (1980). Learned helplessness in humans: An attributional analysis. In J. Garber & M. E. Seligman (Eds.), *Human helplessness: Theory and applications* (pp. 3–34). New York: Academic Press.

Algozzine, B., & Ysseldyke, J. E. (1983). Learning disabilities as a subset of school failure and the over-sophistication of a concept. *Exceptional Children, 50,* 242–246.

Algozzine, B., Ysseldyke, J. E., & Christenson, S. (1983). An analysis of the incidence of special class placement: The masses are burgeoning. *Journal of Special Education, 17,* 141–147.

Allington, R. L. (1980). Teaching reading in compensatory classes: A descriptive summary. *Reading Teacher, 34,* 178–183.

Allington, R. L. (1982). The persistence of teacher beliefs in the perceptual deficit hypothesis. *Elementary School Journal, 82,* 351–359.

Allington, R. L. (1983). The reading instruction provided readers of differing ability. *Elementary School Journal, 83*, 548–559.

Allington, R. L. (1986). Policy constraints and effective compensatory reading instruction: A review. In J. Hoffman (Ed.), *Effective teaching of reading and research and practice* (pp. 261–289). Newark, DE: International Reading Association.

Allington, R. L., & Johnston, P. H. (1989). Coordination, collaboration, and consistency: The redesign of compensatory and special education interventions. In R. Slavin, N. Madden, & N. Karweit (Eds.), *Preventing school failure: Effective programs for students at risk* (pp. 320–354). Boston: Allyn-Bacon.

Allington, R. L., & McGill-Franzen, A. (1989a). Different programs, indifferent instruction. In A. Gartner & D. Lipsky (Eds.), *Beyond separate education* (pp. 75–98). Baltimore: Brookes.

Allington, R. L., & McGill-Franzen, A. (1989b). School response to reading failure: Chapter I and special education students in grades 2, 4, and 8. *Elementary School Journal, 89*, 529–542.

Allington, R. L., Stuetzel, H., Shake, M. C., & Lamarche, S. (1986). What is remedial reading? A descriptive study. *Reading Research and Instruction, 26*, 15–30.

Ames, C., & Ames, R. (1984). Goal structures and motivation. *Elementary School Journal, 85*, 39–52.

Ames, R. (1983). Help-seeking and achievement orientation: Perspectives from attribution theory. In B. M. DePaulo, N. Nadler, & J. D. Fisher (Eds.), *New directions in helping* (pp. 165–188). New York: Academic Press.

Andrews, G. R., & Debus, R. L. (1978). Persistence and the causal perception of failure: Modifying cognitive attributions. *Journal of Educational Psychology, 70*, 154–166.

Anderson, R. C., Mason, J., & Shirey, L. (1984). The reading group: An experimental investigation of a labyrinth. *Reading Research Quarterly, 20*, 6–38.

Anderson, R. C., Wilson, P., & Fielding, L. (1988). Growth in reading and how children spend their time outside of school. *Reading Research Quarterly, 23*, 285–303.

Arter, J. A., & Jenkins, J. R. (1977). Examining the benefits and prevalence of modality considerations in special education. *Journal of Special Education, 11*, 281–298.

Arter, J. A., & Jenkins, J. R. (1979). Differential diagnosis—prescriptive teaching: A critical appraisal. *Review of Education Research, 49*, 517–555.

Au, K. H. (1981). Participation structures in a reading lesson with Hawaiian children: Analysis of a culturally appropriate instructional event. *Anthropology and Education Quarterly, 11*, 91–115.

Au, K. H., & Jordan, C. (1981). Teaching reading to Hawaiian children: Finding a culturally appropriate solution. In H. Treuba, G. Guthrie, & K. Au (Eds.), *Culture and the bilingual classroom: Studies in classroom ethnography*. Rawley, MA: Newbury House.

Barr, R. (1974–1975). The effect of instruction from a sociological perspective. *Journal of Reading Behavior, 16*, 375–389.

Birman, B. F., Orland, M. E., Jung, R. K., Anson, R. J., Garcia, G. N., Moore, M. T., Funkhouser, J. E., Morrison, D. R., Turnbull, B. J., & Reisner, E. R. (1987). *The current operation of the Chapter I program: Final report from the National Assessment of Chapter I*. Washington, DC: U.S. Government Printing Office.

Blau, H., & Blau, H. (1968). A theory of learning to read. *Reading Teacher, 22*, 126–129.

Bloom, B. (1984). The 2 sigma problem: The search for methods of group instruction as effective as one-to-one tutoring. *Educational Researcher, 13*(6), 4–17.

Bowles, S., & Gintin, H. (1976). *Schooling in capitalist America*. New York: Basic Books.

Brown, A. L. (1980). Metacognitive development and reading. In R. Spiro, B. Bruce, & W. F. Brewer (Eds.), *Theoretical issues in reading comprehension* (pp. 453–481). Hillsdale, NJ: Erlbaum.

Burns, R. B., & Lash, A. A. (1988). Nine seventh-grade teachers' knowledge and planning of problem-solving instruction. *Elementary School Journal, 88*, 369–386.

Bussis, A. M., Chittenden, E. A., Amarel, M., & Kalusner, E. (1985). *Inquiry into meaning: An investigation of learning to read*. Hillsdale, NJ: Erlbaum.

Byers, P., & Byers, H. (1972). Nonverbal communication and the education of children. In C. Cazden, V. John, & D. Hymes (Eds.), *Functions of language in the classroom*. New York: Teachers College Press.

Calfee, R. C., & Drum, P. (1979). *Teaching reading in compensatory classes*. Newark, DE: International Reading Association.

Carbo, M. (1987). Reading styles research: "What works" isn't always phonics. *Phi Delta Kappan, 68*, 431–435.

Carter, L. F. (1984). The sustaining effects study of compensatory and elementary education. *Educational Researcher, 12*, 4–13.

Cazden, C. B. (1988a). *Classroom discourse: The language of teaching and learning*. Portsmouth, NH: Heinemann.

Cazden, C. B. (1988b). *Interactions between Maori children and Pakeha teachers*. Auckland, NZ: Auckland Reading Association.

Cazden, C. B., & Leggett, E. L. (1981). Culturally responsive education: Recommendations for achieving Lau remedies II. In H. Trueba, G. Guthrie, & K. Au (Eds.), *Culture and the bilingual classroom: Studies in classroom ethnography* (pp. 69–86). Rowley, MA: Newbury House.

Challman, R. C. (1939). Personality adjustment and remedial reading. *Journal of the Exceptional Child, 6*, 7–12.

Chapin, M., & Dyck, D. (1976). Persistence in children's reading behavior as a function of N length and attribution retraining. *Journal of Abnormal Psychology, 85,* 511–515.

Chomsky, C. (1970). Reading, writing, and phonolgy. *Harvard Educational Review, 40,* 287–309.

Clay, M. M. (1979). *Reading: The patterning of complex behaviour.* Exeter, NH: Heinemann.

Clay, M. M. (1985). *The early detection of reading difficulties* (3rd ed.). Portsmouth, NH: Heinemann.

Clay, M. M., & Cazden, C. B. (in press). A Vygotskyian interpretation of Reading Recovery. In Moll, L. C. (Ed.), *Vygotsky and education: Instructional implications and applications of socio-historical psychology.* New York: Cambridge University Press.

Cole, M., & Griffin, P. (1986). A sociohistorical approach to remediation. In S. deCastell, A. Luke, & K. Egan (Eds.), *Literacy, society, and schooling: A reader* (pp. 110–131). New York: Cambridge University Press.

Coles, G. (1987). *The learning mystique: A critical look at learning disabilities.* New York: Pantheon.

Comer, J. P. (1988). Educating poor minority children. *Scientific American, 259,* 42–48.

Cooley, W. W. (1981). Effectiveness in compensatory education. *Educational Leadership, 38,* 298–301.

Cooley, W. W., & Leinhardt, G. (1980). The instructional dimension study. *Educational Evaluation and Policy Analysis, 2,* 7–25.

Cooper, H. (1979). Pygmalion grows up: A model for teacher expectation, communication, and performance influence. *Review of Educational Research, 49,* 389–410.

Crawford, J., Kimball, G. H., & Patrick, A. (1984). *Differences and similarities in teaching effectiveness findings between regular classroom instruction and Chapter 1 compensatory instruction.* Paper presented at the AERA annual meeting, New Orleans, April.

Critchley, M. (1964). *Developmental dyslexia.* London: Heinemann.

Cronbach, L. J., & Snow, R. E. (1977). *Aptitudes and instructional methods.* New York: Irvington.

Cummins, J. (1986). Empowering minority students: A framework for intervention. *Harvard Educational Review, 56,* 18–36.

Csikszentmihalyi, M. (1977). *Beyond boredom and anxiety.* San Francisco: Jossey-Bass.

Danner, F., Hiebert, E., & Winograd, P. N. (1983, April). *Children's understanding of text difficulty.* Paper presented at the annual meeting of the American Educational Research Association, New Orleans.

DeFord, D. E. (1985). Validating the construct of theoretical orientation in reading instruction. *Reading Research Quarterly, 20,* 351–367.

Delpit, L. D. (1988). The silenced dialogue: Power and pedagogy in educating other people's children. *Harvard Educational Review, 58*(3), 280–298.

Denham, C., & Liberman, A. (1980). *Time to learn.* Washington, DC: U.S. Government Printing Office (1980–695–717).

Diener, C. I., & Dweck, C. (1978). An analysis of learned helplessness: II. The processing of success. *Journal of Personality and Social Psychology, 39,* 940–952.

Dolch, E. W. (1931). *The psychology and teaching of reading.* Champaign, IL: Garrard.

Dolch, E. W. (1948). *Helping handicapped children in school.* Champaign, IL: Garrard.

Donaldson, Margaret (1978). *Children's minds.* New York: Norton.

Doss, D., & Holley, F. (1982). *A cause for national pause: Title 1 schoolwide projects.* Paper presented at the annual meeting of the American Educational Research Association, New York.

Duffy, G. G., Roehler, L., Sivan, E., Rackliffe, G., Book, C., Meloth, M., Vavrus, L., Wesselman, R., Putnam, J., & Bassiri, D. (1987). The effects of explaining reasoning associated with using reading strategies. *Reading Research Quarterly, 22,* 347–367.

Eder, D., & Felmlee, D. (1984). The development of attention norms in ability groups. In P. L. Peterson, L. C. Wilkinson, & M. Hallinan (Eds.), *The social context of instruction: Group organization as group processes.* New York: Academic Press.

Fernald, G. M. (1943). *Remedial techniques in basic school subjects.* New York: McGraw-Hill.

Fernald, G. M., & Keller, H. B. (1921). The effect of kinesthetic factors in the development of word recognition. *Journal of Educational Research, 4,* 369.

Forbes, R. H. (1984). *Academic achievement of historically lower performing students during the 1970's.* Paper presented at the annual meeting of the American Educational Research Association, New Orleans.

Foster, S. G. (1984). Rise in learning-disabled pupils fuels concern in states, districts. *Education Week, 3,* 1, 18.

Fraatz, J. M. B. (1987). *The politics of reading: Power, opportunity and prospects for change in America's public schools.* New York: Teachers College.

Gambrell, L., Wilson, R., & Gannt, W. (1981). Classroom observations of task-attending behaviors of good and poor readers. *Journal of Educational Research, 74,* 400–404.

Gartner, A., & Lipsky, D. K. (1987). Beyond special education: Toward a quality system for all students. *Harvard Educational Review, 57,* 367–395.

Gates, A. I. (1927). *The improvement of reading: A program of diagnostic and remedial methods.* New York: Macmillan.

Gates, A. I. (1937). Diagnosis and treatment of extreme cases of reading disability. In W. S. Gray (Ed.), *The teaching of reading (Thirty-Sixth Yearbook, pt. 1).* Chicago: National Society for the Study of Education.

Gillingham, A. (1932). Detailed description of remedial work for reading, spelling and penmanship. In S. B. Childs (Ed.), *Education and specific language disability: The papers of Anna Gillingam* (pp. 111–146). Pomfret, CT: Orton Society.

Gillingham, A. (1956). The prevention of scholastic failure due to specific language disability. In S. B. Childs

(Ed.), *Education and specific language disability: The papers of Anna Gillingam* (pp. 183–190). Pomfret, CT: Orton Society.

Gillingham, A., & Stillman, B. W. (1936). Remedial work for spelling and penmanship. In S. B. Childs (Ed.), *Education and specific language disability: The papers of Anna Gillingam* (pp. 157–182). Pomfret, CT: Orton Society.

Giroux, H. A. (1981). *Ideology culture and the process of schooling.* Philadelphia, PA: Temple University Press.

Glass, G. V. (1986). The effectiveness of special education. *Policy Studies Review, 2,* 65–78.

Good, T. (1983). Research on classroom teaching. In L. S. Shulman & G. Sykes (Eds.), *Handbook of teaching and policy.* White Plains, NY: Longman.

Graves, D. H. (1983). *Writing: Teachers and children at work.* Exeter, NH: Heinemann.

Gray, C. T. (1922). *Deficiences in reading ability: Their diagnosis and treatment.* Boston: Heath.

Gray, W. S. (1922). *Remedial cases in reading: Their diagnosis and treatment.* Chicago: University of Chicago Press.

Guthrie, J. T., Seifert, M., & Kline, L. W. (1978). Clues from research on programs for poor readers. In S. Jay Samuels (Ed.), *What research has to say about reading instruction.* Newark, DE: International Reading Association.

Harris, A. J., & Serwer, B. L. (1966). The CRAFT project: Instructional time in reading research. *Reading Research Quarterly, 2,* 27–57.

Haynes, M. C., & Jenkins, J. R. (1986). Reading instruction in special education resource rooms. *American Educational Research Journal, 23,* 161–190.

Hiebert, E. H. (1983). An examination of ability grouping for reading instruction. *Reading Research Quarterly, 18,* 231–255.

Hinshelwood, J. (1917). *Congenital word blindness.* London: H. K. Lewis.

Holmes, C. T., & Matthews, K. M. (1984). The effects of non-promotion on elementary and junior high school pupils: A meta-analysis. *Review of Educational Research, 54,* 225–236.

Jenkins, J. R. (1987). Similarities in the achievement levels of learning disabled and remedial students. *Counterpoint, 7,* 16.

Jenkins, J. R., Pious, C., & Peterson, D. (1988). Categorical programs for remedial and handicapped students: Issues of validity. *Exceptional Children, 55,* 147–158.

Johnson, D., & Johnson, R. (1975). *Learning together and alone: Cooperation, competition, and individualization.* Englewood Cliffs, NJ: Prentice-Hall.

Johnston, P. H. (1987a). Assessing the process, and the process of assessment, in the language arts. In J. Squire (Ed.), *The dynamics of language learning: Research in the language arts.* Urbana, IL: National Council of Teachers of English.

Johnston, P. H. (1987b). Teachers as evaluation experts. *Reading Teacher, 40*(8), 744–748.

Johnston, P. H., Allington, R. L., & Afflerbach, P. (1985). Congruence of classroom and remedial reading instruction. *Elementary School Journal, 85,* 465–478.

Johnston, P. H., & Winograd, P. N. (1985). Passive failure in reading. *Journal of Reading Behavior, 17,* 279–301.

Jorgenson, G. W. (1977). Relationship of classroom behavior to the accuracy of the match between material difficulty and student ability. *Journal of Educational Psychology, 69,* 24–32.

Juel, C. (1988). Learning to read and write: A longitudinal study of 54 children from first through fourth grades. *Journal of Educational Psychology, 80,* 437–447.

Kavale, K. A., & Forness, S. R. (1987). Substance over style: Assessing the efficacy of modality testing and teaching. *Exceptional Children, 54,* 228–239.

Kennedy, M. M., Jung, R. K., & Orland, M. E. (1986). *Poverty, achievement, and the distribution of compensatory education services.* Washington, DC: Office of Educational Research and Improvement, U.S. Department of Education.

Kiesling, H. (1978). Productivity of instructional time by mode of instruction for students at varying levels of reading skill. *Reading Research Quarterly, 13,* 554–582.

Kimbrough, J., & Hill, P. T. (1981). *The aggregate effects of federal education programs.* Santa Monica, CA: Rand.

Kirk, S. A. (1940). *Teaching reading to slow-learning children.* Boston: Houghton Mifflin.

Labov, W. (1982). Competing value systems in the inner-city schools. In P. Gilmore & A. Glathorn (Eds.) *Children in and out of school: Ethnography and education.* Washington, DC: Center for Applied Linguistics.

Larrivee, B. (1985). *Effective teaching for successful mainstreaming.* White Plains, NY: Longman.

Lee, G. V., Rowan, B., Allington, R. L., Anderson, L. W., Bossert, S. T., Harnischfeger, A., & Stallings, J. A. (1986). *The management and delivery of instructional services to Chapter 1 students: Case studies of twelve schools.* San Francisco: Far West Laboratory for Educational Research and Development.

Leinhardt, G. (1980). Transition rooms: Promoting maturation or reducing education? *Journal of Educational Psychology, 72,* 55–61.

Leinhardt, G., Bickel, W., & Pallay, A. (1982). Unlabelled but still entitled: Toward more effective remediation. *Teachers College Record, 84,* 391–422.

Leinhardt, G., & Pallay, A. (1982). Restrictive educational settings: Exile or haven? *Review of Educational Research, 52,* 557–578

Leinhardt, G., Zigmond, N., & Cooley, William. (1981). Reading instruction and its effects. *American Educational Research Journal, 18,* 343–361.

Light, R. J., & Smith, P. V. (1971). Accumulating evidence: Procedures for resolving contradictions among different studies. *Harvard Educational Review, 41,* 429–471.

McDermott, R. P. (1974). Achieving school failure: An anthropological approach to illiteracy and social stratification. In G. Spindler (Ed.), *Educational and cultural process* (pp. 82–188). New York: Holt, Rinehart & Winston.

McDermott, R. P., & Aron, J. (1978). Pirandello in the classroom: On the possibility of equal educational opportunity in American culture. In M. Reynolds (Ed.), *Future of Education* (pp. 41–64). Reston, VA: Council for Exceptional Children.

McGill-Franzen, A. (1987). Failure to learn to read: Formulating a policy problem. *Reading Research Quarterly, 22,* 475–490.

McGill-Franzen, A., & Allington, R. L. (1990). Comprehension and coherence: neglected elements of literacy instruction in remedial and resource room services. *Journal of Reading, Writing, and Learning Disabilities, 6,* 149–180.

McLaughlin, M. W. (1982). States and the new federalism. *Harvard Educational Review, 52,* 564–583.

McNaughton, S. (1981). The influence of immediate teacher correction on self-corrections and proficient oral reading. *Journal of Reading Behavior, 13,* 367–371.

Meents, C. K. (1989). Attention deficit disorder: A review of the literature. *Psychology in the Schools, 26,* 168–178.

Messick, S. (1984). Assessment in context: Appraising student performance in relation to instructional quality. *Educational Researcher, 13,* 3–8.

Mehan, H., Hartweck, A., & Meihls, J. L. (1986). *Handicapping the handicapped: Decision making in students' educational careers.* Stanford, CA: Stanford University Press.

Miller, A. (1981). Conceptual matching models and interactional research in education. *Review of Educational Research, 51,* 33–84.

Monroe, M. (1936). *Children who cannot read.* Chicago: University of Chicago Press.

Moore, D., Hyde, A., Blair, K., & Weitzman, S. (1981). *Student classification and the right to read.* Chicago: Designs for Change.

Morgan, W. P. (1896). A case of congenital word-blindness. *British Medical Journal, 2,* 1378.

Morsink, C. V., Soar, R. S., Soar, R. M., & Thomas, R. (1986). Research on teaching: Opening the door to special education classrooms. *Exceptional Children, 53,* 32–40.

Nicholls, J. G. (1984). Achievement motivation: Conceptions of ability, subjective experience, task choice, and performance. *Psychological Review, 91,* 328–346.

Nicholls, J. G. (1987, April). Motivation, values, and education. Paper presented at the annual meeting of the American Educational Research Association, Washington, DC.

Office of Research, Evaluation, and Assessment (1989). *Looking ahead: 1989 citywide reading scores.* New York: New York City Board of Education.

Pelosi, P. L. (1977). The roots of reading diagnosis. In H. Alan Robinson (Ed.), *Reading and writing instruction in the United States: Historical trends* (pp. 69–75). Newark, DE: International Reading Association.

Philips, S. U. (1983). *The invisible culture: Communication in classroom and community on the Warm Springs Indian Reservation.* White Plains, NY: Longman.

Pinnel, G. S. (1989). Success of at-risk children in a program that combines writing and reading. In J. M. Mason (Ed.), *Reading and writing connections.* Boston: Allyn & Bacon.

Postman, N. (1970). The politics of reading. *Harvard Educational Review, 40,* 244–252.

Pugach, M. C., & Johnson, L. J. (1987, April). *Systematic teacher dialogue as a prereferral intervention: Self-appraisal through peer collaboration.* Paper presented at the annual meeting of the American Educational Research Association, Washington, DC.

Quirk, T. J., Trisman, D. A., Nalin, K., & Weinberg, S. (1975). Classroom behavior of teachers during compensatory reading instruction. *Journal of Educational Research, 68,* 185–192.

Quirk, T. J., Trismen, D. A., Weinberg, S. F., & Nalin, K. B. (1976). Attending behavior during reading instruction. *Reading Teacher, 29,* 640–646.

Reynolds, M. C., Wang, M. C., & Walberg, H. J. (1987). The necessary restructuring of special and regular education. *Exceptional Children, 53,* 391–398.

Robinson, H. M. (1946). *Why pupils fail in reading.* Chicago: University of Chicago Press.

Rosenblatt, L. M. (1978). *The reader, the text, the poem.* Carbondale, IL: Southern Illinois University Press.

Rosenshine, B. V., & Stevens, R. (1984). Review of teaching styles and pupil progress. In P. D. Pearson, R. Barr, M. L. Kamil, & P. Mosenthal (Eds.), *Handbook of reading research* (Vol. 1, pp. 745–798). White Plains, NY: Longman.

Rosenthal, R., & Jacobson, L. (1968). *Pygmalion in the classroom.* New York: Holt, Rinehart, & Winston.

Rowan, B. & Guthrie, L. F. (1989). The quality of Chapter I instruction: Results from a study of twenty-four schools. In R. Slavin, N. Karweit, & N. Madden (Eds.), *Effective programs for students at risk* (pp. 195–219). Needham Heights, MA: Allyn-Bacon.

Sammarco, J. (1984). *Joint problem-solving activity in mother-child dyads: A comparative study of normally achieving and language-disordered preschoolers.* Unpublished doctoral dissertation, Northwestern University.

Sarason, S. B. (1971). *The culture of the school and the problem of change.* Boston: Allyn & Bacon.

Schweinhart, L. J., Weikart, D. P., & Larner, M. B. (1986). Consequences of three preschool curriculum models through age 15. *Early Childhood Education Quarterly, 1,* 15–45.

Shepard, L. A., & Smith, M. L. (1986). Synthesis of research on school readiness and kindergarten retention, *Educational Leadership, 44,* 78–86.

Shepard, L. A., Smith, M. L., & Vojir, C. P. (1983). Characteristics of pupils identified as learning disabled. *American Educational Research Journal, 20,* 309–331.

Singer, J. D., & Butler, J. S. (1987). The Education for All Handicapped Children Act: Schools as agents of social reform. *Harvard Educational Review, 57,* 125–152.

Slavin, R. E. (1984). Students motivating students to excel: Cooperative incentives, cooperative tasks, and student achievement. *Elementary School Journal, 85*(1), 53–64.

Slavin, R. E. (1987a). A theory of school and classroom organization. *Educational Psychologist, 22,* 89–108.

Slavin, R. E. (1987b). Making Chapter I make a difference. *Phi Delta Kappan, 69,* 110–119.

Smith, M. L., & Shepard, L. A. (1988). Kindergarten readiness and retention: A qualitative study of teachers' beliefs and practices. *American Educational Research Journal, 25,* 307–333.

Smith, N. B. (1965). *American reading instruction.* Newark, DE: International Reading Association.

Stainback, W., & Stainback, S. (1984). A rationale for the merger of special and regular education. *Exceptional Children, 51,* 102–111.

Stanley, S. O., & Greenwood, C. R. (1983). How much "opportunity to respond" does the minority disadvantaged student receive in school? *Exceptional Children, 49,* 370–373.

Stanovich, K. E. (1986). Matthew effects in reading: Some consequences of individual differences in the acquisition of literacy. *Reading Research Quarterly, 21,* 360–407.

Stonehill, R. J., & Anderson, J. I. (1982). *An evaluation of ESEA Title 1: Program operations and educational effects. Report to Congress.* Washington, DC: U.S. Department of Education, Office of Planning, Budget, and Evaluation.

Tarver, S. G., & Dawson, M. M. (1978). Modality preference and the teaching of reading: A review. *Journal of Learning Disabilities, 11,* 5–17.

Teale, W. H., & Sulzby, E. (1987). *Emergent literacy: Writing and reading.* Norwood, NJ: Ablex.

Thurlow, M. L., Ysseldyke, J. E., Graden, J., & Algozzine, B. (1984). Opportunity to learn for LD students receiving different levels of special education services. *Learning Disability Quarterly, 7,* 55–67.

Timar, T. B., & Kirp. D. L. (1987). Educational reform and institutional competence. *Harvard Educational Review, 57,* 308–330.

Top, B. L., & Osguthorpe, R. T. (1987). Reverse-role tutoring: The effects of handicapped students tutoring regular class students. *Elementary School Journal, 87*(4), 413–425.

Torgeson, J. K. (1977). The role of nonspecific factors in the task performance of learning disabled children: A theoretical assessment. *Journal of Learning disabilities, 10,* 27–34.

Torgesen, J. K. (1982). The learning-disabled child as an inactive learner. *Topics in Learning and Learning Disabilities, 2,* 45–52.

Uhl, W. L. (1916). The use of results of reading tests as bases for planning remedial work. *Elementary School Journal, 17,* 273–280.

Vanecko, J. J., Ames, N. L., with Archambault, Francis X. (1980). *Who benefits from federal education dollars?* Cambridge, MA: ABT Books.

Vellutino, F. R. (1987). Dyslexia. *Scientific American, 256,* 34–41.

Walmsley, S. A., & Walp, T. P. (1990). Toward an integrated language arts curriculum in elementary school: Philosophy, practice and implications. *Elementary School Journal, 90,* 257–294.

Wang, M. (1980). *Evaluating the effectiveness of compensatory education.* Paper presented at the American Educational Research Association, Boston.

Wang, M. C., & Reynolds, M. C. (1985). Avoiding the "Catch 22" in special education reform. *Exceptional Children, 51,* 497–502.

Wang, M. C., Reynolds, M. C., & Walberg, H. J. (1987). *Handbook of special education: Vol. 1, Research and practice.* New York: Pergamon Press.

Whipple, G. M. (1925). *Report of the National Committee on Reading (Twenty-Fourth Yearbook, Part 1, National Society for the Study of Education),* Chicago.

Wiley, D. E. & Harnischfeger, A. (1974). Explosion of a myth: Quantity of schooling and exposure to instruction, major educational vehicles. *Educational Researcher, 3,* 7–12.

Will, M. (1986). *Educating students with learning problems—A shared responsibility.* Office of Special Education and Rehabilitation Services. Washington, DC: U.S. Department of Education.

Willis, P. E. (1977). *Learning to labour: How working-class kids get working-class jobs.* Farnborough, Eng.: Saxon House.

Winfield, L. (1986). Teacher beliefs toward academically at-risk students in inner-city schools. *Urban Review, 18,* 254–268.

Winograd, P. N., & Paris, S. G. (1988). A cognitive and motivational agenda for reading instruction. *Educational Leadership, 46,* 30–36.

Woolfolk, A. E., & Brooks, D. M. (1985). The influence of teachers' nonverbal behaviors on students' perceptions and performance. *Elementary School Journal, 85,* 513–528.

Ysseldyke, J. E. (1973). Diagnostic-prescriptive teaching: The search for aptitude-treatment interactions. In L. Mann & D. Sbatino (Eds.). *The first review of special education.* Philadelphia: JSE Press.

Ysseldyke, J. E., & Algozzine, B. (1982a). *Critical issues in special and remedial education.* Boston: Houghton Mifflin.

Ysseldyke, J. E., & Algozzine, B. (1982b). Where to begin diagnosing reading problems. *Topics in Learning and Learning Disabilities, 2,* 60–69.

Ysseldyke, J. E., Algozzine, B., & Epps, S. (1983). A local and empirical analysis of current practice in classifying students as handicapped. *Exceptional Children, 50,* 160–166.

Ysseldyke, J. E., Algozzine, B., Shinn, M. R., & McGue, M. (1982). Similarities and differences between low achievers and students classified as learning disabled. *Journal of Special Education, 16,* 73–85.

Ysseldyke, J. E., Thurlow, M. L., Mecklenburg, C., & Graden, J. (1984). Opportunity to learn for regular and special education students during reading instruction. *Remedial and Special Education, 5,* 29–37.

Zigmond, N., Vallecorsa, A., & Leinhardt, G. (1980). Reading instruction for students with learning disabilities. *Topics in Language Disorders, 1,* 89–98.

EPILOGUE: UNDERSTANDING PROGRESS IN READING RESEARCH

Peter B. Mosenthal
and Michael L. Kamil

MAPPING THE TERRITORY OF READING

A handbook is a unique literary genre. Like a map, it summarizes the territory that a discipline claims to address; the borders of this map define the breadth of a field; the details of the map define the depth. In comparing handbooks from different disciplines, we can see what territories are unique to a discipline and what territories are claimed by competing disciplines. As successive handbook editions appear within a field of inquiry, different maps of this discipline's territory are presented; new landmarks of thought are included; old landmarks are dropped, modified, or left untouched. In this regard, different handbook editions serve to chronicle the changes in what a field chooses to include and exclude in defining its territory.

As readers, we bring many of the same expectations to new editions of handbooks that we do to new maps. One expectation is that the territories of our discipline and road system are forever changing. The expansion of new road systems and the warning sign "Construction Ahead" remind us of the changes continually taking place in the territory through which we travel. The yearly addition of new journals and the increased number of professional publications are harbingers of the more fundamental changes at work to create the need for the new "map" provided by a new handbook.

We also expect that changes in a territory usually represent changes for the better. These changes are "new" and, therefore, represent "improvements" in our territory's landscape. As these improvements accumulate, they are perceived to reach a level of "significance." At this point, we say that "progress" has been achieved!

Purpose of This Chapter

As readers of the second volume of the *Handbook of Reading Research*, we bring our own personal expectations of what should be included in this latest map of the reading field. More importantly, as we read the *Handbook*, we bring our own individual notions of which changes in the reading territory have been for the better. Some of us will agree and others will disagree that the changes really represent "significant" improvements in the reading field. And upon completing the *Handbook*, some of us will believe, and some of us won't, that progress has truly taken place in the territory known as the "reading field" since the publication of the first *Handbook of Reading Research* (Pearson, Barr, Kamil, & Mosenthal, 1984).

Interestingly enough, although we, as individuals, have views about what the territory of reading is and what it should be, we, as a discipline, have given little attention to answering the question "What constitutes progress in reading research?" To answer this question, we, as researchers, need a framework for discussing and debating this question. Without such a framework, we have no basis as a community for deciding what reading research should be and how we get to there from where we are.

As Laudan (1977) and Toulmin (1983) have noted, disciplines that fail to debate the nature of progress fail to control their destiny. Change, in the absence of understanding progress, can only be "reactive, reflexive, undirected, and irrational." In reactive change, there is no understanding of how territories should be transformed so that change is "for the better."

In contrast to the reactive approach to progress is the "proactive approach" (Laudan, 1977; Mosenthal, 1987). In this approach, the possible goals for change are first delineated. Next, discussion and debate focus on which of these goals is most desirable. Means for achieving these goals are considered and agreed upon. Finally, the community adopts these means in light of the expected goals. The result is planned change where the outcomes of progress are "proactive, reflective, directed, and rational" (Kelly, 1980). Although this approach to progress does not always result in significantly improved road systems, the likelihood of this approach succeeding is much higher than it is for the reactive approach.

In the absence of frameworks for understanding progress in reading, changes in this field have tended to be more reactive, reflexive, undirected, and irrational than proactive, reflective, directed, and rational. If we, as reading researchers and practitioners, hope to improve our field—rather than simply change it over time—we need to heed Laudan (1977) and Toulmin's (1983) advice; we, as a community, need to come together to discuss and debate what we mean by progress.

To this end, we need to understand what we are attempting to achieve by engaging in reading research; we need to discuss and debate the question "What are our goals for doing reading research?" Concomitantly, we need to understand the consequences of choosing one goal over another; and we need to decide the criteria for choosing among competing goals, so that we can give priority to our desired outcomes. Finally, we need to understand the various means that may help us realize our goals. Once we have decided these issues, we will then have a basis for determining whether changes constitute real progress.

In light of researchers' reactive approach to bringing about change, the primary purpose of this chapter is to raise the question "What constitutes progress in reading research?" More specifically, the intended contribution of this chapter is not so much to provide a framework for addressing this question but, rather, to place this question in the collective conscience of reading researchers and practitioners. It is the authors' hope that the issue of what constitutes progress in reading research will prove to be a topic worthy of consideration in all future handbooks. It is as Ayn Rand noted, "We have freedom of choice but not freedom from choice." If we, as reading researchers and practitioners, are to choose our field's future widely, we need to consider the issue of progress today rather than tomorrow.

Overview

There are five parts to this chapter. Part One begins by noting that there are two principal ways we can map the territory of reading: by using either "descriptive" or "operational definitions." Descriptive definitions use semantic features to define reading; operational definitions use semantic features in relation to a set of subjects, materials, and administration and scoring procedures. A distinction is drawn between "partially specified" and "fully specified" descriptive and operational definitions. The former use just a few major semantic features; the latter identify every detail possible. Part One concludes by arguing that progress in reading research involves the process of changing partially specified definitions of reading.

In Part Two, Foucault's (1972) work is reviewed as a framework for analyzing progress in reading research. This approach argues that in order to understand progress, we need to understand: (1) how different speech communities interpret definitions of a phenomenon; (2) the rhetorical rules that different communities of reading researchers abide by to frame their definitions of reading; and (3) the change mechanisms that different reading research communities employ to ensure their role as authorities within a discipline.

In Parts Three and Four, the "validating" and "interpretive" approaches (cf, Biddle & Anderson, 1986; Erickson, 1986; Shulman, 1986; Soltis, 1984) to progress are discussed, respectively. Each approach is analyzed in light of Foucault's (1972) three dimensions of understanding progress. In Part Five, factors that influence how the reading field promotes progress are considered. The chapter concludes with the plea for other reading researchers to look beyond the questions "What is reading?" and "What are possible definitions of reading?" in order to consider an even more important question: "How should reading be defined and who should define it?"

PART I: DEFINING READING AND PROGRESS: DESCRIPTIVE DEFINITIONS OF READING

There are four elements to any definition: (1) the phenomenon, (2) the observers, (3) the phenomenon's label, and (4) clarifying features. The phenomenon is the thing being defined. Observers are the people who experience this phenomenon firsthand. The label is the name that the observers give to the phenomenon that they observed. Finally, clarifying features are notable characteristics that epitomize the relationship between the phenomenon and its label. Taken together, these four elements make up the Definition Square of the phenomenon that we are attempting to define (see Figure 1a). In order to understand any definition adequately, we need to understand how these four elements relate one to the other.

Defining Reading Using the Definition Square

To understand how the Definition Square relates to definitions of reading, consider the following definition from Harris & Sipay (1980):

> Reading is a complex progress in which the recognition and comprehension of written symbols are influenced by readers' perceptual skills, decoding skills, experience, language backgrounds, mind sets, and reasoning abilities as they anticipate meaning on the basis of what has been read. (p. 10)

This definition is recast in light of the Definition Square in Figure 1b. The phenomenon being observed is *reading*. The observers are Harris and Sipay. The phenomenon they have observed is *reading*; they use the label "reading" to refer to this phenomenon. The most important feature of reading that they have identified is "complex process." They then go on to identify additional characteristics that, in turn, define "complex process." These include "recognition of written symbols" and "comprehension of written symbols."

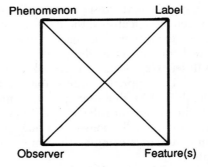

FIGURE 1a   The Definition Square

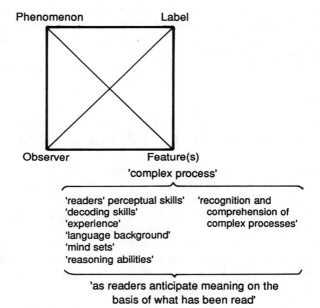

FIGURE 1b   Harris and Sipay's (1980) definition
analyzed in terms of the Definition Square

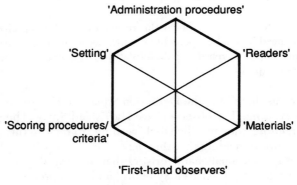

FIGURE 1c   The Operational Hexagon

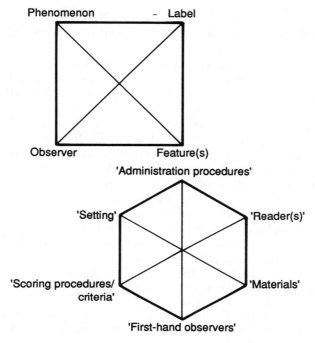

FIGURE 1d   The Operational Hexagon in the
context of the Definition Square

But Harris and Sipay do not end their definition of reading here. They then note that the processes of "recognition" and "comprehension" are influenced by other features, including: "perceptual skills," "decoding skills," "experience," "language backgrounds," "mind sets," and "reasoning abilities." These features are said to influence "recognition" and "comprehension" at a particular time, that is, when "readers anticipate meaning on the basis of what has been read."

Partially versus Fully Specified Descriptive Definitions

When researchers use the Definition Square, they are creating "descriptive definitions" (Mosenthal, 1984a, 1984b; Rudner, 1966) so as to identify the essential elements of some phenomenon-word relation (e.g., the phenomenon *reading* and the word "reading"). The purpose of creating descriptive definitions is to clarify and simplify our understanding of words and the things they represent (Wilson, 1969). By defining features (such as "complex process") with simpler terms (such as "comprehension of written symbols"), we arrive at a more precise understanding of the *reading*-"reading" relation (Rudner, 1966).

Because reading researchers experience reading differently, they identify different features as epitomizing the *reading*-"reading" relation. To illustrate this, consider the following definitions:

Reading is the ability to decode written symbols into spoken sounds (Gough, 1972).

Reading is the ability to do well on a standardized reading test (Perfetti, Goldman, & Hogaboam, 1979).

Reading is the ability to complete one's income tax form (Northcutt, 1975).

Reading is the ability to adopt a perspective (Anderson & Pichert, 1978).

Reading is the ability to reduce uncertainty (Smith, 1971).

Reading is the ability to recognize inconsistent information (Markman, 1979).

Note that each of these well-known descriptive definitions includes a different set of features; each focuses on a different aspect of the *reading*-"reading" relation. In addition to these definitions, we could list many more that would include still different features. The problem is: "How do we know what features to use to define the *reading*-'reading' relation?" "Given the different descriptive definitions of reading, which one is best?" "Should we change them to make them 'better' still? If so, why?"

To understand the answers to these questions is to understand progress in reading research. We will address these questions in Part Two of this chapter. However, it is important to note here that these questions arise because all descriptive definitions are "partially specified." Let's consider what this means.

As Rudner (1966) reminds us, no descriptive definition in science can include all the possible features of a phenomenon-word relation. If one could, then it would be "fully specified." Such a definition of reading would include all the features that observers of the *reading*-"reading" relation have identified, are currently identifying, and will identify in future research. Apart from the fact that a fully specified descriptive definition of most phenomena-word relation is physically impossible to create—given the large number of features associated with them—such a definition would fail to meet science's objective of "simplicity," that is, to convey the essence of the relation using the smallest number of features possible (Hempel, 1966; Rudner, 1966).

Summary

There are many partially specified descriptive definitions of reading, some using very different sets of features to characterize the relation between the phenomenon *reading* and the word "reading." To define reading, we must choose a few features from the universe of all possible features that make up a hypothetical "fully specified descriptive definition of reading."

But on what basis do we choose one set of features over another? As Mitroff and Sagasti (1973) have argued, this question is the most fundamental that a discipline could ask. Yet this question has received little if any attention in reading research. We will return to this question in discussing the two approaches to progress in Parts Three and Four.

OPERATIONAL DEFINITIONS OF READING

The Six Essential Elements of Operational Definitions

In addition to using descriptive definitions to define the *reading*-"reading" relation, researchers also use "operational definitions" (Bridgman, 1978; Hempel, 1966), which have two advantages: (1) they help us render unobservable phenomena, such as *reading*, observable, and (2) they allow observation to be more precise and reliable by specifying a set of replicable conditions that elicit a behavior. Should this behavior meet a specified criterion, it qualifies to be called "reading" (Bridgman, 1978; Hempel, 1966; Rudner, 1966).

There are six "essential" elements to an operational definition: (1) an observer observing the behavior of (2) at least one "reader" whose behavior has been elicited by (3) a set of materials (4) administered in a particular modality (e.g., reading or listening), using a fixed set of procedures in (5) a given location or setting. The observer determines (6), by following a set of scoring procedures, whether the observed groups' behaviors meet a set of criteria that would qualify this behavior as representing a particular phenomenon-word relation. Taken together, these six elements can be combined to form the Operational Hexagon shown in Figure 1c. (see p. 1016).

Defining Reading Using the Operational Hexagon

The six elements of the Operational Hexagon are nothing more than features that we might associate with any descriptive definition of reading. In other words, operational definitions are really a type of descriptive definition that includes the six essential elements of the Operational Hexagon. (This is illustrated in Figure 1d; see p. 1017.) In turn, researchers further define each of these six elements using descriptive definitions that establish the conditions by which a reading behavior is observed.

If we look closely at the operational definitions in the Methods sections of reading research studies, such as the one below, we find reading being defined in terms of the six elements (or features) of the Operational Hexagon. First, we find *group(s) of learners (or readers)* described in the Subjects section. The *materials*, used as stimuli, are delineated in the Materials section. The *administration procedures* are discussed in the section with the same name. The *scoring procedures* and *scoring criteria* are described either in a separate section entitled Scoring Procedures and Criteria or else are mentioned in the Administration Procedures section. Also, often noted in the Administration Procedures section is a brief description of the *observer*, who administers the materials, and the *setting*. This last element refers to where the materials are presented (e.g., a classroom or at home) and whether the materials are administered individually or by group.

To better understand this, consider the following operational definition excerpted from the Methods section of a study by Rickards and Slife (1987) and slightly revised for purposes of this chapter:*

Subjects

Introductory psychology students ($N = 210$) volunteered to take the Dogmatism Scale (Form E) for experimental credit. From the upper and lower quartiles of the score on the Dogmatism Scale, 44 high and 44 low dogmatic subjects were selected for the experiment.

Approximately half of the high and low dogmatics were randomly assigned to read either a passage having a collection rhetorical structure or one having a comparison rhetorical structure.

Materials

Both prose passages were taken from those developed and analyzed by Meyer and Freedle (1984). These investigators originally wrote four passages, which they labeled with the following headings: collection, comparison, causation, and problem/solution. Only the comparison and collection passages were employed in the present investigation . . .

The Dogmatism Scale (Form E) used here consisted of 40 items, with each item being answered in terms of the strength of agreement ($+1$, $+2$, $+3$) or disagreement (-1, -2, -3) with the statement posed. For example, 'The United States and Russia have just about nothing in common,' or 'In a discussion, I often find it necessary to repeat myself several times to make sure I am being understood.'

*"Interaction of dogmatism and rhetorical structure in text recall" by John Rickards and Brent Slife, *American Educational Research Journal*, 24, 635–641. Copyright © 1987 by the American Educational Research Association. Adopted by permission of the publishers.

The 77 subjects were randomly assigned to four groups so that high and low dogmatics were approximately equally represented in each group. One of the researchers of this study administered the stimuli to all four groups on four different occasions. The first and last groups read the comparison passage, whereas the second and third groups read the collection passage, all in one evening.

While seated in a small classroom, each group of subjects read one of the passages. After reading, subjects were asked to write down everything they could recall, using either their own words or the words from the passage. They were requested to write complete sentences rather than to merely list ideas remembered. The instructions used were identical to those of Meyer and Freedle (1984).

Scoring Procedures and Criteria

Recall protocols were scored for idea units recalled as well as for rhetorical structure used by the subjects to organize their protocols. The protocols were scored for the presence or absence of the 58 identical content units and relationship units in the content structure of the two passages. The scoring procedure used was the same as that employed by Meyer and Freedle (1984), in which they obtained 99% agreement by two independent raters . . .

Each recall protocol was examined for the degree of presence of the rhetorical structure given to the learner according to the method employed by Meyer and Freedle (1984). Essentially, the scorer diagrammed the rhetorical structure of each protocol, then classified it as either the same or different from the one given in the text. (pp. 636–638)

Note that the elements of the Observational Hexagon are descriptively defined in Richards and Slife's (1987) operational definition in the following manner. The *firsthand observer* was one of the experimenters who administered the materials and procedures; a *secondhand observer* was the second experimenter who observed and coded the data once it had been collected. The *groups of learners*, whose recall and dogmatic behaviors were observed, consisted of introductory psychology students who performed at the high and low ends of a dogmatism scale, randomly assigned to one of four treatment groups, with 22 students in a group.

The *materials* consisted of two prose passages, one representing a "comparison" structure, the other a "collection" structure. The *administration procedures* required the learners to complete the Dogmatism Scale (Form E) and later read and recall in writing everything they could remember. The groups were administered the stimuli on different occasions on the same day. The *setting* was a small classroom.

The *scoring procedures* involved diagramming the rhetorical structure of each protocol and then matching this structure against that of the corresponding stimulus. Finally, the *scoring criteria* involved the number of idea units recalled as well as whether the rhetorical structure of the recall was the same as that of the stimulus.

Partially versus Fully Specified Operational Definitions

The importance of operational definitions is that they represent a convention for descriptively defining the *reading*-"reading" relationship in research. In fact, following in the tradition of Bridgman (1927), the specification of these six elements, or features, is regarded as a necessary standard if we are to arrive at an "adequate" operational definition of any phenomenon—including reading (Bridgman, 1978; Hempel, 1966).

Interestingly enough, if we were to look at all descriptive and operational definitions of reading, we would find that the features in these definitions can all be subsumed under one or more of the elements in the Operational Hexagon (Mosenthal, 1984a, 1984b). In this regard, the Operational Hexagon approximates both a fully specified, descriptive definition and an operational definition of reading.

The advantage of operational over descriptive definitions is that we know ahead of time what superordinate features of a definition of reading are—namely, the six elements of the Operational Hexagon. However, once we have identified our six essential elements, we are back to the problem of descriptively and, in turn, operationally defining each element. At this point, we encounter the problem we faced earlier in creating a descriptive definition of the *reading*-"reading" relation; only this time, we must define the *materials*-"materials" relation, the *administration procedures*-"administration procedures" relation, the *reader*-"reader" relation, and so forth for all the elements of the Operational Hexagon.

Summary

Although operational definitions provide us with a standard for descriptively defining and observing reading, we find ourselves back at the partial specification problem of choosing features to define each of the elements of the Operational Hexagon. Once again we face this question: "What features should we include to characterize the observer, the group(s) of readers, the materials, the administration procedures, the setting, and scoring procedures and criteria?" Again, because we, as researchers, have neglected to discuss and debate this issue, we have failed to consider one of the most fundamental questions underlying inquiry in reading (and social science) research. And having failed in this, we have ignored what we mean by progress in reading research. We turn to this issue next.

PART II: FOUCAULT'S APPROACH TO UNDERSTANDING PROGRESS

The question of what constitutes progress in science has been addressed in long-standing debates (e.g., Bartley, 1962; Bunge, 1967; Kuhn, 1970; Lakotos, 1970; Laudan, 1977; Popkewitz, 1984; Popper, 1968, 1972). As Weimer (1979) has noted, these debates have focused on the issue of whether or not researchers have "achieved a theory of rationality (or rational inquiry) that would render the practice of science both a rational form of inquiry and, hence, a legitimate source of knowledge" (p. 3).

While this debate has raised important issues of what constitutes legitimate knowledge, the debate has been couched in varied terms; at times in abstract or even metaphysical rhetoric (Bartley, 1962); at times in reference to different logic systems (Popper, 1968); or framed as the problem of choosing among alternative research methodolgies (Borg & Gall, 1989; Shulman, 1986). Critics (e.g., Churchman, 1979; Foucault, 1972; Mitroff & Sagasti, 1973; Shapiro, 1981) have argued that debates about progress have not enhanced our understanding of the issues since there has been little consensus on basic terms like "truth," "theory," "proof," "knowledge," "authority," "problem solving," "inquiry," and "model." Given this failure of philosophers of science to come to a common understanding of fundamental terms, debate at larger rhetorical levels has not been particularly productive. As Mitroff and Sagasti (1973) noted:

> In many respects, the most troublesome problems of any science centre around its most basic terms and fundamental concepts, and not around its more sophisticated concerns. Indeed to the extent that everything either follows from or is based on a discipline's basic terms and fundamental concepts, problems at a higher level can always be traced back to problems at a more fundamental level. (p. 117)

Following Foucault's (1972) suggestion, a more productive way to study progress in a discipline is to determine how different "speech communities" or researchers assign meaning to the phenomenon-word relation central to their field of study. According to the French sociolinguist and critical theorist Foucault, a speech community is a group of people who share the same interpretation of some phenomenon-word relation. This speech community abides by a set of constitutive rules that (1) delimit what features may be included in a definition of the phenomenon-word relation and (2) constrict the range of rhetorical structures used to justify the selection of these features.

Having agreed upon a set of constitutive rules for formulating definitions, members of a research community enter a linguistic system that already contains "the objects one can speak about and the relations one can invoke." The more a definition conforms to and promotes the favored features and rhetorical framework of a speech community, the more likely this speech community is to regard this definition as representing "progress."

While understanding different speech communities' discursive practices is important for understanding progress, Foucault (1972) goes on to argue that an even more important consideration is understanding how different speech communities obtain and exercise power in order to persuade others of the legitimacy of their definition. Shapiro (1981), in citing Foucault, notes this important dimension of speech communities as follows:

> To ask the meaning of the statements that comprise a discourse, for Foucault, is to ask, among other things, "what is the status of the individuals who alone have the right, sanctioned by law or tradition, juridically defined or spontaneously accepted, to proffer such a discourse." (p. 151)

Thus, according to Foucault, definitions of reading cannot be put forth by just anybody; rather, definitions are the "property" of a defined speech community that is perceived by other authorities as having the right to make and maintain definitions.

As Foucault (1972) has documented, different speech communities compete socially, economically, and politically with one another to be statutorily recognized as the legitimate authority for defining some phenomenon-word relation. Whichever speech community is so recognized, its definition is viewed as representing the "greatest progress." In this regard, understanding progress involves understanding how different speech communities initiate change by persuading others to believe in and abide by their discursive practices. Shapiro (1981) argues that

> the meanings of statements and the discourses in which they are deployed create positions for persons. Because of this, the analysis of the development of various discourses is, at the same time, the analysis of the development of various social, political, economic, and administrative institutions and processes in the society in which these discourses occur. The discourses are, in effect, "practices" precisely because they reflect and guide relationships among persons. (p. 155)

In other words, if we are to understand progress, we need to understand the social-change mechanisms that different speech communities of reading research use to advance their perceived legitimacy.

Summary

According to Foucault (1972), progress in a discipline can best be understood in terms of the linguistic, social, and political aspects of the discursive practices of different speech communities that make up this discipline. Because speech communities have different interpretations of what a phenomenon-word relation means, they have different notions of what constitutes an "ideal" definition of the relationship. To understand progress in reading research thus involves understanding how the different communities of researchers interpret definitions of the *reading*-"reading" relation.

In addition, speech communities have different constitutive rules that they use to create "ideal" rhetorical structures for framing their definitions. Thus, to understand progress in reading research, we need to understand the rules and rhetorical structures that the different communities of reading researchers use to frame their definitions.

Finally, speech communities use different change mechanisms to ensure that they are recognized as the authority for defining some phenomenon-word relation. Hence, to understand progress in reading research, we need to understand how reading's different speech communities implement change in a way that best promotes the legitimacy of their discursive practices.

In Parts Three and Four, we turn to these three dimensions of progress as they relate to two speech communities of reading researchers.

PART III: THE VALIDATING APPROACH

To date, the largest community of reading researchers have abided by the "validating approach" to progress (Shannon, 1989). This approach operates under the assumptions that definitions of reading reflect facts about the phenomenon, reading. Moreover, this approach assumes that these facts have little to do with how reading is observed and who does the observing. On the other hand, another group of researchers, who comprise the second largest reading research community, have adopted an "interpretive approach" to progress. This approach assumes that definitions of reading are not facts but a list of features descriptive of the behaviors of readers reading at a particular point in space/time. In this section we consider the validating approach.

What Definitions of Reading Refer To

The validating approach to progress is grounded in "literal-correspondence theory." According to this theory (Bernstein, 1983; Cicourel, 1974; Guba & Lincoln, 1982; Mervis, 1980), there exists an ideal descriptive definition that best characterizes some phenomenon-word relation. This ideal definition consists of a set of critical cause-and-effect features. Cause features bring about a change in a phenomenon's state and/or process. Effect features represent outcomes, or consequences, which, in turn, represent a new state or an altered process (Krathwohl, 1985). Taken together, cause-and-effect features make up critical cause-effect relations.

The cause-effect relations in a validating study represent "facts" about some phenomenon that are assumed to exist independent of observers' beliefs and their means of observation. Further, the facts are social to the extent that other observers who view the same phenomenon would "experience" (or identify) the same critical features defining the cause-effect relation (Firestone, 1987).

The purpose in creating definitions in the validating approach to progress is to predict a set of outcomes relative to a set of causal conditions. These conditions are established by an operational definition. These causal conditions are arrived at through conventions of experimental or correlational designs (Campbell & Stanley, 1966; Chronbach, 1975), which are used to reduce error variance and to maximize the strength of a predicted outcome (Calfee & Piontkowski, 1984).

TABLE 1   The mean number of propositions recalled
by high dogmatics and low dogmatics by collection
and comparison structures

	COLLECTION	COMPARISON
HIGH DOGMATICS	30.94	35.40
LOW DOGMATICS	32.89	33.82

In validating studies, critical cause-effect relations are usually identified in contingency tables, such as the one in Table 1. In simple contingency tables, the causal variables are often listed in a row and the effect variables in a column. The strength of a relationship is reported as a mean number in the row-by-column intersection. Often some measure of variance, such as standard deviations, is presented along with each cell mean.

Table 1 summarizes one set of findings from the Rickards and Slife (1987) study cited earlier. In it, we see that the researchers identified two critical causal features, "degree of dogmatism" and "type of rhetorical structure," and one critical effect feature, "amount of propositions recalled." Subordinate critical causal features included "high dogmatics," "low dogmatics," "collection rhetorical structure," and "comparison rhetorical structure."

Recasting Rickards and Slife's (1987) contingency table in terms of the Definition Square, we would identify "the influence of degree of dogmatism and type of rhetorical structure on recall of text propositions" as representing the first critical feature in defining the *reading*-"reading" relationship. Next, we would find a list of possible cause-effect relations that make up the subordinate features mentioned above.

Discursive Practices

Within the validating approach to progress, two principal classes of rhetorical structures can be identified: "analyzing" and "synthesizing." Included among the latter are "taxonomies" and "models" (Rudner, 1966), which synthesize cause-and-effect features from individual studies into broader categories. Although taxonomies and models serve as important rhetorical devices in advancing progress under the validating approach, they are not considered in this chapter because of space limitations and because much attention has already been given to them (e.g., see Massaro, 1984; Samuels & Kamil, 1984). With this disclaimer aside, let us turn our attention to "analyzing frameworks."

Although analyzing frameworks include a variety of rhetorical designs (Borg & Gall, 1989; Kamil, 1984; Kamil, Langer, & Shannahan, 1985), the primary purpose of these designs is to help researchers establish "theories" of a phenomenon. In turn, theories serve as the basic building blocks that give rise to "lines of research" and that make synthesis possible. Suppe (1974) describes this importance of theories in the validating approach to progress this way:

> If any problem in the philosophy of science can justifiably be claimed the most central or important, it is that of the nature or structure of scientific theories. For theories are the vehicle of scientific knowledge, and one way or another become involved in most aspects of the scientific enterprise. . . . It is only a slight exaggeration to claim that a philosophy of science is little more than an analysis of theories and their roles in the scientific enterprise. A philosophy of science's analysis of the structure of theories is thus its keystone. : . . (p. iii)

Although the nature of theories has been debated (e.g., Biddle & Anderson, 1986; Campbell, 1921), their rhetorical structure and constitutive rules have not been well specified. In the next two sections we attempt to describe the constitutive rules that validating researchers use to formulate the rationale and Methods section of reading theories.

Constitutive Rules of the Rationale Section

As noted earlier, the rationale section of a research article includes a partially specified descriptive definition of some phenomenon-word relationship that is intrinsic to the theory being tested. More often than not, this descriptive definition is an elaboration of the article's title, which identifies the features in the cause-effect relation.

To illustrate this, consider the title from Rickards and Slife's (1987) study, "Interaction of Dogmatism and Rhetorical Structure in Text Recall." The title suggests that among the list of superordinate features, the most important causative feature is "degree of dogmatism by type of rhetorical structure." Likewise, among the list of subordinate features, the most important causative features are those suggesting an interaction between "dogmatism" and "rhetorical structure type." This title implies that the causative variables representing an interaction between features most significantly affect "text recall."

The rationale section of an article often restates the title as a question. The underlying form of this question is: "An important yet little understood question is 'What is the relationship between CAUSE X and EFFECT Y?' " In reading, the importance of this question and the cause-effect relation are discussed—if at all—in terms of reading instruction or evaluation problems. In Rickards and Slife's (1987) study, the underlying question can be stated as : "An important yet little understood question is 'What is the relation between (1) dogmatism and rhetorical structure (CAUSE) and (2) text recall (EFFECT)?' " These authors ignore the issue of why this question is important.

Although justifying a question's importance is not a necessary condition for a theory, justifying why a question is "little understood" is. In reading theories (as in most social-science theories), this justification is always made in reference to an "external validity" argument. There are five steps in this argument; these steps represent constitutive rules to the extent that each must be followed to create a "well-formed" descriptive definition. Consider these steps in turn; excerpts from Rickards and Slife's (1987) study are used to illustrate each.

In the first step, researchers identify an existing theory or model and its underlying processes. For example, Rickards and Slife (1987) begin their external validity argument by identifying Meyer's 1984 text-processing model and by mentioning the processes "identifying," "encoding," and "generating":

> According to Meyer's (1984) model of text processing, the primary activity of the skilled reader is to identify the superordinate, rhetorical structure of the passage being read. Once selected, this structure or schema is used "to encode text and generate expectations for ensuing text." (p. 11)

In the second step, researchers identify the operational conditions that influence a theory's basic processes. For instance, in this step, Rickards and Slife (1987) identify two types of rhetorical structures influencing how text is encoded and remembered.

> Rhetorical structures vary considerably in terms of their degree of organization. For example, the least organized rhetorical structure, the *collection* type, consists of a list of points grouped by association, such as a set of attributes, or by sequence, as in a time sequence. The more highly organized *comparison* rhetorical structure, on the other hand,

involves the presentation of similarities and differences in the form of a favored view and an opposing one with an explanation of the favored view. (p. 635)

In the third step, researchers identify Foundation Study A. They first summarize a set of findings (along with their bridge principles) that relate specifically to what was tested in this study. For example, Rickards and Slife (1987) identify Meyer and Freedle's 1984 study as their Foundation Study A. They then present a set of findings and an explanation (or set of bridge principles) of why collection and comparison produce different effects:

Findings

Not surprisingly, Meyer and Freedle (1984) found that the more organized rhetorical structures (such as the *comparison* type) produced significantly more recall of passage material than the least organized structure (the *collection* type).

Bridge Principles

They reasoned that the *comparison* structure's superiority was due to the fact that it contained many more slots or variables to be filled in by the (reader) as he or she proceeded through the passage, thereby providing an organizing framework for encoding and retrieval. (pp. 635–636)

Next, researchers present a second set of findings. In discussing these findings, researchers identify a set of bridge principles that are implied but not directly tied to what was tested in the Foundation Study A. In this regard, the researchers introduce a new construct, or variable, which was not in the original theory or model. For instance, in discussing the type of rhetorical structure that readers used to recall either a collection or comparison, Rickards and Slife introduce the construct of cognitive style; this construct was not part of Meyer's original 1984 model:

Findings

These investigators also found that 100% of those who had received the comparison passage and 78% of those who had been given the collection passage used the respective structure of the original passage to organize their recall protocols.

Bridge Principles

Since recall protocols tend to match text structure, it would seem that (readers) should retain most when the rhetorical structure suits their particular strategic tendencies. Meyer's model posits such an interaction between "text variables" and "reader . . . variables," such as "processing style" or "cognitive style." (pp. 636)

In the fourth step, researchers argue that although the implied construct is consistent with Foundation Study A's bridge principle, it was not tested; at this point, researchers discuss how the operational conditions of this construct in Foundation Study B produced an outcome similar to the one found in Foundation Study A.

For example, having introduced the new construct "cognitive style," Rickards and Slife argue that both Meyer and Freedle's study (i.e., Study A) had the same outcome as Rokeach's 1960 study—namely, both studied information-processing effects. They identify the operational conditions used to measure the cause and effect in Rokeach's study:

Work on cognitive style represents at attempt to integrate cognition and personality. That is, differences on some personality-related factors are said to be systematically related to differences in the way in which information is processed. For example, Rokeach's Dogmatism Scale attempts to measure the degree to which one can incorporate new information in the form of new beliefs into his or her existing cognitive structure, specifically his or her belief system. Those who score high ("closed-minded" learners) on the 40-item paper-and-pencil test tend to reject new beliefs, and those who score low ("open-minded" learners) typically accept them (see Rokeach, 1960; Goldstein & Glackman, 1978). (p. 636)

At this point in the argument, Rickards and Slife have descriptively defined "cognitive style" in terms of "dogmatism." To make the point that dogmatism influences information processing, they cite several studies where this has been shown:

There is considerable evidence that dogmatism has quite pervasive effects on information processing. Early work by Restle, Andrews, and Rokeach (1964) suggested that high dogmatics were rote learners and low dogmatics were conceptual learners. Further research, using a variety of learning tasks, has demonstrated that high dogmatics use less search time in information search situations (Ballard, 1979), employ simpler information processing strategies (Brightman & Urban, 1974), and are less able to solve paper-and-pencil problem solving tasks (Kemp, 1960, 1962) than low dogmatics. These differences have occurred even though "the correlation between scores on the Dogmatism Scale and intelligence is typically close to zero" (Rokeach, 1960, p. 407). (p. 636)

Finally, in step five, researchers predict how the new construct or variable identified in Study B will influence the outcome identified in both Studies A and B. Here researchers make more explicit the untested bridge principle identified in step three; they do this by explaining how the contrastive features that make up the new variable differentially influence the outcome.

For instance, in step three, Rickards and Slife posited that readers' recalls would vary depending upon the interaction between cognitive style and rhetorical structure. In making their predictions, these researchers describe explicitly how this interaction would vary depending upon whether readers were high or low dogmatics and whether they were reading a text organized as a collection or as a comparison:

Since recall protocols tend to match the rhetorical structure presented, to the degree that high dogmatics engage in simple rote learning strategies, they should recall more with the collection rhetorical structure; and, to the degree that low dogmatics employ more complex conceptual learning strategies, they should recall more with the comparison rhetorical structure. Thus, we predict an interaction between dogmatism and rhetorical structure in text. (p. 636)

In carrying out the above five steps, validating researchers argue that although Study A was an adequate test of a theory, the theory's external validity could be extended by adding a variable (or set of contrasting features) from Study B. If this new variable by itself, or in interaction with an original variable from Study A, proves significant, then researchers can claim that the external validity of the theory underlying Study A has been extended.

Constitutive Rules of the Methods Section

To demonstrate the effect of the new variable, validating researchers replicate the operational conditions in Study A, adding only the new causative features from Study B. This process of creating a new theoretical study by adding one variable to an existing study's operational definition represents "recombinant change," that is, the whole of

Study A's Methods section is maintained while different causative features from other studies are merely added to one or more of the essential elements.

To illustrate this, let us compare Rickards and Slife's (1987) operational definition from Part I to the one described in Meyer and Freedle's (1984) study. Both studies used: (1) similar *readers*—adults attending college classes who volunteered to participate in the experiment; (2) the same *materials* and *mode*—a collection and comparison passage presented aurally; (3) the same *administration procedures*—using the same recall directives. (4) Both studies were conducted in a similar *setting*—a small room with group administration, and (5) the *observer* was one of the experimenters. Finally, (6) the *scoring procedures* and *scoring criteria* were the same—recall protocols were scored in terms of the number of idea units recalled and whether the subjects' rhetorical structures matched those of the text. In sum, both studies instantiated the Operational Hexagon in such a way that the descriptive definition of each essential element contained the same features.

The only two significant differences between the two studies were as follows: (1) Meyer and Freedle used four contrasting features ("comparison," "causation," "problem/solution," and "collection"), whereas Rickards and Slife used two ("comparison" and "collection"). More importantly, (2) Meyer and Freedle defined the reader element in terms of the feature "adults," whereas Rickards and Slife, in drawing upon Rokeach's (1960) study, defined the reader element in terms of the contrasting causative feature "high-dogmatism" vs. "low-dogmatism."

Implications for Progress

As noted above, theory serves as an important rhetorical framework for validating researchers. This framework provides a basis for systematically extending one study by adding to it contrasting causative features from a second. In recombining features, the primary purpose is to demonstrate the internal validity of a primary cause-effect relation under a variety of observation conditions. Although secondary cause-effect relations (e.g., dogmatism in Rickards and Slife's study) may be identified as significant, they in no way diminish the status of the primary cause-effect relation (i.e., rhetorical structure type in Meyer and Freedle's study) in a given theory (such as Meyer's, 1984). Because of the way rhetorical arguments are structured, secondary cause-effect relations must always be justified in terms of the bridge principles associated with the theory of the primary cause-effect relation. In this regard, the extent to which the secondary cause-effect relation is validated (either as a main effect or as an interaction) is viewed as simply a logical extension of Study A's theory.

As such, researchers engaged in validating reading view progress as improvements in the ability to predict an outcome of reading relative to a set of causal conditions. This involves the process of creating a "line of research" wherein a "primary" cause-effect relation is systematically tested and shown to be valid under a range of different operational conditions. The greater this range of conditions is, the greater the "external validity" (Krathwohl, 1985) of this definition of reading.

This view of promoting progress by developing a systematically validated line of research has been described by Hull (1943):

> Progress . . . will consist in the laborious writing, one by one, of hundreds of equations; in the experimental determination, one by one, of hundreds of empirical constants contained in the equations; in the devising of practically usable units in which to measure the quantities expressed in the equations . . . in the rigorous deduction, one by one, of thousands of theorems and corollaries from the primary definitions and equations, in the meticulous performance of thousands of critical quantitative experiments. (pp. 400–401)

Consistent with this view is the emphasis on meta-analysis (Glass, McGaw, & Smith, 1981; Slavin, 1986), which attempts to establish empirical relations among studies that investigate the same superordinate cause-effect relation but use a variety of different operational conditions.

Finally, the view that progress is synonymous with a line of research has been consistently reflected in the work of historians (e.g., Boring, 1950; Watson, 1963) who portray the history of disciplines as linear developments through the logical extension of theories (see Mosenthal, 1988, for further discussion of how this applies to reading). Weimer (1979) refers to these historians as "cumulative record theorists":

> Cumulative record theorists write history backward rather than forward; they refer only to that part of prior theory and the work of past scientists that can readily be viewed as contributions to present problems and positions of the theorists' own substantive points of view, as determined by the research tradition in which they operate. . . . Science is seen as cumulative and directed to the present, simply because it is written to seem continuous and cumulative. This contributes to the invisibility of scientific revolutions; occurrences that are inherently revolutionary in nature are customarily reviewed by the scientist and historian alike not as revolutions but merely as additions to scientific knowledge. Both the historical remarks of practicing scientists and the accounts of historians are geared to portray past achievements as continuous with the ongoing normal science puzzle-solving tradition. (p. 229)

By engaging in recombinant theory building, validating researchers promote progress in a way that is consistent with Kuhn's (1970) notion of "normal science" and Feyerabend's (1965) "theoretical monism." The basic goal of normal science and theoretical monism is to further refine existing theories of a phenomenon-word relation.

Concomitant with this perspective is the notion that progress is made as new contrastive causative features are validated through the use of recombinant operational definitions; that is, the theory is refined experimentally by testing new operational features to determine whether they can extend a theory's external validity. To preserve the integrity of the theory and be consistent with the dictates of normal science, these features are added to the descriptive definition under the conditions that: (1) they do not require a change in interpretation of the theory's superordinate features (or "primitive terms"); (2) they are validated using the theory's critical operational definition; and (3) they do not require a change in the theory's bridge principles (Hempel, 1966).

Promoting Change

Just as there are well-defined rhetorical structures and constitutive rules that provide validating researchers with a framework for developing lines of research, there are well-defined rules for translating research into practice. As Popkewitz (1984) and others (e.g., Kelly, 1980; Schon, 1983) have argued, these rules represent logical extensions of how validating researchers understand causal change:

> [Validating researchers believe that both science and change are] concerned with the appropriate application of technique to realize defined goals and under given conditions. Theories of change, as theories of learning, are to be oriented towards appropriate means for achieving some pre-established criterion. The purpose of the science of change is to explain, order, and analyze the components without judging their final normative appropriateness. *Change theories assume a neutrality towards the "product" being introduced or*

the organizational goals. The professional-scientist is to provide "objective" knowledge to be used by policy-makers. With this assumption of purpose are other paradigmatic commitments, such as seeking universal and formalized knowledge, adopting the notion of social system in which interacting variables can be studied as distinct and independent entities, and the disinterest of science to the goals of the system. (p. 133, our emphasis)

Underlying this approach to change is the notion of "expert." As Foucault (1972) suggests, this notion is really a sociopolitical concept. An expert is one who is both socially recognized by and engages in the practices of a predominant speech community. This community is predominant to the extent that it is recognized by both practitioners and policymakers as the true (or legitimate) authority within a discipline.

In the speech community of validating researchers, experts are those who have mastered the rhetorical structures and constitutive rules for formulating theories, taxonomies, and models. Because these structures and rules are foreign to practitioners and policymakers, two distinct roles emerge in any profession: that of the expert researcher who diagnoses and solves the problems of practice, and that of the lay practitioner, who "furnishes the researcher with problems for study and with tests of the utility of research results" (Schon, 1983, p. 26) (see also Kamil, 1984).

Because validating researchers compete against speech communities representing alternative approaches to progress, these researchers argue the superiority of their assumptions and methods. In addition, these researchers develop public forums, such as journals, which admit only research that conforms to their conventions (Shannon, 1989).

Within the broader community of validating researchers can be found "subspeech communities." These usually form around a particular individual or set of individuals who have identified a widely accepted line of research. Subspeech communities work to heighten their authority, as perceived by practitioners and policymakers, by creating their own public forums, such as books and specialized conferences and workshops.

The extent to which researchers belong to a dominant speech community and subspeech community is the extent to which they are viewed by practitioners and policymakers as "experts." Achieving this status is the first step in bringing about "improved change" in the validating approach to progress. To understand this, we need to understand how validating researchers implement change in policy and practice.

As Popkewitz (1984) suggests, there are four steps. First, researchers become recognized as experts by engaging in the practices of the dominant community and by identifying a line of research that represents a series of recombinant, operational definition studies that have extended a theory. Second, based on the "findings" of these studies (in terms of the modified theory's descriptive definition), instructional programs and evaluation methods are developed and packaged for use by practitioners and policymakers. Third, in the dissemination (diffusion) stage, experts market the products developed. This is usually done through demonstrations, training programs, and advertisements. Finally, in the fourth phase, users adopt or install the product, replacing their programs with the "new and improved" ones developed by the "leading experts" (Schon, 1983).

In sum, in the validating approach, progress involves defining practitioners' and policymakers' problems and developing solutions to them. Definitions of these problems are often framed in a manner consistent with the rhetorical structure and constitutive rules of theories and in terms of the cause-effect relationship of a leading theory. Practitioners and policymakers further this process by adopting and implementing these solutions (Mosenthal, 1984b).

PART IV: THE INTERPRETIVE APPROACH

What Definitions of Reading Refer To

The interpretive approach to progress is based on the belief of "family resemblances" (McCutcheon, 1981; Schutz, 1971; Wittgenstein, 1958). As Wittgenstein argued, rarely does one instance of a phenomenon, labeled by one general term, have a set of identical features to a second instance. Rather, varied instances of a phenomenon have overlapping features representing a set of "family resemblances" (Cantor & Mischel, 1979; Mervis, 1980; Rosch & Mervis, 1975) or shared critical features.

What features are viewed as overlapping depends upon the meaning, values, and uses people assign to instances (Erickson, 1986; Mehan & Wood, 1975). Thus, to understand a phenomenon such as *reading*, interpretive researchers do not study the *reading*-"reading" relation per se; rather, they focus on how "participant observers" assign meaning in a particular instance (Mehan, 1979; Michel, 1988). This means that there are often two sets of observers in an interpretive study. One set is the native observers who assign some meaning, value, or use to the phenomenon as they experience it in different situations; the other consists of the researchers who observe the native observers.

Depending upon their tradition, interpretive researchers disagree on the extent to which native observers will perceive overlapping features (Jacob, 1987, 1988). At one extreme are symbolic interactionists (e.g., Blumer, 1969; Manis & Meltzer, 1978; Rose, 1962), who assume that critical features vary from local situation to local situation; in Blumer's (1969) words: "The actor selects, checks, suspends, regroups, and transforms the meanings in the light of the situation in which he is placed and the direction of his action" (p. 5). Hence, in this tradition, native observers are believed to notice few overlapping critical features from instance to instance.

A less relativistic position has been taken by other interpretivists, such as cognitive anthropologists (e.g., Spradley, 1980; Tyler, 1969) and ethnographers (e.g., Erickson & Mohatt, 1982; Goodenough, 1981; Mehan & Wood, 1975; Pelto & Pelto, 1977), who argue that individuals share a rather large, common core of critical features because they all "attempt to understand human society through the concept of culture." Because culture represents a "shared pattern for behavior," participants within a society often assign the same meanings, values, and uses to common phenomena. In this sense, culture, in cognitive terms, represents "learned and shared standards for perceiving, believing, acting, and evaluating the actions of others" (Goodenough, 1981, pp. 62ff).

Given that culture, however broadly defined, represents a "web of significance" spun by participants, interpretive researchers attempt to discover how individuals collectively assign meaning, values, and uses to phenomena. Here is how Geertz (1973) describes this process of interpretive researchers trying to understand the meaning of a group of "meaning makers":

> Interpretive explanation . . . trains its attention on what institutions, actions, images, utterances, events, customs, all the usual objects of social scientific interest, mean to those whose institutions, actions, customs, and so on they are. As a result, it issues not in laws like Boyle's, or forces like Volta's, or mechanisms like Darwin's, but in constructions like Burkhardt's, Weber's or Freud's: systematic unpackings of the conceptual world. . . .
>
> The manner of these constructions itself varies: Burkhardt portrays, Weber models, Freud diagnoses. But they all represent attempts to formulate how this people or that . . . makes sense to itself and, understanding that, what we understand about social order,

historical change, or psychic functioning in general. Inquiry is directed at cases or sets of cases, and toward the particular features that mark them off; but its aims are as far-reaching as those of mechanics or physiology: to distinguish the materials of human experience. (p. 21)

Independent of their assumptions about common-core, critical features, interpretive researchers attempt to advance understanding in science by observing a phenomenon from a variety of perspectives at different points in space and time. Each of these observations is intended to yield a "thick description" or detailed listing of descriptive features that define the phenomenon (McCutcheon, 1981). As more and more observations are made of different instances over time, more overlapping features can be identified. These "concrete universal" features are distinguished from "local" features, which are unique to a particular instance. The overlapping features will be grouped by "theme" or "taxonomic category." From the interpretive researchers' perspectives, these themes and categories represent the "improved" descriptive definition of the phenomenon being studied (Miles & Huberman, 1984; Mosenthal 1985b).

In interpretive reading studies, themes and taxonomic categories are often reported in terms of different cultural practices, or functions of reading (e.g., Heath, 1980; Scribner & Cole, 1981; Taylor & Dorsey-Gaines, 1988; Teale, 1986); or different perceptions of reading (e.g., Harste, Burke, & Woodward, 1982, Michel, 1988); or the different ways teachers and students socially negotiate reading in classrooms (Au, 1980; Cazden, 1979; Green & Wallat, 1981; McDermott, 1985). In some cases, themes and taxonomic categories are summarized in contingency tables (see Erickson, 1986, for further discussion). Rather than identify critical cause-effect features, these tables serve primarily to list the major themes or categories and provide a way of organizing their descriptive definitions and relevant examples.

More often than not, interpretive researchers simply list their themes or taxonomic categories by name. After each listing, a descriptive definition of each "name" is provided, along with examples that illustrate particular instances. These examples may be extensive or limited; they may include vignettes, direct quotes, or listings of objects or actions.

Heath (1980) succinctly illustrates this typical way of reporting interpretive findings. In her study of the literacy practices of 90 individuals in "an all-black working-class community in the Southeastern United States," she identified the following "seven types of uses of literacy." (Note that after each category label, she provides a descriptive definition and a series of object examples):*

1. *Instrumental.* Literacy provided information about the practical problems of daily life (price tags, checks, bills, advertisements, street signs, and house numbers).
2. *Social-interactional.* Literacy provided information pertinent to social relationships (greeting cards, cartoons, bumper stickers, posters, letters, newspaper features, recipes).
3. *News-related.* Literacy provided information about third parties or distant events (newspaper items, political flyers, messages from local city offices about incidents of vandalism, etc.)
4. *Memory-supportive.* Literacy served as a memory aid (messages written on calendars, address and telephone books, inoculation records).

---

*All the extracts from Heath (1980) reproduced in this chapter come from "The functions and uses of literacy" by Shirley Brice Heath, *Journal of Communication,* 30(1), 123–133. Copyright © 1980 by the *Journal of Communication.* Used with permission.

5. *Substitutes for oral messages.* Literacy was used when direct oral communication was not possible or would prove embarrassing (notes for tardiness to school, message left by parent for child coming home after parent left for work).
6. *Provision of permanent record.* Literacy was used when legal records were necessary or required by other institutions (birth certificates, loan notes, tax forms).
7. *Confirmation.* Literacy provided support for attitudes or ideas already held, as in settling disagreements or for one's own reassurance (brochures on cars, directions for putting items together, the Bible). (pp. 128–129)

Note that in contrast to validating researchers who organize their definitions in terms of cause-and-effect features, Heath organizes hers under the simple category "practices."

Discursive Practices

In a recent essay, Erickson (1986) has suggested that interpretive studies should include nine main elements:

1. Empirical assertions
2. Analytic narrative vignettes
3. Quotes from field notes
4. Quotes from interviews
5. Synoptic data reports (maps, frequency tables, figures)
6. Interpretive commentary framing particular description
7. Interpretive commentary framing general description
8. Theoretical discussion
9. Report of the natural history of inquiry in the study (p. 145)

Although these elements provide some understanding of the content of interpretive studies, they offer little insight into the nature of interpretive researchers' rhetorical arguments and constitutive rules. In light of this, let us consider these arguments and rules using Heath's 1980 and 1983 studies as examples.

As with the validating approach, the interpretive approach makes use of analyzing and synthesizing frameworks for structuring its definitions. However, the interpretive approach uses descriptive taxonomies, as its basic rhetorical form in both its analysis and synthesis of findings (Mosenthal, 1985a). For analysis, a taxonomy is presented that summarizes the detailed observations of native observers in a particular social situation. For synthesis, taxonomies from different analytical studies are compared and contrasted. The purpose for comparing and contrasting taxonomies is to demonstrate how one social group differs from another in terms of its perceptions, values, or practices. For purposes of this chapter, we will consider only descriptive taxonomies used as analyzing frameworks.

Like validating researchers, interpretive researchers are interested in achieving "internal validity" (Krathwohl, 1985). However, internal validity has a different meaning in each case. For interpretive researchers, internal validity refers to the extent to which the general themes or taxonomic categories used to classify a set of observations adequately cover all instances in a "mutually exclusive fashion." That is, there is no overlap—the observations include features unique to each theme or category. The features observed are said to stand in "complementary distribution" (Fodor, Bever, & Garrett, 1974), such that an observation classified by one theme or category shares no features with observations classified by other themes or categories.

There are four parts to descriptive taxonomies, as there are to a theory held by validating researchers. Three are similar: (1) an elaborate descriptive definition; (2) an operational definition; and (3) a set of bridge principles that describe the relation between the generalized themes or taxonomies and particular observational instances. The fourth part differs. For interpretive researchers, the fourth part is a (4) taxonomy of themes or categories that summarize the many instances of recorded observations.

As noted earlier, interpretive studies usually focus on the perceptions, values, and practices of one or more social groups. These dimensions may be discussed as they characterize a group, as they constitute a comparison/contrast between groups, or as they define a series of social interactions. In many instances, whether an interpretive study addresses perceptions, values, or practices is made clear from the study's title, as is the nature of the social group being studied.

To illustrate this, consider the title from Heath's (1980) study, "The Functions and Uses of Literacy." This title suggests that the focus of her study is on practices rather than on the perceptions and values of a social group. However, what is missing from the title is any mention of the social group whose literacy practices are being described.

Constitutive Rules of the Rationale Section

As in theoretical studies, the rationale section of a descriptive taxonomy often restates the title as a question. The underlying form of this question in interpretive studies is: "An important yet little understood question is 'What are the [perceptions] [values] [practices] of social group(s) X (and Y)?' " Unlike validating studies, which often ignore the issue of why a research question is important, interpretive studies always address this issue (Merton, 1959). In most instances, importance is argued in terms of social implications for a particular collection of individuals.

If the focus of the study is on individuals, the social implications are discussed in terms of individual differences; if the focus of the study is on groups, such as disadvantaged readers or a minority community, the social implications are discussed at the societal or cultural level.

For instance, in Heath's (1980) study, the underlying question she addresses can be restated thus: "An important yet little understood question is, 'What are the functions and uses of literacy in the all-black, working-class community located somewhere in the Southeastern United States?' " Heath argues the importance of this question by discussing the consequences of literacy's social functions, first from a historical point of view:

> A number of historians have asked of social groups in certain places and times: What does it matter whether or not a person can read? What social consequences does literacy have for the group? What responses have societies made to the introduction of writing systems or print? Some unexpected patterns have emerged from the attempts to answer these questions. For example, knowledge of the possibility of written language (or the possibilities of print) does not in itself insure that writing and reading will be adopted. Further, even in societies in which writing systems and/or print have been accepted, the uses of literacy have often been very much circumscribed, because only a small elite or particular craftsmen have had access to literacy. Finally, a restricted literate class can increase the range of functions of written language *without* increasing the size of the literate population. (p. 124)

Heath then discusses the importance of literacy's functions in society from a cultural point of view. She includes the following observations:

> Traditionally, the functions and uses of literacy have been examined at the level of the society. Kroeber (1948) traced the invention and diffusion of writing systems. Goody and Watt (1963) . . . suggested that the advent of alphabetic writing systems and the spread of literacy changed forms of social and individual memory of past events and useful informa-

tion. Others . . . have proposed that societies also developed certain logical operations which led them to be able to classify and categorize the world about them in new ways. (p. 125)

Heath next argues the importance of literacy to the community. This argument of importance is also used to establish her argument of "little understood."

In descriptive taxonomies, the argument of "little understood" is established as follows. First, a series of findings are cited that justify studying the perceptions, values, or practices of a set of individuals or a group. These findings, more often than not, are included in the argument of why a research question is important. Second, the argument is made that although these perceptions, values, or practices have been demonstrated to characterize one set of individuals or a group, they have not been investigated with respect to a "favorite" set of individuals or social group. This makes the research question of what characterizes the perceptions, values, or practices of individuals or a group "little understood." Hence, the purpose of the interpretive study is to address this question.

To illustrate this argument, let us return to Heath's (1980) study. She establishes her "little understood" argument in two places. The first occurs after the above quote. Note that her argument can be identified as it is preceded by the concessive "however":

> However, studies of single societies . . . or communities have found that the functions of literacy suggested by Goody, Havelock, and others cannot be universally attributed, and that the methods of learning literacy skills, as well as their consequences, vary considerably across societies. For example, literacy may decline if it becomes non-functional in a society, or if the goals it has been thought to accomplish are not achieved. For example, in cargo cults, the millenarian movements which grew up in New Guinea and Melanesia at various times during the twentieth century, members were initially anxious to have their young and old learn to read for the economic and religious benefits promised by missionaries. However, when the population recognized that they remained poor despite their sons' learning to read and write, they withdrew from literacy and maintained it for only select purposes in religious ceremonies. . . . (p. 125)

Having established that "functions of literacy . . . vary considerably across societies," Heath establishes a more precise "little understood" argument as it applies to black communities in particular. She embeds this "little understood" argument (beginning with "however" in the quote below) within an appeal for the importance of the research question:

> Since reading varies in its functions and uses across history and cultures, it must also vary across contexts of use as defined by particular communities. For example, the highly publicized 'Black English' court decision in the case of *Martin Luther King Jr. Elementary School Children* v. *Ann Arbor School District Board* held that the school should provide appropriate models for students to follow in developing images of themselves as readers. The school's responsibility was seen as particularly important for those students whose parents and/or siblings did not read at home and did not view reading as having a positive effect on their lives. The expert witnesses and the court decision assumed here that children who were not successful readers by school standards were not exposed to types of reading and writing at home which could be transferred to their school experience. *However*, we know very little about the actual types, functions, or uses of literacy in the homes of these children, or in constant television homes or, in general, in the homes of non-skilled or semi-skilled workers (p. 126)

Thus, given that "we know very little about the actual types, functions, or uses of literacy in the homes of these children," the purpose of Heath's study was to define the literacy practices of a black community.

The third part of interpretive researchers' "little understood" argument establishes that since little is known about a set of individuals' or a social group's perceptions, values, or practices, a qualitative study of some sort is needed to "discover" the critical features.

In her study, Heath (1980) develops this line of argument as follows:

> Numerous surveys have characterized the kinds of reading promoted in the homes of successful academically oriented families and industrialized, urbanized populations . . . , but even these surveys provide only a limited picture of reading habits. In particular, we expect surveys by questionnaire to tell us little about the actual reading and writing of lower-class or working-class families. Recently, ethnographers of education . . . have suggested that participation and observation in the lives of social groups can provide a more comprehensive picture of the uses of literacy and its component skills. (p. 127).

In some instances, interpretive researchers, at this point in their rationale section, provide a brief overview of their observation procedures and discuss the underlying bridge principles. In other cases, as in Heath's (1980) study, observation procedures and bridge principles are mentioned in the Methods and Results sections, respectively.

Constitutive Rules of the Methods Section

In contrast to validating studies, which use contrasting causal features in their operational definition, interpretive studies use only descriptive, noncausal features. More often than not, when studying a community or society, interpretive researchers use descriptive features to characterize in great detail: the setting; the learners (or native observers whose perceptions, values, or practices are being studied); and the interaction between the researcher and the native observers. Often a detailed history of the setting and learners is provided; a brief historical account of how the researcher gained entry into a community and developed a collaborative relationship with local informants is also chronicled. Finally, the range of observation procedures (which correspond with "administration procedures" in the Operational Hexagon) are described in significant detail, as are the means for recording these procedures (which correspond with "scoring procedures" in the Operational Hexagon). In many instances, accounts of these aspects of the Operational Hexagon are written in narrative rather than expository format (Bogdan & Biklen, 1982).

In returning to Heath (1980) for an illustration of how the Operational Hexagon is instantiated in an interpretive study, we find ourselves referred to Heath's (1983) larger work in which the 1980 study was based. In it, we find entire chapters on each of these topics: a history of the two communities studied with maps and photographs of the people and communities; how she gained access to these communities; and descriptions of her primary informants and other residents. In order to maintain a "narrative focus," Heath details most of her observation and data reduction procedures in the footnotes at the end of the book.

The bridge principles in interpretive studies are mentioned either in the rationale or the Results section. Their rhetorical form is quite simple. The argument leading to a set of bridge principles is first established in the rationale, where interpretive researchers stake the claim that the perceptions, values, or practices of a social group are unique (recall Heath's uniqueness argument above). In the Methods or Results section, specific examples of this uniqueness are enumerated. This uniqueness is then summarized in the form of themes or taxonomic categories.

In sum, bridge principles are built on the assumption that the particular social group is unique in its perceptions, values, or practices. Interpretive researchers identify and describe in detail particular instances. These instances are then restated in more general terms, reifying the notion of uniqueness. Finally, themes or taxonomic categories are created that epitomize the specific instances of observed unique features.

Heath (1980) illustrates the preceding constitutive rules for developing bridge principles as follows. First, in the rationale section, she stakes the claim that functions and uses of literacy "must" differ from community to community because "reading varies in its functions and uses across history and cultures." In her Methods section, she provides instances of her participants' unique reading behaviors; for example:

> [Children] learned names of cereals or meanings of railroad names, not because they were pointed out each time or because their letters were sounded out, but because of their juxtaposition with a spoken word or an action which carried meaning. (p. 128)

Heath next summarizes what it is that makes these behaviors unique:

> These children's methods of dealing with print were different from those encouraged by parents whose reading goals for their children are oriented to school success. Similarly, adults in this community used literacy in ways that differed from those of academically motivated parents. Among these adults, reading, in fact, was often interpreted as an indication that one had not succeeded socially. . . . Written materials were often used in connection with oral explanation, narratives, and jokes about what the written materials meant or did not mean. The authority of the materials was established through social negotiation by the readers.

Following this general statement, Heath presents the "seven types of uses of literacy" cited above.

Implications for Progress

For interpretive researchers, research promotes progress by: (1) helping others understand particular individuals, especially those who tend to be ignored socially or (2) making transparent the social interactions that undermine how people relate and communicate with one another (Shapiro, 1981). The assumption is that by identifying the plight of those who have been ignored (or mistreated) by our social institutions, they will be "given voice" and, consequently, will be legitimized as a group. In giving voice, interpretive researchers, in turn, set themselves up as potential spokespersons (or "brokers," cf. Heath, 1983) for particular individuals or social groups, or as mediators between groups with conflicting perspectives, values, or practices (Popkewitz, 1984).

In this regard, although interpretive researchers talk about uncovering universal themes and taxonomic categories that apply to a broad range of people in different social situations, the focus of their research is more on the socially neglected individual or group—for example, the disadvantaged—or on groups in social conflict. Interestingly enough, interpretive researchers consider individuals to be unique in terms of their level of social neglect or misrepresentation. For instance, some interpretive reading researchers (e.g., Johnston, 1985; Taylor & Dorsey-Gaines, 1988) define social problems at the individual level, others (Au & Mason, 1981; McDermott, 1985; Mehan, 1979) at the reading group or class level, and still others (Heath, 1980; Ogbu, 1983; Rist, 1970; Scribner & Cole, 1981) in units as large as a social system, community, racial group, or entire society.

At the rhetorical level, interpretive researchers describe an individual's or group's uniqueness using taxonomies of themes or categories. When they use these taxonomies to compare one social group with another, the superordinate categories remain across groups but the descriptive features of the categories differ. Thus, although Heath (1983, 1986) describes how white and a black communities use literacy in terms of the same seven superordinate categories, she identifies different features that make up the descriptive definitions of these categories by community type.

Given their intent to describe the unique characteristics of different individuals and social groups, interpretive researchers tend to pursue the development of new taxonomies of perceptions, values, and practices rather than promote extensions of existing taxonomies. In this sense, they engage in what Kuhn (1970) calls "extraordinary science" and Feyerabend (1965) calls "theoretical pluralism." Progress in research is achieved as the uniqueness of an ever-widening number of socially/politically neglected groups is documented. By bringing the uniqueness of these groups to the collective conscience of the public and policymakers, interpretive researchers achieve progress. They promote both "individual legitimacy" and "community" (Popkewitz, 1984).

Individual legitimacy emphasizes that individuals or groups maintain pluralistic beliefs and should be given the right to determine their own rules for defining appropriate behavior. Popkewitz (1984) emphasizes this dimension or progress as follows:

> The pluralistic perspective found in [the interpretive approach to progress] gives emphasis to the possibility that important social commitments in American life can be fulfilled. The legitimacy of many different systems of social meaning establishes a sentiment that, while there may be efforts towards conformity within the larger society, there is an opportunity for individuals to create their own, unique environments and to engage in an active public life. Pluralism reinforces a belief in the individual self-activation by its attention to the role of small interest groups in achieving the good life. There is also a relativism, in that it considers no one way of life or view better than others and thus relies upon the marketplace of competing interests to produce consensus. (p. 100)

"Community," on the other hand, acknowledges that individuals interact in social groups. They must learn to work together to build consensus through negotiation, creating rules and identifying norms that reflect a common set of perceptions, values, and practices that define this group as a community, society, or culture. Through this commonality, individuals support the social order through an agreed-upon set of constitutive rules (Mehan, 1979; Popkewitz, 1984).

Promoting Change

Unlike researchers in the validating approach who function as "experts" in the change process, researchers in the interpretive approach function as spokespersons or mediators. In the role of spokesperson, they attempt to bring about social change by publicizing a neglected group's plight (e.g., McDermott, 1985; Rist, 1970) or by lobbying to rectify its social plight economically or politically (Johnston, 1985).

In the role of mediator, interpretive researchers focus on the process of change and not on its outcome. This process approach typically involves the steps associated with "problem solving" (Popkewitz, 1984). First, the interpretive researchers identify the "unique" social groups that together define a community (e.g., a classroom, a school, or a school district). These groups are unique to the extent that they differ in terms of their perceptions, values, or practices.

Next, interpretive researchers establish a forum for dialogue among the different social groups. In this forum, the participants may be taught principles of negotiation or cooperation (Goodlad, 1975); or they may be taught principles of ethnographic research so that they become more tolerant of alternative views (Heath, 1983).

In the third stage, consensus is developed among the different social groups. This consensus takes the form of binding constitutive rules that define the goals and social interactions among the respective groups within the community.

Finally, the constitutive rules are implemented and the social groups' behaviors are evaluated as they comply with these rules. These rules are continually renegotiated in an effort to maintain a focus on the process of problem solving rather than on its product (Popkewitz, 1984).

Thus, the mediating approach for bringing about change is really an attempt to recognize both the "individual legitimacy" and "community" dimensions of any organization. When all individuals are given the opportunity to participate in the problem-solving process, each individual is given voice. By emphasizing the importance of consensus and the need to comply socially with constitutive rules, the interpretive researcher helps individuals become aware of the importance of their immediate community.

PART V: EXTERNAL LIMITATIONS
AND BOUNDARY CONDITIONS OF PROGRESS

At the outset of this chapter, we began by saying that, as reading researchers, we have "freedom of choice but not freedom from choice" in how we define reading. However, by adopting a Foucaultian perspective, we soon tempered this claim by arguing that different discourse practices severely constrain the range of discursive practices in which reading researchers might engage. We have spent the better part of this chapter describing and illustrating these conventions and their constraints, as they are manifested in published research reports.

However, there are a variety of other constraints that reading researchers must face in conducting research (cf. Krathwohl, 1985). These constraints include: (1) university, (2) commercial, (3) research funding, and (4) educational inertia. These often influence which approach to progress researchers might select. Within the validating approach, these constraints might further determine what theory and framing study is adopted as the basis for a study or line of research. Within the interpretive approach, these constraints might further determine which social groups are studied and which themes or taxonomic categories are used to frame the data.

University Constraints

University constraints often play an important role in determining what approach to progress reading researchers adopt. Most research in reading is conducted as part of the professional obligations of university professors, with very little being conducted by corporations (although some is funded by not-for-profit organizations).

A major concern of most individuals at universities is with acquiring tenure. The official criteria for achieving tenure at most universities involve the trichotomy of research, teaching, and service. Universities say that the three are equally important; however, it is clear that research is more equal than the other two. This is certainly true at many research-oriented private universities and at land-grant state universities. But even at universities that espouse a clear commitment to teaching, scholarly publication tends to provide an "added advantage" in climbing the tenure ladder.

In order to produce the necessary volume of research, assistant professors can be tempted by the expediency of choosing validating research over interpretive research.

Because it provides for a ready-made set of variables and operational conditions, validating research often yields highly predictable (and publishable) results at much less the effort than might be the case for interpretive research. While this strategy of selecting an approach to progress to ensure tenure may serve the individual's interest, it may not be the approach that reflects the researcher's true orientation toward progress. Nor is it likely to provide the field with the widest perspective for understanding the phenomena it claims to study.

Commercial Constraints

A second constraint arises over the potential conflict between the research and application phases of progress. Many reading researchers have found themselves identified as having particular insights into the production of instructional materials, due to the current emphasis on instructional, classroom-based research. Researchers are being asked to turn their often inchoate ideas into products long before these ideas have been sufficiently tested or validated. Consequently, a great potential exists for a conflict of interest between the financial and the scientific. For example, a researcher who suddenly discovers (or even merely strongly suspects) that a line of research has been flawed after many "successes" in classroom settings might be reluctant to publicize it if the work might lead (or had previously led) to a financial involvement with a company producing certain materials.

Other areas of reading are also involved. There are many researchers involved in teacher training, program evaluation, and large-scale assessments, for instance, who translate a line of research into "products." Whenever the translators and the researchers are the same people, a potential conflict of interest is present. Progress in research may be hindered if the conflict does arise and is resolved "against" the scientific aspects.

The financial involvement is not only a matter of producing or consulting on the production of educational materials. It is also another part of the tenure process. Finding that many of one's previous works are worthless might not lead to a positive decision by tenure committees. It is difficult to assess this as well as other influences on scientific progress—there are clearly no objective measures in these matters. However, the potential for interference with a "free market" of ideas is obviously present. The financial risk associated with losing a job may represent a strong influence on the choice of conduct and interpretation of research.

Research Funding

Another constraint on how progress transpires in reading is research funding. The general costs of conducting research are greater than can be handled by individuals. That leaves most of the funds in the hands of governmental agencies, private foundations, or corporations. The danger in a limited number of sources for funds is that there can potentially be restrictions (intentional or unintentional) on the number of different ideas or perspectives that can be funded. In science, however, the greater the diversity there is in research perspective, the greater the probability of progress.

At times the same point of view about what is appropriate might be adopted by all (or most) of the funding agencies. This is particularly detrimental if that perspective later proves to be incorrect. Not only will progress within an approach have been slowed, but valuable resources will have been wasted. A corollary is that research may be concentrated in the laboratories of only a few researchers. This thwarts the potential of younger researchers, many of whom have not learned to play the funding game.

Educational Inertia

Finally, there is a social or political inertia that impedes progress. Education often works the way it does simply by custom. Research is not always deemed necessary and is consequently not a priority. Finances may be limited; some inertia is related to other factors like power. In any event, the linkage between this inertia in education practice and a slowing of progress in research is relatively direct. Without a perceived need for research to solve problems, there is little demand for research funding.

Practitioners are often too demanding of "product" to be satisfied with a partially specified answer to a problem from researchers. Despite the very current attempts to translate research into practice, there is not a general acceptance of the premise that research will lead to solutions to educational problems. What is needed is more knowledge on both sides—more complete specification of the research answers and more tolerance of the partially specified answers.

None of this is to be taken as suggesting that progress in the validating or interpretive approach will absolutely be stopped by any of these factors. Rather, these constraints have the potential to determine the type of progress that is pursued and its rate within the two approaches. There is also the possibility that the influences might exert forces in the "correct" direction and that progress will be unimpeded in one or both approaches. Most important is to recognize that these boundary conditions and limitations on progress exist. We must strive to minimize their negative possibilities—however they are defined by the reading research community at large.

SUMMARY AND CONCLUSIONS

Two approaches to progress in reading research have been considered: the validating and the interpretive. Each represents a different set of assumptions of what a map of reading represents. For validating researchers, descriptive definitions have features that are assumed to characterize objectively the causes and effects of reading phenomena. For interpretive researchers, descriptive definitions are socially constructed. Their features tend to vary from individual to individual, group to group.

Validating researchers follow the rhetorical framework of theories. Constitutive rules for achieving partial specification require that validating researchers use recombinant procedures for modifying a favored operational definition in a systematic, normal-science fashion. Among the elements of the Operational Hexagon, validating reading researchers most typically identify contrasting causative features in terms of learner (e.g., schema, metacognitive strategies), materials (e.g., rhetorical structures), or administration procedures (e.g., question types) elements. Often little if any mention is made of the larger context in which the research occurs.

In contrast, interpretive researchers organize their definitions of reading in terms of taxonomies consisting of themes or superordinate categories. Their constitutive rules for achieving partial specification require that they begin by identifying a set of individuals or a social group whose situation reflects a "social problem." These rules further require interpretive researchers to identify new superordinate or subordinate features in their taxonomies in order to establish the uniqueness of the individuals or group. Such rules are carried out consistent with revolutionary science. Among the elements of the Operational Hexagon that interpretive researchers most often emphasize are the setting and the interactions among the observer, the learners (or native observers), and the administration procedures.

Progress for validating researchers is measured in terms of the length of a research line that an individual or speech community of researchers has created. This line establishes the integrity of the individual or speech community as being "the expert, the authority." Theoretical accounts published by these experts, because they are the "newest" and have well-established internal validity, are regarded by practitioners as being the most "improved." This, in turn, suggests that these accounts represent the greatest "progress" in a field to date.

Progress for interpretive researchers is measured in terms of social or political action. By bringing a group's plight to the public's attention, interpretive researchers attempt to improve the collective good of this group through community reaction and support. By identifying differences in perceptions, values, or practices among group members, interpretive researchers serve as brokers or negotiators so that some resolution between these differences is forthcoming.

In promoting progress, validating researchers use their expert status to promote change through a "center-to-periphery" strategy (Popkewitz, 1984) by which they create an account of reading and then convince various clients (through marketing) that this is the account to be followed and implemented. In contrast, interpretive researchers promote progress using a "problem-solving" approach to change (Popkewitz, 1984), identifying different perceptions, values, or practices among groups within a community. They then establish a forum where members of the different groups are made aware of their mutual differences. Discussion ensues with an expectation of compromise, thus producing a negotiated set of working principles that incorporate the discussants' varied perspectives, values, and practices.

In sum, each of these approaches involves different interpretations of what a definition of reading represents; each uses a different rhetoric structure and a different set of constitutive rules for defining reading; each has a different interpretation of what progress means in terms both of outcomes and of how these outcomes should be achieved. And each lends itself to different institutional constraints.

Having drawn the lines between these two approaches to progress, we, in essence, have attempted to raise an "important yet little understood question" that both validating and interpretive reading researchers have largely ignored. To date, reading researchers have tended to focus on the question "What is reading?" In part, each of the individual contributors to this volume provides significant and timely answers to this question. Taken as a whole, the chapters of these contributors also address a second question: "What are possible definitions of reading?" To understand the answers to this question is to understand the breadth of the reading field.

However, two questions have been largely ignored by the reading research community; these include: "*How should* reading be defined?" and "*Who should* define reading?" Concomitant with these are the questions: "Given the possible definitions of reading, which one(s) is (are) best?" "And given different speech communities of reading researchers, who should have the ultimate authority to decide the answers?" To understand the answers to these questions is to understand progress.

Rather than provide explicit answers to these questions, we have attempted to highlight their importance and why they are little understood. Perhaps if other researchers and practitioners begin to pursue these questions, they will provide a "truly improved" basis for understanding the reading field. And, in pursuing these questions, perhaps a new dimension of thinking about reading will be added to our research endeavors, much like water flowing into Kazantzakis's (1965) proverbial river bed:

Reality . . . does not exist independent of (wo)man, completed and ready; it comes with (wo)man's collaboration, and is proportionate to (wo)man's worth. If we open a river bed by writing or acting, reality may flow into that river bed, into a course it would not have taken had we not intervened. We do not bear the full responsibility naturally, but we do bear a great part. (p. 386)

NOTES

[a]The authors gratefully acknowledge the help from Janet Binkley, Claudia Gentile, P. David Pearson, David Krathwohl, and Claire Putala who read earlier versions of this chapter.

[b]As Ornstein (1972) has noted, it is precisely this "linear" way of thinking that enables validating researchers to conceptualize causality:

Causality can be inferred only within a linear mode of temporal consciousness. The information-processing of this mode breaks the flow of events into serial lists which can be sequentially analyzed, studied, and manipulated. Succession and duration are the underpinnings of causality, for without a concept of past and future, or discrete events following each other temporally, it would be impossible to perform scientifically meaningful analysis. Together with language and mathematics, this linear construction of temporal experience constitutes the essence of the active mode of consciousness. (p. 100)

REFERENCES

Anderson, R. C., & Pichert, J. W. (1978). Recall of previously unrecallable information following a shift in perspective. *Journal of Verbal Learning and Verbal Behavior, 17*, 1–12.

Au, K. H. (1980). Participation structures in a reading lesson with Hawaiian children: Analysis of a culturally appropriate instructional event. *Anthropology Quarterly, 11*, 91–115.

Au, K. H., & Mason, J. (1981). Social organizational factors in learning to read: The balance of rights hypothesis. *Reading Research Quarterly, 17*, 115–152.

Bartley, W. W., III. (1962). *The retreat to commitment.* New York: Knopf.

Bernstein, R. (1983). *Beyond objectivism and relativism.* Philadelphia: University of Pennsylvania Press.

Biddle, B. J., & Anderson, D. S. (1986). Theory, methods, knowledge, and research on teaching. In M. C. Wittrock (Ed.), *Handbook of research on teaching* (3rd ed.) (pp. 230–252). New York: Macmillan.

Blumer, H. (1969). *Symbolic interactionism.* Englewood Cliffs, NJ: Prentice-Hall.

Bogdan, R. D., & Biklen, S. K. (1982). *Qualitative research for education: An introduction to theory and methods.* Boston: Allyn & Bacon.

Borg, W. R., & Gail, M. D. (1989). *Educational research: An introduction* (5th ed.). White Plains, NY: Longman.

Boring, E. G. (1950). *A history of experimental psychology* (2nd ed.). New York: Appleton-Century-Crofts.

Bridgman, P. W. (1927). *The logic of modern physics.* New York: Macmillan.

Bridgman, P. W. (1978). Operationism. In W. G. Hardy (Ed.), *Language, thought, and experience: A tapestry of the dimensions of reading* (pp. 51–59). Baltimore: University Park Press.

Bunge, M. (1967). *Scientific research* (Vols. I, II). New York: Springer-Verlag.

Calfee, R., & Piontkowski, D. (1984). Design and analysis of experiments. In P. D. Pearson, R. Barr, M. L. Kamil, & P. Mosenthal (Eds.), *Handbook of reading research* (Vol. 1) (pp. 63–90). White Plains, NY: Longman.

Campbell, D. T., & Stanley, J. C. (1966). *Experimental and quasi-experimental designs for research.* Chicago: Rand McNally.

Cantor, N., & Mischel, W. (1979). Prototypes in person perception. *Advances in experimental social psychology, 12*, 3–52.

Cazden, C. B. (1979). Learning to read in classroom interaction. In L. B. Resnick & P. A. Weaver (Eds.), *Theory and practice of early reading* (Vol. 3) (pp. 295–306). Hillsdale, NJ: Erlbaum.

Chronbach, L. J. (1975). Beyond the two disciplines of scientific psychology. *American Psychologist, 30*, 116–127.

Churchman, C. W. (1979). *The systems approach and its enemies.* New York: Basic Books.

Cicourel, A. V. (1974). *Cognitive sociology: Language and meaning in social interaction.* New York: Free Press.

Erickson, F. (1986). Qualitative methods in research on teaching. In M. C. Wittrock (Ed.), *Handbook of research on teaching* (3rd ed.) (pp. 119–161). New York: Macmillan.

Erickson, F., & Mohatt, G. (1982). Cultural organization of participant structures in two classrooms of Indian students. In G. D. Spindler (Ed.), *Doing ethnography of schooling: Educational anthropology in action* (pp. 132–174). New York: Holt, Rinehart, & Winston.

Feyerabend, P. (1965). Problems of empiricism. In R. Colodny (Ed.), *Beyond the edge of certainty: Essays in contemporary science and philosophy* (pp. 145–276). Englewood Cliffs, NJ: Prentice-Hall.

Firestone, W. A. (1987). Meaning in method: The rhetoric of quantitative and qualitative research. *Educational Researcher, 16*, 16–21.

Fodor, J. A., Bever, T. G., & Garrett, M. F. (1974). *The psychology of language.* New York: McGraw-Hill.

Foucault, M. (1972). *The archaeology of knowledge* (A. M. S. Smith, Trans.). New York: Random House.

Geertz, C. (1973). Thick description: Toward an interpretive theory of culture. In C. Geertz, *The interpretation of cultures* (pp. 3–30). New York: Basic Books.

Glass, G., McGaw, B., & Smith, M. L. (1981). *Meta-analysis in social research.* Beverly Hills, CA: Sage.

Goodenough, W. (1981). *Culture, language, and society.* Menlo Park, CA: Benjamin-Cummings.

Goodlad, J. (1975). *The dynamics of educational change: Towards responsive schools.* New York: McGraw-Hill.

Gough, P. B. (1972). One second of reading. In J. F. Kavanagh & J. G. Mattingly (Eds.), *Language by ear and by eye: The relationship between speech and reading* (pp. 331–358). Cambridge, MA: MIT Press.

Green, J. L., & Wallat, C. (1981). Mapping instructional conversations: A sociolinguistic ethnography. In J. L. Green & C. Wallat (Eds.), *Ethnography and language in educational settings* (pp. 161–205). Norwood, NJ: Ablex.

Guba, E., & Lincoln, Y. (1982). Epistemological and methodological bases of naturalistic inquiry. *Educational Communication and Technology Journal, 30,* 233–252.

Harris, A. J., & Sipay, E. R. (1980). *How to increase reading ability: A guide to developmental and remedial methods* (7th ed.). White Plains, NY: Longman.

Harste, J. C., Burke, C. L., & Woodward, V. A. (1982). Children's language and world: Initial encounters with print. In J. A. Langer & M. T. Smith-Burke (Eds.), *Reader meets author/bridging the gap* (pp. 105–131). Newark, DE: International Reading Association.

Heath, S. B. (1980). The functions and uses of literacy. *Journal of Communication, 30,* 123–133.

Heath, S. B. (1983). *Ways with words: Language, life, and work in communities and classrooms.* London: Cambridge University Press.

Heath, S. B. (1986). Critical factors in literacy development. In S. DeCastell, A. Luke, & K. Egan (Eds.), *Literacy, society, and schooling* (pp. 209–229). Cambridge: Cambridge University Press.

Hempel, C. G. (1966). *Philosophy of natural science.* Englewood Cliffs, NJ: Prentice-Hall.

Hull, C. L. (1943). *Principles of behavior.* New York: Appleton.

Jacob, E. (1987). Traditions of qualitative research: A review. *Review of Educational Research, 57,* 1–50.

Jacob, E. (1988). Clarifying qualitative research: A focus on traditions. *Educational Researcher, 17,* 16–19, 22–24.

Johnston, P. H. (1985). Understanding reading disability: A case study approach. *Harvard Educational Review, 55,* 153–177.

Kamil, M. L. (1984). Current traditions of reading research. In P. D. Pearson, R. Barr, M. L. Kamil, & P. Mosenthal (Eds.), *Handbook of reading research* (Vol. 1) (pp. 39–62). White Plains, NY: Longman.

Kamil, M. L., Langer, J. A., & Shanahan, T. (1985). *Understanding reading and writing research.* Boston: Allyn & Bacon.

Kazantzakis, N. (1965). *Report to Greco.* New York: Simon & Schuster.

Kelly, R. M. (1980). Ideology, effectiveness, and public sector productivity: With illustrations from the field of higher education. *Journal of Social Issues, 36,* 76–95.

Krathwohl, D. R. (1985). *Social and behavioral science research.* San Francisco: Jossey-Bass.

Kuhn, T. S. (1970). *The structure of scientific revolutions* (2nd ed.). Chicago: University of Chicago Press.

Lakotos, I. (1970). Falsification and the methodology of scientific research programmes. In I. Lakatos & A. Musgrave (Eds.), *Criticism and the growth of knowledge* (pp. 91–196). Cambridge: Cambridge University Press.

Laudan, L. (1977). *Progress and its problems.* Berkeley: University of California Press.

McCutcheon, G. (1981). On the interpretation of classroom observations. *Educational Researcher, 10,* 5–10.

McDermott, R. P. (1985). Achieving school failure: An anthropological approach to illiteracy and social stratification. Reprinted in H. Singer & R. B. Ruddell (Eds.), *Theoretical models and processes of reading* (pp. 558–594). (3rd ed.). Newark, DE: International Reading Association. (Originally published in 1974.)

Manis, J., & Meltzer, B. (Eds.) (1978). *Symbolic interaction: A reader in social psychology* (3rd ed.). London: Routledge & Kegan Paul.

Markman, E. M. (1979). Realizing that you don't understand: Elementary school children's awareness of inconsistencies. *Child Development, 50,* 643–655.

Massaro, D. W. (1984). Building and testing models of reading processes. In P. D. Pearson, R. Barr, M. L. Kamil, & P. Mosenthal (Eds.), *Handbook of reading research* (Vol. 1, pp. 111–146). White Plains, NY: Longman.

Mehan, H. (1979). *Learning lessons: Social organization in the classroom.* Cambridge, MA: Harvard University Press.

Mehan, H., & Wood, H. (1975). *The reality of ethnomethodology.* New York: Wiley.

Merton, R. K. (1959). Notes on problems finding in sociology. In R. K. Merton, L. Broom, & L. S. Cottrell, Jr. (Eds), *Sociology today* (pp. ix–xxxiv). New York: Basic Books.

Mervis, C. B. (1980). Category structure and the development of categorization. In R. J. Spiro, B. C. Bruce, & W. F. Brewer (Eds.), *Theoretical issues in reading comprehension* (pp. 279–301). Hillsdale, NJ: Erlbaum.

Meyer, B. J. F. (1984). Text dimensions and cognitive processing. In H. Mandl, N. L. Stein, & T. Trabasso (Eds.), *Learning and comprehension of text* (pp. 3–51). Hillsdale, NJ: Erlbaum.

Meyer, B. J. F., & Freedle, R. O. (1984). Effects of discourse type on recall. *American Educational Research Journal, 21,* 121–143.

Michel, P. A. (1988). *Children's perceptions of reading.* Unpublished doctoral dissertation, Syracuse University, Syracuse, NY.

Miles, M. B., & Huberman, A. M. (1984). Drawing valid meaning from qualitative data: Toward a shared craft. *Educational Researcher, 13,* 4–11.

Mitroff, I. I., & Sagasti, F. (1973). Epistemology as general systems theory: An approach to the design of complex decision-making experiments. *Philosophy of Social Sciences, 3,* 117–134.

Mosenthal, P. B. (1984a). Defining reading program effectiveness: An ideological perspective. *Poetics, 13,* 195–216.

Mosenthal, P. B. (1984b). The problem of partial specification in translating reading research into practice. *Elementary School Journal, 85,* 199–227.

Mosenthal, P. B. (1985a). Defining the expository discourse continuum: Towards a taxonomy of expository text types. *Poetics, 14,* 387–414.

Mosenthal, P. B. (1985b). Defining progress in educational research. *Educational Researcher, 14,* 3–9.

Mostenthal, P. B. (1987). Rational and irrational approaches to understanding reading. *Reading Teacher, 40,* 570–572.

Mosenthal, P. B. (1988). Understanding the histories of reading. *Reading Teacher, 42,* 64–65.

Northcutt, N. (1975). *Adult functional competence: A report to the Office of Education Dissemination Review Panel.* Austin: University of Texas.

Ogbu, J. U. (1983). Literacy and schooling in subordinate cultures: The case of black Americans. In D. P. Resnick (Ed.), *Literacy in historical perspective* (pp. 129–153). Washington, D.C.: Library of Congress.

Ornstein, R. E. (1972). *The psychology of consciousness.* New York: Penguin Books.

Pearson, P. D., Barr, R., Kamil, M. L., & Mosenthal, P. (1984). *Handbook of Reading Research.* (Vol. 1). White Plains, NY: Longman.

Pelto, P., & Pelto, G. (1977). *Anthropological research: The structure of inquiry.* New York: Harcourt Brace.

Perfetti, C. A., Goldman, S. R., & Hogaboam, T. W. (1979). Reading skill and the identification of words in discourse context. *Memory & Cognition, 7,* 273–282.

Popkewitz, T. S. (1984). *Paradigm and ideology in educational research: The social functions of the intellectual.* New York: Falmer Press.

Popper, K. R. (1968). *Conjectures and refutations in the growth of scientific knowledge.* New York: Harper Torchbooks.

Popper, K. R. (1972). *Objective knowledge.* Oxford: Oxford University Press.

Rickards, J. P., & Slife, B. D. (1987). Interaction of dogmatism and rhetorical structure in text recall. *American Educational Research Journal, 24,* 635–641.

Rist, R. (1970). Student social class and teacher expectation. *Harvard Educational Review, 40,* 411–451.

Rokeach, M . (1960). *The open and closed mind.* New York: Basic Books.

Rosch, E., & Mervis, C. B. (1975). Family resemblances: Studies in the internal structure of categories. *Cognitive Psychology, 7,* 573–605.

Rose, A. (1962). A systematic summary of symbolic interaction theory. In A. Rose (Ed.), *Human behavior and social processes* (pp. 3–19). Boston: Houghton Mifflin.

Rudner, R. S. (1966) *Philosophy of social science.* Englewood Cliffs, NJ: Prentice-Hall.

Samuels, S. J., & Kamil, M. L. (1984). Models of the reading process. In P. D. Pearson, R. Barr, M. L. Kamil, & P. Mosenthal (Eds.), *Handbook of reading research* (Vol. 1) (pp. 185–224). White Plains, NY: Longman.

Schon, D. A. (1983). *The reflective practitioner: How professionals think in action.* New York: Basic Books.

Schutz, A. (1971). *Collected papers I: The problem of social reality.* The Hague: Martinus Nijhoff.

Scribner, S., & Cole, M. (1981). *The psychology of literacy.* Cambridge, MA: Harvard University Press.

Shannon, P. (1989). Paradigmatic diversity within the reading research community. *Journal of Reading Behavior, 21,* 97–107.

Shapiro, M. J. (1981). *Language and political understanding: The politics of discursive practices.* New Haven, CT: Yale University Press.

Shulman, L. S. (1986). Paradigms and research programs in the study of teaching: A contemporary perspective. In M. C. Wittrock (Ed.), *Handbook of research on teaching* (3rd ed.) (pp. 3–36). New York: Macmillan.

Slavin, R. E. (1986). Best-evidence synthesis: Why less is more. *Educational Researcher, 16,* 15–16.

Smith, F. (1971). *Understanding reading.* New York: Holt, Rinehart, & Winston.

Soltis, J. F. (1984). On the nature of educational research. *Educational Researcher, 13,* 5–10.

Spradley, J. P. (1980). *Participant observation.* New York: Holt.

Suppe, F. (1974). Editor's introduction. In F. Suppe (Ed.), *The structure of scientific theories* (pp. i–xvi). Urbana: University of Illinois Press.

Taylor, D., & Dorsey-Gaines, C. (1988). *Growing up literate: Learning from inner-city families.* Portsmouth, NH: Heinemann.

Teale, W. H. (1986). Home background and young children's literacy development. In W. H. Teale & E. Sulzby (Eds.), *Emergent literacy: Writing and reading* (pp. 173–206). Norwood, N.J.: Ablex.

Toulmin, S. (1983). The construal of reality: Criticism in modern and post modern science. In W. J. T. Mitchell (Ed.), *The politics of interpretation* (pp. 99–117). Chicago: University of Chicago Press.

Tyler, S. (1969). Introduction. In S. Tyler (Ed.), *Cognitive anthropology* (pp. 1–23). New York: Holt, Rinehart, & Winston.
Watson, R. I. (1963). *The great psychologists.* Philadelphia: Lippincott.
Weimer, W. B. (1979). *Notes on the methodology of scientific research.* Hillsdale, NJ: Erlbaum.
Wilson, J. (1969). *Language and the pursuit of truth.* London: Cambridge University Press.
Wittgenstein, L. (1958). *Philosophical investigations* (G. E. M. Anscombe, Trans.). New York: Macmillan.

AUTHOR INDEX

Slater, W. H., 133, 264, 792, 794, 827, 832, 957, 958, 960, 961

Slaughter, D. T., 15

Slavin, R. E., 14, 623, 630, 668, 839, 840, 866, 867, 869, 870, 875, 878, 893, 894–895, 900, 945, 988–989, 991, 997, 998, 1029

Sleeter, C. E., 969, 971, 972, 973

Sless, D., 344

Slife, B. D., 1019–1020, 1024, 1025–1028

Slobin, D. I., 790

Slocum, T. A., 803

Smid, K., 954, 956, 962–963

Smiley, S. S., 526–527, 532, 612, 954

Smillie, R. J., 682

Smith, A. E., 959, 962

Smith, B. B., 678

Smith, B. O., 13

Smith, C. R., 311, 320

Smith, D. A., 864, 865, 867

Smith, D. H., 49

Smith, E., 645

Smith, E. E., 174, 195, 218, 220, 223–224, 225, 837–838, 867

Smith, E. R., 285, 295

Smith, F., 255, 257, 258, 265, 266, 313, 423, 430, 514, 517, 523, 679, 762, 763–764, 836, 850, 965, 966, 968, 1018

Smith, F. L., Jr., 969

Smith, G., 517

Smith, G. H., 87

Smith, H., 584

Smith, I. M., 654, 666

Smith, L., 474, 629, 634, 971, 973

Smith, L. C., 965

Smith, M., 149, 150, 152, 818, 935

Smith, M. E., 792, 794

Smith, M. K., 792, 794, 795

Smith, M. L., 988, 990, 1029

Smith, M. M., 367

Smith, N. B., 121, 122, 149, 297, 887, 888, 913, 914, 985, 986

Smith, P. V., 988–989

Smith, R., 256

Smith, R. J., 954, 956

Smith, S., 344

Smith, S. D., 603

Smith, S. T., 589

Smith, T., 840–841

Smitherman, G., 13

Smolensky, P., 439

Smolkin, L. B., 731–732

Smothergill, D. W., 423

Smout, T. C., 57, 61

Snow, C. E., 271, 616, 628, 731–732, 734, 738, 746

Snow, R. E., 284, 298, 995

Snowling, M., 431, 521

Snyder, B. L., 818, 866, 878

Snyder, C. R., 505

Soar, R. M., 926, 988, 991

Soar, R. S., 926, 988, 991

Soderberg, I., 325

Soderberg, R., 77

Soderbergh, R., 771–772, 773

Sokal, M. M., 282, 285

Solso, R. L., 406

Soltis, J., 161, 162, 163, 164

Soltis, J. F., 1015

Soltow, L., 58

Sorensen, A. B., 893, 896–897, 902, 903

Sorter, J., 830, 958, 959, 961

Soter, A., 268–269

Sours, M. A., 737–738, 740, 741, 749–750

Souther, A. F., 774

Southgate, V., 77, 80, 82, 85, 86

Southwest Regional Laboratories, 128–129

Spache, G. D., 314

Spade, J. Z., 903, 904

Spalten, E., 581

Sparks, P. E., 917

Spaulding, N. B., 122–123

Spearrit, D., 805

Speece, D. L., 550–551

Speer, J. R., 619

Spekman, N. J., 958, 961

Spencer, H., 342, 343, 344, 345–346

Spenser, F., 960

Sperber, R. D., 500, 503

Sperling, G., 517

Sperry, L. L., 183, 185–188, 507

Sperry, R. W., 600

Spiegel, D. L., 80, 85, 86, 822

Spilich, G. J., 196, 236, 241, 530

Spiroff, J., 78

Spiro, R. J., 160, 171, 433, 531, 561, 720–721

Spivey, N. N., 270, 284

Spoehr, K. T., 220, 222, 223–224, 225

Spolsky, B., 101

Spradley, J. P., 1031

Spratt, J. E., 38

Spring, C., 395, 403

Spufford, M., 47, 54, 55, 61

Squire, J. R., 79, 80, 84, 124, 126, 135, 138, 139, 140, 153, 251, 284, 286, 302, 456, 457, 460, 463, 815, 819, 951

Stacy, E. W., 651

Staczek, J. J., 101

Stahl, N. A., 960

Stahl, S. A., 130, 138, 615, 719, 720, 805, 806, 807, 809, 833, 834, 867, 869

Stainback, S., 988

Stainback, W., 988

Stake, R. E., 966, 969, 971, 972

Stallings, J., 861, 893, 899, 928, 993

Stamm, E. G., 435

Stamm, K. R., 69, 72, 75

Stammer, J., 389

Stanley, G., 517

Stanley, J. C., 818–819, 1023

Stanley, S. O., 992

Stanovich, K. E., 386, 399, 418–419, 420, 423, 424, 425, 427, 428, 429, 430, 431, 432, 433, 434, 435, 436, 438, 442, 519–520, 521, 523, 524, 526, 548, 549, 562, 584, 588, 747, 759, 770, 774, 776, 861, 938, 993, 1000

Starr, K., 241–242

Stauffer, R. G., 246, 611, 738

Stayrook, N., 861

Stedman, L. C., 288, 677, 952

Steele, J. M., 106–107

Steenwyck, F. L., 257–258, 833, 834

Steffeusen, M., 461

Steger, J. A., 584, 585

Steiger, J. H., 653

Stein, M., 136, 137, 795, 798, 799, 800, 801, 809

Stein, N. L., 171, 174, 179–180, 183, 184, 284, 295, 821

Steinbach, R., 20, 872, 876–877

Steinbellner, L. L., 79

Steinberg, E., 473

Steinberg, S. H., 28

Stephens, Diane, 690

Sterling, T. D., 430–431

Sternberg, S., 443

Sternberg, R. J., 21, 428, 525, 531, 551, 803, 809

Stern, C., 102

Stevens, D., 298–299, 870

Stevens, E., 58

Stevens, K. W., 500, 695, 697

Stevens, R., 863, 930, 995

Stevens, R. J., 623, 840, 868, 869, 870, 875, 878, 900

Stevens, Wallace, 22

Stevenson, 472

Steward, J., 737–738

Steward, M., 138

Stewart, D., 8

Stewart, J., 957

Stewart, R. A., 970

Stibbe, M. A., 802–803

Stiggins, R. J., 286, 288, 296

Stillman, B. W., 987, 998

Stillman, P. R., 21, 297

Stipek, D., 625, 629

Stitch, T. G., 76, 139, 211, 419, 526, 669, 670, 671, 672, 676, 677, 679–680, 683, 684

SUBJECT INDEX

Ability, 558, 630–631, 816–817, 819, 829, 926, 936–937, 960, 961–962, 1004–1005. *See also* Grouping of students

Abstractness, 693–694, 701, 702, 719

Access: and adults, 520; and comprehension, 520, 529; and context, 523; and individual differences, 519, 520, 522, 523, 524, 529; and phonological recoding, 522; and reading words, 384, 387, 394, 401, 402, 405, 411; to literacy, 557–558; and word identification, 573, 595; and word recognition, 419, 433–438, 440–444, 514, 519, 520, 522, 523, 524

Access structure, 357, 365–370, 372, 373

Achievement: and basal readers, 126; and classroom climate, 926; and comprehension instruction, 844; and emergent literacy, 736; and individual differences, 512; and knowledge, 479; and linguistic diversity, 102, 106, 107; and literary activities, 80, 85–86; and literary response, 479; and questions, 871; reading, 86, 87, 88; and reading words, 386–387, 402, 406; and the reading-writing relationship, 247–248, 256–258; and secondary school reading, 952; and strategic reading, 617; and teachers' instructional actions, 871, 874, 875. *See also* Assessment; Grouping of students; Reading Acquisition; Standardized tests

Active involvement, 836–839, 847

Activities, 745, 749, 865–866

Adults: and access, 520; and cognition, 518; and comprehension, 419, 526; and emergent literacy, 747; and individual differences, 518, 519, 520, 524, 526; and listening, 419; literary activities of, 68–76; and reading acquisition, 767–768, 774; and reading disability, 560; and strategic reading, 612; and word identification, 593, 595–597; and word recognition, 419, 427, 432, 433, 434, 442, 443, 519, 520, 524. *See also* Workplace literacy

Advance organizers, 954, 960

Aesthetic reading, 994

Affect: and cognition, 554, 555; and computers, 332; and grouping of students, 894; and literary response, 476–477, 478–479; and narratives, 175–176, 185, 189, 196–201; and reading disability, 554, 555; and remediation, 999; and secondary school reading, 971; and typography, 344; and word identification, 576–577

Alaska/Alaskans, 71–72, 97, 98, 108

Alphabet: and reading acquisition, 764–768, 774, 781–782; and reading words, 384, 387, 390–398, 405, 411–412; and word identification, 576, 587–588, 590

American Indians, 97, 98, 101

American Sign Language, 99–100

Analogy, 385–386, 387, 408–411, 962

Applied psychology, 341–346

Applied research, 292

Apprenticeships, 842–843, 849, 850, 852, 862

Arbitrariness, 350–354

Argentina, 739

Argument structure, 357–338, 362, 364

Artificial intelligence, 174, 430, 547

Artificial lighting, 51

Aspectual reading, 747

Assessment: assumptions about, 479–480; and basic skills, 284; and comprehension, 479, 490, 633–634; conceptual foundations of, 283–284; and critical literacy, 284; and the curriculum, 287–291, 297–301; and decision making, 286–287, 293; definition of, 283–284; and discussion, 294, 298–299; externally-mandated, 285–291; and instruction, 287–291, 297–301, 633–634; internal, 291–301; internal, 286–287, 293; and interviews, 294–295, 299; and inventories, 294–295, 299; and knowledge, 472–474, 479; and literary response, 473–474, 479–480; methods of, 285–286, 292–293; a model of reading, 284–302; needed research about reading, 301–302; normative/individualized views of, 479–480; and observation, 295–296, 299–300; and performance assessment, 296–297, 300; purpose of, 285, 291–292; and questions, 294, 298–299; and remediation, 988, 990, 998, 1003, 1006; and standardized tests, 281–291, 301–302; and strategic reading, 633–634; and teachers' roles, 287–291, 294–301; tiers of, 282–283; and vocabulary, 795–798, 801, 808–809; and writing, 296–297, 300. *See also* Assessment; Multiple-choice tests

Assisted performance, 862

Associative learning, 577–578, 581, 599–600

Assumptions, 475–480

Attention, 576–577, 582, 599–600, 601–602, 657, 994–995

Austria, 86

Authenticity, 847–850

Authentic texts, 850

Automaticity: and comprehension, 492, 504–506, 508; definition of, 862; and mental models, 504–506; and reading acquisition, 767, 770, 783; and teachers' instructional actions, 862; and word meaning, 715; and word recognition, 423–430, 437–438, 439, 443

Basal readers: and achievement, 126; and comprehension, 126, 824, 851; and the content of student books, 125–126; difficulty of, 126–127, 133; emergence of, 122–123; and grouping of students, 888; and instructional design, 129–130; publishing of, 123–125, 137,